Medical Law and Ethics

Medical Law and Ethics

Second Edition

JONATHAN HERRING

Fellow in Law
Exeter College, University of Oxford

OXFORD
UNIVERSITY PRESS

OXFORD

UNIVERSITY PRESS

Great Clarendon Street, Oxford OX2 6DP

Oxford University Press is a department of the University of Oxford.
It furthers the University's objective of excellence in research, scholarship,
and education by publishing worldwide in

Oxford New York

Auckland Cape Town Dar es Salaam Hong Kong Karachi
Kuala Lumpur Madrid Melbourne Mexico City Nairobi
New Delhi Shanghai Taipei Toronto

With offices in

Argentina Austria Brazil Chile Czech Republic France Greece
Guatemala Hungary Italy Japan Poland Portugal Singapore
South Korea Switzerland Thailand Turkey Ukraine Vietnam

Oxford is a registered trade mark of Oxford University Press
in the UK and in certain other countries

Published in the United States
by Oxford University Press Inc., New York

First edition 2006
Second edition 2008

British Library Cataloguing in Publication Data

Data available

Library of Congress Cataloging in Publication Data
Herring, Jonathan.
    Medical law and ethics / Jonathan Herring. – 2nd ed.
       p. cm.
    Includes bibliographical references and index.
    ISBN 978–0–19–923066–2
  1. Medical laws and legislation. 2. Medical ethics. 3. Medical laws
and legislation–Great Britain. 4. Medical ethics–Great Britain. I. Title.
    K3601.H47 2008
    344.04'1–dc22   2008011163

Typeset by Newgen Imaging Systems (P) Ltd., Chennai, India
Printed in Great Britain
on acid-free paper by
Ashford Colour Press Ltd, Gosport, Hampshire

ISBN 978–0–19–923066–2

10 9 8 7 6 5 4 3 2 1

To Mog

Preface

This book is designed to provide readers with coverage not only of medical law, but also the context, philosophical, social, and political, within which the law operates. It attempts to take the 'ethics' part of a Medical Law and Ethics course as seriously as the legal part. Although, therefore, there is extensive reference to legal material, there is also a substantial reference to writings from non-legal perspectives. In doing this I am all too aware that I have only been able to present, in some cases, the merest outline of a rich vein of material from non-legal disciplines. It would be absurd in a book of this length to suggest that the reader can be provided with an in depth guide to all that philosophers, sociologists, or theologians, for example, might have to say about medicine. I hope that I have provided enough to excite the interest of the reader and at least indicate the variety of perspectives with which it is possible to view the subject. There is ample further reading, both at the end of chapters and in the bibliography for readers to undertake their own studies.

With the use of various boxes in some chapters I have sought to highlight feminist and theological perspectives on particular questions. Readers of drafts of the book have complained that this either gives undue prominence to these perspectives, or sidelines them. I intend neither, but merely to break up the text and provide space for readers to think about what might, or might not, be an interesting viewpoint. It need hardly be said that feminist perspectives are represented throughout the text and not limited to points made in these boxes.

While writing the book I have been greatly aided by anonymous referees inveigled upon by Oxford University Press to comment on draft chapters. Their comments were invaluable. I have also been fortunate to have the support of many colleagues and friends during the writing of this book: Shazia Choudhry, John Eekelaar, Sandy Fredman, Michelle Madden Dempsey, and Elaine Palser, to mention just a few. Ruth Ballantyne at Oxford University Press has been an encouraging and supportive editor and I am grateful for her efforts. Above all I am thankful to my family. To my children, Laurel, Joanna, and Darcy who entertained me greatly when not writing, and forcefully encouraged me to get to my computer and not bother them whenever something worth watching came up on CBeebies. And to my wife Kirsten whose love and care are boundless.

15 November 2007

Contents

Detailed Contents

Table of Cases

Table of Statutes

Table of Statutory Instruments

Table of European and International Materials

1 Ethics and Medical Law

INTRODUCTION

Medical law is undergoing massive change. Rapid scientific advances mean that law-yers and ethicists are constantly required to face new issues. More significantly our attitude towards our health, health services, and the medical professions is changing. There was a time when doctors were given a 'godlike' status and were held in the high-est of esteem; and patients were intended to be, well, patient: passive and submissive. The following exchange exemplifies this well:

DOCTOR: [reading case notes] Ah, I see you've a boy and a girl
PATIENT: No, two girls.
DOCTOR: Really, are you sure? Thought it said...[checks in case notes] oh
            no, you're quite right, two girls.[1]

But this has changed. Doctors are no longer regarded as infallible and beyond question-ing. Doctors, especially General Practitioners, regard their job as working *with* patients to find out what is the best treatment for them. The doctor–patient relationship has, according to some become closer to that of consumer and supplier.[2] The doctor is not regarded as similar to a 'family friend' but the relationship has become more formal and structured.[3] Another change is that the hierarchy amongst medical professionals is being challenged with the nursing profession carrying out an increasing range of tasks. Patients have ready access to health care information, via the internet especially. I am sure I am not alone in checking up what my doctor says with information available on the net. All of these changes have, as we shall see, had a significant impact on legal and ethical approaches to medicine.

1 What is medical law?

A Secretary of State for Health once said: 'The only place for a lawyer in the NHS is on the operating table'.[4] This is wishful thinking. The law has much to say about the treat-ment of those who are ill, but the definition of medical law as an academic discipline is controversial. Two leading experts in the field have suggested:

We see [medical law] as essentially concerned with the relationship between health care professionals (particularly doctors and to a lesser extent hospitals or other institutions) and patients.[5]

[1] Oakley (1980: 41).   [2] Tallis (2004).   [3] Cockerham (2001).
[4] Frank Dobson quoted in Brazier and Glover (2000).
[5] Kennedy and Grubb (2000: 5).

Others have regarded this definition as too narrow. First, in that it emphasizes doctors and does not give sufficient regard to the role of other health care professionals. Second, by focusing on the doctor–patient relationship this does not attach sufficient weight to issues surrounding the provision of health care services, such as rationing; structural issues within the NHS; or issues concerning public health.[6] And what about the crucial role played by those caring for relatives and friends at home?[7] There is no natural place to draw the boundaries between what is and is not medical law. Those sympathetic to these points sometimes prefer to talk health care law, rather than medical law. Although this book does look at these broader issues it uses the term medical law because that is still what the subject is popularly called.

Medical law is made up of bits from a large number of different branches of law: criminal law, human rights law, tort law, contract law, property law, family law and public law. One commentator has suggested a medical lawyer needs to be a 'Jacqui of all trades'.[8] Another commentator has called medical law 'an academic version of the cuckoo'.[9] Indeed until fairly recently medical law was not really studied as a subject in its own right. However, it has now been acknowledged as such.

The relationship between law and medicine is interesting. In the past it was character-ized as one of mutual deference. Medical decisions were regarded as clinical matters best reached by the experts and anyone seeking to challenge a doctor's decision in the court faced an uphill struggle. However, more recently the relationship has changed, as the quote from the Secretary of State indicates. Courts, it seems, are a little more willing to accept challenges to the decision of a doctor. As Lord Steyn recently declared: 'In Medical Law paternalism no longer rules.'[10] Doctors too, it appears, seem grateful that courts are willing to resolve cases of ethical complexity.

In no small part the relationship between doctors and lawyers has been affected by a series of scandals affecting the medical profession. As Margaret Brazier put it recently:

> There must be many days when dedicated nurses and doctors dread opening their daily newspaper, if they have the time to read a newspaper. Consider what the news may be. A nurse is convicted of murdering four of her child patients. Another nurse goes to jail for attempting to murder 'inconvenient' elderly patients whom she considered to be 'bed-blockers'. At least two gynecologists are struck off the register after a history of incredible incompetence, arrogance and appalling discourtesy to patients. General prac-titioners are convicted of sexually abusing patients over several years. Heart surgeons at Bristol are found to have continued to operate on children despite ample evidence that they were incurring higher mortality and morbidity rates than their peers elsewhere. Revelations in Bristol and Liverpool spark controversy over the widespread retention of human body parts without consent from the deceased or their families. And the Shipman Inquiry concluded that Harold Shipman murdered at least 215 of his patients. The cumulative picture of professionals who pose a danger to their patients erodes public trust.[11]

All of this has meant that doctors are no longer on the pedestal that once they were. Patients now have rights and this is reflected in the jargon used within the NHS where

---

[6] Montgomery (2003: 1).   [7] Herring (2007a).
[8] Sheldon and Thomson (1998: 5).   [9] Wicks (2007: 1).
[10] *Chester v Afshar* [2004] UKHL 41, para 16.   [11] Brazier (2005a: 12).

services are to be 'patient-led'. However, the fact that a recent Healthcare Commission report said the NHS was still centred around the needs of staff rather than patients suggests the reality is yet to match the rhetoric.[12]

The link between medical law and medical ethics[13] is also revealing.[14] It might be thought that the two would be closely connected.[15] After all the courts would be unlikely to make an order which required a health care professional to act in a way which was unethical. But that is to overlook several points. One is that something may be unethical, but not illegal.[16] To be discourteous to a patient may be unethical, but it would not necessarily be illegal. The law sets down minimally acceptable standards, while ethical approaches may include deciding what would be the ideal way for a person to behave. Similarly something may give rise to a legal sanction but not be unethical. For example, a doctor acting for a private patient may breach a contract in deciding not to treat that patient. There may be an ethical reason for this (eg that there was another patient in urgent need), but that would not necessarily justify the breach of contract in the eyes of the law. Nevertheless the courts have been willing to accept that, particularly in controversial cases where they are being asked to decide what treatment a patient should receive, ethical issues will play an important role in deciding how the court will reach a decision. Hoffman LJ, in a case concerning the treatment of a patient suffering from persistent vegetative state, stated:

> This is not an area [in] which any difference can be allowed to exist between what is legal and what is morally right. The decision of the court should be able to carry conviction with the ordinary person as being based not merely on legal precedent but also upon acceptable ethical values.[17]

However, this has proved difficult for the courts. In that same case in the House of Lords, Lord Browne-Wilkinson questioned whether complex moral issues would be better resolved in Parliament rather than the courts.[18] In *Re A (Children) (Conjoined Twins: Surgical Separation)*[19] Ward LJ, in a case concerning the separation of conjoined twins, stated:

> In this case the right answer is not at all as easy to find. I freely confess to having found it exceptionally difficult to decide—difficult because of the scale of the tragedy for the parents and the twins, difficult for the seemingly irreconcilable conflicts of moral and ethical values and difficult because the search for settled legal principle has been especially arduous and conducted under real pressure of time.

It is interesting to note the way that in some cases the ethical issues have come to dominate the courts' reasoning;[20] while others (while potentially raising moral issues) are

---

12 Healthcare Commission (2004a).
13 Some writers prefer to use the term bioethics, rather than medical ethics. The argument for doing so is that some controversial ethical issues concern practices in laboratories (eg stem cell research) rather than the practice of medicine.
14 See the stimulating discussion in Miola (2007).
15 SeeVeitch (2006) who argues that it is important to realize the power of law.
16 Ferguson (2002).
17 *Airedale NHS Trust Respondents v Bland* [1993] 1 All ER 821, 850.
18 [1989] 1 All ER 821, 878.   19 [2001] Fam 147,151.
20 See eg *Gillick v West Norfolk AHA* [1985] 3 All ER 402.

dealt with on a more traditional legal basis using principle of statutory interpretation or precedent.[21]

2 The nature of illness

It is surprisingly difficult to define illness or disease.[22] Many definitions are too broad. Consider the following suggested in one medical textbook:

> Disease is any disturbance of the structure or function of the body or any of its parts; an imbalance between the individual and his environment; a lack of perfect health.[23]

The problem with this is that it would include as a disease clipping toenails or being tied to a chair.

The difficulty is in finding a definition which is not overbroad or too narrow or too vague. Perhaps the problem lies in society itself. We ourselves do not agree about what disease is. Are baldness or infertility or hypochondria diseases? An outcry erupted when a Scottish surgeon amputated below the knee two patients suffering from apotemnophilis, described as a psychological condition involving a fixation that you are meant to be an amputee. Their doctors were concerned that without the operation the patients would hack off their own legs. Is this a proper use of medical services? Many people think not, but as Brazier and Glover note surgery to treat gender disyphoria is generally accepted, even where that involves removal of unwanted parts of the body.[24] Is penile dysfunction a medical condition for which drugs such as Viagra are medical treatments, but cosmetic surgery not?

It is clear then that social factors change what is perceived as an illness. Homosexuality was regarded as a psychological illness by the American Psychiatric Association until 1973[25] and only in recent times have dyslexia and ME been widely accepted as medical conditions. Anyone seeking to come up with a definition of disease or ill health would need to consider the following issues:

(i) Does the notion of a disease carry a judgment that the condition is undesirable?

When we use the word disease, do we include within it an assessment that the condition is one people would rather not have, or is it a neutral condition?[26] For example, would it be wrong to refer to double jointedness as a disease because it is not normally regarded as a bad thing to be double jointed? Or is disease to be used as simply a word to indicate that someone has a condition that is not 'normal' for humans, without any connotation that the condition is undesirable? But if so, would we be committed to saying that the body of a well trained athlete is diseased because it is abnormal? Although most people would think that the natural meaning of disease is that the condition is undesirable, to take that view renders defining disease much more problematic because there is little agreement within society about what conditions are undesirable.

---

[21] See eg *R (Quintavelle) v Secretary of State for Health* [2003] UKHL 13. See Montgomery (2006) for a further discussion of this.

[22] Fitzpatrick (2003) and Mackenzie and Cox (2007)

[23] Peery and Miller (1971).   [24] Brazier and Glover (2000).

[25] Hart and Wellings (2002).   [26] The issue is considered in depth in Fulford (2001).

(ii) The 'disability debate'

Some have argued that disability and disease need to be treated differently. The Union of Physically Impaired People Against Segregation has stated:

> In our view it is society which disables physically impaired people. Disability is something imposed on top of our impairments by the way we are unnecessarily isolated and excluded from full participation in society.[27]

In other words what renders disability a disadvantage is society's response to people's condition not the condition itself. There is much truth in this, but it may be said to overstate the position. Although the disadvantages of being deaf or blind, say, can be ameliorated by society's action, at root there is a harm that these people suffer that cannot be made up for, however hard society tries.[28] Putting subtitles on television programmes can ameliorate some of the disadvantages that deaf people may face in watching television, but that will never fully compensate for not being able to hear.[29]

(iii) The mind/body debate

The cause of some illness and treatments is unknown. Some people claim that certain illnesses are 'all in the head'.[30] Although this is often a comment made by those ignorant about a particular condition (eg ME or chronic fatigue syndrome) there can be an element of truth. As Kay Toombs has pointed out, when a person is diagnosed with a terminal condition their life is changed forever. Even if there are no noticeable symptoms present the person's body becomes regarded by them as diseased and a person's attitude to their body completely changes.[31] Indeed with increasing awareness of genetic make-up and genetic predisposition to certain conditions this may have increasing significance.

Linked to this issue is whether the body is seen in a mechanical way or social way. Is 'illness' or 'disease' to be regarded as essentially a malfunctioning of a machine (the body)? In that case disease will be defined in a way that requires an identified malfunction. Or is disease to be regarded in social model: not necessarily a scientific concept with a biological explanation, but the understanding by an individual and a society that a particular condition is to be judged as a disease?[32] Ian Kennedy has argued that labelling a condition an illness is a choice based on social and political judgment.[33]

(iv) Is health a negative or positive concept?

The World Health Organization has described health as 'a state of complete physical, mental and social well-being and not merely the absence of disease and infirmity'.[34] Crucially this defines health in a way which is more than the absence of illness, but in a positive way involving well-being.[35] To many this is too broad a definition. To expect medicine to limit pain is a tall order. To expect it to make people happy is an unattainable goal.

---

[27] Quoted in Fulcher and Scott (2003: 288).   [28] Harris (2001).
[29] Sheldon and Wilkinson (2001).
[30] For a useful discussion of this see Cooper (2002).
[31] Toombs (1999).   [32] See the discussion in Montgomery (2003: 2–4).
[33] Kennedy (1981: 7–8).   [34] Scully (2004).   [35] Scambler (2003c).

3 The scope of medicine

The meaning of illness leads us to a wider debate on what health care should be aiming to do. Indeed it is unclear what ultimate ideal medicine is striving to achieve.[36] Is it a life without illness or death? Would that be a life we would want? If the promotion of health is the main goal of medicine it is clear that it has a fairly small role in achieving that goal:

> The best estimates are that health services affect about 10 per cent of the usual indices for measuring health...the remaining 90 per cent are determined by factors over which doctors have little or no control: individual life-style, social conditions and physical environment.[37]

Alan Cribb[38] has written of the 'diffusion of the health agenda' with notions of the proper scope of 'medicine' expanding and becoming complex. Issues such as obesity, stress, or behaviour problems in children are now regarded as medical issues, while in the past they would not have been seen as something with which doctors or the NHS should be concerned. Defining the scope of medicine raises a number of issues:

3.1 Prevention

One question is whether medicine should be regarded as simply about dealing with illness, or whether it should cover prevention? From the point of view of the NHS vast sums of money could be saved if the public took greater care of its health, and of course most patients would rather take steps to avoid falling ill than deal with illness once it has arisen. Indeed it might be thought to be difficult to object to health prevention. However, concern has been expressed at the way that matters that might normally be regarded as private (eg individual's diets, amount of exercise, alcohol consumption) are regarded as 'health issues', and can then become transformed into public issues.[39] Is it any of a doctor's business what a patient's eating or sexual habits are?[40] This issue is discussed further in Chapter 11.

3.2 Non-diseases

One concern that is expressed by the medical profession and its critics is that an ever increasing range of problems are being regarded as requiring medical treatment. GPs complain that their assistance is being sought by patients for a range of non-diseases. The British Medical Journal carried out a survey to find which were the most common 'non-diseases' and the following 20 came out top.

(1) Ageing

(2) Work

(3) Boredom

(4) Bags under eyes

---

[36] Greaves (2002).   [37] Hunter (1997: 18).   [38] Cribb (2005: Chap 1).
[39] Miles (1991: 183).   [40] Hart and Wellings (2002).

(5) Ignorance

(6) Baldness

(7) Freckles

(8) Big ears

(9) Grey or white hair

(10) Ugliness

(11) Childbirth

(12) Allergy to the 21st Century

(13) Jet lag

(14) Unhappiness

(15) Cellulite

(16) Hangover

(17) Anxiety about penis size/penis envy

(18) Pregnancy

(19) Road rage

(20) Loneliness

Indeed doctors report a great pressure from patients to make some kind of diagnosis and offer a prescription, even where in truth there is nothing seriously wrong with the individual, or there is but there is no precise cause of the problem.[41]

Claims of over-medicalization are also made against the pharmaceutical industry.[42] An argument is sometimes made that drugs firms are particularly keen to promote the recognition of certain conditions as diseases because this will lead to a greater market for their products.[43] This is linked to wider concerns about medical research, and the impact that large drugs companies' financial support of research have on the research agenda.[44] Supporters may reply that if medicine can improve the lives of the shy, those with anxiety about penis size and so forth, why should it not do so? Whether or not these are diseases is an interesting intellectual question, but if 'treatment' is available, why should doctors not provide it?[45]

Another point that might be made here is the division between what is regarded as a disease by patient and doctor; indeed, more widely, how disease is understood and experienced differently by the medical profession and by a patient.[46]

3.3 Anti-medicine

Although at first sight a campaign to oppose medicine might seem to have as much chance of success as a campaign to ban bannoffee pie, there is more to the argument than first appears. The leading anti-medic is Ivan Illich.

There are a number of aspects to his argument. His first and most interesting point is that part of being human is to cope with illness, pain, and death. In the past societies

---

[41] Wade and Halligan (2004).   [42] Hart (1998).
[43] Moynihan, Heath, and Henry (2002) provide some fascinating examples of how the drugs industry has helped create a market for some of its products.
[44] BBC Newsonline (17 May 2005).   [45] Anon (2003a).   [46] Toombs (1999).

and individuals found a way of coping with and understanding these issues. Now that we have lost those coping strategies we seek medical treatment for every pain and illness, and death is regarded as the ultimate evil to be avoided at all costs. He argues the loss of these coping mechanisms has diminished our humanity and impoverished our society. Illich puts it like this:

> More and more people subconsciously know that they are sick and tired of their jobs and of their leisure passivities, but they want to hear the lie that physical illness relieves them of social and political responsibilities. They want their doctor to act as lawyer and priest. As a lawyer, the doctor exempts the patient from his normal duties and enables him to cash in on the insurance fund he was forced to build. As a priest, he becomes the patient's accomplice in creating the myth that he is an innocent victim of biological mechanisms rather than lazy, greedy, or envious deserter of a social struggle over the tools of production. . . .[47]

Illich also emphasizes the harm that medicine can cause. One in ten people will suffer some harm in hospital. One report suggested that 70,000 patients a year die partly as a result of 'adverse events' they suffer in hospital.[48] The scares surrounding MSRA have brought the dangers of hospital treatment to the public consciousness.

In addition, Illich makes the point, alluded to already, that medicine is ever encroaching in treating normal aspects of life as illness. Some have claimed that 'attention deficit disorder' is a condition created so that rambunctious children can be sedated and more easily controlled and the conscience of their parents appeased.[49] Claims of this kind are made in particular in relation to the treatment of mental illness, where some claim traditional medical responses have little effect.[50] Indeed Amartya Sen provides evidence that the more a society spends on health care the more are its citizens likely to regard themselves as sick.[51] The fact that there is evidence of discrimination in the provision of care to women and the aged may support claims that medical provision is driven more by market forces than an assessment of need.[52]

Others have pointed out that increasing medicalization enables moral judgments to be made on people. For example, it has been suggested that the current war on 'obesity' is often used as a thinly disguised attack on a 'collapse of moral values and family life'.[53] Attacks on individuals' way of life which would normally be regarded as inappropriate are legitimated by being labelled as 'health promotion'. A similar point might be made about responses to dramatic increases in sexually transmitted diseases.[54] Of course many others argue that educating people about the dangers of obesity and unsafe sexual behaviour, and informing them of ways of living healthier lifestyles, is not only proper but morally required. There have even been claims that obesity could bankrupt the NHS.[55] These are perhaps modern day examples of what Foucault called 'biopolitics' in his study of the way that, over history, medicine has been used by the state to justify exercising power over people and keeping surveillance over them.[56]

All of these points are important, but Illich's critics argue that at most they point to the dangers of over-medicalization rather than providing a case against all medicine.

[47] Quoted in Smith (2002b).
[48] BBC Newsonline (2 March 2001).
[49] Scully (2004).
[50] Read, Mosher, and Bentall (2004).
[51] Sen (2002).
[52] Dodds (2005).
[53] Gard and Wright (2005).
[54] Hart and Wellings (2002).
[55] BBC Newsonline (15 December 2006).
[56] Armstrong (2004).

Not to provide someone in severe pain with medical treatment and telling them to rely on their own and society's coping mechanisms is not likely to prove a popular suggestion. Indeed it is notable that although Illich is eloquent on the flaws in current medicine he has written less on what its alternatives are.[57]

4 The sociological impact of being ill

Sociologists have done much work on the concept of illness and the consequences for a person being declared 'ill' by a doctor. This, it is said, permits a person to adopt the 'sick role'.[58] They become exempt from some of the normal responsibilities of life: work, domestic chores, even politeness. But they take on responsibilities: they must follow the advice of doctors and must try to get better. Much opprobrium falls on those who do not fall into this model: eg those who go to work and do not seek medical advice, even though they are sick, or those who act as if they are sick when they are not (eg taking a 'sicky'[59] (claiming a day off work, claiming untruthfully to be ill)). This said, the 'sick role' may be culturally specific and different communities take a different approach to what is appropriate for a sick person to do.[60]

This analysis is particularly useful in relation to conditions about which there is scepticism as to whether they are 'real' illnesses or not. For example, although widely accepted as a recognized condition, some experts still dispute the diagnosis of dyslexia;[61] only recently has evidence emerged concerning the biological causes of ME (also known as Chronic Fatigue syndrome) which may assist in that condition having wider acceptance as a 'proper' illness.[62] As sufferers of these conditions will be aware, while they are regarded as 'not really diseases' questions will be raised as to whether they are simply malingerers or 'making it all up'. Once the condition is scientifically recognized then support and encouragement is more readily available.

5 Health statistics

Of course, to provide a complete picture of the nation's health would require a lengthy document, but here are some statistics to give you a flavour:

- In 2005, 59 per cent of adults said they had good health, 27 per cent reported they had fairly good health, and 14 per cent said their health was not good.[63] In 2005 14 per cent of adults and children saw an NHS GP in the 14 days before the interview.[64]

- Smoking is the single greatest cause of preventable illness and premature death: 27 per cent of men and 24 per cent of women are cigarette smokers.[65]

- The most common reasons for people claiming long-term sickness benefit is depression.[66]

- Research has suggested that by 2010 three-quarters of us will be overweight.[67]

---

[57] Moynihan (2002).   [58] Scambler (2003).   [59] BBC Newsonline (8 May 2005).
[60] Quah (2001).   [61] BBC Newsonline (2 September 2005).
[62] Action for ME (2005).   [63] National Statistics (2006)
[64] National Statistics (2006).   [65] DoH (2006c).
[66] BBC Newsonline (8 April 2005).
[67] BBC Newsonline (13 June 2005b).

- One in ten children and one in twelve adults suffer from asthma.[68]

- Hospital Accident and Emergency Departments have to deal with over one million accidents, ranging from falls (the most common cause) to the 'ignition or melting of nightwear' (22 cases per year).[69]

- Forty-two per cent of men and 26 per cent of women said they drank alcohol on at least three days a week. Forty-seven per cent of men and 30 per cent of women interviewed in a Government report had exceeded the recommended daily alcohol intake at least one day in the past week. Thirty-six per cent of male and 22 per cent of female drinkers had exceeded twice the recommended daily limit in the previous week.[70]

- The proportion of men with a medically desirable body mass index decreased from 41 per cent in 1993 to 32.2 per cent in 2005. For women the decrease was from 49.5 per cent to 40.7 per cent. The proportion of men categorized as obese increased between those dates from 13.2 per cent to 23.1 per cent; for women the increase was from 16.4 per cent to 24.8 per cent.[71]

6 General ethical principles: introduction

6.1 What is medical ethics?

The British Medical Association has defined medical ethics as 'the application of ethical reasoning to medical decision making'. This leaves unanswered the question what are ethics? As might be imagined this could be the topic of several books. It might be thought that ethics is all about finding principles that can govern a good life. Of course even that will not be agreed on by everyone. Should ethics be concerned with principles for a 'good life' or 'not a bad life'? After all there are many different views of what makes a life good.

The significance attached to medical ethics has increased for a number of reasons. One powerful influence was the discovery that during World War II Nazi doctors had carried out 'medical research' on Jewish people and others without their consent. This revealed quite clearly how horrors can be committed in the name of medicine. It was clear that trusting doctors to act professionally was not protecting patients' rights. Also, as already mentioned, the decreasing trust in the medical profession led to an increasing desire to ensure that doctors were acting ethically.

Bioethics have received contributions from a variety of disciplines: philosophers, sociologists, lawyers, theologians, economists, and anthropologists have all contributed to the writings around the topic. David Benatar[72] argues that bioethics should be regarded as a branch of philosophy and not include aspects of anthropology, sociology and the like; although the wide range of disciplines writing in this field leads to a rich variety of material, the relationship between the disciplines can be problematic, especially where there are differences in terminology and uncertainty over the role different disciplines should play within bioethics.[73] This led José Miola to describe contemporary medical ethics as 'an amorphous, incoherent and fragmented collection of discourse rather than a "structured conscience" for the medical profession'.[74]

---

[68] Asthma UK (2005).   [69] BBC Newsonline (29 March 2005).
[70] DoH (2005d).   [71] DoH (2006c).   [72] Benatar (2006a).
[73] DeVries (2004).   [74] Miola (2007: 54).

6.2 Consequentialism and deontology

An important divide among those approaching medical ethics is between those who support consequentialism and those who support deontology. We shall look at what these mean in a moment, but before doing so it is important to realize that many writers reject either of these schools of thought and seek to develop a 'third way', and there are those who seek to develop a combination of both approaches.

The basic difference between the two approaches is as follows:

- *Consequentialism.* This approach judges whether an action is ethically right or wrong by the consequences it produces. A consequentialist will say that an action is right if all things considered the consequences are good, but wrong if they are bad.

- *Deontological absolutism.* This approach holds that certain things are right or wrong regardless of the consequences.

An example which shows the difference between the approaches might be a man who is asked by a friend whether he likes an outfit she has just bought. He does not. A consequentialist would weigh up the benefits of telling the truth (she will be upset; she may lose self-confidence) with the disadvantages of not telling the truth (if she finds out he lied she may not trust him in the future). Such a balance might well lead to the conclusion he should untruthfully say he likes the dress. A deontological approach might take the line that telling the truth is an important moral principle and even if the consequences will be bad, a person should be honest.

Let us have a look at these two approaches in a little more detail:

6.2.1 Consequentialism

Consequentialism stresses that in assessing the morality of an action one must judge the consequences of it. You must weigh up all of the good and all of the bad consequences of each alternative course of action. Quite simply if one is faced with two alternative courses of action you should choose the one which has the best overall consequences. You should consider each person who may be affected and be sure not to count one person's interests as more important than another's.

The attraction of this approach is that it is 'common sense' and how most of us make decisions in day-to-day life. When faced with alternatives we naturally look at the consequences. In choosing between two flavours of yoghurt you will ask which will give me greater pleasure? Or in choosing a present for a friend: which will they enjoy more? Many people might hope it would be the approach a doctor would use in deciding which treatment to give a patient. There are, however, problems with consequentialism.

One is that consequentialism is based on deciding which result will produce the most 'good'. But what is 'good'? A popular consequentialist theory is utilitarianism. This argues that the most important good is that people be happy or have pleasure. Therefore in making ethical judgments we should ask which act will most increase the sum of human happiness? We see this in some medical cases where courts have to consider whether to permit the non-treatment of a seriously ill baby. The courts have held that it is better that the baby die than carry on living with a painful existence. But is pleasure all there is to life? What about other goods? Would we really enjoy a life which was nothing but pleasure? Would we regard a good life as one full only of pleasure?[75] Utilitarianism is

[75] Smart (1993).

not the only version of consequentialism on offer. Other forms are willing to include values such as friendship, trust and health in their calculation of what makes a consequence good or bad. The difficulty, though, is finding agreement over what is 'good' once you leave out happiness. We might, for example, take the view that what is good for a person is what that person thinks is good for them.[76] But that robs utilitarianism of some of its practical usefulness: how can I judge how to act if I do not know whether those affected will regard themselves as benefited or harmed by my actions?

Consequentialism also faces the problem of unpredictability. We often do not know what the consequences of our acts are. In such a case, can they be used as a guide as to the morality of our actions?

Another problem is: 'good' for whom? Earlier I suggested that in choosing which flavour yoghurt I should decide which I will enjoy more, but is the utilitarian calculation that straightforward? Should a consequentialist consider factors such as fair trade issues? Or the fact this is the last yoghurt of that flavour in the supermarket and there may be others who have even stronger views than me on yoghurt flavour? More seriously, when deciding about medical treatment for a patient is it just a question of what is best for this patient or for all patients in the NHS? Or indeed all patients in the world? Once we start to consider every conceivable consequence of our actions decision-making starts to become very complex.

Another problem is motivation: should utilitarians be concerned by motivations? Consider a gynaecologist who finds sexual pleasure in carrying out intimate examinations, although he does his job well. If we just focus on the consequences of his actions we may describe them as good. But many people would feel his motivations are relevant in assessing the ethics of his behaviour. Under a traditional consequentialist model his motivation would be irrelevant.

A major problem for consequentialism is that it can produce a result which many feel instinctively is wrong. Let us imagine a doctor who has four patients all in desperate need of transplant organs without which they will die. Could a doctor kill a nurse and use her organs to save the life of the patients and then argue under a consequentialist approach she had done more good than harm in killing one person to save four and hence her actions were justified? Some utilitarians feel that this is an acceptable result. To deal with concerns of this kind, some utilitarians have developed a version of utilitarianism known as 'rule utilitarianism'.

Rule utilitarianism suggests we should adopt the set of rules which govern how we act which will, if followed, produce the best outcome. Rule consequentialism asks 'Which general rules will promote the best consequences in the long term, assuming that everyone accepts and complies with them?'[77] So, even if in the particular case following the rule will not produce the best outcome, if having the strict rule produces overall the best for society we should adopt it. For example, it might be said that doctors should keep confidential information given to them by patients. Even though there may be individual cases where it would produce a better outcome to make that information public, the rule of medical confidentiality produces generally good outcomes, in enabling people to be frank with their medical advisers. Although rule utilitarianism is popular it has difficulties. It is problematic for an individual seeking guidance on what to do in her particular situation. Working out the consequences of alternative courses of action as required for 'act utilitarianism' is difficult enough; attempting to work out what general

---

[76] Singer (1994).   [77] Glennon (2005: 10).

rule to apply in cases of this kind would be very complex. Further, there is the issue of whether within 'rule utilitarianism' the rules have exceptions and if so how these exceptions are to be calculated.[78]

6.2.2 Deontology

A deontological theory holds that certain kinds of actions are good, not because of the consequences they produce, but because they are good and right in themselves. We should tell the truth not because that makes people happy or gives them pleasure, but because truth-telling is the right thing to do. We have a duty to tell the truth. Immanuel Kant is widely regarded as a leading exponent of this thinking. He regarded as a key maxim that no one should be treated merely as a means to an end. A person should not be used merely to help others. We should not therefore use someone in a human research project without their consent, even if using them will produce all kinds of good (eg finding a cure for a terrible illness). Deontologists are keen to point out that some of the atrocities carried out in the name of medicine (eg research by Nazi doctors on non-consenting people) have been justified in the name of utilitarianism. Deontology could never justify such actions.

Key to deontological theories is the principle that you cannot justify the breach of a deontological principle just by referring to the consequences. It is not permissible to kill an innocent person, even if by doing so you save four lives. Some deontologists will say that all or some deontological principles are absolute: that there are no circumstances in which a deontological principle can be breached. For example, under the European Convention on Human Rights (ECHR) torture can never be justified. Others will accept that if there are overwhelmingly good consequences a breach may be justified. So although you should not normally torture someone, if they have placed a bomb in central London it might be appropriate to torture them to find out where it was and thereby save many lives. Deontologists can also claim to have the benefit of clarity. However complex the issue may appear, if there is a clear deontological principle (eg you must not treat a patient without her or his consent) then this provides the guidance without the need to look further.

Deontologists often place much weight on duties. They emphasize that the duties parents owe to their children, or physicians to their patients, are overlooked in utilitarian approaches. When making a decision about your children you must take into account the duties you owe them, not just the consequences for all children. If three people are in danger in a fire parents are expected to rescue their own child first, even if that means the other two are likely to perish.

An issue over which there is much disagreement is how we decide what the principles are. To those with religious beliefs the principles of good or bad behaviour come from God. Others claim that there are things which are naturally right or wrong and which require no justification as such. They may point out, for example, in every society incest is regarded as wrong. Even though there may be no consequentialist justification for this, it seems to be part of human nature to recognise the wrongness of incest. Some claim that there are goods that are 'self-evident': truth, knowledge, friendship, for example. Others have sought to appeal to some form of 'social contract' under which every member of society can be taken to have agreed to abide by certain principles.

---

[78] Hence Lyons (1965) argues that rule utilitarianism becomes, in effect, act utilitarianism.

Key to Kant's version of deontology is the notion of personhood. A moral person must construct their own moral law which will guide their action. Hence his famous prohibition against treating people as a means to an end and not an end in themselves. You should not treat someone in a way which is contrary to their wishes. Some have suggested that this is reflected in the principle that you should treat others as you would like to be treated yourself.[79]

Deontology is seen as an important response to consequentialism. It avoids the unpleasant consequences that consequentialism might be thought to justify, such as permitting a doctor to kill a nurse and use her organs to save the lives of four patients. That would not be permitted in deontological thinking because the doctor would be using the nurse as a means to an end. The thinking also fits in well with many current concepts of human rights, although Kant placed far more emphasis on obligations than on rights. Indeed there is a division amongst deontologists between those who would emphasize rights and those who emphasize obligations.[80]

The difficulties facing deontologists particularly relate to how we define the most important obligation. If two moral people profoundly disagree about what the rights or obligations require, how can they resolve this debate? Consequentialists can debate with each other about the benefits and disadvantages of acting in a certain way, but there seems no way forward for disputing deontologists. Further, as already indicated above, there is dispute over whether deontological principles are absolute, and if they are not in what circumstances they may be infringed. One solution to this dilemma is to try to locate within society an acceptance of how moral principles should be ranked. But in an increasingly multi-religious, multi-cultural society this becomes increasingly difficult.

6.2.3 *Mixing consequentialism and deontology*

The distinction between consequentialism and deontology, although important and useful, is not as clear cut as may at first appear. Deontologists often accept that consequentialism is an appropriate approach where there is no absolute principle to apply. Further, there is much debate over how we decide which principles should be deontological absolutes. One possibility is to adopt those that will produce the best society. For example, we might decide that people should always keep their promises because a truthful society is better than one in which lies are told. But this uses consequentialist reasoning to decide what the deontological absolutes are. Deontological theories may also face difficulties where two principles clash, and then some will turn to consequentialist reasoning to decide which principle to follow.

Consequentialists are not immune from seeking to use deontological approaches too. They may hold on to a principle such as the sanctity of life and claim that even if it appears that there would be more good than harm from killing this individual, the impact on society as a whole, over time, of not respecting the sanctity of life will be to society's detriment. Peter Singer, a leading consequentialist, has argued that we should start with 'utilitarianism' as a 'first base'. Only if there are good reasons should we be persuaded to accept any 'non-utilitarian morals rules or ideals'.

Doug Morrison[81] has complained that in the context of medical ethics neither consequentialism nor deontology appear appropriate. Consequentialism appears to place too little weight on the right of autonomy, and would permit a doctor to carry out treatment

---

[79] Morrison (2005).   [80] Morrison (2005).   [81] Morrison (2005).

on a patient without their consent if the overall consequences of the treatment were beneficial. On the other hand deontology, by regarding as irrelevant the consequences of actions, ignores the importance medical practice inevitably places on the consequences of alternative forms of medical treatment. Morrison promotes a hybrid approach which involves both looking at the consequence of the action and the rights and duties of those involved, and strikes an appropriate balance between them.

To many, especially those of a philosophical bent, this attempt to 'have one's cake and eat it' is unacceptable. Consequentialism and deontology are two very different approaches to a problem and in difficult cases lead to dramatically different approaches. Taking both perspectives into account will do nothing to assist the medical professional in the most complex cases where clear guidance is needed.

6.3 The role of intuition in medical ethics

What role should intuition play in medical ethics? As we shall see in Chapter 6 a respectable philosophical case can be made for arguing that someone only becomes a person and therefore entitled to human rights when they are several months old. This argument is used to justify abortion, but it would also justify the killing of newborn babies. To many this consequence is so revolting that intuitively it must be rejected. However logical and clear the argumentation, 'our hearts' tell us that 'our heads' have got something wrong. Many react in this way to human cloning or the creation of human–animal hybrids; even though it is not possible to explain why, it just feels wrong. But is it legitimate to rely on this kind of intuitive reasoning? Or should medical ethicists only be considering rational arguments?

The BMA has suggested that conscience and intuition can be useful components of ethical guidance, even if dangerous when used alone.[82] In practice a doctor required to make an urgent ethical decision is likely to rule on her or his intuition and it may be argued that this is right. Indeed ethical guidance issued to medical professionals which goes against the dictates of their conscience is unlikely to be respected or effective.[83] As one of the BMA's ethical advisers put it:

> Doctors also want guidance that seems to them to be intuitively correct and consistent with what they understand to be the core purposes of medicine. Moral justifications for various actions are rehearsed but practical solutions sometimes arise quite unexpectedly from intuition or a doctor's hunch that an improbable solution could work, rather than solely from rational analysis.[84]

Others are more sceptical about encouraging doctors to rely on intuition. Indeed some of the recent scandals, for example those involving the retention of the body parts of children, involved medical professionals acting in a way which doctors felt was entirely proper, but was regarded as unacceptable by the general public.

6.4 Universalism

A common theme among ethical thinking is universalism. This means that ethical principles should apply to everyone. The point is that when you claim an ethical principle you are not saying 'this is a principle which seems to work well for me in my life', but

---

[82] Sommerville (2003).   [83] Fulford (2005).   [84] Sommerville (2003: 282).

making a wider claim about principles which should govern everyone's life.[85] This is not to say it must be a principle everyone in the world agrees with, but it is a principle which is not based on your own personal likes or dislikes.

6.5 Practical ethics

Many bioethicists believe that ethical approaches to medicine must be practical. They must develop ways of reaching decisions about complex issues which can be used by medical professionals. A method of approach to ethical issues which is so complex that it can only be understood by a small group of fellow ethicists, and is too sophisticated to be of use 'on the wards', may be seen as of limited use. This in part explains the popularity of principlism (which we shall discuss shortly), with its four key principles which the BMA, for example, says can be easily used by medical professionals working in the field.[86]

There are other points about practicality. It is arguable that medical ethics must reflect the moral values which are regarded as generally acceptable amongst health care professionals and indeed society as a whole. Seeking to impose an ethical code on health care professionals which they would regard as requiring them to act immorally, or to act in a way which society would treat with repugnance, is unlikely to be acceptable or practically used.[87] This might explain why, although ethicists fiercely disagree on how to approach ethical issues, there are in fact relatively few cases where there is genuine disagreement on what should be done. Where there are such issues the debate is fierce, but it should never be forgotten that, in the vast majority of interactions between a patient and medical professional, the ethically appropriate course of action will be agreed by nearly everyone.

6.6 What can we expect from medical ethics?

There is some debate among medical ethicists about what we can expect from medical ethics. Some are highly sceptical of any claim that someone is an expert in medical ethics. What makes a person an expert on whether an embryo has a right to life? Or whether the sale of organs is ethical? While we may be willing to accept that some people are experts in their knowledge of facts, can anyone claim to have expertise on ethics? While many of us would be willing to accept that a professor in physics would have a better chance than us in calculating the speed of light, would we agree that a professor in bioethics is more likely than us to know whether euthanasia is morally acceptable or not? Anne Maclean, critical of the writing of philosophers claiming to provide the 'correct answer' to morally controversial issues, writes:

> [P]hilosophy as such delivers no verdict upon moral issues; there is no unique set of moral principles which philosophy as such underwrites and no question, therefore, of using that set to uncover the answers which philosophy gives to moral questions. When bioethicists deliver a verdict upon the moral issues raised by medical practice, it is their own verdict they deliver and not the verdict of philosophy itself; it is their voice we hear and not the voice of reason or rationality.[88]

---

[85] Singer (1979: 10).   [86] Sommerville (2003).
[87] Sommerville (2003).   [88] Maclean (1995: 5).

This scepticism may reveal a misunderstanding of how many medical ethicists would understand their role. They would argue it is not to provide the right answer but to assist in clear thinking: to set out arguments which are logically coherent and consistent with the facts and to point out logical or philosophical flaws in the arguments of others. So although the ethicist may not have greater claim to producing the right answer, she or he might claim to have a better chance of producing a logically and morally coherent one. While therefore it might be unreasonable to turn to medical ethicists to produce the 'correct' answer, it may be reasonable to expect assistance in thinking through the issues with sensitivity, logic, and clear-headedness. John Harris has, for example, been sceptical of relying on polls of members of the public to ascertain the correct response to controversial issues. He argues most people are ignorant of the facts and do not think out their arguments coherently. A good ethicist is therefore more likely to reach the correct answer than the person in the street. But is that simply intellectual snobbery?

These debates create a particular problem for medical law. Is the law to be based on ethical principles? If so whose ethical principles should be followed—those of the majority of the population, or those of the best medical ethicist in the land? Jonathan Montgomery, in a sensitive discussion of these issues, talks of the problem of the legitimacy of medical law. He concludes:

> The key to the legitimacy problem in the modern context is to see medical law as a tool to ensure the recognition that its subject matter is morally charged and to protect the ability of individuals to grapple with the ethical issues that arise. It maintains the preconditions for moral agency. To impose a particular moral position will usually be to deny people who think differently the possibility of working through their own ethical responsibilities. It would consequently foster the view that the questions were not ethical so much as a matter of compliance with societal requirements. Medical law needs to make clear that its protagonists are morally accountable for their decisions and not merely following rules set down by others. In that sense the legitimacy of medical law lies in its attempt to preserve the possibility of morality, not to enforce a particular version of the 'good'.[89]

6.7 Bioethics 'as entertainment'

An uncomfortable claim that can be legitimately levelled against Western bioethics is that, in focusing on the intellectually interesting issues surrounding abortion, euthanasia, and cutting edge technologies, the really important issues concerning health have received no coverage. As Leigh Turner puts it:

> Many of the questions that bioethicists address only make sense within the context of wealthy developed nations. Some of the favourite topics of bioethicists seem trivial compared with the important health issues facing people in the world's poor countries and in impoverished regions in rich countries.[90]

One response is that the issues concerning world poverty are simply too large to be discussed in the context of a course on medical law or ethics. But even looking within the UK, it is arguable that bioethicists' focus has been narrow: much is written on how to appropriately ration limited medical resources, but little on why there are only limited

---

[89] Montgomery (2006b: 14).   [90] Turner (2004: 175).

resources available; much on the importance of autonomy, but little on the illiteracy and lack of education that makes autonomy a problematic concept on the ground.[91]

7 The notion of rights

Much of the legal thinking and writing in medical law is now put in terms of rights.[92] This is partly because of the impact of the Human Rights Act 1998, but also reflects the power of patient's rights to challenge the paternalism of the medical profession which has been so prevalent until fairly recently.[93] A rights based approach focuses on the interests of the individual and is designed to protect the individual from improper claims that harming them is justified in the interests of society or the interests of others. As we have seen, utilitarianism can be criticized for permitting one person to be seriously harmed if it can be said that the benefits outweigh the costs. A rights based approach seeks to prevent this happening, or at least put limits on when it can happen. The use of human rights talk is, however, not without difficulty. A number of general points about the nature of rights need to be made first.

7.1 Absolute v conditional rights

An absolute right is one that cannot be infringed, whatever the circumstances. As already mentioned, the ECHR article 3 states that there is an absolute right not to suffer torture. Other rights in the ECHR are conditional in that there are circumstances in which the right can be infringed. Under article 8, for example, there is a right to respect for one's private life, but that can be interfered with under paragraph 2 if necessary in the interests of others.

7.2 Rights and obligations

A hotly disputed issue in jurisprudence is whether it is possible to have a right without an obligation; in other words whether one can claim a right to X, without someone else being under an obligation to supply X. If the two are inevitably linked then any right to a 'right to health care' must be matched by a clear statement as to who has the obligation to supply that 'health care'.

7.3 Positive and negative rights

Traditionally human rights have focused more on negative rights (prohibiting people acting in a certain way towards you) than on positive rights (requiring people to act in certain ways towards you). So, although the negative right not to have treatment given to you which you do not want is a strongly protected right, the positive right to receive treatment which you do want is protected to a far less extent, if at all. Derek Morgan has argued that in the context of a socialized medical system, positive rights must be treated

---

[91] Koch (2003).
[92] Wicks (2007). Although see Benatar (2006a) who discusses the dangers of seeing all medical issues in terms of rights and duties.
[93] Garwood-Gowers and Tingle (2001).

with much caution because respecting the positive rights of one person is likely to interfere with the rights of another.[94] As Lord Walker has put it:

> There is no general human right to good physical and mental health any more than there
> is a human right to expect (rather than to pursue) happiness.[95]

7.4 What rights are relevant in medical law?

As we go through the book various rights will be explained, but here we will mention a
few of the most important.

(i) The right of autonomy

The right of autonomy plays a huge role in medical law writing and indeed in court
judgments. In essence the right of autonomy is the right to decide what medical treatment you receive. To be honest talk of the 'right to autonomy' is misleading. As already
indicated, whilst your decision about not receiving treatment is strongly protected in
the law, your decision as to what treatment you would like need not be followed. It may,
therefore, be more accurate to describe this as the right to bodily integrity, rather than
the right to autonomy.

(ii) The right to dignity

As Roger Brownsword[96] has usefully noted that the notion of 'dignity' is used by different people writing in this area in disparate ways. He distinguishes the use of human
dignity as empowerment and as a constraint. Dignity as empowerment sees human dignity as a powerful source of rights. It requires the respecting of individual's choices and
empowering them to live an autonomous life.

Dignity as constraint is less straightforward. Brownsword suggests that the notion
appeals to a coalition of Kantians, Catholics, and communitarians. This view rejects the
argument that respecting an individual's autonomy is necessary to respect their dignity.

Respecting a person's dignity requires more than respecting their choices. Holders of
the view of dignity as constraint might therefore argue that an individual should not be
able to sell their organs because to do so is to demean their dignity as humans. Similarly
allowing couples and researchers to clone humans would contradict human dignity.
Dignity here is talking about what a community or society regards as special about
individuals. Brownsword uses an example of a French case[97] which concerned a police
order prohibiting a 'dwarf-throwing' competition, which involved, as the title suggests,
a 'game' involving participants throwing people of restricted growth. Although all
involved were consenting to the game, and it might therefore be said to be an infringement of their autonomy and therefore dignity not to allow them to perform, it could
also be argued that the 'game' dehumanized the participant and did not respect their
humanity and their dignity.

(iii) The right to life

The right to life for many people is the key human right which must trump all others.
However, there is great debate over the meaning of life and what it means to respect the

---

94 Morgan (2001: chapter 1).
95 R (Razgar) v Secretary of State for the Home Department [2004] UKHL 27, para 34.
96 Brownsword (2003a).
97 Ville d'Aix-en-Provence, 1996 Dalloz 177 (Conseil d'Etat) req. nos. 143–578.

right to life. These issues particularly come to a head in the context of euthanasia and abortion and we will be considering them in Chapters 6 and 9.

EUROPEAN ANGLES

Claims that patients have rights have been strengthened since the passing of the Human Rights Act 1998. This protects individuals' rights under the ECHR. That convention sets out the minimum standards of treatment under the law that people are entitled to expect. There are two important aspects of the Human Rights Act. First, the rights in the Act (which are essentially the rights protected in the European Convention on Human Rights) are directly enforceable against public authorities (eg local authorities) and all public authorities must act in a way that is compatible with these rights unless required to do so by other legislation.[98] The court is a public authority and hence it is generally thought that no court order should infringe an individual's rights as defined in the Human Rights Act, unless compelled to do so by other legislation. Secondly, under section 3 of the Human Rights Act all legislation is to be interpreted, if at all possible, in line with Convention rights. If it is not possible to interpret the legislation in accordance with these rights, then the legislation should be enforced as it stands and a declaration of incompatibility issued: this requires Parliament to confirm or amend the offending legislation. In interpreting the extent of the rights protected in the Human Rights Act, the decisions of the European Court of Human Rights and European Commission will be taken into account by the courts. The possible relevance of rights under the Act will be considered at the relevant points throughout this book.

Patients can also claims rights directly under European law against the State or public bodies. These include rights emanating from the European Treaty.[99] Again we will be considering these at various points throughout this book.

8 Patients' obligations

Much has been written on patients' rights; rather less on patients' duties.[100] The issue of patients' duties arises in a number of contexts. In Chapter 2 when we consider medical rationing we will consider an argument that where limited resources are available a patient who is responsible for their medical condition or has failed to act responsibly in relation to it should be disadvantaged in rationing decisions. Another context is whether infected people have a moral obligation not to infect others.[101] One controversial issue is whether someone who is HIV positive but has unprotected sexual relations with another and as a result infects them should be liable under the criminal law.[102]

Concern that the 'rights of patients' have become too dominant can even be found among the judiciary. Kay J in *R v Collins and Ashworth HA ex p Brady* stated:

> . . . it would seem to me a matter of deep regret if the law has developed to a point in this area where the rights of patients count for everything and other ethical values and institutional integrity count for nothing.[103]

---

[98] Human Rights Act 1998, s 6.

[99] The UK has not signed the European Convention on Human Rights and Biomedicine.

[100] Brazier (2006); Iltis and Rasmussen (2005) and Buetow and Elwyn (2006).

[101] See the discussion in Harris and Holm (1995).

[102] See the discussion in eg Weait (2007).   [103] [2000] Lloyds Rep Med 355.

Of course, there will be many who are convinced that we still have a long way to go if we are to properly protect patient's rights.

9 Principlism

One of the most influential approaches to bioethics is known as Principlism. It is known as this because it is based on a set of principles which can be applied to any bioethical issue. The most influential book advocating this is *Principles of Biomedical Ethics* by Tom Beauchamp and James Childress.[104] This book has formed the basis of much teaching on medical ethics and is widely respected and used within the medical profession. A leading ethicist has even suggested Beauchamp and Childress be given a Nobel prize for their work![105]

They advocate an approach which is based on four principles:

- Respect for Autonomy
- Non-malfeasance
- Beneficence
- Justice

We shall be examining the exact meaning of these terms shortly.

Beauchamp and Childress argue that these four principles represent a 'common morality':[106] principles which are respected within societies generally around the world. They argue that the best way to approach ethical problems is to apply each of these principles to it and if they recommend different courses of action to weigh up the different principles. Although they regard all four principles as of equal value it is clear that a special place is held for autonomy. Indeed Raamon Gillon, a leading supporter in the UK of Beauchamp and Childress's work, has argued that autonomy is the 'first among equals'.[107] It might be considered that in many cases these principles will conflict, but Beauchamp and Childress believe that once the principles are precisely defined and specified then the degree of conflict is far less than may be thought. But where there is a conflict principlism offers no ready solution to how they should be resolved. As Beauchamp and Childress emphasize they are presenting a framework for identifying the moral issues, rather than providing the answer.[108]

Principlism is regarded as having a number of benefits. First it provides an accessible and usable approach. Medical professionals can use it in a practical context. It provides a coherent way to address problems in which most of the important issues are likely to be raised. Indeed supporters claim that all the relevant ethical issues will be raised by a proper consideration of the four principles.[109] Second, it is claimed that these principles are culturally neutral and could be accepted worldwide because they are not based on a particular religious faith or cultural norm. Thirdly the use of the four principles ensures a degree of consistency, in that all cases will be approached in the same way when it comes to balancing the different principles. Fourth, its supporters see it as a strong counter to moral relativism, a view that there are no right or wrong answers to ethical

---

[104] Beauchamp and Childress (2003).   [105] Gillon (2003).
[106] Beauchamp and Childress (2003: 5).
[107] Gillon (2003). For a strong rejection of this view see Dawson and Garrard (2006).
[108] Beauchamp and Childress (2003: 15).   [109] Gillon (2003).

issues. The four principles are those that principlists believe everyone can agree with. Fifthly, the approach is flexible enough to enable ethicists coming from a wide range of perspectives to use it. Even if they might disagree with the balancing of the different principles they are able to agree on the basic approach to these issues.

It is time to look in more detail at the four principles promoted by Beauchamp and Childress:

9.1 Autonomy

We shall be looking at the principle of autonomy in depth in Chapter 4. Here we will consider some of the main issues concerning it.

Autonomy has become the premier principle in medical ethics. To many commentators it should be regarded as the primary medical principle. It is never right for a doctor to impose treatment upon a patient treatment without the patient's consent, unless necessary to prevent harm to others. The whole notion of autonomy, the right to decide how we wish to live our lives, is seen as a fundamental aspect of our humanity. To respect autonomy is to accept a person who has a right to hold views, make choices, and take actions based on personal values and beliefs. To override a person's wishes is to treat that person as a means to reach other people's ends. The decision of a Jehovah's Witness who refuses a blood transfusion, even though without it she or he will die, must be respected. An individual doctor may believe their decision to be utter folly, but the decision is for them and them alone.

Beauchamp and Childress explain the principle in this way:

> To respect an autonomous agent, is at a minimum to acknowledge that person's right to hold views, to make choices, and to take actions based on personal values and beliefs. Such respect involves respectful action, not merely a respectful attitude.... Respect, on this account involves acknowledging decision-making rights and enabling people to act autonomously, whereas disrespect for autonomy involves attitudes and actions that ignore, insult, or demean others' rights of autonomy.[110]

In fact the so-called 'right to autonomy' is perhaps mislabelled in the medical context. A patient does not have a right to decide which medical treatment she or he will be given. A patient has no right to demand that she or he be given cosmetic surgery. A health care professional may refuse because she or he does not want to provide the treatment or because rationing of health care resources means it is not available. What is really being claimed here is a right of 'bodily integrity': a right not to have something done to your body without your consent.

Autonomy does not require the respect of every choice, but only of choices which are competent. A young child's refusal to receive an injection can, therefore, be overridden if she or he is not able to understand the issues. Similarly the refusal to consent to treatment of a person suffering from such severe mental illnesses that they are incompetent can be overridden. But care must be taken with competence. It must not be thought that because a person's decision is foolish that the person is therefore incompetent.

The importance attached to autonomy has grown in recent years. In part this reflects the growth of rights. We no longer regard ourselves as subjects of a higher authority, but as individuals with rights. In the medical sphere doctors are no longer held in

---

[110] Beauchamp and Childress (2003: 63).

unquestioning respect and reverence. Trust that 'doctor knows best' has weakened.[111] The scandals affecting the medical professions already mentioned and the increase in knowledge about medical matters the lay person has, or can acquire, has also led to rejection of the view that a patient should simply lie back and accept whatever the doctor recommends.

As we shall see in Chapter 4, not everyone approves of the weight which has become attached to autonomy, and others have proposed alternatives to the traditional under-standing of autonomy.

9.2 The principle of non-malfeasance

At its core the principle of non-malfeasance asserts that one person should not cause harm to others. For medical professionals there is the well-established principle: *Primum non nocere*, above all do no harm. The Hippocratic oath states: 'I will use treatment to help the sick according to my ability and judgment, but I will never use it to injure or wrong them.'[112] As Beauchamp and Childress put it: 'The principle of non-malfeasance asserts an obligation not to inflict harm on others.'[113]

The importance of this principle is that it urges against harming one patient to help another. This point can be demonstrated by an American case: *McFall v Shimp*.[114] McFall needed a bone marrow transplant to improve his chances of survival from a serious med-ical condition. McFall's cousin, Shimp, was found to be compatible for donation. Shimp, having initially indicated that he would be willing to donate bone marrow, changed his mind and decided against it. McFall sought an order that Shimp had to donate. The court refused. The decision could be seen as support for the principle of non-malfeasance. It would be wrong to harm Shimp by taking the bone marrow without his consent, even thought it would be being done for a good motive: saving McFall's life.

Notice, however, that this principle would not be infringed if Shimp had consented to the bone marrow transplant. Although he would have suffered a harm in a sense (there would be physical pain involved in the donation), because he consented to it, it would not be seen as a wrong against him. So what counts as harm is determined by the individual concerned. This then forms a strong link to the idea of autonomy. Where the patient consents to the treatment and the doctor provides it the non-malfeasance prin-ciple is not infringed.

But it must be questioned whether this last point is always true. If a patient asks a doc-tor to provide treatment which is manifestly harmful to the patient (eg remove a limb when there is no medical reason for doing so), can a doctor rely on the principle of non-malfeasance to refuse to perform the treatment? Some commentators believe that under the principle 'harm' must not always be given the meaning the patient would give it, particularly where the patient's views as to harm are out of line with generally accepted norms in society.

Beauchamp and Childress suggest that there are limits to the principle of non-malfea-sance and that if a harm done to one person is very minor and it is done to save another's life then that may be justifiable.[115] However, those who take a strict line on autonomy would not be willing to even make this concession.

---

[111] O'Neill (2002).

[113] Beauchamp and Childress (2003: 113).

[115] Beauchamp and Childress (2003: 119).

[112] Beauchamp and Childress (2003: 113).

[114] Pa. D. & C. 3d90 (1978).

9.3 The principle of beneficence

This is the principle that medical professionals must do good for their patients. They must cure any disease or injury where possible and avoid the infliction of pain where possible. As the Hippocratic oath puts it: the physician promises to 'follow that system of regime which according to my ability and judgment I consider for the benefit of my patient'.

It may be that doctors are under a special duty to put the interests of patients above even their own interests and that is of a higher level than that imposed on individuals in other professions.[116] Others, however, point out that in many professions professionals are expected to put their clients' interests first, even if that involves self-sacrifice.[117] Why, even lawyers have been known to leave their beds to attend clients detained in police cells in the middle of the night. So whether the principle of beneficence here is a special obligation for doctors or one that is found in many other situations is a matter for debate.

The principle of beneficence is not unproblematic. Simply stated it might suggest a paternalistic approach: the doctor decides what is best and provides that for the patient. However, many commentators argue that in deciding what is best for the patient the health care professional should take the competent patient's views as to what is best for him or herself. So a doctor who does not impose treatment on a Jehovah's Witness who is refusing to consent to a life-saving blood transfusion can be said to be complying with the principle, because she or he is acting in the best way for the patient, as the patient understands that to be.

This principle focuses on the positive ethical obligations owed in the medical context. We have already discussed the principle of non-malfeasance which requires us not to harm others. The principle of beneficence deals with when we are required positively to help others. It must be stated straight away that in general the law rarely requires one person to do something to assist another.[118] There is much in the general law which prohibits one person harming another, and providing sanctions where such harm is caused; but rarely is one person compelled to provide benefits to another. Society may want and even encourage people to assist others, but generally it does not compel them to do so. But in ethics, the principle of seeking to benefit others, or at least doing an act which causes greater good than harm is one that is central to many people's ethical thinking. In short, then, the principle of beneficence is an important one in ethical thought, but is rarely a legally enforced one.

9.4 Justice

The meaning of justice is contested. It is often expressed in terms of what is fair, equitable, or reasonable. In the context of health care, justice becomes particularly significant in the area of allocation of resources. Where there are not enough funds to be able to provide everyone with the health care they would like, we need a just way of deciding who should be treated and how. We shall be looking at this issue in Chapter 2.

At the heart of most theories of justice is the principle of formal equality: all equals should be treated equally and unequals should be treated unequally. The principle, so baldly stated, is perhaps uncontroversial. Its application causes the difficulties: how do we know if two people are equal? How do we know if treatment is equal?

---

[116] Gillon (1985: 73).   [117] Downie (1988).   [118] Foot (1976).

Another aspect of justice that is relevant to health care is whether there is equal access to medical treatment. There are concerns that certain sections of the community find it difficult to access certain forms of treatment.[119] Also, when considering issues of public health it is apparent that those in lower socio-economic groups and certain ethnic groups suffer worse health than those in higher ones.[120] This raises important questions about the justice of health.

9.5 Critics of principlism

It may be fair to say that the most vehement criticism against principlism is not levelled at the approach as it is developed to a high degree of sophistication by Beauchamp and Childress in their book, but at the way it has been used and developed in practice. A simplistic understanding of the principles and applying them in a naïve way can lead to simplistic lines of thought.[121] The approach is also open to misuse because stated baldly the principles are open to a wide variety of meanings. Although in their book they provide much guidance as to the meaning of the terms involved, it is arguable then in a summary form that the notion of beneficence, for example, can mean pretty much whatever you want it to.[122]

To some the principles are simply liable to lead to contradiction. The principle of doing one's best for one's patient (beneficence and non-malfeasance) are simply antithetical to autonomy and justice. Autonomy only means something when the wishes of the patient are not in line with what the doctor wishes to do, but then the clash between the principles is set up. As we have seen this need not be so. If beneficence is understood in terms of how the patient regards their best treatment, the potential conflict is lessened. However, that approach leads to a danger that malfeasance and beneficence lose any meaning. If harm or benefit to a patient is to be determined by the patient then the concepts become the same as autonomy.

Another objection is the lack of a clearer way of balancing the principles when they do clash. The difficulty for Beauchamp and Childress is that if they do indicate that in the event of a clash one particular principle trumps the others, this would undermine their claim that the four principles are of equal value. But critics argue that there is a need for a unifying moral theory to justify these four principles and which would then provide a way of reconciling them in the event of a clash. This leads some critics to argue that autonomy should be recognized as the primary principle. In fact Beauchamp and Childress do give some guidance for cases where it is necessary to infringe one principle in order to abide by another. They argue that this is only justifiable where the moral objective sought is realistic; no morally preferable alternative is available; the infringement is the least possible and the health care professional must act to minimize the effects of the infringement. Further we should remember that Beauchamp and Childress do not claim that principlism provides answers, rather it provides an effective way of approaching an issue.[123] But this then leads some commentators to argue there is simply not enough in the Beauchamp and Childress approach to deal with genuinely difficult cases.[124] Callahan, however, has argued that the way principlism is in fact used,

[119] Higgs (2003).   [120] Scambler and Blane (2003) and Hillier (2003).
[121] Campbell (2005).   [122] Clouser and Gert (1990).
[123] Beauchamp (1995).   [124] Holm (1995).

autonomy ends up winning in any conflict between the principles—and that renders it objectionable to those who are concerned by an overemphasis on autonomy.[125]

A final objection is that using the four principles is simply too narrow. John Harris suggests it causes 'sterility and uniformity of approach of a quite mindbogglingly boring kind'.[126] Although he accepts that reference to the four principles would be a useful 'checklist' in ethical discussion, they must not be regarded as the final word, and that there are a host of other issues and arguments that must be considered, even though they do not fit within the four principles approach. Supporters of principlism claim that any relevant ethical argument can be made in the context of one of the four principles. Even if this is true Harris's point may be that squeezing arguments into one of the four boxes confines them and may be artificial. An argument must be analysed and considered for what it is, rather than seeking to pigeon hole it into one of the four principles.[127]

10 Hermeneutics

The hermeneutic process is based on listening.[128] Where there is disagreement between a patient and a medical professional about a course of treatment it encourages those involved to talk to each other and listen to the 'stories' each have to tell.[129] The aim is that by listening to each other the parties can begin to work out for themselves the ethical problems and produce a shared understanding of the situation. In colloquial terms each party can find out where the other is 'coming from'. This is not, then, an approach to ethics which suggests there are right answers or even general principles to apply, but rather that the solution is the one which is right for the people involved.

To many this is idealistic. Not only is there rarely enough time to engage in this kind of dialogue, it is also only effective where all parties are willing to engage in the process. If there is a belligerent patient then the approach has nothing to offer. Further, where no solution can be found the approach offers no resolution.[130] It may be that in a few cases it will enable the parties to develop a solution which is nuanced to respond to the special features of the problems as perceived by the parties.

11 Casuistry

Casuistry emphasizes that each case has its own unique circumstances and facts. Rather than starting with grand principles and applying them to the case at hand (as principlism does), casuists argue we should start with the facts of the particular case and seek to find a resolution by comparing or contrasting other cases.[131] Lawyers will have some familiarity with this because this is similar to the doctrine of precedent used in the common law. Lawyers tend to argue about whether the case at hand is similar to or distinct from earlier cases in which the law has been set down, rather than working from broad principles. The building blocks of the casuist approach are cases on which there would be a

---

125 Callahan (2003).   126 Harris (2003c).
127 See further Downie and Macnaughton (2007: chap 1).
128 Boyd (2005).   129 Boyd (2005); Hudson Jones (1999).
130 Beauchamp (2004).
131 Jones (1986). See also the dispute between Lawlor (2007) and Benatar (2007) over whether studying general ethical theories is useful in teaching medical ethics.

high degree of agreement among people as to the correct approach. Casuists emphasize that principles cannot be found or established outside the context of a particular factual situation.

12 Feminist medical ethics

No account of medical ethics would be complete without a consideration of feminist approaches to the question of medical ethics.[132] It would be wrong to think there is 'one' feminist approach to medical ethics[133] and indeed there is fierce debate among feminists on some of the issues. It would also be wrong to see feminist ethics as simply looking at medical law with a single issue in mind.[134] What makes an approach feminist? Susan Wolf suggests that:

> feminist work takes gender and sex as centrally important analytic categories, seeks to understand their operation in the world, and strives to change the distribution and use of power to stop the oppression of women.[135]

Much work has been done to argue that medicine has become a way of controlling and exercising power over women.[136] For example, the 'medicalization of childbirth', it has been claimed, has led to a loss in control for women over the birthing process.[137] Similarly the characterization of abortion as a medical issue has meant it has been seen as one over which doctors should make decisions, rather than the women concerned.

Feminists are keen to point out the inequalities in health care provision.[138] Feminist work has shown the lack of research into diseases which affect women particularly and how women's medical conditions are belittled or regarded as non-medical. By contrast other normal aspects of women's lives (such as menstruation) are treated as illnesses.[139]

Feminist ethics has also been keen to emphasize how male norms can be used in a medical context to deprive women of power.[140] Women who are regarded as acting 'emotionally' are improperly treated as incompetent and therefore can be subjected to medical treatment against their will.[141] For example, there have been several cases where women in labour have been regarded as incompetent to make decisions about the treatment of their pregnancy.

Feminists have also worked on developing different ethical approaches to medical issues. Particularly influential has been the 'ethic of care'.[142] This approach is critical of traditional bioethics with its focus on rights and individual autonomy. Instead it focuses on relationships and care. Rather than valuing individual freedom it values the interdependency and mutuality in relationships. Susan Wolf has argued:

> By depicting the moral community as a set of atomistic and self-serving individuals, it [liberal individualism] strips away relationships that are morally central. This not only is impoverished, but may also be harmful, because it encourages disregard of those bonds.

---

132 Wolf (1996); Lindemann Nelson (2007).   133 Wolf (1996: 5); Roberts (1996).
134 Pattinson (2006: 12) describes the feminist approach as 'issue-perspective bioethics', but that fails to recognize the richness and diversity offered by feminism.
135 Wolf (1996: 8).   136 Foster (1995); Davis (1988).
137 Hoffman (2005); Nettleton (2001).
138 Rogers (2006); Mahowald (2006); Scambler (2003).
139 Purdy (1996).   140 Sherwin (1996).
141 Lupton (1994).   142 See Held (2006); Herring (2007a).

It is also inaccurate; developing children as well as full-grown adults are profoundly interdependent. Indeed, we are so interdependent that we cannot even understand the terms of moral debate without some community process and shared understanding.[143]

Sometimes it is said that there is a difference between male forms of reasoning (focusing on individual rights) and female forms of reasoning (focusing on relationships), but this may be an unnecessarily antagonistic way of putting it.[144]

Ethics of care approaches have, inevitably, received their fair share of criticism. First, it has been argued by feminists that its glorification of caring and dependency is likely to be harmful to women. The role of women as carers and dependants has been one which has led to oppression and subordination of women.[145] To elevate and promote that is harmful. Supporters of ethics of care would reply that the way ahead for women is not to seek to live the lives of independent, autonomous, un-obligated individuals which some men appear to, but rather to promote those values of care and dependency.

A second concern is that the notion of care is too vague.[146] It might be pointed out that not all caring relationships are good ones: they may involve manipulation and oppression. Without a far clearer concept of what good care is, it cannot form the basis of an ethical approach. Many supporters of an ethic of care would accept that more work needs to be done to 'flesh' out the concept and that it is in relatively early days of development.[147]

13 Virtue ethics

Virtue ethics goes back to the writings of Socrates and Aristotle. Virtue ethics emphasizes that in assessing what is the morally correct thing to do it is not the consequences of your actions that matter, but rather the attitudes (virtues) motivating your actions.[148] It is character of an individual not the consequences of their actions which is more important. Virtues are good habits which will direct human nature towards good actions. Rachels suggests that a virtue is 'a trait of character, manifested in habitual action, that it is good for a person to have'.[149] We therefore require of our health care professionals that they act compassionately, honestly, fairly and with diligence. Some professionals might find this attractive. In the heat of the hospital faced with an appalling ethical dilemma they may not be confident of choosing the right course of action, but they may be confident that their decision was based on compassion and kindness.[150]

Virtue ethicists disagree over the extent to which consequences can be used to assess the appropriateness of an act. Some argue that consequences are irrelevant so that a well-motivated act cannot be wrong regardless of the consequences.[151] Others argue that the bad consequence can render an act wrongful. Similarly there is a dispute over whether an ill-motivated act which produces a good result can be regarded as right. What all virtue

---

143 Wolf (1996: 17–18).

144 When Gilligan's research has been replicated in other countries the distinction between male and female has not been found: Vikan, Camino and Biaggio (2005). The different approaches may therefore reflect cultural differences to approaching ethical issues as much as gender based ones.

145 Wolf (1996: 9).   146 Allmark (2002).   147 Smart and Neale (1999).

148 Pellegino (1995); Gardiner (2003).   149 Rachels (1999).

150 See Jackson (2006) for a developed account of medical ethics using a virtue based account.

151 Macintyre (1984).

ethicists do agree is that the motivation is a crucial element in any moral assessment. Philippa Foot explains:

> Men and women need to be industrious and tenacious of purpose not only so as to be able to house, clothe and feed themselves, but also to pursue human ends having to do with love and friendship. They need the ability to form family ties, friendships and special relations with neighbours. They also need codes of conduct. And how could they have all these things without virtues such as loyalty, fairness, kindness and in certain circumstances obedience?[152]

One concern with virtue ethics is how we should decide what are good virtues. In such a diverse society there is no agreement on what a good person is like, there are many different ideas of what makes a good life. It may be that in our society keeping fit or eating moderately would be regarded as a virtue, but it is unclear whether in other societies this would be so. But virtue ethicists often argue that there are moral values which are essential for any decent society: love, friendship, truth telling, faithfulness, and wisdom would be accepted around the world as virtues.[153] But others claim that without considering the consequences of having a particular disposition it is not possible to ascertain whether a disposition is good.

Some critics complain that focusing on virtues could uphold unacceptable activities as moral. The suicide bomber may be said to show great courage and steadfastness of purpose, yet the consequences of his or her action reveal it to be clearly immoral. This has led many to recommend an approach that considers both virtues and Beauchamp and Childress's four principles.[154] Indeed Beauchamp and Childress[155] list five focal virtues: compassion, discernment, trustworthiness, integrity and conscientiousness, but argue that those would be displayed by any doctor following their four principles.

14 Communitarian ethics

Communitarian ethicists are critical of the overemphasis on individualism within much current bioethics.[156] Too much weight has been placed on the rights of individuals and too little on individuals' responsibilities and the interests of the wider community.[157] As members of society we have an obligation to make some sacrifices in order to promote it, and we should have no objection because it is only as a member of society that we can flourish as an individual. Communitarians are therefore more willing to allow acts to be done without the consent of an individual if necessary to further the interests of society. Some communitarians therefore support the use of organs from the deceased for transplant purposes, regardless of the views of the deceased.

Communitarians emphasize that living in a decent community and society is key to good life. When, therefore, we consider an issue such as whether a person should be allowed to sell their kidneys, seeing the issue in terms of the rights of the different people involved is to ignore what communitarians suggest is a key question: is kidney selling compatible with a decent society?[158]

---

152 Foot (2001).
154 Campbell (2003), Gillon (2003).
156 Callahan (2003).
158 Callahan (2003).

153 Nussbaum (1988); Olkin (1998).
155 Beauchamp and Childress (2003: 32–35).
157 See English, Mussell, Sheather, and Sommerville (2006).

Critics might pick up on this last point and argue that a decent society is one that respects individuals' rights.[159] If this is correct we may be back with the individualist approach to rights that communitarianism was seeking to oppose. Critics also point to the dangers of being willing to interfere with individuals' rights 'for the greater good'. While this might sound attractive, this kind of reasoning has been used by all kinds of oppressive regimes. In particular there is a danger that promoting the interests of the community will work against the interests of those on the edges of society who may be its most vulnerable members.[160] Critics also argue that the notion that determines 'the interests of the community' has become impossible given the wide range of groups within society.

15 Theology

It might be thought inappropriate to discuss theology in a book on medical law and ethics. True, some individuals might be influenced by their religious beliefs in deciding what treatment they wish to receive, but should theology have any role to play when deciding what the law should be or what ethical standards should govern the behaviour of doctors generally?

The justifications put forward by those who promote theological ideas in medical law and ethics include the following. First, it is argued that in the UK, even though the percentage of people attending religious services may not be great, there is still a high percentage of people who regard themselves as religious. Indeed one large scale survey recently found that in the UK 53 per cent of people described themselves as Christian and 6 per cent as belonging to some other religious faith.[161] However vaguely they may understand the concept, it seems that many people have some appreciation of the spiritual. If medical law and ethics are to reflect the attitudes of society then arguably something spiritual needs to be part of that. Critics would respond by arguing that even if there is a majority of people who have some kind of religious belief, these are so diverse and so vague as to be of little relevance. That said, English law does have some roots in Christian theology and remarkably in 2005 a BBC survey found that 61 per cent of people believe Britain's laws should respect, and be influenced by, religious values.[162]

Second, it might be argued that some theological points of view, although supportable by theological arguments can also be supported rationally.[163] These arguments should then be considered alongside other 'rational' arguments. Indeed there is dispute among those writing from a religious perspective over whether their arguments should be put in explicitly religious terms when entering a public debate, or whether the arguments should be put in non-religious terms, so that they can be weighed alongside other non-religious arguments.[164]

A third point is that religious ideas do play a very important role in many people's lives and even if that is only so for a small minority of individuals, medical professionals will be faced with religious patients and an awareness and discussion of their approaches is useful.

---

[159] Childress and Bernheim (2003).   [160] Parker (2002).

[161] Tearfund (2007). 7.6 million adults were said to attend church at least one a month.

[162] BBC Newsonline (17 July 2005).

[163] Eg Ramsey (1970), which although written from a religious perspective has proved highly influential on secular bioethics.

[164] Messer (2002).

A fourth point is that a religious perspective can offer a challenging alternative to orthodox approaches to medical ethics and in considering and replying to them the secular view can be clarified and strengthened. There is, however, a difficulty here. Many religious arguments are based on precepts which may not be readily open to challenge and negotiation. A person who believes euthanasia is immoral because it is prohibited in a holy text is not going to receive much from, or be able to negotiate with, secular ethicists, unless the validity of the holy text is open to debate.[165]

The difficulty is that a full appreciation of most religious views requires an in depth understanding of the theology underpinning that religion, which in the case of many religions has been developed to a high degree of sophistication. Nevertheless there are themes which appear to unite the world's religions. There is a strong line taken on the sanctity of life. Life is seen as a precious gift from God which should not be readily taken away. This leads to a strong line often being taken against abortion and euthanasia. There is also a strong emphasis on the values of love and compassion, which can resonate with virtue ethics. The notion of humans being stewards of the world, placed by God to look after it, is a theme which is found in many religions' thought. However, how this works out in bioethics is hotly debated. Some religious people are very wary of new medical techniques which are regarded as 'playing God', while others argue that God has given humans the talents and abilities to develop new technologies and therefore they should be used where to do so would prevent suffering and promote good.[166]

In *Re A (Children) (Conjoined Twins: Surgical Separation)*[167] the Court of Appeal took the unusual step of allowing the Roman Catholic Archbishop of Westminster to make written submissions to the court. This has proved controversial. On the one hand there are those who argue that the church, just like anyone else, has the right to participate in a court case. As long as religious groups are not seeking to 'insinuate doctrine under the guise of legal argument' there is no objection.[168] Harris and Holm[169] accept that religious groups can be involved in court cases and public debates, although their arguments must be based on rational argument supported by evidence rather than prejudice. Some argue that while religious leaders may be entitled to direct how their followers should act, should they try to enforce their views on others?[170] Supporters of religious involvement might argue that religious groups, just as anyone else, can make arguments about what makes a good society and about the moral values that underpin our community. Such contributions, they argue, may be useful to courts and policy makers.[171] Indeed some writing from a religious perspective have argued that religions should not seek to actively influence legal or political decisions for fear of being seen as imposing their beliefs on others.[172]

16 Relativism

Moral relativism or pluralism argues that there are many different answers to complex moral issues and that it would be wrong to suggest that one view is necessarily superior to another. In short there are no 'right answers'. Basically you choose the option which

---

[165] See eg Padela (2007) making this point from an Islamic perspective.
[166] Daar and Khitamy (2001).   [167] [2000] 4 All ER 985.
[168] Skene and Parker (2002).   [169] Harris and Holm (2002).
[170] Charlesworth (2004).   [171] Gormally (2002).   [172] Coady (2002).

seems to work best for the particular case you are dealing with.[173] In fact there are few absolute moral relativists. To say whether rape is wrong is a matter of opinion appears a rather extreme view. Opponents (moral objectivists) reject such approaches arguing that there are moral absolutes. Although the men charged with child abuse on the isle of Pitcairn might have tried to claim that within their culture sexual relations with children were widespread, that did not and should not have rendered their actions morally permissible.[174] The growth of international conventions on bioethical issues indicates that consensus can be reached over fundamental principles.[175]

There is a further point here. Are the medical ethics developed in the West also based on a 'Western Mindset'? We tend to focus on individual rights and concepts of community, tradition, and relationships may be neglected. Are these ethical principles no more than a reflection of certain Western norms, based on an assumption that the individualist lifestyles of the West are best?[176]

Complex issues also arise in relation to 'medical' practices which are acceptable in some cultures but not particularly dominant in the UK. The government has, for example, through the Female Genital Mutilation Act 2003, rendered female circumcision illegal, even though it is regarded as acceptable in some cultures. No doubt medical practices that take place in the UK would be unacceptable elsewhere. This raises issues surrounding the right to 'impose' a dominant cultural view on a minority group and further issues surround moral pluralism.[177] This issue can be exaggerated—there are in reality few issues on which in the field of bioethics there are significant cultural differences of an ethical kind, even if the way of reasoning may not be the same.

Childress and Beauchamp argued that their four key principles which we outlined earlier represented a 'common morality' upon which all right thinking people would agree. But there is debate over whether there is a 'common morality'.[178] Some argue that there are basic principles upon which all thoughtful people agree: lying is wrong, killing is worse.[179] Others deny that even killing is universally regarded as wrong. They argue the research has simply not been done to prove that these prohibitions are universally accepted. However, to conduct such research would be enormously complex.[180] Another response may be that even if there are some very general principles on which there is universal agreement once you move from the general to the precise the consensus breaks down. For example, even if there were agreement that life is precious, there would be no agreement on when it is legitimate to wage war. So the 'common morality' is of little practical use.

17 Pragmatism

Pragmatism seeks to develop an approach which starts from actual experiences and develops approaches that are rooted in real life.[181] There is no interest among pragmatists for grand ethical theories but rather for the problems that patients and medical

---

[173] As Pattinson (2006: 4) points out a true moral relativist would not even accept that you must respect other people's point of view, because that would be state a moral absolute.

[174] BBC Newsonline (29 September 2004).

[175] See Harris (2000: 380) for a sceptical look at the international agreement.

[176] Bowman (2004).   [177] The issue is well discussed in Charlesworth (2004).

[178] Veatch (2003b).   [179] Beauchamp (2003).   [180] Beauchamp (2003).

[181] Bellantoni (2003); Hester (2003).

professionals face in real life. The emphasis is on exploring how they see, understand and interpret the issues, rather than engage in the fine language of the philosophers. The aim is to find approaches that have been found workable through prior practice and are acceptable to those concerned.[182]

QUESTIONS

1. Do you think medical lawyers need medical ethics?

2. Is cosmetic surgery a proper use of medicine? Should it be outlawed?

3. Some commentators (BBC Newsonline, 14 March 2007) have argued that behaviour of children which in the past was simply described as 'naughty' is now often labelled as exhibiting signs of a medical condition (eg attention deficit disorder). Do you think that in this area we are having an increasing awareness of the impact of people's health on their behaviour, or is this a way of excusing bad behaviour?

4. Consider how the different ethical approaches would deal with a case where a father wanted to donate his heart to his daughter who needed a heart transplant, even though the result would be that the father would die.

5. Should religious reasoning ever be relevant to those developing medical law or ethics?

6. 3.7 million people care for sick relatives or friends, with 1.7 million spending more than 20 hours a week caring, all unpaid. These figures exceed the workforce of the NHS. Should medical law and ethics pay far more attention to the work of carers than the 'professionals'?

7. Some commentators (eg MacKenzie (2007)) have complained that medical ethics focuses exclusively on issues concerning the permissibility of certain medical activities. However, this leaves out a consideration of emotions such as regret or guilt. Some things are permissible, but regrettable. Do you agree that permissibility should only be one issue for ethicists to consider?

8. Many commentators have noted the increased commercialization of medicine (eg Reiman (2007)). Do commercial pressures pose a greater threat to good medical practice than ignorance of ethical matters?

9. José Miola (2007: 1) suggests that the volume of writing on medical ethics has 'not made medical ethics more effective but, rather, has allowed the various discourses to cancel each other out, leaving a regulatory vacuum to be filled by the conscience of the individual medical practitioner'. Is there a danger that there are so many different ethical theories that medical ethics are of no use to the practitioner? If so, what should be done about it?

---

[182] McGee (2003).

FURTHER READING

For general books on medical ethics see:

Beauchamp, T. and Childress, J. (2003) *Principles of Biomedical Ethics* (OUP).

Fulford, K., Dickenson, D. and Murray, T. (2002) *Healthcare Ethics and Human Values* (Blackwell).

Glannon, W. (2005) *Biomedical Ethics* (OUP).

Hope, T. (2005) *A very short introduction to medical ethics* (OUP).

Jonsen, A. (2003) *The Birth of Bioethics* (OUP).

Miola, J. (2007) *Medical Ethics and Medical Law* (Hart).

For feminist approaches to medical ethics see:

Bridgeman, J. and Millns, A. (1998) *Feminist Perspectives on Law* (Sweet and Maxwell).

Mahowald, M. (2006) *Bioethics and Women* (OUP).

Morris, A. and Nott, J. (2002) *Well women: women's access to health care* (OUP).

Sheldon, S. and Thomson, M. (eds) *Feminist Perspectives on Healthcare Law* (Cavendish).

Tong, R. (1997) *Feminist Approaches to Bioethics: Theoretical Reflections and Practical Applications* (Westview Press).

For religious perspectives see:

Cromwell, S. (2003) *Hindu Bioethics in the Twenty-First Century* (NYU Press).

Keown, D. (1995) *Buddhism and Bioethics* (Macmillan).

Lammers, M. and Verhey, A. (eds) (1998) *On Moral Medicine* (Eerdmans).

Messer, N. (2002) *Theological Issues in Bioethics* (Darton Longman and Todd).

Padela, A. (2007) 'Islamic medical ethics: a primer' *Bioethics* 21: 169.

Sinclair, D. (2005) *Jewish Medical Ethics* (OUP).

Smith II, G. (2005) *The Christian Religion and Biotechnology* (Springer).

Tsai, D. (2005) 'The bioethical principles and Confucius' moral philosophy' *Journal of Medical Ethics* 31: 159.

On virtue ethics see:

Jackson, J. (2006) *Ethics in Medicine* (Polity Press).

Hursthouse, R. (1999) *On Virtue Ethics* (OUP).

On relativism see:

Harman, G. and Thompson, J.J. (1996) *Moral Relativism and Moral Objectivity* (Blackwell).

2 The Structure of the NHS and the Rationing of Health Care Resources

INTRODUCTION

The National Health Service has been described as Britain's best loved institution.[1] Tony Blair has claimed that is one of the country's greatest achievements.[2] It is not only of great national importance, but it is also the scene of huge political controversy and regularly appears at election times as one of the issues voters feel most strongly about.[3] The World Health Organization has said it is one of the best in the world.[4]

This chapter will be looking at the structure of the NHS and some of the key issues facing those dealing with its management.[5] Although the structure of the NHS and the way the money allocated to the NHS is distributed and spent may not at first sight appear the most fascinating of topics, in fact there are a large number of important and interesting issues that are raised. To discuss properly the structures of the NHS and all the surrounding issues would take, at least, a substantial book in itself. This chapter therefore will briefly summarize the structure of this vast institution and then select some of the most topical issues facing it.

The first point to emphasize is that the NHS is, quite simply, enormous. Consider these statistics:

- In 2007–08 the total expenditure on the NHS was £90 billion. The Government has announced that this will increase to £110 billion by 2010–11.[6]

- This is not to mention private health care where in 2005 the total spending among the general public exceeded £10,500 million.

- In 2006 there were 10.7 million people admitted to NHS hospitals. There are some 300 million consultations with a GP each year.[7]

- The number of NHS prescriptions dispensed in 2006 was 834.4 million, or 13.9 items per head of population.[8]

- In March 2006 there were 1,338,000 NHS staff.[9]

---

[1] Hewitt (2005).   [2] DoH (2004a).
[3] Cowling (2005).   [4] NHS (2007c).
[5] The National Health Service Act 2006 provides the statutory basis of the NHS.
[6] HM Treasury (2007).   [7] DoH (2005b: para 7.19).
[8] Association of the British Pharmaceutical Industry (2007).
[9] Information Centre (2007b).

- In 2006 £1,982 was spent by the Government per person per year on the NHS.[10]
- In 2006 UK health expenditure was 9.4 per cent of GDP, placing the UK in the mid range of OECD countries.[11]

1 What are the principles underpinning the NHS?

The Government has set out the core principles underlying the NHS.[12] These are:

(1) The NHS will provide a universal service for all based on clinical need, not ability to pay.

(2) The NHS will provide a comprehensive range of services.

(3) The NHS will shape its services around the needs and preferences of individual patients, their families, and their carers.

(4) The NHS will respond to the different needs of different populations.

(5) The NHS will work continuously to improve the quality of services and to minimise errors

(6) The NHS will support and value its staff.

(7) Public funds for health care will be devoted solely to NHS patients.

(8) The NHS will work with others to ensure a seamless service for patients.

(9) The NHS will help to keep people healthy and work to reduce health inequalities.

(10) The NHS will respect the confidentiality of individual patients and provide open access to information about services, treatment, and performance.

In summarizing the modern NHS the Secretary of State for Health has described the service as:

> An NHS which is fair to all of us and personal to each of us by offering *everyone* the same access to, and the power to choose from, a wide range of services of high quality, based on clinical need, not ability to pay.[13]

The Chief Executive of the NHS, with a more open acknowledgement of financial reality, has stated its aims to be:

> to promote health, reduce health inequalities, and deliver the best possible care for the population with the resources available.[14]

In delivering these aims the NHS accepts that it is facing challenges. The Department of Health sees these as the major ones:

- Rising expectations: the NHS is delivering shorter waiting times and better services, but is still some way short of providing people with the control, choice, and convenience they expect in other parts of their lives.

- Demographics: an aging population, with increasing numbers of people with long-term conditions, requires the NHS, in partnership with local authorities and others,

---

[10] Association of the British Pharmaceutical Industry (2007). Although the amount spent per person on particular services can vary enormously between primary care trusts (PCTs) (see King's Fund (2006)).
[11] Association of the British Pharmaceutical Industry (2007).
[12] NHS (2007b).   [13] DoH (2004a: 7).   [14] DoH (2006b: 1).

to focus more on promoting good health, well-being and independence.[15] This has implications for how services are organized.

- Changes in medical technology: these are transforming the ability of the NHS to prevent, cure, and manage disease, but are also creating new costs and a need to change the way services are configured.

- Variations in quality, safety, access, and value for money: in a national health service, people are rightly concerned about ongoing variations in the care on offer in different parts of the country.[16]

To meet these challenges the Department of Health promises:

- more choice and voice for patients, giving patients real power, backed up by strong commissioning;

- more diverse providers, with more freedom to innovate and improve services, and more competition on quality;

- financial incentives to improve care and promote sound financial management and best value;

- national standards and regulation to guarantee quality, safety, and equity;

- sustained focus on information management and technology to underpin the reforms and deliver better, safer care.[17]

2 The structure of the NHS

The structure of the NHS differs between England, Wales, Scotland, and Northern Ireland. This chapter will look only at England.[18] To describe the structure of the NHS is not an easy task. Partly because it is labyrinthine, and partly because the NHS is undergoing enormous structural changes with bodies being created, merged, and destroyed at an astonishing rate. The structures of the NHS are undergoing these fundamental changes following an important Government Paper, *Shifting the Balance of Power*, which is designed to create a service centred around patients. The Government is also in the midst of rearranging the 'arms length bodies' which play a crucial role in the governance of the NHS.

At a basic level it is possible to examine the structure as consisting of four levels:

(1) Policy making and centralized planning. This task is carried out primarily by the Department of Health.

(2) Supervision, inspection, and regulation. This task is now often carried out by 'arms length bodies'. These bodies are created by and are responsible to the Department of Health but are independent of it.

(3) Service commissioners. These bodies decide which health services are 'purchased' and from whom. This is carried out by, for example, Primary Care Trusts (PCTs). They have the responsibility for assessing the health needs of people in their area and ensuring that their needs are appropriately met.

---

[15] See Wanlass (2006) for a detailed discussion of the health care needs of older people.
[16] DoH (2006b: 5).   [17] DoH (2006b: 5).   [18] Webster (1998).

(4) Health care providers. These are those on the front line who are directly provide the health care to patients and include, for example, doctors and nurses.

We will now look at these different groups of bodies in more detail.

3 Policy and central planning in the NHS

3.1 Parliament

It is, of course, Parliament that approves the allocation of funds to the NHS via taxation. The Secretary of Health is accountable to Parliament for the performance of the NHS in England. There are also three Parliamentary Select Committees who can make inquiries and produce reports in relation to the NHS. These are:

- the *Health Committee* which examines the Department of Health's expenditure, administration and policymaking;
- the *Public Accounts Committee* which ensures that the NHS is running economically, effectively, and efficiently;
- the *Public Administration Committee* which scrutinizes the Health Service Commissioner's reports;

3.2 The Department of Health (DoH)

Under the Ministry of Health Act, section 2 the Secretary of State for Health is bound to:

> Secure the preparation, effective carrying out and coordination of measures conducive to the health of people . . . including measures for the prevention and cure of diseases . . . the treatment of physical and mental defects, the treatment and care of the blind, the initiation and direction of research, the collection, preparation, publication and dissemination of information and statistics relating thereto, and the training of persons for health services.

The Department's role has been defined as including:

- setting overall direction and leading transformation of the NHS and social care;
- setting national standards to improve quality of services;
- securing resources and making investment decisions to ensure that the NHS and social care are able to deliver services;
- working with key partners[19] to ensure quality of services . . .[20]

The DoH's overall aim is to improve the overall health and well-being of the public. To carry out this role, the Department is organized into three Business Groups, who are responsible for Health and Social Care Standards and Quality; Health and Social Care Delivery; and Strategy and Business Development.

---

[19] Eg Strategic Health Authorities, the Commission for Health Audit and Improvement, and the Commission for Social Care Inspection.
[20] NHS (2005a).

In a recent review of the NHS the BMA has complained that there is too much political interference within the NHS. They call for the NHS to become free from extensive Government interference and suggest:

> The Department of Health should review its changed role following the establishment of a constitution for the NHS, a board of governors, and the executive management board. Its primary role will be to provide adequate resources to deliver the constitution and to focus on public and population health and work to diminish health inequalities.[21]

Given the fact that the NHS remains a highly sensitive topic in political terms it is unlikely we will see the Department of Health withdrawing from management of the NHS to such an extent.

4 Quality control: regulation and inspection

There are a group of bodies whose primary responsibility is what might broadly be called 'quality control'. They issue regulation and guidance on particular areas. These may be backed up by inspections or looser forms of enforcement. Their primary role is to ensure the provision of health services of a consistently high standard. The Health and Social Care Bill 2007 will merge the functions of the existing Healthcare Commission, the Commission for Social Care Inspection, and the Mental Health Act Commission into a new super-regulator called the Care Quality Commission. The Healthcare Commission carries out an annual 'health check' on NHS Trusts. It also undertakes investigations where there are particular issues of concern. In 2007 it reported that 'On the new four-point scale, 36% were rated "good" and 4% were rated "excellent" for their quality of services. In addition, 15% of all trusts were rated "excellent" or "good" for their use of resources'.[22] As these results show, the Commission does not readily hand out 'high marks'.

5 Commissioning and planning services

5.1 Strategic Health Authorities (SHAs)

SHAs are responsible for ensuring that the health service needs of the people in their area are met. In this regard they must, as part of the NHS Plan, enter an Annual Delivery Agreement for health with the DoH for their area and seek to ensure the targets set out in that agreement are met. Their main responsibilites are:

* developing plans for improving health services in their local area;
* making sure local health services are of a high quality and are performing well;
* increasing the capacity of local health services—so they can provide more services;
* making sure national priorities—for example, programmes for improving cancer services—are integrated into local health service plans.[23]

---

21 BMA (2007a: 12).   22 Healthcare Commission (2007b).   23 NHS (2005a).

5.2 Primary Care Trusts (PCTs)

PCTs have been described as the 'main engines of the Modern NHS'[24] and this is reflected in the fact that they receive 75 per cent of the NHS budget. They are responsible for finding out what the health needs of their particular area are, deciding which needs should be met and how. They will commission health care providers to meet those needs as appropriate.

5.3 Special health authorities

Special health authorities are those which provide health services to the whole of England.[25] They are therefore to be contrasted with local health authorities who concentrate on particular areas of the country. The NHS Institute for Innovation and Improvement is one, as is the National Blood Authority.

5.4 Social services departments

The provision of social services (as opposed to health care) is the responsibility of the local authority. They can either provide the services themselves or purchase them from other providers. The distinction between social services and health care is a problematic one, as we shall see. Social services cover assistance in living independently and will cover provision of 'meals on wheels'; assistance in washing; and sheltered accommodation, for example. These are not regarded as health care.

6 The provision of services

The providers of services are those who provide the hands-on care of patients within the NHS. 'Primary care' is the term used for the services provided by those people who are the normal first port of call in the case of a medical problem. They include GPs (general practitioner doctors); opticians; dentists; pharmacists; and NHS Direct (a phone service). All those offering primary care are managed by PCTs. 'Secondary care' is the care to which a patient may be sent by a primary carer. It involves acute and specialist services. PCTs are (confusingly!) responsible for planning secondary care. They must decide which services should be commissioned to meet people's needs. The main bodies providing care include the following.

6.1 NHS Trusts

NHS Trusts are responsible for the provision of health services in their area. NHS Trusts were created by the NHS and Community Care Act 1990. That statute set out their responsibilities:

- their functions must be carried out 'effectively, efficiently and economically';[26]
- their revenue must cover outgoings taking one financial year with another;[27]
- they must achieve any financial objectives as may be set by the DoH.[28]

---

[24] Montgomery (2003: 85).   [25] They are set up under the NHS Act 1977, s 11.
[26] NHS Act 1977, Sch 2, para 6(1).   [27] NHS Act 1977, s 10(1).   [28] NHS Act 1977, s 10(2).

Although Trusts are accountable to the Secretary of State and must comply with directions on matters such as staffing, they are intended to have a wider degree of freedom than they did in the earlier history of the NHS. NHS Trusts are allowed to offer private health care or offer extra amenities for NHS patients for a charge.[29] They may also borrow money within annually agreed limits. Any income generated must be spent within the Trust's statutory powers and so the trust cannot make a profit as such.

6.2 Foundation Trusts

These trusts are recent creations, with the first being established in April 2004 under the Health and Social Care (Community Health and Standards) Act 2003. They are 'independent public benefit corporations',[30] although they are not permitted to make a profit. They are run by a Board of Governors made up of local managers, staff, and members of the public. Foundation Trusts have far more financial and organizational freedom than other NHS Trusts. This freedom is meant to mean that they can best meet the particular needs of people in their area. Such trusts are, of course, still within the NHS and are subject to performance inspections. The intention is that by 2008 all NHS hospitals will have attained Foundation Trust status.

6.3 Care Trusts

As already indicated, one of the organizational problems which has bedevilled the NHS is providing a seamless service for patients between health care and social services. This becomes particularly acute where a patient no longer needs hospital care but is not able to live independently. There can then be a tension between the NHS and local authority social service departments as to who provides the care the individual may need. The Health Act 1999 created general duties of cooperation allowing local authorities and NHS bodies to pool budgets and facilitate integration. Now it is possible for local authorities and the NHS to consolidate into a single organization, known as a Care Trust.[31] The aim of a Care Trust is to integrate the provision of social care and health care and bring to an end the 'war' between the NHS and social services departments over which aspect of care each organization is responsible for. There are only a small number of Care Trusts that have been created to date.

6.4 GPs

GPs are doctors who look after the health of those who are listed with them. As well as providing general health advice and prescribing medicines, they can also carry out simple surgical operations and give vaccinations. GPs will often work with a team of health care professionals including nurses, midwives, and physiotherapists. If the GP is not able to deal with a patient's problem she or he will refer the patient to a hospital for tests or treatment, which may involve a meeting with a specialist consultant. Around 75 per cent of the NHS budget is allocated to Primary Care.[32]

---

[29] Health and Social Care Act 2001, Sch 2.   [30] DoH (2005b: para 5.16).
[31] Introduced by the Health and Social Care Act 2001.
[32] Brazier and Cave (2007: 21).

6.5 The independent sector

Of course health and social care purchasers can contract with providers from the independent sector. All providers of independent health and social care must be licensed under the Care Standards Act 2000. All independent hospitals and care homes must register with the National Care Standards Commission.[33] Once registered they must comply with national minimum standards and associated regulations. These are policed by regular inspections. The Commission can revoke a registration, if necessary, by application to a magistrate.[34]

6.6 Mental Health Trusts

Basic mental health services can be provided through primary care services, such as GPs. This might include counselling and other psychological therapies. More specialist care is provided for by Mental Health Trusts or the social services department of the local authority.

6.7 NHS Direct

This is a free confidential telephone service providing medical advice.

6.8 Children's Trusts

Following the Government's Green Paper, *Every Child Matters*, the Government has announced that children's health, education, and social services will be integrated into a single organization, to be known as a Children's Trust. At present these trusts are being run at a pilot level.

6.9 Ambulance Trusts

These are responsible for organizing the ambulance services in their area.

7 Structural issues

We will now briefly look at some of the structural issues facing the NHS.

7.1 The provider/purchaser distinction

An important distinction is drawn between the commissioning of services and the provision of services. The concept was introduced under the Conservative Governments of the 1990s with the creation of the 'internal market'. The idea behind it is that, by giving a PCT the power to decide from whom to purchase the health services needed, the health care providers will strive to offer an excellent service to ensure that they are selected. In short, it creates a form of competition between health care providers seeking to provide better services than each other. This, it was hoped, would drive up the

---

[33] Care Standards Act 2000, s 6.   [34] Care Standards Act 2000, s 20.

standards within the NHS. The present Labour Government has, however, sought to distance itself from the notion of competition and instead prefers to use the concept of partnership, the idea being that health service commissioners and health service providers work together in partnership to meet the needs of the people in a particular area. Even with 'partnership' there is still the threat that if a health service provider is not providing services of the required standard then the health service commissioners will look elsewhere. The use of partnership rather than competition is more about changing the atmosphere of relationships between providers and commissioners than changing the central idea that providers should keep striving to offer a high level of service. Under the NHS reforms currently under consideration patients will start to play some role as commissioners. In the past patients would have had no choice within the NHS other than to accept the services offered by their GP. The proposal is that if local services cannot offer treatment within six months patients can choose alternative providers, including the private sector.[35]

7.2 The use of Arm's Length Bodies (ALBs)

As can be seen from the list of bodies involved in the structure of the NHS Arm's Length Bodies (ALBs) play a significant role. These are commissions, institutes, and authorities who are separate from Government but are answerable to it, and are in charge of regulating particular areas. Although the list is long it is shorter than it would have been but for a recent review of ALBs, which reduced their number in a bid to save some half a billion pounds in the time period 2003–2008.[36] In 2003/04 there were 38 ALBs, who spent a total of £4.8 billion, including operating costs of £1.8 billion.[37] The review found a widespread perception in the NHS that the ALBs were associated with a considerable level of bureaucracy. The review has therefore proposed a reduction in the number of ALBs to 20, as well as cuts in their budget.

Supporters of ALBs emphasize that they enable the regulation of sensitive areas of health care to be provided free from political interference. Take, for example, the Human Fertilisation and Embryology Authority which must issue guidance on sensitive issues relating to embryo research and advances in reproductive technology. If the issue were to be decided by the Government this would create concerns that the regulation would reflect what the Government would think was acceptable to the general public, rather than what was scientifically and ethically appropriate. But opponents of ALBs may claim that this is precisely the problem with them. It is claimed that these bodies are not accountable and are made up of professionals working in the area who are out of touch with the feeling and thoughts of ordinary people.

7.3 Decentralization

One of the key themes in the current NHS is to devolve power to local PCTs and front line staff.[38] The argument is that front line staff are in the best position to know what patients in their area of the country need and how best to meet those needs. The independence given to PCTs is seen as key to enabling local NHS bodies to meet needs in their area. The DoH has said it will provide resources and 'lead the transformation', but

---

[35] DoH (2003c).   [36] DoH (2005b para 1.29).   [37] DoH (2004e).   [38] DoH (2001c).

that it will not seek to manage at a hands-on level.[39] As one document put it, 'it will steer more and row less'.[40]

An important part of the move to decentralization is the use of Foundation Trust hospitals, which have significantly greater freedom over their budgets than the NHS Trust hospitals. The aim is that by 2008 all NHS hospitals will have reached Foundation Trust status. The claimed benefit of the status is that NHS Foundation Trusts will be able to provide relevant care for their patients because they have been set free from government control.[41] But, there are some concerns about Foundation status. Some of those awarded the status have failed subsequently to achieve the required 'star status' and the restrictions on not making profits have been criticized by some. The strength of these concerns is reflected by the fact that the Healthcare Commission has been asked to examine the experiences of the first 20 Foundation Trust hospitals.

One of the consequences of decentralization is a difference in practice between different PCTs. A 2006 King's Fund Report found that, for example, while Islington PCT spent £406 per head on mental health services, Bracknell Forest PCT spent only £56.[42] This is a huge difference and presumably there were other services that Bracknell were paying for instead that Islington were not.

7.4 'Democratic accountability'

Another theme in the structure of the NHS is democratic accountability. This is the notion that the public itself should have the opportunity to direct the future of the NHS and call it to account in areas where it is failing. The Health and Social Care Act 2000, section 11 therefore places a duty on NHS Trusts, PCTs, and Strategic Health Authorities to make arrangements to involve, and consult, patients and the public in service planning and operation, and in the development of proposals for changes.

One of the major ways this is done is through the Patient and Public Interest Forums, but evidence from these indicates the difficulties in the notion of democratic accountability. Claims have been made that it has been very difficult to find members of the public who are willing to be involved in forums, and one commentator has suggested that 'many of the forums are virtually inactive'.[43]

7.5 Change

The pace of change in the structures and workings of the NHS is remarkable. Bodies are created and removed with remarkable speed. One leading commentator has stated that since 1982 there has been some kind of 'organisational upheaval' almost every year.[44] To some this may indicate how seriously governments have been taking the need to improve the quality of service offered by the NHS. Others have claimed that institutional reform has been a smokescreen for hiding really important issues,[45] in particular that the supply of NHS services depends increasingly on private providers, rather than public bodies. One important consequence of this is that the Human Rights Act only applies to a public authority and it has been held that a private care home is not a public authority for these purposes.[46] This means that a patient in an NHS care home can rely

---

[39] DoH (2001c).   [40] DoH (2001c: 9).   [41] Monitor (2005).
[42] King's Fund (2006).   [43] Lewis (2005: 1).   [44] Newdick (2005: 67).
[45] Klein and Williams (2000).   [46] *YL v Birmingham CC* [2007] UKHL 27.

on the Human Rights Act 1998 if their rights have been interfered with; but a patient in a private care home may not be able to.

7.6 Money

Like it or not, money is central to the way the NHS operates. Despite increased funding of the NHS in recent years there still appear to be serious financial difficulties facing many parts of the NHS. A report by the think-tank the King's Fund noted:

> By 2007/8, annual spend will be 40 per cent higher in real terms than it was five years earlier. But despite the increased funding, the NHS is in deficit. In 2005/6 NHS trusts in aggregate overspent by more than £1.2 billion, and the NHS as a whole overspent by more than £500 million. More than 60 trusts incurred significant deficits, and stories of staff reductions, service cutbacks and ward closures are widespread.[47]

It is not possible here to discuss all of the issues facing the NHS. What follows are, however, some selected topics that are of particular interest and controversy.

8 Public health: infectious diseases

The main legislation controlling the behaviour of infectious diseases is surprisingly old, being the National Assistance Acts of 1948 and 1951 and the Public Health (Control of Diseases) Act 1984.[48] It is notable how much of the responsibility for control of infectious diseases rests with local authorities, rather than central government, and that the emphasis is on protection of the public rather than upon individual human rights. The legislation must be construed with the Human Rights Act very much in mind and so any public authority exercising the powers must act in a way which is compatible with an individual's human rights if possible.

The Public Health Act 1984 gives local authorities powers to control the spread of diseases. The list of diseases covered in the Act is: cholera, plague, relapsing fever, smallpox, and typhus. These are known as 'notifiable diseases'. The list has been added to by the Secretary of State[49] and now includes over 20 diseases including AIDS, leprosy, malaria, and rabies. The powers to control diseases include the following.

8.1 Notification

Under the 1984 Public Health Act a doctor must notify the local authority of anyone whom she or he suspects of having a notifiable disease. If the doctor does not notify 'forthwith' then in theory a criminal prosecution could follow. The local authority is required to notify the Health Authority within 48 hours. For some diseases (eg rabies) the Government's Chief Medical Officer must be notified immediately.

8.2 Investigative powers

In order to acquire information needed to tackle notifiable diseases there are obligations on occupiers of premises, employers, and head teachers to provide information that is

---

[47] Palmer (2006: xv).   [48] See DoH (2007a) for proposals for reform of the law.
[49] Under powers given by the Public Health (Infectious Diseases) Regulations 1988 (SI 1988/1546).

reasonably required of them by a local authority's medical officer. Most dramatically there is power to compel someone to undergo compulsory medical examination under order from a Justice of the Peace under the Public Health Act 1984, section 35. The order can only be made if:

(a) there is reason to believe that the person is or has been suffering from a 'notifiable disease' or carries an organism capable of causing a disease;

(b) it is in the interests of the person, her or his family, or the public that the person be examined; and

(c) the doctor treating the person (if there is one) consents to the making of the order.

If this seems draconian, worse follows. The order can be made *ex parte*[50] (ie at a hearing of which the individual has no notice) and can be made in relation to a group of people if it is thought one of them has the disease.[51] If an order is made then there is a power to enter private premises to carry out the examination.[52]

8.3 Powers to remove, isolate, and detain

In an extreme case there are powers to detain an individual in hospital in the name of public health, even without that person's consent. These powers are found in the Public Health (Control of Disease) Act 1984. The National Assistance Act 1948, National Assistance (Amendment) Act 1951, and Mental Health Act 1983 provide powers where the primary concern is for the care of the individual, rather than the prevention of the spread of disease. For example, section 37 of the 1984 Act authorizes a magistrate to order that a person with a notifiable disease to be removed to hospital. There are three requirements that must be satisfied before such an order can be made:

(a) proper precautions to prevent the spread of diseases cannot be (or are not being) taken;

(b) the absence of precautions means that there is a serious risk of infection to others;[53] and

(c) suitable hospital accommodation is available.

The order can be made *ex parte* (ie without the person having an opportunity to put their side of the case). There are also provisions which can prevent a person suffering from a notifiable disease from using public transport, public libraries, or schools.[54] It may be that some of these provisions fail to adequately protect the rights under article 5 of the European Convention on Human Rights (ECHR).[55]

---

[50] Once the order has been made an appeal can be made to the Crown Court against it: Public Health (Control of Disease) Act 1984, s 67.

[51] Public Health (Infectious Diseases) Act 1984, s 36.

[52] Ss 35(2) and 36(2). There are further powers to order examinations of those in specific jobs such as midwives or dairy workers.

[53] Montgomery (2003: 31) notes that there is an ambiguity here over whether it is the risk or the severity of harm that is taken into account in assessing the risk as dangerous.

[54] Public Health (Control of Diseases) Act 1984, ss 20–25.

[55] *Enhorn v Sweden* [2005] ECHR 56529/00, discussed in Martin (2006).

8.4 Vaccination

Immunization programmes are now a widely accepted part of the medical treatment of children. Such programmes have been a highly effective response to smallpox and other illnesses. However, in the UK, concerns over the MMR vaccine in particular have seen a drop in the number of children being vaccinated. As that controversy has highlighted, vaccinations are not compulsory and parents are free to decide not to have their children vaccinated. In *Re B (A Child) (Immunisation)*[56] the children's parents (who had separated) could not decide whether or not have their children vaccinated and the issue was brought to court. The Court of Appeal decided that the question was simply one of what was in the child's welfare. Having heard expert evidence they concluded that it would be in the child's interests to be vaccinated.

8.5 Compulsory care

There are very few circumstances in which people are forced to receive treatment against their wishes. There is a special regime for those with mental health problems which will be discussed in Chapter 10. Here we will focus on the compulsory treatment of people for public health concerns. The following appear to be the only circumstances in which a person can be forced to receive treatment in order to protect the public health:

(i) *Infectious diseases.* The Public Health (Control of Disease) Act 1984, section 13 permits the Secretary of State to make regulations 'with a view to the treatment of persons affected with an epidemic, endemic or infectious disease'. There is some debate whether this enables the Secretary of State to issue regulations permitting compulsory treatment. Kennedy and Grubb[57] argue not, on the basis that the wording is ambiguous, and given the well established common law right to refuse treatment (now reinforced by the Human Rights Act 1998) such rights could not be overridden without the most explicit statutory provision.

(ii) *Cleansing of vermin.* Under the Public Health Act 1936, section 85 a person may be cleansed of vermin under a court order, compulsorily, as long as the court is satisfied that it is necessary to cleanse the person.

(iii) *National Assistance Act 1948.* Section 47 allows people who are suffering from 'grave chronic disease', or are 'aged, infirm or physically incapacitated', and are living in 'insanitary conditions' to be removed if they are not able to provide proper care and attention for themselves and are not receiving that from others. However the section only authorizes the person to be removed to a hospital. There is no explicit power to permit compulsory treatment.

(iv) *Fluoridation.* Fluoride can be added to water, especially to assist in the dental health of children. This is widely seen as the most effective way of promoting children's dental health. However, this is controversial as it means fluoride is added to the water supply for the whole community. The complaint is that fluoridation makes it very difficult for someone who did not want to drink fluoride to avoid it. The Water Industry Act 1991, sections 87–91 permit water suppliers to add fluoride when asked to do so by a health authority. However, water suppliers are not required to do so. Since 1985 there have been no new fluoridation schemes.[58] This is in part due to privatization. Private

---

[56] [2003] 3 FCR 156.   [57] Kennedy and Grubb (2000: 909).   [58] DoH (1999a: para 9.19).

companies do not want the 'hassle' of fluoridation and the aggravation they may receive from customers who object.[59] Further, any proposal to fluoridate must go through a public consultation process. Those groups opposed to fluoridation can dominate any consultation process.

The issue of the non-consensual treatment and detention of patients raises important human rights issues. The ECHR, article 5(1)(c) specifically permits the lawful detention of a person to prevent the spread of infectious diseases. However, the infringement of human rights must be justified in the name of public health, necessary in a democratic society, and be proportionate.[60] If any of the powers mentioned above are to be used it will need to be shown, therefore, that there are no less coercive means of preserving the public health, and that the danger to the public is sufficiently serious as to justify the interference with human rights.

The spread of HIV has given the issue of controlling infectious diseases a particular contemporary resonance. In the debate a number of issues have been raised. It is not possible here to canvass all of the issues this important debate raises. The further reading will direct you to where to look for an in-depth discussion. One issue is whether or not there should be compulsory testing among everyone or certain groups of people. To test someone against their wishes appears to be contrary to fundamental principles of medical law and ethics. However, compulsory testing may be seen by some as essential if the Government is to have clear picture of the extent of HIV infection and even to ensure the safe treatment of a patient. So far the Government had not permitted widespread non-consensual testing for HIV, although it has authorized the anonymized non-consensual testing of blood of those attending antenatal and STD clinics. Further, some of the powers under the Public Health Act 1984 now apply to AIDS, and compulsory examination and removal to hospital are theoretically possible. Given that with responsible behaviour it is possible for an HIV positive person to be non-contagious these are controversial provisions, which have been described as permitting 'drastic interventions into the liberty of those who have or are suspected to have HIV'.[61] There is no reported case in which these powers have been used.

Another issue is that recent developments in criminal law mean that if X, knowing that he is HIV positive, has sexual relations with Y, without Y consenting to sexual relations aware of X's condition, then X can be guilty of inflicting grievous bodily harm if Y becomes infected as a result.[62] In effect this requires a person who is aware that she or he is infectious to inform her or his sexual partners of their condition before sexual activity. To some this is an effective means of promoting public health and protects the sexual and bodily autonomy rights of individuals.[63] To others this is an improper interference with the sexual freedom of those who are HIV positive and may discourage people from taking tests to discover whether they are positive.[64]

---

[59] See *R v Northumbrian Water Ltd ex p Newcastle and North Tyneside HA* [1999] Env LR 715 for an example of a legal challenge to proposed fluoridation.
[60] *Acmanne v Belgium* (1984) 40 D&R 251.   [61] Montgomery (2003: 35).
[62] The offence is under the Offences Against the Person Act 1861, s 20: *R v Dica* [2004] 3 All ER 593.
[63] Herring (2005).   [64] Weait (2005).

9 Public health: prevention

The traditional approach to medicine has been reactive: to diagnose the sick and offer them treatment. Increasingly the importance of preventative measures has been emphasized. Hence the NHS sees itself not only as offering treatment to the ill, but seeking to promote good health for the general public.[65] In economic terms this makes sense. If the Government can reduce the incidence of illness or accident there will be less call on the NHS's resources. Obesity, smoking, increasing drug and alcohol misuse, and sexually transmitted diseases all add to the pressure on the NHS.[66] Without preventative health the NHS would simply be overwhelmed by the needs of those suffering 'preventable illnesses'.[67] Indeed under article 11 of the European Social Charter the Government is required to remove the causes of ill-health, prevent disease, and advise individuals on how to look after their own health.

It is also interesting that the notion of public health has been developing. In the past its goal was simply trying to reduce the death rates among the general population. However, consider the World Health Organization's definition of health:

> a state of complete physical, mental and social well-being and not merely the absence of disease or infirmity.[68]

With this in mind actions which can be said to be public health issues could include things like the provision of recreation and park facilities which might never have been included in earlier understandings of the term.

But the key issue in public health is the role the Government should play in some of the major public health issues: smoking, obesity, and alcohol misuse, for example. Should the Government be actively seeking to prevent unhealthy lifestyle choices or is that too interventionist and rather should the Government's role be to encourage and enable people to live more healthily? There are some areas where it appears less controversial for the Government to intervene in the name of public health. Environmental issues are one. Clean air[69] and water[70] are, of course, essential to the nation's good health. But in areas such as diet, where the Government is seen as too interventionist, it is said by some that we are suffering under a 'nanny state'.

There are two issues here. The first is practical. There is a limit to what the Government can do in some areas. Programmes of vaccination and sanitation can be relatively easy to implement. But even if the Government wanted to force everyone to eat five portions of fresh fruit and vegetables a day, that would be almost impossible to implement. Second, is the theoretical issue, which concerns the extent to which it is the role of the Government to influence people's lifestyle choices. It has been said we have a 'new public health'.[71] Rather than the Government seeking to force people to adopt healthier lifestyles, much more effort is put into persuading individuals to take responsibility for their own health and make 'healthy choices'.[72] A recent Government Paper, *Saving Lives: Our Healthier Nation*, suggests that there needs to be a 'national contract' between individuals, communities, and Government to reduce death rates and improve health. The Government

---

[65] DoH (2005d).
[66] DoH (2005d); Foresight (2007).
[67] Wanless (2006).
[68] WHO (1948).
[69] Clean Air Act 1993 and Environment Act 1995.
[70] Water Industry Act 1991.
[71] Ashton and Seymour (1988: chapter 2).
[72] Calman et al (2004).

is seeking to avoid claims that it is encouraging a 'nanny state',[73] while not standing by as the health of the nation deteriorates and the burden on the NHS increases. The NHS Modernisation Board in 2005 stated:[74]

> The prime responsibility for improving the health of the public does not rest with the NHS, nor with the Government, but with the public themselves. However, it is wrong to say that Government has no role; it must provide clear information, helping more people to make healthy choices, by creating a supportive environment in which they can be helped to stop smoking, improve their diets and take more exercise.

To some critics, however, these ways of presenting public health issues, focussing on individual responsibility, hide an important point and that is that political and social factors play a crucial role in people's health. Poverty levels and socio-economic groupings can have a huge impact on an individual's health. The emphasis on helping people to be healthy ignores these and can be said to be an attempt to shift responsibility for health away from Government and towards individuals.[75]

It should also be remembered that although health is an important value for other people there are other things in our lives that we care about: liberty, autonomy, happiness etc. So health should never be regarded as a value worth pursing at all costs.[76]

TO PONDER

Obesity

There is widespread acceptance that obesity is a problem. Most adults in England are overweight and one in five (around 8 million individuals) are obese. It has been estimated that by 2050 60 per cent of men and 50 per cent of women will be obese (Foresight (2007)). At a simple level the cause is seen as an increasingly sedentary lifestyle, and poor eating patterns. However, in fact a host of more complex factors are behind these statistics. Obesity, it has been said, causes 30,000 deaths a year and shortens life expectancy by nine years. It has been estimated that the annual cost to the NHS of obesity is half a billion pounds (Committee of Public Accounts (2005)). Of course not everyone accepts that there is an 'epidemic' of obesity (Social Issues Research Centre (2005)). What is the Government to do?

In the Government's White Paper on Public Health (*Making Healthy Choices Easier*) three core principles were identified (para 5.101):

- **informed choice:** Government providing support through credible information to allow people to make their own decisions about choices that impact on their health;

- **personalization:** supporting people to make healthy choices, especially for deprived groups and communities; and

- **working together:** through effective partnerships across communities.

This is a delicate balance between encouraging people to adopt healthier lifestyles without being seen to be bossy. Consider the following statement by Tessa Jowell, a health minister (2004):

> We do however live in a time where there is an almost allergic reaction to any suggestion that Government can or should influence private behaviour (and obesity is a function of

---

[73] King's Fund (2004).   [74] Modernisation Board (2005).
[75] Rees Jones (2003).   [76] Häyry (2006).

private behaviour)...Providing people with the means to understand and take informed decisions; removing some of the obstacles to changing behaviour that may be beyond the means of individuals; getting out the wider considerations and context—that is not being a nanny state, but the enabling role of good Government.

Some of the tensions between these aims can be seen in the proposals in the Government's White Paper on Public Health designed to combat obesity:

- a new health advice service called Health Direct to be available over the phone, internet and digital TV;
- a personal health guide and NHS health trainer for everybody;
- working with the food and drink industry to develop voluntary codes on food and drink promotion to children. If these are not satisfactory the Government will introduce legislation;
- traffic light labelling for supermarket foods indicating how healthy they are;
- giving pregnant women vouchers enabling them to buy fresh fruit and vegetables, milk, and infant formula;
- encouraging children to cycle to school;
- monitoring the nutritional value of school meals through the school inspection regime.

Note how it seems more acceptable to be 'nannying' to children than adults.

10 Rationing

It would be wonderful if everyone who needed medical treatment could receive it. However, there appears to be a widespread consensus that to do so is simply not feasible. There are not enough medical professionals and not enough money to provide a comprehensive service.[77] It would simply bankrupt the NHS to give every person the treatment they wanted. One survey of a PCT in the NHS found that the panel which made decisions about funding new treatments was faced with applications that would have cost £44 million, but had only £5 million available.[78] As a result some means must be found to restrict access and decide, given the limited funds available, who should receive which treatment. This is generally known as rationing.

The question, from a legal perspective, can be looked at in two ways. One is to focus on health care authorities and ask in what ways is it lawful for them to restrict access to health care and how they should make rationing decisions. The other is to focus on patients and to ask whether we have a right to health care treatment and if so of what kind. This is not to ask the same question in a different way. Consider a case where a cash-strapped health authority fails to provide urgent health care treatment to a patient on economic grounds. It may be found that the individual's right to health care was infringed, but that the health authority acted reasonably in allocating its resources in the way it did. In such a case the claim may be better made against the Government in failing to provide sufficient funding for Trusts to be able to provide the care required. There could also be a case where a patient was denied health care and, although the court did

---

[77] See Light (1997) for an argument that this assumption should be challenged.
[78] Iqbal, Pryce, and Afza (2006). They also discuss how in practice PCTs make rationing decisions.

not think that there was a right to the kind of care in question, that the health authority had acted improperly in allocating resources in such a way.

10.1 What does rationing mean?

Rationing is said to occur where there is only a limited resource of health care and the decision is made to offer it to some people, but not others. Rationing does not therefore arise where a patient is not offered treatment because it is not clinically effective.

A central issue in rationing is the definition of a health care need. If a person who has no health care need, then denying them 'treatment' does not really involve rationing. However, the notion of 'need' is unclear. Andreas Hasman, Tony Hope, and Lars Østerdal[79] have suggested three possible meanings of need in this context. One definition of need is that the patient is below an accepted state of well-being and there is a treatment which can improve their condition. A second is that there is a need if a treatment will raise the patient's well-being from below a certain threshold to above it. A third is that a treatment will offer a patient a significant increase in well-being. It is rarely articulated which of these three is taken to be a need.

Rationing within the NHS can happen at three levels. First, there is the decision as to how much money the Government allocates to health, as opposed to other calls on public expenditure. Second, there is the decision as to how money will be allocated to different bodies within the NHS. Third, there is the decision by the bodies as to how the money will be spent to meet the needs of different people in their area.

10.2 The law on rationing

10.2.1 Statute

The National Health Services Act 1977 obliges the Secretary of State in section 3 to promote:

> a comprehensive health service designed to secure improvements in (a) in the physical and mental health of the people of [England and Wales], and (b) in the prevention, diagnosis and treatment of illness.

In *R v Secretary of State for Social Services ex p Hinks*[80] the Court of Appeal emphasized that even where the Secretary of State for Health had a duty under the NHS Act 1977, section 3 to provide services (in that case orthopaedic surgery), the duty was to provide the services 'to such an extent as he considers necessary to meet all reasonable requirements such as can be provided within the resources available'.[81] It is therefore clear that it is permissible to take into account financial considerations when deciding whether to offer treatment to a particular patient or group of patients.[82]

Throughout the 1977 Act the following phrase appears: 'to such extent as he [the Secretary of State] considers necessary to meet all reasonable requirements'. This applies to, *inter alia*, duties to provide hospital accommodation and medical, dental nursing, and ambulance services. This makes the enforcement of the Secretary of State's obligations difficult. It would be very difficult to show that the Secretary of State had breached

---

[79] Hasman, Hope, and Østerdal (2006).   [80] (1980) 1 BMLR 93.   [81] Ibid, at 95.
[82] *R v Sheffield HA ex p Seale* [1995] 25 BMLR 1.

her or his statutory duty by failing to provide a service which she or he thought reasonable. One of the few duties not so limited is the requirement to provide for the medical examination and care of state school pupils at appropriate intervals (section 3(1)).

So it is very unlikely that the Secretary of State would be found to be in breach of a statutory duty. Even if she or he was, the mode of enforcement would be by a claim for breach of statutory duty. However, in *Re HIV Haemophiliac Litigation*[83] the Court of Appeal accepted that the 1977 NHS Act did not provide the basis of an action for breach of statutory duty.[84] All of this indicates that a claimant seeking to challenge a rationing decision is unlikely to have much joy basing her or his claim on breach of statutory duty under the 1977 NHS Act.

There is a duty on PCTs to arrange GP, dental ophthalmic, and pharmaceutical services.[85] They must ensure that everyone can find a GP and deal with complaints about their GP that cannot be resolved within practices. Under regulations, the role of a GP is to give patients on their lists 'all necessary and appropriate personal medical services of the type usually provided by a general medical practitioner'.[86] This is not a very precise duty and again it would only be in cases involving the most blatant of failures that the duty could be enforced.

10.2.2 *European law*

EUROPEAN ANGLES

Claims under European law have been considered in the following case which discusses whether a patient who is refused treatment, or who faces a lengthy delay in obtaining treatment, can seek to have the operation conducted in another European Country and require payment for it from the NHS.

KEY CASE   R (on the application of Watts v Bedford Primary Care Trust and Secretary of State for Health 2003 EWHC 2228 and [2004] EWCA 166 and Case C-372/04)

Ms Watts suffered constant hip pain and had limited mobility, caused by osteoarthritis. She was on an NHS waiting list for a hip replacement and given a waiting time of approximately one year. She applied to have the operation performed in France using the form E112 procedure under article 22 of Regulation 1408/71, which conferred a right to be treated in another Member State at public expense where such treatment was not available within the time normally necessary for obtaining the treatment in the Member State of residence. The PCT refused. One of the reasons given was that because she would receive the operation within the normal waiting time she would not suffer undue delay.

---

[83] (1990) 41 BMLR 171. See also the House of Lords decision in *X v Bedfordshire* [1995] 3 All ER 353 where it was noted that there has never been a case of a successful claim for breach of statutory duty in legislation dealing with social welfare issues.

[84] Although see *R v Ealing DHA ex p Fox* [1993] 3 All ER 170 in which, *obiter*, it was suggested that mental patients could rely on the NHS Act 1977, s 3(1) for an action in breach of statutory duty.

[85] NHS Act 1977, ss 29, 35, 38, and 41.

[86] NHS (General Medical Services) Regulations 1992, Sch 2, para 12(1).

In her application to the High Court she sought to rely, *inter alia*, on article 49 EC and article 22 of Regulation 1408/71. It is useful to look at both the first instance and the Court of Appeal decision.

Mumby J: In relation to the article 49 (providing a freedom to obtain services) claim Mumby J held that the article did apply to medical and hospital services, although following the decision of the ECJ in *Geraets-Smits v Peerbooms* [2001] ECR I–5363, such a claim could only succeed if there was prior authorization for the treatment from the UK. But the payments only had to be made if there was not effective treatment available in her home country without 'undue delay'. In so holding he rejected an argument that *Geraets-Smits* did not apply in countries where health care was funded through general taxation. Justice Mumby rejected the PCT's interpretation of undue delay being 'a normal waiting time' for the country in question, but held that the concept required a consideration of what was reasonable bearing in mind whether the patient was in pain, whether there had been repeated delays in treatment, and whether the patient would suffer deterioration if the treatment was delayed. Taking these factors into account a delay of three to fourth months was not undue. He did suggest (at para 158) that a delay of a year leaving a patient in considerable pain and with mobility difficulties could be regarded as undue.

In relation to article 22 of Regulation 1408/71 the availability of treatment 'within the time normally necessary for obtaining the treatment in the Member State of residence' referred to normal within the NHS. Her delay was not abnormal by the standards of the NHS. So that claim failed too.

Court of Appeal: The Secretary of State appealed against Mumby J's decision, arguing that rulings of the European Court of Justice which had held that institutions providing medical services in one Member State might be obliged to reimburse the cost of a patient's treatment in another Member State did not apply to the NHS. Alternatively, if that case law was applicable to the NHS, he argued that the concept of 'undue delay' should be interpreted by reference to a properly operated NHS.

The Court of Appeal confirmed Mumby J's ruling that article 49 EC did apply to NHS Treatment. The decision in *Muller-Faure* [2004] 2 CMLR 33 applied to a State-funded NHS as to other forms of health systems in Europe.

The proviso in article 22 of Regulation 1408/71 that a person should be authorized to go to another Member State for treatment applied where she or he could not be given such treatment 'within the time normally necessary for obtaining the treatment in question in the Member State of residence, taking account of his current state of health and the probable course of the disease' this did not require a consideration of 'normal waiting times'. Rather it focused on clinical judgment and the impact of the delay on the particular individual concerned.

The Court of Appeal went on to explain that although these findings represented the current law they created considerable problems for the UK, with its NHS system. It sought a preliminary ruling from the European Court clarifying the application of article 49 EC and article 22 of Regulation 1408/71 in the light of the specific features of the NHS. A ruling would also be sought as to the basis on which the NHS was obliged to pay or reimburse costs if it authorized medical treatment for a patient in another Member State.

ECJ: The ECJ started their analysis by emphasizing that a UK citizen could only require the NHS to fund overseas treatment if the NHS had given its authorization to the treatment. In deciding whether to give authorization the NHS had to take into account the clinical needs of the patient. In particular an objective assessment had to be made of the patient's medical condition, the history and probable course of their illness, the degree of pain they were in, and/or the nature of their disability. If the treatment could only be offered within the NHS after an unacceptable delay then the NHS had to authorize treatment overseas. Whether the delay was unacceptable or not depended on the clinical factors just listed. Economic factors and budgetary constraints were not relevant considerations.

The impact of this decision is, therefore, that a patient can require the NHS to fund treatment overseas if treatment on the NHS will only become available after an unacceptable delay.[87] It is not open to the NHS to claim that the delay is acceptable given the monetary difficulties facing an NHS Trust. Trusts will now need to set up schemes to deal with applications for those seeking authorization for funding for treatment in other European Countries. Such a scheme will have to be non-discriminatory and readily accessible.[88] It is likely that this decision will assist those patients with sufficient education and articulacy to make the relevant claim. Cynics might see it as providing an effective way of jumping the queue to treatment for the middle classes. Christopher Newdick complains that 'then those willing and able to travel abroad will have greater access to expensive treatments than those who are too ill, old or disabled to travel'.[89]

10.2.3 *Judicial review*

The most common way of using the courts to challenge a rationing decision is judicial review.[90] Such attempts have rarely succeeded. There are three main bases on which judicial review can be sought:

(i) The decision was illegal. For example, that it was a decision the PCT had no power to make.

(ii) The decision was irrational or unreasonable. Unreasonable in the context of judicial review has a special meaning: it must be shown that the decision was so unreasonable that no reasonable decision maker would have made it.

(iii) There was procedural impropriety in the making of the decision.[91]

Most applications in this context will involve the unreasonableness ground. As already indicated this is difficult to prove because it is not enough to show the decision was not the best one that could be made, but rather one that no reasonable decision maker could have made. The following are some of the key points that emerge from the case law:

(i) Although there is a statutory duty to provide medical treatment, that is not an absolute duty, because resources are finite.[92] In *R v North and East Devon Health Authority ex p Coughlan*[93] the Court of Appeal said that, in exercising judgments about resource allocation, the Secretary of State for Health (and therefore all bodies which took their powers from him) had

> to bear in mind the comprehensive service which he is under a duty to promote. . . . However, as long as he pays due regard to that duty, the fact that the service will not be comprehensive does not mean that he is necessarily contravening [his statutory duty]. The truth is that, while he has the duty to continue to provide a comprehensive free health service and he must never. . . . disregard that duty, a comprehensive health service may never, for human, financial and other resource reasons, be achievable. . . . In exercising his judgment

---

[87] See McHale (2007) for a useful analysis of the decision.
[88] McHale (2007).   [89] Newdick (2007: 244).
[90] In *R (on the application of Cavanagh) v Health Service Commissioner* (2005) 91 BMLR 40 it was held that the Health Service Commissioner could not hear a complaint about a rationing decision.
[91] The detail of the law generally on judicial review can be found in textbooks on administrative law.
[92] In *R v Secretary of State for Social Services and others ex p Hincks* (1980) 1 BMLR 93.
[93] [2000] 3 All ER 850.

the Secretary of State is entitled to take into account the resources available to him and the demands on those services.

(ii) A fixed policy that is not responsive to the needs of individuals may be unlawful. In *R v NW Lancashire HA ex p A*[94] a rigid policy against funding gender reassignment surgery was found to be unlawful, as it fettered the discretion of the authority and failed to enable it to consider the individual facts of each case. Of course a policy which stated that generally a certain kind of treatment would not be available would be permissible, as long as each case was considered individually.

(iii) Patients should have a chance to explain why they should be given treatment and to hear why they are being denied it.[95] This does not mean that the patient should be able to directly address the decision maker, but that the patient's views must be properly considered.[96]

(iv) A successful judicial review challenge could be brought if, in reaching its decision, the NHS body had taken into account irrelevant considerations or failed to take into account relevant considerations. It is clear that the likelihood of success of the treatment[97] and NICE guidelines would be relevant factors. So in *R v Derbyshire HA ex p Fisher*[98] it was found to be improper to fail to follow an NHS circular without explanation. Obviously a decision which was based on sex or race would also be unlawful. It is less clear whether age would be an impermissible factor. It certainly could be taken into account if a patient's age meant that the treatment was less likely to be effective. We shall consider this issue in more detail later in this chapter.

(v) If a public body has created a legitimate expectation that a certain form of treatment will be provided, and unfairly alters its policies to the disadvantage of those who have relied on the expectation, then a successful claim could be sought. In *R v North and East Devon HA ex p Coughlan*[99] it was found that the applicant had been assured by the Health Authority that she would have a home for life in a residential facility managed by the Health Authority. Her legitimate expectation rendered the later decision to close the facility unlawful.

(vi) It is unlikely that a clinical assessment concerning treatment will be found unreasonable. In *R v Secretary of State for Social Services ex p Walker*[100] the applicant was the mother of a child who needed an operation to rectify a congenital heart defect. The difficulty was that there was a shortage of beds on a neonatal unit. Other children kept being assessed to be in greater need than the applicant's child and she sought to challenge the health authority's decisions. The Court of Appeal accepted that the local authority had acted properly in preferring to give cots to the most urgent cases. This was, in effect, a clinical decision and not open to challenge in the courts. Similarly courts will not force doctors to provide care that in their clinical judgement they think inappropriate.[101]

(vii) It is not yet clear how the Disability Discrimination Act 1995 will impact on rationing decisions. The Act makes it illegal for service providers to discriminate on the basis of a disability. That is a 'physical or mental impairment which has a substantial and long-term adverse effect on [a person's] ability to carry out normal day-to-day activities'.[102]

94 [2000] 2 FCR 525.
95 *R v Ethical Committee of St Mary's Hospital ex p Harriott* [1988] 1 FLR 512.
96 *R v Cambridge DHA ex p B* [1995] 2 All ER 129.
97 *R v Sheffield HA ex p Seale* (1994) 25 BMLR 1.   98 [1997] 8 Med LR 327.
99 [2000] 3 All ER 850.   100 (1987) 3 B MLR 32.
101 *R v Ealing DA ex p Fox* [1993] 3 All ER 170.   102 Disability Discrimination Act 1995, s 1(1).

This would mean, for example, that it would be unlawful for a health authority not to allocate resources to someone to deal with a physical problem simply on the grounds that they suffered from a mental illness.

(viii) Financial considerations can be taken into account in deciding whether to offer treatment. The courts have tended to take the view that it is appropriate for health authorities in deciding whether to offer treatments to take into account their limited resources.[103] When doing that it is for the health authorities and not the courts to make the assessment.[104] The question of the relevance of financial considerations came dramatically to a head in the following case:

KEY CASE   R v Cambridge HA ex p B [1995] 2 All ER 129

B was a ten year old girl with leukaemia. A bone-marrow transplant had been attempted but it was unsuccessful. Doctors in London and Cambridge believed she had only six to eight weeks to live and that any further treatment would be inappropriate. However, B's father did not accept this assessment and found a professor in London and doctors in the United States who would have offered the girl further treatment. The professor admitted that his proposal of chemotherapy and a possible second transplant was experimental and not standard. The Health Authority supported the decision not to offer further treatment. They explained: 'the substantial expenditure on treatment with such a small prospect of success would not be an effective use of resources'. The father sought judicial review of the decision. At first instance before Laws J he succeeded. Justice Laws emphasized the girl's right to life under article 2 of the European Convention on Human Rights. This meant that compelling reasons had to be provided to justify preferring the needs of other patients over her. Simply stating that resources were limited was not sufficient, the health authority had to state explicitly which other calls on its funds meant that it was not able to offer her treatment.

The Health Authority was, however, successful in its appeal to the Court of Appeal. The Court emphasized it was not for the courts to look at the merits of the local authority's decision. It was not the courts' job to assess whether the local authority's distribution of resources was appropriate. Sir Thomas Bingham held:

> Difficult and agonizing judgements have to be made as to how a limited budget is best allocated to the maximum advantage of the maximum of patients. That is not a judgement which the court can make.

The case is fascinating for its contrast between the approaches of Laws J at first instance and the Court of Appeal.[105] The Court of Appeal used the standard unreasonableness test. They found that sensitive decisions on resource allocations can only in exceptional cases be said to be unreasonable. This was not such an exceptional case. The main point for the Court of Appeal was that the court should in cases of judicial review not be considering the merits of the decision, but rather the process by which it was reached. Justice

---

[103] *R v Secretary of State for Social Services ex p Hincks* (1980) 1 BMLR 93, *R v Sheffield HA ex p Seale* [1995] 25 BMLR 1.

[104] *R v Secretary of State for Social Services ex p Walker* (1987) 3 BMLR 32. See for further discussion King (2007).

[105] Mullender (1996), O'Sullivan (1998).

Laws by contrast regarded the unreasonableness test as inappropriate in cases like this where there are fundamental human rights at stake; here the right to life.

The progress of the case following the Court of Appeal's judgment is revealing. B's father took her to the United States and she received treatment which was paid for by an anonymous donor. The early signs were promising: B's leukaemia went into remission,[106] but several months later she fell ill again and died in May 1996. Whether this vindicated the health authority's view that the treatment was not clinically appropriate, or B's father's views that the treatment enabled her to have several more happy months of life, something on which no value can be placed, is a matter of debate.

However, the decision in B may suggest that it is very unlikely that a rationing decision will successfully be challenged before the courts. It is worth remembering the decision in *R v NW Lancashire HA ex p A and G*[107] where the Court of Appeal held the decision to bar funding of gender reassignment surgery to be unlawful. There Auld LJ stated:[108]

> ...in establishing priorities—comparing the respective needs of patients suffering from different illnesses and determining the respective strengths of their claims to treatment—it is vital: for (1) an authority accurately to assess the nature and seriousness of each type of illness, (2) to determine the effectiveness of various forms of treatment for it and (3) to give proper effect to that assessment and that determination in the application of its policy.

It is not quite clear whether Auld LJ was intending to suggest that a health authority which failed to consider these factors would be acting lawfully and could be subject to judicial review; or whether he was merely indicating good practice. If he was suggesting that a failure to follow this advice could lead to a successful legal challenge then this suggests a far greater willingness by the Court of Appeal to examine the reasoning process by which a rationing decision was made than appeared in B.

KEY CASE   R (Rogers) v Swindon NHS Primary Care Trust [2006] EWCA Civ 392

Anne-Marie Rogers sought a judicial review of the decision of her PCT to refuse to fund her treatment with Herceptin (an unlicenced drug). She had breast cancer. Her consultant had advised her that she had a 25 per cent chance of remaining free from cancer in the next years, but a 57 per cent chance of dying. Initial trials of Herceptin had suggested considerable benefit in the kind of cancer Ms Rogers suffered from. Initially she paid for the drug herself, but when she lacked funds she asked her PCT to fund it. Their policy was only to fund the treatment where there were exceptional personal or clinical circumstances. They determined that there were none in her case.

The Court of Appeal held that the policy of only funding the drug in exceptional circumstances was legal only if the policy maker had envisaged what kind of cases would be exceptional. If in fact it was not possible to imagine such exceptional circumstances the policy was in fact one of complete refusal and this would be irrational, because it failed to take into account each individual case (*R v North Lancashire ex p G*[109] was followed). The court found that the reality here was that among those patients for whom the drug would be appropriate there was no rational basis for distinguishing

---

106   BMA (2004: 156).   107   [1999] L l Rep Med 399.
108   At 408.   109   [2000] 2 FCR 525.

between those patients on the basis of personal or clinical grounds. Ms Rogers could not be said to be any less exceptional than anyone else in her medical condition. The policy had made no mention of costs being a factor to be taken into account. Therefore the policy was irrational and unlawful. The court added that because there were comparatively few patients for whom the drug would be appropriate there was no danger that the PCT would be flooded with claims.

It is important to appreciate that it was central to the court's reasoning that the Trust had declared that costs were not a relevant factor.[110] The Court of Appeal appeared to conclude that if the PCT had openly said that budgetary considerations would be a factor in deciding whether the drug could be granted then it would be permissible to deny a patient the drug on the grounds of cost. The decision is not, then, a decision saying that cancer patients have a right to drugs which will help them. It is rather a decision that rationing decisions must be made openly. If the truth is that the PCT cannot afford to give the drug to a patient it must be open about the relevance of the cost issue. Interestingly Sir Anthony Clarke[111] suggested that it might be appropriate in such a case to decide that a drug could be funded for a mother caring for a disabled son, but not a woman with no dependants.[112]

A similar point can be made about *R (Otley) v Barking & Dagenham NHS PCT*[113] in which Victoria Otley's NHS Trust refused to fund a treatment using an anti-cancer drug (Avastin). She sought a judicial review of that decision. The decision not to fund her treatment was made by a panel of the Trust. The panel had received a report which recommended the drug in Ms Otley's case. However a member of the panel noted that in research studies Avastin had not been used as part of a cocktail of drugs. On appeal it was held that the panel had failed to give sufficient weight to fact that this regime of drugs was the only set of drugs available. Although the chance that Avastin could lengthen her life by more than a few months was slim, this was an important chance that she should be allowed to have. The court emphasized that this was not a decision which had been made on the basis of scarce resources.

What is clear is that the courts are unlikely to find a particular rationing policy unlawful on the basis of it being unreasonable. An application is more likely to succeed where the complaint is essentially procedural: the proper reasons for the decision are not given, the policy was misapplied, or the applicant's individual circumstances were not taken into account. Ironically this may mean it is far harder to challenge the decision of a Trust which boldly states: 'we cannot afford your treatment—there are other needier patients' than a trust who tries to hind behind a formula based on exceptional cases. Christopher Newdick[114] thinks it is not difficult for a court to find a procedural flaw if it wants to allow an application. By contrast Charles Foster[115] thinks it is now easy for a Trust to ensure they comply with the law. One way of reading the decisions of the courts in this

---

[110] According to Newdick (2007) this was because they had misunderstood statements made by the Secretary of State for Health who had stated that women should not be denied access to breast cancer treatment due to cost.

[111] At para 77.

[112] See also *R (Gordon) v Bromley PCT* [2006] EWHC 2462 at para 41 where care for young children was mentioned as a possible exceptional circumstance.

[113] [2007] EWHC 1927 (Admin).   [114] Newdick (2007: 244).   [115] Foster (2007).

area is that they want Trusts to be completely honest and open about the rationing decisions that they make.[116] If treatment cannot be afforded the Trust should say so and not hide behind clever rhetoric.

10.2.4 Should the courts be more interventionist?

Supporters of a conservative role for the courts will emphasize how the courts are ill equipped to make rationing decisions, not just because, arguably, they lack the skills, but more importantly because they lack the information. They will be aware of the situation of the applicant, but they will not know about the other patients needing treatment. As Christopher Newdick asks:

> during litigation on behalf of an individual patient, who will speak for the large numbers of patients who are not party to the dispute but who may be affected by its outcome, and for those particular patients whose operations will have to be cancelled if someone else is treated first?[117]

Bingham MR has made the point this way, in *R v Cambridge Health Authority ex p B*:[118]

> I have no doubt that in a perfect world any treatment which a patient, or a patient's family, sought would be provided if doctors were willing to give it, no matter how much it cost, particularly when a life was potentially at stake. It would, however, in my view, be shutting one's eyes to the real world if the court were to proceed on the basis that we do live in such a world. It is common knowledge that health authorities of all kinds are constantly pressed to make ends meet. They cannot pay their nurses as much as they would like; they cannot provide all the treatments they would like; they cannot purchase all the extremely expensive medical equipment they would like; they cannot carry out all the research they would like; they cannot build all the hospitals and specialist units they would like. Difficult and agonising judgments have to be made as to how a limited budget is best allocated to the maximum advantage of the maximum number of patients. That is not a judgment which the court can make.

Opponents will emphasize the rights of individuals to treatment, especially where it is life-saving treatment. Where life-saving treatment is being denied simply to say 'it's too expensive' is too easy. The courts are entitled to know exactly why it is too expensive, exactly what would be lost if the treatment was provided. Only then can an effective protection of individual patients' human rights be protected.

10.2.5 Human Rights Act 1998

A patient could seek to bring in aid her or his rights under the European Convention on Human Rights.[119] This could either be as an aspect of a claim for judicial review, or a freestanding application under the Human Rights Act 1998, sections 6 and 7.[120] There are four main articles that might be relied upon, although, as we will see, only rarely will

---

116 See also *R (Linda Gordon) v Bromley NHS Primary Care Trust* [2006] EWHC 2462 (Admin) where Ousley J complained that the trust had failed to make it clear why it was refusing treatment.
117 Newdick (2005: 99).   118 [1995] 1 WLR 898, at 906C.   119 MacLean (2001).
120 There is no right under common law to receive treatment: *Re J (A Minor) (Wardship: Medical Treatment)* [1990] 3 All ER 930.

they provide the basis of a right to treatment:[121]

- *Article 2: the right to life.* A person seeking life-saving treatment under the NHS might claim that not to provide them with it would infringe their right to life. The difficulty with such an argument is that although article 2 does protect the right to life, this has not been interpreted to mean that a person is entitled to every form of medical treatment they need to keep alive.[122] After all, in most cases it is likely that life-saving treatment is not being offered to person A in order to provide life-saving treatment to person B. In such a case it cannot be that both A and B's article 2 rights entitle them to the treatment.

- *Article 3: protection from torture or inhuman or degrading treatment.* It might be argued by an applicant that not being provided treatment leaves that individual in such a state of health that she or he is suffering inhuman or degrading treatment. Such an argument also faces difficulties. Like article 2, article 3 does not entitle a person to all forms of treatment that might avoid degradation.[123] However, if a patient in hospital was inadequately fed or washed and this caused the patient to suffer, for example, malnutrition or serious bed sores this might infringe article 3. It might be argued that although article 3 does not give an automatic right to treatment it at least gives a right to basic care. Of course article 3 only applies where the state of health of the individual is of sufficient seriousness to amount to inhuman or degrading treatment.[124]

- *Article 8: right to private life.* It might be argued that the right to respect for one's private life could include a right to receive the treatment one wants.[125] However, in *North West Lancashire v A D and G* it was held that article 8 could not be relied upon to found a right to receive treatment.[126]

- *Article 14: protection from discrimination.* This is perhaps potentially the most promising line of argument for an applicant who can claim that the allocation of resources has been discriminatory on the basis of grounds such as race, sex, or religious belief. It would, of course, be surprising if a health authority were to do that. But there are two categories of cases which deserve greater attention. The first is age. Article 14 does not list age as an unacceptable ground of discrimination, but the list of factors are seen only as examples. The courts have been willing to add, for example, sexual orientation. If age were added then a claim could be brought if a patient felt she or he was denied treatment that a younger person in her or his shoes would have had. The second is disability. Again this is not a factor mentioned in article 14, but the courts may be willing to add it in. Could it be said that a decision not to give a donated kidney to a child suffering from Down's Syndrome who needed a kidney transplant, but to give it instead to a 'healthy' child, amounted to discriminatory conduct?

If age and disability discrimination were held to fall under article 14 then the key issue would be whether or not the decision was 'objectively justifiable', because if it was then the decision could not be challenged. A strong case for justification may be if the disability or age meant that the likely success of the treatment was less. If, for example, a

---

[121] Foster (2007).   [122] Maclean (2000).

[123] *R v North West Lancashire Health Authority ex p A* [2000] 1 WLR 977, at 1000G (Buxton LJ).

[124] *R (on the application of Yvonne Watts) v Bedford Primary Care Trust and Secretary of State for Health* [2003] EWHC 2228.

[125] Epstein (1997) fiercely rejects claims to a right to medical treatment.

[126] [2000] 2 FCR 525. See also *R (on the application of Yvonne Watts) v Bedford Primary Care Trust and Secretary of State for Health* [2003] EWHC 2228.

donated organ was not given to a 70-year-old but given to a young man on the basis that the 70-year-old was less likely to survive the transplantation procedure than the young man then that would provide a justification. We will consider issues surrounding age discrimination later in this chapter.

10.2.6 *European Charter of Fundamental Rights*

EUROPEAN ANGLES

Under article 35 of the EU Charter of Fundamental Rights there is the following right:

Everyone has the right of access to preventative health care and the right to benefit from medical treatment under the conditions established by national laws and practices.

This leaves much to the discretion of individual countries to set the limits of this right.

10.2.7 *Negligence*

An action in negligence could be brought against a local authority if it was claimed that harm had been caused to a patient as a result of a negligently made rationing decision. One issue in such a claim would be whether in making resource allocations decisions the health authority owes a duty of care to patients. This will depend on whether it is just and reasonable to impose a duty of care on the public authority in question. The key case on this is *DHSS v Kinnear*[127] where the plaintiff claimed to have suffered brain damage as a result of vaccinations. Justice Stuart-Smith drew a distinction between operational issues which could be the subject of a tortious claim and a policy decision which could not be challenged by the law of tort. So in this case the policy of encouraging vaccinations could not be challenged. However, an allegation that misleading advice had been given about the manner and circumstances in which vaccinations should be provided could be challenged in the courts. This makes it extremely unlikely that an action could succeed in negligence to challenge a decision about resource allocation. A greater chance of success might meet a claim that, having decided to allocate resources in a particular way, it implemented that decision ineffectively. Even then the courts might take the view that it would not be just and reasonable to impose a duty of care on local authorities given the availability of alternative complaint mechanisms available, and given the impact on the NHS of having to deal with a large number of claims.[128]

A claim of negligence could be brought against the individual health care professional based on the fact she or he improperly rationed health care resources. A court, when considering whether an individual professional is negligent, is likely to take into account that rationing decisions are normally taken at a higher level than an individual doctor.[129] However, a professional who decided not to offer a patient treatment based on a rationing ground which was in defiance of her or his NHS Trust's guidelines might face a challenge on the basis of negligence.

---

[127] (1984) 134 NLJ 886.   [128] *X v Bedfordshire* [1995] 3 All ER 353.
[129] Witting (2000).

10.3 How does the NHS ration at present?

Successive governments have been adamant that there is no such thing as rationing within the NHS. Tony Blair himself has stated 'if you are ill or injured there will be a National Health Service there to help; and access to it will be based on need and need alone'.[130] However, as the Bristol Inquiry said:

> Governments of the day have made claims for the NHS which were not capable of being met on the resources available. The public has been led to believe that the NHS could meet their legitimate needs, whereas it is patently clear that it could not. Healthcare professionals, doctors, nurses, managers, and others, have been caught between the growing disillusion of the public on the one hand and the tendency of governments to point to them as a scapegoat for a failing service on the other...The NHS was represented as a comprehensive service which met all the needs of the public. Patently it did not do so...[131]

Whatever politicians may say it is clear that when deciding what treatment a patient should be given NHS Trusts and doctors themselves are influenced by the monetary restrictions facing the NHS. Even if not done explicitly, the limits on resources mean that some patients are denied treatment that might be clinically desirable. So where and how does rationing occur?

(i) The Government

At one level the amount of money allocated by the Treasury to the Department of Health, and the taxation levels set by the Government, play an important role in determining the amount of money the NHS has to use in offering treatments to patients.

(ii) Clinicians

Medical professionals themselves ration. Perhaps unconsciously, the decision may be made that the treatment is not 'worth while' for this patient, or she or he is not considered an urgent case. In fact, there is very little evidence about the way that 'clinical' decisions can in reality be rationing. It has been said that 'deterrence, delay deflection, denial and dilution' of care all play their part.[132] Indeed financial incentives are offered to some front line staff to discourage 'excessive' use of NHS resources.[133] The benefit to politicians of clinical judgment is that it:

> renders the process of rationing as if it were politically invisible, by fragmenting it across space and time into individualised and private transactions between doctors and patients. The result was that the NHS was able to maintain the fiction of meeting everyone's needs.[134]

(iii) NICE

The most overt way in which rationing decisions are made is through the guidance issued by NICE (the National Institute for Health and Clinical Excellence). This guidance can recommend that treatments are not made available or only made available to certain categories of patients within the NHS. We will look further at the work of this body below.

---

[130] NHS (1997). [131] The Bristol Royal Infirmary Inquiry (2001: para 31).
[132] Newdick (2005: 50). [133] Ashworth (2004). [134] Harrison (1998: 18).

(iv) Waiting lists

Another significant means of restricting access to treatment is the waiting list. A patient is not denied treatment outright, but must wait. Many Trusts have systems where urgent cases can be speeded to the top of the list. Further, it is not uncommon for patients to be told of the delay under the NHS and then, if they are able to afford it, seek speedier treatment under the private health schemes.

10.4 National Institute for Health and Clinical Excellence (NICE)

In the past rationing was done informally and often in a hidden way. Individual doctors and health authorities would make decisions about what treatments were 'appropriate' for patients. These were often presented as clinical decisions about what was best for a patient, even if in fact the decision was solely, or partly, influenced by economic considerations.[135] One of the consequences of this was that the availability of treatment differed widely in various parts of the country.[136] This became known as the 'postcode lottery'. It led to a growing sense of unease, with important decisions about the allocation of health care resources being made in private, without full information and little or no accountability.

It was partly as a result of these concerns that the National Institute for Health and Clinical Excellence (NICE) was created. The then Health Secretary stated that NICE 'will help to bring order and rationality to a system that all too often has appeared arbitrary and unfair'.[137] This body now plays an important role in the rationing of health care within the NHS. One of its primary roles is said to be as follows:

> The Institute will promote clinical excellence and the effective use of available resources in the NHS through the development and dissemination of guidelines for the management of certain diseases or conditions, guidance on the appropriate use of particular interventions, audit methodologies and the dissemination of these to support frontline staff and patients.[138]

The official role of NICE is to establish and set uniform standards regarding treatment across the NHS. It will determine the effectiveness and appropriateness of treatments being offered on the NHS. For example, if it is believed that a new drug will provide an effective treatment for a particular condition that drug will be examined by NICE, who will consider its effectiveness and cost in deciding whether to recommend that the drug be made available on the NHS, not available at all, or available only to a certain class of patients. When its advice is not to prescribe a particular drug on the grounds of its cost, in effect this is rationing. Of course, it is not quite this straightforward because NICE will be looking at all kinds of factors when considering whether to recommend a drug. The chair of NICE has listed factors that would be taken into account:[139]

- The clinical needs of patients in relation to other available technologies: this is obviously an overriding issue, and the evidence base for clinical effectiveness is crucial.

- The NHS's priorities: this is a relative, and not an absolute, criterion.

- The broad balance between benefits and costs: this incorporates both clinical and cost effectiveness.

---

135 Schmidt (2004).   136 House of Commons Health Committee (1995).
137 Milburn (1999).   138 NICE (1999).   139 NICE (1999).

- The potential impact on other NHS resources: this is particularly relevant where there are potential 'knock on' effects for other parts of the service.

- The encouragement of innovation.

- Guidance from ministers on the resources available[140] but, he added, he had never received guidance from ministers on the resources available.

A decision not to recommend a drug or treatment will not be based on the straightforward argument, 'it's too expensive', but rather on a complex combination of clinical and economic factors. In theory a drug company or individual could seek judicial review of a decision of NICE, but it is difficult to imagine the decision of such an august body concerning such a delicate and complex issue being found unreasonable.[141]

NICE's role in assessing new treatments involves a number of factors. The first is in determining the effectiveness of the new treatments. It appears to be generally accepted that NICE carries out this technical side of its job well, using experts in relevant fields to assess proposed treatments and emphasizing the importance of evidence-based medicine. The second is in calculating the cost-effectiveness of the products. It is in this regard that greater concerns have arisen.

It is, perhaps misleading to emphasize the role of NICE as rationing treatment. In fact there are far more instances of NICE recommending treatment than suggesting it should not be available. Indeed, as one commentator has pointed out, although NICE has received plaudits, these have not come from NHS Trusts grateful at the amount of money saved as a result of NICE's work.[142] Indeed this point highlights a real difficulty for NICE's role. It considers whether or not to approve a particular drug or treatment in isolation. It has no way of knowing which treatments a Trust will have to stop providing in order to follow NICE guidance. The difficulty therefore is that NICE cannot know whether the treatments which Trusts might forgo are more efficient or effective than the ones it is promoting.[143]

The exact status and effect of guidance issued by NICE is unclear. A number of questions arise, which are explored below.

10.4.1 *Are NICE guidelines meant to be binding on Trusts or clinicians?*

NICE has emphasized that what it issues is 'guidance' and therefore cannot be binding on particular health care professionals.[144] It explains:

> Once NICE publishes clinical guidance, health professionals and the organizations that employ them are expected to take it fully into account when deciding what treatments to give people. However, NICE guidance does not replace the knowledge and skills of individual health professionals who treat patients; it is still up to them to make decisions about a particular patient in consultation with the patient and/or their guardian or carer when appropriate.[145]

---

[140] NICE (2000).

[141] In *R v Secretary of State for Health ex p Pfizer* [1999] Ll Rep Med 289 a successful challenge was made to the means by which the Secretary of State sought to ration the use of Viagra within the NHS. See *Eisai v NICE* [2007] EWHC 1941 (Admin) for a largely unsuccessful challenge.

[142] Campbell (2003).　　[143] Harris (2007).

[144] See Iqbal, Pryce, and Afza (2006) for a discussion of the ways that in practice, local priorities and NICE guidelines may be in tension.

[145] NICE (2005: 4).

That said, if a patient is refused treatment which has been recommended by NICE then the professional could face a claim of negligence unless she or he had strong reasons why the patient should not receive that treatment.

Since January 2002, NHS Trusts have been required to provide funding for medicines and treatments recommended by NICE and this is to be taken into account when general annual budgets are set out. However, making the money available and ensuring that NICE guidance is followed are not the same thing.[146] As we shall see shortly, in fact it is clear that NICE guidance is not always followed by NHS Trusts.

What if the NICE guidelines recommend that a drug not be used, is that binding? In *R v Secretary of State for Health ex p Pfizer*[147] it was held that Health Circular 1998/158 which stated that Viagra (sildenafil) should only be made available in exceptional circumstances in the NHS was unlawful. This was because it was seen as an improper interference in a doctor's professional judgment.

10.4.2 *Are Trusts in fact following NICE guidelines?*

As already indicated, following NICE guidance is not mandatory. This has led to varying levels of compliance with NICE guidance among NHS Trusts.[148] When the Audit Commission looked into the compliance with NICE guidance[149] it found that 33 per cent of responding NHS bodies said that they had not been able to fund full compliance with NICE guidance. It found that NICE guidance was not integrated into financial planning decisions in a routine way. The Audit Commission concluded that it was not cost difficulties that prevented NICE guidance from being followed, but rather poor management.

10.4.3 *To what extent is NICE meant to look at economics?*

One of the complaints about the work of NICE is that it focuses on the cost-effectiveness of the drug or proposed treatment in the abstract and decides whether it provides good value for money.[150] But being one step apart from the NHS Trusts it does not consider how the Trusts are to afford the implementation of the guidance. To be blunt if a new drug is approved by NICE and a Trust adopts that drug the money to pay for it must come from somewhere. NICE might reassure us that the drug is cost-effective, but it does not (of course) tell a Trust what it should cut from its expenditure when adopting the drug. This has led some to claim that the work of NICE has skewed priorities for Trusts. They are keen to follow NICE guidance but in so doing they may be cutting back on other equally valuable treatments that NICE is yet to consider.[151] Of course NICE does consider the question of overall resource implication in the abstract. As Professor Rawlins, chair of NICE, put it:

> The Institute will have to take into account the NHS's broad clinical priorities and the broad balance between benefits and costs. The Institute will have to take into account guidance from Ministers on the resources likely to be available; and the Institute will have to ensure that the technology represents an effective use of available resources.[152]

---

[146] Syrett (2003).
[147] (1999) 51 BMLR 189.
[148] Eg, in relation to cancer, see National Audit Office (2005b).
[149] National Audit Office (2005b).
[150] WHO (2003: 6).
[151] WHO (2003: 6).
[152] Rawlins (2004).

NICE has also emphasized that it makes decisions about whether or not a treatment is cost-effective. It does not determine whether or not the treatment is affordable. That, it seems, is regarded as primarily an issue for the Government.[153] It has been estimated that the first 22 treatments approved by NICE will have cost £200 million, around 0.5 per cent of the annual NHS spending.[154] Not surprisingly there have been concerns that attempts to comply with NICE guidance is putting financial strains on Trusts.[155]

10.4.4 *What is the relationship between NICE and the Government?*

The exact relationship between the Government and NICE is delicate. On the one hand NICE can be convenient for the Government. When NICE decides not to approve a new expensive drug for a particular illness the 'flack' is directed towards NICE, rather than the Government. Indeed it has been suggested that the creation of NICE is part of a strategy of blame avoidance and blame diffusion within the NHS.[156] However on occasion the Government will want to appear to be taking an active approach to a health problem. Hence we saw, in August 2005, NICE being ordered by a government minister to fast track an assessment of Herceptin, a drug designed to treat breast cancer,[157] and in 2002 the Government's announcement that it would provide a form of funding for a drug to treat Multiple Sclerosis, despite NICE's original decision that it was not cost effective.[158]

In relation to fertility treatment, although NICE recommended three cycles, the Department of Health has stated that Trusts are only required to offer one, while they work towards meeting the NICE guidance. As no deadline has been issued for meeting the NICE guidance it could be argued that the Department has substituted its own view for that of NICE.[159]

NICE, however, insists that it is free from Government intervention and pressure from industry.[160] However the success of campaigns by manufacturers (eg Glaxo-Wellcome on zanamivir) and pressure groups (the Multiple Sclerosis Society on beta-interferon and glatiramer acetate), causing a reversal of an initial decision by NICE, has indicated to some commentators that NICE is not immune from outside pressure.[161] Significantly the Bristol Infirmary Inquiry suggested that NICE be kept clearly separate from the Department of Health.[162] However, NICE itself believes that its status as an NHS body helps give it legitimacy.[163]

10.4.5 *How transparent is NICE?*

There have been concerns expressed that the process by which NICE makes guidance lacks transparency.[164] In particular there are concerns from patient groups that it is unclear how their representations are taken into account and precisely what factors NICE is using to make its decisions.[165] That said, the NICE website[166] is replete with policies, procedures, and decisions, and it has a 'communication strategy' to ensure it

---

[153] NICE (2000). [154] Raftery (2001). [155] BBC Newsonline (22 July 2004).
[156] Klein (2001). [157] BBC Newsonline (21 July 2005).
[158] Mayor (2001). [159] McMillan (2003b). [160] NICE (2002b: 1).
[161] Rodwin (2001: 442).
[162] Bristol Royal Infirmary Inquiry (2001: para 24.38). [163] NICE (2002b).
[164] NICE judgments can be subject to judicial review: see *Eisai v NICE* [2007] EWHC 1941 (Admin).
[165] Smith (2000: 1364); also Cookson, McDaid, and Maynard (2001).
[166] <http://www.nice.org.uk>.

communicates effectively with stakeholders. Despite this there appears to be an unwillingness to accept that the decision-making process is as transparent as it appears. In part the lack of confidence that some have in NICE may be due to the fact that NICE (perhaps inevitably) must conclude that a medicine either is or is not effective, when in reality the issue is far more complex than that. As Smith suggests, NICE's problems are down to its willingness:

> to give the impression that if the evidence supports a treatment then it's made available and if it doesn't it isn't. In other words, the whole messy problem of deciding which interventions to make available can be decided with some data and a computer. It's a technical problem. This lie corrupts the concept of evidence-based medicine . . . The evidence supports decision-making, but the evidence can't make the decision. The values of the patient or the community must be part of the decision.[167]

One way NICE has sought to respond to such concerns is to make greater use of the Partners' Councils which seek to represent the views of the general public. The difficulty is that the more weight that is given to the views of the general public the less weight NICE's guidance will carry as an in-depth independent scientific assessment on the effectiveness of medicine.

10.4.6 *How does NICE decide whether a treatment is cost effective?*

NICE in assessing cost-effectiveness places much weight on quality adjusted life years (QALY). This is a very popular way of deciding how medical treatments should be rationed. We will consider this concept in more detail shortly when we consider how health care services should be rationed.

10.5 **How should health care be rationed?**

Ethicists interested in this area enjoy conundrums of this kind:

TO PONDER

There are three patients in your care. There is only enough money available to fund one of them. Which will you fund?

(i) Alf is a newborn. He has a serious disability and needs intensive care to be kept alive. The likelihood of him surviving into his twenties is moderate and even if he does he will be seriously disabled. Without the treatment he will die.

(ii) Steve is a student who is suffering serious liver failure following excessive drinking for many years. A liver transplant and further treatment is required. If successful, and if he gives up drinking, there is no reason why he should not expect to have a normal life expectancy. Without the treatment he will die.

(iii) Wendy is young mother caring for two toddlers. She has developed a form of cancer. With the treatment it is estimated she will live another ten years, without the treatment she will die a painful death within the next few months.

---

[167] Smith (2000: 1364).

Of course, it is rare that choices facing medical professionals are so stark but the discussion of such hypotheticals helps to bring out some of the key issues. Below are some possible responses to them.

10.5.1 *'Treat all of them'*

To most people the initial response to a hypothetical scenario such as those outlined above is that we should fund all of their treatment. What sort of a society do we live in if we cannot provide treatment to all of these people? Those tempted by such a response might suggest that we need to determine what kind of health service is the minimally decent we would want and to set taxation accordingly. If people realize that without higher taxation people would die they would pay. It is, of course, not that straightforward. What this point emphasizes, however, is that at the end of the day if rationing decisions produce unacceptable results, the answer may be to increase funding for the NHS, rather than try and tweak further the rationing system.

10.5.2 *'There is no answer'*

An acceptable answer to these dilemmas is that there is no correct answer. A perfectly legitimate case can be made for Alf, Steve, and Wendy. All we can ask of the health service is that the way these decisions are made should be open, accessible, and there is a means of challenging any decision made.[168] Although these values are important many people would not find it acceptable if the NHS funded cosmetic surgery but not cancer treatment, however open, accessible, and open to review the system was. It may be correct there is no 'right' answer, but that does not mean there are no 'wrong' answers.

10.5.3 *A rights perspective*

To some we have a human right to a minimally decent standard of health care and that would include providing life saving treatment. Alf, Steve, and Wendy all have a right to receive treatment. Of course where the treatment is not life-saving there may either be no right to it at all, or the rights of individuals will need to be pitted against each other. This perspective has resonance in a legal age focused on rights. However, it does not really provide an answer to the difficult questions. If in our scenario there simply is not enough money, how are these rights to life to be weighed? And in the case of non-life-threatening conditions, a rights approach, without more, does little to indicate how the rights in question are to be balanced. So we need something more to assist us in balancing rights.

10.5.4 *Need*

Another 'simple' solution is to base rationing on the basis of need: resources should go to the patient who needs them most. But this leaves open the question of need:[169] which of Alf, Steven, and Wendy is in greater need? We need a more sophisticated concept than 'need' to help us.

10.5.5 *QALY*

Quality Adjusted Life Years (QALY) is probably the most popular way of analysing the cost-effectiveness of treatments and is widely used in decision-making in rationing. It is

---

[168] Smith II (2002).   [169] NHS Management Executive (1991).

used by NICE,[170] and therefore we shall pay particular attention to this concept. QALY, as used in rationing decisions requires an assessment of three factors:

- How many years extra life will the treatment provide this patient?
- What will the quality of those extra years be?
- How expensive is the treatment?

A treatment that provides a year of perfect health scores as one; however, a year of less than perfect health will score less than one. Death is equivalent to zero. In some schemes is it possible to have a state of health worse than death and this may achieve a negative score. Under QALY, therefore, a treatment which provided a patient with an extra year of perfect health would be preferred to a treatment which provided a patient with an extra year, but a year of pain and low life quality. A treatment which offered a large number of QALY for a small amount of money would be highly cost effective, while one that produced a low number of QALY for a large amount of money would not be.

Someone required to ration health services can therefore examine a range of different services and consider how many QALY for how much money is offered. The following figures have been suggested in one book as the cost per QALY:[171]

Hospital dialysis for end-stage renal disease for patients aged 55–64 years (compared with no treatment)	£45,000
Coronary artery bypass graft for patients with mild angina (compared with medical management)	£26,000
Breast cancer screening programme	£6,800
Cervical cancer screening (women aged 20–59 years)	£200

The main benefit of QALY is its ability to provide a way of considering not only the length of time that a patient gains, but also the quality of that life. It provides a unit which enables those at the policy level to compare contrasting treatments for a particular medical condition. Clearly in considering alternative treatments for, say, back pain, a Trust will be attracted to using that treatment which offers the lowest cost for each QALY. It also provides a way of comparing different treatments for different conditions where a health service is having to choose between funding them.

How do NICE use QALYs? Professor Rawlins, chair of NICE in 2002, argued that if the QALY value was over the range £25,000–£35,000 there needed to be special reasons for regarding the treatment as cost effective.[172] He gave as examples of special reasons: particular features of the condition, wider societal costs and benefits, and the innovative nature of the technology.

10.5.6 Problems with QALY

The use of QALY has not proved uncontroversial. Here are some of the objections that are made:

(i) One objection to the use of QALY is the difficulty in the calculation. How is it possible to assess the quality of a person's life?[173] How can you compare being confined

---

170 Fox-Rushby (2002).   171 Hope, Savulescu and Hendrick (2003: Chap 13, table 13.2).
172 Rawlins (2004).   173 Malek (2003); Kamm (1993: 233–330).

to a wheel chair to being blind? Is it really possible to put a figure on such things? The difficulty is that what gives our lives quality differs greatly from person to person.[174] If a person loses the use of a finger and a treatment is available which could restore its use how do we assess the added quality of restoring use of a finger? For some people the loss of use of a finger will matter very little, to another, a musician for example, it might hugely affect their quality of life. An attempt could be made to assess an average improvement in quality of life but this could be complex.[175] How are we to assess the improvement in quality of life produced by cosmetic surgery? In one quality-of-life study, a group of persons who won the lottery had similar quality-of-life ratings one year after winning as did a group of persons who had become paraplegic.[176] Can anyone really know how bad certain conditions are if they do not suffer from them?[177]

(ii) The QALY approach can produce unacceptable results. In particular it places no weight on concepts such as dignity. A severely mentally ill person with no real awareness of what is happening to them could be left in appalling circumstances on the basis that to offer them basic care would not improve their quality of life, because they lack awareness of their condition.

(iii) A particular concern is that QALY works harshly against older people. An older person who has a low life expectancy will find it much harder, if not impossible, to show a higher number of QALY than a younger person if facing a similar illness. Indeed they are unlikely to be able to compete with a child with a much less serious illness. There are also concerns that there are difficulties in that it may work against people who are seriously ill, for whom all treatment can offer is a slight increase of life expectancy or a small increase in pleasure.

There is also a danger that it draws no distinction between giving one person 40 QALY and four people 10 QALY. It has been therefore described by John Harris as a 'life-threatening device' in that it prefers life years over individual lives.[178] Some have argued that taking age into account in effect amounts to age discrimination.[179] There are two responses that supporters make to this kind of argument.

First, it may be that it is age discrimination, but that is perfectly acceptable. Surely most people would agree that, if we had no choice but to save the life of ten eight-year-olds or ten 80-year-olds we should prefer the former option.[180] Was not the death of the Queen Mother, although sad, far less of a tragedy than the death of the much younger Lady Diana? There must be few grandparents who, faced with the awful alternative of either dying themselves or have their grandchild die, would not think it preferable that they were the ones to go.[181] Any age discrimination might be justified on the basis of an argument that the loss to the 80-year-old of the short period of life is less than the loss of many years for the young person.[182] The discrimination is not on grounds of age but on an assessment of the loss for the individual.

A second response might be to deny that there is age discrimination here. In a QALY approach the distinction is not based on age as such but rather the number of future years a person is predicted to live. QALY draws no distinction between a 20-year-old with a terminal illness and short life expectancy and an 80-year-old with the same illness and life expectancy. Indeed this has even led one commentator to suggest that the

---

[174] Cookson (2005).   [175] Hausman (2006).   [176] Brickman and Coates (1978).

[177] Goold (1996).   [178] Harris (1987).   [179] Keown (2002).

[180] Nord (1999).   [181] Shaw (1994).   [182] Sunstein (2004).

QALY is 'not ageist enough'[183] because we should in the example given prefer giving a 20-year-old a few extra months, rather than the 80-year-old.

Note, however, that no distinction on age would arise if treatment is on-going (eg the taking of medication). This is because although a younger person taking the medication would live for longer than the older person taking the medication, the costs of medicating the younger would be proportionately much higher.

There is less dispute over cases where age is deemed relevant because it impacts on the likely success of any treatment.

Opponents of age as a relevant factor argue that it is simply unjust to value the life of an older person as being of less value than the life of a younger person: both lives are equally precious. The use of age reinforces the all too common perception in our society that the elderly are a 'waste of space'. We must respect and value old age and this means offering the same treatment we would to a younger person. John Harris has argued that age offers an utterly arbitrary criterion. As he points out if there is a fire in a lecture theatre do we really think we should try and get the 19-year-olds out before the 20-year-olds?[184]

NICE has made it clear that 'health should not be valued more highly in some age groups than others' but that 'where age is an indictor of benefit or risk, age discrimination is appropriate.'[185]

(iv) It has been argued that QALY will work against the interests of the disabled.[186] If two people who suffer from a condition are being considered and one has a disability and the other has not, it is arguable that the impact of the treatment on the non-disabled person will be greater because it will restore them to full health, and therefore their QALY will be higher. For example, it has been claimed that in deciding who should receive donated hearts Down's Syndrome children have been overlooked in favour of 'normal' children.[187] There are many to whom that is unacceptable, but it could be said to be justified on a QALY basis if Down's Syndrome children are thought to have a lower quality of life than other children.

(v) It might be argued that QALY is too individualistic in focusing just on the impact of the treatment on the individual patient.[188] When considering a patient the improvement in the patient's quality of life alone is considered and the impact on their carers counts for nothing. It may be that, for example, a drug which prevents incontinence might not hugely improve the quality of life for the patient, but have a dramatic impact on the quality of life for their carer. Others strongly object to arguments of this kind. If we start to take into account not only the individual patient but all those they care for, the task of comparing treatments would become highly complex.

(vi) It has been claimed that QALY inevitably cause us to weigh up the worth of different people, something that is ethically inappropriate. Muireann Quigley[189] argues:

> If I need to decide whether to give a treatment to either patient A or patient B and I utilise the QALY, then I am effectively balancing the improvement (or deterioration) in the quality of A's life multiplied by the number of life-years he gains (or loses) against the same calculation for B. The best score will determine which person will be the most cost effective to treat from my limited resources. Unfortunately, what we are doing when we

183 Lockwood (1988).   184 Harris (1992: 87).   185 NICE (2005a).
186 Harris (1987) and Harris (2001).   187 Savulescu (2001b).
188 Herring (2008).   189 Quigley (2007b: 465).

engage in this type of calculation, in particular, is making value judgements about the lives of those two patients (identifiable or not), because the result is that their lives and health are given lower priority.

Others disagree and insist that QALYs are contrasting treatments, rather than people.[190] Even if Quigley is correct, it may be that the weighing up of the value of the lives of patients is an inevitable part of rationing, rather than being a unique aspect of QALYs.

NICE, in making its guidance will take into account the QALY of treatments.[191] It has been suggested that treatment which costs more than £30,000 per QALY will not be approved,[192] although NICE has denied there is such a strict cut off.[193] Its guidance suggests that above £30,000 per QALY the case has to be 'increasingly strong' if the treatment is to be approved.[194] In respect of one cancer drug, NICE approved its use after the manufacturer said that the NHS would be refunded in cases where the drug did not benefit a patient.[195] Such deals will increase the cost-effectiveness of some drugs.

10.5.7 *Daniel Callahan*

Daniel Callahan has recommended an approach which suggests that we need to provide for each person a fair rationing of health care across their lives. He suggests that our society has become obsessed with avoiding death and that we need to find again the notion of an acceptable death. There comes a point in people's lives when death should be regarded as an acceptable event. At that point the use of health care resources to assist such a person to keep on living should not be used. This might be in one's late 70s or early 80s.[196] If people were to choose whether they would rather have money spent on them if they fell ill when young or when old they would prefer to have the treatment they needed when young. Another author with a similar approach has suggested that there comes a point where a person has had a 'fair innings',[197] and it is right to focus health care resources on those who have been unlucky enough to face the possibility of not having a normal life span, rather than those who have already had such a life.

His proposal has proved highly controversial.[198] Although Callahan appears to believe his proposal would solve the funding crises facing health care it should be pointed out that, even if only very limited health care was offered to those over 80, it is unlikely that it would resolve our rationing problems, the savings by doing that would not be sufficient.[199]

One objection to his approach is that it proposes one particular view of life: an active youth and middle age, followed by an old age of little worth. Many people may regard life like that, but many don't. Many look forward to old age as a time of rest and respect. In other words he imposes on everyone one particular vision of how to live a life on everyone, and it is one that many people feel does not show a sufficient respect for old age. It has also been pointed out that the proposal is likely to work against the interests of women, as a far higher percentage of women than men reach the age of 80.[200]

---

[190] Claxton and Culyer (2006). [191] NICE (2004).
[192] NICE (2002b); Kmietowicz (2001). Raftery (2001) notes an exception to this rule for treatment of motor neurone disease, which had a cost per QALY of £34,000–£44,000.
[193] NICE (2002b).
[194] NICE (2004b: 6.2.6.1 and 6.2.1) although some commentators suggest that in fact looking at their decisions it appears to be closer to £35,000–40,000 (Devlin and Parkin (2003)).
[195] BBC Newsonline (3 June 2007).   [196] Callahan (1990a).   [197] Williams (1997).
[198] Cohen-Almagor (2002b).   [199] Beauchamp and Childress (2003: 262).
[200] Dixon (1994).

10.5.8 *Equality of treatment*

John Harris[201] argues that each citizen has an equal claim to having her or his individual health needs met. Those who are old or disabled or have a poor prognosis of health have no less a right to health services than anyone else. The primary goal, he argues, must be to save lives. He thinks it utterly wrong that that the life of an ill and expensive-to-treat person could be sacrificed under a QALY scheme to improve, by a small amount, the health of a large number of young healthy people. He argues:

> The principal objective of the NHS should be to protect the life and health of each citizen impartially and to offer beneficial health care on the basis of individual need, so that each has an equal chance of flourishing to the extent that their personal health status permits.[202]

Where it is not possible to save everyone's life with the resources available he recommends allocation should be decided by a lottery and in that way there is no suggestion that one person's life is regarded as more valuable than that of another.

This approach, based on equality of access, appears to reject even placing weight on the likelihood of success of treatment. That appears counter-intuitive. To allocate a scarce organ to a person for whom it is likely to fail when there are others needing the organ who have a good chance of thriving with it seems difficult to justify. Critics argue that this could lead simply to a squandering of resources.[203] To provide treatments to those with only a few months to live and deny the same treatment to a person with many years of life ahead of them is likely to increase social costs and costs for the NHS.

10.5.9 *Rawlsian approach*

John Rawls' 'original position' approach has been advocated by some as a solution to the rationing dilemma. His approach involves a 'thought experiment' in which free and equal citizens negotiate about the world in which they are to live. They have a 'veil of ignorance', meaning that they do not know what kind of life they will have or what position they will be in. How would they decide how health resources should be allocated? Would they agree that young people should have a primary call on resources, fearing that they may appear in the world as a young person with a serious medical condition?[204]

This is an attractive way of considering the problem. However there are difficulties with it. As already mentioned it is extremely difficult for such a negotiation to take place without a full knowledge of what suffering from various treatments would be like. How can this hypothetical group decide whether money is better spent providing treatments for arthritis or depression without having experienced the conditions? In any event predicting how people in the thought experiment would decide to ration treatment is problematic.

10.5.10 *Asking the general public*

One solution to the difficulties facing rationing would be to fall back on democracy.[205] Should we simply obtain the views of the general public and follow their assessments as

---

[201] Harris (1997) and Harris (2005c). See Claxton and Culyer (2006) for a powerful rejoinder to Harris's views.
[202] Harris (1997: 670).   [203] McKie et al (2002).   [204] Daniels (1985) thinks it would.
[205] Nord (1999); Cookson and Dolan (1999).

to how priorities in the NHS should be ranked? Notably NICE seeks the views of the general public through its Citizens' Councils when setting their guidance.[206] The rather limited surveys that have been carried out do provide some clear messages: the young should be given priority over the old; those with dependants (eg children) preferred over those without; and those who have looked after their own health should be given higher priority than those who have not.[207]

There are, however, grave concerns about putting too much weight on public surveys of this kind. Can members of the public really understand what it is like to suffer from multiple sclerosis, infertility, or gender identity dysphoria, for example, without personal experience? There is a concern that prejudice, rather than reason will dominate some of the decisions.[208]

10.5.11 *Oregon*

Much attention has been paid to the rationing system developed in Oregon for Medicaid, in the United States. The basis of the scheme could be found in the Basic Health Services Act 1989. The Act created the Oregon Health Services Commission which ranked services that would constitute the decent minimum coverage. The ranking was determined by questioning citizens to consider which treatments were seen as having greater social value. The goal was to fund as many of these priority services as possible. The Commission produced a list of procedures based on quality of wellbeing after treatment and cost effectiveness. The list was controversial and produced some results that appeared arbitrary. The initial list contained 709 treatments, although this has increased over time. They were ranked according to the benefits to the population. Having established the ranking the funds available were allocated to the treatment starting with those at the top of the list. It was found that only the first 587 treatments were available. All treatments lower on the list were not available.[209]

Of course the list is highly controversial and inevitably some people would argue that some things should be higher than others on the list. The first list produced treatment for thumb sucking and tooth capping as having higher priority than for ectopic pregnancy, cystic fibrosis, AIDS,[210] and appendectomy.[211] Other difficulties arose in that, if a patient was suffering from a number of illnesses which, combined, posed a serious risk to her or his well-being, but all of them fell below the cut off point no treatment could be offered. It was therefore said by some to be too strict a restriction on clinical judgment.[212]

The scheme was arranged to enable all eligible people needing treatment to receive procedures as far down the list as possible given the budget set for health care. It faced difficulties in that the number of people eligible to receive treatment exceeded expectation. The scheme was designed to deal with pressure on the budget by reducing the treatments available, rather than reducing the number of people eligible. However, a dramatic increase in the number eligible meant that there needed to be a change in the

---

[206] Davies (2005) examines their work.

[207] Charny et al (1989) and Williams (1997 and 2001). Although Cookson et al (1999) indicated a greater divergence among public opinion over the relevance of 'fault'.

[208] Price (2000b).

[209] For the latest proposal in relation to the scheme see Oregon Health Services Commission (2007).

[210] Tengs et al (1996).   [211] Schmidt (2004).

[212] See Newdick (2005: Chap 8) for a useful discussion.

eligibility criteria. There are still a number of procedures that are not available. These include incapacitating hernias, tonsillectomy, and adenoidectomy.[213]

10.5.12 *Patient choice*

One interesting option is to seek to develop a range of schemes of rationing and allow patients to select the scheme that they prefer.[214] So, the arrangement may be that at 18 you must choose from a variety of options.[215] If you are not concerned about being denied treatment in old age you may opt to be part of a scheme in which rationing decisions do take account of age. If, on the other hand, you wanted a scheme under which every effort was made to postpone death even in old age, you may prefer to opt for a scheme that is willing to invest money in treatments at the end of life. The difficulties with such a proposal are that people will need to make the choice without sufficient information available to them.[216] There would also be difficulties with the treatment of children, but they could be exempt from the scheme.

TO PONDER

Waste in the NHS

With all the talk of rationing it is important to find waste in the NHS (Chief Medical Officer (2006b)). Like all large organizations cynical critics can find mystifying examples of wastefulness in the NHS:

- Terence Hope, a brain surgeon, was suspended on full pay of £80,000 a year after being accused of not paying for an extra helping of soup at the canteen at Queen's Medical Centre, Nottingham, in 2004. He claimed he was only collecting some extra croutons. His suspension was to enable a full investigation to take place. Several operations had to be postponed.

- In 2003 a lap dancer earning £500 a night was give cosmetic breast surgery on the NHS. This was justified on the basis that she was suffering from depression.

- The NHS spent £40,000 on a 'patient experience definition' of what makes a good experience for a patient. The result explained that the sick want to get better. As Lib Dem health spokesman Paul Burstow said, 'Taxpayers will find it difficult to understand why £40,000 has been spent on common-sense definitions.'

- In 2005 the Serious Fraud Squad (Guardian (2005)) started an investigation into companies which may have defrauded the NHS of hundreds of millions of pounds.

- In 2006 it has been claimed that the NHS spent £172 million on external management consultants (BBC Newsonline 12 September 2006).

10.6 **Controversies over rationing**

10.6.1 *Drawing a distinction between treatment for ill health and life style enhancement*

To some rationing in the NHS would be easier if a clear distinction was drawn between treatment for ill-health and 'life-style enhancement'.[217] It is argued that is not the job

---

213 Health Economics Research (1999); Oregon Department of Administrative Services (1999).
214 A useful discussion of these can be found in Attell-Thompson (2005).
215 The scheme could apply to younger people if parents were permitted to make choices for them.
216 Rai (1997).   217 See Chap 1 for a further discussion on what health or sickness means.

of the NHS to make people happier, but just to improve ill health.[218] Hence, even if cosmetic surgery makes people happier it should not be available on the NHS because it is not curing an illness. More controversial examples may be: not providing gender reassignment surgery, obesity treatment, or treatment for erectile problems on the NHS. However, as these examples demonstrate, the line between treatment and enhancement is not easy to draw. The Court of Appeal in *R v NW Lancashire HA ex p A*[219] explained that gender reassignment surgery is an effective treatment for a recognized medical condition. The better view is that far from being a 'lifestyle choice' the surgery is needed to treat a genuine medical condition.

10.6.2 *The Hippocratic Oath*

It has been suggested that there is a tension between the obligation a doctor has under the Hippocratic Oath and the concept of rationing.[220] Under the Hippocratic Oath doctors promise:

> I will follow that system of regimen which, according to my ability and judgment, I consider for the benefit of my patients.

But how does a doctor do that if the rationing system in place means that she or he is not permitted to provide the best treatment? It may be that in this regard the Hippocratic Oath is outdated. The GMC guidance is notably more cautious, stating that doctors 'provide effective treatments based on the best available evidence but also requiring them to 'make efficient use of the resources available'.[221] As this indicates, with limited health resources it simply is not always possible to give every patient the best available treatment. If that is inconsistent with the Hippocratic Oath then it needs updating.

10.6.3 *Rationing and 'clinical judgment'*

One of the objections that has been made about NICE is that it attacks medical professionals' clinical judgment. In telling them when a treatment is appropriate this challenges the assessment of the professional as to the best treatment available to the patient. As we have seen, NICE insists that its guidance is not meant to restrict the freedom of doctors in individual cases, although it would be a brave doctor who departed from the guidance without a 'reasonable justification'.[222] Christopher Newdick has argued that we need to be wary about the term 'clinical judgment'. He looks at the rates of hysterectomies per 100,000 population in various countries and finds the following: US—700; Canada—600; UK—250; and Norway—110. He argues that the difference in these rates cannot be put down to 'clinical judgment' in particular cases. The figures 'call out for an explanation'. They certainly suggest that either, in some countries some women are receiving unnecessary hysterectomies, or that in others they are not receiving them when they are required. Saying that something is clinically required may, therefore, reflect as much a social judgment as a medical one.

---

[218] Gilbert, Walley, and New (2000).   [219] [2000] 2 FCR 525.
[220] Newdick (2005: 17).   [221] GMC (2007).
[222] See Bristol Infirmary Inquiry (2001: 30) which suggested retraining may be needed for professionals who regularly breach NICE guidance without a reasonable justification.

10.6.4 *Fault of the patient?*

It has been estimated that in the developed world a third of all diseases can be attributed to a 'lifestyle choice' involving: tobacco, alcohol, blood pressure, cholesterol, and obesity. In making a rationing decision should we draw any distinction based on whether a patient has brought about the condition upon themselves?[223] Should we be more willing to give treatment for heart disease to a patient who has caused her or his condition by smoking, than to one who bears no responsibility?[224] If a doctor arrives at the scene of a car crash and there are two patients both of whom urgently need her or his attention should she or he focus on the innocent pedestrian rather than the drunk driver? Many people instinctively feel that an 'innocent' patient deserves preferential treatment as regards the 'blameworthy' treatment in rationing decisions.

The difficulty is in deciding the extent to which someone can be blamed for their condition. Is a lawyer who suffers a cardiac disorder due to overwork and stress to be blamed for not having a more sensible work–life balance? Is a firefighter who suffers an injury while putting out a blaze to be blamed for taking on such a risky occupation? The difficulties in making these kinds of assessments has caused the GMC to argue: 'You must not refuse or delay treatment because you believe that patients' actions have contributed to their condition'.[225] NICE[226] states that an injury or illness being self-inflicted should not be a reason for denying treatment, but it can be taken into account in deciding whether treatment will be effective. But others argue that if we acknowledge a right to health care with that should come responsibilities to take care of your health. It is possible, through your irresponsible actions, to forfeit your right to health care. An alternative response to someone sympathetic to these arguments is to say that we should tax 'dangerous' activities such as smoking or drinking and use the revenue to treat the illnesses caused. In that case the cost incurred by the dangerous activity is shared among all those who engage in it and not just those who are 'unlucky' enough to fall ill.[227] Alan Cribb argues that we need to develop a network of health obligations which are connected to entitlements.[228]

It is generally accepted that there is a legitimate way in which prior fault can be relevant in a rationing decision, and that is where it might affect the effectiveness of a treatment. A heavy drinker who requires liver treatment, but is unwilling to cease drinking, may be denied treatment on the basis that the treatment is unlikely to be effective. This is the line NICE has taken: that 'prior fault' should not be relevant, unless it affects the future effectiveness of the treatment.[229]

10.6.5 *Is the contribution a patient can or will make to society relevant?*

In allocating health care resources, is it appropriate to consider the contribution a person has or will make to society? If the choice is between offering treatment to a middle aged leading scientist who has made a major breakthrough in research into the treatment of cancer, or a person who is long-term unemployed, should those factors be taken

---

[223] For discussions of this issue see Cappelen and Norheim (2005); and Underwood and Bailey (1993).
[224] Underwood and Bailey (1993).   [225] GMC (2007).
[226] NICE (2005a: principle 10). For criticism of this approach see Holm (2006) who asks if sports people should not be allowed to have surgery as they are likely to continue playing sport and impede their recovery.
[227] Cappelen and Norheim (2005).   [228] Cribb (2005: Chap 6).   [229] NICE (2005a).

into account? Or what about the fact that one patient has young children to care for, who will be devastated by her death, and another is a single person with no dependents? The general view seems to be that these are not factors that can legitimately be taken into account. NICE has made it clear that social class or position in life should not be a relevant factor in deciding what treatment should be offered.[230] To start to consider whether a patient is more worthy than another is to open a Pandora's box of complex issues and will inevitably lead to claims of improper discrimination. On the other hand, simply to consider the cost-benefit analysis of treatment in terms of the individuals, and without a consideration of the wider interests of the community and those with whom they are in relationships, might be said to take an improperly individualist view of the world.

10.6.6 *Gender*

Of course, there is near universal agreement that it would be improper in the allocation of health care resources that sex should be a relevant categorization. However, as has been pointed out, using age as a category is in effect a form of sex discrimination as among the very elderly there are far more women than men.[231]

It has also been argued that the individualist approach of QALY, focusing on the impact of treatment on the patient, without a consideration of the effect of a rationing decision on a carer, works against the interests of women, who undertake the majority of caring work.[232]

10.6.7 *The many or the few?*

Imagine that we have a patient who is in urgent need of medical treatment without which she or he will die. The treatment will cost half a million pounds. The same money could be used to institute a screening process for cholesterol problems which, it is predicted, will save ten lives. If the choice must be made between the two, which is to be preferred?[233] A QALY approach would prefer the screening programmes because for the same amount of money a large number of lives would be saved. Yet in fact within the NHS large sums of money are spent to save an individual's life, at the expense of preventative health campaigns. It is not just in the NHS where this occurs. Large sums are willingly spent in a bid to rescue a sailor lost at sea or a miner trapped in a mine, whereas similar sums are not available to institute road safety measures which might save a larger number of lives. To some this is illogical. These decisions are based on emotion: we see the face of the person who needs the treatment, or the lost sailor, but we do not know the identity of those whose lives will be saved by the screening campaign or the road safety campaign. We feel compelled to rescue those whose identity we know about, and feel no compassion for the unidentified others who will die without the preventative steps. But many argue that is wrong and we should feel just as strongly about those unknown number of people whose lives are lost through a failure to fund a preventative illness campaign as we do about those we see in desperate need.

---

[230] NICE (2005a).   [231] Lindemann Nelson (2007).
[232] Whitty (1998).   [233] Hope (2005: Chap 3).

A SHOCK TO THE SYSTEM

NICE's controversies

The World Health Organization found that NICE was far less conservative in recommending treatments than similar organizations in Canada, Australia, the Netherlands, and Italy (WHO (2003)). However, this has not stopped there being outcries about some of NICE's decisions. Here are a selection.

- In 2001 NICE considered a group of drugs used in the treatment of patients suffering Alzheimer's disease. It recommended their use for a specific group of sufferers. In March 2005 it published an appraisal document looking at the effectiveness and cost-effectiveness of the drugs. The appraisal recommends that none of these drugs should be used, although patients already receiving one of the drugs '...may be continued on therapy...until it is considered appropriate to stop' (NICE (2005): 1.3). Predictably this caused an outraged response among patients, carers, and professionals (Holm (2005)). The reasoning behind NICE's prelimary conclusions were essentially economical. The cost per QALY for the drug was £40,000–£50,000. Holm (2005) argues that NICE's approach in respect of these drugs has failed to give sufficient weight to the impact on a spouse or partner caring for someone with Alzheimer's. Further anger greeted the announcement in July 2005 that NICE would need further time to consider the question of these drugs. A judicial challenge to the NICE ruling failed (*Eisai v NICE* [2007] EWHC 1941 (Admin)).

- In June 2000 NICE recommended that the drug Beta Interferon should be given to every patient with multiple sclerosis. This was in response to pressure from patients after initially recommending the drug not be used.

- In 2002 a decision was made to limit the number of drugs available for treating people with advanced colorectal cancer.

- In 2005 a new drug (Xeloda) became available for the treatment of bowel cancer. Although the drug was being used in Scotland, NICE stated it would not be able to consider it until May 2006, over a year later (BBC Newsonline 9 August 2005).

- In August 2002, NICE came under fire again after it recommended that the drug Glivec should only be given to a handful of patients with leukaemia. It later changed its mind.

11 Improving quality: targets

One of the main ways that the Government has sought to improve the services provided by the NHS has been through the use of targets. A huge range of issues from reducing suicide rates to waiting times has been subject to targets.[234] Great pressure is placed upon NHS bodies to meet these. Where they are met the Government naturally seeks to claim credit for a very tangible benefit of the extra funding it has put into the NHS. We will not here consider in detail what these targets are or the extent to which they have or have not been met.[235] Rather we shall look briefly at whether targets are a useful way of improving the quality of NHS performance.[236]

The use of targets does provide a very concrete measure of improvement. Without them politicians may fear that the money given to the NHS will go into a 'black hole',

---

234 DoH (2000d).   235 See King's Fund (2005).   236 Leatherman and Sutherland (2005).

and there will be no measure of improvement to which politicians can point and say: 'that outcome has resulted from the improvements we have made'. Of course, where, for example, patients have received treatment more quickly because of waiting list targets, the patient benefits.

There are, however, concerns over the use of targets. The Audit Commission emphasizes that targets must be 'the means not the end'.[237] The danger with targets is that the obsession becomes being able to fill in the form at the end of the day saying that the target has been reached, rather than actually improving the service offered. It has been found that some Trusts have found ways of technically meeting waiting list targets (eg by cancelling operation appointments on the day in question) which have ended up harming patients, even if appearing to meet the targets.[238] There is also a concern that targets can obscure the real priorities of the NHS. There is a concern that management cultures can become obsessed with meeting targets and overlook the real goals of the NHS.[239] In particular there is a concern that aspects of the NHS for which there are not targets can be ignored in the drive to meet the targets set by Government.[240] Some targets have been found to be unrealistic or only achievable by skewing clinical priorities.[241] For example, it has been claimed that clinicians have been required to see non-urgent patients before urgent ones in order to meet waiting list targets. This can lead to low staff morale and frustration with the 'targeting culture'.

The DoH has recognized some of these concerns and has announced a reduction in the number of targets and focusing on 'key outcome standards' (eg a reduction in the number of deaths from breast cancer) rather than focusing on particular aspects of the service (eg waiting times for those needing breast screening).[242]

12 Charging: community v health care

As mentioned at the start of this chapter, one of the precepts of the NHS is that it should be free at the point of delivery. Services must be free of charge unless there is express legal provision saying they may be made.[243] There is, for example, provision to require payment for wigs, drugs, and optical and dental appliances. This makes the definition of what is a service that can be expected of the NHS crucial, because if a service does not fall under the purview of the NHS, it may be subject to charging.

The area where this issue has come to a head is in respect of the distinction between community care and health care. The NHS and Community Care Act 1990 requires local authorities to prepare and publish plans for community care services in their area. Community care includes the provision of accommodation for adults who cannot look after themselves;[244] services for adults who suffer certain disabilities;[245] services to promote the welfare of elderly people;[246] and services for those who have been discharged from mental health services.[247] The kinds of services involved might include the adaptation of homes, the provision of equipment and home help etc. Under the NHS and Community Care Act 1990, section 47 local authorities are required to assess the needs

---

[237] Audit Commission (2003).   [238] Audit Commission (2003).
[239] Audit Commission (2003).   [240] Audit Commission (2003).
[241] Newdick (2005: 71).   [242] DoH (2002f).
[243] NHS Act 1977, s 1(2). See Road Traffic Charges Act 1999 which permits the NHS to recover costs in relation to treatment following road traffic accidents.
[244] National Assistance Act 1948, s 21.   [245] National Assistance Act 1948, s 29.
[246] Health Services and Public Health Act 1968, s 45.   [247] Mental Health Act 1983, s 117.

of anyone who may appear to be in need of community care services and to decide whether such services should be provided.[248] Those who are blind, deaf, dumb, or substantially and permanently handicapped by illness, injury, or congenital disability are entitled to be involved in the assessment process under the Disabled Persons (Services Consultation and Representation) Act 1986 and can make representations in response to the assessment.

It is important to realize that the NHS and Community Care Act 1990, although conferring a right to assessment, does not guarantee that those services will be provided. In the case of disabled clients, and those who are blind, deaf, dumb, or substantially and permanently handicapped by illness, injury, or congenital disability there is a duty on local authorities to provide services necessary to meet the individual's need under the Chronically Sick and Disabled Persons Act 1970. However, for others it would be possible for the local authority to assess a person as in need of services, but then decline to provide them. However, if that were to happen then judicial review may succeed if the decision not to provide services is found unreasonable.

Even if the local authority decides to offer community care services, they are not free of charge, and the local authority can require the client to pay as much of the cost of the services as is reasonable.[249] This means that there is often means testing in the case of services provided at home. The distinction thus created between health care services, which are free at the point of delivery, and community care which is not is one that is hotly debated, not least because it is such a hard one to draw. In *R v North and East Devon HA ex p Coughlan*[250] it was decided to close a residential unit for those with severe disabilities. This meant that Ms Coughlan, a resident, would be transferred from the NHS to local authority services, and that meant she would be liable to contribute to the cost of care. The key point before the Court of Appeal was that under the NHS Act 1977 all nursing care had to be provided and funded by the NHS. However the Court of Appeal thought that nursing care in this context did not include all after-care. The Court of Appeal identified two categories of person who should receive care at NHS expense: (i) those whose needs were so great that they should be regarded as the responsibility of the health authority, rather than the social services; and (ii) those who have additional requirements beyond the need for basic services. Now the Health and Social Care Act 2001, section 49 provides that nursing care cannot be charged for by a local authority. This is defined as being care given by, or planned and supervised by, a registered nurse, unless it cannot be said to be required for a person. The section states:

(1) Nothing in the enactments relating to the provision of community care services shall authorise or require a local authority, in or in connection with the provision of any such services, to—

(a) provide for any person, or

(b) arrange for any person to be provided with,
nursing care by a registered nurse.

(2) In this section 'nursing care by a registered nurse' means any services provided by a registered nurse and involving—

---

[248] If someone is being cared for by an unpaid carer (eg a spouse) then the carer can ask the local authority, when carrying out its assessment, to consider her or his ability to continue to provide the care.
[249] Health and Social Services and Social Security Adjudications Act 1983, s 17.
[250] [2000] 3 All ER 850.

(a) the provision of care, or

(b) the planning, supervision or delegation of the provision of care,

other than any services which, having regard to their nature and the circumstances in which they are provided, do not need to be provided by a registered nurse.

Local authorities' criteria for payment, with this section in mind, have been described as 'confusing and unsettled'.[251] The problems were highlighted by a series of complaints heard by the Health Service Ombudsman in 2003 and 2004.[252] The investigation of those complaints made it clear that some disabled people were wrongly denied funding. The Ombudsman found evidence of delays and difficulties in interpreting eligibility criteria for full funding. Reviews were carried out improperly, and even where it was found that money was due to individuals there were delays in making restitution. The Ombudsman found in over half of the cases examined that assessment had not been carried out properly. Similar problems were found in the Department of Health's own study of the issue.[253] The Ombudsman has sought to visit each local authority to discuss improved good practice in this area.

REALITY CHECK

Confusion over payment for care

The following is a typical case dealt with by the Ombudsman.

Mrs P's husband was diagnosed with Parkinson's Disease in 1985 and his wife cared for him at home until early 2003 with the help of support services. However, following a stay in hospital, Mr P was discharged into a nursing home. His wife was sent a bill for his care by the PCT but she argued that, as her husband's need was primarily for health care and he had complex needs, he should qualify for fully funded NHS continuing care. The PCT told her that Mr P did not meet the criteria for full funding but did not say how this decision had been reached. In a letter to Mrs P the PCT's Continuing Care manager said that if Mr P had been eligible for continuing care NHS staff would have said so. However, Mr P had never been assessed for continuing care. Department of Health guidance requires that all patients needing long-term care should have a continuing care assessment before being discharged from hospital—whether to a care home or to their own home. The patient and their family should be informed about the outcome and given the opportunity to make a formal appeal. None of this happened in Mr P's case. Instead, Mr P had been awarded the highest band of 'free' nursing care, a separate funding stream to cover only the nursing element for those needing care who do not meet the criteria for full continuing care funding (Registered Nursing Care Contribution, RNCC). Sadly, Mr P's condition was terminal. A continuing care assessment was finally carried out on 9 June 2003 and the PCT then decided that he was eligible for full funding. Mr P died on 26 June 2003. Mrs P complained to the Ombudsman that she did not understand why her husband qualified for the last two weeks of his life but not for the six weeks prior to the assessment. The Ombudsman expressed concerns about the review undertaken by the PCT and the contradictory and unclear letters sent to Mrs P by the PCT. She recommended that a proper review should be carried out. This was undertaken and Mr P was found to have been eligible for full funding for the whole period.

[251] Newdick (2005: 118).
[252] Parliamentary and National Health Services Ombudsman (2005).   [253] DoH (2004m).

> Mrs P was given a full apology for the distress she had been caused, and payment to cover the whole period during which her husband had been in the nursing home.
>
> Parliamentary and National Health Services Ombudsman Annual report 2004–05 (2005).

13 Health inequalities

A major concern is inequalities in the level of health across the UK.[254] There are notable disparities in the general quality of people's health in different parts of the country and among different social, ethnic, and economic groups.[255] There are also differences in the quality of NHS service offered.[256] The following figures demonstrate this:

- One report shows that in September 2004, 7 per cent of patients in Scotland and 9 per cent of patients in England had waited for more than six months for an operation. In Wales the figure was 36 per cent.[257]
- In some areas there are five times the number of people per GP than in others.[258]
- The National Audit Office's examination of cancer treatment in England found wide variation in cancer mortality rates, with higher rates in areas with highest levels of deprivation.[259]
- Children from 'manual work' social backgrounds are 1.5 times as likely to die during infancy as those from 'non-manual work' social backgrounds.[260]
- Those living in wealthier parts of the country can expect to live between seven and eight years longer than those is less affluent areas.[261] Glasgow had the worst life expectancy, 72.9 years, compared to Kensington and Chelsea in London with 82.4.[262]
- Infant mortality rates in the poorest parts of the country were 19 per cent higher than the general population.[263] The rate of infant deaths is 70 per cent higher in the West Midlands than in the South East.[264]
- A Health Care Commission Report found that some groups got 'a worse deal' from healthcare services than others, especially travellers, homeless people, those with learning difficulties, and those who live in poorer parts of the community.[265]

The Government states it is determined to reduce these inequalities.[266] Specifically it has a target to reduce inequalities in the levels of infant mortality and life expectancy by 2010.[267]

14 Choice

'Choice' has become one of the 'buzz words' of the modern NHS. The emphasis on choice has been seen by many as an emphasis on consumerism within the NHS.[268] It reflects what might be seen as a shift from seeing the patient as the 'recipient' of care, to

---

254 Cribb (2005); Leatherman and Sutherland (2005).   255 Graham (2002).
256 Davey Smith et al (2002).   257 IPPR (2006).
258 BBC Newsonline (2 February 2005).   259 National Audit Office (2004).
260 NHS Confederation (2007).   261 BBC Newsonline (11 August 2005).
262 BBC Newsonline (29 April 2005).   263 BBC Newsonline (11 August 2005).
264 NHS Confederation (2007)   265 Healthcare Commission (2005).
266 DoH (2005c).   267 DoH (2005c).   268 Harrison and Ahmad (2000).

treating her or him as a consumer who chooses what services she or he wants. Supporters argue that increased choice will lead to increased satisfaction as individuals get the treatment they really want, and improved quality of services as health care providers vie to be the providers of choice for patients.

The Government has clearly emphasized the importance of choice in its NHS Improvement plan:

> Patients' desire for high-quality personalized care will drive the new system. Giving people greater personal choice will give them control over these issues, allowing patients to call the shots about the time and place of their care, and empowering them to personalize their care to ensure the quality and convenience that they want.[269]

The plan was that by the end of 2005 patients would have the right to choose from four or five different health care providers; and from 2008 they have the right to choose from any provider. Under the new computer system patients will have access to their own 'Health space' where they can note individual preferences about their care.[270] There is to be increased access to information to enable 'shared decision-making between patient and clinical team over treatment and care'.[271] We are moving towards a 'patient-led NHS'.[272]

Some of this may frighten some patients. They want to go to the doctor and be told what treatment is best for them and for the doctor to make the necessary arrangements. To be involved in 'shared decision-making' may not be what they want at all. Others, maybe those with access to the internet and other health care resources, will have strong views on how they want their health problems to be dealt with and will find the new approach liberating.

At first giving patients choice may appear to be an inevitable good, but this is not beyond dispute.[273] Providing a choice will cost money and that raises the question about its cost-effectiveness. Also, offering a choice means we must accept that on occasion the wrong choice will be made. It might also be argued that it is a little misleading to talk about choice when, given rationing within the NHS, the choices of an individual patient must be weighed against the interests of the general public. Can we really allow patients to choose treatments under the NHS which are not cost-effective? Will that not amount to a waste of previous NHS resources? Surely we cannot let one patient's choice mean another is denied treatment they need? There are also concerns that choice empowers the educated middle class, who are in a better position to make 'choices' and to insist that their wishes are met; and conversely disadvantages weaker members of society, who are not in a position to make a choice, or do not have the voice to insist upon it. Exercising choice may require having the means to travel to a hospital far from one's home, and this may not be possible for those with low incomes. Indeed if a majority of people in an area with a struggling hospital choose to go elsewhere for treatment, this may lead to the closing of the hospital and the restriction of choice for those less able to travel. These arguments may not mean that choice should not be a relevant goal for the NHS, but that respecting choice can carry expenses and dangers, and steps may need to be taken to limit them.

---

[269] DoH (2004f: 11).   [270] DoH (2004f: 12).   [271] DoH (2000d: 5).
[272] DoH (2005a).   [273] King's Fund (2003b).

15 Regulation by professional or NHS bodies

It is not possible to provide a complete guide to the regulatory work done in the nature of regulation by professional or NHS bodies.[274] These bodies have all reviewed their regulation of professionals particularly following the Bristol Inquiry. There it was said: 'We cannot say that the external system for assuring and monitoring the quality of care was inadequate. There was, in truth, no such system'.[275] It will only be possible to highlight the work done by a sample of bodies:

15.1 The Department of Health

The Department of Health will discipline those involved in professional or personal misconduct.[276] NHS Trusts will be responsible for disciplinary investigations and proceedings involving members of their staff.

15.2 The National Patient Safety Agency

This is a special health authority which has responsibility for co-ordinating efforts to learn from adverse events and 'near misses'. It collects data on these and finds information from other countries and other industries. It seeks to ensure that the lessons that can be learned are learned and that practical steps are put in place to ensure that risks are eliminated or diminished.

This authority assists local NHS bodies to deal with 'performance problems'.[277] These are concerns about the outcomes of cases in which particular medical professionals have been involved. It promotes local and national procedures which are aimed at preventing, identifying, and resolving 'performance problems'. It also provides advice in assisting individual doctors and dentists to improve their practice. The Agency may refer cases to the GMC or other professional body where there are serious concerns.

15.3 The General Medical Council (GMC)

Although we shall look at the GMC, this is by way of an example; there are similar bodies with similar powers over a range of medical professionals. Section 1A of the Medical Act 1983 states the primary role of the GMC:

> The main objective of the General Council in exercising their functions is to protect, promote and maintain the safety of the public.

As we shall see there have been claims that it is the interests of doctors rather than the public which has dominated the concerns of the GMC. The GMC has the job of keeping a register of medical practitioners.[278] In fact the law on this is rather lax. It is not an offence to practise medicine if you are not registered, indeed you do not even have to be qualified.[279] However, if you falsely represent yourself as being a qualified or registered

[274] See Glynne and Gomez (2005).   [275] Bristol Royal Infirmary Inquiry (2001: 8).
[276] DoH (2005g).
[277] This work used to be done by the National Clinical Assessment Authority, which is now part of the National Patient Safety Agency.
[278] Medical Act 1983.   [279] Brazier and Cave (2007: 6).

doctor then an offence is committed under the Medical Act 1983.[280] It is likely that the courts will find that a person who sets themselves up as a doctor is impliedly representing themselves to be qualified. However, if someone is open about being unqualified (eg they claim to be an alternative health practitioner) then people are free to trust their care to them and no offence is committed.

The GMC, as already indicated, has come under fire in recent years, particularly following three enquiries which highlighted the problems over the GMC's supervision of the medical profession:

- *The Shipman Inquiry.* This will be discussed in Chapter 8. The fifth report of the Shipman Inquiry observes how complaints procedures could have prevented Dr Shipman from killing. The inquiry held that the GMC was not to blame for the events. It was proposed that a new database be created to store all the known information about doctors, including records of disciplinary action by employers, information held by the GMC, and the Criminal Records Bureau.

- *The Ayling Inquiry.* In 2000 a GP, Clifford Ayling, from Folkestone was convicted on 12 counts of indecent assault on women patients. The GMC removed him from the Medical Register. Dame Anna Pauffley chaired a public inquiry into the case. Despite complaints raised by patients it had taken a long time for an effective response—there appeared a widespread reluctance to believe that the complaints could be true.

- *The Neale Inquiry.* Richard Neale, a former gynaecologist, was erased from the Medical Register in July 2000 for poor standards of care. Although the GMC had been notified of action taken by Canadian Authorities, the GMC took no action in response to concerns over this doctor. The GMC admitted to the inquiry that this was 'extraordinary and inexplicable'.

In response to these cases the GMC has created a new procedure which is as follows: when a complaint is received it will be investigated by two case examiners: one medical and one lay. This is intended to enable a rapid response to concerns. If they are unable to agree, the Investigation Committee of the GMC will consider the complaint. If the investigators decide there is a need to act quickly to protect the public, then the case can be referred to an Interim Orders Panel who can take action pending a full hearing. When the investigation is complete a Fitness to Practice Panel will conduct a full hearing. The Panel will contain independent panellists who will be specially trained. The Panel can prevent a doctor from practising medicine or place restrictions on the kind of work she or he does. The doctor can be erased from the medical register, meaning that she or he will be excluded from the medical profession. Only in exceptional circumstances will an excluded doctor be restored to the register. A doctor can be suspended so that she or he cannot practice for the period of the suspension. A warning can be issued where there is a significant departure from good medical practice, but not such as to warrant removal from the register. The Panel must provide reasons for its decision.[281] A doctor can appeal to the High Court. The Council for the Regulation of Healthcare Professionals can appeal against a decision which it regards as imposing too lenient a punishment.[282]

[280] The deception may be sufficient to negate consent to any procedure and therefore render it an assault (*R v Tabassum* [2000] Ll Rep Med 404).
[281] *Threlfall v General Optical Council* [2004] EWHC 2683.
[282] *Council for the Regulation of Healthcare Professionals v GMC* [2005] EWHC 579.

The GMC is also taking pro-active measures to try to highlight doctors who may pose a risk to patients. They will be asking all doctors to give details about their practice. If they are not in an 'approved environment' (eg the supervision of their work is very limited) the GMC will take further steps to ensure there is monitoring of what they do.[283] The GMC will also do much more to ensure there is effective sharing of information between the NHS and other employers about concerns over professionals.

Complaints made to the GMC have increased almost 15-fold, since 1990.[284] This increase suggests a growing willingness to lodge a complaint against doctors and may be interpreted as indicating decreasing deference to the medical profession. This may also suggest that there are inadequacies in the informal complaints process.

A report by the Chief Medical Officer[285] recently recommended substantial reform to the current system of professional regulation. It was noted that once a doctor achieved independent practice there was never formal assessment of their competence, while an airline pilot might expect to be assessed about 100 times during their career. Further, the report noted that the GMC was too secretive and 'too tolerant of sub-standard practice'.[286] The report accepted that part of the problem with the current climate is that:

> A culture of blame and retribution has dominated the approach to this whole field so that it has been difficult to draw a distinction between genuine misconduct, individual failure, human error provoked by weak systems, and untoward outcomes which were not the result of any specific failure. An 'off with their heads' approach to every problem will ultimately make healthcare and medical practice more dangerous, since no one will admit their own mistakes, nor will they want to condemn a colleague's career to ruin.[287]

However, the report concluded that the GMC (and equivalent professional bodies) should retain their functioning of regulating conduct. It recommended significant reforms to the way complaints are dealt with and hearings conducted.

A report issued by the Department of Health[288] recommended that an independent body carry out adjudications of whether a doctor was fit to practice. This set out the principles which should govern the regulation of medical professionals:

- First, the body's overriding interest should be the safety and quality of the care that patients receive from health professionals.

- Second, professional regulation needs to sustain the confidence of both the public and healthcare professions through demonstrable impartiality. Regulators need to be independent of Government, the professionals themselves, employers, educators, and all the other interest groups involved in health care.

- Third, professional regulation should be as much about sustaining, improving, and assuring the professional standards of the overwhelming majority of health professionals, as it is about identifying and addressing poor practice or bad behaviour.

- Fourth, professional regulation should not create unnecessary burdens, but be proportionate to the risks it addresses and the benefits it brings.

- Finally, a system is needed that ensures the strength and integrity of health professionals within the UK, but is sufficiently flexible to work effectively for the different

---

[283] GMC (2005).   [284] MDU (2004).   [285] Chief Medical Officer (2006a).
[286] Chief Medical Officer (2006a: para 60).   [287] Chief Medical Officer (2006a: xii).
[288] DoH (2007c).

health needs and health care approaches within and outwith the NHS, and to adapt to future changes.

A central proposed change is that regulatory councils have a majority of members who are not members of the profession and that their members are appointed independently. The aim of this measure is to avoid perceptions of bias that are currently all too prevalent. There are also proposals that all doctors will need to re-licence and can do so only having shown they are fit to continue practicing.

QUESTIONS

1. 'To the seventy-six-year old woman with liver failure, we must say: "For all your children and grandchildren, we can't spend this much on you." To the patient with one heart transplant: "I'm sorry but we can't afford to give you more than one heart because it costs too much and because another person awaits the next heart". To life long smokers: "Sorry, no lung transplants. You could have stopped smoking". Do you think, as Pence (2002: 110) indicates in this quotation, that we need to be more blunt about rationing? If we do, do you agree with his comments?

2. Having read this chapter do you think we need to spend more on the NHS? What do you think of Belshaw's (2005: 48) point: 'Hardly anyone thinks that we should put all our money into the health service, and none at all into pizzas, or holidays, or schools.'?

3. What role should age take in rationing decisions? In an ICM Poll carried out for NICE, people were asked on a scale of one to ten 'How important do you think the age of the patient should be when deciding what treatments can be given on the NHS'; there was no consensus. But when asked 'If extra money became available for the NHS, how would you prioritise where the money should go? Young children? People of working age? People over the age of 65?' the responses were 45 per cent for children, 19 per cent for those of working age, and 12 per cent for people over 65.

4. Do you think that it can never be right to give someone a multiple organ donation (ie a donation of two organs at the same time)? The argument being that the two organs could have saved the lives of two people and so should never be used to save just one (Menzel (1994)).

5. If you were allowed to create your own rationing system for your own heathcare what things would you want and not want to receive treatment for?

6. Porter (1997: 718) wrote: 'It is endemic to a system in which an expanding medical establishment faced with a healthier population, is driven to medicalizing normal events like menopause, converting risks into diseases, and treating trivial complaints with fancy procedures. Doctors and "consumers" are becoming locked within a fantasy that everyone has something wrong with them, everyone and everything can be cured.' Do you agree?

7. In 2005 a nurse was told by her health authority that it did not offer Herceptin, a drug to treat breast cancer. After great media interest and the intervention of the Department of Health, the health authority said that it now regarded her case as exceptional and that she would receive the drug (BBC Newsonline, 3 October 2005). Is it right for politicians to intervene in cases like this?

FURTHER READING

On rationing generally see:

Butler, J. (1999) *The Ethics of Health Care Rationing: Principles and Practices* (Cassell).

Cookson, R. and Dolan, P. (2000) 'Principles of Justice in health care rationing' *Journal of Medical Ethics* 26: 323.

Coulter, A. and Ham, C. (eds) (2000) *Global Challenge of Healthcare Rationing* (Oxford University Press).

McLachlan, H. (2005) 'Justice and the NHS: a comment on Culyer' *Journal of Medical Ethics* 31: 379.

Newdick, C. (2005) *Who Should We Treat?* (Oxford University Press).

Rhodes, R. Battin, M., and Silvers, A. (2005) *Medicine and Social Justice* (Oxford University Press).

Smith II, G. (2002) 'Distributive justice and health care' *Journal of Contemporary Health Law and Policy* 18: 421.

Sunstein, C. (2004) 'Lives, life-years, and willingness to pay' *Columbia Law Review* 104: 205.

On the work of NICE see:

Claxton, K. and Culyer, A. (2006) 'Wickedness or folly? The ethics of NICE's decisions' *Journal of Medical Ethics* 32: 375.

Claxton, K and Culyer, A. (2007) 'Rights, responsibilities and NICE: a rejoinder to Harris' *Journal of Medical Ethics* 33: 462.

Harris, J. (2005c) 'It's not NICE to discriminate' *Journal of Medical Ethics* 31: 373.

Harris, J. (2006) 'NICE is not cost effective' *Journal of Medical Ethics* 32: 378.

Rawlins, M. (2004) 'National Institute for Clinical Excellence and its value judgments' *British Medical Journal* 329: 224.

Syrett, K. (2002) 'NICE work: Rationing, Review and the "legitimacy problem" in the new NHS' *Medical Law Review* 10.

Syrett, K. (2005) 'Does it Pay to be NICE?' in A. Garwood-Gowers, J. Tingle, and K. Wheat (eds) *Contemporary Issues in Healthcare Law and Ethics* (Elsevier).

Syrett, K. (2006) 'Deconstructing Deliberation in the Appraisal of Medical Technologies: NICEly does it?' *Modern Law Review* 69: 869.

On Oregon see:

Oregon Health Services Commission (2007) *Prioritization of Health Services* (Oregon Health Services Commission).

On public health see:

Rees Jones, I. (2003) 'Health Promotion and the New Public Health' in G. Scambler (ed) *Sociology As Applied to Medicine* (Saunders).

On rights under EU law see:

Jervey, T. and McHale, J. (2004) *Health Law and the European Union* (Cambridge University Press).

On professional and government regulation see:

DoH (2005g) *Maintaining High Professional Standards in the Modern NHS* (DoH).

Montgomery, J. (1998) 'Professional Regulation a gendered phenomenon' in S. Sheldon and P. Thomson (ed) *Feminist Perspective on Healthcare Law* (Cavendish).

Quick, O. (2006a) 'Outing medical errors: Questions of trust and responsibility' *Medical Law Review* 14: 22.

3 Medical Negligence

INTRODUCTION

Although this chapter is going to discuss medical negligence and mishaps, it should be emphasized at the outset that for most people their experience of medicine is positive. In the 2006 Healthcare Commission Patient Survey[1] 90 per cent of adult inpatients described the care they had received in hospital as excellent, very good, or good. Inevitably the cases where things go wrong are those that grab the attention and lead to the involvement of lawyers. But even where they do go wrong only exceptionally is this the result of maliciousness. In a report on inadequate treatment at Bristol Royal Infirmary it was said:

> A tragedy took place. But it was a tragedy born of high hopes and ambitions, and peopled by dedicated, hard-working people. The hopes were too high; the ambitions too ambitious.[2]

There are few things a patient awaiting treatment fears more than that the intervention, far from improving their condition, will make it worse. Similarly there are few things medical professionals fear more than that something will go wrong in their dealings with their patient, leaving the patient harmed. When something goes wrong in the medical context it seems natural in our society that legal consequences will follow. If there is a very serious lapse of standards it is possible that criminal proceedings can be brought against a health care professional. More often there is the possibility of an action in tort or contract. Such legal proceedings perform a variety of functions: they ensure that the person injured as a result of negligence receives compensation for their losses; they (where successful) provide a public statement of the wrong-doing of the professional, thereby providing a way of holding professionals accountable for their actions; and they provide a deterrent against bad medical practice. The problem is that these different functions are not always compatible. There may be a case where, although the professional behaved wrongly and deserves censure, it is not possible (or desirable) to identify the loss to the claimant. There may be other cases where it would be desirable to compensate a patient for her or his loss, but blame cannot fairly be attributed to a particular individual. There is, further, the difficulty that requiring an NHS trust to pay compensation to one patient may mean that NHS resources are taken away from other patients.

Even if the wisdom of paying damages in cases of negligence is accepted we have the issue of how to set the standard of acceptable medical practice. Set it too high and the NHS may be flooded with claims and doctors may resort to 'defensive medicine' out of fear of potential litigation. Set it too low and patients will find it impossible to get compensation for their injuries.

---

[1] Healthcare Commission (2007a).   [2] Bristol Royal Infirmary Inquiry (2001: 2).

It is difficult to find an accurate picture of the number of 'adverse' incidents involving the medical professions in England and Wales.[3] Only a tiny proportion of these actually reach the court and so reading court reports will not provide an accurate picture. One study suggested that 11 per cent of patients in hospital experienced an adverse event, of which over a half were preventable if ordinary standards of care had been used.[4] It has been estimated that there are 450,000 adverse events each year in the NHS which caused harm to patients, including 63,000 deaths. Of the total number of adverse events 135,000 were due to medical negligence.[5] The Government's own report estimates that 10 per cent of hospital admissions lead to some kind of adverse event and that 5 per cent of the population have experienced an adverse medical event at some point.[6] Of that 5 per cent one third claimed the event had had a permanent impact on their health. In the year ending 31 March 2007 there were 1.4 million 'patient safety' incidents reported to the National Patient Safety Agency, of which three quarters occurred in hospitals.[7] In 2005, 1,804 serious incidents were reported as resulting in death, with 576 of these cases being avoidable.

In order to have a complete picture of medical malpractice it might be necessary not only to look at reported 'adverse events' but also figures such as the following:

- only 76 per cent of patients talking to a GP had definitely understood the answer to their questions;[8]

- a third of NHS staff would not want to be patients in their own hospitals;[9]

- in 2004, 44 per cent of NHS staff reporting witnessing an error or near error;[10]

- the BMA admits that one in 15 doctors could be abusing drugs or alcohol.[11]

1 The law and medical malpractice: an overview

Imagine a medical professional has clearly harmed a patient through negligent conduct. What legal consequences may follow?

(i) A criminal prosecution. The most likely criminal charge would be for gross negligence manslaughter.[12] A doctor who operated on a patient without his or her consent could also face a charge of battery. In a case of sexual misconduct an offence under the Sexual Offences Act 2003 could be made out. Remember that criminal prosecutions (unlike civil actions) do not require the consent of the victim to be brought. It is, of course, very rare for doctors to face criminal prosecutions for actions performed in their professional capacity.[13]

(ii) A civil action. The claimant could sue for damages relying on the tort of negligence or (in the case of private medical treatment) breach of contract.

---

[3] See Quick (2006a) for further discussion of the statistics.
[4] Vincent, Neale and Woloshynowych (2001).   [5] Towse et al (2004).
[6] Chief Medical Officer (2001: 8). See also National Audit Office (2005a).
[7] National Patient Safety Agency (2007). See DoH (2006d) on how the NHS seeks to learn from mistakes.
[8] Healthcare Commission (2004a).   [9] BBC Newsonline (15 June 2004).
[10] Healthcare Commission (2004c).   [11] BBC Newsonline (13 June 2005c).
[12] *R v Adomako* [1995] 1 AC 171.
[13] An NHS Trusts could also face criminal proceedings under, eg, health and safety legislation: *R v Southampton University Hospital NHS Trust* [2006] EWCA Crim 2971.

(iii) Professional disciplinary proceedings or the NHS complaints procedure. A complaint about a medical professional could be investigated by the relevant professional body and/or by the NHS itself. These procedures may result in a variety of punishments of the professional, but will not provide compensation to the individual victim.

2 Criminal law

A doctor can be guilty of a criminal offence against a patient in the same way as anyone else. For example, if a doctor intentionally cut a patient without his or her consent, this could amount to an assault. Of course, it is rare for a doctor to deliberately harm a patient in this way.[14]

Perhaps of greater concern to most doctors is the possibility of gross negligence manslaughter. This offence is discussed at page 444. Notably, a medical professional can be convicted of gross negligence manslaughter without proof that she or he intended or foresaw the harm. It is rare for there to be a manslaughter case involving medical professionals, although such prosecutions do appear to be on the increase. In the period 1970 to 1990 there were four prosecutions, from 1990 to 1999 there were 17, but from 2000 to 2006 there appear to have been 64.[15]

3 The law of negligence

The majority of litigation following medical malpractice is brought under the tort of negligence. In order to succeed the claimant will need to prove three things:

(1) The professional who is being sued owed the claimant a duty of care.

(2) The professional breached the duty of care.

(3) The breach of duty of care caused the claimant loss.

We will need to look at each of these requirements separately.

3.1 The duty of care

The duty of care is normally easily established. The basic approach in the law of tort is that you owe a duty of care to anyone you may reasonably foreseeably injure. There is little difficulty in finding that all staff in a hospital owe a duty of care to patients in the hospital. In General Practice doctors owe a duty of care to those on their lists. More difficult is whether a doctor owes a duty of care to a person who falls ill in a public place in the presence of the doctor, or whether a duty of care is owed by a medical professional to the relatives of a patient. Such cases would be dealt with using the general principles of negligence which would focus on the following questions:

(i) *Was it reasonably foreseeable that the defendant's actions would cause the victim harm?* If not, then there is no duty of care. So a doctor who prescribes medicine to a

---

[14] Although sexual assaults in the course of treatment are more common. See eg *R v Kumar* [2006] EWCA Crim 1946.
[15] Quick (2006b).

patient would not be found to owe a duty of care to the patient's grand-niece who subsequently found the medicine bottle and ate the tablets. The grand-niece's actions would not be reasonably foreseeable.

(ii) *Is there a sufficiently close relationship between the defendant and the patient?*
This is a rather vague concept but the discussion of four scenarios may clarify the concept. First, in *Goodwill v BPAS*[16] it was held that a doctor did not owe a duty of care, in giving contraceptive advice to a patient, towards people the patient may in the future engage in sexual relations with. The doctor may, however, in such a case owe a duty to care to the patient's spouse. The difference is that doctors giving contraceptive advice to patients whom they know are married will clearly have the spouse in their contemplation when giving the advice. But doctors will have no awareness at all of potential future sexual partners of a single patient. Second, in *West Bromwich Albion v El-Safty*[17] it was held that a surgeon treating a football player did not owe a duty of care to his club, so as to be liable for financial losses suffered by the club when the player was treated negligently. The Court of Appeal emphasized that at no point had the surgeon assumed responsibility for the financial well-being of the club. It might have been different if the club had employed the surgeon, warning him of the financial consequences if the treatment was ineffective. Third, in *Farraj v King's Healthcare NHS Trust*[18] it was held that a private laboratory that conducted some tests on a patient's material on behalf of an NHS hospital owed the patient a duty of care. The laboratory had not communicated with the patient, but knew that the results passed on to the hospital would be used to make decisions about treatment. Fourth, if a medical professional walks past a road traffic accident and fails to offer assistance that will not amount to breach of a duty of care,[19] although it might infringe professional good practice.[20] There is an important limitation on this and that is where health care professionals' contract of employment requires them to offer assistance. GPs, for example, are required to provide services to those in their practice area in need of care following an accident or emergency.[21] Therefore if a GP came across a car accident and notices that one of her or his patients was involved in the accident then it might constitute a breach of contract for the GP not to provide or summon assistance.[22] It should also be noted that if doctors do decide to help people involved in accidents they owe them a duty of care and can be held liable in tort if they are negligent, although in one case it was suggested that in such a case a doctor would only be liable if she or he made the patient's condition worse, but not if she or he failed to provide treatment which should have been provided.[23] It has been suggested that this potential liability for assisting someone at the scene of an accident is a discouragement for a doctor to be a 'Good Samaritan',[24] although a survey of GPs found little evidence that they were put off assisting others for fear of litigation.[25]

(iii) *Is there a public policy reason which argues against a duty of care being found?*
It is well established in tort law that a duty of care only exists where it is 'just and

---

[16] [1996] 2 All ER 161.   [17] [2006] EWCA Civ 1299.   [18] [2006] EWHC 1228 (QB).
[19] *F v West Berkshire HA* [1989] 2 All ER 545, 567.   [20] GMC (2007: para 11).
[21] NHS (General Medical Services) Regulations 1992 (SI 1992/635). Similarly an accident and emergency department at a hospital owes a duty of care to any patient who arrives at its premises (*Barnett v Chelsea and Kensington* [1969] 1 QB 428).
[22] A member of an ambulance crew called to the scene of an accident would owe a duty of care to those injured: *Kent v Griffiths (No 3)* [2001] QB 36. See further Williams (2007).
[23] Stuart-Smith LJ in *Capital and Counties v Hants CC* [1997] 2 All ER 865 and *Powell v Boldaz* [1997] 39 BMLR 35.
[24] Brazier (2003b: 141); K. Williams (2001).   [25] Williams (2003).

reasonable' to impose one. If a hospital released an outpatient who had a history of violence and harmed a member of the public it is likely the court would refuse to find a duty
of care owed by the hospital to the general public.[26] It would not be just and reasonable
to require every NHS trust to detain any outpatient who could pose a risk to others.

Although most cases have involved a claim that a particular medical professional was
negligent, it may be possible to claim that the NHS or the PCT was negligent. This
might be appropriate where the negligence lies in the way the hospital was managed
or staffing issues addressed, rather than the conduct of a particular person. This was
acknowledged in *A (A Child) v Ministry of Defence*[27] where it was recognized that an
NHS Trust owed a duty of care to provide a safe and satisfactory medical service to a
patient.[28]

3.2 The breach of the duty

Having established that the defendant owed the victim a duty of care the next question
is whether the professional breached that duty. Normally in the law of negligence the
question is whether it is shown on the balance of probabilities that the defendant acted
as a reasonable person would. In the medical context it is more complicated. The leading
decision is *Bolam v Friern HMC* where in a controversial statement it was held:

> A doctor is not guilty of negligence if he has acted in accordance with a practice accepted
> as proper by a responsible body of medical men skilled in that particular art.[29]

The test applies not only to doctors but to any health care professional. Although con-
troversial, the test has been approved by the House of Lords in several cases: *Maynard v
West Midlands RHA*,[30] *Whitehouse v Jordan*,[31] *Sidaway v Bethlem RHG*,[32] and *Bolitho v
Hackney HA*,[33] so there is no doubt it represents the present law.

The effect of the *Bolam* decision is that it is difficult to show a doctor breached the
duty of care. It will not be enough to introduce evidence from an expert witness that she
or he would not have carried out the procedure in the way the defendant did. It would
be necessary to show that there is no responsible body of medical opinion that would
have approved of acting in that way. All the defendant would need to do to win the case
would be to find an acknowledged expert to agree that the way the defendant dealt with
the patient was within the range of acceptable practice.[34] It should be emphasized that
the question is not whether the defendant was acting in the ideal way but that their
actions were above the minimal acceptable practice. Therefore, even if it is shown that
the professional made a misdiagnosis, this does not mean it was negligent.[35] Similarly,
a failure to give information about an alternative treatment which was available will not
necessarily be regarded as negligent if it is in accordance with acceptable practice.[36]

The logic behind the *Bolam* test was explained by the House of Lords in *Maynard v
West Midlands RHA*.[37] There the House of Lords held that a judge is not in a position

---

[26] *Palmer v Tees HA* [1999] Ll Rep Med 359.
[27] [2004] EWCA 641. See also *Garcia v St Mary's NHS Trust* [2006] EWHC 2314 (QBD).
[28] Beswick (2007).   [29] [1957] 2 All ER 118, 121.   [30] [1985] 1 All ER 635.
[31] [1981] 1 All ER 267.   [32] [1985] 1 All ER 643.   [33] [1997] 4 All ER 771.
[34] *Bellarby v Worthing & Southlands Hospitals NHS Trust* [2005] EWHC 2089.
[35] *Whitehouse v Jordan* [1981] 1 WLR 246.
[36] *Thompson v Blake-James* [1998] Lloyd's Rep Med 187.   [37] [1985] 1 All ER 635.

to choose between the views of competing medical expert opinions. So as long as there is a competent school of thought that believed the defendant's actions were reasonable the judge will find the defendant had not been negligent.

Having grasped the basic idea of the *Bolam* test, we need to make a few more detailed points about its operation:

(i) A doctor is to be judged on the state of knowledge at the time of the incident. So if, by the time of the hearing, it was generally accepted that treatment of the type given by the defendant was improper, but at the time when she or he acted there was a respectable body of opinion that the treatment was acceptable, the defendant will not be negligent.[38] Further a doctor will not be expected to have read and digested research which has only just become available. So a doctor was not negligent because she failed to read an article in a medical journal published six months earlier[39] or did not use a piece of equipment which was not widely available.[40] It is arguable that the existence of the internet, making research more readily available, will mean that doctors will be expected to be more up to date than they were in the past.

(ii) To have a defence, all a defendant need show is that her or his conduct would be thought acceptable by a respected body of opinion. It does not need to be a substantial body of opinion.[41] Therefore if a respectable medical expert gives evidence that what the defendant doctor did was an appropriate way of dealing with the case it is unlikely that the claimant will succeed. In *Maynard v West Midlands RHA*[42] the House of Lords criticized a judge at first instance who had heard two competing experts on what course of action was appropriate and had attempted to decide whose evidence was preferable. It was emphasized that it was not for the judge to weigh up competing bodies of professional opinion. Under the *Bolam* test, once it is found that the defendant's course of action was approved of by a responsible body of medical opinion, that was enough to show that there was no negligence. The point was dramatically demonstrated in *Defreitas v O'Brien*[43] where the evidence was that just four or five specialist neuroscientists would endorse the defendant's way of dealing with the case. Still that was sufficient to amount to a body of responsible opinion and so there was no negligence.

The law's approach however is less clear cut after the House of Lords decision in *Bolitho v City & Hackney Health Authority*[44] and in particular the following *dicta* of Lord Browne-Wilkinson:

> ...the court has to be satisfied that the exponents of the body of opinion relied on can demonstrate that such opinion has a logical basis. In particular, in cases involving, as they so often do, the weighing up of risks against benefits, the judge before accepting a body of opinion as being reasonable, responsible or respectable will need to be satisfied that, in forming their views, the experts have directed their minds to the questions of comparative risks and benefits and have reached a defensible conclusion on the matter.[45]

This led one leading academic critic of the *Bolam* test to exclaim 'Eureka!'.[46] What excited this response is that Lord Browne-Wilkinson's *dicta* suggests that simply because a medical expert declares that what the defendant did was acceptable it does not mean

---

[38] *Roe v Minister of Health* [1954] 2 All ER 131.

[39] *Crawford v Board of Governors of Charing Cross Hospital The Times*, 8 December 1953.

[40] *Whiteford v Hunter* (1950) 94 SJ 758.   [41] *Defreitas v O'Brien* [1995] 2 Med LR 155.

[42] [1984] 1 WLR 634.   [43] [1993] 4 Med LR 281.

[44] [1998] AC 232.   [45] At 242.   [46] Grubb (1998a: 38). See also Teff (1998).

that the judge must accept that the defendant was not negligent. Judges must satisfy themselves that the evidence had a 'logical basis'. To some this has marked a radical change in the courts' approach. Now judges will seriously examine a claim that the defendant acted in accordance with a responsible body of medical opinion and will not just accept the say so of a fellow doctor. Indeed, it might be said that the phrase 'defensible' position requires the judge to give careful scrutiny to the evidence supporting the competing views on the legitimacy of the defendant's conduct.[47]

However, other commentators do not believe that Lord Browne-Wilkinson's *dicta* had a dramatic impact on the law because any judicial scrutiny of medical expert opinion will be minimal. It would require a bizarre case for a medical specialist to have an illogical view and not to have considered the benefits and disadvantages of her or his approach. Indeed Lord Brown-Wilkinson accepted that '. . . in the vast majority of cases the fact that distinguished experts in the field are of a particular opinion will demonstrate the reasonableness of that opinion'. So, it is argued, even if the judge is to take a slightly harder look at claims of the defendant's expert witnesses, it is highly unlikely the judge will declare them illogical or 'unrespectable'.

So what of the cases following *Bolitho*: how have they interpreted Lord Browne-Wilkinson's comments?[48] One notable point is that many of the cases after *Bolitho* do not cite the case and simply refer to the *Bolam* test. This itself indicates that the courts might not regard *Bolitho* as having made a change of any great significance. But of those cases which do cite *Bolitho* it is possible to find some which suggest it has had a significant impact on the degree of scrutiny with which judges will examine the views of the experts. Contrast these three cases:

- In *Marriott v West Midlands Health Authority*[49] a GP called on the claimant who had suffered a fall. The GP prescribed painkillers. He did not suggest a full neurological examination. Expert evidence was given that as the risk that the patient had a blood clot on the brain following the fall was so small it was not negligent not to seek further tests. However the trial judge, supported by the Court of Appeal, in considering this evidence held that although the risk of a clot was small the consequences for the patient if there were a clot were so serious that the only reasonable course of action was to require tests. In other words, although there was evidence that some experts regarded it as unnecessary to carry out the tests, such an approach was held to be irresponsible by the court. This indicates *Bolitho* does authorize a judge to consider carefully the views of medical experts and where appropriate deem them irresponsible.[50]

- In *Wisniewski v Central Manchester Health Authority*[51] it was claimed that there was medical negligence in the management of the claimant mother's pregnancy. In particular it was argued that there should have been further investigations of abnormalities in the fetal heart beat. Further investigations would have resulted in an earlier Caesarean section intervention which would have avoided the injuries the claimant suffered. There was conflicting evidence as to whether there was a responsible body of skilled medical opinion that would not have sought further investigations. The trial

---

[47] See the discussion in Lord Woolf (2001) and Lord Irvine (1999).
[48] A useful analysis of the post-*Bolitho* case law can be found in Maclean (2002).
[49] [1999] Ll Med Rep 23. See also *Penney v East Kent AHA* [2000] Ll Rep Med 41, *Reynolds v North Tyneside HA* [2002] Ll Rep Med 453.
[50] *Townsend v Worcester DHA* [1995] BMLR 31 and *Bouchta v Swindon* [1996] Med LR 62.
[51] [1998] Ll Rep Med 223.

judge held that there no such body of opinion. One argument on appeal was that the judge had wrongly substituted his own assessment of what was the appropriate course of action, rather than correctly applying the *Bolam* test. That argument succeeded. It was held that the judge had heard eminent and impressive experts stating that there was a responsible body of opinion which would not have undertaken further investigations. Only rarely could a judge declare that the views of experts could not be supported logically.[52] Brook LJ stated: 'It is quite impossible for a court to hold that the views sincerely held by doctors of such eminence cannot logically be supported at all.'[53]

- In *Burne v A*[54] a mother telephoned a doctor concerned about her child. The alleged negligence was that the GP had failed to ask the mother about symptoms which would have revealed a blockage in a shunt which had been inserted into his head to help drain fluid from the brain (something the GP knew about). Instead the doctor just listened to the symptoms the mother listed. The experts before the trial judge said that the doctor did not act improperly in simply taking into account what he had been told by the mother and was not required to ask about specific symptoms. The judge hearing the case found that despite what the experts said about accepted practice there was no reason or logic behind not asking specific questions which might reveal symptoms when it was known that the child had a shunt, which if it was blocked would produce serious medical problems.[55] On appeal Sedley LJ thought it was understandable that the judge thought it unacceptable that the medical profession thought it was unnecessary to ask specific questions of this kind. However, he ordered a retrial because the judge had not given the experts an adequate opportunity to explain and defend common practice. Ward LJ added that a judge was not free to ignore the views of experts on what was acceptable practice and rely on 'common sense' without giving the experts the chance to explain themselves. This case is notable for its acceptance that a judge could reject the views of the experts on what is a responsible course of conduct, but before doing so the experts must be given the chance of justifying the practice.

At present, therefore, there is conflicting case law on the correct reading of *Bolitho*. Silber J has suggested it would 'very seldom be right' for a judge to regard competent medical expert's views as unreasonable.[56] The Court of Appeal in applying *Bolitho* to a case involving vets said that to call an expert's view unreasonable or illogical was 'extreme'.[57] If a judge does decide to reject an expert's view on a responsible body of medical opinion a careful explanation is required.[58] However, more recently, in *Smith v Southampton University Hospital NHS Trust*[59] the Court of Appeal said that if there is a conflict

---

[52] See also *Briody v St Helen's & Knowsley AHA* [1999] Ll Rep Med 185.

[53] *Wisniewski v Central Manchester Health Authority* [1998] Ll Rep Med 223, 237 (Brook LJ). See *Zarb v Odetoyinbo* [2006] EWHC 2880 (QB) where reference was made to the qualifications and writings of an expert in concluding his view could not be said to be irresponsible.

[54] [2006] EWCA Civ 24.

[55] In this particular case the mother had not specifically mentioned that the child was irritable and drowsy which would have indicated a shunt problem.

[56] *M (A Child by his Mother) v Blackpool Victoria Hospital NHS Trust* [2003] EWHC 1744.

[57] *Calver v Westwood Veterinary Group* (2001) 58 BMLR 194, para 34. See also *Cowley v Cheshire and Merseyside Strategic Health* [2007] EWHC 48 (QB) where Forbes J held it would be rare for an expert's views not to be found to represent a responsible body of opinion.

[58] *Elaine Ruth Glicksman v Redbridge NHS Trust* [2001] EWCA Civ 1097.

[59] [2007] EWCA Civ 387.

between experts on whether the conduct of defendant was in accordance with a respectable body of opinion, the judge must explain which expert is preferred and why. It is not enough just to say that the expert saying that the defendant was not negligent was a responsible expert.[60] It has been suggested that courts will be more willing to find an expert's view not to represent a responsible school of thought where the medical issue is not complex, or technical, but is an issue on which an ordinary person can consider the matter.[61]

(iii) The standard of care a professional is expected to exercise is that of those in the speciality or profession involved. A general practitioner is to be assessed by the skills expected of a general practitioner not a specialist consultant.[62] Similarly a practitioner in traditional Chinese herbal medicine was not expected to meet the standard of a practitioner in orthodox medicine.[63] So a GP or alternative medicine specialist would not be negligent in failing to diagnose a condition which would only be apparent to a specialist in the field. However, a GP in such a case may be found negligent in not referring a patient with unusual symptoms for a consultation or at least a follow-up appointment.[64] Further it would be negligent for a general practitioner to attempt a medical procedure which should only be attempted by a specialist in a particular field.[65]

This also means that if a person is acting in a particular capacity then she or he must exercise the skill expected of such a person. The fact she or he is inexperienced,[66] or a student,[67] or aged is irrelevant. However, an inexperienced member of staff might not be negligent if she or he is following the advice of a more experience colleague. In *Wilsher v Essex AHA*[68] a house officer inserted a catheter into a vein, rather than an artery. He asked his senior registrar to check what he had done and the registrar approved it. The registrar was found to be negligent, but the house officer not. It should not be thought, however, that it is automatically a defence for a health care professional to say that they were 'only following orders' from a more senior practitioner. First, the court may find that there was a duty on the junior professional to check that they had correctly understood the instructions. This might be particularly so where the instruction appears unusual. Secondly, there may come a point where the instruction is so blatantly wrong that the health care professional should not follow it.[69] So a pharmacist who failed to seek confirmation of a prescription that was patently wrong was found to be negligent.[70] It is also interesting to note that in *Antoniades v East Sussex Hospitals NHS Trust*[71] the court found that the way that a team of doctors worked together had produced a negligent level of care. The team leader was found to have been negligent in having inadequately trained his team in how to deal with the kind of case they had to deal with.

(iv) The court will take into account the situation in which professionals find themselves. So, if a doctor is faced with an emergency the law generally accepts that she or he

---

[60] *Hanson v Airedale Hospital NHS Trust* (QBD) [2003] CLY 2989.

[61] *French v Thames Valley Strategic Health Authority* [2005] EWHC 459, para 112.

[62] *Stockdale v Nicholls* [1993] 4 Med LR 190.

[63] *Shakoor v Situ (trading as Eternal Health Co)* [2000] 4 All ER 181.

[64] *Judge v Huntingdon HA* [1995] 6 Med LR 223.

[65] *Defreitas v O'Brien* [1993] 4 Med LR 281.

[66] *Jones v Manchester Corporation* [1952] 2 All ER 125.

[67] This is assumed to be the law as it is in line with the general approach in the law on tort; on learner drivers see *Nettleship v Weston* [1971] 3 All ER 581 on learner drivers.   [68] [1986] 3 All ER 801.

[69] Montgomery (2003: 179), although there seems little case law to support this.

[70] *Horton v Evans* [2006] EWHC 2808 (QB); *Dwyer v Roderick* (1983) 127 SJ 806.

[71] [2007] EWHC 517 (QB).

will not necessarily be able to demonstrate the same level of skill as if faced with a case with plenty of time to decide what to do.

A doctor's liability will depend on the information provided by a patient. So if a patient does not give a doctor the necessary information it is unlikely that a negligence action will lie. So if a doctor is not told about a crucial symptom then the patient will have an uphill task establishing a negligence action. However, a doctor in an emergency room who failed to diagnose the broken ribs of a drunken man who had been involved in an accident involving a car was found to be negligent. Although the man had not mentioned any pain, his drunkenness would have dulled any pain and the doctor should have appreciated that.[72]

(v) It is unclear the extent to which lack of resources will be a defence to a claim of negligence.[73] In *Garcia v St Mary's NHS Trust*[74] it was claimed that the NHS Trust had been negligent in setting staffing levels and arranging work practices. Their failures in those areas, it was alleged, had caused the patient to receive an inadequate level of care. This claim failed. In deciding that the level of provision was not negligent under the *Bolam* standard, the point was made that budget restrictions inevitably affected staffing levels and work practices. The issue of the rationing of medical resources is considered further in Chapter 2.

(vi) If a hospital has an official protocol or policy from which a health care professional has departed this will assist in demonstrating that the professional has been negligent. The courts appear to have taken the approach that in such a case unless the professional can provide good reasons for departing from the standard practice then she or he will be found negligent.[75] On the other hand, it should not be thought that following an official protocol or policy will necessarily provide a full defence. This is particularly where to do so would clearly harm the patient.[76] Further, a failure to follow NICE guidelines, especially where the deviation is significant, may be taken as good evidence of a breach of a duty of care.[77] Similarly failure to follow guidelines issued by professional bodies may also be taken as evidence that there was a breach of a *Bolam* duty.[78]

(vii) The doctrine of *res ipsa loquitur* (the thing speaks for itself) may be relied upon in some cases. Essentially this doctrine is used where, although the claimant cannot directly prove medical negligence, she or he claims that it is obvious from the fact of the injury and its circumstances that there was negligence. Lord Denning in *Cassidy v Ministry of Health*[79] considered a case where a patient went in for an operation with two stiff fingers and came out with four stiff fingers. Although the plaintiff could not prove there had been negligence Lord Denning thought that the plaintiff was entitled to say to the defendant 'explain my injuries if you can'. In effect then because the circumstances clearly indicated that something went wrong (even though it was not clear exactly what). Where it is unclear whether an injury was caused by an act of negligence rather than a non-negligent cause the doctrine cannot help.[80] Recently Hobhouse LJ stated:

> . . . that the expression *res ipsa loquitur* should be dropped from the litigator's vocabulary and replaced by the phrase 'a prima facie case'. *Res ipsa loquitur* is not a principle of law: it

---

[72] *Wood v Thurston The Times*, 25 May 1951.
[73] Witting (2001).   [74] [2006] EWHC 2314 (QBD).
[75] *Clark v Maclennan* [1983] 1 All ER 416.
[76] *Barnet v Chelsea and Kensington HMC* [1968] 1 All ER 1068.
[77] *West Bromwich Albion v El-Safty* [2006] EWCA 1299.
[78] Samanta, Mello, Foster, Tingle and Samanta (2006).   [79] [1954] 2 KB 343.
[80] *Howard v Wessex RHA* (QBD) 21 July 1993.

does not relate to or raise any presumption. It is merely a guide to help to identify when a prima facie case is being made out. Where expert and factual evidence has been called on both sides at a trial its usefulness will normally have long since been exhausted.[81]

Latham LJ in *Lillywhite v University College London Hospitals' NHS Trust*[82] held that the doctrine of *res ipsa loquitur* would only rarely be useful where a court had heard full evidence from all sides. In that case an experienced consultant carried out an ultrasound on a foetus. The consultant had noted three structures of the fetal brain as being present, when in fact they were not. The majority of the Court of Appeal held that this error meant the doctor had a heavy burden of showing he had acted with reasonable care and skill. There was no need to rely on a special doctrine to reach this conclusion.

(viii) Under section 1 of the 2006 Compensation Act 2006:

A court considering a claim in negligence or breach of statutory duty may, in determining whether the defendant should have taken particular steps to meet a standard of care (whether by taking precautions against a risk or otherwise), have regard to whether a requirement to take those steps might—

(a) prevent a desirable activity from being undertaken at all, to a particular extent or in a particular way, or

(b) discourage persons from undertaking functions in connection with a desirable activity.

Brazier and Cave doubt this section, which applies to tort law generally, will have any effect on clinical negligence.[83] This is probably true; although a court may refer to this section if a doctor is claiming that she or he was attempting to pioneer a ground-breaking new form of treatment, which in retrospect it has turned out to ineffective.

3.3 Causation

Simply showing that a health care professional has been negligent does not mean that the claimant has won her or his case. It must also be shown that the negligence caused the victim's injuries.[84] The basic test for causation is known as the 'but for' test. This simply asks whether 'but for' the defendant's negligence the patient would have suffered an injury. In some cases this is straightforward. If in error a doctor removes the healthy rather than diseased kidney it is obvious that the doctor's negligence caused the loss of the kidney. However, where the claim is that the defendant's negligence meant that the patient's disease was not diagnosed or treated properly it is necessary to show that if the professional had acted properly:

 (i) the disease would have been diagnosed; and

 (ii) it would have been possible to treat the patient so that her or his condition would have improved.

In *Barnett v Chelsea and Kensington HMC*[85] a doctor refused to see a man who turned up at casualty complaining of stomach pains. The man died shortly afterwards. It was

---

[81] *Ratcliffe v Plymouth and Torbay HA* [1998] 4 Med LR 162, 190. Although see *Richards v Swansea NHS Trust* [2007] EWHC 487 (QB) where the doctrine was referred to uncritically.

[82] [2005] EWCA Civ 1466.   [83] Brazier and Cave (2007: 160).

[84] See *Thomson v Bradford* [2005] EWCA Civ 1439 where, although there was fault in the advice given by the doctor, that fault did not cause the loss.

[85] [1968] 1 All ER 1068.

clear that the doctor was negligent in refusing to see the patient. However, the evidence suggested that even if the doctor had seen the man there was nothing the doctor would have been able to do to save his life. Therefore although there was negligence it could not be said to have caused the injury. That case was, in a way, an easy one. In other cases it will be far more difficult to show whether the patient's condition would have been apparent from a proper examination or whether any treatment would have improved the patient's condition.[86] There are some complex issues that can arise where the defendant is not shown to have definitely caused the harm but to have been a possible cause or to have exposed the claimant to a risk. A number of different situations need to be distinguished.

3.3.1 *Where it is unclear whether the injury suffered was caused by the defendant or some other cause*

In *Wilsher v Essex*[87] it was unclear whether the blindness suffered by a child was caused by the negligent care given him or by his premature birth. The House of Lords confirmed that it had to be shown on the balance of probabilities that the harm was caused by the negligence of the defendant. This could not be demonstrated on the facts and so the action failed.

This may be a special rule for medical law cases. In *Fairchild v Glenhaven Funeral Services*[88] workers who had been exposed to asbestos suffered from mesothelioma. The workers had worked for a variety of employers and, of course, it was not possible to establish which employer's asbestos dust had caused the injury. It was held that all the employers were liable as they had all materially increased the risk of harm to the employees. But in so doing the House of Lords approved the *Wilsher* decision. Lord Hoffman referred to the 'massive increase in the liability of the National Health Service' had *Wilsher* been decided differently.[89] This suggests that there may be policy reasons why the courts will take a strict approach to causation in medical negligence cases.

3.3.2 *Cases where the alleged negligence is that the defendant failed to examine the claimant*

The facts of *Bolitho v City & Hackney HA*[90] demonstrate another difficulty with causation. There a child had breathing difficulties. Although the paediatric registrar was called she failed to attend until too late. The evidence was that if she had examined the boy within a reasonable time and put him on an intubater he would not have suffered the serious injuries that he did. However, one argument put before the House of Lords was that it had not been shown that the negligence caused the death because, if the registrar had attended, she might have decided not to place the child on an intubater. The House of Lords held that it was necessary to ask two questions. First, what would the registrar have recommended if she had attended on the boy? This was a factual question which just required the court to predict how the registrar would have acted. If the answer was that she would have used the intubator then it was shown that negligence caused the injuries. If the answer was that she would not then the second question was whether it would have been negligent for her to do so (using the *Bolam* test). If it would have been negligent then again the injuries would be caused by her negligence. For the

---

[86] See also *Kay v Ayrshire and Arran Health Board* [1987] 1 All ER 417.
[87] *Wilsher v Essex AHA* [1988] 1 All ER 871.   [88] [2002] Ll Rep Med 361.
[89] Para 69.   [90] [1997] 4 All ER 771.

registrar to have a defence on the causation ground it would be necessary to show that if she had attended on the child she would not have used the intubator and that it would not have been negligent for her to make that decision. On the facts of the case the House of Lords held causation not to be established because there was evidence that using an intubator on as young a child as the claimant carried serious risks, and that therefore the registrar would not have used it and it would not have been negligent for her to make that decision.

By contrast in *Gouldsmith v Mid-Staffordshire*[91] a doctor failed to refer a patient to a specialist unit for treatment on her finger. It was not known who at the unit would have seen the patient but it was found to be more likely than not that if she had been referred she would have received treatment because that was normal practice. If she had received treatment the injuries to her finger would not have occurred. That being the case there was no need to ask whether it would be negligent for the specialists not to offer treatment.[92] In a dissenting judgment Kay LJ thought that it was wrong to distinguish a case where you knew exactly who would have treated the patient (eg *Bolitho*) and a case (eg *Gouldsmith*) where it was not known who would seen the patient. He thought it inappropriate that in *Gouldsmith* a claimant only needed to show that it was more likely than not that a surgeon would provide the treatment. He thought a claimant should show that it was more likely than not that the actual physician who would have seen him would have provided the treatment. However, as Kay LJ acknowledged, that would prove very difficult for a patient, because they could not know which doctor they would see. The majority in *Gouldsmith*, then, held that where the alleged negligence is a failure to refer a patient, and it is not known to whom they would be referred, you imagine a hypothetical expert in the field and consider whether it was more likely than not that they would treat the patient.

3.3.3 *Depriving the claimant of a chance of treatment*

What if the evidence shows that if properly cared for the claimant's illness would have been diagnosed, and she or he would have been offered treatment which might have cured her or his condition, but the defendant failed to diagnose the claimant's condition and so deprived her or him of the chance of treatment?[93]

The following three cases are crucial to the understanding of this complex area of the law.

KEY CASE   Hotson v E Berkshire [1987] AC 750

A boy, aged 13, fell out of a tree, injured his hip and was taken to hospital. He argued that if his condition has been properly diagnosed when he arrived at the hospital he would have been offered a treatment. That treatment would have had a 25 per cent chance of providing a recovery. Because his condition was not properly diagnosed he was not given the treatment and lost his chance of recovery. He suffered a vascular necrosis of the epiphysis, involving disability of the hip joint with the

---

91 [2007] EWCA Civ 397.
92 See also *Carter v Basildon & Thurrock University Hospitals* [2007] EWHC 1882 (QB).
93 For a sophisticated analysis of the law and the issues raised in such cases see Khoury (2006).

virtual certainty that osteoarthritis would later develop. The trial judge granted him 25 per cent of the damages he would have received if the health authority was fully responsible for the hip condition. The House of Lords held this approach wrong. As a general rule damages could only be awarded if it could be shown that, if the patient had been properly diagnosed, there was available treatment which would probably have worked (ie had a greater than 50 per cent chance of success). Quite simply the plaintiff had failed to show on the balance of probabilities that, had the health authority not been negligent, he would not have suffered the injury. In fact, as there was only a 25 per cent chance of success, if the boy had been given the correct treatment he may still have suffered the injuries from which he was presently suffering.

Lord Mackay and Lord Bridge, however, refused to rule that the loss of a less than 50 per cent chance of a full recovery was never recoverable. They did not indicate in what kinds of cases they thought it might be.

KEY CASE   Chester v Afshar [2004] UKHL 41

Ms Chester suffered severe pain in her back. She was referred to Mr Afshar, an eminent consultant neurosurgeon. Mr Afshar recommended surgery, but failed to warn Ms Chester of the 1–2 per cent risk of significant nerve damage which was an inevitable risk of the surgery. Ms Chester agreed to the operation and although it was performed properly the risk of nerve damage materialized and she was left partially paralysed. The trial judge found that had Mr Afshar informed Ms Chester of the risk she would not have consented to the operation at that time, but would have sought a further opinion. However, on receiving the further opinion she would have consented to the treatment probably with Mr Afshar at a later date. The trial judge held that it had therefore been shown there was a causal link between the surgeon's advice and the loss to the patient. The case went up to the House of Lords.

By a majority of three to two their Lordships found in favour of Ms Chester. It was held that where a patient had not been warned about a risk of injury and as a result of that failure underwent the operation which she would not have undertaken *at that time* if she had been properly informed, a patient was entitled to compensation. It was not necessary for Ms Chester to show that she would never have consented to the kind of operation at any time in the future, only that she would not have consented to the operation that took place. The majority accepted that on conventional causation principles the decision could not be supported. This was because it was found that had she been properly informed of the risks Ms Chester would have agreed to the operation, although at a later date. She would therefore have been undertaking an operation with exactly the same chance of causing her an injury as the operation she undertook. Lord Steyn emphasized that, even if the risk of the injury occurring was the same whenever she undertook the operation, she would not have suffered exactly the same injury at the same time that she did if the proper information had been given. In any event, whatever the arguments over causation, Lord Steyn believed that justice required a modification of the normal approach to causation. The duty on doctors to warn patients of risks was important because it protected the rights of patients to make informed choices about whether, and when and by whom, to be operated upon. To leave the patient who was not informed about the risk when they would not have immediately consented to the operation would render the duty meaningless. As Lord Hope put it:

> The function of the law is to protect the patient's right to choose. If it is to fulfil that function it must ensure that the duty to inform is respected by the doctor. It will fail to do this if an appropriate remedy cannot be given if the duty is breached and the very risk that the patient should have been told about occurs and she suffers injury. (para 56)

Lord Walker for the majority accepted that the conclusion of the majority was more about policy than the principles of causation. But the majority were not ignoring causation altogether:

> ...if a taxi-driver drives too fast and the cab is hit by a falling tree, injuring the passenger, it is sheer coincidence. The driver might equally well have avoided the tree by driving too fast, and the passenger might have been injured if the driver was observing the speed limit. But to my mind the present case does not fall into that category. Bare 'but for' causation is powerfully reinforced by the fact that the misfortune which befell the claimant was the very misfortune which was the focus of the surgeon's duty to warn. (para 94)

The point of Lord Walker's analogy is that 'but for' causation is not sufficient, as otherwise the taxi driver would be liable. But in *Chester*, the risk was within the scope of the duty, and it was fair to hold the surgeon responsible for it.

The views of the dissenting judges were summarized by Lord Bingham in the following passage:

> A defendant is bound to compensate the claimant for the damage which his or her negligence has caused the claimant. But the corollaries are also true: a claimant is not entitled to be compensated, and a defendant is not bound to compensate the claimant, for damage not caused by the negligence complained of. The patient's right to be appropriately warned is an important right, which few doctors in the current legal and social climate would consciously or deliberately violate. I do not for my part think that the law should seek to reinforce that right by providing for the payment of potentially very large damages by a defendant whose violation of that right is not shown to have worsened the physical condition of the claimant. (para 9)

In such a case, he argued, one could not claim to have been caused a loss due to not being given the correct odds.

KEY CASE   Gregg v Scott [2005] UKHL 2

Mr Gregg visited Doctor Scott because he had a lump under his arm. Scott negligently misdiagnosed the lump as benign. One year later it was discovered that Gregg suffered from cancer of the lymph gland. As a result he had to undergo chemotherapy and was left with a poor prognosis. Gregg alleged that had Scott properly diagnosed his condition when he saw him there would have been a much greater chance of being cured. At trial the judge held that his chances of surviving for more than 10 years were now 25 per cent but would have been 42 per cent had he been properly diagnosed early on and treatment begun then. However, the judge held that even if properly diagnosed it would have been more likely than not that there would not have been a cure. It had not therefore been shown that the negligence caused a loss. The Court of Appeal dismissed Gregg's appeal and the case went to the House of Lords. Their Lordships divided three to two and took eight months to produce their judgments after hearing the arguments. As that suggests, the judgment was controversial.

The majority dismissed Gregg's appeal. It had not been shown that on the balance of probabilities the delay in the treatment had caused a loss. Even if there had been no negligence the most likely outcome would have been that the claimant would suffer the loss he did. The loss of a chance of a more favourable outcome could not be sued for in tort. The minority, by contrast, regarded the significant reduction in the possibility of survival to be a loss for which the claimant should be compensated.

It is worth summarizing the judgments of each of their Lordships:

Lord Hoffmann (majority): argued that the most likely future for Gregg was that he would die within 10 years. This would have been true even if the correct diagnosis had been made early on. The likelihood was, therefore, that the negligence had not affected the outcome for him. To allow people to claim for the loss of a chance would be a radical change in tort law and should be made by legislation not judicial decision. The impact of such a change of the law on the NHS and insurers would be enormous. It would be improper for the House of Lords to make such a potentially significant change.

Lord Phillips (majority): noted that, whatever the statistics, Mr Gregg had, by the time their Lordships heard the case, survived nine years and his chances of survival were 'climbing daily'. It therefore seemed that the lack of early intervention had not caused a premature demise. In other words the chance of survival, given he had lived to read the House of Lords' judgments, were higher than they had been at trial. He suggested that the issue should be seen simply as one of causation, and percentages only became relevant in deciding the effect of the negligence. As a matter of causation what mattered was whether or not on the balance of probability it had been shown that negligence had caused loss. Here on the balance of probability the negligence had not caused loss. He accepted this might be seen as unfair but: 'A robust test which produces rough justice may be preferable to a test that on occasion will be difficult, if not impossible, to apply in practice.' Using this robust test which produced rough justice was justifiable on policy grounds and because of the need to retain coherence in the common law. Lord Phillips appeared to leave open a case where the defendant's negligence had meant the loss of a possible cure and the claimant had in fact gone on to suffer the illness.

Baroness Hale of Richmond (majority): Tort law was not about the punishment of wrongdoing but rather the compensation of injury. She was concerned that a loss of a chance approach would enable a claim to be made even where no harm had in fact occurred. She thought 'almost any claim' could be reformulated to be the loss of a chance. It had not here been shown in this case that on the balance of probabilities the delay in treatment caused the spread of cancer. She pointed out that under a loss of a chance approach some claimants would win, but others would lose. The winners would be those who could only show a less than 50 per cent chance of succeeding, but the losers would be those who could show an 80 per cent chance of recovery. They would be losers because under the present system they would recover 100 per cent of their presumed loss, whereas under the 'loss of a chance' scheme they would recover only 80 per cent of their loss. To move to a loss of a chance scheme would mean that trials and negotiations would become far more complex.

Lord Hope (dissenting): argued that this case was significantly different from *Hotson*. In that case the boy had already been injured and there was no doubt that the cause of the injury was the fall. In Gregg's case the injury was in the future. Treatment would be preventing the injury arising, rather than seeking to cure or mitigate it. He referred to a number of cases where the loss of a chance (eg the loss of the prospect of promotion) was recoverable in tort law. He argued that where there was a significant reduction of the prospects of a successful outcome then there should be compensation. This should be calculated on the assumption of the certainty of complete recovery when the negligence took place and a discount to reflect the actual prospects of recovery at the time of the case. He also argued that there could be no doubt that negligence had caused the growth in tumour. If the growth in tumour had increased the chances of suffering cancer he should recover for that.

Lord Nicholls (dissenting): was highly critical of the view of the majority that if it could be shown that on the balance of probability the negligence did cause the injury then damages are recoverable, but if not there would be no damages. He said:

> This surely cannot be the state of the law today. It would be irrational and indefensible. The
> loss of a 45 per cent prospect of recovery is just as much a real loss for a patient as the loss of

a 55 per cent prospect of recovery. In both cases the doctor was in breach of his duty to his patient. In both cases the patient was worse off. He lost something of importance and value. But, it is said, in one case the patient has a remedy, in the other he does not. (para 3).

He also voiced the concern that if a doctor could show that the correct treatment only provided a less than 50 per cent chance of recovery then there was no recovery. This would leave a doctor's duty of care to her or his patient 'hollow' (para 4). He argued that a claimant who lost a 40 per cent chance of recovery should receive 40 per cent of the damages that would be awarded if the claimant had been able to show the defendant was 100 per cent responsible for the injuries, although he thought that damages should be awarded where a patient had a 'reasonable prospect' of recovery and then negligence had reduced these by a 'significant extent'. As to concerns about the financial burdens this might impose on the NHS he described these as speculative and argued that it was for Parliament to amend the law if the burden proved to be too great, not for the courts to deny a valid claim due to financial concerns.

The current law after these cases appears to be this:

- A claimant will only succeed if she or he can show that on the balance of probability the defendant's act caused the claimant's loss. So, if the claimant was only able to show that it was 40 per cent likely that the defendant's act had caused the harm the claimant would fail.[94]

- If the claimant has suffered a harm for which the defendant negligently fails to offer treatment or diagnose it needs to be shown that it would be more likely than not that if the treatment had been offered the claimant would not have suffered the harm.[95]

- In exceptional cases, even if it cannot be shown that the outcome was caused by the defendant's negligence, damages can be awarded.[96] If it can be shown that a medical professional negligently failed to warn of a risk and as a result the claimant agreed to undergo an operation when, if properly advised, she or he would not have agreed to undergo that particular operation at that time, then a claim can be established.[97]

There are a number of issues raised by these cases including the following:[98]

(i) Is the law of medical negligence about punishing the wrongdoing of the defendant or compensating the harm to the victim? In *Chester v Afshar*[99] the House of Lords emphasized the importance of the patient's bodily integrity and the importance of using tort law to uphold patients' rights of information.[100] One way of reading the case is to suggest that the courts were wanting to punish the wrongdoing of the doctor, even

---

[94] *Hotson v E Berkshire* [1987] AC 750.

[95] *Hotson v E Berkshire* [1987] AC 750; *Anderson v Milton Keynes General NHS Trust* [2006] EWHC 2249.

[96] Hoffman (2005); *Fairchild v Glenhaven Funeral Services Ltd* [2003] 1 AC 32. See further Compensation Act 2006, s 3 and *Barker v Corus (UK) Plc* [2006] UKHL 20.

[97] *Chester v Afshar* [2004] UKHL 41.

[98] Stapleton (2005 and 2006); Hoffman (2005); Peel (2005); Spencer (2005); Porat and Stein (2001).

[99] [2004] UKHL 41.

[100] In *Beary v Pall Mall Investments* [2005] EWCA Civ 415 *Chester v Afshar* was said not to be a case of general application in negligence cases. This suggests it represents a special rule of medical negligence cases.

though the loss to the claimant was difficult to identify.[101] Notably in *Gregg v Scott*[102] talk of patients' rights played a far less prominent role than it had in *Chester*.[103] In *Fairchild v Glenhaven Funeral Services*[104] Lord Bingham approved the following extra-judicial comment of McLachlin J:[105]

> Tort law is about compensating those who are wrongfully injured. But even more funda-mentally, it is about recognizing and righting wrongful conduct by one person or a group of persons that harms others. If tort law becomes incapable of recognizing important wrongs, and hence incapable of righting them, victims will be left with a sense of griev-ance and the public will be left with a feeling that justice is not what it should be.

The right of a patient to be fully informed of risks was seen as of sufficient importance to justify a departure from the traditional approach to causation in *Chester*, but the right of the patient to receive non-negligent diagnosis was not in *Gregg*.[106] It is not clear that the right to be fully informed is more important than the right to be given non-negligent treatment: would most patients not prefer to receive non-negligent treatment, but with-out full information, rather than fully informed negligent treatment? Indeed Sarah Green[107] argues that the claim in *Gregg* could have been characterized as one where he was not informed of the risks of treatment/non-treatment and there is no justifiable way of distinguishing the kinds of claims in the cases.

(ii) The problems of over-/under-compensation. In a case such as *Gregg v Scott*[108] involving loss of a chance, their Lordships were aware that whatever conclusion they reached it could be seen as a case of over- or under-compensation. It may be that Mr Gregg would go on to live into his 90s, in which case any award would have to com-pensate him for a loss he did not suffer. On the other hand if he were to deteriorate shortly after the House of Lords judgment and die and if the early diagnosis would have led to a course of treatment which would have cured his condition (something we will never know) then he clearly did suffer a loss, for which he would have been given no compensation.

(iii) The law after *Gregg v Scott* draws an important distinction between a case where the defendant's negligent misdiagnosis reduces the claimant's chance of recovery from 60 per cent to 40 per cent and a case where it causes a reduction from 30 per cent to 10 per cent. In the former cases damages can be recovered, but not the latter. In both cases there is a reduction of 20 per cent in the chance of recovery. Should there be any differ-ence between them?

---

[101] In *Clough v First Choice Holidays and Flights Ltd* [2006] EWCA Civ 15, *Chester v Afshar* [2004] UKHL 41 was described as a 'policy decision' and not of relevance to personal injury cases generally (although see *Mountford v Newlands School* [2007] EWCA Civ 21 where it was held to apply outside the medical context).
[102] [2005] UKHL 2.
[103] See further *Johnston v NEI International* [2007] UKHL 39 where *Gregg* was applied and no mention was made of *Chester*.
[104] [2002] Ll Rep Med 361, para 11.   [105] McLachlin J (1998: 16).
[106] See Palmboom et al (2007) for a survey which suggests there is little consensus among doctors as to which risks should be disclosed. Many doctors questioned thought to some extent it depended on the char-acteristics of the patient.
[107] Green (2006).   [108] [2005] UKHL 2.

3.4 Damages

If the defendant has succeeded on all the issues discussed above she or he is entitled to damages. In tort the basic principle is that the claimant should be put back in the position she or he was in before the negligent act was committed. The aim of damages, then, is not to punish the defendant or reflect the gravity of her or his wrongdoing, but to compensate the claimant for her or his losses. In the case of a financial loss this is straightforward, but where the injuries are physical it is far more difficult.

Medical cases will use the same principles in relation to damages that are used generally in tort. Books on Tort Law should be consulted to give the details on this. The following is a very brief summary of the law of damages. A claim can include the following elements:

(i) 'Fair and reasonable' compensation for the injury suffered. It is not really possible to put a figure on the financial sum to compensate for, say, the loss of a finger. The law has dealt with this by developing a tariff which sets out sums of money for particular kinds of injury. Although arbitrary, such a tariff does at least create consistency.[109]

(ii) Damages can be granted for pain and suffering. The Court of Appeal in *Heil v Rankin*[110] has recently looked again at these and agreed with Law Commission[111] proposals that the levels set then were too low. Although they were conscious of the potential impact of greatly increasing levels on the NHS, they increased the levels by 50 per cent.

(iii) Loss of amenity. This covers the inability of the claimant to engage in activities which previously she or he had been able to engage in.

(iv) Expenses incurred as a result of the injuries. Any extra costs that have been incurred can be recovered. This can include a claim for private medical costs, even if the same treatment was available for free on the NHS.[112]

(v) Loss of earnings suffered as a result of the harm up to the date of the hearing.

(vi) Future losses. This will involve an element of guesswork as it requires the court to calculate what expenses and loss of earnings the claimant will suffer in the future.[113] This may also involve an estimate as to how long the claimant will live.

Having calculated this total there may be a reduction in two cases. First, where the claimant was contributorily negligent. This would arise where it was found that the negligence of both the patient and the doctor contributed to the injury. For example, if a patient failed to disclose an important medical fact to her or his doctor, the doctor failed to check it, and as a result of the ignorance of the fact prescribed medication which harmed the patient, then possibly both the patient and doctor could be regarded as negligent. In such a case the level of damages paid by the doctor will be reduced by the percentage it is thought that the patient contributed through her or his negligence. So if the patient and doctor were equally blameworthy the damages would be halved.

---

109 See Bagshaw and McBride (2005: Part III) for a further discussion.
110 [2000] 3 All ER 138.   111 Law Commission Report No 257 (1999).
112 NHS Law Reform (Personal Injuries) Act 1948, s 2(4); see eg *H v Thompson Holidays* [2007] EWHC 850 (QB).
113 See eg *Appleton v El Safty* [2007] EWHC 631 (QB) where it was necessary to predict how a professional footballer's career might develop.

The second way that the damages payable may be reduced is where the patient has failed to mitigate her or his loss. This means that the patient has failed to undertake reasonable steps which would reduce or limit the harm she or he is suffering. This would arise, for example, where the patient has failed to undertake subsequent treatment which would have ameliorated her or his condition.[114]

3.5 Damages for secondary victims

The law is generally reluctant to allow a claim in tort to be brought by someone who is not directly injured by the negligence, but is affected by the injuries of others.[115] The general position is that a 'secondary' victim (ie a person who did not themselves suffer a physical injury) cannot sue for the psychological distress they suffer because of what has happened to another. However, this is subject to two important exceptions:

(i) Where the claimant has witnessed what has happened to her or his relative then she or he may be able to claim damages, but only when what it witnessed is exceptionally horrifying.[116] Margaret Brazier and Emma Cave suggest that a husband who is present and watches his wife screaming in agony because she is awake during a Caesarean section due to a failure in anaesthetic may succeed in a claim for negligence.[117]

(ii) If the relative is told in a negligent way about what has happened and this causes a psychological injury a claim may succeed. If a parent is told that her or his child has unexpectedly died on the operating table in a callous way, and as a result a psychological illness is suffered, then damages may be available. In a way this is a case where the relative is a 'direct' victim of the negligence of the medical professional.[118]

3.6 The controversial nature of damages awarded

There is no doubt that the way damages are awarded can produce astonishingly unfair results. A parent losing a child is given £10,000 bereavement damages.[119] This cannot be adequate compensation for the loss. But there again, can any sum truly represent such a loss? Is £150,000 damages adequate for a patient paralysed from the waist down by negligence? Also one's job can profoundly affect the level of damages awarded. Two people may suffer the same injury, but if one loses their employment as a result they will receive significantly more than the other who does not. Even when the claimant is a seriously injured child, the court will attempt to calculate how much income the child would be likely to make when they grow up. The child of two barristers who is seriously injured could expect to receive significantly more than the child of an unemployed single parent. The levels of award in horrific cases can be very high: they regularly exceed £3 million.[120] Should one's income or socio-economic background really be relevant in assessing the amount of damages? Or is this an appropriate way of assessing the genuine loss of a party?

---

[114] *Geest Plc v Monica Lansiquot* (2002) 1 WLR 1311.
[115] Extensive discussion of this issue can be found in Case (2004).
[116] *Ward v Leeds Teaching Hospitals NHS Trust* [2004] EWHC 2106.
[117] Brazier and Cave (2007: 158). The court was generous in *Froggatt v Chesterfield NHS Trust* [2002] All ER (D) 218 where a husband obtained damages after he was shocked on seeing his wife naked following an unnecessary mastectomy (following a negligent and false diagnosis of breast cancer).
[118] See Mulheron (2007) for further discussion.
[119] Brazier and Cave (2007: 201).   [120] Brazier and Cave (2007: 201).

Consider also the case of Hollie Calladine[121] where a child suffered brain damage and was awarded £700,000. Tragically days later she unexpectedly died. The hospital was unable to recover the damages paid. Although the money had been ordered on the basis that it was required to meet the costs of raising Hollie as a seriously disabled child, the parents could keep it. On the other hand, had the award been much lower based on the assumption that she only had a year to live, but in fact she lived much longer she would not have been able to seek to return to court to ask for more. It is common for it to become apparent over time that the level of damages which appeared reasonable at the time of the trial was, in retrospect, too little or too much.

One solution to that difficulty is to use structured settlements.[122] These involve an initial capital sum which covers the losses which have already occurred and are quantifiable. For future costs a sum is paid to purchase an annuity; this will produce flexible sums of money to cover the losses as they transpire. The amounts paid out could therefore increase or decrease with those expected if the claimant's condition improves or worsens over time. There is no power yet for courts to order structured settlements but they can be entered into if both parties consent. They are not popular with some claimants because claimants lose control over their award and are constantly having their medical progress checked. Another option is to order an interim payment which can be increased if the applicant is later able to show losses higher than those originally envisaged.[123]

3.7 The limitation period

The law of limitation may bar a claim in some cases. If the case involves personal injury then the action must be commenced within three years of the date of the negligence or the date on which the defendant realized that an action could be brought (note that special rules apply to minors).[124] If the loss claimed was purely financial, ie contractual, then the limitation period is six years, rather than three.[125]

The reasoning behind the limitation restrictions is that a medical professional should not have a potential claim hanging over them for years ahead. Of course, the disadvantage is that a claimant may have a serious injury for which they deserve compensation, but for which no action is brought. There is, however, a discretion in the court to extend the limitation period.[126] This can be used to permit a claim to be brought out of time if there is a good reason for the claim being brought late and neither party will be prejudiced by the lateness of the claim.

3.8 Who should be sued?

If a patient has suffered harm as a result of medical malpractice she or he has a number of people whom she or he could sue:

(i) She or he could sue the medical professional individually.

(ii) She or he could sue the employer of the professional (eg the NHS Trust or hospital) relying on the doctrine of vicarious liability.

(iii) She or he could sue the provider unit directly for their own negligence.

---

121 Hopwood (2001: 191–2).
122 See *A v B NHS Hospital* [2006] EWHC 2833 (Admin) for a case where a lump sum was seen as preferable to periodic payments. Periodic payments can be ordered under the Damages Act 1996, s 2.
123 *H v Thompson Holidays* [2007] EWHC 850 (QB).
124 Limitation Act 1980, s 11.   125 Limitation Act 1980, s 2.   126 Limitation Act 1980, s 33.

The options (ii) and (iii) may not be obvious. Under the doctrine of vicarious liability an employer is liable for the negligence of their employees who are acting in the course of their employment. In theory, if an NHS Trust or health authority is sued on the basis of vicarious liability the body could recover the damages paid out from the negligent professional concerned.[127] However, the NHS has declared that it will not do this.[128] Further, the NHS has agreed to meet the costs of litigation against medical staff. So rather than staff having to arrange their own insurance, the NHS takes on that responsibility. General Practitioners, however, remain responsible for meeting their own costs and must maintain insurance cover.[129] This has led to a growing effort in the NHS to avoid the risk of accidents and avoid litigation. Risk management has become a 'buzzword'.

The doctrine of vicarious liability need not involve any evidence that the employers were themselves negligent. Under direct liability (option (iii) above) the claim is that the providers themselves were negligent (eg in failing to ensure that there were sufficient numbers of adequately trained staff).[130] In such a case it may be that none of the staff were negligent (they all did they best they could) and yet the Trust was. Other examples of direct liability might be if there were no proper procedures to check that equipment was working properly or that staff were not properly kept up to date with medical developments.[131] Although the courts are yet to give full consideration to the question, it seems that when considering whether a NHS Trust is negligent the *Bolam* test will not apply. In other words, a hospital will not necessarily have a defence simply because they are acting at a level other hospitals act, if the judge decided those standards to be unreasonable.[132]

If a court has decided that both an individual doctor and her or his hospital are negligent who is to pay the damages? It seems that the court will focus on the extent to which the doctor was able to avoid the harm to the patient, in the context of her or his working environment. So if a junior doctor is negligent, but it is found that they were receiving an inadequate level of support and supervision then the hospital may be required to pay the bulk of the damages.[133]

A primary care trust could be sued. There is an argument that a primary care trust owes a duty of care to ensure that there is reasonable provision for all the patients in their area. If through negligence a primary care trust failed to ensure that a patient received a reasonable level of care then a tortious action could be brought. In *A (A Child) v Ministry of Defence*[134] it was recognized that an NHS Trust owed a duty of care to provide a safe and satisfactory medical service to a patient.[135]

The most likely scenario where this could arise is where a patient is told that they cannot be given an operation until a long time in the future. It may be that the claim will fail if the PCT can show that they acted reasonably in allocating the resources available to them, but it might succeed if it could be shown the delay in treatment was due to negligence (eg the timetabling of operations was organized in an irresponsible way). An NHS patient who is referred to a private hospital for treatment within the NHS will still

---

[127] See Brazier and Beswick (2006).   [128] NHS Executive (1996).
[129] NHS Executive (1996).   [130] *Godden v Kent and Medway SHA* [2004] EWHC 1629.
[131] *Blyth v Bloomsbury HA* [1993] 4 Med LR 151.
[132] *Bull v Devon AHA* [1993] 4 Med LR 117.
[133] *Jones v Manchester Corporation* [1952] 2 All ER 125.
[134] [2004] EWCA 641. See also *Garcia v St Mary's NHS Trust* [2006] EWHC 2314 (QBD).
[135] Beswick (2007).

be able to sue the NHS for any negligence that takes place in the private hospital.[136] A patient of the NHS should not lose a legal remedy because of how the NHS decided to deliver its services. In such a case the NHS will often seek an indemnity for the money it has paid out from the private institution.

3.9 Apportionment

If two medical professionals' negligence has caused the injury to the patient then the principle of apportionment may come into play. The claimant can receive the whole of the damages from either of the defendants. It is up to that defendant to sue the other for reimbursement of their share. The damages will be divided according to the degree of responsibility for the accident.[137] In fact the NHS indemnity means that NHS staff will not be individually liable and so apportionment is rarely an issue except in general practice or where the patient has been treated by the NHS and another medical provider.

4 The law of contract

There is no contract between an NHS patient and the NHS or its staff.[138] Therefore NHS patients cannot sue for breach of contract if their doctor mistreats them. However, a private patient can sue their medical professionals for breach of contract. That said, normally whenever a breach of contract could be established so could a negligence claim. It is not impossible that a contract between a doctor and private patient will require the doctor to exercise a higher standard of care than that imposed by negligence, but it would be unusual. Certainly the courts have been very reluctant to interpret a contract as a guarantee that the procedure will be a success.[139]

5 Why do people sue?

There is much talk in the media of a 'compensation culture'; the House of Commons Constitutional Affairs Committee[140] investigated the claims that people will use the slightest opportunity to sue in the hope of making a fast buck. The committee found that the compensation culture was a myth. However, the belief it existed created inappropriate risk aversion which had harmful effects. The Committee stated: 'Risk aversion has a number of complex causes, including advertising by claims management companies, selective media reporting, a lack of information about how the law works and, on occasion, a lack of common sense amongst those who implement health and safety guidelines'.[141] Research suggests that, at least in the medical field, the motivations of those suing is not simply trying to obtain money; they are far more complicated.[142] In a

---

136 *M v Calderdale Health Authority* [1998] Ll Rep Med 157; *Farraj v King's Healthcare NHS Trust* [2006] EWHC 1228 (QB).
137 Civil Liability (Contribution) Act 1978.
138 *Reynolds v The Health First Medical Group* [2000] Ll Rep Med 240.
139 *Thake v Maurice* [1986] 1 All ER 497.
140 House of Commons Constitutional Affairs Committee (2006).
141 House of Commons Constitutional Affairs Committee (2006: 1).
142 Morris (2007).

leading survey[143] it was found that a majority of those suing were more concerned with getting an acceptance of fault; an assurance that the errors would not be repeated in the future; or a fuller investigation of what had happened. Just under half were concerned with receiving an explanation, an apology, and ensuring that the professionals understood what had happened to them. Only about a third said that they were concerned with money.[144] In a study for the Department of Health it was found that only 11 per cent of those making complaints were seeking money,[145] although that rose to 35 per cent where serious injuries were involved. That said, it may be that these points cannot be separated from money. Will an apology which is not backed up by a payment of money be regarded as a 'cheap and easy' apology and not genuine? Will patients only believe that lessons have been learned if payment is required to provide a financial incentive not to repeat the mistake?

There is also the difficulty that for medical professionals having a complaint made against them can be seen as an attack on their professional integrity. This leads to a defensive response to such complaints, which in turn can exacerbate the patients' feelings that they are not being listened to or are not being shown respect.[146]

6 Medical malpractice litigation in practice

The number of cases of alleged medical malpractice which actually reach the court is, of course, small. Of cases handled by the NHS Litigation Authority 96 per cent were settled without going to court. Most cases end before they reach the courts at the negotiation stage. Practically, therefore, what happens at the negotiation stage is more important than what happens in the court room, although some lawyers argue that the two cannot be easily separated: lawyers bargain 'in the shadow of the law'.[147] What order the lawyers believe a court will make plays an important role in deciding whether to accept/reject an offer made by the other side.

In recent years more has been done to attempt to regulate the negotiations that take place before court proceedings are started. Following an investigation of the civil justice system by Lord Woolf in 1998, Civil Procedure Rules were introduced giving judges greater power to manage cases and to control and prevent misuse of expert evidence. The Rules encourage greater openness and attempt to keep negotiations moving. There are now 'fast track procedures' for claims worth between £1 and £15,000. Such cases ought to be dealt with within 30 weeks.

7 Costs

The payment of legal costs is a crucial aspect of litigation. In 2005/06 the NHS Litigation Authority spent £132,737,180 on legal costs connected to medical negligence litigation.[148] A person who has suffered an injury as a result of medical malpractice may well be deterred from suing because they are unable to pay for the legal costs in bringing the action. Indeed a defendant may prefer to settle the case rather than take the

---

[143] Mulcahy, Selwood, and Nettern (1999: fig 2.1) and Mulcahy (2003).
[144] For similar findings see Woolf (2001).   [145] Chief Medical Officer (2003: 75).
[146] Mulcahy (2003).   [147] Mulcahy (2003).
[148] NHS Litigation Authority (2007).

issue to court for fear of the lawyers' costs involved. Certainly it would be a brave person on an average income who brought a medical negligence case.[149]

For some claimants the availability of legal aid will assist, but their financial resources must be very limited indeed for them to be entitled to it; significantly children's financial position is assessed separately from their parents and so children are normally eligible for legal aid. Even if financially entitled to it, legal aid will only be granted to someone who has an arguable case. In 2006/07 only 3,724 new cases of clinical negligence were funded by the Legal Services Commission.[150]

The availability of legal aid can be said to have a negative impact on cases. First, if a person is not funding their own litigation then they may be thought to have a greater incentive to pursue unmeritorious litigation. Indeed there is some evidence that a very high number of legally aided cases are unsuccessful.[151] Whether that is due to the Legal Services Commission not properly 'weeding out' weak cases or whether it shows the difficulties in assessing the strength of claims until they have been heard in court is debated. In 2006/07 only 15 per cent of completed cases funded by the Legal Services Commission were said to be successful.[152] Second, normally if a party loses in litigation the other party will be required to pay the successful party's legal costs. In the case of a legally aided claimant this is not possible.[153] Although the Legal Services Commission could be required to pay a hospital's costs this would be exceptional.[154] So in relation to small claims, a health authority is likely to think that paying the sum demanded will cost less money than seeking to defend the claim in court, thereby incurring legal costs greater than the sum demanded and which they will not be able to recoup.

For those who cannot afford legal aid, the alternative is likely to be a conditional fee arrangement.[155] This introduced the possibility for lawyers to take on a case on the basis that if it is lost then the client will face no charge, while if the case is won the lawyer will charge more than she or he would if the client were paying lawyers' fees in the normal way. From the lawyers' point of view this is a kind of gamble. They could do very well if the case is won, but lose out significantly if the case fails. From the clients' point of view the option is risk free in the sense that they cannot be financially out of pocket as least as regards their own lawyer's fees; they could still face an order to pay the legal costs of the other side. However, they must realize that if they succeed in their litigation they will see less of the damages than they would have done if they paid the lawyer at the traditional hourly rate approach. Although it was feared by some that conditional fee arrangements would mean that there would be a flood of litigation in the medical context, in fact lawyers have been reluctant to take on risky cases for fear of having to do an enormous amount of work for no pay.[156]

---

[149] Newdick (2005: 130).

[150] Legal Services Commission (2007).

[151] Forty-one per cent of cases handled by the NHS Litigation Authority were dropped by the applicant, although we do not know the reasons.

[152] Legal Services Commission (2007).

[153] Jandoo and Harland (1984) claim that this has caused health authorities to settle cases they would be expected to win in court.

[154] *R v Greenwich LBC ex p Lovelace (No 2)* [1991] 3 WLR 1015.

[155] This became possible after the Courts and Legal Services Act 1990. The House of Commons Constitutional Affairs Committee (2006) found no evidence that the advent of conditional fees increased rates of litigation.

[156] Peynser (1995).

8 Criticisms of the current legal position

There is a widespread perception that medical negligence litigation is unsatisfactory.[157] Mason and Laurie summarize some of the concerns in this way:

> Both sides—if one should talk of sides in this matter—see the current system of compensation for medical injury as being slow, traumatic and socially expensive, one from which it is often only the lawyers who profit. There must be a better way of dealing with this issue—a way which provides reasonably efficient compensation without destroying the doctor-patient relationship and without diverting health-targeted funds from hospitals and patient care into legal fees and damages.[158]

One survey found that 70 per cent of claimants said they were totally or very dissatisfied with the claims process. There was a similar percentage even among claimants who succeeded in obtaining an award.[159] Of course, among the medical professions there is a similar deep disquiet about the way the law operates in this area.[160] Medical litigation appears to demoralize medical professionals; provides patients with stress rather than compensation; and constitutes an enormous expense for limited NHS resources.

8.1 Criticisms of the *Bolam* test

The *Bolam* test has generated much criticism. Here are some of the objections to it.

(i) The test means that the medical profession, rather than the courts set the legal standard required of doctors. In all other professions it is no defence for an individual to show that others would have acted in the same way. A driver sued for negligence will have no defence if she or he can show that many other respectable drivers drive as badly as she or he did. It is the law, not drivers, who set the standard expected of them. In other words negligence here appears not to be setting standards to which health professionals should strive to meet, but rather is describing the standards which are in fact practised. The need for the law rather than the medical profession to set standards of good practice is highlighted by the scandals at Bristol and Alder Hey.[161]

(ii) *Bolam* has put an almost impossible burden on claimants. They can only be confident that they have a strong case if they interview every expert in the relevant field and are told by each one that the alleged conduct is negligent. The defendant, by contrast, needs only find one respected expert to have a good chance of success. Critics claim that the law appears to be more concerned with protecting the reputation of the professional than ensuring that patients receive compensation if they have been badly treated.[162] Even where causation is demonstrated the restrictive approach to 'loss of a chance' claims means that still no damages may be available.

(iii) Being a doctor is a well paid and highly respected profession. Society is, therefore, entitled to expect high standards from those working in the field. The *Bolam* test does not reflect the justifiable expectations of the general public. The *Bolam* test is not used in respect of other professionals, such as solicitors.[163]

---

[157] Simanowitz (1995); Lord Woolf (2001).   [158] Mason and Laurie (2003: 297).
[159] Mulcahy et al (1999: 11).   [160] BMA (2001).
[161] Brazier and Miola (2000).   [162] Sheldon (1998); Montgomery (1989).
[163] *Edward Wong v Johnson Stokes and Master* [1984] AC 296.

(iv) To be found negligent under the *Bolam* test is a serious indictment of a medical professional. Any expert giving evidence for the claimant is going to have to state not only that they would not have done as the defendant did, but none of their colleagues would have done. It is not surprising that at one time it was difficult to find expert witnesses who would give such evidence. Apparently this has become less difficult,[164] although there are concerns that this is because of the increasing number of 'professional expert witnesses'.

(v) Only 15 per cent of legally aided cases succeed.[165] This may suggest that the Legal Services Commission is funding too many weak cases. Alternatively it may demonstrate that the adjudication of the claim is making it too difficult to establish a successful case.[166]

Of course *Bolam* has its supporters too. Here are some of the points they might make:

(i) If a judge is faced with two groups of expert medical opinion which disagree on the correct approach to deal with a particular kind of case it is impossible for the judge to choose between them. *Bolam* relieves the judge of such a task, because as long as the defendant was acting in line with a responsible body of medical opinion she or he has a defence. This is preferable to a judge making an 'amateur' assessment of the two views.

(ii) The decision discourages excessive litigation. If we departed from the *Bolam* test we would face an avalanche of litigation. It would be far too easy to bring a negligence claim if all that was required was to find a doctor who disagreed with the way a colleague dealt with a case. The potential extra costs to the NHS if it was even easier to sue than at present would lead to a negative impact on the resources available to the NHS.

(iii) *Bolam* enables innovative and exciting medical practice. Without it all doctors, fearing litigation, will follow the officially approved line, and will no longer be willing to try innovative medicine.[167] Under *Bolam,* if they can show there were other respected colleagues who thought the innovative treatment was worth trying they will have no fear of a successful negligence claim.

(iv) The case of Wendy Savage could be used to support the *Bolam* test.[168] There Dr Savage sought to develop a women-centred approach to gynaecology. In various ways this was contrary to the traditional approach (which nowadays would be regarded as highly paternalistic). Complaints about her were unfounded; although her 'women-centred approach' was a minority view it could be said to represent a responsible body of medical opinion.

8.2 Is there a litigation crisis?

There are certainly many who claim that the NHS is facing a litigation crisis. The NHS, it is suggested, is being crippled by the increasing cost of litigation. Something has to be done to stem the tide. But others feel that such claims are greatly exaggerated.[169] It is even suggested that 'the litigation crisis' is a myth relied upon by the medical profession to avoid proper legal scrutiny.[170]

---

164 Brazier and Cave (2007: 197).   165 Legal Services Commission (2007).
166 Brazier and Cave (2007: ch 8).   167 Brazier and Miola (2000).
168 Sheldon (1998).   169 Kennedy (1987).   170 Simanowitz (1998).

Payments made by the NHS Litigation Authority in respect of negligence claims against the NHS were £432 million in 2003/04, but by 2006/07 this had increased to £613 million.[171]

In 2006/07, the NHS Litigation Authority, which handles most claims of negligence against the NHS, recorded 5,426 claims of clinical negligence and 3,293 claims of non-clinical negligence against NHS bodies. This was a drop from the figures of 5,697 claims of clinical negligence and 3,497 claims of non-clinical negligence in 2005/06.[172] £579.3 million was paid out in connection with clinical negligence claims in 2006/07. That figure is the cost to the NHS of both compensation payments and legal fees connected with litigation. The estimated liabilities for the NHS for future years is £9.22 billion.[173] Of cases taken to court by the NHS, the NHS won 67 per cent of cases, while 29 per cent were settled in favour of the applicant.

One point worth emphasizing is this: there appear now to be about 5,500 claims per year against the NHS—given that there are over a million adverse events a year that patients suffer while in the care of the NHS, the number of claims might be thought to be rather modest.[174]

The Better Regulation Task Force, looking at the alleged litigation crisis concluded:

> The compensation culture is a myth; but the cost of this belief is very real.[175]

Their point was that people fear litigation and this makes them over-cautious, even though in fact the chances of successful litigation being brought are low. They point out that although the newspapers often report 'absurd' cases where claimants have succeeded, they rarely report the far more common cases where litigation has not succeeded. They do, however, express concerns over the working of the claims management firms which offer 'no win, no fee', and there are allegations that some encourage claims in the hope that a settlement will be reached to avoid the hassle of litigation. However, studies show that there has not been an increase in litigation since 2000.[176] Indeed Annette Morris[177] has suggested the mistaken belief that there is a 'compensation culture' has put some people off pursuing legitimate claims.

Despite the alleged growth in litigation it should not be forgotten that, as Margot Brazier has pointed out:

> Even today patients leaving NHS hospitals are more likely to return with a box of chocolates for the staff than with a claim form![178]

8.3 Costs and time

We have already referred to the substantial sums involved in payments out for compensation for medical injuries. These figures may be shocking in themselves but it is even more so when it is realized that the costs of litigation regularly exceed the amount recovered. The National Audit Office Report suggested that in 65 per cent of claims below £50,000 costs exceeded the compensation awarded to the patient.[179] So money is removed from the strapped NHS and given, not to a suffering patient, but to the lawyers.

[171] NHSLA (2007).   [172] NHS Litigation Authority (2007).
[173] NHS Litigation Authority (2007).   [174] Leigh (2004).
[175] Better Regulation Task Force (2004: 3). [176] A. Morris (2007).   [177] A. Morris (2007).
[178] Brazier (2003b: 171).   [179] National Audit Office (2001b).

Not only is litigation expensive; it is slow. In 2003 it was said that the average reso-lution time for cases under £30,000 was eight months.[180] For cases of over £10,000 the average length is one and a half years, but that is still much shorter than the five and a half years such cases took in 1999. Nevertheless complex cases can still take many years to resolve. Not only does this mean that claimants have to wait a long time for the money to compensate them for their loss, with the stress involved in negotiations and litigation, but also that medical professionals have a long wait before they can 'clear their name'.

8.4 The impact of medical negligence litigation on doctors

There is evidence of the powerful negative impact on doctors of complaints.[181] Perhaps not surprisingly, studies have shown that doctors tend to regard complaints as chal-lenges to their competence, rather than revealing an issue that is troubling the com-plainant.[182] Thirty-eight per cent of doctors facing a medical negligence complaint are said to suffer clinical depression.[183] Fear of litigation and media vilification of doc-tors are cited as reasons for low job satisfaction among many doctors.[184] All NHS Trusts have now joined the Clinical Negligence Scheme for Trusts, which is a pooling arrangement between NHS Trusts designed to spread the cost of any especially large negligence award.[185]

A separate point is that damages awarded against an NHS doctor will come out of the NHS budget, rather than the doctor's own pocket. This fact deters some from suing because well-minded individuals may not want to be seen to be taking money from the cash-strapped NHS. It also means that as a means of publicly blaming the negligent pro-fessional the legal system works poorly. The negligent doctor suffers no financial loss. A further point is that those cases which go to court and make the headlines tend to be those where the negligence is more borderline. In cases of blatant negligence the NHS is likely to settle. Indeed in cases of the most serious negligence where the patient is killed the damages are likely to be much less than where the negligence may be less gross, but causes a permanent disability.

In a more general way it has been said that the existence of negligence litigation harms the doctor–patient relationship. For example, if something has gone wrong with the patient's treatment doctors may avoid explaining about why she or he has suffered, or why or how an injury has occurred for fear that anything they say will lead to litigation if seen as an admission of blame.[186] The Kennedy Report recommended that there should be a duty of candour to inform a patient if a harmful event had occurred.[187] Indeed, there is some old authority for the view that failure to inform a patient of an accident is negligent. In *Gerber v Pines*[188] a doctor failed to tell a patient that the needle had broken off in the course of an injection. Although the fact that the needle broke was not due to negligence, the failure of the doctor to tell the patient what had happened was held to be negligent.[189]

---

[180] Leigh (2004).   [181] Kaplan and Hepworth (2004).
[182] Allsop and Mulcahy (1998).   [183] Chief Medical Officer (2003: 43).
[184] Chief Medical Officer (2003: 44).
[185] Brazier and Cave (2007: 187). Members of the scheme must agree to comply with risk managements procedures.
[186] Simanowitz (1987).   [187] Bristol Royal Infirmary Inquiry (2001: Recommendation 33).
[188] (1933) 79 SJ 13.
[189] There is *obiter* support for this, perhaps, in *Naylor v Preston* [1987] 2 All ER 353, 360.

The National Health Services Litigation Authority has taken control of large claims and those which raise novel or contentious cases. It has even suggested that the existence of this body 'show a corporatist, centralist, conception of how the litigation game should be played'.[190] One consequence of this might be that the NHS Litigation Authority is more concerned in dealing with the complaint in a cost effective way than 'clearing the name' of the doctor against whom a complaint has been made. Although settling a claim early may be efficient, for the doctor wrongly complained against settlement can be regarded as an acknowledgement that she or he was at fault.

8.5 Defensive medicine

It is often claimed that the fear of malpractice litigation leads to defensive medicine.[191] Although this is a common complaint, it is not quite clear what 'defensive medicine' actually is. Fear of litigation can lead to some good practices: better record keeping, politeness in dealing with patients, clearer communication, and double checking. On the other hand there is a concern that doctors are over-cautious, ordering tests that are not necessary or asking for second opinions where that is inappropriate.[192] What cannot be known is whether changing practices are due to a fear of litigation or an improving safety culture. Research by Dingwall has shown that although the rise in rates of Caesarean section operations has been blamed on defensive medicine, similar rises have been found in countries with very little malpractice litigation.[193]

9 Learning lessons

One concern about the current approach to clinical negligence litigation is that the focus is so much on deciding who is to blame and whether there was negligence that the learning of lessons is forgotten. The NHS has sought to address this with a document entitled, *An Organisation with a Memory*.[194] This report, in line with much current thinking on accident prevention, contends that steps can be taken to reduce the possibility of mistakes being made in the treatment a patient receives.[195] Part of accident prevention is seeking to identify individuals, units, processes, or equipment whose performance is below that which the public is entitled to expect. Another part is to identify the circumstances and pressures that lead someone to make a mistake. This is based on the view that 'accidents' are more often caused by mistakes in the system than by the faults of individuals.[196]

One major problem is a reluctance on the part of staff to report accidents or near accidents, particularly where doing so will be seen as a complaint against a colleague. This has led to some recommending that it should be possible to make anonymous reports about the conduct of others. This should remove the concern that one's name will forever be on a file associated with that complaint. Of course, such a suggestion may be seen by some as being contrary to the principles of natural justice. If a complaint has

---

[190] Montgomery (2003: 200).
[191] Jones and Morris (1989). Indeed this led to the passing of the Compensation Act 2006.
[192] Kessler et al (2006).   [193] Dingwall (1995).
[194] DoH (2000c). See DoH (2006d) for recent developments in developing this project.
[195] Runciman, Merry, McCall Smith (2001).
[196] IOM Committee (1999). For further discussion of this see Quick (2006a).

been made about a professional she or he should be entitled to know who has made the complaint. There is a concern that it is only possible to properly learn from mistakes if a full investigation is undertaken surrounding the events, but that is only possible where the identity of the complainant is known. Australian experience, however, suggests that only rarely do complainants misrepresent what happened.[197]

There is a concern that negligence-based compensation discourages openness.[198] A doctor who has made an error is likely to want to avoid the stigma of a finding of negligence, and the harm that will be done to their professional reputation. This may be particularly so where a junior employee has concerns about a more senior employee.[199] This secrecy is likely to mean that it is more difficult for claimants who should be entitled to damages to be awarded them.

Investigations by the Commission for Health Improvement[200] into adverse events have indicated a number of factors that are liable to create dangers to patients. They are predictable: staff shortages; reliance on agency or locum staff; poor team working; ineffective risk management, including inadequate incident reporting; financial problems in the services; inadequate training and supervision of staff; and the service having a low national profile. In over half their investigations the bodies concerned were under severe financial pressure. It has now become a major aim of the NHS to avoid accidents to patients and considerable effort is being put into developing risk management strategies to avoid adverse events occurring.[201]

As mentioned at the start of this chapter, some patients who have suffered as a result of medical malpractice are not particularly concerned about getting money, but are more interested in receiving an apology, explanation, and assurance that such mistakes will not happen again. Such patients may be attracted by the possibility of using the hospital complaints procedures. For many years there has been dissatisfaction with the complaints procedures available within the NHS. The NHS has created a range of bodies designed to deal with complaints procedures and minimize medical accidents. These include most significantly:

- The National Patient Safety Agency
- The National Clinical Assessment Authority
- The Commission for Healthcare Audit and Inspection.

10 The NHS Redress Act 2006

In the light of the complaints about the current system it is not surprising that the Government has sought reform. It has identified the following as the major flaws with the current system:[202]

(i) the current system is perceived to be complex and slow;

(ii) the current system is costly both in terms of legal fees and diverting clinical staff from clinical care; there is a negative effect on NHS staff morale and on public confidence;

[197] Runciman, Merry, McCall Smith (2001).   [198] Bristol Royal Infirmary Report (2001).

[199] Burrows (2001).   [200] Healthcare Commission (2004a).

[201] NHS Litigation Authority (2004).

[202] See Parliamentary and Health Services Ombudsman (2007); NHS Ombudsman (2005); Healthcare Commission (2004a).

(iii) patients are dissatisfied with the lack of explanations and apologies or reassurance that action has been taken to prevent the same incident happening to another patient; and

(iv) the system encourages defensiveness and secrecy in the NHS, which stands in the way of learning and improvement in the health service.

Here we will consider the option favoured by the Government set out in the NHS Redress Act 2006.[203] We will later be considering a more radical option: a 'no fault' system.

The NHS Redress Act 2006 is designed to deal particularly with claims of less than £20,000, and gives patients an alternative to litigation. The scheme will require the providers and commissioners of hospital services with a 'consistent, speedy and appropriate response to clinical negligence'.[204] The scheme will be funded by the NHS Litigation Authority which will have responsibility for overseeing the financial compensation. All members of the scheme must report to the NHS Litigation Authority cases which fall within the scheme and they will determine whether there is liability and the appropriate remedy, be that payment of compensation, an investigation, an apology, or remedial care. The Act allows the Secretary of State to create this 'scheme', but its details are yet to be announced. The Government has indicated that the levels of compensation will be 'broadly equivalent' to those awarded in a court.[205] The Chief Medical Officer in his 2003 paper suggested an award should only be available if there are 'serious shortcomings'.[206] It is not yet clear whether a similar term will be used in the Redress Scheme.

Interestingly the Government has indicated that it expects the scheme initially to attract higher costs because more patients will receive compensation. However, it believes over time these costs will be offset by the saving in legal costs because there will be fewer cases resorting to litigation. The Government also argues that the scheme will attempt to move away from focusing on attributing blame and instead focus on preventing harm, reducing risks, and learning from mistakes. This will, in the long term, reduce the number of incidents and therefore the costs of claims for the NHS. The Government has indicated that the annual cost of the scheme will be between £3.2 million and £11.2 million per year.[207]

One important point is that the Government explains that the NHS Redress Scheme is meant to be additional to court procedures and not to replace them,[208] so a patient who is harmed in hospital can still use the court system, rather than the Redress Scheme. However, if an offer is accepted under the Redress Scheme legal proceedings could not be brought in connection with the same incident. It may be just a matter of time before the Redress Scheme replaces the court procedure, at least in cases of smaller financial value. Indeed, it appears that the Government expects people who use the scheme will not need the assistance of a solicitor, although an applicant will be entitled to have an offer independently evaluated by a solicitor, without charge to the applicant. This will mean that if successful the scheme will provide redress for people who otherwise would not have been able to bring a legal action.

The lack of detail on the scheme means it is hard to predict how well it will work. There are certainly concerns that people who currently use the courts will continue to

---

[203] The Act builds on Chief Medical Officer (2003).   [204] DoH (2005g).
[205] DoH (2005g: 4).   [206] Chapstick (2004).
[207] House of Commons Constitutional Affairs Committee (2006).   [208] DoH (2005g: 3).

do so and the scheme will only attract those who otherwise could not afford litigation. If this fear proves founded, it will certainly not be saving costs. A rather different concern is that the scheme will be administered by the NHS Litigation Authority and may not, therefore, appear impartial.[209] Brazier and Cave have also suggested that the scheme may do little more than 'formalise what already happens'.[210]

11 No fault

A more radical alternative is to move towards a no fault scheme.[211] Imagine two patients left paralysed after an operation. In one case it is shown that the paralysis was caused by a surgeon's negligence, in the other there was no negligence and the patient was just unlucky, it was one of those rare cases where paralysis just happens. Is it correct that one patient should receive substantial compensation and the other nothing? In other words should compensation following injuries suffered in the course of medical treatment be due regardless of the question of whether there was negligence? The line between negligence and no negligence is difficult. In many cases, to classify the case as negligent would be unfair to the doctor. But to classify the case as not negligent and therefore attracting no compensation also seems unfair.

This leads some to argue that we need a system in which compensation is paid to those who suffer due to mishaps during medical treatment, regardless of whether these are a result of negligence or not. A patient who suffers an 'adverse event' while receiving medical care should receive compensation even if there was no negligence. This would mean that, for example, if the patient was one of the unlucky few to suffer an adverse reaction to a drug which was properly prescribed, compensation would be available, even if the doctor could not be blamed for prescribing it.

11.1 The 'no fault scheme' in New Zealand

Any country considering moving to a no fault scheme for clinical negligence is likely to turn to New Zealand.[212] The Scheme is administered by the Accident Rehabilitation and Compensation Corporation (ACC). It is designed to compensate anyone who has suffered a personal injury due to an accident. The scheme is not designed to compensate for disease, infection, or aging. In the clinical context the Injury Prevention, Rehabilitation and Compensation Amendment Act (No 2) 2005[213] permits compensation to be paid for 'treatment injury'.[214] This covers injuries caused by medical treatment where they are

> not a necessary part, or ordinary consequence, of the treatment, taking into account all the circumstances of the treatment, including—
>
> (i) the person's underlying health condition at the time of the treatment; and
>
> (ii) the clinical knowledge at the time of the treatment.[215]

---

209 Brazier and Cave (2007: 236).   210 Brazier and Cave (2007: 238).
211 Not that the Vaccine Damage Payments Act 1979 creates a no fault compensation scheme in respect of injuries caused by vaccinations performed by the NHS.
212 'No fault schemes' can also be found in Finland, Sweden, and France.
213 See Oliphant (2007) for a useful analysis of the law.
214 This phrase replaced the term 'medical misadventure' which had been used under the previous legislation.
215 Injury Prevention, Rehabilitation and Compensation Amendment Act (No 2) 2005, s 32.

This does not cover the normal consequences of a treatment (eg a scar left after surgery), but rather unexpected consequences of surgery. Notably, unlike English law, there is no need to show that the doctor behaved negligently. But the notion of 'treatment injury' is not as broad as might at first appear. Section 32(2) explains:

(2) 'Treatment injury' does not include the following kinds of personal injury:

(a) personal injury that is wholly or substantially caused by a person's underlying health condition;

(b) personal injury that is solely attributable to a resource allocation decision;

(c) personal injury that is a result of a person unreasonably withholding or delaying their consent to undergo treatment . . .

Ken Oliphant states that the 2005 Act has simplified the scheme meaning that more claims are made, fewer are rejected, and claims are dealt with more speedily.[216] Critics complain that the system fails to bring those medical professionals who have behaved badly to account. No distinction is drawn in the scheme between cases where the professional behaved badly and where there was simply an unfortunate misadventure.[217]

The New Zealand scheme records high rates of consumer satisfaction of 84 per cent.[218] The ACC not only works to compensate injuries but also works to prevent accidents. In 2004 it spent $30 million on accident prevention work generally.

11.2 Arguments in favour of no fault

Many of the advantages of a no fault scheme appear obvious. The proposal has the great attraction of simplicity. Gone would be the difficulties in proving that a professional breached the duty of care. Gone would be feeling of animosity created by the adversarial nature of legal proceedings and we could expect cases to be dealt with significantly quicker. The following passage from the Bristol Inquiry Report sets out the case for moving away from clinical negligence and putting in its place a no fault scheme:

The system of clinical negligence litigation is now ripe to review. . . . We take the view that it will not be possible to achieve an environment of full, open reporting within the NHS when, outside it, there exists a litigation system the incentives of which press in the opposite direction. We believe that the way forward lies in the abolition of clinical negligence litigation, taking clinical error out of the courts and the tort system. It should be replaced by effective systems for identifying, analysing, learning from and preventing errors . . .

A further concern with the current system is that it may allocate blame unfairly.[219] By isolating the individual professional and considering whether she or he is to blame overlooks the institutional failures that are regarded by some experts on accidents to be more often the true cause.[220] As Merry and McCall Smith argue:

Even removing the individual without correcting the system simply creates a situation where his or her replacement will be vulnerable to a recurrence of the same problem.[221]

---

[216] Oliphant (2007).
[217] Critical comments about the scheme can be found in Merry and McCall Smith (2001: 244).
[218] ACC (2004).   [219] Merry and McCall Smith (2001: Chap 1).
[220] Merry and McCall Smith (2001: 11).   [221] Merry and McCall Smith (2001: 15).

11.3 Argument against no fault

The following are some of the main objections to a no fault system:

• If the scheme is not going to compensate people just because they are ill it would need to draw a distinction between people who were ill, and those who were suffering as a result of medical treatment in some sense going wrong. However, that would create disputes and complexity. Whether a particular harm is a natural progression of the illness, a justifiable side effect of successful treatment, or a result of a mishap may be contested. Indeed in many cases it may bring back to the fore the question of whether or not the doctor was at fault. The claim that a 'no fault' system is easier and cheaper may, therefore, prove to be unfounded.

• A 'no fault' system would be extremely expensive. The Chief Medical Officer estimated that 'even with a 25 per cent reduction in the current level of compensation the cost of a true no-fault compensation scheme would vary between £1.6 billion per year...to almost £28 billion...This compares with £400 million spent on clinical negligence in 2000–01'.[222]

• There is a concern that a no fault scheme will lead to less accountability. If one of the aims of tort law is to identify wrongdoers then a 'no fault' scheme would lose that. Should the NHS be held liable in respect of a loss even if was not preventable?[223] Do we not need to hold medical professionals accountable for their bad behaviour and create a deterrent against negligence?

11.4 No compensation scheme

Most of the discussion surrounding the present law has concerned debates over whether we should move towards a no fault system of compensation. But there is an argument for moving in a different direction and moving towards abolishing compensation payments. Imagine a patient is harmed as a result of negligent treatment by a doctor. Certainly that patient should receive treatment for their current condition—but should they receive money from NHS funds? Might not that money be better spent treating another patient in a worse medical condition than the patient? Is it right that money needed to develop treatment for life saving illnesses should be taken from NHS funds and given to one person to make up for their 'pain and suffering' as a result of a botched operation? John Harris, for one, thinks not necessarily.[224] At the very least he proposes a cap on the level of damages that may be awarded because otherwise a single person can receive a larger portion of NHS funds than other equally needy and deserving patients. He suggests that payment of compensation should only be made where there is no more urgent call on those NHS resources. One might think that that will rarely if ever be the case.

12 Matters other than compensation

In *Making Amends,* the Chief Medical Officer emphasizes the importance of not regarding the payment of compensation the only response to a medical mishap:

> The individual who has suffered harm as a result of the health care they have received must get an apology, a clear explanation of what went wrong, treatment and care, and

---

[222] Chief Medical Officer (2003: 112).   [223] Towse et al (2004).   [224] Harris (1997).

where appropriate, financial compensation. The NHS must also ensure that such bad experiences of the individual are learned from so that future NHS patients throughout the country benefit from reduced risks and safer care. The primary aim must be to reduce the number of medical errors that occur.[225]

He points out that too often these issues are lost in the heat of the litigation battle:

Legal proceedings for medical injury frequently progress in an atmosphere of confrontation, acrimony, misunderstanding and bitterness. The emphasis is on revealing as little as possible about what went wrong, defining clinical decisions that were taken and only reluctantly releasing information. In the past, cases have taken too long to settle. In smaller value claims the legal costs have been disproportionate to the damages awarded. In larger value claims there can be lengthy and expensive disputes about the component parts of any lump sum payment and the anticipated life span of the victim.[226]

13 Medicines and law

13.1 The licensing of medicines

The Medicine Act 1968 deals with the development, manufacture, distribution, and importation of medicines. Under the statute the Secretary of State for Health is responsible for licensing drugs. However, she or he exercises those powers through the Medicines and Health Care Products Regulatory Agency (MHRA), the Royal Pharmaceutical Society, and other bodies.

Of course before medicines are licensed for use they must go through a thorough testing process. The first stage will normally involve animals.[227] The second will be on healthy human volunteers and will attempt to ascertain how much of the drug a human being can take before it becomes intolerable. Thirdly the drug is tested on sufferers of the relevant illness to see whether the drugs have clinical effects. Fourthly trials are used to compare the effectiveness of the drugs compared with other remedies (Chapter 11 discusses the law regulating research).

The trials on patients must take place with a special licence. Before importing, marketing, selling, or supplying the drug, the company will need a product licence from the MHRA. Before granting a licence the following factors should be considered: the safety of the drug; the efficacy of the drug in respect of the purpose for which it is to be administered; and the quality of the drug, having regard to its method of manufacture and the proposals for its distribution.[228] Whether there are other drugs which are as effective or more so is irrelevant. The product licence lasts for five years and the clinical trial certificate for two. At the end of these periods there must be an application for renewal of licence. If the product can no longer be regarded as safe or efficacious then the licence can be revoked. Once a licence is issued then the MHRA must be informed by the holder of the licence of any information suggesting that the information on which the licence was granted was inaccurate. The licence holder must keep a record of any evidence of adverse side effects of the medicine.[229]

---

[225] Chief Medical Officer (2003: 7).   [226] Chief Medical Officer (2003: 7).
[227] These are regulated under the Animals (Scientific Procedures) Act 1986.
[228] Medicine Act 1968, s 19.
[229] Medicines (Standard Provisions for Licences and Certificates) Regulations 1971 SI 1971/972.

EUROPEAN ANGLES

It is likely that eventually regulation of drugs will be taken over by a European-wide system. There is already a European Medicines Agency and its Committee for Proprietary of Medicinal Products has the power to licence medicines across Europe. The Committee has two delegates from each Member State. The committee gives provisional approval for a medicine after which Member States have 28 days to comment before a final decision is made.

The procedure of approval of medicines has given rise to concern in some quarters. For some the procedure is too cumbersome and can lead to long delays before much needed drugs are made available to the general public. Indeed the National Institute for Health and Clinical Excellence (NICE) has announced that a fast track scheme will be introduced to enable the licensing of urgently needed drugs.[230]

One, as yet unresolved, question is whether if a harmful drug was given a licence a patient who suffered from the drug could bring a claim against the Government, arguing that it was negligent to grant the licence. It is unlikely that a court would think it 'just fair and reasonable' to impose a duty of care on the MHRA.[231]

13.2 The marketing and use of medicines

There are also a special set of laws designed to ensure that patients are properly informed about their medicines. These require labels to accurately describe the product; instructions concerning the medicines; any special warnings; labels to make it clear how the product is to be taken; and appropriate packaging, including the need for child-resistant containers.[232]

There are also regulations to restrict advertising of medicines. There is a specific offence of issuing misleading advertisements in connection with medicines.[233] There are a variety of legislative provisions which control the use of medicines. The Medicines Act 1968 divides medicines into three categories: medicines that can only be available if prescribed by a doctor;[234] medicines that can only be supplied by a pharmacist, but which do not require a doctor's prescription; medicines which can be available generally.

13.3 Compensation for drug causing injury in tort

If a manufacturer produced a medicine which harms people who use it, then an action in negligence can be brought against the manufacturer.[235] It would be necessary to show that the manufacturer had not taken reasonable care in the production of the drug and that this caused the patient's injuries. It may be claimed that the failure to take reasonable care occurred in the design, manufacture, labelling, or marketing of the drug. It is often difficult to know whether the injury was caused by the drug or the medical

---

[230] BBC Newsonline (22 September 2005).   [231] Brazier (2003b: Chap 10).

[232] The details of the law can be found in Applebe and Wingfield (2005).

[233] Medicine Act 1968, s 93. See also Medicines (Advertising) Regulations 1994 SI 1994/1932.

[234] Although these are generally available in a hospital if a doctor or dentist has written a direction for their use.

[235] See Newdick (1995).

condition. There can also be difficulties in obtaining information about the production process of the drug, as this can be seen as confidential information.

Rather than relying on negligence it is easier for a claimant to use the Consumer Protection Act 1987 (CPA). The Act is designed to make it easier for patients to sue the producer of a drug they believed injured them. To win a case under the CPA the patient would need to show:

(i) the product was defective; and

(ii) the defect caused the damage.

The patient can sue the producer or the person who supplied the drug unless they can identify who produced it. This avoids the problem of a patient who has suffered harm because of a drug whose origins have been disguised. The Act covers products which include medicine and medical devices. It is unclear whether it includes blood, tissue, or organs. Crucially, there is no need to show that a producer was negligent.

Section 3(1) states:

> …there is a defect in a product…if the safety of the product is not such as persons generally are entitled to expect…

In deciding whether that is so the judge can take into account all the relevant factors including:

(a) the manner in which, and purposes for which, the product has been marketed, its get-up, the use of any mark in relation to the product, and any instructions for, or warnings with respect to, the doing of anything with or in relation to the product;

(b) what might reasonably be expected to be done with or in relation to the product; and

(c) the time when the product was supplied by its producer to another (section 3(2)).

The notion of the product being defective is difficult in the case of a drug. Many drugs carry unavoidable side-effects, which can be unpleasant, but that does not, of course, make the drug defective. A court may want to weigh up the benefits the drug supplies with its harmful side effects to decide whether or not the product is defective. Further a drug's effectiveness may vary from individual to individual, as may its side effects. If a drug has highly unpleasant side effects for one person but for thousands of others it provides a cure against an illness does it mean that the drug is defective? The answer to this question will depend on the seriousness of the disease the drug combats, the severity of the side effects, and the frequency with which those side effects occur. A drug which was effective in combating cancer which had a small side effect of producing skin blemishes would hardly be described as defective. A product designed to deal with the symptoms of the 'common cold' which had a high risk of causing liver failure certainly would be. It may be that, if there is an identified group of people to whom the product is dangerous (eg pregnant women), then the matter can be dealt with by the clearest of warnings that the product should not be used by that group of people. Another difficult issue is where the company is aware that their product carries a risk for some patients but does everything it can to make that risk clear to patients and doctors. Could the drug company say we left the decision of whether to run the risk to patients and their doctors?

The manufacturers will have a defence if they can show that the state of scientific knowledge at the time of production was such that they could not reasonably have been expected to discover the defect. The Consumer Protection Act, section 4(1)(e) puts it like this:

> the state of scientific and technical knowledge was not such that a producer of products of the same description as the product in question might be expected to have discovered the defect.

A leading case interpreting this defence in the medical context is the following:

KEY CASE   A v National Blood Authority [2001] 3 All ER 289

The claimants were patients who had been infected with the hepatitis C virus after they had received blood transfusions. They brought proceedings against the National Blood Authority under the Consumer Protection Act 1987. It was agreed that blood fell within the definition of product in the Act. It was held that in deciding whether a product was defective the 'legitimate expectations' of the public were a relevant consideration. Here it was held that people expected blood used for blood transfusions to be clean. The defendants had tried to argue that it was not possible to test the blood for all contamination and therefore the public ought not to expect blood always to be clean. However the judge held that if the public were not informed of the risks of contaminated blood they were entitled to assume that the blood was clean. If the public expectation was based on false assumptions then it was for the producer to 'reformulate' those expectations.

The blood authority argued that they could rely on the development risks defence. It was argued that at the relevant time there were no effective tests to screen blood for hepatitis C and that manufacturers of analogous products were aware of and been able to eliminate the risks. The judge rejected these arguments and ruled in favour of the claimants. The question was whether or not the risk was known about, not whether the risk could be eliminated. Here the fact the risk was known about was enough to mean that the defence was not available, even though with the knowledge available at that time the only thing the manufacturer could do about the risk was to warn patients of it.

The appropriateness of the CPA's 'development defence' has concerned some commentators. Its justification is that without it drugs companies might be deterred from seeking to develop new drugs and this will stifle innovation. Brazier has responded to such arguments thus: 'Germany, which boasts a thriving pharmaceutical industry, rejected the development risks defence specifically with regard to drugs while adopting it in relation to other products. Germany did not want to become a testing ground for risky drugs. Does Britain?'[236]

The main benefit, then, of using the CPA is that rather than the burden being on the claimant to show that the producer was negligent, the burden is on the producer to show that they were not negligent. However the Act does not mean everything is 'plain sailing' for a claimant:

- An action can only be brought in the first ten years of the drug being available on the market.

- The drug manufacturer has a defence if they can show the 'developments risks' defence.

---

[236] Brazier (2003b: 213).

- A drug company, unlike a manufacturer of other products, is likely to fight litigation fiercely. This is because if it is shown that the manufacturer of a lawn mower, for example, produced a faulty product which harmed a purchaser, this is likely to be a one-off case. However, if a drug is found to be defective then it is likely the company will face a multitude of claims.

- The biggest hurdle is that it must be shown that the drug caused the injury. It is, for example, difficult to show that a fetal abnormality is caused by a drug rather than a genetic problem. It must also be shown that the drug was taken properly and the problems did not therefore result from, for example, the patient taking inappropriate amounts of the drug.

- Even if it is shown that a drug did cause an injury it is difficult to know whether this is because of the drug. For example, it might be that the drug is not defective if it provides a cure for the vast majority of people, although it has undesirable consequences for a small number of people. If you are one of the unlucky few you will have difficulty in demonstrating that the drug was defective.

13.4 **An action for breach of contract**

Where a consumer purchases a medicine from a shop or pharmacy and the medicine causes an injury, an action can be brought against the shop or pharmacy for breach of contract. This claim cannot be used by a patient acquiring drugs on prescription. Even if they have to apply the prescription charge they are not, technically, buying the drug. The benefit of suing in contract is that because of the Sale of Goods Act 1979, the following terms ill be implied: that the goods must be of satisfactory quality (ie that they are of the standard that a reasonable person would regard as satisfactory) and must be reasonably fit for the purpose for which they are sold. Note that the action will be brought against the seller, not the manufacturer of the goods. All that needs to be shown is that the goods breached one of the terms of the contract; it is no defence for the pharmacist to argue that she or he had no way of knowing that the product was defective. Notice also that the action is only available for the purchaser. If it is a member of the purchaser's family who is harmed as a result they will probably not be able to sue in contract but may have a remedy in tort.

14 **Conclusion**

This chapter has considered the legal consequences that can flow when a patient suffers harm in the course of medical treatment. There is widespread dissatisfaction with the current approach as it appears a cumbersome and costly process—costly both in financial and emotional terms for all involved. However, there are difficulties with the alternatives. Finding a system which holds people who have behaved wrongly responsible for their actions, but which also encourages openness and the NHS to learn from past mistakes has, so far proved elusive.[237] Perhaps it is an impossibility.

---

[237] See DoH (2007e) for the latest proposals.

QUESTIONS

1. Should it be assumed that the increasing level of litigation is bad for the NHS? Could it not be that this will lead to increasing safety standards and a lower number of mishaps?

2. Should we take a positive view of mistakes? Merry and McCall Smith (2001: 71) argue: 'The inevitability of human error should be seen not so much as evidence of a primary human weakness, but rather as an inevitable concomitant of our impressive cognitive ability and evolutionary success.'

3. Is there a problem with labelling a professional as 'negligent' on the basis of a single incident and not to consider the individual's whole career?

4. Studies have suggested that overwork and lack of sleep are a major cause of errors in the NHS (Merry and McCall Smith (2001: 115). Would we rather medical professionals worked less, saw fewer patients, leading to longer delays, but made fewer mistakes?

5. The Healthcare Commission (2005) tells us that 6 per cent of admissions to NHS hospitals result from adverse drugs reactions. Do we too readily accept that drugs are the solutions to medical problems? Should a drug which will have such an adverse reaction that it requires treatment in a hospital ever be authorized?

6. Consider whether a no fault scheme would in the long term be beneficial for (a) those injured in the course of receiving medical treatment; and (b) medical professionals.

FURTHER READING

Bartlett, P. (1997) 'Doctors as fiduciaries; Equitable regulation of the doctor-patient relationship' *Medical Law Review* 193.

Brazier, M. and Miola, J. (2000) 'Bye-Bye Bolam: A Medical Litigation Revolution' *Medical Law Review* 85.

Cane, P. (2006) *Atiyah's Accidents, Compensation and the Law* (Butterworths).

Green, S. (2006) 'Coherence of medical negligence cases: A game of doctors and purses' *Medical Law Review* 14: 1.

Khoury, L. (2006) *Uncertain Causation in Medical Liability* (Hart).

Merry, A. and McCall Smith, A. (2001) *Errors, Medicare and the Law* (Cambridge University Press).

Miola, J. (2007) *Medical Ethics and Medical Law* (Hart), Chap 4.

Samanta, A., Mello, M., Foster, C., Tingle, J., and Samanta, J. (2006) 'The role of clinical guidelines in medical negligence litigation: a shift from the Bolam standard?' *Medical Law Review* 14: 321.

Teff, H. (1998) 'The standard of care in medical negligence—Moving on from Bolam' *Oxford Journal of Legal Studies* 18: 473.

Woolf, Lord (2001) 'Are the Courts Excessively Deferential to the Medical Profession?' *Medical Law Review* 9: 1–16.

4 Consent to Treatment

INTRODUCTION

It is a fundamental principle of medical law and ethics that before treating a competent patient a medical professional should get the patient's consent.[1] Gone are the days when a 'trust me, I'm a doctor' approach justified imposing treatment on a patient. Now it is the patient, rather than the doctor, who has the final say on whether a proposed treatment can go ahead. This 'principle of autonomy' involves complex issues: What does consent mean? Does the consent need to be 'informed'? Are there any circumstances in which it is permissible to treat patients without their consent? Of course consent is not only a legal requirement, in many cases it will be clinical one. Forcing a treatment on an unwilling patient is likely to be counter-productive. The consent requirement also protects the rights of patients. Lord Steyn in a recent House of Lords decision, *Chester v Afshar*, explained:

> A rule requiring a doctor to abstain from performing an operation without the informed consent of a patient serves two purposes. It tends to avoid the occurrence of the particular physical injury the risk of which a patient is not prepared to accept. It also ensures that due respect is given to the autonomy and dignity of each patient.[2]

Indeed it might be said that to operate on a competent patient without her or his consent would be to contravene a patient's right not to suffer torture or inhuman or degrading treatment contrary to article 3 of the European Convention on Human Rights.[3]

The basic legal starting point is that a health professional who intentionally or recklessly touches a patient without her or his consent is committing a crime (a battery) and a tort (trespass to the person and/or negligence[4]). To be acting lawfully in touching a patient the professional needs a defence or what the Court of Appeal has called a legal 'flak jacket'.[5] There are three such flak jackets available:

- the consent of the patient;
- the consent of another person who is authorized to consent on the patient's behalf (eg the consent of a parent for treatment of a child);
- the defence of necessity.

We will be looking at the meaning of these and when they can be relied upon later in this chapter.

---

[1] See, eg, the extensive discussion in *Re B (Consent To Treatment: Capacity)* [2002] EWHC 429, [2002] 1 FLR 1090.

[2] [2004] UKHL 41, para 18.

[3] *R (on the application of N) v Dr M, A NHS Trust and Dr O* [2002] EWHC 1911.

[4] *Sidaway v Bethlem RHG* [1985] 1 All ER 643.

[5] *Re W* [1992] 4 All ER 627, 633.

Without one of these flak jackets, touching a competent patient without their consent will be unlawful. As the Court of Appeal recently made clear in *R (on the application of Burke) v GMC*:

> Where a competent patient makes it clear that he does not wish to receive treatment which is, objectively, in his medical best interests, it is unlawful for doctors to administer that treatment. Personal autonomy or the right of self determination prevails.[6]

This is so even if there is strong evidence that the operation is in the best interests of the patient.[7] This point was dramatically made in *S v St George's*[8] where a woman in labour was told that she needed a Caesarean section and that without such an operation she and the foetus she was carrying would die. Despite her refusal to consent, the operation was carried out. The Court of Appeal held this to be unlawful. Great weight was placed on the importance of the right to bodily integrity. Not even the fact that she and the foetus would die without the operation provided a good enough reason to justify carrying out the Caesarean without her consent. Despite these points, as we shall see, many academics have criticized the law for prioritizing the wish to protect health care professionals from legal actions over protecting the right of the patient not to be given treatment to which they have not consented.[9]

Although the law takes seriously the right to be able to refuse treatment, it does not follow that if a patient wishes to receive treatment she or he must be given it. As the Court of Appeal in *R (on the application of Burke) v GMC* put it:

> Autonomy and the right of self-determination do not entitle the patient to insist on receiving a particular medical treatment regardless of the nature of the treatment. Insofar as a doctor has a legal obligation to provide treatment this cannot be founded simply upon the fact that the patient demands it. The source of the duty lies elsewhere.[10]

This chapter will start by considering the legal consequences of treating a patient without consent and will consider the meaning of consent. It will then look at the position of patients who lack the capacity to consent.

1 The legal consequences of illegal treatment without consent

Technically a medical professional who intentionally or recklessly touches a patient without consent could be charged with the criminal offence of battery. However, it is in fact very unlikely that that would happen, unless she or he was acting maliciously, for example, where the act involved a sexual assault.[11] Far more likely are legal proceedings in the law of tort. The proceedings could be brought under the tort of battery or the tort of negligence. It appears from the reported cases that negligence is used by far the

---

[6] *R (on the application of Burke) v GMC* [2005] 3 FCR 169, para 30.
[7] *Williamson v East London and City HA* (1998) 41 BMLR 85.
[8] [1998] 3 All ER 673.   [9] Montgomery (1988) and Harrington (1996).
[10] [2005] 3 FCR 169, para 31.   [11] *R v Healy* [2003] 2 Cr App R (S) 87.

most often.[12] Indeed it has been suggested that the tort of battery should play only a very limited role in these cases.[13]

There is a crucial difference between battery and negligence. In the tort of battery the claim is that the patient did not consent to the touching. In the case of negligence the claim is that, even though there may have been apparent consent, the doctor acted negligently in failing to provide a sufficient amount of information or making a misrepresentation concerning the treatment or the patient's condition.

There are some important differences between the tort of battery and the tort of negligence. These include the following:

(i) Negligence focuses on the question whether the medical professional acted in accordance with an accepted body of medical opinion, whereas battery focuses on the question whether the patient consented. So, in a case where a patient agreed to an operation, after being only given very limited information about it, if the case were considered under battery the key issue would be: 'did the patient consent in broad terms to the nature of the procedure, given his or her limited understanding of what was entailed?';[14] whereas under negligence it would be: 'was the information provided by the professional the amount of information considered appropriate by a respectable body of medical opinion?'. It would also need to be shown that if the correct information had been given the patient would not have gone ahead with that operation.[15] As can be seen the battery approach is more focused on the protection of the patient's rights to make decisions about her or his treatment, while the negligence approach is focused on ensuring that doctors follow an established body of medical opinion.

(ii) To succeed in a claim of negligence it must be shown that the patient suffered some harm. Therefore, if a doctor operates on a patient without her or his consent and can show that the operation benefited the patient then only nominal damages will be awarded if the claim is brought in negligence. By contrast in a case of battery there is no need to show that a patient suffered loss because the battery will be in itself a legal wrong. But even then the damages may be very low. In *Ms B v An NHS Trust*,[16] where a woman was given life-supporting treatment against her wishes, only £100 was awarded for the battery.

(iii) It will be a defence to a negligence claim based on non-disclosure of information to show that had the doctor fully informed the patient, the patient would have consented to the operation she or he received. This is because it could not be shown that the negligence (the failure to properly inform the patient about the operation) caused any harm. This would not provide a defence in a battery claim, if it was established that the victim had not consented.

(iv) Punitive damages can be awarded in a battery case, but not a negligence case.[17] If punitive damages are awarded the professional will not only have to pay for the losses suffered by the claimant, but a judge can award, in addition, a further sum by way of punishment of the defendant.

---

[12] Eg *Chatterton v Gerson* [1981] 1 All ER 257; *Freeman v Home Office* [1984] 1 All ER 1036; *Sidaway v Bethlem RHG* [1985] 1 All ER 643; *Williamson v East London & City HA* (1997) 41 BMLR 85; *Blyth v Bloomsbury AHA* [1993] 4 Med LR 151.

[13] The case law is discussed in Feng (1987) and Brazier (1987).

[14] *Chatterton v Gerson* [1981] 1 All ER 643.

[15] *Chester v Afshar* [2004] UKHL 41.   [16] [2002] 2 FCR 1.

[17] *Appleton and Others v Garrett* (1997) 34 BMLR 23.

(v) In a battery case all the loss flowing from the operation performed without consent can be recovered in a damages award, but in a negligence case only the foreseeable losses can be claimed.

(vi) A battery is only committed if there is a touching. Margaret Brazier and Emma Cave suggest 'A patient who agreed to take a drug orally, having been totally misled as to the nature of the drug, could not sue in battery'.[18] In such a case a negligence claim would still lie.

2 Who must provide the consent?

To answer this question it is necessary to distinguish cases of competent adults, incompetent adults, competent children, and incompetent children.

2.1 Competent adults

Where the patient is a competent adult only that person can consent. There is no doctrine of consent by proxy in English medical law. So, for example, it is not possible for a wife to consent on behalf of her husband. It is now accepted that a competent patient can provide an advance directive: this is a document (normally) which sets out what treatment a patient would or would not consent to in the event that she or he becomes incompetent.[19] Jehovah's Witnesses might, for example, want to sign an advance directive stating that if they are brought into a hospital unconscious they do not wish to receive blood transfusions, even if that is necessary to save their life.

The Mental Health Act 1983 authorizes the treatment of mental disorder in certain circumstances, even where the patient is not consenting. We shall discuss this legislation in detail in Chapter 10, but it is worth noting here that the courts have given treatment of mental disorder a fairly wide meaning. It has, for example, been held to cover forced feeding,[20] although whether such an interpretation withstands challenge under the Human Rights Act 1998 remains to be seen.

2.2 Incompetent adults

The law on the medical treatment of incompetent adults is surprisingly restrictive. Where the patient is an incompetent adult a relative does not automatically have the power to consent on her or his behalf. So if a woman collapses unconscious after a stroke, her husband cannot necessarily consent to treatment on her behalf. The medical professionals can provide the treatment which is in the best interests of a patient. Of course, often the medical professionals would want to discuss an incompetent person's medical treatment with relatives, but at the end of the day it is the medical team which decides what medical treatment is necessary. The practice that was common at one time of asking relatives of incompetent patients to sign consent forms has been criticized in Department of Health guidelines.[21]

The Mental Capacity Act (MCA) enables a competent adult (P) to create an enduring power of attorney which enables its donee (ie the person appointed to act under the

---

[18] Brazier and Cave (2007: 101).
[19] *R (on the application of Burke) v GMC* [2004] EWHC (Admin) 1879, para 44.
[20] *B v Croydon HA* [1995] 1 All ER 683.   [21] DoH (2001b: para 6).

enduring power of attorney) to make decisions on P's behalf when P become incompetent.[22] The MCA also enables the court to appoint a deputy to make certain decisions on behalf of a person who has become incompetent.[23] Perhaps most significantly, the Act allows competent people to create advance decisions rejecting treatment in the event that they become incompetent.[24] If the patient then becomes incompetent the advance decision must be respected. We shall be discussing these provisions of the MCA in much more detail later in this chapter.

A relative who is unhappy with the way a patient is being cared for can seek a court declaration as to the legality of the treatment. If there is a medical emergency and there is not time to seek court approval a medical professional may be able to rely on the defence of necessity. However, this is only possible where the treatment provided is in the best interests of the patient and the patient is not competent. So if a mother and child were both unconscious following an accident, and the child urgently needed blood and a doctor wanted to take it from her or his mother, it would not be possible to do that under the defence of necessity because the treatment would not be for the benefit of the mother.[25]

2.3 Incompetent children

If a child is incompetent then consent for treatment can be provided by anyone with parental responsibility for the child.[26] All mothers have parental responsibility for their children, but not all fathers. Fathers who are married to the mother or are registered on the child's birth certificate do, but otherwise a father will need to enter a Parental Responsibility Agreement with the child's mother or apply to the court for a Parental Responsibility Order or Residence Order. It is also possible for someone who is not a parent to acquire parental responsibility if she or he is granted a residence order in relation to the child (ie that the court has ordered that the child will live with them).[27]

2.4 Competent children

If a child is mature enough to be able to consent then she or he can provide effective consent to treatment. We will examine later how the court decides whether a child has sufficient maturity. It should also be noted that simply because the child is sufficiently mature to consent, this does not mean that those with parental responsibility cannot make decisions for the child. As we shall see, a doctor can treat a competent child who is objecting if the doctor has the consent of someone with parental responsibility for the child.

3 Who has the burden of proving consent?

If a criminal charge is brought, the prosecution will need to prove beyond reasonable doubt that the victim did not consent. Remarkably the legal position on who has the burden of proving consent in civil proceedings is unclear. Kennedy and Grubb[28]

---

[22] MCA 2005, s 9.   [23] MCA 2005, s 19.
[24] MCA 2005, s 24.   [25] Re F [1990] 2 AC 1.
[26] DoH (2001a) states that only parent with parental responsibility can consent.
[27] Children Act 1989, s 4. The law is discussed in detail in Herring (2007b: Chap 5).
[28] Kennedy and Grubb (2000).

suggest that consent is a defence a medical professional may raise to what will otherwise be a tort and therefore it is for the medical professional to prove that there was consent.[29] Certainly a medical professional is well advised to have evidence of consent before embarking on risky or controversial treatment.

4 What is consent?

In order for there to be an effective consent to treatment it is not enough just to show the patient said the word 'yes'. There must be a genuine agreement to receive the treatment.[30] It is, therefore, necessary to show that:

- the person is competent;
- the person is sufficiently informed;
- the person is not subject to coercion or undue influence.

These elements need to be looked at further.

4.1 Competence

A patient must be competent in order to be able to provide legally effective consent.[31] The Mental Capacity Act (MCA), section 1(2) makes it clear that a medical professional should presume that a patient is competent, unless there is evidence that she or he is not.[32] If the case comes to court the burden is on the doctor to demonstrate that the patient lacks capacity on the balance of probabilities.[33] But what exactly does it mean to say that the patient is incompetent? The MCA, section 2(1) states:

> . . . a person lacks capacity in relation to a matter if at the material time he is unable to make a decision for himself in relation to the matter because of an impairment of, or a disturbance in the functioning of, the mind or brain.

The Code of Practice lists the following as examples of conditions which might involve an impairment or disturbance of the functioning of the brain:

- conditions associated with some forms of mental illness;
- dementia;
- significant learning disabilities;
- the long-term effects of brain damage;
- physical or medical conditions that cause confusion, drowsiness, or loss of consciousness;
- delirium;

---

[29] *R (on the application of N) v Dr M, A NHS Trust* [2002] EWHC 1911.

[30] It is generally accepted that what counts as consent for the purposes of the law does not necessarily reflect how consent would be understood by philosophers and others. For further discussion see Epstein (2006).

[31] S. Lee (1987). Gunn (1994) and Devereux (2006) provide a useful discussion of the meaning of incapacity.

[32] *R v Sullivan* [1984] AC 156, 170–1.

[33] *R (on the application of N) v Dr M, A NHS Trust* [2002] EWHC 1911.

- concussion following a head injury; and
- the symptoms of alcohol or drug use.[34]

So, for a person to be incompetent it must be shown that she or he is unable to make a decision for her or himself. Section 3(1) explains:

> ... a person is unable to make a decision for himself if he is unable—
>
> (a) to understand the information relevant to the decision,
>
> (b) to retain that information,
>
> (c) to use or weigh that information as part of the process of making the decision, or
>
> (d) to communicate his decision (whether by talking, using sign language or any other means.

As this indicates, there are a number of ways a person may be said to be unable to make a decision. It may be a case of lack of comprehension: the person is not capable of understanding their condition or the proposed treatment or the consequences of not receiving treatment.[35] A patient may be found to have sufficient understanding to be able to consent to a minor straightforward piece of medical treatment, but not have sufficient understanding to be able to consent to a far more complex procedure.[36] The MCA, however, emphasizes that a patient should not be treated as lacking capacity 'unless all practical steps to help him' reach capacity 'have been taken without success'.[37] Further under section 2(2):

> A person is not to be regarded as unable to understand the information to a decision if he is able to understand an explanation of it given to him in a way that is appropriate to his circumstances (using simple language, visual aids or any other means).

To be competent the patient must also be able to use the information, weigh it, and be able to make a decision. This means that even though a patient may fully understand the issues involved, if she or he is in such a panic that she or he is unable to process the knowledge to reach a decision then she or he will be incompetent. In *Bolton Hospitals NHS Trust v O*[38] a pregnant woman needed a Caesarean section operation without which her life, and that of the life of the child she was carrying were in danger. She consented to the Caesarean section, but on four occasions when she was taken to the operating theatre in a panic she withdrew her consent. She was found to be incompetent on the basis that her refusal was not the result of reasoned decision and the court declared it lawful to perform the operation. The decision was made before the MCA came into force, but a similar conclusion would probably be reached under the Act.

The MCA, section 1(4) states that: 'A person is not to be treated as unable to make a decision merely because he makes an unwise decision'.[39] However, as *Re B (Consent To Treatment: Capacity)*[40] (a case decided before the MCA) made clear, although patients

---

[34] Department of Constitutional Affairs (DCA) (2007: para 4.12).   [35] MCA 2005, s 2(4).

[36] A point emphasized in *Re W* [2002] EWHC 901 and *Gillick v West Norfolk and Wisbech Area Health Authority and Another* [1986] AC 112, 169 and 186. See also DCA (2007: Chap 4).

[37] See DCA (2007: para 2.6) for a further discussion of what might be involved.

[38] [2003] 1 FLR 824.

[39] Despite the clear statement of this principle commentators have claimed that the judges have done exactly this to ensure patients receive the treatment they need: Montgomery (2000); Harrington (1996).

[40] [2002] EWHC 429, [2002] 1 FLR 1090.

must not be found incompetent because their decisions appear irrational, if the irrationality reveals that the patient is incapable of weighing up the issues or appreciate the consequences of their decisions then that may mean that they are incompetent. There is a careful line to be trod between not allowing this line of reasoning: this decision is irrational therefore the patient is incompetent; but permitting the reasoning: this decision is irrational because the individual is not able to properly weigh up the different issues.[41] As was emphasized in *Re B*:

> The doctors must not allow their emotional reaction to or strong disagreement with the decision of the patient to cloud their judgment in answering the primary question whether the patient has the mental capacity to make the decision.[42]

As was explained there, a decision which appears irrational to a health care professional may make perfect sense in the context of the patient's religious and personal beliefs. It is important to note that the MCA does not require a person to believe the information that they have been told, simply to understand it. However, as the Code of Practice indicates, there will inevitably be concerns that a person lacks capacity if they repeatedly make 'unwise decisions that put them at significant risk of harm or exploitation' or make 'a particular unwise decision that is obviously irrational or out of character'.[43]

In order to show that a person lacks capacity under the MCA it is not enough just to show that they are unable to make a decision for themselves; it must be shown that this is as a result of an impairment of or disturbance in the functioning of the mind or the brain. The significance of this is that a patient has capacity if there is no mental impairment or disturbance, however impaired their reasoning process may have been. So, for example, patients with no mental impairment who refuse all treatment because of their religious beliefs that God will cure them will not lack capacity, even if the doctors try to argue that they do not properly understand the reality of their situation. However, this provision could cause problems if a person is unable to communicate due to a muscular disease or severe physical pain. In such a case the person could not really be said to be suffering a mental impairment and so would be competent, but unable to communicate a decision.[44]

It must be emphasized that before the MCA the courts had not taken a very strict approach to the definition of competence. It is likely that a similar approach will be taken with the MCA. In *Re JT (Adult: Refusal of Medical Treatment)*[45] even though the patient suffered from a severe learning difficulty and was being detained under the Mental Health Act 1983 she had sufficient mental competence to refuse treatment for kidney failure. She understood that without the treatment she would die and had made a calm and rational decision. The low hurdle of consent can be seen from the following case.[46]

KEY CASE   Re C (Adult: Refusal of Treatment) [1994] 1 WLR 290 (FD)

C was a patient at Broadmoor and had been diagnosed as suffering from paranoid schizophrenia. One of his delusional beliefs was that he was a great doctor who had a 100 per cent success rate with

41 See Savulescu and Momeyer (1997) who insist that a patient's decision must be based on rational belief if it is to be respected.
42 *Re B (Consent to Treatment: Capacity)* [2002] EWHC 429, [2002] 1 FLR 1090.
43 DCA (2007: para 2.11).   44 Bartlett (2005: 27).   45 [1998] 1 FLR 48.
46 For an interesting discussion see Stauch (1995).

patients with damaged limbs. He suffered an injury to his foot which became gangrenous. He was told that there was an 85 per cent chance that he would die without an amputation. C opposed the treatment believing that God did not want him to have his foot amputated. Although he accepted that the doctors believed he was going to die, he did not agree with them.

Thorpe J held there were three aspects to competence: 'first, comprehending and retaining treatment information, second believing it and, third, weighing it in the balance to arrive at choice.' Applying that to this case he held: 'I am satisfied that he has understood and retained the relevant treatment information, that in his own way he believes it, and that in the same fashion he has arrived at a clear choice.' The doctors were therefore not permitted to operate on his foot without his consent, even if that were to lead to his death.

No operation was performed, but he managed to live and his foot largely recovered (Stauch and Wheat (2004: 122)).

It was crucial in this case that C understood the doctors' diagnosis and their proposed treatment.[47] It was simply that he believed that he (and God) knew better. The case can, on that basis, be contrasted with *R (on the application of N) v Dr M, A NHS Trust and Dr O*[48] where a patient believed that doctors wanted to give her drugs in order to induce her to believe she was a man. In fact they wished to give her anti-psychotic medicine. She was found incompetent because she did not understand the nature of the proposed treatment. A similar result would be found under the MCA because her lack of understanding would mean that she could not make a decision for herself and this would be due to her mental impairment.

A further point on competence is that the MCA makes special provision to ensure that patients are not assessed as lacking capacity in a prejudicial way. Section 2(3) states:

A lack of capacity cannot be established merely by reference to—

(a) a person's age or appearance, or

(b) a condition of his, or an aspect of his behaviour, which might lead others to make unjustified assumptions about him.

This is designed to ensure that a patient who appears unkempt or disordered is not assessed as lacking capacity purely on that basis.[49] The use of the word 'merely' is perhaps surprising because it suggests prejudicial attitudes can be a factor taken into account in assessing capacity.[50]

The Code of Practice makes it clear that those assessing capacity may not be professionals; it could be a family member caring for the individual. Therefore, if a person is caring for someone suffering with dementia who needs a bath, but that person is refusing, then the bath can be given if the person lacks capacity and the bath is in their best interests. Carers may find this concerning because if they get the assessment wrong and in fact the person does have capacity, in theory this could be a crime. Some comfort

---

[47] van Staden and Krüger (2003) state that a person cannot be competent if he is unable to appreciate the need for treatment.
[48] [2002] EWHC 1911.
[49] DCA (2007: para 4.8) also warns against assuming incapacity where someone has an appearance which includes features of Down's Syndrome.
[50] Bartlett (2005: 28).

can be found in section 5(1) of the MCA where it states that the Act applies where a person has reasonable grounds for deciding a person lacks capacity, even if in fact that person does not. Presumably in deciding whether or not there are reasonable grounds the court will take into account whether the person making the decision is an expert or not.[51] However, section 5(1) only applies where the decision relates to care or treatment.[52] That would very probably not include financial decisions.

4.2 The patient must be 'sufficiently informed'

The law in England and Wales does not recognize the so-called 'doctrine of informed consent' which states that a patient can only provide effective consent if given the relevant and necessary information to make a proper decision. All that is required is that the patient must understand 'in broad terms the nature of the procedure which is intended'.[53]

It is important at this point to distinguish two claims that patients may make in relation to a case where they claim that they were not given the appropriate amount of information:

(a) They could claim that they did not consent to a procedure because they did so only on the basis of false or inadequate information. This could be a claim in tort for battery or negligence. It can also result in criminal proceedings.

(b) They could claim that they did consent to the procedure but that the medical professional was negligent in not informing them of all the risks. This would be a claim in the tort of negligence.

We will examine cases of type (b) later, because they are not claims of non-consent as such but rather complaints that the doctor failed to provide the amount of information required.

Cases of type (a) are rare and are limited to the few situations in which the courts accept that an apparent consent was negated by misrepresentation or a failure to inform. The clearest instances are where an apparent consent is negated by fraud. One such case is *Appleton v Garrett*[54] where a dentist was found to have deliberately misinformed his patients in order to persuade them to agree to unnecessary treatment for financial gain.

Consent has also been held to be negated in the following circumstances:

- misrepresentation of the nature of the proposed treatment;[55]

- misrepresentation of the nature of the patient's present condition;

- a deliberate withholding of information.[56]

In *Potts v NWRHA*[57] a woman consented to the giving of what was described as a routine post-natal vaccination. In fact it was a long-acting contraceptive. There was no difficulty in deciding that the treatment was not consented to and so amounted to a battery. Less straightforward was *R v Tabaussum*[58] where it was said that a deception either as to the nature or quality of the act could negate consent. In that case women agreed to breast examinations on the understanding that they were being performed for

---

[51] See further DCA (2007: Chap 4).   [52] See DCA(2007: Chap 6).
[53] *Chatterton v Gerson* [1981] 1 All ER 257, 265. For further discussion see E. Jackson (2006).
[54] (1995) 34 BMLR 23.
[55] *Freeman v Home Office* [1984] 1 All ER 1036.   [56] *Chatterton v Gerson* [1981] 1 All ER 257.
[57] *The Guardian* 23 July 1983.   [58] [2000] L l Rep Med 404.

educational purposes whereas, in fact, they were being carried out for the defendant's own purposes (presumably sexual). Although the nature of the touching (ie where he touched her) was consented to by the defendant, the quality of the acts were different. Touching motivated by sexual purposes has a different quality to touching for non-sexual purposes. He was therefore convicted of criminal offences of battery.

A deception as to the identity of the person providing the treatment can negate the apparent consent, but a deception as to the qualities of the person do not. The distinction was revealed in the case of *R v Richardson*[59] where Diane Richardson had been removed from the list of the Dental Register, but continued to provide treatment to the patients. The patients had not been deceived either as to the nature of the treatment or as to the identity of the person (she was the very Diane Richardson they thought she was). Their mistake was as to one of her attributes, not her identity. However, the case has been criticized on the basis that a person receiving medical treatment may be far more concerned about whether or not the individual was medically qualified, than whether it was Dr X or Dr Y.[60]

4.3 The patient must be free from coercion or undue influence

Even if a patient is competent and she or he is aware of the crucial issues if her or his consent is not given freely it will not be legally valid consent.[61] It is rare for this issue to arise and it is difficult to demonstrate that an apparent consent was only given under coercion or undue influence. In *Freeman v Home Office*[62] it was held that the fact a prisoner felt he had no option but to submit to the prison medical officer's proposed treatment did not mean he was not validly consenting. The court pointed out that he had not in any way been threatened or physically restrained. In *Mrs U v Centre for Reproductive Medicine*[63] a man amended a form dealing with the infertility treatment he was receiving with his wife to read that his sperm could not be used after his death. When he died his wife sought to claim that her husband had only amended the form because he was under pressure from a nurse. It was held by the Court of Appeal that this was not a case where it was believable that he had signed the form under undue influence. He may have felt under pressure to sign the amendment, but he did not lack the ability to make his own decision. The following comment of Butler Sloss P was approved:

> when one stands back and looks at the facts of this case, it seems to me that it is difficult to say that an able, intelligent, educated man of 47, with a responsible job and in good health, could have his will overborne so that the act of altering the form and initialling the alterations was done in circumstances in which Mr U no longer thought and decided for himself.

A useful case where apparent consent was found not to be given freely is as follows:

KEY CASE Re T [1992] 4 All ER 649

The case concerned a young woman (T) who had been raised as a Jehovah's Witness, but had not become an official member of that religion as an adult. T was taken to hospital after a car accident.

[59] [1998] 43 BMLR 21.   [60] Herring (2005).   [61] Pattinson (2002a).
[62] [1984] 1 All ER 1036.   [63] [2002]Ll R Med 259.

> She was so badly injured that she needed a blood transfusion. Her mother, a Jehovah's Witness, came to see her in hospital and after that visit 'out of the blue' T announced that she did not wish to have a blood transfusion. T's boyfriend and father brought a court action claiming that T's views about the blood transfusion were not her own, but she had been pressurized by her mother.
>
> The Court of Appeal stated that a patient's consent or refusal to treatment could be incompetent if his or her will had been overborne by another's influence. The key question was whether the patient's decision was an independent one: had the outside influence caused the patient 'to depart from her own wishes to such an extent that the law regards it as undue'. Although there was no evidence of what the mother said to the daughter, the Court found that her refusal of a blood transfusion was not an expression of an independent decision. This conclusion was reached in part because T was in a weakened state through pain, tiredness, and the effect of medication, and partly because the closeness of T to her mother meant that the mother was in a position where she could exercise undue influence. It was also emphasized that the mother, as a committed Jehovah's Witness, would have very much wanted her daughter to refuse the blood transfusion. Having found T's refusal to consent to treatment was not competent the correct approach was for doctors to be authorized to treat the patient in a way which would promote her best interests. In this case that meant that T could be given the blood transfusions.

The decision has been criticized by some on the basis that it appears to set a higher hurdle for competence when a patient is refusing, rather than giving consent. If in *T* the patient had decided to agree to a blood transfusion after speaking to her mother, having previously opposed the treatment, it is hard to believe that anyone would have suggested that there had been undue influence.[64] There has also been concern expressed at the weight the court placed on pain, confusion, and the effects of medication.[65] If these are seen as rendering someone incompetent then many patients in hospital could be said to be incompetent. Notably in *NHS Trust v T*[66] it was held that only where confusion, shock, fatigue, pain, or drugs 'completely erode capacity' should it be found there is no consent.

4.4 The form of the consent

A consent does not need to be in any particular form. There is no legal distinction between written or oral consent. Although in the case of major surgery it is common to ask a patient to sign a consent form, this is not, strictly speaking, necessary. The precise nature of the consent has been described as 'pure window dressing'.[67] The benefit of having a signed form is that it can specify precisely what the patient has been told and what they have consented to. It should also be noted that consent is an ongoing concept and a professional should obtain consent for each medical procedure, rather than rely on the fact that the patient has consented to similar procedures in the past.[68]

Consent can also be express or implied. An example of implied consent would be where a doctor proposes giving an injection and the patient says nothing but rolls up the sleeve of his shirt and presents his arm to the doctor. Although the patient has not

---

64 Feldman (2002: 282).   65 Feldman (2002: 282).   66 [2004] EWHC 1279.
67 *Taylor v Shropshire Health Authority* [1998] Ll Rep Med 395.
68 *Bartley v Studd*, unreported but discussed in Dyer (1997).

actually said 'yes', his actions indicate that he is consenting. Of course, express written consent is the most undisputable form of consent and so the safest course of action is to ask a patient to sign a consent form.[69] The NHS Executive has produced a set of model consent forms which can be used. However, it should be emphasized that even if a patient has signed the form, if there is no true consent the form itself will not provide a defence.[70] It is still open, for example, for a patient to argue that she or he had been misled as to the nature of the proposed treatment or that she or he lacked the capacity to consent. Where a patient has not signed a consent form, or the form is amended without her or his signed authorization, the doctor is leaving her or himself open to claims that the procedures were not consented to.[71]

One important point is that consent is a 'positive' notion. The legal issue is whether or not the patient consented to the procedure, not whether the patient failed to oppose the treatment.[72] So, using the example above, if the doctor proposes an injection and the patient sits in the surgery impassively and the doctor injects the patient then it is not clear there is consent. It is true the patient did not object to the proposal, but that is insufficient to amount to consent. The doctor would have to argue that the patient's failure to get out of the way as she or he approached with a needle amount to implied consent. Whether a court would be willing to accept implied consent from an omission is highly debatable.

The following is a commonly used consent form:

[NHS organization name]
consent form 1

Patient agreement to investigation or treatment
Patient details (or pre-printed label)

Patient's surname/family name. _____

Patient's first names. _____

Date of birth. _____

Responsible health professional. _____

Job title. _____

NHS number (or other identifier). _____

☐ Male   ☐ Female

Special requirements. _____

(e.g. other language/other communication method)

To be retained in patient's notes

---

69 DoH (2001a).
70 DoH (2001b: 11); *Chatterton v Gerson* [1981] 1 All ER 257.
71 See eg *Williamson v East London and City HA and Others* [1998] Ll Rep Med 6.
72 *St George's Healthcare Trust v S* [1998] 3 All ER 673.

Patient identifier/label

Name of proposed procedure or course of treatment (**include brief explanation if medical term not clear**)

_____

_____

_____

_____

Statement of health professional (**to be filled in by health professional with appropriate knowledge of proposed procedure, as specified in consent policy**)

I have explained the procedure to the patient. In particular, I have explained:

The intended benefits _____

_____

_____

Serious or frequently occurring risks.

_____

_____

_____

Any extra procedures which may become necessary during the procedure

☐   blood transfusion.

☐   other procedure (please specify). _____

_____

I have also discussed what the procedure is likely to involve, the benefits and risks of any available alternative treatments (including no treatment) and any particular concerns of this patient.

☐   The following leaflet/tape has been provided

This procedure will involve:

☐ general and/or regional anaesthesia   ☐ local anaesthesia   ☐ sedation

Signed: _____   Date _____

Name (PRINT) _____   Job title _____

Contact details (if patient wishes to discuss options later) _____

Statement of interpreter (where appropriate)

I have interpreted the information above to the patient to the best of my ability and in a way in which I believe s/he can understand.

Signed _____   Date _____

Name (PRINT) _____

Top copy accepted by patient: yes/no (please ring)

Statement of patient   Patient identifier/label

Please read this form carefully. If your treatment has been planned in advance, you should already have your own copy of page 2 which describes the benefits and risks of the proposed treatment. If not, you will be offered a copy now. If you have any further questions, do ask—we are here to help you. You have the right to change your mind at any time, including after you have signed this form.

I **agree** to the procedure or course of treatment described on this form.

I **understand** that you cannot give me a guarantee that a particular person will perform the procedure. The person will, however, have appropriate experience.

I **understand** that I will have the opportunity to discuss the details of anaesthesia with an anaesthetist before the procedure, unless the urgency of my situation prevents this. (This only applies to patients having general or regional anaesthesia.)

I **understand** that any procedure in addition to those described on this form will only be carried out if it is necessary to save my life or to prevent serious harm to my health.

I **have been told** about additional procedures which may become necessary during my treatment. I have listed below any procedures **which I do not wish to be carried out** without further discussion.

_____

_____

_____

_____

_____

Patient's signature. _____   Date _____

Name (PRINT) _____

A witness should sign below if the patient is unable to sign but has indicated his or her consent. Young people/children may also like a parent to sign here (see notes).

Signature _____   Date _____

Name (PRINT) _____

Confirmation of consent (to be completed by a health professional when the patient is admitted for the procedure, if the patient has signed the form in advance)

On behalf of the team treating the patient, I have confirmed with the patient that s/he has no further questions and wishes the procedure to go ahead.

Signature _____   Date _____

Name (PRINT) _____   Jobtitle _____

Important notes: (tick if applicable)

☐   See also advance directive/living will (eg Jehovah's Witness form)

☐   Patient has withdrawn consent (ask patient to sign/date here)

4.5 How precise must the consent be?

We do not have clear guidance from the courts on how precise consent must be. This issue tends to arise where it has not been possible to diagnose precisely the patient's problem. Then a physician may decide that an operation is required to investigate and diagnose the problem. Only once the patient is opened up in the operating theatre will it be clear what operation needs to be done. Of course if the patient consents to a range of alternative operations and the surgeon performs one of those there is no difficulty in finding consent. More difficult is consent of the most general kind: 'operate on me and do whatever is necessary'. It is not clear whether such a broad consent would be effective, there may need to be at least some reference to the kinds of surgery that would be envisioned.[73]

One particular issue surrounds testing a patient's blood for the HIV virus.[74] If a patient had in a general way agreed for 'blood tests' to be carried out, would this be sufficient to authorize an HIV test? Some argue that because of the special significance that attaches to a diagnosis of being HIV positive it is important to insist that a patient has consented with full appreciation of the ramifications.[75] Others argue that as long as the patient has consented to the taking and testing of blood it should not be necessary to have consent for every single test that may be carried out.[76] It may be that the key issue is whether HIV should be regarded as similar to other tests, in which case it might be said the general consent covers them, or whether HIV tests should be regarded as special, with specific rules. Notably the Department of Health has taken the view that specific consent should be sought in respect of an HIV test.[77]

Another scenario which can arise is if, while carrying out one operation, it becomes apparent to the physician that another operation is required. Should the physician wait until the patient recovers from the anaesthetic and get their consent or can the physician assume that the patient would want the surgeon to operate? One controversial area is where a surgeon is performing an operation on a woman and discovers that there are good medical reasons for performing a hysterectomy. Although there is no clear ruling on this kind of case, it would appear that the physician must obtain consent for each procedure she or he carries out. Consent to operation A is not consent to operation B. For example, there is an old case which makes it clear that consent to an abortion does not include consent to a sterilization.[78] However, if all the physician does is a minor deviation from the consented to procedure, implied consent may be found. In *Davis v Barking, Havering and Brentwood HA*[79] a claimant failed in her action for damages based on her claim that she had not consented to a specific form of anaesthetic known as a caudal block. Her claim failed because she had signed a form agreeing to the performance of an operation and 'such further or alternative operative measures as may be found necessary during the course of the above-mentioned operation and to the administration of general, local or other anaesthetics for any of these purposes'. The anaesthetic was administered as a part of the operation to which she had consented.

It should be noted that if, in the course of one operation, there is a medical emergency requiring a medical procedure, the doctor can operate on the patient without her or his consent, and is protected by the defence of medical necessity.

---

[73] Montgomery (2003: 236).   [74] Keown (1989b).
[75] Kennedy and Grubb (2000).   [76] Mason and Laurie (2006: 388).
[77] DoH (1996b). For a full discussion of the issues see Bennett (2007).
[78] *Cull v Royal Surrey County Hospital* (1932).   [79] [1993]4 Med LR 85.

5 Actions in negligence based on a failure to provide sufficient information

Even though a patient may have been provided with sufficient information to consent to a procedure she or he may claim that the doctor was negligent in failing to provide her or him with the appropriate level of information. In such a case the claim should be brought in negligence. Such claims raise a number of issues:

5.1 How much information must be provided?

It should be made clear at the outset that English law does not recognize the doctrine of 'informed consent' as is understood in other countries.[80] The doctrine suggests that patients are only taken to consent if they are aware of all the relevant and necessary information to make an informed decision. The approach of the English law is found in the following leading case:

KEY CASE   Sidaway v Bethlem RHG [1985] 1 All ER 653

During an operation to relieve a trapped nerve Mrs Sidaway's spinal cord was damaged and she was left paralysed. She brought legal proceedings against the hospital, not on the basis that the operation was performed negligently, but on the basis that the risks connected with the operation were not explained to her. The case was heard on the basis that the surgeon had not told Mrs Sidaway the risks of paralysis that the operation carried. Expert witnesses at the trial said at the time of the operation some but not all neurosurgeons would have regarded it as acceptable not to tell a patient about the risks of paralysis. Although all of their Lordships agreed that Mrs Sidaway's action should fail, each of the judges who wrote full judgments provided a different explanation:

* Lord Diplock held that the case should be approached in the same way as other medical negligence cases. A medical professional would not be acting negligently if he or she was acting in accordance with a respectable body of medical opinion (the *Bolam* test). In other words a doctor would only be negligent if her or his failure to disclose the information would be unacceptable to all responsible practitioners in the relevant specialty. That was not the case here and so the doctor had not been negligent.

* Lord Bridge (with whom Lord Keith agreed) also held that the *Bolam* test guided the issue: was there a respectable body of opinion which would have agreed with not telling the patient the information? If so, the doctor was not negligent. However, Lord Bridge went on to add two qualifications which he stated indicated that his approach did not mean that the law was simply handing over the scope of disclosure to the medical profession. First, the court would be astute to ascertain whether or not there was a body of medical opinion which approved of non-disclosure. In particular he emphasized that if experts disagreed over whether or not there was such a body of opinion a judge would need to decide which expert's view was preferable. Secondly, he indicated that even if there was an established body of opinion of medical opinion in favour of non-disclosure

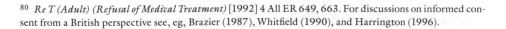

[80] *Re T (Adult) (Refusal of Medical Treatment)* [1992] 4 All ER 649, 663. For discussions on informed consent from a British perspective see, eg, Brazier (1987), Whitfield (1990), and Harrington (1996).

it was open for a judge to hold it unacceptable and hence not responsible. He suggested that not to disclose a serious risk could be negligent, even if thought acceptable by a respectable body of opinion: not disclosing a 10 per cent risk of a stroke was his example. He appears therefore to be suggesting that although generally the *Bolam* test would apply in non-disclosure of risk cases there might be some circumstances in which the court would automatically find that non-disclosure of serious risks would amount to negligence, whatever the views of the medical experts. Applying his approach to the case at hand, as there was a responsible body of opinion which supported the non-disclosure and, as the risk was very small, the doctor was not negligent.

- Lord Templeman held that the views of professional bodies of opinion were irrelevant. He regarded the doctor as under a duty to inform patients as to the nature of the operation and any risks that were special to the patient (eg if because the patient had a heart condition the operation was riskier to that patient than it would be to others). However, having told the patient about the operation it was up to the patient to ask any particular concerns they had. He argued that in this case the doctor's explanation of what the operation entailed would have made it clear that there were risks of injuries to the spine. Mrs Sidaway had chosen not to ask for more information and so there was no duty to provide any. Indeed Lord Templeman pointed out that patients often do not want to hear about all the possible risks their surgery carries and are often content to leave decision-making to their doctors. He argued that giving a patient too much information would impair their ability to reach a decision as much as too little. The patient was entitled to enough information to reach a balanced decision, but no more. Here she was given enough information.

- Lord Scarman emphasized that patients have a right to decide whether or not to receive medical treatment. To give effect to this right a patient had a right to be given all material information necessary to make the decision. To decide whether information was material he proposed the 'prudent patient test': if a reasonable person in the patient's shoes would have regarded the information as significant, the patient had a right to know it. But, and this is a big 'but', he went on to say that health care professionals could rely on a defence of 'therapeutic privilege': this permitted doctors not to disclose a risk if that disclosure would seriously harm the health (including mental health) of the patient. Applying this approach to this case, although Mrs Sidaway had the right to know about the risk, the doctor was entitled not to tell her on the basis that to inform her of the risk would cause her serious distress.

As can be seen it is not easy to determine the scope of the decision in *Sidaway*. Lords Diplock, Bridge, and Keith appear to see the *Bolam* test as providing the key to the issue, although the latter two leave open the possibility of the court overruling a body of medical opinion in an extreme case. Indeed, apart from Lord Diplock, all the judges were concerned that just using the *Bolam* test might lead to too little protection of patients' rights. It is not surprising therefore that much rests on the subsequent interpretation of the case.

In the early years after *Sidaway* the courts appeared to accept Lord Diplock's speech as providing the guidance and so there was a simple application of the *Bolam* test.[81] However in *Pearce v United Bristol Healthcare NHS Trust*[82] Lord Woolf MR preferred to emphasize Lord Bridge's speech which he thought enshrined the clearest expression of the majority view, particularly in light of the reconsideration of the *Bolam* test in *Bolitho v City & Hackney HA*.[83] Lord Woolf emphasized that Lord Bridge, in applying

---

[81] Eg *Gold v Haringey HA* [1987] 2 All ER 888.   [82] (1998) 48 BMLR 118.   [83] [1998] AC 232.

the *Bolam* test in the context of revealing information, had emphasized that the issue was not simply a matter of medical judgment. The medical opinion to justify non-disclosure had to be both 'reasonable' and 'responsible'. Lord Woolf went on to explain that this meant:

> If there is a significant risk which would affect the judgement of the reasonable patient, then in the normal course it is the responsibility of a doctor to inform the patient of that significant risk, if the information is needed so that the patient can determine for him or herself as to what course he or she should adopt.

This formulation is reminiscent of Lord Scarman's 'prudent patient' test. There are two important points to make about Lord Woolf's approach. The first is that the obligation is only to inform of *significant* risks. In *Pearce* itself, the court accepted the views of the doctor's medical experts that the risk was not significant. However, in the one reported decision[84] where such negligence was found, the judge took the view that the body of medical opinion that claimed it was not necessary to warn of a risk of impotence which accompanied an operation was neither reasonable nor responsible.[85] A survey of doctors has indicated little agreement over which risks are sufficiently serious to require disclosure to a patient.[86]

The second point is that Lord Woolf indicated that a doctor had to inform patients of significant risks 'in the normal course of events'. This suggests that there are some circumstances in which it may not be appropriate to inform the patient of significant risks. Unfortunately he did not elaborate on what those might be. It may be he had in mind cases where informing the patient of the risks would cause the patient to suffer such panic as to amount to a harm.

In a recent *dicta* Lord Steyn in *Chester v Afshar*[87] put the duty of the professional in terms which did not refer to the *Bolam* test:

> A surgeon owes a legal duty to a patient to warn him or her in general terms of possible serious risks involved in the procedure. The only qualification is that there may be wholly exceptional cases where objectively in the best interests of the patient the surgeon may be excused from giving a warning....In modern law medical paternalism no longer rules and a patient has a prima facie right to be informed by a surgeon of a small, but well established, risk of serious injury as a result of surgery.[88]

The lack of reference to the *Bolam* approach here may simply be because he assumed that no responsible body of medical opinion would think it inappropriate to disclose a serious risk to a patient.

It appears therefore that generally if a doctor is following a responsible body of medical opinion in not disclosing a particular risk she or he will not be negligent.[89] However, the courts have left open the possibility that where the risk is a serious one it could not be a responsible view not to disclose the risk,[90] unless to do so would cause a serious harm to the patient. The Department of Health suggests a patient should be presumed

---

[84] *Smith v Tunbridge Wells HA* [1994] 5 Med LR 334.
[85] The surgeon claimed he had warned of the risk, but this was not believed.
[86] Palmboom et al (2007).   [87] [2004] UKHL 41.   [88] Para 16.
[89] In *Gold v Haringey HA* [1994] 5 Med LR 3 34 the Court of Appeal rejected any distinction in the disclosure requirements in cases of therapeutic and non-therapeutic treatment.
[90] *Newbury v Bath DHA* (1998) 47 BMLR 138.

to want to know of all relevant risks.[91] It has also stated:

> It is now clear that the courts will be the final arbiter of what constitutes responsible practice, although the standards set by the health professions for their members will still be influential.[92]

A few other points about the information which needs to be provided by a doctor should be made. First, in *Smith v Tunbridge Wells Health Authority*[93] it was held that the doctor's duty is not only to inform the patient but also to take reasonable steps to ensure that the patient understands what she or he is consenting to. A doctor cannot, therefore, seek to claim she or he informed a patient of the relevant risks by taking out a medical textbook and reading a page at great speed![94] On the other hand only reasonable steps have to be taken. The doctor does not need to be absolutely sure that the information has been understood.[95] Secondly, there are some risks which are so obvious that they do not need to be explicitly explained to patient. There is no need, for example, to warn a patient that surgery will produce a scar![96] Thirdly, Lord Walker in *Chester v Afshar*[97] emphasized that a patient had the right to be told not only about the treatment being offered, but also alternative or variant treatments that could be used.

5.2 Where the patient has asked a question about a particular issue

So far we have been looking at cases concerning the duty on doctors to inform patients about a medical procedure. But what about cases where the patient, having heard the doctor's description of the proposed treatment, asks particular questions? In *Sidaway*[98] Lords Diplock and Bridge indicated that cases where specific questions were asked by patients were different from the standard cases where no questions are asked. Lord Bridge suggested that if a question was asked the doctor's duty was 'to answer both truthfully and as fully as the questioner requires'.[99] However that statement was *obiter*. The only other case to discuss the issue in detail is *Blyth v Bloomsbury HA*,[100] although again the discussion was *obiter*: on the facts that the patient had not asked any questions. There, the Court of Appeal stated that where questions were asked, the *Bolam* test applies. In other words, if a question was asked, as long as a doctor gives a response which would be considered appropriate by a responsible body of medical opinion that will not be negligent, even if that answer was not 'full'.

It may not be safe to assume that *Blyth* represents the current law until there is a clearer statement from the courts. Some commentators argue that applying the *Bolam* test would mean that patients can be lied to, if that was thought to be appropriate by a responsible body of opinion.[101] However, leaving aside the question of whether a responsible body of medical opinion would hold that, it should not be forgotten that fraudulently obtained consent is not valid consent. It is suggested that if the issue comes before a court it is likely that a distinction will be drawn between cases where a doctor has given an incomplete answer, and where a false answer has been given. The former, if thought

91 DoH (2001c: 11).   92 DoH (2001c: 4).   93 [1994] 5 Med LR 334 at 339.
94 Giving a patient a leaflet specifically written for patients, which sets out clearly the information, may well be sufficient: *Al Hamwi v Johnston* [2005] EWHC 206.
95 *Al Hamwi v Johnston* [2005] EWHC 206. See criticism of the law in Miola (2007).
96 Browne Wilkinson LJ in *Sidaway v Bethlem Royal Hospital* (CA) [1984] 1 All ER 1018, 1034.
97 At para 95.   98 At 659 and 661.   99 At 661.
100 [1993] 4 Med LR 151.   101 Montgomery (2003: 249).

appropriate by a respectable body of medical opinion, may well not be negligent, but the latter will always be, unless there are very strong clinical reasons.

5.3 Bringing a successful legal claim where the patient has not been sufficiently warned of risks

Even if the patient is able to prove that the information she or he was given was inadequate, she or he will still face an uphill task in claiming damages. This is because she or he must show that as a result of the negligence she or he suffered a loss. Therefore, if a patient is not told about the risks of an operation, and the operation is performed, and fortunately the risk does not materialize, there is no possibility of obtaining substantial damages against the surgeon. Even if the patient does suffer from the risk the case is not clear cut. Cannot the surgeon argue: even if I had told the patient she or he would have consented to the operation and suffered the harm? In other words the injury would have occurred even if fuller information had been provided. The validity of such an argument was raised in the following important decision:

KEY CASE   Chester v Afshar [2004] 4 All ER 587

Ms Chester, a journalist, was suffering from persistent lower back pain. She consulted Mr Afshar, a consultant neurosurgeon. During the consultation he advised surgery to remove three spinal disks. Ms Chester agreed to undergo the operation with Mr Afshar at the next available opportunity which was a few days later. What was said at the consultation was in dispute. The trial judge preferred the evidence of Ms Chester who explained that she had concerns about the risks of the proposed operation but that all Mr Afshar had said about the dangers of the operation was that he 'hadn't crippled anybody yet'. It was common ground that it was accepted practice amongst specialists in the field to warn patients due to undergo this operation about the risk of paralysis which could result. There was a 1–2 per cent chance of the risk developing in an operation of this kind. When Mr Afshar carried out the operation in what was found to be an entirely appropriate way Ms Chester suffered from severe pain and motor impairment as a result.

The key issue before the House of Lords was that Ms Chester stated that if she had been told about the risks connected with the operation she would not have consented to undergo the procedure immediately, but would have sought a second or even third opinion. For Mr Afshar it was argued that Ms Chester had no claim. Mr Afshar had not operated negligently and although he should have informed her of the risk, even if he had informed her of the risk she would still have undergone the operation. Although she would not have had the operation at the same time as she did, she would have (she accepted) had the operation at some point. The operation would have carried the same risk of the paralysis developing as it did when she undertook it. In other words Ms Chester was in no worse position as a result of the failure to inform her of the risks, than she would have been if she had been told of the risks.

The majority of the House of Lords rejected this argument. It was held that there was a specific loss for Ms Chester: she had lost the chance of having the operation on another day when she might not have developed the paralysis. The majority focused on the policy that doctors had to be liable if they failed to respect their patient's rights to know about the risks attendant on the operation. Even if there were difficulties in establishing causation, a doctor who had not properly informed a patient about risks should be liable to pay damages to the patient.

The minority applied the traditional causation principle. Lord Bingham did not accept that it was just for a claimant to be awarded a substantial level of damages when it could not be shown that she or he was any worse off as a result of the negligence. Lord Hoffman said that the operation in this case could be analogized to a game of roulette. The chances of winning (or losing) were the same whichever day someone played. It was the same with the chances of the operation causing paralysis. Ms Chester's paralysis could not therefore be said to have resulted from Mr Afshar's negligence.

This decision is significant. It would not have been particularly controversial if the facts of the case had indicated that if she had been informed of the risks Ms Chester would not have had the operation. Then it would have been easy to show that the defendant's negligence had caused her loss. However, here, as the majority accepted, it was difficult to identify a loss which had resulted from the failure to inform her of the risks. At the heart of the majority's judgment is a finding that Mr Afshar's negligence should not go unpunished. Lord Hope emphasized that the law of tort in this area had the function of protecting patients' rights (to choose whether or not to have treatment). He explained (at para 54):

> If it is to fulfil that function it must ensure that the duty to inform is respected by the doctor. It will fail to do this if an appropriate remedy is not given if the duty is breached and the very risk that the patient should have been informed about occurs and she suffers injury.

But notice that the majority did not throw causation entirely out of the window. If the evidence had indicated that had she been informed of the risk she would still have agreed to the operation at the time and place where she had it, then there would have been no claim. Her evidence indicated that if told of the risk she would have sought a second opinion and therefore had the operation at a later time.

The difficulty facing the majority and minority in the case was this: the real loss to the patient was the loss of the opportunity to make an informed decision for herself; an infringement of her rights of autonomy and right to human dignity. Such 'ephemeral' losses are not recognized as wrong in tort law. To award her nothing would be to show lack of respect for these losses, but to award her the losses which flowed from her injuries seemed to the minority to award her too much.

6 Professional guidelines

The Department of Health's *Good Practice in Consent* opens with a powerful statement of the importance of obtaining the patient's consent:

> Patients have a fundamental legal and ethical right to determine what happens to their own bodies. Valid consent to treatment is therefore absolutely central in all forms of healthcare, from providing personal care to undertaking major surgery. Seeking consent is also a matter of common courtesy between health professionals and patients.[102]

---

[102] DoH (2001c: 9).

The General Medical Council[103] has suggested the following matters should be disclosed by doctors when discussing proposed treatment with a patient:

- details of the diagnosis, and prognosis, and the likely prognosis if the condition is left untreated;

- uncertainties about the diagnosis including options for further investigation prior to treatment;

- options for treatment or management of the condition, including the option not to treat;

- the purpose of a proposed investigation or treatment; details of the procedures or therapies involved, including subsidiary treatment such as methods of pain relief; how the patient should prepare for the procedure; and details of what the patient might experience during or after the procedure including common and serious side effects;

- for each option, explanations of the likely benefits and the probabilities of success; and discussion of any serious or frequently occurring risks, and of any lifestyle changes which may be caused by, or necessitated by, the treatment;

- advice about whether a proposed treatment is experimental;

- how and when the patient's condition and any side effects will be monitored or re-assessed;

- the name of the doctor who will have overall responsibility for the treatment and, where appropriate, names of the senior members of her or his team;

- whether doctors in training will be involved, and the extent to which students may be involved in an investigation or treatment;

- a reminder that patients can change their minds about a decision at any time;

- a reminder that patients have a right to seek a second opinion;

- where applicable, details of costs or charges which the patient may have to meet.[104]

Significantly the guidance emphasizes that it is not enough to ensure this advice is provided—attempts must be made to make sure it is understood. The patient may need to be given written information and enough time to reach a decision. The patient's family may need to be involved. The Guidance accepts that there may be circumstances in which it is legitimate to withhold information on significant risks, but this should be limited to cases where providing the information would cause the patient 'serious harm'. The Guidance indicates that refusing treatment or becoming upset would not be sufficient to amount to 'serious harm'.

The BMA's guidance is in similar terms. However, it makes the point that the patient can be overburdened with information:

> There is inevitably a degree of selectivity about the amount of information patients are given. It would be overly burdensome on both patients and health services for every detail to be explained, and patients are extremely unlikely to want this. It is, however, important that patients can be confident that the information they will be given is that which is likely to be relevant to them, and understand that they may always ask for more details or explanation if they wish.[105]

---

[103] GMC (1998).   [104] Paras 4–5.   [105] BMA and Law Society (2004: 79).

The Guidance offered by the Royal College of Surgeons also requires surgeons to:

> ensure that patients, including children, are given information about the treatment proposed, any alternatives and the main risks, side effects and complications when the decision to operate is made.[106]

These Guidelines may be thought to go further than the legal requirements. Indeed one leading commentator has suggested that 'the law has failed patients but that the professions have taken steps to plug the gap that the judges have left'.[107]

7 The non-consenting competent patient

As we have seen already it is a fundamental legal principle that a doctor cannot provide treatment without the consent of a competent patient. However there are some very limited circumstances in which it is permissible to infringe that right:

(i) It is not an offence to touch someone without their consent if that touching is 'physical contact which is generally acceptable in the ordinary conduct of daily life'.[108] Therefore a doctor who gave her patient a welcoming handshake or a nurse who gave a nervous patient a reassuring pat on the arm would not be committing an offence even if the patient had not consented. However, this would be a limited exception and could not be used to provide a justification for medical treatment. It has been suggested that it could justify some basic nursing care such as dressing and feeding.[109] However, it is hard to see how these touchings could be described as an aspect of the ordinary conduct of daily life.

(ii) There has been some debate over whether it is possible to force treatment on a non-consenting patient on the grounds of public policy. If there is such a power, it would require the most unusual of circumstances. In *Robb v Home Office*[110] a prisoner went on hunger strike. The case raised the question of whether it was lawful to force feed the prisoner. Lord Justice Thorpe accepted that there was a clash between the right of self determination and four state interests: (1) preserving life; (2) preventing suicide; (3) maintaining the integrity of the medical profession; and (4) protecting innocent third parties. But all of the state interests yielded to the right of self-determination. It will be recalled that in *St George's NHS Healthcare Trust v S*[111] the preservation of the life of the woman and her foetus were insufficient grounds to justify operating on her without her consent. However, the courts have generally stood back from saying it is never permissible to provide medical treatment against the wishes of a competent person. If a terrible disease took a grip on the population threatening to kill thousands of people it is not difficult to believe that the court would permit the taking of blood from a person who appeared to have an antibody. Also, perhaps, if in order to a save another person's life a very minor invasion of another person was required (eg the taking of a hair) a court might be tempted to authorize it. We have little case law on such scenarios,

---

106 Royal College of Surgeons (2002: 4.1).
107 Montgomery (2003: 251). He develops his argument in Montgomery (2000).
108 *Collins v Wilcock* [1984] 3 All ER 374.
109 DoH (2001a: para 19.2) suggests that 'basic care' falls within this exception and that it is not possible to refuse to consent to this.
110 *Secretary of State v Robb* [1995] 1 All ER 677.   111 [1998] 3 All ER 673.

but what can be said is that if there can be a public policy justification to justify non-consensual treatment, it will only arise in unusual situations.[112]

(iii) If a patient is suffering from a 'notifiable disease' (eg cholera, typhus) she or he can be ordered to be detailed by a magistrate under the Public Health (Control of Disease) Act 1984. The Public Health (Infectious Diseases) Regulations 1985 give magistrates powers to order compulsory detention of people known or suspected to have AIDS.[113]

(iv) If a person is trying to commit suicide it is generally thought to be lawful to seek to prevent that happening. In *R v Collins and Ashworth Hospital ex p Brady*,[114] *obiter*, it was suggested that it was lawful to prevent suicide. This issue is discussed in Chapter 9.

8 The treatment of incompetent patients

The treatment of a patient lacking capacity is now governed by the MCA 2005. The Act only applies to those over the age of 16.[115] It will be remembered that the Act makes it clear that a patient should be presumed to be competent.[116] If a person is not competent then generally a decision can be made on their behalf, as we shall discuss shortly. But first it should be noted that there are some things that it is not possible to provide consent for on behalf of a person lacking capacity. These are listed in section 27:

• consenting to marriage or a civil partnership;

• consenting to have sexual relations;

• consenting to a decree of divorce on the basis of two years' separation;

• consenting to the dissolution of a civil partnership;

• consenting to a child being placed for adoption or the making of an adoption order;

• discharging parental responsibility for a child in matters not relating to the child's property; or

• giving consent under the Human Fertilisation and Embryology Act 1990.[117]

If the issue concerns something else and the patient is incompetent then the following questions must be considered:

(1) Has the patient created an effective advance decision (sometimes called a 'living will') which refuses the treatment in question? If so the advance decision must be respected.

(2) Has the patient effectively created a lasting power of attorney (LPA)? If so the donee of the LPA may be able to make the decision.

(3) Has the court appointed a deputy? If so the deputy in some cases can make the decision.

[112] Skegg (1985: 110–16).
[113] Brazier and Cave (2007: 150) state that only one person has ever been detained under these provisions.
[114] [2000] Ll Rep Med 355.
[115] Although the offence of ill-treatment or wilful neglect of a person lacking capacity in s 44 has no age limit. Also in s 18(3) there is power for the court to deal with the property of an incapable minor.
[116] MCA 2005, s 1(2).
[117] See also s 27 preventing voting on behalf of a person lacking capacity and s 28 preventing consent to mental disorder treatment for a person detained under the Mental Health Act 1983.

(4) If there is no effective advance decision and no LPA or deputy who can make the decision then the question is whether the treatment is in the best interests of the patient.

We need therefore to consider the four scenarios separately.

8.1 Advance decisions

An advance decision is defined in section 24 thus:

'Advance Decision' means a decision made by a person ('P'), after he has reached 18 and when he has capacity to do so, that if—

(a) at a later time and in such circumstances as he may specify, a specified treatment is proposed to be carried out or continued by a person providing health care for him, and

(b) at that time he lacks capacity to consent to the carrying out or continuation of the treatment,

the specified treatment is not to be carried out or continued.

A number of points should be noted about this definition. First, the advance decision is only effective if P (the patient) was over 18 and competent when she or he made it. Second, the advance decision is only to be relevant if the patient lacks capacity to consent to the treatment. So if a patient has signed an advance decision refusing to consent to a blood transfusion, but at the time is competent and consents then the advance decision should be ignored.[118] Third the definition of advance decisions only allows 'negative' decisions; decisions to refuse treatment. An advance decision cannot be used to compel a medical professional to provide treatment. The definition of advance decision covers both treatment and the continuation of treatment. An advance decision could, therefore, indicate that P is willing to receive treatment, but only for a certain period of time.

If the advance decision does reject life-saving treatment it must be in writing and signed by P and witnessed by a third party.[119] Otherwise the decision does not need to be in writing.

Section 25 explains how an advance decision may be invalid. This is where P, with capacity, has withdrawn the advance decision; where P has created an LPA after making the advance decision and given the LPA the power to make the decision in question; or where P has done anything else which is clearly inconsistent with the directive in the advance decision. In *HE v A Hospital NHS Trust*,[120] a case decided before the MCA came into force, a patient had signed an advance decision indicating that she did not want to be given a blood transfusion, even if without it she would die. At the time she signed the decision she was a Jehovah's Witness. She later needed a blood transfusion, but the court heard evidence that she was no longer an active Jehovah's Witness and had indeed become engaged to be married to a Muslim. It was held that this, along with other evidence, indicated that the advance decision should be ignored. It is likely that a similar result would have been reached had the case been heard under the MCA. In *HE v A Hospital NHS Trust*[121] it was held that in the case of life-saving treatment, where it was unclear whether the advance decision was applicable, there should be a presumption

---

[118] MCA 2005, s 25(3).   [119] S 25(6).
[120] [2003] EWHC 1017 (Fam).   [121] [2003] EWHC 1017 (Fam).

in favour of life. There is no such explicit presumption in the MCA. However, a court may be reluctant to rely on an advance decision refusing life-saving treatment if there is any evidence that P has acted in a way which indicates that the refusal no longer represents her or his wishes.[122] Section 25(4), it must be admitted, is vague. Is a marriage, birth of a child, or a change in a religious behaviour inconsistent with a prior advance decision to refuse life-saving treatment? Another issue which is not clearly resolved is whether the behaviour of P after losing capacity can be behaviour inconsistent with an earlier advance decision.

It is also important to emphasize that the advance decision is only relevant if it specifies the treatment in question, or 'there are reasonable grounds for believing that circumstances exist which P did not anticipate at the time of the advance decision, and which would have affected his decision had he anticipated them'.[123] This means that advance decisions will have to be drafted with sufficient precision to cover the treatment in question. Further there will no doubt be challenges to advance decisions on the basis that patients had not anticipated important factors when they made them. In relation to advance decisions rejecting life-saving treatments, P needs to make a statement in the decision to the effect that the decision is to be respected even if her or his life is at risk.[124]

The MCA, section 26(1) explains:

If P has made an advance decision which is—

(a) valid, and

(b) applicable to the treatment,

the decision has the effect as if he had made it, and had had capacity to make it, at the time when the question arises whether the treatment should be carried out or continued.

This means that if P has a valid and applicable advance decision which rejects treatment, the medical professional should not provide it. If she or he does then there is the potential for a criminal or tortious action. However under section 26(2): 'A person does not incur liability for carrying out or continuing the treatment unless, at the time, he is satisfied that an advance decision exists which is valid and applicable to the treatment.' Section 26(3) in similar terms provides a defence to someone who withdraws or withholds treatment believing (incorrectly) that there is a valid advance decision requiring this. Notably both these defences appear to be in subjective terms. In other words if the professional provides treatment believing there to be no advance decision she or he would not face legal consequences, even though it would have been easy for them to find out about the decision.[125] It might be argued that doctors should be required to take reasonable steps to find out whether there was an effective advance decision. Parliament clearly decided that that could be too onerous an obligation on medical staff. If there are doubts over the validity or applicability of an advance decision, an application to court can be made for a declaration.[126]

It should be emphasized again that an advance decision cannot permit a medical professional to do an act which would hasten the death of P. Nor can the advance decision

---

[122] However, see Michalowski (2005) who argues the courts should not be too willing to overrule an advance directive refusing life saving treatment.

[123] MCA 2005, s 25(4).   [124] MCA 2005, s 25(5).

[125] Michalowski (2005) is concerned that this provision gives inadequate protection to the right to refuse treatment by means of an advance directive.

[126] MCA 2005, s 26(5).

prevent a medical professional giving treatment which is permitted under Part IV of the Mental Health Act 1983, even without the consent of the patient. We will consider this in Chapter 10, but in very broad terms, this covers treatment for a mental disorder which is necessary for the protection of the patient or other people.

In the Law Commission's draft of the Bill[127] there would have been a presumption that an advance decision refusing life-saving treatment would not apply if P was pregnant with a viable foetus. There is no such provision in the Act. However, if the advance decision is not explicit, then a court might be tempted to conclude that 'there are reasonable grounds for believing that circumstances exist which P did not anticipate at the time of the advance decision and which would have affected [her] decision had [she] anticipated them'.[128] In other words when creating the advance decision she did not consider whether she wanted it to apply if she were pregnant. If the advance decision makes it clear that it is to apply whether or not P is pregnant then this argument would not be available and the directive, if valid, would need to be applied.

8.2 Lasting powers of attorney

If someone wants someone else to make decisions on their behalf when they become incompetent they can make a lasting power of attorney (LPA) under the MCA, section 9.[129] The donee or donees of the LPA can make decisions for general matters relating to someone's welfare, including some medical decisions. In order to execute an LPA the person (P) must be over 18 years old and have capacity to do so.[130] There are strict regulations as to the formalities surrounding the LPA and its registration. These are set out in the MCA, Schedule 1. If they are not complied with the LPA will be ineffective.

The donee of the LPA must be over 18. It is possible to appoint more than one LPA. Unless the LPA says so, where more than one donee is appointed, they are to act jointly.[131] In other words all of them must agree on the decision in question before using the LPA. An LPA can be revoked at any time if P has the capacity to do so.[132]

Where an LPA has been validly appointed and the donee has the power to make decisions about P's personal welfare, then this can extend to giving or refusing the carrying out of health care. However, this is subject to an important restriction in that the donee must make the decision based on what would be in P's best interests, as described in section 4 (which will be discussed below). Donees of LPAs may be reassured that if they reasonably believe that their decision will promote P's best interests, but a court subsequently concludes that it did not, they will not face legal actions in tort or the criminal law.[133] Under section 11(8) the LPA has no power to 'authorise the giving or refusal of consent to the carrying out or continuation of life-sustaining treatment, unless the instrument contains specific provision to that effect'. So if P wants her or his donee to be able to refuse to consent to life-sustaining treatment the LPA must specifically state this.

The concept of an LPA is not without difficulty. First, there is substantial evidence to indicate that people are very bad at predicting what decisions another person would make.[134] This is so even where the people know each other very well. So people may be

---

[127] Law Commission Report 231 (1995: para 5.26).
[128] MCA 2005, s 25(4).   [129] See also Department of Constitutional Affairs (DCA) (2007: Chap 7).
[130] MCA 2005, s 9.   [131] MCA 2005, s 9(5).   [132] MCA 2005, s 13(2).
[133] MCA 2005, s 4(9).   [134] The evidence is discussed and summarized in Wrigley (2007).

mistaken if they think that appointing a good friend or partner will mean that the decisions they would have taken will be repeated. Second, it is important to note that the donee of the power of attorney does not have the role they might think they have. They cannot simply ask themselves 'what decision would X have made'; rather they must make the decision which is in the best interests of the individual. It is not clear that donors and donees of LPAs will appreciate that this distinction could be significant in a case where what the donor would have decided would be something against their best interests.

8.3 Deputies

Under section 16 if P lacks capacity in relation to a matter concerning her or his personal welfare (eg a health issue) then the court can make the decision on P's behalf, or decide to appoint a deputy to make decisions on P's behalf. In deciding whether to appoint a deputy the court should consider whether to do so would be in P's best interests (considering the factors in section 4 which we shall be looking at shortly) and also the following principles:

(a) a decision by the court is to be preferred to the appointment of a deputy to make a decision; and

(b) the powers conferred on a deputy should be as limited in scope and duration as is reasonably practicable in the circumstances.

This suggests that where there is a 'one-off' decision to be made about P it is unlikely to be appropriate to appoint a deputy. Where decisions need to be made about P on a regular basis then a deputy may be more suitable. A deputy must be over the age of 18 and have consented to take on the role.[135] The court can appoint more than one deputy. The court can revoke the appointment of a deputy.[136]

A deputy has the power to give or refuse consent to medical treatment.[137] However, the deputy has no authority to act if 'he knows or has reasonable grounds for believing that P has capacity in relation to the matter'.[138] A further important restriction is that 'a deputy may not refuse to consent to the carrying out or continuation of life-sustaining treatment in relation to P'.[139] The deputy is required to act in accordance with the best interests of the patient as set out in section 4.[140]

8.4 Court decision based on best interests

An application can be made to court in respect of any person who lacks capacity. The court can make a declaration as to the lawfulness of any act concerning the individual. The decision will be made based on what is in the best interests of the patient, as that is understood under section 4.

8.5 The best interests of the person

If an advance decision is valid and applicable, it must be respected; the issue of what is in P's best interests does not arise. However, where a court or donee of an LPA or deputy

---

[135] MCA 2005, s 19.   [136] MCA 2005, s 16(8).   [137] MCA 2005, s 16.
[138] MCA 2005, s 20(1).   [139] MCA 2005, s 20(5).
[140] MCA 2005, s 4(9) offers her or him protection from legal consequences if he reasonably, but wrongly, makes a decision which she or he believes is in the patient's best interests.

or a person caring for or providing treatment to P is making a decision concerning P, the decision must be made based on what is in P's best interests.[141] Section 1(6) emphasizes that:

> Before the act, is done, or decision is made, regard must be had to whether the purpose for which it is needed can be effectively achieved in a way that is less restrictive of the person's rights and freedom of action.

So whenever a decision is being made about an incompetent patient it is not enough just to show that the action is in P's best interests; it must be shown there is not an equally good way of promoting P's interests which is less invasive of her or his rights or freedom.

The MCA, section 4 states that, in deciding what is in a patient's best interests, the court or deputy must consider all the relevant circumstances, including the following factors:

(i) '(a) whether it is likely that the person will at some time have capacity in relation to the matter in question, and (b) if it appears likely that he will, when that is likely to be.'[142] Clearly if the person is soon to regain capacity it may be better, if possible, to postpone making a decision so she or he can make it for her or himself.

(ii) The decision maker must 'so far as reasonably practicable, permit and encourage the person to participate, or to improve his ability to participate, as fully as possible in any act done for him and any decision affecting him'.[143] This is a recognition that even if it is not possible for the person to make a decision for her or himself, she or he should still be involved to a reasonable extent in the decision-making process and her or his views listened to.

(iii) The decision maker must consider, so far as is reasonably ascertainable: '(a) the person's past and present wishes and feelings (and, in particular, any relevant written statement made by him when he had capacity), (b) the beliefs and values that would be likely to influence his decision if he had capacity, and (c) the other factors that he would be likely to consider if he were able to do so.'[144] It should be emphasized that the MCA does not adopt a substituted judgment test (see page 181 below). In other words it does not require decision makers to make their decision based on what they guess the person would have decided if she or he had been competent. However, as these factors make clear, the views of the person while competent and assessment of what decision she or he would have made if competent can be taken into account in deciding what are in her or his best interests. In *Ashan v Universities Hospital Leicester*[145] a dispute arose in the context of a tort case over the care of a Muslim woman who had been seriously injured and was unaware of what has happening to her. Her family wanted her to be cared for in accordance with the Muslim tradition, but this would be more expensive than other care. The defendant argued that, as she had no awareness of what was happening to her, it was not in her best interests to receive Muslim care. This was firmly rejected by Hegarty J:

> I do not think for one moment that a reasonable member of the public would consider that the religious beliefs of an individual and her family should simply be disregarded

---

[141] MCA 2005, s 1(5).   [142] MCA 2005, s 4(3).   [143] MCA 2005, s 4(4).
[144] MCA 2005, s 4(6). See Miola (2007: Chap 6) who argues that simply requiring that these factors be taken into account offers little guidance or control for the decision maker.
[145] [2006] EWHC 2624 (QB).

in deciding how she should be cared for in the unhappy event of supervening mental incapacity. On the contrary, I would have thought that most reasonable people would expect, in the event of some catastrophe of that kind, that they would be cared for, as far as practicable, in such a way as to ensure that they were treated with due regard for their personal dignity and with proper respect for their religious beliefs.

(iv) The decision maker should, if practical and appropriate, consider the views of: '(a) anyone named by the person as someone to be consulted on the matter in question or on matters of that kind, (b) anyone engaged in caring for the person or interested in his welfare, (c) any donee of a lasting power of attorney granted by the person, and (d) any deputy appointed for the person by the court, as to what would be in the patients best interests.' The decision maker may choose to consult a wider group of people than this, but is not required to do so.[146] It is unclear how much weight should be placed on the views of a family. If P's family are all Jehovah's Witnesses and oppose the required blood transfusion should their views carry the day? Probably not; the views of family members are only one factor and in such a case it would hard to see P's death as in P's best interests, as that term is generally understood in society. In *A Local Authority v E and others*[147] it was held that although there is no presumption that a person lacking capacity is better off cared for by their family than an in institution, 'nevertheless the normal assumption that mentally incapacitated adults who have been looked after within their family will be better off if they continue to be looked after within the family rather than by the state'.[148]

There are two factors which the decision maker should not take into account:

(i) A decision as to what is in a person's best interests should not be made merely on the basis of: '(a) the person's age or appearance, or (b) a condition of his, or an aspect of his behaviour, which might lead others to make unjustified assumptions about what might be in his best interests.' This might be most relevant in combating assumptions about older people and what is best for them.

(ii) Section 4(5) states: 'Where the determination relates to life-sustaining treatment [the decision maker] must not, in considering whether the treatment is in the best interests of the person concerned, be motivated by a desire to bring about his death.'[149] Life-sustaining treatment is defined as 'treatment which in the view of the person providing the health care for the person concerned is necessary to sustain life'. Section 4(5) is in line generally with the law relating to end of life decisions, namely that a medical professional should not do an act intending that the person die. However, it extends it to the withholding or withdrawing of treatment. Notably by referring to motive, rather than intention, it is made clear that withdrawing treatment which it is foreseen will lead to death, but is not motivated by the desire to produce death, is permitted. John Coggon, in criticizing this provision, argues that where a doctor is providing what is regarded as appropriate treatment it should be irrelevant what his or her intention is.[150] Perhaps with such concerns in mind the Code of Practice states:

> Importantly, section 4(5) cannot be interpreted to mean that doctors are under an obligation to provide, or to continue to provide, life-sustaining treatment where that treatment is not in the best interests of the person, even where the person's death is foreseen.[151]

---

[146] DCA (2007: para 4.23).   [147] [2007] EWHC 2396 (Fam).   [148] Para 66.
[149] Coggon (2006) provides a useful discussion of the provision.
[150] Coggon (2006).   [151] DCA (2007: para 5.33).

The section 4 factors have been described as 'open ended' and 'quite broad'.[152] This is probably inevitable. People, their circumstances, their families and beliefs are so different that it would be difficult to produce a more concrete list that would not lead to undesirable results in some cases. However, the looseness of the definition of best interests means it will be very difficult to challenge a decision maker's determination as to what is in P's best interests.

Several cases prior to the implementation of the Act have recommended that judges adopt a 'balance sheet'[153] whereby all the factors for and against the proposed order are listed. These are weighed up to decide what is in a patient's best interests. The Code of Practice states:

> When working out what is in the best interests of the person who lacks capacity to make a decision or act for themselves, decision makers must take into account all relevant factors that it would be reasonable to consider, not just those that they think are important. They must not act or make a decision based on what they would want to do if they were the person who lacked capacity.[154]

Where an incompetent patient is opposing treatment, articles 3 and 8 of the European Convention may become relevant. These require the state to protect the patient from torture or inhuman or degrading treatment. In *Herczegfalvy v Austria*[155] the European Court held: 'as a general rule, treatment which is a therapeutic necessity cannot be regarded as inhuman or degrading. The court must nevertheless satisfy itself that the medical necessity has been convincingly shown to exist'.

This indicates that as long as the treatment is necessary and therapeutic it will not infringe article 3. However, in *R (on the application of N) v Dr M, A NHS Trust and Dr O*[156] it was explained that to force medical treatment on an incompetent patient therefore contravenes article 3 unless it was convincingly shown that the treatment was a medical necessity. Simply to show that there was a responsible body of medical opinion in favour of the medical treatment would be insufficient.

The vagueness of the criteria might also lead to a challenge under the Human Rights Act 1998. In *Kawka v Poland*,[157] which considered the circumstances in which an incompetent person can be deprived of their liberty, the European Court emphasized that the criteria for deprivation needed to be clearly defined and foreseeable in application. The European Court in *HL v UK*[158] emphasized the need for substantive criteria to justify an infringement of article 5. However, as already mentioned, it is difficult to imagine that a more concrete appropriate law could be devised. The MCA has certainly given the concept of 'best interests' a clearer meaning than it had under the common law.

In applying the best interests test it should not be thought that this will mean that it is always in a patient's best interests to receive life-saving treatment. *In R (on the application of Burke) v GMC* the Court of Appeal explained:

> The courts have accepted that where life involves an extreme degree of pain, discomfort or indignity to a patient, who is sentient but not competent and who has manifested no wish to be kept alive, these circumstances may absolve the doctors of the positive duty to keep the patient alive. Equally the courts have recognised that there may be no duty

---

152 Bartlett (2005: 35–6).
153 Eg *A Local Authority v E and others* [2007] EWHC 2396 (Fam).   154 DCA (2007: para 5.7).
155 50 EHRR 437, at para 82.   156 [2002] EWHC 1911.
157 [2001] ECHR 4.   158 (2005) EHRR 32, para 124.

to keep alive a patient who is in a persistent vegetative state ('PVS'). In each of these examples the facts of the individual case may make it difficult to decide whether the duty to keep the patient alive persists.[159]

The Court of Appeal rejected the view that it would only be in a patient's best interests to withdraw life-sustaining treatment if the patient's life was intolerable. It was simply a question of what was in the best interests of the patient. It also made clear that if a doctor is unsure about the legality of withdrawing life-sustaining treatment a court declaration can be sought, but there is no obligation on her or him to do so. Where a patient is in persistent vegetative state it is good practice, but not obligatory.[160]

One issue is whether it can be said to be in a patient's best interests to act in a way which is primarily designed to help another. It may be thought that it cannot. But the following case indicates that there are ways of finding such altruistic behaviour to be in P's best interests:

KEY CASE   Re Y (Mental Patient: Bone Marrow Donation) [1997] 2 FCR 172

Y (aged 25) was severely mentally and physically handicapped. She lived in a community home but was regularly visited by her mother. Y's sister suffered from a bone disorder and her only real prospect of recovery was a bone marrow donation. Y was in medical terms a suitable donor but due to her disabilities was unable to consent. The sister sought a declaration authorizing the harvesting of bone marrow.

Connell J granted the declaration. The basis of the reasoning was that by making the donation to her sister this would benefit Y's mother who was very important to Y's well-being. Y's mother was in ill-health, partly due to anxiety concerning the sister's state of health. There was some evidence that if the sister were to die this would be fatal to the mother. If she were to die this would severely distress Y. Also it was held that Y would receive an emotional, psychological, and social benefit from the operation. Justice Connell indicated that the fact that the operation required Y to suffer only a 'minimal detriment' was an important aspect of the decision to authorize the harvesting.

Indeed it has been argued that it is not in a patient's interest to live in a relationship in which no account is taken of the interests of their carer, especially where that carer is a member of their family. Few people would be happy with the idea that if they were to fall incompetent a decision would have to be made if it benefited them a little bit, even if that caused grave harm to the person caring for them.[161]

8.6 Independent mental capacity advocates

The MCA, section 35 creates the post of independent mental health advocates (IMHAs). IHMAs will be created by health authorities. Their functions will be governed by detailed regulations.[162] Their role is set out in section 36. They are to be used where there is no person other than a professional carer who it would be appropriate to consult

[159] [2005] 3 FCR 169, para 33.
[160] *R (on the application of Burke) v GMC* [2005] 3 FCR 169, para 80.
[161] Herring (2008). See also the discussion in DCA (2007: Chap 5)
[162] These were not available at the time of writing.

concerning P's interests. It involves providing support to the person lacking capacity and ascertaining their wishes and feelings. They can ask for further medical opinions relating to the person and obtain other information. The regulations will provide that the advocates can challenge any medical decision made concerning a person lacking capacity. Under section 37 if it is proposed to provide 'serious medical treatment'[163] then an IHMA must be appointed to represent P, unless the treatment is required urgently.

9 Consent of children

9.1 Who can consent for the medical treatment of children

A child is any person under the age of 18.[164] As indicated above it could be both a tort or a criminal offence for a doctor to treat a child without 'the flak jacket of consent'. This 'flak jacket' can be provided by any of the following.

(i) A child aged 16 or 17

The Family Law Reform Act 1969, section 8 states that a child aged 16 or 17 can consent to 'treatment' and that such consent is to be treated in the same way an adult's consent would be. Treatment includes diagnosis and procedures ancillary to treatment (such as the administration of anaesthetics).[165] However, it may not cover every 'medical procedure'. Cosmetic surgery, tissue donation, or research are very unlikely to be classified as 'treatment'. If the procedure is not treatment 16- and 17-year-olds can consent if the can show they are 'Gillick competent',[166] a concept we shall discuss next.

(ii) A 'Gillick competent child'

If the child can show that she or he has sufficient maturity to make the decision in question then the child can provide legal consent for the medical procedure. Such a child is known as a 'Gillick competent child', after the decision in *Gillick v W Norfolk AHA*[167] which first acknowledged the notion of a competent child (the case is discussed in detail below). To be *Gillick* competent the child must have 'sufficient understanding and intelligence to enable him or her to understand fully what is proposed'.[168] If doctors or courts are deciding whether a child is competent they will consider the following points:

(a) The child must understand the medical issues. As with adults the child must understand the proposed treatment, the consequences of not having treatment, and the effect of treatment. This means the more complex the medical procedure the harder it will be for a child to show she or he is competent.[169] In *Re E*[170] a Jehovah's Witness child refused a blood transfusion. He was held to be incompetent because he did not understand the slow and painful process of his death were he not to receive the blood transfusion. A similar point has been made in several cases involving children refusing life-saving treatment.[171] These cases have been criticized on the basis that the children

---

[163] The phrase will be defined in the regulations.

[164] Family Law Reform Act 1969, s 1.   [165] Family Law Reform Act 1969, s 8(2).

[166] Family Law Reform Act 1969, s 8(3) explicitly preserves the common law on the consent of children.

[167] [1985] 3 All ER 402.   [168] At 423, per Lord Scarman.

[169] BMA and Law Society (2004:134).   [170] [1993] 1 FLR 386.   [171] *Re S* [1994] 2 FLR 1065.

have not known of the nature of their death because the doctors decided they would be too distressed to be told. To find a child not competent because she or he does not know information which doctors have decided not to provide is difficult to defend. As Montgomery puts it: 'it is the refusal of the adults to allow her to be informed that rendered her incompetent, not her ability to comprehend.'[172]

(b) The child must understand the 'moral and family' issues involved.[173] Although the courts have emphasized this the Department of Health's and British Medical Association's guidance do not mention the need for the child to be morally mature.[174] Perhaps it is assumed that if the child has the mental capacity to understand the medical issues involved she or he will also be aware of the key moral issues.

(c) The child need only have the maturity needed to consent to the particular issue in question. In other words a child may be mature enough to consent to a straightforward procedure, but not to consent to a far more complex one.[175]

(d) If the child is fluctuating between competence and incompetence she or he should be treated as incompetent.[176] The primary concern here is to ensure the law is workable. A hospital caring for a teenager who is competent to consent one moment, but incompetent the next would be in a difficult position if they had to continually assess the child every time there is a need to treat her or him.

(e) The court will need to be persuaded that the child is sufficiently mature to reach her or his own decision and not merely be repeating the views of her or his parents. This consideration has been particularly pertinent where the courts have felt that a child with a strict religious upbringing has not been made sufficiently aware of a variety of ways of understanding the world and so is not sufficiently competent.[177] In *Re S*,[178] for example, a 15-year-old Jehovah's Witness refused a blood transfusion. She was not, however, able to explain clearly why she objected to the transfusion. The court was not confident that she was sufficiently competent to make the decision for herself. In *Re L* an expert felt able to say that a 14-year-old Jehovah Witness's religious views were merely a reflection of her parents' and local church's, even though he had not actually seen the girl.

(f) In assessing whether a child is competent or not the court should not reason that because the decision is 'wrong' the child must be incompetent.[179]

It is not yet clear what the position would be if a doctor assessed a child as competent and performed treatment on her or him, but the court subsequently assessed her or him as incompetent. Kennedy has suggested that if a medical professional assessed a child as competent in good faith then the court would not hold the doctor to have committed a criminal offence.[180] It is less clear whether her or his wrong assessment would provide a defence in civil law. In cases involving adults a court has been willing to award damages where the professionals were found to have wrongly assessed a patient as incompetent.[181]

---

172 Montgomery (2003: 292)
173 At 424 (Lord Scarman). But see Montgomery (2003: 290) who is not persuaded that this is required.
174 DoH (2001c); BMA (2001).   175 *Re R* [1991] 4 All ER 177.
176 *Re R* [1991] 4 All ER 177.   177 *Re L* [1999] 2 FLR 1097.
178 [1993] 1 FLR 376.   179 *South Glamorgan CC v B* [1993] 1 FLR 574.
180 Kennedy (1991a: 107).   181 *St George's Healthcare Trust v S* [1998] 3 All ER 673.

(iii) *The consent of a person with parental responsibility for the child*

A person with parental responsibility can consent to treatment for her or his child. See page 137 for a list of who has parental responsibility.

(iv) *An order of the court*

A court can make an order authorizing medical treatment either under the Children Act 1989, section 8 or under its inherent jurisdiction. It would also be possible for the court to order that a certain kind of treatment not be given to a child. If an application is brought under either jurisdiction the court will make the order which best promotes the welfare of the child.[182]

(v) *The defence of necessity*

Where a child needs urgent medical treatment to avoid death or serious harm the doctor may perform that treatment even without the protection of a court order or parental consent. This is so in the case of life-saving treatment even if the parent objects.[183] However, the defence may only be available if there was not sufficient time to enable the doctor to get the consent of a parent or the court. It must be admitted that the doctrine of necessity is of uncertain scope. Whether it can be used to justify medical treatment for non-serious conditions is open to debate. For example, if a child in hospital cut a finger and a nurse wanted to put a plaster on the small cut must she or he first obtain the consent of the parents? And if the parents cannot be contacted must an application to court be made? Lavery has suggested that necessity can be used to justify routine medical treatment.[184] This would seem a sensible suggestion, although there is no clear judicial support for it.

(vi) *Children Act 1989, section 3(5)*

The Children Act 1989, section 3(5) states that a person with care of a child may do:

> what is reasonable in all the circumstances of the case for the purpose of safeguarding or promoting the child's welfare.

In *B v B*[185] it was suggested that this could include the power to consent to medical treatment. But the extent to which this is true is unclear. It may well cover someone putting a plaster on a minor cut, but most commentators take the view that the section cannot be used to authorize treatment to which a parent objects or major irreversible surgery.

9.2 Disagreements between the decision makers

9.2.1 *Doctors and parents or children*

It is important to appreciate that simply because a parent or competent child has consented to a treatment does not mean that the doctor must provide the treatment. So even though a doctor may decide that a child seeking cosmetic surgery is competent this does not mean that the doctor must provide that treatment.[186] A court cannot require

---

182 Children Act 1989, s 1.   183 Eg *Re O* [1993] 2 FLR 149.
184 Lavery (1990).   185 [1992] FLR 327.
186 See eg *Re R* [1991] 4 All ER 177 at 184; *Re C (Detention: Medical Treatment)* [1997] 2 FLR 180.

a doctor to treat a child in a way the doctor believed appropriate. However, if a medical team wish to perform an operation they need the consent of either the person with parental responsibility *or* a *Gillick* competent child. Failing either of these they need to apply for court authorization to do so, unless there is a medical emergency requiring an operation on the child and there is no time to apply to court.[187] It should be borne in mind that in an emergency it is normally possible to find a judge to hear a case within an hour. The court will make the order which will best promote the welfare of the child.

9.2.2 If the child and parents disagree

The approach taken by the Court of Appeal in *Re R*[188] and *Re W*[189] is that a doctor only needs one 'flak jacket' as protection from potential legal protection. This means a doctor can provide treatment in any of the following situations:

- The *Gillick* competent child consents, but the parents object.

- A parent with parental responsibility consents, but the *Gillick* competent child objects.[190]

- The court authorizes the treatment, despite the objections of parent and child.

If necessary a reasonable level of force can be used to ensure that the treatment is given to a child who is objecting.[191]

In a recent decision (*R (Axon) v Secretary of State for Health*)[192] Silber J suggested that once a child becomes *Gillick* competent the parent loses any right under the Human Rights Act 1998 to family life and to make any decisions for the child. It would be reading too much into this to conclude the courts will not follow *Re R*[193] and *Re W*,[194] but it suggests that the courts are becoming more open to arguments based on the rights of children.[195]

The law as set out in *Re R* and *Re W* is highly contentious. It appears to fly in the face of children's rights. To take an extreme example, it would mean that if a competent pregnant 15-year-old did not want an abortion, but her parents did, the doctor could lawfully carry out the termination of the pregnancy. We shall return to these issues later in this chapter. But it should be noted that what the law is saying is that a doctor may, not must, treat a child if a parent objects. In the scenario mentioned above, it is extremely unlikely that a doctor would be willing to perform an operation on a non-consenting teenager. So, in practice it may be that the concerns that children's rights will be readily overridden are overstated.[196] Indeed, if a parent can be said to be exercising parental responsibility in a way which positively harms the child then arguably it is ineffective. We shall return to the ethical issues raised here later in this chapter.

---

[187] *Glass v UK* [2004] 1 FCR 553 and *Royal Wolverhampton Hospitals NHS Trust v E and RB* [2000] 1 FLR 953.

[188] *Re R* [1991] 4 All ER 177.   [189] [1992] 4 All ER 627.

[190] The Court of Appeal makes it so clear that this is the law that in *Northamptonshire HA v Official Solicitor and Governors of St Andrew's Hospital* [1994] 1 FLR 162 it awarded costs against a local authority which sought court approval for treating a child who objected to treatment, but whose parents consented. It was so clear that the local authority could rely on the parental consent that the application for a court order was unnecessary.

[191] *Re C (Detention: Medical Treatment)* [1997] 2 FLR 180.

[192] [2006] EWHC 37 (Admin).   [193] *Re R* [1991] 4 All ER 177.

[194] [1992] 4 All ER 627.   [195] Taylor (2007).

[196] For a discussion of whether this position can be challenged under the Human Rights Act see Michalowski (2001).

9.2.3 *If the parents disagree*

The Children Act 1989, section 2(7) implies that one parent with parental responsibility can act alone and consent to treatment, without consulting or having to reach an agreement with the other parent. However, the courts have stated that in relation to important issues parents must consult. It is not clear precisely what issues might be regarded as important issues. In *Re J* [197] it was held that circumcision was one such issue, as was the decision not to give a child the MMR vaccine in *Re B*.[198] No doubt, abortion and cosmetic surgery would also be included. What these cases indicate is that parents with parental responsibility should consult, and if they are unable to reach an agreement an application should be made to the court to determine the issue.[199]

9.2.4 *Where the courts and parents disagree*

If there is a dispute over the correct medical treatment for the child then the court must simply decide what is in the best interests of the child.[200] The court can override the views of the child and/or parent if they do not accord with the welfare of the child.[201] As Ward J has put it:

> Parents may be free to become martyrs themselves, but it does not follow that they are free in identical circumstances to make martyrs of their children.[202]

In cases where the welfare decision is very finely balanced the court may decide that the parental views tip the balance in favour of making the order they are seeking.[203] However a court will not compel a doctor to act in a way which is against their clinical judgment.[204] In *The NHS Trust v A*[205] Holman J summarized the law's approach to taking into account the views of parents:

> The views and opinions of both the doctors and the parents must be carefully considered. Where, as in this case, the parents spend a great deal of time with their child, their views may have particular value because they know the patient and how he reacts so well; although the court needs to be mindful that the views of any parents may, very understandably, be coloured by their own emotion or sentiment. It is important to stress that the reference is to the views and opinions of the parents. Their own wishes, however understandable in human terms, are wholly irrelevant to consideration of the objective best interests of the child save to the extent in any given case that they may illuminate the quality and value to the child of the child/parent relationship.[206]

9.3 Limits on parental consent

Are there some medical procedures that cannot be consented to by a parent? It appears that there are some procedures which cannot be performed on children without court approval. Unfortunately there is very little guidance on the issue. It has been suggested

---

197 [2000] 1 FLR 571.   198 [2003] EWCA 1148.

199 The application would be under Children Act 1989, s 8.

200 Children Act 1989, s 1.   201 See eg *Re C (A Child) (HIV Testing)* [2000] Fam 48.

202 *Re E* [1993] 1 FLR 386.

203 This may be the explanation for *Re T (A Minor) (Wardship: Medical Treatment)* [1997] 1 WLR 424.

204 *R (on the application of Burke) v GMC* [2005] 3 FCR 169.

205 [2007] EWHC 1696 (Fam).   206 Para 40.

that the following may be operations which require the consent of the court:

* Sterilizations carried out for non-therapeutic reasons.[207]

* Refusal of life-saving treatment. If a parent refuses to consent to life-saving treatment it has been argued that the doctor should obtain court approval before following the parent's views.[208]

* Abortion.[209]

* Donation of non-regenerative tissue.[210]

In the absence of a clear legal ruling, if a doctor is unsure about the advisability of an operation, court approval should be sought. This might be so in a case where controversial cosmetic surgery is sought.

10 Treatment which cannot be consented to

There are two important points to make here. First, it is often emphasized that simply because a competent patient wants treatment does not mean that she or he has a right to it.[211] A doctor is at liberty to refuse to provide a treatment however keenly the patient wants it.[212] It has been said that courts will not force medical professionals to provide treatment they do not want to provide.[213] Such a view might be open to challenge under the Human Rights Act.[214] We discussed this issue in Chapter 2.

Second, even though a patient and a doctor agree on a form of surgery the law may prohibit the operation. There may be some public policy objection to a proposed procedure which would render it illegal. The leading case on this is *R v Brown*[215] where the House of Lords held that it was unlawful to cause someone actual bodily harm, or more serious injury, unless there was a public policy argument in favour of the conduct, even if the 'victim' was consenting. In that case a group of men were convicted of criminal offences of violence even though their 'victims' had willingly consented to the actions as part of a sado-masochistic encounter. Clearly, in most cases of orthodox medical treatment there will be no difficulty in showing that a particular treatment was in the public interest.[216] However, if a modern artist asked a doctor to cut off her leg so that she could use it in a new exhibit, it would probably be illegal for a doctor to perform the amputation. The issue very much turns on current social attitudes. There is now little doubt that sterilization operations,[217] sex change operations,[218] organ transplants,[219] and circumcision of males are lawful.[220] Less clear

---

[207] *Re B* [1987] 2 All ER 206, 214 (Lord Templeman).
[208] Bevan (1989: 25–6).
[209] *Re P (A Minor)* (1982) 8 LGR 301.
[210] *Re F* [1989] 2 FLR 376, at 390 (Lord Donnaldson MR) and at 440 (Neill LJ).
[211] MacLean (2001).
[212] *Re J (A Minor) (Wardship: Medical Treatment)* [1990] 3 All ER 930.
[213] *Re C (A Minor)* [1998] LL Rep Med 1.   [214] MacLean (2001).
[215] [1993] 2 All ER 75.   [216] *R v Brown* [1993] 2 All ER 75, 109–10.
[217] *Gold v Haringey HA* [1987] 2 All ER 888.   [218] Gender Recognition Act 2004.
[219] Human Organ Transplants 1989.
[220] *Re J* [2000] 1 FCR 305. Circumcision of females is prohibited by the Female Genital Mutilation Act 2003.

is the following:

TO PONDER

Consider the following case referred to in BMA and Law Society (2004: 94). If the doctors had operated would they have committed an offence?

In 2000, 55-year-old Gregg Furth, a psychoanalyst from New York, travelled to the UK to see psychiatrists and the surgeon who had previously amputated the healthy legs of two men with body dysmorphic disorder. Since before he was ten years old, Mr Furth could recall feeling that the lower part of his right leg was not part of his body. Since then he constantly thought about being without that part of his leg and had searched for many years to find a surgeon willing to amputate it. Mr Furth had undergone many years of therapy but had not been able to repress the feelings he had about his leg. He was assessed by two psychiatrists in the UK, both of whom confirmed that he was competent to make the decision and was suffering from body dysmorphic disorder. Both psychiatrists recommended him for amputation and the surgeon agreed to carry out the procedure. Shortly before the operation was due to take place, however, the hospital withdrew its permission for any more operations of this type to be undertaken on its premises.[221]

11 Ethics and autonomy

For many medical ethicists autonomy has become the most fundamental ethical principle in the medical arena. For too long patients have been treated by medical professionals as 'objects to be mended'. By emphasizing the principle of autonomy we can move from a 'doctor knows best' perspective to an approach which recognizes the rights of the patient.[222] After all it is the patient's body, even if the doctor does know best. The emphasis on patients' rights may have been fuelled by the decrease in trust in the medical profession.[223] In recent years there have been a growing body of writing concerned by the pre-eminence of autonomy in medical ethics. There are some who, while recognizing the importance of autonomy, claim that it should not block out consideration of other important values. There are others who argue that, although autonomy is important, the concept of autonomy traditionally used by commentators is an inappropriate one and alternative ways of understanding autonomy have been proposed.

Before looking at the views of those troubled by the pre-eminence of autonomy it is useful to expound the principle of autonomy and why it is valued:

11.1 The importance of autonomy

In 1914 the highly respected American judge, Cardozo J, recognized the importance of autonomy:[224]

> Every human being of adult years and sound mind has a right to determine what shall be done with his own body; and a surgeon who performs an operation without his patient's consent, commits an assault.

---

221 See further Schramme (2007) who discusses the legality of 'extreme bodily modification'.
222 P. Foster (1998).   223 See Chap 1.
224 *Schloendorff v New York Hospital* (1914) 105 NE 92.

However, much as the medical profession might believe a procedure to be in a patient's best interests, or even may be morally required of a patient, it is still seen as morally wrong to force that treatment on the patient. It must be that patient's choice to receive the treatment. Professor Kennedy[225] has put the point eloquently:

> if the beliefs and values of the patient, though incomprehensible to others, are of long standing and have formed the basis for all the patient's decisions about his life, there is a strong argument to suggest that the doctor should respect and give effect to a patient's decision based on them.... To argue otherwise would effectively be to rob the a patient of his right to his own personality which may be far more serious and destructive than anything that could follow from the patient's decision as regards a particular proposed treatment.

It is also perhaps notable that the rise of autonomy has been matched with a lack of confidence about declaring what is or is not in a person's best interests. With an increasing lack of trust in medical expertise and a breakdown in agreed moral values it has become highly controversial to declare what is or is not in a patient's interests. To replace such paternalism with an assessment of what the patient consents to avoids controversial judgments.[226] Hence we have the 'triumph of autonomy'.[227]

Supporters of autonomy emphasize the value that each of us puts on being in control of our destiny and being able to decide how to live out our version of the 'good life'.[228] One person may want to dedicate their life to the watching of football and the drinking of beer. To others that may be a bad way of life, but we must respect each person's decision as to how they wish to live their life, unless that causes harm to others. The idea of someone else coming along and telling you what to do with your life, and how to live, is repellent to most people.

11.2 Challenges to the pre-eminence of autonomy

We should start by emphasizing that nowadays few people reject the importance of autonomy. The dispute is over whether it should be the sole or primary ethical principle governing medical ethics.

A number of challenges have been made to the paramountcy of autonomy. First, some critics have suggested that it should not be held that all autonomous decisions demand respect. John Keown argues:[229]

> The capacity to choose brings with it the responsibility of making not just any old choice, but choices that do in fact promote, rather than undermine, human flourishing. Given the legitimate diversity of lifestyles and life-choices which are consistent with human flourishing, many choices are consistent with human well-being. We should, therefore, think carefully before restricting another's autonomy. But it is difficult to see why patently immoral choices, choices clearly inconsistent with human well-being, merit any respect. In other words, an exercise of autonomy merits respect only when it is exercised in accordance with a framework of sound moral values.

Supporters of autonomy would reply that the difficulty with such an argument is in identifying what decisions are 'consistent with human flourishing'. This has a different

---

[225] Kennedy (1991a: 56). [226] Bailey-Harris (2000).
[227] Beauchamp and Childress (2003: 61). [228] See further Chap 1.
[229] Keown (2002: 53). See West (1985) for a similar argument from a feminist perspective.

meaning for different people. Some people might say train spotting is inconsistent with that aim, but it is an activity greatly valued by some. Should we not leave each person to work out their own version of human flourishing? On the other hand does Keown not have a point: just because a decision is made autonomously does not mean it is a valuable one deserving of great respect? Is the decision to spend a life reading pornography one deserving of respect? As Onora O'Neill has pointed out, letting people act out their autonomous wishes can lead to disastrous result.[230] Indeed it is notable that even those taking a strong autonomy-based line scrutinize very carefully the competency of a person who is wanting to make a decision which will cause a serious harm.[231]

A second challenge to the pre-eminence of autonomy is the argument that autonomy is very much a western, perhaps even north American way of looking at the world. The 'American dream' promotes the freedom of all individuals to seek the best for themselves. But other societies have placed great weight on co-operation and the pursuit of community goals. In other words there is a danger that we elevate an American value into a high ethical principle without regard to its cultural roots.[232] Indeed this point can be developed further. If you choose to live your life according to certain moral values and seek to live in a community which holds fast to certain principles, these will involve restrictions on your choice. There can therefore be a tension between retaining free choice and respecting autonomy (in the sense of building up a system of values to live by as part of your vision of the good life).[233]

A third challenge is that the emphasis on autonomy overlooks other important values.[234] There is a danger that autonomy ignores issues of obligations owed to others, the pursuit of community goals, notions of justice in health care decisions, and the importance of relationships in the lives of others. Some who make this suggestion have promoted the notion of 'relational autonomy', a concept that will be explored later.

A fourth challenge is to question to what extent health care decisions can be said to be autonomous. We shall consider the reality of 'consent giving' shortly, but there it will be noted that often patients are willing to agree to whatever is suggested by their expert doctor. 'Rituals of consent' have replaced true autonomous decision making, it is suggested.[235] A rather different point is that whether a patient consents or not may depend on a host of factors which do not reflect a real choice by them. In one study patients were offered two alternative treatments and were told of the percentages of people who survived the treatments; 18 per cent of people selected the first treatment. The same group were then offered the two treatments and were told the percentage of people who died (ie the same statistic just presented differently). This time 44 per cent of people selected the first treatment.[236] In other words, although it may appear that a patient is exercising their autonomy in fact the choice they make may be influenced by a host of external factors.

A fifth challenge follows from the point just made. Onora O'Neill suggests that what we really value in health care decisions is not the ability to make decisions for ourselves, but rather trust in our medical advisers.[237] Faced with the alternative of having a deceitful doctor advising you, but who left you with the ultimate decision as to the appropriate course or a trustworthy doctor who left you with no choice, which would you prefer? With this in mind she argues that trust is a more important value than autonomy in

---

230 O'Neill (2002: 20).
231 Flamme and Forster (2000). The view is rejected by Beauchamp and Childress (2003: 76).
232 Holm (1995).   233 Montgomery (2006).   234 McCall Smith (1997).
235 Tauber (2003: 484).   236 Schwab (2007).   237 O'Neill (2002); Sirrat and Gill (2005).

medical decision making. We need to be taking steps to reinforce trust between patient and doctor, rather than emphasize patient autonomy. But many might feel that we need both: both trust and respect of autonomy.

A final point is that although the right not to be touched without your consent is treasured in medical law, in other areas of law it is not regarded as a sacrosanct principle. For example it is possible to touch another without their consent in the following cases: intimate searches by police of suspects without their consent;[238] carrying out tests on people with certain infectious diseases;[239] and acts of violence in self defence or the prevention of crime. Does the fact the right to bodily integrity can be infringed in these cases but not the medical context show that the principle has been elevated to too high a pedestal in medical law? Or is it that in medical law there is (unlike these other areas) no higher value that trumps the right not to be touched without consent?

11.3 Alternative versions of autonomy: relational autonomy

In light of these criticisms some have argued that, rather than abandon autonomy, we need to find a new way of understanding it. One of the most popular is the notion of relational autonomy.[240] At the heart of this approach is a rejection of the idea that we live our lives as unconnected individuals. The traditional notion of autonomy promotes the concept of an isolated patient deciding for himself what is in his best interests (the image of 'the male in the prime of his life'[241]), whereas in fact we live lives based on inter-dependant relationships.[242] We need therefore to recognize that for most patients the question is not simply 'what is best for me?', but rather, 'given the responsibilities I owe to those in relationships with me and the responsibilities owed to me by others, what is the most appropriate course of action?'[243] We need a vision of autonomy that promotes the values of love, loyalty, friendship, and care.[244] We need to examine a patient's choice in light of the relationships within which they live and the feelings of worry, concern for others, and obligation that they may have.[245]

Some supporters of traditional autonomy argue that supporters of relational autonomy have misunderstood traditional liberal autonomy, and it was never intended as an individualistic concept. Indeed liberals accept that for many individuals the meaning of their lives is shaped by their relationships and communities.[246] However, there is a danger within relational autonomy that the wishes of the individual can be too easily overridden by the needs of their 'community'. Christman has argued:

> Just as conceiving of persons as denuded of social relations denies the importance of such relations to the self-understandings of many of us at various times in our lives, to define persons as necessarily related in particular ways similarly denies the reality of change over time, variability in self-conception, and multiplicities of identity characteristic of modern populations.[247]

In particular there is a concern that relational autonomy could be used to reinforce the traditional caring roles that women have played in our society or trap individuals into decisions prescribed by a culture to which they do not subscribe.[248]

---

[238] Police and Criminal Evidence Act 1984, s 55.
[239] Public Health (Control of Diseases) Act 1984, ss 35–6.
[240] Dochin (2001); Agich (2003).   [241] Dochin (2001).
[242] Herring (2000: 278).   [243] West (1997).   [244] Mackenzie and Stoljar (2000).
[245] Dodds (2000).   [246] Singer (1993).
[247] Christman (2004: 145). See also Tauber (2003).   [248] MacKinnon (1987).

11.4 Autonomy in practice

To some, although the theoretical case for emphasizing autonomy is strong, there are inevitable difficulties when the concept is put into practice. Following a diagnosis and suggestion of treatment very few patients will disagree with the proposal. Patients may consent but feel that they have no real choice. Those who are weaker, less articulate, or more malleable than others can have their autonomy 'used against them'. One sociologist has written of 'the modern clinical ritual of trust'[249] whereby a patient is given information about an operation to which a patient accedes with little understanding of what is proposed or even an appreciation that she or he has a choice. In other words, despite grand visions of autonomy, in practice, far from being an expression of a patient's image of the good life for themselves, consent is little more than a formality.

Further, there are real difficulties facing a medical professional who wants to ensure that her or his patient makes a truly knowledgeable choice about treatment. There are problems in explaining complex medical issues in terms comprehensible to a lay person. There is some research which suggests that patients remember or understand little of what they have agreed to,[250] even when extraordinary efforts are made to ensure that patients are adequately informed.[251] Understandably it is frustrating for a professional when a patient trying to decide about treatment becomes obsessed with an 'irrational fear' of a minute risk associated with a treatment. Not surprisingly (and arguably quite properly) medical professionals in such cases can put considerable pressure on patients to agree to treatment.[252] It should not be forgotten that we require medical professionals to deal with a large number of patients in a short space of time. There is often simply not the time to go through all the details and complex issues surrounding every treatment.[253] Some patients in the face of a large amount of information find it impossible to make a decision because they are unable to comprehend the nature of risks and to weigh them up.[254]

Some have pointed out the difficulty in deciding what a patient's true wishes are. Take *Re MB*[255] where due to a needle phobia a woman refused to consent to a Caesarean section which she wanted and was necessary in order to save her life and that of the baby. The Court of Appeal stated that to force the injection on her against her wishes would be to infringe her autonomy, although it was permissible in that case because she was not competent. But was this a correct classification of her wishes? The difficulty was that in that case she had contradictory wishes: to have the Caesarean section operation, but not to have the injection. To not give her the injection would respect one decision, but thwart the other. Indeed there is an argument that in such a case the court should seek to ascertain, between the two conflicting decisions, which is closer to the individual's sense of identity. In *Re MB* if such an approach was taken surely the desire to remain alive and give birth to a healthy baby was more important to her than the wish to avoid the prick of a needle.[256] The issue could be put in these terms: should her wishes and beliefs as experienced over a considerable time be given less weight than the momentary decision to reject the injection in a moment of anguish?

It should also be emphasized that a surprising number of patients do not want to make decisions about their medical treatment. They are happy for doctors to make decisions for them.[257] The emphasis on autonomy may therefore be one which does not

249 Wolpe (1998).   250 Cassileth et al (1980).   251 Schneider and Farrell (2000).
252 Culver and Gert (1982).   253 Tallis (2004: Chap 5).   254 Pierce (1993).
255 [1997] 2 FCR 541.   256 Herring (2000).   257 Schneider (1998).

accord with the attitudes of a large section of patients. As Schneider put it:

> While patients largely wish to be informed about their medical circumstances, a substantial number of them do not want to make their own medical decisions, or perhaps even to participate in those decisions in any very significant way.[258]

Childress and Beauchamp have responded to such an argument by saying that if a patient wants decisions about their medical care to be made by a family member or doctor this is a perfectly proper exercise of autonomy and needs to be respected like any other exercise of autonomy.[259]

A rather different concern about the emphasis on autonomy in practice is that now medical professionals must spend a considerable amount of time giving mini-seminars to patients on alternatives forms of treatment, and the risks associated with them. This is time which could, it is suggested by some, be better spent on treatment. It leads to patients being over-burdened with information they do not understand because doctors are in terror of being sued for failing to give patients sufficient information, although, as Jones has pointed out, doctors have only faced 30 reported cases involving non-provision of information in the 14 years since *Sidaway*, of which only seven were successful.[260] This suggests any fear of litigation is exaggerated.

Another practical concern is that patients are too readily found to be competent. One study found 50 patients in an acute medical ward to be mentally incapable of consenting to treatment, but only 12 of these cases were recognized as incompetent by the medical staff. This indicates that a significant number of patients are being treated as competent when in fact they are not, and this means that incompetent consent is being used to authorize their treatment.[261]

11.5 Informed consent: theoretical issues

To some commentators a case can only be made for giving pre-eminence to autonomy if we are strict about what consent is. To allow autonomy to triumph over principles of beneficence we need to be strict about what counts as consent. It must be a 'rich' understanding of the term: a fully informed and genuine choice, free from improper pressure.[262] If this is accepted there is a paradox here: the greater the weight attached to autonomy, the stricter the requirements for consent need to be, and so the fewer the number of people who are covered by the principle and therefore the more who are regarded as incompetent and treated on a paternalistic basis.

Many accept that given the importance attached to autonomy we should require doctors to ensure that their patients understand fully the issues surrounding medical treatment. Requiring simply that the patient says 'yes' or 'no' is a meaningless charade unless the 'yes' or 'no' is a reflection of a true expression of the patient's will, being aware of the important issues. The jargon often used is that we need to show that patient has given 'informed consent'.[263] There is no universal agreement as to its meaning, but it has been defined in the following way:

> An informed consent is that consent which is obtained after the patient has been adequately instructed about the ratio of risk and benefit involved in the procedure as compared to alternative procedures or none at all.

---

[258] Schneider (1998: xi).   [259] Childress and Beauchamp (2003: 63).
[260] Jones (1999).   [261] Raymont (2004).   [262] Herring (2000).
[263] For a useful discussion see Skegg (1999).

On the other hand there is a delicate balance here. It might be argued that the more information that is given to a patient the more likely it is that the patient will become confused and find it more and more difficult to make an effective decision. On the other hand too little information and the consent, with no real awareness of what is being proposed, can be regarded as ethically worthless.

There is perhaps a further issue here which is that medical decisions can be extremely difficult. The diagnosis of a condition may be uncertain and the outcome of an operation may be unknown. Especially with cutting edge medicine, a surgeon may be struggling to advise a patient on the basis of unreliable data. Understandably doctors in such cases may not want to tell the truth. 'We do not really know what is wrong with you and we are not sure whether this operation will work' is hardly likely to generate consent from the patient or inspire confidence.[264]

Onora O'Neill has suggested that the best reason for requiring informed consent is that it provides patients with protection against being deceived or coerced.[265] She rejects the idea that requiring informed consent should be about protecting people's right to autonomy. She argues:

> Informed consent procedures protect choices that are timid, conventional, and lacking in individual autonomy (variously conceived) just as much as they protect choices that are self assertive, self knowing, critically reflective, and bursting with individual autonomy (variously conceived).[266]

The significance of this approach is revealed when we consider a patient who tells her or his doctor that she or he does not want to know all the details of the operation, but only the barest outline, and that she or he does not want to know about all the things that could go wrong. In such a case a traditional approach to informed consent may suggest that the fact she or he is not aware of all of the key issues surrounding the treatment means that she or he is not sufficiently informed and therefore there is no consent. However, on O'Neill's approach, as she or he has not been deceived or coerced there can said to be a valid consent. She also makes the point that requiring a patient to understand all of the key factors may not be what the patient wants. As she points out, often people are too mentally impaired or confused to understand treatment and 'even in the maturity of our faculties we may find it quite taxing to give informed consent to complex medical treatment when feeling lousy'.[267]

 FEMINIST PERSPECTIVE

Consent

Feminist writers on consent have tended to fall into one of three camps, although many feminists see strengths in all three positions (see Tong (1996)).

First, there are those who greatly welcome the emphasis on autonomy, believing that in the past women were too easily seen as subject to the paternalistic power of medicine (Jackson (2001: Chapter 1)). Women were regarded as incapable of making decisions for themselves

---

[264] Schneider (1998).

[265] O'Neill (2003). Although see Sokol (2006) for a discussion of how difficult it can be to define deception in this context.

[266] O'Neill (2003).   [267] O'Neill (2003).

and wise doctors were needed to make decisions for them. Autonomy should therefore be welcomed as giving women a voice in their treatment and providing them with power in the medical context.

Second, many of those supporting the notion of 'relational autonomy' mentioned above have
written from a feminist perspective (Sherwin (1998); Mackenzie and Stoljar (2000)). Traditional
visions of autonomy have been seen as 'masculine' by emphasizing values of independence and
self-sufficiency that are alien to the lives of many women (Fineman (2004)). By contrast the
emphasis that relational autonomy places on the values of relationship, care, and interdependence reflects the values that matter to many women.

Thirdly, there are feminists who feel that both of the positions mentioned so far fail to recognize the social context within which women make medical decisions (Oshana (1998)). The
oppressive circumstances of women's lives and the social expectations placed on women can
lead them to make sacrificial decisions. Until there is greater equality between men and women
there is a danger that women's autonomy will be used against them.

12 Ethics and best interests

As we have seen, if a patient is incompetent to make a medical decision, the key principle
is that the medical team must act in the patient's best interests. At first sight this may
seem such an obviously sensible approach that it is difficult to disagree with it, and that
even if one did there are few effective alternatives. However, as we shall see, the issue is
not as straightforward as may at first appear.

12.1 Criticisms of the best interests principle

There are a number of criticisms of the best interests principle. Many centre around the
vagueness which surrounds the concept of best interests. It has been described as 'empty
rhetoric'.[268] Specifically concerns have been expressed that the phrase is so vague that it
can mean whatever one wants it to mean. The judge or medical professional can declare
treatment to be in a patient's best interests, with that being no more than a reflection
of one person's views. Supporters of the best interests standard might accept that there
is an element of subjective evaluation in the assessment, but argue that in fact there is
widespread agreement about what are the good things in life. Although there are cases
where what is in a patient's best interests may be contested, those are rare and are likely
to be difficult cases whatever standard is used.

There is also some debate over whether the best interests standard should take into
account the values and principles of the individual person. If a health care team is dealing with an incompetent Jehovah's Witness would it be correct to say that for that person
it is in their best interests not to receive a life-saving blood transfusion? Or should our
assessment of best interests be objective and take no account of the particular characteristics of the individual?

Some have criticized the best interests principle for being unduly individualistic. When
making decisions for an incompetent person is it not permissible to take any account of
the interests of the incompetent person's relatives and family? What should happen if a

---

[268] Kennedy (1991a: 90).

relative of an incompetent patient will die without blood or even a kidney taken from the patient? The law's best interests principle would appear to suggest that such acts of altruism should not be forced on an incompetent person.[269] However, as was indicated in *Re Y (Adult Patient) (Transplant: Bone Marrow)*[270] (discussed at page 165), it could be lawful under the best interests principle if it is possible to find a tangible benefit from the sacrifice, for example, if the patient has a close relationship with the individual in need of the donation). More controversially it might be argued that, even if the patient does not have a close relationship with the relative, if the 'donation' means the patient will receive more care and attention from her family, because they are grateful for the sacrifice she or he has made and feel an increased obligation towards her, this could be said to be in her or his best interests. It is unlikely that a claim that such a donation will increase her or his standing within her or his community or family (if that produces no tangible benefit) would be sufficient. Similarly arguments that the incompetent patient is benefiting from a family or society that values and promotes altruism and so the patient should play their part in such a giving and taking if they are able to, is likely to be regarded as too remote.[271] John Robertson has suggested that as altruism is widely practised in our society and something that people find valuable and rewarding,[272] we can assume that altruism is beneficial to people generally and therefore to the incompetent person. But is it, in fact, true that altruism in the medical context is widespread?

Opponents of these kinds of arguments are deeply wary of using incompetent people as a means of assisting another person. We would not force a competent person to act altruistically without her or his consent, nor should we with an incompetent person.[273]

12.2 Who should decide what is in the patient's best interests?

The law takes the view that medical professionals, and ultimately the court, should decide what is in a patient's best interests. This is disputed by some. Although a medical professional may have expertise in medical issues they will not know a patient's religious or ethical views, nor what they found pleasurable in life.[274]

Some have argued that the relatives of the patient are better placed to decide what is in the best interests of the individual in question than the medical team.[275] There again it might be thought that relatives lack the emotional detachment to make an effective assessment of a patient's best interests. Indeed relatives might even have conflicting interests in reaching decisions over a relative (eg financial concerns over the cost of care). Also, the assumption that family members know a patient better than anyone else is often untrue. A patient's flatmate may know her or him better than her or his brother, for example.

Another alternative decision maker would be an ethics committee. This could intervene where there is a dispute between the family and the physician. Such a committee could be comprised of lay members and medical professionals, and act as representatives of the wider community in the way a jury does in a criminal trial. There are, however, concerns that such committees act without the procedural safeguards that courts have.

---

[269] See Cantor (2005: Chap 5).   [270] [1997] Fam 110.
[271] For a very useful discussion of these arguments see Lewis (2002).
[272] Robertson (1997).   [273] Lewis (2002) contrast Herring (2008).
[274] Veatch (2000).   [275] Fan and Tao (2004).

12.3 Substituted judgment

An alternative to the 'best interests' test which has received support in some quarters is the notion of substituted judgment which it is a particularly influential concept in American medical law. This requires the decision maker to decide what the incompetent individual would have wanted had she or he been able to make a decision. This involves the decision maker considering whether the person had made comments about how they would like to have been treated if they were to become incompetent. The individual's religious or ethical views may be taken as indictors as to the kind of decision the person would have made, if competent. Supporters claim that this approach maximizes autonomy in that it means we are seeking, as best we can, to determine the decision of the individual over their health care.

Critics argue that such a test places undue weight on comments made by an individual maybe years previously. A dinner conversation in which a person said she or he 'never wanted to live as a vegetable' can suddenly becomes the key element in a health care decision years later. Worse than this, it can encourage deception with relatives being encouraged to 'recall' the wishes of the individual. The huge controversy in the United States concerning whether to stop nutrition for Terri Schiavo[276] centred in part on disputed claims over what she may or may not have said many years previously. Dresser has claimed that the substitute judgment approach 'is indeterminate enough to permit almost any treatment option preferred by a patient's family, guardian, or physician'.[277]

TO PONDER

Information about fatal conditions

As has been clear throughout this chapter the right of autonomy plays a central role in medical law and ethics. It is proudly declared that patients should be the ones who decide what treatment they should be given, and should be informed about their treatment. But is this always what the general public actually want? One issue which generates controversy is what a medical professional should do if she or he discovers that her or his patient is suffering from a fatal condition?

One survey (Ajaj, Singh, and Abdulla (2001)) of elderly people found that 80 per cent said that they would rather not be told if it was discovered that they were suffering from cancer. It seems that people would rather have a few weeks or months of blissful ignorance than to spend the time in terror of the potential impact of the disease. Yet despite such surveys, when asked in general terms, patients do support a right to know of their medical condition (Sullivan, Menapace, and White (2001)). The difficulty is, of course, for every patient where there is a wish for blissful ignorance, there is another patient who would value the time to prepare for their death and 'put their affairs in order'.

A survey of physicians found a notable minority of physicians not telling patients of their life-threatening conditions, with a quarter saying they only told patients of life-threatening conditions 50–90 per cent of the time. Over half of those questioned said that they explained a patient's condition in only general terms (Sullivan, Menapace and White (2001)). Another survey found that where a doctor did tell a patient of a diagnosis of a terminal illness they were deliberately over-optimistic in their discussion of the prognosis and that that was in fact welcomed by patients (The, Hak, Koëter, van der Wal, (2000)).

[276] Koch (2005) discusses this case.   [277] Dresser (1994).

13 Ethical issues surrounding advance directives

Is it appropriate to pay heed to advance directives (known as advance decisions in the MCA)? A competent person, fearing incompetence, might, quite properly, seek to determine how she or he will be treated in the future when incompetent. Such an action can be seen as an attempt to ensure that what happens to them at the end of their lives is a fitting end to the vision of the good life they have set for themselves and sought to live by.[278] As Dworkin has put it: 'they want their deaths, if possible, to express and in that way vividly to confirm the values they believe most important'.[279] Controversially Dworkin goes on to say that even if the incompetent person is stating that she or he does want treatment these wishes are experimental (short-term) interests and can be overridden in the name of protecting the critical (long-term) interests of the earlier competent person. Even ignoring this more controversial suggestion, where there is a clear advance directive it might be thought obvious to prefer the expressed wishes of the patient, rather than someone else's view about what is best for her or him.

It is not that straightforward, however. There are three main points that are made by opponents of advance directives. Some claim that the person who makes the advance directive is not the same person as the person who is subsequently incompetent. We are, it is said, a collection and continuity of memories and life stories.[280] In the case of an Alzheimer's patient, although their body remains same, the loss of memory or connection with relatives or friends means that, with the onset of Alzheimer's, a new person has come into being. Or at least there has been such a change of personality and personhood that the competent person is no longer empowered to speak on behalf of the incompetent.[281] Therefore the advance directive made when competent should not have force. Robertson[282] writes as follows:

> The values and interests of the competent person no longer are relevant to someone who has lost the rational structure on which those values and interests rested. Unless we are to view competently held values and interests as extending even into situations in which, because of incompetency, they can no longer have meaning, it matters not that as a competent person the individual would not wish to be maintained in a debilitated or disabled state. If the person is no longer competent enough to appreciate the degree of divergence from her previous activity that produced the choice against treatment, the prior directive does not represent her current interests merely because a competent directive was issued.

Dworkin has replied to such arguments that even if there is some validity in the claim that the person has changed since developing Alzheimer's, their 'critical interests' remain.[283] Critical interests are those things which are fundamental to our life story (important relationships, career goals etc.) Being able to determine how the final chapter of our life is to be played out, if we become incompetent, is a critical interest. We should, therefore, through advance directives, be able to restrict how we are to be treated if incompetent.

---

278 Dworkin (1993).
279 Dworkin (1993: 211). Dresser (1995) is doubtful people have such a developed view of the story of their lives.
280 This is developed from the theories of Parfitt (1984), Dresser (1994), Dresser (1995), Rich (1998).
281 Dworkin (1993: 554); Buchanan and Brock (1990:152–89). See also Quante (1999).
282 Robertson (1991: 7).   283 Buchanan (1998).

Dresser responds by saying that if a person has lost the capacity to understand their critical interests they should not be given weight.[284] Another line of response to the 'personality change' argument is that to her or his friends and family the Alzheimer's patient has not changed her or his identity.[285] The notion that we are only our memories is unduly focused on an individual picture of person identity and does not place the individual in the community of their friends and relatives.[286] A more extreme response is to claim that an incompetent person has no interests in receiving life-sustaining treatment and therefore can, in compliance with an advance directive, be permitted to die.[287] The interests of a competent person in knowing that their wishes will be fulfilled is greater than the interests the incompetent person has in being kept alive.

Secondly, and more straightforwardly, there is a question mark over whether it is possible for us to predict how we would like to be treated when we suffer incompetence.[288] We may imagine suffering from Alzheimer's would be an horrific experience, and yet many sufferers appear to be happy. Are we confident that the person who made the advance directive had sufficient information about what experiencing the condition would be like?[289] People's reaction to death and dying when they are healthy can be very different when actually faced with death as an imminent reality.[290] Indeed evidence suggests that people are likely to underestimate the strength of their desire for medical intervention. Indeed it is difficult to imagine all the possible scenarios one might find oneself in.[291] You might decide that you would rather die quickly if suffering from a prolonged illness, but would that be your view if, by intervention, you could be kept alive long enough to see your first grandchild? Further, there are difficulties in determining whether we can be confident that a directive made years previously represents the most recent views of the patient. Notably the BMA does not encourage people to make advance directives, pointing to the possibility of them being misinterpreted.[292]

Thirdly, some argue that even if an advance directive can be seen as having some weight, our primary obligation towards the incompetent person is to show compassion and to seek their best interests. That principle cannot be challenged by using a directive.[293] Supporters of advance directives could reply that the person, in making the directive, has considered whether, when incompetent, they wished to be treated on the basis of compassion, or under the terms of their directive and have chosen the latter. Rebecca Dresser argues that we must focus on the interests of the incompetent patient, not the person they once were. She argues:

> ...the law must also ensure that the present patient does not simply disappear in the shadow of the person she once was. The law must ensure that someone looks carefully at the patient whose fate is now in question. It is the best interests standard that shines the brightest light on the patient in the present.... Courts should not permit competent persons to exercise tyranny over their lives as incompetent patients.

---

[284] Dresser (2003).

[285] This might mean that there is a difference if the 'second person' is regarded as a non-person (eg they are PVS) rather than being a different person (Holland (2003)).

[286] Kuczewski (1994).   [287] Kuhse (1999).

[288] Fagerlin and Schneider (2004) suggest that in the United States medical professionals regularly ignore living wills because they are not certain the individual imagined themselves to be in the position in which they have ended up.

[289] Dresser (2003).   [290] Ryan (2000).   [291] Ryan (2000).

[292] BMA and Law Society (2004: 113).   [293] Dresser (1994).

If the decision is made to respect advance directives there is a further question as to how far they should be taken. Generally it is thought that a directive should be treated in the same way as an expression of a competent person. In other words it cannot compel doctors to provide a certain form of treatment, but it can restrict what may be done to her or him. Some, however, have questioned whether an advance directive can direct altruistic behaviour. For example, if a patient signed a directive stating that in the event of a relative of hers or his requiring a kidney she or he would be willing to donate one, even if she or he was incompetent, could such a directive could be relied upon? One view is that there is no reason why not, given that a competent person would be allowed to make such a donation.[294] Others think that an advance directive cannot be used to authorize treatment which is not in a patient's best interests.[295] Alistair Maclean[296] has drawn an analogy between the competent person making the advance directive and their future demented selves; and a parent making a decision for a child. Although he emphasizes the analogy is not exact, he suggests an advance directive should be followed, but that it should be open to challenge if doing so will cause serious harm to the demented person; just as we allow people to challenge the decisions of a parent which will cause serious harm to the child.

In all of the debate over advance directives it should not be forgotten that in fact few people do try and make advance directives. This may well be because they do not like to think about death or serious illness.[297] Alternatively it may be that many people are simply happy for decisions concerning their medical treatment to be made by their doctors and family should they become incompetent.[298]

14 Autonomy and the medical professional–patient relationship

The law's approach to medical decision making has an impact on the relationship between the medical professional and her or his patient. Myfanwy Morgan[299] has suggested four models of the doctor–patient relationship:

- *A paternalist relationship.* The physician controls the relationship and decides what is best for the patients.
- *A relationship of mutuality.* The doctor and patient are equal partners engaged in a sharing of information and ideas designed to produce the best treatment for the patient.
- *A consumerist relationship.* The patient is the active and dominant party, demanding treatment and assistance from a doctor whose primary role is to meet the requests of the patient.
- *A relationship of default.* Here neither party takes a leading role. This normally leads to a non-productive result of the encounter.

As can be seen an autonomy model could fit within either the mutuality or consumerist model.

---

294 Lewis (2002).   295 Law Commission Report 231 (1995) at 5.13.
296 Maclean (2006).   297 Stern (1994).   298 Dresser (1995).   299 Morgan (2003).

Several legal commentators have suggested that a useful model of doctor–patient relationships would be to regard the doctor as a fiduciary. Andrew Grubb defines a fiduciary relationship in these terms:

> It arises when a person (the beneficiary) entrusts another (the fiduciary) with a power which may affect the beneficiary's interests and which is to be exclusively exercised for the beneficiary benefit.[300]

The advantage of this model is that it recognizes the reality that the medical professional has the power of knowledge and authority in the relationship. It emphasizes the obligations that that power carries and insists that it is used for the benefit of the patient.

One important benefit of the emphasis placed on the importance of autonomy is that it has greatly improved communication between medical professionals and patients. Rather than decreeing from on high the appropriate treatment, the professional is required to enter into a dialogue with the patient.[301] As Jay Katz has put it:

> Ultimately disclosure and consent seek to pierce the isolation, to eliminate the feelings of abandonment, and to reverse the lack of control that patients now experience so often in their interactions with physicians. Put affirmatively, disclosure and consent seek to safeguard patients' integrity that, illness notwithstanding, doctors can either help restore or undermine further; or put another way, disclosure and consent seek to protect patients from the ravages and pain of abandonment.[302]

15 The ethics of child treatment

When the decision in *Gillick* was handed down it was interpreted by some as heralding the emergence of children's rights in the medical arena.[303] In recognizing that a competent child was able to give legally recognized consent to receive contraceptive advice and treatment, the case was interpreted by some as meaning that mature children had the same rights to make decisions about their medical treatment as did adults. However, *Gillick* must now be considered in the light of subsequent decisions of the Court of Appeal, which have emphasized that even although the *Gillick* competent child can provide a legally effective consent to treatment (and in that way she or he is treated like an adult), if she or he refuses treatment then (unlike adults) consent can be provided by another: a person with parental responsibility, or the courts.

To many the current law is illogical.[304] To say to a child: 'you are mature enough to be able to make a decision about your treatment and we will respect your decision if you consent, but if you refuse we will enable your decision to be readily overridden' is illogical. If a child is competent to decide about medical treatment then that is so whether the child says yes or no. It is almost as if the law is saying to children we will respect your right to autonomy but only if you give the right answer!

To others the law does have a certain logic.[305] Rather than seeing *Gillick* as a case about giving children the right to make medical decisions for themselves, the decision should be seen as about preventing Mrs Gillick from depriving her daughters of access to needed medical treatment. Her veto of treatment could be overridden by the competent

[300] Grubb (2004) and Bartlett (1997).   [301] Katz (2002).   [302] Katz (2002: 208).
[303] Eekelaar (1986).   [304] Eg Bainham (1992).   [305] Lowe and Juss (1993).

consent of one of her daughters.[306] The principle underlying the law, then, is that if a doctor believes a child needs medical treatment, then the law should make it as easy as possible for the doctor to give it. This is done by enabling the doctor to provide the treatment providing she or he has the consent of either a person with parental responsibility, or a *Gillick* competent child, or a court. Seen this way the law is simply promoting what is seen as the guiding principle in relation to children in the law: that the child's welfare should be promoted. However, this principle is not unproblematic. As Andrew Bainham points out:

> The courts are much inclined to speak of the welfare principle as an absolute standard and an unproblematic concept which can act as a panacea for all ills affecting children. This is not altogether surprising since it is they who get to define this content in any given situation.[307]

The debate can appear, then, as a clash between 'child liberationists' who would like to see the law recognize that children have the same rights as adults, and 'child paternalists' who see the law's paramount role as the protection of children's best interests. It appears that the majority of commentators reject 'the extremes' of child liberation or paternalism, and instead seek to develop a model which acknowledges both a child's right to be protected from harm and a child's right to make decisions for her or himself. One theory, which has received widespread support, is that proposed by John Eekelaar.[308] He has developed an approach to children's rights which requires the law to protect three different interests that a child has:

(1) *Basic interests.* These are interests that are central to a child's well-being. They would include the feeding, housing and clothing of a child. Basic interests also include promotion of the child's physical, emotional, and intellectual care.

(2) *Developmental interests.* These are the interests that a child has to enable her or him to develop as a person. Interests in education or socialization may be included here.

(3) *Autonomy interests.* These are the interests that children have in being permitted to make decisions for themselves.

Eekelaar goes on to argue that, where there is a clash between the autonomy interests and the other two, the developmental or basic interests would trump the autonomy interest. In other words, children have an interest in being able to make decisions for themselves unless such a decision would infringe their basic or developmental interests. Children would therefore be able to make what adults might think as 'bad decisions', but only as long as those are not such bad decisions that they interfere with matters that are central to a child's well-being. This is because the law should seek children to develop into adults with maximum autonomy and maximum ability to decide how to live their lives. In other words an infringement on a child's autonomy in childhood is justified if necessary in order to maximize autonomy later in life. Applied to this context it would mean that children can be prevented from refusing life-saving treatment or treatment without which they would suffer debilitating conditions, because to do so will increase their autonomy when they become adults.

---

[306] It should be emphasized that there was no question in the case that one of her daughters would actually be seeking contraceptive treatment.
[307] Bainham (1987: 339).   [308] Eekelaar (1986) and Eekelaar (1994).

Where there is a dispute between parents and doctors over medical treatment for children the parties will, of course, attempt to reach a compromise. If necessary the courts will be required to resolve the dispute using the welfare principle as the guiding rule. When making such decisions the courts have emphasized that they will place weight on the views of parents, but the guiding principle will be what is in the welfare of the child.[309] Indeed occasionally there have been cases where the views of the parents have played a critical role in the court's decision.[310] This has been criticized by some as not protecting children's rights.[311] To allow a parent's views to change what would otherwise be ordered in the best interests of the child is unjustifiable.[312] To others it is a recognition that a child is a member of a family and her or his welfare is to some extent tied up with the family's.[313]

The decisions of the courts about whether a child is *Gillick* competent have been criticized by many commentators. It is said by some that the law improperly sets far higher standards of competence for children than it does for adults.[314] Others have claimed that if a child is making a decision with which the court disagrees then the court declares the child incompetent, whereas if the court agrees with the child then the child is declared competent. There is a particular concern that where a child is expressing religious views as the basis for her or his refusal to consent to treatment the courts are sceptical and are likely to regard the child as incompetent. The judges have stated that they respect teenagers' profession of religious belief, but then state that the child may reject their religion when they are older[315] or that the child, having been brought up within a religion, does not have a wide enough experience of the world to enable him or her to be competent.

The most common criticism amongst academics of the current law is that it pays inadequate regard to the rights of children. Indeed a case can be made for saying the current law does not sufficiently protect the rights of competent minors under the European Convention on Human Rights, article 8. But in the media a common complaint is that it pays too little regard to the rights of the parent. In May 2004 there was uproar when it was reported that a 14-year-old girl had had an abortion without her mother's knowledge. The fact that a child could consent to treatment without her parent's permission was seen as an attack on family values.

16 Conclusion

This chapter started with the relatively straightforward proposition that a medical professional should not treat a patient without her or his consent. However, it has become apparent that the law on consent is far from straightforward. The exact meaning of capacity to consent is a delicate issue: if too strict a line is taken then we rob a large number of people of their rights of autonomy; but if too liberal a line is taken we may end up attaching great weight to the statements of people who have little understanding of what the issues are. It is one thing to let a competent patient die if they have rejected life-saving treatment, after a careful consideration of the issues; it is another where the person's rejection is little more than a confused and frightened 'no' without

---

[309] *Re A (Conjoined Twins: Medical Treatment)* [2001] 1 FLR 1, 49E.
[310] *Re T (A Minor) (Wardship: Medical Treatment)* [1997] 2 FCR 363.
[311] Freeman (2000).   [312] Freeman (2000).
[313] See the useful discussion of these issues in Bridge (2002).
[314] Bridgeman (1998).   [315] *Re E* (1990) 9 BMLR 1, 8.

a real understanding of what is going on. Further, the chapter has explored the difficulties in deciding how decisions should be made in relation to those who are incompetent. For incompetent children this involves a delicate balance between the rights of children and those of their parents. For incompetent adults the Mental Capacity Act 2005 has emphasized the best interests test, but has largely left open the question of how a person's best interests are ascertained. That is a question, no doubt, the courts will be required to address very soon.

QUESTIONS

1. Consider the following comment of Lord Diplock's in *Sidaway*, explaining why he opposed requiring informed consent: 'the only effect of mention of risks can have on the patient's mind, if...any at all, can be in the direction of deterring the patient from undergoing the treatment which in the expert opinion of the doctor is in the patient's best interests to undergo.'

2. Many competent people do not do everything they should to promote their health (eg they fail to ensure they have regular dental check-ups). Should we impose on those who lack mental capacity higher standards of care than most people choose for themselves?

3. In *Re E* a 15-year-old Jehovah's Witness refused to consent to a blood transfusion. The transfusions were, nevertheless, authorized by a court. After nearly three years of non-consensual transfusions he reached the age of majority, and his views had to be respected. He died. Does this tell us that the law on children's refusal of medical treatment is wrong? Or that the law on adults is?

4. 'It is one thing to respect a refusal of treatment based on a religious conviction of a devout patient who has long held their religious beliefs. It is another to require us, as the courts have declared, to accept a decision made for "no reason at all"' (Stauch (1998: 76). Does the law pay too much respect to decisions which appear to defy logic?

5. Does the law improperly assume that a decision maker is competent or is not? Would it not be more appropriate to recognize that there is a scale of competence with decisions falling at different places along that line? The weight attached to a decision could then depend on where on the scale of competence the decision maker lay.

6. Is it correct to emphasize the 'principle of autonomy' given that although great respect is paid to a patient's refusal to consent to treatment, little legal weight attaches to the right to receive treatment one desires? (See Graber and Tansey (2005) for a discussion of this issue).

7. 'Healing, as we define it, is a form of assistance in making the patient whole again by working through her or his body. If the values of patient welfare and patient autonomy remain in conflict, then authentic healing cannot take place. A physician, therefore, must become both a moderate autonomist and a moderate welfarist' (Pelligrino and Thomasma (1988: 32)). Is a compromise view of this kind between a welfarist and autonomist approach workable?

8. In May 2005 (BBC Newsonline 9 May 2005) it was disclosed that that a man who had refused treatment for tuberculosis had gone on to infect twelve other people with the disease. The Government announced it would review whether the law needed to be changed to permit the forceful treatment of people with certain infectious diseases. What do you think the Government should do?

9. Would an approach based on patient request, rather than consent better protect patients? This would envisage informed patients requesting certain forms of treatment from their doctors, rather than patients having to consent to medical professionals' suggestions? See Habiba (2000) for discussion of this.

10. Should doctors perform circumcision on boys where that is not clinically required, but the parents want it? If parents wanted the tips of a finger removed would we allow doctors to operate to remove that? Is it any different whether the parents are acting for religious or aesthetic reasons? See Fox and Thomson (2005) for a discussion of this question.

11. In early 2007 (BBC Newsonline 4 January 2007) much media attention was paid to an American couple who had decided to keep their severely disabled daughter 'child sized' by giving her drugs. This would avoid her having periods and make caring easier. Should the doctor have been willing to go along with the parents' wishes? Or is this a case where making her care easier so she can stay at home is more important than her interests in growing up?

FURTHER READING

For a discussion of the capacity of children to consent see:

Alderson, P. (1993) *Children's Consent to Surgery* (Open University Press).

Bainham, A. (2005) *The Modern Law of Children* (Jordans), Chap 8.

Bridge, C. (2002) 'Religion, Culture and the Body of the Child' in *Body Lore and Laws* (Hart).

For issues surrounding autonomy see:

Bailey-Harris, R. (2000) 'Patient Autonomy—A Turn in the Tide?' in M. Freeman and A. Lewis (eds) *Law and Medicine* (Oxford University Press).

Beyleveld, D. and Brownsword, R. (2007) *Consent in the Law* (Hart).

Harrington, J. (1996) 'Privileging the Medical Norms: Liberalism, Self-Determination and Refusal of Treatment' *Legal Studies* 16: 348.

Jones, M. (1999) 'Informed Consent and Other Fairy Stories' *Medical Law Review* 7: 103.

McCall Smith, A. (1997) 'Beyond Autonomy' *Journal of Contemporary Health Law and Policy* 14: 23.

O'Neill, O. (2002) *Autonomy and Trust in Bioethics* (Cambridge University Press).

Tauber, A. (2003) 'Sick autonomy' *Perspectives in Biology and Medicine* 46: 484.

For ethical and legal issues surrounding advance directives see:

Dresser, R. (2003) 'Precommitment: a misguided strategy for securing death with dignity' *Texas Law Review* 81: 1823.

Maclean, A. (2006) 'Advance directives, future selves and decision-making' *Medical Law Review* 14: 291.

Michalowski, S. (2005) 'Advance refusals of life-sustaining medical treatment: The relativity of an absolute right' *Modern Law Review* 68: 958.

For the treatment of incompetent patients see:

Buchanan, A. and Brock, C. (1990) *Deciding for Others. The Ethics of Surrogate Decision Making* (Cambridge University Press).

Cantor, N. (2005) *Making Medical Decisions for the Profoundly Mentally Disabled* (MIT Press).

Garwood-Gowers, A. (2005) 'The proper limits for medical intervention that harms the therapeutic interests of incompetents' in A. Garwood-Gowers, J. Tingel, and K. Wheat (eds) *Contemporary Issues in Healthcare Law and Ethics* (Elsevier).

Lewis, P. (2002) 'Procedures that are against the medical interests of the incompetent person' *Oxford Journal of Legal Studies* 12: 575.

For the leading work on relational autonomy see:

Mackenzie, C. and Stoljar, N. (2000) *Relational Autonomy* (Oxford University Press).

5 Confidentiality

INTRODUCTION

It might, at first, be thought that the issue of medical confidentiality is straightforward. Health care professionals should always keep secret their patients' confidential information and it is as simple as that. As Lord Phillips MR in *Ashworth Security Hospital v MGN Ltd*[1] stated:

> It is well settled that there is an abiding obligation of confidentiality as between doctor and patient, and in my view when a patient enters a hospital for treatment, whether he be a model citizen or murderer, he is entitled to be confident that details about his condition and treatment remain between himself and those who treat him.

However, as we shall see the issue is complex. Modern health care systems would be unworkable if a doctor never passed on medical information about patients to other medical professionals. Also a moment's thought will be able to conjure up situations where even information given in confidence to a doctor should be revealed. For example, if a father confesses to his doctor that he is abusing his child, is the doctor to do nothing?[2]

Current medical practice has certainly made the issue of confidentiality more complex. A patient in a hospital is likely to be treated by a large number of health care professionals each dealing with different aspects of her or his treatment. Each one may need to have access to her or his medical records. Also internal and external audits of NHS Trusts may require managers to have access to at least parts of a patient's medical records to be able to ensure high standards of treatment are being offered. Further, the inevitable increase in use of computer technology in relation to patients' records, while easing the passing of information to those who need to know, makes protecting confidentiality more complex.[3]

Despite these modern pressures on confidentiality the notion that a doctor should not improperly divulge sensitive information about her or his patient is deeply ingrained. The Hippocratic Oath states:

> Whatsoever things I see or hear concerning the life of men, in my attendance on the sick or even apart therefrom, which ought not to be noised abroad, I will keep silence thereon, counting such things to be as sacred secrets.[4]

---

[1] [2000] 1 WLR 515, at 527.

[2] A doctor who did nothing after receiving a report of abuse in 1975 was found not to be negligent when assessed by the standards of doctors at that time *C v Dr AJ Cairns* [2003] Lloyds Rep Med 90. The judgment assumes that things would be very different today.

[3] HM Government (2007b) promotes the use of electronic health records (see also Cambridge Health Informatics Ltd (2001a)).

[4] Kennedy and Grubb (2000: 1047).

The World Medical Association's International Code of Medical Ethics[5] declares:

A doctor shall preserve absolute secrecy on all he knows about his patient because of the confidence entrusted to him.

Confidentiality is seen as an essential aspect of effective medical treatment. As the British Medical Association (BMA) has put it:

Frank and open exchange between health professional and patients is the ideal and patients need to feel that their privacy will be respected before they can enter into such an exchange.[6]

Indeed it is difficult to find anyone working in the medical field who believes that confidentiality is unimportant, even though there are certainly disputes over when confidentiality can properly be breached. However, as we will see later in this chapter, although the principle of confidentiality has received much praise, some believe it is honoured as much in the breach as in the observance. There have even been complaints that medical ethicists themselves in their writings have discussed individual patient's cases, thereby failing to pay sufficient attention to issues of confidentiality.[7]

One important point which is now being taken seriously in the NHS is that confidentiality is not just a negative concept: the obligation on staff not to reveal information. It also contains a positive obligation: the NHS must take steps to ensure that confidential information is not revealed. This has led to some to shift the focus of the discussion away from confidentiality and instead on to the notion of data protection.[8] The emphasis reflects the view that the greater threat to medically sensitive information is not doctors selling our health records to the tabloid press, but hackers entering NHS computers and accessing private information. NHS authorities and trusts are required to appoint Caldicott Guardians[9] whose job it is to ensure the protection of confidential information within their organization.

The General Medical Council (GMC) has also issued strict guidelines in relation to confidentiality based on the following principles:[10]

Patients have a right to expect that information about them will be held in confidence by their doctors. Confidentiality is central to trust between doctors and patients. Without assurances about confidentiality, patients may be reluctant to give doctors the information they need in order to provide good care. If you are asked to provide information about patients you must:

- inform patients about the disclosure, or check that they have already received information about it;
- anonymize data where unidentifiable data will serve the purpose;
- be satisfied that patients know about disclosures necessary to provide their care, or for local clinical audit of that care, that they can object to these disclosures if they wish;
- seek patients' express consent to disclosure of information, where identifiable data is needed for any purpose other than the provision of care or for clinical audit—save in the exceptional circumstances described in this booklet;
- keep disclosures to the minimum necessary; and

---

5 Quoted in Beauchamp and Childress (2003: 304).   6 BMA (2004: 165).
7 Rogers and Draper (2003).   8 Montgomery (2003: 252).
9 Named after the report which recommended them: Caldicott (1997).
10 GMC (2004).

- keep up to date with and observe the requirements of statute and common law, including data protection legislation.

The Department of Health has recently published guidelines on the issue of confidentiality within the NHS. But notice in this opening statement how the emphasis is more on fairness of dealing with information, rather than keeping it confidential:

> The NHS is committed to the delivery of a first class confidential service. This means ensuring that all patient information is processed fairly, lawfully and as transparently as possible so that the public:
>
> - understand the reasons for processing personal information;
> - give their consent for the disclosure and use of their personal information;
> - gain trust in the way the NHS handles information; and
> - understand their rights to access information held about them.[11]

These principles and the duties of confidentiality apply to all NHS staff, including volunteer helpers,[12] not just to doctors.

1 The legal basis of confidentiality

Perhaps surprisingly the legal basis of a medical professional's duty of confidentiality is far from clear. There is not a single statute or common law body of laws governing confidentiality.[13] A medical professional who improperly discloses private information can be found to have acted illegally on the basis of a wide range of legal obligations, as follows.

1.1 Contract law

It might be said that to reveal a patient's confidential information is a breach of contract with the patient. However, there is no contract between an NHS patient and anyone caring for them. A court might find a special implied contract but the general view is that that is unlikely. A contract claim would, however, have a greater chance of success in a case involving a private patient.

A breach of contract claim could also arise if (as is likely) infringing patient confidentiality was a breach of the health care professional's contract of employment.[14] The claim and any remedy would, however, only be open to the employer, not the patient.[15]

1.2 Tort law

Revealing confidential information could amount to negligence. It is well established that keeping a patient's affairs private is part of reasonable care. A claim could be brought against a medical professional in tort if either the professional revealed the protected information, or failed to take reasonable steps to ensure that others did not get hold

---

[11] DoH (2003a: 4).   [12] DoH (2003a: 16).
[13] Law Commission Report 110 (1981) recommended the creation of a new statutory tort of breach of confidence, but the proposal was never taken up.
[14] *X v Y* [1988] 2 All ER 649.
[15] Unless a patient could claim under the Contracts (Rights of Third Parties) Act 1999.

of it.[16] The difficulty in such a claim is, however, damages. Generally in tort damages are only available for financial or physical loss. Feelings of embarrassment, for example, would not be a recognized form of financial loss in tort law. Therefore, even if a successful claim could be brought in negligence only very limited damages might be available.

If the released information was untrue and led to reasonable people thinking less of the patient then a claim could be brought in defamation. However, this will only assist a patient if the information disclosed is false. Reassuringly for doctors they also have a defence of 'qualified privilege' if they reasonably believed their statement to be true and have communicated with a person who has a legitimate interest in the relevant information.[17] This would be relevant in a case where a doctor supplied information in a medical questionnaire for an insurance company which was reasonably believed to be correct, but which was, in fact, not.

Some have suggested that very soon the courts will recognize a new tort of breach of privacy. The argument has gained particular weight following the enactment of the Human Rights Act 1998. The issue has recently been considered by the House of Lords in *Wainwright v Home Office*[18] who confirmed the orthodox position that in English tort law there is not a tort of infringing privacy. However, the case has not resolved all debate over the issue because their Lordships left to another day the question of whether the Human Rights Act could be relied upon to extend the existing tort law to ensure privacy was protected. Lord Nicholls in *Campbell v MGN*[19] referred to the tort of misusing private information. However, this tort was identical to the equitable obligation of confidence and other of their Lordships preferred to describe it in terms of an equitable obligation, rather than a tort.

1.3 Equitable obligations of confidence

Often the best option for a patient who wishes to commence a legal claim in respect of a revelation of medical information is to rely on the equitable obligation to respect confidential information. In order for information to be protected by equitable obligations of confidence four criteria need to be satisfied:[20]

(i) The information must be of a personal, private, or intimate nature.[21] The test for this is whether the person whom the information concerns had a reasonable expectation that the information would be kept private.[22] This will generally be true of medical information. This requirement indicates that if a doctor were to reveal a trivial piece of information (eg what colour socks a patient was wearing) this may be regarded as not protected by confidence. However, it should be noted that the BMA has suggested that even the fact a patient visited a doctor should be regarded as confidential information.[23] Lady Hale in *Campbell v MGN* surprisingly stated:

> Not every statement about a person's health will carry the badge of confidentiality or risk doing harm to that person's physical or moral integrity. The privacy interest in the fact

---

[16] *Swinney v Chief Constable of the Northumbria Police* [1996] 3 All ER 449.
[17] Brazier and Cave (2007: 86).   [18] [2003] 3 WLR 1337.   [19] Para 15.
[20] The leading book on breach of confidence is Gurry (1985).
[21] *Stephens v Avery* [1988] 2 All ER 477; *Campbell v MGN* [2004] UKHL 22.
[22] *Campbell v MGN* [2004] UKHL 22 (Lord Nicholls (para 21), Lady Hale (para 137)). Lord Hope preferred the test whether it would cause the victim 'substantial offence' (para 92); but this test was rejected by Lord Hoffman (at para 22) and Lady Hale (at para 135).
[23] BMA (2004: 167).

that a public figure has a cold or a broken leg is unlikely to be strong enough to justify restricting the press's freedom to report it. What harm could it possibly do?[24]

This statement might be read as suggesting that minor medical complaints are not to be regarded as confidential. However it is better understood as a statement that, with minor medical complaints, it will not be particularly difficult to find public interest reasons (eg freedom of the press) that justify breaching the confidence.

(ii) The information must be imparted in circumstances imposing an obligation of confidence.[25] It used to be thought that there needed to be shown that there was a confidential relationship between the parties such as doctor–patient or husband–wife, but now it is clear that all that is required is that a person receives information which she or he knows, or ought to know, is fairly and reasonably to be regarded as confidential or private.[26] There is therefore little doubt that information provided to a doctor by a patient would satisfy this criterion. Indeed even words spoken in group therapy sessions have been said to be bound by confidence in this regard.[27] The duty of confidence will also apply to someone who discovers information and it is clear that the person whom it concerns had a reasonable expectation that it would be kept private.[28] So if a doctor told his wife about a patient's medical condition she would also be bound by the duty of confidence because she would be aware that the information was confidential in its nature. Similarly, if a member of the public found medical notes which had been accidentally left on a park bench the member of the public would be required to keep the information confidential.

(iii) It may be necessary to show that someone will suffer as a result of the release of confidential information about them. This was the basis of the reasoning in *R v Department of Health ex p Source Informatics Ltd*[29] which held that the release of anonymized medical information was not a breach of confidentiality. However, it is not clear whether this represents the law because Lord Keith in *A-G v Guardian (No 2)*[30] suggests that even if no one individual suffered a specific detriment in relation to the revelation, there could be a public interest that supported confidentiality. In other words even if the revelation did not itself harm a particular person if it could be said to have caused a public harm (eg to lead to a lack of trust in doctors) this could be sufficient to justify protecting the information in equity.[31] Hence it is widely accepted that even if a patient has died a doctor ought not to make public details of their medical conditions.

(iv) Confidence will be breached if only an unauthorized person sees it. It is not necessary to show that the information was made public.[32]

The leading case on breach of confidence is now *Campbell v MGN*.[33] Their Lordships emphasized that the right to respect for private and family life under the European

---

[24] *Campbell v MGN* [2004] UKHL 22, para 157.
[25] Lord Hoffman in *Wainwright v Home Office* [2003] 3 WLR 1337, para 29 stated that to establish a breach of confidence it was no longer necessary to show that the parties were in a confidential relationship.
[26] *Campbell v MGN* [2004] UKHL 22, para 14 (Lord Nicholls), para 85 (Lord Hope). See also *CC v AB* [2006] EWHC 3083 (QB) where information about an adulterous affair was seen as protected in equity.
[27] *Venables v MGN* [2001] 1 All ER 908.
[28] Lord Goff of Chieveley in *Attorney General v Guardian Newspapers Ltd (No 2)* [1990] 1 AC 109, 281.
[29] [2000] 1 All ER 786.   [30] [1988] 3 All ER 545.
[31] *Stone v South East Strategic Health Authority* [2006] EWHC 1668 (Admin); *Ashworth v MGN* [2001] 1 All ER 191.
[32] *A-G v Guardian (No 2)* [1990] 1 AC 109, 260.   [33] [2004] UKHL 22.

Convention on Human Rights, article 8 should now be regarded as underpinning the protection of confidentiality.[34] Protection of confidential information is about respecting the autonomy and dignity of individuals.[35] This meant that in deciding whether the information is protected by the law it would be necessary to consider whether the information is protected under article 8 and then whether infringement of the confidence is justified under paragraph 8.2.[36]

KEY CASE   Campbell v MGN [2004] UKHL 22

Naomi Campbell (and as Baroness Hale pointed out 'Even the judges know who Naomi Campbell is') was photographed leaving a meeting of Narcotics Anonymous. The Daily Mirror published the photographs accompanied by an article praising Ms Campbell's battle with drug addiction and giving details about her treatment. Naomi Campbell sued for breach of confidence. She won at first instance, lost in the Court of Appeal, but won again in the House of Lords. She was awarded £2,500 damages plus £1,000 aggravated damages.

The speeches in the House of Lords, unfortunately, are unclear on the basis of the award. Lord Nicholls talked of the tort of misuse of private information. However, Lord Hoffman, Lord Hope, and Baroness Hale all talked of equitable breach of confidence. Lord Hoffman also mentioned a new common law right to protect private information. Lord Carswell talked in general terms about a right to confidentiality but it is not clear what kind of right he was talking about. This lack of certainty is explicable because none of their Lordships suggested that the law differed depending on what classification was used. They were united in agreeing that the law would protect an improper revelation of confidential information, be that through tort, equity, or some unclassified right.

The first issue was whether details about Naomi Campbell's attendance at Narcotics Anonymous meetings were confidential. Lord Hoffman explained that the protection of confidential information was about 'the right to control the dissemination of information about one's private life and the right to the esteem and respect of other people'. Their Lordships explained that in considering what information was confidential, consideration would be given to the European Convention on Human Rights, article 8 and the right to respect for private life. In deciding whether information was confidential Lord Hope suggested: 'the broad test is whether disclosure of the information about the individual ("A") would give substantial offence to A, assuming that A was placed in similar circumstances and was a person of ordinary sensibilities.' However Lord Hoffman and Baroness Hale did not approve of this test. They preferred to ask whether a person would have a reasonable expectation that the information would be kept confidential.

Applying this test to the facts of the case their Lordships agreed that *prima facie* the fact that someone was receiving treatment for drug addiction would be confidential information. However, in this case Naomi Campbell had made various public statements to the effect that she (unlike many other models) did not take drugs. By so doing she had made her drug-taking a public matter and so no longer confidential. Alternatively her statements created sufficient public interest to justify the press correcting the misleading impression she had created. But the majority of their Lordships then held that her statements did not mean that every aspect of her drug-taking and treatment was now public information. The time, place, and form of drug therapy was still confidential. To the minority (Lords Nicholls and Hoffman) the article was essentially about Campbell's treatment for drug addiction

---

[34] See also *R (on the application of B) v Stafford Combined Court* [2006] EWHC 1645 (Admin).

[35] *Campbell v MGN* [2004] UKHL 22, para 53 (Lord Hoffman).

[36] See eg Lord Nicholls, para 17.

and that was not private because she had chosen to make that issue a public one. The information about where and when she was attending treatment was 'unremarkable and consequential' (in Lord Nicholls's view). To the majority, revealing the fact she was attending Narcotics Anonymous was analogous to informing the public of what medical treatment a celebrity was receiving, which was clearly protected information.

Having decided that the taking of photographs and publication of the story was in breach of confidence the next question was whether there was a public interest (including freedom of the press) which justified the infringement. Quite simply this involved a balancing exercise between the right to respect for private life under the European Convention on Human Rights, article 8 and right to freedom of expression under article 10:

> the right to privacy which lies at the heart of an action for breach of confidence has to be balanced against the right of the media to impart information to the public. And the right of the media to impart information to the public has to be balanced in its turn against the respect that must be given to private life.

In making this balancing exercise Baroness Hale, for one did not have great sympathy for either side: 'Put crudely, it is a prima donna celebrity against a celebrity-exploiting tabloid newspaper.' And this might explain why even though the majority sided with Campbell the level of damages was small. What seemed to have influenced the majority was that a recovering drug addict is in a vulnerable position, needing all the support she can get. The publication of information about her treatment was likely to distress her at what might be a particularly vulnerable time. There was little public interest in the story and therefore the right to privacy trumped the right to freedom of expression.

The main disadvantage in relying on the equitable remedy is in relation to the remedies a court can grant. The primary remedy is an injunction. A court may be willing to prevent a disclosure of confidential information through an injunction if that is necessary in the public interest.[37] This is, of course, only useful to someone who is aware that there is about to be a revelation of confidential information and provides little assistance in a case where the revelation has already been made. It used to be thought that damages were not available. However, the Court of Appeal in *Cornelius v de Taranto*[38] upheld an award of damages for breach of confidence and, of course, the House of Lords in *Campbell* did likewise. In neither case were the sums awarded very large. If the person breaching confidence thereby acquires a profit it may be she or he can be made liable to account for those profits to the victim.[39]

1.4 Ownership

It could be argued that a patient owns her or his medical information and therefore can bring a property claim if the information is revealed to others. But in *R v Department of Health ex p Source Informatics Ltd*[40] the Court of Appeal rejected an argument that a patient owns the information about themselves. Indeed, the general view seems to be that it is the NHS Trust which owns the records its staff makes.[41] The Trust (rather than

---

37 *W v Egdell [1990]* 1 All ER 855.   38 [2001] 68 BMLR 62.
39 *Blake v Attorney-General* [2003] 1 WLR 625 and see the discussion in Feldman (2002: 619).
40 *R v Department of Health exp Source Informatics Ltd* [2000] 1 All ER 786.
41 *R v Department of Health ex p Source Informatics Ltd* [2000] 1 All ER 786.

the staff) therefore can control the access to that information. That said in *R v Mid-Glamorgan FHSA ex p Martin*[42] it was emphasized that simply because someone owns records does not mean that they have the right to do what they want with them.

1.5 Criminal law

It has long been held that information is not property which is capable of being stolen.[43] However, the paper on which a medical report is contained could be. So, a doctor who handed over a piece of paper with a medical record or an X-ray to a journalist could be guilty of theft, not of the information, but of the piece of paper on which it was written. If the doctor telephoned a journalist and read out a medical record there could be no theft conviction. The Computer Misuse Act 1990 also criminalizes 'hacking' into a database to access confidential information. Notably, an offence under that Act is committed by staff who have access to some parts of a database but who access parts to which they are not authorized.[44] This means that a health professional is guilty of an offence under the Act if he accesses his hospital's database to discover information about a celebrity who is not his patient.

1.6 Human rights

The Human Rights Act, as discussed in Chapter 1, affects the law in two ways. It can be used to direct the interpretation of statute or develop the common law. Plus it provides a cause of action in its own right.

1.6.1 Interpretation of statutes and common law

The European Convention on Human Rights, article 8 which protects the right to respect for private and family life also protects confidential information.[45] As the European Court of Human Rights in *Z v Finland*[46] explained:

> The protection of personal data, not least medical data, is of fundamental importance to a person's enjoyment of his or her right to respect for private and family life as guaranteed by article 8 of the Convention...Without such protection, those in need of medical assistance may be deterred from revealing such information of a personal and intimate nature as may be necessary in order to receive appropriate treatment and, even, from seeking such assistance thereby endangering their own health and, in the case of transmissible diseases, that of the community.

It is now arguable that when the courts are interpreting statute or the common law they should as far as possible do so in a way which is compatible with the protection of confidential information as required under article 8. Indeed we have seen in *Campbell v MGN* that the House of Lords relied on the European Convention on Human Rights in determining the extent of the confidentiality, and in balancing the right to privacy and the right to freedom of expression. It should not be forgotten that it is permissible to infringe the right to respect for private life if one of the interests listed in article 8(2) is threatened. This will mean that it will only be permissible to disclose confidential

---

[42] [1995] 1 All ER 356.   [43] *Oxford v Moss* (1978) 68 Cr App R 183.

[44] *R v Bow Street Metropolitan Stipendiary Magistrate ex p Government of the USA* [2000] 2 AC 216.

[45] Phillipson (2003). See further Wicks (2007: Chap 6).   [46] (1998) 25 EHRR 371, paras 95–6.

information if to do so is 'necessary in a democratic society' in the interests of 'national security, public safety or the economic well-being of the country, for the prevention of disorder or crime, for the protection of health and morals, or for the protection of the rights and freedoms of others'. This offers a stronger protection for individual rights of privacy than might at first be apparent. First, the word 'necessary' means not just reasonable or convenient, but that there is some pressing social requirement. Second, the European Court of Human Rights has interpreted the provision to emphasize the notion of proportionality. This means that the extent to which the confidence is interfered with must be the minimum required to protect the countervailing interest. In other words, even if the interests of the protection of public health may justify interfering with the confidentiality of part of someone's medical records, it may not justify revealing them all.

In *Z v Finland*[47] a husband was being prosecuted for a crime. The prosecuting authorities needed to establish when he became aware of his HIV-positive status. The police relied upon his wife's medical records for this purpose. The wife unsuccessfully complained to the European Court that her human rights had been infringed. A number of important points come out of the decision. First, the court indicated that some kinds of medical information were more sensitive than others; information about HIV status was particularly sensitive. The implication is that the more intimate the information, the stronger the countervailing interests had to be to justify revealing it. Second, the court held that accessing her medical records was justified in the name of pursuing criminal proceedings for a serious offence, but that that did not justify making her medical records public. It should have been possible for the evidence to have been made available in the trial without her right to respect for her private life being invaded. In other words the extent of the invasion of her confidence was disproportionate.

In *MS v Sweden*[48] the applicant applied for compensation for an industrial injury from social insurance benefits. The Social Insurance Office were sent information in her health records, including an abortion she had had as a result of the injuries. It was held this did not infringe her article 8 rights; the infringement of her rights of privacy were justifiably infringed in the name of checking the accuracy of the data. The officer checking the information was required to maintain the confidentiality of the information. One point that seemed to be given attention by the court was that she had chosen to apply for the benefit and had therefore raised publicly the state of her health.

1.6.2 *Remedies under the Human Rights Act 1998*

The Human Rights Act 1998, section 7 allows someone to sue a public authority which has infringed their convention rights. Section 8 permits the court to award damages on such an application. This would clearly enable a person whose records have been improperly revealed to others by the NHS to bring an application against the NHS under the Human Rights Act.

1.7 **Statutory obligations**

There are a number of statutes which impose particular obligations in relation to confidential information. The Data Protection Act 1998 is the most significant, although

---

[47] (1997) 5 BMLR 107.   [48] (1998) 45 BMLR 1.

there are a host of other statutory instruments and provisions which impose duties of confidentiality in particular circumstances.[49] For example, a medical professional cannot disclose information about a patient's attendance at a fertility clinic[50] or genitourinary medicine clinic,[51] even to the patient's GP, without the express consent of the patient.

1.8 Professional disciplinary procedures

As well as the law, a variety of professional bodies have issued guidelines on confidentiality. These include the BMA,[52] the GMC,[53] and the Nursing and Midwifery Council.[54] The NHS has also issued its own code on confidentiality.[55] These guidelines are clearer and more accessible to health care professionals than the law. No doubt most professionals simply ensure that they are following the relevant professional guidelines, rather than attempting to understand the legal position. They make the assumption that if they are following the guidelines they are acting lawfully. This is probably a reasonable assumption to make. Notably the courts have on occasion relied upon the professional guidelines when deciding what the legal position was.[56] This is understandable if the basis of confidentiality is the tort of negligence, which places much weight on the accepted professional standards. If the law is based on human rights or equitable obligation of confidence, it is arguable that it is wrong to assume that following professional guidelines will necessarily provide a defence to any legal action. That said it is difficult to imagine that a judge would ever penalize a professional who had followed her or his professional guidelines. So, although not technically law, these guidelines are likely to play a significant role in the interpretation of the law on confidential information in this context. We will now introduce four of the most important guidelines.

1.8.1 The Nursing and Midwifery Council

The Nursing and Midwifery Council provides guidance on confidentiality in their *Code of Professional Conduct*.[57] It emphasizes that: 'You must treat information about patients and clients as confidential and use it only for the purposes for which it was given'.[58] It states that disclosure of patients' information should not take place without their consent, with two exceptions:

- it can be justified in the public interest (usually where disclosure is essential to protect the patient or client or someone else from the risk of significant harm);
- it is required by law or by order of a court.[59]

1.8.2 The General Medical Council

The Guidelines issued by the General Medical Council (GMC) also emphasize the importance of ensuring that confidences are respected.[60] It regards the consent of the

---

[49] Eg NHS (Venereal Diseases) Regulations 1974, SI 1974/29; NHS Trusts and Primary Care Trusts (Sexually Transmitted Diseases) Directions 2000.
[50] Human Fertilisation and Embryology Act 1990, as amended by the Human Fertilisation Embryology (Disclosure of Information) Act 1992.
[51] National Health Service (Venereal Diseases) Regulations 1974, SI 1974/29.
[52] BMA (2004).   [53] GMC (2004).   [54] Nursing and Midwifery Council (2002).
[55] DoH (2003a).   [56] *Re C* [1996] 1 FCR 605, *W v Edgell* [1990] 1 All ER 835.
[57] Nursing and Midwifery Council (2002).   [58] Para 5.1.   [59] Para 5.3.   [60] GMC (2004).

patient as the primary exception to the principle that confidential information must be kept secret. However, it also accepts that where secrecy would risk death or serious harm to the patient or another person, disclosure is permitted. The GMC guidance emphasizes that patients should be told at the outset how information about them is to be used. If a patient refuses to permit the sharing of their records with others caring for them this must be respected.

The GMC suggests that a disclosure of confidential information is only exceptionally justifiable:

> Personal information may be disclosed in the public interest, without the patient's consent, and in exceptional cases where patients have withheld consent, where the benefits to an individual or to society of the disclosure outweigh the public and the patient's interest in keeping the information confidential. In all cases where you consider disclosing information without consent from the patient, you must weigh the possible harm (both to the patient, and the overall trust between doctors and patients) against the benefits which are likely to arise from the release of information.[61]

1.8.3 *NHS guidelines*

The Department of Health has issued a code of practice designed to ensure the protection of confidential information. At the heart of the guidance is the following principle:

> Patients entrust us with, or allow us to gather, sensitive information relating to their health and other matters as part of their seeking treatment. They do so in confidence and they have the legitimate expectation that staff will respect their privacy and act appropriately. In some circumstances patients may lack the competence to extend this trust, or may be unconscious, but this does not diminish the duty of confidence. It is essential, if the legal requirements are to be met and the trust of patients is to be retained, that the NHS provides, and is seen to provide, a confidential service. What this entails is described in more detail in subsequent sections of this document, but a key guiding principle is that a patient's health records are made by the health service to support that patient's healthcare.[62]

The Code makes it clear that duties of confidentiality apply not just to doctors but also that:

- all NHS bodies and those carrying out functions on behalf of the NHS have a common law duty of confidence to patients, and a duty to support professional ethical standards of confidentiality;
- everyone working for or with the NHS who records, handles, stores, or otherwise comes across information has a personal common law duty of confidence to patients and to her or his employer. This applies equally to those, such as students or trainees, on temporary placements;
- health professionals have, by virtue of professional regulation, an ethical duty of confidence which, when considering whether information should be passed on, includes paying special regard to the health needs of the patient and to her or his wishes;
- other individuals and agencies to whom information is passed legitimately may use it only as authorized for specific purposes and possibly subject to particular conditions.[63]

---

[61] GMC (2004: 22).   [62] DoH (2003a: 7).   [63] DoH (2003: 4.1).

1.8.4 *The British Medical Association*

The BMA sees the importance of confidentiality from a broad perspective. Its guidance on confidentiality opens with the following statement:

> Respect for privacy allows people time and space to express their thoughts and feelings without fear of being misunderstood or judged by unsympathetic third parties. It has been described as being essential for 'sexual, religious, and imaginative impulses to flourish' as well as necessary for people making important life choices such as those related to medical treatment. Despite this, people are often interested in the private lives of others. In medicine, others—typically relatives or employer—sometimes believe that it is important for the protection of their own interests to discover information about patients. Health professionals' duties of confidentiality prevent such access without patients' consent.[64]

However, the guidance goes on to emphasize that confidentiality is not an absolute right and can be breached in order to protect the rights of others or the public interest.[65]

1.9 Comments on the law

It must be admitted that the law in this area is not very satisfactory. There have been few cases governing the issue and there appear to be large number of branches of the law that govern the area. A number of points can, however, be made to reassure the reader. The first is that, as already indicated, professional bodies have provided fairly clear guidance on the obligations of confidentiality and the courts are likely, in areas of doubt, to ensure that the law coincides with professional guidance. Second, the courts have indicated that when considering the legal position of confidence, whether the obligation is seen as emanating from contract, tort, or equity, the extent of the obligation will be the same.[66] Third, the paucity of case law may indicate that this is not an area where clear legal regulation is required, professional responsibilities appear to adequately protect patients' confidentiality. However, it might be that lack of clarity discourages people from bringing legal proceedings.

 REALITY CHECK

Confidentiality in practice

As we have seen, in theory the law takes breaches of confidentiality seriously, but in real life how well is confidentiality protected?

According to David Stone, 'many observers would say that, at ground level, the rights and duties arising from patient confidentiality are honoured more in the breach than the observance' (Stone (2001: 132)). As he points out, such a large number of people will have access to the records that they cannot realistically be described as private. One writer explains that at least 25 and possibly 100 health care professionals and administrative personnel at one university hospital deal with a particular patient's records (Gillon (1986: 109)). But this kind of use of information is probably not objected to by many people.

---

[64] BMA (2004: 165).   [65] BMA (2004: 166).   [66] Montgomery (2003: 262).

The kind of case which is more likely to give concerns to members of the public is the following mundane case:

> Over a golf match between a dentist and a GP the two men discovered they shared a patient. The GP told the dentist that the patient had had an abortion. The dentist told his wife, who told a friend. The friend mentioned it to the patient (mentioned by BMA (2004:167)).

It is this kind of revelation of personal information to a person's social circle which is the main concern of many patients (Siegler (1982)). Another kind of incident which raises ire in the media is the finding of confidential medical reports in public waste bins or on the street (see eg BBC Newsonline (9 December 2003)).

Interestingly people in one survey were not particularly concerned about doctors seeing their medical records, but were unhappy about receptionists receiving it (NHS Information Authority (2002: 6)).

An Observer investigation (Browne (2000)) discovered some troubling breaches of confidentiality including the following:

- A 68-year-old man was refused a place in a care home when social services found from his medical records that he was gay.

- A man found out that his niece had a secret abortion when the company he worked for was asked to do a financial audit of the local health authority. He told her parents, who were very religious.

- A woman was sacked after her GP sent her records to her employer. The notes revealed that she had a history of mental health problems.

- An MP was sent the medical records of a constituent without her consent. She found out only when the MP passed on the records to her.

A survey by the Audit Commission in 1995 revealed rather lax attitudes when it looked at hospital records. The report stated: 'In nearly two thirds of the hospitals visited case notes were taken out of the hospital by clinical staff for research and other purposes. They had been known to be left under the doormat in doctors' residences and in the boots of cars. In one instance a doctor sold his car with patients' case notes still in the boot' (Audit Commission (1995: 31)). It may be that, since the report, attitudes within the NHS towards confidentiality have changed. As already mentioned there has been in recent years a moving away from seeing confidentiality as a negative concept ('don't reveal private information') to data protection as a positive concept ('make sure that private information does not become public'). The NHS has talked about the need to create a 'Confidentiality culture' (NHS Information Authority (2002: 6)). However there is at least anecdotal evidence that doctors are often overheard discussing patients' personal medical details on trains (Hendricks (2003)) at parties (Weiss (1982)) and in lifts (Vigod, Bell, and Bohnen (2003)). Interestingly the NHS code on confidentiality has seen it necessary to spell out the requirement not to discuss patients' confidential information in public places (DoH (2003a)). Another concern in a study is the willingness of GP surgeries to reveal personal information about patients to telephone callers, without checking their identity (Sokol and Car (2006); Russell (2003): 25 out of 46 surgeries gave out contact details of patients without checking the identity of the caller).

Interestingly from the perspective of NHS workers one of the main challenges in relation to medical records is not the problem in keeping the records private, but the burden of complying with requests for medical records from solicitors or others pursuing personal injury claims on people's behalf (Research Works Ltd (2004)).

One final point; in hospital many consultations on the ward take place with only the flimsiest of curtains between patients. These may offer the pretence of privacy, but it is difficult to believe that they ensure that conversations are not overheard.

2 Defences to alleged breach of confidentiality?

It is arguable that the easiest way to look at the law is to consider what defences someone might raise to a claim that they wrongfully revealed confidential information and that is how we shall proceed.

2.1 The information is not confidential

It may be argued that the information lacks any element of confidentiality. Really this is not a defence to a breach of confidence claim, but rather an argument that the information is not protected by the law on breach of confidence. In the House of Lords decision in *Campbell* it was held that information is confidential if someone had a reasonable expectation that it would be kept confidential. It is generally thought that information can acquire its confidentiality from two sources:

 (i) The information is given in the context of a relationship which is of a kind is based on an assumption of confidentiality. There is little doubt that the doctor–patient relationship is of this kind.

 (ii) The information is itself of a private and intimate kind and therefore must be kept confidential.

It should be noted that information can be regarded as confidential if it falls in either of these categories.

There are two main issues of dispute. What if information given to a health care professional by a patient is trivial. For example, if a law professor tells her or his doctor that she or he loves the television programme *Big Brother* and the doctor tells her or his friend, could this be regarded as a breach of confidence, even though love of *Big Brother* is not a particularly intimate piece of information? Is the fact that the doctor acquired the information as a result of the confidential relationship between them enough to render the information confidential?[67] In *R (on the application of Stevens) v Plymouth*[68] it was suggested that 'straightforward descriptions of everyday life' of a patient would not be regarded as confidential. On the other hand in *Ashworth Hospital Authority v MGN Ltd*[69] an argument that information about a patient was too trivial to be protected by confidentiality was rejected, on the basis that confidentiality contained a subjective element. In other words, a person would be entitled to regard a piece of medical information about themselves as sensitive, even if most people would not regard it as particularly private. Of course if the information revealed is not particularly damaging, there is unlikely to be a legal remedy of any significance, even if technically there is a breach

---

[67] BMA (2004: 167) suggests that even if the information is not 'medical' it can still be regarded as confidential.
[68] [2002] 1WLR 2483.
[69] [2001] 2 All ER 991. See further *Mersey NHS Trust v Ackroyd* [2007] EWCA Civ 101.

of confidence. The professional guidance is not in agreement. The GMC guidelines state that 'patients have a right to expect that information about them will be held in confidence by their doctors'.[70] This appears to relate to all information a patient gives a doctor. The BMA guidelines state that 'all information collected in the context of health care' is covered.[71] The NHS code states: 'A duty of confidence arises where one person discloses information to another . . . in circumstances where it is reasonable to expect that the information will be held in confidence'.[72] This might be read as suggesting trivial or non-intimate information can be revealed.

Second, what if a doctor is given information when she or he is not acting in her or his professional capacity? It is generally thought that if a doctor is given private information as a doctor it must be kept confidential.[73] For example, if a person at a party takes a doctor aside and asks for some medical advice then what the person says should be kept confidential. But if the doctor is given information, not as a doctor, but as a piece of gossip between friends, (for example, she or he is told a neighbour is having an affair) this will not necessarily attract confidentiality, but may do so if it is the kind of information which a reasonable person would expect to be kept confidential.[74] Some commentators argue that if the neighbour, or the person telling the doctor, was a patient of hers or his that would change the issue and the information would then become confidential.

2.2 The information is no longer confidential

Even if it is accepted that the information was confidential, it might be argued that the information has lost its confidential nature. Confidentiality can be lost if the information has become public. If, therefore, a patient has revealed her or his medical condition to the press, there can be no complaint if the doctor subsequently reveals that same information.[75] Remember, in *MGN v Campbell*,[76] by making public statements that she did not take drugs it was suggested that Naomi Campbell had made some information about her drug-taking non-confidential. As that case shows, however, just because some knowledge about a medical condition has been made public does not mean that others are free to reveal everything relating to the condition and its treatment. Less straightforwardly in *Stone v South East Strategic Health Authority*[77] a convicted murderer was found through his crimes to have put himself in the public domain and hence weaken the protection of his right to respect for privacy over his medical information.

2.3 The disclosure does not breach the confidentiality

Even though it is admitted that there has been a disclosure of confidential information it might be argued that the disclosure was not in breach of the obligation not to disclose. There are two main situations in which such a claim could be made:

(i) Consent. Fairly obviously if the patient is happy for information to be disclosed, then there is no breach of confidence. A husband may, for example, ask a doctor to

---

[70] GMC (2004: 1).
[73] Kennedy and Grubb (2000: 1062).
[75] See also *Douglas v Hello!* [2001] 1 WLR 992.
[77] [2006] EWHC 1668 (Admin).

[71] BMA (2004: 167).   [72] DoH (2003: 7).
[74] BMA (2004: 167) leaves the question open.
[76] [2004] UKHL 22.

discuss his medical condition with his wife. The GMC in its guidance states:

> When seeking express consent to disclosure you must make sure that patients are given enough information on which to base their decision, the reasons for the disclosure and the likely consequences of the disclosure. You should also explain how much information will be disclosed and to whom it will be given.[78]

(ii) In a highly controversial decision it was held that the release of confidential information in an anonymized form was not in breach of a duty of confidentiality. It is worth considering the decision in further detail.

KEY CASE R v Department of Health ex p Source Informatics Ltd [2001] QB 424 (CA)

Source Informatics Ltd were in the business of selling medical information to pharmaceutical companies. They started a scheme under which GPs and pharmacists would pass to them information about drugs prescribed for patients. This information included the doctor's name, and the amount and name of drug prescribed. The name of the patient was removed from any information passed on. The GPs and pharmacists were given a small sum of money for doing this. The Department of Health issued guidelines that passing on this information (even with the patient's name removed) breached the professional's confidentiality to patients. Source Informatics Ltd sought a judicial ruling on the Department of Health's guidelines. The Court of Appeal held that even though the patients had not consented to the passing of their medical information, because the information was anonymized there was no breach of confidentiality. Nor could the patient claim any property in the prescription forms from which the information was taken or the information itself.

The key passage in the judgment is as follows:

> the confidant is placed under a duty of good faith to the confider and the touchstone by which to judge the scope of his duty and whether or not it has been fulfilled or breached is his own conscience, no more and no less. One asks, therefore, on the facts of this case: would a reasonable pharmacist's conscience be troubled by the proposed use to be made of patients' prescriptions? Would he think that by entering Source's scheme he was breaking his customers' confidence, making unconscientious use of the information they provide? (Simon Brown LJ, at para 31).

The answer to the questions in the Court of Appeal's view was clearly no. There was no identifying information and therefore the patient's privacy was not infringed and therefore the doctors and pharmacists were not acting in breach of their duty of good faith.

The decision in *R v Department of Health ex p Source Informatics Ltd*[79] is highly controversial. It is important to separate out two questions here. The first is whether the disclosure of anonymized medical information is in breach of confidence. The second is whether the disclosure is justified if necessary to the public interest, for the purposes of medical research. The controversy surrounds the former issue. The Court of Appeal's approach is that because no one can know whose medical details are being looked at there can be no harm, no invasion of privacy, and therefore no wrong is committed.[80]

---

[78] GMC (2004: para 16).   [79] [2000] 1 All ER 786.
[80] O'Neill (2003) and Warnock (1998).

However that is debatable. If a nude photograph of a person was published in a news-paper without their consent, with their face obscured so they could not be identified, that person may well feel wronged, even though no one would know it was them. Their private and intimate space had been invaded, even if no one else but them realized it. Could not the same thing be said about someone's private medical details? The decision has also been criticized on the basis that it appears to suggest that a breach of confidence is only a wrong if there is unfairness or loss to someone, rather than seeing the breach of confidential information being a *prima facie* wrong for which a justification must be produced.[81]

The Court of Appeal's assumption was that the general public would not object to their medical information being used if it was anonymized. That assumption is con-testable. In fact the research shows a mixed picture with some surveys suggesting the general public have no such objection and others that they do.[82] The decision also pro-vides no option for a person who objects to their information being used for the basis of particular kinds of research. A patient may have strong moral objections to research in relation to contraception or which involves animals, and yet have no power to object to their medical information for use in such research.[83] A person's information may also be used in a way that (indirectly) harms them. Their anonymized information might, for example, show that people of a particular ethnic or cultural group were more susceptible to a certain disease and such a finding could have negative impacts for all members of that group, for example making it difficult for them to obtain mortgages.[84]

Data which contains the postcode (but not the name) of the patient is regarded by some people as anonymous.[85] The postcode is useful if research is being carried out in an attempt to ascertain whether certain conditions are more prevalent in particular parts of the country. However some argued that it can be all too easy to discover the identity of a person given their postcode and a few pieces of health information.[86] Critics reply that it is fanciful that someone will seek to discover the identity of individuals from amongst a mass of research data.

The most fundamental aspect of the decision in *Source Informatics* is its shift in focus from protection of confidential information to fairness of use. As long as the user can show they were acting in good faith with personal information they are not acting in breach of confidence. This shift from protecting the privacy of the patient, to focusing on the conscience of the user could be highly significant.[87] The decision could even be read as shifting the burden from the user, to show they had justifiable reasons for using the confidential information to the patient, being required to show the use was in bad faith. The potential impact of the decision is therefore enormous. However the traditional approach that people have a right to have their private information protected underpins the professional guidance that has been issued, and the Data Protection Act must still be followed.[88] Also the emphasis Lord Hoffman in *Campbell v MGN*[89] placed on the right

[81] Mason and Laurie (2006: 280). For criticism of its interpretation of the Data Protection Act see Beyleveld and Histed (2000).

[82] Research by Willison, Kashavjee, Nair, Goldsmith, Holbrook (2003) found that patients drew no dis-tinction between identifiable and anonymous data. But NHS Information Authority (2002) found patients happy not to be asked for consent if the information was anonymized. Morgan (2001) found 61 per cent of his sample did not want their medical details used for research even if it was anonymized.

[83] Chester (2003).   [84] Gostin (1995: 521).

[85] GMC (2004) suggests that to be anonymized information it must not contain a full postcode.

[86] Chester (2003).   [87] See the discussion in Laurie (2002: 224).

[88] Laurie (2002: 228).   [89] [2004] UKHL 22, para 51.

to privacy and autonomy as underlying the law on protection of confidential information suggests a very different approach from that promoted by *Source Informatics*.

Those keen to emphasize the importance of confidentiality can try to take a more positive spin on the decision in *Source Informatics*. The Department of Health Guidelines state that if information is disclosed it should be anonymized if possible.[90] A person wishing to reveal personal medical information must now first show that there are sufficient reasons for making the disclosure, and secondly show why the disclosure cannot be made with the information first anonymized. This is most significant in the area of the use of medical information in research, where it might be thought that only exceptionally would anonymous information not be sufficient for the task at hand. However, there can be difficulties in using anonymous data for research purposes, because it can be harder to ensure there are no duplicates.[91]

2.4 Consent

As already indicated there is no breach of confidence if the patient has consented to the release of the information. In fact it is rare for patients to be asked explicitly whether they consent to others seeing their information. This is because often medical professionals rely on implied consent.[92] When patients agree to be referred to a consultant by a GP, although they do not in so many words consent to the disclosure to the consultant of their medical history, they do by implication.[93] As we shall see this 'implied consent' can be taken to authorize the use of information to a wide range of medical personnel.[94] So more generally, patients who give information to their doctors are presumed to consent to the information being provided to others in the health care system in the course of normal medical practice.[95] However, the current GMC guidance clearly states that express consent should be obtained for the sharing of information amongst a health team:

> Most people understand and accept that information must be shared within the health care team in order to provide their care. You should make sure that patients are aware that personal information about them will be shared within the health care team, unless they object, and of the reasons for this.[96]

Although this might be best practice it is likely that a court would accept that a patient impliedly consents to their information being shared amongst a health team if they had voiced no objection to this. The difficulty with using the implied consent model to such a wide range of medical professionals is that it assumes that a patient is aware that the information will be shared.[97] Although this is plausible in relation to a sharing of information between the doctors who are actually dealing with the patient, the justification has been said by the Department of Health also to cover sharing information in the context of, *inter alia*, clinical audit, investigating complaints,[98] monitoring public

---

[90] DoH (2004b: 4.5).   [91] Chalmers and Muir (2003).   [92] BMA (2004: 177).
[93] But, a consultant should not pass on a report to a GP against the wishes of a patient: *Birmingham CC v O* [1983] 1 All ER 497.
[94] BMA (2004: 180).   [95] Information Commissioner (2002).
[96] GMC (2004: para 10).
[97] The Royal College of General Practitioners (2000: 1) is concerned about the reliance on implied consent.
[98] A GP about whom there has been a complaint by a patient can look only at the parts of the patient's medical records that relate to the complaint: DoH (1996a).

health and research.[99] Is it not a fiction to say that the patient 'consents' to such use of information? This is especially so in circumstances where the revealing of information is not directly related to their treatment, but includes managers looking at the general running of the hospital.[100] Also, if implied consent is the basis of the law here, does that mean that patients who state that they do not want their records to be viewed by anyone except the medical staff attending them must have those wishes respected?

Such concerns about an implied consent model could lead us in two directions:

(i) We should continue to accept that consent is the basis of the justification, but we need to make sure patients are aware how widely their information will be distributed within the NHS and give them an opportunity to object to some of the uses.[101] If they do object then their wishes must be respected. The GMC has accepted this approach. Its guidance in relation to clinical audits explains:

13. ...Where an audit is to be undertaken by the team which provided care, or those working to support them, such as clinical audit staff, you may disclose identifiable information, provided you are satisfied that patients:

• have been informed that their data may be disclosed for clinical audit, and their right to object to the disclosure; and

• have not objected.

14. If a patient does object you should explain why information is needed and how this may benefit their care. If it is not possible to provide safe care without disclosing information for audit, you should explain this to the patient and the options open to them.

Similar guidance is issued in relation to research.[102]

(ii) The alternative approach (which we will consider below) would be to abandon the implied consent model as too artificial and instead suggest that revelation to workers in the health care system should be seen as justified in the public interest.

2.5 'The proper working of the hospital'

As we have seen, in a modern hospital medical information about patients is shared among a bewildering number of people. Accountability, monitoring, and research may require confidential information to be processed by many within a hospital.[103] The breach of confidentiality could be justified on the basis that it is an essential part of the working of a modern national health care system.[104] As such it is justifiable in the public interest that a patient's medical information be available to any worker in the NHS who has a legitimate interest in viewing it. If such a justification were supported then arguably, even if a patient objected, public policy would justify the disclosure. In terms of article 8 of the European Convention on Human Rights it could be said that the breach of the patient's rights under article 8(1) is justified as necessary in the interests of the state under article 8(2).

---

99 DoH (1996a).   100 See the discussion in Cambridge Health Informatics Ltd (2001b).
101 Some steps in this regard are mentioned in DoH (1996a). See also GMC (2004: para 1) and British Psychological Society (2002).
102 DoH (2003a: para 12).
103 DoH (1996a: para 1.2). Even the Commission for Health Care Audit and Inspection has the power to look at unanonymized data (Dyer (2003)).
104 BMA (2004: 180).

There is little explicit legal support for this approach. In *R v Department of Health, ex p Source Informatics Ltd*[105] Simon Brown LJ suggested that using confidential information for legitimate NHS purposes was legitimate, even if done against a patient's wishes. However, he left open the question of whether this was because there was no breach of confidence, or because there was a public interest justifying the breach. There are also cases in banking law which have accepted an argument that confidential information can be used within a bank if necessary to enable the proper workings of the bank.[106]

2.6 A threat of serious harm to others

Threats of serious harm to others can justify revealing confidential information.[107] There have been few cases dealing with this justification and so it is difficult to state the law with certainty. The most obvious explanation for this exception is that there is a public interest in protecting innocent people from harm, and that this outweighs the public interest in protecting confidences. An alternative could be based on the principle that those who seek the protection of equity must have 'clean hands'. If a patient poses a risk to others she or he thereby forfeits the protection of the law on confidence. However, the equitable principle is founded on the notion of conscience and thus cannot explain why a patient who, through no fault of her or his own, poses a risk to others should lose the protection of the law. So the obvious explanation is the most popular one: given the choice between respecting confidentiality or protecting someone from death or serious harm a medical professional should choose the latter. It is not surprising that this exception is not controversial either among most ethicists,[108] practitioners, or members of the public.[109]

What is, however, a matter of some debate is how serious the harm to others must be before a breach of confidentiality is justified. The GMC advice is that there must be a serious risk of death or serious harm.[110] The British Psychological Society's guidelines for psychologists requires only a 'risk of harm'.[111] The Department of Health guidelines suggest:

> Murder, manslaughter, rape, treason, kidnapping, child abuse or other cases where individuals have suffered serious harm may all warrant breaching confidentiality. Serious harm to the security of the state or to public order and crimes that involve substantial financial gain or loss will also generally fall within this category. In contrast, theft, fraud, or damage to property where loss or damage is less substantial would generally not warrant breach of confidence.

The BMA guidance suggests that a risk of assault or a road traffic accident are sufficient to justify disclosure of confidential information, but not just a financial loss.[112] However, it went on to point out that this division between a threat of harm to person and property is not that straightforward. Serious fraud of the NHS delays treatment for patients and can thereby be said to cause physical harm.

---

[105] [2000] 1 All ER 786.
[106] *Tournier v National Provincial and Union Bank of England* [1924] 1 KB 461.
[107] For a rejection of this claim on ethical grounds see Kipnis (2006).
[108] Morgan (2001: 166) thinks it will be very rare that the threat will be of sufficiently serious harm.
[109] Jones (2003).
[110] GMC (2004: para 22). BMA (2004: 190) suggest that serious harm can include psychological harm.
[111] British Psychological Society (2002: 4).   [112] BMA (2004: 190).

The problem, as the BMA has pointed out, is that it is difficult for a medical professional to know whether the risk to others would be judged sufficiently serious to justify
an interference until the courts rule on the issue. This can leave the professional in an
'invidious position'.[113]

The leading case on this exception is *W v Egdell*:[114]

KEY CASE   W v Edgell [1990] 1 All ER 835

W had been convicted of manslaughter in connection with some extremely violent killings of five
people. He was being detained in a secure hospital under the Mental Health Act 1983. Dr Edgell
was asked to prepare a report for a mental health review tribunal which was considering whether W
should be released. The doctor's report indicated that W was extremely dangerous. He went on to
say that those caring for him did not appear to appreciate his dangerousness, particularly his interest
in high explosives. When W's solicitors saw the report they decided to drop their application to the
tribunal. Dr Egdell wanted to send a copy of his report to the Home Office and the medical director
of the hospital caring for W. W applied to stop him disclosing the report. The Court of Appeal held
that the disclosure of the report to those parties was justified. The Home Office and the hospital staff
were not aware of W's dangerousness and the public interest justified the disclosure. It was legitimate
to breach confidence where there was a real risk of significant harm to others.

Importantly Bingham LJ emphasized that the court was not saying that W's confidentiality was not
protected at all: '[Dr Egdell] could not lawfully sell the contents of his report to a newspaper... Nor
could he without a breach of the law as well as professional etiquette, discuss the case in a learned
article or in his memoirs or in gossiping with friends, unless he took appropriate steps to conceal the
identity of W.'

This case reveals some important limitations on the justification based on a threat of
death or serious harm to another:

(i) It must be shown that there is a real and serious risk of danger to the public. The
risk must be of significant harm, probably of a physical kind, to a victim. Also that
risk must be a serious possibility and not merely a fanciful one.

(ii) The risk must be an ongoing one.[115] The fact that there was in the past a risk to the
public would not, it seems, be sufficient.[116]

(iii) The disclosure had to be to appropriate people with a legitimate interest in the matter. In *W v Egdell* the Court of Appeal approved of the disclosure to the hospital
and the Home Office. A disclosure to members of the press would probably not be
regarded as lawful. However, there might be cases where revealing information to
the public would be appropriate (eg if a dangerous patient escaped from a secure
hospital). Disclosure of confidential information to regulatory bodies such as the

---

[113] BMA (2004: 190).   [114] [1990] 1 All ER 835.
[115] *R v Harrison* [2000] WL1026999 held that a doctor owed no duty of confidentiality in respect of threats
to kill made by a defendant. See also *R v Kennedy* [1999] 1 Cr App R 54.
[116] *Schering Chemicals v Falkman Ltd* [1981] 2 All ER 321.

GMC is permissible if to do so is necessary to enable them to ensure that the public is protected from professional misconduct.[117]

(iv) Any disclosure must be restricted to the minimum necessary to protect the public.[118] To use the example just mentioned, if a dangerous patient escaped from a secure hospital, although it may be justifiable to inform the public that the patient posed a particular risk, for example towards elderly women, it would not be necessary for all of his medical history or details to be made public. However, in *Stone v South East Strategic Health Authority*[119] it was held that partial disclosure of the report which contained details of a convicted murderer's mental health would be misleading and so the full report should be made available.

What is the position where a patient has informed her or his doctor that he or she intends to kill or cause serious harm to another and the doctor decides to keep quiet about this? If the patient does go on to kill or cause serious harm can the doctor be sued? An American decision, *Tarasoff v The Regents of the University of California*[120] discusses the issue.

P was receiving therapy at a hospital in the University of California at Berkeley. He told his therapist, a Doctor Moore, that he was going to kill his former girlfriend, Tatiana Tarasoff when she returned from her holidays. The doctor informed the police, who detained P, but released him when he promised not to harm Tatiana. The doctor took no steps to warn Tatiana herself. P killed Tatiana on her return from her holidays. The Supreme Court of California, by a majority, held that Dr Moore owed Tatiana a duty of care. Where a doctor is aware that one of her or his patients poses a serious danger of violence to another she or he incurs an obligation to use reasonable care to protect the intended victim. He had failed to do this. It is far from clear whether that decision would be followed in England and Wales. The general view seems to be that it would not[121] because normally in tort law someone is not responsible for the acts of a third party.[122] In *Palmer v Tees Health Authority*[123] it was held that a health authority who were caring for a man did not owe a duty of care to a woman he killed. One of the reasons given was that there was no way the Health Authority could foresee that their patient would kill this woman. This might suggest that the case would be decided differently if he posed a risk to an identifiable individual.

2.7 Child protection

In a similar vein to the exception just mentioned, confidence can be breached if there is evidence that a patient may have been abusing a child.[124] The GMC has suggested that not only may doctors make a disclosure in order to protect a child from abuse, but that they *must* do so:

> If you believe a patient to be a victim of neglect or physical, sexual or emotional abuse and that the patient cannot give or withhold consent to disclosure, you must give information

[117] *Re A (A Minor) (Disclosure of Medical Records to GMC)* [1999] 1 FCR 30; *Woogar v Chief Constable of Sussex Police & UKCC* [1999] 1 LMLR 335.

[118] *X v Y* [1988] 2 All ER 649.   [119] [2006] EWHC 1668 (Admin).

[120] (1976) 17 Cal (3d) 358.   [121] Miers (1996); Morris and Ashead (1997).

[122] *Smith v Littlewoods* [1987] AC 241.   [123] [2000] PIQR1.

[124] *Re M* [1990] 1 All ER 205, 213. DoH (1999a: para 7.27).

promptly to an appropriate responsible person or statutory agency, where you believe that the disclosure is in the patient's best interests. If, for any reason, you believe that disclosure of information is not in the best interests of an abused or neglected patient, you should discuss the issues with an experienced colleague. If you decide not to disclose information, you must be prepared to justify your decision.[125]

This also could be justified in terms of article 8, in that the patient's rights under that article are properly infringed because to do so is necessary in the interests of others (ie the child).

2.8 Assisting police investigations

Perhaps surprisingly, there is no general obligation on health processionals to disclose confidential information even if requested to do so by the police.[126] There are a few specific circumstances where they must. They are bound to provide the police, on request, with any information that would identify a driver alleged to have committed a traffic offence.[127] Even if not specifically requested, they are bound to disclose to the police suspicions that a person has been involved in terrorist activities.[128] It should be added that medical professionals should not obstruct a police investigation, but that offence will not be committed by failing to answer police questions, provided they have a lawful excuse (eg that the information requested is confidential).[129]

Although there are only limited circumstances in which there is a *duty to* disclose information there are circumstances in which the information *may* be disclosed. The Crime and Disorder Act 1998, section 115 permits the disclosure of confidential information to, *inter alia*, a Chief Officer of Police. However, this power should only be used where the patient has consented or there is a strong public interest for doing so.

The BMA and Department of Health[130] have suggested that doctors should consider disclosing information where all of the following are true:

- The offence is grave (eg murder, manslaughter, rape, hostage-taking, causing death by dangerous driving).

- The prevention or detection of the crime will be seriously delayed or prejudiced without the disclosure.

- The disclosed information will only be used for the detection and prosecution of the alleged criminal.

- Any material released will be destroyed once it has been used.

Lord Denning in *Initial Services Ltd v Putterill*[131] appeared to suggest that disclosure of any crime committed or contemplated is permitted. If this is correct it means that a doctor who discloses information concerning a minor crime is not acting illegally, but is acting contrary to professional guidance. That said, until we have further guidance, it is not safe to declare with confidence what the law is.

---

[125] GMC (2004: para 29). Although Montgomery (2003: 269–71) questions the source of the legal obligation.

[126] *Sykes v DPP* [1962] AC 528, 564 (Lord Denning).   [127] Road Traffic Act 1988, s 172.

[128] Terrorism Act 2000, ss 19 and 20.   [129] *Rice v Connolly* [1966] 2 All ER 649.

[130] BMA (2004: 23–4) and DoH (1996a).   [131] [1968] 1 QB 396, 405.

2.9 Public debate and press freedom

Can a breach of confidentiality be justified on the basis that the disclosure is in the public interest because it promotes public debate? Two cases which show the issues well are *H (A Healthcare Worker) v Associated Newspapers Ltd* and *N (A Health Authority) and X v Y.*

KEY CASE   X v Y [1988] 2 All ER 649

A newspaper discovered that two doctors were being treated for AIDS. A hospital sought an injunction to prevent the publication of the information. The newspaper accepted that it had obtained the information in breach of confidence, but argued that it was important that there was a public debate over the issue. The judge argued that the public interest (which was not to be confused with things in which the public were interested) had to be weighed against: (i) the principle that hospital records should remain confidential; (ii) the public interest that employees should not be encouraged to disclose confidential information to newspapers (in other words prohibiting the publication might deter employees from passing on confidential information to newspapers in the future); (iii) the public interest in ensuring that AIDS sufferers could use hospitals without fear that their condition will be made public. Taking these factors into account the judge concluded that the newspaper should not publish the information. The judge noted that there was already wide-ranging debate about AIDS and the information in question would add little to it.

KEY CASE   H (A Healthcare Worker) v Associated Newspapers Ltd and N (A Health Authority) [2002] LLMLR 210 (CA)

H, a health care professional tested positive for HIV. The health authority (N) proposed to notify all his patients and invite them to undergo an HIV test if they wished. H sought an injunction to prevent N from notifying his patients. He argued that the risk to patients of HIV was very low and insufficient to justify a breach in his confidentiality. The *Mail on Sunday* got to hear about the dispute and H successfully applied for an injunction to prevent the publication of any details identifying him, his speciality, or N. On the hearing for the full injunction Gross J upheld the ban on publishing H's identity, but would have allowed the naming of N and H's specialism. H appealed to the Court of Appeal, arguing that it would be easy for people knowing his specialism and the name of the health authority to discover his identity. The Court of Appeal held that H's name and N's identity should be kept secret. They accepted the argument that H's identity would otherwise be too readily discovered. In particular they were concerned that his patients would discover the news before being contacted by N and being offered the appropriate counselling. However, H's specialism could be named, because that raised particular issues which were relevant to a legitimate debate about the risks of HIV.

It is a notable aspect of *H (a Health Care Worker) v Associate Newspapers Ltd* that the court attached particular significance to the protection of press freedom guaranteed by the European Convention on Human Rights, article 10. This right led the court to require clear harms to justify an interference with this right:

> We would view with concern any attempt to invoke the power of the court to grant an injunction restraining freedom of expression merely on the ground that release of

information would give rise to administrative problems and a drain on resources. Such consequences are the price which has to be paid, from time to time, for freedom of expression in a democratic society.

In weighing up the freedom of expression and protection of privacy in a case where medical records have been improperly acquired the court should consider *both* the interests of the individual patient and the interests of the hospital in ensuring the confidentiality of its records.[132]

2.10 For the best interests of an incompetent person

If a person is incompetent then it is generally thought that it is permissible to disclose confidential health information to those caring for her or him or others if that was necessary for her or his proper care.[133] However this exception should be interpreted strictly. As the BMA have stressed, just because a patient is incompetent this should not lessen the protection that is accorded to her or his right of confidentiality.[134]

2.11 Discovery

If a person is bringing or plans to bring legal proceedings against another she or he can apply for all relevant information to be disclosed. However this is not an absolute right.

In *D v NSPCC*[135] the plaintiff sought from the NSPCC documents indicating the name of the person who had alleged that she had been committing child abuse. The court refused to order disclosure of the information. It was felt that it was necessary to weigh up the plaintiff's interest in discovering her accusers, so that she could if appropriate bring legal proceedings against them, with the public interest in encouraging people who have suspicions about child abuse to alert appropriate authorities, without fear that doing so could lead to legal proceedings being taken against them. The balance fell against ordering disclosure. The same approach might be taken if a person was seeking another's medical records for the purposes of using it in litigation: would the interest in protecting confidentiality outweigh the importance of enabling a person to have access to relevant documents in the course of legal proceedings? The reasoning in *D v NSPCC* would not be directly applicable because the issue there was a special immunity known as 'Crown Immunity' which applied to bodies acting in the public interest. Nevertheless a similar approach may well be adopted by the courts when considering infringement of an individual's rights of confidentiality.

If a health professional is called to court in a case as a witness and is asked about confidential information then she or he can ask to be permitted to decline to answer the question on the basis that it would involve breaking confidence. However, if the judge states that the information must be provided it would be a contempt of court by the professional not to provide the information. In *AB v Glasgow and West of Scotland Blood Transfusion Service*[136] a Scottish court refused to require a doctor to name a donor who had supplied infected blood as part of a blood donation. The concern about the impact

[132] *Ashworth Hospital Authority v MGN* [2002] UKHL 29; [2002] 4 All ER 193.
[133] *F v W Berkshire HA* [1989] 2 All ER 545.   [134] BMA (2004: 178).   [135] [1978] AC 171.
[136] (1989) 15 BMLR 91 (Scottish Court of Session (Outer House)).

of discouraging blood donation was held to outweigh the importance of the information for the case.

2.12 Good faith disclosure

The Court of Appeal in *R v Department of Health ex p Source Informatics Ltd*[137] suggested that there is only a breach of confidence if the breach affects the conscience of the discloser.[138] In other words if the revelation of the secret information is in good faith then there is no breach of confidence. It is not clear, however, that this represents the law. It does not sit easily with *Swinney v Chief Constable of Northumbria Police*[139] which suggests that a breach of confidence does not need to be deliberate and can be negligent.[140] More significantly Lord Hoffman in *Campbell v MGN* in the House of Lords stated that the modern understanding of breach of confidence was that it was not based on a 'good faith' requirement imposed upon the recipient of the information, but rather it focussed on the protection of human dignity and autonomy of the person the information concerned.[141]

2.13 Other public interest reasons

The exceptions mentioned so far can be said to be justifiable in the public interest. There may be in addition to those already discussed a 'catch all exception' that a breach of confidence can be justified in the public interest. The GMC give an example of 'where a colleague, who is also a patient, is placing patients at risk as a result of illness or other medical condition'.[142] When relying on the general public interest the medical professional must be persuaded that it is necessary to reveal non-anonymized data and that it is not practical to obtain the consent of the patient.[143]

In *R v Crozier*[144] a psychiatrist instructed by the defendant in an attempted murder case disclosed his report to the prosecution after a judge sentenced the defendant to prison, not having been told of the report. Once the judge was informed about the report the defendant was sentenced to a hospital order and orders were made under the Mental Health Act 1983. The court held this disclosure was justified in the general public interest in ensuring appropriate sentences were imposed in criminal cases.[145] In *R (Axon) v Secretary of State*[146] Silber J rejected an argument that there was a public interest in infringing a child's right to confidentiality in order to inform their parents that the child was seeking an abortion. Indeed Silber J suggested quite the reverse; the public interest was in respecting the confidentiality of the information.

---

137 [2000] 1 All ER 786.
138 The role of conscience in breach of confidence was also emphasized in *Campbell v MGN* in the Court of Appeal [2003] QB 633 and *Stephens v Avery* [1988] 2 All ER 477.
139 [1996] 3 All ER 449.
140 See also Grubb (2000) who questions this part of the judgment.
141 *Campbell v MGN* [2004] UKHL 22, para 51.   142 GMC (2004: para 37).
143 GMC (2004: para 1).   144 (1990) 12 Cr App R (S) 206.
145 Disclosure of medical reports might also be justifiable in order to protect the economic well-being of the country: *MS v Sweden* (1997) 45 BMLR 133.
146 [2006] EWHC 37 (Admin).

2.14 Special statutory provisions

There are special statutory provisions which permit or even require confidential information to be disclosed. To give a couple of examples: a doctor treating a drug addict must
give details about the person to the Home Office;[147] and the Public Health (Control of
Disease) Act 1984 states that cholera, plague, relapsing fever, smallpox, and typhus shall
be notifiable diseases, which means that if a doctor finds a patient with such a disease she
or he must notify the Government. Similarly some kinds of venereal disease[148] and food
poisoning are notifiable. The Government has been under pressure to add HIV/AIDS
to the list of notifiable diseases, but has declined to do so.[149] The argument is that HIV/
AIDS is nothing like as infectious as, for example, cholera, and indeed with responsible
behaviour poses no risk to others. It is therefore in the public interest to encourage
people to receive medical treatment for suspected AIDS and not be deterred by any
mandatory reporting requirement. Controversially details of terminations of pregnancies under the Abortion Act 1967 must be given to the Chief Medical Officer.[150] Since
2002 only a patient's NHS number, date of birth, and full postcode are required, not
her or his name.[151]

The Health and Social Care Act 2001, section 60(1) permits the disclosure of medical
information for research purposes without a patient's consent. This provision provides:

> The Secretary of State may by regulation make such provision for and in connection with
> requiring or regulating the processing of prescribed patient information for medical
> purposes as he considers necessary or expedient—
>
> (a) in the interest of improving patient care, or
>
> (b) in the public interest.

This is a controversial provision because potentially it provides a significant inroad into
protection of medical confidentiality. Regulations under the Act state: 'Anything done
by a person, that is necessary for the purposes of processing patient information in
accordance with these Regulations shall be taken to be lawfully done despite any obligation of confidence owed by that person in respect of it'.[152]

Much depends on what kind of regulations will be issued by the Secretary of State.
She or he must consult with a Patient Information Advisory Group before issuing any
regulation.[153]

The Patient Information Advisory Group[154] has the job of overseeing arrangements
created under section 60. It has made it clear that section 60 will not be allowed to
be used just in order to make access to medical data easier. It will have to be shown
that there is no other practical way to get to the data and that it is not possible to use
anonymized data. Between July 2005 and June 2006 there were 42 applications and
approval was given to 37.

Section 60 has been criticized. The BMA has complained that it is 'very general' and
more guidance is required on how to apply it. It is justified by others on the basis that,

---

[147] Misuses of Drugs (Notification of Supply to Addicts) Regulations 1973, SI 1973/799.
[148] *Lee v South West Thames RHA* [1985] 2 All ER 385.
[149] See Keown (1989a) for a summary of the arguments.
[150] Abortion Regulations 1991, SI 1992/499.   [151] DoH (2002a).
[152] Health Service (Control of Patient Information) Regulations 2002, SI 2002/1438.
[153] See Health Service (Control of Patient Information) Regulations 2002, SI 2002/1438.
[154] Patient Advisory Group (2007).

if large scale research needs to be carried out, it is not practical to obtain the consent of each and every person. If that was done and only the information of those who consented could be used this would skew the sample. On the other hand, researchers have complained that the procedures to obtain approval to carry out large scale studies are 'sluggish' and an improper restriction on research.[155]

2.15 Extent of disclosure

One point which has already been emphasized at several points bears repeating, and that is that even if there is a justifiable ground for disclosure it must be shown that:

(i) The person to whom the disclosure was made was an appropriate person.[156] So although in a certain case disclosure to the police may have been justified, if the disclosure was to a journalist this may be unlawful.[157]

(ii) The disclosure was to the minimum amount necessary under the justification. In other words if anonymized disclosure would have adequately protected the public interest then only anonymized disclosure is permitted.

3 The Data Protection Act

The Data Protection Act 1998[158] covers the processing of personal data. The Act is not restricted to computerized records; it covers all personal data stored in systems (be they electronic or on paper) that enable information about someone to be readily accessible. At the heart of the Act are eight cardinal principles which are set out in Schedule 1, Part 1 of the Act:

(1) Personal data shall be processed fairly and lawfully and, in particular, shall not be processed unless—

   (a) at least one of the conditions in Schedule 2 is met, and

   (b) in the case of sensitive personal data, at least on of the conditions in Schedule 3 is also met.

(2) Personal data shall be obtained only for one or more specified and lawful purposes, and shall not be further processed in any manner incompatible with that purpose or those purposes.

(3) Personal data shall be adequate, relevant and not excessive in relation to the purpose or purposes for which they are processed.

(4) Personal data shall be accurate and, where necessary, kept up to date.

(5) Personal data processed for any purpose or purposes shall not be kept for longer than is necessary for that purpose for those purposes.

---

155 Turnberg (2003).
156 In *Woolgar v CC of Sussex Police* [1999] Lloyds Rep Med 335 the police contacted the UKCC (the nurse's professional body) after they had concerns over her behaviour.
157 Although on whether a journalist is required to reveal his or her sources see *Mersey NHS Trust v Ackroyd* [2007] EWCA Civ 101; discussed in Sandland (2007).
158 The Data Protection Act 1998 was passed to give effect to the European Directive on Personal Data 1995 (EC Directive 95/46/EC).

(6) Personal data shall be processed in accordance with the rights of data subjects under this Act.

(7) Appropriate technical and organizational measures shall be taken against unauthorized or unlawful processing of personal data and against accidental loss or destruction of, or damage to, personal data.

(8) Personal data shall not be transferred to a country or territory outside the European Economic Area unless that country or territory ensure an adequate level of protection for the rights and freedoms of data subsection relation to the processing of personal data.

Health records are classified as 'sensitive personal data' and are subject to special protection. A health record is defined as:

any record which:

(a) consists of information relating to the physical or mental health or condition of an individual, and

(b) has been made by or on behalf of a health professional in connection with the care of an individual.[159]

All information in health records is regarded as sensitive personal data, whether it relates to minor injuries or much more intimate information.[160] Sensitive personal data can only be 'processed' (eg consulted or used) if a series of special conditions are met. These include the following:[161]

(a) The patient has given explicit consent to the information being used.

(b) It is necessary to process the information to protect the vital interests of the patient.

(c) Where the data is in the public domain.

(d) A health care organization or professional needs to use the information to obtain legal advice or in the course of legal proceedings.

(e) The processing of the information is necessary for the purposes of statutory or government functions.

(f) It is necessary for medical purposes and the information is used by a healthcare professional.

(g) Processing of medical data or data relating to ethnic origin for monitoring purposes.

(h) Processing in the substantial public interest, necessary for the purpose of research whose object is not to support decisions with respect to any particular data subject otherwise than with the explicit consent of the data subject and which is unlikely to cause substantial damage or substantial distress to the data subject or any other person.[162]

It is the responsibility of the 'data controller' to ensure that these obligations are complied with. However all those who use protected information are required to comply with the terms of the legislation. Anyone who obtains or discloses information without

---

[159] S 68(2).   [160] Information Commissioner (2002).
[161] The full list is to be found in Data Protection Act 1998, Schs 1 and 3.
[162] The Data Protection (Processing of Sensitive Personal Data) Order 2000 added (g) and (h).

the consent of the data controller commits an offence.[163] If a person has suffered damage or loss as a result of a violation of the Data Protection Act she or he can receive compensation. There is also an obligation on health organizations to protect the security of health records. The Information Commissioner has the power to issue an enforcement notice requiring specific steps be taken to ensure compliance of data.[164] Individuals can ask the Information Commissioner to assess whether the Act is being complied with.[165] It is a criminal offence to fail to comply with a notice.[166] The Information Commissioner also has the function of preparing good practice guidance.[167]

4 Problem issues

We now look at some particular areas in relation to confidentiality which have proved particularly controversial.

4.1 Genetic information: informing relatives

Genetic information has become increasingly important and the extent to which it should be kept confidential is a highly topical issue.[168] Consider the following two scenarios which indicate why the issue can be complex:

(i) A couple are considering having a child but are aware that there may be genetic diseases in the family history. They seek medical advice on what risks there are that any child of theirs will inherit a condition. The doctor to properly advise them will need the medical history of their parents. If the couple's parents refuse to cooperate, can the doctor access the parents' notes so as to advise the couple?

(ii) In treating X a doctor discovers that X suffers from a genetically inherited illness and therefore it is likely that X's relatives do too. The doctor wishes to advise the relatives of that risk, but X objects to this. If the doctor went ahead and informed the relatives would the doctor be infringing X's rights to confidentiality?

It is notable that in both these cases if the doctor maintains confidentiality she or he is not thereby putting people at risk of harm; rather she or he is denying them the option of treatment or advice which might otherwise have been available. Montgomery[169] suggests that, going back to first legal principles, the law does not normally require people to provide benefits to others, but simply not to harm them. This might suggest that the law would require confidentiality to be preserved. He goes on to suggest, however, that this might be a situation where the law should depart from its normal approach, and adopt a less individualistic approach. With similar ideas in mind Loane Skene[170] has contrasted two approaches that could be taken to this topic:

(i) A legal approach. This emphasizes individual rights of privacy of particular patients.

---

[163] S 55.   [164] S 40.   [165] S 42.   [166] S 55.
[167] S 51(3). Information Commissioner (2002). See also Health and Social Care Act 2001, s 60 which permits the making of regulations in relation to using information to pursue the public interest where the information is kept anonymous.
[168] Gilbar (2005); Pullen (1990); Nuffield Council on Bioethics (1993); Genetic Interest Group (1998).
[169] Montgomery (2003: 277).   [170] Skene (1998).

(ii) A family approach.[171] This focuses on the care of patients with genetic illness. It places less weight on individual rights and emphasizes the concerns of the community and families. Patients should be treated as members of a family, not as isolated individuals.

One question which is immediately raised is whether the issues surrounding genetic information are any different from other medical information. Loane Skene suggests a number of differences including the following:

• For genetic tests to be accurate it is necessary to test members of the patient's family.

• The issue of consent to the tests is complex because the results will not be certain and will be predictive of an illness perhaps quite some time in the future.

• There may be significant social and legal consequences which flow from a test.

• The result of the test may have significance for other members of the family.[172]

Gostin and Hodge[173] are critical of any attempt to provide special protection for genetic information. They argue that a genetic predisposition to a particular illness is no different from a predisposition to an illness that a person might have from other causes. They go on to argue that it would be quite wrong if the legal position in relation to a woman whose breast cancer was linked to genetic factors was any different from a woman whose breast cancer was due to other factors. One response to this is that it is not the position of the woman which is different, but the claims, if any, that can be made by her relatives. Another point to emphasize is that it is far more likely that women will receive genetic tests and so any obligation to share that information with wider family members will fall disproportionately on women.[174]

Schedule 4, paragraph 9 of the Human Tissue Act 2004 permits the Human Tissue Authority to authorize the use of X's tissue to obtain medical information which will be used for the benefit of X's relative, even if X did not consent.[175] We do not know yet whether the Authority will authorize such use and if it will, what conditions might be attached. Further, the courts are yet to discuss the issues relating to genetic confidentiality and families. So all it is possible to do at the moment is outline a number of ways the law could address the issue.

4.1.1 *The traditional confidentiality approach*

It could be argued that issues surrounding genetics should be addressed in line with the normal rules on breaching confidentiality.[176] This would suggest that only where there is a high risk of significant harm to another is it proper to breach confidentiality.[177] So the arguments in favour of informing a patient's relatives are stronger the greater the risk of the relative suffering from the illness; the greater its severity; and the more likely it is that having the information will enable the relative to receive effective treatment for the condition.[178]

---

[171] Skene (1998) described this as a medical approach but in Skene (2001) stated that she preferred the term family approach.

[172] But see Mason and Laurie (2006: 207) for an argument that other kinds of medical test results can also carry significance for family members.

[173] Gostin and Hodge (1999).   [174] Melo-Martín (2006).

[175] Lucassen and Kaye (2006) discuss the issue in depth.   [176] Bell and Bennett (2001).

[177] Grubb (1999) suggests that the courts at some point will recognize a legal duty on doctors to tell relatives in such a case.

[178] Ngwana and Chadwick (1993).

Laurie[179] has suggested that, in considering disclosure of genetic information to a relative, the following factors should be considered:

- the availability of a therapy or cure;
- the severity of the condition and the likelihood of onset;
- the nature of the genetic disease;
- the nature of any further testing which might be required;
- the nature of the information to be disclosed;
- the nature of the request (for example, testing for the individual's health or for diagnostic purposes for a relative);
- the question of whether disclosure can further a legitimate public interest;
- the question of how the individual might react if offered unsolicited information (for example, whether any advance directive has been made).

Critics of the traditional approach claim that it is individualistic and fails to take into account that we are not isolated people but live in a web of family relationships.[180] Most people would want family members to whom they were close to be told of medical information that was relevant.[181] Informing family members will support and encourage family bonds, whereas the individualist traditional approach threatens them. However, it should be born in mind that what we are discussing here is whether a doctor should provide information to a patient's family against the patient's wishes. Where the patient is happy for her or his family to be informed, there are no particular legal difficulties.

4.1.2 A Human Rights Act approach

A similar solution could be reached if the issue was examined from the perspective of the Human Rights Act 1998. A patient would have the right for her or his genetic information to be kept secret under article 8,[182] but that right could be interfered with if necessary to protect the interests of others as set out in article 8(2). It should be emphasized that the infringement can only be justified under article 8(2) if it is in accordance with the law. So anyone seeking to rely on article 8(2) to justify an interference in someone's rights of confidentiality would need to point to a statutory or common law permission to do so. It is likely that only if another was going to suffer a serious harm would the breach of private life involved in breaching genetic confidentiality be justified. It might be argued that as genetic information might be regarded as even more private, more connected with the most intimate part of person, that even stronger reasons are required to justify its disclosure than is normally required to justify disclosure of medical information.

4.1.3 The right not to know

Laurie has emphasized that as well the patient having a right of confidentiality the court should also take into account that the relative could claim a right not to know the information. The 'right not to know' has been recognized in the Convention for the Protection of Human Rights and Dignity of the Human Being with regard to the

---

[179] Laurie (2002).   [180] Gilbar (2004).   [181] Benson and Britten (1996).
[182] *A London Borough Council v (1) Mr & Mrs N* [2005] EWHC 1676.

Application of Biology and Medicine, of which article 10(2) states:

> Everyone is entitled to know any information collected about his or her health. However, the wishes of individuals not to be so informed shall be observed.

At first, the notion of a right not to know sounds strange.[183] But imagine this: you have a 10 per cent chance that you will develop a genetic disease to which there is no known cure or treatment. If you are told this your life might be blighted by the knowledge, living in terror of this illness, seeing signs of it in every twinge or strange feeling in your body, and you might never develop the disease. With this in mind you might, quite rationally, decide that it would have been better for you not to know of this genetic risk. It is, therefore, rational for someone to say 'I do not want to be told of risks of illnesses, unless that knowledge will enable me to take preventative action'.[184] Of course, it would also be rational to say that you would want to know of risks so that you can plan your life accordingly.[185] The difficulty is, of course, that most people do not think about the issue. We end up usually trying to guess whether or not a person would want to be told about a certain risk. To overcome this problem Laurie proposes that we focus on the right of privacy rather than a right not to know.[186] This idea is one we will look at later.

4.1.4 A property approach

A very different approach would be to say that a person's genetic data belongs not just to themselves, but also to their relatives.[187] There is some research suggesting that this is how such information is understood by members of the public.[188] After all, a person's genetic information can say as much about their relatives as it does about themselves. In the terms of the Data Protection Act 1998 a daughter, for example, can claim that information held about her mother is information held about her.

4.1.5 A duty approach

Another solution would be to insist on the preservation of medical confidentiality, but place a legal duty on the person tested to inform her or his family of any risks they face in the light of the test. The NHS could even consider making it a condition of genetic testing that the patient agree that relatives will be informed of any relevant information.[189] However, the approach suffers from the difficulty that we do not normally require people to bear such a duty to warn relatives of dangers to their health.[190] There is no obligation on someone to warn their sister of the dangers of smoking. Gilbar[191] has suggested that before testing is carried out all family members who may be affected should agree whether or not they wish to be informed of the results.

---

[183] Takala (1999).

[184] See Andrews (2001: 31–40) for evidence that after being informed of a risk of serious illness patients suffer psychological illness. One study (Almqvist (1999)) found that suicide rates among those informed they have Huntingdon Disease is 10 times higher than the United States' average. Levitt (1999) studies the impact on the sense of self caused by knowledge of a predisposition towards a particular illness.

[185] Hietala et al (1995).   [186] Laurie (2002). See also Ngwena and Chadwick (1993).

[187] *R v Department of Health ex p Source Informatics Ltd* [2000] 1 All ER 786 suggests that a patient does not 'own' his or her medical information.

[188] Kent (2003).   [189] Genetic Interest Group (1998).

[190] King (1999).   [191] Gilbar (2004 and 2005).

4.1.6 *The public health approach*

Gostin and Hodge[192] have argued that the collection, study, and dissemination of genetic information can achieve important public health goals. The more we can learn about the genetic causes of various diseases the more we can do to put in place programmes of education or treatment to prevent or ameliorate these illnesses. There are therefore dangers that in treating genetic information as some kind of especially privileged information we shall lose out on a host of gains. As they ask:

> '[I]s the value of collecting genetic information so important to the achievement of communal goods that the law ought not to promise absolute or even significant levels of privacy? Perhaps the law should simply require that genetic data be acquired, used, and disclosed in orderly and just ways, consistent with the values of individuals and communities.'

4.2 **Genetic privacy: Insurance**

Another controversial issue concerning genetic information is its use for insurance purposes.[193] An insurance company offering someone life insurance would dearly want to know genetic information about that person, so that a precise calculation can be made as to whether they are a good or a bad risk for life insurance purposes. However, if genetic information were to be made available to insurers this would mean that some people would, in effect, be unable to acquire life insurance. This would also probably mean that they would not be able to take out a mortgage. Being denied life insurance, then, can have a severe impact on someone's life.[194] Concerns of this kind led the Human Genetics Commission in May 2001 to impose a three-year moratorium preventing insurers seeking access to genetic test results,[195] where the figure involved was less than £500,000. The Association of British Insurers, which represents the majority of insurance companies, has voluntarily agreed a five-year ban on requesting genetic information for other policies.[196] The Human Genetic Commission has asked the Government to pass legislation specifically to protect genetic privacy, and outlaw discrimination on the grounds of genetic make-up.[197]

In many ways the issue over insurance depends on what values should underlie life insurance. Is our society one which is willing for the majority of people to pay slightly higher life insurance premiums, so that genetic information can be kept confidential? Or do we believe that each person is entitled to be assessed for life insurance on their own merits? This will mean that those with a genetic make-up predisposing them to various illnesses will have to pay much higher premiums, and those with 'healthy' genetic make-up paying slightly lower premiums.[198] One MORI poll suggests that four out of five members of the general public thought that genetic information should not be used for insurance purposes.[199]

---

[192] Gostin and Hodge (1999).   [193] McGlennan (2000).   [194] Laurie (2002: 138).

[195] There is one exception and that is for tests relating to Huntington Chorea. DoH (2000f).

[196] Laurie (2002: 137).

[197] Disability Discrimination Act 1995 does something to protect discrimination on the grounds of genetic background. At present there is no evidence that people are discriminated against in the area of insurance in relation to genetic make-up: Low and Juss (1993).

[198] Rothstein (1998).   [199] MORI (2001 para 7.2).

4.3 HIV status: informing partners

Of course if a patient tests HIV positive her or his physician will recommend that she or he avoid unprotected sexual intercourse and other practices that could involve the transmission of AIDS.[200] But what if the patient refuses to agree and refuses to inform her or his partner of the HIV status? In such a case should the physician inform the partner of the patient's status without her or his consent? To do so would, of course, be a clear breach of confidence, but may enable the partner to take precautions which would avoid her or him acquiring the virus. Not surprisingly, this is a highly controversial issue.[201]

Montgomery[202] suggests we apply the basic principles on confidentiality. As HIV infection is a serious harm it is justifiable to reveal a person's HIV status if (a) there is a real risk to the person to be informed, and (b) the disclosure is the only practical way of protecting them. The General Medical Council has advised that informing others who are at serious risk of infection from a patient is justifiable, even if the patient refuses to consent to others being informed.[203] However, their advice is put in terms of it being permissible to tell others, rather than there being a duty to tell others.[204] It is arguable that this puts a doctor's duty in terms that are too weak.[205] Although normally one person is not liable in tort or criminal law for a wrong committed by another,[206] now there is a duty on the state under the Human Rights Act to protect citizens' lives under article 2 and to protect citizens from torture or inhuman or degrading treatment under article 3. This may *require* the NHS to inform relatives who are known to be at risk of being infected with HIV.[207] But is it reasonable to permit disclosure of confidential information in this case when so often the fact a person could possibly infect others (eg because they have chickenpox) is not disclosed?

What is often overlooked in this debate is that it is a serious criminal offence for someone who is aware that she or he is HIV positive to infect a partner by engaging in sexual relations without informing her or his partner of the risk.[208] There seems to be an arguable case for saying that a doctor should 'shout' a warning to protect a victim from a foreseeable crime.[209] Another way of seeing the issue is to argue that the commission of the offence (or perhaps threat to commit the offence) by the patient justifies the loss of a right of confidentiality. However, a court might decide that if the doctor was convinced there was a serious risk to the girlfriend she or he ought at least to inform the police. The issue might also be regarded differently if the partner is also the doctor's patient.[210] Feminists in particular have been keen to argue in favour of a right to inform third parties. It has been claimed that women are more likely than men to be the ones who are not informed by their HIV positive partners.[211] However, there are also concerns that

---

[200] Some studies indicate promises made by a patient that she or he will tell his partner cannot be relied upon: Landis, Schoenbach, and Weber (1992).
[201] See for example BMA (2004); Gostin and Hodge (1998); DoH (1993); GMC (1993); Boyd (1992); and Gillon (1987).
[202] Montgomery (2003: 269).
[203] Although a doctor should inform her or his patient if she or he has done this: GMC (1997).
[204] This was said to be the law in Jones (1996: paras 2.77–2.86).
[205] See *Reisner v Regents of the University of California* [1997] Med L Rev 25. For further discussion see M. Jones (1990).
[206] *Smith v Littlewoods* [1987] 1 All ER 710.   [207] Eg *Osman v UK* [1999] 1 FLR 193.
[208] *R v Dica* [2004] EWCA Crim 1231.
[209] Khan, Robson, and Swift (2002: 13) argue that a doctor may, but does not have to, inform the partner.
[210] Mason and Laurie (2006: 268).   [211] Gostin and Hodge (1998).

revealing HIV status is likely to lead to domestic violence.[212] Further, is society entitled to place an obligation on HIV positive people and infringe their confidentiality rights, given its inadequate support for them?[213]

The case against the doctor informing the partner is an argument that confidentiality must be taken seriously. In our society someone's HIV status can be particularly sensitive information.[214] The revelation by someone of their HIV status to their partner is an intimate matter which should be left to the individuals themselves. Another concern focuses on the practical issues. Mason and Laurie argue:

> The crucial dilemma here is whether relaxation of the confidentiality rule would lead to failure to seek advice and treatment and hence to the spread of the disease, or whether the imposition of absolute secrecy improperly denies others the opportunity to avoid the risk of exposure to infection or the benefits of early therapy where exposure has occurred.[215]

The argument could be made that although warning the partner may save that person's life, if the informing of partners becomes standard practice that might deter people from seeking medical advice in connection with HIV which in the long run might lead to a loss of even more lives.[216]

A slightly different scenario involves health care workers who are HIV positive.[217] It is generally thought that health workers who are HIV positive pose a very low risk to patients and therefore disclosure of their status to the public is not justified.[218] However, if the health care worker is a surgeon, there is a risk with some kinds of operations that if the surgeon cut her or himself then the disease could be spread. In such a case the GMC advises a surgeon to avoid such operations and if a surgeon does not then her or his colleagues must inform the relevant regulatory authority and appropriate person in the health worker's authority.[219]

4.4 Domestic violence and child abuse

What if a patient reveals that she or her children are being the victims of abuse from her partner?[220] There seems to be near universal agreement that in the case of child abuse the doctor must break confidence if that is necessary to protect the children. Where the adult patient is her- or himself the victim of abuse the position is more debatable. The advice from the GMC is:

> If you believe a patient to be a victim of neglect or physical, sexual or emotional abuse and that the patient cannot give or withhold consent to disclosure, you must give information promptly to an appropriate responsible person or statutory agency, where you believe that the disclosure is in the patient's best interests. If, for any reason, you believe that disclosure of information is not in the best interests of an abused or neglected patient, you should discuss the issues with an experienced colleague. If you decide not to disclose information, you must be prepared to justify your decision.[221]

---

212 North and Rothenburg (1994).   213 Holm (2001).
214 This was accepted by the European Court of Human Rights in *Z v Finland* (1997) 25 EHRR 371.
215 Mason and Laurie (2006: 265).   216 Micholowski (2004: 29).
217 See Burrows (2001) for a general discussion about health care workers who pose a risk to patients.
218 There are only two reported cases of a health care worker infecting a patient: Mason and Laurie (2006: 266).
219 See now the guidance in DoH (2002b: Chap 8).   220 Jecker (1993).
221 GMC (2004: para 29). This passage is approved by the BMA (2004: 195).

4.5 Confidentiality and child patients

The issue of confidentiality and children was considered in Chapter 4.[222] Young people aged 16 or 17 are regarded as adults for purposes of consent to treatment, and are therefore entitled to the same duty of confidence as adults.[223] The Data Protection (Subject Access Modification) (Health) Order 2000[224] states that competent children can prevent their records being disclosed to parents, where they are able to appreciate the nature of the application for access to the records.

Children under 16 who have the capacity and understanding to take decisions about their own treatment are entitled also to decide whether personal information may be passed on, and generally to have their confidence respected (eg they may be receiving treatment or counselling which they do not wish their parents to know about). In other instances, decisions to pass on personal information may be taken by a person with parental responsibility in consultation with the health professionals involved.[225]

More problematic are cases where the child who is not competent to consent to treatment asks the doctor not to tell her or his parents. There is no clear case law authority. There is much to be said for the view[226] that the key question is whether the child is competent to reach a decision about confidentiality. Just because a child is not competent to decide about a medical treatment does not mean that the child is not competent enough to reach a decision about whether or not her or his parents should be informed. If the child is competent to decide that the parents should not be involved the doctor must follow their wishes. However, it has also been suggested that if a child is incompetent to reach the medical decision then there is no duty of confidentiality. Kennedy,[227] supporting this view, argues that the basis of the obligation of confidence is about enabling autonomous decision making. If the child is unable to make the decision then autonomy is not at issue. However, there is an argument that confidentiality is not about autonomy but privacy rights and these rights exist whether or not the person is autonomous.[228]

4.6 Medical research

The use of medical information has been mentioned already. The basic approach is that where possible, the consent of patients involved should be obtained.[229] Where that is impractical (for example where a large sample is required) then anonymized data should be used. Only those personal identifiers (eg postcode) which are essential to the research should be in the data. The MRC has legal advice that under common law it may be permissible to disclose confidential information for research purposes considering the following factors: necessity (there are no other ways of doing the study); sensitivity (was it particularly sensitive information?); importance of research; safeguards (eg limit disclosure to the smallest group possible); independent review; expectations (have people been given the opportunity to object, if not, consent?). Interestingly there are also complaints from some in the research community about the poor quality of medical notes that are kept by the NHS.[230]

---

[222] For a discussion of confidentiality issues and patients suffering mental illness see Cordess (2001).

[223] *Torbay Borough Council v MGN* [2003] EWHC 2927 (Fam). Although research by Rae, Sullivan, Razo, George, and Ramirez (2002) suggests that American psychologists are willing to break confidence in relation to adolescent patients far more readily than they would in respect of adults.

[224] SI 2000/413, art 5.   [225] DoH (2004b: 4.10).   [226] Montgomery (1987).

[227] Kennedy (1991a: 111–17).   [228] Loughrey (2003).

[229] Medical Research Council (2004a: 9).   [230] Medical Research Council (2004a: 5).

5 Legal remedies in confidentiality cases

Few cases on confidentiality appear in the law reports. This is primarily because of the limited nature of the remedies available.[231] There are basically two on offer:

- damages;
- an injunction to prevent publication.

The problem is that damages are only rarely available if there has not been a financial loss to the patient. However, rarely is there a pecuniary loss to the patient.[232] The revelation of medical information may cause embarrassment and loss of social standing, but rarely financial loss. Notably in the *Campbell* case discussed above only £2,500 damages plus £1,000 aggravated damages were awarded. Injunctions to prevent publication are only useful where it is known that the information is about to be revealed. In most cases the patient only learns of the breach of confidentiality when it is too late. Even where it is not too late the claimant will face an uphill task persuading the court that her or his right to respect for private life justifies an infringement of the freedom of the press. It may be argued that the present inadequacies of legal remedies are incompatible with an individual's rights under the European Convention on Human Rights, articles 6 and 8 and so open to challenge through the Human Rights Act 1998.

If someone does breach confidentiality it is more likely that the remedy against them will be disciplinary procedures brought by their employers and professional bodies. For such procedures there is no need to show that the patient suffered a financial loss as a result. It has been suggested that the fact that confidentiality is widely respected is not due to the availability of legal remedies, but rather the widespread acceptance of its ethical basis among those working in medicine.

6 Access to information

A doctor must maintain medical records as part of care for her or his patients. So far we have been discussing the obligation on doctors to keep a patient's records secret, but a patient may also want to see the information kept about her or him. There is no common law right to see your health care information,[233] but there are various statutory rights to see the information.

6.1 The statutory provisions of access to records

The Data Protection Act 1998 is, by far the most important piece of legislation governing this area, but others will be briefly mentioned first. It should also be noted that article 8 of the European Convention on Human Rights protects the right of access to

---

[231] Stauch and Tingle (2002: 260).

[232] *Cornelius vde Taranto* [2001] 68 BMLR 62.

[233] *R v Mid-Glamorgan FHSA ex p Martin* [1995] 1 All ER 356, criticized in Dermot Feenan (1996). See also *Breen v Williams* (1996) 70 ALJR 772 and *McInerney v MacDonald* (1992) 93 DLR (4th) 415 for Australian and Canadian decisions providing alternative approaches to rights of access to medical records.

medical records and therefore legislation should be interpreted in a way which is compatible with that right.[234]

(1) *Supreme Court Act 1981.* If a person has commenced or is likely to commence litigation which has some prospect of success then they have a right to 'discovery' of relevant evidence, including documents. These can include medical records. If disclosure would harm a patient then they can be shown only to the patient's medical advisers.[235]

(2) *Access to Medical Reports Act 1988.* This Act applies to reports supplied by a medical practitioner for the purposes of insurance or employment. The subject of such a report has the right to see them, veto their release, and to append comments if they believe the reports are inaccurate. Doctors are entitled to refuse access if there are concerns that to do so would be likely to cause serious harm to the physical or mental health of the person seeking it or to others; or to protect a doctor's informant.

(3) *Access to Health Records Act 1990.* The 1990 Act gives right of access to patients to all manual health records since 1 November 1991. The 1998 Data Protection Act has in fact rendered the 1990 Act obsolete, except in relation to deceased persons, who are not covered by the 1998 Act.

(4) *Data Protection Act 1998.* Patients have rights of access to their health records under the Data Protection Act 1998, sections 7 and 8. A person can discover if their personal data is being processed, a description of the data, the purposes for which it is being processed and the classes of people to whom it will be disclosed. Most significantly they are entitled to a copy of their records in an 'intelligible form'. This includes, where necessary, an explanation of any terms used.[236] Once they have seen their records patients are entitled to require the data controller to stop processing the information if to do so would cause substantial and unwarranted distress to the patient or another.[237] The patient has the right to have the information rectified if it is wrong.[238]

There are two important limitations on the right of access under the Data Protection Act and they are:

(i) where the disclosure would cause serious harm to the physical or mental health of the patient or another.[239] A health care professional must confirm that this applies. The BMA guidance suggests that it will be 'extremely rare' for this exception to apply;[240]

(ii) if the data disclosed would reveal information about another person; so if on a man's medical records there was a statement about his wife's concerns about him, that section of the record could not be revealed.

Normally, of course, another person cannot use the Act to obtain the record of another. However, a parent with parental responsibility can obtain the records of their child or a person managing the affairs of an incompetent person can access the relevant files unless

---

[234] *McGinley and Egan v UK* (1998) 27 EHRR1.   [235] S 33(2).
[236] S 8(2). In some areas patients are entitled to access their records via the internet (BBC Newsonline (9 December 2003).
[237] S 10.   [238] S 14.
[239] Data Protection (Subject Access Modification) (Health) Order 2000 413, art 5.
[240] BMA (2004: 217).

the patients have provided information in the expectation that it will not be disclosed. So if a child has seen a doctor on her or his own and talks on the basis that her or his parents will not find out what she or he says, then this need not be disclosed.

The leading case on common law rights of access to medical records is the following:

KEY CASE   R v Mid Glamorgan Health Services ex p Martin [1995] 1 All ER 356

Martin sought from the medical authorities all his personal health and social work records which had been made while he had been a patient at a number of different hospitals. The hospitals concerned were willing to disclose the records to Mr Martin's medical advisers but not to him directly.

It was held by the Court of Appeal that health authorities and doctors owned the medical notes. They could deny a patient access to the notes if that was in her or his best interests. This might be, for example, if disclosure could be detrimental to the patient's health. The offer to disclose the notes to Mr Martin's medical advisers was the most that could be expected. Sir Roger Parker LJ stated:

> I regard as untenable the proposition that, at common law, a doctor or health authority has an absolute property in medical records of a patient, if this means, which it appears to do, that either could make what use of them he or it chose. Information given to a doctor by a patient or a third party is given in confidence and the absolute property rights are therefore necessarily qualified by the obligations arising out of that situation.

But he regarded as equally untenable that a patient had an unfettered right of access to her or his records. He then stated:

> In my view the circumstances in which a patient or former patient is entitled to demand access to his medical history as set out in the records will be infinitely various, and it is neither desirable nor possible for this or any court to attempt to set out the scope of the duty to afford access or, its obverse, the scope of the patient's rights to demand access. Each case must depend on its own facts.

The lawyers were only permitted to use the documents for the purposes of advising on and undertaking legal proceedings.

6.2 Should there be a right to see one's medical records?

Those who support such a right claim four particular benefits:[241]

(i) *The accuracy and general quality of records would improve.* Certainly there are concerns about the quality of information in medical records.[242] If a patient could check records, then this would be one way of improving the accuracy of records. It might also means that the records would be more efficiently kept and would not include inappropriate comments about patients.[243] The press is often full of reports of offensive remarks being made in people's medical records. The BMA records a case where a medical record

---

[241] Gilhooley and McGhee (1991).
[242] Information Policy Unit (2004). The National Patient Safety Agency Plan 2003–04 found 1,742 incidents where patients had suffered as a result of bad medical records.
[243] BMA (2004: 199).

originally referred to a patient as a 'silly old bat', although this was altered to read 'still holds bottle'.[244]

(ii) *Relief of patient's anxiety*. Some patients are convinced that they are suffering from illnesses that they are not, or that their doctors are hiding the truth from them. A right to access their health information may allay such fears.

(iii) *Improve communication*. If patients are entitled to see their health care information then the records will need to be presented in a clear way which is readily understandable to patients. This might be in the best interests of everyone.

(iv) *Increase trust*. Openness in dealings between patients and their doctors may persuade patients to be more open with doctors and doctors more open with patients.

There are, however, those who are opposed to opening up medical records.[245] It is argued that inevitably they contain complex medical terminology and too easily lead to misconceptions and may even exacerbate an over-anxious patient. It is feared that doctors may then have to become involved in lengthy discussions explaining the records to their patient. It may, of course, be regarded as a good thing that doctors explain to patients the details of their medical conditions.

REALITY CHECK

Medical acronyms

It should not be thought that medical records will only contain medical information. A BBC Newsonline (18 August 2003) report found the following acronyms used in people's records:

CTD—Circling the Drain (a patient expected to die soon)

GLM—Good looking Mum

GPO—Good for Parts Only

TEETH—Tried Everything Else, Try Homeopathy

UBI—Unexplained Beer Injury

NFN—Normal for Norfolk

FLK—Funny Looking Kid

GROLIES—Guardian Reader Of Low Intelligence in Ethnic Skirt

TTFO—roughly translated as 'Told To Go Away'

LOBNH—Lights On But Nobody Home

'Pumpkin Positive'—which refers to the implication that a penlight shone into the patient's mouth would encounter a brain so small that the whole head would light up.

7 The ethical issues

We have so far concentrated on the legal position. This is generally based on the assumption that medical professionals should not breach confidence. But what are the ethical arguments that might support such an assumption?

---

[244] BMA (2004: 218). No doubt there are worse things written on medical records.
[245] Ross (1986).

7.1 Arguments in favour of confidentiality

7.1.1 *Consequentialist arguments*

These arguments rely on the benefits and disadvantages that flow from confidentiality. It is argued that by promising confidentiality patients will be willing to be completely honest with their doctors and discuss all their symptoms and past history.[246] This will mean that the best diagnosis and treatment can be offered. This will benefit both patients and the general public. It will also ensure that there is an efficient and organized health system. Murphy has argued in favour of confidentiality because it encourages 'talk' between the patient and the medical professional. In other words it encourages a model whereby the doctor and patient discuss and agree on an appropriate course of treatment, rather than the doctor providing a monologue setting out the problem and proposed solution, which the patient must simply accept or reject. All of the arguments in this paragraph assume that patients are aware of the obligations of confidence under which medical professionals operate and rely on them. Whether this is true is a matter of debate.

7.1.2 *Deontological arguments*

Confidentiality is a fundamental principle that should be respected. It has been argued: 'The right to control who knows the things about us which we regard as private is integral to our sense of self and sense of identity'.[247] Others ground the right in terms of the right to autonomy: that people should have the ability to live their lives as they choose. This is possible only if private matters are being kept secret by those to whom they are divulged. Capron argues that a breach of confidence involves a lack of respect for reserve and solitude.[248] Others emphasize not privacy, but fidelity. In other words a breach of confidence is quite simply a breach of a promise.[249] The obligation of confidence can also be seen as a reflection of the fact that patients must submit themselves and their futures to the professional.[250]

7.1.3 *Public/private benefits*

As can be seen from the points above, some arguments in favour of confidentiality are in terms of the public good: it aids an effective health care system. When confidentiality is broken not only does that harm the individual concerned, it has an impact on the general public's willingness to trust medical professionals and this can harm the health of the nation.[251] Other arguments focus more on the 'private' issues: the rights and harms of the particular individual concerned.

It is of course quite possible to claim that there are both public and private claims that can be made in favour of confidentiality and it would be wrong to emphasize one more than the other.[252] In other words when a doctor breaks a duty of confidentiality not only is there a wrong done to the individual patient, but there is a public harm because patients generally lose trust in the medical profession. Until recently the case

---

[246] There are psychological studies which support the argument that guaranteeing confidentiality will lead to greater honesty and openness: McMahan and Knowles (1995); Woods and McNamara (1980).

[247] O'Brien and Chantler (2003).   [248] Capron (1991).

[249] Beauchamp and Childress (2003: 307–10).   [250] Sokolowski (1991).

[251] Hall (2002) emphasizes the importance of trust in good medical practice.

[252] Childress and Beauchamp (2003: 307–10).

law on the equitable protection of confidential information emphasized the public inter-est in protecting confidential information as more important than the private interest in maintaining confidence.[253] However, it may be that the understanding on the basis of confidentiality has shifted after the Human Rights Act 1998. Indeed the House of Lords in *Campbell v MGN*[254] held that privacy, dignity, and autonomy provided the basis of medical confidentiality. It is arguable that the recognition of confidentiality as a private right will make it more difficult to justify a disclosure on the basis of the public interest.[255] If confidentiality is seen as being in the public interest it is easier to justify an infringement by reference to other public interest claims than it would be if the claim was seen as being a private individual's right.[256] Also if put in terms of the public benefit there are concerns that some groups of people could claim to have a stronger claim than others.[257] It could, for example, be argued that it is more in the national interest that medical records of top politicians be kept confidential, than of benefit claimants.[258]

7.2 Arguments against confidentiality

There are very few people who actually believe that confidentiality does not deserve protection at all. But there is a considerable body of opinion who believe that far too much respect is paid to the notion of confidentiality. Paterson argued that the emphasis on confidentiality was an interference with research.[259] Indeed the impact on research has led some to claim that 'privacy is bad for your health'.[260] Professor Gostin has put the problem well:

> Because significant levels of privacy cannot realistically be achieved within the health information infrastructure currently envisaged by policymakers, we confront a hard choice: should we sharply limit the systematic collection of identifiable health care data in order to achieve reasonable levels of informational privacy? The result of that choice would be to reduce considerably the social good that would be achieved from the thoughtful use of health data. Alternatively, we may decide that the value of informa-tion collection is so important to the achievement of societal aspirations for health that the law ought not promise absolute or even significant levels of privacy at all, but rather should require that the data be used only for authorized and limited purposes.[261]

He argues that in a modern health care system the notion of confidentiality between patient and doctor is outdated. We have instead to focus on protection of records and ensuring that that any medical data (however acquired) is used for proper purposes.

Rubinstein[262] makes the point that emphasizing confidentiality too strongly carries risks:

> Inherent in the privacy advocates' rejection of the public duty paradigm is a refusal to recognize, in exchange for the vast improvements in medical care, a correlative respon-sibility on the part of the individual, as a potential consumer of health care services,

---

[253] *W v Egdell* [1990] 1 All ER 836; *X v Y* [1988] 2 All ER 649.
[254] [2004] UKHL 22.   [255] Lee (1994: 291).
[256] Lee (1994: 292).   [257] Murphy (1998).
[258] Roberts (1996) is concerned how easily the medical confidentiality of benefit claimants is infringed in America.
[259] Paterson (2001); Al-Shahi, R. and Warlow, C. (2000).
[260] O'Grady and Nolan (2004).   [261] Gostin (1995: 454).   [262] Rubinstein (1999: 227).

toward the community. As individuals rely on their right to be let alone, they shift the burden on others in the community to accept the responsibility for providing the data needed to advance medical and health policy information. Their individualist vision threatens the entire community, because when particular segments of the community opt out of participation as data subjects, the resulting value of the research is questionable, and many worthwhile protocols could be abandoned on that basis. Thus, a policy that requires consent before each use of health data might have unintended and undesirable consequences for our medical care and health policy.

7.3 Public views

Surveys among the general public in relation to confidentiality might make depressing reading for those who are concerned about the present protection of confidential information. First, the surveys suggest the public has high confidence in the way the NHS protects confidentiality.[263] Second, the surveys suggest that people are not particularly concerned about the fact a large number of people within the NHS may need access to their data,[264] although there is much unease about information being given to people outside the NHS.[265]

However, the picture is more complicated than this. Although the public are pleased with the way their medical records are kept secret, in fact the general public have little idea how the information is in fact used.[266] For example only 16 per cent of those questioned in one large survey realized that their information could be revealed to hospital managers. Further surveys indicate that when the public are asked if they are happy for their medical details to be used in 'medical research' there is much unease, although they tend to be much happier when asked if they would be willing for their records to be used in a particular project (eg to research the causes of cancer).[267] A team researching asthma and angina who decided to write to individuals asking consent to use their medical records found that 9.8 per cent refused. This indicates that that an assumption that nearly everyone wants to help in medical research is ill founded, even when the research might be regarded as uncontroversial.[268]

Surveys do give us some picture of what kind of medical issues people are particularly sensitive about. Not surprisingly they are termination of pregnancy and mental health issues.[269] This might support an argument that medical records should be divided up into general records, readily available for anyone in the NHS with a legitimate reason for seeing it, and a sensitive part which could only be examined on a 'need to know' basis. One study looked at this option and found much support among the general public, but 60 per cent said they would want information to be put in the sensitive part.[270]

---

263 National Health Service Information Authority (2002).
264 Adams, Budden, Hoare and Sanderson (2004).
265 NHS Information Authority (2002) and van de Creek, Miars, and Herzog (1987).
266 National Health Service Information Authority (2002).
267 The Welcome Trust and Medical Research Council (2001).
268 Baker, Shields, Stevenson, Fraser, and Stone (2000).
269 National Health Service Information Authority (2002).
270 National Health Service Information Authority (2002).

8 Informational privacy

Laurie[271] has argued that the law should move away from focusing on the notion of confidentiality and instead focus on the right to informational privacy.[272] He explains the difference between the two concepts in this way:

> Informational privacy is concerned with the control of personal information and with preventing access to that information by others. An invasion of informational privacy occurs when any unauthorized disclosure of information takes place. Confidentiality is a subset of this privacy interest, and is breached when confidential information which is the subject of the relationship is released to parties outside the relationship without authorization. Informational privacy is wider than this in that it requires no relationship to exist.[273]

Laurie sees privacy as creating and respecting a 'state of separateness' for individuals; 'the protection of a private sphere around oneself'.[274] It is important for people living in society to have their 'own space'. This may involve a physical space, but also a psychological one. This is only possible if people are able to control who has access to information about them and what information they find out about themselves. Laurie is aware this might sound as if he is advocating a highly individualist vision of society which pays no attention to relationships between people. However, he says that the protection of privacy is important to enable relationships to flourish.[275]

So what exactly is the difference between confidentiality and informational privacy? The differences appear to include the following:

(i) The classic definition of confidentiality requires there to be a confidential relationship between the parties. It therefore does not readily apply where a party acquires private information about another outside the context of such a relationship. There are no such difficulties for the notion of informational privacy which does not depend on any kind of relationship.[276]

(ii) The idea that a party has a right not to know a piece of information can be readily included within the notion of informational privacy. It cannot easily fit into the notion of breach of confidence.

(iii) Laurie suggests that an understanding of a right to information privacy when combined with a proprietal right over medical information about a person will give a person appropriate control over their medical details. In particular it will mean that a person can have on-going control over how their records are used. He is concerned that with breach of confidence once consent is given for the public use of the information then the protection is lost.

---

[271] Laurie (2002: Chap 7).
[272] For further discussion on the nature of privacy see Neill (2002).
[273] Mason and Laurie (2006: 224).
[274] Laurie (2002: 128).
[275] See Andorno (2004) who develops the right not to know from autonomy rather than privacy.
[276] Micholowski (2004: 16–18).

A SHOCK TO THE SYSTEM

The following shows that it is possible to respect confidentiality too much.

In January 1999 Maine in the USA enacted a strict law prohibiting the passing of medical information without a patient's written consent (see C. Scott (2000)). Heavy fines would be placed on those who violated the rules. The law was soon found to be impracticable: relatives of patients who telephoned for updates could not be told; florists found it impossible to deliver flowers; priests could not discover the whereabouts of patients to administer religious rites; doctors found it difficult to consult over problems with patients; delays occurred because labs refused to give the results of tests over the telephone.

There is also some evidence that following the Data Protection Act 1998 some health care trusts became so nervous of infringing that Act that they refused to provide information to outside bodies, even where to do so would be uncontroversial (Boyd (2003)).

9 Conclusion

A survey of patients across European countries found that they regarded confidentiality as 'very important' and one of their highest priorities when consulting doctors.[277] And, if the professional guidelines are anything to go by, health care workers take the duty of confidentiality seriously. Yet there is little doubt that medical confidentiality is under threat. In practice the flimsy curtain in hospitals with medical notes at the end of a bed mean that in that setting confidentiality is little protected.[278] The desire to ensure the NHS is run effectively and efficiently means that managers and administrators need to have access to records to an extent never needed before. Further, computerization of health records will inevitably increase and with it the difficulties of ensuring that the information is kept secure.[279] Insurance companies seek ever more intimate medical information about people seeking life insurance.[280] It is not surprising that some commentators have described confidentiality as a 'decrepit concept'.[281]

This ambiguity over the notion of confidentiality is also found in the shift of language in some court cases[282] and professional guidance[283] from talk of a duty of confidentiality to a discussion of the fairness of use of information. Maybe this is realistic: the NHS cannot promise that your information will not be disclosed to anyone else, but it can promise that your information will be dealt with fairly. But there are influences the other way. The Human Rights Act 1998 appears to classify protection of private information as a human right.[284] Especially in the area of genetic information there is widespread unease about the way such information is used. Also, there is increasing concern at the lack of trust between patients and doctors which is central to an effective health care system. A reaffirmation of the importance of confidentiality could be seen as one way of restoring that trust.[285]

---

[277] Grol et al (1999).   [278] Okino Sawada et al (1996).
[279] Gostin, Hodge and Burghardt (2002). For the latest developments see HM Government (2007b).
[280] Royal College of General Practitioners (2000) are concerned about this.
[281] Siegler (1982).   [282] *R v Department of Health exp Source Informatics Ltd* [2000] 1 All ER 786.
[283] NHS (2007b: 1).
[284] Evans and Harris (2004) are concerned at the shift away from protecting confidentiality as a right.
[285] Clarke (2002).

QUESTIONS

1. Proposals to take DNA profiles of every baby born in the UK have been rejected by the Human Genetic Commission (BBC Newsonline (31 March 2005)). What ethical issues would be raised by such a database? (See Gibbons (2007)).

2. There are plans for all medical records within the NHS to be computerized. Is this a concern? How should the balance be struck between the importance of keeping information confidential and ensuring that medical professionals have ready access to the medical information necessary to treat a patient?

3. Should the law do more to distinguish between different kinds of medical information? It might, for example, be argued that we could distinguish non-intimate medical information (eg the fact a person has broken a leg) from intimate information (eg the fact a person has had an abortion). Would that be a useful distinction?

4. Can you think of any medical information about yourself that you would rather not know? How can the law respect that wish?

5. Does it matter whether the protection of medical confidential information is regarded as a matter of private rights or public interest or both?

FURTHER READING

Generally on the protection of confidential medical information see:

Andorno, R. (2004) 'The right not to know: an autonomy based approach' *Journal of Medical Ethics* 30: 435.

Case, P. (2003) 'Confidence matters: The rise and fall of informational autonomy in medical law' *Medical Law Review* 11: 208.

Kipnis, K (2006) 'A defense of unqualified medical confidentiality' *American Journal of Bioethics* 6: 7.

Michalowski, S. (2004) *Medical Confidentiality and Crime* (Oxford University Press).

Moreham, N. (2005) 'Privacy in the common law: a doctrinal and theoretical analysis' *Law Quarterly Review* 121: 628.

Pattenden, R. (2003) *The Law on Professional Client Confidentiality* (Oxford University Press).

Skene, L. (2001) 'Genetic Secrets and the Family' *Medical Law Review* 9: 162.

On the protection of genetic information see:

Canadian Biotechnology Advisory Committee (2004) *Protecting Privacy in an Age of Genetic Information* (CBAC).

Gilbar, R. (2005) *The Status of the Family in Law and Bioethics: The Genetic Context* (Ashgate).

Laurie, G. (2002) *Genetic Privacy: A Challenge to Medico-Legal Norms* (Cambridge University Press).

6 Contraception, Abortion, and Pregnancy

INTRODUCTION

Few topics arouse greater passion than those surrounding abortion and the regulation of pregnancy. In the United States, the issue of abortion is of enormous political significance; in Britain less so, although it was raised in the 2005 election. Whether as a political matter, or a moral one, it creates heated argument. The reason is that for those on either side of the debate the stakes could hardly be higher. On the one hand there are those who regard abortion as the murder of the most innocent and vulnerable human beings. On the other, there are those who claim that access to abortion is a crucial part of the battle towards women's equality and is a fundamental human right. For them, abortion and fertility decisions should be made by the woman alone, and should not be interfered with by the state.

The law, as we shall see, seeks to strike a somewhat uneasy balance between recognizing that the foetus has some interests; reinforcing medical control over pregnancy and birth control; and protecting the rights of the pregnant woman. In all of the fascinating theoretical debate it must not be forgotten that these issues affects millions of women in the UK. A recent poll suggested that in the UK nearly 40 per cent of pregnancies were unplanned.[1]

Before looking at the issue of abortion, we will consider contraception.

1 Contraception: its use and function

Many people have claimed that the wide availability of effective contraception has done more to emancipate woman than any other social development. Women's control over their fertility is now sometimes taken for granted. In England and Wales the majority of women under 50 (76 per cent) are using contraception. The most popular method was the contraceptive pill (27 per cent) followed by the male condom (22 per cent).[2] Access to effective contraception is regarded by some as a fundamental human right.[3] This is, however, a western perspective. Worldwide it has been said that there is a global shortage of contraception and many people see increasing its availability as a major aspect of improving conditions in developing countries.[4]

The most common forms of contraception are:

- the condom;
- intra-uterine device (IUD);

[1] BBC Newsonline (16 March 2004). [2] National Statistics (2007a).
[3] Kirilova Eriksson (1993). [4] AGI and UNFPA (2004).

- injectable contraceptives;
- the female contraceptive pill;
- sterilization;
- natural methods.[5]

It is not emphasized often enough that there are serious disadvantages to all of these forms of contraception. In a survey covering seven countries a substantial majority of women were dissatisfied with all the available methods of contraception.[6] Two leading clinical experts working in the UK have stated: 'there is a real need for new methods of contraception to be developed that are more effective, easier to use, and safer than existing methods'.[7] It is remarkable that the most commonly used method of birth control worldwide is sterilization.[8] New techniques of sterilization have meant the operation is less invasive and is highly reliable, yet its permanence and degree of invasion mean it is hardly ideal. Although it is possible to try and reverse sterilization, it involves major surgery and is not always successful.[9] In one US study 26 per cent of those sterilized (both men and women) regretted the operation, stating that they now wanted to be able to have children. In the case of those under 30 at the time of the operation the figure rose to a remarkable 42 per cent.[10]

The other forms of contraception also have disadvantages. The pill, although popular, can carry unpleasant side effects, and there have been persistent concerns with long-term health risks associated with it. The pill has been linked to breast cancer, cervical cancer,[11] and thrombosis.[12] That said, many believe that these risks are overstated.[13] Certainly the pill has been used for over 40 years, without there being a clearly established link between the pill and illness for most women. The other disadvantage of the pill is that it requires users to ensure they take the pill daily. Some people find the discipline required to remember to do this challenging.[14]

A major problem with all forms of contraception is reliability. The success rates of the different forms of contraception vary. One study by the respected Alan Guttmacher Institute found the following percentages of those using these methods who became pregnant in the first year of use:[15]

- withdrawal 15–28 per cent;
- rhythm 14–57 per cent;
- spermicide 13–55 per cent;
- condom 6–51 per cent;
- pill 3–27 per cent;
- female sterilization 0.5 per cent;
- male sterilization 0.1–0.2 per cent.

---

[5] These are methods which do not use devices or medication but depend on ensuring that sexual intercourse is at a time when the woman is not fertile or requiring the man to withdraw before ejaculation.
[6] Snow et al (1996: 8).   [7] Baird and Glasier (1999: 969).
[8] Blank (1991: 16).   [9] Blank (1991: 31–3).   [10] Blank (1991: 28).
[11] BBC Newsonline (4 April 2003).   [12] Grabrick et al (2000).
[13] Baird and Glasier (1999: 969) claim that the pill has an excellent safety record.
[14] Baird and Glasier (1999: 970) believe that in due course a 'once a month' pill will be developed.
[15] Alan Guttmacher Institute (2004: 16).

One practical consequence of these failure rates is that in about three quarters of pregnancies ended by abortion the woman was using some form of contraception at the time of conception.[16] The National Institute for Clinical Excellence (NICE) has recommended that wider use be made of reversible long acting contraception.[17]

Fifty-two per cent of all women aged 16–49 are using some form of non-surgical contraception, the most popular being the contraceptive pill, with 25 per cent of women in that age group using it. Of men aged 16–49, 17 per cent had been surgically sterilized, as had 11 per cent of women.[18] Twenty-one per cent of women were using long acting reversible contraception.[19] Despite a widespread perception of sexual promiscuity a major government survey found that of those aged 16–69, 74 per cent of men had had only one sexual partner in the year prior to the interview and 13 per cent had had no sexual partners.[20] For women the corresponding statistics were 78 per cent and 10 per cent. It is notable that of those seeking advice from NHS contraceptive clinics 91 per cent were women.[21] Sadly, contraception still seems to be regarded as largely a 'woman's responsibility'.

2 The availability of contraception

In 1925 the House of Lords held in a libel action that to describe contraception as 'monstrous and revolting to human nature'[22] was a fair comment. Lord Denning in *Bravery v Bravery*[23] suggested that a sterilization which is done 'so as to enable a man to have the pleasure of sexual intercourse, without shouldering the public interest attaching to it' was contrary to public policy and degrading to the man. But the judges gradually moved with the times and Lord Scarman in *Gillick v West Norfolk and Wisbech HA* held that contraceptive medical treatment is 'recognized as a legitimate and beneficial treatment in cases where it is medically indicated...'.[24] There would be widespread agreement with Mumby J's statement in *R (Smeaton) v The Secretary of State for Health et al*:

> It is, as it seems to me, for individual men and woman, acting in what they believe to be good conscience, applying those standards which they think appropriate, and in consultation with appropriate professional (and, if they wish, spiritual) advisers, to decide whether or not to use IUDs, the pill, the mini-pill and the morning-after pill. It is no business of government, judges or the law.[25]

In fact the law does regard contraception as part of the state's business. Contraceptives are medical products which must be licensed by the Medicines Control Agency of the European Evaluation of Medicinal Products before use.[26] Also, the National Health Service Act 1977, section 5(1)(b) places a duty upon the Secretary of State

> to arrange, to such extent as he considers necessary to meet all reasonable requirement in England and Wales, for the giving of advice on contraception, the medical examination

---

[16] *R (John Smeaton on Behalf of SPUC) v The Secretary of State for Health et al* [2002] 2 FCR 193, para 215.
[17] NICE (2005b).   [18] National Statistics (2004: vii).   [19] NHS (2007a).
[20] Office of National Statistics (2007a).   [21] NHS (2007a).
[22] *Sutherland v Stopes* [1925] AC 45.
[23] [1954] 1 WLR 1169. The other members of the Court of Appeal were not in agreement with his comments.
[24] [1985] 3 All ER 402, 418.   [25] [2002] 2 FCR 193, para 396.
[26] Medicine Act 1968, s 19; Medicines for Human Use Regulations, SI 1994/3144 and EC Council Directive 65/65/EEC.

of persons seeking advice on contraception, the treatment of such persons and the supply of contraceptive substances and appliances.

In effect it means that anyone should be able to access contraception.

It must not, however, be thought that there are no barriers to accessing contraceptive treatment. First, the oral contraceptive pill is only available under prescription. This is because, for people with certain medical conditions, it can carry serious side effects and it is thought that the pill should only be used under medical supervision. However, condoms and, significantly, post-coital contraception is available over the counter at a pharmacy. The second barrier is cost: although contraception provided under prescription is free, as is contraception (including condoms) provided at family planning clinics, when purchased at a supermarket a packet of 20 condoms can cost around £15.00. Although to many these barriers appear small, as we shall see, to some young people they are significant.

Sterilizations are available on the NHS although about one third are carried out privately. In 1999 there were 64,422 vasectomies and 41,300 tubal occlusions. The number of sterilizations for women carried out on the NHS has dramatically fallen from 49,000 in 1995–06 to 18,400 in 2004–05. This might be explained by an increase in the use of vasectomies by men and a growing use of long-acting contraceptives.[27] One explanation is the growing awareness that tubal occlusion has a much higher failure rate (1 in 200 in a person's lifetime) than vasectomy.

There is also widespread use of 'emergency contraception'. In the General Household Survey of 1998, 10 per cent of women aged 16–49 stated that they had used emergency contraception at least two years prior to interview.[28] Research suggests that users of emergency hormonal contraception are not using it as an alternative to other methods.[29] It is available from a pharmacist without a prescription to over 16-year-olds.[30]

3 Teenage pregnancy rates

In England and Wales there were 82,941 teenage conceptions for women under the age of 18 in 2002 and 15,778 conceptions for under 16s.[31] About 56,000 children are born to teenage mothers a year.[32] Less than one third of young people under the age of 16 have sexual intercourse, but of those that do half do not use contraception.[33] One recent study found that 25 per cent of people did not use contraception during their first experience of sexual intercourse.[34] If these figures sound high, it is because they are. England and Wales has the highest teenage pregnancy and teenage parenthood rates in Europe,[35] the highest by some distance. The teenage pregnancy rate is twice that of Germany, three times that of France, and six times that of the Netherlands. This has

[27] National Statistics (2007a).   [28] Office of National Statistics (1998).

[29] Glasier and Baird (1998).

[30] The Prescription Only Medicines (Human Use) Amendment (No 3) Order 2000, SI 2000/3231 pilot schemes to make free morning-after pills available to under 16-year-olds from pharmacists are being expanded: 'Morning-after Pill scheme grows' BBC Newsonline 9 February 2004.

[31] Uren, Sheers, and Dattani (2007: 34).   [32] Social Exclusion Unit (1999: 6).

[33] Social Exclusion Unit (1999: 6).   [34] BBC Newsonline (2 July 2007).

[35] Social Exclusion Unit (1999). But the birth rate is not as high as in Canada, New Zealand, or the United States.

been recognized as a major social problem which the Government has sought to address through the Social Exclusion Unit.[36]

The concerns about the high levels of teenage pregnancy have been powerfully voiced by former Prime Minister Tony Blair:

> Teenage mothers are less likely to finish their education, less likely to find a good job, and more likely to end up both as single parents and bringing up their children in poverty. The children themselves run a much greater risk of poor health, and have a much higher chance of becoming teenage mothers themselves. Our failure to tackle this problem has cost the teenagers, their children and this country dear... As a country, we can't afford to continue to ignore this shameful record.[37]

This negative picture of teenage pregnancy is not one shared by all. Indeed many teenage mothers are pleased with the pregnancy and regard it as a fulfilling addition to their lives.

3.1 Causes of teenage pregnancy

Why are so many young women getting pregnant? Here are some suggestions.

3.1.1 *Social deprivation*

To many commentators teenage pregnancy is related to social deprivation.[38] As one government report put it, some teenagers 'see no reason not to get pregnant'.[39] There is indeed a strong correlation between those areas of the country marked by social deprivation and those in which there is a high rate of teenage pregnancy.[40] Poorer areas of the UK have up to six times the birth and conception rates of the most affluent.[41] Uran et al[42] point out: 'In 2004, the most deprived 20 per cent of local authorities in England had, on average, an under 18 conception rate of 56 conceptions per 1,000 females aged 15–17, compared to 25 per 1,000 in the 20 per cent least deprived'. The reasons given for teenagers choosing to become pregnant often relate to hopes that child raising will give them new opportunities in life.[43] It may well be that these youngsters believe having a baby to look after offers them a greater chance of fulfilment than attempting to pursue education or paid employment. Maybe they are right. Caring for a baby may well be more satisfying that taking a low paid job in a burger bar. Indeed in one study a clear majority of young mothers who had chosen to become pregnant reported that having a child had improved the quality of their life.[44]

3.1.2 *Inadequate sex education*

Another cause of teenage pregnancy according to some is inadequate sex education. There is certainly much dissatisfaction with the sex education offered at schools. Jackson, after

---

[36] Lee et al (2004: 2) complain that it is often just assumed that teenage pregnancy is 'a problem' without any clear evidence of its harms. They point out that in fact young women are less likely to get pregnant and less likely to give birth than 30 years ago (2004: 1).

[37] Social Exclusion Unit (1999: 3).

[38] See eg Uren, Sheers, and Dattani (2007); Cater and Coleman (2006); Lee, Clements, Ingham, and Stone (2004).

[39] Social Exclusion Unit (1999: 7).   [40] Cater and Coleman (2006)

[41] Social Exclusion Unit (1999: 20).   [42] Uren, Sheers, and Dattani (2007: 34).

[43] Cater and Coleman (2006).   [44] Ibid.

looking carefully at the empirical evidence, concludes that 'many teenagers consider their sex education to have been almost entirely without utility'.[45] Some people believe that sex education encourages young people to engage in sexual activity at an early age and so it should be restricted. This is a minority view. The Government's view in 1999 was:

> good, comprehensive sex and relationships education does not make young people more likely to start sex. Indeed it can help them delay starting sex and make them more likely to use contraceptives when they do.[46]

This view is supported by much empirical evidence.[47] However, about one per cent of parents[48] exercise their right to withdraw their children from sex education under the Education Act 1996, section 405, probably concerned that the classes will encourage sexual activity.[49] This is a controversial provision. To some the section protects the rights of parents to decide how to educate and raise their children. To others it denies children the right to proper sex education.[50]

Whatever the reasons there is a 'considerable level of ignorance and misinformation' about sex and its consequences.[51] One study found that one in ten girls had not been told about periods before they started and one quarter of teenagers thought that the contraceptive pill protected against sexually transmitted diseases.[52] However, despite this another survey found not one young person who was not aware that it was necessary to use contraception in order to avoid pregnancy.[53] Information about sex appears usually to be obtained from older siblings or friends, rather than schools or parents.[54] As one group of researchers put it: 'Much information is passed through a form of Chinese whispers, with accurate information confused by embarrassment and bravado'.[55] Depressingly, many young men cite pornography as a major source of sex education.[56]

3.1.3 *The difficulty of accessing contraception and contraceptive advice*

The BMA has acknowledged that there is a 'clear need' to improve access to contraception.[57] Although contraception is widely available, young people find it difficult to access it. Why is this? One explanation is ignorance. Teenagers may not be aware that the pill is available free from their GP. In particular they might believe that, because sexual relations between those under 16 is a criminal offence, contraception is not available to those under that age or that they might even be reported to the police for seeking it.[58] Interestingly one survey of sexually active young people found that all the under 16-year-olds who were on the pill had asked their GPs for the pill in order to deal with painful periods, rather than admitting the real reason.[59]

A second explanation surrounds confidentiality. Although the legal position is that a doctor must keep confidential a request from a child for contraception,[60] this may not

---

[45] Jackson (2000: 17) referring to Yamey (1999).   [46] Social Exclusion Unit (1999: 37).

[47] Grunseit and Kippax (1994) and Ingham, Clement, and Gillibrand (2000).

[48] Social Exclusion Unit (1999: 39).

[49] Although parents are not permitted to withdraw their children from those aspects of sex and health education which form part of the National Curriculum.

[50] Bainham (1996).   [51] Social Exclusion Unit (1999: 36).

[52] Social Exclusion Unit (1999: 37).   [53] Counterpoint Research (2001: 8–9).

[54] Counterpoint Research (2001: 14).   [55] Winn et al (1998: 24).

[56] Gelder (2002: 6).   [57] BMA (2004: 228).

[58] Social Exclusion Unit (1999: 53).   [59] Counterpoint Research (2001: 8–9).

[60] Although perhaps not if, for example, the request reveals that the child is being abused.

be appreciated by teenagers.[61] The child may be concerned that the doctor will inform her or his parents. More practical concerns over confidentiality may arise, especially in a rural community where an unaccompanied visit by a child to a doctor is likely to be noticed by someone who knows the child's parents.[62]

The third explanation is practical difficulties in actually getting to the doctor. This has led to some schools offering contraceptive advice by school nurses, including the dispensing of the 'morning after pill'. Young people report finding GP and clinic opening hours restrictive, their locales difficult to get to, and their atmosphere intimidating. It was for this reason partly that buying contraceptives from chemists and supermarkets was more popular than obtaining them from clinics.

A fourth point is that many young people appear to find the present methods of contraception distasteful. It seems they dislike the current alternatives because they carried health risks, were smelly, involved rubber or cream, or interrupted sex.[63] They were also perceived to be expensive, although as already mentioned in fact contraception is available free on the NHS.

Finally, there appears also to be a need not only for accessing contraception, but also training in how to use it. Several studies have found complaints from women that their partners do not know how to put on condoms,[64] and that men are deterred from using them because they are not confident that they will be able to put them on properly.[65] There may also be evidence for this in a finding that 80 per cent of pregnant teenagers claimed to have been using contraception at the time of conception.[66]

3.1.4 *Peer pressure and social expectation*

There is a widespread impression that peer pressure and social expectation pressurizes some young people into sexual relations. These are, in part, created by the belief among young people that a majority of teenagers are having sexual intercourse. In fact just under a third of young people have had sexual intercourse by their 16th birthday.[67] When asked for the reason why they engaged in their first incidence of sexual intercourse, only 17 per cent of boys and 38 per cent of girls gave 'love' as the reason. Curiosity topped the bill for boys and a desire to lose virginity for girls.[68]

3.1.5 *Social benefits*

The tabloid press are keen to suggest that many young women choose to get pregnant in order to 'jump' the housing ladder and access the variety of social benefits available to parents. The Government's report into teenage pregnancy found no evidence to support such a claim and describes it as improbable.[69]

3.1.6 *Alcohol and drugs*

It would be difficult to underestimate the significance that alcohol or drugs can play in early unprotected sexual intercourse.[70] In one study of Scottish young people who had

---

[61] For evidence that young people are deterred from seeking advice because of confidentiality concerns: Carlisle et al (2007).

[62] Counterpoint Research (2001: 11). See also Independent Advisory Group on Teenage Pregnancy (2005).

[63] Counterpoint Research (2001: 9).   [64] Counterpoint Research (2001: 23).

[65] The study is referred to at Social Exclusion Unit (1999: 50).

[66] Pearson et al (1995).   [67] British Market Research Bureau (2003: 10).

[68] Wellings et al (1994).   [69] Social Exclusion Unit (1999: 27).

[70] Alcohol Concern (2002).

had sexual intercourse it was found that 259 of the men (out of 631) said that they were drunk or stoned at the time of their first sexual intercourse, and 226 (out of 260) of the women.[71] Revealingly one set of interviews with young men revealed that on nights out they wanted to 'get out of it' and alcohol, drugs, and sex were all part of that. They stated that contraception appeared adult and responsible and was therefore contrary to their mood.[72] A recent study suggested that 14 per cent of people were under the influence of drink or drugs when they first had sex.[73]

As can be seen there are a multitude of different factors which may explain the high levels of teenage pregnancy in England and Wales. The difficulty is that, as one young person explaining why they had not used contraception said: 'sex is not a rational process'.[74] However much education and encouragement to use contraception is placed on young people, for them sex is often on the spur of the moment. That said, as the statistics from other countries show, it should certainly be possible to lower the rate of teenage pregnancy, even if it is not clear how to do so.

3.2 What can be done to help?

The Government's Health Development Agency has accepted that anti-poverty strategies are more likely to have a longer term influence than any other efforts that may be used to try and reduce the teenage pregnancy rate.[75] But if we wait until the removal of social inequality before the problem is dealt with we will wait a very long time. Recently Beverly Hughes, a Health Minister, said that there is a limit to what the Government can do to reduce teenage pregnancy, and that the parents of teenagers must play their part in reducing the rate.[76]

Much attention is understandably placed on sex education. While there is widespread dissatisfaction with the old-fashioned form of sex education which focused on the mechanics of sexual activity without providing a wider context, there is less agreement on the way ahead. A large number of different schemes and proposals have been made. These include giving young people relationship skills; emphasizing the stress of looking after a baby;[77] focusing on the needs and concerns of young men;[78] encouraging and enabling children to talk with their parents;[79] and using older children to teach younger ones responsible attitudes and behaviour concerning sexual relations.[80] Perhaps the most controversial issue in sex education is whether young people should be encouraged not to engage in sexual intercourse or whether the decision should be left to the young people without a line being taken. Supporters of an abstinence approach argue abstinence is the only 100 per cent certain way of ensuring that one does not become a teenage parent or acquire a sexually transmitted disease. Of course, some will argue that sexual experimentation among teenagers is normal and beneficial, and the issue of sexual behaviour has to be worked out by each person for her or himself. The 'just say no' message may be seen as adults 'preaching to' young people and will have little effect.[81]

---

[71] Wight et al (2003).   [72] Counterpoint Research (2001: 9).
[73] BBC Newsonline (2 July 2007).   [74] Counterpoint Research (2001: 19).
[75] Health Development Agency (2001: 3). For assessment of the Government's work see Independent Advisory Group on Teenage Pregnancy (2005).
[76] BBC Newsonline (26 May 2005).   [77] Cramb (1998).
[78] Gelder (2002: 15).   [79] Health Development Agency (2001: 5).
[80] Counterpoint Research (2001: 13).
[81] Teenage Pregnancy Unit (2000). Evidence from the US queries the effectiveness of these abstinence programmes: Underhill et al (2007).

3.3 Conclusion

In 1999 the Government launched a cross-government teenage pregnancy strategy with a target of halving the under-18 conception rate in England by 2010 with an interim target of a 15 per cent reduction by 2004 (a target that was not reached).[82] In 2007 the Government stated that the conception rate had been reduced by 11.8 per cent.[83] It is notable that the target set by the Government was to reduce the teenage conception, rather than teenage birth rates. This may be because of the political furore which would be likely to result if the Government were seen to be 'encouraging' abortions. The Government's strategy is being masterminded by the Teenage Pregnancy Unit. There are three basic pillars to their approach:

- a national campaign to mobilize every section of the community to achieve agreed goals (including a media campaign);
- better prevention through better education about sex and relationships, clearer messages about contraception, and special attention to at-risk groups; and
- better support for teenage parents.[84]

The success of the programme is debated. Between 1998 and 2005 the conception rate for under-18s in England fell by 11.8 per cent.[85] The birth rate for that time period fell by 19 per cent. The current figures show that 41.1 out of every 1,000 women aged 16 or 17 will conceive and 7.8 for every 1,000 girls aged 13 to 15.[86] The percentage of 16–17-year-old women on the pill rose from 17 per cent in 1998–99 to 24 per cent 2002–03.[87]

4 Abortion and contraception

At the heart of the legal regulation of fertility is a distinction between abortion and contraception. If a technique is classified as producing an abortion or miscarriage its regulation is entirely different from where it is classified as a contraceptive. As we shall see later in this chapter there is a host of detailed regulations governing abortion. The following recent decision is now the leading authority on the distinction.[88]

KEY CASE   R (John Smeaton on Behalf of SPUC) v The Secretary of State for Health et al [2002] 2 FCR 193

The SPUC (Society of the Protection of the Unborn Child) sought to challenge the legality of The Prescription Only Medicines (Human Use) Amendment (No 3) Order 2000, SI 2000/3231 which permitted the sale of the morning-after pill without prescription. The 1861 Offences Against the

---

82 DoH (2000b).   83 DoH (2007d).
84 DoH (2007d) provides the detail in this.
85 DoH (2007d). Although Family and Youth Concerns (2004) argue that areas of the country which have been the focus of Government efforts have in fact seen rises in the rates of teenage pregnancy.
86 Teenage Pregnancy Unit (2007).   87 National Statistics(2004).
88 See Keown (2005a) for a critique of this decision.

Person Act, sections 58 and 59 (creating the offence of procuring a miscarriage) mean that substances which cause miscarriage or abortion may be administered only if two doctors certify that the conditions set out in the 1967 Abortion Act are satisfied. Otherwise, the use of such substances is in principle potentially criminal. The question for the court was whether the morning-after pill is such a substance. If it was then it is an offence for a pharmacist to provide it and an offence for the woman to take it, unless all the formalities required by the Abortion Act were complied with.

To answer the question Mumby J explained the 'medical facts':

> Put very simply, there are two key stages in the biological process following sexual intercourse:
>
> (i) The first is fertilization. This takes place after the man's sperm and the woman's egg have met in the fallopian tube. It is a process which commences hours, or even days, after sexual intercourse. The process itself takes many hours.
>
> (ii) The other key stage is implantation. This takes place after the fertilized egg has moved into the womb. It involves a process by which the fertilized egg physically attaches itself to the wall of the womb. The process does not start until, at the earliest, some four days after the commencement of fertilization. The process of implantation itself takes some days.'

SPUC argued that any procedure that caused the loss of a fertilized egg was procuring a 'miscarriage' and that contraception involved procedures which prevented fertilization. So their argument was that something that prevented a fertilized egg implanting itself in the wall of the womb is an abortifacient and not a contraceptive. The morning-after pill (and indeed the normal contraceptive pill) operate in some cases to prevent fertilization and in others to prevent implantation. However, the morning-after pill (and the normal pill) cannot work once the fertilized eggs are implanted.

SPUC argued that the word miscarriage, at least as understood in 1861, included preventing implantation. The aim of Parliament in 1861 was to prohibit all attempts to abort from the moment of fertilization. This argument was rejected by Mumby J for two main reasons:

(i) As a matter of law, the decision must ultimately turn not on what the word 'miscarriage' was understood to mean in 1861 but rather on what it means today.

(ii) Whatever it may or may not have meant in 1861 the word 'miscarriage' today means the termination of an established pregnancy, and there is no established pregnancy prior to implantation. There is no miscarriage if a fertilized egg is lost prior to implantation. Current medical understanding of what is meant by 'miscarriage' excludes results brought about by the pill, the mini-pill or the morning-after pill. That is also, I should add, the current understanding of the word 'miscarriage' when used by lay people in its popular sense.

It followed that SPUC's arguments failed and the morning-after pill was a form of contraceptive and not abortion for the purposes of the legislative scheme.

Part of Mumby J's reasoning was based on the social benefits of the availability of emergency contraception. He accepted the point: 'Emergency contraception is safe, simple and effective. Abortion is both medically and psychologically invasive.' All the evidence was that if emergency contraception was not available the number of abortions would greatly increase and this, he thought, would be a bad thing. Also he pointed out if the SPUC's arguments were accepted then use of the contraceptive pill itself where it operated to prevent implantation (as opposed to conception) would be criminal. The pill was used by millions of women and it could not be Parliament's intention that its use was unlawful.

The effect, then, of Mumby J's judgment is that the line between contraception and abortion is not pre- and post-conception, but before and after implantation.[89]

5 Contraception and children

We have already indicated that a doctor is permitted to provide contraceptive advice to under-16-year-olds. However, the position is not quite as straightforward as stated. The leading decision on the issue is *Gillick v West Norfolk & Wisbech AHA*:

KEY CASE   Gillick v West Norfolk & Wisbech AHA [1986] AC 112

Mrs Gillick sought to challenge the legality of a Department of Health Circular which permitted doctors to provide contraceptive advice and treatment to under-16-year-olds without parental permission. The House of Lords held that it was lawful for a doctor to do so providing the child is sufficiently mature to understand the medical, social, and family issues involved, and the child can provide an effective consent. Therefore maturity and the ability to understand the issues determined whether a person was competent, rather than age. The majority emphasized that even if a child's parents do not want the child to have contraceptive advice, it was still open to a doctor to provide the advice if the child was competent to make the decision. Some commentators have seen a distinction between the approach of Lord Fraser and Lord Scarman in the case. Lord Fraser emphasized that the doctor can only treat a *Gillick* competent child with contraceptive treatment if to do so would be in her best interests. However Lord Scarman makes no reference to best interests. It may be that Lord Scarman made no reference to this because he thought it self evident that a doctor would only act in a way that benefited her or his patient. An alternative interpretation is that there is a difference: Lord Scarman thought that a doctor could treat a competent child seeking treatment unless to do so would harm the child; while Lord Fraser thought the doctor would have to be convinced that the treatment benefited the child.

Their Lordships dealt with two other issues. First, it was emphasized that a doctor owes a child patient a duty of confidentiality. The doctor should not inform the child's parents of the visit. Secondly, their Lordships responded to an argument that the provision of contraception to an underage person could be regarded as a criminal offence of assisting in the commission of a child sex offence. The House of Lords held that the doctor could not be guilty of an offence because she or he did not intend the child to engage in sexual intercourse. Although a controversial piece of reasoning, this issue has now been addressed by the Sexual Offences Act 2003 and so it is not necessary to consider this aspect of their Lordship's judgment further.

As *Gillick* makes clear, a doctor can provide contraceptive advice and treatment to an under-16-year-old if the child has sufficient maturity and intelligence to understand the issues involved and is therefore competent to give consent to the treatment provided. There may also, it appears from Lord Fraser's speech, be a requirement that any treatment provided is in the child's interests. As the House of Lords appeared to approve of the general social policy of making contraception available to competent sexually active

[89] There is some debate whether menstrual abstraction should be regarded as a form of abortion: Bridgeman and Millns (1998: 241–8).

minors, it may be thought to unnecessarily complicate a GP's job to consider whether or not the contraception was in the child's interests. There have been reports of children as young as ten being given the contraceptive pill.[90]

There is still the issue of potential criminal liability as an accessory to a sexual offence. This is addressed in the Sexual Offences Act 2003. The concern is that by providing contraception a doctor might be said to be aiding or abetting the commission of a child abuse offence. Section 73 of the Act states:[91]

(1) A person is not guilty of aiding, abetting or counselling the commission against a child of an offence to which this section applies if he acts for the purpose of—

(a) protecting the child from sexually transmitted infection,

(b) protecting the physical safety of the child,

(c) preventing the child from becoming pregnant, or

(d) promoting the child's emotional well-being by the giving of advice,

and not for the purpose of obtaining sexual gratification or for the purpose of causing or encouraging the activity constituting the offence or the child's participation in it.

This makes it clear that if a doctor is acting to protect the child's health she or he will not be guilty of an accessory to sex offence against the child if she or he provides contraceptive advice or treatment.

The BMA has provided guidance for doctors dealing with young people on contraception issues. It suggests that doctor should encourage under-16-year olds to discuss the issue with their parents, and emphasizes that the doctor is permitted to give advice and treatment even without parental consent if the young person has sufficient understanding of the relevant issues.[92] The Department of Heath's *Best Practice Guidance for Doctors and Other Health Care Professionals on the Provision of Advice and Treatment to Young People under 16 on Contraception, Sexual and Reproductive Health*[93] admits that concerns over confidentiality can be the biggest deterrent to seeking contraception by young people. The Guidance emphasizes the importance of respecting confidentiality, even if the doctor decides that the child is not sufficiently competent to receive advice. Only where there is evidence that the child is suffering serious harm (eg she or he is being sexually abused) should the doctor breach confidence. Although publication of the guidance might do something[94] to encourage young people to see their GPs, their concerns over confidentiality also include 'gossipy receptionists' and receiving doctor's letters in the post which their parents might see. The Guidance may not assuage such fears.[95]

6 Sterilization and the incompetent

Is it ever appropriate to sterilize a person without their consent? At first this appears an horrific suggestion but it is a reasonably common practice. In the not too distant past it was part of eugenics, whereby it was thought appropriate to sterilize 'undesirables'

---

[90] BBC Newsonline (9 May 2005). [91] See also s 16(3).

[92] BMA (2004: 225). [93] DoH (2004i).

[94] Young people are not known as the most avid readers of Department of Health circulars!

[95] Brook Advisory Centres (1999).

to prevent them reproducing children who would be similarly undesirable. Eugenics was seen as a way of ensuring only the best kind of human beings survived. This kind of thinking was revealed by the judgment of Justice Oliver Wendell Holmes in *Buck v Bell*:[96]

> It is better for all the world if instead of waiting to execute degenerate offspring for crime, or to let them starve for their imbecility, society can prevent those who are manifestly unfit from continuing their kind.

Few were more enthusiastic about eugenic sterilization than the Nazi regime, sterilizing up to 3.5 million people.[97] Nowadays few people openly support eugenics, but it is thought appropriate to sterilize incompetent people because to do so would be in their best interests.

6.1 The law and sterilization of incompetent people

The legal position on sterilization is as follows. If a doctor wishes to sterilize a patient the normal rules on consent apply. So if the patient is an adult and competent she or he cannot be sterilized without consent.[98] If a patient is incompetent and a doctor believes that a sterilization would be in the patient's best interests and is the least intrusive way of protecting their interests then the sterilization can be performed.[99] Approval of the court must be obtained first.[100] This will now be governed by the Mental Capacity Act 2005. In determining whether a sterilization is in a patient's best interests under section 4, the Mental Capacity Act Code of Practice[101] states that the courts should follow the approach they have developed in the earlier case law which was also based on ascertaining the best interests of the patient. However, the House of Lords in *F v W Berkshire HA*[102] emphasized that if the sterilization is for non-therapeutic reasons (ie it is not required to treat a medical condition) then a court declaration that the sterilization would be lawful should be sought.[103] In the case of a child this could be an application made under the Children Act 1989 or under the wardship jurisdiction. In the cases of an incompetent adult the court can declare a sterilization lawful under the Mental Capacity Act 2005, section 15. There is no need to obtain court authorization if there are therapeutic reasons for the sterilization (eg to deal with excessive menstruation), as long as the sterilization is the least intrusive way of dealing with the medical problem.[104]

It is not quite clear what the legal position is where a doctor fails to obtain a court order authorizing sterilization where it is not therapeutic. Technically, the court order made in this kind of case is a formal declaration that the procedure is lawful. In other words it does not render a procedure lawful, it simply confirms the legal position. It may therefore be that a doctor who fails to obtain a court order will be breaching professional

---

[96] US 200 (1927), at 207.   [97] Lombardo (1996: 12).

[98] The test of capacity to consent to or refuse treatment is set out in *Re MB (Medical Treatment)* [1997] 2 FLR 426, 437, see Chap 4.

[99] This is now emphasized by the Mental Capacity Act 2005, s 1(6).

[100] DCA (2007: para 8.18).   [101] DCA (2007: para 8.22).   [102] [1989] 2 All ER 545.

[103] *Practice Note (Official Solicitor: Declaratory Proceedings: Medical and Welfare Decisions for Adults who Lack Capacity)* [2001] 2 FLR 158.

[104] *F v F* (1991) 7 BMLR 135, *Re SL (Adult Patient) (Medical Treatment)* [2000] 1 FCR 361. If the case is near the boundary line between therapeutic and non-therapeutic it should be referred to the court: *Re S (Sterilisation)* [2000] 2 FLR 389, 405.

guidelines, but otherwise will only be acting criminally if it could be shown that the procedure was not in the patient's best interests.

Where an application is made to authorize a sterilization, the decision will be made simply on the basis of what is in the best interests of the patient.

This approach was established in the following case:

KEY CASE   Re B (A Minor) (Wardship: Sterilization) [1988] AC 199

The House of Lords were faced in this case with a 17-year-old with the mental age of a child aged five or six. The issue before them was the legality of her proposed sterilization. Their Lordships held that the key question was simply what was in her best interests. Lord Hailsham, giving the leading judgment, focused on the terror and distress the 17-year-old would face were she to become pregnant. He stated that she had no maternal instincts and that she would not be able to care for the child. Lord Bridge was careful to emphasize that the case was not based on eugenics. He stated that the only consideration was what was in B's best interests. In taking this line he rejected the approach of the Canadian Supreme Court in *Re Eve* [1986] 2 SCR 388.

Re Eve concerned the proposed sterilization of Eve, a 21-year-old woman. She suffered from learning difficulties and had struck up a friendship with a man. The point was made that the only reason for the operation was to prevent Eve becoming pregnant. The Court was heavily influenced by concerns that sterilization may be used for eugenic reasons. It was emphasized that Eve was no more likely to suffer from a pregnancy than other women. The personal hygiene problems associated with menstruation were troublesome but no more so than other matters of personal hygiene. The Court emphasized the point that the operation was irreversible. Maintaining the physical integrity of a human being ranked highly. A non-therapeutic sterilization was a 'grave intrusion' on a person's rights. It could therefore never be lawful.

This approach was rejected by Lord Bridge on the basis that this approach could require a court to make an order which was not in a patient's best interests. This was unacceptable.

> This sweeping generalization [that non-therapeutic sterilizations should not be performed] seems to me, with respect, to be entirely unhelpful. To say that the court can never authorize sterilization of a ward as being in her best interests would be patently wrong. To say that it can only do so if the operation is 'therapeutic' as opposed to 'non-therapeutic' is to divert attention from the true issue, which is whether the operation is in the ward's best interests, and remove it to an area of arid semantic debate as to where the line is to be drawn ([1998] 2 All ER 206, 217).

The courts have emphasized that because the best interests are to be the sole consideration there are two considerations which should not be taken into account:

• The interests of those people who are caring for the patient.[105] So, for example, an argument by those caring for a mentally ill woman that sterilization should be performed because of the extra burdens the carers would face were she to become pregnant could not be a reason for providing sterilization. That said, the court might consider an argument that the burdens of supervising the woman who was not sterilized would

---

[105] *Re B* [1987] 2 All ER 206. Although in *Re HG* [1993] 1 FLR 588 the 'legitimate concerns' of the patients' carers were a relevant consideration.

be so great that the carers would fall ill and be unable to offer care. It should also be noted that the court will often be given information from which they decide what is in a patient's best interests by her or his carers. This might be thought to give them 'power' to present the image of the patient to the court in a way which is likely to lead to the order they are seeking being made.

- The courts will not take into account eugenic considerations.[106] So the fact that the person might have a disabled child is not a relevant consideration.[107]

These are the factors which are not taken into account, but what is to be considered? In *Re F (A Mental Patient: Sterilization)*[108] it was emphasized by the House of Lords that the 'best interests' test was not the same as the *Bolam* test. In other words it would not be enough to show that there was a respectable body of medical opinion in support of sterilization, but the court had to be persuaded considering all the arguments that the procedure would be in the patient's best interests.[109]

In deciding whether the operation is in the best interests of an individual the court will consider not only the medical issues but also the broader ethical, social, moral and welfare considerations.[110] The Practice Direction which sets out the procedures where decisions are being made for patients who lack capacity suggests that: 'The court will wish to prepare a balance sheet listing the advantages and disadvantages of the procedure for the patient. If potential advantages and disadvantages are to be relied on then the court will wish to assess in percentage terms the likelihood of them in fact occurring'.[111] Having prepared the balance sheet the court will be in a position to determine what is in a patient's best interests. In deciding whether or not to authorize the sterilization the following factors have been mentioned by the courts:[112]

- The professional opinion. Rarely will the court decline to authorize the sterilization where it has the approval of all of the professionals involved. In the few cases where the court has refused to grant a declaration the professional opinion has been divided.[113] However, the Court of Appeal has recently emphasized that it is for the court, not the doctors, to decide what is in the best interests of the patient.[114]

- Sterilization will only be approved if it is a 'last resort'.[115] This is because forcing sterilizations on incompetent people infringes their rights under the European Convention, articles 3 or 8.[116] So, if the court is to be persuaded that sterilization is appropriate because a pregnancy would be too distressing for the patient, then it will need to be shown that

---

[106] *Re B* [1987] 2 All ER 206.
[107] *Re X (Adult Sterilisation)* [1998] 2 FLR 1124, 1129. *Practice Note (Official Solicitor: Declaratory Proceedings: Medical and Welfare Decisions for Adults who Lack Capacity)* [2001] 2 FLR 158, appendix 1.
[108] [1990] 2 AC 1.
[109] This was recently reiterated in *Re A (Medical Treatment: Male Sterilization)* (2000) 53 BMLR 66 and *SL v SL* [2000] 2 FCR 452.
[110] *Re S (Sterilisation: Patient's Best Interests)* [2000] 2 FLR 389, 401.
[111] This is adopting the approach proposed by Thorpe LJ in *Re A (Male Sterilisation)* [2000] 1 FLR 549, 560.
[112] In *Re S (Sterilisation: Patient's Best Interests)* [2000] 2 FLR 389, 403 it was held that best interests test was the same as the welfare test used in wardship.
[113] Eg *Re D* [1976] 1 All ER 326; *Re LC* [1997] 2 FLR 258 (where the patient's key social worker opposed the operation).
[114] *Re A (Medical Treatment; Male Sterilisation)* [2000] 1 FCR 193.
[115] Lord Oliver *Re B* [1987] 2 All ER 206, 218.
[116] *Re A (Medical Treatment: Male Sterilisation)* [2000] 1 FCR 193.

alternative means of avoiding pregnancy are not appropriate.[117] Therefore, successful applications tend to include evidence that the contraceptive pill is not appropriate for some reason.[118] However, the courts do not appear to be at all strict on this ground. In *Re* P,[119] although the patient was successfully using an oral contraceptive at the time of the hearing, sterilization was approved because it was felt that there was a risk she might not take the pill regularly in the future. A court may be persuaded that the controlling of severe menstrual bleedings justifies sterilization rather than other forms of contraception.[120]

- The court will need to be persuaded that any alleged risk of pregnancy is not fanciful.[121] Applications are, therefore, often supported by evidence that the patient is showing an interest in members of the opposite sex, or is involved in an intimate relationship, or even that she is 'attractive'.[122] The practice direction states that there should be evidence that the person is capable of conceiving.[123] However, again, some of the older decisions do not take this point particularly seriously.[124] In *Re* W[125] it was held that the risk of pregnancy was slight, but the sterilization was approved because it was supported by the medical experts. In *Re HG*[126] sterilization was approved even though there was no evidence that the woman was sexually active. More recent decisions seem to take a stricter line.[127] In *Re LC*[128] Thorpe LJ refused to approve of a proposed sterilization because he believed the patient's carers were constantly supervising her and therefore she was adequately protected from the risk of pregnancy.[129]

- The ability of the person to care for any child born following a pregnancy is a factor sometimes mentioned by the court.[130] This is said to be relevant where the child will have to be removed from the patient soon after birth and that to do so would cause the patient great distress.

6.2 Criticisms of the courts' approach

There have been many who have been critical of the courts' approach to these cases. Their objections include the following:

- The courts are too readily finding a patient to be incompetent.[131] In *Re* P[132] the judge accepted that P might have the mental capacity to marry, but she did not have the

---

[117] *Practice Note (Official Solicitor: Declaratory Proceedings: Medical and Welfare Decisions for Adults who Lack Capacity)* [2001] 2 FLR 158.

[118] In *Re P (A Minor) (Wardship: Sterilisation)* [1989] 1 FLR 182 the fact that the kind of sterilization performed was reversible was a relevant consideration.

[119] [1989] 1 FLR 182.

[120] *Re Z (Medical Treatment: Hysterectomy)* [2000] 1 FCR 274. There it was said that her periods brought her nothing but pain and discomfort. But is there anything unusual in that?

[121] Montgomery (2003: 400).

[122] *Re P (A Minor) (Wardship: Sterilisation)* [1989] 1 FLR 182 and *SL v SL* [2000] 2 FCR 452.

[123] Appendix 1, para 3.

[124] *Re W (Patient Sterilisation)* [1993] 1 FLR381; *Re P (A Minor) (Wardship: Sterilisation)* [1989] 1 FLR 82; *Re HG* [1993] 1 FLR 588.

[125] [1993] 1 FLR 381.   [126] [1993] 1 FLR 588.

[127] *Re S (Medical Treatment: Adult Sterilisation)* [1998] 1 FLR994; *Re LC (Medical Treatment: Sterilisation)* [1997] 2 FLR 258.

[128] [1997] 2 FLR 258.

[129] See also *Re S* [1998] 1 FLR 944 where a sterilization was not approved because there was insufficient proof of a risk of pregnancy.

[130] *Re X* [1999] 3 FCR 426; *Re M (A Minor) (Wardship: Serilisation)* [1988] 2 FLR 997.

[131] Jackson (2001; 54); Lee and Morgan (1988).   [132] [1989] 1 FLR 182.

mental capacity to decide about a sterilization. This appears out of line with the normal approach to consent in medical law where even people with some mental difficulties are permitted to make decisions for themselves, providing they have a basic understanding of the issues. There have been particular concerns that pregnant women have been too readily found to be incompetent.[133]

• The courts are simply too ready to declare a sterilization to be a last resort. Although the courts say that they will only authorize a sterilization as a last resort, in fact the courts are far more willing to grant sterilizations than might appear from their rhetoric.[134] For example, as Jackson, points out, it is surprising that the courts have authorized sterilizations without requiring evidence that the individual is fertile.[135]

• The law puts much weight on the distinction between a therapeutic and non-therapeutic sterilization. This distinction is not always an easy one to draw.[136] In some cases the courts have accepted as a reason for sterilization the distress caused by menstruation. Some commentators have firmly rejected the view that menstruation should be regarded in this way as an illness.[137]

• The 'best interests' rhetoric is so vague that it enables a judge to reach a decision based on her or his own values.[138] It therefore fails to protect adequately patient's rights.

• Montgomery has argued that 'eugenic' arguments have been 'introduced through the back door'. He points to Re M[139] where Bush J held that as there was a 50 per cent chance that the patient, were she to become pregnant, would conceive a child suffering a mental handicap, and that if so she would have to have an abortion and this would cause her harm. Justice Bush insisted that this was not a eugenic argument because it was based on concerns about the patient's welfare. However to Montgomery this method of reasoning has become a 'routine means of bypassing the restriction on eugenic considerations'.[140]

• Brazier and Cave[141] have expressed the concern that sterilization of the mentally ill provides an easy means of covering up sexual abuse. In institutional settings it is difficult to ensure that there is no sexual abuse between patients, or between staff and patients, and there are concerns that it is even routine. Sterilization means that staff do not need to be overly concerned about the issue as it is unlikely to come to light through pregnancies. They suggest that proper policing of institutions should mean that sexual abuse is avoided and that therefore there is much less need for sterilization.[142]

• The law fails to pay sufficient attention to the fact that any case of involuntary birth control violates a person's freedom to make reproductive choices for themselves.[143] Emily Jackson argues:

> My argument is, however, that honourable intentions will invariably fail to offer adequate justification for the non-consensual and permanent removal of an individual's reproductive capacity. That the sterilization of mentally incapacitated women without their consent is not generally perceived to be an egregious and violatory act reflects, I argue, a

---

[133] See eg Re MB (Medical Treatment) [1997] 2 FLR 426.
[134] Montgomery (1989).   [135] Jackson (2001: 63).   [136] Hale (1996: 25).
[137] Cica (1993).   [138] Peterson (1996: 64).   [139] [1988] 2 FLR 497.
[140] Montgomery (2003: 400).   [141] Brazier and Cave (2007: 287).
[142] Indeed sterilization offers no protection from sexually transmitted diseases.
[143] Jackson (2001: 42).

web of negative assumptions about the sexuality and possible future maternity of women with mental disabilities.[144]

Notably one study found that 68 per cent of mentally handicapped women disapproved of their sterilization and felt stigmatized and degraded.[145]

● The law purports to be gender neutral. However, it is difficult to justify the sterilization of a man as being in his best interests, there being no danger of pregnancy for him.[146] This makes it far easier for the courts to authorize the sterilization of women than men. This might be said to be an example of double standards.

Underlying many of the criticisms is the view that to sterilize a person without their consent is a major invasion of their rights and dignity.[147] Freeman refers to:

> The rights we have we have simply by virtue of being human. The right to reproduce is one of these rights. Involuntary sterilization, save where it is carried out for exclusively medical reasons, denies an aspect of humanity.[148]

Only in the most unusual of cases will that be justifiable. A representative of MENCAP is reported as saying of the *Re B* decision that now mentally disabled girls have been reduced to the status of pets who can be neutered at will.[149] However, to supporters of the current law's approach the loss of ability to reproduce is hardly a grave invasion of a person's rights if they are unable to appreciate the nature of the right or be able to exercise it in a responsible way. It is easy to take the high moral ground and demand respect for the rights of the mentally incompetent. However, that may leave them and their carers to suffer the consequences of unwanted and distressing pregnancies. Should the courts pay more attention to the high minded musings of theoreticians or the wishes of those caring for the mentally disordered day-by-day?[150] Some commentators have suggested that the reality is that if we take a strict line in protecting the rights of reproductive freedom and do not sterilize that will lead to an infringement of the freedom of movement and association of mentally ill people. This is because if they are not sterilized they will need to be supervised and have their movements restricted to a far greater extent that if they were sterilized.[151] This in turn leads to a debate over the importance of reproductive freedom. Is the ability a key aspect of a woman's identity? Or is that to reinforce childbearing as part of an essential part of being a woman? Or is the law here enforcing a construction of idealized motherhood, with only the 'good mothers' being permitted to reproduce?[152]

7 Tort liability and contraception

A number of tort law issues can arise in connection with contraception. They include the following.

---

[144] Jackson (2001: 55).   [145] Cepko (1993).
[146] *Re A (Medical Treatment: Male Sterilisation)* [2000] 1 FCR 193.
[147] Cleveland (1997).   [148] Freeman (1988).
[149] Brian Rix, quoted in Brazier and Cave (2007: 285).
[150] Scott (1986). See Scroggie (1998) for a sympathetic look at why parents seek sterilization for their mentally disordered children.
[151] Keywood (1998).   [152] Bridgeman and Millns (1998: 342).

7.1 Contraception and side-effects

A doctor prescribes the pill without warning of potential side effects. This is, *prima facie*, negligent.[153] However, if a patient claims that taking the pill has caused them to suffer medical conditions about which they were not informed, they face an uphill task in establishing that the pill caused the medical condition.[154]

7.2 Defective contraception

In *Richardson v LRC Products*[155] a condom split and a woman who became pregnant as a result failed in her action against the manufacturer. She claimed that the condom was a defective product. The claim failed for three reasons. First it had not been shown that the product was defective in the sense that it failed to provide the protection which 'persons generally are entitled to expect'.[156] Justice Kennedy pointed out that people were not entitled to expect any method of contraception would be 100 per cent effective. Secondly, that she had known the condom had broken, but not taken the morning-after pill. Thirdly, that the *McFarlane*[157] decision (see below) had made it clear that damages were not available for raising a child.

7.3 Mistaken sterilization

In *Devi v West Midlands AHA*[158] a woman went into hospital for a minor gynaecological procedure. By mistake she was sterilized. Her religion outlawed sterilization or contraception. She received £4,000 for the loss of the ability to conceive and £2,700 for the neurosis caused by the knowledge of what had been done to her. In *Biles v Barking HA*[159] where a women was wrongly advised that she needed a sterilization she was awarded £45,000. This award in part was to fund IVF treatment.

7.4 Negligence in sterilization

If a patient is sterilized in a defective way, then has sexual intercourse, leading to a pregnancy, can legal proceedings be brought against the doctor? There are quite a number of difficulties which would face such a claim.

First, it would need to be shown that the failed operation cause the pregnancy. This is normally easily shown. It might be argued that the sexual intercourse, rather than the failed sterilization caused the pregnancy, but the courts have not accepted such arguments, unless at the time of the sexual intercourse the applicant was aware that the sterilization was not effective.[160] The courts have also firmly rejected an argument that if a woman becomes pregnant following a failed sterilization she has a duty to have an abortion and if she chooses not to then she cannot sue.[161]

---

153 *Pearce v United Bristol Healthcare NHS Trust* [1999] PIQR 53.
154 *Vadera v Shaw* (1999) 45 BMLR 162.   155 [2000] Ll Med Rep 280.
156 The wording of s 3 of the 1987 Consumer Protection Act.
157 *Mc Farlane v Tayside Health Board* [1999] 4 WLR 1301.
158 (1981) Unreported.   159 (1986) Unreported.
160 *Sabri-Tabrizi v Lothian Health Board* [1998] BMLR 190, a Scottish case, but one that is likely to be followed south of the border.
161 *Emeh v Kensington, Chelsea and Fulham Area Health Authority* [1984] 3 All ER 1044, 1053; *Mc Farlane v Tayside Health Board* [1999] 4 WLR 1301 at 1301 (Lord Slynn) and 1317 (Lord Steyn).

Secondly, it would need to be shown that the doctor owed the claimant a duty of care. There would be no difficulty if the doctor treated the woman herself or her and her partner together. Where it was the woman's partner whose vasectomy was unsuccessful it needs to be shown that the doctor who carried out the operation owed the woman a duty of care. This will be shown if the doctor is aware that the woman is a partner of the patient. However in *Goodwill v BPAS*[162] a doctor was held not to owe a duty of care to a woman who started a relationship with the man three years after the operation.

Next, it would need to be shown that the doctor was negligent. Two claims could be made here. It could be said that the procedure was negligently performed. The normal law governing whether the performance of an operation was negligent would apply (see Chapter 3). Alternatively it might be claimed that the doctor had made a negligent mis-statement. This may be an assurance that the operation has been a success when it was not, or a failure to encourage the parties to use contraception until tests have confirmed that the operation is a success, or a failure to warn the parties of the small risk that the operation has not succeeded. In the case of such claims the normal test for deciding whether a failure to give medical information was negligent will apply: was the risk such that no responsible body of medical opinion would have failed to give a warning, or is the risk so substantial that the court feels that whatever medical opinion may be it is one of which a patient should be warned?[163] It is established that it is not negligent for a doctor not to warn a couple of the one in 2,000 chance that a sterilization operation of men will reverse itself years later.[164] Professional bodies have stated that women should be warned of the one in 200 risk that sterilization will not work.[165]

Thirdly, it would need to be shown that the claimant had suffered a loss. This has proved the most difficult issue. If the woman miscarries or suffers a stillbirth, she will be able to claim for her pain and suffering, although the sums awarded will not be high. If she decides to have an abortion, she could claim for medical expenses connected with the abortion and for pain and suffering and any loss of income. Again the sum awarded is unlikely to be high. The greatest difficulty comes with cases where the woman gives birth.

A child cannot bring a 'wrongful life' claim. In other words it is not possible for the child to sue the doctor who negligently performed the sterilization. In essence the courts have found morally repugnant the claim that a child should not have been born.[166] This is so even where the child has been born seriously disabled.

The woman can seek damages for the pregnancy and birth if it was her steriliza-tion which failed. This can include medical expenses and money to compensate for the pain and suffering in connection with pregnancy and childbirth In *Walkin v South Manchester Health Authority*[167] it was confirmed that a pregnancy could be regarded as a personal injury (although Roch LJ had 'some difficulty'[168] with that conclusion). A loss of earnings can also be claimed. Similarly she can recover for expenses associated with the birth.

But what about the costs of raising the child? Generally the courts have been extremely reluctant to award damages for the raising of the child. There are a number of reasons

---

[162] [1996] 1 WLR 1397.
[163] *Sidaway v Board of Governors Bethlem* [1985] AC 871 and *Pearce v United Bristol Healthcare NHS Trust* [1999] PIQR 53.
[164] *Newell v Goldenberg* [1995] Med LR 6.   [165] RCOG (1999).
[166] *MacKay v Essex Area Health Authority* [1982] QB 1166.
[167] [1995] 1 WLR 1543.   [168] At 1553.

for this: it might harm the child to find out that their birth led to litigation rather than happiness;[169] there is a public policy against describing the birth of a child as a loss to parents because it is not possible or desirable to weigh up the joy the child will bring its parents with the costs of parenthood. The leading case is *Mcfarlane v Tayside Health Board*[170] which classified the claim for child-rearing costs as a claim for pure economic loss and the normal rules of tort which applied to such claims should be used. This required proof that the loss be foreseeable, that there be a relationship of sufficient proximity between doctor and claimant and that it should be fair, just, and reasonable to impose a duty of care in the circumstances. The House of Lords decided that it would not be fair, just, or reasonable to impose a duty of care in such a case. At the heart of their reasoning was a moral judgment that the birth of a child should be regarded as a blessing and joy, not a harm. As Lord Millett put it:

> if the law regards an event as beneficial, plaintiffs cannot make it a matter for compensa-
> tion merely by saying that it is an event they did not want to happen. In this branch of the
> law at least, plaintiffs are not normally allowed, by a process of subjective devaluation, to
> make a detriment out of a benefit.[171]

This reasoning has been criticized.[172] Emily Jackson argues: 'Where a patient has decided to have an operation in order to irrevocably remove the possibility of concep-tion, it seems perverse to argue that they should regard the failure of this surgery as a blessing'.[173]

A second strand of reasoning is that the level of damages that would be awarded would be out of proportion for the wrongdoing of the doctor.[174] While it is true that the amount of money required to raise a child could be substantial, the argument is not one that is normally used in tort law. A driver who through a moment of carelessness renders another a paraplegic will not be heard to say that the level of damages necessary to compensate the victim is out of proportion to the degree of negligence. But it may be that behind this point is a point of public policy. Weir points out that if such claims are allowed we 'transfer to reluctant parents for the upbringing of healthy brats the resources needed by hospitals to cure the sick'.[175] While this is true, this kind of argu-ment could be used to deny nearly any claim against the NHS brought by a patient who has suffered loss at the hands of a negligent medical staff.

Subsequently in *Greenfield v Irwin*[176] an attempt to claim that the HRA required English law to provide compensation for raising the child was rejected. It was also argued that, even if there could be no claim for the costs of raising the child, a claim could be made for the loss of earnings caused by a parent giving up work to raise the child. This argument was unsuccessful too.

In *Rees v Darlington Memorial Hospital NHS Trust*[177] a negligently performed steril-ization was performed on a woman with a severe visual impairment. A healthy child was born. *McFarlane* was unsuccessfully challenged in the House of Lords. Unanimously it was decided that it would be wrong to reverse a House of Lords decision only four years after it had been made. It was agreed by all their Lordships that sterilization cases were a special exception to the normal rules of tort law. Lord Bingham for the majority was willing to award £15,000 for the affront to the woman's autonomy caused by the

---

[169] [1997] SL 211, Lord Gill. [170] [1999] 3 WLR 1301. [171] At 1346.
[172] Priaulx (2007a: Chap 1). [173] Jackson (2001: 35–6). [174] Lord Clyde at 1340.
[175] Weir (2000b: 131). [176] [2001] 1 WLR 1279. [177] [2004] AC 309.

sterilization. This was not money to compensate for the expense of raising the child, but for her loss of opportunity to live her life in the way she wished and planned. The fact that the mother was disabled was not a reason for departing from the approach taken in *McFarlane*.

But what if the child was born disabled? The House of Lords in *McFarlane* expressly left this issue open. In *Parkinson v St James*[178] a woman gave birth to a disabled child following a negligent sterilization operation. In a notable speech by Hale LJ the emphasis was placed on the fact that to cause a woman to become pregnant against her will was an invasion of bodily integrity. This interference with personal autonomy would continue while the mother raised the disabled child. In the light of *McFarlane* the Court of Appeal were willing to award damages for the costs over and above the costs of raising a non-disabled child. It must be admitted that the arguments used in Hale LJ's judgment would point to an overruling of *McFarlane*. In *Rees* the House of Lords considered the *Parkinson* decision. Lords Steyn, Hope, and Hutton approved of the decision. Lords Bingham and Nicholls disapproved it. Lord Scott thought the decision was wrong on its facts in that he thought that damages should only be awarded if the sterilization had been requested specifically to avoid the birth of a disabled child. Lord Millett did not express a view. So the correctness of the approach in *Parkinson* is unclear.[179]

In *Groom v Selby*[180] a woman was sterilized, although the clinician failed to notice she was pregnant at the time. By the time the pregnancy was spotted it was too late (in her view) to have an abortion. The child was born healthy but three weeks after the birth developed meningitis, due to an infection picked up during the birth. The Court of Appeal followed the *Parkinson* approach and awarded damages for the raising of the disabled child.

8 Ethical issues concerning contraception

Many of the ethical issues relating to contraception are tied up with one's response to the question: when does life begin? Contraceptives which cause the destruction of a fertilized egg are rejected as immoral by those who see fertilization as the beginning of human life. We shall be discussing the question of when life begins when we look at abortion. Much of the writing specifically on contraception has been written from a feminist or religious perspective. We shall consider these next:

FEMINIST PERSPECTIVES

To many feminists contraception has been heralded as a major contribution to women's liberation. Birstow, writing 'in praise of the Pill', stated:

> Whatever the Pill's faults, 50 years on from the time it was first synthesised it remains the best form of contraception that we have; and it seems unlikely that, without it, the struggle for women's equality would have come so far, so fast.

---

[178] [2002] QB 266.   [179] See Priaulx (2004) for an interesting discussion of the issues raised.
[180] (2002) 64 BMLR 47.

Contraception has done much to give women freedom over their lives. The ability to control whether and when to have children is treasured by many women.

However, contraception is not without its feminist critics. We have already noted that there are concerns over the health risks associated with the pill, and developing better forms of contraception appears to be low on the list of priorities for medical research. A different concern is that contraception can be seen as of benefit to men in that it renders women sexually available without men having to bear the financial cost of child support. Pollock argues that current forms of contraception make women available for men's pleasure, through contraception which poses a risk to women's health (Pollock (1985: 66)).

It has been suggested that women who use contraception can be stigmatized in a way which works against women's interests. MacKinnon writes:

> Using contraception means acknowledging and planning the possibility of intercourse, accepting one's sexual availability, and appearing non-spontaneous. It means appearing available to male incursions (MacKinnon (1987: 95)).

Gilder has argued that men are yet to grasp the psychological impact of birth control:

> few males have come to psychological terms with the existing birth control technology; few recognize the extent to which it shifts the balance of sexual power further in favour of women. A man quite simply cannot now father a baby unless his wife is fully and deliberately agreeable ... Throughout the centuries, men could imagine their sexual organs as profoundly powerful instruments ... Male potency was not simply a matter of erectile reliability; it was a full weapon of procreation. Women viewed male potency with some awe, and males were affirmed by this response. This masculine attribute is now completely lost. The male penis is no longer a decisive organ in itself ... A man's penis becomes an empty plaything unless a woman deliberately decides to admit a man's paternity. (Gilder (1986: 106))

 A VIEW FROM ABOVE

Religious views on contraception

Many religions have no objection to contraception. The most vocal opposition to it comes from the Roman Catholic Church which has consistently opposed the use of artificial means of contraception. Pope Paul VI explained:

> God has wisely disposed natural laws and rhythms of fecundity which, of themselves, cause a separation in the succession of births ... [This teaching] is founded upon the inseparable connection, willed by God and unable to be broken by man on his own initiative, between the two meanings of the conjugal act: the unitive meaning and the procreative meaning. (Pope Paul VI (1968))

The Roman Catholic Church does, however, permit the use of natural birth control methods such as *coitus interruptus* and other natural methods of birth control. To some the distinction drawn between 'natural' and 'unnatural' methods of contraception is artificial (Moore (2001: 163) and Bovens (2007) suggests that even using the 'rhythm method' can be said to cause the destruction of embryos).

The argument behind the church's approach is that the purpose of sexual intercourse should not be pleasure but the production of children. Gormally explains:

if I engage in contraceptive intercourse I undermine in myself the disposition to recognise that the good of sex is essentially connected with children. I act on the assumption that it has a separate meaning which makes good and adequate sense of it. This is to act as if there is a true good of sexual activity apart from marriage. (Gormally (1997b: 1))

Some Catholic writers have argued that contraception should be regarded as a decision against the coming into being of a new life, which is a decision against a basic human good (Grisez, Boyle, Finnis, and May (1988)). But others have responded to this by saying that to many people the use of contraception is about deciding when it would be the right time to produce a new life, rather than a decision against life (Moore (2001: 167)). The Catholic view has also been objected to on the basis that it would appear to say there is nothing good about sex between an infertile couple or a same-sex couple.

Although this is the official teaching of the church there is evidence that in fact most Roman Catholics do practice artificial means of contraception (Sander (1993)). Further the teaching has been criticized by leading Catholic theologians (Barth (1998) and Burtchaell (1998)). The official teaching has been strongly criticized by those who say that it works particularly harshly in developing countries where condom use needs to be encouraged to prevent the spread of HIV and to control population growth (Curran (1982)). Nevertheless the Papacy has taken a firm line against contraception, and its prohibition remains the formal teaching of the Church.

The Islamic view of birth control is hotly debated (Deuraseh (2003)). At the strict end there is a ban on all use of contraceptives (Ebrahim (2000)), while at the more liberal end there is less opposition. However, most Muslim traditions do emphasize that procreation within marriage is a religious duty and therefore sterilization is nearly always objected to by Muslims.

Jewish approaches to contraception are also divided. The Orthodox position is that male contraception (eg the condom) is not permitted but female contraception may be permitted for health reasons (eg danger to the health of the mother or potential child). Conservative and Reform views tend to have no opposition to the use of contraception between married couples.

9 Introduction to abortion

Abortion is one of the most controversial issues of our time. This is in a way surprising given that it is, in the words of one leading commentator, 'a simple, routine and frequently performed operation'.[181] Indeed it is estimated that 35–40 per cent of all women in England will have at least one abortion during their lives.[182] But to some commentators abortion has become too readily available, with women treating 'babies like bad teeth to be jerked out just because they cause suffering'.[183] According to the most vehement opponents of abortion we are witnessing via abortion the mass murder of the most vulnerable members of our societies (unborn children). To others abortion is a fundamental human right which is an essential aspect of the move towards greater equality between men and women. To force a woman to go through with a pregnancy against her wishes would be the most profound violation of her body and autonomy.

We tend in the UK to take abortion and good maternity care for granted. It has been estimated that worldwide 70,000 women die a year from unsafe abortions.[184] Of all

---

[181] Jackson (2002: 72).
[182] Furedi (1998: 161). RCOGa (2001) estimate that at least a third of pregnancies will end in abortion.
[183] Knight HC deb vol 732 cl 1100 (22 July 1966).
[184] International Planned Parenthood Federation (2003: 7).

pregnancies worldwide it is thought that 22 per cent are ended by abortion and 15 per cent by miscarriage.[185] So under two-thirds of pregnancies worldwide lead to a birth.

The forms of abortion include the following:

- *The abortion pill.* This drug (mifepristone) is taken in early pregnancy and procures a miscarriage by blocking the hormone needed to enable a fertilized egg to implant.

- *The 'morning-after pill'.* This pill is similar to the normal contraceptive pill, but contains a much higher dose of female hormones. It needs to be taken within 72 hours of sexual intercourse. The pill can operate as a contraceptive by preventing or delaying ovulation or as an abortion by preventing the egg implanting. Note that in legal terms this is a form of contraception rather than abortion.[186]

- *Intra-uterine device.* This is a 'mechanical' device which must be fitted up to five days after sex.

- *Vacuum aspiration abortion.* A tube is inserted through the cervix up into the womb. The tube is used to suck out the contents of the womb, thereby destroying the foetus.

- *Evacuation and curettage.* Here the woman's cervical canal is enlarged and the womb then emptied by suction or scraped out with a currette.

- *Intact dilation and extraction ('partial birth abortion').* The foetus is extracted into the vagina and the contents of the skull are sucked out. This kills the foetus. The body is then removed.

REALITY CHECK

In 2006 there were 197,700 abortions for women resident in England and Wales. This means that 18.3 women in every 1,000 had an abortion in that year. The number of abortions was the highest recorded number since records began in 1968. The age group with the highest rate of abortions was those aged 19. Just over 3 per cent of women in that age bracket had an abortion in 2006. The abortion rate for under-16-year-olds was 3.9 per 1,000.

However it would be misleading to think that abortions were restricted to young single women. Seventeen per cent of women having abortions were married and 47 per cent had previously had a pregnancy which had resulted in a birth.

Eighty-seven per cent of abortions were funded by the NHS, but 55 per cent of those abortions were carried out in private establishments, under an NHS contract.

Eighty-nine per cent of all abortions were carried within 13 weeks of gestation and 68 per cent under 10 weeks. The most common ground for abortion was the Abortion Act 1967, section 1(1)(c): risk to the mother's health, with 95 per cent of all abortions being under that ground, while 1 per cent were based on the risk that the child would be born handicapped, most of which were chromosomal abnormalities or congenital malformations. Around 30 per cent of abortions involved the use or drugs (eg Mifepristone) rather than surgery. This is an increase from 19 per cent in 2004.

All of these statistics come from the National Statistics (2007a).

---

[185] Alan Guttmacher Institute (1998).
[186] *R (John Smeaton on Behalf of SPUC) v The Secretary of State for Health et al* [2002] 2 FCR 193.

10 Abortion: the law

The legal attitude to abortion is that it is a criminal offence, although the Abortion Act 1967 provides an extensive defence to any criminal charge.

10.1 Criminal offences

The starting point for the law on abortion is the criminal law.[187] Most abortions will be a criminal offence unless there is a statutory or common law defence. The criminal offences in relation to abortion are the following:

(i) Offences Against the Person Act 1861, section 58.

Every woman, being with child, who, with intent to procure her own miscarriage, shall unlawfully administer to herself any poison or other noxious thing, or shall unlawfully use any instrument or other means whatsoever with the like intent and whosoever, with intent to procure the miscarriage of any woman, whether she be or not with child, shall unlawfully administer to her or cause to be taken by her any poison or other noxious thing, or shall unlawfully use any instrument or other means whatsoever with the like intent, shall be guilty of an offence, and being convicted thereof shall be liable to imprisonment.

There are a number of points to notice about this section. The first is that the offence can be committed by the pregnant woman or by someone else. The second is that if the woman is being charged she must actually be 'with child', but if another person is charged there is no need to show the woman is 'with child'. This means that if a woman who is not in fact pregnant, but believes herself to be, consults a friend and together they attempt to use an instrument to procure a miscarriage then the friend,[188] but not the woman, could be guilty of the offence.[189] The third is that the offence is only committed where the defendant intended to procure a miscarriage. So a pregnant woman who takes illegal drugs, foreseeing that by doing so she may cause a miscarriage, but not wanting to, will not commit the offence.

(ii) Offences Against the Person Act 1861, section 59

Whosoever shall unlawfully supply or procure any poison or other noxious thing, or any instrument or thing whatsoever, knowing that the same is intended to be unlawfully used or employed with intent to procure the miscarriage of any woman, whether she be or not be with child, shall be guilty of an offence and being convicted thereof shall be liable to imprisonment for a term not exceeding five years.

This offence prohibits the supply of drugs, substances, or instruments for use in unlawful abortions. Notice that for this offence there is no need to show that the woman was actually pregnant.

---

[187] For a discussion of the law see Keown (1988) and Grubb (1990).
[188] *R v Price* [1968] 2 All ER 282.
[189] An argument could be made that in such a case the woman has committed an attempted offence.

(iii) Infant Life Preservation Act, section 1

(1)

(a) Subject as hereinafter in this subsection provided, any person who, with intent to destroy the life of a child capable of being born alive, by any wilful act causes a child to die before it has an existence independent of its mother, will be guilty of felony, to whit of child destruction, and shall be liable on conviction thereof on indictment to penal servitude for life. Provided that no person shall be found guilty of an offence under this section unless it is proved that the act which caused the death of the child was not done in good faith for the purpose only of preserving the life of the mother.

(2) For the purpose of this Act, evidence that a woman had at any material time been pregnant for a period of 28 weeks or more shall be prima facie proof that she was at the time pregnant of a child capable of being born alive...

These offences can be committed by anyone including the pregnant woman, a doctor, or anyone else, such as the boyfriend of the mother. This offence can only be committed where the foetus is 'capable of being born alive'. It will be noted that under subsection (2) a foetus of 28 weeks or older is presumed to be capable of being born alive. This is only a presumption and could be rebutted if it could be shown that, for example, an older foetus was not actually capable of being born alive or that a younger one was. According to Jonathan Montgomery it is generally assumed in medical circles that foetuses of 24 weeks are capable of being born alive.[190] The phrase 'capable of being born alive' was defined in *Rance v Mid-Downs HA* as 'breathing and living by its breathing through its own lungs alone, without deriving any of its living or power of living by or through the connection to its mother'.[191]

10.2 Common law defences

In *R v Bourne*[192] it was accepted that there was a defence of necessity for a doctor facing a criminal charge of procuring a miscarriage. The case involved a well-known surgeon who performed an abortion without charge on a girl who was 14 and had been violently raped. The doctor gave evidence that he only performed the operation after being persuaded that the girl was pregnant as a result of the rape and that she would become a 'mental wreck' if she were required to go through with the procedure. Justice Macnaughten at the Central Criminal Court concluded that if the jury was persuaded that the doctor performed the operation in good faith in order to save the girl's life then it was entitled to acquit him. He went on to say that if the probable consequence of the pregnancy was to make a woman a physical or mental wreck then the performance of the abortion can be said to be done in order to preserve her life. As a result of his direction the jury acquitted the doctor. The decision left the law in a somewhat uncertain state in that it was unclear how the phrase 'in order to save a woman's life' was to be interpreted. Disputes over the extent of the common law defence are of little importance now because it will not be wider than those provided in the Abortion Act 1967. In other words whenever the common law defence of necessity provides a defence so does the Abortion Act 1967.

---

190 Montgomery (2003: 391).   191 [1991] 1 All ER 1230.   192 [1939] 1 KB 687.

10.3 **The Abortion Act 1967**

The Abortion Act 1967 sets out the circumstances in which an abortion is legal. There are special rules in cases where an abortion is urgent,[193] but normally there are four requirements:

(i) Abortions may only be carried out under the authority of a registered medical practitioner. In fact all that the Act requires is that the doctor, having decided that the grounds for the termination are made out and deciding on the method of abortion, is on call and is responsible for the woman's treatment throughout the procedure. Other health professionals, such as nurses, can carry out the actual abortion.[194]

(ii) Abortions can only be carried out in an NHS hospital or another approved place (eg a private clinic).[195]

(iii) Two medical practitioners must agree that one of the statutory grounds permitting abortion is made out.[196] We will examine these in detail shortly.

(iv) All abortions must be notified to the relevant authorities. Certificates have been produced on which the doctors must set out their opinions as to the grounds which justify the abortion. There are further forms relating to the abortion requiring details about the method of abortion used.[197]

The statutory grounds are the most contentious requirements, but before looking at them it is worth noting the following general points:

• The Abortion Act does not on its face provide a 'right to abortion' in any sense. A woman can only have an abortion if two doctors are satisfied that the grounds for an abortion are made out. The Act does not recognize that because a woman has chosen to have an abortion her choice must be respected.

• The Act focuses on the opinion of the doctors. It is not in fact necessary to show that one of the statutory grounds was actually made out, it is sufficient that the doctors were of the opinion it was. In other words, if the doctors in good faith mistakenly believed that one of the grounds existed when it did not, the abortion will still be lawful. This emphasizes that abortion is seen as a medical decision.[198] If the doctors are persuaded an abortion is appropriate it is not for non-medical people to seek to challenge that decision. Indeed George Baker P stated:

[N]ot only would it be bold and brave judge . . . who would seek to interfere with the discretion of doctors under the [Abortion Act 1967], but I think it would really be a foolish judge who would try to do any such thing, unless possibly there is clear bad faith and an obvious attempt to perpetrate a criminal offence.[199]

• It is extremely difficult to show that an abortion was illegal because it is necessary to show that the doctor did not believe that one of the statutory grounds was made out. One of the very few cases where a conviction has been upheld was *R v Smith*[200] where

---

[193] Abortion Act 1967, s 1(4).   [194] *RCN v DHSS* [1981] 1 All ER 545.

[195] Abortion Act 1967, s 1(3).

[196] House of Commons Science and Technology Committee (2007) suggested that the law should be changed so that only one signature should be required.

[197] Abortion Regulations 1991, SI 1991/499.   [198] Grubb (1990).

[199] *Paton v BPAS* [1978] 2 All ER 992, *C v S* [1987] 1 All ER 1230.

a doctor carried out a private abortion. The evidence suggested that he had made no internal examination of the patient and had not inquired into her personal history or situation. The only entry in the doctor's notes was that she was depressed. It was not clear if the doctor who had given the second opinion had even examined the patient. The jury convicted on the basis that the doctors had not in good faith formed the opinion that the termination was justified under one of the statutory grounds.

The statutory grounds for an abortion are found in section 1 of the Abortion Act, as amended by the Human Fertilisation and Embryology Act 1990[201] which states:

(1) Subject to the provisions of this section, a person shall not be guilty of an offence under the law relating to abortion when a pregnancy is terminated by a registered medical practitioner if two registered medical practitioners are of the opinion formed in good faith—

(a) that the pregnancy has not exceeded its twenty-fourth week and that the continuance of the pregnancy would involve risk, greater than if the pregnancy were terminated, of injury to the physical or mental health of the pregnant woman or any existing children of her family; or

(b) that the termination of is necessary to prevent grave permanent injury to the physical or mental health of the pregnant woman; or

(c) that the continuance of the pregnancy would involve risk to the life of the pregnant woman, greater than if the pregnancy were terminated; or

(d) that there is a substantial risk that if the child were born it would suffer from physical or mental abnormalities as to be seriously handicapped.

(2) In determining whether the continuance of a pregnancy would involve such risk of injury to health as is mentioned in paragraph (a) or (b) of subsection (1) of this section, account may be taken of the pregnant woman's actual or reasonably foreseeable environment...

We shall look at the four individual grounds in more detail:

(a) *Section 1(1)(a): 'that the pregnancy has not exceeded its twenty-fourth week and that the continuance of the pregnancy would involve risk, greater than if the pregnancy were terminated, of injury to the physical or mental health of the pregnant woman or any existing children of her family'.*

Two things are required here. First, that the two registered medical practitioners are of the opinion that there is risk to the physical or mental health of the pregnant woman or her existing children, and secondly, that the risk of harm is greater than that which would occur if the pregnancy were terminated.

What is 'mental health' in this context? This is unclear. It clearly includes recognized mental conditions, such as depression. But would it include emotional upset? Also unclear is the meaning of risk. Does the possibility of a mental condition have to be likely or just a possibility? Until we have some decisions of the court we do not know the answers to these questions.

---

[200] [1974] 1 All ER 376.
[201] The Termination of Pregnancy (Counselling and Miscellaneous Provisions) Bill 2007 would have restricted access to abortion and required counselling before an abortion but it was defeated by 182 votes to 107.

Section 1(2) states that in considering the risk to physical or mental health the woman's 'actual and foreseeable environment' in relation to the risk can be taken into account.[202] If the woman is a teenager with limited family or social support this would be an important factor to consider. It has even been suggested that it would permit an abortion to be carried out on the basis of the sex of the foetus if serious social or cultural harm would be caused to a woman by the birth of a child of a particular sex and that this could be said to have an adverse impact on her mental health.[203] Such a suggestion is, however, controversial.

The reference to the health of the pregnant woman's existing children is interesting. What is envisaged is a case where the woman's care for her newborn will mean that her existing children's physical or mental health will be affected. This might most readily be demonstrated where the mother has a severely disabled child who requires continuous care which might be severely affected by any new child. There is debate over what is meant by children of the pregnant woman's family. The use of this phrase, rather than 'any children of the pregnant woman', suggests that the mother's step-children could be included; indeed perhaps any children living with her.

Section 1(1)(a) can only be relied upon if the pregnancy has not exceeded its twenty-fourth week.[204] In practice it can be difficult to find doctors willing to perform an operation on this ground where the pregnancy exceeds 16 weeks.[205] But when does this time period run from? Kennedy and Grubb suggest four different times when the 'clock could start running':

(i) The first day of the woman's last period.

(ii) The date of conception (up to 14 days later than (i)).

(iii) The date of implantation (up to 10 days later than (i)).

(iv) The date of the woman's first missed period (about four weeks after (i)).

None of these is entirely satisfactory. Approaches (ii), (iii), and (iv) all suffer from uncertainty because we cannot be sure precisely when they occur. If a court was required to face this issue a number of approaches could be taken. One would be to consider what method most medical practitioners use for assessing the length of the pregnancy. This would lead to support for approach (i).[206] An alternative way of finding an answer is to ask why Parliament chose this 24-week time limit. The answer appears to be that Parliament believed that 24 weeks from conception was the time at which a child would be capable of surviving if born.[207] This leads Murphy to support (ii);[208] although arguably Murphy's view appears to be better designed to date the foetus, than date of the pregnancy. A further difficulty with this argument is that it is nowadays thought that 22 weeks or less is the date at which a foetus can be viable. Kennedy and Grubb argue in favour of (iii).[209] They suggest that (i) leads to the 'absurd conclusion' that a woman is pregnant from the moment she missed her last period which cannot be true. Secondly, as the statute deals with criminal liability it would be wrong to interpret any ambiguity in a way which works against a potential defendant.

---

[202] S 1(2).   [203] Morgan (1998).
[204] The House of Commons Science and Technology Committee (2007) decided that there was no recent medical evidence to justify reducing this time period.
[205] Furedi (2000).   [206] Montgomery (2003: 386) supports this approach.
[207] House of Commons Science and Technology Committee (2007).   [208] Murphy (1991).
[209] Kennedy and Grubb (2000: 1423). See also Grubb (1991).

(b) *'that the termination is necessary to prevent grave permanent injury to the physical or mental health of the pregnant woman'*.

It should be noted that this ground is significantly harder to prove than (a). Although both involve mental and physical harms (b) is harder to satisfy in three ways:

(i) The harm must be grave.

(ii) The harm must be permanent.

(iii) The harm must be an injury.

The fact this ground is significantly harder to prove reflects the fact that under it an abortion can be carried out 24 weeks or more after the pregnancy commences. Remember that the Act does not require a doctor to show that the abortion was actually necessary to prevent the injury, but that the doctors in good faith believed that it was. Subsection (b) is different from (a) in that it does not specifically require the doctor to decide that the risks of continuing the pregnancy are greater than the risks of an abortion. However, the word 'necessary' is important here. If the risks of an abortion are greater than the risks of the pregnancy continuing it can hardly be said that the abortion is necessary to prevent a grave and permanent injury.

(c) *'that the continuance of the pregnancy would involve risk to the life of the pregnant woman, greater than if the pregnancy were terminated'*.

This ground justifies an abortion where the medical practitioners believe that the pregnancy involves a risk to life of the woman. It therefore is not necessary to show that continuing the pregnancy will lead to the death of the woman, only that it might and that an abortion will reduce any risks to the woman's life.

(d) *'that there is a substantial risk that if the child were born it would suffer from physical or mental abnormalities as to be seriously handicapped'*.

Notably this ground has no time limit and therefore it is permissible for a very late abortion to be performed on this basis.[210] This ground could be explained on two bases. First, on the well-being of the child: it could be argued that if the child will suffer appalling handicaps it would be better for the child not to be born.[211] However, it may be noted that serious handicaps may fall well short of those we might consider appalling. Secondly, that raising a severely disabled child will impose such heavy burdens on parents that they should not be compelled to take them on.

It should be emphasized that the risk must be substantial and the handicap must be serious. This limits the width of the ground. The meaning of 'substantial' is disputed. Gillian Douglas has suggested that in considering whether the risk is substantial consideration can be given to the severity of the disability being faced.[212] Others claim that it would be strange if the meaning of 'substantial' altered depending on the nature of the disability. The Guidance issued by the Royal College of Obstetricians and Gynaecologists[213] suggests that substantial only means that it is more likely than not that the child will suffer from a serious handicap. It is also unclear whether the woman's view on whether the disability would be serious are relevant.[214] One study found a wide variation among those practising in the field over the relevance of the mother's view and how severe the disability needed to be to fall within subsection (d).[215]

---

[210] DoH (2007b) discloses that 2,036 abortions were carried out under this ground in 2006.

[211] *Mackay v Essex AHA* [1982] QB 1166.   [212] Douglas (1991: 94).

[213] Royal College of Obstetricians and Gynaecologists (1996: para 3.2.1).   [214] Scott (2005).

[215] Statham, Solomou, and Green (2006).

The Guidance also gives some suggestions on what might be regarded as a serious handicap. They include the following:

(3) Assisted performance. Includes the need for a helping hand (ie the individual can perform the activity or sustain the behaviour, whether augmented by aids or not, only with some assistance from another person).

(4) Dependent performance. Includes complete dependence on the presence of another person (ie the individual can perform the activity or sustain the behaviour, but only when someone is with him most of the time.)[216]

Kennedy and Grubb suggest that this definition of serious handicap is 'broad'.[217] The ground has been relied upon to justify the abortion of a foetus that would have been born with a cleft palate.[218] The BMA suggest that in deciding whether this ground is made out the doctor should consider: 'the probability of effective treatment, either in utero or after birth; the child's probable potential for self awareness and potential ability to communicate with others, the suffering that would be experienced by the child when born or by the people caring for the child'.[219] Morgan, arguing for a narrow interpretation of this ground, suggests that consideration could properly be given to the case law on severely disabled newborns and the circumstances in which it is legitimate not to offer them treatment.[220] There has also been some debate whether a more serious handicap is required if the pregnancy is very well developed, while a less serious handicap would suffice earlier on.[221]

10.4 Emergency abortions

Under the Abortion Act, section 1(4):

Subsection (3) of this section, and so much of subsection (1) as relates to the opinion of two registered medical practitioners, shall not apply to the termination of a pregnancy by a registered medical practitioner in a case where he is of the opinion, formed in good faith, that the termination is immediately necessary to save the life or to prevent grave permanent injury to the physical or mental health of the pregnant woman.

This covers situations where there is a medical emergency and the abortion must be carried out immediately to prevent injury to the physical or mental health of the woman. In such a case the termination can be carried out by one doctor and the abortion need not take place in an approved place.

---

[216] Royal College of Obstetricians and Gynaecologists (1996).
[217] Kennedy and Grubb (2000: 1424).
[218] A cleft palate is described by the Cleft Lip and Palate Association (2005) in these terms: 'A cleft palate occurs when the roof of the mouth has not joined completely. The back of the palate (towards the throat) is called the soft palate and the front (towards the mouth) is known as the hard palate. If you feel the inside of your mouth with your tongue, you will be able to notice the difference between the soft and the hard palate. A cleft palate can range from just an opening at the back of the soft palate to a nearly complete separation of the roof of the mouth (soft and hard palate)'. The condition can cause problems with breast feeding, hearing and speech. Surgery is often performed to amend the appearance of a person suffering from a cleft lip and/or palate.
[219] BMA (2004: 242).
[220] Although it might even be argued that an even stricter approach is called for in those cases because abortion involves an act killing the foetus, rather than the withdrawal of treatment (Stauch and Wheat (2004): 451).
[221] RCOG (1998).

10.5 Where abortions can take place

Section 1(3) of the 1967 Act states:

> Except as provided by subsection (4) of this section, any treatment for the termination of pregnancy must be carried out in hospital vested in a Primary Care Trust or the Secretary of State for the purposes of his functions under the National Health Services Act 1977 or the National Health Services (Scotland) Act 1978 or in a hospital vested in National Health Service trust or in a place approved for the purposes of this section by the Secretary of State.

This means that an abortion, even if based on one of the permitted grounds, will be illegal if the abortion does not take place in one of the permitted places. A private clinic requires the approval of the Secretary of State to carry out abortions. There is a licensing procedure.[222] Specific approval is required if abortions are required for pregnancy after the 20th week. Abortions after the 24th week can only be carried out in an NHS institution.

These provisions are straightforward, although complexities arise concerning the 'morning-after' drug RU-486, known as Mifepristone. This drugs blocks progesterone (the female hormone) and that causes the surface of the endometrium to be shed and prevent implantation. However, the drug can also be taken to dislodge a fertilized egg which has implanted. Following *Smeaton*[223] it can, therefore, operate as a form of abortion. The drug has been licensed although its conditions require that it can only be administered at a hospital. The problem is that the pill is normally given to the woman at a hospital who will take it and leave about two hours later. The drug will take effect up to 48 hours later. The question is whether her 'treatment' is taking place in a licensed place. It could be said in this context that the treatment is simply the taking of the pill, in which case the Abortion Act is being complied with. However, it could also be argued that the treatment lasts for the whole of the period of time during which the pill is having an effect on her. If so there is a danger that the drug would fall foul of the Abortion Act if the woman leaves the hospital within 48 hours of taking the pill. Kennedy and Grubb take this interpretation and suggest as the only solution, apart from statutory amendment, would be for the Secretary of State for Health to declare everywhere a licensed place for treatment![224] Of course such a proposal would undermine the purpose of the regulation which is to ensure that abortions are carried out in a safe environment.

10.6 'Abortions' which fail or where the patient is in fact not pregnant

It might be thought the Abortion Act 1967 must provide protection from criminal liability where the requirements of the Act are complied with, but the attempted abortion fails, or it turns out that the patient is in fact not pregnant.[225] However this is far from straightforward. The difficulty is that the Abortion Act 1967 provides protection in cases 'where the pregnancy is terminated'. Discussing these words, *obiter*, in the *Royal College of Nursing* case Lord Wilberforce took the view that it was fanciful

---

222 DoH (1994).
223 *R (John Smeaton on Behalf of SPUC) v The Secretary of State for Health et al* [2002] 2 FCR 193.
224 A woman could be required to remain in hospital while the pill is having its effect, but this would negate many of its benefits.
225 In such cases those involved could face a charge of attempting to procure a miscarriage.

to think Parliament intended the 1967 Abortion Act to cover unsuccessful abortion or attempted abortions where there is no pregnancy. However, Lord Diplock thought that it could not have been the intention of Parliament to render criminal those who are involved in an abortion, where the abortion is unsuccessful. Lord Edmund-Davis thought that such cases would not be criminal, but not on the basis that they would be covered by the Abortion Act 1967, but that they would not be guilty of an offence under the Offences Against the Person Act. Whether a court follows Lord Diplock or Lord Edmund-Davis's reasoning it is hard to imagine a court convicting someone involved in an attempted abortion which would have been lawful if it had resulted in a successful pregnancy termination.

10.7 Selective reduction

There is much debate over the legality of selective reduction. This procedure takes place in cases where a woman is pregnant with multiple embryos, and one or more of those embryos are destroyed in order to allow the others to develop healthily or in order to preserve the health of the woman. It is particularly common where a number of embryos have been implanted in a woman as part of infertility treatment. As we shall see in Chapter 6, the maximum number of embryos which can be implanted in infertility treatment is three. A crucial point to notice is that when selective reduction is performed the destroyed foetus becomes absorbed into the mother's body and is not expelled.

There are two issues here. The first is whether the procedure constitutes a miscarriage and is therefore potentially an offence contrary to the Offences Against the Person Act 1861, section 58. It is arguable that the natural meaning of miscarriage is that the foetus is expelled from the mother and therefore a selective reduction would not be a miscarriage. John Keown has argued that it is.[226] He argues that the meaning of miscarriage relates not to the destination of the foetal remains, but rather to the failure of gestation.

Even if the procedure falls within the Act there is an argument that it is covered by the 1967 Act. Section 5(2) of the 1967 Act, as amended by the 1990 Act, states

> For the purposes of the law relating to abortion, anything done with intent to procure a woman's miscarriage (or, in the case of a woman carrying more than one foetus, her miscarriage of any foetus) is unlawfully done unless authorized by section 2 of this Act and, in the case of a woman carrying more than one foetus, anything done with intent to procure her miscarriage of any foetus is authorized by that section if
>
> (a) the ground for termination of the pregnancy specified in subsection (1)(d) of that section applies in relation to any foetus and the thing is done for the purpose of procuring the miscarriage of that foetus, or
>
> (b) any of the other grounds for termination of the pregnancy specified in that section applies.

This means that foetal reduction is permissible if it falls under the foetal abnormality ground or where there is a risk to the mother without the reduction. Kennedy and Grubb take the view that section 5(2) does not permit an abortion on the ground that it being a multiple pregnancy increases the risk to the foetuses the mother carries, but

---

226 Keown (1987). See also Price (1988).

arguably a risk that the foetuses will be lost is nearly always a risk of causing harm to the mother.

10.8 Abortions where the child is born alive

If the abortion procedure fails and a child is born alive then the doctors must act reasonably towards her or him. Remember to be 'born alive' means that the child must be outside the mother and capable of independent existence. Indeed to kill the child once born alive could be murder.[227] Failing to provide the born child with a reasonable level of medical care might lead to a murder or manslaughter conviction.

10.9 Reporting of abortions

The Abortion Regulations 1991, SI 1991/499 provide the forms that need to be completed by the practitioners involved with an abortion. One interesting point revealed by these forms is that their format permits the two medical practitioners to state different grounds for the abortion. In other words it indicates the abortion is lawful if the two practitioners agree that one of the statutory grounds is made out, even if they cannot agree which one. The Abortion (Amendment) (England) Regulations 2002 introduced a change to the form which means that rather than the patient's name being put on the form her patient identity number and postcode are used. The forms are used to collate statistics on abortion, although it is not quite clear why this should be needed. There are no other operations where the Government centrally collects information of this kind. Even with this regulation it might be felt that patients' confidentiality is inadequately protected.

10.10 The involvement of non-doctors in abortions

In *Royal College of Nursing of the UK v NHSS*[228] the issue was the meaning of 'when a pregnancy is terminated by a registered medical practitioner'. The majority of their Lordships took the view that the Act was designed to ensure that the abortion is carried out with all proper skill and in hygienic conditions. However the statute did not require the doctor to do everything with her or his hands. Lord Diplock explained: 'the requirements of the subsection are satisfied when the treatment for termination of a pregnancy is one prescribed by a registered medical practitioner carried out in accordance with his direction and of which a registered medical practitioner remains in charge throughout.'

There is a problem here with the drug RU-486 mentioned earlier. If the woman takes the drug, is the termination 'by a medical practitioner'? The problem is particularly in cases where the miscarriage produced by the drug occurs at home.[229] However, relying on the *Royal College of Nursing* case it could be argued that if the woman is taking the

---

[227] As Stauch and Wheat (2004: 473) emphasize the Abortion Act provides no defence to a charge of murder or manslaughter.
[228] [1981] AC 800.
[229] There is some evidence that women would like to have the option of a 'home abortion' (see Hamoda et al (2005)). The House of Commons Science and Technology Committee (2007) argued that this should be permitted.

medication under the guidance of the doctor, this should be regarded as analogous to other situations such as nurses carrying out her or his instructions.

10.11 Conscientious objection

Of course abortion is a highly controversial issue. Inevitably there will be medical practitioners who have moral objections to the procedure.[230] The Abortion Act, section 4 makes it clear that if someone has a conscientious objection to abortion they are not under a legal duty to participate in any treatment authorized by the Act. This is subject to some limitations. First, it should be noticed that section 4 does not affect the duty of a doctor to perform an abortion if that is necessary to save the life or prevent permanent injury to the physical or mental health of a pregnant woman. So if a patient's life is in danger or she is at risk of serious injury the doctor's conscience does not provide a defence to any legal action which may result from her or him not acting. Of course, in many cases, a doctor with a conscientious objection in such a case will be able to find a colleague to carry out any necessary surgery. Secondly, the Act does not remove the duty on a doctor to advise. Therefore if a patient visits a GP wanting to discuss an abortion, but the GP has contentious objections to abortions, she or he should still refer the patient to another practitioner.[231] Thirdly, section 4 does not affect the duties owed to those who have had an abortion. For example, if due to a negligently performed abortion a woman required a blood transfusion, a doctor could not refuse to participate in the blood transfusion because of his objections to abortion.

The leading case on section 4 is the following:

KEY CASE   Janaway v Salford AHA [1989] AC 537 (HL)

The applicant was employed as a secretary at a Health Centre. She was a Roman Catholic and refused to type a letter referring a patient to a consultant for a possible abortion. She was disciplined for failing to carry out her instructions and in due course her employment was terminated. She applied for judicial review and sought to quash the decision to dismiss her and a declaration that she was entitled to refuse to participate in typing work if it was connected to an abortion. She argued that but for the Abortion Act she could have been, in typing the letter, liable as an accessory to the offence of procuring a miscarriage. The Act would have provided her with a defence to such a charge and therefore she was acting in a way authorized by the Act. But if so she was entitled to rely on section 4. Their Lordships dismissed the application, holding that the use of the words 'in any treatment under the Act' indicated that section 4 only applies to 'actually taking part in the treatment'. Had Parliament intended the section to apply to people such as the applicant, Lord Keith suggested, the word treatment would not have been used and instead section 4 would have referred to 'anything authorized by the Act'.

The working of the conscience clause was considered by the Social Services Committee of the House of Lords.[232] It found conflicting evidence over its operation. There was

---

[230] The BMA (2004) says that it is neutral on the ethical debate surrounding abortion.
[231] *Barr v Matthews* (1999) 52 BMLR 217, although it is unclear whether this is a legal duty.
[232] Social Services Committee (1990).

evidence that in some areas of the country so many staff refused to participate in abortions that that abortions could not effectively be provided under the NHS. In other places staff were unable to use the clause because of the pressure of other colleagues and managers.

10.12 Actions to prevent abortion

If a person wishes to oppose an abortion are they able to seek an injunction to prevent it being performed? It appears not. The leading decisions are as follows:

(i) In *Paton v Trustees of the British Pregnancy Advisory Service*[233] a husband sought an injunction to prevent his wife from having an abortion without his consent. Sir George Baker held that the father had no right to such an injunction. Indeed he noted that the 1967 Act did not even require a father to be consulted or notified before an abortion took place. He did not, however, rule out the possibility that a court might order an abortion not to take place where a doctor was clearly acting in bad faith. Mr Paton also sought to argue that even if he did not have standing to prevent the abortion as the father he could intervene to prevent it on behalf of the foetus. This argument failed because the foetus was said not to have any legal standing in the eyes of the law.

(ii) In *C v S*[234] a man sought to prevent his partner having an abortion. The approach in *Paton* was followed, with Sir John Donaldson MR stating that even where it was claimed that the abortion would be illegal (ie the doctor was acting in bad faith) the matter should be left to the Director of Public Prosecutions or the Attorney-General.[235] The court also rejected the man's attempt to claim to represent the foetus on the ground that the foetus could not be a party to the proceedings. He failed in the English Courts and took the case to the European Courts. The European Commission of Human Rights held that not only did he have no right to prevent the abortion, a father did not even have a right to be notified that an abortion was going to take place. Even if the failure to notify him amounted to an interference with his rights to respect for his family life under article 8(1) such interference could be justified under article 8(2) as necessary to protect the rights of the mother.

(iii) In *Jepson v The Chief Constable of West Mercia Police Constabulary*[236] a curate-learned of a case where an abortion had been carried out on the disability ground. The alleged 'serious disability' was that the foetus suffered from a cleft lip. She notified the Crown Prosecution Service, who, after an investigation, decided not to prosecute. She sought a judicial review of the decision. She was given leave to bring the application. The CPS in the face of her application decided to re-investigate the case but decided, after a thorough review, that there was no evidence that the doctors concerned had not formed in good faith the view that the child would be seriously handicapped.[237]

These cases demonstrate that if someone wishes to object to an abortion being performed it is highly unlikely that they will be found to have standing to bring the matter

---

[233] [1979] QB 276.   [234] [1988] QB 135.

[235] In a Canadian decision *(League for Life in Manitoba Ltd) v Morgentaler* [1985] 4 WWR 633 it was held that a pro-life pressure group did not have standing to bring an application to prevent a doctor performing abortions.

[236] [2003] EWHC 3318.   [237] Scott (2005) discusses in detail the issues raised by this case.

before the court, be they claiming in their own right (eg as a 'father' of the foetus), or claiming on behalf of the foetus. Any challenge to the legality of an abortion should be brought by the Attorney-General or the Crown Prosecution Service. If an individual wishes to challenge a decision not to prosecute then judicial review of that decision is a possibility.

10.13 Abortion and incompetent adults

What is the position where the pregnant woman is incompetent and not able to decide whether or not she wants an abortion? The issue is resolved by applying the normal legal principles in relation to incompetent people. The doctor can perform the abortion if that is in the best interests of the patient. It is not required to obtain a court order before carrying out the operation,[238] although if there is a division among medical opinion[239] or perhaps if the incompetent person or her family is strongly opposed to an abortion it might be appropriate to seek a court order.[240] In *Re SS (Adult: Medical Treatment)*[241] a schizophrenic woman (S) who was 24 weeks pregnant was being detained under the Mental Health Act 1983. She had had four children previously. There was conflicting evidence over whether it was in S's best interests to have an abortion or continue the pregnancy. S was strongly in favour of a termination. S would not be able to look after any child born and so it would be likely that the child would be removed. Justice Wall in deciding against an abortion placed weight on the fact that S was nearly 24 weeks pregnant[242] which meant that abortion procedure would be painful and traumatic, especially if done without the patient's understanding. He took the view that this would be more traumatic than giving birth and having the baby removed.

One controversial issue is whether a pregnant woman in a coma can be kept on a life support machine solely for the purposes of allowing her foetus to be kept alive and in due course born.[243] To some, once the mother had died, she has no interests[244] or she has some interests and these are outweighed by the interests of the unborn child. To others to permit the mother to be kept alive in this way is an affront to her dignity; to use her as little more than a 'fetal container'.[245] Yet another view is that the key issue should be what the woman's wishes were while alive. If this approach is taken some argue that, especially if the pregnancy is well advanced, it can be presumed that the mother wanted to take the pregnancy to term if she had not made her views known in advance.[246]

10.14 Abortion and minors

Where the pregnant woman is under 16 the normal rules in relation to medical treatment of children apply. This means that if the child is assessed to be *Gillick* competent

---

[238] *Re SG* [1993] 4 Med LR 75.

[239] *Re SS (Adult: Medical Treatment)* [2002] 1 FCR 73.

[240] Stauch and Wheat (2004: 232).   [241] [2002] 1 FCR 73.

[242] At para 62 Wall J was critical of the fact that the pregnancy had been allowed to develop so far before seeking court involvement.

[243] For a recent example of this in the United States see BBC Newsonline (2 September 2004). A thorough discussion of the issue can be found in Sperling (2006) and Peart et al (2000).

[244] De Gama (1998) strongly rejects such a claim.   [245] Purdy (1990).

[246] Sperling (2006) argues we should require very strong evidence that this was what the woman wanted before relying on this argument.

and consents it is permissible for a doctor to perform the operation on her if she or he assesses that to be in the interests of the child. There is no need for the doctor to obtain parental consent. This was confirmed in *R (Axon) v Secretary of State*[247] where a mother claimed that she had a right under the Human Rights Act to be informed or consulted if her daughter sought an abortion. Indeed Silber J held that a young person seeking advice from a doctor on reproductive issues has a strong right of confidentiality. Further there was an important public interest in ensuring young people had access to confidential abortion and contraceptive advice. The Department of Health[248] has issued guidelines which recommend that doctors encourage children to discuss the issue with their parents, relative, or other responsible adult.[249] However, the guidance makes it clear that this is not a requirement.

Technically, if the child is judged *Gillick* competent and does not want an abortion, it is permissible for a doctor to still carry out the abortion if that is consented to by someone who has parental responsibility for her, and the doctor assesses the abortion to be in the girl's best interests. It is hoped that no doctor would want to perform an abortion in such a case. What if the girl is incompetent? The issue then is simply whether the doctor believes the abortion is in the best interests of the patient. If she or he does and someone with parental responsibility for the child consents then there is no need for the doctor to obtain the approval of the court before doing so.

10.15 Discussion of abortion law in UK

There are a number of themes which run through the legal treatment of abortion. One is the medicalized model of abortion: the judgment of doctors is key to the legality of abortion procedures. As Sheldon puts it:

> if the law aims to protect and entrench any rights it is not those of the woman (nor indeed those of the foetus) but rather those of the doctor.[250]

Indeed the wording of the Act does not even require the woman to consent to the abortion. By contrast in other countries abortion is seen as a private matter for the woman alone.[251] The historical explanation of the English abortion law can be found in the debates surrounding the Abortion Act 1967. As Sheldon's analysis of these demonstrates, much weight was placed by campaigners in favour of the Act on the image of a woman at the end of her tether desperate for an abortion without which she and her family may be plunged into despair.[252] This image meant that the woman was regarded as barely competent and therefore the doctor had to be the one to decide that the abortion was appropriate and help make the decision for the confused woman. In fact Sheldon[253] goes so far as to claim that far from being a liberalizing measure the 1967 Act was about putting in place a more rigorous and subtle system of medical control over women's fertility. She argues that the Act means that the abortion decision is made by the doctor. She argues that the decision should be made by the woman: 'any system of abortion must decide on one person who should be empowered to make such a decision.

---

[247] [2006] EWHC 37 (Admin), discussed in Bridgeman (2006) and Taylor (2007).
[248] DoH (2004b).
[249] Herring (1997b) provides arguments in favour of such an approach.   [250] Sheldon (1997: 42).
[251] Lee (2003). In *Mackay v Essex AHA* [1982] QB 1168 CA at 1180 Griffiths LJ said the medical profession was under a duty to advise a woman of 'her right to have an abortion and the pros and cons of doing so'.
[252] Sheldon (1997: 38–41).   [253] Sheldon (1997: 30).

It seems to me that this can only be the pregnant woman'.[254] Marie Fox[255] has made the interesting point that regarding abortion as a medical issue has had one benefit for pregnant women in that it has produced an obstacle for men seeking to challenge the legality of an abortion. The matter is one for medical experts, rather than lay people and so any outsider seeking to challenge abortion is unlikely to succeed.

Despite these points there is general agreement that in practice a woman who is seeking an abortion, at least in the first three months of pregnancy, will face few obstacles to obtaining one.[256] Many doctors appear to operate on the principle that if a woman wants an abortion she should have one. To some, then, the criticisms of Sheldon and others fail to appreciate that the Act is in a sense a benign fiction. Whatever the Act says, in truth a woman who wants an abortion, at least in the first three months, will get one. But such points may overlook the symbolic power of the wording of the Act. Abortion is not widely seen as an entitlement, and, if anything, carries stigma. Interestingly in a major research project looking at why pregnant teenagers reach a decision over abortion the researchers found that most made the decision on the basis of what was best for the unborn child. In other words the abortion decision was seen by these young women not as a matter of their rights, but rather in terms of what was best for the unborn child.[257] The message still sent is that pregnant women are not able to make decisions about their own bodies and this reinforces medical power.[258] As Sheldon points out the meeting between the pregnant woman and her doctor is one that is pervaded with the doctor's power:

> first at the level of a technical control of the means of avoiding reproduction, secondly at the level of decisional control—policing who should (and who should not) be allowed the possibility of an abortion, thirdly at the level of paternalistic control (where the benevolent doctor will enforce her views through "persuasion"), and lastly at the level of a normalising control exercised in the medical interview over women seeking abortion.[259]

A different interpretation of the Abortion Act is that its regulation is surprisingly loose. The decisions are made in private; there are no prior notification requirements; and there are very limited grounds upon which a legal challenge can be made to the decision of the patient. It can be argued that the Act was specifically designed to enable the routine use of abortion in an attempt to reduce the number of 'unwanted children'.

11 Abortion: the reality

In 2006, 87 per cent of abortions were funded by the NHS, although over half of these were contracted out to an agency.[260] Thirteen per cent of abortions were performed in the private sector. However, the rate of use of NHS facilities varies around the country. In Kensington and Chelsea 45 per cent of abortions were private in 2006, while in Doncaster the figure was 3 per cent. It has been claimed that better-off women are

---

[254] Sheldon (1997: 4).   [255] Fox (1998).
[256] Lee (2002) argues that after 16 weeks few doctors are willing to agree to an abortion and in many areas only a few will terminate pregnancies after the 12th week.
[257] Lee, Clements, Ingham, and Stone (2004: 16).   [258] Lee (2002).
[259] Sheldon (1997: 73). Contrast Wyatt (2000) who sees in abortion cases doctors working with pregnant woman on an expert–expert level to reach an appropriate decision for the woman.
[260] DoH (2007b).

encouraged to use private facilities.[261] However, abortions cost the NHS about £300 each on average, so there are hardly huge sums of money to save here.[262] Much of the study on the availability and experience of abortion has been undertaken in respect of teenagers. This is because of the concerns that surround teenage parenthood that we mentioned earlier in this chapter. Around half of pregnant teenagers decide to have an abortion.[263] However, the proportion of teenagers having abortions varies in different parts of the country. The lowest number of abortions are performed in the most socially disadvantaged areas, even though those areas have the highest pregnancy rate. For example, in Derwentside (County Durham) the proportion of pregnancies ending in abortion was below 18 per cent, compared with 76 per cent in Eden (Cumbria).[264]

By far the most common ground for an abortion is section 1(1)(a): the risk to physical or mental health. In 2006 97 per cent of the abortions were performed on that ground.[265] This has led some to claim that in effect there is abortion 'on demand'.[266] Some doctors have even argued that because carrying a pregnancy to term always carries health risks it is arguable that there is always less risk to a woman's health in a termination than with continuation of the pregnancy. Whether such an argument would be accepted by a court is a matter of debate.[267] But if it were it would suggest that the grounds for a lawful abortion exist in the first 24 weeks of every pregnancy.

As we have seen, English and Welsh law does not recognize a right to abortion on demand. However, it would be accurate to state that while the law enables there to be abortion on demand, it does not ensure there is. A woman can only have an abortion if she can find a doctor who is willing to comply with her wishes.[268] There is little difficulty for a woman who is able to afford private medical treatment. If a woman is relying on the NHS then the limited number of doctors in her vicinity could mean that if a couple of them are unwilling to agree to her request for an abortion (for example because they have conscientious objection to such a procedure) then her choices become limited. Of course with some perseverance and determination every woman in the UK can find a doctor relatively close by who will be willing to arrange the abortion, but for some that may require quite some effort at a vulnerable stage of their lives. Sheldon argues that doctors' views still play a significant role in restricting or enabling access to abortion.[269]

Despite the generally widespread availability of abortion those who are supporters of abortion provision still have concerns over the quality of it. Their concerns include the following:

• *Availability.* There appear to be few problems with women wanting an abortion but finding it unavailable. However, there can be difficulties where an abortion is sought after the first trimester (ie first three months). Then the number of NHS facilities willing to provide an abortion was smaller and some women have to travel long distances to access them.

• *Delay.* There is some evidence of lengthy delays in some abortion cases.[270] It was recently reported that in some cases women have had to wait up to seven weeks for an

[261] Abortion Law Reform Association (1997).   [262] BPAS (1999).   [263] DoH (2007d).
[264] Lee, Clements, Ingham, and Stone (2004).   [265] DoH (2007b).
[266] Lord Denning MR in *RCN v DHSS* [1981] 1 All ER 545, 554.
[267] Sheldon (1997: 53–74).   [268] Clarke (1989).   [269] Sheldon (1997).
[270] Lee, Clements, Ingham, and Stone (2004: 3).

abortion.[271] The Government recommendation is that there should be no longer than a three-week wait.[272]

- *Counselling and attitudes of health care professionals.* One report looking at young women's experiences with abortion services found that generally the professionals they encountered were non-judgmental and respectful of their choice. However a minority complained about being 'over counselled' about the pros and cons of the abortion decision, although others complained that there was not enough time to talk about their decision.[273] In one case a young woman complained that her GP had tried to change her mind about having an abortion.[274] In fact a slightly more common complaint was of GPs encouraging those who did not want to have an abortion to consider one.[275]

- *Scanning.* Being required to go through a scan prior to the abortion was disturbing for some mothers.[276] Understandably for some this was seen as a way of criticizing the decision they had made.

- *Place of abortions.* In one study 56 per cent of health authorities' abortion patients were dealt with in gynaecological units which also dealt with women giving birth.[277] Not surprisingly this is distressing for women undergoing an abortion.

12 The legal status of the foetus

English law is clear that a foetus is not a person until it is born. Baker P went further and stated:

> The foetus cannot, in English law, in my view, have any right of its own at least until its born and has a separate existence from the mother.[278]

But that does not mean that a foetus is 'a nothing'. In *Attorney-General's Reference (No 3 of 1994)*[279] the House of Lords rejected an argument proposed by the Court of Appeal that a foetus should be regarded as part of the mother, equivalent to a leg or an arm. Instead Lord Mustill declared that a foetus is a unique organism. This, of course, leaves much to question. The courts, perhaps understandably, have sought to avoid the controversial issue of the status of the foetus and tend to talk more about what a foetus is not rather than what a foetus is, but it seems we can say the following:

(i) The foetus is not a person. Only at the point of birth does the foetus become a person. But once the child is born she or he can sue for injuries suffering while she or he was a foetus.[280]

(ii) The foetus does not have rights that can be enforced by other people.[281]

(iii) The foetus is not simply part of the mother.[282]

---

[271] BBC Newsonline (22 January 2007). See also Abortion Rights (2004).   [272] DoH (2003c).
[273] Lee, Clements, Ingham, and Stone (2004: 27).
[274] Lee, Clements, Ingham, and Stone (2004: 27). See also *Saxby v Morgan* [1997] 8 Med LR 293.
[275] Lee, Clements, Ingham, and Stone (2004: 27).
[276] Lee, Clements, Ingham, and Stone (2004: 35).
[277] RCOG (2001a).   [278] *Paton v BPAS* [1978] 2 All ER 987, 989.   [279] [1998] AC 245.
[280] Under Congenital Disabilities (Civil Liability) Act 1976. In *Buton v Islington HA* [1993] QB 204 it was explained that the foetus's potential claim crystallizes at birth.
[281] BMA (2004: 227).   [282] *Attorney-General's Reference (No 3 of 1994)* [1998] AC 245.

(iv) In *St George's Healthcare NHS Trust v S*[283] Judge LJ stated that a 36-week-old foetus is 'not nothing: it is not lifeless and is certainly human'.[284]

(v) It is not possible to bring proceedings 'in the name of the foetus'.[285]

(vi) A foetus cannot be made a ward of court.[286]

(vii) The foetus has interests which are protected by the law.[287]

(viii) A foetus could not be abducted. So a man could not prevent a pregnant woman from travelling out of the country.[288]

The following cases give a flavour of how the courts deal with the foetus:

(i) *Evans*. The Court of Appeal heard a dispute over what should happen to a frozen embryo created using the gametes of a couple who were undergoing assisted reproductive treatment. The case is discussed in detail at page 330. Essentially the man wanted the embryo destroyed, while the woman wanted to keep the embryo. The woman sought to argue that the rights of the embryo should be taken into account in their dispute. Lord Justice Thorpe felt that the position in English law was so clear that he did not even need to hear the barristers' arguments on the issue:

> In our domestic law it has been repeatedly held that a foetus prior to the moment of birth does not have independent rights or interests: see *Re F (In Utero)* [1988] (Fam) 122 and *Re MB (Medical Treatment)* (1997) 2 FLR 426. Thus even more clearly can there be no independent rights or interests in stored embryos. In this respect our law is not inconsistent with the decisions of the ECHR. Article 2 protects the right to life. No Convention jurisprudence extends the right to an embryo, much less to one which at the material point of time is non-viable.

It is possible that Thorpe LJ dealt with this issue a little too quickly. Although it is clearly established that the foetus has no interests that can trump the rights of autonomy or bodily integrity of the mother (as the cases he cites shows) this does not mean that the foetus has no rights at all.

(ii) *Attorney-General's Reference (No 3 of 1994)*.[289] The case involved a man who stabbed a pregnant woman, injuring her and her foetus. The child was subsequently born, lived for a short while, and then died. The man was charged with murder. The House of Lords emphasized that murder involved the killing of a human being. Therefore the killing of a foetus was not murder. However once the foetus was born alive it was a person. The man had therefore in this case killed a person. He was not guilty of murder, because he lacked the necessary intention to kill or cause grievous bodily harm to the victim, but could be guilty of manslaughter. Lord Mustill had the following to say about a foetus. He first rejected the view expressed in the Court of Appeal that the foetus

283 (1998) 44 BMLR 160.

284 For discussion and criticism of this comment see Fovargue and Miola (1998).

285 *Paton v BPAS* [1979] QB 276.

286 *Re F (In Utero)* [1988] Fam 122 CA. The reasoning is neatly summarized by Staughton LJ who explained that wardship is about the court taking over care of the child, but 'The court cannot care for a child, or order that others should do so, until the child is born; only the mother can'.

287 Judge LJ in *St George's NHS Trust v S* (1998) 44 BMLR 160. See also *R v Gibson* [1990] 2 QB 619 where an artist who displayed two earrings created from freeze dried human foetuses of 3–4 months duration was convicted of the offence of a conspiracy to outrage public decency.

288 *Re J* [2006] EWHC 2199 (Fam).   289 [1998] AC 245.

should be regarded as part of the mother:

> The emotional bond between the mother and her unborn child was also of a very special kind. But the relationship was one of bond, not of identity. The mother and the foetus were two distinct organisms living symbiotically, not a single organism with two aspects. The mother's leg was part of the mother; the foetus was not.

He went on to say:

> ...the foetus does not (for the purposes of the law of homicide and violent crime) have any relevant type of personality but is an organism sui generis lacking at this stage the entire range of characteristics both of the mother to which it is physically linked and of the complete human being which it will later become.... I would, therefore, reject the reasoning which assumes that since (in the eyes of English law) the foetus does not have the attributes which make it a 'person' it must be an adjunct of the mother. Eschewing all religious and political debate I would say that the foetus is neither. It is a unique organism.[290]

There has been much debate over whether the foetus can claim protection under the European Convention on Human Rights.[291] The issue has recently been considered in the following case:

KEY CASE Vo v France [2004] 2 FCR 577 (ECtHR)

Ms Vo attended a routine antenatal appointment. Due to a mix-up over names a doctor thought she was present for the removal of a contraceptive coil. In attempting this procedure he ruptured her amniotic sac and as a result the pregnancy had to be terminated. The doctor was charged with negligently injuring or killing the foetus. Under French law the courts found that he could not be guilty of criminal offences against the foetus. The case was brought before the European Court of Human Rights. The claim was the absence of a criminal remedy to punish the unintentional destruction of the foetus meant that the foetus's right to life under article 2 of the European Convention was inadequately protected.

The majority (14 to 3) found that French law did not violate the foetus's rights under article 2. The majority, however, refused to make a clear ruling on the status of the foetus under the Convention. It was confirmed, as had been held in previous cases, that the foetus was not a person and so was not directly protected by article 2. However, it was left as an open question whether the foetus could claim a version of right to life under article 2. The court explained that even if the foetus did have such a right, it would be limited by the mother's rights and interests. The majority took the view that when the right to life begins and becomes protected by the Convention it comes within 'the margin of appreciation' and that each European Country can decide the legal status of the foetus for itself. This meant that although it was not contrary to Convention for French law not to protect the foetus in criminal law, it would also not be contrary to the Convention for another country to protect the foetus. However, the European Court held that there was common ground between European States that the potentiality of the foetus and its capacity to become a person required protection in the

---

[290] At 256–7.
[291] Stauch (2001); *Paton v UK* (1980) EHRR 408 EcomHR and *Open Door Counselling and Dublin Well Woman v Ireland* (1992) 18 BMLR 1 EctHR.

name of human dignity. The majority went on to suggest that even if article 2 was held to protect the foetus, still its rights were not improperly interfered with by not providing a criminal offence, because the foetus could be protected under the civil law.

In dissenting speeches judges criticized the majority for not being willing to make a clear finding on whether or not the foetus was protected within article 2. They were adamant that it would be perfectly possible to hold that a foetus was protected under article 2, but still uphold a right to abortion. It could, for example, be argued that a case where a pregnant woman harms her foetus is entirely different from where a third party does so (Judge Rees). Judge Rees argued that the civil law protection was inadequate. Judge Mularoni pointed out that if the foetus did not have any rights then there would be no need for there to be special legislative provisions relating to abortion. The fact that all European countries had such legislation indicated that there was a consensus that the foetus had some kind of rights.

The failure of the Court to make a determinative ruling on the status of the foetus has led one commentator[292] to state that 'the reader is likely to feel, by analogy, that it had been a long journey to the pub with no beer'. As he points out, English law at present has produced the odd result that if a foetus is so badly injured that the foetus dies in the womb there is no murder or manslaughter, but if the foetus is less seriously injured and is able to be born alive, but then dies from her or his injuries then there could be an offence of murder or manslaughter. Katherine O'Donovan[293] criticizes the decision for being overly concerned with the interface with abortion law. She sees the case as involving an interference with the woman's right to bodily integrity, given that this was a wanted pregnancy. Such a wrong to the mother should be recognized in the law, she argues.

13 Abortion ethics

13.1 Introduction

Few areas of medical law and ethics are more controversial than abortion. Many people fall into one of two camps:

- Those who emphasize a 'woman's right to choose' whether or not to terminate her pregnancy. To them abortion is a fundamental aspect of personal freedom to decide what happens to a person's body.

- Those who emphasize a right to life of the unborn child. To them abortion is tantamount to a murder.

Hence we have the well-known division between the pro-choicers and the pro-lifers.

As may appear from this summary it is often difficult for the two camps to reach any consensus. They appear to be emphasizing two utterly different principles. Public debates on abortion can sometimes appear to involve each side simply repeating to the other their key principles. The entrenchment is enhanced by the fear that both sides have in 'giving an inch'. Once a pro-lifer agrees there may be some cases in which abortion is

---

[292] Mason (2005: 106).   [293] O'Donovan (2006).

legitimate it becomes difficult for her or him to still maintain that the life of the foetus is as valuable as a life of an adult. Similarly once a pro-choicer accepts that sometimes a woman should not be permitted to abort she or he is taken to admit that it is not simply a matter of choice for a woman.[294]

Before going any further it is worth emphasizing that this is an area of the law where some commentators distinguish between what is moral and what should be illegal. It is, for example, a perfectly respectable view to believe that abortion is (or nearly always is) immoral, but that the law should leave the choice up to the individual.[295] There are plenty of examples of where the law permits individuals to act in a way which might be regarded as being immoral. A far rarer view would be that abortion is morally justified, but should be illegal. That view might be supported by someone who believes that the state needs to increase its population, or that the claims of infertile couples wishing to adopt outweigh the rights of pregnant women. That said, for many people the moral and legal positions are interlinked. If you believe that a foetus is a person, it is difficult to then explain why you think that person can be lawfully killed.

As already indicated one's starting point in looking at the debate depends on one's view of the issue. Pro-lifers would want to start with the right to life of the foetus, and pro-choicers with the right to choice of the woman. We will start by looking at the position of the foetus, because if you conclude that the foetus has no right to life or no interests to be protected that is practically the end of the debate.

13.2 The status of the foetus

What status should the foetus have? Before looking at some of the answers to that question we must point out that many people object to it. They argue that you cannot look at the foetus without looking at the woman as well. We should be asking what status the pregnant woman and foetus have together. Even if it is the wrong question, it is one about which there has been much discussion, and so we will address it: what status should the foetus have?

Before looking at the answers to this question it is appropriate to have a woefully brief biology lesson. Conception takes place while the sperm enters the ova (egg). Conception (or fertilization) actually takes quite some time later (up to 24 hours). The conceptus then moves from the fallopian tube to the womb and attaches to the womb. This is sometimes known as implantation. The next point of significance occurs about 14 days after the conception and is known as a 'primitive streak'. Another time of significance is viability. This is when the foetus is capable of living outside of the mother. This with present technology can be at 22 weeks. At about 26 weeks a foetus is capable of experiencing pain and has basic responses to external stimuli.[296] Birth normally occurs about 42 weeks after conception.

Before looking at these views it might be worth drawing a distinction between saying a foetus is human and saying it is a person.[297] There seems to be general agreement that the foetus is living (it is growing and developing) and that it is human (it can hardly be said to belong to another species). The debate is over whether the foetus is regarded as a person.

---

[294] Hursthouse (1987).   [295] Boonin (2002: 5).
[296] Wyatt (2000: 1).   [297] Fortin (1988).

We will now consider some of the views as to the status of the foetus:

13.2.1 *The foetus is a person from the moment of conception*

This is a view taken by many people opposing abortion, especially those writing from a religious perspective. However, it also has its supporters who have no explicit religious affiliation. We will now only consider the secular reasoning that supports the view that the foetus is a person from the moment of conception.

It is important to look at three kinds of argument that can be made about conception being the start of personhood. First, it can be claimed that the foetus is a person at the point of conception. Second, it can be claimed that at the point of conception the foetus is not yet a person but has the potential to be a person and therefore should be treated in the same way as a person. Thirdly, it can be claimed that because we do not know when life begins, the safest assumption is that life begins at conception. One common argument in favour of regarding a foetus as a person from the moment of conception is that at that point the entire genetic make-up of the person is complete.[298] Apart from growing and developing there is nothing that will be added or taken away in genetic terms from a person.[299] Opponents may reply that in fact it is not until the forming of the primitive streak that this is so.

A slightly different argument is that apart from conception there is no other clear point in time at which it is possible to say that a foetus's personhood beings. Koop[300] writes as follows: 'My question to my pro-abortion friend who will not kill a new born baby is this: 'Would you kill this infant a minute before he was born, or a minute before that, or a minute before that, or a minute before that?' Such an argument assumes that there must be a clear point in time at which a foetus becomes a person and that conception provides the clearest place to draw the line. There is no other point in foetal development which is as dramatic as conception and as clear an indicator of the beginning of life.

Another point that is made in favour of conception as being the start of life is that the embryo has within it all the genetic material it needs to develop into a human being.[301] The embryo is the same physical organism that develops into a person. Against such an argument it could be said that a corpse is the same human organism that the alive person was. However, we do not attach the same moral status to a corpse and a live person.[302] The fact that the embryo can be said to be the same organism as the person it grows into does not, therefore, mean it must be given the same moral status.

One reply to such an argument is that we should not assume that there needs to be a clear moment in time when life begins. We know there is a difference between day and night, even though there are times of the day when it is unclear whether night has started or finished. But in response it might be said that while it might be easily accepted that daytime and night-time are relative concepts we believe that something either is or is not a person; that an entity either does or does not have a right to life.[303] Another criticism that could be used against an argument like that made by Koop is that in fact conception is not the 'bright line' event that it is sometimes portrayed to be. Rather conception and fertilization take place over a period of time (normally about 22 hours) and it might be as difficult to pinpoint the moment during the conception process at which

---

298 Noonan (1970).   299 Finnis (1995b).   300 Koop (1978: 9).
301 Lee (2004).   302 Reiman (2007).   303 Boonin (2002: 35).

personhood begins as it is for other theories to pinpoint when life begins.[304] Another argument against this 'line drawing' argument is to ask whether it is sensible to draw a distinction between the sperm and egg a few seconds before fertilization and the conceptus produced shortly afterwards.

Those who disagree with the argument that personhood begins at conception, as well as making the responses mentioned already, could also make the following argument: 'it is striking that the usual fate of the fertilized human egg is to die'.[305] It has been estimated that fewer than 15 per cent of fertilized eggs will result in a birth.[306] This might be taken as an argument that setting personhood at conception means that the vast majority of people die within a few days. Some see this as a strong argument against conception being the start of personhood. However, in reply to such points it has been asked: would we say that in an impoverished country where there was an infant mortality rate of 90 per cent that the children born were of lower moral status than where there was a much lower rate?[307]

Some argue that even if life does not begin at conception an embryo has moral value on account of its symbolic status. It represents the beginning of a human life, and is therefore deserving of respect, even if it is not actually yet a human.[308] Lisa Bortolotti and John Harris[309] reject such arguments, claiming that the embryo is not in itself of value, even if you think it represents something valuable (eg life). It therefore does not itself have moral value.

A final point to note is that if personhood starts at conception then many forms of contraception would become immoral, namely all those which operate after conception, including the contraceptive pill. It would also mean that all forms of embryo research and IVF practices which involved discarding embryos would probably be immoral. Such consequences lead some to argue that we cannot accept this conception view. But if the view is correct should we shy away from it because of its 'undesirable consequences'?

13.2.2 *The foetus has moral claims based on its potential*

A different kind of argument in favour of treating the foetus as a person from the moment of conception is that even accepting that at conception a foetus is not a person it has the potential to become a person. We must therefore respect the foetus, not for what it is, but for what it has the potential to become. By killing foetuses you are depriving them of the future lives they would have. The deprivation of future life is what is the essential wrong in killing. We must therefore treat the foetus as a person.[310] Christopher Nobbs[311] has developed a version of this argument suggesting that the greater the likelihood the foetus will become a person the greater value it has. Hence less value attaches to a conceptus and much more value to a foetus just prior to birth.[312]

Inevitably such an argument has its critics. We do not normally treat someone who has the potential to be something as if they have acquired it. You might have the potential to qualify as a doctor, but that does not mean we should treat you as a qualified doctor.

---

[304] Williams (1994). N. Ford (2002: 55) simply responds that it is at the end of fertilization that personhood begins. See further Eberl (2000 and 2007) and in response Deckers (2007a).

[305] The words of Professor Brown reported in *Smeaton* [2002] 2 FCR 193, at para 129.

[306] Harris (2003a).   [307] Beckwith (2005).   [308] Steinbock (1992).

[309] Bortolotti and Harris (2006).

[310] Marquis (2006, 2002, and 1989); Wilkins (1993); and P. Lee (1996 and 2007). For a rejection of the argument see Savulescu (2002b).

[311] Nobbs (2007).   [312] See also Card (2006).

There is a distinction, of course, in that a foetus (barring something unexpected) will certainly develop naturally into a person. It is not inevitable that you will develop into a doctor. Further, whether it is wrong to deprive someone of a future about which they have no awareness is debatable.[313] It is arguable that it is worse to kill a human with a self-conscious future than to kill one who has no such awareness.[314] This would suggest that although killing a foetus may be a wrong it is not as wrong as killing a child or adult.[315] But if a person who has no awareness of the value of their future cannot be killed does that mean a person in a temporary coma (or in a depressed suicidal state) has no right not to be killed?

A different reply to the potentiality argument is that it could apply to a couple who have undergone IVF treatment and decide not to use their stored gametes to produce an embryo, or even a couple who decide not to have sex at a time when a woman was fertile. These couples too could be said to have deprived someone of a future,[316] although it might be said in reply that in such a case an identified individual is not deprived of a future.[317]

Of course the potentiality view is criticized by those who are adamant that a foetus is a person from conception. Finnis argues: 'he or she is a human being and human person with potential, not merely potential human person or potential human being'.[318]

13.2.3 Playing it safe

This argument is probably best considered when all of the arguments over the status of the foetus have been considered. But it will be discussed here because it is a powerful argument in favour of emphasizing conception. Let us imagine you have read all the writings on the status of the foetus, and your conclusion is simply that you do not know whether the foetus is a person or not, you might have sympathy with Brazier's comments:

> Perception of the status of the embryo derives in many cases from the presence or absence of religious belief.…The dispute reaches stalemate…The humanity of the embryo is unproven and unprovable. But that acts both ways. Just as I cannot prove that humanity was divinely created and that each and every one of us possesses an immortal soul, so it cannot be proved that it is not so.[319]

If we do not know when a foetus becomes a person it is possible that a foetus is a person at conception, is it not better to resolve the doubt in favour of life? In other words is it far better to treat a non-person as a person than to treat a person as a non-person? In reply it might be asked whether this is a strong enough justification to compel a woman to go through an unwanted pregnancy with all the bodily invasion and loss of autonomy that results.

---

[313] M. Brown (2000). Stretton (2000) argues that something cannot have intrinsic value if it is not valued by other people.

[314] McMahan (2002).

[315] Dworkin (1993: 19) argues: 'Whether abortion is against the interests of a foetus must depend on whether the foetus itself has interests at the time the abortion is performed, not whether interests will develop if no abortion takes place.'

[316] Savulescu (2002b).   [317] Marquis (2006).

[318] Finnis (1994: 14).   [319] Brazier (1990a: 134).

13.2.4 *The foetus becomes a person at 14 days*

Those who support the view that the foetus becomes a person at 14 days (when the primitive streak appears) tend to support it with the kind of arguments that have been made above in relation to relying on conception.[320] However, they argue that it is at 14 days rather than conception that the embryo becomes a distinct entity.[321] It is, for example, not until 14 days that it is clear whether the embryo will divide and form two people (twins). It is only then that we can be confident that we have, at least in genetic terms, an identified person. One difficulty with this view is that it does not provide a precise moment in time at which human life starts. The exact moment of the primitive streak is unclear.

13.2.5 *Quickening/human appearance*

Historically the moment the foetus 'quickened' was regarded as of moral and social significance. This was the time the mother could feel the foetus moving inside her. This was seen by some as the moment life begins. With modern technology and scans it is possible to see images of the foetus at an early stage. Expectant mothers looking at books with pictures of how their foetus might look are understandably excited at the stage (normally about eight weeks) when the foetus starts to look recognizably human. Much was made of recent pictures appearing[322] to show a foetus waving and smiling. Nowadays, although these points in time are no doubt of emotional importance, few people suggest that they should carry moral significance.[323]

13.2.6 *The foetus becomes a person at viability*

To some commentators it is the moment of viability which is crucial.[324] That is the moment at which the foetus becomes capable of existing independently of the mother (with appropriate medical support); in other words the time at which, if prematurely born, the child would be capable of living and which is currently about 22 weeks.[325] The significance that may be attached to viability can result from two different kinds of arguments:

(i) At viability the foetus becomes a person.

(ii) At viability the mother is entitled to withdraw her support of the foetus (she can have the foetus removed) but not in such a way as to kill the foetus.

We will focus on the first argument here. The second kind of argument is an argument about the responsibility of the mother to the foetus, rather than the moral status of the foetus as such.

The notion of viability is seen as important by some because it marks the transition from being a human entity dependant another for survival, to being someone capable of independent life. The foetus has at that point sufficient independence to be regarded as clearly separate from the mother.

---

[320] Nathanson (1979: 216).
[321] McMahan (2002: 82). Warnock (1998: 64) sees the development of the primitive streak at 14 days, as signalling that it acquires a special moral status, although not personhood.
[322] Kirklin (2004) claims that these images are in a way deceptive.
[323] Gillon (2001a).   [324] Eg Lee et al (2005).
[325] As Gillon (1989) points out technology with artificial incubators could develop so that from conception a foetus could be deemed viable.

The notion of viability as a criterion for life is not without its critics. Some are simply critical of uncertainty. It can be very difficult to know whether a foetus could survive outside the mother.[326] Others argue that it might mean that the moment at which a foetus becomes a person depends when in history and even where in the world you live. A 26-week-old foetus may be viable in Britain, but would not be in a developing country with limited medical facilities. Should the moral status of the foetus depend on where in the planet the mother is?[327] A further argument concerns the meaning of viability. A premature foetus may be viable if placed in an incubator and is receiving full time nursing care, but such a baby is utterly dependant on others to provide the essentials for life. Being completely independent from others is in fact not possible (if ever) until the child is several years old.

13.2.7 *The foetus becomes a person at sentience*

A popular approach is to argue that a foetus becomes a person when it develops sentience or is capable of sensation[328] or desires.[329] This may be around 20–24 weeks, although this is debated.[330] One way of justifying this approach is to argue that we should base our approach to the question 'when does life begin' on the question 'when does life end?' There is much support for the view that brain death (the cessation of brain activity) should be the mark of death. If so, it is arguable that life should therefore be said to begin at the point when brain activity starts.[331] John Harris has put the argument this way:

> I argue that the moral status of the embryo and indeed of any individual is determined by its possession of those features which make normal adult human individuals morally more important than sheep or goats or embryos.[332]

As we shall see such an approach could, in fact, also lead to the view that life does not begin until some time after birth. What makes someone a person is not merely sensation or sentience (an animal can experience these), but rather being a 'rational self-conscious being' and that does not start until some time after birth. We will discuss this view below. From a different perspective is the argument that a person's life should be valued not for what they do or think, but for what they are: a living person. Indeed it has been suggested that seeing brain activity as being the start of life creates an artificial divide between the brain and the body. There is also a concern voiced by some that if sentience is seen as the criterion for life, then as foetal science develops it may be that foetal sentience will be found to start at an earlier and earlier point in time.

13.2.8 *The foetus becomes a person at birth*

There is no doubt that birth is a dramatic event in human life. To some it is the most natural moment to see the foetus as having its own existence. It is the point at which the child becomes an entirely separate entity from the mother.

There are others, however, who see birth as essentially an arbitrary occasion. It is clearly of great significance to the mother and her relationship to the foetus, but does

---

[326] Cave (2004: 15).   [327] Watt (2002b) develops this argument.
[328] Martin (2006).
[329] Steinbock (1992: 5). Martin (2006) contains a detailed discussion of when foetuses can feel pain.
[330] Boonin (2002).   [331] Savulescu (2002b).   [332] Harris (1998: 79).

it alter the status of the foetus? Why does a 30-week-old foetus who has been born and kept alive in an incubator have a different moral status from a 30-week-old foetus which is yet to be born? Where they are living is different, but should that alter their moral status? In response it might be said that the law often has to use apparently arbitrary points in time to ascribe statuses (eg an 18th birthday).[333]

13.2.9 *Personhood does not begin until some time after birth*

One view which appears to have growing support is the view that someone is not a person until they are 'a rational and self-conscious being'. This means that a foetus is not a person. Nor indeed is a newborn infant.[334] Kuhse and Singer have written:

> We must recall however, that when we kill a new-born infant there is no person whose life has begun. When I think of myself as the person I now am, I realise that I did not come into existence until sometime after my birth.[335]

The shocking conclusion, if this argument were accepted, would be that infanticide (the killing of babies) is permissible. To many the shock is such that the argument must immediately be rejected.[336] However, there is undoubtedly a logic to the argument. If we are looking at what makes an entity distinctly human the traditional religious answer would be: a soul. But if that view is rejected it is difficult not to conclude that capacities such as rationality and self-consciousness are the most obvious hallmark of people.[337] Yet newborn babies appear to lack these. Is therefore our rejection of infanticide based on a failure to think clearly and on sentimental attachments to babies? Or is it that the supporters of such a view have taken their logic to extremes? Anne Maclean argues that:

> We treat babies in certain ways and not in others; not for example, as if their lives were at our disposal. Bioethicists demand for what reason we do so, but there is no reason—or, to put the same point differently, their being babies is the reason, all the reason in the world.[338]

Jeff McMahan,[339] taking a view similar to that of Kuhse and Singer, argues those suffering severe mental illness do not have the status of people, as they lack an awareness of self or an ability to think rationally. Eva Feder Kittay[340] argues that such arguments involve 'creating a category of moral status extended to certain human beings (along with unspecified, hypothetical others) based on intrinsic valued properties but denied to other human beings is dangerously close to the harmful exclusions of racism and pernicious nationalism'.

13.2.10 *Gradualist view*

A popular answer to the status of the foetus is an attempt to move away from having to locate a point in time at which the foetus becomes a person. Instead we should recognize that the status of the foetus changes during pregnancy.[341] It has a special status

[333] Norrie (2000: 226).   [334] Tooley (1983).   [335] Kuhse and Singer (1985: 133).

[336] Maclean (1993: 22).

[337] Lockwood (1985: 10). J. Harris (1999) suggests that to be a person you must be capable of valuing your own existence.

[338] Maclean (1993: 36).   [339] McMahan (2002).

[340] Feder Kittay (2005: 131).   [341] Eg Feinberg (1992: 49).

which means it is more than merely a bit of human tissue, but is less than a person. The older the foetus, the greater the respect due to it.[342] The Polkinghorne Committee argued for 'a special status for the living human foetus at every stage of its development which we wish to characterize as a profound respect based on its potential to develop into a fully formed human being'.[343] Others talk of the foetus moving from being a human organism, to a human being to being a person.[344] Indeed it has been argued that we should not base our discussion around what is or is not a person but rather about the moral relevance of particular characteristics.[345]

Such arguments seek to drive a middle way between saying that a foetus is a person or a nothing, but rather that a foetus is somewhere in-between. Some add that such a view enables us to say that as the foetus grows older the foetus acquires an increasing measure of respect until it reaches the status of a person.[346] Mackenzie[347] argues that this accords with the experiences of pregnant women which change as their pregnancy progresses:

> Firstly, from the perspective of the woman, the foetus becomes more and more physically differentiated from her as her own body boundaries alter. Secondly, this gradual physical differentiation . . . is paralleled by and gives rise to a gradual psychic differentiation, in the experience of the woman, between herself and the foetus . . . Thirdly, physical and psychic differentiation are usually accompanied by an increasing emotional attachment of the woman to the foetus, an attachment which is based both in her physical connection with the foetus and in anticipation of her future relationship with a separate being who is also intimately related to her.[348]

This middle view of the foetus might be said to accord with the real views of many of the protagonists in the debate.[349] Many staunch pro-lifers are willing to concede that abortion might be permissible following a rape and many staunch pro-choicers would be unhappy with the idea of a woman carrying out an abortion at 38 weeks without a good reason. Does this not suggest that in fact many pro-lifers do accept that foetal life is not exactly equal to adult life and that many pro-choicers do accept that foetal life has at least some value? As Wolf points out many people's attitudes to foetuses depends on whether the foetus is wanted:

> So what will it be: Wanted fetuses are charming, complex, REM-dreaming little beings whose profile on the sonogram looks just like Daddy, but unwanted ones are mere 'uterine material?'[350]

13.2.11 *The relationship view*

To another group of commentators much of the discussion on the status of the foetus is misguided. We cannot consider the status of the foetus in isolation from the woman. She is not simply a foetal container.[351] Rather our discussion should focus on the relationship between the mother and foetus: they are both two and one.[352] Any dealings

---

[342] BMA (2004: 228).

[343] Polkinghorne (1989).

[345] Beauchamp (1999).

[347] Mackenzie (1992: 148–9).

[349] Quinn (1984).

[351] Annas (1986).

[344] This approach is discussed in Fortin (1988).

[346] See the discussion in Sanger (2004).

[348] See further Stychin (1998).

[350] Wolf (1995: 4).

[352] Seymour (2000); Herring (2000).

with the foetus must be mediated by the woman.[353] Dworkin puts it this way:

> her foetus in not merely 'in her' as an inanimate object might be, or something live but
> alien that has been transplanted into her body. It is 'of her and is hers more than any-
> one's' because it is, more than anyone else's, her creation and her responsibility; it is alive
> because she has made it come alive.[354]

Seymour argues that instead we need to emphasize the relationship between the foetus
and woman. She explains that the key feature of the relationship approach:

> its emphases on the shared needs and interdependence of the woman and her foe-
> tus, whose relationship is seen as characterized by '[c]onnectedness, mutuality, and
> reciprocity'.[355]

The alternative, she suggests, involves setting up the interests of the foetus in conflict
with the interests of the mother.[356] Catherine Mackinnon argues '[T]he only point of
recognizing fetal personhood, or a separate fetal entity, is to assert the interests of the
fetus *against* the pregnant woman'[357] Mackinnon, however, also argues that it is wrong
to see the foetus as simply like a body part of a woman: 'Physically, no body part take as
much and contributes as little. The fetus does not exist to serve the woman as her body
parts do...No other body part gets up and walks away on its own eventually.'[358] We
need an approach that recognizes the intimacy of the relationship between the two. As
Dawn Johnsen points out, there are dangers with presenting the interests of the foetus
and the woman as separate: '[b]y creating an adversarial relationship between a woman
and her fetus, the state provides itself with a powerful means of controlling women's
behaviour during pregnancy, thereby threatening women's fundamental rights'.[359]

Opponents of the relationship approach argue that to focus on the relationship
between the two rather than separate out the interest, despite its worthy aims, is misguided. How can we discuss the maternal–foetal relationship in any meaningful way
without deciding whether a foetus should be regarded as equivalent to a strand of her
hair,[360] or has the same status as an adult person. Others are concerned that emphasis
on the relationship rather than the interests of those involved might too easily lead to
an overriding of the woman's rights, especially given the strong image that motherhood
holds in our society.[361]

Certainly it is true that the relationship approach does not necessarily point in a particular direction in the abortion debate and could even be used to support abortion.
Petcheksy argues:

> A feminist challenge to fetocentrism has to assert that, while some fetuses may become at
> some point transplantable, no fetus is actually viable. Fetuses are biologically dependent
> on a pregnant woman and will be physically and socially dependant on her after birth.
> This dependence provides the basis for both her moral obligation to regard the fetus
> with care and her moral right to decide whether to keep it.[362]

---

[353] Gallagher (1987); Gibson (2007).   [354] Dworkin (1993: 55).
[355] Seymour (2000: 190, quoting L De Gama (1993: 114, 115)).
[356] Jackson has objected to the phrase 'maternal–foetal' conflict on the basis that the pregnant woman is
not yet a mother and because there is rarely a conflict between the two but rather between the mother and
a third party.
[357] Mackinnon (1991: 1315).   [358] Mackinnon (1991: 1316).   [359] Johnsen (1986: 599).
[360] Warren (1973) suggests that abortion is morally equivalent to cutting one's hair.
[361] Fovargue (2002).   [362] Petcheksy (1984: xii).

The relationship approach has received some support from pro-life feminists. They emphasize what are seen as the feminist values of nurturing, caring, and the value of life.[363] Wolf-Devine argues that there is:

> a prima facie inconsistency between the ethics of care and abortion. Quite simply, abortion is a failure to care for one living being who exists in a particularly intimate relationship to oneself. If empathy, nurturance, and taking responsibility for caring for others are characteristic of the feminine voice, then abortion does not appear to be a feminine response to an unwanted pregnancy.[364]

13.2.12 Property model

This model sees the foetus as the property of the mother. Mary Ford explains the benefits of this approach:

> By treating the foetus as the property of the pregnant woman, it allows us to understand why the law should only protect the foetus against the actions of third parties, and not against the actions of the woman herself. Within a property framework, she is entitled to dispose of her property without legal interference, and she is also entitled to seek compensation from—and criminal sanctions for—those who interfere with her property.[365]

She denies that this approach leads to the conclusion the foetus has no interests. By regarding it as a piece of property it is recognized as having value and having interests that should be protected by the law. However, harms to the foetus are seen as harms to the mother. A problem with this approach is that it may not accord with any women's own understanding of pregnancy. At least in the case of a wanted pregnancy few woman will regard their foetuses as analogous to their microwaves. Although one response to that would be that no legal approach can hope to properly capture the experience of pregnancy.

13.2.13 Conclusions on the moral status of the foetus

It is tempting to conclude that all of the theories outlined above have 'problems'.[366] Some lead to what would be widely regarded as undesirable consequences: such as the legality of infanticide or the illegality of the contraceptive pill; others appear to rest on uncertain or arbitrary distinctions: whether the foetus is born or the current state of technology. In the end the question of when life begins depends on what meaning and value you give to life, and as there are so many answers to those questions, it is not surprising that there is such dispute over when life begins. The problem is that compromise is hard to find. Suzanne Gibson[367] suggests: 'Ethically acceptable uses of the embryo have to be worked out in a way that acknowledges that the human embryo is both something that may well have considerable moral status and something that may well not have considerable moral status... Just as we should approach the use and destruction of the human embryo with 'fear and trembling' so too should we approach the prevention of its use in the same way.' That shows a sensitivity and respect to both sides of the debate, but does it get anywhere?

---

363 Castonguay (1999) and Maloney (1995).
364 Wolf-Devine (1989).   365 Ford (2005b: 263).
366 Gillon (2001a).   367 Gibson (2007: 377).

13.3 **The right to choose**

Many pro-choicers reject the argument that the foetus has any rights or interests until birth and argue that what is important is the right of autonomy of the woman. Such a view is relatively straightforward: if a foetus has no interests of its own until birth then it is difficult to think of any convincing arguments that would justify denying that women have a right to abortion.

More difficult is the position of a person who wishes to argue that a foetus is a person or has rights to be treated in the same way as a person, but the rights of the foetus are trumped by the woman's right to autonomy or bodily integrity. The debates over the legitimacy of such a view have been dominated by a hugely influential article by Judith Jarvis Thomson.

13.3.1 *Jarvis Thomson's violinist*

At the heart of Thomson's article is the following hypothetical example:

> You wake up in the morning and find yourself back to back in bed with an unconscious violinist. A famous unconscious violinist. He has been found to have a fatal kidney ailment, and the Society of Music Lovers has canvassed all the available medical records and found that you alone have the right blood type to help. They have therefore kidnapped you, and last night the violinist's circulatory system was plugged into yours, so that your kidneys can be used to extract poisons from his blood as well as your own. The director of the hospital now tells you, 'look, we're sorry the Society of Music Lovers did this to you—we would never have permitted it if we had known. But still, they did it, and the violinist is now plugged into you. To unplug you would be to kill him. But never mind, it's only for nine months. By then he will have recovered from his ailment, and can safely be unplugged from you'.[368]

Thomson assumes that you will say that you are entitled to unplug yourself. She expects you would agree that if you were an extremely virtuous person you may be willing to make the sacrifice and remain plugged but that is something that you should not be legally compelled to be. Many people have accepted this analysis. Thomson then argues that if you agree you must agree that abortion likewise is permissible. In the same way you think that your right to bodily integrity means that you do not have to remain plugged to the violinist, you should also think that you do not have to remain pregnant. If, however, you feel that the person plugged into the violinist should not be permitted to unplug themselves then the article offers you no arguments in favour of abortion.

Many have found Thomson's argument highly persuasive. But also there are many who seek to distinguish her scenario from the abortion debate.[369] Some of the points they make are as follows.

Thomson's analogy involves a person who is kidnapped and forced into being linked up to the violinist. This is only analogous to pregnancy following rape.[370] So some commentators have taken the view that whilst Thomson's analogy creates a powerful case to justify abortion in the case of rape, it is unconvincing in other cases.[371]

---

[368] Thomson (1971: 132).   [369] Wiland (2000) provides a useful summary.
[370] Tooley (1983: 45).   [371] Meilaender (1998).

Thomson foresees this objection and produces another analogy:

> Suppose it were like this: people-seeds drift about in the air like pollen, and if you open your windows, one may drift in and take root in your carpets or upholstery. You don't want children, so you fix up your windows with fine mesh screens, the very best you can buy. As can happen, however, and on very, very rare occasions does happen, one of the screens is defective; and a seeds drifts in and takes root. Does the person-plant who now develops have a right to the use of your house? Surely not—despite the fact that you voluntarily opened your windows, you knowingly kept carpets and upholstered furniture, and you knew that screens were sometimes defective.

Here Thomson is arguing that a woman should not be regarded as responsible for the foetus's vulnerable position where she has taken precautions against the child being born.[372] She argues that a foetus has no rights to use a woman's body without her consent.[373] In cases of contraceptive failure clearly the woman has not consented.

Some commentators do not find this seed analogy very convincing. Meilaender argues that the womb is the natural place for a foetus to be, it cannot be seen as similar to an invader or intruder.[374] Others reply that the fact a woman has known that using contraception is not 100 per cent reliable means that she has undertaken the risk of pregnancy and so is responsible for the foetus.[375] Warren[376] modifies Thomson's violinist analogy to one where you have joined the society of music lovers and accepted that in the event of a violinist's illness there will be a lottery and you will have a one in 100 chance of having to be plugged into the violinist for nine months. In such a case if you are selected you are morally bound to remain plugged in because you took on the responsibility by joining the club. Similarly if you decided to engage in sexual intercourse you voluntarily undertake the risk of pregnancy. But others are not convinced by this. It can be argued that you cannot in advance give away your right to bodily integrity.[377] Just because a person agreed to provide ten sessions of bone marrow transplant treatment does not mean we would force her or him to do so if she or he changed her or his mind mid-way through.[378] Boonin[379] suggests that in the end this comes down to a question of society's conventions: do we as a society agree that a woman who engages in sexual intercourse thereby takes on the responsibility for any foetus thereby created? He suggests we do not. But not everyone will agree. In part the question is whether the personal and societal benefits of sexual freedom outweigh the harms of unwanted pregnancy that result.

Another distinction between Thomson's violinist analogy and abortion is that in the case of the violinist by unplugging yourself you are letting the violinist die,[380] while in some methods of abortion you are killing the foetus (eg by cutting it up).[381] The validity of this argument depends in part on whether you think there is a difference between an act and an omission. The arguments concerning this distinction are found at page 488. As we noted there are many philosophers who find the distinction one of little or no moral significance, although it plays an important role in the law.

---

[372] Thomson does not make it clear how she would deal with a case where a woman had sexual intercourse without using contraception.

[373] Thompson (1971: 138).   [374] Meilaender (1998).

[375] See the discussion at Steinbock (1992: 78).   [376] Warren (1973).

[377] Long (1993: 189).   [378] Kamm (1992).   [379] Boonin (2002: 164).

[380] But Tooley (1983: 43) argues that unplugging is an act.

[381] Brody (1975: 27–30); Alward (2002). It may be argued that in other forms of abortion (which just involve prising the foetus away from the womb thereby creating a miscarriage) the analogy would be convincing.

To some the crucial distinction between pregnancy and the violinist analogy is that the violinist is a stranger to you, while the woman is no stranger to her foetus. The argument here is that a stranger owes no duty to another. To use yet another of Thomson's analogies:

> If I am sick unto death, and the only thing that will save my life is the touch of Henry Fonda's cold hand on my fevered brow, then all the same, I have no right to be given the touch of Henry Fonda's cool hand on my fevered brow.[382]

However parents, unlike strangers, do owe a duty to act reasonably in order to protect their children from danger.[383] Pro-choicers might respond to such an argument by saying that even parents are not required to give a kidney or even blood if necessary to save the child's life, although a pro-lifer might want to argue that we should compel parents to offer life-saving treatment to their children.[384]

Another distinction some seek to make surrounds the concept of intention. In the case of the violinist when you unplug yourself you do not intend to kill the violinist.[385] You would be delighted if somehow he managed to survive, although you realize that is unlikely. However in the case of abortion most procedures are done with the purpose of killing the foetus. If the foetus survives *in utero* the abortion will be regarded as a failure. Even if the woman does not want the baby to die she is consenting to a process which will inevitably result in the foetus's death.[386] Such an argument relies on the doctrine of double effect which we shall discuss at page 487 and the controversial distinction between foresight and intention. Also, it appears arguable that at least some women having an abortion would be happy if the foetus were born alive, as long as they were no longer pregnant. Presumably some would then consent to adoption.

Interestingly Thomson's article has also been criticized by those who are pro-choice. These critics have made the following arguments:

(i) The article does not emphasize the fact that only women get pregnant. In other words the violinist analogy overlooks the point that abortion can be justified as part of the equality between the sexes. To look at abortion without looking generally at the position of women and mothers in society is to miss much of the context within which the abortion debate must take place.[387]

(ii) Thomson appears to accept that it is selfish to abort. Her argument is that the law does not expect people to be 'Good Samaritans' and go the extra mile for other people. Rather the law requires that we are 'minimally decent Samaritans'. This implied criticism of those who choose to have abortions is objected to by some.[388]

(iii) Thomson is wrong to assume that it is wrong to detach oneself from the violinist. Kamm has argued that unplugging the violinist simply returns him to the position he would have been in before he came into contact with you. This was support to which he had no right. So by unplugging him you are not harming him, but returning him to the position he was initially.[389] Similarly in relation to abortion no wrong is done to the foetus through abortion: the foetus is simply returned to the position it would have been in without the woman's sustenance.

---

382 Thomson (1973: 31).   383 Beckwith (1992).
384 See the discussion in Shrage (2003: 63).
385 Finnis (1973). See by way of reply, Thomson (1973).
386 Lee (1996).   387 Markowitz (1990).
388 Markowitz (1990).   389 Kamm (1992).

(iv) Thomson's article is based on the assumption that a foetus is a person, an assumption Thomson makes absolutely clear that she is only making for the purpose of the article. But some pro-choice critics think she moves too quickly from accepting that the foetus is a person to saying that a foetus has a right to life. It is arguable that if a person's existence is dependant on the body of another that person cannot assert their right to life against the other. The foetus's life is dependant on the mother's support and this is something to which it has no right;[390] although it may be replied, as has been already argued, that a woman who engages in intercourse thereby accepts a risk that a foetus will be created and therefore has responsibilities towards it.[391]

13.3.2 *Self-defence/duty to rescue*

One theme underlying the debate surrounding the Thomson article which is worth bringing out more clearly is whether abortion should be regarded as a 'failure to rescue' the foetus or a killing of it in self-defence. If one regards abortion as a positive action which kills the foetus then the analogy will be with self-defence; while if abortion is seen as a withdrawal of support this will be regarded as failure to aid and the analogy will be with rescue. It may be necessary to draw a distinction between the forms of abortion. If abortion is seen as a failure to rescue it is harder to justify its criminalization than if it is seen as an act of killing done in self-defence.

At first, the idea that abortion can be regarded as an act of self-defence might seem strange. The argument is that the woman is defending herself against the pain, injuries, indignities, and bodily intrusion which can accompany a pregnancy. McDonagh writes: 'A woman's bodily integrity and liberty is just as violated by preborn life that implants itself, using and transforming her body for nine long months without consent, as she is when a born person massively imposes on her body and liberty without consent, as in rape, kidnapping, slavery, and battery'.[392] Such an argument has difficulties. Normally killing in self-defence is only justified to avoid a threat of death or very serious injury, and it may be questioned whether the effects of pregnancy are sufficiently grave to justify a killing. Further, at the time of the abortion the threat is not of imminent harm as is normally required for the operation of the defence. Finally, self-defence normally involves a defence against a blameworthy aggressor and the foetus, it might be thought, is hardly that. Can the foetus be regarded as posing an unjust threat to the woman? That is alien to most women's understanding and experience of pregnancy.[393] Or should we ask whether it would be unjust not to permit the mother to expel the risk posed by the foetus?

If abortion becomes more a question of whether the woman is under a duty to rescue it appears easier to justify abortion. Even though generally English law does require parents to rescue their children the degree of physical invasion involved in pregnancy is unlike any normal obligation to rescue. Indeed we do not require parents to donate a kidney that their child needs.[394] Should we therefore require a woman to go through her pregnancy?

---

390 Kamm (1992)   391 McMahan (2002).   392 McDonagh (1996: 169).
393 Shrage (2003: 68).   394 Scott (2002: 90).

13.3.3 *Dworkin*

Ronald Dworkin has suggested that despite appearances there is less disagreement between the 'pro-choice' and 'pro-life' camps than might at first appear.[395] He starts by claiming that those in both camps 'overstate' their position. Pro-choicers do not believe that a foetus is a 'nothing' that has no moral value, nor do most pro-lifers really believe that the death of a foetus is as serious as the death of person. Although they do not realize it, both camps are emphasizing the sacredness of life, albeit different aspects of life's sacredness. He suggests that there are two things that make life sacred. There is the natural investment in life and the human investment in life. He explains that by the natural investment in life he is thinking of the wonder and awe created by new life represented by the evolutionary process (or, if you prefer, the creative power of God). By contrast the human investment is the effort and love put into a life by the person themselves and by other people. This is why he suggests we see the death of an elderly person as less of a tragedy than the death of a teenager. The elderly person has seen a return for the investment they and others have put into their life through the richness of experience they have enjoyed during their life. On the other hand in relation to the teenager the return on the investment has only just begun.

He thinks this distinction between the different kind of investment in life is key to the divisions over the abortion debate. He argues:

> If you believe that the natural investment in a human life is transcendently important, that the gift of life itself is infinitely more significant than anything the person whose life it is may do for himself, important though that may be, you will also believe that a deliberate premature death is the greatest frustration of life possible, no matter how limited or crippled or unsuccessful the continued life would be. On the other hand, if you assign much greater relative importance to the human contribution to life's creative value, then you will consider the frustration of that contribution to be a more serious evil, and will accordingly see more point in deciding that life should end before further significant human investment is doomed to frustration.[396]

Dworkin sees the key question as being: 'Is the frustration of a biological life, which wastes human life, nevertheless sometimes justified in order to avoid frustrating a human contribution to that life or to other people's lives, which would be a different kind of waste?'[397]

Although many have found Dworkin's contribution to the debate extremely useful it has, of course, not produced universal agreement. It would be surprising if Dworkin had managed to articulate the issue in such a way that those who had been warring over the issue for so long 'laid down their arms' in realization that their only real disagreement was over the nature of the concept of sanctity. Those who take a 'pro-life' view find that Dworkin too easily dismisses their argument.[398] Certainly his view that most pro-lifers would accept that abortion in a case of rape is permissible overlooks the firm line consistently taken against abortion in such circumstances by the Roman Catholic Church (arguably the most influential body in the pro-life movement) that even in the case of rape abortion is impermissible.[399] Keown argues that Dworkin's view appears to suggest that lives with greater investment in them are of more value than those without. That would suggest that the life of a newborn baby who required intensive care

---

[395] Dworkin (1993).   [396] Dworkin (1993).   [397] Dworkin (1993).
[398] Bradley (1993).   [399] Kingston (1996).

by a substantial number of people would be of greater value than a healthy newborn because of the greater investment into her or his life. Could that be correct, he asks?[400] Dworkin's idea of 'investment', however, includes not only matters of input, but also 'added value' and therefore he could distinguish the life of the baby in intensive care and the 'normal' baby.

Those who take more of a pro-choice line have expressed concern that his emphasis on the value of the foetus is misplaced. No doubt the human foetus creates feelings of awe and wonder, but so too does the human egg or sperm and yet these are not seen as having some special sacred position.[401]

13.3.4 Privacy, equality, or bodily integrity

So far we have been a little vague on the question of precisely what right or rights of the woman it is said justify overriding the interests, if any, of the foetus. Three candidates are most often promoted:

- *The right to privacy.* This is the argument that the issue of abortion should be a private issue for the woman herself. It involves grave moral, social, and personal issues which are for her, and no one else, to decide.[402]

- *The right to bodily integrity.* This focuses on the extent to which pregnancy can be said to constitute a bodily invasion of the woman. A pregnant woman, like anyone else has the right to control what happens to her body; abortion is a central part of this right. Indeed it could be claimed that being forced to continue a pregnancy against your wishes amounts to torture or inhuman or degrading treatment.[403]

- *The right to equality.* Abortion plays a central role in tackling the disadvantages that women faced when compared to men. The significance of abortion can only be appreciated when seen in the context of the oppression and restriction of women. Catherine MacKinnon puts it this way: 'abortion promises to women sex with men on the same reproductive terms as men have sex with women'.[404]

Pro-choice advocates have disagreed over which right it is best to emphasize. Some of the issues in that debate will be discussed now.

The benefit of the privacy approach is that it emphasizes that the abortion decision is for the woman alone.[405] The views of the father of the foetus, her doctor, or indeed the 'moral majority' are irrelevant. Indeed it is a common argument of the pro-choice camp that the pro-life supporters are seeking to impose their religious beliefs on others. However, some have seen weaknesses with the privacy approach. First, it does not appear to require the state to ensure there are proper abortion facilities.[406] If abortion is a private matter, then its obligations can be limited to not prohibiting women from attending abortion, it would not mean that the state was required to ensure that abortions were available.[407] By contrast, if abortion was seen as an aspect of equality or bodily integrity

---

[400] Keown (1994b: 675).   [401] Boonin (2002: 31).

[402] In *Tysiac v Poland* (2007) the European Court of Human Rights accepted that not permitting abortion could interfere with a woman's right to private life.

[403] Although in *Tysiac v Poland* (2007) 22 BHRC 155 a woman who was denied an abortion, despite pregnancy posing a serious risk to her eyesight (a risk which materialized in severely impaired eyesight), was held not to have had her article 3 rights interfered with.

[404] Mackinnon (1987: 99).   [405] Fox (1998b).   [406] Mackinnon (1987: 96–7).

[407] Clarke (1989); Kingdom (1991).

it is easier to establish an obligation on the state to provide abortion facilities. Second, simply regarding the issue as one of choice appears to underplay the issues involved. Abortion is not just a 'lifestyle choice'; it concerns matters intimately involved with the body of the woman. This is a factor that the right to bodily integrity emphasizes. Thirdly, to see the issue simply as one of privacy ignores the fact that the issue of abortion is one that is of especial significance *to women*. Indeed to many commentators it is not possible to understand the issues surrounding abortion without appreciating the wider forms of oppression women live under.[408] As Bridgeman puts it:

> Neither the unpleasant side effects nor risks to health of contraception, the lack of social provision to assist in the cost of bringing up a child which forces a woman to choose to abort, nor the physical and emotional pain of high-tech, low-success fertility treatments are acknowledged. The focus upon choice makes the circumstances in which women make decisions about pregnancy and child birth irrelevant.[409]

Some pro-choice advocates dislike the emphasis on rights. We have already mentioned the relationship-based perspective on abortion which seeks to emphasize the relationship between the foetus and the mother. Such a view is concerned that a strong emphasis on rights is liable to underplay the importance of the foetus. Himmelweit stated:

> Their [rights] ultimate flaw resides in the inability of a liberal rights position to cope with caring, interdependent relationships. This means that a position which is based on the individual rights of the woman alone, inevitably appears self-centred and inhumane. Basing the claim for access to abortion on women's individual rights has forced feminists to maintain a hopelessly insensitive position on the status of the foetus.[410]

13.4 Is criminalizing abortion practically desirable?

Even a hardened opponent of abortion could take the view that making it illegal would, in fact, do little to stop the practice. Rendering abortion illegal would simply send the practice underground. For example, although in Chile abortion is officially illegal it has been estimated that up to 300,000 illegal abortions are performed each year.[411] The concern is that these backstreet abortions are likely to endanger women's lives and open them up to exploitation. In Nepal it is estimated that six women die each day as a result of illegal abortions[412] and that worldwide 80,000 maternal deaths a year result from illegal abortions.[413] So, to some, whatever the moral arguments, the practical consequences of rendering abortion illegal would be so disastrous that we should not go down that route. However, those who take a strict pro-life view might argue that if rendering abortion illegal meant that only a few hundred fewer abortions were carried out, that would be worth doing even if it also meant some women dying in illegal abortions.[414]

13.5 The role of 'fathers' in abortion

As we have seen the law has granted 'fathers' few rights in the abortion debate. They do not even have a right to be consulted, let alone veto, an abortion decision. Their legal

---

[408] Thomson (1998).   [409] Bridgeman (1998: 86).
[410] Himmelweit (1998: 49).   [411] Cases-Becerra (1997).   [412] IPPF (1999).
[413] Alan Guttmacher Institute (1998).   [414] Watt (2000b).

position is no stronger if they seek to institute legal proceedings in the name of the foe-tus, rather than their own. Most commentators accept that this is correct. Feminists in particular have emphasized that the decision should be one for the woman alone. However, it might be argued that if we wish to encourage fathers to play a larger role in contraception and the raising of children then fairness requires an acknowledgement of their interests in the abortion decision. This has led one leading feminist commen-tator to suggest that men should at least play a role in the counselling process.[415] When considering the strength of these arguments it should be borne in mind that pregnant women are at greater risk of violence from their partners than non-pregnant women.

A VIEW FROM ABOVE

Religious perspectives on abortion

The Roman Catholic Church and many other Christian denominations have taken a strong line against abortion, with Pope Paul VI calling abortion an 'abominable crime' (Pope Paul VI (1977)). For them personhood begins at 'ensoulment' the moment an entity develops a soul (Moreland and Rae (2000)). This is usually taken to be at conception. However, it should be noted that at different points in history Christian theologians have pointed to different stages of pregnancy as being the moment of ensoulment (Maguire and Burtchaell (1998)). The one con-cession that the Catholic Church is willing to make in the context of abortion is if there is a very serious threat to the mother's life if the pregnancy continues then abortion is permissible (see Lee (2004)). The Anglican Church is generally opposed to abortion, but states that there may be a few strictly limited cases in which abortion is morally preferable (Church of England (2005)).

Islam also takes a strong view against abortion. An embryo from conception is seen as having a right to life and hence abortion is murder (Ebrahim (2000)). An interesting side consequence of this view is that if a pregnant woman is given a death sentence that must be postponed until after she has given birth (Ebrahim (2000)). Some Muslims take a more moderate view, accept-ing that although abortion is wrong it may be permissible, or at least not punishable, early in the pregnancy.

Judaism has generally taken a less strict line against abortion (Sinclair (2003: chapter 1)). This is, in part, because in Jewish thought it is not until birth (or at least until the greater part of the child is outside the mother) that the foetus becomes a person. Although not regarded as a person, there is still an offence of foeticide, which is normally regarded as an offence that a third party commits if, for example, he or she causes a mother to miscarry. Of course, there are many writing from a Jewish perspective who oppose abortion.

There is some debate over the appropriate Buddhist approach to abortion. It appears that the majority view is that life begins at the moment of rebirth: when a previous life enters the embryo. This is widely taken to be at conception (Keown (2002: chapter 1)). Others think that life does not begin until much later and that Buddhists should not object to abortion (LaFleur (1992).

Hindus generally oppose abortion as it is seen as contravening the principle of ahimsa (non-violence). The general approach is that the course of action which will do least harm to the mother, the father, the foetus, and society should be chosen. There may, therefore, be circum-stances in which abortion is permitted. It should also be noted that among Hindus in India abortion appears widespread.

[415] Fox (1998b).

PUBLIC OPINION

A survey in 2002 (Marie Stopes International (2002)) found that 88 per cent stated that the choice over abortion should rest with the woman alone (although this included 17 per cent who also said that the consent of her partner should also be required). Seventy-six per cent of those questioned said that they agreed with the statement that all women should have the right to abortion. Only 11 per cent of those questioned disagreed with that statement. A MORI poll in 2006 found a small drop in the percentage who agreed that a woman who wanted an abortion should not be required to continued with the pregnancy. Eighteen per cent disagreed with the statement. Fifty-nine per cent thought that abortion should be available to all who want it (BPAS (2006)). An opinion poll for Abortion Rights in 2007 found that 77 per cent of those questioned supported a woman's right to choose an abortion in the first three months of the pregnancy. Only 3 per cent agreed with the statement that 'under no circumstances would it be acceptable to have an abortion' (Abortion Rights (2007)), while an opinion poll for LIFE found that 68 per cent of those questioned supported 'a substantial reduction in the upper time limit for abortion to around 13 weeks' (Pro-Life Alliance).

A survey of GPs in 2007 produced some surprising results. Twenty-four per cent of GPs questioned said they would not sign abortion referral forms, and 19 per cent did not believe abortion should be legal (*The Guardian* (3 May 2007)).

14 Particularly controversial abortions

Let us assume for now that the pro-choice arguments have been found most persuasive. Does this mean that every abortion must be lawful, or are there special arguments in relation to particular kinds of abortion? The following are regarded as particularly problematic kinds of abortion.

14.1 Late abortions

Late abortions can be seen as particularly controversial for a number of reasons.[416] First, for those who regard personhood as beginning at viability or sentience then by the time of a late abortion the foetus may have become a person. Second, it would be possible to take the view that although a nine-month pregnancy is demanding too great a sacrifice of woman who is unwilling to make it, if the pregnancy is well advanced and there are only a few weeks left, it may not be an inappropriate burden to place on a woman to save the life of the foetus. Thirdly, it could be claimed that there comes a point where the woman by delaying an abortion has waived her right to an abortion.[417] Finally if the foetus is viable it can be claimed that although the woman has the right to withdraw her support and nurturance she has no right to kill the foetus. However, for pro-choice advocates, however far along the pregnancy it is still the woman who should choose what happens during the pregnancy and whether a termination is appropriate.[418]

---

[416] See *Gonzales v Carhart* 550 US (2007) where the US Supreme Court permitted a state to render unlawful a form of abortion used in late pregnancy.

[417] See the discussion in Regan (1979).

[418] See Lee (2007) for a powerful consideration of current debates over later abortions.

14.2 **Abortion and disability**

If a woman learns that the child she is carrying is severely disabled she may decide to have an abortion.[419] Many people will find such a decision understandable. However, the issue is a controversial one, especially if the disability is not severe. Imagine a woman who finds that the foetus she is carrying suffers from Down's syndrome and opts for an abortion. Is she not thereby saying that Down's syndrome children are better off dead?[420] If so, is such a view not deeply offensive to those suffering from the syndrome, and a law which respects such a decision (by permitting abortion) equally offensive? If we would not permit someone to abort on sexist grounds (eg because they did not want to have a girl) should we permit abortion decisions which are based on discriminatory attitudes towards disability? Interestingly amongst younger people in particular disability is not regarded as an acceptable reason for termination. In one survey only 11.4 per cent of young people thought Down's syndrome an acceptable reason for termination.[421] Only 47 per cent of those aged 15–24 thought physical handicap an acceptable reason for abortion.[422]

We have already mentioned that in the past abortion of disabled foetuses was justified on eugenic grounds. Our society now firmly rejects such eugenic arguments. However, there is a concern that in the past we practised public eugenics and now we practise private eugenics.[423] In other words although the establishment does not seek to prevent the birth of disabled people directly, by encouraging expectant mothers to undergo tests for foetal abnormality and make abortion readily available if a disability is discovered, in effect eugenics is being practiced.[424] There are also concerns that once a test reveals an abnormality people feel pressurized to have a termination.[425] There is some research that medical professionals advising women in these cases overemphasize the difficulties connected with raising a disabled child.[426] Some disability groups point to what they regard as the disparity between the effort and funding put into prenatal testing for disability and that put into improving the lot of disabled people.[427] Nor is it just serious disabilities that are involved here. We have already mentioned a case where abortion was performed because the foetus had a cleft lip, and some foresee a time where fixation with personal appearance will mean that even the most 'trivial blemish' will be regarded as a reason for abortion.[428]

Some argue that disability is a social construct and should never be perceived as a ground for abortion. It is not the person's body that is the problem; it is society's failure to provide properly for disabled people. This argument was raised and discussed in Chapter 1. The point here would be that allowing abortion on the disability ground would be relying on a distinction (between disability and health) without meaning. Notably there is research suggesting that parents of disabled children are more worried about the social stigma attached to disability, than the impact of the physical limitations.

---

[419] Sheldon and Wilkinson (2001) note that there are 1,500–2,000 abortion per year on this ground.
[420] Field (1993). See also Lindemann Nelson (2007); Mahowald (2007); Asch and Wasserman (2007).
[421] Lee and Davey (1998: 21).   [422] Furedi (1998: 166).   [423] Parens and Asch (2000).
[424] Field (1993).   [425] Tomlinson (1999).
[426] Alderson (2002 and 2002). Scott (2003: 321) argues for a serious look at the way the news about the diagnosis of a pre-natal screening is presented to parents.
[427] Shakespeare (1999).
[428] Gosden (1999: xiv) This is just implausible according to Jackson (2001: 97). Williams, Alderson, and Farsides (2002) found a variety of practices among doctors as to whether to tell parents if a very minor condition had been revealed. The majority felt that they should tell parents all relevant information.

In supporting the permissibility of abortion on the grounds of foetal disability Jackson argues:

> Disability should not be a legitimate reason for choosing between people, but a fetus does not have legal personality and so rules that prohibit discrimination cannot be said to apply in utero. It is perfectly plausible to think that a disability makes a life less satisfying without believing that a person with that disability is less valuable.[429]

Furedi and Lee argue:

> A woman who opts for this kind of abortion is not making a social or political statement about the abnormality, or about people with that disability. She is making a statement about herself; what she feels she can cope with and what she wants.[430]

In other words the abortion decision should simply be regarded as the mother's choice.[431] Priaulx[432] argues that there should be no discrimination between a woman carrying a late term healthy foetus and a late term foetus suffering disability. Both women should have equal control over their pregnancy.

Those who oppose the foetal disability ground could argue that it should be removed from the list of circumstances in the Abortion Act in which abortion is illegal. Alternatively it might be argued that these arguments show the difficulties that can arise once the reasons behind a woman's abortion decision are opened up to scrutiny from other parties. This leads to the argument that, therefore, it would be better to allow a woman to abort, without any consideration of the reasons behind her decision.[433]

14.3 Abortion and sex selection

What about the decision to abort a foetus on the basis of its sex?[434] An abortion may be carried out solely on the basis of the sex of the foetus if it complies with the Abortion Act, section 1(1)(a). It would have to be argued that having a child of the 'wrong sex' would harm the mother's mental health. Morgan[435] estimates that in the UK up to 100 abortions each year are carried out due to foetal sex alone. Worldwide it appears there is a preference for boys.[436] It has been suggested that India is 40 million women short of the number that a normal sex ratio would produce.[437] Should the law take the view that although generally abortion may be regarded as a private decision of the woman, where she reaches her decision for reasons which amount to discrimination on the grounds of sex she should not be permitted to abort?[438] Notably there is an increasing reluctance in some hospitals to tell a woman the sex of the baby she is carrying for fear that the information could be used as the basis for an abortion decision. Emily Jackson insists that the abortion decision is for the woman to take and even if it is one of which we do not approve that does not mean she should be compelled to carry on an unwanted pregnancy.[439] The correct response to the issue of sex selection, she argues, is to educate

---

[429] Jackson (2001: 98).   [430] Furedi and Lee (2001) and Furedi (2001).

[431] Scott (2003).   [432] Priaulx (2007b).   [433] Savelscu (2000a).

[434] Sex is now identifiable at 12 weeks: Gosden (1999).   [435] Morgan (2001).

[436] Jackson (2001: 107–9).   [437] Gosden (1999: 47).

[438] Moazam (2004) provides an interesting discussion of the difficulties feminists find in dealing with this issue.

[439] Jackson (2001: 110). As she points out it would be easy to invent a different reason for an abortion if she was told that the foetus's sex was an unacceptable reason. See also Zilberberg (2007).

people against it. To Derek Morgan, however, to allow sex to form a basis of an abortion decision is to violate a fundamental principal of equality between men and women.[440] Others question whether women who choose to abort on the basis of sex selection are making a genuinely autonomous choice.[441]

15 Pregnancy and childbirth

There have been great medical advances in the treatment of pregnancy and foetal medicine. In the past pregnancy and childbirth carried a significant risk of death, and indeed it still does in many parts of the world. But in the UK pregnancy for most women carries few risks and the number of children lost during pregnancy or childbirth has decreased. That said, a recent report found that between 2002 and 2005 ten women in one hospital had died during or shortly after childbirth, largely due to poor communications and staff cuts.[442] The advances in foetal medicine have been remarkable. Further, in recent years, there has been an emphasis on social support for pregnant women. Pregnant women are exempt from prescription charges during pregnancy and for 12 months after birth. Classes, obstetric services, and a wide range of support services are available during pregnancy, birth, and its aftermath.[443] Pregnant woman are offered some protection under employment law, which, for example, makes it illegal for an employer to dismiss a female worker on the grounds that she is pregnant. However, with modern day medical approaches to pregnancy come some concerns.

First, the ability of medicine to provide treatment and even surgery for the foetus has encouraged the notion that the foetus, like the mother, is a patient. Some are concerned that in so doing the mother's interests are easily lost.[444] A focus on the interests of the foetus alone easily leads to a model that promotes the maternal–foetal conflict. On the other hand foetal medicine has meant the birth of healthy (or healthier) babies for women wanting to give birth. It has also led to a wider social awareness of factors that can harm a foetus, such as pollution and cigarette smoke.[445]

Second, there is a concern over the 'medicalization' of pregnancy. In 2005/06 only 47 per cent of deliveries were 'normal' (defined as those without surgical intervention, use of instruments, induction, epidural, or general anaesthetic).[446] Some argue that pregnancy which should be a natural, straightforward process has been 'pathologized' into a kind of illness. Ann Oakley writes:

> when antenatal care began [its purpose] was to screen a population of basically normal pregnant women in order to pick up the few who were at risk of disease or death. Today the situation is reversed, and the object of antenatal care is to screen a population suffering from the pathology of pregnancy for the few women who are normal enough to give birth with the minimum of midwifery attention.[447]

---

440 Morgan (2001).   441 Rogers, Ballantyne, and Draper (2007).
442 Healthcare Commission (2006).
443 Although Jackson (2001: 116) states that there are regional variations in the standards of obstetric services available.
444 McLean (1999: 48).
445 There is evidence that a child is able to suffer pain at least by the 26th week of gestation (Wyatt (2000: 1)).
446 Richardson and Mmata (2007: vii).   447 Oakley (1984: 213).

Pregnant women must regularly meet with medical professionals who will be monitoring them and encouraging or discouraging certain forms of behaviour. Despite the movement in support of natural child births' and home births fewer than 4 per cent of births take place at home.[448] Although women are usually encouraged to 'take control' of the birthing process, this is often presented as being the doctor letting her do so.[449] All of this disempowers the woman. The perception created is that she lacks the expertise and technology to deal with her pregnancy and needs health care professionals to assist her. Again these concerns need to be weighed up against the benefits of the medical supervision in terms of improved health of the mother and baby.[450] The delicate balance between advising, supporting, and empowering is a difficult one to make. The Department of Health's document *Changing Childbirth* puts it this way:

> The woman must be the focus of maternity care. She should be able to feel that she is in control of what is happening to her and be able to make decisions about her care, based on her needs, having discussed matters fully with the professionals involved.[451]

Many feel this is a statement of ideal rather than of practice.[452]

Third, there is a particular concern at the rate of pregnancies which end in a Caesarean section operation (23.5 per cent in 2005/06).[453] The rate recommended by the World Health Organization is 10–15 per cent.[454] The national Caesarean section rate has been increasing over the years, although it varies from 10 per cent to 65 per cent depending on where in the country a person is.[455] The general view appears to be that what has changed is not the medical condition of pregnant women, but a number of factors.[456] One is fear of litigation. Where there are complications during birth it is often seen as 'safer' to immediately perform a Caesarean section than to allow the birth to continue. It is also quicker, cheaper, and easier to perform a Caesarean section than to assist a woman through what might be a painful and lengthy natural birth. The popular press has even suggested that some women request a Caesarean section to avoid the pain of labour: they are 'too posh to push'.[457] This appears to be a myth with no empirical support, but it is noticeable that the two most expensive private maternity hospitals do have some of the highest rates of Caesarean sections (at 34 per cent and 38 per cent).[458] The Maternity Care Working Party points out:

> The NHS pays a high price for this trend towards surgical birth. But women and their families pay an even higher price in the form of delayed postnatal recovery, increased risks, and post-surgical discomfort and fatigue.[459]

NICE has now issued guidance on the use of Caesarean sections and has emphasized that maternal preference of itself is an insufficient reason to justify the operation. The aim of the guidance is to reduce the number of Caesarean section operations.

---

[448] Richardson and Mmata (2007: vii), but there is wide variation around the country.

[449] Jackson (2001: 118).

[450] Fitzpatrick (2003) is a little sceptical about the benefits that such treatments offer.

[451] DoH (1989).

[452] For a recent survey of women's unhappy experiences during childbirth see BBC Newsonline (13 June 2005a).

[453] NICE (2004c).   [454] RCOG (2001a).   [455] NICE (2004c).

[456] Nordic countries have been able to reduce their Caesarean rate significantly, without harmful consequences (RCOG (2001a).

[457] Fitzsimons (2001) is highly critical of such claims.

[458] Jackson (2001: 117).   [459] Maternity Care Working Party (2001: 6).

A fourth issue is the widespread use of prenatal tests.[460] Fewer than one per cent of British pregnant women receive no prenatal tests[461] and research indicated that many women do not realize that routine screening is optional.[462] The explicit aim of the tests is to ascertain whether there are abnormalities or concerns with the foetus. On the one hand there are those who argue that the primary purpose of the tests is to enable a couple to abort a child whom it is predicted will be disabled. This raises the issue of abortion and disabled foetuses, which we discussed earlier. On the other hand there are those whose concern is that the tests and particularly scans are really designed to emphasize to the mother that she is carrying 'a child', and thereby reinforce the huge number of concerns about what an expectant mother should or should not eat or do.[463] This all increases medical control over pregnant women. On the other hand all of these concerns must be weighed up against the improvements in the health of newborn babies, which for many women is crucial. Many pregnant women will want to know what they can do or avoid doing to improve the health of their foetus.

16 Regulating pregnant women

We now know that a foetus can be harmed by the conduct of the mother during pregnancy. For example, inappropriate use of alcohol, illegal drugs, and food can damage a foetus.[464] Less well known is that the father's behaviour can affect the foetus. If, for example, before intercourse he had been misusing drugs this can damage his sperm and thereby cause harm to any child born. Further, environmental factors, such as pollution or the cleanliness of hospitals,[465] can harm a child before birth. Should we seek to limit other people's behaviour in order to protect the foetus? It is the mother on whom most attention has been focused (a point noteworthy in itself).[466] Should we, for example, imprison a drug-using mother to ensure that her unborn child does not suffer from the consequences of her drug use, as has happened in the United States?[467]

Perhaps the first point to make is that the idea that inappropriate drug or alcohol use leads to harm to the foetus is a little simplistic. Research[468] has shown that 70.9 per cent of 'poor' women drinking more than three units of alcohol a day gave birth to a child suffering from foetal alcohol syndrome, while for wealthier people the rate was 4.5 per cent. This suggests that there is more to foetal alcohol syndrome than simply misuse of alcohol. But that should not distract from the fact that drug and alcohol misuse by pregnant women can harm their foetuses.

---

[460] Although there have been concerns expressed over adverse consequences of ultrasound there is no conclusive evidence of any.
[461] Graham et al (2000: 157).
[462] Kolker and Burke (1994: 5). The Human Genetics Commission(2006) emphasizes how important it is that women realize screening is optional.
[463] Jackson (2001: 121).
[464] See Seymour (2000: 223) for a useful summary of the ways maternal behaviour can cause harm to the foetus. It is well established that smoking during pregnancy can harm the foetus (Hultman et al (1999)). More controversial are suggestions that a vegetarian diet (North and Golding (2000)) or depression (Hultman et al 1999) are harmful.
[465] BBC Newsonline (18 July 2005) highlights concerns over the state of maternity wards.
[466] Meredith (2005).
[467] Cave (2004: chapter 3) provides a useful discussion of the use of the criminal law in the United States in these kinds of cases.
[468] Bingol et al (1987).

It might be thought that if you take the view that the foetus does not become a person until birth (or afterwards) the issue is straightforward; the foetus cannot make any claims on the woman. However, this would be too quick. First, even if the foetus is not a person you might still believe it has interests that deserve protection.[469] Second, it might be argued that even if intervention is not justified in the name of the foetus, protection is justified in the name of preventing harm to the child who will be born and suffer from the effects of the woman's action during pregnancy. Third, it might be argued that there are broad social objectives, such as saving expenses for the NHS, that justify intervention.

Let us assume that we have a clearly established harm, be that to the foetus or the child who will later be born. Does that justify imposing legal restrictions on the woman's lifestyle? Those who argue not tend to use three types of argument. The first is that because of the closeness of the relationship between the woman and the foetus—all the sacrifices that the woman has and will make for the foetus—the law cannot demand anything more from her.[470] As Eekelaar[471] notes, there is an important difference between parents of children and pregnant women here. With parents—if their lifestyle choices are harming children—the criminal law may be appropriate. This is because we can say to a parent of a child: you are free to live your life in this way if you choose, but if you do then you must ensure your child is cared for by someone else (eg by asking the local authority or a relative to care for the child). But for a pregnant woman there is not this option (unless you are attracted by the argument that the woman has the option to abort if she wishes to continue her alcohol intake, for example). But this still leaves Scott arguing that a woman cannot refuse to have treatment for the foetus's benefit if she is refusing for a trivial reason.[472]

A second argument is that such legal intervention would be counter-productive. If a pregnant woman who was taking drugs or excessive alcohol knew that she was thereby committing an offence she may decide not to seek medical help at all. Further, it is unlikely that many addicted to alcohol or drugs would change their behaviour in the light of potential criminal sanctions. Robertson[473] asks: what kind of society do we want?

> In the worse-case scenario, special pregnancy police will be commissioned to monitor women for pregnancies, and then survey their behaviour; if they err, they are stigmatised, shamed, fined or incarcerated.

A third argument is to emphasize that the legal response to such arguments appears to have been especially directed towards women. Men whose lifestyles have meant that their sperm is 'damaged' and thereby harm the child escape liability.[474] The wider ways in which society may be said to cause harm to foetuses often go unchallenged, although it has even been reported that makers of French wine are facing legal action in connection with children born with birth defects, based on the fact their products do not contain clear warnings about the dangers of drinking alcohol while pregnant.[475]

[469] Norrie (2000: 227) points out that things can be protected even though they are not people, and even if they do not have interests (e.g. listed buildings).

[470] Herring (2000: 281).

[471] Eekelaar (1988). See also the reasoning of the Canadian Supreme Court in *Winnipeg Child and Family Services v G* 1997 152 DLR 193.

[472] Scott (2003: 114).   [473] Robertson (1994b: 180).

[474] Daniels and Golden (2000) discuss in detail the ways that fathers can harm their offspring through their lifestyle choices prior to conception.

[475] Burgermeister (2004).

In conclusion, many writers have accepted there is an argument that a pregnant woman is under a moral obligation not to engage in behaviour which will cause avoidable harm to the child once born.[476] But few British academic commentators have argued that that duty should be turned into a legal one.[477] The strongest legal response would be for the removal of child at birth, the justification being that the behaviour of the woman during pregnancy indicates that she poses a risk to the wellbeing of the child after birth.[478] It is through education, encouragement, and support that we are more likely to prevent these kinds of harmful behaviour than through the criminal law.[479] Finally, it should not be forgotten that in the words of one obstetrician most pregnant women 'would cut off their heads to save their babies'.[480]

17 Caesarean section cases

One topic which has attracted much attention from commentators and courts is the issue of enforced Caesarean sections.[481] The kind of case under discussion is one where the pregnant woman in labour is told that without a Caesarean section her life and that of the foetus are in severe danger. The woman is, however, adamant that she does not want the operation. Some first instance decisions have indicated that an operation could be performed.[482] The legal position now clear after the judgments of the Court of Appeal in *Re MB (An Adult: Medical Treatment)*[483] and *St George's Health Care NHS Trust v S*.[484]

KEY CASE   St George's Healthcare NHS Trust v S [1998] 3 All ER 673

S was 35 weeks pregnant and suffering from various complications including pre-eclampsia. She was told that she needed to have a Caesarean section operation. She was adamant that she wanted the child to be born naturally, even if that meant that she and/or the child would die. Her doctors were clear that she was competent to make decisions. Nevertheless the hospital detained her under the Mental Health Act 1983, section 2. An application by the NHS trust to a court seeking authorization of the operation against her consent was made and Hogg J granted the declaration sought. A baby girl was born as a result. S did not seek to resist the performance of the operation because to do so would be undignified. S sought judicial review of the hospital's actions and appealed against Hogg J's decision.

The Court of Appeal allowed the appeal and declared that the detention and administration of treatment had been unlawful. Judge LJ warned of the dangers in concluding that a patient was incompetent or mentally ill simply because of her decision appeared irrational or bizarre. Her depression

---

[476] But note Jackson (2001: 115) view: 'Every pregnant woman should . . . be allowed to decide for herself the nature and the scope of the obligations she chooses to assume towards her developing fetus'.
[477] Cave (2004); Seymour (2000: 239); Norrie (2000); Brazier (1999b).
[478] *D v Berkshire* CC [1987] 1 All ER 29.   [479] Cave (2004: Chap 6).
[480] Quoted in Rhoden (1987: 1959).
[481] Much has been written on these cases, including Scott (2002); Wells (1998); Herring (2000); Brazier (1997); Plummer (1988); Draper (1996); Widdett and Thomson (1997); and Weaver (2002).
[482] Wells (1998: 250).   [483] [1997] 2 FLR 426, discussed in Michalowski (1999).
[484] [1998] 3 WLR 936.

was not a mental condition of the kind required for the Mental Health Act. Having found that S was competent the Court of Appeal found the case in legal terms straightforward. Lord Justice Judge explained:

> [I]n our judgment while pregnancy increases the personal responsibility of a woman it does not diminish her entitlement to decide whether or not to undergo medical treatment. Although human, and protected by the law in a number of different ways...an unborn child is not a separate person from its mother. Its need for medical assistance does not prevail over her rights. She is entitled, not to be forced to submit to an invasion of her body against her will, whether her own life or that of her unborn child depends on it. Her right is not reduced or diminished merely because her decisions to exercise it may appear morally repugnant. ([1998] 3 All ER 673, 692).

Therefore if a competent pregnant woman refuses to consent to medical intervention it cannot be imposed upon her even if without it she and the foetus will die.

So the first question in the legal analysis is whether the woman is competent. If she is and refuses to consent to the Caesarean section then it is illegal to perform it and a court will not authorize its performance. The courts have explicitly rejected an argument that it is lawful to carry out the operation in such a case in order to save the life of the foetus. If the woman is not competent then doctors can carry out the operation having regard to the best interests of the woman. The interests of the foetus are not to be taken into account. There will be little difficulty, therefore, ordering the Caesarean section if that is necessary to save the incompetent women's life. But if the benefit of the Caesarean section is solely for the benefit of the foetus then it may not be performed.

The law as set out above therefore emphasizes the importance the law attached to the autonomy of the pregnant woman. Whether or not autonomy should be granted such pre-eminence is a matter for debate which we discussed in Chapter 4. The current state of the law raises concerns from a variety of perspectives:

(i) Some commentators have complained that the courts too easily find a woman undergoing labour to be incompetent. The courts have been willing to find a woman incompetent because of the emotional stress and pain of labour.[485] As almost any labour involves stress and pain it might be thought that this, in effect, will mean that every woman in labour can be found incompetent. Indeed some have argued that the construction of motherhood is such that any pregnant woman who does not want to consent to an operation to save her foetus's life will be regarded as incompetent.[486] This means that a pregnant woman has a harder task in establishing competency than a man.[487] Further, some women may not realize that they can say no.[488] If so, the loud trumpeting by the courts of autonomy will mean little. On the other hand it has also been argued that if the principle of autonomy is to be elevated to the extent that respecting it can mean the death of the woman and her foetus then the law should ensure that the refusal of life-saving treatment is a fully free and informed decision.[489]

---

[485] *Rochdale v C* [1997] 1 FCR 274 and Widdett and Thomson (1997).
[486] Diduck (1993) expresses concerns that any woman who is not acting as the idealized 'mother' is therefore incompetent.
[487] Widdett and Thomson (1997).   [488] Donohoe (1996).   [489] Herring (2000).

(ii) In many of the cases where the court has ordered that the Caesarean section go ahead despite the opposition of the woman she has afterwards expressed great gratitude that the courts reached the decision that they did.[490] Does this demonstrate that there are dangers that the present law places too much weight on the 'momentary' wishes of the woman?[491] Or is this argument too easy a way of justifying paternalism?

(iii) There have been grave concerns that judges are often faced with these cases at a stage they have become an emergency and so have little time to properly assess the issues.[492]

(iv) To some the emphasis on the right of the pregnant woman overlooks her responsibilities. Kluge[493] writes:

> By voluntarily allowing the fetus to become a person, possessed of a right to life, the mother had de facto accepted the conditions accompanying that action—which is to say, since she was aware of the dependent nature of the fetuses and children (or ought to have been thus aware) she had, through her action, voluntarily accepted the responsibilities attendant on the fact of such dependence and thereby has de facto subordinated her right to otherwise unhindered autonomy, to the right to life of the fetus.

But Scott[494] replies that 'a woman who elects not to abort and thereby chooses to carry a fetus to term is not at the same time undertaking to do *whatever* is required to prevent harm to the fetus and ensure that it is live-born and in good health, notwithstanding her moral duties to do all she can'.

(v) As already mentioned the courts, when considering the best interests of the incompetent patient will not consider the interests of the foetus. Some think the court, however, needs to take on board the point that if the mother has taken the pregnancy through to the stage of labour she can be taken to have wanted the foetus to be born alive, and that therefore in that sense the interests of the foetus should be considered, because the foetus's welfare is important to the mother's well-being.[495]

But, even in the light of these concerns, given the current law on consent the present law should not be surprising. If a six-year-old child needs a donor kidney, a parent cannot be compelled against their wishes to provide one. Indeed, if the child only needs some blood a parent could not be compelled to donate that. So why should a pregnant woman be required to undergo a Caesarean section operation for the foetus?

18 Conclusions

Your views on the topics discussed will determine what you regard as the main theme of this chapter. To some we have seen the shocking failure of our legal system to protect the most vulnerable members of our society (unborn children) from being killed. To others we have seen the struggle for control over women's bodies, especially during pregnancy.

---

[490] Eg *Re L (Patient: Non-consensual Treatment)* [1997] 2 FLR 837.
[491] See the discussion at Wells (1998: 250).   [492] Wells (1998: 62).
[493] Kluge (1998: 205). See also Robertson (1983: 456).   [494] Scott (2002: 273).
[495] Jackson (2001: 136) is critical of the willingness of the courts to order Caesarean sections where the patient is incompetent, especially where the decisions appear to have taken into account the wellbeing of the foetus. In reply it could be argued that a pregnant woman who has carried her pregnancy to labour can be taken to wish, if possible, for the birth of a healthy child (Herring (2000: 277)).

Although women now have some control over their reproductive bodies this control is said by some only to be to the extent that it is permitted by the male-dominated legal or medical establishment.[496] For those seeking a middle path of respecting the interests of the foetus and the rights of the mother, the exact balance appears elusive and uneasy.

QUESTIONS

1. 'Choosing to carry a pregnancy to term and give birth to a child is undoubtedly one of the most significant decisions a woman will ever take, and it is not, in my opinion, one that anyone else should be able to either veto, or force upon her.' (Jackson (2001: 71)). Do you think this is a guiding principle which should be applied to all of the topics discussed in this chapter?

2. Apparently some clinics will now offer 'lunchtime abortions' where women can spend just an hour or two in a clinic during the procedure. Is this shocking or an important stage towards recognizing the right to abortion?

3. 'Some argue that civilized society can be judged by its attitude to the "unborn child". We believe it can also be judged by its attitude to women.' (Furedi (2001)). What do you think?

4. 'And suppose we've let him be born in the first place, not plucked him out, or sucked him out, untimely ripped from the womb. Many of us have a death like this on our conscience: the children that might have been, the embryos. A murdered foetus: not to be equated with a murdered child. And yet, and yet. There are no weighing-scales for the guilty heart' (B. Morrison (1997: 55–6)). Do you think there needs to be a greater awareness from all those affected by the trauma aroused by the abortion debate? Or should the message be that abortion is a simple standard medical procedure?

5. Ronald Dworkin (1993: 57) a leading supporter of abortion rights argues that 'in a better society, which supported child rearing as enthusiastically as it discourages abortion, the status of a fetus probably would change, because women's sense of pregnancy and motherhood as creative would be more genuine and less compromised, and the inherent value of their own lives less threatened'. Do you agree?

6. In the popular literature a common pro-life argument is to point out that in line with current medical practice, it is likely that Beethoven would have been aborted. What geniuses are being lost to the human race through the practice of abortion? Hare (1975) makes the point in a more personal way: we are glad we were not aborted and so we should not abort others. Harris replies: 'To choose not to have a child with inherited syphilis is not to decide that the world would be better off without Beethoven. It is as senseless to bemoan the fact that we have elected not to create "a Beethoven" as it would be to celebrate the fact that, by practicing contraception, we have just prevented the birth of a Hitler' (Harris (2001)). Are these profitable lines of argument?

7. Deckers (2007b) argues that we would not permit a parent of a severely disabled child to kill them in order to avoid the years of caring that would be required, and so we

---

[496] Thomson (1998).

should not allow the pregnant woman to kill the foetus. Do you find this a convincing analogy?

8. It has been reported that in the US a woman refused to agree to a Caesarean section and as a result the foetus died. She was prosecuted with murder. Is that a justifiable approach for the court to take?

9. If a woman is offered a scan, but through medical negligence she is not told of an apparent disability, should she be able to claim damages based on the argument that had she known of the child's disability she would have had an abortion? This issue is discussed in detail in Scott (2003).

10. Is there an argument that a foetus who is wanted by the woman and which she intends to carry until birth has moral status, but the unwanted foetus has no moral status? See the discussion in Harman (1999).

11. For those who believe an embryo has some kind of moral status there are some difficult questions which will arise in the future. What status should be attached to an entity which is a mixture of human and non-human gametes; or a creation which is a bit of embryo (eg a 'headless clone'? See Watt (2007) for a discussion).

12. If there was a fire in a fertility clinic and it was only possible to save either a two-month-old baby or 100 frozen embryos, would not even the most ardent pro-lifer save the baby? Does this not show that in fact pro-lifers do not really think that embryos have an equal right to life as babies? See Deckers (2007c) for a discussion of such a scenario.

FURTHER READING

For book-length discussion of abortion see:

Boonin, D. (2002) *A Defense of Abortion* (Cambridge University Press).

Dworkin, R. (1993) *Life's Dominion* (Harper Collins).

Lee, E. (2002) *Abortion: Whose Right?* (Hodder and Stoughton).

Sanger, A. (2004) *Beyond Choice* (Public Affairs).

Sheldon, S. (1997) *Beyond Control Medical Power and Abortion Law* (Pluto).

Leading articles on abortion include:

Thomson, J. (1971) 'A defense of abortion' *Philosophy and Public Affairs* 1: 47.

Finnis, J. (1973) 'The Rights and Wrongs of Abortion' *Philosophy and Public Affairs* 2: 117.

Mackenzie, C. (1992) 'Abortion and Embodiment' *Australasian Journal of Philosophy* 70: 136.

Marquis, D. (2006) 'Abortion and the beginning and end of human life' *Journal of Law, Medicine and Ethics* 17.

Scott, R. (2005) 'Interpreting the Disability Ground of the Abortion Act' *Cambridge Law Journal* 64: 388.

For discussion of the regulation of pregnancy see:

Cave, E. (2004) *The Mother of All Crimes* (Ashgate).

Meredith, S. (2005) *Policing Pregnancy: The Law and Ethics of Obstetric Conflict* (Ashgate).

Seymour, J. (2000) *Childbirth and the Law* (Oxford University Press).

Sperling, D. (2006) *Management of Post-Mortem Pregnancy: Legal and Philosophical Aspects* (Aldershot).

The status of the foetus is examined in:

Brazier, M. (1988) 'Embryo's "Rights": Abortion and Research' in M. Freeman (ed), *Medicine, Ethics and Law* (Stevens).

Ford, M. (2005b) 'A property model of pregnancy' *International Journal of Law in Context* 1: 261.

Ford, N. (2002) *The Prenatal Person* (Blackwell).

Mason, K. (2005) 'What is in a name? The Vagaries of Vo v France' *Child and Family Law Quarterly* 16: 97.

Morgan, L.M. and Michaels, M.W. (1999) *Fetal Subjects, Feminist Positions* (University of Pennsylvania Press).

Warren, M. (1997) *Moral Status: Obligations to Persons and their Living Things* (Oxford University Press).

Compulsory sterilization is considered in:

Freeman, M. (1988) 'Sterilising the mentally handicapped' in M. Freeman (ed) *Medicine, Ethics and the Law* (Stevans).

Keywood, K. (2002) 'Disabling Sex: Some Legal Thinking about Sterilisation, Learning Disability and Embodiment', in A. Morris and S. Nott (eds), *The Gendered Nature of Health Care Provision* (Dartmouth).

Negligent sterilization and wrongful birth is discussed in:

Priaulx, N. (2007a) *The Harm Paradox: Tort Law and the Unwanted Child in an Era of Choice* (Routledge).

7 Reproduction

INTRODUCTION

We live in interesting times. Consider some of these recent headlines:

- Mixed-sex human embryo created[1]
- Twins born to own gran fly home[2]
- Girl could give birth to sister[3]
- Mother, 53, has baby for daughter[4]
- UK considers bulk sperm imports[5]
- Yes to cloning with two mothers[6]
- Woman, 67, to be 'oldest mum yet'[7]
- UK scientists clone human embryo[8]
- Lords back 'designer baby' choice[9]
- Male pregnancy now an option, Beijing surgeon says[10]
- Gay couple become fathers[11]
- Sperm ships for fertility seekers[12]
- Briton becomes new mother at 62[13]
- The genius sperm bank[14]

Such headlines generate a range of responses. Some are terrified, some amused, and others impressed with the wonders of modern science. What is clear is that the days when there was one 'simple' way of producing children are long past. Technological advances have given us a wide range of options for creating children. The first 'test tube baby' was born in 1978, but now in the UK one in 80 children born is a result of medically assisted conception.[15] With the scientific developments have come a host of complex legal and ethical difficulties. These will be considered in this chapter. The starting point however, is the issue of infertility, for it is that which has spurred the technological advances.

---

[1] BBC Newsonline (3 July 2003).
[2] BBC Newsonline (26 July 2004).
[3] BBC Newsonline (3 July 2007).
[4] BBC Newsonline (30 September 2005).
[5] BBC Newsonline (21 October 2003).
[6] BBC Newsonline (8 September 2005).
[7] BBC Newsonline (3 May 2005).
[8] BBC Newsonline (20 May 2005).
[9] BBC Newsonline (28 April 2005).
[10] Eastday.com (29 May 2002).
[11] BBC Newsonline (12 December 1999).
[12] BBC Newsonline (16 September 2005).
[13] BBC Newsonline (8 July 2006).
[14] BBC Newsonline (15 June 2006)
[15] Jackson (2001: 161).

1 Infertility

1.1 What is infertility?

A common definition of infertility is that a couple have failed to conceive after 12 months of unprotected sexual intercourse or have suffered three or more miscarriages or still births.[16] However, the World Health Organization suggests there should be two years of unprotected sexual intercourse without conception before an infertility diagnosis is made. Indeed it is notable that half of those couples who have had unprotected sexual intercourse for 12 months in an unsuccessful attempt to have a child in fact are able to go on to have children without medical intervention.[17] This has led some to claim that the 'assisted reproduction industry' uses an unduly broad definition of infertility in order to increase the number of potential clients.[18] That said, it should be noted that the age of the couple can have a significant impact on the chances of success of assisted reproductive treatment and a couple who delays seeking assistance might be reducing their chance of the treatment working.

1.2 What are the rates of infertility?

It has been stated that one in four heterosexual couples will experience infertility for at least a year at some point while of reproductive age,[19] although others claim the figure is more like one in six or seven.[20] Over 30,000 couples receive infertility treatment each year in the UK. In 2004 10,175 children were born using IVF and 750 children were born using donated sperm; this amounted to around 1 per cent of all births.[21]

1.3 What are the causes of infertility?

The exact cause of infertility is unknown. According to the National Institute of Clinical Excellence (NICE) in 27 per cent of cases the medical cause is ovulatory disorders; in 14 per cent tubal damages; in 19 per cent low sperm count or quality; and in 30 per cent of cases it is not possible to identify a physical cause. The Human Fertilisation and Embryology Authority (HFEA) states that in 49 per cent of cases the medical cause of the infertility rests with the man,[22] and there is some evidence that this figure is increasing.[23] What is unknown is what causes these problems to arise. There is, no doubt, a plethora of different reasons ranging from obesity;[24] smoking; heavy alcohol use;[25] tight underwear; using laptops;[26] hot baths;[27] to delaying the age at which women seek to start a family.[28]

A controversial issue is whether we are seeing an increase in rates of infertility. NICE claim that although an increasing number of people are seeking medical assistance with

---

[16] Jackson (2001: 162).   [17] Jackson (2001: 162).   [18] Faludi (1992: 47).
[19] Gunnell and Ewings (1994).
[20] National Collaborating Centre for Women's and Children's Health (2004); Riley (2007); HFEA (2007b).
[21] HFEA (2007b).   [22] HFEA (2005b).
[23] BBC Newsonline (23 June 2005).   [24] BBC Newsonline (23 June 2005).
[25] National Collaborating Centre for Women's and Children's Health (2004).
[26] BBC Newsonline (5 March 2007).   [27] BBC Newsonline (5 March 2007).
[28] Templeton (2000).

infertility problems that does not mean that we are witnessing an increase in infertility. However, some studies do provide evidence of declining fertility. A study looking at the sperm counts of men attending a regional fertility clinic in Aberdeen who fell within the band of men with 'normal sperm concentration' found a 29 per cent decrease in sperm counts from 1989 to 2002.[29] More research needs to be done to obtain a clearer picture.

1.4 Responses to infertility

Some people find unwanted childlessness profoundly distressing. The lengths people are willing to go to financially, emotionally, and physically in order to have a child using assisted reproduction demonstrates that vividly. This is particularly so given the low rates of success of many forms of reproductive assistance. Donor insemination, for example, has a failure rate of around 90 per cent. The Canadian Royal Commission referred to some experiences felt by those who were infertile:

> There is often a loss of self-esteem mixed with feelings of grief, anger, and sometimes guilt about the source of the infertility. Many also experience a sense of isolation from family members and friends. People told us that infertility is not something that is easy to deal with and move on from, because having children is so firmly embedded in the everyday social and family interactions in which most of us take part. As friends and siblings go through life, milestones in their children's lives—school events, graduations, weddings, the birth of grandchildren—continuously remind those without children of their childlessness.[30]

Others have written that for infertile couples: 'The painful gap occupied by the fantasy baby haunts their daily relationship.'[31] Some women regard it as one of their primary roles to produce and raise children, and infertility is, in a sense, a failure to be a 'real woman'. Men similarly regard infertility as a lack of manliness.[32] The sadness is that many infertile couples would make wonderful parents. As Wall J noted:

> The Family Division, unfortunately, is all used to the fact that nature often makes most fecund those least able properly to exercise parental responsibility, whilst at the same time denying parenthood to those who would undertake it conscientiously.[33]

It must be emphasized that many people do not regard infertility as a tragedy. They may have no wish to have children; infertility may even be a boon as it avoids the difficulties of contraception. Others accept infertility as their 'lot' without feeling childlessness as a huge loss. Certainly there are many who would fiercely reject the idea that women should regard reproduction as a primary role or that fertility should be needed by men as a confirmation of their sexual identity.[34] As this indicates, it is perhaps dangerous to categorize 'infertility' as a straightforward concept. Its meaning, impact, and treatment, if any, will vary from person to person.[35] Fertility has social consequences too. Even today some commentators bemoan the low numbers of children being born in the UK

---

[29] British Fertility Society (2004).
[30] Canadian Royal Commission on New Reproductive Technologies (1993: 171).
[31] Raphael-Leff (2002).
[32] *Evans v Amicus Healthcare Ltd and others* [2003] 3 FCR 577, para 318.
[33] Hardy and Yolanda Makuch (2001).   [34] Morgan (1998).   [35] Phillips (2002).

and argue that something must be done to increase the birth rate.[36] Yet others argue it is immoral and irrational to want to have children.[37]

The strength of feeling that infertility can create means that access to assisted reproduction becomes highly sought after. Wealth and power comes to the physicians who are able to provide treatment, who are able to provide life itself.[38] In the past infertility carried a stigma of mysteriousness. Was the infertility a sign that the couple had not pleased 'the gods'? Now it normally has a medical explanation it has lost that stigma, although it has been suggested a new kind of stigma attaches to those who are infertile but do not seek treatment or for whom treatment does not work.[39] Certainly there is a greater degree of openness than there was in the past.

2 The concept of reproductive autonomy

Key to the theoretical disputes surrounding the issue of reproductive technology is the concept of reproductive autonomy.[40] Unfortunately, although it is a phrase which is much bandied about, it can have multiple meanings. First it is necessary to distinguish between the right to reproductive liberty and the right to reproductive autonomy. These two ideas, although both sometimes called 'reproductive autonomy', are best kept separate:

• *Reproductive liberty.*[41] This is the idea that one's reproductive choices (when, where, how, with whom to have children) should be a private matter in which the state should not interfere. It would therefore be wrong of the state to seek to prevent a woman from reproducing on the grounds that it thought she would be bad mother. Likewise it would be wrong of the state to prevent a couple seeking access to IVF treatment on the basis that the state believed they would make inadequate parents. It is also used to support a woman's right to abortion. However, reproductive liberty is essentially a negative concept: it prevents the state from interfering in people's reproductive choices. It does not give people rights to treatment, for example.

• *Reproductive autonomy.* This shares all ideas contained within the notion of reproductive liberty but goes further. Decisions about whether or not to have children are profoundly important and intimate for individuals, and for many are central to how they wish to live their lives. The state should, therefore, so far as practical, assist couples who need treatment or help to have children. Infertility, in this way, may be seen as analogous to a serious disease, which the NHS has an obligation to treat. This concept then places positive obligations on the state to provide treatment for those suffering from infertility. Notice that even in its strongest manifestation the right to reproductive autonomy is not a right to a child but a right of access to facilities so that one can try and have a child.

As will be appreciated, these concepts of reproductive liberty or autonomy cover a wide range of reproductive issues: from contraception to abortion; from cloning to sex selection of embryo for implantation.

We need to look a little more at some of the arguments that might be used to justify reproductive liberty or autonomy.

---

[36] Häyry (2004).   [37] Heitman (2002).   [38] Heitman (2002).
[39] Jackson (2001: chapter 1).   [40] Purdy (2006); Robertson (1986).
[41] Harris (1998).

2.1 Arguments in favour of reproductive autonomy or liberty

(i) *The harm principle.* This principle developed from the writings of John Stuart Mill has received widespread support. At its simplest it declares that the state should accept as lawful any activity unless it causes harm to others, even if it is regarded as immoral. This principle would support non-intervention by the state unless it could be shown that the reproductive choice would harm someone else. For example, making reproductive cloning illegal could be supported under this principle if it harmed people, but not on the basis that it was 'unnatural' or 'immoral'.[42]

(ii) *Discrimination: the principle of equal treatment.* This holds that there should be no disadvantage suffered by those who are infertile as compared to fertile couples. This principle leads John Harris to argue:

> It seems invidious to require that people who need assistance with procreation to meet tests to which those who need no such assistance are not subjected. If we are serious that people demonstrate their adequacy as parents *in advance* of being permitted to procreate, then we should license all parents. Since we are evidently not serious about this, we should not discriminate against those who need assistance with procreation.[43]

Part of the debate concerning this issue is the argument made by some that infertility should be regarded as a kind of disability.[44] The argument is that infertility is a disease which impairs normal functioning.[45] The state should do all it can to limit the negative impact of this disability. But to some, being unable to have a child is not a disability. We might like to be good looking, have fast cars or a big house, but that does not mean we have a right to them, even if we want them very much; similarly, we are not 'disabled' if we are not able to have a child.[46] To suggest so is to reinforce the view that child bearing is an essential role of womanhood, some argue. Baroness Mary Warnock has sought to develop a moderate position: that there is no right to fertility treatment, but that for some infertility creates a great need, and therefore an expectation, but not a right, that that medical need will be met by the NHS.[47]

(iii) *The intimate nature of the procreation question.* Those supporting the right to procreative autonomy often emphasize how important reproductive decisions are to individuals.[48] They are, it has been said, similar to rights to freedom of religion or freedom of speech because they involve issues of a profound kind that go to individuals' sense of identity.[49]

Orna O'Neill has argued that the analogy with freedom of speech or religion is misleading because reproduction involves the creation of another person and therefore the interests of that person must inevitably come into play in the formation and boundaries of any alleged right.[50]

---

[42] See Blackford (2006) for an attempt to give some philosophical meat to the notion that a practice is unnatural.

[43] Burley (1998).   [44] RCOG (1999).   [45] Brazier (1998: 75).

[46] Warnock (2002: 50).   [47] Robertson (1994b) and Walker (2003).

[48] Robertson (1994) and Walker (2003).   [49] See Alghrani and Harris (2006).

[50] O'Neill (2002).

The significance of procreation may also be reflected in the European Convention on Human Rights, article 12 where it is said:

Men and women of marriageable age have the right to marry and to found a family, according to the national laws governing the exercise of this right.[51]

The Court of Appeal *R v Secretary of State for the Home Dept ex p Mellor*[52] held that this article did not give an absolute right to assisted reproductive services or impose obligations on the state to provide them. Rather, they suggested that access to reproductive services should be regarded as a benefit offered by the state. This approach was confirmed as legitimate in the European Court of Human Rights in *Dickson v UK*.[53]

(iv) *Reproductive autonomy or liberty*. As already indicated, there is a dispute between views which see reproductive rights as negative (preventing the state from interfering in reproductive decisions) and those which see them as positive (the state must as far as is reasonable enable people to carry out their reproductive choices by supplying services and support). It must be admitted that even the most ardent supporters of the reproductive autonomy rights do not claim that these are absolute rights.[54] A person's reproductive choice may need to be limited in the name of countervailing interest. If, for example, there were other more pressing calls on NHS resources it may not be possible to provide NHS fertility treatment to all who need it. This, however, leaves open the question of how strong this right is. In other words: what degree of public interest will justify an interference in it?

2.2 Arguments against reproductive autonomy or liberty

There are those who reject the arguments put forward by those supporting reproductive autonomy rights. These objections can be divided between those who object to assisted reproductive techniques (ARTs) generally, and those who object on other grounds—the latter of these will be considered first.[55]

Conservatives might accept that reproductive choices are valuable and important, but only within the context of marriage. To reproduce outside that context (eg a single woman wanting to raise a child) is irresponsible. It is a choice which does not deserve the respect which is due to a right. Supporters of such an approach would accept the idea of 'reproductive liberty', but restrict it to those seeking to raise children in a traditional context of marriage. O'Neill would not go that far, but argues against a right to procreate willy-nilly. She writes:

Reproduction aims to create a dependent being, and reproductive decisions are irresponsible unless those who make them can reasonably offer adequate and lasting care and support to the hoped-for child.[56]

If an individual wishes to procreate, but has no intention to take responsibility for the resulting child, then there is no right to do that.[57]

---

[51] The rights could also be said to be an aspect of someone's private life and so protected by the right to respect for private and family life in article 8: Blyth (2003).

[52] [2001] 2 FCR 153.   [53] Application No 44362/04 (2006), discussed in Codd (2007).

[54] Robertson (1994).

[55] See also Laing and Oderberg (2005) who argue that the harms to society caused by assisted reproduction mean that the state is not required to provide reproductive services.

[56] O'Neill (2002: 62).   [57] O'Neill (1979).

Some have questioned whether the right to reproductive autonomy is problematic given the limited claim men have to such a right. A father, unlike a mother, is not recognized as having anything approaching a right to 'abort' (see Chapter 6). His 'procreative rights' (ie ability to decide whether or not to become a father) stop immediately following sexual intercourse. On the other hand, this argument may just show that any procreative rights are not the only rights that can come into play here. For example, the woman's right to bodily integrity may trump the father's procreative autonomy rights. But Margaret Brazier asks us to question whether, if we are unwilling to accept giving equal reproductive autonomy choices to both men and women, the notion of reproductive autonomy should be promoted.[58]

One difficulty over the right to procreative freedom is where the corresponding duty lies. If we have a right to reproduce on whom does the burden to meet that right fall? Surely the Government is not under a duty to run a national stud and/or surrogacy service! However, one reply is that it is perfectly proper that one can have a right to something, even if there is no corresponding duty. Elaine Sutherland suggests that such a right should be understood as a right not to be deprived of the opportunity to procreate.[59] But putting it that way looks more like procreative liberty rather than procreative right.

3 Criticisms of assisted reproduction

To many the 'miracle' of assisted reproduction has brought enormous joy into their lives through a child they thought that they would never have had. It might be thought difficult to object to procedures which create new life and produce such happiness, yet the main objections to assisted reproduction are as follows.

3.1 Unnaturalness

One complaint is that assisted reproduction is unnatural. It is 'playing God' and interfering in nature's most precious activity: the creation of life.[60] Life and its beginnings should be kept as a mysterious and sacred process, rather than babies being designed or produced.[61] Babies should be gifts not products to be created or destroyed at will. As one group of Catholic bishops put it: 'Increasingly, children are seen as the object of "consumer choices", rather than as new human beings to be accepted unconditionally.'[62] Jacqueline Laing and David Oderberg argue that assisted reproduction commodifies life.[63]

To supporters of ART these points are vague and/or meaningless. As Jackson points out, it is common for couples to deliberately have sexual intercourse at the time of ovulation in order to increase the chances of conception. This 'designing' of the production of children is not objected to. Indeed a lot of medicine can be seen as an interference in what would otherwise be a 'natural' process.

The Roman Catholic Church's objection to assisted reproduction is based particularly on the separation of sex and conception. It teaches that children should be 'brought

---

[58] Brazier (1998).   [59] Sutherland (2003).   [60] Watt (2002a).
[61] Gormally (2004).   [62] Catholic Bishop's Conference (2004).
[63] Laing and Oderberg (2005).

about as the fruit of the conjugal act specific to the love between spouses'.[64] Critics might argue that a couple attending regular courses of assisted reproductive treatment may be demonstrating their love just as powerfully as through sexual intercourse. They argue that the Roman Catholic Church's view is based on a particular theological understanding of the sexual act and if that is not accepted by the wider community then it should form no part of the general law.

3.2 Harm to the embryo

Many forms of ART involve the creation of a number of embryos from which two are normally selected and implanted. Where the treatment is successful, or the couple decide to stop the treatment, this leaves spare embryos, which if not used, are destroyed. This is strongly objected to by those who regard embryos as having a right to life or having a profound symbolic importance.[65] Of course, it would be possible to meet this concern. Regulations could permit only the creation of single embryos which would then have to be immediately placed in a woman. This would mean that there would be no need to store and then destroy embryos. However, that would greatly reduce the chances of the procedure working. Alternatively, all spare embryos could be made available for donation to other couples.[66]

3.3 Donated sperm

Some concerns focus on the use of donated sperm in some forms of ART.[67] The objections centre on the separation between the social and genetic fatherhood.[68] To set about deliberately generating a situation in which the child will be raised by a man who is not their biological father is seen as departing too greatly from the traditional setting in which children should be raised. However, many children nowadays are raised by a man who is not their genetic father (but a step-father). There is no evidence that such children suffer greatly from this (as opposed to the separation of their parents).

3.4 'Child welfare'

There are those who are convinced that children born as a result of ART will suffer harms in a variety of ways.[69] There are medical dangers for IVF children, most of which result from the greatly increased chances of multiple births when assisted reproduction is used. There are also, it is said, dangers that children will suffer psychological damage when they discover the unusual circumstances of their conception. It is sometimes said to be harmful for children to be born with no clear familial identity or sense of kinship.[70] In fact, it is far from clear what the dangers of IVF are,[71] but the rather limited

---

[64] Congregation for the Doctrine of the Faith (1990: 28).
[65] Catholic Bishop's Conference (2004: para 8). For a rejection of the symbolic significance of embryos see Bortolotti and Harris (2006).
[66] Savulescu (2003a).
[67] It should be noted that only 2,951 out of 40,115 cycles of treatment involved the use of donated sperm in 2004 (HFEA (2007b)).
[68] Giesen (1997: 260).   [69] Rosato (2004).   [70] Laing (2006).
[71] The research is summarized in Medical Research Council (2004a).

data to date does not prove that children born using ART suffer psychologically or physically.[72]

3.5 Adoption

An argument made more in the media than in academic circles is that it is improper for couples to use assisted reproduction when there are so many children who need to be adopted, having been abandoned by their parents. Apart from the fact that in the UK at least there are in fact very few babies available for adoption, the argument could be used for fertile couples as well. Rather than having a child through sexual intercourse, they should be adopting. This seems an argument against anyone producing children, not assisted reproduction in particular.

3.6 The cost of failure

The public image of IVF is the joyful production of a new 'miracle baby'. This public face masks much private grief. There are official figures on the number of children born using assisted reproduction, but none on the number of couples for whom the experience has produced only false hopes, huge expense, deeply invasive procedures, and unbearable sadness.[73] It must not be forgotten that the rates of success of assisted reproduction are not high. Indeed the Medical Research Council has accepted that we need much more research than we have to date on the effectiveness and safety of ART.[74] It is remarkable that ART has become so widespread without a firmer research basis. From 1 April 2003 to 31 March 2004 there were 38,264 cycles of treatment given to 29, 668 women. This led to 8,251 births of 10,242 children. The birth rate per cycle for IVF was therefore 21.6 per cent,[75] although the success rate varies by age. For those under 35, the success rate is 28.1 per cent, while for those over 44 it drops to 1.4 per cent. Although some 25 per cent of IVF is provided on the NHS (see below) the majority of people pay for it privately. It costs around £8,000 per cycle.[76]

Even where successful there is the risk with ART of multiple pregnancy, and with it the extra risks to women and children. Over half of all children born using ART are twins or triplets.[77] Although they no doubt bring delight, the burdens on parents raising multiple birth children is considerable. In particular, multiple births have higher rates of miscarriage, abnormality, prenatal death, and prematurity. This produces greater strain on the couple, neonatal services, and expenses for the NHS.[78] The HFEA code now says that only two embryos should be transferred if the woman is under 40 or three if she is over 40.[79] There is a delicate balance here between increasing the chances of success of the treatment, and decreasing the chances of multiple births. The Government has indicated that we should be moving to the transference of a single embryo being the norm.[80]

---

[72] Brewaeys, et al (1997); Golombok et al (1996).   [73] Franklin (1997).
[74] Medical Research Council (2004a).   [75] Riley (2007: 83).   [76] HFEA (2007b).
[77] Medical Research Council (2004a).   [78] Price (1993).
[79] HFEA (2007c: G.8.5). This policy was challenged in the courts, but upheld: R *(on the application of Assisted Reproduction and Gynaecology Centre) v Human Fertilisation and Embryology Authority* [2002] EWCA Civ 20 [2003] 1 FCR 266.
[80] DoH (2005f: 18).

Are the risks of ART worth taking? To supporters this is all a matter of choice for the people concerned. As long as people are aware of the risks involved it is up to them whether to take them or not.

Assisted reproduction

Perhaps not surprisingly there is no single 'feminist' response to assisted reproduction. The response from radical feminists has tended to oppose assisted reproductive techniques and we will examine that first, although as we shall see other feminists have been more supportive.

Feminists are concerned that ART reinforces the message that a woman's primary purpose is to be a mother. It perpetuates the message that reproduction is essential for women, and that invasive procedures are justifiable if a woman is unable to meet that role. As Callahan and Roberts (1996: 1211) put it:

> reproduction-assisting technologies…contribute to the subordination of women by continuing to tie the value of women to reproduction…

If a woman is infertile the message of society should not be 'you must get that fixed' but rather 'that is unimportant'. Women's desperation to use assisted reproduction simply reflects wider society's assumptions about the role of women. We need to challenge those assumptions, not reinforce them. If we lived in a society where childlessness was a 'respectable' choice, we could be confident about women's choice to use assisted reproduction (Maclean (1993): 30). As Emily Jackson (2001) points out, however, although it is often said women who use assisted reproduction are not 'genuinely' consenting, we do not tend to say the same thing about women who conceive 'naturally'. Is this not a further example of double standards? Is not the choice to have a child through assisted reproduction as open to societal pressure as any decision to have children?

There is concern about the power that assisted reproductive technology gives to the medical professionals (often male). Rosi Braidotti (1994: 88) suggests that:

> the test-tube babies of today mark the long-term triumph of the alchemists' dream of dominating nature thorough their self-inseminating, masturbatory practices…

Even if that is a bit much, there is a widespread feeling among women receiving ART that they end up with their bodies being treated as laboratories (Corea (1985)). All indignities and pain involved in using the woman's body are justifiable for the ultimate goal of producing a child. And it *is* normally women's bodies that suffer all the invasion, even where the cause of the infertility rests with the man, and such invasion is normally at the hand of male doctors. As Corea (1985: 4) states:

> Reproductive technology is a product of the male reality. The values expressed in the technology—objectification, domination—are typical of male culture. The technology is male-generated and buttresses male power over women…

Of course not all feminists agree with such arguments; some argue that they lead to an argument that no woman should decide to have children. Does a fertile woman having sexual intercourse reinforce the mother role any more or less than a woman having assisted reproduction?

Another feminist response is that opposition to ART is voiced by feminist intellectuals who are not listening to what women actually want. Listening to our infertile sisters, some feminists argue, will lead us to appreciate their needs and position much better. ART has done much to improve the reproductive options for women. Increasing reproductive autonomy for women, it is said, cannot amount to being anti-feminist.

Some feminists also see great hope in assisted reproduction as a means of challenging the traditional image of a family. ART offers single women and lesbian couples the hope of having a child which would otherwise not be possible (Lublin (1998)). Indeed a feminist opposing assisted reproduction may end up in the uncomfortable position of having to accept that the only legitimate way to conceive children is through male–female sexual relations.

Another feminist argument used against assisted reproduction is that it reflects a preoccupation with the genetic link. What drives some couples (and especially fathers) to use assisted reproduction is the desire to have a child which is 'their own'; in other words has a genetic link to them. Some feminists suggest we need to challenge this argument that it is genetics that makes someone a parent: they argue that it is day-to-day caring that makes someone a parent, whereas others feel that this is to ignore the powerful feelings that some people have concerning the genetic link.

Perhaps, then, for feminists the advances of ART are a 'double edged sword' (Stanworth (1988): 16). Do we respect women's wishes to have children and promote their reproductive autonomy or do we reject such desires as a result of patriarchal thinking? As has been suggested reproductive technologies are the wrong responses to the wrong problems (Smart (1993): 223–4). The problem for a feminist response to infertility is that feminism would not want to support the situation that our society is currently in: one in which childlessness is regarded as an unattractive option, especially for women, and in which great store is placed on genetic links. Certainly if we are to take the notion of reproductive autonomy seriously the option of childlessness needs to be as facilitated as much as the option of child rearing.

4 The different techniques

We will only discuss here the lawful techniques that are available. Reproductive cloning is presently illegal, but will be discussed later in this chapter.

4.1 Cryopreservation

Sperm eggs and embryos can be frozen. This means that donors' sperm can be tested or embryos frozen so that they can be implanted at the optimum time in a woman's cycle. It is also used for individuals who are about to undergo surgery or treatment which will render them infertile, so that they can keep the option of reproduction in the future. The freezing of eggs carries serious risks of failure, although technological advances are improving the success rate of doing so.[81]

4.2 Intrauterine (or Assisted) Insemination by Husband/Partner (AIH/AIP)

Here a husband or partner's sperm is placed inside the woman where it fertilizes an egg. The technology available through ICSI (see below) means that it is now rarely used, unless the man's sperm has been frozen in advance. Assisted insemination with sperm

---

[81] BBC Newsonline (29 May 2005).

of a living husband or partner is specifically excluded from the kinds of treatment which require a licence under the Human Fertilisation and Embryology Act 1990.

4.3 Donor Insemination (DI)

This is used where the woman has no partner, or her partner is infertile. It involves the insemination of sperm from a donor into a woman, via her vagina into the cervical canal or into the uterus itself. It is normally used as a last resort. The use of ICSI means that even low quality sperm can now be used where in the past donor insemination would have been the only option. It has a live birth rate of about 10–12 per cent with each attempt in women under 30 years, and 9 per cent in women aged 35–39 years.[82]

4.4 Egg (Oocyte) donation

Egg donation is necessary where the woman has no healthy eggs. A woman willing to donate eggs will have hormonal treatment and then eggs will be surgically retrieved from her. This is an uncomfortable and invasive procedure, certainly more so than the donation of sperm. The donated eggs can be fertilized with the sperm of the woman's partner or donated sperm and are then put into her uterus. Oocyte donation has a live birth rate of 25–40 per cent with each attempt (eggs donated by women under 36 years).[83]

4.5 In Vitro Fertilization (IVF)

Here hormonal treatment is used to stimulate the over-production of eggs. These are removed from the ovarian follcules and placed in a culture which matures them further. Then in a Petri dish they are fertilized with sperm (that of her partner or donated sperm) and the resulting zygotes are either frozen or placed back into the woman's uterus. Each year there are some 35,000 cycles of IVF and 18.2 per cent of these lead to a live birth.[84] The overall live birth rate per treatment cycle is 21.8 per cent (25.1 per cent for women aged less than 38 years). If frozen embryos are used the success rate is about 12 per cent per treatment cycle. After five attempts, just over half of women aged under 34 years will have conceived.[85] These success rates appear slightly lower than those in some other European Countries.[86]

4.6 Gamete Intra-Fallopian Transfer (GIFT)

Here eggs are retrieved as in IVF, but the eggs are mixed with sperm and returned to the fallopian tubes, with the intent that fertilization will take place there. Technically this procedure does not require a licence, but will very rarely be attempted in unlicensed clinics. GIFT has a pregnancy rate of 25–30 per cent in any one treatment cycle.[87]

---

[82] HFEA (2004b).   [83] HFEA (2004b).   [84] HFEA (2000b).
[85] HFEA (2004a) and (2004b).   [86] Nyboe Andersen et al (2004).
[87] HFEA (2004a).

4.7 Intra-Cytoplasmic Sperm Injection (ICSI) and Sub-Zonal Insemination (SUZI)

This involves the injection of a single sperm into an egg with a very fine needle. If fertilization is successful the fertilized egg is then transferred to the woman's uterus in same way as IVF. ICSI is particularly useful where the sperm cannot naturally penetrate the egg or where it is of poor mobility. ICSI now accounts for 44 per cent of all IVF treatment.[88] There have, however, been some concerns raised about whether there are higher levels of abnormalities involving children born as a result of this procedure.[89] SUZI is a similar procedure but involves micro injections of a small number of sperm. The overall live birth rate per embryo transfer for ICSI is 28.7 per cent (25.7 per cent for women over 38 years).[90]

4.8 In Vitro Maturation (IVM)

This is a new form of treatment which has only been used occasionally in England. It involves removing an immature egg from a woman's ovaries and then maturing it in a laboratory before being fertilized and then returned to the woman's womb.

5 Regulation

Assisted Reproductive Technologies (ARTs) are regulated by the Human Fertilisation and Embryology Act 1990 (HFE Act), which created the Human Fertilisation and Embryology Authority (HFEA). The HFEA issues guidance on ARTs and licenses their use.[91]

In this country we have become quite used to the idea that scientists wishing to carry out reproductive treatment or research require a licence from a government agency, but from a worldwide perspective it is a controversial stance to take. The idea of the Government restricting what scientists can or cannot research, or what treatments a doctor can offer a patient, are seen in some countries as improper government intrusion. Nevertheless the UK's regulation of this area is well established and is regarded by many in the world as a model system.[92] But what is the justification for regulation?

It is easy to forget that when the 1990 Act was passed ARTs were controversial and there was widespread mistrust and uncertainty at what was being done. The regulation of the HFEA meant that reassurance could be given that scientists would not be allowed to create 'Frankenstein's children'. The HFEA would be inspecting what happened in laboratories, and those wishing to conduct research and practice in the area would need approval. The HFEA has meant that reproductive medicine has been able to expand with a respectable image. It is interesting to consider the position in Italy, where initially assisted reproduction was largely unregulated, but following a number of scandals involving allegedly improper behaviour by doctors working in the area the Italian Government passed legislation which is highly restrictive about what doctors can do in the field of ART.

The advantage of regulation is that it provides a flexible approach to this controversial area. The HFEA can respond reasonably quickly to advances in medical technology or

---

88 HFEA (2007b).   89 Meschede and Horst (1997).   90 HFEA (2004b).
91 Montgomery (1990).   92 Deech (2003).

novel moral issues, whereas it can be slow for Parliament to pass legislation in response to changing circumstances. The HFEA is also able to provide regulation which is free from political pressure: it is less likely to be influenced by a campaign from the tabloid press than politicians might. Veronica English has listed what she regards as the four main advantages of having regulation under a body like the HFEA; it:

(i) protects patients;

(ii) allays public concerns;

(iii) provides an environment within which scientific progress can flourish; and

(iv) protects IVF practitioners against claims of unethical behaviour.[93]

Martin Johnson has listed the parties whose interests regulation needs to protect:

(i) the embryo *in vitro*;

(ii) children deriving from these embryos;

(iii) patients (especially women, but also partners, donors, surrogates);

(iv) society (the public interest);

(v) the health team (doctors, counsellors, nurses, and biomedical scientists).[94]

Johnson is concerned that the interests of the embryo have come to dominate the issue of regulation, without proper thought being given to what regulation is seeking to achieve and how the different interests can be balanced.

The disadvantages of regulation include the dangers of 'slippery slopes': by considering each new case 'on its merits' there is a danger that the wider picture will be lost. An apparently reasonable decision will be made on each occasion, with the change made from previous cases being minimal, but we will end up at a place we did not want to be. There are also claims that the HFEA is not adequately responsive to public opinion and there is no way of readily holding it to account for its decisions. Finally, there are the costs of regulation which ultimately are passed on to the consumer and this may increase the number of people for whom ART is not available for financial reasons.

EUROPEAN ANGLES

In addition to the HFE Act, regulation is provided by the EC Tissues and Cells Directive.[95] The Directive introduced common safety and quality standards and inspections to facilitate the easier exchange of tissues and cells (including human gametes) between Member States. Notably the directive covers all dealings with gametes and is therefore wider than the HFE Act. It covers, for example, internet services which offer to deliver fresh sperm. The primary aim of the directive is to deal with the distribution of gametes across Europe. It therefore requires there to be a system for tracing gametes and requires regulation of imports of gametes to ensure their quality. The detail of the directive is yet to be worked out. The HFEA intends a single inspection regime which will ensure clinics are complying with the requirements of the directive as well as the HFE Act.[96]

---

[93] English (2006: 3048). [94] Johnson (2007).
[95] Directive 2004/23/EC. [96] HFEA (2006).

The HFEA has two primary purposes: to ensure assisted reproductive treatment and research is ethical and safe. The Authority produces guidelines which govern licensed clinics. It does not normally consider individual cases, unless they raise particularly complex problems. There are 20 members of the Authority appointed by the UK Health Ministers, made up of both lay and medically qualified individuals. They operate as a licensing body for clinics who wish to offer ARTs and for researchers wishing to conduct research on embryos. A clinic which receives a licence will face a full inspection at least every three years and interim inspections on other occasions. Licensed clinics must abide by codes of practice issued by the HFEA.[97]

It is possible to divide up activities in the areas of ART and research into three categories:

(i) those that are unlawful;

(ii) those that are only lawful if the clinic has a licence in respect of those activities;

(iii) those which are lawful and do not require a licence.

We shall look at these separate categories.

5.1 Activities prohibited by the HFE Act

The HFE Act renders certain activities unlawful and does not permit the HFEA to license them. They include the following:

- An embryo cannot be stored for more than 14 days after the mixing of the gametes (at which time the primative streak will have appeared).[98] This means that although research can take place on embryos up until the 14th day, the HFEA has no power to authorize the storage of an embryo beyond that time.
- It is unlawful to place a non-human embryo in a woman.[99]
- It is unlawful to place in a woman any non-human gametes.[100]
- It is unlawful to place a human embryo in a non-human animal.[101]
- The use of eggs taken from embryos in fertility treatment is forbidden.[102]
- It is unlawful to replace the nucleus of an embryo with a nucleus taken from a cell of any person or embryo.[103] This is often known as cloning.

Keeping or using an embryo under any circumstances in which regulations prohibit its keeping or use is unlawful.[104] It is unlawful to alter the genetic structure of any cell while it forms part of an embryo.[105]

5.2 Activities only permitted if performed under a licence

The HFE Act also outlaws certain activities, although it enables the HFEA to provide a licence for them which renders them lawful.

---

[97] HFEA (2007c).   [98] HFE Act 1990, s 4(3).   [99] HFE Act 1990, s 3(2).
[100] HFE Act 1990, s 3(2).   [101] HFE Act 1990, s 3(3).   [102] HFE Act 1990, s 3A.
[103] Human Reproductive Cloning Act 2001, s 1.
[104] HFE Act 1990, s 4(2).   [105] HFE Act 1990, para 1(4), Sch 2.

- The storage of an embryo is only lawful[106] if carried out under a licence issued by the HFEA.[107]

- The storage and use of gametes can only be lawfully carried out under a licence issued by the HFEA.[108]

5.3 Activities which do not require a licence

There are of course other activities involving assisted reproduction which do not require a licence. This is any process which does not involve the creation of an embryo outside the human body or the storage of any gametes. 'Do it yourself insemination' using fresh sperm and a turkey baster (or similar instrument) is not subject to regulation. Nor is GIFT. This is because it would not involve the storage of sperm, nor does it involve the creation of an embryo outside the woman. So the work of 'Man Not Included'[109] in which women can order fresh sperm from the internet and it is delivered to their door is not covered by the HFE Act. Similarly if a lesbian couple advertized for a man to give some of his sperm and one did so, that would not be covered by the Act. It would of course be difficult to police a law which made it illegal for someone to give someone else their fresh sperm.

The exclusion of these activities may be questioned. The work, for example, of 'Man Not Included' might be said to raise some of the concerns and issues which are said to justify the regulation of licensed clinics. It may be that the EU Tissue Directive will regulate their activities.[110] Indeed the Government has initiated consultation to discuss whether such internet services should be regulated and if so how.[111]

5.4 The paramountcy of consent

A key principle in the HFE Act is that gametes or embryos may not be used without the consent of the provider(s). So, if a couple have had embryos frozen these can only be stored with the couple's consent. If they ask for the embryo to be destroyed then it would be unlawful for the clinic not to do so. However there is a maximum limit on the storage of embryos and gametes. This is five years for embryos and ten years for gametes.[112] However, in both cases this can be extended if there are special circumstances. For example, if a 20-year-old woman is facing medical treatment which is likely to render her infertile and she therefore decides to have some of her eggs frozen, she is entitled to keep them for longer than the five years.[113]

The most controversial issue surrounding consent is where a couple have created frozen embryos but disagree over whether or not the embryo should be destroyed.[114] That

---

[106] It is a criminal offence: HFE Act 1990, s 41.   [107] HFE Act 1990, ss 3 and 4.

[108] S 4 prohibits the storage and use of human gametes. There are special exemptions where the storage of gametes is for the researching or developing of pharmaceutical and contraceptive products, or for teaching: Human Fertilisation and Embryology (Special Exemptions) Regs 1991.

[109] Try www.mannotincluded.com.

[110] House of Commons Science and Technology Committee (2005: para 86).

[111] DoH (2005e: 16).   [112] HFE Act 1990, s 14.

[113] Human Fertilisation and Embryology (Statutory Storage Period) Regulations 1991 SI 1991/1540; Human Fertilisation and Embryology (Statutory Storage Period for Embryos) Regulations 1996 SI 1996/375.

[114] Shenfield (2000); Daar (1999).

issue was addressed in the following controversial case:

KEY CASE   Evans v Amicus Healthcare Ltd and others [2004] 3 All ER 1025

In October 2001 Natalie Evans and Howard Johnston, who were engaged, underwent IVF treatment. It was discovered that Natalie Evans had tumours on her ovaries. Her ovaries had to be removed as soon as possible and she was required to make a decision quickly on whether she wanted any ova removed and frozen. There were three main options: either that she freeze her ova; that her eggs be fertilized with donated sperm and frozen; or that her ova be fertilized with Mr Johnston's sperm and then frozen. She chose the last option, a decision she would subsequently deeply regret. There were two main reasons for it. The first was that ova do not freeze well and many do not survive. The second was that Mr Johnston assured her that he wanted to be the father of her children; that they were not going to split up; and that she should not be negative. Six eggs were harvested, fertilized, and frozen. Later that month her ovaries were removed. In May 2002 the couple separated and Mr Johnston wrote to the clinic asking them to destroy the embryos. Ms Evans sought an order preventing their destruction.

The Court of Appeal found the case straightforward in legal terms and decided against Ms Evans and authorized the destruction of the embryos. The decision was reached primarily on the basis of the interpretation of the HFE Act. That Act makes it clear that a licensed clinic is only permitted to store an embryo which has been brought about *in vitro* if there is effective consent by each person whose gametes were used to bring about the creation of the embryo (HFE Act, Sch 3, paras 6(3), 8(2)). Although Mr Johnson had consented to the original storage of the sperm and its use in fertilizing the egg, he had now withdrawn his consent and so the clinic was no longer permitted to store it. Lord Justice Thorpe explained: 'the clear policy of the Act is to ensure continuing consent from the commencement of treatment to the point of implant' (para 37). The Court of Appeal also emphasized the fact that the consent form signed by Mr Johnston and Ms Evans stated that the embryo could be used for the treatment of 'myself [Ms Evans] together with a named partner [Mr Johnston]', clearly indicating that they were agreeing to treatment as a couple.

It was not just the wording of the statutory provisions which convinced the Court of Appeal that this was the correct interpretation of the Act. They emphasized that there were two principles underlying the Act:

(i) The welfare of any child born by treatment was to be of fundamental importance.

(ii) Licensed clinics were only able to store gametes with their providers' informed consent, which was capable of being withdrawn at any point prior to the transfer of the embryos to the woman receiving treatment.

Both of these principles supported the conclusion that the embryos should be destroyed. As to the first, it was not in the child's interests to be born to a father who did not want the child to be born. As to the second, it clearly required the destruction of the embryo.

The Court of Appeal also considered whether the Human Rights Act 1998 required the Court to re-interpret the HFE Act in a way which was consistent with the parties' rights under the European Convention on Human Rights. The Court quickly concluded that the embryo had no rights under the Convention. As to the article 8 rights to respect private and family life it was noted that Ms Evans's right to reproduce had to be balanced against Mr Johnston's right not to reproduce. This was problematic because it involved 'a balance to be struck between two entirely incommensurable things' (para 66). In essence the Court of Appeal felt that the HFE Act had taken a reasonable approach between balancing these rights and so it could not be said to be incompatible with the

Convention, although had the Act permitted Ms Evans to implant the embryo this too might have been compatible with the Convention.

The Court divided on whether the law discriminated against Ms Evans on the grounds of disability (her infertility). In essence the argument was that for a fertile woman once the man has given his sperm he has no right to stop the birth of the child which may result. The HFE Act meant that an infertile woman faced the risk that the man who provided the sperm could prevent the birth of the child. Arden J accepted this argument. Thorpe and Sedley LJ thought that this did not constitute discrimination, arguing 'it is not the Act which discriminates against Ms Evans on this ground [infertility]. It is the Act which, conditionally, seeks to reverse nature's discrimination. What are under attack in these proceedings are the conditions on which it does so' (para 72). However all three agreed that even if there was discrimination it was justifiable in order to protect Mr Johnston's rights.

Ms Evans took her case to the European Court of Human Rights and the Grand Chamber. Both courts accepted that Ms Evans's right to private life under article 8 was applicable to the case. The court explained that this case involved 'sensitive moral and ethical issues' and that there was 'no clear common ground amongst the member states' (at [62]). This meant that states had a wide margin of appreciation of this issue. The UK law, in not allowing Ms Evans to implant the embryo, did not infringe the Convention, although neither would a law which would have allowed her to use the embryo. The European Courts accepted that in this case there was a clash between the article 8 rights of Mr Johnson and of Ms Evans. In essence, Ms Evans was asserting the right to be a parent and Mr Johnson the right not to be a parent. The UK law had struck a balance between these two rights which could not be said to exceed their margin of appreciation. It was important in cases of this kind that there was legal certainty and that there was public confidence in the provision of assisted reproductive services. Both of these policies justified the UK's approach.

The case, as an interpretation of the HFE Act, was relatively uncontroversial. However, the human rights issues were less straightforward. The Court of Appeal's conclusion that the article 8 rights of Ms Evans and Mr Johnston were approximately equal is also controversial. Although both the alleged right to implant the embryo and thereby become a mother and the alleged right to destroy the embryo and thereby avoid becoming a father could be said to be an aspect of the right to respect for private and family life under article 8, but this did not mean that the alleged rights were equal. Many people will agree with Thorpe LJ that these were incommensurate. Only the most hard-hearted can fail to find sympathy with Ms Evans being denied the only chance she had to have a child of her own. But many will also sympathize with Mr Johnston's principled objection to becoming a father against his wishes. One could go back to what is at the heart of the rights claimed here. In essence this is the right of autonomy: the right to live your life as you wish. It is common to talk in terms of encouraging people to find and live out their version of the 'good life' free from interference from the state. This provides us some benchmark against which to measure these competing rights. Would it be a greater setback to their version of living their 'good life' for Ms Evans to be denied having the child she so desperately wanted, or for Mr Johnston to have to live his life knowing there was a child of his whom he did not know and in whose life he was not able to play an effective role?[115]

---

[115] C. Morris (2007); Lind (2006); Alghrani (2005); and Sheldon (2004) discuss the reasoning in the cases.

What the case most certainly demonstrates is the importance of ensuring that couples are properly counselled before embarking on treatment, to ensure they have considered the consequences of the forms they are signing. The Government has recently announced that there will be a consultation over whether the law needs to be altered in the way it deals with cases such as *Evans*.

6 Criticisms of HFEA

We will now consider the criticisms that have been made of the HFEA. Although they amount to a long list it should be emphasized at the start that in fact the HFEA has many supporters. It has overseen the regulation of a highly controversial and rapidly expanding area of science, without obviously losing the support of the general public or Parliament.[116] Indeed it is cited around the world as a model of regulation. So although more space will be dedicated to its criticisms than its praises, that reveals the fact that critics tend to be more vocal than supporters.

6.1 Quality control concerns

There is a wide variation in the success rates of different clinics around the country. This has led to complaints that the HFEA is failing to ensure there is sufficiently high quality across the board and is failing to advise patients of the differences in services offered. An HFEA report found the average success rate for IVF for women under 35 to be just 27.6 per cent, but that some clinics were achieving success rates at double this level and others at significantly below. Of course, such statistics must be treated with some caution. Some clinics may be willing to take on couples who are 'difficult cases' with a low chance of success and others may be more strict in their selection criteria. There may also be other socio-economic factors that influence a clinic's success rate. A low rate does not necessarily indicate bad practice. That said, the levels of difference are so great that it is difficult to avoid the conclusion that there must be a difference in the quality of service being offered. The HFEA has admitted that until its recent report there had not been sufficient information for patients to make an informed decision about which clinic to use for treatment.[117]

6.2 'Adverse events'

There have been a number of 'adverse events' at licensed clinics. In 2004 an Independent Review was carried out into four of these.[118] The report found that the HFEA's relationship with clinics had developed a culture in which it had become difficult for the licensing committees to censure centres who were not complying with guidelines. The report suggested, *inter alia*, the use of external specialist inspectors to assist in the inspection process. As this report indicates, there are concerns about the effectiveness of the inspection system.[119]

---

116 See Callus (2007) on attitudes among the general public towards the HFEA.
117 BBC Newsonline (24 May 2005).   118 Toft (2004).
119 Some examples are found in House of Commons Science and Technology Committee (2005: 227–8).

6.3 'Pro-life concerns'

Predictably the HFEA has been criticized by pro-life groups for not adequately promoting respect for the embryo.[120] It has been too ready to permit research and ART that involves the destruction of embryos which are regarded by many as having a right to life. The complaint is sometimes made that HFEA is under the thumb of scientists wishing to make ever greater advances, without protecting the interests of the unborn child.

6.4 Restrictions on research

From another perspective the HFEA has been criticized for being too restrictive. A leading critic from this point of view has been Lord Robert Winston who has described the HFEA as 'incompetent'.[121] He has complained about the organization being too bureaucratic and hindering research.[122] For example, he states that his clinic, which handles just over 1,000 patients a year, has to employ two people full time just to deal with the paperwork required by the HFEA. The HFEA's investigations are haphazard, he complains, with the same procedures being praised by one inspection team and then criticized by another.[123] It is perhaps fair to add that these kinds of complaints echo those made by any professional subject to outside inspection.

6.5 The membership of the authority

There are concerns about the membership of the Authority.[124] The chair must be a lay person (ie someone not involved in reproductive medicine) and there must be a lay majority on the Authority. There are between six and nine professional members of the Authority, but that means that there are restrictions on the range of expertise. It has been noted, for example, that for much of the time the HFEA has not had a clinical embryologist as a member.[125] That said, the number of lay members means that a wider range of different perspectives can be brought to issues.

6.6 A conflict in roles

There are concerns that the HFEA is in the difficult position of both regulating and advising clinics. The HFEA is required both to enforce the provisions of the HFE Act and issue regulations, while at the same time advising the Government whether there are problems with the legislation.[126] This is seen as particularly problematic because one of the requirements to be a member of the HFEA is that one is broadly sympathetic to the aims of the HFE Act.

---

[120] SPUC (2000).   [121] BBC Newsonline (10 December 2004).
[122] Winston (2005).   [123] Winston (2005).
[124] The HFE Act, Sch 1 sets out the requirements of membership.
[125] House of Commons Science and Technology Committee (2005: para 196).
[126] House of Commons Science and Technology Committee (2005: para 209).

6.7 Reform of the HFEA

In the light of these and other criticisms the House of Commons Select Committee (by a bare majority) recommended radical reform:

> We propose that the current regulatory model, which provides the HFEA with a large amount of policy-making flexibility, should be replaced with a system which devolves clinical decision-making and technical standards down to patients and professionals while at the same time strengthening Parliamentary and ethical oversight. This system has three strands: a dedicated Government regulator to ensure high standards of treatment; professional regulation to ensure the highest level of conduct by practitioners; and a system of ethical oversight.[127]

The Government has responded to this report by indicating a willingness to reform the HFE Act, but not in such a liberal way as recommended by the Committee.

7 Access to treatment

If we were to take the right to reproductive autonomy seriously then any person who came forward for treatment would have a right to it unless there were very strong reasons why they should not.[128] In fact in England and Wales there are a number of barriers to accessing treatment and we shall consider these now:[129]

7.1 Financial restrictions

Perhaps the major bar to ART at present is financial. The NHS provision of assisted reproduction is patchy and presently there is no consistent approach taken.[130] In 2006 only 25 per cent of IVF treatment was funded by the NHS. In many areas the NHS offers no assisted reproductive treatment and therefore couples seeking it must use the private sector. Of course that is only an option for those with the funds to pay for it. At around £8,000 for a cycle of IVF it is not cheap.[131] Even where the treatment is offered on the NHS there can be significant waiting times. Indeed the Government has admitted that whether or not one receives ART under the NHS can be a 'postcode lottery'.[132] At present three out of four couples receiving IVF treatment pay for it.[133]

The National Institute for Health and Clinical Excellence (NICE) has looked at the issue of provision of assisted reproductive services in the NHS and has recommend that a woman who satisfies the following two criteria should be offered up to three cycles of IVF:

- she is aged between 23 and 39 years at the time of treatment;
- she has an identified cause for fertility problems (such as azoospermia or bilateral tubal occlusion) or infertility of at least three years' duration.

To satisfy this requirement will impose a significant financial burden on primary care trusts. The Department of Health has taken the view that it is not possible to meet the

---

[127] House of Commons Science and Technology Committee (2005: para 390).
[128] Peterson (2005b).   [129] See Riley (2007).   [130] Riley (2007).
[131] HFEA (2007d); Riley (2007: 84).   [132] DoH (2000d).
[133] BBC Newsonline (30 June 2004).

NICE recommendations immediately, but that each primary care trust should offer:

- all women aged 23–39 years who meet the NICE clinical criteria a minimum of one full cycle of IVF from April 2005. In the longer term it is expected that primary care trusts will progress towards fully implementing NICE guidance;
- priority should be given to couples who do not already have a child living with them.

The reference to meeting the NICE guidelines only in the 'longer term' will worry some and indicates that the Government is not willing to put in the funding to ensure that infertile couples should receive the treatment NICE suggests they should. Indeed press reports suggest that ten Primary Care Trusts are still not funding any ART[134] and many are failing to follow the NICE guidance.[135] An issue not directly addressed by the Department of Health announcement is waiting times. In 2005 a survey found that in one in ten primary health care trusts, waiting times for ART were over two years.[136] In only one in ten was it one year or less. Another concern is that some clinics who were offering a better service than the DoH suggestions had reduced their service to be in line with the DoH guidelines.[137]

Critics of the ready availability of fertility treatment will point to the fact that the amount of fertility treatment offered in the UK is falling behind other Northern European Countries. During 2000 there were 580 cycles of fertility treatment per million people. In other Northern European countries it was 1,057 per million.[138] Indeed it has been suggested that we may well witness a growth in 'fertility tourism' as IVF treatment in other countries is reported to be significantly cheaper than the UK.[139]

Even the most ardent supporter of reproductive autonomy would accept that it is not realistic for the NHS to offer unlimited reproductive treatment to everyone who wants it. Emily Jackson asks simply that any restrictions be reasonable and fair.[140] Margaret Brazier reminds us that calls for reproductive autonomy must be matched by other calls on NHS resources:

> one woman's right to reproduce would have to be weighed against her mother's right to preventive care to ensure breast cancer is detected early enough, against her grandmother's need for a hip-replacement, against perhaps her great grandmother's life itself.[141]

As this quote indicates, there is a real danger that for all the bold talk of reproductive autonomy it may not be affordable by the NHS. Then the right of reproductive autonomy in this context will join that shameful list of rights that are rights for the rich alone. And if they are rights for the rich alone should they be called rights at all?

7.2 The welfare of the child

Before a clinic can provide infertility treatment to a couple or individual it must consider the HFE Act, section 13(5), which states:

> A woman shall not be provided with treatment services unless account has been taken of the welfare of any child who may be born as a result of the treatment (including the need of that child for a father), and of any other child who may be affected by the birth.

---

[134] BBC Newsonline (19 July 2005).
[135] BBC Newsonline (6 August 2007). HM Government (2007a) has announced it will be monitoring the provision of IVF around the country.
[136] BBC Newsonline (1 April 2005).   [137] Barron (2005).   [138] ESHRE (2004).
[139] Pennings (2002: 337); Blyth and Farrand (2005).
[140] Jackson (2001: 196).   [141] Brazier (1998: 74).

In 2005 the HFEA[142] produced guidance which made it clear that clinics should only refuse treatment if the child is likely to be at risk of serious harm. Factors that can be considered include whether the woman or her partner have convictions related to harming children; whether there is a history of violence within the family; the mental and physical health of the woman and her partner (if any); and any alcohol or drug misuse. The Government intends to remove the reference to the need for a father in the Human Fertilisation and Embryology Bill 2007. The 2007 code no longer requires clinics to consider the stability of the relationship and the age of the parties.[143]

For supporters of reproductive autonomy rights these provisions are objectionable. A number of objections are made:

(i) They require the clinic to assess the parental fitness of infertile individuals wanting to have children when we do not do this for couples who wish to have children by sexual intercourse. There is in this way an improper discrimination against infertile people.

(ii) Section 13(5) is based on an assumption, which some believe unfounded, that a child has a need for a father.[144] This discriminates against lesbian couples and single women seeking treatment, it is claimed.[145]

(iii) It requires the clinic to ask an unanswerable question: how can anyone know whether someone else will make a good parent or not? This is guesswork and the test is simply an invitation to prejudice. In any event clinicians are not social workers and have no training in assessing parenting skills. Even if they did have the skills, how are they to get evidence to make an effective decision?

(iv) The test is meaningless. How can it not be in the interests of the child to be born?[146] Perhaps if the child's life was destined to be a short life full of pain, but in such a case no clinic would offer treatment. The section does not explain precisely what the clinic is meant to be asking itself. The section states that the child's welfare need only be taken into account; it is not a 'paramount consideration' as is often the case in child law.[147] This seems to suggest that it might be appropriate to give treatment even if in some sense this was not in any potential child's interests. But can that have been Parliament's intention?

(v) There appear to be inconsistencies in the way that the provision is interpreted by clinics.[148] Some use it to justify a policy of not offering treatment to single women; others do not so interpret it.

(vi) The provisions appear to be rarely used to deny treatment. It has been reported that clinics have used this provision in between 0 and 0.3 per cent of cases to deny treatment.[149]

---

[142] HFEA (2005b).   [143] HFEA (2007c).

[144] HM Government (2007a) on reviewing the evidence found that it was the quality of the parenting, rather than the gender of the parent that mattered to the child.

[145] See Riley (2007: 87) for some evidence of discrimination against lesbian couples.

[146] Indeed at least one philosopher argues it is true of everyone that it would have been better for them not to have existed (Benatar (2006b)).

[147] Children Act 1989, s 1.

[148] House of Commons Science and Technology Committee (2005: 95); HFEA (2004a: 8); Douglas (1993).

[149] House of Commons Science and Technology Committee (2005: 96).

The logic of the arguments in favour of reproductive autonomy would be that there should be no restrictions on who can receive reproductive assistance. So even if there was a couple seeking treatment with a history of child abuse they should receive treatment. After all if they were fertile there would be nothing the state could do to stop them having children. Of course, in such a case, the baby may be removed from the couple at birth. Hence Emily Jackson has written:

> if we respect the procreative choices of alcoholics, and people with record of violence and abuse, even when we know that their children are likely to be disadvantaged, is it disingenuous to require infertile people to satisfy a conceptually incoherent version of the welfare principle prior to reproducing?[150]

Opponents of reproductive autonomy question whether it can be right to deliberately provide treatment to a couple knowing that their child will be removed from them soon after birth. We do not prevent utterly unsuitable people from conceiving children naturally because we cannot: but where we can, we should.

To others the present law is too weak to be of use. Some support a far stricter approach on who can receive assisted reproductive help. As in adoption, we should be confident that the couple are in a stable relationship and are fit to raise the child well. Others reject the analogy with adoption. In adoption the state has taken into its care a child whose parents cannot care for her or him and is looking for alternative carers. In such a scenario the state has a responsibility to find the best possible carers. In the case of assisted reproductive treatment there is no equivalent responsibility on the state. The analogy should be with children conceived by sexual intercourse where there is no attempt to regulate who can become a parent.

7.3 Single women

Should ART be offered to a single woman who has no partner at present and is intending to raise the child alone? A single woman may need assistance due to infertility problems of her own, or because she does not want to have sexual relations with a man. The HFEA has suggested that treatment can be offered, even in 'rare cases' with embryo donation.[151] The HFEA suggests that embryo donation to a single woman might be appropriate where a couple have successfully had IVF treatment and wish to give some of their surplus embryos to a single female friend of theirs; or where a couple have frozen embryos using their gametes, but their relationship has broken down and the man is happy for the woman to be given the embryos on the basis that he is not to be treated as the father. As shall be seen later, a child born using ART to a single woman may well have no father in the eyes of the law.

One issue is whether a child born to a single parent will suffer psychologically more than a child raised by two parents. Such a question is difficult to resolve on the statistics. It does seem to be true that children raised by single parents do less well than children raised by two according to a variety of indicators. However, this may be simply due to the economic and social deprivations suffered by many lone parents.[152] Further, there is clear evidence that children who are raised by a couple whose relationship is bad will suffer greatly. There are also those who are convinced that children will suffer without

---

[150] Jackson (2001: 195).   [151] HFEA (2003).

[152] HFEA (2004a: 5); MacCallum and Golombok (2004).

a clear male role model in their lives,[153] although even if a couple are married there is no reason to assume that the marriage will survive and that the husband will continue to provide a role model. It is worth noting that in the Parliamentary debates over the HFE Act a proposal that infertility treatment should only be offered to married couples was only defeated by one vote. Lord Walker in *Re D* stated that clinics were 'rightly cautious about providing assisted conception services for unmarried women'.[154] The Government has recently declared that as a general rule it is better for a child to be raised by two parents.[155] Of course to supporters of reproductive autonomy the key point would be that a woman can conceive a child through a one night stand and intend to raise it on her own without there being any state interference with that right. If a woman needs or wants ART to do the same, she should receive it.

7.4 Lesbian couples

When the HFE Act was passed the possibility of a lesbian couple receiving ART was a highly controversial issue. It is less so now. The Adoption and Children Act 2002 permits same-sex couples to adopt a child and the Civil Partnership Act 2005 provide official recognition for same-sex relationships. Evidence suggests that children raised in lesbian households do not suffer as compared with children raised in opposite sex couples.[156] That said, most of the studies have involved relatively small numbers of children and it would be wrong to suggest the case has been made beyond reasonable doubt. Interestingly one study found that children benefited from a greater degree of involvement from the mother's partner than on average a child raised by an opposite sex couple received from her or his father.[157] Although it is clear that some clinics do offer lesbian couples ART, there is evidence that some lesbian couples are deterred from approaching clinics for fear of how they will be treated and prefer to use unregulated methods.[158] In part this fear may spring from the existence of the HFE Act, section 13(5), which, it will be remembered, requires the clinic to consider the child's 'need' of a father. Further, the lesbian partner of a woman who becomes pregnant using ART will not be recognized as a parent of the child in the way that a male partner would be. The Government has initiated a consultation on whether the law on that needs to be changed.[159]

7.5 Age

There is some debate over whether or not age should be a factor in deciding whether or not to offer treatment.[160] The HFEA Code of Practice states simply that 'the age, health and ability to provide for the needs of a child/children'[161] should be taken into account. The NICE guidance recommendations only apply to women aged below 39. However, one survey found that only 35 per cent of clinics used that age as their upper age limit for offering treatment.[162] It is clear that most clinics will not offer treatment to older women and particularly post-menopausal women. In *R v Sheffield AHA ex p Seale*[163] it

---

[153] Catholic Bishops' Conference (2004).
[154] *In re D (A Child Appearing by her Guardian ad Litem)* [2005] UKHL 33, para 35.
[155] DoH (2005f: 28).   [156] Brewaeys (2003).   [157] Brewaeys et al (1997).
[158] Wallbank (2004).   [159] DoH (2005f: 62).
[160] See Cutas (2007) and Biggs (2007b) of a discussion of the issues raised by enabling older women to become mothers.
[161] Para 3.12.   [162] Brown (2005).   [163] (1994) 25 BMLR 1.

was held that a ban on women over 35 receiving ART was justified on the basis that the chances of treatment being successful decreased once a woman was over that age. There are reports of a woman aged 67 become a mother using ART in Romania.[164]

It is important to distinguish two reasons why age may be relevant. The first is that the chances of success of assisted reproductive services greatly reduce as age increases.[165] The second is that any child born may suffer from having a parent older than normal. Robert Winston has suggested:

> Children should reasonably expect that their parents should be young enough to indulge in the pursuits which are all part of growing up with their family.[166]

Critics respond that there are no such considerations when a couple is seeking to have a child 'naturally'. No one questions whether they are too old to have children. In particular men have been known to father children at a great age. Mine worker Les Colley is said to have fathered a child at 93. This is rarely seen as irresponsible, but rather a sign of their continuing virility. Indeed it has been pointed out that not many decades ago a woman's average life expectancy was 47 and so there was by no means a guarantee that a mother would live to see her child's teenage years.[167] Would we say it was immoral for mothers in that era to give birth?

A factor which has received less attention is young women seeking ART. Apparently teenagers have been seeking ART, having not been able to conceive after over two years of sexual activity.[168] Notably the NICE guidelines put the lower age at which their guidelines should apply at 23.

7.6 Genetic conditions

If the parents suffer from a genetic condition and if granted ART there is, say, a 25 per cent or 50 per cent chance that the child born will inherit the condition, does that justify not providing the couple with treatment? It is unlikely that a clinic would be willing to offer them treatment. Again the point could be made that if they were fertile there would be no restriction on them producing a child through sexual intercourse; should there be one imposed because they need medical assistance? Certainly some commentators have suggested that it would be immoral to have a child, knowing that child was likely to suffer from a disadvantageous genetic condition.[169]

7.7 Revisiting the welfare question

The HFEA has announced a review of the operation of the welfare test in the HFE Act. There are four alternatives, although the HFEA is only considering the first three:

(i) *The maximum welfare principle.* This is an approach which suggests that medical professionals should not intentionally help others to bring a child into the world unless there are ideal circumstances, or at least a very good chance that the child will live a happy life with no foreseeable disadvantages. This approach would be seen as similar to that used when selecting parents to adopt a child.

---

[164] Cutas (2007).   [165] De Wert (1998).
[166] Quoted in Harris (1999: 20). Harris comments that he expects the remark would be offensive to disabled parents.
[167] Jackson (1999).   [168] Anon (2004a).   [169] Purdy (1999).

(ii) *Reasonable welfare principle*. Assisted conception should be offered when the child born will have a reasonably happy life.

(iii) *Minimum threshold principle*. A doctor should only deny treatment if the quality of the child's life fell below a minimum threshold of acceptability. It might, for example, be that where a child would suffer significant harm if born, then treatment should not be offered.[170]

(iv) *No welfare test*. It would be wrong ever to deny treatment to a couple based on the welfare of the future child. This is not a criterion used to prevent fertile couples having children and so it should not be used to prevent infertile ones.

8 Parentage

8.1 The legal position

In family law the rules as to who is the parent of a child used to be relatively straightforward.[171] The woman who gives birth to the child is the mother and the man presumed to be the genetic father was the father. The presumptions used in relation to paternity (that the husband of the mother was the father of the child) are less important now that DNA tests can be performed if there is any question over paternity. However, these rules do not operate satisfactorily in the context of assisted reproduction and so the HFE Act developed some special rules in relation to paternity.[172] These can be summarized as follows:

(i) The mother is the woman who gives birth to the child even if she became pregnant using donated eggs.[173] So even though the woman does not have a genetic link to the child the fact she has carried the child through pregnancy and given birth entitles her to be the mother. In a case involving donated eggs the donor will have no legal rights in respect of the child.

(ii) Who is the child's father in cases involving donated sperm? We need to consider three categories of men in a case where a woman gives birth using donated sperm:

(a) *The sperm donor*. Where a donor's gametes are used in accordance with his consent, as required by schedule 3, he is not to be treated as the father of the child: HFE Act, section 28(6)(a). A sperm donor therefore need not fear potential claims under the Child Support Act or other parental liabilities.

(b) *The husband of the woman*.[174] Under the HFE Act, section 28(2) if a married women gives birth using donated sperm then her husband will be treated in law as the father of the child unless he can prove:

(1) he is not the genetic father of the child and

(2) he did not consent to the placing of the embryo into her.

---

[170] See Blyth (2007) who promotes this approach relying on the ECHR.

[171] In family law an important distinction is drawn between being a parent and having parental responsibility. Here we are simply considering who will be regarded as a parent.

[172] Bridge (1999) provides a useful discussion of the rules of paternity.

[173] HFE Act 1990, s 27(1) .

[174] These rules cannot apply if the marriage is void or a non-marriage: *J v C (Void Marriage: Status of Children)* [2006] 2 FLR 1098.

As the standard practice for clinics is to require the written consent of a married patient's husband it will be very rare for a husband not to be treated as a father under this provision.[175]

(c) *The partner of the woman*. If a man is receiving treatment services together with a woman using donated sperm, that man will be treated as the father of the child. The phrase 'receiving treatment services together' does not require that the man actually receive medical treatment, but rather that he and the woman attend the clinic as part of a joint enterprise to produce a child together.[176] This provision can only be relied upon where the couple have attended a licensed clinic.[177]

(iii) A child can be legally fatherless. If a child is born with the use of donated sperm and the mother is unmarried and without a partner then the child will have no father. However, Hale LJ in *Re R (a Child)*[178] said that it is in a child's interests, if possible to have a father. Not least, perhaps, so that the child will have a greater chance of receiving adequate child support.

(iv) A child cannot have more than one mother or one father (save in the case of adoption). The HFE Act, section 28(4) makes it clear that where the husband or partner of the woman is treated as the father, no other man will be the father.

The two leading case interpreting these provisions are the following, which demonstrate the complexities which can result:

KEY CASE   Leeds Teaching Hospital v A [2003] 1 FLR 1091

Mr and Mrs A and Mr and Mrs B both attended an assisted conception clinic in Leeds to receive infertility treatment. For both couples the intention was to use the eggs of the wife and inject into them the sperm of the husband. Due to a mistake Mrs A's eggs were mixed with Mr B's sperm. The resulting embryo was placed in Mrs A and healthy twins born. The mix up with the sperm came to light because Mr A and Mrs A were white, while Mr and Mrs B were black. DNA tests confirmed that Mr B was the genetic father of the twins. Mr B had no contact with the twins and did not wish to play an active role in their lives. Mr A, however, was happy to perform the role as father and wished to be legally recognized as such.

The key question for the court was who should be regarded as the child's father. At the heart of Dame Butler-Sloss's reasoning is the holding that as a basic principle the genetic father of a child is the legal father of the child, unless there is a statutory provision which displaces that principle. This meant that Mr B was to be regarded as the father of the child unless there was a provision in the HFE Act which led the court to conclude otherwise.

The court first considered Mr B's position and considered whether he could claim not to be a father because he was a sperm donor under section 28(6)(a). The difficulty the court found in accepting this argument was that the section only applies where the sperm is used in accordance with the donor's

---

[175] This provision appears from its wording only to apply to cases where donated sperm is used within a licensed clinic. However, Lloyd LJ in *Re N (a child)* [2007] EWCA Civ 1053 seemed to think it could apply in a case outside the context of licensed treatment, but he was not supported by the two other judges in the Court of Appeal.

[176] *In re D (A Child Appearing by her Guardian ad Litem)* [2005] UKHL 33.

[177] *U v W* [1998] 1 FCR 526.   [178] [2003] 1 FCR 481 para 27.

consent. In this case it had not been: he had consented to the use of his sperm to fertilize one of his wife's eggs. He therefore could not rely on section 28(6)(a).

The court then considered whether Mr A could claim to be the father relying on section 28(2). He was, after all, the husband of the mother and he had consented to her receiving the treatment. However, the court rejected this argument. Although he had consented to her receiving treatment, he had not consented to her receiving *this treatment* (ie an embryo using another man's sperm). He therefore could not claim to be the father under section 28(2).

What about Mr A claiming to be the father under section 28(3) based on the fact he was receiving treatment services together with his wife? Dame Butler Sloss concluded that section 28(3) only applied to unmarried couples and so could not be relied upon by Mr A.

This led to the conclusion that Mr B was the legal father of the child. Mr and Mrs A were, however, free to adopt the child, terminating Mr B's parental status.

KEY CASE   In re D (A Child Appearing by her Guardian ad Litem) [2005] UKHL 33

The mother, D, gave birth to a daughter, R. D's former partner, B, promptly made an application for contact and parental responsibility orders in respect of the child. D had initially attended the clinic with B as her partner and they had been approved for treatment together. They signed forms accepting that they would be receiving treatment services together. Subsequently D and B separated, but the clinic was not informed of this and they continued to provide assisted reproductive services to D. D formed a relationship with S and he supported her through the next stages of the treatment and was still with her. A key question for the House of Lords was whether B was R's father, relying on section 28(3).

The first question for their Lordships was the meaning of 'receiving treatment services together'. Lord Hope explained that the phrase 'treatment services together' did not require the man to be receiving medical treatment himself. Rather 'that this is in reality a joint enterprise—that the treatment is being sought by the woman and the man together because they both wish to receive the benefit of the treatment to bring a child into being jointly as their child' (para 11).

The next question for their Lordships was, for the purposes of section 28(3), when did the couple need to show they were receiving treatment services together: when the couple were approved for treatment by the clinic or when the embryo was implanted into D?

Lord Hope answered that question in this way:

> The language of the subsection tells us that the man shall be treated as the father if the embryo or the sperm and eggs 'were placed' in the woman, or she 'was' artificially inseminated, 'in the course of treatment services provided for her and the man together. These words make it plain that the point of time is the time when the embryo or the sperm and eggs were placed in the woman or she was artificially inseminated.

This meant that although B could claim he was receiving treatment services together with D when they first approached the clinic, he was not at the crucial time when the embryo or sperm and eggs were placed into D.

There was, however, a further question: in considering whether D and B were receiving treatment services together at the time of implantation, from whose perspective do we consider this? The argument on B's behalf was that from the clinic's understanding they were still treating D and B as a couple, even at the time of implantation.

Lord Hope rejected this argument and held that:

> whether the treatment services were being provided for the woman and the man together at the relevant time simply raises a question of fact which must be determined by the judge in the light of all the evidence. The perspective of the clients is therefore to be treated as part of the relevant evidence. So too is the perspective of the provider of the services, as demonstrated by the records which the provider has kept as required by the licensing authority. Neither has any priority over the other in terms of the statute. Each is as vulnerable to human error, deceit, mistake or misunderstanding as the other. To elevate one over the other when the statute does not clearly require this would be to create an unnecessary gloss. It could result in a decision which was imposed on the man by default and which, when looked at in the light of all the evidence, was quite wrong. (para 19)

On the facts of this case D and B were no longer a couple and could not be said to be receiving treatment services together. Lord Walker accepted that the test was not as certain as an approach which looked at the paperwork which had been signed, but stated:

> But important though legal certainty is, it is even more important that the very significant legal relationship of parenthood should not be based on a fiction (especially if the fiction involves a measure of deception by the mother). (para 42)

So, it was S who was R's father, because he had been receiving treatment services with the defendant at the time of the implementation.

The result in the *Re D* decision may be regarded as common sense: to regard B as the father when he would have neither a genetic tie nor be involved in the upbringing of the child would seem nonsensical. However, there are some concerns about the case.[179] The clinic here had assessed the couple (D and B) and decided it was appropriate to offer them treatment together. We do not know whether the clinic would have permitted D alone to receive treatment, nor whether they would have offered treatment to D and S. Her failure to tell the clinic of her separation meant the clinic was deprived of the chance to assess the couple.[180] On the other hand, as we have seen, many commentators take the view that it would be improper to refuse to permit a woman to receive treatment simply because she was unpartnered.

8.2 What should make someone a parent?

The rules on assisted reproduction and parenthood are controversial and highlight the complex issue of what makes someone a parent.[181] There are four main theories:

(i) *Genetic link*. There are those who argue that we should take a strict approach and declare that a parent is the person with the genetic link to the child. That would mean that the sperm donor was the child of the father. Some may find that unpalatable but quite simply that is the truth. As Daniel Callahan has put it: 'Fatherhood, because it is a biological condition, cannot be abrogated by personal desires or legal decisions.'[182]

179 Fovargue (2006).   180 Lind (2003).
181 See Horsey (2007) for a useful discussion.   182 Callahan (1992a: 739).

Supporters of this view would object to the allocation of parenthood in the HFE Act. They would suggest that husbands and partners of women who become pregnant using donated sperm should be given parental responsibility, but not receive the status of being a parent.

A slightly different argument is that we have responsibilities towards our genetic off-spring. A sperm donor who therefore gives his sperm with no concern about any result-ing child is not showing sufficient respect for this moral responsibility.[183] The HFE Act encourages such irresponsibility. However, it might be thought that in giving sperm to a responsible licensed clinic, a donor can be confident that it will be used to assist a couple who desire a child and will care for her or him.

(ii) *Social parenthood*. There are those who argue that what makes someone a parent is not a mere biological link, but rather the day-to-day caring for the child: washing, feeding, clothing, and educating the child. It is the doing of the work of parenthood that earns the title of parent, not the genetic link which may indicate no more than a 'one night stand'. This approach would generally be supportive of the provisions in the HFE Act. For example, we can presume that the husband or partner of a woman under-going IVF will undertake some of the jobs of parenthood, while the sperm donor will not. To declare the husband the father is therefore justifiable.

(iii) *The intended parent*. There are those who argue that the person who is intended by those involved to be the parent should be the parent.[184] Again this theory can be used to explain some of the provisions in the HFE Act. The sperm donor is not intended by anyone involved to be the father, while the husband or partner is. The HFE Act can be said to ensure that the intended father is the father. Critics of this approach criticize its vagueness. You cannot decide to become a parent of a child just by intending to do so.

(iv) *Causation*. Rebecca Probert[185] has argued that those who are the primary cause of the child or who are best held as being responsible for the production of the child should be regarded as the parents. She accepts there may be many causers of a child: a sperm donor; the medical team; the couple seeking treatment. However, she regards the couple as being the primary causes and therefore being regarded as parents of a child born using donated sperm.

The complex notions of what is a parent may be threatened by yet further technological advances. Reproductive cloning and the use of artificial gametes[186] provide the possibil-ity of children being born genetically related to two people of the same sex, or indeed of being genetically related to only one person or more than two people. Our 'cereal box' family assumption that each child has one mother and one father may not last very long.

9 The Diane Blood case

Perhaps the case involving the HFEA which hit the headlines and generated more fur-ore than any other was that involving Diane Blood.[187]

---

183 Benatar (1999) and see the reply in Bayne (2003).   184 L. Hill (1991).
185 Probert (2004).   186 Newson and Smajdor (2005).
187 Morgan and Lee (1997).

KEY CASE R v Human Fertilisation and Embryology Authority ex p Blood [1997] 2 All ER 687 (CA)

Diane Blood and her husband had been trying for a child, when Mr Blood contracted meningitis and fell into a coma. Mrs Blood asked doctors to remove his sperm so that she could use it to have his child. The sperm was removed from the comatose Mr Blood shortly before his death but the HFEA refused to permit Mrs Blood to use it to have a child. The HFEA emphasized that under the HFE Act a person's gametes could only be used with her or his consent and that Mr Blood had never consented to the posthumous use of his sperm. Mrs Blood claimed that Mr Blood would have wanted his sperm to be removed had he known of the circumstances; after all they were seeking fertility treatment at the time of his death. However, the HFEA insisted that the HFE Act required written consent, indeed this is clear from Schedule 3, paragraphs 1 and 8. Mrs Blood then sought permission that she remove his sperm from the country so that she could use it in a clinic overseas and become pregnant there. The HFEA also refused to allow her to do that as that would be to allow her to circumvent the provisions of the HFE Act. When she challenged the HFEA's decision in court the HFEA's stance was upheld in relation to the decision that she should not be allowed to use her husband's sperm in the UK. However, the refusal to allow her to take the sperm overseas was overruled. She was entitled to take the sperm overseas under her rights regarding the free movement of goods under article 59 (as it was then) of the EC Treaty.

This she did and after receiving fertility treatment gave birth to two sons. She then started a campaign to be permitted to register Mr Blood as the father. She was eventually permitted to do this following the Human Fertilisation and Embryology (Deceased Fathers) Act 2003.

Some have argued that Mrs Blood's argument carried weight, that taking sperm from a comatose man is hardly a great wrong to him: he will not be aware of what has happened and that it is a reasonable presumption that if he had been able to express his views he would have consented.[188] Others, however, argue that a great wrong was done to Mr Blood when his sperm was removed without his consent. Had someone managed to remove sperm from a sleeping man without his consent this would be regarded as a serious wrong. It should be not different because Mr Blood was comatose rather than asleep.[189]

10 Gamete donation: anonymity

An issue of great controversy is whether children born using donated sperm should be able to discover the identity of the sperm donor.[190] Until recently such children only had access to the most limited of information: a child could discover whether she or he was born as a result of donated gametes and whether she or he was related to a person she or he intended to marry.[191] However the Human Fertilisation and Embryology Authority

---

[188] Harris (1998).   [189] The issue is debated in Orr and Siegler (2002) and Parker (2004).

[190] Blyth et al (1998).

[191] For donations since 1 July 2004 a wider range of non-identifying information such as hair colour can be provided. HM Government (2007a) proposes a change to the law to permit cohabiting couples to discover if they are born using the same donor's sperm.

(Disclosure of Donor Information) Regulations 2004[192] have provided children with access to a far greater range of information. However the regulations will only apply prospectively: to all donations from 1 April 2005. Children born as a result of donations after that date can apply, once they have reached the age of 18, to discover identifying information including:

- the donor's name (and name at birth, if different) and address;
- the donor's date of birth and the town or district of birth;
- the appearance of the donor;
- a short statement about the donor.

The regulations will *not* render a sperm or egg donor a parent in the eyes of the law, *nor* will they mean that they become liable for child support or take on other financial responsibilities. All they mean is that her or his identity can be discovered by a child.

This change in the law may not have as great an impact as may be thought. This is because children have no right to be told that they were born as a result of IVF.[193] Of course, if a child does not know she or he has been born using donated sperm she or he will not realize she or he could request the identify of the sperm donor. In fact, very few children are told about their genetic origins. In one study 8.6 per cent of children born using donated sperm had been told of that fact.[194] Where egg donation is involved there may be a greater degree of sharing of information not least because almost one third of egg donors are known to the couple before the donation.[195] The Government recently rejected calls to require parents to state on a child's birth certificate if the child was born using donated sperm.[196]

There are in fact some question marks over the position of those who donated before April 2005. Although the HFE Act appears to protect their anonymity there is an argument that children have rights under the Human Rights Act 1998 to identifying information. In *R (on the application of Rose) v Secretary of State for Health*[197] the court accepted that children born as a result of assisted reproduction had a right under article 8 ECHR to discover information about their genetic parentage. However a gamete donor who donated with the promise of anonymity also had a right under article 8 to protect their anonymity. The court was not required at that hearing to decide how these rights could be balanced. It is by no means clear how such a balancing exercise would be resolved by the courts.

The arguments in favour of allowing children access to the identity of their sperm donor 'fathers' or egg donor 'mothers' include the following:

(i) The identity of one's genetic parents forms a key part of many people's sense of themselves. This is reflected in, for example, the extent to which adopted people will try and find their genetic parents. Children born using donated sperm have spoken of being incomplete without the full knowledge of their genetic origins. However, it is not clear from research whether giving identifying information creates the feelings of

---

[192] SI 2004/1511.
[193] The Human Fertilisation and Embryology Bill 2007 will not as currently drafted change this. HM Government (2007a) preferred education of parents of the benefits of telling their children rather than compulsion.
[194] Golombok (2002).   [195] Abdallah et al (1998).
[196] BBC Newsonline (8 October 2007).   [197] [2002]3 FCR 731.

completeness that these individuals hope for.[198] The stories of donation are not likely to be as dramatic as those surrounding adoption, but are more likely to reveal a student donating sperm to generate beer money.[199]

(ii) A person's genetic background can nowadays contain important medical information. Denying access to information identifying a sperm donor would deprive an individual about important information about their medical background. However, it may be that the medical information could be provided in a way which would not reveal the identity of the donor, in the sense of giving their name.

(iii) Children have a right not be deceived as to their genetic origins. John Eekelaar has asked whether anyone would like to be brought up deceived as to their genetic origins.[200] He thinks not. On the other hand one might argue that there are occasions in which we would rather not know the truth. Would one want to know the genetic truth if it would destroy the image of the happy childhood one has grown up with?

(iv) There does appear amongst the general public a genuine concern that a child born using donated sperm might meet and fall in love with someone born from sperm from the same donor (a blood half-brother or sister).[201] Although this fear may be generated more by the stories of soap operas than statistics, openness about genetic background would alleviate this concern.

The arguments against allowing children access to the information include the following:

(i) Donors have a right of privacy. It is noticeable that the new regulations will only apply prospectively and so donors who in the past donated on the understanding that their identity would be kept secret will have their rights respected, unless the Human Rights Act 1998 provides a challenge. In future donors will be made aware that children born using their sperm will be able to discover their identity and so donors can hardly claim an infringement of rights if the information is disclosed.

(ii) Couples who used donated sperm may be very wary about their children being able to discover their genetic origins. Such information may undermine family relationships if the child does not regard her or his legal father as her or his 'real father'.[202] There was evidence that when Sweden changed its law removing the anonymity of sperm donors a large number of Swedish couples went abroad to countries which retained the anonymity.[203] Indeed the Select Committee of the House of Commons heard that of the 260 children born to Swedes each year using ART 200 are conceived abroad.[204] Of course, whether the wishes of infertile couples should trump the 'rights of the child to know her genetic origins' is a matter of debate.

(iii) The removal of anonymity would create a significant disincentive for people to donate. Supporters of the new regulations claim that although the kinds of people who wish to donate may change there will not be a significant drop in the numbers donating. This can be a problem in particular because at present there are attempts to 'match' the donor and the infertile person so that the donor and person will be from the same ethnic

---

[198] Turner and Coyle (2001) and McWhinnie (2001).
[199] Deech (1998).   [200] Eekelaar (1994).
[201] Edwards (1999).   [202] Roberts (2000).
[203] Jackson (2001: 213). It has been claimed that ships will be moored off British waters offering insemination for those wishing to use 'anonymous sperm' BBC Newsonline (16 September 2005).
[204] House of Commons Science and Technology Committee (2005: para 154).

group and even (apparently) the same hair colour.[205] It appears there has been a significant drop in the number of donors coming forward from the time the Department of Health announced its proposals in relation to anonymity.[206] One clinic has reported a drop from 27 donors to one from 1992 to 2000.[207] The number of men donating sperm has reportedly fallen from 544 in 1991/92, to 222 in 2002/03. The Government has produced a publicity campaign to encourage new people to come forward to donate gametes. It is entitled 'give life, give hope'. The campaign cost £300,000 but produced only 486 calls to the telephone number given for those interested in donating.[208] However, in the year ending 13 March 2006 there was a 6 per cent increase in the number of men registering as sperm donors.[209] Still, the HFEA accepts there are severe shortages of sperm and eggs and long delays.[210] In 2006 there were 295 registered sperm donors. This was an increase on the 2004 figure of 247 but below the rates in 2001 of 328.[211] The HFEA have said that a single donor should not provide gametes for more than ten children.[212] It is too early to know if the controversial 'give a toss' campaign, aimed at finding a new batch of sperm donors, has been successful. One option that has been mooted involves bulk imports of sperm from Denmark.[213] If the beer adverts are correct and the Danes get nasty when learning of the export of their beer who knows what their reaction will be if they get to hear of this!

(iv) There are those who argue that we should reject the idea that genetic parenthood is of importance. What makes a parent is not a genetic link, which may be at most the result of the most casual of relationships, but rather the day-to-day hands-on aspect of parenting. A man with no genetic link to a child can be just as good a father as one who has none.[214] To encourage people to think that genetic links are important is to encourage an outdated idea of parenthood. Feelings of being incomplete without knowledge of one's genetic identity are social constructions and need to be challenged not pampered.[215] As Harris points out any two people share 99.90 per cent of their genes; indeed we share 50 per cent of our genes with bananas. The notion that one's genetic link with one's parents is of significance must therefore be challenged. However, whether socially conditioned or not and however illogical or not, the strong desire for knowledge of children born using donated sperm cannot be denied.

11 Payment for gamete donation

The HFEA does not prohibit the payment or giving of benefit in return for gametes but it is only permitted if authorized by directions issued by the HFEA. The HFEA has recommended that donors can receive payment in kind in the form of discounts for assisted reproductive services.[216] Sperm donors are normally paid (97 per cent of clinics paid sperm donors in one survey), while egg donors are normally not.[217] £15 is apparently the norm for sperm donors.[218] However the EU Tissues and Cells Directive requires that gametes should only be supplied on a not-for-profit basis. Article 12 of the

---

[205] Anon (2004a).
[206] House of Commons Science and Technology Committee (2005: para 152).
[207] Anon (2005).   [208] The Daily Telegraph (2005).   [209] HFEA (2007a).
[210] HFEA (2005).   [211] HFEA (2007e).   [212] HFEA (2005c).
[213] BBC (21 October 2003).   [214] Golombok et al (2005).   [215] Harris (2003a).
[216] HFEA (2005c).   [217] Stauch and Wheat (2004: 406).   [218] Jackson (2001: 218).

Directive says that 'donors may receive compensation which is strictly limited to making good the expenses and inconveniences related to the donation'. But it also requires Member States to 'endeavour to ensure voluntary and unpaid donations of tissues and cells'. So it may be that in the future payment as such will cease, although compensation for inconvenience will be available. On the other hand, the HFEA has indicated that it supports planned increases in payments to donors of sperm and eggs to £250, in order to increase supply.[219]

There has been some debate over whether donors of gametes should be paid.[220] It is noticeable that the role of payment plays a startlingly different role depending on whether donors are male or female. Seventy-one per cent of sperm donors in one survey reported being influenced by payments, while almost all of the egg donors were influenced solely by a desire to help others.[221] The small amount of money available may reflect the fact that the typical sperm donor is a student wanting extra beer money,[222] whereas the typical egg donor knows someone who has infertility problems and is wanting to help them or others like them.

The reason for paying donors is principally that without them the number of donors of sperm would fall. It has been suggested that 80 per cent of sperm donors would stop donating if there was no payment.[223] It may be, however, that if the change in the rules on anonymity means that a different kind of person donates, then they will be less interested in payment. Indeed in Sweden where anonymity was lifted a recent survey suggested that the new crop of donors is not motivated by payment.[224]

If a woman seeking IVF is unable to afford the treatment she may be asked whether she is interested in donating her eggs in return for a reduction of the costs of the IVF treatment. Critics claim that calling this 'egg sharing' disguises the reality that this is payment for eggs.[225] There are also, it is claimed, a host of potential psychological difficulties with the idea. What if the woman engages in egg sharing and, while her treatment is unsuccessful, the treatment using her eggs succeeds for someone else? Despite these concerns one study found that 65 per cent of women who had engaged in egg sharing would be willing to do it again.[226] However, one might be concerned at the 35 per cent who would not.

12 Surrogacy

12.1 The definition of surrogacy

Surrogacy was defined in the Warnock Report as 'the practice whereby one woman carries a child for another with the intention that the child should be handed over after birth'.[227] In practice the child is handed over within a day of the birth.[228] A distinction is often made between a partial and full surrogacy. In a partial surrogacy the eggs of the commissioning mother are fertilized and place into the surrogate, whereas in full surrogacy the surrogate mother's eggs are used and so she is both the genetic and gestational mother. One writer has claimed that there are 100 surrogate births a year.[229]

[219] BBC Newsonline (6 October 2005).   [220] Daniels (2000); Draper (2007).
[221] Cook and Golombok (1996).   [222] British Fertility Society (1996).
[223] HFEA (1996).   [224] Lalos et al (2003).   [225] Lieberman (2005).
[226] Ahuja et al (1997).   [227] Warnock (1984: para 8.1).
[228] Jadva et al (2003) and MacCallum et al (2003).   [229] Laurance (2000).

12.2 Is surrogacy legal?

It is not illegal to enter a surrogacy arrangement, but there are a series of criminal offences connected with surrogacy:

- It is unlawful to negotiate or arrange a surrogacy arrangement on a commercial basis.[230] This does not prevent non-commercial groups facilitating surrogacy arrangements and there are some organizations that do that. These offences cannot be committed by the surrogate mother or commissioning parents.[231] The offences could be committed by a commercial organisation seeking to facilitate surrogacy arrangements.

- It is unlawful for anyone to advertise surrogacy services.[232]

- It is unlawful to make an offer that constitutes a reward or profit for the gestational mother, although she can be offered payment of expenses.[233]

Essentially, then, if a surrogacy arrangement is organized by an individual or a non-commercial body and there is no payment, surrogacy is legally permitted. However, even then the surrogacy arrangement is not enforceable. The Surrogacy Arrangement Act 1985, section 1A makes this absolutely clear:

> No surrogacy arrangement is enforceable by or against any of the persons making it.

It may be that those involved in a surrogacy arrangement wish to use a licensed clinic to assist in the conception. This is permissible but the HFEA code of practice is fairly strict. The clinic should only be involved in assisting a surrogacy arrangement if it is physically impossible or highly undesirable for medical reasons for the commissioning mother to carry the child.[234] So a clinic cannot assist a commissioning mother who wishes to use a surrogate to avoid the burdens of pregnancy. The clinic should also ensure that the parties are aware of the legal issues; consider whether there is likely to be a dispute concerning the child; and take into account the likely effect of the arrangement upon the child or a child of the family.[235]

The realities of surrogacy in Britain are that in most cases payments are made and these range from £10,000 to £15,000. Most surrogate mothers are on income support and most commissioning couples are comparatively wealthy.[236] In the US, by contrast, surrogacy is a booming commercial business, with commissioning couples being charged anywhere from $22,000 to $65,000.[237]

12.3 What is the legal position if a child is born under a surrogacy arrangement?

When a child is born using surrogacy the parental issues are dealt with as follows. The mother is the woman who carried the child.[238] The commissioning mother is not the mother, even if her eggs were used. The father will be the genetic father, unless he is a

---

[230] Surrogacy Arrangements Act 1985, s 2(1).
[231] Surrogacy Arrangements Act 1985, s 2(2).
[232] Surrogacy Arrangements Act 1985, s 3.
[233] *Re C (Application by Mr and Mrs X)* [2002] FL 351.
[234] Para 3.16.   [235] Brinsden et al (2000).
[236] Brazier (1999c: 180).   [237] Blyth and Potter (2003: 9).
[238] Contrast the position in California (*Johnson v Calvert* 286 Cal Repr 369, 372 Cal Ct App) where the commissioning couple were said to be the parents.

sperm donor. In *Re Q (A Minor) (Parental Order)*[239] an argument that the commissioning man was receiving treatment services with the surrogate mother and was therefore the father under the HFE Act, section 28 was rejected.

If the child is handed over and the commissioning parents wish to become recognized as the parents they have two main options: adoption or a parental order. A parental order can be applied for under the Human Fertilisation and Embryology Act 1990, section 30. To obtain the order the following must be shown:

(i) Either the sperm, or eggs, or both, came from the commissioning husband or wife.

(ii) The treatment that resulted in the pregnancy was provided by a licensed clinic.

(iii) The applicants must be married.

(iv) The applicants must both be over 18.

(v) At least one of the applicants must be domiciled in the UK.

(vi) The child must, at the time of the order, live with the applicants.

(vii) The order must be made within six months of the child's birth.

(viii) The father[240] must give full and unconditional consent to the making of the order.

(ix) The gestational mother must give her full and unconditional consent to the making of the order, at least six weeks after the birth.

(x) The husband of the woman who gave birth to the child must give his full and unconditional consent.

(xi) Money or other benefits must not have been given to the surrogate mother, unless they amount to reasonable expenses,[241] or the court has retrospectively authorized the payments. In *Re C*[242] a parental order was made even though £12,000 had been paid. It was held that the commissioning couple had been honest and the sum was not disproportionate as compensation for her expenses and loss of earnings.

(xii) The pregnancy was not the result of sexual intercourse between the surrogate mother and male applicant.

(xiii) The court must decide to make the order with the child's welfare being the first consideration.[243]

This is a highly restrictive list of requirements. Most notably the applicants must be married[244] and at least one of them have a genetic link to the child. If any of the above criteria are not met then the applicants might consider adoption. An adoption order can be made even if the applicants are unmarried or a same-sex couple and there is no need to show any genetic link. However, they will need to be approved by an adoption agency as suitable adoptors. Of course what can happen is that the child is handed over and the commissioning couple then do nothing to regularize their position and the matter only

---

[239] [1996] 1 FLR 369.
[240] This includes someone who is a father by virtue of s 28(2) or (3) of HFE Act 1990.
[241] This could include loss of earnings, maternity clothes etc.   [242] [2002] 1 FLR 909.
[243] Parental Orders (Human Fertilisation and Embryology) Regulations 1994, Sch 1.
[244] DoH (2006f) proposes reform to allow a same-sex couple to obtain a parental order.

comes to a court's attention some years later. In such a case the court is unlikely to want to change the residence of the child, unless there are serious concerns.[245] The Brazier Report suggested that 'a substantial proportion of commissioning couples are failing to apply to the courts to become legal parents of the child'.[246]

In the event of a dispute between the commissioning couple and the surrogate over who should care for the child, the matter is likely to be brought before the court by means of an application for a residence order[247] (ie an order determining where the child should live). The court will make the order based on what will best promote the child's welfare.[248] Where the child has lived to date is likely to be an important factor. If the surrogate has given birth to the child and cared for the child since birth, it is unlikely that the court would order the child be handed over to the commissioning couple, unless there is evidence that the surrogate mother poses a serious risk to the child.[249] On the other hand, if the surrogate has handed over the child to the commissioning couple and then some time later changed her mind and sought a court order that the child be returned to her, it is unlikely she would succeed.[250]

12.4 The arguments in favour of surrogacy

These are some of the most popular arguments used in favour of surrogacy:

(i) The main argument in favour of surrogacy is autonomy. If a woman wishes to be a surrogate mother why should she not be allowed to be?[251] She is not harming anyone else. Quite the opposite, her actions will bring great joy to the commissioning couple.

(ii) Surrogacy is inevitable and has occurred since biblical times. If it were outlawed this would simply lead to a black market in surrogacy. It is better to permit it and regulate it, rather than send it underground.[252]

(iii) Surrogacy widens the variety of family forms. Gay couples can now arrange for the production of a child; a single man can arrange for a child to born for him to care for; and grandparents can use the sperm of their deceased son to produce the grandchildren they would otherwise never have.[253] Of course whether these kinds of developments are a welcome break from the traditional nuclear family, or a misuse of technology, is a matter for debate. As Cook, Day Sclater, and Kaganas put it:

> Surrogacy, then, perhaps more than any other reproductive practice, throws into sharp relief our anxieties about the future(s) of the family. It threatens accepted views of what a family is, of gender-appropriate parental behaviour, and of our ideas of what is natural in the realm of reproductive behaviour.[254]

---

[245] *Re H (A Minor)(S. 37 Direction)* [1993] 2 FLR 541.

[246] Para 5.7.   [247] Children Act 1989, s 8.

[248] *Re N (a child)* [2007] EWCA Civ 1053.   [249] *A v C* [1985] FLR 445.

[250] *Re ME (Adoption; Surrogacy)* [1995] 2 FLR 789.   [251] Freeman (1999).

[252] Freeman (1999: 10).   [253] Laurance (2000).

[254] Cook, Day Sclater, and Kaganas (2003: 5). See also Mackenzie (2007).

12.5 The arguments against surrogacy

These are some of the most common arguments raised against surrogacy:

(i) The situation is potentially harmful to children in that it is liable to produce litigation over them.[255] A surrogate mother may form a strong attachment to the child and be unwilling to hand the child over. Whether that is likely to happen may be questioned: two studies of surrogate mothers found a significant majority saying they felt no special bond between them and the child.[256] Further, from the limited data on surrogacy in the UK it appears that disputes over a child are rare[257] and so far there have been no reported cases in the UK of a commissioning couple refusing to accept a baby.[258]

(ii) Surrogacy exploits surrogates.[259] There is evidence, especially in the USA where large sums are paid to commercial surrogate companies, that surrogate mothers are required to undertake risky work for inadequate care.[260] It has even been said to be analogous to slavery.[261] In the Warnock Report it was argued 'it is inconsistent with human dignity that a woman should use her uterus for financial profit'.[262] However, supporters of surrogacy might point out that we do generally allow people to do things that we think foolish or even exploitative.[263] Many of these concerns are based on the view that for a woman to give up a baby to whom she has just given birth is unnatural and that she would only do so if desperate for money.

(iii) An argument specifically against the paying of surrogates is that the practice becomes too close to 'baby selling'. This may be seen as objectionable in itself; supporters argue that once the child discovers the circumstances of her or his birth she or he will be greatly distressed. It might also be said to transform surrogacy from essentially an altruistic exercise into a commercial one.[264] Michael Freeman has said that payment to a surrogate is not buying children, but recompense for 'a potentially risky, time consuming and uncomfortable process'.[265] We pay the medical staff who enable the surrogacy, why should we not pay the woman who carries the child?

12.6 The Brazier review

Margaret Brazier chaired a review into surrogacy in 1997. It considered in particular whether mothers should be allowed to receive payment, whether an agency should be created to regulate surrogacy arrangements, and whether there was a need for legislative change. Its main findings were:

(i) Surrogacy contracts should continue to be unenforceable.

(ii) Only legitimate and proven expenses should be paid to a surrogate mother. If illegitimate expenses were paid then a parental order should not be made.

---

[255] Eg *W v H (Child Abduction: Surrogacy) (No 2)* [2002] 2 FLR 252.
[256] Jadva et al (2003) and MacCallum et al (2003).
[257] Dodd (2003) find only 2 per cent of surrogacy cases in which there were disputes; Brazier (2003b: 3.38) found between 4–5 per cent.
[258] van der Akker (1999).
[259] The arguments receive careful analysis in Callahan and Roberts (1996) and Purdy (1989).
[260] Ince (1984).   [261] Roberts (1986).   [262] Warnock (1984: 45).
[263] Steinbock (1988: 44).   [264] Brazier (1999c: 345).   [265] Freeman (1999: 9).

(iii) All surrogacy agencies should be registered with the Department of Health but no commercial agency should be allowed.

(iv) There should be a code of practice issued which governs the practice of surrogacy agencies.

The report proved controversial and the Government has not taken any steps to implement it. The Government has recently initiated a consultation exercise which will include questioning whether the law on surrogacy needs to be reformed.[266] It seems there is widespread agreement that there should be some kind of regulation.[267] Surrogacy carries at least as many risks as IVF and yet is unregulated, at least when performed outside of a clinic. What has proved elusive is a form of regulation which is acceptable to all. Should surrogacy be promoted, tolerated, or discouraged? Should we regard the commissioning couple as the parents of the child from the moment of birth? Unfortunately it may take a scandal to spur the Government into regulation and the resolving of these questions.

13 PGD (Pre-implantation Genetic Diagnosis)

The usual procedures for couples using IVF is to create a number of embryos and implant them two at a time into the woman. The question we will consider here is whether it is permissible to select from the embryos created which will be implanted. There is generally no objection to a selection being made on the basis of which embryos are most likely to survive to birth; but more controversially a couple who are at risk of having a child with a genetic disability may wish to select an embryo which does not carry that disability. This requires an assessment of the different embryos to see if they carry the desirable or undesirable characteristic. This is known technically as PGD (Preimplantation Genetic Diagnosis) and requires a licence from the HFEA. The practice is controversial and the HFEA will only allow it for a strict set of reasons.[268]

Supporters for PGD make some of the following arguments. First, some argue that the question of which embryos a woman chooses to implant should be up to her. It is an aspect of her reproductive autonomy.[269] No one should prevent a woman selecting her embryos as she chooses, just as no one could interfere with the decisions of a woman to have sexual relations with a dark haired man in the hope the baby born would have dark hair. Secondly, there are those who argue that zygotes have no moral status and therefore decisions about them and their disposal carry no weight.[270] Third, there are those who argue that there is a basic moral obligation to avoid harm to others. If, therefore, it is possible to choose an embryo which will not suffer the harm of having an undesirable characteristic to her or his parents we should do so. Indeed there is even an argument that genetic screening should be compulsory in order to ensure a disadvantaged child is not born.[271]

The reasons why PGD may be used vary and as they raise slightly different arguments it is worth considering them separately.

---

[266] DoH (2005e).

[267] Warnock (1984: 8.18) expressed the concern that regulation might be seen as official endorsement.

[268] See the discussion in Gavaghan (2007) and Scott (2006).

[269] Harris (1998: 133).   [270] Holm (1998).   [271] BBC Newsonline (19 May 2005c).

13.1 Disability

The HFEA allows couples to select embryos if there is a risk of serious disability.[272] Since 1990 only 500 cases involving PGD have taken place.[273] At first it might be argued that it should be unproblematic that a couple select from their embryos those which have no sign of disability. A couple may be particularly tempted to do this if they suffer from a genetic condition and there is a risk that any child of theirs might inherit it. Indeed if a woman can abort a foetus which is suffering a severe disability there would be little logic in not permitting her to choose not to select one.

But reflection will reveal that the issue is not as straightforward as may at first appear. If a couple choose from their embryos those which do not carry a gene for, say, cystic fibrosis we can presume that those embryos carrying this gene will be discarded. But what does that say about the attitude revealed towards people suffering from cystic fibrosis? Is it not revealing a discriminatory attitude: in the most obvious way, the statement is that a life with cystic fibrosis is not worth as much as a fully healthy person's life? Should we allow couples to exhibit such an attitude and allow medical staff to act on it?[274] Or, rather, is it the message that is being sent by a society which encourages the use of tests for disability which is most concerning?[275] Does it not perpetuate the promotion of the myth of idealism as to human nature: that any child which is not perfect can be rejected by a parent. However, it might be replied that it is proper to seek to ensure that those with disabilities are not disadvantaged, while at the same time seeking to prevent disabilities where possible.[276] A parent may therefore legitimately prefer a child without that disadvantage than a child with. There is, after all, a difference between saying a life with a characteristic is one that is not worth living, and saying that it would be better not to have that characteristic. Adrienne Asche has argued that parents should be given full information about the characteristics of the embryos and allowed to choose. She objects to the fact that particular characteristics (ie those connected with 'disability') are selected and highlighted as disadvantages, and suggests that all the facts about each embryo should be given to parents to let them make a choice, without indicating that medicine regards some characteristics as harmful and others as not.[277]

Even more controversial is a question whether a couple should be allowed to choose to have the embryos which carry a disability. Say, for example, a deaf couple wished to select an embryo which was likely to be born deaf, rather than a child who could hear. Should that be permitted?[278] Supporters of a strong right to procreative autonomy might be compelled to say 'yes'. After all a person could, by selecting a sexual partner, seek to increase the chances of a child having a disability and that could not be prevented. To others, deliberately choosing a child who will be at a disadvantage when compared to other children is simply wrong. The debate centres on what can be regarded as an acceptable range of conditions to produce a person with. There is little consensus on that.[279]

13.2 Sex selection

The HFEA does not allow embryo selection on the basis of sex unless there is a genetic illness related to sex and therefore the sex selection is done in order to avoid a risk

---

[272] For a discussion of how practitioners understand this see Scott, Williams, Ehrich, and Farside(2007).
[273] House of Commons Science and Technology Committee (2005: 108).
[274] Kaplan (1999); Peterson (2005a).   [275] Asch and Wasserman (2007).
[276] Asche (2003); Mahowald (2007).   [277] Asche (2003).
[278] Anstey (2002).   [279] See the useful discussion in Hull (2006).

of a particular condition. The HFEA will not accept sex selection for social reasons.[280] These would include 'family balancing' (to have a family which has children of both sexes) or to replace a dead child with a child of the same sex. However, the Government has announced that a consultation exercise will consider whether sex selection should ever be permitted for social reasons.[281]

Supporters of reproductive autonomy argue that sex selection should be permitted as an aspect of a person's right to control their reproduction.[282] After all there are all kinds of folklaws about what to do if one wants a boy or a girl when engaging in sexual intercourse. No one suggests that it is improper to try to use them.

The objections to sex selection include the following:

(i) Demographic impact. The concern is that the ratio between male and female will skewed. In some countries (India and China are often given as examples) the ratio of boys to girls is 107: 100 or even higher and this is said to be caused by the abortion of girls.[283] However, there is no reason to believe that sex selection would lead to such a skew in the UK. Indeed it is perfectly possible that couples would prefer girls to boys. In any event there would only be a noticeable demographical impact if a large number of parents engaged in sex selection, and this is unlikely.

(ii) International implications. There is a concern that if sex selection were to be permitted in the UK it would make it difficult for the UK to object to the procedure in other countries where it was used in an unacceptable way.

(iii) Psychosocial impacts. There is a concern that a child born as a result of sex selection will suffer psychological problems. She or he may fear that they were selected only on account of their sex.[284] We simply do not know if children would have these feelings, or if they did whether that would be harmful.

(iv) Sex discrimination.[285] There is an argument that allowing people to choose the sex of their child will pander to their sexist beliefs and attitudes. People should be encouraged to accept children regardless of their sex.

(v) Public opinion. The HFEA report found widespread feeling among the members of public consulted against sex selection. Eighty per cent of those questioned thought that people should not be allowed to select on the basis of sex for social reasons.[286] A common feeling was that parents should love their children whatever their characteristics.[287]

The following case demonstrates how cases of sex selection can give rise to complex issues:

---

[280] See Seavillekein and Sherwin (2007) for a disturbing account of the range of sex selection services available from the internet and internationally.
[281] DoH (2005e).   [282] McCarthy (2001).
[283] House of Commons Science and Technology Committee (2005: 135).
[284] Baldwin (2005) and see the reply by Harris (2005b).
[285] Dickens (2002); Robertson (2003).   [286] HEFA (2004b: 25).
[287] See Herrisone-Kelly (2007) for a discussion of such arguments.

REALITY CHECK

The Masterton case

'Alan and Louise Masterton from Monifieth near Dundee lost their youngest child, a three year old daughter Nicole, in 1999, in a bonfire accident. The loss was particularly tragic because they had been trying for 15 years to have a girl and Nicole's arrival was therefore a huge joy. The Mastertons, who have four sons, campaigned for the right to rebuild their family with a daughter. They were adamant that they did not want to replace Nicole, but did want a daughter. Louise Masterton had been sterilized after Nicole's birth. The Mastertons wanted the HFEA to permit them to undergo IVF and use PGD to ensure they had a daughter. The HFEA would only consider the issue if a clinic applied for a licence. However the Mastertons could find no clinic who would take them on. The Mastertons eventually travelled to Italy and spent £30,000 on IVF treatment but unfortunately they were only able to produce a male embryo who they donated to another couple. Female embryos which were implanted were lost. In 2001 the HFEA did apologize to the Mastertons for mishandling their case. They should in the unusual circumstances of the case consider the couple's direct appeal to them.' (BMA 2004: 297)

13.3 'Trivial reasons'

What about selection for reasons that appear 'trivial': hair or eye colour for example? In one sense it may be argued that this is more acceptable. Say a parent selected an embryo child on the basis that they wanted a curly haired child rather than a straight haired one, it could not be suggested that this indicates a view that children with straight hair have lives not worth living, or be an expression of a prejudicial attitude, in the way a decision based on disability can be perceived. To Harris such choices can be left to parents:

> It seems to me to come to this: either such traits as hair colour, eye colour, gender, and the like are important or they are not. If they are not important why not let people choose? And if they are important, can it be right to leave such important matters to chance?[288]

It should be added that at present it is not technically possible to use PGD to select for traits such as intelligence, height, hair colour, or sexuality, although it might be possible in the future.[289] In response Scott[290] has argued that while parents have legitimate interests in avoiding a child who will be born seriously impaired, their interests are not seriously implicated where the decision is over insignificant matters. Indeed allowing parents to make decisions over trivial matters could lead to a shallow view of what parenthood is about or create unrealistic expectations in parents about what their children will be like. Either of these would harm children.

13.4 Saviour siblings

The emotive term 'saviour siblings' has come to be used for cases where parents of a sick child wish to have another child whose tissue can be used to provide a treatment for the condition of their sick sibling. The following case highlights some of the issues involved.

---

[288] Harris (1999: 29).
[289] House of Commons Science and Technology Committee (2005: 143).   [290] Scott (2006).

KEY CASE   Quintavalle (on behalf of Comment on Reproductive Ethics) (Appellant) v HFEA [2005] UKHL 28

The House of Lords were asked to consider the legality of the HFEA's licence to permit a clinic to use H LA typing to test embryos to know whether the embryo would have stem cells which could provide a cure for Zain. Under the HFE Act 1990, section 3(1) it is a criminal offence to bring about the creation of an embryo, except under licence from the HFEA. The proposed treatment involved the creation and use of an embryo and required a licence which the authority granted. The granting of the licence was challenged in the court by CORE. Their application succeeded before Maurice J, but failed before the Court of Appeal and the House of Lords.

   The key provision was the HFE Act, section 11 which permitted the HFEA to license certain activities. In Schedule 2, paragraph 1(3) these included '(d) practices designed to secure that embryos are in a suitable condition to be placed in a woman or to determine whether embryos are suitable for that purpose'. The HFEA argued successfully before their Lordships that the word 'suitable' meant 'suitable for the woman to whom the services are provided'. Mrs Hashmi was entitled to regard an embryo as only suitable if it was compatible for treatment with Zain. CORE argued that this is too wide an interpretation provision and would allow the HFEA to license treatment to test for a whole range of idiosyncratic wishes, such as hair colour. The interpretation of paragraph 1(3) advanced by CORE was that suitable meant that the child would be healthy and free from abnormalities. This would allow PGD to test for abnormalities but not to test for whether the child's tissue matched a sibling's. This argument was rejected. First, it was pointed out that although the HFEA's interpretation meant a licence could be given for frivolous reasons, there was no reason to believe the HFEA would grant such a licence. Secondly, and more importantly, the HFE Act was designed to leave these complex moral issues with the HFEA. The Act was structured by outlawing some things (eg the cloning of an embryo), but in others leaving them open to the HFEA to license if it thought appropriate. The issue in this case was not outlawed specifically in the Act and therefore was licensable by the HFEA. If Parliament felt that the HFEA was using its powers improperly it was for Parliament to reform the HFEA.

   It is worth emphasizing that the House of Lords approached this case addressing the narrow legal issue of whether the HFEA had statutory authority to license the treatment. The ethics of it, or whether it would be lawful to use the tissue of any resulting child, were not considered in any detail.

The HFEA introduced a new code of practice to deal with such cases in 2007. PGD to enable the selection of a suitable embryo to be a 'saviour sibling' will only be permitted to provide treatment for a life-threatening or serious condition.[291] When deciding the appropriateness of preimplantation tissue typing in any particular situation consideration should given to the condition of the affected child, including:

(a) the degree of suffering associated with the condition of the affected child; and

(b) the speed of degeneration in progressive disorders; and

(c) the extent of any intellectual impairment; and

(d) the prognosis for the affected child in relation to all treatment options available; and

[291] HFEA (2007c: para G.12.5).

(e) the availability of alternative sources of tissue for the treatment of the affected child, now and in the future; and

(f) the availability of effective therapy for the affected child, now and in the future.

Consideration should also be given to the possible consequences for any child who may be born as a result, including:

(a) any risks associated with embryo biopsy for the child who may be born; and

(b) the likely long-term emotional and psychological implications for the child who may be born; and

(c) whether the treatment of the affected child is likely to require intrusive surgery for the child to be born (and whether this is likely to be repeated); and

(d) any complications or predispositions for the child who may be born associated with the tissue type to be selected.

Consideration should also be given to the family circumstances of the people seeking treatment, including:

(a) the previous reproductive experience of those seeking treatment; and

(b) the views of the people seeking treatment and of the affected child about the condition of the affected child; and

(c) the likelihood of a successful outcome, taking into account the reproductive circumstances of the patients (ie the number of embryos likely to be available for testing in each treatment cycle, the number likely to be suitable for transfer, whether carrier embryos may be transferred, the number of cycles likely to be undertaken) and the likely outcome of treatment for the affected child; and

(d) the consequences of an unsuccessful outcome; and

(e) the demands of IVF/preimplantation testing treatment on the family whilst caring for an affected child; and

(f) the extent of social support available; and

(g) the family circumstances of the people seeking treatment.[292]

If the Human Fertilisation and Embryology Bill is enacted then it will permit the creation of saviour siblings in order to treat life-threatening or serious conditions.[293]

Critics of 'saviour siblings' claim that it involves bringing a person into being for the sole purpose of assisting their sibling. This infringes the principle that people should not be used solely as a means to an end. Supporters could reply to this in two ways. One would be to argue that in fact to save the life of one's sibling is beneficial to the donor, or at least not harmful to them.[294] Alternatively, they could argue that it is extremely unlikely that parents would treat the saviour sibling simply as a source of tissue. It would be hard to believe that parents would 'discard' a saviour sibling once treatment of the existing child had been effective. The child is being created to be loved in her or his own right as well as assisting the sibling. A slightly different argument is that child when older might perceive her or himself as having been created as merely a means to save her or his sibling. This could cause psychological problems, particularly so if the matching

---

[292] HFEA (2007c: para G.12.5.6–8).   [293] HM Government (2007a).   [294] Spriggs (2005).

had not worked out.[295] Again, these may be dangers and we do not know how likely they are to be. The 'saviour sibling' might just as well feel delighted that she or he were able to save or attempt to save another life and regard it as having enriched her or his or her won life. John Harris has argued that guesses about possible emotional harms for the 'saviour sibling' do not justify denying treatment which would save a life.[296] Another issue which the courts may need to address at some point is the legal liability that could arise if a 'saviour sibling' that is created but does not provide a cure.[297]

14 Cloning

14.1 Introduction to cloning

Cloning raises high emotions. To some extending the possibilities of human reproduction beyond normal sexual intercourse is terrifying, raising profound questions about our identity. To others, cloning provides exciting possibilities of enabling couples who would be unable to have them otherwise to have children, and offers the hope of a treatment for diseases for which at present there is no hope of a cure. Now that the cloning of people is feasible and there have been some claims that humans have been cloned,[298] predictions about the effect of cloning have moved well beyond the realm of science fiction. But the question of whether or not to clone is one that has attracted much attention and this has led in many cases to a polarization of views.

14.2 The definition of cloning

The United States' President's Commission on Bioethics[299] defined cloning in this way:

> The asexual production of a new human organism that is, at all stages of development, genetically virtually identical to a currently existing or previously existing human being. It would be accomplished by introducing the nuclear material of a human somatic cell (donor) into an oocyte (egg) whose own nucleus has been removed or inactivated, yielding a product that has a human genetic constitution virtually identical to the donor of the somatic cell.

A clone, then, is a group of cells that have identical DNA sequences to the 'parent' group of cells. Almost all the clones that have been produced so far are not true clones, because their non-chromosomal (mitochondrial) DNA are different from that of the 'parent' even though their chromosomal DNA are identical. Clones are currently created by cell nucleus replacement (CNR). This involves a nucleus from a cell being placed into an egg, thereby activating it. Cloning therefore opens up a number of reproductive possibilities. Because sperm is not required it offers hope for a man who wants to have genetic offspring, but is unable to produce sperm. It would also enable a lesbian couple to produce a child genetically related to them both.

---

[295] Delatycki (2005).   [296] Harris (2002).
[297] See Chico (2006) for a discussion of the issues which could arise.
[298] BBC Newsonline (19 May 2005b). Certainly a monkey embryo has been cloned and this means that human reproductive cloning is not far off (BBC Newsonline (14 November 2007)).
[299] United States' President's Commission on Bioethics (2002).

It is common to draw a distinction between reproductive and therapeutic cloning. Although the same process is used to create an embryo in each case the difference lies in the motivation behind the processes:

- *Reproductive cloning.* Here the aim is produce a child. Having produced the cloned embryo the plan would be to transplant it into the womb to develop.

- *Therapeutic cloning.* Here there is no intent to produce a child. The cloned embryo is created in order to produce cells that will be transplanted into someone who suffers from some kind of disability or condition. The cloned embryo may also be created for research purposes.

14.3 Legal responses to human cloning

Under the HFE Act CNR can only be performed with a licence. This was decided by the House of Lords in *R (on behalf of Bruno Quintavalle on behalf of Pro-life Alliance) v the Secretary of State for Health.*[300] But reproductive cloning has now been banned by the Human Reproductive Cloning Act 2001. The core provision in section 1(1) is self-explanatory:

> A person who places in a woman a human embryo which has been created otherwise than by fertilisation is guilty of an offence.

The criminal offence carries a maximum sentence of ten years. This legislation does not prohibit the creation of a cloned embryo, but only the placing of such an embryo into a woman. Therapeutic cloning and cloning for research is, therefore, permitted if licensed by the HFEA. The 2001 Act appears straightforward, but as technologies develop there is little doubt it will need to be reconsidered. There are two issues in particular which may need to be addressed:

(i) The legislation only prohibits the placing of such an embryo in a woman. This appears to permit the placing of a cloned embryo into an artificial uterine environment; or even the placing of such an embryo in a male, if ever attempts were made to enable men to provide a gestational base for an embryo.[301]

(ii) There may be some concerns that the legislation prohibits the placing in a woman of *an embryo.* It is not impossible that a scientist would wish to create from manipulated sperm and eggs a clump of cells that are not embryos (at least in the sense of being capable of developing into a human). These cells could conceivably grow and provide replacement tissues or organs for therapeutic purposes. The Act may not prohibit the insertion of such a clump of cells into a woman.

As these examples demonstrate, there are difficulties facing any state which wishes to pass legislation which prohibits human cloning. Technological advances can quickly render legislative attempts to ban cloning outdated. Further, national based bars will be of little use without an international ban.[302]

---

[300] [2003] UKHL 13, criticized in Morgan and Ford (2004).
[301] Herring and Chau (2002).
[302] See the Council of Europe's *Additional Protocol to the Convention for the Protection of Human Rights and the Dignity of the Human Being with Regard to Application of Biology and Medicine on the Prohibition of Cloning Human Beings and* UNESCO's *Universal Declaration on the Human Genome and Human Rights.*

14.4 Arguments in favour of reproductive cloning

The key argument in favour of permitting cloning is reproductive autonomy, a concept with which we are now familiar. If we accept that people have free choice over when and how to reproduce, cloning should be open to them, unless there are some powerful state interests against allowing it.[303] The arguments over cloning, therefore, tend to have centred on the strengths or weaknesses of the arguments against it.

Supporters of reproductive cloning argue that cloning enables people to have children, who otherwise would be unable to do so. Couples who otherwise would have to use donated gametes can have a child who is genetically related to both of them. Lesbian couples, in particular, might for this reason welcome the technology. It would even be possible for a woman to use a cell from her own body to implant into one of her own eggs.[304] Although the media might portray cloning as being used by people trying to produce the 'perfect baby' in reality it is more likely to be used for couples for whom reproductive cloning offers the only hope of a child.

14.5 Arguments against cloning

Here we will examine the arguments that have been made against cloning. It will be emphasized that the arguments are stronger against some forms of cloning than others.

(i) It is widely accepted that to attempt human cloning with the present state of scientific knowledge would pose unacceptable risks.[305] The rates of miscarriages in attempted cloning of animals have been high[306] and there is a real risk that any child successfully produced would suffer from illnesses or diseases. However, it may be just a matter of time before the success rate of gestation improves and concerns over the future of cloned children would be overcome. Harris rejects the arguments that at present the dangers of reproductive cloning are too great to authorize it. He points out that with normal sexual intercourse 80 per cent of fertilized eggs 'die' and between 3 and 5 per cent of embryos have an abnormality.[307] In the light of such statistics he suggests the chances of reproductive cloning producing a healthy child do not look too bad. Lane argues that as long as the products of human cloning would have a minimally decent life cloning should be permitted, even if they would be likely to suffer some form of disability.[308] Perhaps a more common view is that until the rates of disability likely to result from cloning are similar to those associated with traditional sexual reproduction, human cloning to produce a child should not be attempted.

(ii) From an evolutionary perspective it is possible to argue that cloning will limit the genetic diversity of the gene pool, rendering the human race more susceptible to extinction by a particular disease or virus.[309] This argument, however, would only carry weight if cloning became the primary means of reproduction. Even if cloning is permitted the number of cloned people is likely to remain small and so the impact of cloning on the human gene pool will be minimal.

(iii) Some commentators have claimed that one has a right to be genetically unique.[310] Jim McLean has stated:

303 Foley (2002).
306 Golton and Doyal (1998).
309 Gardner (2003).
304 Harris (2002: 81).
307 Harris (2001: 111).
310 Eg Williamson (1999).
305 DoH (2005e).
308 Lane (2007).

[a]n artificially cloned human being would have been denied the right to be the product of a genetic blueprint having two different sources.[311]

The argument is that each person has a right to have their own genetic make-up, which is independent of others. This is because our genetic make-up is regarded as the core to our humanity.[312] To ensure an individual's unique status and separateness from their parents it is crucial that a child is a combination of genetic material from both parents.[313]

To some commentators, however, such a claimed right to genetic uniqueness is difficult to justify. Nature itself permits individuals to share DNA: identical twins for example.[314] Further, the idea that one cannot have a unique personality, identity, and character because another person shares one's genes is unconvincing, again as twins show.[315]

In response to these points the genetic identity argument could be rephrased. Andre Rose has expressed concern that cloning 'confuses the intergenerational structure of the family'.[316]

The House of Lords Committee put it this way:

If the cell nucleus from the father were used, for example, the child would be the genetic son of its grandparents, the genetic sibling of its uncles and aunts and the genetic uncle of its cousins. The range of ambiguities introduced into family relationships by cloning from a close relative would be large and the possibility for emotional confusion and uncertainty—not only on the part of the cloned child—considerable.

(iv) Some have argued that children have the right to choose an open future. Even if there is no biological reason for this[317] a cloned person may believe that they are genetically pre-ordained to be like their clone.[318] The pressure that a cloned person will feel to be like, or indeed unlike, their clone will deprive them of their right to be an individual and live out their own version of life. In reply it might be said that even a child born using normal reproduction may feel destined to have some of their parents' characteristics and pressure to follow, or not follow, their parents' footsteps. Sean Pattinson argues that although reproductive cloning itself does not harm an individual, behaviour after the birth, eg in pressurizing the clone to behave in a particular way, would.[319] He argues therefore that this argument is not against reproductive cloning per se, but against treating the clones, once born, in a particular way. Again the example of twins could be brought up: pressures that one twin may feel to be like (or unlike) their twin are not regarded as some kind of infringement of their human rights.[320]

(v) Some suggest that cloning is likely to work against the interests of women.[321] The argument is that cloning is likely to be particularly attractive to infertile men. The risks, pains, and discomfort of ova stimulation, ova retrieval, and embryo transfer necessary for cloning will all fall on women, in addition, of course, to the burdens of gestation and childbirth. It has been claimed that for each human cloning attempt there will be a need for several hundred ova,[322] and there is a high risk of late foetal deaths in cloned embryos.[323] All of these will impose extra burdens on women. There are also wider

---

[311] McLean (1998: 26).   [312] Kass (1998).   [313] Meilaender (1998).
[314] Harris (2004b).   [315] Prainsack and Spector (2006).   [316] Rose (1999).
[317] Savulsecu (2005).   [318] Holm (1998).   [319] Pattinson (2002b).
[320] As Harris (2005a: 35) points out one in 270 births is a twin.
[321] Mahowald (2006).   [322] National Academy of Sciences (2002).
[323] Smolin (2002).

concerns that reproductive technologies such as cloning increase and perpetuate the exercise of medical and patriarchal power over women's bodies.[324]

Such concerns, however, must be weighed against the strong desire of women to have children for whom cloning may be the only option, such as lesbian couples. To address these concerns, supporters of cloning may call for regulation to ensure that women do not become only 'vessels' in the hands of medical professionals, but there is nothing in the nature of human cloning which necessarily demeans women.

(vi) A study of public attitudes to cloning found a widespread feeling that the practice of cloning was unnatural.[325] It would disrupt a child's lineage which is an important part of identity. Helen Watt has said that children would be treated more like products whose genetic make-up is selected in advance rather than as a gift.[326] Leon Kass has argued that society's natural repugnance of cloning reflects a sound intuition concerning the profound principles of things that people hold dear.[327] Supporters of cloning have questions whether merely feelings of disgust per se are sufficient to justify outlawing an activity. Feelings of repugnance which are not supported by moral arguments should not form the basis of law.[328]

(vii) One way of dealing with questions of this kind is to ask whether a child would choose to be born cloned. Sonia Harris-Short argues that people would not.[329] The question could, however be phrased: would you rather be born cloned than not exist at all?

The answer to that question is likely to be yes. Burley and Harris suggest that only if the harms could be said to blight the life of the child could they be said to justify prohibiting cloning.[330]

 A VIEW FROM ABOVE

Religious views on cloning

Some of the most vocal opponents of human reproductive cloning have been those writing from a religious perspective. Indeed the religious concerns on this issue reflect the objections that many religious people have to the whole area of assisted reproductive treatment.

There are a set of concerns based on the sanctity of life doctrine and the belief that life starts from conception. This leads to a rejection of any method of reproduction that involves the destruction of, or lack of respect for, the embryo (see Ibrahim (2000), who emphasizes this point from an Islamic perspective). These issues are discussed in detail in Chapter 8 so they will not be repeated here.

Those writing from a religious perspective are often concerned with the way reproductive technologies and in particular cloning involve playing God. Some emphasize that God intended reproduction to take place through sexual intercourse between married people. Attempting to create children in other ways is an unnatural effort to thwart the divine plan. Richardson (1998), for example, argues that God intended reproduction to involve the co-operation of two parties in an act of mutual love and cloning undermines that. There are also concerns that cloning will challenge the notion that each person has been created by God as part of his plan (see Fadel (2002)). ART and cloning are seen as ways in which children become regarded as commodities to be bought or produced, rather than gifts from God.

---

324 Petchesky (1979).   325 The Wellcome Trust (1998: 13–14).
326 See also Finnis (1998a).   327 Kass (1998).   328 Tribe (1998); Rao (2002).
329 Harris-Short (2004).   330 Burley and Harris (1999).

However, others do not see it in this way and argue that God gave talent to individuals so that they can be used to better the lot of humankind. There should be no more objection to medicine being used to cure infertility than there is in dealing with other forms of illness. ART should be regarded as a gift from God rather than a challenge to God's purposes. Indeed it may be said to fulfil the Biblical command to 'be fruitful and multiply'. Such reasoning is found particularly among Jewish scholars (Dorff (1998)).

15 Therapeutic cloning and embryo research

We will discuss therapeutic cloning and embryo research together as they raise similar issues. Both involve the creation of an embryo in order to assist in research, or to assist the treatment of others. The first question to consider is the definition of an embryo.

15.1 Defining an embryo

Human cloning has challenged the legal definition of an embryo. The Human Fertilisation and Embryology Act 1990, section 1 defines an embryo:

(1) In this Act, except where otherwise stated—

   (a) embryo means a live human embryo where fertilisation is complete, and

   (b) references to an embryo include an ovum in the process of fertilisation and, for this purpose, fertilisation is not complete until the appearance of a two cell zygote.

(2) The Act, so far as it governs bringing about the creation of an embryo, applies only to bringing about the creation of an embryo outside the human body.

This definition is rather unhelpful. It focuses on the manner in which the organism comes into being, rather than being a description of what the organism is.[331] This is a peculiar way of defining the embryo because, surely, it is the potential of an embryo to develop into a human being, rather than the process by which the embryo was created, which gives the embryo any special moral or scientific significance.

In *R (on behalf of Bruno Quintavalle on behalf of Pro-life Alliance) v The Secretary of State for Health*[332] the Court of Appeal and House of Lords unanimously decided that the definition of embryo in the HFEA, section 1 did include a cloned embryo. As Lord Millett put it, CNR embryos

> are in all respects save the method of their creation indistinguishable from other embryos. They are alive and human, and accordingly possess all the features which Parliament evidently considered make it desirable to regulate their use for treatment or research.[333]

Section 1 was therefore treated as only supplying the definition of an embryo where the embryo was created by fertilization. In effect there is no definition of an embryo where the embryo was created without fertilization. The Government has indicated that it believes

---

[331] The Human Fertilisation and Embryology Bill proposes an amendment to this definition to include 'an egg that is in the process of fertilization or is undergoing any other process that is capable of resulting in an embryo' (cl 14).
[332] [2002] EWCA Civ 29 and [2003] 2 AC 687.   [333] Para 49.

that there needs to be new legislation to make clear that all human embryos are within the scope of regulation under HFEA.[334] This will be done if the Human Fertilisation and Embryology Bill becomes law. It will not permit reproductive cloning.[335]

15.2 The status of the embryo

This issue has already been extensively discussed in Chapter 6. It will be recalled that there are a wide variety of views on the moral status of the embryo,[336] ranging from the point of view that an embryo is a person with as much of a right to life as any other human being, through to the view that the embryo is no more than a collection of cells of no particular moral significance.

The HFE Act allows research to be licensed on embryos until the formation of the primitive streak. That is taken to occur no less than 14 days after fertilization. Baroness Warnock, whose report led to the HFE Act, has explained her view in this way:

> before fourteen days, the embryo, or pre-embryo as it was scientifically known, was a loose cluster of first two, then four, then sixteen cells, undifferentiated. An undifferentiated cell could develop into any of the types of cell that go to make up the human body, and some of them would not become part of the embryo at all, but would form the placenta or the umbilical cord. After fourteen days, there begin to appear the first traces of what will become the central nervous system of the embryo, the primitive streak.[337]

The 14-day period has also been supported on the basis that it is close to the time when the embryo may be able to experience pain.[338] It is also the time at which the embryo is a coherent entity and it is clear that there are not going to be twins.

The HFE Act imposes a number of important restrictions on the use of embryos in research. These include the following:

(i) An embryo cannot be stored or used for research after the primitive streak which is taken to be 14 days from the mixing of gametes.[339]

(ii) The use or storage of an embryo requires a licence and licences can only be issued by the HFEA for certain purposes[340] including: promoting advances in treatment of infertility, miscarriages, contraception, or causes of congenital diseases.[341] The Human Fertilisation and Embryology (Research Purposes) Regulations 2001 have added three new purposes to the original five set out in the Act: increasing knowledge about the development of embryos; increasing knowledge about serious disease; or enabling any such knowledge to be applied in developing treatments for serious disease.

(iii) It is not permitted to mix human and animal gametes or to place a human embryo in a non-human animal.[342]

(iv) The HFEA will only consider licences for research if a Research Ethics Committee has approved the research.

---

[334] DoH (2005f).   [335] HM Government (2007a).
[336] See, eg, Polkinghorne (2004) and Brooke (2004). For a discussion on whether cloning has altered the debate over the moral status of the embryo see Cameron and Williamson (2005) and Harris and Santon (2005).
[337] Warnock (2002: 35).   [338] Warnock (1984: 11.19–21).
[339] HFE Act 1990, s 3(3)(a) and (4).   [340] These are listed in HFE Act 1990, Sch 2, para 3.
[341] HFE Act 1990, Sch 2, para 3(2).   [342] S 3(3)(b) and (d).

Controversially the HFE Act permits research not only using embryos which are 'spare' following infertility treatment, but also on embryos which are specifically created for research.[343] The significance of this is that it permits research into therapeutic cloning.

Most people who support research involving embryos, including the Warnock Committee whose report underpins the HFE Act, require that embryos be treated with respect. Many will share John Polkinghorne's view:

> The very early embryo is entitled to a deep moral respect because of its potential humanity, so that it is not just a speck of protoplasm that you can do what you like with and then flush it down the sink; but it is not yet fully a human being.[344]

However, deep moral respect is a troublesome concept in this context.[345] In what way is it respectful of an embryo to carry out experiments on it and then discard it? The House of Lords Select Committee on Stem Cell Research recently concluded that the HFE Act does demonstrate respect for the embryo used in research, for example by only allowing embryo research to be performed where no alternative means is available and only for one of the permitted purposes.[346]

John Harris makes the point that 'nature' itself is no great respecter of embryos. He points out that for every successful pregnancy involving natural sexual intercourse five embryos are lost or miscarried.

> One obvious and inescapable conclusion is that God and/or nature has ordained that 'spare' embryos be produced for almost every pregnancy, and that most of these will have to die in order that a sibling embryo can come to birth. Thus the sacrifice of embryos seems to be an inescapable and inevitable part of the process of procreation.[347]

15.3 Should the law permit the use of embryos in research? If so when?

Generally the issues here are similar to those discussed in Chapter 6.[348] Those that take a strong 'pro-life' view will often oppose embryo research, while those being more 'pro-choice' will support it.[349] But for some the link between the issues is not straightforward. Consider these views:

(i) *The agnostic.* If a person is wholly undecided about the status of the embryo then a perfectly respectable position for them to take would be this: 'I cannot oppose abortion because it would be wrong for me to require a woman to undergo a pregnancy against her wishes and the interference in her rights that would constitute, based on my doubts over the correct status of the foetus. On the other hand in relation to embryo research because no one else's rights are being infringed my doubts predominate and lead me to argue that research should not be carried out on embryos.' Note, however, that the assumption that no one else's right are interfered with if embryo research is prohibited

---

[343] Notably the European Bioethics Convention, art 18 does not permit states to create embryos specifically for research and that is a major reason why the UK has not signed this Convention.
[344] Polkinghorne (2004: 594).   [345] See eg Brazier (1999a); Brownsword (2003c).
[346] Brownsword (2002).   [347] Harris (2002: 129).
[348] See Harman (2007) for a useful discussion of the differences in the issues raised in embryo research and abortion.
[349] Although see Deckers (2007b) for further discussion.

might be challenged. Are the interests of those whose diseases would be cured if embryo research was carried out not interfered with if research is banned?

(ii) *The aborted foetus.* A strong opponent of abortion may still be able to justify research on an aborted foetus. Although she or he may regard the abortion as abhorrent, it might be arguable that as it has happened at least some good should come out of the tragedy and if medicine can be advanced by research on the aborted embryo so be it.[350] Of course this would restrict the kind of research that could be performed.

(iii) *The potentiality argument.* One of the arguments that a foetus deserves moral respect is that 'left to its own devices' the embryo would become a human being. Abortion is wrong because it interferes with the potential person. Arguably an embryo created in a lab is in a different position. It will not develop into a person if left alone. This could lead someone to conclude that the moral status of the embryo in the womb is not the same as the embryo in 'the test tube'.[351]

15.4 Therapeutic cloning

Therapeutic cloning is the cloning of an embryo to make the cells, tissue, or organs of that embryo compatible with a proposed recipient. The intention normally is that the embryo will never develop beyond the 14 days mentioned in the HFE Act. The technology offers potential treatments for diseases such as diabetes, Alzheimer's, and Parkinson's diseases.[352] The controversial nature of the procedure is immediately apparent because it involves the creation and use of embryos merely to provide genetic material for a person and then be disposed of.[353]

One greatly disputed issue is whether it is necessary to use embryonic tissue for therapeutic cloning. Some people argue that developing stem cells lines from the umbilical cords of children at birth or from the tissue of adults, is just as effective.[354] There is no consensus on the question, although most of the research in the area appears to be being conducted on embryonic tissue.

15.5 Human Fertilisation and Embryology Bill

At the time of writing Parliament is debating the Human Fertilisation and Embryology Bill 2007, which has proved a controversial piece of legislation.[355] The Government has declared that the principles behind the reforms are:

- to ensure that legitimate medical and scientific applications of human reproductive technologies can continue to flourish;

- to promote public confidence in the development and use of human reproductive technologies through effective regulatory controls applicable to them;

- to secure that regulatory controls accord with better regulation principles and encourage best regulatory practice.[356]

---

[350] Harris (1998a).   [351] Agar (2007). See also the disussion in Brazier (2006b).
[352] DoH (2003c).   [353] Halliday (2004).   [354] Catholic Bishops' Conference (2004).
[355] The original proposals are in DoH (2006f). These were considered in a Parliamentary Committee (Joint Committee (2007)), in light of whose report the Government made changes to the Bill (HM Government (2007a)).
[356] DoH (2006f: para 2.2).

The Bill contains the following proposals:

- The Bill will seek to ensure that all research conducted on embryos is regulated. Currently the definition of embryo in the HFE Act is such that some modern techniques of creating them could fall outside the scope of the Act.

- The Bill will not permit couples to select embryos on the basis of sex, unless there are medical reasons for doing so. The Draft Bill proposes that a licence can only be granted if 'there is a significant risk that a person with the abnormality will have or develop a serious physical or mental disability, a serious illness or any other serious medical condition' (Schedule 2, 3(2)). Unlike the HFEA Code of Practice the parents' views on whether the condition will be serious is not mentioned. The Bill will permit the creation of 'saviour siblings' in order to treat a life-threatening or serious illness.[357]

- The Bill will amend the law so that a same-sex couple who have a child using assisted conception can both be recognized as parents of the child born.

- The requirement in the HFEA that in deciding whether to provide licensed treatment the clinic consider the need for a father of any child created will be abolished.

- There will be an extension of the kinds of research permitted.[358] Most controversially this includes permitting the creation of hybrid embryo. Some such research had already been approved in principle by the HFEA following a public consultation which found 61 per cent of those questioned approved of their creation if they were useful in understanding diseases.[359] Originally the Bill had only permitted licensing the creation of cytoplasmic embryos. However, the Government now says that it will permit the HFEA to license the creation of full hybrids, which will contain genetic material from both humans and animals. The Government announcement states:

  The Bill will now bring the following inter-species embryos within the scope of the regulator, where licences may permit their creation subject to the requirement that the project is necessary or desirable for the purposes described in legislation:

  - 'True' hybrids—embryos created by the mixing of human and animal gametes.

  - 'Cytoplasmic hybrid' embryos—embryos created by the insertion of a human nucleus into an enucleated animal egg.

  - Human transgenic embryos—human embryos modified by the addition of animal DNA.

  - Human–animal chimera embryos—embryos created by the addition of animal cells to a human embryo.[360]

- The original draft of the Bill proposed merging the HTA and HFEA, but this was rejected by a Parliamentary Committee and later dropped by the Government.[361]

- The Bill will not permit cloning. In particular it will not permit fertilizing an egg with genetic material from another woman to produce a child who is related only to two women.[362]

---

[357] HM Government (2007a: para 42).
[358] Joint Committee (2007) proposed giving HFEA more powers to license research and to have greater powers for setting its remit. The Government (HM Government (2007a) rejected this believing it would leave the HFEA lacking accountability.
[359] HFEA (2007f). [360] HM Government (2007a: para 34).
[361] HM Government (2007a). [362] HM Government (2007a).

16 Eugenics

So far we have been discussing circumstances in which a couple select an embryo from the embryos their gametes have produced. But now we will discuss whether it is permissible for a couple to manipulate the genetic make-up of an embryo before it is implanted. It is common to draw a distinction between manipulation that is designed to remove a genetic abnormality so that the embryo has an average health; and where the manipulation is designed to enhance the embryo's characteristics (eg to make the embryo especially intelligent or strong). Amongst the general public there appears to be much more sympathy for couples who wish to give birth to children who do not have disabilities or disorders than couples who wish their child to have some enhanced characteristic.[363]

The law is clear: the HFEA is not permitted to grant a licence authorizing the alteration of the genetic structure of a cell which forms part of an embryo.[364] To do so would be illegal. The HFE Act, Schedule 2, paragraph 3(4) does permit regulations to be passed by Parliament which allow the alteration of the genetic structure of embryonic cells, but only for the purposes of research.

Not only is genetic modification of embryos therefore against the law, the technology to do so is at a very early stage. However, as it advances the issue is likely to become controversial. If the law was to be relaxed, one option would be to draw the distinction mentioned above: allowing the removal of disadvantages, but prohibiting the enhancement.[365] This, however, assumes we can agree on what an advantage or disadvantage is.[366] Whether being gay, religious, or temperamental are beneficial or negative characteristics is a matter on which there is no consensus.

Another alternative would be to give parents the choice: they can determine whatever changes to their children's genetic structure that they wish.[367] This would permit a couple to amend their child's genetic structure to be deaf, for example. Many would find that repugnant but the strict logic of a reproductive autonomy rights perspective would support it. Some have reached an almost opposite conclusion, that there is a duty to engage in genetic intervention to prevent or ameliorate serious disability or illness.[368] Julian Savulescu goes even further and promotes what he calls 'procreative beneficence' which urges parents to select the best children that they produce.[369] Critics of such a view might argue that this assumes we can determine what is good or not for a person; that having lives and personalities which are a mixture of good and bad make our existence more rewarding; that it will lead to children suffering from the over-hyped expectations of the their parents; and that it overlooks the importance of wider societal influences on what makes a good life.[370]

Overhanging this whole debate are concerns about eugenics[371] and particularly memories of the Nazi regime's desire to produce a pure Aryan race. This is seen as so revolting to many that any procedure that begins to raise the spectre of such a desire must be prohibited. Another concern about allowing enhancement is that it might produce injustices if there is not equal access to the possibilities offered. As Walter Glannon puts it:

---

363 Richards (1999).
365 Farrelly (2004); Pattinson (2002b: 103).
367 Savulescu (2001c).
369 Savulescu (2001c and 2006).

364 HFE Act 1990, Sch 2, para 1(4).
366 Buchanan et al (2000).
368 Buchanan et al (2000).
370 Parker (2007).   371 Glover (1998).

it would involve unfair access to enhancement technology based on ability to pay; it would involve an unacceptable social cost in the form of mental impairment as a side-effect in some people; it would threaten to undermine equality as one of the bases of self-respect, social stability and solidarity; and it would threaten to undermine individual autonomy and responsibility.[372]

Imagine a world in which every person was genetically engineered to be perfect physical and intellectual specimens. Would the human race be any the happier or better off? Some, indeed, have suggested part of the joy and value in life is the struggle to reach physical or intellectual heights. If we are born with these what will people do with their lives?[373]

QUESTIONS

1. Should people be allowed to buy children? Many people find the notion repugnant, but for many expensive IVF or surrogacy is the only way to have children. Are these people, in effect, buying children? Or what about reports of churches offering pregnant women considering abortion money to persuade them to carry the child to term and then arrange adoption? (Compare Brazier (1999c) and Landes and Posner (1978) on this issue).

2. It has been suggested that in our society choosing to be childless is regarded as an act of unimaginable selfishness (Callahan and Roberts (1996: 1225). Do you agree? Is it selfish not to have children? There is even an argument that it is morally indefensible to have children, the argument being that not having children means leaving the situation morally neutral. Having children is more likely to produce unhappiness than happiness. It is therefore immoral to have children and immoral to provide services to help people have children (see Häyry (2004) and Bennett (2004)). Are you persuaded?

3. Consider for example this case: a women aged 62 went to Los Angeles and used IVF to become pregnant with her brother's sperm. Apparently this was an attempt to win a dispute over an inheritance with other members of her family (Warnock (2002: 48). Does this indicate that any claim to reproductive autonomy must have some limits?

4. Agar (2004: 1) tells of a repository of the sperm and eggs of the most able and active individuals from around the world. These are then available for sale or research. Should there be more of this? Why should we not only use the gametes which contain the very best genetic material?

5. 'Even if our genes could be manipulated to make our behaviour conform to a morally perfect course of action in every situation, it is unlikely that we would want it. Most of us would rather make autonomous choices that turned out not to lead to the best course of action. This is because of the importance of moral growth and maturity that come with making choices under uncertainty. The disposition that we cultivate on our own, imperfect as they are, make our lives valuable to use.' (Glannon (2005: 113)). Do you agree? Is this a convincing argument against attempts to 'improve' embryos?

[372] Glannon (2001: 107).   [373] Holland (2003: 152).

6. According to a recent study one in 25 men are raising children to whom they are not genetically related, but believe they are (Ives and Draper (2005)). Does that matter? Why should it matter to someone whether the man who has acted throughout that person's life as a father was genetically related to them?

7. Is there any weight in the argument that because there is so much money available surrounding ART, with private clinics charging large sums there is a danger that the 'reproductive industry' is exaggerating its success rates? (Callahan and Roberts (1996)). Why else is there so little information about success rates? Why is there so little effort put into finding ways that couples can avoid becoming infertile?

8. One of the difficulties facing the HFEA is that as Brazier has pointed out: 'British law...displays contradictions, no single, coherent, philosophy underpins the law's response to reproductive medicine' (Brazier 1999c: 197). She points out that the embryo is seen as deserving of respect, and yet at least until the 14th day she wonders whether it is 'in reality treated differently from laboratory artefacts?' (Brazier (1999c: 198)). Is it possible to respect a foetus and permit its destruction?

9. Devolder and Savulescu (2006) argue that reproductive cloning should not be permitted, but there is a moral duty to research therapeutic cloning. Would you agree?

FURTHER READING

On the general issues raised in this chapter see:

Alghrani, A. and Harris, J. 'Reproductive liberty: should the foundation of families be regulated' *Child and Family Law Quarterly* 18: 191.

Deech, R.and Smajdor, A. (2007) *From IVF to Immortality* (Oxford University Press).

Gunning, J. and Stoke, H. (2003) *The Regulation of Assisted Reproductive Technology* (Ashgate).

Harris, J. and Holm, S. (2004) *The Future of Reproduction* (Oxford University Press).

Horsey, K. and Biggs, H. (eds) (2007) *Human Fertilization and Embryology: Reproducing Regulation* (Routledge).

Jackson, E. (2001) *Regulating Reproduction* (Hart).

Laing, J and Oderberg, D. (2005) 'Artificial reproduction, the welfare principle, and the common good' *Medical Law Review* 13: 328.

Lublin, N. (1998) *Pandora's box: Feminism Confronts Reproductive Technology* (Rowman and Littlefield).

On cloning see:

Harris, J. (2004b) *On Cloning* (Routledge).

Klotzo, J. (2004) *A Clone of Your Own* (Oxford University Press).

Macintosh, K. (2005) *Illegal Human Beings* (Cambridge University Press).

President's Council on Bioethics (2002) *Human Cloning and Human Dignity* (Washington).

On genetic enhancement/selection issues see:

Agar, N. (2004) *Liberal Eugenics* (Cambridge University Press).

Buchanan, A., Brock, D, Daniels, N. and Wikler, D. (2000) *From Chance to Choice* (Cambridge University Press).

Freeman, M. (2006) 'Saviour siblings' in S. McLean (ed) *First Do no Harm* (Ashgate).

Gavaghan, C. (2007) *Defending the Genetic Supermarket* (Cambridge University Press).

Haker, H. and Beyeveld, D. (2000) *The Ethics of Genetics in Human Reproduction* (Ashgate).

Parnes, E. (2000) *Enhancing Human Traits* (Georgetown University Press).

Pattinson, S. (2002b) *Influencing Traits Before Birth* (Dartmouth).

Savulescu, J. (2006) 'In defence of procreative beneficence' *Journal of Medical Ethics* 33: 284.

8 Organ Donation and the Ownership of Body Parts

INTRODUCTION

In 2001 for several weeks two news stories were prominent in the media. Both involved showing crying parents torn with love for their children. One involved parents who had discovered that parts of their children had been removed after death without consent and stored for research purposes. To them the bodies of their children had been defiled and abused without their permission. The other story concerned parents of seriously ill children in urgent need of a transplant, without which the children would die; they wereappealing for people to donate organs.[1] These two news stories capture some of the issues in this chapter. On the one hand there is an acceptance of the importance of retaining bodily integrity, even of a deceased person, but on the other there is the urgent need for organs to be transplanted and bodily material to be used for research so that cures for diseases can be found.

Until very recently it was the topic of organ donation which dominated the debates over the legal regulation of bodily parts and products. Although organ donation is still a very important topic a host of other issues have risen to prominence in recent years: Does a patient have any control over bodily material removed during an operation? If a scientist uses bodily samples to develop a wealth-creating discovery, do the people from whom the samples originate have any claim to the proceeds? Can, and should, it be possible to patent DNA sequences?

The starting point for the issues raised concerning the legal regulation of bodily material is now the Human Tissue Act 2004.

1 Human Tissue Act 2004

The Human Tissue Act 2004 was passed following the scandals at Bristol Royal Infirmary and the Royal Liverpool Children's Hospital (Alder Hey) in 1999–2000, the details of which were revealed in the Kennedy and Redfern Inquiries. What was discovered was that the retention of body parts and organs from dead children was common and widespread. This was often done without the consent or knowledge of the parents. On some occasions parents were misled as to what they were consenting to or, where they agreed to a post mortem subject to certain conditions, these conditions were sometimes ignored. Some parents had agreed to the retention of 'tissue' understanding that to refer to tiny pieces of a child's body, not appreciating that in medical circles the term was taken to include whole organs.

---

[1] Herring (2002: 43).

The public outrage at what had happened was enormous. Margaret Brazier and Emma Cave describe it in this way:

> In some cases infants were literally stripped of all their organs and what was returned to their families was an 'empty shell'. In a horrifying number of cases organs and tissue retained were simply stored. They were put to no good use. In some of the most tragic instances the whole of a foetus or still born infant was kept and stored in pots.[2]

The doctors concerned believed that there was nothing improper in what they were doing. The removal of organs and bodily material can be justified on a number of medical grounds: it may be necessary to establish the cause of death; to diagnose the diseases from which the patient was suffering; to discover whether there were environmental causes of death; to ensure that any lessons in relation to treatment of the relevant condition are learnt.[3] It is useful for doctors to have a collection of organs and body parts to refer to in the course of research, education, or preparing for other operations. It would, of course, be helpful for a surgeon about to operate on a heart with a particular abnormality to have a look at a heart with a similar abnormality in a collection of stored samples. Further, banks of samples of bodily material can assist in research which seeks to discover what, if any, genetic form may predispose someone toward a particular disease.[4] As the Chief Medical Officers has pointed out:

> There have been many occasions in the past where the study of tissue after death had led to discoveries in medical science which have resulted in the saving of lives and the relief of suffering. This has particularly been so in the field of cancer research.[5]

In addition to the belief that the retention of organs was important for the progression of science it was thought that to ask parents' permission to do so would have only added to the parents' distress. The views of the hospitals involved were described in the Kennedy Report as 'institutional paternalism'.[6] It seems there was an element of 'what they don't know won't hurt them' in the surgeons' attitude. But also, a genuine belief that whether parents buried the whole of their child's body or most of it would not really bother parents. Why waste a good example of a deformed heart by burying it when it could be used to save lives and progress science?

Outrage greeted the disclosures of what had been done in the two hospitals, which was regarded by many, and particularly the parents involved, as utterly unacceptable.[7] Worse was to follow. A census carried out by the Chief Medical Officer for England (2000) and the *Isaacs Report* (2003) found that the kinds of practices at Alder Hey and Bristol were widespread across the country. It was discovered that there were 54,000 organs and body parts of children or foetuses retained, mostly without proper consent having being obtained.[8]

As well as disclosing the practice of organ retention, the reports also found the law to be unclear and inconsistent. It became apparent that new legislation was required. The Human Tissue Act 2004 built on advice from the Chief Medical Officer in *The Removal*,

---

[2] Brazier and Cave (2007: 470).   [3] Chief Medical Officer (2001: 5).
[4] Chief Medical Officer (2001: 5).   [5] Chief Medical Officer (2001: 6).
[6] Morrison (2005) provides a useful guide to the attitudes and reasoning that permitted the scandals to occur.
[7] Retained Organs Commission (2004: para 2).   [8] DoH (2001h).

Retention and Use of Human Organs and Tissue from Post Mortem Examination[9] and a Government consultation document, *Human Bodies, Human Choices*.[10]

In the past it appeared to be accepted that bodily material could be retained unless there was an objection from the individual or a child's parents.[11] At the heart of the Act is the notion of consent. Bodily material can only be retained or used with the consent of the individual, or in the case of children their parents. The point being this: it may be that many people will share the attitude that the doctors had in these case. Why does it matter very much if a little bit of a body is retained for the benefit of science? But some people do object. There are, for example, those with religious beliefs that demand that a body be buried whole. To them it can matter enormously whether the body is buried complete.

In any event, to obtain consent reveals a proper respect for the deceased and their family. Interestingly many of the parents involved in the scandals stated that they would have consented had they been asked. Their objection was that the doctors had treated the bodies of the children with contempt by plundering them for organs without seeking anyone's consent.[12] As one father, Paul Bradley, put it:

> ...we feel it was criminal, what was done. It is how we felt, that it was very contemptuous what was done, to the dignity of our child that her body has been, as we see it, invaded and body parts stolen...[13]

As Mavis Maclean[14] has emphasized, for a parent who has seen their child die in hospital the feelings of hopelessness and guilt can be enormous. That final duty of the parent, to ensure a proper burial of their child, becomes the most painful and important of tasks. To be prevented from doing that properly, because the body of the child has been decimated, can create feelings of failure, anger, and violation. To discover that parts of their children's bodies were put in yellow sacks and put into a tip revealed an attitude that the bodies of loved ones are rubbish.[15]

Others have written of the way that the removal and retention of body parts without consent was a mutilation of the image of the deceased. This, perhaps, explained why there was the gulf between the doctors involved, who saw nothing wrong in what they were doing, and the relatives. To the doctors the bodies were just cadavers which would, in all likelihood, be cremated; while to relatives the bodies were the images of the recently deceased. As the BMA has put it:

> In simplistic terms, doctors were portrayed as treating cadavers as useful objects, whereas to the relatives they were still people.[16]

Of course, the need for consent is by no means the only lesson to be learned from the scandals. The improved need for counselling following bereavement, and training for medical staff in dealing with recently bereaved people, was also revealed. More needs to be done to explain the functions and purposes of post mortems.

But it was the need to obtain consent before removing and retaining bodily material which became the bedrock for the Human Tissue Act 2004.[17] The Government Paper, *Human Bodies, Human Choices* suggested that the following principles (developed by

---

9 Chief Medical Officer (2001).   10 DoH (2002e).
11 *AB v Leeds Teaching Hospital NHS Trust* [2004] EWHC 644.
12 Brazier and Cave (2007: 471).   13 Maclean (2001: 80).   14 Maclean (2001: 80).
15 Chief Medical Officer (2001: 18).   16 BMA (2004: 417).   17 DoH (2002e: para 1.19).

the Chief Medical Officer) should underpin the law and practice in this area:

- *Respect:* treating the person who has died and their families with dignity and respect.

- *Understanding:* realizing that to many parents and families, their love and feelings of responsibility for the person who has died are as strong as they were in life.

- *Informed consent:* ensuring that permission is sought and given on the basis that a person is exercising fully informed choice; consent is a process, not a 'one off' event.

- *Time and space:* recognizing that a family member may need time to consider whether to agree to a post mortem examination and to consider donation of tissue and organs, and will not wish to feel under pressure to agree in the moments after death.

- *Skill and sensitivity:* NHS staff must be sensitive to the needs of the relatives of someone who has died and sufficient staff skilled in bereavement counselling must be available.

- *Information:* much better information is required, both generally by the public and specifically for relatives who are recently bereaved, about post mortems and the use of tissue after death. Relatives may also require information about the progress of research involving donated material.

- *Cultural competence:* attitudes to post mortem examination, burial, and the use of organs and tissues after death differ greatly between different religious and cultural groups; health professionals need to be aware of these factors and respond to them with sensitivity.

- *A gift relationship:* the emphasis in all present legislation and guidance is on 'taking' and 'retaining'. The balance should be shifted to 'donation', so that tissue or organs are given as a gift to help others and recognized as deserving of gratitude towards those making donations.[18]

1.1 The coverage of the Act

The Government has explained the purpose of the Human Tissue Act 2004 (HTAct) in the following way:

> The purpose of the Act is to provide a consistent legislative framework for issues relating to whole body donation and the taking, storage and use of human organs and tissue. It will make consent the fundamental principle underpinning the lawful storage and use of human bodies, body parts, organs and tissue and the removal of material from the bodies of deceased persons. It will set up an over-arching authority which is intended to rationalise existing regulation of activities like transplantation and anatomical examination, and will introduce regulation of other activities like *post mortem* examinations, and the storage of human material for education, training and research. It is intended to achieve a balance between the rights and expectations of individuals and families, and broader considerations, such as the importance of research, education, training, pathology and public health surveillance to the population as a whole.[19]

---

[18] DoH (2002e: para 2.3).   [19] DoH (2004f: para 5).

The Act is restricted in its general coverage in four important ways:

• Part I of the Act does not apply to the removal of human material from humans, but rather the storage and use of the material.[20] The Act is not designed to deal with complaints that a doctor improperly performed an operation (which are covered by the tort of negligence), but rather the way material is stored or used, after removal.

• The Act only deals with certain kinds of human material. It does not deal with other animals, nor with some kinds of human material (eg sperm, eggs, embryos). It does not cover photographs or other images of human material.[21]

• The Act only deals with the storage and use of human material for particular purposes.

• Part 1 of the Act is not intended to affect the way a coroner carries out her or his duties.[22]

1.2 Section 1: lawfully storing or using bodily material

The HTAct opens with a definition of what can lawfully be done with relevant materials (ie certain bodily materials).

The Act makes it lawful to do any of the following:

• store or use a whole body;

• remove, store, or use human material from a deceased person;

• store and use human material from living people.

Providing:

• there is the necessary consent;

• the act was done for a 'schedule 1 purpose'.

We need to clarify some of the terms used in this summary.

1.2.1 *Human material*

The Act governs 'relevant material.' Under the HTAct, section 53 relevant material is tissue, cells, and organs of human beings, excluding gametes, embryos outside the body, hair and nails from a living person. Cell lines are also excluded by virtue of section 54(7), as is any other human material created outside the human body.

1.2.2 *Appropriate consent*

Consent must be given to the storage or use for the particular purpose in question.[23] So, for example, the fact there is appropriate consent for the storage of an organ for the purposes of transplantation does not authorize the storage of the organ for research. However, if a patient is willing for their material to be used in 'research' it is not necessary to obtain their consent for every individual research project.[24]

---

[20] S 9.   [21] Human Tissue Authority (2006d: para 14).   [22] S 11.
[23] See McHale (2006a) for a useful discussion of the notion of appropriate consent.
[24] Lord Warner (2004).

What does consent mean in this context? Positive consent is required. A failure to object is insufficient.[25] Whether a person has capacity to consent is governed by the general law on consent, as discussed in Chapter 4. The Code of Practice states:

> To give consent, patients (or the person with parental responsibility) must understand the nature and purpose of what is proposed and be able to make a balanced judgement. They should be told of any 'material' or 'significant' risks inherent in the way the sample will be obtained, how the tissue will be used and any possible implications of its use, eg, genetic tests.

But who can give consent?

(i) Adults

Under the HTAct, section 3, in the case of competent adults appropriate consent can only be provided by the individual themselves. The normal law on consent as set out in Chapter 3 applies. The Human Tissue Authority (HTA)'s Code states that 'consent must be given 'voluntarily by an appropriately informed person who has capacity'.[26]

(ii) Deceased adults

In the case of a deceased adult the consent or non-consent of the deceased can come from three sources:

• *The deceased.* If the deceased has made clear her or his views then those determine the question. Where the use of human tissue involves storage for the purposes of public display or anatomical examination there must be consent in writing.[27] However, for all other activities under the Act there is no need for the decision to be in writing. The decision must have been in force immediately before she or he died. So, for example, if the deceased had indicated that she or he was happy for her or his body to be used for medical research, but shortly before her or his death indicated that that was not her or his wish then there would be no effective consent.

• *An appointed representative.* If the person has died without expressing a decision about how her or his bodily material is to be used and she or he has appointed a 'representative' they can make decisions on her or his behalf. The appointment must comply with the requirements in section 4. The representative can be appointed orally or in writing (eg under a will).

• *The person in the closest 'qualifying relationship'.* If the person has died without expressing a decision and has not appointed a personal representative then the person who is in the closest 'qualifying relationship' can make the decision. Section 27(4) ranks the qualifying relations in this order: (a) spouse or partner; (b) parent or child; (c) brother or sister; (d) grandparent or grandchild; (e) child of a person falling within paragraph (c); (f) stepfather or stepmother; (g) half-brother or half-sister; (h) friend of longstanding. If there are two people of the same rank, then only the consent of one is required.[28]

---

[25] Human Tissue Authority (2007d: para 17).   [26] Human Tissue Authority (2007d: para 31).

[27] HTACt 2004, s 2(5). See Human Tissue Authority (2006a) for guidance on public display.

[28] In HM Government (2007a) it was acknowledged that the absence of aunts and uncles from this list was causing problems in practice. The Government said it would be considering the issue.

(iii) Children

The law on consent in relation to children[29] is set out in the HTAct, section 2. If the child is competent[30] then she or he may consent. Indeed a competent child can make an advance decision concerning her or his consent and such a decision must be respected.[31] If not competent then a person with parental responsibility[32] will be able to consent for the child.[33] Thus a parent with parental responsibility could consent that her or his child's organs be used for transplant, but only where the competent child had not expressed her or his views.[34] If the child has died without anyone having parental responsibility then someone in a 'qualifying relationship' can consent to the removal of the material and its storage and use.[35]

(iv) Incapacitated Adults

Where an adult is incapacitated, consent can be deemed in certain circumstances under the Human Tissue Act 2004 (Persons who Lack Capacity to Consent and Transplants) Regulations 2006. These are explained in the HTA's Code of Practice thus:

- Storage and use of relevant material for certain scheduled purposes by a person who is acting in what s/he reasonably believes to be in the best interests of the person lacking capacity from whose body the material came. The scheduled purposes provided for under the Regulations are obtaining scientific or medical information about a living or deceased person which may be relevant to another (including a future person) and transplantation.

- Storage and use of relevant material from a person who lacks capacity for the purposes of a clinical trial authorized and conducted in accordance with the clinical trials Regulations.

- Where it is consistent with sections 30–34 of MCA 2005, allowing for the storage and use of relevant material from persons lacking capacity for research in circumstances provided for in that Act.[36]

1.2.3 A Schedule 1 purpose

A person's act is made lawful by the HTAct, section 1 if she or he is acting for a 'Schedule 1 purpose'. The schedule divides these purposes into two parts. We shall see why shortly.

PART 1

1 Anatomical examination.

2 Determining the cause of death.

3 Establishing after a person's death the efficacy of any drug or other treatment administered to him.

---

[29] Children are people under the age of 18.
[30] Competence is not defined, although presumably the *Gillick* competence test will be used (see Chap 3).
[31] Where the consent concerns anatomical examination or public display the child's consent must be in writing and witnessed.
[32] Chapter 3 explains who has parental responsibility for a child.
[33] A person with parental responsibility cannot consent to the use of a child's body for use as an anatomical examination, only the child herself.
[34] Human Tissue Authority (2007d: para 43).   [35] S 2(7).
[36] Human Tissue Authority (2007d: para 40)

4 Obtaining scientific or medical information about a living or deceased person which may be relevant to any other person (including a future person).

5 Public display.

6 Research in connection with disorders, or the functioning, of the human body.

7 Transplantation.

PART 2

8 Clinical audit.

9 Education or training relating to human health.

10 Performance assessment.

11 Public health monitoring.

12 Quality assurance.

The following can be done with appropriate consent for any of the twelve purposes:

(i) the storage of the body of a deceased person (excluding anatomical examination).

(ii) the removal from the body of a deceased person of any 'relevant material' of which the body consists or which it contains.

The following can be done with appropriate consent for a purpose in Part 1 of Schedule 1:

the storage or use of any 'relevant material' which has come from a human body.

The following can be done for a purpose in Part 2 of Schedule 2, even without consent:

the storage or use of any 'relevant material' which has come from the body of a deceased person.

It should be noted that there are special provisions dealing with the storage of bodies for anatomical examinations.[37]

Where a person is using bodily material for a purpose other than approved in Schedule 1 then, according to the explanatory notes, the Act does not apply. So an artist removing part of a corpse to use in a sculpture will not have done an act covered by the 2004 Act. The Act will not render such an act legal or illegal. However, she or he could still be guilty of, for example, the offence of theft.

1.3 Storage and use of human material without consent

A key principle in the Act is that someone's relevant material can only be used with their consent. But there are eight situations where it is lawful to store and use human material even though there is no consent. These are the following.

(i) A Schedule 1, Part II purpose (eg education, training, and audit)
As already mentioned there is no need for 'appropriate consent' where human material from a live person is stored for a purpose in Part II of Schedule 1 of the Act; that is if it is stored or used in connection with clinical audit, education and training in relation to

---

[37] HTAct 2004, s 1(2) and (3).

human health, performance assessment, public health monitoring, or quality control. Research is not included in this list, although the line between research and education and training may be blurred. The reason for these exceptions is that the use of material for these purposes is seen as intrinsic to the proper conduct of the patient's treatment or the health of the nation.[38] Note that the exception does not apply to human material taken from a deceased person.

(ii) The Human Tissue Authority can deem consent

The Human Tissue Authority has power to deem that there is consent where it is not possible to trace the individual from whom the material originated.[39] The Authority is only likely to use this power where tissue relating to a relative of a patient could be used for genetic testing purposes to assist in the diagnosis or treatment of a patient. It has the power to deem consent where it is satisfied that material has come from the body of a living person; that it is in the interests of another person to obtain scientific or medical information about the individual; and that there is no reason to believe that the individual has died, or made a decision not to consent to the use of material. There is also power for the authority to deem consent where reasonable attempts have been made to get a person to decide what they want to happen to their human material and the individual has not made a decision.

(iii) A High Court Order

A High Court can order that appropriate consent is to be deemed for 'research purposes in connection with disorders, or the functioning of the human body'.[40] These orders can cover the storage of the body of a living or a deceased person and the removal and use of 'relevant material' from a body. The order will be made if it is in the public interest. However, the Government has stated that this power is to be used only in the most exceptional of cases.[41]

(iv) Storage for research purposes

If 'relevant material' from living bodies is stored for the purpose of research in connection with disorders or the functioning of the human body, then consent is not required, providing (i) the research has been ethically approved in line with regulations issued by the Secretary of State, and (ii) the material has been anonomized so that it is not possible to identify the person from whom the material originates.[42] This is an extremely important provision. Notably it permits the use of material for research, even where the patient positively objects. Hopefully where a patient has voiced an objection the researchers will choose not to use their material. Note that this does not justify the removal of material without the consent of the patient. It therefore covers material that has been removed with consent, for example, material removed during an operation.

(v) Surplus material

If material has been removed in the course of treatment, diagnostic tests, or research then that material can be dealt with as waste and there is no need to obtain consent before disposing of it.[43] So a tumour removed in the course of an operation can be disposed of without the explicit consent of the patient. It will be taken that consent to the operation will include consent to the disposal of the tumour.

---

[38] DoH (2004f: para 13). McHale (2006a) discusses whether a person whose material is used for research without their consent can claim interference with their human rights.

[39] HTAct 2004, s 7. [40] HTAct 2004, s 7(4). [41] Price (2005a: 801).

[42] HTAct 2004, s 1(7)–(9). [43] HTAct 2004, s 44.

(vi) Imported material

Consent is not required where the body or material has been imported from overseas.[44] If, therefore, a hospital receives a consignment of organs for research purposes from, say, Denmark, it is not for the English hospital to ensure it has consent from those from whom the organs originated. It is presumed that the law regulating the country of origin will provide adequate protection for their citizen's rights.

(vii) Existing holdings

If a hospital or surgeon has bodies or material which were held for a Schedule 1 purpose immediately before the Act came into force, consent is not required.[45] A Code of Practice will be issued by the Human Tissue Authority to deal with the storage, use, and disposal of existing holdings.

(viii) Coroners' activities

The functions of the Coroner are not covered by the Act. A Coroner may, therefore, authorize the retention of organs without complying with the provisions of the 2004 Act.

As can be seen from this list there are a large number of exceptions to the principle that a person's bodily material cannot be used without their consent.

1.4 The creation of the Human Tissue Authority

The Human Tissue Act, Part 2 sets up the Human Tissue Authority (HTA) whose remit will cover the removal, use, storage, and disposal of human material.[46] The Authority will set up a licensing scheme under which a licence will be required for a range of activities connected with human tissue. It will be an offence to conduct the activities without a licence.[47] The Authority will also produce codes of practice in connection with dealings with human tissue. The HTA will have no power over actions performed for criminal justice purposes, such as coroner's post mortems.[48]

The HTA's remit includes:

- storage and use of human bodies and tissue, and removal of tissue from human bodies, for scheduled purposes;

- import and export of bodies and human tissue for scheduled purposes; and

- disposal of human tissue, including imported tissue, following its use in medical treatment or for scheduled purposes.

In 2007 it was proposed that the HTA would merge with the Human Fertilisation and Embryology Authority to form the Regulatory Authority for Fertility and Tissue (RAFT), however, that proposal has been abandoned. It is expected that regulation of the use of cell lines for therapeutic use will be added to the HTA's remit. Blood and its derivatives are excluded from the remit of the HTA because they are dealt with by the National Blood Service.[49]

---

[44] Special provisions mean that a body or material which is exported and then imported cannot rely on this exception, otherwise this could provide too ready a way round the terms of the Act.

[45] HTAct 2004, s 9(4).

[46] Human Tissue Authority (2007a) describes the recent work of the Authority.

[47] Human Tissue Authority (2007a) reports that over 500 licences have been granted.

[48] HTAct 2004 s 39.

[49] For an excellent analysis of the regulation of blood donation see Farrell (2006).

In respect of the matters within its remit the HTA will be required to do the following:

- Provide information for the general public and the Secretary of State.
- Issue codes of practice. These cover, amongst other things, consent; communicating with relatives post mortem; import and export; disposal of tissue.
- Licensing. A number of activities in relation to human tissue can only be performed with a licence. Anyone seeking a licence will have to apply to the HTA who will be in charge of the licensing system. The activities requiring a licence include the following:
  — storage and use of human bodies for anatomical examination and related research;[50]
  — the carrying out of post mortem examinations, including removal and retention of human tissue;
  — removal of human tissue from the body of a deceased person for other scheduled purposes, except transplantation;
  — storage and use of human bodies or parts for public display;
  — storage of human tissue for other scheduled purposes, for example, human tissue banking for transplant purposes or research.
- The HTA will have the job of carrying out inspections to ensure that the terms of the Human Tissue Act and the conditions of any licences are being complied with. The HTA will be required to ensure that licensing and inspection are 'proportionate' and not unduly 'burdensome'. The HTA is given flexibility to decide how to carry out its duties of inspection and licensing.

1.5 Criminal offences

There are several criminal offences created by the HTAct.

1.5.1 *Failure to obtain 'appropriate consent'*

Section 5 states:

(1) A person commits an offence if, without appropriate consent, he does an activity to which subsection (1), (2) or (3) of section 1 applies, unless he reasonably believes—

(a) that he does the activity with appropriate consent, or

(b) that what he does is not an activity to which the subsection applies.

Section 1 was described above and covers storage or use of a whole body or bodily material; or removal, storage, or use of human material from a deceased person. This means that it would now be a criminal offence for a doctor to retain a child's organs without consent: the kind of behaviour at Alder Hey which caused such uproar. The maximum sentence for this offence is three years, regarded as very high by some, but thought by the Government to be appropriate in the most flagrant of breaches.[51]

---

[50] Previously licensed by Her Majesty's Inspector of Anatomy under the Anatomy Act 1984.
[51] Price (2005a: 809).

The defence of 'reasonable belief' is important. It would mean that if, for example, a doctor was convinced by a written document that a patient had consented to the use of her or his body, but in fact that document was forged, the doctor could not be prosecuted. Of course, what will amount to a reasonable belief will depend on the circumstances.

1.5.2 A false representation of consent

It is an offence for anyone to falsely represent that there is 'appropriate consent' or that an activity does not require consent for the purposes of the Act, if the person knows the representation to be false, or does not believe it to be true.[52]

1.5.3 Failure to obtain a death certificate

It is a criminal offence for someone to store or use a body for anatomical examination without a death certificate.[53] There is a defence for someone who believes that there is a death certificate, or that she or he is doing something not covered by the Act.

1.5.4 Using or storing donated material for an improper purpose

A person who uses or stores donated material commits an offence unless it was done for one of the following purposes:

- the purposes detailed in Schedule 1;
- medical diagnosis or treatment;
- decent disposal;
- for purposes specified in regulations made by the Secretary of State.[54]

There is a defence if a person reasonably believes that she or he was not dealing with donated material.[55]

1.5.5 Analysis of DNA without consent

A offence is committed if a person has any bodily material intending that the DNA is to be analysed without 'qualifying consent' unless the results are for an 'excepted purpose'.[56] There are four 'excepted purposes'. These are:

- General excepted purposes:
  - (a) the medical diagnosis or treatment of the person whose body manufactured the DNA;
  - (b) the purposes or functions of a coroner;
  - (c) the purposes or functions of a procurator fiscal in connection with the investigation of deaths;
  - (d) the prevention or detection of a crime;
  - (e) the conduct of a prosecution;
  - (f) the purposes of national security;
  - (g) implementing an order or direction of a court or tribunal, including one outside the United Kingdom.

---

[52] HTAct 2004, s 5(2).   [53] HTAct 2004, s 5(4).   [54] HTAct 2004, s 8.
[55] HTAct 2004, s 8(2).   [56] HTAct 2004, s 45.

- Under order of the High Court for the purposes of medical research.

- There are complex provisions allowing analysis for certain purposes in respect of existing holdings.

- Where the bodily material is taken from a living person, the DNA can be used without consent for, *inter alia*:

    (a) research;

    (b) clinical audit;

    (c) education;

    (d) performance assessment;

    (e) under direction from the Human Tissue Authority;[57]

    (f) for the benefit of another person.[58]

1.5.6 *Trafficking human tissue for transplantation*

There are offences connected with the selling or trafficking human tissue for transplantation.[59] We will be considering these in greater detail below.

1.5.7 *Unlicensed activities*

Carrying out licensable activities without holding a licence from the HTA is an offence.[60] There are also lesser related offences such as failing to produce records or obstructing the Authority in carrying out its powers or responsibilities.[61]

1.6 Miscellaneous provisions

- Section 43 makes it clear that it is lawful for hospital authorities to take steps to preserve the organs of deceased persons whilst appropriate consent to transplantation is sought.[62]

- Section 44 provides for disposal of human material which is no longer to be retained.

- Section 47 creates a power for certain national museums to transfer human remains out of their collections if they think it appropriate to do so.

2 Comments on the Human Tissue Act 2004

The Human Tissue Act 2004 is attempting to strike a delicate balance. On the one hand it recognizes the importance of ensuring that there is effective consent to the removal and use of human tissue. On the other hand there is a recognition that the use of human

---

[57] See Human Tissue Authority (2006c) for when direction may be given. These cover where it is not possible to find the indviduals whose DNA is in question or reasonable efforts have been made to get someone to decide whether to permit use of the DNA but they have not been able to make a decision.

[58] The Human Tissue Act 2004 (Persons who Lack Capacity to Consent and Transplants) Regulations 2006 provide exceptions where the individual lacks capacity.

[59] HTAct 2004, s 32.   [60] HTAct 2004, s 16.   [61] HTAct 2004, s 16.

[62] For objections that this section inadequately protects autonomy and is a back door to presumed consent donation, see Bell (2006).

tissue is enormously important for research into medical illnesses and for training.[63] The need to restore public trust into genetic research and the collection of human biological samples[64] must not be bought at the cost of severely hampering research into fatal diseases.

While in its draft form the Act went through a number of amendments in its passage through Parliament. Many of these amendments were inserted in response to concerns by scientists and medical professionals that the burdens placed on them were too great.[65] Nevertheless there have been criticisms which have been made about the legislation and ambiguities that have been noted. These include the following:

2.1 What is a criminal offence?

There is an ambiguity that unfortunately strikes at the heart of the HTAct. As we have seen, section 5(1) states:

A person commits an offence if, without appropriate consent, he does an activity to which subsection (1), (2) or (3) of section 1 applies. . . .

Section 1(1) opens:

(1) The following activities shall be lawful if done with appropriate consent—

(a) the storage of the body of a deceased person for use for a purpose specified in Schedule 1, other than anatomical examination. . . .

The ambiguity arises in a scenario where a person is storing the body of a deceased person for a purpose not listed in Schedule 1 (eg to turn a body into a private art exhibit). Whether this is an offence or not turns on the meaning of 'an activity to which subsection (1) applies'. In section 1(1)(a), for example, is the activity simply the storage of a body of a deceased person, in which case the defendant would be guilty; or is the activity 'storage of a deceased person for a Schedule 1 purpose', in which case the defendant is not guilty of the offence under section 5.

The Department of Health's Guide to the Act describes the offences in these terms: 'removing, storing or using human tissue for scheduled purposes, without appropriate consent'.[66] This would appear to suggest that if the actions are done for a purpose not included within Schedule 1 then there is no offence committed under the HTAct, although there may be some other criminal offence (eg theft) but, as we shall see, the circumstances in which some other offence may be committed are unclear. On the other hand it may be questionable whether there is much sense in making doctors who remove tissues from cadavers for research without consent guilty of an offence, but people who remove bits of bodies for prurient interest possibly not guilty of any offence.

Further the use of the word 'lawful' in section 1 is unclear. Presumably the section means the Act will not be unlawful as contrary to the other provisions of the Act and does not mean that an act under section 1 cannot be unlawful under other legislation or other parts of the law (eg the law of negligence or the Data Protection Act).[67]

63 Genetic Interest Group (2004).
64 Medical Research Council (2000) and Human Genetics Commission (2006).
65 For research on how the legislation might affect the day-to-day work of professionals see McLean et al (2006) and Wilton (2007).
66 DoH (2005m).   67 Zimmern, Hall, and Liddell (2004).

2.2 The meaning of consent

Although consent is a central concept in the Act it is not defined.[68] The concept is therefore likely to have the meaning which it normally has in medical law and which we discussed in Chapter 4. As we have seen, many commentators argue that the law is not strict enough regarding the amount of information that must be provided before consent is effective (there is no requirement of 'informed consent' of the kind required in some jurisdictions). The Human Tissue Authority may well produce guidance on what level of information must be provided for consent to be effective. If this is done then that will do much to clarify the law. But there have been complaints that the definition of consent does not appear on the face of the Act.[69]

2.3 Exceptions to the consent principle

It might be thought from the furore that followed the various scandals preceding the Act, and some of the rhetoric from the Government in connection with the Act, that we would have a clear principle that body organs and materials can only be retained with consent. Although this appears as a cardinal principle the number of exceptions to it means that its paramountcy is greatly weakened. We cannot say to patients 'no human material can be taken from your body without your consent'; we can only say 'no human material can be taken from your body without your consent, unless it is permitted under the HTAct'. Notably a person's material can be used without their consent for training, audit, or teaching. The justification of the exception (that it is 'considered intrinsic to the proper conduct of a patient's treatment or are necessary for the public health of the nation') will not convince everyone.[70] And why is research not regarded as 'necessary for the public health of the nation'?[71] Is there a clear distinction between education and research?[72] The distinction is made more complex by the fact that under section 1(7)–(9) use of material for research without consent is permitted if the factors mentioned there (most significantly anonomization of any sample and approval by a Research Ethics Committee[73]) are met.

There is perhaps also a question mark over the distinction here between the bodies of the dead and the living. Why is it lawful to use material from living bodies for teaching purposes (without explicit consent) but unlawful to do the same thing with material from a cadaver? Of course, with the scandals in mind the Government had at the forefront of their mind the position of parents and the bodies of their children; but is there a logical distinction between the living and the dead?

2.4 Rights or utility

One way of examining what happened at Alder Hey and Bristol is that doctors were relying on utilitarian reasoning: it will be for the greatest good to remove the tissue and not tell parents what has happened; rather than a rights-based approach: recognizing the rights of individuals to have control over their bodily material.[74] The Human Tissue Act

---

[68] Nuffield Council (2004).   [69] Parry, Zimmern, Hall, and Liddel (2004: 5).
[70] DoH (2004f: para 13).   [71] Parry et al (2004).   [72] MRC (2004a, para 1).
[73] Zimmern, Hall, and Liddell (2004) question whether RECs have sufficient resources to deal with the increased workload that will result from this.
[74] Morrison (2005).

can be seen as a form of compromise between a rights-based approach and a utilitarian approach. Although at first the statute appears to grant clear rights that material cannot be stored or used without an individual's consent, the number of exceptions to this, many of them justified in the name of the public good, indicate the impact of utilitarian reasoning. It may be claimed that this balancing between the rights of individuals and the public good of research (for example) is necessary.[75] Of course, another argument is that any rights analysis requires the rights of the community to be balanced against the interests of the general community: see the European Convention on Human Rights (ECHR), article 8 for example.

2.5 Is the Act practical?

There will be some who feel that the HTAct fails to appreciate the difficulties in discussing these issues with grief-fuelled family members. To approach relatives soon after the death of a child to discuss in detail post mortem examinations and research on removed organs cannot be done in a way that does not appear callous and insensitive. The obtaining of consent may be an ideal we should strive for, but at the 'coal face' it is far from straightforward. One point worth making here is that, although organ transplant decisions will need to be taken very soon after death, decisions over post mortem are much less time-sensitive. This may make more realistic the possibility of sensitively obtained consent.[76]

With such concerns in mind one suggestion that was made was that the Act should have focused on authorization, rather than consent.[77] The argument is that a parent may feel uncomfortable consenting to the invasion and retention of organs and body parts from their child. However, they will feel less perturbed by simply permitting the procedure to go ahead. The word authorization is also thought by some to be more appropriate in the case of children: parents should be permitted to authorize treatment, but cannot be said to consent as it is not their bodily material. Some might think that the subtle distinction between authorization and consent might trouble the academic lawyer, but it is unlikely to be appreciated by a grieving parent.

A different point is that if the requirement as to what constitutes consent becomes too bureaucratic and onerous, this will stifle important medical research.[78] At the very least the existence of the criminal offences in this area may produce an atmosphere of excessive caution.[79] If consent is too difficult to acquire, there will be fewer bodily materials available for research, and the advance of science will be slowed.

2.6 The role of parents

One of the themes that emerged from the various scandals was the importance attached to parents being involved in decisions concerning the bodies of their deceased children. It has generally been assumed that they should be. But is this any more than sentiment? Should the views of parents on what should happen to their children's bodies hamper the advance of science? Brazier has provided some powerful arguments for paying

---

[75] Morrison (2005).   [76] Morrison (2005: 187).
[77] The arguments are discussed in Brazier (2003a).
[78] Nuffield Council (2004).   [79] Parry et al (2004).

respect to the views of parents:

(1) The child is 'theirs'. She or he belongs to them. Her or his body belongs to them. They are still parents, albeit bereaved parents.

(2) They are the guardians of the family's values, be they religious or cultural imperatives, or simply personal convictions.

(3) Robbed of their child, parents need the means to come to terms with the loss of all the joys of parenthood. They need some means of regaining control.

(4) The parents' own mental health and emotional wellbeing are at stake.

(5) The physical body of a beloved child remains fixed in the mind. Rationally parents know the child does not suffer or bleed. In the imagination, nightmares haunt their sleep.[80]

To others, although it is understandable that we feel enormous sympathy with grieving parents, the law has to rise above 'mere emotion'. Is it right that the particular wishes of parents trump the public interest in carrying out research into childhood illnesses, which in the long term might save the lives of other children? After all the feelings of grieving parents are not of such legal weight as to prevent a post mortem. Is it obvious that post mortems are more in the public interest than research into childhood illness?[81] Consider these comments from some leading scientists made about the Human Tissue Bill:

> We regret that the Government, in its proper concern for the distress caused to individuals by unacceptable activities at Alder Hey and Bristol, has sought to pass a Bill that fails to provide a proper balance between the needs and rights of individuals and those of the community. We believe that changes will be needed if the Bill is to strike a fair balance between the requirements of individual patients and individual citizens, and those of public health and the public interest.[82]

In stronger terms John Harris has written of the 'quite absurd, if understandable, preoccupation with reverence and respect for bodily tissue that has come to dominate discussions of retained tissues and organs in the wake of the Alder Hey revelations'.[83]

2.7 The definition of human material

Some concern has been expressed at the broad definition of human material in the HTAct. Although there may be widespread acceptance that the removal of organs from cadavers without appropriate consent should be unlawful, should we say the same thing about a minute amount of tissue to be placed on a slide. Would parents of the children involved in the scandals have felt any shock at discovering a tiny portion of cells are removed?[84] It can be argued that the Act should have drawn a distinction between a sample (a tiny piece of human material) and organs or large pieces of material.

2.8 Ownership of bodily material

The HTAct does not directly address the question of whether a person owns bodily material once it has been removed. The focus is on consent rather than property rights

---

[80] Brazier (2003a: 30).   [81] See the arguments of Harris (2002).   [82] Parry et al (2004: para 1.5).
[83] Harris (2002: 546).   [84] Skene (2002); Mason and Laurie (2001).

as the guiding principle behind the Act. The implication of the need for consent, and especially the fact that in some circumstances material can be removed without consent, might be that a person does not own bodily material taken from them during a medical procedure, but if that it is correct it might have been desirable for the Act to say so explicitly.

Section 32(9) refers to human material which has become property by the application of human skill. Unfortunately it fails to give guidance as to when human material can become property and if so who owns it. This is particularly disappointing given that the Act is intended to provide a comprehensive framework for issues relating to the use and storage of bodily material. Whether one can be said to own one's body or parts of it is a vexed legal and ethical issue and one to which we shall be returning later in this chapter.

2.9 Conditional consent

It has already been mentioned that the Act fails to clarify what 'consent' means for the purpose of the Act. In particular it is unclear whether a patient can give 'conditional consent'. A Roman Catholic might, for example, be happy for her or his human material to be used for research as long as the research does not involve embryos or concern contraception. Could he or she consent with such a proviso? Until we have guidance from the Human Tissue Authority we do not know.

2.10 Should the deceased's wishes carry any weight?

It is generally thought that in relation to cadavers the wishes of the deceased, if expressed, should be followed. If a person has made it clear that on death they do not want their bodies used for medical research their wishes should be respected. This principle is reflected in the HTAct. However, that view is not held universally. John Harris has argued that although a person may have an interest in what happens to their body after their death, that interest should carry only a little weight. In short this is because after death a person cannot be harmed: they no longer exist and although their interests persist, because the infringement to those interests cannot harm the person (because the person no longer exists) the interests are weak.[85] Given the enormous benefits of medical research, the public interest in enabling researchers to use material from cadavers should outweigh the value of following an individual's wishes. He goes on to argue that we regularly dispose of parts of our bodily tissue through bowel movements, combing hair, menstruation etc. We should be no more concerned about bits of our bodily material being taken by doctors than we are with these losses of human material. Harris accepts that there are interests in ensuring that the bodies are disposed of in a way which poses no health risk; that respects public decency; and attaches appropriate weight to the legitimate interests of the deceased. But there are no further interests than these.

In reply to Harris' arguments Brazier has suggested that Harris's views are driven by a 'cold rationality'.[86] She starts by making the point that it is easy to over-egg the claims for research. Many of the organs removed in the Alder Hey and Bristol scandals were simply being stored and not, in fact, being used for ground-breaking research. But at the heart of her argument is that people's views (or the views of their relatives) about how

---

[85] Harris (2002: 537).   [86] Brazier (2002: 551).

they wish their bodies to be treated after death, deserve the highest respect. Their views may represent powerful religious beliefs. As she points out, Judaism, Islam, and some Christian traditions have particular requirements in relation to the disposal of bodies. To prevent the burial of bodies in line with these religious beliefs (by authorizing removal of body parts without consent) would infringe religious rights.[87] As she says, to some an improper burial will mean awful consequences in the afterlife: 'It is easy to mock such beliefs from an atheist, agnostic or liberal viewpoint. The pain such a belief must produce is acute and life-destroying.'[88]

But it is not only religious sensibilities that concern Brazier. Many people, however 'irrationally', have strong views about how bodies are treated on death:

> The image of the newly dead person remains fixed in the minds of most bereaved families. Mutilation of the body becomes a mutilation of that image. Reason may tell the family that a dead child could not suffer when organs were removed. Grief coupled with imagination may overpower reasons. Families grieve differently just as they live their lives differently. Respect for family life requires respect for such differences.[89]

To Harris, feelings of this kind are simply irrational and, although deserving of respect, should not lead us to adopt laws which hinder important medical progress. To Brazier, Harris is seeking to impose his view of the world on everyone.

Brazier points out that we allow people to decide where their property should go on their death, through a will, even if they wish to leave their money to a cause many people would think irrational. Should we not let people make the same decision about their bodies? She is willing to agree that it is good for people to altruistically donate their body to medical science, but she points out that we do not force people to be altruistic while they are alive, and so we should not do so when they die. She argues that to ignore a person's wishes about their body does cause them harm:

> We live in a world where our welfare depends on the mutual love and solace our families and friends provide for us. We live in the knowledge of death's inevitability. How we will be treated after our death affects our welfare in life.[90]

3 Transplanting of organs

3.1 Introduction

It is useful to start with a brief outline on some of the technical issues relating to organ donation. First, it is necessary to distinguish between the following:

(i) *Live organ donation.* An organ is taken from a live person and given to another. Clearly the kinds of organs where this is possible are limited. A popular one is a kidney.

(ii) *Cadaver organ donation.* Here an organ is taken form a person shortly after death and transplanted into another.

(iii) *Xenotransplantation.* Here an organ is taken from another animal and used in a human.

---

[87] Brazier (2002: 560).   [88] Brazier (2002: 560).
[89] Brazier (2002: 566).   [90] Brazier (2002: 566).

(iv) *Genetically created organs.* Scientists are presently working on this technology. The hope is that at some point in time an organ can be created in a laboratory from a person's own genetic material, that can be used to be placed into a person.

(v) *Artificial organs.* Some work is being done to create robotic/mechanical organs for transplant, with some success.[91]

From a medical perspective organ transplants are often a last resort because of the difficulties that can arise in the course of a transplantation. The medical problems include:

(i) *Rejection of the transplanted organ by the host.* It is a natural reaction of a body to reject tissue which is not genetically the host's. This can to some extent be controlled by medicine. Xenotransplantation causes particular problems in this regard. It also means that donors are generally sought who are genetically a close match to the recipient of the organ.

(ii) *The donated organs must be healthy.* This is an obvious point but has important ramifications in the case of cadaver organ donation. In order to ensure that the organ is as healthy as possible it is desirable to remove the organ from the donor as soon as possible after death. This creates practical difficulties. Some have claimed that organs have been from people who have not technically died in order to ensure that their organs are usable, and there is even debate over whether the meaning of death is influenced by when it is most appropriate to remove organs for transplantation. A further issue is that where relatives have to be consulted over donation they have to make a decision shortly after the death of their loved one, at a time when they are so full of grief that they may not be able to make a clear headed decision.[92]

(iii) The organs must be preserved between the time of removal and the time of being placed into the recipient.

 REALITY CHECK

Some statistics on organ donation

The number of transplants In 2006–07 3,086 organs were transplanted and 2,402 people had their sight restored through a cornea transplant. The organs came from 1,495 donors. The vast majority of organs came from deceased people. There were 690 live organ transplants, the number which has increased from 461 in 2004 (UK Transplant (2007)).

Research suggests that there is a wide variance in the number of organs donated in different parts of the country and in the rate of donation among different ethnic groups (Wight, Jakubovic, Walters, Maheswaran, White, Lennon (2004)).

It was reported that the organs of one woman who died were able to help 20 different seriously ill people (BBC Newsonline 9 February 2005).

Would-be donors There has been a push to increase the number of names on the NHS Organ Donor Register. There are now 14,201,229 people on the NHS Organ Donation Register. (UK Transplant (2007)).

---

[91] BBC Newsonline (1 June 2005).
[92] UK Transplant (2007) reports that 41% of relatives refuse to consent to transplantation when approached. See also Barber et al (2006).

Those needing organs Official figures suggest that by March 2007 there were 7,234 patients on the 'waiting list' for organ transplants. Unfortunately in 2006–07 459 patients died while waiting for their transplants. (UK Transplant (2007)).

Success rate of organ transplant For transplants during calendar years 1999–2001 in adult recipients, the five-year kidney transplant survival rates are 83 per cent and 89 per cent for cadaveric heartbeating and living donation, respectively. The five-year heart transplant survival rate is 69 per cent, that for lung transplantation is 53 per cent, and for liver transplantation the survival rate is 86 per cent (UK Transplant (2007)).

Technology in this area is ever advancing. It was reported that a woman was cured of diabetes after a donor transplant of insulin producing cells (BBC Newsonline 19 April 2005).

3.2 Living donors: the law

If a living donor wishes to donate regenerative tissue (eg blood or bone marrow) there are few legal or ethical objections to this.[93] The main legal issue is whether or not there is genuine consent to the donation. Where, however non-regenerative donation (eg a kidney) is involved the issue is more problematic. Our discussion will therefore focus on those cases.

There are three important legal principles here:

- It is not permissible to consent to a procedure which causes death or serious injury.[94] Therefore a parent cannot donate a heart to a child, assuming the parent will die as a result of the donation. Donation of a single kidney, a segment of a liver, or a lobe of a lung will be permissible if the donor is in good health.

- There must be consent to the procedure. The donor must understand fully the processes involved. In the case of an incompetent patient the donation will only be permitted if it can be shown to be in that person's best interests.[95] It is doubtful whether it could ever be shown that the donation of an organ would be in an incompetent person's interests. As we shall see the terms of the Human Organ Transplants Act 1989 mean that if the donation is to someone not genetically related to the donor it is extremely unlikely that it would be lawful for an incompetent person to donate.

- The procedure must be permissible under the Human Tissue Act 2004.[96]

This final element requires elaboration. The Human Tissue Act 2004, section 33 states:

(1) Subject to subsections (3) and (5), a person commits an offence if—

(a) he removes any transplantable material from the body of a living person intending that the material be used for the purpose of transplantation, and

(b) when he removes the material, he knows, or might reasonably be expected to know, that the person from whose body he removes the material is alive.

(2) Subject to subsections (3) and (5), a person commits an offence if—

---

[93] There has been an increase in the number of live kidney donors and these now represent a quarter of all kidney donation (UK Transplant (2007)).
[94] Law Commission Consultation Paper 139 (1995: para 8.32).
[95] Mental Capacity Act 2005, s 4.
[96] Human Tissue Authority (2006b) provides an accessible summary of the law.

(a) he uses for the purpose of transplantation any transplantable material which has come from the body of a living person, and

(b) when he does so, he knows, or might reasonably be expected to know, that the transplantable material has come from the body of a living person.

(3) The Secretary of State may by regulations provide that subsection (1) or (2) shall not apply in a case where—

    (a) the Authority is satisfied—

        (i) hat no reward has been or is to be given in contravention of section 32, and

        (ii) that such other conditions as are specified in the regulations are satisfied, and

    (b) such other requirements as are specified in the regulations are complied with.

As this section makes clear, the starting point is that it is illegal both to remove an organ from a living person to transplant into another, and to use the organ which has been removed illegally from a living person. To do so could lead to a criminal conviction. However, the removal and use of the organ can be lawful if (1) there are no payments, and (2) the regulations required by the Human Tissue Authority have been satisfied. These two requirements need further clarification.

(i) The organ must not have been subject to 'commercial dealing' of the kind prohibited by section 32. We will be looking at this provision later in this chapter.

(ii) The Human Tissue Authority will issue regulations concerning live donations. The code of practice provides a lengthy list of issues that must be discussed with the proposed donor. These include the risks involved in the donation and the fact that there is no guarantee that the recipient will benefit from being given the organ.[97] Where the donor is genetically or emotionally related to the recipient, provided they have been given the necessary information and have met with a clinician and an independent assessor, then the donation can go ahead without the specific approval of the HTA. Where, however, the donor is not genetically or emotionally related to the recipient there is a need for approval from an HTA panel.[98] The code suggests that a psychiatrist must meet with the donor and ensure there is genuine consent to the donation.

3.3 Children donating organs

There is no case law which deals specifically with this question. The Human Tissue Act 2004 itself provides no specific guidance. The HTA has issued a Code of Practice. There it is said that living donations from children will be extremely rare.[99] Any donation from a child must be approved by a Panel of the HTA.

Looking at the legal issues there is no direct authority on the issue. It is therefore necessary to deal with it as a matter of first principle. It is necessary to distinguish between cases where the child is *Gillick* competent and where the child is not.[100]

(i) The child is not Gillick competent

The general position of the law and indeed that in the HTAct is that a person with parental responsibility can consent to a medical procedure for a child. Can a parent

---

[97] Human Tissue Authority (2006b).   [98] Human Tissue Authority (2006b).

[99] Human Tissue Authority (2006b: para 30).   [100] Herring (2007b: Chap 8).

consent to an organ donation? The Code of Practice says that they can only do so where the donation will be in the child's best interests.[101] Some have argued not because the donation may be said not to be in the child's best interests. There are two responses that could be made to this argument.

The first response is to suggest that in a particular case the donation could be in the child's best interests. If, for example, the donation was to a sister with whom the child had a close bond, and if without the donation the sister would die, the courts would have little difficulty in finding that the welfare of the child would be promoted by the donation. This argument may be more difficult to run where the relationship between the child and recipient was more distant. Or when the child is a newborn sibling can it be said that the benefit that the child will gain in the future from the relation with the sibling justifies a donation now?

A second response is to suggest that the law does not compel a parent to exercise parental responsibility in a way which is harmful to a child. For example, no parent will be said to be acting illegally if they feed their child unhealthy food, even though to do so would be in the child's best interests. As long as the child is not caused significant harm parents are generally permitted to raise their children as they see fit. In reply it may be said that an organ donation involves major surgery and would amount to significant harm.

(ii) Where the child is Gillick competent

As we discussed in Chapter 3 where a child has sufficient capacity to understand the issues she or he is able to give effective consent to medical treatment. Can this extend to organ donation? One view is that a *Gillick* competent child should be treated in the same way as an adult for these purposes. Lord Donaldson appeared to suggest in *Re W (A Minor) (Medical Treatment)*[102] that a *Gillick* competent child could consent to an organ donation. However, he limited that statement by saying that he thought it improbable that a teenager would be competent to take such a serious decision[103] and also that it was 'inconceivable' that a doctor would want to remove a child's organs without the parents' consent.[104] He also thought it 'inconceivable' that an organ would be removed for donation if a child opposed the taking.[105] The provisions in the HTAct 2004 dealing with children consenting to the removal of tissue generally allows a competent child to consent, and does not allow those with parental responsibility to have a say unless the child is incompetent. The Code of Practice issued by the HTA states that a *Gillick* competent child can consent to organ donation.[106] It suggests that good practice would be to involve the child's family in the decision-making process. The implication seems to be that a parent would not have a veto over a *Gillick* competent child's wish to donate.

The House of Lords in *Hashmi*[107] approved of a decision of the HFEA that it was permissible to screen embryos to see if they would have matching tissue for a bone marrow or umbilical cord transplant. Although not addressing directly the legality of taking the

---

101 Human Tissue Authority (2007e: para 30).   102 [1992] 4 All ER 627, 639.
103 At 635.   104 At 635.
105 At 635. But see *Re M (Child: Refusal of Medical Treatment)* [1999] 2 FLR 1097 where a 15½-year-old refused to consent to receiving a donated heart. Her refusal was overridden and the operation authorized by the courts.
106 HTA (2006e).
107 *Quintavalle (on behalf of Comment on Reproductive Ethics) v Human Fertilisation and Embryology Authority* [2005] UKHL 28.

marrow or cord for transplant the authorization of the screening would appear to imply that any subsequent donation could be regarded as lawful.

(iii) 16- and 17-year-olds

A 16- or 17-year-old is able to consent to 'treatment' by means of the Family Law Reform Act 1969, section 8(1) without needing to show that she or he is *Gillick* competent. It is not clear whether treatment would cover a donation. In *Re W (A Minor) (Medical Treatment)*[108] Lord Donaldson appeared to suggest it could not. He suggested that in the case of organ donation a person with parental responsibility would need to consent or it would need to be shown that the teenager was *Gillick* competent.

So working from first principles it appears that it may in some cases be lawful for a competent child to donate an organ. However, it is clear that in practice it is very rare for a child's organs to be used,[109] although it is fairly common for blood or skin to be donated by children.[110] Where donated material is taken its use is restricted to close relatives, such as siblings.[111] It is notable that the World Health Organization[112] has suggested that there should be a blanket ban on the use of minors as organ donors. In practice it seems in the UK that child donors are virtually unheard of. In the Eurotransplant catchment area only five minor living donors have been used.[113] Many would agree with Garwood-Gowers:

> Perhaps the only circumstances in which the incompetent minor should be used...is where the donation is a necessity, such as because it is the only feasible option for preserving the life or well-being of a prospective recipient who is a key component in the incompetent minor's own-wellbeing.[114]

The BMA take a slightly less positive attitude: only in 'truly exceptional circumstances' should children be considered as donors.[115] What is agreed by nearly all commentators is that it would be improper to force a child to donate an organ against her or his wishes, whether she or he is competent or not. Such an action is likely to infringe the child's rights under the Human Rights Act.[116]

3.4 Incompetent donors

What about the position of an incompetent adult (including a patient in PVS)?

The Human Tissue Act, section 6 explains that if an adult lacks capacity to consent to the use of storage of material for the purposes of transplantation her or his consent can be deemed in certain circumstances. The donation would also require the approval of the Court,[117] and would require the approval of a panel of at least three members of the HTA where there is no effective consent in place.

The general position on the treatment of incompetent people is covered by the Mental Capacity Act 2005 (MCAct), which is discussed in detail in Chapter 4. We shall here briefly explain how that Act deals with organ donation.

---

[108] [1992] 4 All ER 627. [109] Garwood-Gowers (1999: 122).
[110] Brazier (2003a: 423). [111] Ross (1993).
[112] WHO (1994) has suggested that there should be a blanket ban on the use of minors as organ donors.
[113] Garwood-Gowers (1999: 122). [114] Garwood-Gowers (1999: 145).
[115] BMA (2004: 93). [116] Garwood-Gowers (2001).
[117] Human Tissue Act 2004 (Persons who Lack Capacity to Consent and Transplants) Regulations 2006; see Human Tissue Authority (2006e).

There are three ways by which the removal and transplantation of an organ or bodily material can be authorized from an incompetent person.

(i) An advance directive

If the incompetent person made an advance decision authorizing the transplantation of the organ, it will be possible to rely on that as consent to the donation. However the 2005 MCAct states that an advance decision can only relate to refusal of treatment.

(ii) An enduring power of attorney

The incompetent person may have signed an enduring power of attorney which has authorized someone to make decisions concerning her or his welfare and the attorney has approved of the proposed removal of material for donation. However, as with advance decisions, the legislation only permits the donee of the power of attorney to authorize treatment and donation of bodily material may not be treatment. Further the donee can only authorize things which are in the best interests of the patient and it will be rare for a donation to be regarded as in the patient's best interests.

(iii) The best interests of the patient

The key principle is found in the Mental Capacity Act 2005, section 1(5):

> An act done, or decision made, under this Act for or on behalf of a person who lacks capacity must be done, or made, in his best interests.

So the basic proposition of law is that material can be taken from a person for donation to another if it is in that individual's best interests.

But can it ever be in someone's best interests to donate material? The leading case on the donation of bodily material prior to the passing of the 2004 Act was *Re* Y.[118] That case is discussed in detail at page 165. There Connell J accepted that it was in a patient's best interests to donate bone marrow to his sibling on the basis that otherwise the sibling might fall seriously ill or die and this would impact on the level of care and support Y's mother would be able to offer Y, although it should be emphasized that the case involved bone marrow, and Connell J was doubtful that his judgment would act as a useful precedent where more invasive surgery was required, as would be the case in a kidney donation, for example.

To some people, in the absence of an advance directive or the decision of an appointed attorney it is not permissible to use the organs or bodily material of an incompetent person, that is, to use the incompetent person as a means of helping another. Ethically it cannot be right to use such people for the benefit of others; it is simply 'exploitation'.[119] As we have seen in Chapter 3 arguments can be made that there are benefits to an incapacitated person from donation: they may be receiving care or benefit from a relationship with the donee of the material; they may receive better care as a result of the donation; it might even be claimed that allowing them to participate in the 'good' of donation is beneficial for their lives. In response others have claimed that forced altruism is not altruism.[120]

3.5 Living donors: ethical issues

To some the low levels of live organ donations (we have the lowest in Europe[121]) are shocking. Quite simply people are dying because of our reluctance to welcome and

---

[118] The case is discussed in Feenan (1997) and Mumford (1998).
[119] Keown and Gormally (1999).   [120] Keown (1997b).   [121] Choudhry et al (2003).

encourage live organ donations. In clinical terms the likelihood of a successful transplant appears higher where the donor is a live donor[122] and there is even evidence that recipients prefer to receive organs from live donors rather than cadavers.[123] Indeed one leading commentator has suggested that live donor transplants should no longer be regarded as a last resort but should become a major source of organs.[124] In May 2005 the Government announced a drive to increase live organ donation, although this was said to be restricted to donations between loved ones.[125]

Despite these arguments in favour of encouraging live organ donations, the subject raises some complex ethical issues including the following.

3.5.1 *Are there any limits to the donation of organs?*

Should the law allow someone to donate an organ if in so doing they are liable to suffer a serious injury or even death? Normally in the criminal law a person is not permitted to consent to a serious injury unless there is a good reason to do so. Does this pose a problem for live kidney donations? Not necessarily. First, the risk of injury with live donations is small; reported death rates range from 0.03–0.06 per cent. The rate of complications for nephrectomy is 2 per cent and wound pain is 3.2 per cent. In fact overall donors who successfully complete the evaluation for living kidney transplant have an above average life expectancy.[126] Great psychological benefits have been found to result from successful donation, although where the recipient dies after the donation, then there can be psychological harm for the donor.[127] In one survey of live donors only three of the 84 donors questioned said they would not go through with the donation if they had their time again.[128] Second, the serious injuries are being caused for a good reason: to save the life of another. We permit people to suffer serious injuries in the name of boxing and bungee jumping; should we not allow them to do so in the name of saving a life?

But, how far can we take this? Consider the following:

TO PONDER

Donating everything?

The BMA report the following:

Surgeon's refusal to meet a patient's request. Mr P had two sons, aged 33 and 29. Both sons had Alport's syndrome, an inherited condition that causes kidney failure. Mr P successfully donated a kidney to his younger son. His older son, R, received a cadaveric kidney, but the transplant failed. As it had been a poor match, R developed antibodies that made him incompatible with 96 per cent of the population. Finding a suitable kidney was therefore extremely unlikely, unless his parents were suitable donors. Mrs P was told that she was not suitable. Mr P wanted to donate his second kidney to R.

Mr P argued it would be better for him to be on dialysis than his son. He was retired and prepared for the lifestyle change that dialysis would bring. Despite finding support from some doctors, Mr P's request was turned down by three transplant teams. Some of the deliberations of the third were filmed and shown on television.

---

122 Garwood-Gowers (1999: 37); Nicholson and Bradley (1999).
123 Kranenburg et al (2005).   124 Garwood-Gowers (1999: 206).
125 BBC Newsonline (30 May 2005).   126 ULTRA (2003).
127 Garwood-Gowers (1999: 49).   128 Garwood-Gowers (1999: 37).

> Members of the transplant team had mixed views about Mr P's request. Some understood and felt they would want to do the same for their own children. Although some believed that the benefits were one sided, others agreed that there could be emotional benefits for Mr and Mrs P if the transplant was a success for R. There were also concerns about the impact on the family (the younger brother was opposed to the operation) and about how R in particular would feel about the effects on his father's length and quality of life. The resource implications of ending up with two people on dialysis rather than one if the transplant was not successful were also discussed.
>
> The decision rested with the transplant surgeon. Although he knew that Mr P understood the nature and implications of his request, and that he could see ethical and rational justifications for the operation taking place, he knew that ultimately he would feel unable to perform the operation. Mr P was therefore turned down.
>
> As a last resort, Mrs P was tested again to see if she might be a match. Although she had been rejected several times in the past, she was found to be a match (BMA (2004: 91)).

It would even be possible to imagine a more extreme case: a parent wanting to donate a heart to her or his child. That would, of course, entail the death of the parent. But what justification is there for preventing a person who has freely chosen to act in what many would regard to be a virtuous way which causes no harm to anyone else?[129]

The answer, which will not convince everyone, is that it will infringe the principle of beneficence: that doctors should do no harm.[130] As Austen Garwood-Gowers puts it:

> The justification for law stepping in is not to prevent people voluntarily assuming risk but to prevent others from using the fact that a person has consented as a basis for mutilating them.[131]

In other words it is not wrong for a parent to wish to save their child's life by donating a heart, but it is wrong for the medical team to rely on that consent to justify their procedure.

3.5.2 The importance of a genetic relationship?

Before the 2004 Human Tissue Act a clear distinction existed between live donors who were genetically linked to the recipient and those who were not. In short, the assumption was that those who were not genetically related to the recipient were likely to be improperly motivated, probably by money, and so great caution was required. By contrast, with a genetically related donor we could assume that the donation was motivated by altruism and so was subject to less scrutiny. This attitude is reflected in the World Health Organization's Guiding Principles on Human Organ Transplantation:

> Organs for transplantation should be removed preferably from the bodies of deceased persons. However, adult living persons may donate organs, but in general such donors should be genetically related to the recipients. Exceptions may be made in the case of transplantation of bone marrow and other acceptable regenerative tissues. (Guiding Principle 3)

Not everyone is attracted to the distinction. It has been pointed out that even if the donor is genetically related to the recipient, genuine consent may not be present. Indeed

---

[129] Glannon and Ross (2002).   [130] Nys (1996).   [131] Garwood-Gowers (1999: 62).

an argument can be made that emotional pressure can be much greater than that created by the offer of money.[132] Further, it is perfectly possible for a stranger to be willing to donate out of a genuine spirit of altruism, rather it being inevitably a matter of money. For example, a group calling themselves the 'Jesus Christians', see donation of organs to strangers as an important part of showing their love for their fellow human beings and have complained at the difficulties their members have faced in seeking to donate organs in the UK.[133] Such arguments have led some to claim that we should welcome donations from live donors whether there is a genetic link or not.[134] The British Transplant Society and Renal Association have supported live donations, providing the risk to the donors is low; they are fully informed; they consent voluntarily and without coercion or the offer of money; and the transplant procedure has a good chance of proving effective.[135]

3.5.3 *The distinction between regenerative and non-regenerative organs*

To the law and to many commentators there is an important distinction to be drawn between the donation of regenerative and non-regenerative parts. The donation of bodily material which will automatically be replaced (eg blood or bone marrow) is much less controversial than the donation of an organ which is not replenished (eg a kidney). This means that there is much less regulation of blood and marrow donation, and the law is happier about authorizing blood or bone marrow donation from incompetent people.[136] A few commentators have found the distinction unconvincing. They point out that even non-regenerative organs are constantly changing and remaking themselves.[137] That said, the loss of a kidney can have potential long term health impact which could not be analogous to the loss of a pint of blood.

3.5.4 *Payment*

If we are going to permit live donation should we accept payment? This is an issue to which we will return shortly, where we will discuss the commercialization of the body generally. As we shall see, it is illegal and contrary to professional guidance to be involved in the sale of organs.[138]

For now we shall just note that it certainly seems possible to buy organs if one is willing to do so. The ban on the commercial selling of organs in 1989 followed the discovery that kidneys purchased from donors in Turkey were being transplanted to recipients in the UK. Apparently it is possible to find kidneys for sale on the internet, with prices up to £100,000.[139] They have even appeared on eBay (the internet auction site).[140] UK doctors have been struck off for trying to arrange organ sales.[141] A journalist who placed an advert on the internet purporting to be desperately seeking a kidney, claimed to have been inundated with replies from people both in the UK and the States.[142] Many of the respondents were in need of medical treatment themselves and were willing to sell a kidney to pay for it. In many developing countries it is claimed there is a flourishing

---

132 Biller-Andorno and Schauenberg (2001).   133 Ronson (2002).
134 See Roff (2007) who discusses the motives of unrelated organ donors and argues for a greater acceptance that there can be genuinely altruistic motives.
135 BMA and Law Society (2004: 93). British Transplant Society (2000).
136 See Farrell (2006) for a discussion of the regulation of blood donation.
137 Herring (2002: 55).   138 GMC (1992: 2).
139 Hayward and O'Hanlon (2003).   140 BBC Newsonline (26 April 2004).
141 O. Dyer (2002).   142 Hayward and O'Hanlon (2003).

trade in organs. In 2007 a man was given a suspended sentence after trying to sell his kidney for £24,000.[143]

3.5.5 *Compulsory organ donation*

Should we compel people to be organ donors against their will? At first sight the idea seems preposterous: would it not be a monstrous suggestion that people could be killed without their consent so that their organs could be used to save the lives of others? Let us imagine Alfred is in urgent need of a heart transplant and Bertha in need of a lung transplant. We could kill Charles and use his heart and lungs to save Alfred and Bertha's lives. Is this not justifiable on the basis that it is better to kill one person in order to save two lives? John Harris, in his article 'The Survival Lottery'[144] suggests that the proposal would be acceptable if Charles is selected by random (eg by a computer). In response to the argument that it cannot be right to kill an innocent person, he replies that it is wrong to let two innocent people die. In our scenario Alfred and Bertha are as innocent as Charles. This point causes him to accept that a person may not be able to receive an organ under this scheme if they are responsible for the failure of their organs (eg through excessive drinking of alcohol).

His proposal has not exactly received universal acclaim, and one can hardly envisage it being part of a political party's manifesto. Nevertheless an explanation of what is wrong with it has proved harder to articulate. One response is to draw the distinction between killing someone and letting people die. It is wrong to let Alfred and Bertha die for want of an organ, but a greater wrong is done to Charles by killing him. It could be put in terms of human rights: we have a right not to be killed, but not necessarily a right to receive life-saving treatments. These distinctions turn on the difference between doing an act which kills and an omission which fails to save a patient. As we will see in Chapter 9 this distinction is a controversial one and one which is rejected by others.

Harris's argument is utilitarian and a different response would be to challenge it on its own terms. Although saving the two lives at the cost of one would initially appear to produce a utilitarian benefit, it might be argued that the impact on society of this scheme, with citizens constantly in fear that their 'number may be up', will be such as to outweigh the benefits. Harris suggests that this concern is fanciful: more people are killed in cars than would be under his proposal and people do not appear to be too concerned about that. In any event the scheme could be promoted in a way which encourages people to make sacrifices for others.

3.6 Organ transplants from the dead

From April 2006 this area of the law will be governed by the Human Tissue Act 2004. As we have seen section 1 of the Act permits the removal, storage, and use of organs for transplantation from a deceased person as long as there is 'appropriate consent'.[145] In order to decide this point it is necessary to consider the following questions:

(1) Has the deceased made a decision whether or not to consent to the transplant which was in force immediately before her or his death? This decision can be oral or

---

[143] BBC Newsonline (11 May 2007).
[144] Harris (1975). See Øverland (2007) for a discussion of the different forms such a lottery could take.
[145] S 3 defines appropriate consent.

in writing.[146] If the deceased has made a decision then that must be respected. So, for example, if the deceased has made it clear that she or he wants to donate her or his organs her or his relative cannot prevent them being removed for that purpose. Similarly, if the deceased has made it clear that she or he does not want her or his organs used her or his family cannot override those wishes.[147]

(2) If the deceased has left no views then the next question is: Has the deceased nominated a representative to make decisions? Section 4 of the Act sets out the circumstances in which the nomination can be made. This can be made orally or in writing. If made orally it must be in the presence of two or more witnesses; if in writing it must be signed and witnessed.[148] The representative can make the decision in relation to transplant. The representative must be an adult[149] and can if she or he wishes renounce her or his appointment.[150] If two or more people are appointed as nominated representative then it is only necessary to have the consent of one of them, unless the terms of the appointment made it clear that they had to act jointly.[151]

(3) If the deceased has not made a decision and not nominated a representative or the representative is not able to give consent then the person who stood in the closest 'qualifying relationship' to the deceased immediately before her or his death can make the decision.[152] Section 27(4) ranks the qualifying relations in this order: (a) spouse or partner; (b) parent or child; (c) brother or sister; (d) grandparent or grandchild; (e) child of a person falling within paragraph (c); (f) stepfather or stepmother; (g) half-brother or half-sister; (h) friend of longstanding. The person who is highest up the list immediately before the death of the deceased can make the decision. This means if there is a dispute between the spouse and parent of the deceased, the spouse will be able to make the decision. If the relationship of each of two or more persons to the person concerned is accorded equal highest ranking it is sufficient to obtain the consent of any of them.[153] So if the brother and sister of the deceased were the two people highest in the list, and the brother wanted to approve a donation and the sister did not, the donation could go ahead.

Note the following points about this list. First, notice that the question is the relationship immediately before the death. This means a former spouse will not fall within the 'spouse' category. Second, there is no position for a step-child. Third, the category of 'friend of longstanding' means that there who will be few deceased who will have no one who falls into this category.

It will be a criminal offence attracting a maximum prison sentence of three years if a surgeon performs an organ transplant from a deceased person without the necessary consent.[154] However it will be a defence if the person concerned reasonably believed that the appropriate consent had been given.[155] So, if a surgeon relied on the consent of a deceased person's spouse to remove an organ for transplant, unaware that in fact the deceased had made a written statement not wanting her or his organs removed for transplant, she or he could rely on this defence. But she or he would only succeed if it was reasonable to believe there was no written statement. This is problematic: to what

---

[146] It seems there are no formal requirements in this regard: there is no need for the consent to be in writing (for example) as there is where the tissue is to be used where material is for anatomical examination.
[147] Human Tissue Authority (2006d: para 47).
[148] HTAct 2004, s 4. [149] HTAct 2004, s 4(10). [150] HTAct 2004, s 4(9).
[151] HTAct 2004, s 4(6). [152] HTAct 2004, s 3(6). [153] HTAct 2004, s 9(4).
[154] HTAct 2004, s 5(1) and (7). [155] HTAct 2004, s 5(1)(b).

lengths should a surgeon go to find out whether or not there was a binding decision of the deceased or appointment of a representative? How is a surgeon to know who is the closest relative of the deceased? This is especially problematic given that transplant decisions often have to be made very shortly after death. Hopefully the word 'reasonable' will be interpreted in light of the difficult position a surgeon may find her or himself in. One approach that might appeal is to say a surgeon is guilty of an offence only if she or he acts unreasonably.[156]

3.7 Special issues and organ donation

3.7.1 *Conditional donation*

If a person wishes to donate an organ should she or he be permitted to attach conditions as to who should receive it? For example, if a donor stated that she or he was only willing to donate if she or he could be assured that the recipient would be of a certain sex, race, or creed, should her or his proposed donation be rejected?

The official response has been that conditional donation is not permitted. In 2000 it was reported that an organ was accepted by a hospital subject to the condition that it would only be used by a white person. In fact, the person who was 'top of the queue' was a white person and the organ was used for him. In other words this racist condition had not affected how the organ was used. When news of the case emerged the Government declared itself to be shocked and an investigation was undertaken.[157] As a result the Department of Health announced that organs subject to a condition should not be accepted. Certainly if such advice was ignored and a person was not given an organ following the wishes of the donor on account of race, it is likely a successful claim could be made against the Trust under the Human Rights Act 1998.[158]

While many have accepted the Department of Health's approach, it is not without its critics.[159] It certainly seems arguable that where the condition could be met by giving the organ to the person at the 'front of the queue' there should be no objection. The wishes of the donor have not in reality affected the allocation of the organs—should the conditionality of the donation mean the organ goes unused, and as a result people die who would otherwise not die? Indeed we see no difficulty in a person donating an organ and restricting it to a relative.

What is permitted is a 'paired organ exchange'. Imagine Mr A and Mr B both need a kidney. Mrs A is compatible with Mr B and Mrs B is compatible with Mr A. In such a case the couples could agree that in exchange for Mrs A giving her kidney to Mr B, Mrs B will give hers to Mr A. This has been said to be acceptable by the British Transplant Society[160] and there is at least one recorded case of this happening in the UK.[161]

---

[156] Mason and Laurie (2006: 437).   [157] DoH (2000e).

[158] See Pennings (2007) for a philosophical justification for not permitting conditions to be attached to organ donation.

[159] Wilkinson (2003) and Wilkinson (2007a) who argues that a 'racist' condition should be permitted if the organ will not be available to anyone if the condition is not permitted.

[160] British Transplant Society (2005). See also Murphy and Veatch (2006) who discuss an American society whose members agree to donate only to other members.

[161] BBC Newsonline (4 October 2007).

3.7.2 'Beating heart donation'

One issue which can cause problems in practice is where organs are removed from a person who is technically dead (ie brain dead) but has the appearance of being alive because their heart is still beating.[162] A distinction can be drawn between

- *'heart beating' donors*, who have died on a life support system and whose death is established by brain stem criteria; and

- *'non-heart beating' donors*, who are not on life support and whose death is established by the more traditional criteria (ie breathing and heartbeat have ceased).

Underlying the debate over the definition of death is the issue of organ transplantation.[163] The point in time at which death is declared and therefore transplant organs can be removed can be crucial for the quality of the organs. Critics sometimes claim that 'brain stem death' is 'suspiciously convenient'[164] for medical professionals because it readily enables the removal of organs.[165] However, other commentators have complained that the legal definition of death has hindered the policy of encouraging organ transplants.[166] It has been suggested that the question 'when can organs be removed from a living person?' and 'when is a person dead?' are two separate questions.[167] If a person is dying some say their organs should be available for removal even if in fact they have not yet died.[168]

Particular controversy surrounds elective ventilation.[169] This is a technique where a person who is on the point of death is put on a life support machine, for the purpose of preserving their organs for transplantation. But for the possibility of transplantation, life support would not be used. At present this practice is considered unlawful by the Department of Health because the patient is being treated in a particular way which gives them no benefit.[170] Supporters of the practice have suggested that consent to organ donation can be treated as consent to elective ventilation.[171]

3.7.3 The foetus as donor

Can a fetus or neonate be acceptable? The Polkinghorne Report appears to reject the use of a living abortus for transplant purposes. Indeed the foetal organs must be mature and viable if they are to be usable for transplant. Realistically the issue concerns neonates born with fatal conditions who will die within a week or two.

The use of foetal brain transplants has been suggested as a treatment of Parkinson's Disease, however, a moratorium has been called on such research. As the cells could be used on a foetus aged 10–14 weeks the issue is a real one. For some, if good can come of an abortion then it should be done.[172] To others this is an abuse of human dignity.

The arguments made in this area usually match those that have already been made in the context of abortion and experiments on foetuses. There are issues, however,

---

[162] Ducharme (2000).   [163] Campbell (2004).

[164] Holland (2003: 72). See for a wide-ranging discussion Lock (2002). See Machado et al (2007) for a look at the history of the notion of brain death and a convincing argument that the concept was not created to assist transplantation.

[165] Linacre Centre (2002).   [166] Fost (1999).

[167] Truog (1997: 29) suggests organ removal from patients who are 'as good as dead' should be permitted. Truog and Robinson (2003) suggest that organs can be removed from the 'imminently dying'. See the discussion by Veatch (2004) over whether this could ever be acceptable to the general public.

[168] Singer (1995).   [169] Price (1997a).   [170] DoH (2002e: para 13.13).

[171] Kluge (1999).   [172] Robertson (1990).

particularly where a woman becomes pregnant specifically in order to abort the foetus and use its material, although such an event is unlikely. It is generally accepted that foetal material can only be used where the woman consents, and that questions surrounding an abortion must not be connected to issues surrounding the disposal of foetal material.[173]

4 Liability for mishaps from organ transplant

If a person receives an organ which is diseased or otherwise leads to infection of the recipient, is there any legal remedy to the recipient? There is no case law on this issue to date. An action in negligence could certainly been brought if it could be demonstrated that the NHS trust could have discovered the organ's problems through screening procedures. Another possible claim would be under the Consumer Protection Act 1987 because its definition of a 'product' includes human tissue.

5 The lack of organs

For many years now there has been a shortage of organs available for transplant. This has been described as a 'terrible and unnecessary tragedy'.[174] To be blunt many people die because of the shortage of organs. Four hundred and fifty-nine people died in 2006 while on the transplant waiting list. Others will have died without even reaching the waiting list.[175] The following are some of the ways it would be possible to attempt to increase the number of available organs:

(i) *No change.* We should retain the current legal system but do more to increase the numbers of those registering. This could be by public education or even by offering incentives for people to donate. We could also do more to persuade doctors to encourage relatives to consider agreeing to the donation of a deceased's organs.

(ii) *Mandated choice.* This is an approach which requires citizens to indicate what they want to happen to their organs on their death.

(iii) *No choice.* We should move to a system where on death people's organs can be donated regardless of their wishes. This might even involve a system where live organ donation can be used against a person's wishes.

(iv) *Opt out.* We should move to a system whereby it is presumed that a person wishes to donate their organs and if they have not registered an objection their organs be made available for use. In other words we should move from an 'opt in system' (where you opt in to having your organs donated) to an 'opt out system' (where you opt out of having your organs available for transplant).

5.1 Keeping the current system

We could seek to persuade more people to register as willing to donate their organs. This could be done by simply making it easier to register. Some increase in numbers has

---

[173] DoH (2002e: para 15.11).   [174] Harris (2003b).   [175] BMA (2005).

been achieved by allowing people seeking car licences or a Boots 'Advantage card' to indicate that they wish to join the register. There could also be campaigns of persuasion or education to encourage more people to register. The Human Tissue Act, section 34A requires health authorities to promote awareness of the register.

One alternative would be to offer incentives for people to join the register. Those who put their names down as donors would receive priority if they themselves needed an organ.[176] Payment (or tax advantages) for organs might encourage individuals to register as donors, or relatives to consent to organ transplant. There is some debate whether or not payment would be effective.[177]

It has been claimed that part of the blame for the lack of organs lies with health care professionals, who are reluctant to discuss the issue of organ donation with the relatives of a person who has just died. This reticence is, of course, understandable, and asking grieving relatives for consent to donate organs could very easily be seen as callous. Indeed it is difficult to raise the issue without feeling one is placing 'moral blackmail' on the relatives. But the failure to approach relatives early on has led to organs not being available for transplant which might otherwise have been. It has even been suggested that doctors should be legally required to ask relatives of a deceased whose organs would be suitable for transplant.[178]

5.2 Mandated choice

The idea here is that individuals should be required to indicate a choice as to whether or not they wish their organs to be used for transplant purposes after death.[179] It would be possible, for example, to have a box on tax returns, benefits claim forms, or driving licence application forms requiring an individual to make a decision in respect of donation. Supporters for such a proposal point out that far higher numbers of people in surveys say they wish to donate than get around to registering their wish to do so. One difficulty with this proposal would be devising the 'punishment' for those who refuse to express a wish.

5.3 Mandatory donation

We referred earlier to John Harris's radical suggestion for a 'lottery' to provide live organ donors to supply organs. It will therefore be of little surprise to learn that he advocates the removal of organs from a deceased regardless of the views of the deceased and/or her or his relatives.[180] He makes the point that we already override the wishes of a deceased in relation to what happens with their bodies. Post mortems can be carried out on a deceased, whatever objections she or he may have voiced in her or his lifetime. This is justified as being necessary in the interests of the community. If the public interest in post mortems is sufficient to override the deceased's wishes, why is the saving of lives through transplants not sufficient?[181] In reply it is said, to permit the removal of organs against someone's wishes can be a profound violation of their autonomy, especially where their objection is made on the basis of a religious belief.

---

[176] Nadel and Nadel (2005).   [177] Evans (2003).   [178] Chisholm (1988).

[179] Chouhan and Draper (2003).   [180] Harris (2003b).   [181] Harris (2003b).

5.4 'Opt out'

This has been dealt with last because it has received much support, including from the BMA.[182] After Alder Hey some commentators view an opt-out scheme as not politically acceptable.[183] In 2004 the Government made it clear that it was not in favour of an opt-out scheme and a Bill proposing such a scheme was rejected by Parliament.[184] However, it is likely that Parliament will be being asked to consider this option again in the future. Whether we should move to an 'opt out' scheme raises a number of issues.[185]

(i) A moral obligation to donate

One argument is that we should 'presume consent' because it is morally correct that people consent. The Department of Health has argued: 'If you are prepared to consider accepting a transplant for yourself or your family it seems only fair to play your part in being willing to be a donor'.[186] The problem is that the law does not normally compel people to act in a way which is moral. The moral case for giving money to help alleviate the condition of the starving does not lead us to conclude that the Government should force people to donate.

There may be an argument that for family members the situation is different. A parent can be criminally liable for not providing the necessary basics of life to her or his children. Can we extend that to organs?[187] Not automatically. Although parents are required to feed and care for their children this does not extend to invasions of their bodily integrity of the kind required in organ donation.

(ii) 'Presumed consent'

To some an opt-out position is reasonable because we can presume consent. The argument is most commonly made by reference to a number of surveys of public opinion which indicate that while a majority of people would want to donate organs on their death only a minority get round to holding a donor card.[188] It is, therefore, a reasonable presumption that any given person would want their organs used at death. We could therefore have a register for those who *object* to their organs being used post mortem for donation. If a person fails to register an objection we can presume consent.

Critics respond that 'presumed consent' is a misnomer.[189] In a case of presumed consent there is no consent. To remove a person's organ without their explicit consent is unethical. In particular it must be recalled that in a multicultural society, although some people may have no strong views on what happens to their body on death, there are many who have strong religious or cultural influences on what happens after death. To remove organs without explicit consent runs the risk of causing religious or cultural offence.

One way of resolving this debate is to ask: which is worse, not to have your organs removed when you would have wanted them to be (which happens under an opt-in system) or to have your organs removed post mortem when you would not have wanted them to be (which could happen under an opt-out system). To supporters of the 'opt-out' system both are wrong and given that people are dying because of the lack of organs we can presume consent. It is more efficient and cost-effective to maintain a register of the small number who wish to opt out of donation than of the majority who are willing to be donors.[190]

---

[182] BMA (2005).   [183] Chouhan and Draper (2003).
[184] DoH (2004g).   [185] Erin and Harris (1999).   [186] DoH (1999b).
[187] The issues are well discussed in Glannon and Ross (2002) and Spial (2003).
[188] BMA (2005).   [189] Price (2003).   [190] BMA (2005).

(iii) Can the interests of the dead outweigh the interests of the living?

If you take the view that an opt-out system would be improper because it would infringe the rights of the deceased, there is still the question of whether the deceased's interests should outweigh those of the potential recipients of the organ. After all, can ignoring or placing little weight on the wishes of the deceased cause them any harm or loss? Some people believe that the dead have no interests. As Harris has put it:

> The dead person cannot be wronged or harmed by the transplant of their organs 'against their will' for they have no will—they are not there to be harmed.[191]

Others disagree and argue that we do have an interest in how we are treated in our death. To many people our death and burial is the final chapter[192] of our stories. How our death is recalled and commemorated is of great importance.

Ruth Chadwick has argued that respecting the interests of the dead can be seen in terms of respecting the interests of the living:

> Duties regarding the dead could be seen as indirectly duties towards living persons, who certainly do have preferences about how the dead should be treated. The preferences of living persons include both those of the loved ones of a dead person who cannot bear to think of their friend or relative being disfigured in an organ transplant operation, and the preferences of person currently alive who do not like the thought of such procedures being carried out on their own bodies after death.[193]

Harris emphasizes that even if we can claim the dead have interests in how their body will be treated on death, we need to weigh those interests against other interests.[194] He argues:

> We must remember that while the organ donor may have a posthumous preference frustrated, (more of which anon) and her friends and relatives may be distressed and upset, the potential organ recipient stands to lose her very life and her friends and relatives will have grief to add to their distress.[195]

One factor not mentioned by Harris is the feelings of distress all of us might now experience if we knew we would have no control over how our bodies would be used after our death.[196]

(iv) Would an opt-out scheme actually work?

Belgium, Italy, and Greece have all moved to an opt-out scheme and this has increased the number of organs available for transplant.[197] However, the link between an opt-out scheme and increasing organ donation rates is not as straightforward as might at first appear. It is true that in some countries the increase has been dramatic.[198] But when Austria moved to an 'opt out' scheme this had little impact on the number of donations.[199] A move to an opt-out scheme may therefore only have a noticeable impact on donation rates if it has the support of medical professionals and the general public.[200] In some countries with opt-out schemes the consent of family members is still sought and medical teams are reluctant to proceed with transplants against the wishes of a grieving

---

[191] Harris (1984: 119). See also Partridge (1981), Callahan (1987).
[192] Herring (2002: 56).   [193] Chadwick (1994: 58).   [194] Harris (2002).
[195] Harris (2003b).   [196] Hamer and Rivlin (2002).
[197] De Cruz (2001: 552).   [198] Chouhan and Draper (2003).
[199] New et al (1994).   [200] English and Sommerville (2003).

family.[201] It might be argued that it is possible to increase the number of donors without moving to an opt-out scheme. Noticeably, Spain has dramatically increased its rate of organ donors without moving to an 'opt-out scheme'.[202] It must also be remembered that as well as the legal structure a host of other factors can impact on the transplant rate: causes of death;[203] the kinds of organs required; the number of transplant surgeons; and the availability of intensive care beds and staff.[204]

6 The wishes of relatives

Should family members have any say in what happens to a deceased?[205] It is important to realize that family members could be involved in two ways: first, in providing evidence about what the deceased would have wanted; second, the interests they have in their own right. Here we are talking about the second issue. There are two main issues: should the views of relatives be able to outweigh the views of the deceased? And, should the views of relatives be taken into account in a case where the deceased has failed to express any views?[206]

A study published in 2004 revealed that 42 per cent of relatives objected when asked to consent to organ donation.[207] This is notably higher than rates found in the early 1990s and this may be because of the Alder Hey scandal.[208] Brazier has suggested that overriding relatives' wishes in respect of the deceased's body is 'scarcely appropriate' in the light of Alder Hey.[209] It is interesting to note that the BMA now supports a 'soft opt out' system under which it is presumed that a patient does want to consent, but that relatives are given the opportunity to object and if they do the transplant must not go ahead.[210]

This could be justified on the basis that ignoring the wishes of relatives runs the risk of turning public opinion against the transplant system. Further, as UK Transplant has pointed out, often the co-operation of the relatives of the deceased is important in uncovering the medical history of the deceased, which is essential if transplants are to be successful.[211] Also, it has been argued that respecting the wishes of relatives is interconnected with the wishes of the deceased because we can presume the deceased would not want distress caused to her or his relatives.[212] Even if it is accepted that the wishes of the family do carry weight there is still the question of whether they are sufficient to outweigh the interests of the person needing an organ, and their family.[213]

We should bear in mind the fact that some relatives who choose not to donate have feelings of regret later when they are able to think about the issue more calmly.[214]

---

201 De Cruz (2001: 595).   202 English and Sommerville (2003).
203 Some causes of death mean organs are unsuitable for transplant.
204 English and Sommerville (2003).   205 Wilkinson (2007b); Boddington (1998).
206 Haddow (2005) looks at what influences family's attitudes to bodies after death.
207 Parliamentary Office of Science and Technology (2004).
208 Parliamentary Office of Science and Technology (2004).
209 Brazier (2003a: 434).   210 BMA (2005).
211 UK Transplant (2004).   212 Murphy and Younger (2003).
213 Cronin (2007).   214 Sque, Long and Payne (2005).

REALITY CHECK

Public opinion on donation

There is much evidence that most people would be keen for their organs to be used for transplant on their death. According to DoH (2002e): 'repeated surveys for the British Kidney Patient Association have shown nearly 75 per cent of the UK population favour their own and their families' organs being used for transplantation.'

Public support for a shift to an 'opt-out' regime is mixed: A Department of Health poll in 1999 found 50 per cent of respondents favoured the current system, 28 per cent supported a shift to presumed consent, and 22 per cent expressed no preference.

A survey conducted by the NKRF in September 2000 showed that 57 per cent of the British population supported presumed consent. A poll for the BBC's Watchdog Healthcheck programme found 78 per cent in favour of a shift to presumed consent in respect of organ donation (POST (2005)). An NHS Networks (2007) poll found 72 per cent favouring an opt-out system. Another survey also found that 90 per cent of those questioned said that they were willing to donate their organs if they died, but in fact only 50 per cent had registered to donate organs. The most common reason for not registering was not wanting to 'tempt fate' (BBC Newsonline 22 August 2004).

A poll in 2005 (UK Transplant (2005)) showed that over 47 per cent of those questioned did not know their relatives' wishes concerning transplant.

A VIEW FROM ABOVE

Religious views on organ donation

UK Transplant (2004c) in a leaflet written with the support of religious leaders representing Buddhism, Christianity, Hinduism, Islam, Judaism, and Sikhism claims:

All our major religions support the principles of organ donation and transplantation.

Pope John Paul II, in an address to the participants of the Society for Organ Sharing (quoted in UK Transplant (2004)) said:

With the advent of organ transplantation, which began with blood transfusion, man has found a way to give of himself, of his blood and of his body, so that others may continue to live.

Buddhism takes a neutral attitude towards donation. The choice of whether or not to donate is seen as being up to the individual and there is no 'correct' choice. Some Buddhists (especially followers of Tibetan Buddhism) believe that consciousness may stay in the body for a short time after the heart has stopped beating. For them there may be difficulties in organ donation procedures being commenced too soon after death.

Within Judaism there are strong objections to unnecessary interference with a corpse, and there is a need for immediate burial of a complete body. However, the majority view is that organ donation in order to save lives (*pikuach nefesh*) is justifiable. Donation of organs for medical research would be unacceptable.

Islam also takes a strict line against violating a human body. However the 1996 Shariah Council issued a fatwa permitting organ donation on the basis of necessity. It is justifiable as a means of alleviating pain or saving life (See also Aasi (2003)).

> One faith which has serious concerns about organ donation is the Shinto faith. In that faith the notions of purity and wholeness of the physical body are important. From the moment of death the body is seen as impure, and therefore organ donation is normally regarded as inappropriate because it may injure the relationship between the dead person and the bereaved (the *itai*).

7 Xenotransplantation

Xenotransplantation involves the use of the organs of one species to transplant into another.[215] It has been defined by the Department of Health in this way:

> ...any procedure that involves the transplantation, implantation, or infusion into a human recipient of either live tissues or organs retrieved from animals, or, human body fluids, cells, tissue or organs that have undergone ex vivo contact with live non-human animal cells, tissues or organs.[216]

It is at present a complex procedure because of the difficulties of rejection from the recipient. In fact the procedure is still at an experimental stage.[217] Improvements in drugs which suppress the rejection of the host have meant that only in very recent years has xenotransplantation become a realistic possibility.[218] The Department of Health has recently encouraged research into this practice saying: '...it is right to explore the potential of xenotransplantation in a cautious, stepwise fashion...in a controlled research context'.[219]

Anyone who wishes to use xenotransplantation will need the approval of a research ethics committee. They will only give permission where strict guidelines are followed.[220] The fact that one of the most successful cases of xenotransplantation involved a man who received a baboon's liver, but only lived for 70 days[221] demonstrates that to permit the practice would be to make participants 'human guinea pigs' (so to speak). Following technological advances some scientists claim that it is now safe for pig organs to be used in humans; however, so far there have been no xenotransplantation in the UK.[222]

As well as the difficulties in actually succeeding in transplanting an organ, there are concerns about the possibility of transferring viruses to humans, and developing new strains of viruses which may severely impact on the wider community.[223] This is an especially significant issue in relation to the question of consent when people are being involved in medical trials based on xenotransplantation.[224]

A further issue is whether there are some animals which should not be used for transplantation. There is a widespread feeling that organs should not be taken from primates because of their special status, even though they, being closest to humans in biological terms, would be the best donors.[225] The pig has therefore become a popular option. Although there is much debate whether or not non-human animals have rights, it should be remembered that even if they do not, that does not mean they do not have interests which deserve protection.

---

[215] McLean and Williamson (2005), Fovargue (2005) and Anderson (2007) discuss this topic in detail.
[216] DoH (2006a: 1).   [217] Mason and Laurie (2006: 422).
[218] Nuffield Council on Bioethics (1996: 7) suggest that in time the procedure will be technically possible.
[219] DoH (2006a: 2).
[220] DoH (2006a). For criticism of the guidance see McLean and Williamson (2007).
[221] Starlz, Fung, and Tzakis (1993).   [222] BBC Newsonline (1 September 2004).
[223] Muir and Griffin (2001).   [224] McLean and Williamson (2005: Chap 7).
[225] Fox and McHale (1998).

This still leaves some with a profound distaste of the use of an animal's organs to sustain human life. There are of course those who take a strong line on animal rights and object to the eating of animal meat. To those the use of animal organs is likely to be objectionable. It could it be argued that the eating of animal meat is unjustifiable while there are alternative foods, but if xenotransplantation is the only way of saving the life of a human it may be seen as justifiable. Others, by contrast, take the view that eating meat is justifiable, but the use of animal organs is not, seeing one is natural and the other is not. To properly assess this issue it would be necessary to consider the complex issue of animal rights. There is not space to discuss this more, but there is further reading at the end of the chapter on this topic.

8 Selling organs

Should we permit people to sell their organs or body parts? The official response has always been a resounding 'no'. It has been a criminal offence to be involved in the sale of organs for several decades now. Doctors who have been found to be involved in organ selling have been struck off the medical register.[226]

8.1 The criminal offences

The Human Tissue Act 2004 provides an impressive array of offences connected with the commercial dealing of human material for transplantation. Section 32 contains a series of offences connected with dealing with organs for reward:

(1) A person commits an offence if he—

    (a) gives or receives a reward for the supply of, or for an offer to supply, any controlled material;

    (b) seeks to find a person willing to supply any controlled material for reward;

    (c) offers to supply any controlled material for reward;

    (d) initiates or negotiates any arrangement involving the giving of a reward for the supply of, or for an offer to supply, any controlled material;

    (e) takes part in the management or control of a body of persons corporate or unincorporate whose activities consist of or include the initiation or negotiation of such arrangements.

Reward here includes giving a financial or other material advantage. It is not therefore possible to by-pass these provisions by not paying cash but providing property or other economic benefit.

There then follows an offence dealing with advertising and soliciting commercial dealings with human material:

(2) Without prejudice to subsection (1)(b) and (c), a person commits an offence if he causes to be published or distributed, or knowingly publishes or distributes, an advertisement—

    (a) inviting persons to supply, or offering to supply, any controlled material for reward, or

---

[226] Dyer (1990).

(b) indicating that the advertiser is willing to initiate or negotiate any such arrangement as is mentioned in subsection (1)(d).

The prohibitions on payment for organs are not as strict as might first appear. Most importantly in section 32(7) the prohibitions on reward do not apply to expenses incurred in removing, storing, or transporting the organ. Nor does it include payments to cover the loss of earnings of a person donating an organ. It will remain to be seen how generously the terms 'expenses' and 'loss of earnings' might be interpreted.[227] Certainly in the context of similar provisions in relation to surrogacy payments there have been claims that the courts have been very generous in determining the legitimacy of expenses.

The offences are only committed where the controlled material 'consists of or includes human cells', but it must be intended for use in transplantation. It does not include gametes, embryos, or 'material which is the subject of property because of an application of human skill'.[228] This last phrase is problematic because (as we shall see shortly) it is far from clear when material becomes 'the subject of property'. Indeed it is arguable that an organ removed from a person and preserved for later transplant is indeed the subject of property. If this is correct the section will fail to achieve its aim in rendering illegal the sale of organs.

The Human Tissue Authority, under section 32(3), can designate a person who can lawfully engage in trade in human material. For example, presumably the National Blood Service will be permitted to purchase blood from abroad, if necessary.

8.2 Professional guidance

As well as the sale of organs involving a criminal offence it would also breach professional guidance. For example, the Guidance from the GMC is clear:

> In no circumstances may doctors participate in or encourage in any way the trade in human organs from live donors. They must not advertise for donors nor make financial or medical arrangements for people who wish to sell or buy organs.
>
> ...Doctors must also satisfy themselves that consent to a donation has been given without undue influence of any kind, including the offer of a financial or material benefit. A doctor, or another appropriately qualified professional, independent of the transplantation team, must assess the motivation of each donor.

8.3 The ethical issues

Although the legal approach is strict there has been much discussion among ethicists on the issue of organ selling. One starting point is to consider on whom the burden of argument should lie: is it for those who want to permit organ selling to produce arguments as to why it should be allowed; or is it for those who oppose it to produce arguments as to why it should not be permitted? To those who think the sale of organs should be permitted the starting point is autonomy.[229] If someone wishes to sell their organs they should

---

[227] Payments can only be made by a 'proper authority'(eg an NHS Trust) and cannot be made by the relatives of the recipients (Human Tissue Authority (2006e: para 64).
[228] S 32(9)(c).   [229] Stacey Taylor (2005).

be permitted to do so unless there is clear evidence of a harm.[230] As has been argued:

> If the rich are free to engage in dangerous sports for pleasure, or dangerous jobs for high pay, it is difficult to see why the poor who take the lesser risk of kidney selling for greater rewards—perhaps saving relatives' lives or extricating themselves from poverty and debt—should be thought so misguided as to need saving from themselves.[231]

But to others there is such widespread instinctive unease at the sale of organs that we should rely on our 'gut instincts' that organ selling should not be permitted unless justified by a very good reason.

So what are the arguments for and against organ selling?

8.3.1 *Arguments against permitting organ selling*

(i) *Gains for the rich*

There is a concern that once a market for organs is created it will be the wealthy who will be able to purchase organs, and the poor who will go without. Organ distribution will be on the basis of wealth, not need. This is a grave concern, although it should be noted that it would be possible, for example, to only allow the NHS to purchase organs and then to distribute the organs on the basis of need.[232] In other words, it would not be impossible to devise a scheme that offered an incentive to donate, without benefiting the better off. However, requiring all organs to be purchased by the NHS may do nothing to discourage the 'black market' in organs. Another response is that the availability of private medicine already, in effect, offers the rich access to quicker and higher quality treatment, although we don't like to admit that. If money buys you quicker and therefore potentially life-saving cancer treatment, why not organs?

(ii) *Vendors are coerced or do not validly consent to the sale of their organs*

Opponents of a market in organs are concerned that those who sell their organs are often driven to do so by poverty or threats from debt collectors. Any person wanting to sell their kidney must be driven by such desperation that their consent should be regarded as invalid. Supporters of a market tend to make two responses. One is to argue that if the market is made lawful it can be properly regulated and we can make sure that only those who are genuinely consenting donate. The other is to question whether being driven by poverty into selling an organ is properly described as coercion. People often agree to do things they would not otherwise do for money. Many people work because of fear of the poverty they would face if they did not: are they not acting freely? Wilkinson refers to a survey in which 65 per cent of those questioned said they would sleep with a complete stranger for one million pounds.[233] Would we say those people were not acting voluntarily or were being coerced into acting against their will? In contract law, when considering whether or not a person has entered a contract freely or under duress, the question the courts now focus on is the legitimacy of the pressure.[234] This question, rather than asking how pressurized the individual felt, has no uncontroversial answer but focuses the mind on the correct issue.

Sometimes the argument is put in term of autonomy: does allowing organ sales infringe an individual's rights of autonomy? At first this may appear a strange claim: allowing organ sales increases the range of options available to someone. Some philosophers have,

---

[230] Fabre (2006).   [231] Radcliffe-Richards et al (1998).   [232] Harris and Erin (2002).

[233] Wilkinson (2003: 118).   [234] Herring (2002: 53).

however, argued that sometimes giving people an extra choice can inhibit autonomy. That would be where the choice offered is 'self-defeating' in that the result of the choice ends up restricting their lifestyle choices.[235] This raises the issue of whether a sale of one's organ should be regarded as an act which shows disrespect to one's body, or a way of improving one's financial position while saving lives.[236]

(iii) Exploitation

Some are worried about the position of those who are willing to donate for money. Is there not something very wrong with the world that we are content to allow the most impoverished people in the world to sell their organs in an attempt to combat their financial situation? Is that the kind of society we want to live in?

When expressed in its strongest terms, opposition to organ selling sees an analogy between organ selling and slavery. Thomas George writes in these terms:

> The evolution of human civilisation has witnessed several periods of gross exploitation of human beings. Slavery, the extermination of six million Jews, and today the transfer of body parts from one living human being to another, for a financial consideration, are part of a continuum of values which sees some human beings as less valuable than others. It is this value system that those of us who oppose the sale of kidneys, seek to change.[237]

The analogy between slavery, Nazi extermination, and organ selling seems far fetched, to say the least.

(iv) Bodily invasion

It has been suggested that to remove an organ is a *prima facie* wrong as an invasion of bodily integrity. Although this can be justified by the good of altruism, in the case of commercial sale there is no countervailing good.[238] To some this argument is not convincing because it would be possible that a person is selling an organ to obtain money to use for another person's benefit. A person could be selling their kidney in order to pay for their child's medical treatment. In such a case the sale could be regarded as an altruistic act.[239] Indeed it must be rare for someone to sell a kidney to increase their own happiness.

(v) Public opinion

It has been suggested that public opinion is so revolted by the idea of selling organs that the law should match this strong opposition. However, in fact surveys suggest that the opposition may not be as entrenched as assumed. One survey found that between 40 and 50 per cent of those questioned thought it should be permissible to pay for organs.[240] Whatever the figures are, there is a debate over whether feelings of disgust are sufficient to deny treatment to the dying.

(vi) Commercialization of the body

For some the concern is over the commercialization of the body. Allowing body parts to be bought or sold reduces our bodies to the status we accord our cars or televisions.[241] This leads to a devaluation of the body and of human life. The body is seen as simply a collection of parts to be disposed of at will.[242] Is there not something wrong with a

---

[235] Hughes (1998).   [236] Boyle (1999).
[237] George (2005: 1).   [238] Wilkinson (2003b).
[239] Mason and Laurie (2006: 434).   [240] Guttmann and Guttman (1993).
[241] See Bjorkmann (2007) for an argument against selling organs based on virtue ethics.
[242] Cherry (1999: 9).

society where an advert for a kidney appeared on e-bay and was removed by the managers of the website when the bidding reached 5.7 million dollars?[243] To many this is a convincing argument. To others the notion of 'commercialization of the body' is a hopelessly vague notion.[244] It is difficulty to identify a precise harm that it had caused.

(vii) Harm to altruism
The current system of organ donation encourages and celebrates altruism. This is a virtue which we should seek to uphold and there is a danger that if there is a market in organs that fewer people will donate and will instead sell their organs.[245] Stephen Wilkinson responds that it would be wrong to assume that because there is payment, there is no altruism. People often buy raffle tickets to support their favourite charity, they may be motivated both by the desire to give to a worthy cause, as well as the chance of winning. The latter motivation does not negate the former. Similarly the fact the Government provides tax benefits for those who donate to charity is not thought to undermine the altruism of such donors.[246]

8.3.2 Arguments in favour of permitting organ selling

(i) Freedom
A commonly cited argument in favour of organ selling is that it causes no harm and people should be permitted to sell their organs if they wish. It is part of the right of autonomy.[247] We allow people to sell their hair, engage in high risk sports, so why not organ donation. We even permit people to receive payment for things society regards as immoral or improper, such as pornography.

(ii) It increases the number of organs available for transplant
It is claimed that if we permit organ selling, it is likely there will be a larger number of organs available and so lives will be saved.[248] Some have doubted this, however. It is suggested that those who donated in the past out of altruism will be put off donation now that the commerciality has sullied the transplantation scene. Of course this is a matter of guesswork, but the fact that some people are paid to make music does not mean that amateurs are not happy to do so for free. Indeed, as most organ donations are given to relatives, it is unlikely a person will be deterred from giving an organ to a relative due to the payment. Therefore supporters claim it is safe to assume that allowing a market will increase the number of organs available.[249]

(iii) Avoids exploitation
It has been suggested that permitting organ selling avoids exploitation. The present system means that donors who have given a valuable resource receive no payment. The professionals involved in the transplant will all receive payment but the provider of the organ will not.[250] But Hughes has argued that selling organs pre-supposes and reinforces dependency relations.[251]

(iv) Avoids the 'black market'
As organ selling is officially illegal, any market in organs takes place underground in a market which has been described as 'rampant'.[252] This can easily work against the

---

[243] Wilkinson (2003: 107).   [244] De Castro (2003b).   [245] Keown (1997b).
[246] Herring (2002: 55).   [247] Stacey Taylor (2005).   [248] Erin and Harris (2003).
[249] Radcliffe-Richards et al (1998).
[250] Larijani, Zahedi, and Ghafouri-Fard (2004: 2540).   [251] Hughes (1998).
[252] Larijani, Zahedi, and Ghafouri-Fard (2004: 2539).

interests of vulnerable donors who do not complain about bad treatment or non-payment for fear they will be prosecuted for an offence. Creating a market in organs should mean that donors are paid a fair price and regulations can ensure their health needs are protected.[253]

8.3.3 A middle view?

It may be that although organ sales should not be allowed we should be generous in ensuring that expenses of donors are covered. Garwood-Gower suggests that they could include the following:

* the right to fair compensation for the loss of what the material was reasonably worth to the donor and for the pain, intrinsic and non-intrinsic determinants that stem from the donation;
* the right to free medical care and regular check-ups in relation to the donating;
* the right to fair compensation for his or her time involved in donation related activities;
* the right to defrayment/reimbursement of reasonable costs arising in activities pursuant or incidental to the donation;
* the right to compensation for discrimination stemming from having donated...[254]

8.4 Face transplants

Recently several groups of scientists have been able to engage in face transplants. These are used where someone suffers a severe facial disfigurement and a deceased person's face is grafted on in place of their own. To some commentators such transplants do not raise any special legal or ethical issues over and above those that apply to, say, kidney transplants. Michael Freeman and Pauline Jaoude disagree. They argue:

> As an expressive part of our body, it [the face] represents identity in a way no other part of the body does. It is the most intimate, the most individual characteristic of our body. It is what we recognise as ourselves and what others recognise as us.[255]

They fear that it is not possible to give properly informed consent to a face transplant, given that the impact upon one's identity is so significant and the risks of rejection are largely unknown. Further there are concerns about the family of the donor, because there will be a person with a close resemblance to their departed loved one. Finally there are concerns that the effect of face transplants, if they become common, will have on the disfigured community.[256] While all these are legitimate concerns, whether or not they are sufficient to outlaw the practice is very debatable.[257] To some, those objecting to face transplant on ethical grounds are failing to appreciate the pain of facial disfigurement.[258]

---

253 De Castro (2003b).
255 Freeman and Jaoude (2007: 76).
257 Agich and Siemionov (2005).
254 Garwood-Gowers (1999: 192–3).
256 See also Huxtable and Woodley (2005 and 2006).
258 Agich and Siemionov (2005).

9 The living body as property

9.1 The law

There has been much academic discussion over whether it can be said that our bodies are our property.[259] In truth the legal position is far from clear. Gage J recently accepted that English law was uncertain and unclear.[260] The safest thing that can be said is that there are some respects in which the body can be treated as property and other respects where it cannot. There is no coherent picture that can be drawn.

The traditional rule has been that there is no property in the human body. This has been understood to represent the common law,[261] although explicit authority for the proposition is, in fact, limited.[262] However, it has for so long been presumed to be the common law that it would be unlikely that a court would declare the understanding had been wrong.[263]

The law appears rather less reluctant to find that separated body parts or products are property. Hair,[264] blood,[265] and urine[266] have all been found to be property for the purposes of the Theft Act 1968. The following are now the leading cases on this topic:

KEY CASE   R v Kelly [1998] 3 All ER 714

A technician at the Royal College of Surgeons removed body parts from the college and gave them to an artist who used them as moulds for sculptures. The technician and artist were charged with theft but argued that they could not be guilty because corpses or parts of corpses could not be property. The Court of Appeal held that '...parts of a corpse are capable of being property...if they have acquired different attributes by virtue of the application of skill, such as dissection or preservation techniques, for exhibition or teaching purposes' (749). In this case the body parts had been preserved and used as specimens. They therefore had become property and therefore the defendant had committed theft. In fact the Court of Appeal went further and suggested if parts attracted a 'use or significance beyond their mere existence' (570) they could become property.

KEY CASE   Dobson v Northern Tyneside Health Authority [1996] 4 All ER 474

A woman had died from a brain tumour. Her relatives sought to bring an action in negligence against the health authority for failing to diagnose the nature of the deceased's condition. To establish their claim they wanted a sample of the brain. It then transpired that the brain had been removed and

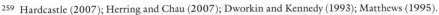

259 Hardcastle (2007); Herring and Chau (2007); Dworkin and Kennedy (1993); Matthews (1995).
260 *AB v Leeds Teaching Hospital NHS Trust* [2004] EWHC 644, [2004] 3 FCR 324, para 135.
261 *Doodeward v Spence* 1908 6 CLR 906, confirmed recently in *AB v Leeds Teaching Hospital NHS Trust* [2004] EWHC 644, [2004] 3 FCR 324.
262 The no property rule is largely *obiter dicta:* Magnusson (1998).
263 DoH (2002e) supports the no property rule.
264 *Director of Public Prosecutions v Smith* [2006] EWHC 94 (Admin); *R v Herbert* (1961) 25 JCL 163.
265 *R v Rothery* [1976] RTR 478.   266 *R v Welsh* [1974] RTR 478.

disposed of. The relatives therefore brought a further claim in the tort of conversion claiming that the hospital had no right of unauthorized disposal. The Court of Appeal found against the relatives. They had no right of possession or ownership in respect of the brain, nor indeed of the corpse. The most that could be said was that an executor or administrator of a deceased person had a limited right to a corpse. That right is only to possess the corpse with a view to its burial or disposal. The next of kin did not even have that limited right.

The Court of Appeal accepted that property rights could arise in respect of body parts where some work or skill differentiated the body or its parts from a corpse in its natural state. Here the brain had simply been removed and preserved in a basic way. It had not been preserved for the purposes of teaching or exhibition. Likewise it had not been changed sufficiently to become property. Where work or skill were used on a body to render it property the body was owned by the person who did the work. Reliance was placed on the view in *Doodeward v Spence* 1908 6 CLR 406 414 of Griffith CJ: 'when a person has by lawful exercise of work or skill so dealt with a human body or part of a human body in his lawful possession that it has acquired some attributes differentiating it from a mere corpse awaiting burial, he acquires a right to retain possession of it, at least as against any person not entitled to have it delivered to him for the purposes of burial.'

These cases leave undecided what kind of skill must be exercised on a part of a body in order for it to acquire the nature of property. The exercise of skill in dissection or preservation may well be sufficient.[267]

In *AB v Teaching Hospital NHS Trust*[268] parents could claim no kind of property rights to material removed from their children in the course of a post mortem. The executors of a hospital can claim lawful possession of a corpse, even though it cannot be owned.[269] Few would claim that the current law on whether and when the body or its parts can be owned is satisfactory. Margaret Brazier expresses her views on the current law as it operated in respect of the organ retention scandals thus:

> The deceased did not own their body and could not bequeath it to their estate. The estate can claim the body for decent disposal, although not necessarily disposal as the deceased would have wished. Parts are taken from the body without either the deceased's of their family's approval. Put to the uses of medicine, these body parts become, as if by magic, property, but property owned by persons unknown, for purposes unforeseen by the deceased. If that represents the law, the law is an ass.[270]

9.2 Commercialization and body: ethical issues

To some to treat the body as other property, as something which can be traded, is to show disrespect to our bodies. Can it be right to suggest that the relationships we have with our televisions should be the same in the eye of the law as that we have we our bodies? To allow the commercialization of bodies is to demean them. One response to this is that it may be demeaning to pay people for body parts, but it may be equally demeaning not to pay them.

---

[267] *AB v Leeds Teaching Hospital NHS Trust* [2004] EWHC 644, [2004] 3 FCR 324.
[268] [2004] EWHC 644, [2004] 3 FCR 324.   [269] Skene (2002).   [270] Brazier (2003a: 563).

One response to these powerful arguments is that, however high minded, they are out of touch with reality. In the Western world biotech scientists and their employers make large sums of money through research on bits of bodies. Why should they make all the gains from the body parts and not the people from whom the samples originated?[271]

The following case raises some of the issues well.

KEY CASE   Moore v Regents of the University of California 793 P 2d 4791990

John Moore, suffering from hairy cell leukaemia, had his spleen removed. Dr Golde discovered that cells from his spleen contained potentially beneficial properties. He developed a cell line from the spleen which he eventually sold for $15 million. The products produced as a result were said to be worth several billion dollars. His research on the spleen was carried out without Moore's consent or knowledge.

Moore brought an action on a claim based on conversion; breach of fiduciary duty; and informed consent. The Californian Supreme Court rejected the conversion claim declaring that there was no precedent on which to base a claim that a person had property rights in their bodies and that it would be inappropriate for the law now to recognize one. Indeed to recognize one would cause difficulties: it would hinder medical research by restricting access to raw materials and lead to a 'litigation lottery'. The prospect of patients 'shopping around' to find who would offer them the best price for their bodily parts or products was not an attractive one. They accepted that he might have a claim for breach of fiduciary duty.

Dissenting from the majority opinion in the *Moore* case, California Supreme Court Justice Mosk argued that the law should at least recognize Moore's 'right to do with his own tissue whatever the defendants [including his doctor and the University] did with it: ie he could have contracted with researchers and pharmaceutical companies to develop and exploit the vast commercial potential of his tissue and its products'.

The issue of whether the body should be regarded as property or whether some other legal regulation should be used has generated much debate from a variety of perspectives. Before exploring them it might be useful to summarize some views that have been expressed on the issue:

(i) We need to assert that we own our bodies. This provides us with a number of important advantages. It means that individuals have control over parts of their bodies when they are removed. It is, for example, possible for a person to sell, bail, or loan body parts. If a body part is wrongfully taken then they (or their representatives) can seek its return. This also means that if profit is made from a body part without a person's permission they can claim compensation for it.

(ii) To regard the body as property is demeaning to the body.[272] There are some things that are too precious to be owned. The principles that should govern bodies are consent, dignity, and respect.[273] These values are not captured by the property model. We need therefore to focus on rights of autonomy or the right to dignified treatment of bodies, rather than property rights.[274]

---

[271] Gold (1996: 37).   [272] Munzer (1994).   [273] Brazier (2003a: 479).
[274] See the discussion in Brownsword (2003c).

(iii) Although there are no moral difficulties to regarding the body as property, there are technical legal ones. To constitute property an item has to possess certain characteristics and be subject to certain kinds of treatment. As bodies are not transferable or divisible we cannot treat them as property. Further, rights of property in law come about in a variety of accepted ways (eg the fruits of labour). So even though we may feel as if our bodies are owned, they cannot be regarded as property in the way that the term has been understood by property law.[275]

We need now to look at some of the issues about which debate has arisen:

9.2.1 *The nature of property*

To some there are technical legal difficulties in declaring that the body is property.[276] This issue is complex and it is not possible to do justice to the notion of property,[277] but a few basic points can be made. The word 'property' is used to describe not only a thing, but also a relationship between a person and a thing. So a book is a piece of property, but to say the book is 'my property' is to describe a structure of legal rights and obligations between me and my book. When a person owns a piece of property, that usually denotes a number of rights or entitlements: eg the right to use or enjoy the property; the right to exclude others from using the property; the right to sell or transfer the property to someone else.[278] 'Full blooded ownership' involves possession of all of these rights. But a lesser form of ownership may involve only some of these rights. Roger Brownsword has argued that the bundles of rights which are most 'proprietal' are the exclusionary ones: those that prevent others taking our property however strong a moral claim they may have (eg permitting someone to not allow a starving person some of their food). These he suggests are very much connected with how we see bodies, in that we firmly reject the notion that other people can make claims over our bodies.

Harris has warned of the dangers of faulty lines of reasoning. Just because the law treats bodies in some ways similar to ownership does not mean that they are property. So, although our bodies are ours because we can do what we want with them and stop others doing things with our bodies, this does not mean we own them. It may just reflect rights to be 'left alone' or rights of bodily integrity, rather than rights of ownership. Further it would be wrong to think that because no one else owns our bodies, we must; because it may be that no one owns our bodies.

To some there is a logical problem in saying that we own ourselves and that there needs to be a clear separation between 'the owner' and 'the owned'. We can only say we own our bodies if we see a clear distinction between 'us' and 'our bodies'.[279] This kind of reasoning leads some to prefer seeing rights in respect of the body flowing from the right of privacy where an interference with the body is an interference with the self and a breach of privacy. Radhika Rao argues:

> Property produces a fragmented relationship between the body and its owner, the person 'inside' the body, in contrast with privacy, which creates an indivisible corporeal identity. By uncoupling the body from the person and undermining the unity of the physical being, the property paradigm facilitates fragmentation of the body itself, both literally and figuratively.

[275] Harris (1996: 59).
[276] Harris (1996).
[277] See further Davies and Naffine (2001).
[278] Harris (1996: 59); Quigley (2007).
[279] Naffine (1997); Morgan (2001: Chap 6).

...Privacy theory, on the other hand, forecloses such bodily fragmentation by identifying the person with his or her physical presence. Hence, privacy shields the individual
against corporeal invasion and alteration and preserves the unity and integrity of the
embodied being.[280]

9.2.2 The Moore decision and control of removed bodily products

The decision in *Moore* (discussed in the box above) has generated much comment in this
debate. To some the case shows the problem with not adopting the property approach.
Vast sums of money were made by the scientists involved, but the person who made
'everything possible' is left with nothing. A property approach would ensure he was
adequately rewarded. The difficulty is that the property approach might ensure he was
over-rewarded. On the facts of that case, if we regarded the sequence as his and therefore he had a claim to the money produced from his property, then in theory he should
be entitled to all the proceeds. Indeed there is a danger that valuable research into stem
cell lines and DNA will be hindered if there is a danger of patients claiming an interest
in the products.[281] Indeed lawyers would have a field day if weeks were spent in court
rooms attempting to ascertain whose bodily material was used in the creation of a particular product.

Skene has summarized the issues that need to be balanced here in this way:

> We need legal principles that promote healthcare, teaching medical research and the
> development of new drugs, but at the same time [we need] to take account of people's
> sensitivity concerning the removal, retention and use of human bodies, excised body
> parts and tissue[282]

She believes the best balance is achieved in relying on autonomy rights rather than property rights in respect of bodily material.

9.2.3 Privacy or property?

As has already been indicated there are two main camps: those who see interests in bodies and bodily material as founded in property rights, and those who see them based
on privacy rights.[283] In many ways there is no difference between the approaches. Both
would have no difficulty in prohibiting the removal of a person's bodily material without
their consent. So what are the practical differences in the approaches? Here are some
possibilities:

(i) Rao, preferring an autonomy based approach as the way of protecting the body,
argues that property rights are useful for protecting market values, but that privacy
rights are appropriate for spiritual ones. Our bodies are not just property: they are the
medium through which we interact with the world. Our relationship with our bodies
is not one of 'having' but rather 'existing'.[284] Our bodies are not like machines which
we can manipulate or discard. Some are not convinced by such arguments. Many items
of property carry values beyond the material wealth they represent: consider wedding
rings for example. As long as we do not regard property as the only way a body is valued

---

[280] Rao (2000: 364).

[281] DoH (2002e: 17.20). See Cohen (2007) for a general discussion of research using stem cells.

[282] Skene (2002: 102–3).

[283] Skene (2002) and Mason and Laurie (2006).   [284] Toombs (1999).

we have few objections.[285] Indeed it is possible to regard something as property even if there are restrictions on access to it or restrictions on sale.[286]

(ii) Skene has argued that property rights are well established and carry strong legal and symbolic protection. The notion of privacy rights is amorphous and less well defined. Those seeking a clear strong protection for rights in the body should prefer property rights.

(iii) It can be argued that privacy is essentially a negative right: it is useful in preventing people acting in a certain way, while property rights give positive rights to act in certain ways. Privacy is effective in protecting the body from physical invasion, whereas property rights provide a freedom to use one's body in whatever way one wishes.

(iv) Some commentators argue that although privacy rights might provide an effective means of protecting interests in the body while the body is intact; once a part of the body has been removed property rights are a more effective means of protection. This is because if an organ has been removed and is used without consent, although that can be regarded as infringement of a property right, it is less clear how such interferences fit within a privacy model. Too often the debate is seen in all or nothing terms. It is quite possible to use both. We might say that we have autonomy rights in respect of the body which are protected, although these are supplemented by property rights in the body.[287]

9.2.4 *The interconnection of bodies*

The autonomy and privacy approaches are based on an assumption that our bodies are ours. This has been challenged as overlooking the extent to which our bodies are interconnected and interdependent.[288] There are certainly ways in which our bodies are interconnected: during pregnancy the bodies of foetus and mother are interdependent; even during childhood the body of the child and parents can be connected: the child is dependant on the parent to do things; but also the parent's body can be connected with the child. In many relations of dependency the bodies of carer and dependant will be in a relationship of interconnection. If the body of the carer is impaired, this will impact on the body of the person receiving care. Further, our bodies are connected with the world around us: our bodies take in food, liquid, and air and these are in due course expelled, often in a modified form. Indeed our bodies are constantly changing: by the time we die there is little of us left which is the same as when we were born.[289] This has led some commentators to argue that the buying, selling, and giving of organs should be understood as natural and normal, and a process in which people should be involved and in which we can assume that they wish to be involved.[290]

Critics of such a view may respond that the examples of bodily interconnection are rare. We do regard our skin as representing an important barrier between ourselves and others. Organ donation is hardly a natural process, because only with the help of powerful drugs are such donations effective.

---

[285] Gold (1996).
[286] Brownsword (2003c).
[287] Mason and Laurie (2006).
[288] Herring and Chau (2007); Herring (2002).
[289] Leder (1999); Shildrick (1997).
[290] Herring (2002).

SHOCK TO THE SYSTEM

BBC Newsonline (2 October 2007) reports the following story. John Wood's barbecue smoker was auctioned off in 2007 after he fell behind with payments for a storage facility in North Carolina. It was bought by Shannon Whisnant. Mr Whisnant found Mr Wood's amputated leg in the smoker, where Mr Wood had put it following an amputation several years earlier. Mr Whisnant started up a business charging adults $3 and children $1 to have a look at the leg. The police took the leg to see if it was connected to a crime and they handed it to a funeral home, for Mr Wood to pick up. Mr Whisnant demanded the leg be returned to him, although Mr Wood said he wanted his leg back. Mr Whisnant suggested a joint custody arrangement, which Wood rejected.

10 Intellectual property

10.1 The law

Should it be possible for an individual to claim intellectual property in bodily material: a patent for a string of DNA perhaps? This is a large topic and it is difficult to appreciate it all without a grounding in the law of intellectual property. It will only be possible to provide a brief introduction to the issues here.

In simple terms if a person makes an invention she or he can seek a patent to protect their discovery. If granted, the patent will prevent anyone else marketing a product using that invention for up to 20 years without the patent holder's permission. In order to obtain the patent it must be shown, *inter alia*, that the invention had novelty. In other words it was not already in the public domain and was not an obvious application of current technology.

Patenting is required because the normal law that protects property rights is not effective in the area of intellectual property. Protection of property rights in a car, for example, can involve rules about someone not touching or interfering with the vehicle. However, with an idea or invention, rules like 'do not touch', 'do not damage' have little meaning.

So can body parts or genetic material be patented? The EU law on this is governed by the EC Directive on the Legal Protection of Biotechnological Inventions 98/44/EC and the European Patent Convention 2000. Article 5 of the Directive states:

(1) The human body, at the various stages of its formation and development, and the simple discovery of one of its elements, including the sequence or partial sequence of a gene, cannot constitute patentable inventions.

(2) An element isolated from the human body or otherwise produced by means of a technical process, including the sequence or partial sequence of a gene, may constitute a patentable invention, even if the structure of that element is identical to that of a natural element.

(3) The industrial application of a sequence or a partial sequence of a gene must be disclosed in the patent application.

The European Patent Convention 1973 which governs the patent in Europe allows a patent to be refused on the grounds that the publication or exploitation of the invention would be contrary to morality. In HARVARD/ONCmouse[291] Harvard University sought to patent a mouse which was genetically engineered with a human cancer gene, meaning that the mouse would inevitably develop cancer. It was argued that a European patent should not be granted because of the suffering of the animal. This was rejected on the basis that the potential cure of cancer was a good enough benefit to outweigh the harm to the mouse. It was also argued that the European Patent Convention (EPO) did not permit patents in respect of 'plants or animal varieties', but the mouse here was held not to be merely an 'animal variety' and not caught by this prohibition. To some the decisions were influenced more by the policy concerns of making Europe an attractive place to do research than a proper consideration of the moral issues.[292] Notably the EPO indicated that had the mouse been developed to establish a 'cure' for hair loss, it would have been unlikely the patent would have been granted.

Potentially of even greater significance is the decision in HOWARD FLOREY/ Relaxim.[293] This concerned H2 Relaxin which is a protein produced naturally by women during childbirth. A company had created this protein artificially and sought to patent it. It was held that the patent should be granted. Arguments that to permit the claim would be to support exploitation and an offence to human dignity were rejected on the basis that only women who consented were required to supply the material. Further, in relation to the argument that DNA is 'life' and so could not patented, the reply was that DNA is a chemical substance which carried genetic information and not life. The patent was allowed because 'no woman is affected in any way by the present patent'.[294]

There is now a Directive of the European Parliament and of the Council on the *Legal Protection of Biotechnological Inventions* No 98/44/EC (6 July 1998). This covers bio-technical patents. It is in rather general terms.[295] Even if the product has moral ques-tionability (such as the ONCOmouse) it is permitted if there is a 'substantial medical benefit' to humanity or animals.

So in English law patenting of human material is permissible if (a) it can be shown there is sufficient novelty and inventive step; and (b) the patent is not seen as objection-able on moral grounds. There is much debate over whether or not the law should allow the patenting of human material. Here are some of the issues.

10.2 Are patents necessary to encourage research and development?

Some object to the very existence of the patenting system. The starting point is that huge amounts of money are to be made in medical drugs. It has been estimated that in 2000 £70 billion was made from the biotechnical industry worldwide. In the UK alone the figure is £9 billion.[296] Although there is profit to be made there is also a need to spend money on developing and researching drugs. The law of patents is designed to ensure that the person (or company) which puts in the money and research time to discover a new drug is the person who reaps the reward for the discovery. Without the law of patents it would be possible for someone to spend a fortune discovering a new drug, but for another company to 'steal' the idea and produce their own version. So if a company believes they have developed a new drug they can apply for a patent which will

---

[291] [1990] EPOR 4 and [1991] EPOR 525.   [292] Mason and Laurie (2006: 465).
[293] [1995] EPOR 541.   [294] At 550.
[295] Indeed it was even challenged as being so vague that it infringed principle of legal certainty. The claim was rejected in *Netherlands v European Parliament* [2002] All ER (EC) 97.
[296] DTI (1999: para 2.1).

grant them a monopoly for up to 20 years. No one else will be allowed to put a similar product onto the market. Supporters of the law of patents means that the system promotes justice by ensuring those who discover the drug receive the rewards, and it also makes economic sense in making it beneficial for companies to research and develop new drugs. Opponents argue that by giving one company a monopoly over production there is no control over the price and this means an extortionate sum can be charged. Or, perhaps even worse, a company may decide not to produce the drug at all.[297] There is, in fact little evidence of companies having patents for life-saving drugs but simply failing to manufacture the drugs. Examples can certainly be found of drugs being produced but being so expensive that they are only available to the very wealthy. The difficulties of third world countries and less well off people in developing countries having access to drugs dealing with HIV/AIDS is a clear example. In 2004 it was reported that in Africa only 440,000 of the six million people needing medication for AIDS were getting it.[298] Patent law can only be said to be responsible for a part of that. The respected charity Médecins Sans Frontières in its report on patents and medicines suggests that patents for 18 essential medicines are providing (or are likely to provide) barriers to those who need the medicines in the developing world.

10.3 Inhibition of future research

There are concerns that a patent over a crucial technique can restrict access to it.[299] The difficulty is that, particularly in the biotechnology area, many advances in medicines have used combinations of previously well known medicines or the application of well known medicines in a new way. The patent system acts to prevent companies trying new combinations of established drugs, or the using established drugs in new ways. Certainly there are particular dangers that an over-broad patent could seriously stifle research. The BMA have neatly summarized the issue:

> In order to provide the maximum benefit for society, therefore, it would appear that some patenting of genetic research may be appropriate and desirable. The crucial issue is to set the threshold at the right level: setting the threshold too low would result in too much being protected but setting it too high would be equally damaging by failing to protect some key inventions.[300]

10.4 Immorality of patenting life

In the area of patenting and biotechnology one key issue is the role that ethical considerations should play. In other words, should there be any discretion to decide not to grant a patent on the basis that the invention is in some way immoral? The Canadian Biotechnology Advisory Committee on Patenting of Higher Life Forms[301] suggested four views that could be taken:

(i) Patent law should only be concerned with economic considerations. Ethical or social concerns were better dealt with by regulation or the criminal law.[302]

---

[297] Nuffield Council on Bioethics (2002).   [298] BBC Newsonline (1 December 2004).
[299] Heller and Eisenberg (1998).   [300] BMA (2001b: 1).
[301] Canadian Biotechnology Advisory Committee on Patenting of Higher Life Forms (2002).
[302] Laurie (1997).

(ii) The patent system should be largely concerned with economic forces, although it has a limited ability to address some ethical issues.

(iii) Ethical and social matters should be given equal consideration when considering patents. The overarching goal of the patent system is to attain overall social good and this should be addressed by the patent system.

(iv) There should be an absolute bar on patents over higher life forms or other sensitive biotech areas, and whatever countervailing economic factors might be brought into play the bar should remain in place.

If it is assumed that ethical issues can legitimately play a role, are there any ethical issues which should inhibit biotech patents? Some would point to the practical issues we have been discussing above as sufficient to demonstrate the harmful effects of granting patents.

Others have relied on deontological arguments against granting patents. A common claim is that it is wrong to 'patent life'.[303] Before exploring this argument in more detail it is useful to distinguish a desire to patent a natural or a modified gene sequence or organism type. The gene sequence or organism type will be modified if a human intervention is a major cause of its existence. This will therefore refer to a gene sequence or organism type that is not normally found in the 'natural' world, but has been created from naturally found sequences, subjected to a process controlled by a human.

Let us consider natural gene sequences and organisms first. Some may object to a patent of a natural gene sequence on the basis that there has been no invention, but at most a discovery. Patents, as described above, are not meant to protect obvious things, but to encourage the invention and exploitation of non-obvious things. If anything, naturally occurring sequences and organisms should be regarded as collective property and cannot be claimed as belonging to any one person. The response to this might be to point out that some gene sequences or organisms, although existing in nature, can only be known about, and their significance appreciated, after a significant amount of time, effort, and money. If the purpose of patents is to encourage scientists and companies to find new medicines and useful products and to develop them, then that is true in the case of hitherto unknown benefits of a particular plant or genetic structures.

Now we shall consider modified organisms. Some will object to the genetic modification of sequences or organisms. Their objection will not be as such to patenting, but the process itself. It is not possible here to enter into the debate about genetic modification. Its key elements are well known. On the one hand there are those who are concerned that by 'meddling' in the natural genetic make-up of products we are 'playing God' and the consequences of our interference are unknown. The consequences of altering these building blocks of products are unknowable and may be irreversible. On the other hand it is claimed that if it is possible to create naturally occurring products which are more desirable (eg more resistant to infection) then we should use our ability to do so. It should also be emphasized that although we have placed weight on the distinction between natural organisms and modified ones the distinction is not straightforward. Some processes, for example, seek to speed up what might otherwise be a natural progression.

One line of argument is that patenting genes is like 'slavery' in that it involves the ownership of people. Stephen Wilkinson rejects this as 'fanciful and rhetorical'.[304] Even

---

[303] Wells (1994).   [304] Wilkinson (2003: 208).

if a company had a patent over part of your DNA make-up they would in no sense own you. All it would mean is that you would be restricted in marketing products that were made from your bodily material. Perhaps the argument is best understood as being about symbolism. DNA has come to occupy a special role in the public imagination. It is not well understood, but perhaps our unique genetic make-up is part of us. Therefore symbolically to own your DNA is to own you.

11 Conclusion

This chapter has involved some profound questions. What is our relationship with our bodies? Are they ours to do with as we please or do we need to protect the 'dignity' of our bodies? As technology develops and it becomes easier to add, extract, and alter not only organs but the genetic basis of our bodies the questions will only increase in complexity. Many people will feel wonder at the advances that are being made, tinged with fear that we might not know all of the consequences of the issues surrounding the transplantation of organs and ownership of bodies.

QUESTIONS

1. Bob Brecher (1994: 1001–2) states: 'However much the Turkish peasant who sold a kidney may have needed the money he was paid; however genuinely he may have wished to exercise his autonomy in this enterprising endeavour...however sincere his wish to benefit his family with the proceeds, and however great their need; nevertheless what he did was wrong.' Do you think it is as simple as that?

2. Why do you think that the Human Tissue Act 2004 did not adopt as an inviolable principle that material from humans could never be removed or stored without valid consent?

3. Price thinks: 'It would appear that the legislature ultimately moored the statutory framework in the [Human Tissue] 2004 Act to a rationale principally based upon the infringement of personal integrity ie to the validity of the consent governing removal of the tissue (further uses are implicitly consented to ie they are "part of the deal" in receiving medical treatment). Arguably however, it is philosophically grounded in property rights and interests, even despite the modifications to the Bill obviating the need for consent, but which in any event only apply to non-identifiable tissue as regards research' (Price (2005a: 817)). Do you agree?

4. Should someone be allowed to donate their heart to their sick child? We glorify those who give up their lives for the sake of others, so why not allow that in the case of organ donation?

5. 'Each person is the morally rightful owner of himself. He possesses over himself, as a matter of moral right, all those rights that a slaveholder has over a complete chattel slave as a matter of legal right, and he is entitled, morally speaking, to dispose over himself in the way such a shareholder is entitled, legally speaking, to dispose over his slave' (Cohen (1986: 109)). Do you agree?

6. Are the objections to patenting genetic material no more than ignorant sentimentality?

7. It is interesting to note that even among those who are willing to donate other organs the rate of cornea donation is low (Kounougeri-Manoledaki (2000)). Why do you think this is? What does this tell us about how people understand different parts of the body?

8. Volokh (2007) has argued that paying for organs should be regarded as a form of self-defence and so be legally and morally permissible. Is that a fair anology?

FURTHER READING

On Xenotransplantation see:

Fovargue, S. (2007) 'Oh pick me, pick me'—Selecting participants for xenotransplant clinical trials' *Medical Law Review* 15: 176.

Fox, M. and McHale, J. (1998) 'Xenotransplantation: The Ethical and Legal Ramifications' *Medical Law Review* 6: 42.

McLean, S. and Williamson, L. (2005) *Xenotransplantation—Law and Ethics* (Ashgate).

On the legal status of the body see:

Bjorkman, B. and Hansson, S. (2006) 'Bodily rights and property rights' *Journal of Medical Ethics* 32: 209.

Beyleveld, D. and Brownsword, R. (2001) *Human Dignity in Bioethics and Biolaw* (Oxford University Press).

Fabre, C. (2006) Whose Body is it Anyway? (Oxford University Press).

Freeman, M. (1997) 'Taking the Body Seriously?' in K. Stern and P. Walsh *Property Rights in the Human Body* (Kings College London).

Hardcastle, R. (2007) *Law and the Human Body* (Hart).

Herring, J. and Chau, P-L (2007) 'My body, your body, our bodies' *Medical Law Review* 15: 34.

Machado, N. (1998) *Using the Bodies of the Dead* (Ashgate).

Nuffield Council on Bioethics (1995) *Human Tissue: Ethical and Legal Issues* (Nuffield Council).

Price, D. (2007) 'Property, harm and the corpse' in Brooks-Gordan, B., Ebtehaj, F., Herring, J., Johnson, M., and Richards, M. (eds) *Death Rights and Rites* (Hart).

Radick, G. (2001) 'Discovering and Patenting Human Genes' in A. Bainham, S. Day Sclater, M. Richards, *Body Lore and Laws* (Hart).

Steiner, H. (1997) 'Property in the body: a philosophical perspective' in K. Stern and P. Walsh (eds) *Property Rights in the Human Body* (King's College London).

On issues surrounding organ donation and sale see:

Andrews, L. and Nelkin, D. (2001a) *Body Bazaar: The Market for Human Tissue* (Crown).

Cherry, M. (2005) *Kidney for Sale by Owner* (Georgetown University Press).

Garwood-Gowers, A. (1999) *Key Legal and Ethical Issues in Living Donor Organ Transplantation* (Ashgate).

Glannon, W. (2003) 'Do the sick have a right to cadaveric organs?' *Journal of Medical Ethics* 29: 153.

Goodwin, M (2007) *Black Markets* (Cambridge University Press).

Price, D. (2000a) *Legal and Ethical Aspects of Organ Transplantation* (Cambridge University Press).

Stacey Taylor, J. (2005) *Stakes and Kidneys: Why Markets in Human Body Parts are Morally Imperative* (Ashgate).

Wilkinson, T. (2005) 'Individual and family consent to organ and tissue donation: is the current position coherent?' *Journal of Medical Ethics* 31: 587.

On organ retention issues and the Human Tissue Act 2004 see:

Brazier, M. (2002) 'Retained Organs: Ethics and Humanity' *Legal Studies* 22, 550.

Harris, J. (2002) 'Law and Regulation of Retained Organs: The ethical issues' *Legal Studies* 527.

Liddell, K. and Hall, A. (2005) 'Beyond Bristol and Alder Hey: the future regulation of human tissue' *Medical Law Review* 13: 170.

Price, D. (2005) 'The Human Tissue Act 2004' *Modern Law Review* 68: 798.

You can register to donate your organs on < http://www.uktransplant.org.uk/ >.

9 Dying and Death

INTRODUCTION

Our attitudes towards death have changed in recent years. In the past, death was simply something that happened to us and had to be accepted. However, with techno- logical developments it has become possible to exercise greater control over our dying. Many people now wish for a quiet, peaceful, controlled death. Crypto-freezing and remarkable medical advances have even meant that it is possible to consider the pos- sibility of immortality.[1] It may soon be possible to say that death is not something that happens to you, but something that you do.[2] But the extent to which people should have control of their or another's death is highly controversial. This chapter focuses on questions such as: Is it permissible for a doctor to kill patients at their request? What about supplying drugs so that patients can kill themselves? Does a person have a right to commit suicide?

Very strong views are held on such questions. The academic debate over the legal and ethical issues is marked by heated exchanges where both sides feel that the other has misrepresented or failed to understand their arguments. More than once in this area, there have been complaints that the normal pleasantries surrounding academic debate have been set aside in the heat of the argument. Euthanasia and the related issues are topics that courts have struggled to deal with, and more than once the House of Lords has called upon Parliament to legislate on the area.[3] It appears that politicians so far have preferred to leave this hot potato with the courts,[4] although one leading lawyer has commented: 'Life and Death are too important to be left even to the judges.'[5]

At the heart of the debate is the nature of death, although that in turn is, to some extent, a debate about the nature of life. To some, death is the ultimate disaster to be avoided at all costs.[6] We must 'rage rage against the dying of the night' as Dylan Thomas put it. By contrast, another commentator has suggested that a good death is one marked by serenity and powerfulness fortified 'by qualities of composure, calm- ness, restraint, reserve and emotions or passions subdued and securely controlled with- out being negated or dissolved'.[7] People's attitudes towards death are often marked by their ethical or religious beliefs. Some therefore regard death as no more than a passage to the start of a joyous afterlife. To others death is the final chapter of their

---

[1] Harris (2004a).

[2] For a discussion of this change in attitude towards death see Battin (1998) and Brooks-Gordan et al (2007).

[3] *Airedale NHS Trust v Bland* [1993] 1 All ER 821, at 880, 885, and 899; *R (On the Application of Pretty) v DPP* [2002] 1 All ER 1, at para 96.

[4] Council of Europe (2003) provides a useful summary of position in the European Countries. Jost and Mendelson (2003) consider the legal position on euthanasia in a variety of jurisdictions.

[5] Beloff (2003: 37). He suggests there is a need for at least a 'legislative steer' (36).

[6] Freud (1911).   [7] Kolnai (1995).

story, which should reflect the values and principles which they have treasured during their lives.[8]

It has become common in recent times to seek a dignified death and this wish is behind some of the writing advocating the legalisation of euthanasia.[9] The kind of death feared by many people was summarized in the *Debate of the Age*:

> Most people fear death, or perhaps more accurately—most people fear dying. The prospect is often one of dying in hospital, perhaps in great pain, wired up to equipment and enduring uncomfortable interventions, suffering indignities and having little or no privacy, being sedated in such a way that there is little or no awareness of circumstances or surroundings, and, no opportunity to say goodbye.[10]

On the other had there are some who complain of the false expectation that we should have a 'dignified death experience'.[11] Death is normally ugly and painful and we should accept this as a fact of life, so to speak. It has been suggested that the wish to promote euthanasia and physician-assisted suicide is a sign of the times reflecting modern obsessions with living a fast pace of life; avoiding relationships of dependency; disliking mystery and ambiguity; and emphasizing costs and efficiency.[12]

Some academics argue that there has been a marked change just in the past century in the way society has responded to death. Until recently death was a public event which affected not only the deceased and their family but which wounded society itself. But now 'society no longer observes a pause; the disappearance of an individual no long affects its continuity';[13] death no longer makes a 'sign'.[14] Others disagree, suggesting that in recent times death has become very much a public issue. For example, looking at news stories and popular dramas on television, death has become public, a 'suppertime experience'.[15] Further, the widespread use of pensions and life insurance requires people as never before to take careful stock of their mortality.[16]

When thinking about death it is easy to see the issue entirely from the perspective of the person dying. Of course death usually brings with it unspeakable grief for those 'left behind'. Seale has written of the responsibility relatives felt for ensuring that the deceased died well.[17] This can be particularly difficult in a case where the loss is not publicly recognized as a death. Miscarriage or still births can have a huge impact on the parents, but this loss is often not formally acknowledged.[18]

REALITY CHECK

Death

There were 502,599 registered deaths in England and Wales in 2006. Of every one million males 7,123 died in 2004, and of every million females 4,989 did (National Statistics (2007b)).

There are clear signs that people are living longer. Allowing for changes in age structure of the population overall, death rates declined from 1993–2002 by 20 per cent for males and 14 per cent

---

[8] For interesting discussions on what might be regarded as a 'good death' see Dekkers, Sandman and Webb (2002) and Bradbury (2000).

[9] Biggs (2001).   [10] Age Concern (1999: 18).   [11] Nuland (1993: xvi).

[12] Mann (1998).   [13] Aries (2000: 10–11).   [14] Aries (1983: 266).

[15] Walter, Littlewood, and Pickering (2000).

[16] A fascinating study of changes in the causes of death during the 20th century can be found in Griffiths and Brock (2004).

[17] Seale (1998).   [18] Biggs (1998).

for females. For children born in 2002 the life expectancy for women was 81, for men it was 76 (National Statistics (2004)). In 1944 the average life expectancy worldwide was 48; by 1995 it was 65. The World Health Organization predicts it will be 73 by the year 2025 (WHO (1998)).

The leading cause of death for both sexes was ischaemic heart diseases, which accounted for approximately one in five male deaths and one in seven female deaths during 2006. Strokes were the second leading cause of death for both sexes (7.8 per cent). Three per cent of all deaths (16,421) were caused by accidents or violence (National Statistics (2007c)). Between 1979 and 2001 the number of alcohol related and drug poisoning related deaths tripled among young men aged 15–44. There were almost 23,000 alcohol-related deaths of people aged 20–64 in England and Wales in 2001–05. There were more than twice as many deaths among men as among women (15,436 and 7,477 respectively) (National Statistics (2007c)). In young men the most common cause of death is suicide (a fifth of all deaths in the 15–44 age group); for young women it is breast cancer (11 per cent of such deaths) (National Statistics (2003)). Biggs (2001: 9) states that 70 per cent of deaths take place in hospitals. A survey of six European countries suggests that between a quarter and a half of deaths in those countries were as a result of 'end of life' decisions by doctors (eg actively terminating life; a decision to withhold treatment or provide drugs, even though death was to be a consequence of the medication) (Van der Heide et al (2003)). Although another study looking at 17 countries found that only 10 per cent of patients had died following a limitation of life-sustaining treatment (Sprung et al (2003)). However, according to a study by Seale (2006) 0.16 per cent of deaths in the UK were a result of voluntary euthanasia and not due to physician-assisted suicide. He noted these figures were far lower than elsewhere in Europe. By contrast 32.8 per cent of deaths followed treatment for pain which also had life-shortening effects.

1 What is death?

1.1 Defining death

Defining death is controversial and problematic.[19] The issue raises fundamental questions about our humanity: What is it to be a person? What are the essential elements of life? There are usually no difficulties in deciding whether a person is dead, even if there is disagreement over when death occurred. However, where a patient is in a state involving an absence of consciousness, but is being artificially sustained, a debate may ensue over whether the person is alive. The issue can become of great practical relevance in the area of organ donation. If the view taken is that organs cannot be removed until the person is dead it is important to know exactly when death occurs. Postponing the removal of organs until a late stage can mean that they cannot be used for transplantation. The issue is also of practical importance when the care of those in permanent comas is considered. If they are dead then there are no legal or ethical difficulties in switching off their life support machines.

1.2 The legal definition of death

It is surprising that the legal definition of death has received very little attention from the courts. In *Bland*[20] Lords Brown-Wilkinson, Goff, and Keith accepted that brain

---

[19] Lizza (2006), Chau and Herring (2007), and Veatch (2005) discusses the issues.
[20] *Airedale NHS Trust v Bland* [1993] 1 All ER 821.

stem death was the definition of death for the purposes of medicine and law. Tony Bland, although suffering Persistent Vegetative State, was not brain stem dead and so was still alive. In *re A*[21] Johnson J held that a child who was on a ventilator and certified as brain stem dead was also legally dead. This was in line with the medical expert opinion, even though the parents took the view that the boy was still alive.[22]

Perhaps the safest statement to make is that at present the legal definition of death is taken to coincide with the medical one.[23] So if the issue is raised a court is very likely to follow the expert medical opinion.[24] The Human Tissue Act 2004, section 26(2) authorizes the Human Tissue Authorities to issue codes of practice which will set out how it will be determined whether a person has died in cases involving transplantation. The problem is that there is some disagreement over what the medical definition of death is.

1.3 Alternative definitions of death

Although English and Welsh doctors and lawyers appear to have adopted brain stem death as the definition of death, it is important to appreciate that this is only one definition that could be taken and it is a controversial one.[25] We shall now look at some of the alternative definitions proposed:

(i) *Brain stem death.* As already indicated brain stem death is widely accepted in the UK as the medical definition of death.[26] It is claimed that a person whose brain stem is dead has ceased to live in anything but a mechanical way.[27] At present the Department of Health's *A Code of Practice for the Diagnosis of Brain Stem Death*[28] sets out in detail the definition of brain stem death. This outlines three requirements that must be met before a doctor makes a diagnosis of brain death:

1. It must be concluded that the coma is not due to reversible causes, such as drug overdose.

2. It must be demonstrated that the several components of the brain stem have all been permanently destroyed. Significantly this includes the respiratory centre.

3. It must be proved that the patient is unable to breathe spontaneously.

The code suggests that two medical practitioners registered for more than five years and specialists in the field should agree that there is brain death, before pronouncement.[29]

A fundamental attack on the concept of brain death is that it elevates the brain to being the essential organ of the person. The body is made up of much more than the

---

[21] [1992] 3 *Medical Law Review* 303.

[22] Mumby J in *R (Smeaton on behalf of SPUC) v The Secretary of State for Health et al* [2002] 2 FCR 193, at para 57 agreed.

[23] So the parents' views on whether a child is dead will not affect the legal analysis: Inwald, Jacobovits, and Petros (2000). See also *Re C (A Minor)(Medical Treatment)* [1998] 1 FLR 384 where the religious views of the parents did not justify ordering continued treatment of the child contrary to the advice of doctors.

[24] Unfortunately there is controversy amongst medics over what the correct definition of death is: see Skegg (1985: Chap 9); Kennedy (1969); Van Tilld and Borouill (1975); Bennion (1994).

[25] For an extensive criticism of the concept of brain stem death see Shewmon (1998).

[26] Pallis and Harley (1996).

[27] Although Karakatsanis and Tsanakas (2002) argue that it is far from proven that the tests for brain stem death show that there is no consciousness.

[28] DoH (1998).

[29] Fost (1999) complains that there is no definite test for brain death. Although see DuBois (2002) who suggests tests based on the absence of activity as indicating death are based on common sense.

brain, opponents point out. To declare the body dead when only part of it (the brain) is not working reveals too narrow an understanding of the body. Veatch imagines a time in the future in which it would be possible to give a person a brain transplant. He suggests that if a brain stem test was to be used this would lead to such a person being classified as dead, even though they would patently be alive.[30] It has also been argued that a person can be classified as brain dead, even though their body is warm and breathing[31] and to do so would create too big a gap between the legal meaning of death and its understanding by lay people.[32]

(ii) *The end of breathing.* At one time death was defined as the moment a patient's heart stopped pumping and breathing ceased. However, medical advances have made this definition of death problematic. It is now clear that the stopping of the heart does not lead to an end of brain activity. The point can also be made that even if respiration has stopped, medical intervention such as the use of a ventilator or electrical stimulation in the case of a heart attack, can save the patient at the door of death.

One prominent supporter of the loss of cardiac function is the Danish Council of Ethics, which preferred it to brain death.[33] The Council took the view that the definition of death is not a technical question, but must be decided in terms of how the community as a whole understands death. It argued that the person in the street would view the stopping of the beating heart as the criterion for death because the heart is widely seen as a symbol of life.[34] So, even if the notion of the beating heart as the key to life is not logically or philosophically justifiable, it is intuitively felt to be the essential mark of life.

(iii) *The end of the organism.* If the body is seen as a 'working organism' with various functions then it might be possible to define death as when that organism ceases to achieve those functions.[35] The functions of the body might include ventilation, circulation, nutrition, and elimination of waste products. Only once all of these are no longer being performed should the body be said to have died. To opponents of this view it treats the body like a piece of machinery; most people regard their bodies as more than an organism that takes in and expels air. Such an approach overlooks what most people regard as most important about their bodies: feelings, thoughts, emotions and the like.

(iv) *Death of every cell.* An extreme view would be to declare that a person has not died until every cell in the body has ceased functioning.[36] This would place the point of death at the state when the body has begun to putrefy. It is unlikely this would be regarded as an acceptable notion by most people.

(v) *Death as a process.* Although most people see death as a moment in time, in medical terms death is better seen as a process. Occasionally there will be a clear instant of death, where, for example, a person is blown up in an explosion. But where death is 'natural' there is no easy cut off point at which we can mark the line between a person who is alive and a person who is dead. As one dying patient put it 'death keeps taking a little bit of me'.[37]

---

[30] Veach (1999: 41) and see the discussion in Biggs (2002: 18–20).
[31] Evans (1993).   [32] Byrne and Rinkowski (1999: 42).
[33] Discussed in Rix (1990), Gillon (1990), and Lamb (1990).
[34] Truog (1997: 29).   [35] Lamb (1985).
[36] It would, for example, be possible to use hypostasis (the moment blood stops circulating) as the moment when death occurs.
[37] Quoted in Kafetz (2002: 536).

Although there is much to be said in favour of this approach it is not a practical one. Aries has argued:

> Death in the hospital is no longer the occasion of a ritual ceremony, over which the dying person presides amidst his assembled relatives and friends. Death is a technical phenomenon obtained by a cessation of care...Indeed in the majority of cases the dying person has already lost consciousness. Death has been dissected, cut to bits by a series of little steps, which finally makes it impossible to know which step was the real death, the one in which consciousness was lost or the one in which breathing stopped. All these little silent deaths have replaced and released the great dramatic act of death, and no one any longer has the strength or patience to wait over a period of weeks for a moment which has lost part of its meaning.[38]

The law, relatives, and professionals require a clear point at time at which someone has died.[39] Proponents of seeing death as a process could, however, suggest that a person could be treated as dead for different purposes at different times. There could be one point in time in the process where a person is declared dead for the purpose of removal of organs for transplant, but another where they are dead for the purposes of burial or cremation.[40]

(vi) *Desoulment.* For those of a religious persuasion death is often defined as the moment the soul[41] leaves the body and moves on to the afterlife. Of course such a definition will be rejected by those who deny the existence of a soul. Even if the existence of a soul is accepted there is a problem in that the moment of desoulment is not apparent to humans. It cannot therefore readily provide a basis of a legal or medical test.

(vii) *Consciousness or social interaction.* To some commentators the definition of death should depend on what we understand it is to be human. TSome define this as a consciousness of one's self or others, and an ability to interact with other people. Supporters of such an approach would argue that a person who has permanently lost the ability to communicate or relate to other people and/or a person who has permanently lost a conscious awareness of themselves or their surroundings, has lost what is essential to being a human. Such an approach would lead to a far wider classification of death than used at present. For example, those suffering from Persistent Vegetative State would be regarded as dead. Even more dramatically it would classify as dead (or at least non-people) huge numbers of people with severe mental conditions.

(viii) *Choose your own.* Bagheri[42] has suggested that because there are so many definitions of death and they all depend on one's theological, spiritual, or political beliefs it is best to let each person decide what they would like the definition of death to be. This has some attractions as a proposal, although one would need to have some 'fall back' position to rely on in cases where the person had failed to indicate what they wanted their definition of death to be. There would also, presumably, be some definitions of death which would be unacceptable, and so not permitted.

(ix) *Avoiding the issue of death.* One response to the difficulties over defining death is to suggest that we need to look at the question differently, avoiding the question

---

[38] Aries (1974: 88).   [39] Stanley (1987).
[40] DuBois (2002) argues that death should be seen as a state not a process or event.
[41] The 'soul', roughly speaking, is the spiritual essence of a person that continues after death.
[42] Bagheri (2007).

of when death occurs. We could, for example, ask: At what point is it appropriate to authorize burials of bodies? When can organs be removed from a body for transplant to another? When can a person whose body is being artificially ventilated have the machine switched off? It would be possible to have different answers to these questions.

1.4 Choosing between the definitions

In choosing between these different definitions it is worth considering the claim by Lamb: 'It is as wrong to treat the living as dead as it is to treat the dead as alive.'[43] The argument is that it is important not only not to put the point of death too early, but also not to put it too late. But not everyone will agree with Lamb's suggestion. Treating a dead person as alive may be a waste of resources, or delay improperly the grieving process for the family; but is it really as serious as burying a person who is alive?

The different definitions of death tend to group into two categories: those that emphasize life as being about conscious awareness; and those that understand the body as a living organism.[44] The problem is that many people regard both understandings of our bodies and lives as valid.[45] One solution could be to accept that we die twice: once when we lose consciousness and once when our biological organism comes to an end.[46] This would be supported by those who argue we are not just minds, nor are we just bodies, we are 'embodied minds'.[47]

Another difference between the definitions may be the viewpoint from which death is appreciated: the dying person or her or his carers. Arguable brain stem death will the point at which the dying person will lose all appreciation of their life, but cessation of breathing will be the point at which the person will appear to have died to on–lookers. However, it should be noted that the stopping of breathing is the most common cause for the brain stem to cease.[48] Indeed Mason and Laurie suggest it would be wrong to see brain stem death and non-breathing as two competing definitions of death. They prefer:

> to visualise the brain, the heart and the lungs as forming a 'cycle of life' which can be broken at any point; looked at in this way, there is no need to speak of two *concepts* of death—that is, cardio respiratory death or brain death; it is simply that different criteria, and different tests, can be used for identifying that the circle has been broken.[49]

A further key issue is who should define death? As already mentioned, so far the English courts have in recent times tended to follow the medical definition of death. Although this is approved of by some lawyers,[50] others have argued that the philosophical and moral arguments must also be taken into account and therefore the courts should not slavishly follow medical opinion.[51]

Finally, in producing a legal definition of death it is necessary to consider not only philosophical considerations, but the test must be usable and one which accords with the general public's understanding of death.[52] In other words it may be that the

---

[43] Lamb (1994: 1028).
[44] Gervais (1986: 15) distinguishes between those who see death as a biological question and those who see it as a moral one.
[45] Holland (2003: 75).   [46] McMahan (1995).
[47] McMahan (2002: 426). See also Shewmon (1998).   [48] Pallis(1990).
[49] Mason and Laurie (2006: 466). See also United States President's Commission (1981).
[50] Kennedy (1969).   [51] Skegg (1974).   [52] Devettere (1990).

philosophically most desirable definition of death is not usable because it cannot be transformed into a clear and practical test.

2 The law and the end of life

This section will seek to set out the law on a range of 'end of life issues' including euthanasia, assisted suicide, and refusal of medical treatment. To understand the legal position it is necessary to look at the criminal law on murder, manslaughter, suicide, and the legal position of patients who are refusing life-saving treatment.[53]

2.1 Murder

To be guilty of murder the jury must be persuaded beyond reasonable doubt that:

 (i) the defendant caused the death of the patient;

 (ii) the defendant intended to cause death or grievous bodily harm;

(iii) the defendant cannot successfully raise a defence.

More needs to be said in medical end-of-life cases about each of these requirements:

2.1.1 *The defendant caused the death of the victim*

In considering whether the defendant caused the death of the victim it is necessary to distinguish cases where it is alleged that it was the act of a defendant which caused the death (eg where the doctor has given a patient a lethal injection) and where it is claimed it was an omission which caused the death (eg the carer of a terminally ill patient fails to resuscitate her or him when she or he slips into unconsciousness).

 (i) *Acts of the defendant causing death.* In a murder case it is necessary to show that the defendant's act was a substantial and operating cause of the death. This means that the doctor's act does not need to be the sole cause of death, but it must be a substantial cause of death.[54] In other words if an autopsy established that a patient died from a combination of a disease and the injection of drugs by a doctor it could still be said that the doctor's act caused the death. This is subject to two caveats. The first is that if the administration of the drug only shortened the victim's life by a few seconds this may not constitute a substantial cause of death. However, as Devlin J put it in the trial of Dr Adams:[55]

> If the acts done are intended to kill and do, in fact kill, it does not matter if a life is cut short by weeks or months, it is just as much murder as if it were cut short by years.

The second caveat is that the courts are reluctant to find 'normal' medical treatment to have broken the chain of causation.[56] Certainly where a defendant has stabbed a victim

---

[53] Biggs (1996) offers a useful summary of the criminal law in this area. There is also health and safety legislation which may be relevant: *R v Southampton University Hospital NHS Trust* [2006] EWCA Crim 2971.

[54] *R v Cheshire* [1991] 3 All ER 670; *R v Mellor* [1996] 2 Cr App R 245.

[55] Discussed in Palmer (1957).

[56] Tur (2002) argues that normal medial treatment does not break the chain in causation and so a doctor following sound medical opinion cannot be said to cause a patient's death.

who has received medical treatment and died, the courts are only likely to be convinced that the stabbing did not cause the victim's death where the medical treatment was 'palpably wrong'.[57]

(ii) *Omissions of the doctor causing death.* If the claim is that it was a doctor's failure to treat a patient which caused the patient's death, the situation is a little more complicated. Generally in the criminal law a defendant is not criminally responsible for an omission. Many criminal lawyers point out that a defendant who walks past a stranger drowning in a pond without offering help will not be criminally responsible for the stranger's death. However, there are occasions where a criminal prosecution may be faced by those who fail to act. These are: where the defendant owes a duty to the victim; the defendant fails to act in accordance with that duty; and had the defendant acted in accordance with the duty the victim would not have died when she or he did.[58]

There is normally no difficulty in establishing that a health care professional owes her or his patient a duty of care.[59] However, less straightforward is the question whether the doctor is acting in accordance with her or his duty in not providing treatment to a dying patient. Normally a doctor will be breaching her or his duty in not providing appropriate medical treatment to a dying patient. However, this is not always so. In the following three situations a doctor will not breach her or his duty by failing to provide treatment to a patient:

(a) If a competent patient does not consent to the treatment a medical professional need not provide it. Indeed it is unlawful to do so.[60] It is well established that patients have a right to refuse treatment, even if as a result the patient will die.[61] This was recently confirmed in *Ms B v An NHS Trust*[62] (see page xxx below). It could be argued that a competent person cannot refuse basic care (such as cleaning or feeding, causing serious harm to the individual). The basis for this view is that there is a public policy objection to a person in a hospital not receiving a decent level of care.[63] Indeed for a person to be denied food or basic cleaning could be said amount to torture and inhuman or degrading treatment and therefore forbidden by article 3 of the European Convention on Human Rights. Others, however, argue that the importance placed by the court on a competent patient's right to refuse treatment is so great that no exceptions to it should be permitted.[64]

(b) A doctor is not required to provide treatment if the treatment is not in the patient's best interests. Of course, only exceptionally will it not be in a patient's interests to receive life-saving treatment.[65] In *Airedale NHS Trust v Bland* Lord Browne Wilkinson[66] stated:

[I]f there comes a stage where the responsible doctor comes to the reasonable conclusion (which accords with the views of a responsible body of medical opinion) that

---

[57] *R v Cheshire* [1991] 3 All ER 670.   [58] *R v Stone and Dobinson* [1977] QB 354.

[59] See Chapter 3.

[60] Grubb (1997) discusses the position of a person with conscientious objection to, for example, switching off a ventilation machine at the request of the patient.

[61] *Re T (Adult Refusal of Medical Treatment)* [1992] 4 All ER 649; *Re MB* [1997] 2 FLR 426. See also the Canadian decision of *Nancy B v Hotel-Dieu de Quebec* (1992) 86 DLR (4th) 385.

[62] [2002] EWHC 429.

[63] Keown (1994a). In *Secretary of State for Home Department v Robb* [1995] 1 All ER 677 it was suggested, *obiter*, that there could be public policy objections that could justify overriding the refusal of a patient for treatment.

[64] Biggs (2001: Chap 1).   [65] *R (Burke) v GMC* [2005] 3 FCR 169.

[66] [1993] 1 All ER 821, at p 882.

further continuance of an intrusive life support system is not in the best interests of the patient, he can no longer lawfully continue that life support system: to do so would constitute the crime of battery and the tort of trespass to the person.

In *Bland* the House of Lords held that the treatment was not in his best interests and so the medical team did not have to provide it.[67] Notice that it was not that the medical treatment was against his best interests, it simply did not promote them. Notice also that it is only legitimate to consider whether the treatment would be in the best interests *of that patient*. The Mental Capacity Act 2005 makes it clear that if the incompetent person has issued an effective advance directive (see Chapter 4) stating that they do not want to be given life-sustaining treatment then it would be unlawful for the medical team to give it. However, as Sabine Michalowski points out, the legal consequences for failing to comply with such a directive are fairly minor.[68]

(c) Where a doctor has to allocate scarce resources between patients and reasonably decides not to offer some patients the resource. The most obvious example of this would be where several patients urgently need a kidney transplant, but only one kidney is available.

In cases involving omissions it can be very difficult to tell in the case of a very sick patient whether they died due to an inappropriate lack of care or from their medical condition.[69]

2.1.2 *The doctor intended death or grievous bodily harm*

Generally in criminal law there are two ways in which a person can be said to intend a result.

(i) *Direct intent.* A person intends a result if it is her or his purpose to produce the result.[70]

(ii) *Indirect or oblique intent.* The test developed in the House of Lords decision in *R v Woollin*[71] is used. The jury is entitled to find that a defendant intended a result if:

(a) the result was virtually certain to result from the defendant's act; and

(b) the defendant realized this.

A doctor who gives a patient a drug in order to kill her or him will intend to kill her or him (direct intent). This is so even if the doctor was motivated by what some people would regard as the 'good' reason of wishing to end the patient's pain. The criminal law in deciding intention is interested in the purpose of the defendant not the reasons she or he had for having that purpose.

If a doctor were to give pain relieving drugs to a patient with the purpose of relieving pain, but was aware that the drugs would shorten the victim's life, then, applying the general criminal law, the jury would be entitled to find, but would not have to find,[72]

---

[67] *Re MB (An Adult: Medical Treatment)* [1997] 2 FCR 541 at 555 emphasizes that a consideration of a patient's best interests includes medical emotional and all other matters relating to the patient's general welfare.

[68] Michalowski (2007). Mental Capacity Act 2005, s 5 provides a defence to a doctor who reasonably believes that a patient is incompetent when they are not.

[69] BBC Newsonline (21 March 2005) provides an example of the difficulties.

[70] Ormerod (2005: 93).   [71] [1999] 1 AC 82.

[72] *R v Matthews and Alleyne* [2003] 2 Cr App R 30.

there was intent. One might predict that few juries would choose to find intent in such a case. As we shall see later, it may in fact be that in this particular kind of case the general law on intent does not apply; instead there may be a special rule that when doctors give pain-relieving medication to relieve pain there is, as a matter of law, no intent.

2.1.3 Defences

To a charge of murder a defendant may seek to raise a variety of defences including self-defence and necessity. The defences which are most likely to arise in the context of a medical case include the following:

(i) *Diminished responsibility.* Under The Homicide Act 1957, section 2(1):

> Where a person kills or is party to the killing of another, he shall not be convicted of murder if he was suffering from such abnormality of mind (whether arising from a condition of arrested or retarded development of mind or any inherent causes or induced by disease or injury) as substantially impaired his mental responsibility for his acts and omissions in doing or being a party to the killing.

The defence is most likely to be relied upon in a case where someone who has been caring for a terminally ill relative is suffering from the exhaustion and stress that 24-hours-a-day care can produce.[73] It should be noticed that this is only a partial defence and so if successful the defendant is still guilty of manslaughter. Significantly this means that the defendant does not have to receive the mandatory life imprisonment that accompanies a murder conviction.[74] It would only be in an unusual case that a medical professional killing one of her or his patients could rely on diminished responsibility.

(ii) *Provocation.* If a defendant can demonstrate that she or he killed while suffering from a loss of self-control as a result of something said or done, and it was reasonable for her or him to do so, then a defence is available.[75] Again this is a partial defence which, if successful, leads to a conviction of manslaughter. In *Cocker*[76] a husband smothered his wife who suffered from a terminal illness and who had been asking him to kill her. He failed in his attempt to use provocation as a defence because it had not been demonstrated that he had lost his self-control when he killed her; quite the opposite he was in complete control.

(iii) *Suicide pact.* If the defendant killed the victim intending to go on and kill her or himself as part of a suicide pact then she or he will have a defence to a charge of murder, but still be guilty of manslaughter.[77] The onus of proof on establishing that the killing was in the course of a suicide pact is on the defendant.

(iv) *Necessity of self-defence.* In the most exceptional of cases it may be permissible to kill one person in order to save another. If one person is attacking or posing a threat to another then force can be used to repel that threat, relying on self-defence or private defence. But otherwise it is not generally permissible to kill one person in order to save others. For example, if a doctor had four patients who were all in need of an organ transplant, without which they would all die, it would not be lawful for the doctor to kill one person, take her or his organs, and use them to save the lives of four of his other patients,

---

[73] Dell (1984). See Innes (2002) discussing the case of a 74-year-old husband who killed his wife who was suffering from motor neurone disease. The judge gave a three year community rehabilitation order after a conviction of manslaughter on the grounds of diminished responsibility.

[74] See *Taylor* [1979] CLY 570, where a man who killed his autistic child was placed on probation.

[75] Homicide Act 1957, s 3.   [76] [1989] Crim LR 740.   [77] Homicide Act 1957, s 4.

even though the doctor might be said to have performed an act which produced a great good (she or he killed one person but saved the life of four). Generally the argument 'I did the lesser of two evils' or 'I produced the greater good' is not a defence in the criminal law. In very exceptional circumstances it might. An exceptional case was *Re A (Conjoined Twins)*[78] where it was held that the defence of necessity provided a defence to a doctor who killed one conjoined twin in order to save the other:

KEY CASE   Re A (Conjoined Twins) [2001] Fam 147 (CA)

Jodie and Mary were born joined together at the pelvis. Jodie was the stronger of the two. Mary's heart and lungs did not function and she was only able to live because she shared a common artery with Jodie. In effect Jodie's heart was pumping for both of them. The medical evidence demonstrated that if they were not separated Jodie's heart would not be able to cope and both twins would die within a few months. However, if an operation was carried out to separate them it was likely that Jodie would be able to live a relatively normal life, although Mary would die almost immediately. The doctors caring for the twins wished to separate them, but the parents objected on religious grounds. The Court of Appeal held that the operation could go ahead.

The starting point was to consider whether or not it would be a criminal offence to carry out the operation. It was held it was not. It was accepted that the doctors carrying out the operation would cause Mary's death. Lord Justices Ward and Brooke held the doctors would also intend to kill Mary because they would have foreseen Mary's death as virtually certain. Lord Justice Robert Walker held that there was no intention because Mary's death was not the purpose of their actions and the doctrine of double effect (see page 463) meant there was no intention. All three members of the Court of Appeal thought that the doctors would have a defence to a charge of murder. Lord Justice Robert Walker relied on the defence of self-defence. Lord Justices Ward and Brooke suggested that on the unusual facts of the case the doctors could rely on the defence of necessity. Although normally it is not a defence to a charge of murder to claim that by killing one person you are saving another person's life, in this 'unique case' it was. What appears to have influenced the Court of Appeal is that although it would not quite be correct to say that Jodie was attacking Mary and therefore self-defence could be relied upon, it was very nearly a case of self-defence. Mary's existence was posing an unjust threat to Jodie's life. It is difficult to draw any hard and fast conclusions from this case about when else a court might recognize a defence of necessity.

Deciding the operation was not a criminal offence was not the end of the case, because the Court still had to decide whether to make a declaration authorizing the operation. The Court of Appeal took the view that the question should be governed by the family law principle: what is in the best interests of the child(ren)? The difficulty here was that at first sight the operation was not in the interests of Mary (it would cause her death), although it was in the interests of Jodie (it would save her life). Lord Justice Robert Walker argued that the operation would be in the interests of both twins. For Mary it offered the prospect of 'bodily integrity' and respected her right to have her body 'whole and intact'. Further, without the operation her life offered only pain and discomfort. However, their other Lordships thought it could not be said that the operation was in Mary's interests. But, in a case where the welfare of two children was directly involved the court could balance the benefits and disadvantages to each and here the advantages to Jodie of a full life over for Mary a small increase in her life expectancy meant that the operation should be performed.

---

[78] A useful collection of academic commentary on this case can be found in Volume 9, number 3 *Medical Law Review* 2001.

(v) *There is no defence of mercy killing.*[79] Some have argued that a relative who kills a terminally ill person for whom they have been caring should be able to rely on a defence of mercy killing, but the law does not recognize such a defence. That said, it is very rare for a case which might be said to be a mercy killing to be brought to court. This is because the Crown Prosecution Service will only bring a prosecution if they believe that to do so will be in the public interest.[80] According to the Home Office, between 1982 and 1991 inclusive only 24 such cases were brought before the court. Only one resulted in a murder conviction. Sixteen resulted in manslaughter convictions, but of those only three went to prison. It has also been suggested that doctors acting in accordance with good medical practice should have a special defence. The courts have not expressly acknowledged such a defence, but some commentators argue that the criminal law would never find a doctor who had followed sound medical practice to have committed an offence.[81] Indeed according to the Home Office in the study just referred to, in not one of the cases was a doctor prosecuted.

2.2 Manslaughter

To be guilty of gross negligence manslaughter it must be shown that:

(i) the defendant owed the victim a duty of care;

(ii) the defendant breached the duty of care;

(iii) the breach caused the death of the victim;

(iv) the breach was so gross as to justify a criminal conviction.[82]

A conviction for gross negligence manslaughter would arise if a health care professional or carer acted or failed to act in an extremely negligent way, so much so that the jury were convinced a criminal conviction was appropriate.[83] A person who was providing treatment or not providing treatment for a dying person in a way regarded as appropriate by a respectable body of opinion would not be acting negligently[84] and so would not be guilty of this offence. It will be noted that there is no need to show an intention to cause injury to the victim.

2.3 Suicide

The law's response to suicide is complex. At one time suicide was a crime and, bizarrely, attempted suicide potentially carried a sentence of capital punishment![85] The present law, as set out in the Suicide Act 1961, is that suicide and attempted suicide are not crimes.[86] The reasoning behind this is that those who have attempted suicide do not

---

[79] *R v Beecham* discussed in Horder (1988). See also *R v Latimer* [2001] 1 SCR 3, where the Supreme Court of Canada upheld the murder conviction of a father who had killed his 12-year-old daughter who was suffering from a severe form of cerebral palsy.

[80] See the case of Rachel Heath whose trial for attempted murder of an elderly cancer patient in her care was abandoned after the judge asked the Crown Prosecution Service to reconsider whether the prosecution was in the public interest. The case is discussed in Biggs (1996).

[81] Tur (2002); Smith (2000b).   [82] *R v Adomako* [1995] 1 AC 171.

[83] See Biggs (2007c) for a discussion of the criminalization of carers in this context.

[84] Using the test set out in *Bolam v Friern* [1957] 1 WLR 582.   [85] Williams (1957: 274).

[86] Suicide Act 1961, s 1; although there have been reports of a woman who repeatedly attempted suicide being given an ASBO (MacDonald (2006)).

need the ministrations of the criminal law, but rather the care of medical and other professionals. However, the Suicide Act does make it an offence to aid, abet, counsel, or procure suicide. So although a patient who took an overdose of tablets in a bid to kill her or himself would not have committed an offence, the physician who gave her or him the tablets might have done so. To understand further the offence of aiding, abetting, counselling, or procuring suicide a number of issues need to be considered.

2.3.1 *What is suicide?*

The general view seems to be that suicide involves a person intentionally killing themselves.[87] There are two main areas of controversy surrounding the legal definition of suicide. The first is whether it includes omissions. If a person refuses life-saving treatment because they want to die, is this suicide?[88] The second is whether a person who acts knowing that death will result, but not acting for the purpose of dying, is committing suicide. The courts are yet to express a clear view on this. Lord Justice Thorpe in *Secretary of State for the Home Department v Robb*[89] argued that a prisoner who went on hunger strike and as a result died did not commit suicide. He did not explain why. It may be because the hunger striker did not intend to die; rather he wanted his complaints to be dealt with. Or it may be because Thorpe LJ thought that suicide required a positive act. Cholbi has suggested we use the category of self-manslaughter to cover those who take a risk of killing themselves, but do not intend to do so.[90]

2.3.2 *What is aiding, abetting, counselling, and procuring suicide?*

For a detailed discussion of these terms a book on criminal law should be consulted.[91] An example of aiding and abetting[92] suicide would be providing equipment or advice that would help someone commit suicide.[93] Counselling suicide involves encouraging and supporting another to commit suicide. Procuring suicide is to produce another's suicide 'by endeavour'.[94] To be guilty of the offence the defendant must intend or foresee that the other will commit suicide as a result of their assistance. The offence is only committed if someone does commit suicide following the defendant's actions. In *A–G v Able*[95] it was suggested that simply writing a book or pamphlet which described ways of committing suicide would not constitute aiding suicide. The decision does not make it quite clear why not, although this might be because it would not be possible for the prosecution to demonstrate that the book has assisted the suicide or that the writer intended to assist the suicide of a particular person. Justice Woolf did make it clear that if it could have been shown that the booklet actively encouraged someone to commit suicide and the author intended people to be encouraged, the offence could be made out.

---

[87] Donnelly (1998) argues that in fact the definition of suicide is a highly complex matter.

[88] Lanham (1990) discusses this in detail. Otlowski (1997: 64) thinks that it is possible to commit suicide by omission.

[89] [1995] Fam 127.   [90] Cholbi (2007). See also Williams (2007: chap 5)

[91] Eg Herring (2006: chap 15).   [92] No one seems quite for sure what abetting means.

[93] Although see *R v Chard* The Times, 23 September 1993, which appears to provide a defence to a doctor who provided tablets to a patient at her request. The trial judge indicated that as the doctor had only given the patient the option of taking her life no offence was committed.

[94] *Attorney-General Reference (No 1 of 1975)* [1975] 2 All ER 686 (CA).   [95] [1984] QB 795.

2.3.3 *Is there a right to commit suicide?*

There has been some debate over whether there is a right to commit suicide. It is true that the Suicide Act means that suicide is no longer a crime, but that does not mean that there is a right to do it.[96] Adultery is not a crime, but there is no right to commit adultery. However, the issue may not be that straightforward because the use of the term 'right' here is ambiguous. It may be helpful to distinguish a claim from a liberty.[97] If you have a liberty to do something you are permitted to engage in the activity without anyone preventing you from doing something. A claim is an entitlement which you can expect another to provide. A child may have a claim against her or his parents for protection and support. Normally in the case of liberty the activity is regarded as permissible, but is not necessarily approved of, whereas with a claim generally it is regarded as proper to expect it. So although there is a liberty for people to read pornography in English law, the law does not regard that as a right. A prisoner could not insist that the authorities give her or him pornography. But she or he would be regarded as having a 'claim right' to food. Using this distinction it is arguable that suicide is not a 'claim right', but might be (like adultery) a 'liberty right'. Indeed it is arguable that the fact that it is an offence for someone to aid or abet suicide indicates that suicide is not regarded as a justifiable activity to which there is a 'claim right'.[98] So perhaps this is a form of conduct which is not quite a criminal offence, but an activity which society does not wish to encourage. In a sense it is unlawful, even if not a criminal offence.

In *G v Central and North West London Mental Health Authority*[99] a depressed woman who was under the care of her local hospital attempted to commit suicide and sued the hospital for failing to protect her from attempting suicide. Notably the claim failed because the authority was found to have acted reasonably, rather than on the basis that they had no right to try and stop her committing suicide.

2.4 Refusal of medical treatment

The basic legal principle is that it is not lawful to administer treatment against the wishes of a competent person. This is so even where without the treatment the patient will die.[100] So if an adult Jehovah's Witness requires a blood transfusion to save her or his life but refuses to consent to it, then it is impermissible to force it on her or him. That would amount to the criminal offence of battery.

It is important to appreciate that this is only true where the patient is competent. So if the physician is convinced that the individual is suffering from such a severe mental condition that she or he is not competent to make the decision, then the doctor can provide the life-saving treatment.[101] If there is any doubt over the patient's competence the guidance of the court could be sought. The courts have recently confirmed the right to refuse medical treatment in a striking case:

---

[96] Keown (2002: 65).   [97] The distinction is usefully explained in Pedain (2003).

[98] *Secretary of State for Home Department v Robb* [1995] 1 All ER 677. See also Price (1996).

[99] [2007] All ER (D) 286 (Oct).   [100] *S v St George's* [1998] 3 All ER 673.

[101] *Re MB (Caesarean Section)* [1997] 2 FCR 541.

KEY CASE   Re B (Adult: Refusal of Medical Treatment) [2002] 2 FCR 1

Ms B, aged 41, suffered a haemorrhage of the spinal column in her neck. Despite several years of treatment her condition worsened and she suffered compete paralysis from the neck down. She became entirely dependant on a ventilator. Subsequently she made it clear that she wanted to have the ventilator turned off, even if that meant that she would die. Her clinicians accepted that Ms B was competent to make the decision, but had grown close to her during the treatment and could not bring themselves to abide by her wishes. Butler Sloss P confirmed that Ms B was competent to make the decision to withdraw treatment. She reiterated the fundamental principle that 'if . . . the patient, having been given the relevant information and offered the available options chooses to refuse, that decision has to be respected by the doctors. Considerations of the best interests of the patient irrelevant' (para 100). The fact the doctors felt that her decision was wrong did not give them a reason to ignore it. Remarkably Butler Sloss P herself added '[Ms B] is clearly a splendid person and it is tragic that someone of her ability has been struck down so cruelly. I hope she will forgive me for saying, diffidently, that if she did reconsider her decision, she would have a lot to offer the community at large' (para 95). Because the doctors had not complied with her wishes they had acted unlawfully and a small amount of damages had to be paid by the NHS. She was transferred to another hospital who were to arrange the termination of the ventilation. Ms B died shortly afterwards.

2.5 The impact of the Human Rights Act

Is the law on euthanasia or assisted suicide liable to challenge under the Human Rights Act?[102] The issue has been considered in the Diane Pretty litigation.

KEY CASE   R (Pretty) v DPP [2002] 1 AC 800; Pretty v UK [2002] 2 FCR 97

Diane Pretty sought confirmation from the Director of Public Prosecutions (DPP) that if her husband were to assist her to commit suicide he would not face prosecution under the Suicide Act 1961, section 2(1). The DPP refused and Ms Pretty sought to challenge his decision in the court. Her case reached the House of Lords and the European Court of Human Rights. At the heart of her case was a claim that the provisions of the Suicide Act infringed her rights under the European Convention on Human Rights. The House of Lords and European Court both rejected her arguments. Part of the decision in the House of Lords was that the DPP had no legal power to issue an immunity of prosecution. For us, greater interest is in the discussion of the human rights issue. Their conclusions were as follows:

(1) *Article 2: the right to life.* It was argued on Ms Pretty's behalf that the right to life in article 2 of the European Convention included a right to control the manner of one's death and therefore a right to commit suicide. The House of Lords and European Court of Human Rights held that article 2 imposed a duty on the state to protect life

[102] See Wicks (2007: chaps 11 and 12).

and this could not be taken to include a right to die. The interpretation sought by Ms Pretty involved too great a stretch of the natural meaning of the words.

(2) *Article 3: the right not to suffer torture or inhuman and degrading treatment.* Ms Pretty argued that by prohibiting her husband from killing her the state was inflicting torture or inhuman or degrading treatment upon her. It was held by the European Court of Human Rights that even if Ms Pretty's medical condition could be said to amount to torture, inhuman or degrading treatment it could not be said that this was inflicted by the state or was as a result of treatment by the state (para 53). The European Court also stated that the right under article 3 had to be read alongside the right to life in article 2. It could not therefore be argued that that a person had the right to be killed or helped to die under article 3 as that would contravene the right to life under article 2.

(3) *Article 8: the right to respect for private and family life.* The argument was that the law on suicide interfered with Ms Pretty's right to respect for private life. The House of Lords held that the right to private and family life did not bear on the right to choose to shorten life. The European Court of Human Rights disagreed and accepted the argument that the right to determine issues surrounding one's death was an aspect of private life. It was stated:

> The very essence of the Convention is respect for human dignity and human freedom. Without in any way negating the principle of sanctity of life protected under the Convention, the Court considers that it is under article 8 that notions of the quality of life take on significance. In an era of growing medical sophistication combined with longer life expectancies, many people are concerned that they should not be forced to linger on in old age or in states of advanced physical or mental decrepitude which conflict with strongly held ideas of self and personal identity (para 65).

Nevertheless they took the view that even if the law on suicide did infringe Ms Pretty's article 8(1) rights, under article 8(2) the interference could be justified as necessary to protect the interests of the state. In particular it enabled the law to ensure that vulnerable people were not taken advantage of by others or manipulated into committing suicide.

(4) *Article 9: the right to freedom of thought, conscience, and religion.* Ms Pretty argued that she was being prevented from exercising her moral conviction that it would be best if her life was brought to an end. This argument was rejected on the basis that she was not being prevented from thinking or believing what she wished. It was permissible to prohibit actions motivated by a person's beliefs; article 9 only dealt with acts prohibiting the manifestation of a person's beliefs.

(5) *Article 14.* It was argued that to allow people who were physically capable of committing suicide to do so, but to prohibit those physically incapable of committing suicide to arrange for another person to do so amounted to discrimination on the grounds of disability contrary to article 14. The European Court accepted that Ms Pretty was discriminated against in this way but held that there were objective and reasonable justifications for the discrimination, namely that any law that permitted assisted suicide could lead to vulnerable people being manipulated into killing themselves.

The Diane Pretty litigation indicates that the present law in the UK on suicide will not be open to challenge on the basis of the European Convention,[103] at least not in the near

---

[103] For discussion of the decision see Keown (2002) and Pedain (2003).

future. However, the decision should not be regarded as an utter defeat for those who seek to promote 'a right to die'.[104] First, it is important to appreciate that the decision was only saying that it was not contrary to the European Convention for a state to prohibit assistance of suicide. It was not saying that it would be contrary to the European Convention for a state to render it lawful. In other words if the Government decided to change the law and legalize the assistance of suicide, this would probably be permitted under the Convention, providing there were adequate safeguards to ensure that vulnerable people's rights to life would not be infringed. Second, the case included high level judicial approval of the argument that if suicide is permitted, then logically it should follow that those who, through their disability, are unable to commit suicide should be entitled to be killed by another. Lord Bingham stated:

> If article 2 does confer a right of self-determination in relation to life and death, and if a person were so gravely disabled as to be unable to perform any act whatsoever to cause his or her own death, it would necessarily follow in logic that such a person would have a right to be killed at the hands of a third party.[105]

Of course such an argument may cut both ways. It may deter a Government that wishes to legalize assisted suicide but not euthanasia from doing so. Third, there is recognition from the European Court of Human Rights that a competent person has a right to refuse life-saving treatment and that this right is protected by the European Convention on Human Rights.[106] Indeed in *R (Burke) v GMC*[107] the Court of Appeal stated that article 3 gave a right to be protected from treatment or a lack of treatment which would result in dying in avoidably distressing circumstances.

The Human Rights Act has also been used to require doctors to provide treatment for patients they might otherwise not have provided. The leading case on this is the following:

KEY CASE   R (Burke) v GMC [2005] 3 FCR 169

Leslie Burke suffered from cerebellar ataxia. This meant that at some point in the future he would require artificial nutrition and hydration (ANH). He sought a declaration from the court to clarify the circumstances in which it would be lawful for doctors to withdraw the feeding and hydration. He was concerned that the Guidance issued by the GMC on withdrawal of artificial feeding and hydration was inconsistent with the law. He did not want artificial feeding and hydration withdrawn if he were to become incompetent. He sought a number of declarations from the court, including most notably the following:

(1) the withholding or withdrawal of artificial nutrition and hydration, leading to death by starvation or thirst would be a breach of Mr Burke's rights under articles 2, 3, and 8 and would be unlawful under domestic law;

(2) where a competent patient requests or where an incompetent patient has, prior to becoming incompetent, made it clear that they would wish to receive artificial nutrition and hydration, the

104 See the general discussion in Du Bois-Pedain (2007); Coggon (2006); Blake (1997); and Sapiro and Ungoed-Thomas (2001). See also *Rodriguez v British Columbia (A-G)* (1993) 83 BCLR (2d) 273 (Can Sup Ct).
105 [2002] 1 All ER 1, at 6–7.   106 Para 63.
107 [2005] 3 FCR 169, discussed in de Cruz (2007).

withholding or withdrawal of artificial nutrition and hydration, leading to death by starvation or thirst would be a breach of their rights under articles 2, 3, or 8 and would be unlawful under domestic law;

(3) the refusal of artificial nutrition and hydration to an incompetent patient would be a breach of article 2 unless providing such artificial nutrition and hydration would amount to degrading treatment contrary to article 3.

The Court of Appeal declined to give the declaration sought. In part this was because he was not presently incompetent and the issue of his medical treatment in the future was a hypothetical question. Instead the Court were adamant that a patient did not have a right to demand whatever treatment she or he wanted. It approved of the following propositions promoted by the GMC.

 (i) The doctor, exercising his professional clinical judgment, decides what treatment options are clinically indicated (ie will provide overall clinical benefit) for her or his patient.
 (ii) She or he then offers those treatment options to the patient in the course of which he explains to him or her the risks, benefits, side effects, etc involved in each of the treatment options.
(iii) The patient then decides whether she or he wishes to accept any of those treatment options and, if so, which one. In the vast majority of cases she or he will, of course, decide which treatment option she or he considers to be in her or his best interests and, in doing so, she or he will or may take into account other, non-clinical, factors. However, she or he can, if she or he wishes, decide to accept (or refuse) the treatment option on the basis of reasons which are irrational or for no reasons at all.
(iv) If she or he chooses one of the treatment options offered to him, the doctor will then proceed to provide it.
 (v) If, however, she or he refuses all of the treatment options offered to her or him and instead informs the doctor that she or he wants a form of treatment which the doctor has not offered him, the doctor will, no doubt, discuss that form of treatment with him or her (assuming that it is a form of treatment known to him or her) but if the doctor concludes that this treatment is not clinically indicated she or he is not required (ie he is under no legal obligation) to provide it to the patient although she or he should offer to arrange a second opinion.

The Court was adamant that a patient had no right to demand treatment on the basis of the right of autonomy. The Court of Appeal explained:

Autonomy and the right of self-determination do not entitle the patient to insist on receiving a particular medical treatment regardless of the nature of the treatment. Insofar as a doctor has a legal obligation to provide treatment this cannot be founded simply upon the fact that the patient demands it. The source of the duty lies elsewhere (para 31).

This, however, did not mean there was not a duty to provide ANH as the Court explained:

Once a patient is accepted into a hospital, the medical staff come under a positive duty at common law to care for the patient....A fundamental aspect of this positive duty of care is a duty to take such steps as are reasonable to keep the patient alive. Where ANH is necessary to keep the patient alive, the duty of care will normally require the doctors to supply ANH (para 32).

However, the Court explained the duty to provide ANH was not an absolute duty. It did not apply where the competent patient refuses ANH or, where the patient is not competent, it is not in the patient's interests to receive ANH. The Court explained:

The courts have accepted that where life involves an extreme degree of pain, discomfort or indignity to a patient, who is sentient but not competent and who has manifested no wish to be kept alive, these circumstances may absolve the doctors of the positive duty to keep the patient alive. Equally the courts have recognised that there may be no duty to keep alive a patient who is in a persistent vegetative state ('PVS') (para 33).

However, this did not apply where the patient was competent and wanting to receive ANH. Withdrawing ANH from a competent patient against her or his wishes would infringe her or his right to life under the European Convention on Human Rights, article 2 and be guilty of murder, except in the unlikely event that ANH would hasten death. If there is doubt over the legality of withdrawing ANH advice can be sought from the court.

Mr Burke took his case to the European Court of Human Rights[108] where he lost. The Court held that if he lost capacity a

> doctor would be obliged to take account of the applicant's previously expressed wishes and those of the persons close to him, as well as the opinions of other medical personnel and, if there was any conflict or doubt as to the applicant's best interests, then to approach a court. This does not, in the Court's view, disclose any lack of due respect for the crucial rights invoked by the applicant.

Commentators have divided on this case. Some commentators have seen the case as correctly upholding the principle that where a patient is incompetent doctors must treat them as promotes their best interests and that a patient cannot require a doctor to treat them in a way which is harmful.[109] Hazel Biggs, on the other hand, sees it as 'a dangerous endorsement of medical paternalism'[110] and fails to appreciate that there can be a variety of different views on what is in a person's best interests. To prefer those of the doctor over the patient themselves is inappropriate.

If there are concerns that a patient will need life-sustaining treatment, but that it might not be appropriate to give it, a 'do not resuscitate notice' may be attached to their notes. This will avoid doctors needing to make a split second decision at a moment of medical crisis. It might be thought obvious that if a patient is still competent they should be consulted before such a notice was attached to their notes, although only 80 per cent of junior doctors thought this was necessary in one survey.[111]

3 Applying the law in difficult cases

We have now summarized some of the key legal principles governing the law in relation to end of life decisions. It is now necessary to consider some particularly complex cases where the law is not always easy to apply. We will look at the administration of pain-relieving drugs; the treatment of severely disabled newborn children; and the position of patients suffering Persistent Vegetative State.[112]

---

[108] *Burke v UK* Application 19807/06.   [109] Gillon (2004).   [110] Biggs (2007a).
[111] Schildmann et al (2006).
[112] One study in New South Wales in Australia suggested that a third of surgeons there were willing to admit to having performed euthanasia (Zinn (2001)). A US study found a much lower figure among American physicians: 6% (Meier (1998)).

3.1 The administration of pain-relieving drugs

It is clear that if a doctor gives a patient drugs in order to kill her or him and death results then that can be murder. Lord Goff in *Bland* reiterated that: 'it is not lawful for a doctor to administer a drug to his patient to bring about his death, even if that course is prompted by the humanitarian desire to end his suffering, however great that suffering may be.'[113] But can a doctor lawfully supply pain-relieving drugs to a terminally ill patient, even if a side-effect of the drugs will be to shorten the patient's life?

3.1.1 *The general principles*

Applying the basic principles outlined above, if the drugs have been a significant cause of death the doctor has committed the *actus reus* of murder. What about the *mens rea*? It will be recalled that a defendant will be taken to intend to kill or cause grievous bodily harm if it was the purpose of the defendant to kill, failing which the jury should be given the direction approved in the House of Lords decision of *Woollin*.[114] If a doctor gave drugs to a patient in order to relieve the patient's pain, but was aware that the patient's life will be shortened by administering, then, applying *Woollin*, the jury would be entitled to find intention, if they wished.

However, there are several judicial pronouncements which suggest that in such a case there is *as a matter of law* no intention;[115] in other words the jury are not permitted to find intention. In *Bland* Lord Goff stated:

> [It is] the established rule that a doctor may, when caring for a patient who is, for example, dying of cancer, lawfully administer painkilling drugs despite the fact that he knows that an incidental effect of that application will be to abbreviate the patient's life…Such a decision may properly be made as part of the care of the living patient, in his best interests; and, on this basis, the treatment will be lawful.[116]

This suggests then that if the doctor is acting in accordance with proper medical practice when prescribing pain-relieving drugs, and is doing so with the purpose of reducing pain not ending life, she or he will not be committing an offence.[117] It may be enough if the doctor simply believes that she or he is acting in accordance with standard medical opinion.[118] It is not clear whether the defence is based on an absence of intention or a special defence; but the courts have never explicitly stated that doctors have a special set of legal rules that apply to them in murder cases.[119]

3.1.2 *The case law*

Looking at cases where doctors have given high quantities of pain-relieving drugs which have resulted in the patient's death two things stand out: first how few prosecutions there

---

[113] [1993] AC 789, 865.   [114] [1999] 1 AC 82.

[115] The legality of providing pain relief even if it shortens a person's life is recognized around the common law world: eg *Washington v Glucksberg* (1997) 50 BMLR 65 (US Sup Ct); *Rodriguez v A-G* [1993] 3 SCR 519 (Canada); Consent to Medical Treatment and Palliative Care Act 1995 s 17 (South Australia).

[116] *Airedale NHS Trust v Bland* [1993] 1 All ER 821, at 868 (Lord Goff).

[117] *Adams* [1957] Crim LR 365, Cox 18 September 1992, unreported. This is also the view of the Attorney-General in evidence to House of Lords Select Committee (2005: 13).

[118] *Moor* 11 May 1999, unreported.

[119] See Tur (2002) for a sophisticated explanation for why doctors following professional guidance should have a defence in these cases.

have been; and second how rarely they result in a conviction. Doctors Carr,[120] Adams,[121] and Moor were all acquitted.[122] It may be that juries are influenced by the kind of attitude expressed by the direction of the judge directing the jury in the trial of Dr Moor:

> You have heard that this defendant is a man of excellent character, not just in the sense that he has no previous convictions but how witnesses have spoken of his many admirable qualities. You may consider it a great irony that a doctor who goes out of his way to care for [the deceased] ends up facing the charge that he does.[123]

It should not be thought that doctors are never convicted in relation to euthanasia. In Cox[124] a doctor injected a lethal amount of potassium chloride in order to kill a patient who was suffering intense pain from rheumatoid arthritis. The expert opinion was that the drug shortened life and otherwise had no analgesic value. The jury convicted Dr Cox of attempted murder. Cox's prosecution involved a number of elements which made it unusual: the patient was not terminally ill; the drugs injected were non-therapeutic (eg they did not lessen pain or treat symptoms), their sole effect was to kill; Cox could not argue that his purpose was to relieve pain. Despite his conviction it is noticeable that the consequences for him were limited. He was lucky to face the charge of attempted murder and not murder because a murder conviction carries the sentence of mandatory life imprisonment. With attempted murder the judge has a discretion, and a suspended sentence was used in this case.[125] Further, the General Medical Council admonished him, but only on the grounds that although he had acted in good faith he had not lived up to the high standards expected of the medical profession. His regional health authority continued to employ him subject to certain restrictions. What seems to have led to the 'weak' response to his conviction is the fact that he was widely regarded as acting out of compassion. Even if his intent was blameworthy, his motivations were not.[126]

REALITY CHECK

The legal position on euthanasia appears straightforward. It is illegal to give a person a lethal dosage of drugs with the intention of killing them. But in practice how often do doctors engage in euthanasia or assisted suicide?

These surveys give some picture:

1. One BMA (1996) survey found that 22 out of 750 doctors said they had actively ended the life of a patient.

2. In a study for BBC Scotland of 1,000 health professionals (McLean and Britton (1996)) 60 per cent reported having treated a patient who had considered suicide; 28 per cent had been asked to provide assistance to suicide; 12 per cent knew a health care professional who had assisted the suicide; 4 per cent admitted having provided information or drugs to do so.

---

[120] Unreported except in the *Sunday Times*, 30 November 1986.
[121] His trial is discussed in Palmer (1957).
[122] See further Kennedy and Grubb (2000: 2115).
[123] Quoted in Dyer (1999).   [124] (1992) 12 BMLR 38.
[125] See also Dr Michael Irwin who gave his friend sleeping pills so the friend could kill himself. Dr Irwin was only cautioned by the police, although he was struck off the register of doctors by the GMC (BBC Newsonline (27 February 2005)).
[126] Boyd (1998).

3 Ward and Tate (1994) reported that 9 per cent of 424 English doctors questioned said that they had taken active steps to bring about the death of a patient who had asked them to do so. Sixty-five per cent would be prepared to withhold or withdraw a treatment from a terminally ill patient knowing the treatment might prolong the patient's life. Thirty-two per cent of NHS doctors confirmed they had complied with a request from a patient to hasten their death.

4 In the Social and Community Planning Research (1996) survey of health care professionals 82 per cent thought that doctors should be allowed to end a person's life when requested; 86 per cent supported the procedure where the patient was comatose or incurably ill patients; while 42 per cent where the patient was in pain, but the illness was not incurable.

5 In a confidential questionnaire one in seven GPs admitted assisting suicide (BBC Newsonline (16 November 1998)). Of those who had, the average number of people assisted was five per GP. More than two-thirds wanted the power to give lethal injections on request.

6 A survey carried out in 2003 by Medix–uk.com reported that of 1,002 UK doctors, 40 per cent said they had been asked by patients to assist in suicide or euthanasia. Fifty-five per cent of doctors thought a person who had a terminal illness and uncontrollable physical suffering should be allowed to engage in physician-assisted suicide (Voluntary Euthanasia Society (2003)).

7 In a survey of 200 GPs in 1997, 46.5 per cent admitted 'easing a patient's death in some way' (Voluntary Euthanasia Society (2003)).

8 In 2002 a motion at the BMA calling for the repeal of the Suicide Act 1961 which prohibits assisted suicide, was defeated, although 44 per cent of doctors voted in favour of this motion (BMA and Law Society (2004)). In 2005 the BMA decided to take a neutral stance on euthanasia issues. However in 2006 (BBC Newsonline (26 June 2006)) this was overturned with 65 per cent of members voting against a motion supporting assisted suicide. A poll of members of the Royal College of Physicians found 73 per cent opposed to changing the current law on euthanasia and assisted suicide (BBC Newsonline (10 May 2006)).

9 According to the Voluntary Euthanasia Society 100,000 people a year are quietly helped to die (Hornell (1999)).

10 Only 5 per cent of a recent study of nurses interviewed agreed with the statement that 'health professionals already quietly help patients on their way' (Nursing Times (2003)).

11 According to Seale (2006), only 4.6 per cent of doctors felt the current law inhibited their preferred way of treating patients and 82 per cent supported the current ban on assisted suicide and euthanasia. Not one GP or hospital doctor said they had taken part in euthanasia or assisted suicide.

Although these statistics do not give an entirely consistent picture, it is clear that most GPs face requests for assistance in dying. Clearly a significant number of GPs are willing to some extent to assist in someone's death, and a much higher number would like to.

3.2 Persistent Vegetative State

What is the legal position of the doctor who switches off the life support machine of a patient who is suffering from Persistent Vegetative State (PVS)?[127] Patients in PVS are

---

[127] The term was coined by Jennett and Plum (1972). See also Cranford and Smith (1987). The exact definition of PVS is controversial, see Grubb et al (1997), Walsh (1999).

not immobile and retain some cranial nerve and spinal reflexes, and these can include visual and auditory stimuli. The degree of responsiveness reflects the degree of vegetativeness. It can never be completely certain that the condition is permanent.

The current legal position can be briefly summarized as follows.[128] Patients suffering from PVS are still alive; they have not yet suffered brain death. The switching off of the life support machine will be regarded as an omission. Although the omission may result in the patient's death it will not be in breach of the doctor's duty to the patient and so no crime is committed.[129] The Mental Capacity Act 2005 requires doctors to comply with any effective applicable advance directive issued by a patient which states that she or he does not wish to receive life-sustaining treatment. If there is no effective advance directive then the test is whether the best interests of the patient require the treatment to be offered. Judicial permission should be obtained before hydration and nutrition are withdrawn from a PVS patient.[130] This is so even if the patient has appointed a donee of a lasting power of attorney. The approach taken in that Act reflects the approach of the House of Lords in *Airedale NHS Trust v Bland*.[131]

KEY CASE   Airedale National Health Service v Bland [1993] AC 789

Tony Bland suffered horrific injuries in the Hillsborough Football Stadium disaster. He had been in a coma for three years and was diagnosed as suffering from PVS. Both his family and medical team sought a declaration from the courts that it was lawful to switch off his life support machinery and cease giving him nutrition and hydration. The judgments in the House of Lords made the following points:

(1) Tony Bland was alive. He was not brain dead, even though he was incapable of interaction with the outside world.

(2) Three out of the five Lordships stated that in the circumstances of this case if the doctors switched off the life support machine then there would be an intention to kill. This appears to be because it would be a virtual certainty that death would follow the switching off of the life support. The other Lordships were silent on the issue.

(3) The withdrawal of treatment would constitute an omission rather than an act. The argument was that by withdrawing treatment Tony Bland was being returned to the position he was in when he first entered the hospital. In other words, after withdrawing the treatment, the total impact of what the doctors had done was nothing. The significance of the behaviour being an omission is that, as described above, the court had then considered whether the omission was in breach of the duty owed by the doctors to Tony Bland.

(4) The House of Lords therefore turned to the question of what duty a doctor owed to a patient in Tony Bland's position. The answer was that the doctors only had to provide him with treatment that was in his best interests. The provision of continued treatment for Tony Bland would not

[128] See BMA (2007b).

[129] A useful discussion can be found in the New Zealand Case *Auckland Area Health Board v A-G* [1993] 1 NZLR 235, [1993] 4 Med LR 239.

[130] DCA (2007: 6.18, 8.18, and 8.19). *Practice Note (Official Solicitor: Declaratory Proceedings: Medical and Welfare Proceedings for Adults Who Lack Capacity)* 28 July 2006, [2006] 2 FLR 373; *Trust A, Trust B, Dr V v Mr M* [2005] EWHC 807 (Fam) at 12.

[131] [1993] 1 All ER 821 (HL), discussed in McGee (2005).

be in his best interests. Continued treatment would not harm him, but would not benefit him according to general medical professional opinion. Therefore there was no breach of the doctors' duty in not treating him. Therefore the doctors could not be said to be committing any offence by switching off the life support machine. Withdrawal of artificial hydration and nutrition was also justifiable because it was part of the general medical treatment being given to Tony Bland, and was not benefiting him.

(5) Lord Browne-Wilkinson was concerned that the issue of the appropriate way to treat PVS patients had fallen to the courts rather than Parliament.

In *A Hospital v SW*[132] Sir Mark Potter confirmed that the Bland decision was still the law, even after the Human Rights Act 1998. He rejected an argument that the withdrawal of hydration from a PVS patient could amount to torture or inhuman or degrading treatment and so infringe article 3 rights.[133] In *Ms D v NHS Trust*[134] a declaration was made permitting doctors not to provide certain forms of life-saving treatment on a PVS patient. The declaration was made despite the objections of the patient's family. Colderidge J explained that it was in Ms D's best interests that she be allowed to die in a dignified way. The approach of the law to PVS patients is controversial and we shall return to the issue later in this chapter (see pages 498–503). To some the requirement of obtaining court approval is little more than a rubber-stamping procedure, designed to calm the consciences of the medical team, rather than to protect the rights of patients with PVS.[135] The legal approach is now backed up by guidance from the British Medical Association, entitled *Withholding and Withdrawing Life-Prolonging Medical Treatment. Guidance for Decision Making.*[136] What is now clear is that the *Bland* ruling applies not only to those in PVS, but those in analogous positions. The 2001 Practice Direction states:

Diagnostic guidelines are not statutory provisions and a precise label may not be of importance. The court's concern is whether there is any awareness whatsoever or any possibility of change...There has as yet been no decided case dealing with the discontinuance of artificial feeding and hydration for an adult patient with any (however minimal) awareness of self or environment.[137]

In *An NHS Trust v J*[138] Sir Mark Potter heard evidence that although the patient was in PVS a new drug offered a 'very slim outside chance' of recovery. He refused to accede to the application of the medical team, supported by the patient's family, that hydration and nutrition be withdrawn. Instead he authorized the use of the drug on an

---

[132] [2007] EWHC 425 (Fam).
[133] See McLean (2006) for further discussion on the political issues association with withdrawal of hydration.
[134] [2005] EWHC 2439 (Fam)   [135] Lewis (2007b).
[136] BMA (1999), criticized in Keown (2000).
[137] *Practice Note (Official Solicitor: Declaratory Proceedings: Medical and Welfare Decisions for Adults Who Lack Capacity)* [2001] 2 FLR 158, quoting, *Re D (Medical Treatment)* [1998] 1 FLR 411, 420 and *Re H (A Patient)* [1998] 2 FLR 36.
[138] [2006] EWHC 3152 (Fam), discussed in Lewis (2007b).

experimental basis, despite the family's opposition. At a later hearing authorization was given to withdraw life-sustaining treatment as the drugs had not produced any increase in awareness.[139]

The best interests test, which will determine how a patient in PVS who has not issued an advance directive should be dealt with, is discussed in Chapter 4.

3.3 Severely disabled adults

What about the medical treatment of adults who are severely disabled, but not suffering from PVS? Arguably being just short of a vegetative state (ie having some awareness of one's condition) may be worse than suffering the full condition.[140] Again the Mental Capacity Act 2005 will govern such cases and the key question will be, in the absence of an effective advance directive, what is in the patient's best interests? There is less case law on these cases than on patients who are suffering PVS. It is clear that it is illegal to do an act with the intention of killing a person, even if that person is suffering from a severe disability. But what about withdrawing treatment? Assuming such a person is not competent to decide for themselves whether treatment should be withdrawn, the question is simply what is in the best interests of the patient. In *Re R (Adult: Medical Treatment)*[141] Justice Taylor held '[t]he correct approach is for the court to judge the quality of life [the patient] would have to endure if given the treatment and decide whether in all the circumstances such a life would be so afflicted as to be intolerable'. In that case the doctors dealing with the patient and his mother agreed that given his severe disabilities, no attempt should be made to resuscitate him in the event of a cardiac arrest. The policy was held to be lawful.[142] In *Re G (Adult incompetent: Withdrawal of Treatment)*[143] the patient was a 45-year-old woman with serious anoxic brain damage. She was being kept alive by artificial nutrition and hydration. Her family stated that she would not have wanted to live like this. One expert stated that she had no reasonable prospect of recovering and she should be allowed to 'die with dignity'. It was held that it was permissible to withdraw feeding.

To critics of such decisions, the courts appear to be becoming increasingly willing to accept that it is in a patient's interests to die, even where a patient is not in particular pain and is well short of being in PVS. Such fears will be exacerbated by the controversial advice of the BMA that patients with dementia or those who have suffered a stroke need not be resuscitated.[144] Also there will be concern that, unlike withdrawal of life-sustaining treatment from non-PVS patients, judicial approval is not required (or at least it is clear it is not in practice sought).[145]

3.4 The treatment of severely disabled children

Few areas of medical practice can be more distressing than cases involving severely disabled babies and young children.[146] The basic legal principles are those with which

---

139 *An NHS Trust v J* [2006] All ER (D) 73 (Dec).   140 Cranford (1996).
141 [1996] 31 BMLR 127.   142 See also *Re D* [1998] 1 FLR 411.
143 (2001) 65 BMLR 6.   144 BMA (2001).   145 Lewis (2007b).
146 See Nuffield Council (2007) for a helpful summary of the issues. An argument can be made that some disabilities are so severe that the sufferer should not even be regarded as a person. See, eg, the discussion in McMahan (2002: 449) of anencephalic infants.

you will now be familiar. It is not permissible to do an act which intentionally causes the death of the patient. However, a doctor may decline to provide treatment to a patient if that is in a patient's best interests and it is in accordance with established medical practice.

The leading case is *Re J (A Minor) (Wardship: Medical Treatment)*,[147] where Taylor LJ made the important point that, in deciding whether or not treatment was in a patient's best interests, it should be remembered that 'even severely handicapped people find a quality of life rewarding which to the unhandicapped may seem manifestly intolerable'. He went on to explain that:

> I consider that the correct approach is for the court to judge the quality of life the child would have to endure if given the treatment and decide whether in all the circumstances such a life would be so afflicted as to be intolerable to that child. I say 'to that child' because the test should not be whether the life would be tolerable to the decider. The test must be whether the child in question, if capable of exercising sound judgment, would consider the life tolerable.

It is notable that in these cases the judiciary appear to be happier than they are in the adult cases in asking more openly whether a life is worth living.[148]

The hardest cases are those where there is a disagreement between the medical teams and the parents. Such cases can be divided into two categories.

(i) The doctors wish to stop treatment, but the parents do not

In *Re C*,[149] C was able to smile at her parents, and able to move her hands laterally, but had a very low life expectancy and little movement. She had to be ventilated to survive. Doctors sought permission to withdraw ventilation arguing that the life-sustaining treatment would do nothing to alleviate her suffering. Her parents wanted the life-sustaining treatment to continue, based in part on their beliefs as Orthodox Jews. Stephen Brown P emphasized that the sole consideration was what was in the best interests of the child: here it was that the medical treatment be withdrawn.

As we have seen, as a general principle of medical law the courts are very reluctant to order doctors to give treatment to patients which doctors do not believe appropriate for the patients.[150] In *Re J*[151] it was suggested that the court would never order a doctor to act in a way she or he thought inappropriate. However in *Portsmouth Hospital NHS Trust ex p Glass*[152] it was suggested that, although doctors could not be dictated to, the issue of the child's best interests was always the paramount consideration. This appeared to suggest that there could be cases where a court could require a doctor to act in a child's best interests. That said, it is unlikely that a judge will rule that the doctors' views on what is in the best interests of a child are wrong.[153]

---

[147] [1990] 3 All ER 930.

[148] See Ford (2005a) for a very helpful discussion on whether painful lives can have value.

[149] [1998] Lloyds Rep Med 1.

[150] *Re J* [1998] 1 FCR 1; *R v Central Birmingham HA ex p Walker* (1987) 3 BMLR 32; *R v Central Birmingham HA ex p Collier* 6 January 1988.

[151] [1998] 1 FCR 1.   [152] [1999] 3 FCR 145.

[153] *R v Cambridge DHA ex p B* [1995] 2 All ER 129. For cases where the views of doctors were preferred over those of parents see, eg: *Re C* [1998] 1 FCR 1; *Royal Wolverhampton NHS Trust v B* [2000] 2 FCR 76; *NHS Trust v D* [2000] 2 FCR 577.

(ii) The parents wish treatment to stop, but the doctors do not

In *Re B*[154] baby Alexandra had Down's syndrome and an intestinal blockage. The blockage could easily be removed in an operation and, had she had not had Down's syndrome, there would have been no doubt that the doctors would have operated. The parents did not want the operation done and were happy for her to die. The Court of Appeal was willing to make the girl a ward of court. It would be in her best interests to receive the treatment. It could hardly be said that after the operation her prognosis was a life full of pain and suffering and that she should die. A key point to remember in this case is that if the parents did not want to raise a child suffering from Down's syndrome they could ask the local authority to find foster carers or adopters who would be willing to do so.

There are reported cases where parents successfully objected to the proposed course of action of a medical team: *Re T*.[155] The boy had suffered from liver failure and the medical team wanted him to have a liver transplant, without which he would die. The parents successfully applied for an order preventing the transplant without their consent. Three factors appear to have been crucial in this case. First, the parents were health care professionals and their views were clearly based on medical reasoning. Second, the parents had recently moved abroad to take up new jobs, the operation would require them to leave their new positions and return to the UK. Third, the Court of Appeal heard medical evidence that if the transplant was to be a success it was essential that the parents were fully involved in the lengthy rehabilitation process that followed the treatment. Butler-Sloss P explained that the child and mother 'were one' for the purpose of the application when considering what order would promote the child's welfare. If the mother did not want to participate in the procedure its chances of success were severely reduced.[156] However it must be emphasized that this case was exceptional; normally the views of medical experts will be preferred to those of parents, even if the parent's views are rational and understandable.[157]

In *An NHS Trust v MB*[158] doctors wished to withdraw ventilation from a child suffering from spinal muscular atrophy (a severe degenerative condition which meant that the child had virtually no movement and was expected to die within the year). The parents successfully argued that the child still had some benefits from life in particular 'the single most important source of pleasure and emotion to a small child: his relationship with his parents and family'. The judge placed much weight on the fact that although he could communicate in a very limited way with them, the evidence suggested he had pleasure from being with them.

So then, in those difficult cases involving severely disabled children the courts usually follow the doctors' opinion. Where the child's future is utterly bleak and the doctors conclude that there is no benefit in continuing treatment then the treatment can be

---

[154] [1990] 3 All ER 927.   [155] [1999] 2 FLR 1004.
[156] In fact after the case the mother changed her mind and consented to the treatment.
[157] *Re MM* [2000] 1 FLR 224; *Re A (Conjoined Twins)* [2000] 4 All ER 961; *The NHS Trust v A* [2007] EWHC 1696 (Fam).
[158] [2006] EWHC 507 (Fam).

withheld, even if the consequence of doing so is that the child will die.[159] The leading case in this area is the following:[160]

KEY CASE   The Charlotte Wyatt Litigation [2005] EWCA 1181

To date there have been six reporting hearings involving the medical treatment of Charlotte Wyatt ([2005] EWHC 2293; [2005] EWCA 1181; [2005] EWHC 693; [2005] EWHC 117; [2004] EWHC 2247; [2006] EWHC 319 (Fam)). Charlotte was born on 21 October 2003. She was born prematurely and since her birth suffered a complex medical history. She has not left hospital and has been seriously ill all her life. There have been a series of disputes between her parents and the medical team over how best Charlotte should be cared for, in particular what should happen if Charlotte acquires an infection which will kill her without ventilation. The doctors opposed ventilation on the basis that it might kill her; that it would deprive her of a peaceful death in her parents' arms; and that it would be extremely painful. It is not possible here to go through in detail all of the medical issues, but it is important to realize that in essence the case was about how and when Charlotte should die, rather than whether she should be allowed to live. Although her parents were praying for a miracle, they accepted that her medical condition at present indicated that she could not be expected to live many years. But the judgments make clear the following points of general application:

(1) 'In the event of an important disagreement between doctors and a child's parents, however, either side can invoke the inherent jurisdiction of the Family Division of the High Court relating to children, and a judge of the Division will decide what course of treatment is in the best interests of the child' ([2005] EWCA 1181, para 3).

(2) In deciding whether life-saving treatment should be given to a severely ill child, the test is whether or not it would be in the child's best interests to receive the treatment. Although asking whether the child's life would be intolerable, were she to live, can be a 'valuable guide' in ascertaining best interests, it does not supplant the best interests. The Court of Appeal explained:

> In making that decision, the welfare of the child is paramount, and the judge must look at the question from the assumed point of view of the patient (*Re J*). There is a strong presumption in favour of a course of action which will prolong life, but that presumption is not irrebuttable (*Re J*). The term 'best interests' encompasses medical, emotional, and all other welfare issues (*Re A*). The court must conduct a balancing exercise in which all the relevant factors are weighed (*Re J*), and a helpful way of undertaking this exercise is to draw up a balance sheet (*Re A*, [2005] EWCA 1181, para 87).

(3) When a doctor is deciding what treatment is in a child's best interests the views of the parents had to be taken into account but would not determine the matter.

In the most recent decision ([2006] EWHC 319 (Fam)) doctors were told that they need not provide ventilation or intubation if that became necessary. The medical evidence showed that such intervention would be unlikely to save her life and could lead to an undignified death. At the time of writing it seems Charlotte is still alive.

---

[159] However see Kuhse (1984) who argues it is cruel to expect a child to live out a short miserable existence rather than kill her or him shortly after birth.
[160] See also *Re Winston-Jones (A Child)* [2004] All ER (D) 313; *Re K* [2006] EWHC 1007 (Fam).

To critics of the courts' approach, asking whether life-saving treatment is in the best interests of a child is little more than a 'empty mantra'.[161] Margaret Brazier has complained that the courts have taken a 'medical' picture of what was best for the child and looked at her through the eyes of the 'professionals'.[162] However, it should be noted that the courts have now made it clear that best interests should not be a consideration only of medical interests.[163] The courts do appear to place greater weight on the views of parents where the professionals accept that they are reasonable views to hold, even if not the views of the doctors.[164] The difficulty is that if we moved to a position where parents' views always carried the day, that would be problematic where parents did *not want* their children to receive treatment which doctors wished to provide. Brazier also notes that although the judge gave careful consideration of the parents' views, the views of the nurses who were actually providing the day-to-day care received little judicial attention. Finally, there is the point that, at least in the Charlotte Wyatt case, the doctors' gloomy prognosis as to how long she had to live in the early cases proved to be wrong and this does nothing to reassure the parents that the 'doctors know best'.

The Nuffield Council on Bioethics[165] have produced a report on the care of very ill babies. They suggest the following questions should be considered when deciding what treatment is in the best interests of the child:

- What degree of pain, suffering and mental distress will the treatment inflict on the child?

- What benefits will the future child get from the treatment, for example, will the child be able to survive independently of life support, be capable of establishing relationships with other people, and be able to experience pleasure of any kind?

- What kind of support is likely to be available to provide the optimum care for the child?

- What are the views and feelings of the parents as to the interests of the baby?

- For how much longer is it likely that the baby will survive if life-sustaining treatment is continued?[166]

They suggest that where the child is less than 23 weeks' gestation normally resuscitation and life-sustaining treatment should not be offered. However, they strongly oppose actively taking steps to end the life of newborns.[167]

A SHOCK TO THE SYSTEM

The Shipman case

In January 2000 Dr Harold Shipman was convicted of the murder of 15 patients. A subsequent inquiry led by Dame Janet Smith found that in fact he had killed 215 between 1975 and 1998 (J Smith (2002)). There were a further 45 deaths about which a suspicion had arisen, but that could not be established as a fact, and 38 cases about which there was so little information

---

161 Brazier (2005b: 415).   162 Brazier (2005b: 416).

163 *The NHS Trust v A* [2007] EWHC 1696 (Fam).

164 Pedain (2005).   165 Nuffield Council on Bioethics (2007).

166 Nuffield Council on Bioethics (2007: para 3.90).

167 For criticism of the report see April and Parker (2007).

the Inquiry could not form a view. Most of his victims were healthy elderly women whom he injected with a lethal combination of drugs during a routine consultation. It is far from clear why he acted in this way.

In sentencing him for his murder convictions Forbes J stated:

> none of your victims realized that yours was not a healing touch. None of them knew that in truth you had brought her death, death which was disguised of the caring attention of a good doctor (quoted J Smith (2002: 1)).

Several things were striking about this case. That a man, thought by many in the town of Hyde where he practiced to be the best doctor in town, and widely respected, could in fact be one of Britain's most prolific mass murderers. The case can be regarded as sending all kinds of messages. Is it the ultimate example of medical arrogance? Only the position of high esteem in which he was held and with which he must have regarded himself can explain why so many crimes could be committed. Does it show the dangers of the kinds of arguments used by some who support euthanasia: is this death with dignity gone mad? Or is this simply one maverick doctor about whom no general lessons can be learned? Shipman killed himself on 13 January 2004 and so the answers will never be known.

Dame Janet Smith's Inquiry calls for changes in registration of births, cremation certificates, tighter controls on drugs provision to doctors, and improved training of coroners in an attempt to ensure that never again could one person kill so many people without suspicions being raised.

4 Ethical issues: euthanasia

We will start with the ethical debates surrounding euthanasia, before turning to assisted suicide and terminating treatment. It is in the debate over euthanasia that many of the ethical issues are made most apparent.

4.1 The heart of the debate

Before getting into the detail of the debate over the issue it is useful to summarize two extreme views on euthanasia:

(i) Supporters of euthanasia. There is nothing more horrific than a slow, pain-filled, undignified death. People faced with such a possibility should have the option of ending their life at a time and in a way of their choosing. We live in a society which emphasizes the right to autonomy: to make decisions over how we live our lives. To render illegal the killing of a person desperate to die is to deny them the power to make one of the most important and intimate decisions of their lives.

(ii) Opponents of euthanasia. To permit one person to kill another is a profound violation of a crucial moral principle: the sanctity of life. To legalize euthanasia is to undermine the principle that all lives are of equal value. Support for euthanasia is premised on the assumption that there are some lives that are not worth living. That implies that there are some lives that are of greater value than others and that is a repugnant idea. Further, any move to change the law will have a particularly harsh impact on vulnerable people who will be easily manipulated into agreeing to euthanasia.

4.2 **Definitions**

Before considering some of the arguments for and against euthanasia, it is necessary to set out some definitions and distinctions. One of the difficulties facing anyone navigating the material in this area is that there is no agreement over many of the key terms. This can lead to arguments where some of the disagreement is caused by alternative understandings of terms such 'euthanasia' and 'sanctity of life'. Inevitably not all of the following distinctions or definitions will be agreed by everyone, but an attempt has been made to use the most widely accepted understanding of these terms.

4.2.1 *Voluntary/non-voluntary/involuntary euthanasia*

To many writing on this topic it is crucial to distinguish between the following:

 (i) *Voluntary euthanasia:* behaviour which caused the patient's death at the patient's request.
 (ii) *Non-voluntary euthanasia:* behaviour which causes euthanasia without the consent *or objection* of the patient (ie where the patient is unable to consent or object).
 (iii) *Involuntary euthanasia:* Where the competent patient has not expressly consented to die, but nevertheless they are killed.

There are few people who accept the justifiability of involuntary euthanasia. Indeed some commentators argue that involuntary euthanasia should be simply described as murder, rather than dignifying it by giving it the label 'euthanasia'.[168]

4.2.2 *Active/passive voluntary euthanasia*

English and Welsh law draws an important distinction between cases where an act or omission causes the death of the patient.[169] To some there is a clear distinction between a case where a doctor deliberately injects a patient with a lethal dose of drugs, and where the doctor decides not to perform an operation which would save the life of a patient or withdraws life-sustaining treatment from a patient. Indeed some suggest that it is only correct to describe as euthanasia cases where a person has done an act.[170] Many others, as we shall see, argue that there is no moral difference between an act and an omission intended to cause death; both should be treated in the same way. They tend to argue that what matters is not how a person kills another (be it by act or omission) but the circumstances in which they act or the intentions with which they act.[171]

4.2.3 *Intention/foresight and the doctrine of double effect*

To some euthanasia only occurs where the actor intends to kill the patient. If, for example, a doctor provides a pain-relieving drug to a patient in order to reduce a patient's suffering, although she or he knows that the drug will also cause the death of a patient, this will not be euthanasia because there is no intent.[172] Other commentators reject a

---

[168] Biggs (2001: 12).   [169] Garrard and Wilkinson (2005) provide a useful discussion.
[170] House of Lords Select Committee on Medical Ethics (1994).
[171] For a useful discussion of such arguments see Dworkin, Frey, and Bok (1998); Kamm (1998) and Brock (1992).
[172] Keown (2002: Chap 2).

distinction between intention and foresight, and argue that if a doctor foresees that her or his treatment will lead to a patient's death, this is equivalent to intention.

Many who support the idea that euthanasia only occurs where there is an intention to kill support the doctrine of double effect. In essence this doctrine holds that in some circumstances a person who is doing an act with the purpose of producing result A, but foreseeing that result B may well result from her or his actions, will be held to intend result A. The exact meaning of the doctrine is disputed. Keown's version quotes four principles that render it permissible to do an act which produces a bad consequence:

(1) the act one is engaged in is not itself bad;

(2) the bad consequence is not a means to the good consequence;

(3) the bad consequence is foreseen but not intended; and

(4) there is sufficiently serious reason for allowing the bad consequence to occur.[173]

Relying on this doctrine, its supporters are able to say that a doctor who gives her or his patient pain-relieving drugs for the purpose of pain relief, but foreseeing that they will also have the effect of killing the patient, will not be said to have intended to kill the patient.

4.2.4 *Justified/excused euthanasia*

Another distinction is between an argument that in cases of euthanasia the act is justified or excused. This distinction (basically[174]) is as follows:

(1) A justification is an argument that the killing was permissible or even morally right.

(2) An excuse admits that the killing was not permissible, but that the actor does not deserve blame.

To most supporters of euthanasia there is a strong case for claiming that killing was justified in some circumstances. Opponents reject an argument that euthanasia is justified. However, some opponents of euthanasia will accept that there may be cases where the killing is excused, for example, where a person, exhausted by the caring of an infirm spouse, kills their partner at their request. Although opponents will argue that such a killing was wrong, we might accept that the killer has an excuse because of the mental strain they were suffering.

4.2.5 *Sanctity of life/vitalism/quality of life*

At the heart of much of the debate on euthanasia is the principle of the sanctity of life. Unfortunately there has been considerable division over what exactly that principle means. It is clear it has been used by judges and commentators to mean very different things.[175] It is perhaps helpful to distinguish the principles of vitalism; sanctity of life; and quality of life.[176]

(1) *Vitalism*. This holds that human life has an absolute moral value. It is never justifiable to kill another person. Doctors should take all reasonable steps to keep humans

---

[173] Keown (2002: 20). See also Gormally (1995).

[174] The concepts are in fact more complex than appear from this outline, see Herring (2006: 668–80).

[175] Keown (1999: 253) sees a collapse of respect for the principle of sanctity of life around the world.

[176] Keown (2002: 43; and 2006c: 109) stresses the importance of this distinction.

alive. It is therefore impermissible for doctors to do an act which causes a patient to die or to fail to take reasonable steps to keep a person alive.

(2) *Sanctity of life*. This also holds that human life is a fundamental basic good. It states that a person should not be intentionally killed, be that through an act or an omission. Sanctity of life seeks to value the good of life itself. That good exists independent of any disability or incapacity. However, the theory can be distinguished from vitalism in two regards:

- First the principle accepts that an act which shortens the life of a patient can be justifiable if it is not done with the intent to kill. It is the intentional killing which is outlawed by the principle and so it would support the doctrine of double effect.

- Second, it may be permissible to withdraw treatment if the reason for doing so is that it offers no hope of benefit. The principle would not, however, justify withdrawal of treatment because the patient's life was not worth living.[177] It does not therefore agree with vitalism that life should be protected at all costs.

(3) *Quality of life*. Here the basic approach is concerned with assessing the worthwhileness of the patient's life. It holds that certain lives are not worth living and that it is therefore right to end them. It rejects the argument put forward by supporters of the sanctity of life approach that there is something good about life in and of itself. By contrast it is claimed that what makes a life good are the experiences of the person and their interaction with others. A life which can no longer be experienced, and in which relationships with others are impossible, is a life that has lost its goodness. Some supporters of this approach would attach great weight to the assessment of the individual themselves as to whether they thought their life still had value.

4.2.6 *The principle of autonomy*

To most supporters of euthanasia the key ethical concept is the principle of autonomy. This is, in simple terms, the argument that people should be permitted to live their lives as they wish, as long as their choices do not harshly impact on others. The alternative, of the Government or other people dictating to us how we should live our lives, is seen by many as unacceptable paternalism. This principle underlies much liberal political thought and was discussed in much greater detail in Chapter 1. To supporters of euthanasia it should dominate the debate on euthanasia: people should be able to choose how to die.

4.2.7 *Ordinary/extraordinary treatment*

To some commentators there is a fundamental distinction to be drawn between ordinary treatment which doctors are obliged to provide to their patients and extraordinary treatment which they are not obliged to provide. Behind this debate is an argument over the lengths to which a doctor need go to delay the death/prolong the life of the patient. This can be said to be justified as part of the need to protect the dignity of the patient: it is undignified for a patient to have every attempt made in a desperate bid to save their life. In *Ms D v NHS Trust*[178] Colderidge J made a declaration that doctors need not

---

177 Keown (2002: 43).   178 [2005] EWHC 2439 (Fam).

provide further life-saving treatments for a PVS patient. He held:

> In my judgement she should be allowed as dignified a passing as is achievable. Some might say that her dignity has already been severely compromised by the progress and incidence of this awful disease. To subject her body to further grossly invasive procedure can only further detract from her dignity.[179]

The distinction might also be justified as a reasonable allocation of resources. It would be foolish to expend substantial resources on treatment which has only a faint chance of saving the life of the patient.

To some commentators, although the distinction is a useful one, the words 'ordinary' or 'extraordinary' are not particularly helpful.[180] It is not whether the treatments are often used or not, it is rather whether the treatment is proportionate or beneficial to the patient. Gerald Kelly, in an oft-quoted statement, has suggested:

> Ordinary means are all medicine, treatments, and operations which offer a reasonable hope of benefit and which can be obtained and used without excessive expense, pain, or other inconvenience. Extraordinary means are all medicines, treatments, and operations, which cannot be obtained or used without excessive expense, pain, or other inconvenience, or which, if used, would not offer a reasonable hope of benefit.[181]

This interpretation suggests that the extraordinary/ordinary distinction is little more than a balancing of the benefits and disadvantages of the treatment, in which case it might be better to use different terminology.

4.2.8 The difference between treatment and basic care

Some commentators argue that there is a crucial distinction between medical treatment and basic care.[182] They take the view that although it may be legitimate to withdraw medical treatment from a patient it is never permissible to withdraw basic care such as feeding or cleaning. The argument is that to deny basic care is undignified and inhumane. So, although a patient has the right to refuse medical treatment, she or he does not have the right to refuse basic care.

4.3 Autonomy

4.3.1 The right to choose the time and manner of your death

As already mentioned the notion of autonomy is that people should be free to lead their lives as they wish and have control over their own bodies. People's decisions on how to live their lives deserve respect, even though other people might think them foolish.[183] A person's decision is respected not because it is a good choice, but because it is their choice.[184] To deny a person the respect for their views is the ultimate denial of respect

---

[179] Para 44.
[180] President's Commission for the Study of Ethical Problems in Medical and Biomedical and Behavioural Research (1983).
[181] Kelly (1951).
[182] Anscombe (1981). Significance was attached to the distinction in the American decision *In the Matter of Quinlan* 70 NJ 10, cert. denied 429 US 922 (1976). Although subsequently the American Supreme Court in *Curzan v Director Missouri Department of Health* 110 SCt 281 (1990) placed little weight on it.
[183] Seale and Addington-Hall (1994) consider the reasons why people wish to die in a particular way.
[184] Pedain (2003: 203).

for that person.[185] Such respect is particularly important in relation to deeply personal or intimate issues such as when to die. Dworkin has written:

> Making someone die in a way that others approve, but he believes a horrifying contradiction of his life, is a devastating, odious form of tyranny.[186]

Each person may have her or his own view of what is a good death: be it struggling to live for as long as possible, or dying before life becomes undignified or full of pain.[187] Each person should be free to select her or his mode of dying, and if that needs the involvement of others they should be free to act as requested without fear of a criminal prosecution. Supporters of euthanasia sometimes claim that those opposing euthanasia are attempting to impose their own ethical or religious beliefs on others.[188]

Dworkin has argued that death is an area where it is particularly important that a person's wishes be followed. He distinguishes two kinds of choices: critical and experimental interests. Experimental interests are the interests we have in things we enjoy doing in and of themselves: eating certain kinds of food for example; and critical interests are part of what we believe make us who we are: a person's religious beliefs or ethical beliefs, for example. It is especially important that critical interests are respected.[189] He argues that how a person dies is of critical interest to most people (their death should 'keep faith' with the way they lived their life) and it is therefore of fundamental importance that their wish is respected.[190] Not all supporters of autonomy are happy with Dworkin's analysis as it appears to leave the door open for someone to say to a person requesting death: 'I know you are now saying you want to die, but a better fit with your life story (your critical interests) would be for you to live longer'.[191]

4.3.2 *Challenging the autonomy argument*

Opponents of euthanasia tend to argue against an approach based on autonomy in one of four ways: either by accepting that autonomy is an important principle but arguing that there are other interests that need to be weighed against it; by saying that in the context of euthanasia it is not possible to be confident that the person has made a genuine free choice; that autonomy cannot be used to justify an act which leads to death; or that the argument proves too much as it would justify euthanasia in circumstances which would be unacceptable. These will be looked at separately.

First, there is the argument that other principles or values can be used to outweigh the principle of autonomy. But what might those be? Here are three possible contenders:

(i) *The right of the patient to choose to die must be counterbalanced against the interests of society as a whole.* Dying is not an individual matter, it has an impact on others and society as a whole. It is, however, difficult to identify precisely the harm that relatives or society as a whole will suffer by permitting euthanasia. Clearly there will be the grief relatives suffer, but how does this compare with the pain of watching someone die in a

---

[185] Harris (1995).   [186] Dworkin (1993: 217).
[187] Logue (1996) discusses the sociological understanding of a good death.
[188] See Williams (2005) and Dworkin et al (1998: 431). This is subject to careful analysis in DuBois (1999).
[189] Dworkin (1998) is therefore critical of the reasoning in *Bland* focussing on Tony Bland's inability to experience anything, rather than considering how his death might fit in with his values (his critical interests).
[190] See Grubb (1997) for further discussion.   [191] Harris (1995).

slow painful way? But is there more? The House of Lords Select Committee[192] held:

> We acknowledge that there are individual cases in which euthanasia may be seen by some to be appropriate. But individual cases cannot reasonably establish the foundation of a policy which would have such serious and widespread repercussions. Moreover dying is not only a personal or individual affair. The death of a person affects the lives of others, often in ways and to an extent which cannot be foreseen. We believe that the issue of euthanasia is one in which the interests of the individual cannot be separated from the interest of society as a whole.[193]

(ii) *This right to die must be balanced against concerns that other patients who do not want to die will be pressurized into saying they do.*[194] In other words it is better to have a legal system that denies some people the right to autonomy to die as they wish, than to have a legal system whereby some people could be killed under the label euthanasia against their wishes. In essence this argument is connected to the 'slippery slope' argument mentioned below. As we shall see, there is heated debate over whether, once voluntary euthanasia is permitted, it is possible to put in place mechanisms which ensure that involuntary euthanasia is not permitted.

(iii) *There is a moral imperative or value which counterbalances the autonomy right.*[195] The argument here is not that there are the interests of others or particular members of society which need to be protected, but there are moral principles which the law should uphold, such as the sanctity of life (to be discussed shortly), even if, in doing so, the autonomy rights of individual members of society are infringed. So, the argument here is not that there are specifically identified harms, but there is damage to the moral fibre of society, which justifies an infringement of people's autonomy.

The second kind of argument that can be made against autonomy in the euthanasia context is that it is not possible to make a fully informed, autonomous choice to die. Because the decision to die is of the utmost gravity and is irreversible we should properly require the highest standards of competence. Some commentators suggest that no person suffering the pain and anguish of being close to death will be sufficiently competent to be able to consent to the treatment;[196] or that patients do not often appreciate the effectiveness of pain relief or the availability of rehabilitative care for those with disabilities or with terminal illness and therefore cannot make a properly informed decision.[197] Indeed there is also some evidence that many of those seeking death are suffering depression and that once medication for depression is provided the numbers of those seeking euthanasia falls (by 99 per cent according to a report produced by the Royal College of Psychiatrists).[198] Further evidence suggests that people with terminal illnesses keep changing their views on whether or not they want

---

[192] House of Lords Select Committee (1993), discussed in Keown (2002: Chap 16).
[193] Para 237.   [194] Mak, Elwyn and Finlay (2003).   [195] Keown (2002: chapter 5).
[196] Grisez and Boyle (1971) and Gordijn, Crul, and Zylicz (2002).
[197] Coleman and Drake (2002) and Woods (2002). Van der Maas, Van Delden, Pijnenborg (1991) found that in their study less than a third of patients who were seeking death retained a wish to die after alternative pain relief had been offered.
[198] Royal College of Psychiatrists (2006: 3). See also Blank et al (2001). Conwell and Caine (1991: 1101) argue that front-line doctors dealing with end of life cases are not well equipped to diagnose or appreciate the impact of depression on a person's decision-making abilities.

assistance in dying.[199] So abiding by a person's wish to die one day may be to work contrary to what their wishes would be the next day. The European Parliamentary Assembly, Committee on Legal Affairs and Human Rights,[200] considering such evidence, stated:

> Medical professionals working within the palliative care sector have emphasised the fragility of patients' desire for death and the rapid changes that, in their experience, may occur in response to good symptom control or psychological interventions. The dangers of acceding to rare requests for voluntary active euthanasia and physician assisted suicide should not be underestimated.

The difficulty with this reasoning is that even at its strongest it may lead us to conclude most people at the point of death lack competence, but it is difficult to believe that everyone will.[201]

Third, some commentators argue there is an irony in using the principle of autonomy in relation to death which is the ultimate loss of the ability to make choices. In other words we encourage autonomy to enable people to live the kind of lives they wish, to flourish and develop as people.[202] Euthanasia, by contrast, is not promoting personality growth; it is the end of the person. It is therefore not possible to justify euthanasia on the basis of autonomy. Alexander McCall Smith[203] has warned against seeing autonomy as a good in and of itself. He says autonomy is a good because it enables us to develop our lives as we wish in connection with other people. Indeed it is notable that we do not abide by the wish of those who desire to sell themselves into slavery. In part this is because such an exercise of autonomy undermines the values of autonomy we treasure.[204] Critics might reply that this overlooks the fact that a way a person dies is regarded by many as an important part of their lives. A good death is seen as a good conclusion to the end of people's lives, fitting in with the values that have determined their life to date. So seen, it is a reasonable aspect of a person's vision of a 'good life'.

A fourth argument against the emphasis placed on autonomy is that most supporters of euthanasia do not believe that anyone who wants to be killed should be allowed to do so. Dworkin, for example, has suggested that euthanasia should only be available for those who are predicted to die within six months.[205] Few supporters of euthanasia would agree that a young man whose girlfriend has just left him and feels life is no longer worth living should be able to walk into a hospital and demand to be killed.[206] But if the principle of autonomy is the guiding light why not? His choices should be respected whether we think it right or wrong.[207] Critics argue that, although it is said that the principle of autonomy is at the heart of the debate, the reality is that supporters of euthanasia only respect the wishes of a person if she or he thinks that the decision is a reasonable one. In other words they will respect the wish to die of people whose lives

---

[199] Chochinov et al (1999) state the will to live is highly unstable among elderly terminal cancer patients. Mak, Elwyn, and Finlay (2003) point out that decisions to want to die may result from a complex set of pressures and assumptions and need to be carefully 'unpicked'.

[200] Para 1 (2003).   [201] See Gorsuch (2000) for a further discussion of competence in this area.

[202] Gormally (1995).   [203] McCall Smith (1997).

[204] But see Singer (2003) who argues the reason for not enforcing slavery is the repugnant enforcement mechanisms which would have to be used.

[205] Dworkin (1998: 1151).

[206] Frileux et al (2003) found that the general public regard euthanasia as more appropriate the older, more ill, and the greater the suffering of the person seeking death.

[207] This argument is developed in Ackernman (1998).

are not worth living.[208] Dworkin has responded to such arguments that:

> We might very well say as a community—we bet we might be wrong, but we bet—that if the teenage lover lives another two years, maybe even two weeks, he will be very glad not to have taken his own life.[209]

But such an argument might be thought to undermine the basis of autonomy which is to let people make decisions for themselves, and not permit others to assume they know what someone really wants.

There is no doubt that the hypothetical example of the lovesick teenager has caused some difficulties for some supporters of euthanasia. But there is a problem here for opponents of euthanasia too. Most opponents of euthanasia support the principle that if a competent person refuses life-saving treatment their wishes should be respected. But why does autonomy dominate when the wish is not to have treatment but not when the patient seeks active intervention to hasten death.[210] This issue raises the extent to which it is justifiable to distinguish an act and an omission. Yet, as we shall see, this is a distinction many philosophers find difficult to maintain.

4.4 The sanctity of life: the key principle or religious mumbo jumbo?

For many opponents of euthanasia, at the heart of the issues surrounding euthanasia is the principle of the sanctity of life. The lives of every member of society should be valued so highly by our society that they should not be intentionally destroyed, even if that is what the particular individual wishes. Supporters argue that once the principle is departed from, it inevitably becomes necessary to value some lives as less than others and not worth living. By contrast, the sanctity of life principle values all human lives equally and emphasizes that killing represents a unique wrong.[211] The House of Lords Select Committee on Medical Ethics[212] concluded that the prohibition on intentional killing was 'the cornerstone of law and of social relationships'.[213]

The principle is supported particularly by those writing from a religious perspective, who often start from the principle that each person has been made in the image of God and is equally precious in God's sight. However the principle is also supported by those of no religious persuasion but who are attracted by its insistence of the equal value of all human life. Somerville[214] emphasizes the importance of the 'secular sacred', respecting the mysteries of life and death, which is of importance to the religious and non-religious. She also emphasizes the 'deeply intuitive sense of relatedness or connectedness to other people and to the world and the universe in which we live',[215] which means that each person's life has value for the whole of society. Allowing death to occur when 'its time has come' is part of recognizing the mystery of life and death.[216] She admits this all sounds rather vague, but insists that this does not detract from the fact it has been intuitively felt to be true by so many people for so long.

Opponents of the principle of sanctity of life generally accept that life is precious and valuable, but they reject the insistence that all life must be valued for its own sake.[217] In

---

[208] Gormally (1997).   [209] Dworkin (1998: 1151).   [210] Eg Keown (2002: Chap 5).

[211] Linacre Centre (1994).   [212] House of Lords Select Committee on Medical Ethics (1993).

[213] See also Special Committee of the Canadian Senate (1995).

[214] Sommerville (2001).   [215] Sommerville (2002: 654).   [216] Sommerville (2001: xiv).

[217] Harris (1984) and Glover (1977).

other words, supporters of euthanasia often take the view that there comes a point where a person's life is so wracked with pain and indignity that its special value has been lost. Rachels,[218] for example, argues that there is a difference between having a life and being alive. To keep a person alive on a life-support machine for years on end, even though there is no prospect of an improvement in her or his condition, is not to value the preciousness of life, but to demean it. Such commentators argue that the sacredness of life turns not on being alive, but on having a life worth living.[219] This is why we regard the death of a person in the full flush of health and youth as a tragedy, but the death of person who months ago ceased to interact with the outside world as almost a blessing.[220]

Ronald Dworkin, considering the position of a patient suffering from Alzheimer's, says that such a person:

> is no longer capable of the acts or attachments that can give [life] value. Value cannot be poured into a life from the outside; it must be generated by the person whose life it is, and this is no longer possible for him.[221]

He sees value in life about making something of one's life and living in earnest. Therefore once a person is in great pain near the end of their life then if, to them, their life has lost its value, then that person's life is no longer of special value and no longer protected by the sanctity of life principle.

We can now specify clearly the difference between supporters and opponents of the sanctity of life view:

• Supporters of sanctity of life argue that life in and of itself is valuable. Even a person in a coma, with no awareness of the outside world and with no friends or relatives to be concerned about them, has value by virtue of being human. To reject such a view leads one to value the lives of disabled people less than others.[222] Finnis[223] claims:

> Human life is indeed the concrete reality of the human person. In sustaining human bodily life, in however impaired a condition, one is sustaining the person whose life it is. In refusing to choose to violate it, one respects the person in the most fundamental and indispensable way.

In other words life is valuable in itself. To value a person's life just for the experiences they have is to adopt a dualist view of existence which draws a sharp distinction between the mind and the body.[224] We cannot treat people like goods which have passed their 'sell by' date.[225]

• Opponents of sanctity of life emphasize that what makes life valuable is the things that people do with it. It is the experiences people have, their relationships and activities which give life meaning. A person with no experiences (or only pain-filled ones) and no capacity for relationships has lost the goodness of life.[226] Of a person suffering from PVS, Harris argues: 'It is a living human body (as in a sense it often is when brain death is diagnosed on a life-support system—it is warm, the blood circulates and so on) but it is not the living body of a person'.[227]

[218] Rachels (1986).   [219] Harris (1995a).   [220] Warnock (1992).
[221] Dworkin (1993: 230).   [222] Ramsay (1978).   [223] Finnis (1995b: 32).
[224] Finnis (1993).   [225] Sommerville (2001: xix).   [226] Glover (1977).
[227] Harris (1995b: 42). See also McMahan (2002).

The principle of sanctity of life has been approved by the judiciary. For example, Lord Goff of Chieveley said in his speech in *Airedale NHS Trust v Bland:*

> ...the fundamental principle is the principle of the sanctity of human life—a principle long recognized not only in our own society but also in most, if not all, civilized societies throughout the modern world....But this principle, fundamental as it is, is not absolute...[228]

However John Keown argues that Lord Goff had wrongly understood sanctity of life to be the same as vitalism.

Supporters of the principle of sanctity of life face a number of difficulties:

(i) Many supporters of sanctity of life support the current legal position that a patient is entitled to refuse life-sustaining treatment. However, this can involve the death of a person. The distinction supporters make is between an act causing a death which is said to infringe the sanctity of life principle and an omission causing death, which does not. Whether the difference between an act and an omission is sufficiently strong to justify such a crucial distinction is a matter of debate.

(ii) Most supporters of the sanctity of life accept that a person can kill another in self-defence. So it is acknowledged that the principle of sanctity of life is not without exceptions: there are competing values which can justify the intentional killing of someone.[229] Why is it, then, that supporters of sanctity of life are not willing to consider any circumstances in which euthanasia is justified? Is it not, for example, possible to say that the life of someone dying in pain is a life which is valued by society, but the on-going pain justifies the end of the life?[230]

(iii) Supporters of the sanctity of life suggest that permitting euthanasia would involve having to accept that some people's lives are not worth living. This can be challenged. McCormick[231] argues it is perfectly possible to say that every person is equally valued, but not every life is, although to say to someone 'we value you, but not your life' will be seen as a contradiction to some.

(iv) Harris[232] points out that most supporters of the principle of sanctity of life believe that human life is precious and more valuable than the life of other animals. However, he argues the one factor that might be said to distinguish a human and other animals is consciousness and interactive abilities. Yet when these are lost, opponents of euthanasia are unable to explain why there is not the end of human life.

Ronald Dworkin[233] has sought to develop an argument that both supporters and opponents of euthanasia in fact respect the sacredness of life, it is just that they are emphasizing different aspects of sacredness. He argues that even supporters of sanctity of life do not treat the death of a seriously ill person as as much of a tragedy as the death of a young person; but likewise opponents of sanctity of life are unwilling to support euthanasia where the person is in good health. He explains this apparent contradiction in this way. He argues that life has value in three ways: subjectively (for the person

---

[228] [1993] AC 789, [1993] 1 All ER 821 at p 864. See also Lord Bingham of Cornhill in *R (Amin) v Secretary of State for the Home Department* [2003] 3 WLR 1169, 1185, para 30; Lord Donaldson MR in *Re J (A Minor) (Wardship: Medical Treatment)* [1990] 3 All ER 930, at 938.
[229] McMahan (2002).   [230] Stauch and Wheat (2004: 669).   [231] McCormick (1998).
[232] Harris (1995b). The debate continues between H. Harris (1995) and Finnis (1995c).
[233] Dworkin (1993).

themselves); instrumentally (it produces useful things for society and other people); and non-instrumentally or intrinsically (it is in and of itself valuable, just as a great painting is[234]). As to the intrinsic value of life, he suggests that this flows from 'two combined and intersecting bases of the sacred: natural and human creation'.[235] By the natural he means that a person's life is the highest product of natural creation: the greatest achievement of God's or evolution's creationary process. A life is, as such, like a great work of art. By human creation he sees the human effort that has been put into the person's life: by their parents, carers, and friends, but ultimately by the individual her or himself. Hence, Dworkin argues, we see the death of a teenager as a waste of human investment and a tragedy, but death after a full life as less so. The difference between those who take a conservative or liberal view on euthanasia depends on the weight placed on the natural creation and the human investment. Those who emphasize natural creation are likely to oppose euthanasia, and those who emphasize the human investment are likely to support it. Dworkin's argument, however, is that most people recognize that life is sacred in both these ways; the argument is over which understanding of sacred should take precedence.[236]

4.5 Dignity

Many commentators supporting euthanasia argue in terms of protecting the dignity of the dying person.[237] In dying, a person gradually loses the control of physical and mental functions, and helplessness and dependence on others increases. In one survey a majority of respondents stated that the one thing worse than death is the distress of loved ones having to care for you over a lengthy period of physical deterioration.[238] It is not simply the inability to care for oneself which is demeaning, but the inability to offer care and support to others. To enable a person to die with dignity, to die before they have reached the stage when they are dependant on others for even the most basic of functions, is an option that people should have a right to take. The concept has even received judicial support. Mumby J in *R (A, B, X and Y) v East Sussex CC and the Disability Rights Commission (No 2)*[239] stated:

> The recognition and protection of human dignity is one of the core values—in truth the core value—of our society and, indeed, of all the societies which are part of the European family of nations and which have embraced the principles of the Convention. It is a core value of the common law, long pre-dating the Convention . . . The invocation of the dignity of the patient in the form of declaration habitually used when the court is exercising its inherent declaratory jurisdiction in relation to the gravely ill or dying is not some meaningless incantation designed to comfort the living or to assuage the consciences of those involved in making life and death decisions: it is a solemn affirmation of the law's and of society's recognition of our humanity and of human dignity as something fundamental.

[234] The point is that people treasure a great painting in itself, not just because it gives people who see it pleasure.
[235] Dworkin (1993: 83).
[236] For challenges to Dworkin's argument see Harris (1995a); Holland (2003: 61–3).
[237] Biggs (2001).   [238] Pearlman et al (1993).
[239] [2003] EWHC 167 (Admin), (2003) 6 CCLR194, at para 86.

Critics of such arguments suggest that the notion of dignity has been barely defined.[240] Even if euthanasia is regarded as dignified for the person who dies, does it respect the dignity of those who have to do the killing or society as a whole? A report by the Linacre Centre[241] suggests that we need to distinguish between two meanings of dignity:

(i) The basic worth that each person has by virtue of being human.

(ii) The quality which some people have because they have shaped their lives to honour what is of true worth.

The report argues that the first sense of dignity cannot be lost, even if a person has lost their mental faculties. Even when suffering in great pain that person has the dignity that comes from being a person. To kill them would not be to respect their dignity in that sense. Amarasekara and Bagaric[242] argue:

> It could be suggested that allowing a patient to die in pain against his or her wish is undignified. But killing a person hardly seems to be according him or her much concern or respect or placing much value on the person's life—it would seem to be the antithesis of respecting one's dignity.

It has also been argued that the notion of dignity has a social dimension.[243] A person's sense of dignity in part depends on how they are treated by society and those they relate to. If a person at the end of their life is feeling undignified this may say as much about our society's attitudes towards the elderly and dying, as it does about an individual's own values.

Critics of the dignity argument also tend to emphasize the benefits of palliative care which, it is claimed, enable a more dignified and good death than that offered through euthanasia.[244] However, supporters of euthanasia will claim it should be for individuals to decide whether palliative care offers them an acceptable alternative to death.[245] Others have characterized the notion of a dignified death as an idealized social construct.[246] Death is nasty and painful normally; to try and pretend that it is not and demand from medics a perfect pain-free death represents the ultimate denial of the reality of death.

4.6 The cruelty argument: 'we put down animals, why not humans?'

In a similar vein to the argument about dignity is the argument concerning cruelty. It is argued that the legalization of euthanasia is all about the alleviation of pain and suffering.[247] We do not let animals suffer painful deaths, we 'put them out of their misery'. Why not do the same in relation to humans?[248] Euthanasia is simply the expression of compassion.[249] Even if not used, the option of euthanasia can be regarded as a comfort to the dying, who can be reassured that if the pain becomes too much they have the

---

[240] Otlowski (2002).

[241] Linacre Centre (1998). See also Gentzler (2003).

[242] Amarasekara and Bagaric (2002).   [243] Pleschberger (2007).

[244] Seale and Addington-Hall (1994) question such arguments.

[245] House of Lords Select Committee (2005: 7).   [246] Nuland (1993: xvi).

[247] Although see Emanuel (1998) for an argument that many of those seeking euthanasia are not those suffering the greatest pain, but those suffering from untreated depression.

[248] Bachelard (2002) rejects this argument on the basis that human fellowship and the impact of death on other people justifies distinguishing the deaths of humans and other animals.

[249] Van Zyl (2000).

option of requesting euthanasia.[250] Singer argues that euthanasia can be supported on the basis of a simple utilitarian calculation.

> if the goods that life holds are, in general, reasons against killing, those reasons lose all their force when it is clear that those killed will not have such goods, or that the goods they have will be outweighed by the bad things that will happen to them.[251]

Critics of euthanasia might reply to such arguments in a number of ways. Of course many will simply reiterate the principle of the sanctity of life. Some will emphasize that arguments based on avoiding pain often show a failure to appreciate the ability of palliative care to deal with pain. Although some supporters of euthanasia reply that even if such pain relief is available in theory, it is often not made available in practice.[252] Some argue that our society has a problem with pain.[253] We have developed a growing intolerance to pain (or the perception of it) and euthanasia is an easy way of avoiding it.[254] In other eras, pain was seen as an accepted part of life, and perhaps even having redemptive qualities. We need to recapture an appreciation of pain. It should also be noted that research suggests that quality of life of those at the end of their lives is less dependant on the level of pain felt than whether they are living with their caregiver, they have social support and a sense of the spiritual.[255]

4.7 Public opinion: 'let the people decide'

It is claimed that public opinion has reached the stage where a clear majority of people accept that euthanasia should be permitted. However, such polls are difficult to interpret and subtle changes in the wording of the questions asked can produce startlingly different results.[256] Polls questioning members of the public and particular professional groups have found the following:

REALITY CHECK

Public opinion on euthanasia

- In a 2002 NOP Poll people were asked: 'Do you think that a person who is suffering unbearably from a terminal illness should be allowed by law to receive medical help to die, if that is what they want, or should the law not allow them medical help to die?' Eighty-one per cent thought that they should be allowed to receive it (Voluntary Euthanasia Society (2003)).

- An Opinion Research Business (2003) poll of 986 doctors found:
  — 74 per cent would refuse to perform assisted suicide even if it were legalized;
  — 56 per cent consider that it would be impossible to set safe bounds to euthanasia;
  — to the question 'As a doctor do you agree with assisted suicide?' 25 per cent agreed, 60 per cent disagreed, and 13 per cent were undecided;

---

[250] Quill (1993) sees the option of euthanasia as empowering for patients.   [251] Singer (2003).
[252] Although the same point can be made to argue that allowing euthanasia will meaning that less effort will be put into ensuring that proper pain relief is available to all: Marquis (1989).
[253] Lavi (2001).   [254] Lavi (2001).   [255] Tang, Aarason, and Forbes (2003).
[256] House of Lords Select Committee on Medical Ethics (1994).

— the number who rejected euthanasia was higher—61 per cent as compared with 22 per cent in favour and 14 per cent undecided;

— not one palliative care doctor who responded to the survey would practice either euthanasia or assisted suicide.

- A survey of geriatricians in the UK 2001 (Clark et al (2001)) found that 81 per cent thought voluntary euthanasia was never justified in ethical terms and even if legal only 13 per cent would be willing to be involved in it. The opposition to assisted suicide was slightly less: 68 per cent opposed physician-assisted death on ethical grounds; but only 12 per cent would be willing to be involved in it.

- A survey of British pharmacists in 2003 (Hackett and Francis (2003)) found that the majority of respondents (83 per cent) reported that, at times, a person had the right to choose their own manner of death; 61 per cent and 53 per cent thought that there should be changes in the law to legalize voluntary euthanasia and physician-assisted suicide. If it were legal to do so, 63 per cent stated that they would be willing to dispense medication for voluntary euthanasia and 64 per cent for physician-assisted suicide.

- A survey of nurses (Nursing Times (2003)) found just over a half were supportive of legalizing assisted suicide, although a third were strongly opposed.

- A 2004 Voluntary Euthanasia Society-sponsored survey suggested that 47 per cent of the population might be prepared to break the current law to assist someone else to take her or his own life in the case of terminal illness and unbearable suffering (House of Lords Select Committee (2005: 72)).

- Chapple, Ziebland, McPherson, and Herxheimer (2006) did a very small-scale study of those close to death and found a clear majority in favour of allowing euthanasia.

- The British Attitudes Survey (Park (2007)) found that 80 per cent say that the law should 'definitely' or 'probably' allow a doctor to end someone's life at the person's request if they have an incurable and painful illness from which they will die; but only 45 per cent still agreed if the illness was one from which they would not die. The survey found that those who attended religious services were far more likely to oppose euthanasia than those who did not.

These surveys show that among the general public the legalization of euthanasia has the support of a majority, but there is notable opposition among some, but not all, professional groups. However, such surveys need to be treated with care. The way questions are put to people in surveys and the public's understanding of the terms used can affect the results obtained (Hagelin et al (2004)).

4.8 Doctor–patient relationship

Some opponents of euthanasia claim that the possibility of euthanasia will undermine the relationship between doctor and patient and disrupt a doctor's healing role.[257] The Hippocratic Oath[258] states 'To please no one will I prescribe a deadly drug, nor give advice which may cause his death'. The World Medical Association reaffirmed its strong belief that euthanasia conflicts with basic principles of good medical practice.[259] The British Medical Association, the Canadian Medical Association, and the American

---

[257] BMA (2004: 396), Kass (1998).   [258] Reproduced in Mason and Laurie (2006).
[259] English, Gardner, Romano-Critchley, and Sommerville (2001).

Medical Association have all voiced their objection to euthanasia.[260] The root of the concern has been vividly expressed by Capron:

> I never want to have to wonder whether the physician coming into my hospital room is wearing the white coat...of a healer—concerned only to relieve my pain and to restore me to health—or the black hood of the executioner.[261]

Hence it is argued that the knowledge that a doctor could kill the patient will undermine the trust that is at the heart of the doctor–patient relationship. Seeking advice from a physician who may be thinking 'it would be best if I gave you a lethal injection and killed you' is a frightening prospect.[262] Although doctors will respect the autonomy rights of a patient this does not mean that a doctor must comply with every patient's request.[263]

Supporters argue that on the contrary it will create a more open and equal relationship between doctor and patient, with the patient being more able to discuss her or his true feelings.[264] The present law may discourage a patient from discussing her or his wish to die with her or his doctor for fear that it would put the doctor in a difficult position. On the other hand, if euthanasia were legal would people be deterred from discussing their pain for fear that the doctor may pressurize them into considering euthanasia? We should remember that at present doctors can give a lethal quantity of drugs so long as they are doing so with the intention of relieving pain, rather than killing. It appears the fact that doctors under the present law are arguably permitted to kill does not appear to undermine the trust between patient and doctor.

4.9 Human Rights: a right to die?

As mentioned earlier, the House of Lords and the European Court of Human Rights in *Pretty v DPP*[265] were adamant that the European Convention on Human Rights gave no right to die or assistance in suicide.[266] The decision is, of course, not without its critics.[267] There are those who are adamant that there is a right to die in the manner of one's choosing. The heart of the argument was expressed by a Canadian judge, Cory J dissenting in *Rodriguez v A-G of British Columbia*:[268]

> Dying is an integral part of living...It follows that the right to die with dignity should be as well protected as is any other aspect of the right to life. State prohibitions that would force a dreadful, painful death on a rational but incapacitated terminally ill patient are an affront to human dignity.

In terms of the European Convention on Human Rights the argument would be that the decision to end one's life is an essential aspect of the right to private and family life.[269] As noted above, in fact the European Court in *Pretty v UK*[270] accepted that choosing the manner of one's death could be included as an aspect of the right to respect

---

[260] BMA (2004); Keown (2002: Chap 18).   [261] Quoted in BMA (2004: 144).

[262] Kass (1998) see also Finnis (1998b).   [263] Kass (1998: 26).

[264] Baumrin (1998) argues retaining the two and a half millennia old tradition of respect for sanctity of life is crucial to retain public confidence in the medical profession.

[265] Boyd (2002).   [266] See Coggon (2006) for an excellent discussion of a right to die with dignity.

[267] Eg Tur (2003a).   [268] (1994) 107 DLR (4th) 342, at 413.

[269] English (2001).   [270] *Pretty v UK* [2002] 2 FCR 517.

for private life,[271] but held that the interests of the state and others justified an interference with that right.

It should not be thought that human rights arguments all point in favour of liberalizing the laws on suicide and euthanasia. The Committee of Legal Affairs and Human Rights[272] in a report generally negative towards euthanasia emphasizes the right to life of the terminally ill. The European Assembly has asked members to uphold the prohibition against intentionally taking the life of terminally ill or dying persons.[273] But some argue that the right to life means the right to a minimally decent life and if a person's life is intolerable their right to life, paradoxically, entitles them to a right to die.[274]

4.10　Duty to die

In a highly controversial article Hardwig[275] has suggested that people may even be under a duty to die. He argues that people must accept that towards the end of their lives when seriously ill they will become a burden on their families and friends.[276] The burdens placed on relatives caring for the elderly can be intolerable. It can have a devastating impact on carers' family lives, job opportunities, and finances. He argues that:

> To think that my loved ones must bear whatever burdens my illness, debility or dying process might impose upon them is to reduce them to means to my well-being. And that would be immoral.

It should be emphasized that Hardwig is discussing a moral obligation, not a legal one. What perhaps his argument overlooks is that this placing of burdens is part of everyday life. The care of children, friends, and partners can place great burdens on people, but these burdens are not necessarily bad. The caring for others is part of the joy and fulfilment of life. Unfortunately, however, our society does far too little to support and enable such caring relationships to be valued.[277]

A slightly different argument, but also controversial, has been put forward by Daniel Callahan. He suggests that once our life's work has been accomplished then we should be willing to accept a natural death. His point is that the death of a young person is regarded as a terrible tragedy; the death of a person in their 80s may be sad, but does not have that element of waste. We need to accept that once a person reaches a certain age they have lived a 'fair innings' and extensive medical intervention to prolong their lives should not take place. He is not advocating euthanasia, but advocating non-intervention in later years.

4.11　Slippery slopes: where will it all end?

A slippery slope argument is that even if it is morally acceptable to permit A, it should not be permitted because it would lead to B which is not morally acceptable.[278] In this

---

[271] Mumby J in *R (Burke) v GMC* [2004] EWHC (Admin) 1879 stated at para 62 'Article 8 embraces such matters as how one chooses to pass the closing days and moments of one's life and how one manages one's death'.

[272] Council of Europe (2003).

[273] See also the European Parliamentary Assembly (2003).　　[274] Grayling (2005).

[275] Hardwig (1997).　　[276] Wilson, Curran, and McPherson (2005).

[277] Warnock (2001) rejects any argument based on a duty to oneself to end the pain.

[278] For detailed analysis of slippery slope arguments generally see Lamb (1988) and Walton (1992).

context the concern is that if voluntary euthanasia is permitted it will be inevitably lead to non-voluntary or involuntary euthanasia.[279] Of course any jurisdiction which decided to permit voluntary euthanasia would be likely to put in place procedures which would be designed to ensure that euthanasia only took place where the patient consented. The question is whether these procedures would be effective.[280] As Penney Lewis points out, in order to succeed, a slippery slope argument would need to show that legalization of voluntary euthanasia or assisted suicide would cause the slippery slope; so it would need to be shown that it was not other social forces that had caused the move to accept non-voluntary euthanasia.[281]

Keown argues that the slippery slope argument can be made in two ways:

(1) As a matter of logic, once voluntary euthanasia is permitted there are no arguments which would justify opposing involuntary euthanasia and so one will lead to another.

(2) As a matter of practice, it is not possible to put in place procedures to ensure that there is no involuntary euthanasia. Indeed, in considering the position in countries where voluntary euthanasia has been allowed, critics claim that there is evidence that involuntary euthanasia has occurred.

Looking first at the argument from a logical perspective, Keown argues that supporters of euthanasia are on the horns of a dilemma. If they accept that autonomy is key, then they should permit a perfectly healthy person who wants to die to receive euthanasia. However, he points out that few supporters of euthanasia would be happy to give euthanasia to a teenager who has been disappointed in love.[282] However, if we only allow euthanasia where the person's decision is 'sensible' (eg where they are in great pain, facing a terminal illness) then this means we have to make a decision that a person is better off dead. Once we are willing to make this kind of assessment when dealing with incompetent people, it follows that we must likewise accept that there are some cases where it is desirable (in the person's best interests) to die. Lillehammer[283] rejects the logic of this argument, saying that it is perfectly coherent to say that euthanasia is only appropriate where both the patient competently seeks euthanasia and such a patient is terminally ill.[284] These two requirements could be seen as 'individually necessary and jointly sufficient'.[285] As Gerald Dworkin puts it: 'This is why the view is called voluntary euthanasia—voluntary to indicate choice of the patient, euthanasia to indicate that the death is "good" '.[286] But this leaves open the question of when the death is 'good'. Most

---

[279] Keown (2002) is a book-length consideration of the 'slippery slope' arguments against euthanasia. For a detailed response see Smith (2005). Interestingly the Board for Social Responsibility of the Church of England (2000) accepts there may be cases where euthanasia is permissible in moral terms, but that it should not be permitted legally, because of concerns that legal regulation would never be able to ensure that only voluntary euthanasia took place.

[280] Dworkin, Frey, and Bok (1998) and Dworkin (1998) argue that when considering the slippery slope argument the burden is on those seeking to advance it because they must justify denying respect of the autonomous decision of a patient wanting help to die.

[281] Lewis (2007a).

[282] For an example of a commentator who does not think suffering should be a requirement before euthanasia is permitted see Varelius (2007).

[283] Lillehammer (2002).

[284] Smith (2005) argues that changes in the law in Holland allowing voluntary euthanasia have not changed the attitudes of the Dutch to involuntary euthanasia.

[285] Lillehammer (2002: 548).   [286] Dworkin (1998: 10).

supporters of euthanasia would accept this is so where a patient is suffering terrible pain and wants to die; but what if they are merely tired of life?[287]

Supporters of euthanasia state that euthanasia is appropriate not where a person's life is valueless, but rather where it has lost its value for that person.[288] Put this way it is claimed that it is possible to argue that a person who is not able to express a view should not be killed as we do not know how they value their life, although that may still leave open the 'best interests' reasoning in *Bland*.

Looking next at the slippery slope argument in the context of practice, the argument here is that whatever safeguards were put in place they would not be effective in ensuring that there was only euthanasia where the patient voluntarily accepted. Battin[289] suggests there are three kinds of abuse that could occur in the context of a legal system which approved of euthanasia:

(1) *Interpersonal abuse*. A person may be encouraged or pressurized into agreeing to be killed. This could be by overt pressure, or by indirect means.

(2) *Professional abuse*. Doctors may not want to waste time in expensive and time con-suming medical procedures, and may encourage patients to agree to euthanasia. Consciously or not a doctor may exaggerate the pain in the future. There may even be concerns that physicians who have made medical mistakes may seek to cover them up by encouraging euthanasia. The concept of doctors trying to manipulate their patients in euthanasia may appear fanciful, but it is not difficult to find examples of doctors who have illegally killed quite a number of their patients.[290]

(3) *Institutional abuse*. The medical and legal structures themselves may encourage the use of euthanasia and manipulate patients into agreeing to be killed.

To consider whether such abuses are realistic concerns or scaremongering we will look at three jurisdictions[291] which have departed from the traditional approach of render-ing illegal euthanasia and assisted suicide: The Netherlands, Belgium, and Oregon.[292] Perhaps predictably supporters of euthanasia argue that these jurisdictions demonstrate that effective safeguards can be put in place, while opponents argue that evidence from these jurisdictions reinforce their concerns.[293]

4.11.1 *The Netherlands*

The Netherlands has legislated to permit euthanasia in certain circumstances.[294] The Termination of Life on Request and Assisted Suicide (Review Procedures) Act amends article 293 of the Penal Code of the Netherlands to read as follows:

---

[287] See for discussion of this Huxtable and Möller (2007).   [288] Harris (1992).

[289] Although Battin (1992) believes that it is possible to put in place safeguards to ensure that these concerns are met.

[290] Kinnell (2000) argues that it is wrong to see Shipman as a special case and controversially claims that the medical profession attracts people who enjoy power of over life and death.

[291] See Lewis (2006) for a discussion of the position in France.

[292] Although there are other countries which permit assisted suicide or euthanasia, eg Rights of the Terminally Ill Act 1995 (Northern Territory (Australia)).

[293] See Gillon (1999b) for an example of a commentator who supports euthanasia in theory but is deeply concerned about the difficulties the Dutch have had in regulating the practice.

[294] Griffiths, Bood, and Weyers (1998).

(1) A person who terminates the life of another person at that other person's express and earnest request is liable to a term of imprisonment of not more than twelve years or a fine of the fifth category.

(2) The offence referred to in the first paragraph shall not be punishable if it has been committed by a physician who has met the requirements of due care . . . and who informs the municipal autopsist of this.

The concept of due care is defined in the legislation in article 2. It requires that the patient's request is voluntary and well-considered. The patient must be suffering in a way which is lasting and unbearable and that there is no prospect of improvement. The patient and doctor must believe that there is no reasonable solution to her or his plight, apart from assisted suicide or euthanasia. The doctor must have consulted an independent physician who has seen the patient and approved of the proposed course of action. The consent of the patient can be by an advance directive (ie a 'living will'), if the patient is no longer capable of expressing her or his wishes.

A House of Lords committee looking at the use of the Dutch law stated:

> Approximately 16 million people live in The Netherlands, of who around 140,000 die every year. We were told that some 9,700 requests for euthanasia are made annually. About 3,800 of these actually receive euthanasia, of which some 300 are assisted suicides. Euthanasia therefore accounts for around 2.5 per cent and assisted suicide 0.2 per cent of all deaths in The Netherlands. In addition to these, there are about 1,000 deaths a year (0.7 per cent of all deaths) where physicians end a patient's life without an explicit request.'[295]

A recent study suggested that in 2005 1.7 per cent of deaths results from euthanasia and 0.1 per cent assisted suicide.[296] Critics[297] point to the following to express their concern over the Dutch scheme:[298]

- There is evidence that doctors were regularly ignoring the formal guidelines set down in the regime.[299] However, most of the evidence relates to behaviour before the Act was fully implemented. The most recent studies show that only around 50 per cent of cases are reported. In fact the number of cases reported has fallen since 2000, although it is unclear whether this is due to a decrease in the incidence of euthanasia, or a decrease in proportion of doctors reporting.[300] Further, the Dutch Government has recognized the problem and recently announced a wider range of penalties for doctors who perform euthanasia but do not comply with the formal requirements.[301] The rate of reporting may be improving. A recent study found that 80.2 per cent of cases were properly reported.[302] That will still be regarded as worryingly low by some.

- Some claim that non–voluntary euthanasia is regularly practised under the Dutch scheme. Finnis,[303] considering the findings of a detailed survey into the operation

---

[295] House of Lords Select Committee (2005: 57).   [296] Van der Heide et al (2007).
[297] Keown (1992), Keown (1995), and Jochemsen and Keown (1999).
[298] Van der Maas, Van Delden, and Pijnenborg (1992) and Van der Maas (1996) are the leading surveys on the practice of euthanasia in Holland. Thomasma et al (1998) provides a detailed consideration of the statistics.
[299] Hendin (1999).   [300] Onwuteaka-Philipsen et al (2005).
[301] Sheldon, T. (2004).   [302] Van der Heide et al (2007).   [303] Finnis (1998b: 1476–7).

of the euthanasia laws, states:

> when you look at those figures, the bottom line is this: we find that not just 1,300 or 2,300 or another 1,000 but 25,306 cases of death were accelerated by medical intervention intended wholly or partly to terminate life...And of these Dutch deaths, well over half, or fifty eight percent—14,691—were without any explicit request.[304]

However, it should be noted that the statistics he refers to include non-treatment decisions and cases of terminal sedation, which do not need to be reported under the Act.

- Evidence of a slippery slope is also said to be found in the fact that respected Dutch medical bodies have suggested there needs to be a debate on whether a patient suffering from severe dementia, even if there are no serious physical symptoms, might be terminated without an advance directive or consent.[305] At present the Act does not apply to such cases.

- The courts and Dutch authorities have been lenient in their treatment of doctors who breach the legal requirements. For example, a Dutch psychiatrist was found by the Dutch authorities to have been justified in assisting in the suicide of a depressed woman who was physically healthy;[306] he was only subject to medical disciplinary proceedings.

- The availability of palliative care and hospices in the Netherlands is said by some to be limited.[307]

- The percentage of Dutch physicians concerned about economic pressures causing patients to seek euthanasia increased from 9 per cent in 1990 to 15 per cent in 2001.[308] It should be noted that this study relates to a time before the Act was implemented.

However, it would be quite wrong to suggest that the Dutch system is without its supporters, indeed some of the leading commentators in the area believe that the Dutch system is a success and reject claims that the system is open to abuse.[309] It has even been argued that rates of involuntary and non-voluntary euthanasia are lower in the Netherlands than other countries because the Dutch law enables people to decide to die before they lose competence[310] and it prevents euthanasia being practised 'underground'.[311] By bringing it out into the open and regulating it, greater protection can be offered against abuses.[312]

---

[304] The detailed analysis behind these claims is discussed in Keown (2002: Part III). Van Delden et al (1993) claim that Keown and others have misinterpreted this data. Keown (2002: 100–1) defends his interpretation. For further discussion of whether there is evidence of non-voluntary and involuntary euthanasia see Pijnenborg, Van der Maas, Van Delden, and Looman (1993).

[305] Hellema (1993).

[306] Mason and Laurie (2006: 607). Keown (2002: 87) refers to a case where euthanasia was carried out because a patient felt his life was 'pointless and empty'. See also Sheldon (2001).

[307] Zyic (1998) and Van Delden (1999), although not everyone agrees with this assessment, see eg Cohen-Almagor (2002a) and Van der Heide et al (2007).

[308] Onwuteaka-Philipsen et al (2003).   [309] Eg, Singer (2003).

[310] Otlowski (2002). Kuhse et al (1997) argue that where euthanasia is not legal there are higher numbers of patients being killed without their consent. They claim that 36.5% of Australian deaths involve intentional killing of patients (by acts or omissions) without the patient's consent. However, their findings have been challenged by Kissane (2002).

[311] Magnusson (2004). Although see Keown (2006b) who is not convinced of the extent to which there is 'underground' euthanasia. In any event he argues there are many criminal laws which are often breached, but that is not an argument for abolishing them.

[312] Kuhse (1998).

Indeed a study of the practice of euthanasia between 1990 and 2001 has shown that in the years 1995 to 2001 the rates of euthanasia were stable, suggesting that the legislation had not created a slippery slope with an ever rising number of incidents of euthanasia.[313] In fact in 2005 there was a reduction in the rates of euthanasia.[314] Further one study showed that 12 per cent of requests for euthanasia were refused by doctors and in 13 per cent of cases patients withdrew their requests after consulting doctors.[315] Supporters and opponents of euthanasia will disagree whether or not these figures show that doctors are effective in determining which cases are suitable for euthanasia or not.[316]

So, the statistics have been interpreted in a number of ways and there is no consensus.[317] A comparison between countries which have legalized assisted dying or euthanasia and counties which have not fails to produce a clear picture of the effect of such legalization.[318] However, it should be noted that some highly respected bodies in considering the Dutch systems have expressed profound misgivings about whether the operation of the law in Holland is adequately protecting vulnerable people. These include: the United Nations Human Rights Committee[319] and the Committee on Legal Affairs and Human Rights of the European Parliament.[320] The latter body stated that the studies:

> have demonstrated a disturbingly high incidence of euthanasia being carried out without the patient's explicit request and an equally disturbing failure by medical professionals to report euthanasia cases to the proper regulatory authority.

These and other problems may explain why so few jurisdictions have implemented similar laws,[321] although a recent study suggested there were no higher rates of assisted suicide among vulnerable groups in Oregon and the Netherlands.[322] Whatever one's interpretation of the statistics, it is surprising that the Dutch legal and medical establishment have not done more to rigorously ensure the legal requirements are complied with and so avoid allegations of malpractice.[323]

4.11.2 *Belgium*

Belgium decriminalized euthanasia in 2002.[324] The law applies only to patients who are over the age of 18, are competent, and are in persistent and unbearable pain or distress, which cannot be alleviated. If they then make an explicit, unambiguous, repeated, and durable request for euthanasia this can be complied with by a doctor. The clinician must provide full information about the patient's condition and tell her of palliative care options. A second doctor must confirm that the suffering is unbearable and that it cannot be alleviated. Further consultations are required where the patient is not terminally

---

[313] Onwuteaka-Philipsen et al (2003) and Downie (2000).   [314] Van der Heide et al (2007).

[315] Jansen-van der Weide, Onwuteaka-Philipsen, and van der Wal, (2005).

[316] Coggon (2007) queries whether debates over empirical evidence can be carried out objectively and therefore questions their usefulness in resolves debates over end of life issues.

[317] Lewis (2007c).   [318] Lewis (2007a).

[319] The United Nations Human Rights Committee (2001). The Dutch Government has promised to undertake further research to see whether the Committee's concerns are justified: Dutch Government (2003).

[320] The Council of Europe (2003: para 1).

[321] Support for the Dutch system can be found in Admiral (1996). But negative reports can be found in Keown (1994 a and b) and Hendin (1998).

[322] Battin et al (2007); Department of Human Services (2007).

[323] Even supporters of the Dutch system have admitted there has been too little compliance with the formal requirements of registration of death (Griffiths et al (1998: 298)).

[324] Gastmans et al (2004) consider the new Belgian law.

ill. In 2004 there were 347 cases of euthanasia in Belgium.[325] One interesting aspect of the Belgian law is that where a patient has been cared for by nurses and/or family members they should be consulted by the doctor.

4.11.3 *Oregon in the United States*

In 1994 Oregon, a state in the United States, passed the Death with Dignity Act 1994.[326] This permitted doctors to provide a patient with a lethal quantity of drugs for the purpose of assisting a patient's suicide. However, this was only permitted in certain carefully proscribed circumstances and it did not permit the doctor to administer the drug her or himself.[327] In other words the legislation permitted physician-assisted suicide, not euthanasia. The patient must be found to be acting voluntarily and be competent.

Since the law was passed 292 people have died. In 1998, 16 Oregonians used physician-assisted suicide. This increased to 27 in 1999, 27 in 2000, 21 in 2001, 38 in 2002, 42 in 2003, and 37 in 2004.[328] There were 46 deaths under the Act in 2006. This means that 1.47 in 1,000 Oregans die through physician-assisted suicide. In 2006 there were 65 prescriptions for lethal medicine under the Act, but only 35 took the medication; 11 others who had been given the medicine in 2006 died without taking it. Disturbingly there were four cases in 2006 where complications arose from unsuccessful attempts to take the medicine.[329]

Some interesting information comes out of Oregon about the kind of people who seek physician-assisted suicide (PAS):

- The most common medical condition among those using to Act to commit suicide were those suffering from cancer.

- The most common reason given for wanting to die was loss of autonomy and not being able to do the things which made life enjoyable and a loss of dignity. Forty-four per cent of those using the Act mentioned fears about being a burden to their family or friends as a major factor leading them to seek suicide.[330] In 2006 44 per cent mentioned concerns about pain relief.

- Between 1998 and 2006 the median age of those seeking PAS was 70. Younger people with terminal illnesses were more likely to seek PAS than older people with terminal illnesses.

- There was no significant difference between rates of men and women seeking PAS. From 1998 to 2006 54 per cent of those who died under the Act were men and 46 per cent women.

- Asian Oregans were three times more likely than white Oregans to seek PAS. Divorced and never married people were two times more likely than married people to do so.

- There was a strong association between having attended higher education and seeking PAS.[331]

---

325 Jackson (2007).   326 Chin et al (1999); Cohen-Almagor and Hartman (2001).
327 Smith II (1996).   328 Dahl and Levy (2006).
329 Department of Human Services (2007).
330 Department of Human Services (2003: 20).
331 Department of Human Services (2007).

So far it does not appear from the evidence that there is widespread abuse of the system,[332] but Bonnie Steinbock believes it as yet unproven whether the benefits of the Oregon system outweigh the disadvantages of potential abuse.[333] In 2006 ten cases were referred to the Board of Medical examiners, with complaints that the paperwork for prescriptions under the Act was inadequately completed. However, in none of those cases was there a finding of unprofessional conduct made.

Before we leave the slippery slope argument we should note that it should not be assumed that countries which outlaw euthanasia are immune from slippery slopes. As the Shipman case shows, even in England an enormous number of patients can be killed without the authorities being alerted.[334]

4.12 Concern over treatment of the vulnerable

Linked to the 'slippery slope' argument is the concern that permitting voluntary euthanasia would work against the interests of vulnerable people.[335] Those people suffering poverty, confusion, or general vulnerability may be pressurized into agreeing to euthanasia against their wishes.[336] Keown[337] has claimed that many people who consent to euthanasia may in fact simply be suffering from severe pain, distress, depression, or 'demoralization',[338] and are therefore not in a position to make a rational decision. It should not be forgotten that people are often expected to take decisions over their medical treatment in the alien environment of hospital without clothes, friends, and support.[339] Indeed, for the less well off the alternatives to euthanasia or assisted suicide may well be less attractive than those well able to afford high quality nursing care.[340] There are concerns that euthanasia will work against the interests of women and those in ethnic minorities.[341] Katrina George lists the following factors as meaning that women's choices about euthanasia may not be voluntary: 'structural inequalities and disparities in power—most evident in women's experience of violence—and social and economic disadvantage and oppressive cultural stereotypes that idealise feminine self-sacrifice and reinforce stereotyped gender roles of passivity and compliance.'[342] No doubt the articulate, well-educated and assertive will be in a position to take informed decisions about whether or not they wish to end their lives, but will the depressed, the despairing, and the poor?[343] Nor should it be forgotten that unscrupulous relatives, concerned that the medical and caring costs will decimate their inheritance, have an interest in encouraging

---

[332] Dahl and Levy (2006).

[333] Steinbock (2005). See also Battin et al (2007).

[334] Thunder (2003).

[335] Brogden (2001) has written of the 'Geronticide', the mass killing of older people. Godiwala (2002) is critical of the way both sides to the debate have sought to use the 'vulnerable' to promote their cause.

[336] Street and Kissane (2000) and Breitbart and Rosenfeld (1999) and Chochinov et al (1999) discuss the psychological issues surrounding consent to euthanasia.

[337] Keown (2002: Chap 5).

[338] The demoralization of terminally ill patients is recognized as a medical condition by some: Kissane et al (2001).

[339] O'Neill (1984).

[340] Godiwala (2002) and Kamisar (1998).

[341] King and Wolf (1998). Dieterle (2007) argues that the evidence from Oregan and the Netherlands does not bear out such concerns.

[342] George (2007: 2–3).

[343] Pacheco et al (2003) are concerned at the numbers of changes of mind among people seeking euthanasia.

euthanasia.[344] This is particularly so given evidence that many people nearing the end of their lives are desperate not to be a burden to their families.[345]

Despite all of these points there is a concern about the validity of consent from vulnerable groups in many kinds of medical treatment, but these do not normally mean that the treatment (if thought useful) is not made available.[346] The argument, to be convincing in and of itself, would also need to show that it would not be possible to protect vulnerable groups from improper manipulation by providing careful independent advice from trained counsellors, for example. It should also be remembered that vulnerable groups should be an issue of concern under the current law, where they can be left without treatment or provided pain relieving (but killing) drugs with little regulation or supervision.[347]

4.13 It happens

It can be argued that the reality is that euthanasia does occur and that it is widely accepted even in countries which, like England, outlaw it. Rather than have a formal legal position which is consistently ignored, it is better to have a legal regulation to ensure there is no improper practice. We saw at page 476 some of the surveys attempting to ascertain the level of euthanasia that takes place. The argument that can be made is that if euthanasia is going to take place—even if it is illegal—it would be better to permit euthanasia but only if, for example, an ethical committee has approved the course of action.[348] Then at least we would have a system of checks and balances on a practice which at present goes ahead without any formal controls at all.

4.14 Can't make up your mind?

You might find that in considering all these arguments you are unable to make your mind up. You see the strength of the argument on either side. Such a reaction has led some commentators to take the view that euthanasia should be regarded as not illegal, but also not something to be encouraged either. Boonin[349] has emphasized that there is a difference between having a right to do something and it being right to do it. He gives the example of there being a right to tell racist jokes,[350] but that no virtuous person would choose to exercise that right. Similarly he argues that, in the context of euthanasia, a strong argument can be made for saying that a person has a right to engage in euthanasia but that no virtuous person would do so. He argues that practising euthanasia can be said to amount to an agreement with the patient that the patient's life is not worth living. He therefore advocates that the law takes a neutral stance on euthanasia: not prohibiting it, but not promoting it either. He backs this up by arguing that otherwise the state will be required to take a stance on the controversial issue of what gives life value, and on such questions the state should remain neutral. To opponents of

---

[344] In *R v McShane* 1977 66 CAR 97 the defendant wanted to persuade her 89-year-old mother to kill herself to get her inheritance. A secret camera installed by police showed the daughter giving her mother drugs in a bag of sweets and pinning on her dress a note saying, 'don't bungle it'.

[345] Biggs (1998). Care Not Killing (2006) argue this is particularly a concern from the Oregon statistics.

[346] Boonin (2000).   [347] Jackson (2007).

[348] Magnusson (2002) examines the extent to which euthanasia is practiced underground in the US and Australia.

[349] Boonin (2000).   [350] Presumably he has in mind the right to free speech.

euthanasia, permitting it, but not encouraging it, is not a 'neutral' stance as it involves the law failing to respect the sanctity of life.

5 Inconsistency in present law

The current law opposing euthanasia and assisted suicide is said by some to be illogical and unsupportable.[351] It is argued that it is based on two unsupportable distinctions: between intention and foresight; and between acts and omissions. We shall consider these separately.

5.1 Intention/foresight

As we have seen, for the law and for many commentators there is an important distinction between intention and foresight.[352] The distinction has been justified on the basis that there is an important difference between aiming to produce a result and being aware that a result is a possible result of one's actions.[353] You may foresee that if you drink too much alcohol you will get a hangover, but that does not mean you intend it; a lecturer may foresee that her or his lecture will confuse her or his students, but this does not mean she or he intends to confuse them. The reasons for which a person acts tell us far more about their personality than the results they foresee when they act.[354] We would, for example, regard a dentist who drilled a tooth foreseeing pain in a quite different light from a dentist who drilled a tooth wanting there to be pain. Most supporters of the distinction between foresight and intention also approve of the doctrine of double effect which sets out the circumstances in which even though a result may be foreseen it is not intended (see page xxx). There is some debate among supporters of double effect whether the doctrine can even be relied upon where a result is inevitable.[355] If a person knows that a consequence will inevitably result from her or his action, can it really be argued that it is not intended? Keown appears to believe that even if the effect is certain, if it is a side consequence it is justifiable and not intended. However others say the doctrine should only be used if the side consequence is highly probable or less.[356]

There are, however, plenty of people who reject the distinction between intent and foresight and the doctrine of double effect.[357] Warnock sees the difference between intention and foresight as 'absurdly pedantic'.[358] Harris[359] has criticized the doctrine for depending too much on how one expresses a problem. He considers a scenario where a group of potholers are trapped and the only way to escape is to move a boulder, but moving the boulder will crush one person to death. You could describe this as 'intending to make an escape route, foreseeing that this will kill someone' or 'intending to make an escape route by killing someone'. He suggests that the morality of an action depends on whether the action judged as a whole was right, not by how one is able to express what one is doing. One way of putting the argument is that we accept consequences in

---

[351] See Williams (2007).
[352] The doctrine of double effect was defined above. See also Somerville (2003: Chap 1).
[353] See eg Keown (2002: Chap 2); Finnis (1991) and Garcia (1997).
[354] Maclean (1992: 90–4).   [355] Huxtable (2004) explores the ambiguities within the concept.
[356] Cantor and Thomas III (2000).
[357] Price (1997b). For an interesting discussion on the concept see Gurnham (2007).
[358] Warnock (2001: 39).   [359] Harris (1984: 44).

packages. If, for example, I need a filling and I go to the dentist I can be said to intend to have the treatment. It is true I do not want the pain, but the pain comes with the treatment, I accept the 'package' (the treatment with the consequential pain) because I decide that even though there is pain it will, in the long term be preferable for me.[360] I cannot say 'I intend to have the filling, but not to experience the pain' because life is not like that.

Harris,[361] responding to the example of the person who drinks, foreseeing but not intending to have a hangover, suggests that even accepting that a person does not intend to have a hangover, they are responsible for it. If, as a result of a hangover, they were unable to work properly the next day then we can justly blame them. He argues in deciding whether or not it is proper to administer a lethal quantity of pain relieving drugs to a terminally ill person, the crucial question should not be what was the doctor's purpose in administering the drugs but whether the person should die.[362] Surely far more important than the doctor's intent are the questions: did the patient consent,[363] or what was the doctor's motivation?

One difficulty for those who wish to emphasize the difference between intent and foresight is its practicability. If a doctor is found to have injected a patient with a lethal amount of a pain relieving drug, how are we to know what was her or his intent or foresight?[364] As the law stands, with its emphasis on intent, only a doctor foolish enough to admit she or he was intending to kill would face prosecution. Further, if a doctor wishes to give a large dose of pain relieving drugs to her or his patient, but seeks her or his lawyer's advice first, is it really sensible that the advice might be 'you can give the injection, but make sure that at the time you are not wanting the death and focus on wanting to relieve pain'? Such concerns have led some to suggest that whatever its merits in terms of ethics, the doctrine does not provide a practical guide to medical practice.

5.2 Acts/omissions

The second controversial distinction at the heart of the present law is a distinction between active and passive euthanasia (those cases where an act of the doctor causes death and those cases where the doctor's omission causes the death). Lord Goff in *Bland* summarized the current law:

> It is not lawful for a doctor to administer a drug to his patient to bring about his death, even though that course is prompted by a humanitarian desire to end his suffering, however great that suffering may be…So to act is to cross the Rubicon which runs between—on the one hand the care of the living patient and on the other hand euthanasia—actively causing his death to avoid or to end his suffering. Euthanasia is not lawful at common law.[365]

This reflects the popular view that the duty not to harm others is stronger than the duty to assist.[366] The distinction can be supported in terms of causation. An omission cannot

---

[360] Shaw (2002) summarizes the criticisms of the doctrine of double effect.
[361] Harris (1995b).   [362] Harris (1995b).
[363] Davies (1988) argues that the difference between murder and euthanasia is the same as the difference between raping and making love: it is the consent of the 'victim' which makes all the difference.
[364] Wilkinson (2000).
[365] [1993] 1 All ER 821, 867. See *Quill v Vacco* (1997) 117 S Ct 2293 where the majority regarded the distinction between assisting suicide and withdrawing life-support as important and logical (2298).
[366] Foot (1976).

cause death; death is caused by the underlying medical condition. An omission may be necessary for a death, while it cannot be sufficient. By contrast an act can take over authorship and full responsibility for what happens.[367] Phillippa Foot poses the question: Are we as much to blame for allowing people in Third World countries to starve to death as we would be for killing them by sending poisoned food? This 'common sense' intuition that there is an important distinction between acts and omissions appears to be one which is shared by many health care professionals working in the field. One survey of UK medical practitioners suggests that 75 per cent accept a moral distinction between active and passive euthanasia as of important moral significance.[368] However much the distinction has been considered to justify and explain at a practical level, it has been far less popular among philosophers.[369] Lord Mustill likewise was not convinced by the distinction drawn between acts and omissions and he feared that after *Bland* the law is 'morally and intellectually misshapen': 'Still, the law is there and we must take it as it stands'.[370] Two leading medical ethicists, Beauchamp and Childress, state: 'the distinction between killing and letting die suffers from vagueness and moral confusion. The language of killing is so thoroughly confusing—causally, legally, and morally—that it can provide little if any help in discussion of assistance in dying'. The specific concerns about it are as follows.

First, the distinction can be said to lead to illogical results. As Lord Goff in *Bland* admitted:

> it can be asked why, if the doctor, by discontinuing treatment, is entitled in consequence to let his patient die, it should not be lawful to put him out of his misery straight away, in a more human manner, by a lethal injection, rather than let him linger on in pain until he dies. But the law does not feel able to authorise euthanasia, even in circumstances such as these, for, once euthanasia is recognised as lawful in these circumstances, it is difficult to see any logical basis for excluding it in others.

Even some opponents of euthanasia are critical of the distinction between acts and omissions. To Keown[371] the focus on acts and omissions avoids the key question: did the doctor intend to produce death? He argues that if a doctor intends to kill this is wrong. Whether the doctor intended to produce death by an act or an omission is just a detail about the method of killing which should not carry moral weight.[372]

Second, it is difficult to know sometimes whether an aspect of one's behaviour is an act or an omission. Is switching off a life support machine an act or an omission?[373] Williams makes the point in this way:[374]

> The question then arises whether stopping a respirator is an act of killing or a decision to let nature take its course? Common sense suggests it is the latter. Suppose that the respirator worked only as long as the doctor turned a handle. If he stopped turning, he would be regarded as merely commencing to omit to save the patient's life. Suppose, alternatively, that the respirator worked electrically but was made to shut itself off it would be an omission. It can make no moral difference that the respirator is constructed to run continuously and has to be stopped. Stopping the respirator is not a positive act of killing the patient, but a decision not to strive any longer to save him.

---

[367] Stauch (2000).   [368] Coulson (1996).
[369] For arguments supporting the distinction between killing and letting die see Callahan (1993) and Kamm (1998).
[370] At page 885.   [371] Keown (2002: 14).   [372] Bennett (1966).
[373] Leng (1982).   [374] Williams (1978: 237).

To some commentators the difficulties in making the distinction between an act and omission reveals that the moral principles governing a doctor's decision should not focus on the distinction between withholding or withdrawing treatment, but rather what duties a physician owes her or his patient.

Third, it is argued by some that omissions cannot cause a result. Logically the absence of an act cannot make something happen. In response others claim that we regularly talk of an omission causing a result. The student failed the exam because she or he failed to work hard enough.[375] In the context of seriously ill patients is there not a difference between letting nature take its course (ie an omission) and doing an act that disrupts the course of events?[376]

Much of the philosophical discussion concerning the distinction between acts and omission has centred around a hypothetical example put forward by James Rachels:[377]

> Smith stands to gain a large inheritance if anything should happen to his six year old cousin. One evening while the child is taking his bath, Smith sneaks into the bathroom and drowns the child, and then arranges things so it will look like an accident. No one is any the wiser, and Smith gets his inheritance.
>
> Jones also stands to gain if anything should happen to his six–year–old cousin. Like Smith, Jones sneaks in to the bathroom planning to drown the child in his bath. However, just as he enters the bathroom Jones sees the child slip, hit his head, and fall face down in the water. Jones is delighted; he stands by, ready to push the child's head under if necessary, but it is not necessary. With only a little thrashing about, the child drowns all by himself, 'accidentally', as Jones watches and does nothing. No one is any the wiser and Jones gets his inheritance.

Rachels argues there is no difference between Smith and Jones in this scenario and this demonstrates that there is no moral difference between an act and omission. He accepts that generally omissions are not blameworthy, but this is because omissions are normally accidental or negligent, whereas actions rarely are.[378] A person rushing past a person drowning in a river is not normally intending that person to die, but a person who pushes another in is. He argues that the significance of his hypothetical example is that both Smith and Jones intend to kill. Where there is no difference in intention he argues that there is no moral difference between what they have done. He goes to point out that killing a child by deliberately starving her or him would be one of the cruellest ways of killing, even though it would be an omission.

Nesbitt provides a powerful repost to Rachels. He argues that he would rather live in a world populated by people who would not rescue him if he were to get into trouble, but would not try to actively kill him, than a world populated by people who would be willing to act to kill. He argues that if Rachels' scenario were modified so that Jones would not have been prepared to push the child's head under if necessary (ie he was only willing to kill by omission) there would be a clear difference between Jones and Smith. This he argues suggests that the difference between acts and omissions is significant. Kuhse responds to this argument by saying that if she was in the process of a painful death she would rather have people who were willing to act to kill her, than those who would stand by. The issue, she argues, is whether the killing is good or not; not whether

---

[375] Garrard and Wilkinson (2005: 66).   [376] McGee (2005).   [377] Rachels (1986: 112).
[378] Actions it is said are also more likely to result in a serious injury than omissions and are more likely to threaten society as a whole: Tooley (1980).

there was an act or an omission.[379] It is the outcome that matters not how the outcome was produced.

There are many problems with the sharp distinction between an act and an omission. Despite these philosophical problems, many argue that the distinction provides a useful guide.[380] It gives doctors who cease treating patients the comfort of saying they did not kill their patients,[381] and also preserves the slippery slope argument. Even if not logical arguably, the distinction is said to be in accordance with many people's intuition.[382] McCall Smith has suggested that despite its theoretical difficulties it provides a basis upon which many people think and act.[383] Leaving aside cases where it is difficult to draw a distinction between an act and an omission, there are few cases where a killing is justified (it may be in self-defence, for example); whereas generally 'letting die' is permissible (we are not responsible for failing to ensure those starving in other countries do not die). Despite the philosophical arguments it should be emphasized that the law takes the distinction between acts and omissions seriously.

5.3 Euthanasia and disabled people

There have been concerns about euthanasia from those writing from a disabilities perspective, in particular that legalizing euthanasia would send the message that the lives of disabled people were not worth living.[384] More often the writings have been concerned about the way the arguments are phrased. The weight placed on autonomy is seen as misplaced by some writers, pointing out that disabled people's autonomy is severely restricted.[385] Others have been concerned that opponents of euthanasia have been too quick to describe disabled people as vulnerable and easily coerced or incompetent.[386] Biggs and Diesfeld, looking at the position of depressed people, are concerned that assisted suicide and euthanasia would only further isolate those suffering with depression, rather than forcing society to properly face up to the challenges offered by depression.[387] A similar point can be made about those suffering from other forms of physical or mental disability.

 A VIEW FROM ABOVE

Theological perspectives on euthanasia

As already indicated, many of those writing from a religious perspective oppose euthanasia. In Judaism, Christianity, Buddhism, Hinduism, and Islam respect is shown to the principle of sanctity of life. Every life is valuable and precious to God. It is easier for a religious person to see the life of a person in, say, PVS, as valuable and precious than it is to someone without faith. The person in PVS is still valued and loved by God and hence is precious, even if no earthly person can relate to her or him. There might be thought to be a slight paradox here. For a non-religious person it might be thought that death is a 'tragedy' and the end of everything; whereas for many

---

[379] Kuhse (1998) and Kuhse and Singer (2001).   [380] Glover (1977: 186–8).

[381] Gillon (1999a).   [382] Gillett (1988).

[383] McCall Smith (1999). Kamisar (1998: 34) refers to the 'deep need' to distinguish between killing and letting die.

[384] Bickenbach (1998).   [385] Bickenbach (1998).   [386] Silvers (1998).

[387] Biggs and Diesfeld (1995: 34).

with a religious belief there is hope of some kind of after life. It might therefore be thought that a religious view would be less concerned about causing death than a non-religious view. The answer to this conundrum appears to be that life, being created by God is of value to God and so must not be taken (Guroian (2002)).

Most Jewish religious scholars draw a sharp distinction between accelerating the death of a dying person, which is prohibited, and removing an impediment to death, which is permitted (Sinclair (2003: 182)). At the heart of the Jewish approach, according to many scholars, is the notion that there is a 'time to die' and that should not be inappropriately delayed nor foreshortened. The difficulty is in defining what is an impediment to death and this has led to some debate over whether and when, for example, life support machines can be switched off (Resnicoff (1999); Kunin (2003)).

Within Christianity it is the Roman Catholic Church which has been most vociferous in its rejection of euthanasia and support for sanctity of life and the principle of double effect (Pontifical Academy for Life (2000)). Indeed that doctrine has its origins in Roman Catholic theology. Many Christian writers from all dominations reject euthanasia and argue that life is a gift from God which we are to treasure and steward, not destroy (Paris and Moreland (1998)). Notably churches have played a significant role in the creation and support of hospices. (Hauerwas (1998: 131)).

Islam also tends to take a strong stance against euthanasia and assisted suicide. The prohibition on the intentional taking of life is emphasized in much Muslim writing. There is an emphasis on the idea of life being given on trust by Allah (Khan (2002)) and therefore not being a person's to dispose of as they wish. Allah will and should control when a person will die (Brockopp (2002)). However, the general Muslim view appears to be that this does not require doctors to provide futile treatment in a desperate bid to save someone's life (Khan (2002)).

Key to Buddhist thinking on this issue is the precept not to take life and the virtue of compassion. The Dalai Lama has stated: 'From a Buddhist point of view, if a dying person has any chance of having positive virtuous thoughts, it is important—and there is a purpose—for them to live even just a few minutes longer' (quoted in Anderson (1992: 36)). To Buddhist thought the moment of death and its quality is important. This leads some Buddhist thinkers to support the hospice model of enabling a calm and controlled dying, without active intervention to hasten death. The idea of meeting death mindfully is seen as important. Others argue that Buddhist tradition is in fact tolerant of suicide and euthanasia where doing so enables a person to have a conscious and dignified death (Becker (1990 and)). However, the majority of Buddhist opinion appears to be that the high value of life placed by Buddhism cannot support euthanasia (Hughes and Keown (1995) and Keown (1999)).

There are two main views on euthanasia that can be found in Hindu thought. Perhaps the majority view is that disturbing the cycle of birth and rebirth by ending a life should be avoided. Indeed this same point would argue against keeping a person on a life-support machine for an unnecessary amount of time. Other Hindus regard ending a painful life as a fulfilment of a moral obligation and therefore not objectionable. Hinduism does in some circumstances allow suicide: prayopavesa. This is only permissible under strict conditions, including that non-violent means of suicide are used. Starvation would be permitted, but not shooting oneself.

FEMINIST PERSPECTIVES

Dying in relationship

Perhaps surprisingly there has been relatively little written on end of life issues from an explicitly feminist perspective. There is, of course, no consistent feminist line opposing or supporting euthanasia and feminists will adopt many of the arguments already mentioned. The distinctively feminist contributions to the debate include the following:

- Wolf (1996: 283) has argued that those factors which are likely to result in requests for suicide (depression, poor pain relief, concern about being a burden on one's family) are more likely to fall on women than men (see further Biggs (2003) and George (2007)). She is concerned therefore that legalizing euthanasia would mean that women would be particularly likely to seek death (see also Callahan (1995), although the evidence from Holland and Oregon does not show significantly higher numbers of women than men seeking death; but contrast Carmel's (2001) study of Israeli women). Wolf is concerned also that physicians, in encouraging patients to consider euthanasia or suicide, may be affected by gendered perceptions. For example, a physician may regard a woman's concern that she will place an impossible burden on her husband as carrying more weight than a husband suggesting that he will be a burden on his wife, because it is seen as a woman's role to be carrying out caring tasks. Others have expressed concerns that women may find it particularly hard to persuade clinicians that they be permitted to utilize euthanasia (Prado (1998)). There is some evidence that generally in medical practice women suffer higher levels of pain, but receive less effective treatment (Hoffmann and Tarzian (2001)).

- Feminist writers have been concerned with the emphasis placed on autonomy by those supporting euthanasia. It has been argued that a woman's request to die must be considered in the context of her history, her intimate relationships, the resources available to her, and the level of care being offered. In the light of these her choices may be profoundly constrained and it cannot be assumed that a wish for death is a fully autonomous choice. Wolf talks of the danger that 'We construct a story that clothes the patient's terrible despair in the glorious mantle of "rights" ' (Wolf (1996: 300)). A call for euthanasia should lead, she suggests to a redoubling of efforts to provide effective pain relief, not acceding to the request. Others have promoted a relational based autonomy, requiring decisions to be considered in the context of a society made up of interdependent people engaging in overlapping enterprises. This led Donchin (2000) to suggest that any death decisions should be made in the context of the family.

- Feminists have also emphasized that much of the writing of legal responses to death have ignored deaths that can have a particularly powerful impact on women: abortion, miscarriage, and neonatal death are often downplayed and there is little support for women affected in these ways (Field, Hockey, and Small (1997: 1–2)).

- Feminists also emphasize that much of the work for caring for the dying is undertaken by women (Biggs (1998: 284). In the heat of the euthanasia debate, the value and significance of this work is often overlooked.

6 Suicide

Durkheim has defined suicide in this way:

> The term suicide is applied to any death which is a direct or indirect result of a positive or negative act accomplished by the victim himself, which he knows should produce this result [death].[388]

As already mentioned, the present law on suicide is that suicide and attempted suicide are not criminal offences, but it is an offence to aid, abet, counsel, and procure

---

[388] Durkheim (1952).

suicide.[389] This leaves suicide rather ambiguous in legal terms.[390] Is there a right to commit suicide? If suicide is lawful can a person lawfully intervene and prevent a person committing suicide?

The legal position appears to be that there is not a right to commit suicide[391] and (therefore) a person can lawfully intervene to prevent a person who is about to commit suicide. The fact that suicide is not a criminal offence does not mean that the law approves of suicide.[392] It is interesting to note that in an inquest there is a presumption against suicide unless that is proved as the cause of death. This indicates an acceptance that a verdict of suicide carries moral opprobrium of some kind.[393] In *R v Collins and another ex p Brady*[394] it was held to be lawful for the prison service to force feed a prisoner who was on hunger strike. The basis of the ruling was that in relation to his eating Brady was not competent. But Maurice Kay J added that a prisoner detained in a secure unit, even if competent, could be force fed. Indeed he mooted the possibility that the prison service would be required to do so. He concluded by saying 'it would seem to me to be a matter for deep regret if the law has developed to a point in this area where the rights of a patient count for everything and other ethical values and institutional integrity count for nothing'.[395] More significantly in *Reeves v Commissioner of the Police of the Metropolis*[396] the House of Lords held that the prison services were under a duty to prevent a sane prisoner committing suicide.[397] Indeed the Commissioner was liable to pay damages to the family of a prisoner who they did not prevent committing suicide.[398] However, the amount of damages was reduced because the prisoner was 50 per cent to blame applying the doctrine of contributory negligence. It is not clear whether the decision applies in other circumstances. Their Lordships saw the duty arising particularly because of the high degree of control that the prison authorities had over the prisoner. It does not, for example, follow that a police officer who came across a person committing suicide in a park would be under a duty to intervene, although there is little doubt the police officer would be permitted to do so.

The most recent decision looking at legal responses to suicide is the following:

KEY CASE   Re Z (An Adult: Capacity) [2004] EWHC 2817

Mrs Z, aged 65, suffered from cerebella ataxia. This was an incurable and terminal condition which caused her to become increasingly disabled. She had become determined that she wanted to commit suicide. She was no longer physically capable of killing herself and so wanted to travel to Switzerland

---

[389] However s 2(4) requires the consent of the DPP to commence any prosecution for assisting suicide which might imply an acceptance by Parliament that there will be cases where assisting suicide should be permitted.

[390] See the discussion in Tur (2003a) and the reply to that article in Calvert-Smith (2003).

[391] *R (On the Application of Pretty) v DPP* [2002] 1 All ER 1 at para 106 (Lord Hope).

[392] *R v Inner W London Coroner ex p De Luca* [1988] 3 All ER 414.

[393] *Re Davies (Deceased)* [1967] 1 All ER 688.   [394] (2000) 58 BMLR 137.

[395] Para 73. In *Hyde v Tameside AHA* The Times, 16 April 1981 Lord Denning claimed that there was a state interest in preventing suicide.

[396] [2000] AC 360.

[397] See also *Selfe v Ilford and District Hospital Management Committee* (1979) 114 Sol Jo 935 for a discussion of a hospital's responsibilities towards suicidal patients.

[398] Wheat (2000).

where assisted suicide was permitted. Her husband, Mr Z, made the travel arrangements and planned to travel with her. When the local authority learned of their plans, they became concerned. Mrs Z's social worker believed Mrs Z to be competent but also was concerned that Mr Z would be committing the criminal offence of aiding and abetting suicide by making the arrangements. The local authority therefore applied to court, seeking to invoke its inherent jurisdiction to prevent Mr Z from removing Mrs Z from the jurisdiction. An interim injunction was ordered until a full hearing could take place.

By the time of the hearing there was evidence which established that Mrs Z had legal capacity to make her own decisions. Justice Hedley lifted the interim injunctions. He held that in cases of this kind the duties of the local authority were:

(i) to investigate the position of a vulnerable adult to consider what was her true position and intention;

(ii) to consider whether she was legally competent to make and carry out her decision and intention;

(iii) to consider whether any other (and if so, what) influence may be operating on her position and intention, and to ensure that she has all relevant information and knows all available options;

(iv) to consider whether she was legally competent to make and carry out her decision and intention;

(v) to consider whether to invoke the inherent jurisdiction of the High Court so that the question of competence could be judicially investigated and determined;

(vi) in the event of the adult not being competent, to provide all such assistance as may be reasonably required both to determine and give effect to her best interests;

(vii) in the event of the adult being competent to allow her in any lawful way to give effect to her decision, although that should not preclude the giving of advice or assistance in accordance with what are perceived to be her best interests;

(viii) where there are reasonable grounds to suspect that the commission of a criminal offence may be involved, to draw that to the attention of the police;

(ix) in very exceptional circumstances, to invoke the jurisdiction of the court under the Local Government Act 1972, section 222 (which enables a local authority to bring proceedings to a court in relation to inhabitant in their area).

Mrs Z was therefore free to go to Switzerland. Justice Hedley stated that, once it was clear that an individual was competent, then the local authority should not interfere, even if that individual was about to commit suicide. As Hedley J put it, having decided that Mrs Z was competent her 'best interests are no business of mine'. Whether Mr Z should be prosecuted for committing an offence was within the jurisdiction of the Crown Prosecution Service.

On the general issue of suicide he explained:

This case affords no basis for trying to ascertain the court's views about the rights or wrongs of suicide, assisted or otherwise. This case simply illustrates that a competent person is entitled to take their own decisions on these matters and that that person alone bears responsibility for any decision so taken. That is the essence of what some will regard as God-given free will and what others will describe as the innate right of self-autonomy (para 21).

The ethical position is less straightforward. The argument in favour of recognizing a right to kill oneself goes back to the principle of autonomy already discussed in this context. Opponents of such a claim have two lines of defence. The first is to accept that theoretically there is a right to commit suicide, but argue that few people who attempt suicide are competent at that point in time.[399] Most are in such a state of despair, or mental illness, that they lack the capacity to make a full, free, and informed choice.[400] The act can therefore be regarded as *prima facie* the act of an incompetent person and therefore others can intervene to protect the individual.[401] Wheat argues: 'It is no interference with autonomy to be given time to make a decision after considered reflection, and to be given the opportunity to investigate the possible alleviation of conditions which are making life intolerable'.[402] A second argument is that even if it is the wish of the person to die at that time, if that wish is no more than a short-term wish out of line with their general views on life, it might be argued that it should not be respected as the wish of an autonomous person.[403] However, it may be replied that there can be cases where a person has made a careful clearly thought-out decision to commit suicide and they cannot be said to be incompetent.

One way the right to commit suicide may be rejected is to argue that an autonomy right in relation to suicide is outweighed by other state interests. To some suicide should be regarded as an immoral act because it involves a conscious rejection of the value of human personhood.[404] Gorsuch[405] argues that suicide is not a harmless act; it leaves behind distraught relatives and friends. The harm caused to others justifies a restriction on people's autonomy. There are also practical concerns that permitting assistance of suicide may permit pressure to be put on vulnerable people to commit suicide. It might also provide a convenient way that would-be murderers could disguise their crime.

REALITY CHECK

The official statistics In the UK there were 5,671 suicides in the year 2005. This accounted for one per cent of all deaths (National Statistics (2007d)). One person dies every two hours from suicide in England (DoH (2002f)). The most common methods were hanging, strangulation, or suffocation. However, 50 per cent of women suicides use overdosing. Only 83 people committed suicide with firearms. The death toll from suicide is double the death toll from road traffic accidents.

Unofficial statistics The figures above are the official statistics and it has been estimated that the true suicide rate is 50–60 per cent higher than the official figure. Coroners are reluctant to record a verdict of suicide unless it is clear that that is what happened. Brock and Griffiths (2003): in 2001 open verdicts accounted for 28 and 38 per cent of suicides for men and women respectively. It has been estimated that there were 140,000 suicide attempts. One in five people who attempt suicide will try again, of whom 10 per cent will succeed.

The Government response Suicide has been recognized as a major public health issue. The Department of Health has issued a programme, *Saving Lives; Our Healthier Nation* designed to reduce the suicide rate as at 1996 by 20 per cent by 2010. By 2006 a 7.4 per cent reduction had been obtained (National Institute for Mental Health in England (2007)).

---

[399] Hill (1994) provides one person's carefully explained reasons for committing suicide.
[400] DoH (1992) suggests that there is 80 times the level of suicide among the mentally ill than the general population. See *R v Collins and Ashworth Authority ex p Brady* (2000) 8 Lloyds Rep Med 355 where it was permissible to force feed a prisoner who had gone on hunger strike but was too mentally ill to be able to make a rational decision.
[401] Hill (1991).   [402] Wheat (2000: 208).   [403] See Kant (1993).
[404] Resnicoff (1999). For a strong case against the right to commit suicide see Velleman (1999).
[405] Gorsuch (2000).

Trends in suicide It is noticeable that 75 per cent of all suicides are committed by males. Research indicates that 70 per cent of suicides suffer from depression. Other indicators of suicide are drug and alcohol misuse, being unmarried, homelessness, and being imprisoned. The rate of suicide among young Asian women is three times that of young white British women (DoH (1999c)).

The picture worldwide In 2000 one million people worldwide died from suicide. Ten to 20 times that number attempted suicide. The rate of suicide varies dramatically across countries from 51.6 per 1,000 population in Lithuania to 4.2 in Paraguay. The United Kingdom at 9.2 would be in the middle of a table of suicide rate. The WHO pinpoints being male, depression, homelessness, schizophrenia, childhood abuse, and sexual orientation as indicators of suicide.

7 Physician-assisted suicide

Physician-assisted suicide involves the giving of assistance by a physician to enable her or his patient to commit suicide.[406] Typically this might involve the provision of drugs to be taken by the patient in such quantities as to enable suicide. A more modern example is to provide a computer operated system by which an individual can direct a computer connected to medical apparatus to administer lethal quantities of drugs.[407] At present it is an offence under the Suicide Act, section 2(1) to aid, abet, counsel, or procure suicide, as discussed above. It should be added that the exact line between assisted suicide and murder is unclear.[408] Michael Freeman[409] has asked whether placing a lethal dosage of medicine in someone's mouth or pushing it to the back of their throat is assisted suicide or murder? If it is not possible to draw a clear line between the two, can a clear legal distinction be drawn? One response to such argument is that often in law it is necessary to draw sharp distinctions and sometimes, wherever the line is drawn, cases can be produced on either side of the line to suggest that distinction is arbitrary. However, such an argument could be made wherever the line between authorized and non-authorized killing/assistance in killing is drawn.

In ethical terms, assisting suicide is regarded by some as less controversial than euthanasia.[410] In particular because it is the victim's decision to commit suicide there can be less doubt that the victim genuinely consented.[411] To some, assisted suicide is permissible based on the right of the patient to commit suicide and does not involve another person.[412] The supplier of the means of suicide is not a direct cause of death in a way a person who injects a lethal drug is.[413] Beauchamp and Childress[414] suggest that it should be accepted that assisted suicide should not be simply permitted in every case where a patient wishes to die. However they suggest that assisted suicide is justified if the following nine conditions are satisfied:

(1) A voluntary request by a competent patient.

(2) An ongoing patient–physician relationship.

---

[406] See Dieterle (2007) for a discussion of the issues raised by physician-assisted suicide.
[407] Biggs (2001: 62).   [408] See Meyers and Mason (1999).   [409] Freeman (2002).
[410] Keown (2002) is sceptical about the difference between physician-assisted suicide and euthanasia.
[411] Deigh (1998). Biggs and Diesfeld (1995) look at the link between depression and suicidal desire.
[412] Lewis (2001) provides a useful discussion of such claims.
[413] Dworkin, Frey, and Bok (1998).   [414] Beauchamp and Childress (2003: 151).

(3) Mutual and informed decision making by patient and physician.

(4) A supportive yet critical and probing environment of decision making.

(5) A considered rejection of alternatives.

(6) Structured consultation with other parties in medicine.

(7) A patient's expression of a durable preference for death.

(8) Unacceptable suffering by the patient.

(9) Use of a means that is as painless and comfortable as possible.

One of the main concerns with a general practice or policy on physician-assisted suicide is that serious abuses might occur. In particular a general policy could be open to abuse of the system by unscrupulous persons. Opponents might point to the activities of Jack Kevorkian, whom the tabloid press have labelled 'Dr Death'. His well-publicized 'death machine' is set up to enable a patient to press a button which would trigger the machine to inject the patient with a drug which caused death. The concern over his practice is that some claim there is inadequate means to ensure that the patient had genuinely decided to die. His practice has received much condemnation,[415] yet also demonstrates that there are people who feel traditional medical practices fail to provide them with the services and supported needed. Clearly Kevorkian was seen as offering a more attractive alternative to that offered by traditional medicine.[416]

8 Incompetent patients

Where an issue arises concerning life-saving treatment and an incompetent person, the first question now is whether the individual has issued an effective advance directive stating that they do not want to receive treatment. If they have, section 24 of the Mental Capacity Act 2005 requires a doctor to abide by that, even if so doing will lead to the death of the patient. An effective advance directive cannot, in this context, be overruled in the name of pursing the patient's best interests. Where, however, the advance directive is ambiguous or there are doubts over its validity it is likely the courts will not give effect to it, where to do so would lead to death.[417] Where an effective advance directive states that the patient does want to receive treatment then following the decision in *R (on the Application of Burke) v GMC*,[418] unless the case is exceptional, the life-saving treatment should be given. An exception would be where giving the treatment requested in the advance directive would kill the patient, or be ineffective but very painful.

If there is no advance directive the law is governed by the Mental Capacity Act 2005. In section 62 the Act makes it clear that it is not intended to change the law on homicide or assisted suicide. Nothing in the Act will authorize a medical professional to do an act which intentionally causes death. The Act makes special provision to deal with 'life-sustaining treatment' defined as 'treatment which in a view of a person providing health care for the person concerned is necessary to sustain life'.[419] When considering such treatment, the key question is the best interests of the patient. This is defined in section 4. The normal approach to ascertaining best interests will be used. That is discussed in Chapter 4. So the views of the doctor will be relevant but will not be determinative.

---

[415] Beauchamp and Childress (2003: 149). He is currently serving a sentence for second degree murder.
[416] McMahan (2002).   [417] Bartlett (2005).   [418] [2005] 3 FCR 169.   [419] S 4(10).

Assuming that the life-sustaining treatment will be regarded as serious treatment for the purposes of section 37, the independent advocate will become involved (see Chapter 4). When considering the best interests of the patient, section 4(5) makes an important point about what factors a doctor should consider:

> Where the determination relates to life-sustaining treatment he must not, in considering whether the treatment is in the best interests of the person concerned, be motivated by a desire to bring about his death.

This reflects the approach of the law that although it may be permissible for a doctor to do an act which she or he foresees may causes death, she or he must not do an act for the purpose of causing death.[420]

If a lasting power of attorney has been made then the attorney can make the decision relating to life-saving treatment, but only if the appointment specifically states that the attorney is to have the decision-making power over such treatment.[421] Court-appointed deputies are required to consent to life-sustaining treatment.[422]

Critics of the current law have made the following points:

(1) The decision places too much weight on the distinction between an act and an omission. Under the present law if the treatment or its withdrawal is classified as an act then the *actus reus* of murder is made out, even if the doctors could have claimed to be acting in accordance with good medical practice. As we have seen, the distinction between acts and omissions is complex. Critics argue that switching off a life-support machine should be regarded as an act; it is after all a positive movement of the doctor. Indeed the House of Lords in *Bland* accepted that if an 'interloper' switched off the life support machine, causing the patient's death, that could be regarded as the *actus reus* of murder.[423] It seems to some odd that the same behaviour can be regarded as an act when done by one person, but an omission if done by another.

(2) The diagnosis of PVS is controversial and difficult.[424] Notably if an application is made to court it is necessary to produce the evidence of two experts in the diagnosis and prognosis of PVS.[425] There are reports of misdiagnosis and even stories of remarkable recovery from the condition.[426] For example, Hillsborough victim Andrew Devine emerged after five years and was able to count and communicate with a buzzer.[427] One study in 1996 found that 43 per cent of PVS cases had been misdiagnosed.[428] However, others claim that it is not justifiable to keep patients alive in the faint hope they may recover. We do not, for example, continue to search for those lost at sea even where there is a slight chance they may be recovered.[429] Two leading commentators have said that the post-*Bland* case law shows 'a disturbing relaxation of the criteria for the diagnosis of the permanent vegetative state and a move towards quality of life standards rather than irrevocable and absolute loss of cognitive function'.[430]

(3) The withdrawal of tube-feeding and hydration has been heavily criticized by some. In *Bland*, their Lordships regarded tube-feeding as medical treatment, rather

---

[420] The provision is discussed in Coggon (2007).   [421] Mental Capacity Act 2005, s 11(8).
[422] Mental Capacity Act 2005, s 20(5).   [423] Kennedy (1977).
[424] *Re A (Adult: Incompetent)* (1997) 38 BMLR 11.
[425] *Practice Note: Official Solicitor; Declaratory Proceedings: Medical and Welfare Decisions for Adults who Lack Capacity* [2001] 2 FLR 158.
[426] Andrews et al (1996).   [427] Dyer (1997c).   [428] Andrews et al (1996).
[429] Brock (1992: 240).   [430] Meyers and Mason (1999: 274).

than basic personal care, and therefore that it could legitimately be withdrawn.[431] The BMA has issued guidance on withholding and withdrawing life-prolonging medical treatment.[432] The guidance takes the view that the artificial provision of food and water counts as medical treatment which can therefore be withdrawn under the *Bland* ruling (if it no longer promotes the best interests of the patient).[433] Keown has argued that although the insertion of the gastrostomy tube would have involved a medical procedure, the pouring of the food down it did not require medical skill and would be analogous to spooning food into someone's mouth.

The distinction between basic and medical care is controversial. The argument that appeared to be accepted in *Bland* was that, even if it is appropriate to remove medication from a patient on the basis that that is in the patient's best interests, it is not appropriate to withdraw basic care, such as feeding or cleaning. The argument in favour of the distinction includes the suggestion that to permit death by starvation shows a serious lack of regard for the patient's comfort and dignity. Further, our society regards starvation as symbolically horrific. Even if there is no logical or moral basis for it, feeding the hungry is seen as a basic human obligation.[434] There are also dangers that permitting the withdrawal of sustenance will lead to a slippery slope, because it will permit the death of a person, not from their illness, but from the lack of basic provision. In other words non-dying patients could be left to starve to death. This is a very different thing from letting a patient die from the disease from which she or he is suffering.

Critics of the distinction[435] argue that the distinction between treatment and basic care is impossible to draw. Take feeding, perhaps a classic example of basic care. If feeding is only possible through machinery or by the application of medical skill, does it become medical treatment?[436] Certainly to the House of Lords in *Bland* there was no distinction to be drawn between the provision of foods by artificial means and medical treatment.[437] Whatever the difficulties in drawing the distinction, to many people there is an intuitive feeling that letting a patient starve to death cannot be seen as proper medical treatment.[438] There is also a concern that the emotive phrase 'starve' is misleading. Beauchamp and Childress state that: 'Malnutrition is not identical with hunger; dehydration is not identical with thirst; and starvation is very different from acute dehydration in a medical setting.'[439] It should also be noted that in a few cases artificial feeding and hydration can worsen a patient's medical condition.[440]

(4) Keown has also criticized the reasoning in *Bland* that because Tony Bland was not capable of experiencing any benefits, he had no interests. He argues a person can benefit through having money put into their bank account even though they are unaware of it. It could not, he says, be said to be in Tony Bland's interests to be used as a sideboard. To

---

[431] Finnis (1993) is highly critical of this reasoning.
[432] BMA (1999). See also GMC (2007) para 81.　　[433] Para 1.2.
[434] Carson (1986) and Callahan (1983).
[435] Beauchamp and Childress (2003: 126).
[436] Keown (1997a) argues this cannot be treatment: 'what is it treating?' he asks.
[437] *Practice Note: Official Solicitor; Declaratory Proceedings: Medical and Welfare Decisions for Adults who Lack Capacity* [2001] 2 FLR 158 para 3. BMA (1999) suggests that artificial nutrition and ventilation can lawfully be withdrawn if they no longer benefit a patient.
[438] See *A Hospital v SW* [2007] EWHC 425 (Fam) where the argument that withdrawal of hydration and nuitrition breached a patient's article 3 rights was rejected.
[439] Beauchamp and Childress (2003: 127).
[440] See the expert evidence given in *R (Burke) v GMC* [2005] 3 FCR 169.

say he has no interests is wrong.[441] However, Keown suggests the better way to reason this point was that this treatment did not provide him with a benefit.[442]

(5) Some commentators[443] have argued that the courts need to be more open and accept that the legal treatment of PVS patients after *Bland* is about sensible use of resources and ending the strain on families and friends which justify the decisions in *Bland*.[444] Morgan, perhaps a little brutally, states, '. . . unpalatable as it is, we must face the fact that Tony Bland is more expensive to maintain in PVS than he is to bury. Fiscally, at least, we save by deciding that Tony Bland has no interests worth further protection, that he is, to all intents and purposes, a wasting asset wasting assets'.[445]

(6) Some commentators argue that PVS sufferers should be regarded as dead. They are unable to experience the things that make us human. Without consciousness they may be alive but they have lost what makes them human.[446] McMahan[447] suggests a PVS patient should be treated in the same way as a corpse. There is none of the goods of life for such a person in the future.

Moving on from PVS patients, what should be done in cases where the patient is incompetent and unable to decide for her or himself whether to die? To opponents of voluntary euthanasia the issue is straightforward; it will be prohibited for anyone to intentionally kill such a patient, just as it would be if they were competently requesting the treatment. But supporters of euthanasia would divide on the issue. Here are some of the responses that could be taken:

(1) The patient should receive such treatment or non-treatment as would best promote the interests of that patient. A patient should not be penalized just because they are not able to make decisions for themselves. If a doctor's assessment of a patient's suffering is such that it is in the patient's interests to stop the suffering, she or he should go ahead and hasten death. In deciding what is in a patient's best interests there is some dispute over what factors can be taken into account: clearly the level of pain and suffering endured,[448] but what about more abstract concepts such as emotional distress? Opponents of such a view claim that here, at last, we see the heart of the argument in favour of euthanasia: some lives are not worth living.[449] They deny it can ever be said that death is in a person's best interests.

(2) The patient should receive such treatment as the patient would have wanted had the patient been competent.[450] This approach asks what the patient would have wanted had she or he been competent. This may involve looking at the ethical, religious, or expressed views of the patient.[451]

(3) Some supporters of euthanasia may take a high view of the importance of sanctity of life and find the balancing of the importance attached to sanctity and the importance

---

[441] See also Boyle (1997).

[442] Keown (2002: 220); Jennet (1997).

[443] Alldridge and Morgan (1992); Wade (2001).

[444] Biggs (2002: 42); Harris (1995a: 18).   [445] Morgan (2001: 220).

[446] Veatch (1993).   [447] McMahan (2002).

[448] *In the Matter of Claire Conroy* (1985) 486 A 2d 1209.

[449] Boddington and Podpadec (2002).

[450] Lords Goffand Mustill in *Airedale NHS Trust v Bland* [1993] 1 All ER 821 went out of their way to reject the substituted judgment test (872–3, 892).

[451] *Re Jobes* (1987) 529 A 2d 434 Garibaldi J.

attached to autonomy a difficult one to strike. They may feel that in a case where the patient's wishes are unknown, sanctity of life should rule the day.

(4) The decision should be taken by the relatives of the person.[452]

At the heart of the Mental Capacity Act 2005 is the question whether or not the treatment is in the best interests of the patient.[453] If it is not then it can be withdrawn. This is often put in terms of the question: 'Is the medical treatment futile?'[454] Sometimes this can be a straightforward question. To give a patient medicine which has no effect will be futile. To give antibiotics to someone suffering from a virus will be futile because antibiotics do not affect viruses.[455] A treatment may also be futile if it has an effect, but that is negative (for example, all it does is increase pain). But the concept of futility is also used where the medicine has an effect. For example, some argue to give medicine to someone suffering PVS may be futile, even if it has an effect on them, if they are unaware of that effect. However, the question: does the medicine have a net benefit? is controversial. Is it of net benefit if the medicine reduces pain, but hastens death? The concern is that to define futility in net terms leads to an irresolvable conflict of views and may not produce a useful concept. In an attempt to resolve this some commentators suggest that futility be defined in terms of reaching a patient's goals.[456] However, this produces a problem in defining the patient's goals. The issue is further complicated once financial considerations are taken into account. If a medicine has a very low chance of success does the fact it is very cheap or very expensive bear on the question whether it is regarded as futile? However, in considering the question of futility it is important to remember that we must ask what the goal is that the treatment is proposing to reach. So a treatment may be futile in relation to one goal (eg pain relief); but not futile to another (keeping a patient alive).[457]

The BMA[458] have listed the following factors to consider when deciding whether prolonging treatment would provide an overall benefit to the patient:

(1) The patient's own wishes and values (where these can be ascertained).

(2) Clinical judgment about the effectiveness of the proposed treatment, including its likely benefits and harms.

(3) The likelihood of the patient experiencing severe unmanageable pain or suffering.

(4) The level of awareness the individual has of her or his existence and surroundings as demonstrated by, for example, an ability to interact with others (however expressed), the capacity for self directed action, or the ability to take control of any aspect of her or his life.

(5) The likelihood and extent of any degree of improvement in the patient's condition if treatment is provided.

(6) Whether the invasiveness of treatment is justified in the circumstances.

(7) The views of the parents, if the patient is a child. .

---

[452] Boozang (1997). Although see the exception in *Re R (Adult: Medical Treatment)* (1996) 31 BMLR 127 where the consent of parents was required before antibiotics were withdrawn from a severely disabled adult.
[453] Winter and Cohen (1999) state that 70% of deaths in intensive care follow a withdrawal of care.
[454] See Mohindra (2007); Janssens et al (2002); Ardagh (2000) and Strasser (1998) for useful discussions of the concept.
[455] Strasser (1998).   [456] Gampel (2006).
[457] Mohindra (2007).   [458] BMA (2004: 356–7).

(8) The views of people who are close to the patient, especially near relatives, partners, and carers, about what the patient is likely to see as beneficial.

There is also the question of appropriate treatment of severely ill newborns. Some commentators have supported the approach taken by the courts in permitting the withdrawal of treatment in cases of very severe disability, suggesting that there is a widespread concern that medicine has become overly interventionist and expending great efforts to keep alive those whose lives will be short and full of pain is an example of inappropriately aggressive medicine. Jonsen and Garland have suggested that aggressive intervention should not be permitted in any of the following circumstances:

(1) The child is unable to survive infancy.

(2) The child is unable to live without severe pain.

(3) The child is unable to participate, at least minimally, in 'the human experience'.[459]

They suggest that to keep severely disabled newborns alive in such cases would be to infringe the principle of non-maleficence. Childress and Beauchamp, broadly supporting this approach, suggest that, for example, children suffering from Tay-Sachs disease, which causes spastic behaviour and dementia, leading to death by age three or four, should be allowed to die. However, Down's syndrome would not be a sufficient reason to allow the newborn to die they suggest. A more extreme view is that 'the loss of life for newly born infants is, other things being equal, much less significant than the loss of life for an older child or adult'.[460] Such an approach suggests that a newborn infant is not yet a person in the full sense of the term, and that therefore we can require less justification for killing or denying treatment than we would in the case of child or adult. This has led some to suggest that, if a parent does not want to raise a disabled child and would prefer the child to die, this provides a good reason for not providing treatment because it would be wrong to force a parent to raise a severely disabled child.[461] However, such an argument overlooks the point that parents are free to ask the local authority to provide care for their child (eg by adoption) and are therefore not compelled to look after her or him.

To others, the law's approach infringes upon the principle of the sanctity of life and the equal valuing of all lives. A short life is still a life to be treasured and valued, and should not readily be discarded as not useful. Critics of the law sometimes warn that there is a danger of such an approach slipping into eugenics, by too easily disposing of those who are not useful to society. Certainly the present law on the treatment of newborns can be criticized for leaving too much to the judgement of parents and clinicians and not ensuring there is an objective assessment of the best treatment for the baby.[462]

9 Refusal of treatment

English law makes it clear that a competent person can refuse treatment even if without the treatment she or he will die.[463] To force such treatment on someone could amount to a battery or a tort. Simply put, we do not have a duty to keep on

---

[459] Jonsen and Garland (1976).   [460] Kuhse and Singer (1985: 151).
[461] Kuhse and Singer (1985).   [462] McLean (1999: 136).
[463] *Re T (Adult: Refusal of Treatment)* [1992] 4 All ER 649 at 652–3; *Airedale NHS Trust v Bland* [1993] 1 All ER 821 at 860 (Lord Keith), 866 (Lord Goff) 881 (Lord Browne-Wilkinson and Mustill (889); *Re AK* [2001] 1 FLR 129.

living.[464] This is as true for pregnant women as anyone else.[465] What are the ethical issues surrounding the decision of a person to forgo medical treatment? A variety of views can be taken:

(1) A competent patient has an absolute right to refuse treatment. This appears to be the position taken by the law. In *S v St George's*[466] the woman was entitled to refuse treatment even though without it she and her unborn child would die. Although the law respects the right to a patient to refuse treatment, it is notable in *Re B*[467] how carefully the court considered the issue of competence.[468] This could be supported on the basis that given the gravity of the consequences we have to ensure that the patient is competent. Especially in an emergency case, there is an argument for performing the necessary treatment and then, with the luxury of time, reconsider the appropriate way of treating the patient.[469]

(2) For some commentators the key ethical issue is whether refusing necessary medical treatment can be regarded as suicide. If it is suicide then there are ethical objections to it, but if it is not then there are not. One view is that the intention of the patient provides the key. If the patient refuses treatment because she or he wants to die then this is suicide, but if the patient does not act with the purpose of killing her or himself (even if death is foreseen) then the act is permissible.[470] A patient who refuses a blood transfusion for religious reasons may be said not to intend her or his death even though she or he may have foreseen it as an inevitable consequence of her or his actions.[471] Clearly in this distinction the doctrine of double effect is being relied upon.

(3) Some commentators argue that the law should be more willing to override the refusal of a competent person of life-saving treatment. To blindly follow the views of a competent patient is to give too much heed to the 'cult of self-determination'.[472] Although to respect the refusal of the patient may be to recognize her or his autonomy, in so doing we ignore other important values, such as the importance attached to life. The courts' response to such arguments has been that the rights of the competent individual to self-determination will normally outweigh the interests of the state in promoting the sanctity of life.[473] In other words the law does not ignore the other values in play in these questions; it simply attaches greater significance to autonomy than to the other values. Particular concerns arise where a person is borderline competent.[474] To return to the scenario of a teenager disappointed in love, if he had a septic cut but refused treatment, should we really stand by and let him die? Indeed it has been suggested that the courts do, in effect, carry out an assessment of the reasonableness of the patient's decision, and where the decision is thought utterly unreasonable then the patient is declared incompetent.[475]

(4) David Shaw[476] has argued that the current law is based on an illogical distinction: euthanasia is not permitted, but patients are entitled to reject life-support. He argues that the body should be seen as a life-support machine for the brain. In the same way

---

[464] Hale (1996: 87).　　[465] *St George's Health Care Trust v S* [1998] 3 All ER 673.
[466] *St George's Health Care Trust v S* [1998] 3 All ER 673.
[467] [2002] EWHC 429.　　[468] Stauch (2002).　　[469] Hale (2003: 7).
[470] Price (1996) argues that under this definition there would be very few suicides.
[471] Gorsuch (2000).　　[472] Mason and Laurie (2006: 552).
[473] *St George's Health Care Trust v S* [1998] 3 All ER 673. Wicks (2001) argues that this is reinforced by the Human Rights Act 1998.
[474] *Re JT* [1998] 1 FLR 48.　　[475] Coleman and Drake (2002).　　[476] Shaw (2007).

that a competent patient has the right to refuse life-support from equipment and can demand that it be switched off, a patient should be permitted to refuse life-support from their body and demand that it be 'switched off'. This view is based on a controversial understanding of the body and requires a separation between brain and bodies which some commentators are unable to accept.

10 Advance directives

Advance directives have been discussed in Chapter 4 and you should read the material on them there. The Mental Capacity Act 2005, section 24 makes it clear that where a person has made an effective advance directive stating that she or he does not consent to treatment then it would be unlawful for a doctor to give that treatment. This is so even if without the treatment, the patient will die. However, an advance directive cannot be made which requires doctors to act in a particular way. In other words an advance directive can state that if the patient is in a certain condition, she or he should not be offered further treatment, but cannot authorize doctors to give the patient a lethal injection. As we saw in Chapter 4 where the advance directive concerns life or death matters, the court will want to be convinced that the directive is effective.

11 Palliative care and hospices

It might be thought from some of the discussion to date that the dying can expect nothing but pain and discomfort. Opponents of euthanasia reject such a view and encourage the use of hospices or palliative care.[477] These emphasize the importance of dying well with a peaceful, contented death and reject attempts to induce an early death by euthanasia. Palliative care emphasizes pain relief and psychological and emotional support to assist in the last stages of life. There is evidence that even those who are suffering appalling disabilities or pain can enjoy life and do no not wish to die through euthanasia.[478] Supporters of palliative care claim that apart from in a very few cases, pain can be controlled to endurable levels.[479] Where pain is utterly unbearable there is always the option of sedation.

The aim of palliative care is to put the patient at the heart of care and to seek to treat the whole person: not just their physical needs, but also their emotional, spiritual, and psychological needs. The aim is to travel with the patient on the journey of the last few days of their life.[480] Palliative care focuses not just on the patient, but her or his family as well.[481] The World Health Organization has described palliative care as:

the active, total care of patients whose disease is not responsive to curative treatment. Control of pain, other symptoms and psychological, social and spiritual problems is paramount. The goal of palliative care is the achievement of the best qualify of life for patients and families.[482]

[477] Have and Clark (2002) argue that the notions of euthanasia and palliative care are generally regarded as incompatible.
[478] Gardner et al (1985). [479] Moreland and Rae (2000).
[480] Schotsmans (2002) discusses the importance of relational care in the context of palliative work.
[481] Gilley (2000) emphasizes the need to assist the partners, relatives and friends of the dying.
[482] Cited Biggs (2001: 38).

A group of European specialists have suggested four goals for palliative care: achieving the best quality of life for patients and relatives; the relief of suffering; enabling the patient to have a 'good death'; and to prevent euthanasia.[483] However, as they admit, these goals may be in conflict and they are rather vague.[484] What is a 'good death', for example, is very much a matter of opinion and for some it requires the use of euthanasia.

The existence of hospice care is often emphasized by those seeking to oppose euthanasia. But to some the provision of hospice care is all well and good, but is of little relevance to the debate over euthanasia. As the leading figure in Brian Clark's play *Whose Life is it Anyway?* states:

> I know that our hospitals are wonderful. I know that many people have succeeded in making good lives with appalling handicaps. I'm happy for them and respect and admire them. But each man must make his own decision. And mine is to die quietly and with as much dignity as I can muster.[485]

Similarly Aneurin Bevan is reported to have stated that he would 'rather be kept alive in the efficient if cold altruism of a large hospital than expire in a gush of sympathy in a small one'.[486]

Supporters of the work of hospices argue that palliative care offers the chance for a person to reconcile themselves to the last phase of her or his life and accept death.[487]

Hospices seek to emphasize that essential to being human are vulnerability, interdependence and the need for care.[488] A high premium is placed on the importance of communicating with the patient.[489] As Dame Cecily Saunders, the founder of the hospice movement, has said:

> To talk of accepting death when its approach has become inevitable is not mere resignation or feeble submission on the part of the patient, nor is it defeatism or neglect on the part of the doctor. For both of them it is the very opposite of doing nothing. Our work...is to alter the character of this inevitable process so that it is not seen as a defeat of living but as a positive achievement in dying; an intensely individual achievement for the patient.[490]

In the UK much work is being done to expand the use of palliative care. At present it has been particularly used among cancer patients, although it is hoped to extend it to other patients soon.[491] There is also an increasing recognition that it is inappropriate to restrict palliative care work to 'hospices', but rather palliative care should be a method of caring for those that are dying be they in a hospice, a hospital, a nursing home, or at home.[492] Indeed many dying people wish to be at home and therefore much effort is currently placed on providing community based palliative care.[493] While such wishes are of course understandable the immense strain that can thereby be placed on carers should not be forgotten.[494] There are also calls for palliative care, particularly with its focus on the

---

[483] Clark, ten Have, and Janssens (2002b).   [484] Clark, ten Have, and Janssens (2002b).
[485] Clark (1979: 76).   [486] Quoted in Saunders (2001: 430).
[487] NHS (2001).   [488] Hermsen and Have (2002).
[489] Blyth (1990).   [490] Saunders (1994: 174).
[491] Field and Addington-Hill (2000). For concern that there is still a lack of palliative care for non-cancer patients see NHS Confederation (2005).
[492] Sindell et al (2000).
[493] NICE (2004a: para ES2); Thomas (2003); Clark, ten Have, and Janssens (2002a).
[494] Scambler (2003b).

person's psychological, spiritual, and emotional side, to be offered from the moment of diagnosis, not just when the person enters what may be the final stages of their life.[495]

The sad truth is that where hospices are not used, the standard of care offered to the dying can be poor. In one leading study of elderly people being cared for in nursing homes, the overall standard of care was described as 'inadequate' and there was persistent overuse of unnecessary drugs and underuse of beneficial drugs.[496] Even those being cared for at home can suffer if their carers do not receive appropriate training.[497] The Government has recently accepted that much needs to be done to improve the standards of palliative care in the UK, even though there have been improvements in recent years.[498]

It is, perhaps, too easy to have an idealistic view of the hospice.[499] It has been claimed that although hospices start out with the best of intentions and practice, all too easily they become dominated by routinization, bureaucracy, professional rivalry, and medicalization.[500] Others complain that the idealism of the founders of the palliative care movement has been replaced with bureaucratic battles and professional rivalries.[501]

It might be thought that no one could doubt the benefits of hospices and palliative care services. However, there is in fact only a little evidence that demonstrates that palliative care and hospices have better outcomes for patients or are cost effective.[502] Indeed some have suggested that the unique features claimed for hospice care are in fact found in ordinary hospital wards[503] and some of the 'bad features' said to be found in hospitals can also be found in hospices.[504] One study suggested that there were only minor differences between hospital and hospice care, and that the differences that existed were only made possible by 'entrance policies' of hospices ensuring that 'difficult patients' were not admitted.[505] That said, few people are willing to suggest that hospices provide a less effective service than hospitals. A thorough survey of the literature on palliative care performed by NICE found very slight benefits for patients from palliative care as opposed to traditional methods of caring, but that palliative care was greatly appreciated by patients and their families.[506]

It has also been argued that the attention paid to hospices has taken attention away from the care provided to dying people not able to find a place in a hospice. Hospices, it has been suggested, provide a high- cost service for a favoured minority of patients.[507] However, that can be taken as an argument for extending the work of hospices and palliative care units. A slightly different complaint is that the hospice movement offers a false vision of death. Hope of a dignified death rarely matches reality. Lawton[508] argues that as the body disintegrates towards the end common symptoms are delirium, urinary and faecal incontinence, sores, and discharges. To offer death with dignity may be to suggest a false picture of what death is like. Despite all these concerns, palliative care is

---

[495] Finlay (2001).   [496] Fahey et al (2003).   [497] NICE (2004b).   [498] DoH (2004m).

[499] Logue argues that although hospice care may be appropriate for some it should not be regarded as the ideal solution for everyone.

[500] See James and Field (1992); McNamara (2004); McNamara (2001); Janssens et al (2002) report a survey of European palliative care workers which found that 50% were concerned about over-medicalization in palliative care.

[501] McNamara (2004).

[502] NICE (2004a: ES 13); Higginson et al (2002); Fordham and Dowrick (1999) are critical of the little research that does suggest the effectiveness of palliative care.

[503] Seale and Kelly (1997), although that study found that relatives of dying patients preferred hospices.

[504] Johnston and Abraham (1995).   [505] Seale (1989).   [506] NICE (2004b).

[507] Douglas (1992).   [508] Lawton (2000).

now widely recognized as a better all round treatment for the dying and their families, and its importance is likely to increase in the years ahead.

REALITY CHECK

Hospice care in the UK

In 2003 there were 170 hospices and palliative care centres in England and 216 in the UK (Hospice Information (2004)). There were 59,000 patients in the UK being cared for by them. In 2003, 29,000 patients being cared for in a hospice or palliative care setting died. There are 51 beds per one million adults in the UK. However the availability of beds in hospices and palliative care centres varies in different parts of the country, as do the extent of the services offered. (NICE (2004a: para ES3)). The average length of stay in the hospice is 13.5 days. There are only 332 palliative community based services and 247 palliative day care centres.

At present 95 per cent of hospice care is funded by charities and voluntary organizations. In 2001 less than a quarter of in-patient hospices were managed by the NHS and of the rest, the NHS provided only a third of the total funding (BMA (2004: 367)). The Government has said it now recognizes the importance of palliative care (DoH (2003b)). In 2006 it was announced there was to be a doubling in the amount of money for palliative care (DoH (2006g)). These measures will be designed to reduce inequalities in accessing specialist palliative care (NHS Information Authority (2002)). There still appears to be a wide disparity in the amount of financial support given by the state to hospices (BBC Newsonline 1 June 2006). The NHS contribution varies between 25 and 60 per cent.

12 Reform of the law

There has been a trickle of private members Bills which have been introduced to amend the law in this area, none of which have been passed.[509] The Assisted Dying for the Terminally Ill Bill 2006 was designed to enable a competent adult who is suffering unbearably as a result of a terminal illness to receive medical assistance to die at his own considered and persistent request. The Bill contained a number of important safeguards,[510] including that the patient is suffering a terminal illness, is in unbearable pain, and has consulted a specialist in palliative medicine. It was finally defeated in the House of Lords in 2006.[511]

By contrast the Medical Treatment (Prevention of Euthanasia) Bill proposed in 1999 states in clause 1:

It shall be unlawful for any person responsible for the care of a patient to withdraw or withhold from the patient medical treatment or sustenance if his purpose or one of his purposes in doing so is to hasten or otherwise cause the death of the patient.

This Bill attempted to tighten the law in that it prevents a doctor withholding treatment from a patient if the purpose is to hasten death. This might outlaw the present treatment of patients suffering from PVS, unless doctors could claim that the treatment is

---

[509] Any reform of the law will need to consider the complex issue of how life insurance will operate in cases of assisted suicide or euthanasia (see Davey and Coggon (2006)).
[510] Although see Keown (2006b) for an argument that the safeguards were inadequate.
[511] See for a discussion of the proposals Keown (2007) opposing the Bill and Smith II (2007) supportive.

withheld not to produce death, but because the treatment is not producing any benefit to the patient. The use of the word 'purpose' rather than 'intend' was designed to make it clear that a doctor who foresaw death being the result of her or his treatment or non-treatment would not be breaking the law if death was not her or his purpose. However, some commentators felt the Bill (if enacted) would have placed doctors in a difficult position.[512]

Of course a strong case can be made for leaving the law as it is.[513] McCall Smith accepts the present law as a satisfactory, if a little untidy, compromise between the different arguments.[514] He even finds the uncertainty in the present law a benefit. Biggs,[515] however, finds the uncertainty and complexity of the law problematic:

> Sophistry and creative legalism may be effective in the court room, but medical practice cannot always be tailored to take advantage of them.[516]

She is particularly critical of the failure of the law to provide clear guidance to those working day-to-day in the area.

13 Conclusion

Our relationship with death is undergoing a remarkable change.[517] Some see an ever-increasing acceptance of the arguments in favour of assisted suicide and euthanasia which will lead to a time when people expect to be in complete control of when and where they die.[518] 'Make a diary date for death now!' may become a popular call, with assisted suicide being the normal preferred method of death.[519] The wish for a dignified death before we become 'unlovable' is a strong one for many.[520] But there are tensions in popular current attitudes towards death. While there appears to be a growing desire for people to be able to control the manner and time of their passing, there is also a growing wish for death to be 'natural'. There is much fear of over-medicalized death and some would agree with Nietzsche that:

> In a certain state it is indecent to go on living. To vegetate on in cowardly dependence on physicians and medicaments after the meaning of life, the right to life, has been lost ought to entail the profound contempt of society.[521]

However, as has been pointed out, many relatives' image of a natural death is only possible with medical intervention.[522] Also, it should not be forgotten that medical advances have done much to improve the quality of people's lives and enable them to live far longer than they would have done in the past.[523] How in the future our society will be meeting these potentially conflicting aims remains to be seen.

Age Concern organized *The Debate of the Age*[524] which set down the following principles of a care of all terminally ill patients:

(1) To know when death is coming, and to understand what can be expected.

(2) To be able to retain control of what happens.

---

[512] Morris (2000).   [513] Arras (1997).   [514] McCall Smith (1997).
[515] Biggs (2001).   [516] Biggs (2001: 5).   [517] Mann (1998).   [518] Battin (1998).
[519] Scambler (2003b).   [520] Sommerville (2002: 40).
[521] Nietzsche (1968: 88).   [522] McNamara (2001) and Seale (2000).
[523] McLean (1999: 142).   [524] Age Concern (1999).

(3) To be afforded dignity and privacy.

(4) To have control over pain relief and other symptom control.

(5) To have choice and control over where death occurs (at home or elsewhere).

(6) To have access to information and expertise of whatever kind is necessary.

(7) To have access to any spiritual or emotional support desired.

(8) To have access to hospice care in any location, not only in hospital.

(9) To have control over who else is present and shares in the end.

(10) To be able to issue advance directives which ensure wishes are respected.

(11) To have time to say goodbye, and control over other aspects of timing, and to be able to leave when it is time to go, and not to have life prolonged pointlessly.

Many of these reflect the goals of palliative care and are principles on which people on all sides of the euthanasia debate can agree.

QUESTIONS

1. 'The ban on assisted suicide is ineffective (a regulated system would stifle more abuse), morally obtuse (it discriminates against the disabled and privileges the incompetent over the competent) and though controversial, out of line with popular opinion (Had Mr Pretty assisted his wife's suicide, would he have been prosecuted? Would a jury have convicted? Would he have been imprisoned?). We can regulate how we die very much better than we currently do.' (Freeman (2002: 270)).
   Do you agree?

2. Remarkably the facts here are not an invented case, but a real one. In *Re C (Adult: Refusal of Treatment)* [1994] 1 WLR 290 C, 68, C was in Broadmoor prison and suffered from delusions, including the fact that he was a renowned vascular surgeon who had pioneered techniques to avoid amputating limbs. He suffered a minor injury, for which he refused treatment. He was warned that without the treatment his leg may require amputation. He refused treatment and when an amputation was required he refused that, even though he was warned that without it he might die. He was held to be competent to refuse the amputation because he understood the basic medical treatment and the consequences of refusal. Is this a case boldly upholding the principle of autonomy? Or does it show that adhering to autonomy overlooks the need to protect the vulnerable from themselves?

3. John Robertson (1997: 342–3): 'As long as we can dress the choice to take life in other clothes, such as refusing treatment or relieving pain, then we can acknowledge it. But naked decisions to take life as such are, to paraphrase T.S. Eliot, too much "reality" to bear openly. We must hide the reality of how we made end of life decisions for fear of what we will find. Yet in doing so, society risks even greater harm. Many persons who need assisted suicide to relieve their suffering will not receive it. Some persons may still receive such assistance covertly, but without the advantages of openly following medical protocols that can assure efficacy and prevent arbitrary and abusive practices... If we practice and tolerate assisted suicide and euthanasia, we certainly need to do it

openly to reassure the public and prevent abuse. At the same time, as T.S. Eliot reminds us, "humankind cannot bear very much reality." We also cannot tolerate the notion that doctors will openly take life, even with proper reporting and bureaucratic over-sight. We are caught in the dilemma that we can permit assisted suicide only by not admitting it...'

Do you agree?

4. 'I think the most honest statement of the issues presented in the physician-assisted suicide cases is this: the Court faced a choice of two lies to countenance. By lie I mean knowing misrepresentation; by countenance to extend approval or toleration. The first lie is that physicians do not already, and regularly, participate in assisting dying patients to end their lives. Every physician I have encountered acknowledges as much; many have written about it....The second lie is that permitting such assistance would not systematically and routinely be used to push dying people into death. The problem is not merely risks of abuse; the problem arises from the inauguration of a regime in which people would have to justify continuing to live....It is better to live with the lie that prohibition works so that, at the margin, those who engage in it do so with trembling.' Minow (1997: 20–22).

Do you agree there are these two lies? If so which is the better to live with?

5. Some doctors are willing to deal with a terminally ill patient in this way: sedate the patient so that she or he has no awareness or feeling and then withdraw food and hydration. Within a few days the patient will die. Is this a more or less acceptable way of treating such patients than giving them a lethal injection which immediately kills them? (This issue is discussed in Williams (2001)). If sedation is the best form of pain relief, should this be given, even if there is no intent to cause the patient's death? (see Broeckaert and Olarte (2002)). See Koch (2005), who discusses the case of Teri Schiavo in the United States, where a sedated patient could be left to 'starve' to death, but could not be killed by a lethal injection.

6. Reg Crew travelled to Switzerland so that he could be given drugs to commit suicide because his doctors in England refused to help (BBC Newsonline (24 January 2003)). Does this indicate that in this age of easy international travel, any attempt to prevent euthanasia or assisted suicide is unlikely to be effective?

7. Shelia McLean writes: 'To allow third parties to decide that life lacks quality for some-one else, for example in the case of the PVS patient, yet at the same time to deny individuals the right to make that decision for themselves, is nothing short of bizarre' (McLean (1999: 158). Do you agree?

8. 'A driver is trapped in a blazing lorry. There is no way in which he can be saved. He will soon burn to death. A friend of the driver is standing by the lorry. This friend has a gun and is a good shot. The driver asks the friend to shoot him dead. It will be less painful for him to be shot than to burn to death' (Hope (2005: 15)). Should the friend shoot the driver? If you answer 'yes' does that mean you must support active euthanasia?

9. One study of medical professionals working in the field found widespread support for the distinctions between acts and omissions and intention and foresight, which many ethicists believe to be misguided (Dickenson (2000)). Does this suggest that medical

ethicists are 'out of touch' or that medical professionals are not thinking clearly about the issues?

10. As forms of computer and mechanically assisted forms of dying become more sophisticated (see Battin (2005: Chapter 15)) will it become harder to distinguish suicide and assisted suicide?

11. Epstein (2007) argues that economic factors in reality play a major role in end of life decisions. Have the ethical debates ignored the significance of monetary issues?

12. Weyers (2006) points to three sociological factors she sees as particularly influencing attitudes in favour of euthanasia: increased individualism; a lessening of the taboos surrounding death; and a shift in power away from doctors and towards patients? Do you agree? Do you see any social forces pushing against liberalizing the law on euthanasia?

FURTHER READING

There is so much that has been written on the issue that the following is only a small selection of the wealth of material.

Some general writings on end of life issues can be found in:

Battin, M. (2005) *Ending Life* (Oxford University Press).

Chau, P-L and Herring, J. (2007) 'The meaning of death' in B. Brooks-Gordan, F.Ebtehaj, J. Herring, M. Johnson, and M. Richards (eds) *Death Rights and Rites* (Hart).

Du Bois-Pedain, A. (2007) 'Is there a Human Right to Die?' in B. Brooks-Gordan, F.Ebtehaj, J. Herring, M. Johnson, and M. Richards (eds) *Death Rights and Rites* (Hart).

Ford, M. (2005a) 'The Personhood Paradox and the "Right to Die"' *Medical Law Review* 13: 80.

Harris, J. (2005e) 'The right to die lives! There is no personhood paradox' *Medical Law Review* 13: 386.

House of Lords Select Committee (2005) *On The Assisted Dying For The Terminally Ill Bill* (TSO).

Lewis, P. (2007) *Assisted Dying and Legal Change* (Oxford University Press).

McGee, A. (2005) 'Finding a way through the ethical and legal maze withdrawal of medical treatment and euthanasia' *Medical Law Review* 3: 357.

McMahan, J. (2002) *The Ethics of Killing* (Oxford University Press).

Otlowski, M. (1997) *Voluntary Euthanasia and the Common Law* (Oxford University Press).

Writing broadly opposing euthanasia includes:

Gorsuch, N. (2006) *The Future of Assisted Suicide and Euthanasia* (Princeton University Press).

Keown, J. (2002) *Euthanasia, Ethics and Public Policy* (Cambridge University Press).

Keown, J. (2006b) *Considering Physician-Assisted Suicide* (Care not Killing).

Sommerville, M. (2001) *Death Talk* (McGillQueen's University Press).

Writing broadly supporting euthanasia includes:

Biggs, H. (2001) *Euthanasia* (Hart).

Cohen-Almagor, R. (2001) *The Right To Die With Dignity* (Rutgers University Press).

Dworkin, R. (1993) *Life's Dominion* (Harper Collins).

Dworkin, R., Nagel, T., Nozick, R., Rawls, J., Scanlon, T., and Jarvis Thomson, J. (1998) 'The Philosophers' Brief' in M. Battin, R. Rhodes and A. Silvers (eds) *Physician Assisted Suicide* (Routledge).

Ost, S. (2004) *An Analytical Study of the Legal, Moral, and Ethical Aspects of the Living Phenomenon of Euthanasia* (Edwin Mellen Press).

Zyl, van, L. (2000) *Death and Compassion* (Ashgate).

For a discussion of the law see:

BMA (2007b) *Withholding and Withdrawing Life-Prolonging Medical Treatment* (BMA).

Coggon, J. (2006) 'Could the right to die with dignity represent a new right to die in English law?' *Medical Law Review* 14: 219.

Hale, B. (2003) 'A Pretty Pass: When is There a Right to Die?' *Common Law World Review* 1.

Pedain, A. (2003) 'The Human Rights Dimension of the Diane Pretty Case' *Cambridge Law Journal* 181.

Williams, G. (2007) *Intention and Causation in Medical Non-Killing* (Routledge).

On the Dutch experiences see:

Battin, M., van der Heide, A., Ganzini, L., van der Wal, G., Onwuteaka- Philipsen, B. (2007) 'Legal physician-assisted dying in Oregon and the Netherlands: evidence concerning the impact on patients in "vulnerable" groups' *Journal of Medical Ethics* 33: 591.

Halliday, S. (2005) 'Regulating active voluntary euthanasia' in A. Garwood-Gowers, J. Tingel and K. Wheat *Contemporary Issues in Healthcare Law and Ethics* (Elsevier).

Smith, S. (2005) 'Evidence for the practical slippery slope in the debate on physician assisted suicide and euthanasia' *Medical Law Review* 13: 17.

On palliative care see:

Randall, F. and Downie, R. (2006) *The Philosophy of Palliative Care* (Oxford University Press).

ten Have, H. and Clarke, D, (eds) *The Ethics of Palliative Care* (Open University Press).

For feminist approaches see:

Biggs, H. (1998) 'I don't want to be a Burden! A feminist reflects on women's experiences of death and dying' in S. Sheldon and M. Thomson (eds) *Feminist Perspectives on Health Care Law* (Cavendish).

Raymond, D. (1999) 'Fatal Practices: A Feminist Analysis of Physician Assisted Suicide and Euthanasia' *Hypatia* 14: 1.

10 Mental Health Law

INTRODUCTION

We should start by asking why there needs to be any special 'mental health law'. After all, we don't have 'broken leg law' or other law designed to deal with particular medical conditions. Indeed, as we shall see, there are those who believe that there should not be a special mental health law, but rather the normal principles of medical law should be applied. There are even those who argue that there is no such thing as mental health, but that is something we will be looking at much later.

The reason why mental health has its own special law is because the law permits the detention and treatment of people who are mentally ill, even if they are competent. This goes against one of our most hallowed principles of medical law: that treatment may not be given to a competent person without their consent. The most common justification provided for infringing this principle is that to do so is necessary to protect the 'general public' from dangerous mentally ill people and/or for the protection of the individual themselves. Whether these are good enough reasons to infringe the fundamental principle is open to debate. The end result of balancing the rights of the mentally ill and the protection of the general public is a law which is complex and, to many, unsatisfactory. But that may be inevitable. As Bartlett and Sandland indicate in the following quotation the rationality of the law may not fit easily into the world of the 'irrational':

> The centrality of a medical model of insanity is asserted, imposing a scientific order onto the profoundly un-ordered world of the mad. While madness is displayed in the form of a disease, sanity is a constraint, both physical and moral, into which the insane person is confined through pressure of the group, the sane. All this is a construction of the reasoned, and reflects the world of the reasoned; to the insane person, it is an alien landscape.[1]

It is, however, unfortunate that the issue of the detention of the 'dangerously mentally ill' has come to dominate the law on mental health. It creates a skewed vision of mental illness in our society. As we shall see shortly, mental illness is widespread and very common. The vast majority of mental illness is treated voluntarily in the community, with no special legal regulation. Indeed a perhaps even larger amount goes unrecognized and untreated. Worries about the detention or rights of the 'dangerous' should not hide the needs of those suffering less dramatic, but still debilitating mental illness.

The popular image of mental illness is a confused one. Images of the 'dangerous lunatic' sit alongside the image of the 'tortured genius'. There is still a strong negative attitude towards mental illness in our society. In a 2007 survey only 78 per cent

---

[1] Bartlett and Sandland (2007: 1).

of people disagreed with the statement: 'people with mental illness are a burden on society'.[2] The survey found that attitudes towards those with mental illness were less positive than they had been in 2000. There is increasing awareness of the agonies of mental illness, but perhaps less of the positive benefits it can bring. To many the mentally ill are to be pitied, rather than valued. But one thing that will be clear as we turn to statistics on mental illness is that the idea that there is a sharp line between 'them' (the mentally ill) and 'us' (the sane) is misleading.[3] We may even be moving towards a time when mental illness is the norm.

1 Statistics on mental health

The level of mental illness is astonishing. Consider the statistics in the following box:

REALITY CHECK

Mental health statistics

- One in six adults will be affected by mental illness each year (Mental Health Foundation (2007)).

- One in three people will suffer mental illness at some point in their lives (DoH (2005d: 1)).

- Depression will affect half of women and a quarter of men before the age of 70 (DoH (2005d: 1)).

- At any point in time 630,000 people are in contact with specialist mental health services. 14,000 people will be being treated under the Mental Health Act (DoH (2005d: 1)).

- In 2006 one in ten children and young people aged 1 to 18 had a clinically recognizable mental disorder; 11 per cent of girls and 3 per cent of boys have committed an act of self harm (BMA (2006)). Twenty per cent of children in families with neither parent working had a clinically recognizable mental disorder. One per cent of children aged 5 to 16 had autistic spectrum disorder. Four per cent of children had an emotional disorder (anxiety or depression) (Office of National Statistics (2005)).

- Mental health problems are estimated to cost the country more than £77 billion a year through the costs of care, economic losses and premature death (Social Exclusion Unit (2005)).

- About a quarter of all suicides had been in contact with mental health services prior to their death. One study of 300 suicides where the individual had been in such contact suggested that 67 of them had been preventable (Laurance (2003: 67)) The UK has one of the highest self harm rates in Europe at 400 per 100,000.[4]

- As at July 2007 there were more than 3,500 people detained in secure hospitals (BBC Newsonline (9 September 2007)).

There has been much debate whether the mental health of the nation is worsening. It is difficult to find statistics which give a definite answer. What we do know is:

- The number of guardianship cases in force at the end of the year 2006 (926) was 7 per cent lower than at its peak in 2000 (Information Centre (2007a)).

---

[2] National Statistics (2007e).   [3] DoH (1999c: 10).   [4] Mental Health Foundation (2007).

- Admissions to hospital under the Mental Health Act have risen by nearly 30 per cent in the ten years prior to 2004 (Kmietowicz (2004)).
- Seventy-two per cent of GPs questioned in a survey in 2004 said that they prescribed more antidepressants than they had five years previously (Bell (2005)).

2 Mental Health Act 1983

We will now look at the Mental Health Act 1983. The Act was recently reformed through the 2007 Mental Health Act, so when reference is made to the Mental Health Act 1983, this is as amended by the 2007 Act. Indeed progress towards reforming the 1983 Act has been going on for over nine years. Lord Steyn in *R (on the application of Munjaz) v Ashworth Hospital Authority* described the Act as 'out of date in its approach'.[5] The 2007 reforms have attempted to make the law more in line with human rights requirements and public expectations. Originally the intention was that the new Act would produce a completely new scheme, but in the end the 2007 Act simply amended aspects of the law as set out in the 1983 Act.

Before looking at the Act it is important to remember that there are two situations involving mentally ill patients where there is normally no need to use the Act and other law can be relied upon:

- If the patient is competent and consents to treatment it can be provided under the normal principles of medical law.
- If the patient is incompetent then treatment which is in the best interests of the patient can be given. This is done under the Mental Capacity Act 2005, discussed in Chapter 4.

The Act is needed particularly where the patient is competent but does not consent to treatment for a mental disorder.

2.1 Involuntary admission to hospital

Most mentally ill patients consent to receiving treatment and there is therefore normally no need to use the Mental Health Act 1983 (MHA). However where it is thought appropriate to provide mental health treatment against the wishes of the patient then the Act becomes relevant. There are three routes to involuntary admission to hospital.

2.1.1 *Section 2: admission for assessment*

An application for an admission for assessment can be made by either the patient's nearest relative[6] or an approved social worker. Two registered medical practitioners[7] must

---

[5] [2005] UKHL 58, para 38.

[6] Under s 26 of the Mental Health Act 1983, 'nearest relative' is spouse (or unmarried persons living together as husband and wife), child, parent, sibling, grandparent, grandchild, uncle or aunt, nephew or niece. Where there are competing claims those higher up the list have priority over those lower down the list. If within the same category, then those relatives of the full blood have priority over those of the half blood and older relatives take priority over their juniors. However, there is one way a relative can 'jump' to the front of the queue. That is that if the patient is living with or being cared for by a relative then they are the 'nearest relative' even if they are not the top of the list.

[7] At least one of the two must have a mental health qualification.

support the application. If necessary, reasonable force can be used to transfer the patient to hospital. The 1983 MHA, section 2(2) states:

> An application for admission for assessment may be made in respect of a patient on the grounds that—
>
> (a) he is suffering from mental disorder of a nature or degree which warrants the detention of the patient in a hospital for assessment (or for assessment followed by medical treatment) for at least a limited period; and
>
> (b) he ought to be so detained in the interests of his own health or safety or with a view to the protection of other persons.

Section 1(2) defines mental disorder as: 'any disorder or disability of the mind'. The draft Code of Practice lists the following as examples of a mental disorder:

- organic mental disorders such as dementia, and including personality and behavioural changes due to brain injury or damage (however acquired);
- mental and behavioural disorders due to psychoactive substance use;
- schizophrenia and other delusional disorders;
- affective disorders, such as depression and bipolar disorder (manic depression);
- neurotic, stress related, and somatoform disorders, such as anxiety, phobic disorders, obsessive compulsive disorders, post-traumatic stress disorder, and hypochondriacal disorders;
- eating disorders, non-organic sleep disorders, and non-organic sexual disorders;
- personality disorders;
- learning disabilities (but see below);
- autistic spectrum disorders (including Asperger's syndrome);
- behavioural and emotional disorders of children and adolescents.[8]

The MCA specifically states that learning disability[9] or alcohol or drug dependency cannot be the sole basis for treating someone as having a mental disorder.[10] The reasoning behind this provision is the history of treating those showing what was regarded as 'immoral' or 'unusual' behaviour as suffering from some kind of mental illness. This does not prevent a person who suffers from a mental illness as well as, say, drug dependency, from being classified as suffering from a mental disorder. However, if the learning disability 'is associated with abnormally aggressive or seriously irresponsible conduct on his part' then it can be regarded as a mental disorder.[11] The term 'irresponsible' is ambiguous. It is suggested that the best interpretation is that it means irresponsible in the sense of liable to cause injury to himself or another, rather than being simply rowdy or disruptive. However, the courts may need to clarify the meaning of that term.

In *R v Mental Health Tribunal for South Thames Region ex p Smith*[12] it was held that the use of the phrase 'nature or degree' meant that a patient who is suffering from a serious mental condition could be detained under section 2 even though the present

---

[8] DoH (2007f).
[9] MHA 1983, s 1(3) defines learning disability as 'a state of arrested or incomplete development of the mind which includes significant impairment of intelligence and social functioning'.
[10] MHA 1983, s 1(3).   [11] MHA 1983, s 1(2A).   [12] (1998) 47 BMLR 104.

manifestations of it are not serious. In that case a schizophrenic patient was not showing dangerous manifestations of his condition at present, but it was likely that he would in the near future.

The patient must be detained 'in the interests of his own health or safety or with a view to the protection of other persons.' It will be noted that this provision covers not only cases where the patient poses a risk to other people but also to her or himself.

Once admitted under section 2, patients can be kept in hospital for assessment for a maximum of 28 days. If a patient is to be kept for longer that must be under section 3 powers (see below). A patient can apply to have her or his case reviewed by a Mental Health Review tribunal during the first 14 days of detention. The nearest relative can discharge the patient on three days' notice, but the Responsible Medical Officer can prevent this. Treatment can only be given for a patient being assessed with her or his consent, unless there is an immediate and serious danger.

As Peter Bartlett has pointed out the criteria for admission under section 2:

> provide little guidance to professionals as to who should, and who should not be admitted. In practice, standards have for some time been a function of professional culture rather than law, coupled with continued chronic under-funding. This latter has placed considerable restrictions on the number of persons confined at a given time, introducing standards indirectly by way of rationing.[13]

The House of Lords has recently considered section 2:[14]

KEY CASE   MH v Secretary of State for Health [2005] UKHL 60

M was severely mentally disabled and was detained in a hospital under section 2 of the Mental Health Act 1983. She had not applied to a Mental Health Review Tribunal within the first 14 days. The hospital wished to arrange for her to be received into their guardianship. Her mother objected, as her nearest relative. The proceedings took longer than expected and so M was detained under section 2 for more than the normal 28 days. M's mother asked that M's case be referred to a Mental Health Tribunal. This the Secretary of State did, but the tribunal decided that M's detention should continue. M sought judicial review. Her main complaints were that section 2 was incompatible with the ECHR, article 5(4) because the burden was on the patient to make an application (to the Mental Health Review Tribunal) to review the detention; where the patient was incapable of exercising this right there was inadequate protection of her or his rights, she argued. She also complained that section 29(4) of the Act was incompatible with article 5(4) of the Convention because it enabled the extension of the period of detention without a review of the lawfulness of the detention.

The House of Lords held that section 2 was not incompatible with the Convention. Every sensible effort should be made to enable a patient to apply to the tribunal if there was reason to think the patient wished to do so. Hospital managers had a statutory duty to take steps to ensure that patients understood their rights. Article 5(4) of the ECHR did not require every detention to be subject to judicial approval. The system tried hard to give patients and relatives easy access to mental health review tribunals. It was true a nearest relative did not have an independent right of application to the tribunal, but there were ways a nearest relative could get the case before a tribunal, as in this case where the assistance of the Secretary of State had been sought. Although it was important to ensure

---

[13] Bartlett (2003a: 331).   [14] See the discussion in Scott-Moncrieff (2006).

that the Convention rights of the mentally ill were 'practical and effective' rather than 'theoretical and illusionary', the protection in place surrounding section 2 were effective.

As to the section 29(4) issue, the patient could request the Secretary of State to refer the patient's case to a Mental Health Review Tribunal or challenge the lawfulness of the decision through judicial review in the courts. There was, therefore, an adequate way of ensuring the detention was appropriate and this rendered the provision compatible with the ECHR, article 5. Their Lordships accepted that section 29(4) was capable of being operated in a way that was compatible with article 5(4). However, the use of the power of the Secretary of State to refer a case to a tribunal could ensure that the power would not be used improperly. If the Secretary of State refused, there was always the option of judicial review.

2.1.2 Emergency admission (section 4)

If there is an emergency a patient can be admitted under section 4 on the recommendation of one doctor. But that doctor must confirm that it is of 'urgent necessity' for the patient to be admitted and detained; *and* that waiting for a second doctor to confirm the need for an admission under section 2 would cause 'undesirable delay'. Remarkably this doctor does not need to be a specialist in mental illness, although (if practical) it should be a doctor who knew the patient beforehand. The maximum length that a person can be detained under section 4 is 72 hours. At the end of that time the patient must be free to go, unless one of the other routes of admission has been invoked. Treatment cannot be provided to a patient detained under section 4 without her or his consent.

Other provisions in the Act can also be relied upon in emergencies. Under the MHA, section 135 a Justice of the Peace may, upon the application of an approved social worker, require the detention in a place of safety for up to 72 hours of mentally disordered individuals who are being ill-treated, neglected, or not kept under proper control, or who are living alone and unable to care for themselves.[15] Section 136 of the MHA allows mentally disordered individuals found by police officers in public places to be removed to a place of safety (eg a hospital) for up to 72 hours if it appears to a police officer that they are in need of immediate care and control.[16]

2.1.3 Admission for treatment (section 3)

Unlike the other two grounds, this ground is designed for longer-term detention. An application can be made by either the patient's nearest relative or an approved social worker.[17] Section 3(2) states:

An application for admission for treatment may be made in respect of a patient on the grounds that—

(a) he is suffering from mental disorder of a nature or degree which makes it appropriate for him to receive medical treatment in a hospital; and

---

[15] *Ward v Metropolitan Police Commissioner and another* [2005] UKHL 32 held that there is no power to insist that named individuals are present when the mentally ill person is detained.
[16] *Seal v Chief Constable of South Wales Police* [2007] UKHL 31.
[17] Where a social worker makes the application, the next of kin must be consulted.

(b) it is necessary for the health or safety of the patient or for the protection of other persons that he should receive such treatment and it cannot be provided unless he is detained under this section; and

(c) appropriate medical treatment is available to him.

These can be separated into three grounds for admission. They are that in the opinion of a medical qualified officer:

(i) The patient is suffering from a mental disorder of a nature which makes it appropriate for her or him to receive medical treatment in a hospital. Section 1(2) defines mental disorder as: 'any disorder or disability of the mind'. Notice that it is insufficient simply to show that a person has a mental disorder: the disorder must be such that it cannot be treated in the community, and hospital treatment is required. The definition of a mental disorder is deliberately broad. There is no need to identify precisely what disorder a person is suffering from.

(ii) It is 'necessary for the health or safety of the patient or for the protection of other persons that he should receive such treatment and it cannot be provided unless he is detained under section three'. As with section 2 a person can be detained either if they are danger to others or themselves. The reference to the requirement that the treatment cannot be provided unless she or he is means that if the patient is competent, and able to consent to the treatment, there is no requirement for her or him to be detained under section 3.

(iii) Appropriate treatment must be available to the patient.[18] The wording of this provision was debated at length in the House of Commons. The issue is how to deal with a patient suffering from a mental disorder where there is no treatment that can be offered to improve, or at least prevent a worsening of, her or his condition. Of course, this may be true of those with the most serious forms of mental illness. Section 145(4) is crucial here. It states that:

Any reference in this Act to medical treatment, in relation to mental disorder, shall be construed as a reference to medical treatment the purpose of which is to alleviate, or prevent a worsening of, the disorder or one or more of its symptoms or manifestations.

This would appear to indicate that if no medical treatment is available to a patient then he cannot be detained under the Act. The reasoning behind this is that if there is nothing that doctors can do to assist a patient they should not be required to simply detain her or him, acting as a 'warehouse' for the untreatable.[19] But that did mean that in theory, at least, a 'dangerous' person could be released because nothing can be done for them. There is some ambiguity under the provisions because the treatment can relate to a manifestation or symptom of the illness, rather than the condition itself. However, it is clear that simply feeding and generally caring for the patient will not amount to medical treatment. Section 145 defines treatment as including 'psychological intervention and specialist mental health habilitation, rehabilitation and care'. Much may depend on whether the courts give the word 'care' a broad or narrow meaning. The

---

[18] Rather unhelpfully, s 3(4) states that references to appropriate medical treatment, in relation to a person suffering from mental disorder, are references to medical treatment which is appropriate in his case, taking into account the nature and degree of the mental disorder and all other circumstances of his case.

[19] The draft Code of Practice (DoH (2007f: para 6.2)) states that the Act should not be used simply to permit preventative detention.

draft Code of Practice emphasizes that a person can properly receive care even if they cannot be cured.[20]

The Mental Health Alliance Foundation has serious concerns about the 'treatability criterion' They argued that 'compulsory mental health treatment [should] be used only where there is no alternative; where it has therapeutic benefit; and when the person concerned is unable to decide for themselves about treatment.'[21] They warned the Bill would lead to the system being clogged up with patients who cannot be treated and should not be being detained. Whether their concerns are valid depends in part on how the 'treatability' criterion is interpreted.

The treatability test under the old law was discussed in *R v Canons Parke MHRT ex p A*[22] where the issue was whether a patient could be detained if the proposed treatment was group therapy, the problem being that the patient had indicated that he did not wish to participate in the session. It was argued that the patient was therefore not treatable. Lord Justice Roch said:[23]

> First, if a tribunal were to be satisfied that the patient's detention in hospital was simply an attempt to coerce the patient into participating in group therapy, then the tribunal would be under a duty to direct discharge. Second, 'treatment in hospital' will satisfy the 'treatability test' although it is unlikely to alleviate the patient's condition, provided that it is likely to prevent a deterioration. Third, 'treatment in hospital' will satisfy the 'treatability test' although it will not immediately alleviate or prevent deterioration in the patient's condition, provided that alleviation or stabilisation is likely in due course. Fourth, the 'treatability test' can still be met although initially there may be some deterioration in the patient's condition, due for example to the patient's initial anger at being detained. Fifth, it must be remembered that medical treatment includes 'nursing and also includes care, habilitation and rehabilitation under medical supervision.' Sixth, the 'treatability test' is satisfied if nursing care etc., is likely to lead to an alleviation of the patient's condition in that the patient is likely to gain an insight into his problem or cease to be unco-operative in his attitude towards treatment which could potentially have a lasting benefit.

Admission for treatment under section 3 is up to six months and can be extended for a second period of six months. It can then be extended a year at a time. It would therefore be possible for someone to be detained under section 3 for the rest of their lives. Renewal simply requires the responsible medical officer to produce a report indicating that:

(i)   the patient suffers from one of the conditions required for section 3;

(ii) that treatment is likely to alleviate or prevent deterioration of that condition *or* that if the patient is suffering a mental illness of severe mental impairment that if discharged the patient is unlikely to be able to care for her or himself, to obtain other care needed, or to guard her or himself against serious exploitation;

(iii) continued treatment is necessary for the health and safety of the patient or others and detention is required.[24]

The possibilities of challenging detention under section 3 are limited. The main form of challenge will be by application to the Mental Health Tribunal. An application for civil

[20] DoH (2007f).   [21] Mental Health Alliance Foundation (2005).
[22] [1994] 2 All ER 659.   [23] At 679–80.   [24] MHA 1983, s 20.

proceedings can be brought to the High Court, but only if leave is obtained first.[25] The 1983 MHA, section 139 states:

> No person shall be liable...to any civil or criminal proceedings...in respect of any act purporting to be done in pursuance of this Act...unless the act was done in bad faith or without reasonable care.

This means that any criminal proceedings or claim in tort is unlikely to succeed if brought in respect of an act done in pursuance of the 1983 Act.

2.2 Detention of patients informally in hospital (section 5)

If a patient is in hospital informally (ie she or he is competent and has consented to receive treatment) then a doctor in charge of the patient can detain the patient for up to 72 hours by reporting to hospital managers that an application for compulsory admission 'ought to be made'. Some nurses can detain an informal patient for up to six hours or until a doctor with authority to detain the patient arrives.

2.3 Treatment

A patient detained under the MHA can consent to treatment if competent. If not competent she or he must be treated in the way which promotes her or his best interests.[26] If competent and refusing then they cannot have treatment imposed upon them, except under Part IV of the Act. Section 63 permits treatment for mental disorder and does not authorize treatment for physical conditions unrelated to the mental disorder. This distinction between treatment for a mental disorder and for other matters has proved problematic.

As the following cases show the courts have given a liberal interpretation to the notion of treatment of the mental condition.

- In *Re KB (Adult) (Mental Patient: Medical Treatment)*[27] it was held that forced feeding could be regarded as medical treatment. The argument that this was not treatment of her mental condition was rejected because it was held that treating the symptoms was part of treating the disorder (anorexia nervosa).

- In *B v Croydon Health Authority*[28] it was held permissible under section 63 to provide forced feeding for a patient suffering 'borderline personality disorder'. The Court of Appeal held that treatments designed to alleviate the consequences of the disorder could be regarded as treatment of the disorder.

- In *Tameside and Glossop Acute Services Trust v CH*[29] a schizophrenic patient was 38 weeks pregnant. There were concerns that she would refuse to consent to a Caesarean section. The court found that the Caesarean section would be treatment and if necessary restraint could be used to carry it out. The argument for this was that an ancillary aim of the Caesarean section was to prevent deterioration of the mother's mental health. This extends further the notion of treatment for a mental disorder to

---

[25] Judicial Review proceedings can be brought: *ex p Waldron* [1986] QB 824. See further Allen (2007).
[26] MCA 2005, s 4. See eg *Trust A and Trust B v H* [2006] EWHC 1230 (Fam).
[27] (1994) 19 BMLR 144.   [28] [1995] Fam 133.   [29] [1996] 1 FCR 753.

treatment designed to deal with physical matters which if untreated would worsen the mental condition of the patient.

- In *Reid v Secretary of State*[30] the House of Lords, considering the similarly worded Scottish mental health legislation, held that 'treatment for the condition' could include treatment that alleviated the symptoms and manifestation of the illness.

- In *R (on the application of B) v Ashworth Hospital Authority*[31] the House of Lords held that it was permissible to provide treatment for any mental disorder from which the individual was suffering, even if it was not the one for which he had been originally detained under the Mental Health Act 1983.[32]

- Following *Norfolk v Norwich Healthcare (NHS) Trust*[33] a reasonable degree of force can be used to require a patient to undergo treatment which is permitted under section 63.

Article 3 of the European Convention on Human Rights would need to be considered here. It prohibits torture and inhuman and degrading treatment.[34] It might be thought that imposing treatment on a patient against her or his wishes would be torture or inhuman or degrading treatment. Certainly it could be, but the courts have accepted that medical treatment of a mental condition will not amount to inhuman or degrading treatment if a therapeutic necessity.[35] This was the line taken by the European Court of Human Rights in *Herczegfalvy v Austria*[36] and has been adopted by the English courts, in, for example, *R (on the application of B) v SS*.[37] However, what these human rights cases emphasize is that if the patient is competent, and does not consent to the treatment, then forcing treatment upon her or him will infringe article 3 unless it is 'convincingly' demonstrated that the treatment is medically necessary. As Collins J put it in *R (on the application of B) v Haddock*:[38] 'the more drastic the treatment, the more the doctor must be satisfied of the need for it'.[39] In *R(N) v M & Others*[40] the Court of Appeal held the following factors to be relevant:

> The answer to that question [whether the treatment is justifiable in the light of article 3] will depend on a number of factors, including (a) how certain is it that the patient does suffer from a treatable mental disorder, (b) how serious a disorder it is, (c) how serious a risk is presented to others, (d) how likely is it that, if the patient does suffer from such a disorder, the proposed treatment will alleviate the condition, (e) how much alleviation is there likely to be, (f) how likely is it that the treatment will have adverse consequences for the patient and (g) how severe may they be?[41]

The Court of Appeal also held that as long as a respectable body of opinion held the treatment was necessary, this rendered it compliant with article 3, even if other doctors might disagree. Article 8 is also relevant, but it would not be infringed if the medical treatment was necessary in the patient's best interests or for the protection of others.[42]

---

[30] [1999] 1 AllER 481.   [31] [2005] 2 All ER 289.
[32] See the discussion of this case in Bartlett (2006).   [33] [1996] 2 FLR 613.
[34] *Savage v South Essex Partnership NHS Foundation Trust* [2006] EWHC 3562 (QB) looked at a claim that a hospital caring under the MHA for a patient who had committed suicide, breached the patient's article 2 rights. It was held that in order for a claim under s 3 of the Human Rights Act 1998 to succeed it needed to be shown that there was gross negligence.
[35] *R (on the application of B) v S* [2006] EWCA Civ 28.
[36] (1993) 15 EHRR 437.   [37] [2005] EWHC 86.   [38] [2005] All ER(D) 309.
[39] Para 13.   [40] [2003] 1 WLR 562.   [41] Para 19.
[42] *R (on the application of PS) v G (Responsible Medical Officer)* [2003] EWHC 2335.

Similarly in *R (on the application of B) v SS and others*[43] the Court of Appeal found that the detention of man suffering from bipolar disorder was justified as necessary for his own and others' protection, and therefore it was permissible to give him treatment, without his consent. It was not necessary to show that the treatment was necessary for his own or others protection. Lord Phillips CJ thought it illogical for it to be compatible with human rights to detain a person suffering mental ill health, but then not to be compatible to give them the treatment they need. As he had been legitimately detained under the Act, doctors were automatically authorized to provide treatment.

Where treatment is being given against the wishes of a competent patient then a second opinion must be obtained from a registered medical practitioner appointed by the Secretary of State (known as a SOAD (a second opinion appointed doctor)), who must consult two persons concerned with the patient's treatment who are not themselves doctors.[44] The patient has the option of taking the matter to a court if she or he disagrees with the decision reached by the doctor. As the Court of Appeal in *R (On the application of B) v Haddock*[45] noted, it will be very rare for a judge to disagree with the opinion of the doctors.

The MHA, section 118 allows the Secretary of State to issue Codes of Practice governing how patients being detained under the Act should be treated. The legal position of these codes was considered in the following decision:

KEY CASE   R (on the application of Munjaz) v Ashworth Hospital Authority [2005] UKHL 58

Munjaz was being detained under the MHA 1983 in a high security mental hospital. He had been placed in seclusion for periods of more than four days, which was in breach of the code of practice issued by the Secretary of State for Health. It was argued that the hospital's use of exclusion was unlawful under UK law and breached articles 3, 5, and 8 of the ECHR.

Their Lordships divided three to two. The majority held that the code of practice amounted to guidance and not instruction. The code could be departed from, but only with great care and where the hospital had cogent reasons for doing so. Here the Trust, in departing from the code, had taken into account three key issues:

(i) The code had been written with mental hospitals generally in mind and not with the special problems facing high security hospitals.

(ii) The code had not recognized that there were patients for whom exclusion for longer than four days would be appropriate.

(iii) The code had made it clear that the Secretary of State's code was guidance and that the final decision of the treatment of patients rested with those with practical care for them.

Lord Bingham, writing for the majority, accepted that the practice of the hospital was to use exclusion only as a last resort and where necessary to protect other patients. The hospital's policy included

[43] [2006] EWCA Civ 28.
[44] MCA 1983, s 58(3)(b). The Secretary of State has issued a Code of Practice under s 118 of the 1983 Act. This governs how the SOAD should carry out this task (para 16.20 et seq). If the patient wishes to challenge the treatment in court both doctors can be required to attend: R *(Wilkinson) v Broadmoor Special Hospital & Others* [2002] 1 WLR 419.
[45] [2005] All ER (D) 309.

sufficient protections to ensure that a patient secluded for more than seven days would not have her or his article 3 rights infringed. He was observed by a nurse every 15 minutes and his condition was regularly reviewed. The policy was an infringement of a patient's article 8(1) rights, but the infringement was justified under article 8(2) as necessary to prevent disorder or crime, for the protection of health or morals, or for the protection of the rights and freedoms of others. The policy was sufficiently precise and accessible to mean the infringement of the article 8(1) rights was in accordance with the law.

Lords Steyn, dissenting, regarded the code as setting down 'minimum centrally imposed safeguards' for vulnerable patients (paragraph 46). For him the judgement of the majority 'permits a lowering of the protection offered by the law to mentally disordered patients. If that is the law, so be it. How society treats mentally disordered people detained in high security hospitals is, however, a measure of how far we have come since the dreadful ways in which such persons were treated in earlier times. For my part, the decision today is a set-back for a modern and just mental health law' (paragraph 48).

2.4 The Mental Health Act Commission

The Commission was created under the MHA, section 121. The Commission's role is to visit hospitals where patients are detained and deal with any complaints that patients have.[46] The Commission also raises issues which have not been specifically mentioned by patients. Their inspections will look generally at conditions in hospitals.

2.5 Regulation of special procedures

The MHA 1983 provides that some kinds of treatment can only be provided if certain special procedures are undertaken. The first are surgical operations that destroy brain tissue or interfere with the brain's function, and hormone implants designed to reduce the male sex drive (section 57(1)). Such treatment can only be given when the patient consents and a second opinion provided by a panel appointed by the Secretary of State (section 57(2)) agrees. The panel can only authorize the treatment if the doctor on the panel certifies that the treatment should be given. That doctor should consult two people, one a nurse and the other neither a nurse nor a doctor, who have been concerned with the patient's treatment.

The second medical procedure for which there is special statutory regulation is electroconvulsive therapy (ECT) which is governed by sections 58 and 58A.[47] ECT can be given if either the patient consents or the patient is found to be incompetent. Where a second opinion is relied upon it must be the opinion of a doctor appointed for the purpose; she or he must certify that the treatment is appropriate bearing in mind the likelihood that it will alleviate or prevent the deterioration of the patient's condition. The fact that ECT can be given against the wishes of a competent patient is highly controversial because the benefits and disadvantages of ECT are hotly debated amongst specialists in the field.

---

[46] Mental Health Act 1983, s 132.
[47] See *R (on the application of JB) v Haddock* [2006] EWCA Civ 961 for a case under the previous law where medication was authorized without consent.

Third, psychiatric drugs can be given for three months. After that time an independent doctor must consider whether the patient should continue to receive them or not (section 58) and reasons for the decision should be provided.[48]

2.6 Discharge under MHA

Detained patients can be discharged if the responsible medical officer believes that it is no longer necessary to detain the patient. Where appropriate a community treatment order can be made (see below).

A patient believing she or he has been improperly detained can bring an action for *habeas corpus*; if this is established then the court will order her or his release. The action is appropriate when there was no legal power to detain the patient. It is not appropriate where there was a legal power to detain the patient but it is claimed that there was an improper exercise of a discretion in deciding whether or not to detain the patient; in the latter claim an application for judicial review could be brought.[49]

There is also the option of using informal procedures which are to be heard by the 'managers' (ie the non-executive directors) of the NHS Trust. A more formal process is the Mental Health Review Tribunal (MHRT). Patients have the right to appeal to a tribunal once for each period of time during which their detention is authorized. The following decision considers further the effect of being discharged by a MHRT:

KEY CASE   R (on the application of von Brandenburg) v East London and the City Mental Health NHS Trust [2004] 2 AC 280

The appellant had been detained in a hospital under the MHA 1983, section 2. He successfully applied to a Mental Health Tribunal for a review of his decision. The tribunal ordered his discharge within eight days, having concluded that he did not suffer from a mental illness. The eight days was to give time for a care plan to be prepared. Before the eight days expired and before the appellant had been discharged, he was readmitted under section 3. The approved social worker argued that the appellant had failed to take his medication and so his mental condition had deteriorated. The appellant challenged his readmission under section 3. The key question for the House of Lords was whether it was lawful to readmit a patient under section 3 when a Mental Health Review Tribunal had ordered his discharge and there was no relevant change of circumstances.

The House of Lords held that:

> an ASW [approved social worker] may not lawfully apply for the admission of a patient whose discharge has been ordered by the decision of a Mental Health Review Tribunal of which the ASW is aware unless the ASW has formed the reasonable and bona fide opinion that he has information not known to the tribunal which puts a significantly different complexion on the case as compared with that which was before the tribunal. (para 10, Lord Bingham)

Where a patient was readmitted it would be helpful if the medical recommendation in support of that identified the new information upon which it was based. There was a limited duty on an ASW to give reasons why there should be readmission. The duty was limited because the disclosure of reasons could be harmful to the patient and so the reasons might have to be given in very general terms.

---

[48]   *R (Wooder) v Feggetter* [2003] QB 219.   [49]   *R v Hallstrom ex p* W [1985] 3 All ER 775.

On the facts, their Lordships thought that the ASW had reasonably and in bona fides concluded that there was further evidence which was not available to the tribunal. The readmission was, therefore, lawful.

2.7 Community Treatment Order

When a patient is discharged, having been detained under the MHA, the clinician can impose a community treatment order under section 17A of the MHA 1983.[50] This will mean the release will be conditional. The order can be made if a clinician and a mental health professional agree that it is appropriate to make an order and that the following conditions in section 17A(5) are made out:

(a) the patient is suffering from mental disorder of a nature or degree which makes it appropriate for him to receive medical treatment;

(b) it is necessary for his health or safety or for the protection of other persons that he should receive such treatment;

(c) subject to his being liable to be recalled as mentioned in paragraph (d) below, such treatment can be provided without his continuing to be detained in a hospital;

(d) it is necessary that the responsible clinician should be able to exercise the power under section 17E(1) below to recall the patient to hospital;[51] and

(e) appropriate medical treatment is available for him.

The conditions placed on the release must be for the following purposes:

(a) ensuring that the patient receives medical treatment;

(b) preventing risk of harm to the patient's health or safety;

(c) protecting other persons.[52]

The conditions can be suspended or varied by the responsible clinician.[53]

The responsible clinician can recall a patient subject to a community treatment patient order as set out under section 17E:

(1) The responsible clinician may recall a community patient to hospital if in his opinion—

    (a) the patient requires medical treatment in hospital for his mental disorder; and

    (b) there would be a risk of harm to the health or safety of the patient or to other persons if the patient were not recalled to hospital for that purpose.

(2) The responsible clinician may also recall a community patient to hospital if the patient fails to comply with a condition specified under section 17B(3) above.

---

[50] This provision was added by the Mental Health Act 2007.
[51] In considering this factor the 'the patient's history of mental disorder and any other relevant factors, what risk there would be of a deterioration of the patient's condition if he were not detained in a hospital' should be taken into account (s 17A(6)).
[52] S 17B(2).   [53] S 17B.

2.8 Guardianship (sections 7–10)

An approved social worker or nearest relative can apply for guardianship.[54] This lasts for up to six months, but can be renewed. Two doctors must confirm that the patient is suffering from mental illness, severe mental impairment, psychotic disorder, or mental impairment of a degree that warrants guardianship and that the guardianship is in the interests of the patient's welfare or for the protection of others. The guardian must be a local social services authority or a person approved by them. Under section 8 the guardian can require the patient to live at a particular place; attend places for the purposes of occupation, training, or medical treatment; or permit a doctor, social worker, or other person specified by the guardian to see the patient. What a guardian cannot do is force the patient to undergo treatment. Guardianship can be discharged by the RMO, the local social service authority, or the nearest relative. The patient can also apply to the MHRT for discharge.

3 Informal treatment

As has already been emphasized, if a patient is competent and consents to treatment then there is no difficulty detaining and treating such a person.[55] However, in *R (on the application of H) v Home Office*[56] it was held that the principle of necessity at common law permitted the detention of a person without capacity, providing force was not required to detain a person. In *HL v UK*[57] it was held by the European Court of Human Rights that this use of necessity was incompatible with the requirements of Article 5.

It has been estimated that about 50,000 people are being detained under the principle of necessity,[58] so the ECHR decision required a change in the law. This was achieved through a new section 64 inserted into the 1983 Mental Health Act by the 2007 Mental Health Act. This deals with patients who are not being formally detained under the Act but are not resistant to receiving treatment for mental disorder. The treatment can certainly be given if the patient has capacity and consents. However, if the patient lack capacity then if the five conditions in section 64(d) are met, a person can provide treatment to them:

(1) The first condition is that, before giving the treatment, the person takes reasonable steps to establish whether the patient lacks capacity to consent to the treatment.

(2) The second condition is that, when giving the treatment, he reasonably believes that the patient lacks capacity to consent to it.

(3) The third condition is that—

   (a) he has no reason to believe that the patient objects to being given the treatment; or

   (b) he does have reason to believe that the patient so objects, but it is not necessary to use force against the patient in order to give the treatment.

(4) The fourth condition is that—

   (a) he is the person in charge of the treatment and an approved clinician; or

   (b) the treatment is given under the direction of that clinician.

---

[54] Richardson (2002).   [55] BMA and Law Society (2004).
[56] [2003] UKHL 59.   [57] 45508/99 (ECtHR).   [58] DoH (2005p).

(5) The fifth condition is that giving the treatment does not conflict with—

    (a) an advance decision which he is satisfied is valid and applicable; or

    (b) a decision made by a donee, deputy or the Court of Protection.

There are several points to emphasize about this provision. First the treatment cannot be given to a non-consenting patient if force is required to give the treatment. If force is required then an application under section 4 should be made. Second, if the individual has made an advance directive or has appointed a donee then these can, in effect, veto the use of section 64.

4 Codes of Practice

The 1983 Act permits the Secretary of State to issue a Code of Practice on how the law is to operate. This was power was introduced through the 2007 Act and so currently only a draft Code is available. Section 118(2)(b) sets out factors that the Secretary of State should take into account when preparing the Codes:

    (a) respect for patients' past and present wishes and feelings;

    (b) respect for diversity generally, including in particular, diversity of religion, culture and sexual orientation (within the meaning of section 35 of the Equality Act 2006);

    (c) minimising restrictions on liberty;

    (d) involvement of patients in planning, developing and delivering care and treatment appropriate to them;

    (e) avoidance of unlawful discrimination;

    (f) effectiveness of treatment;

    (g) views of carers and other interested parties;

    (h) patient wellbeing and safety; and

    (i) public safety.

The Draft Codes of Practice produced in 2007 state the following principles:

Purpose principle
1.2 Decisions under the Act should be taken with a view to minimising the harm done by mental disorder, by maximising the safety and wellbeing (mental and physical) of patients and protecting the public from harm.

Least restrictive alternative principle
1.3 Any intervention without the patient's consent must attempt to minimise the restrictions on the patient's liberty, having regard to the purpose for which they are imposed.

Respect principle
1.4 Decision makers must recognise and respect the diverse needs, values and circumstances of each patient, including their race, religion, culture, gender, age and sexual orientation. They should consider the patient's wishes and feelings (whether expressed at the time or in advance), so far as reasonably ascertainable, and respect those wishes wherever that is practicable and consistent with the purpose of the decision. There must be no unlawful discrimination.

Participation principle

1.5 Patients should be involved, as far as is practicable in the circumstances, in planning and developing their own care to help ensure it is delivered in a way that is as appropriate and effective for them as possible. The involvement of carers, family members and other people who have an interest in the patient's welfare should be encouraged (unless there are particular reasons to the contrary) and their views taken seriously.

Resources principle

1.6 Decision-makers must seek to use the resources available to them and to patients in the most effective, efficient and equitable way. Decision-makers must take account of other people's perspectives on what is required.[59]

5 The reforms to the law in the 2007 Act

5.1 Introduction

The journey to reform of the law on mental health has been a long one. In 1998 the Government announced that it was going to reform the 1983 Mental Health Act. In part this was motivated by a growing acceptance that the current law was not compliant with the requirements of the European Convention on Human Rights. But also there was a perception that it was failing to adequately protect the public from 'dangerously ill' people. The Government White Paper stated:

> The 1983 Act...fails to address the challenge posed by a minority of people with mental disorder who pose a significant risk to others as a result of their disorder. It has failed properly to protect the public, patients, or staff. Severely mentally ill patients have been allowed to lose contact with services once they have been discharged into the community.[60]

There followed a report from an expert committee,[61] a Green Paper, a White Paper, a consultation Bill in 2002, a draft Bill in 2004, a report of the Parliamentary Joint Committee which described the Bill as 'fundamentally flawed', and a lengthy response from the Government to that report. The Bill was redrafted and presented to Parliament in 2006.

One of the difficulties which bedevilled the debate over the reform is: how is it possible to protect the human rights of those with mental illness while adequately protecting the 'general public'? The fact that over 2,000 comments were received on the Government's draft legislation indicates the strength of feeling which the issue raises.

5.2 Key principles

The purpose of the 2007 Act was described as:

> to protect patients and others from any harm that can arise from mental disorder.[62]

This, of course, neatly sidesteps the issue of what should happen when there is a conflict between what is the best treatment for the patient and what is most likely to protect the

---

59 DoH (2007f).   60 DoH (2005d: 1).

61 Richardson (1999).   62 DoH (2004h: para 1.2).

public. Critics, including the Parliamentary Joint Committee, have complained that the Bill attaches too great a weight to the need to protect the public. The Government's response is:

> We consider that the Committee's concerns about the balance of public safety and patient autonomy miss the point that our concern is about the balance between patient and public safety and patient autonomy. The great majority of people with a serious mental disorder are more likely to harm themselves than others, and it is wrong to paint a picture of a government or society obsessed with public safety. The Government's and society's concern is to protect very vulnerable people from harming themselves or, much more occasionally, others. And the concern to ensure that people can get the treatment they need to protect them from harming themselves or others is balanced by a concern to respect patients' rights to make decisions for themselves. . . . We must stress that we see no conflict between protection from harm and ensuring that patient rights are fully and appropriately promoted. The Bill does both.[63]

We have already set out the law as it has been amended by the Act. However, we will now list some of the main changes the 2007 Act made:

- There is a new definition of mental disorder. The legislation will no longer distinguish between different kinds of mental disorder.

- Section 3 is amended to mean that a person can only be detained if there is 'appropriate medical treatment for them'. Previously treatment which would improve, alleviate, or prevent deterioration of their condition was required.

- The Act enables the making of codes of practice.[64]

- The Act creates a power to make community treatment orders.

- The Act provides for the Independent Mental Health Advocacy service which can assist in applications being made to the Tribunal.

- The circumstances in which the use of electro-convulsive therapy can be used are tightened up.[65]

- The Act gives patients the right to make an application to remove their nearest relative if there are reasonable grounds for doing so.

- The Act gives greater powers to mental health professionals who are not psychiatrists by creating a category of 'approve clinician' who can carry out some of the roles that previously only psychiatrists can do.

The proposals created tensions between some of the professional bodies.[66]

5.3 Criticisms of the Act

The Bill during its progress has been subject to a barrage of objections and it is only possible here to mention a few of the main complaints. The further reading provides ample additional material if more is required.

(1) There is no 'treatability' test or 'therapeutic benefit' test. Critics complain that the Act will require doctors to become 'jailors' by taking into hospitals individuals who

---

[63] DoH (2005d: 4).   [64] S 118.   [65] S 58A.   [66] Butcher (2007).

are deemed to be dangerous, but for whom no medical treatment can be offered.[67] As seen above, the Act does in fact require evidence that the individual can be offered treatment, but critics argue that the definition of treatment is so wide (it includes 'care') that the restriction is meaningless. The Joint Committee warned that without a 'treatability' test the Act could be incompatible with the European Convention on Human Rights. However the decision of the European Court of Human Rights in *Hutchinson Reid v UK*[68] held that it is permissible under article 5(e) to detain a mentally disordered person for the purpose of protecting others, even if no treatment is provided.

(2) The Act could lead to an increase in the use of compulsory powers in the community, through the use of the community treatment order.[69] The concern is that a larger section of the mentally ill community will face compulsory powers than do under the current law. Further, the wider use of compulsory powers may challenge the relationship between patients and professionals, with patients being unwilling to discuss the problems they are experiencing with their treatment programme. Supporters of compulsory treatment suggest that it will mean that more patients will be able to leave hospital, albeit under tightly supervised regimes. The Government has emphasized that there will be no forcible treatment of patients in the community.[70]

(3) The over-emphasis on risk. The theme that unites most critics of the Act is that there is too great an emphasis on risk to the 'public' and too little respect for the human rights of mentally ill people in the law. Notably the risk to others in the 'relevant criteria' justifying compulsory detention is not required to be 'serious' or 'grave'.

(4) The absence of provisions addressing problems experienced in getting access to services. Some support groups argue that putting more money and effort into improving the quality of mental services would be a better use of resources than amending the legislation.[71] The Government, however, is adamant that it is improving services and will continue to do so. It was not the purpose of the Act to directly address all of the issues surrounding mental health, it emphasizes.

(5) A fundamental question is whether, if a patient is competent, she or he should be able to be treated against her or his wishes. It is, of course, contrary to general medical law principles that a person should be treated against their wishes. Does this apply to mentally disordered individuals? Some people believe it does and there should be a fundamental principle that, if competent, a person should not be given treatment against her or his wishes. Others believe that a narrow exception should be created in the case of mentally disordered people who pose a serious risk to others. Some would add: or a risk to themselves. Even among supporters of an exception to the principle, there is generally agreement that there should be narrowly defined circumstances.[72]

6 Protection from abuse

Much of the debate in relation to mental health is about protecting the public. However, it is important to appreciate that mentally ill people can be subject to abuse and mistreatment. It is notable how the law has been far more ready to protect the 'general

[67] Richardson (2005).   [68] (2003)37 EHRR 9.
[69] Moncrieff (2003). The arguments are well rehearsed in Pinfold and Bindman (2001) and Canvin, Bartlett, and Pinfold (2004).
[70] DoH (2005d: 19).   [71] Rethink (2005).   [72] Richardson (2005).

public' from the mentally ill than it has been to protect the mentally ill from the 'general public'. The Mental Capacity Act 2005 has enabled orders to be made to protect incompetent people from others seeking to take advantage of them. That Act is discussed in Chapter 3.

7 Human rights

It is clear that the courts, in interpreting the MHA and the common law in cases involving the mentally ill, are paying increasing attention to the European Convention on Human Rights, as they are required to do by the Human Rights Act.[73] The European Court has suggested that due to the vulnerability of mentally ill people, especially those detained in psychiatric hospitals, particular vigilance is required to protect their human rights.[74] The European Convention contains a number of articles that are relevant to the issue:

EUROPEAN ANGLES

Article 5

Article 5 of the European Convention states that:

> Everyone has the right to liberty and security of person. No one shall be deprived of his liberty save in the following cases and in accordance with a procedure prescribed by law.

But this is subject to a number of exceptions. The relevant one for this chapter is (e):

> the lawful detention of person for the prevention of the spreading of infectious diseases, of persons of unsound mind, alcoholics or drug addicts or vagrants.

Winterwerp v The Netherlands[75] set down a number of criteria before the justification in (e) could be satisfied:

(1) The patient must be 'reliably shown' by 'objective medical expertise' to be of 'unsound mind'.[76]

(2) The disorder must be such as to justify detention.

(3) The patient can only be detained while she or he is suffering from the disorder.

The European Court has also emphasized that the detention must be proportionate to the mental condition of the individual.[77]

In *Aerts v Belgium*[78] it was emphasized that the Convention only permits the detention of a mentally ill person for the treatment of that medical condition. If no treatment is available for their condition then article 5(e) does not justify their detention. Detention in a prison in which no treatment was being offered was therefore unlawful. Release is required as soon as the

---

[73] *R (on the application of JB) v Haddock* [2006] EWCA Civ 961. For discussion of the impact of the HRA on mental health law see: Richardson (2005); Fennell (2005); Davidson (2002); and Gostin (2000).

[74] *Herczegfalvy v Austria* (1992) 15 EHRR 437.

[75] (1979) 2 EHRR 387.

[76] In emergencies the ECtHR made it clear detention may be permissible without the evidence being provided.

[77] *Litwa v Poland* (2000) 63 BMLR 199.   [78] (1998) 29 EHRR 50.

person has recovered from the disorder to an extent such that their detention is not justified.[79] Any detention must be subject to regular review to ensure the detention is still justified.[80]

Article 5.4 imposes important procedural safeguards in relation to detention:

> Everyone who is deprived of his liberty by arrest or detention shall be entitled to take proceedings by which the lawfulness of his detention shall be decided speedily by a court and his release ordered if the detention is not lawful.

Under article 5(4) there must be an effective and speedy[81] means of challenging the compulsory admission. This led the Court of Appeal to find that the requirement that a MHRT could only release a patient if it was shown that the criteria for detention were not made out was incompatible with patients' rights under article 5.[82] It should be for the medical authorities to show the criteria existed rather than for the patient to show they did not.[83]

Article 5 is also relevant in a case where the patient's condition no longer justified her or his detention. In *R v Secretary of State for the Home Department and another ex p IH*[84] the House of Lords confirmed that article 5 required that if a patient is no longer suffering from a mental disorder she or he should be released without unreasonable delay. However, they refused to take a more radical interpretation of article 5 and require the release of a patient who could, with appropriate support be released into the community where despite all reasonable endeavours that support could not be provided despite all reasonable endeavours. This applicant took the case to the European Court (*Kolanis v United Kingdom*[85]) where it was held that her mental condition had justified the continued detention. However, the difficulties and delays she had faced in bringing the issue to a court following the failure follow the MHRT (by releasing her conditionally) infringed her rights under article 5(4).

Article 3

Article 3 is also relevant in that it prohibits torture or inhuman or degrading treatment. This could be relevant in two ways. First, it might be argued that any form of compulsory treatment is degrading. Given the widespread practice of non-consensual treatment for mental illness across Europe, a court may well hold that treatment is not inhuman or degrading simply by virtue of being non-consensual. Indeed, as we have seen, the courts have accepted that if the treatment is necessary for the therapeutic treatment of an incompetent person it will not infringe their article 3 rights.[86] However, if the treatment is not necessary for their treatment, it could infringe article 3 if the circumstances in which the compulsory treatment is provided are such that it can be regarded as inhuman and degrading.[87] Unnecessary physical force used against a patient, where the force is not reasonable to give lawful treatment, may also breach article 3.[88]

Second, it might be argued that not to treat someone suffering from a serious mental condition might infringe their article 3 rights.[89] In *Keenan v UK*[90] a suicidal patient who was not given the appropriate care was found to have had his article 3 rights infringed.

---

[79] *Johnson v United Kingdom* (1999) 27 EHRR 440.

[80] *E v Norway* (1994) 17 EHRR 30.

[81] See *R (on the application of C) v Mental Health Review Tribunal* [2002] 1 WLR 176 for a case where the appeals process infringed an applicant's rights by being too slow.

[82] *R (H) v Mental Health Review Tribunal* [2001] 3 WLR 512; *Reid v UK* (2003) 37 EHRR 9.

[83] This is now the law after Mental Health Act 1983 (Remedial) Order 2001 SI 2001/3712.

[84] [2003] UKHL 59.   [85] [2005] All ER(D) 57.

[86] *R (on the application of B) v SS* [2005] EWHC 86.

[87] *R (On the Application of PS) v G (RMO) and W (SOAD)* [2003] EWHC 2335 (Fam).

[88] *Keenan v UK* (2001) EHRR 38.   [89] Wicks (2007).   [90] (2001) 33 EHRR 38.

Article 8

Article 8, with its right to respect for private and family life, is also potentially relevant in the cases involving mentally ordered individuals. However article 8(2) permits an interference with that right if necessary in order to (*inter alia*) protect health or the interests of others. Forced treatment which does not amount to torture or inhuman or degrading treatment may still be unlawful under article 8, if not justified under paragraph 2.[91] There is an argument that if the patient is competent and refusing treatment it should only rarely be found justifiable under paragraph 2.[92] In *R (on the application of O'Reilly) v Blenheim Healthcare Ltd*[93] it was held that passing on confidential information about a mentally disordered patient could infringe that patient's article 8 rights, although on the facts of that case there was no such disclosure, and even if there had been it could have been justified under paragraph 2 as necessary to protect the health of the patient and the safety of others.

---

8 Problems in mental health practice

So far we have been looking at some of the difficulties in the legal regulation of mental health. It is time to look at some of the problems in the practical operation of mental health services.

8.1 Ethnic minority communities

There are serious concerns about the ethnic make up of clients using mental health services.[94] Consider these points:

- People from ethnic minority groups are six times more likely to be detained under the Mental Health Act than white people.[95]

- The prevalence of common mental health problems is fairly similar across different ethnic groups, although rates are higher for Irish men and Pakistani women and lower for Bangladeshi women.[96]

- Poor mental health is particularly acute among refugees, two thirds of whom have experienced anxiety or depression.[97]

- Adults from ethnic minority groups have higher levels of dissatisfaction with mental health statutory services than white people, and are twice as likely to disagree with their diagnosis.

The Government has accepted that there are particular needs and issues relating to the use of mental health services by ethnic minorities and claims to be seeking to address them.[98] One explanation is that we are seeing institutional racism. Particularly in a climate of fear of the 'dangerousness' of mental illness, the stereotypes of violence associated with black men may lead to racist attitudes in making decisions. An alternative

---

[91] *R (Wilkinson) v Broadmoor Special Hospital* [2001] EWCA Civ 1545.
[92] Richardson (2005).   [93] [2005] EWHC 241.
[94] Sainsbury Centre for Mental Health (2005).
[95] Social Exclusion Unit (2005).   [96] Social Exclusion Unit (2005).
[97] Social Exclusion Unit (2005).   [98] Social Exclusion Unit (2005).

explanation is that social deprivation and exclusion is linked to mental illness, and higher rates of this are found among ethnic minority communities.[99]

8.2 Sexuality

There have also been concerns about the treatment of gay and lesbian communities within mental health services.[100] Of course there is historical baggage: it was not too long ago that 'non-orthodox sexuality' was regarded as a form of mental illness. Even today it is claimed that gay, lesbian, and bi-sexual people can face discrimination when being open with mental health professionals about their sexuality. In one study 36 per cent of gay men, 42 per cent of lesbians, and 61 per cent of bisexual women claimed to have faced negative or mixed reactions from mental health professionals.[101]

There are also issues about the difficulties that partners of mentally ill people can face in being recognized as 'nearest relative' of a patient under the Mental Health Act. They will be helped by the decision in *R (on the application of SSG) v Liverpool CC*[102] where it was held that the Human Rights Act required the courts to interpret the phrase 'living together as husband and wife' as covering a same-sex couple.

8.3 Sex and mental health

Feminists in particular have been concerned about the position of women within the mental health system.

 FEMINIST PERSPECTIVES

Mental health

There have been regular complaints of sexism within the mental health system. The variety of claims made about the system demonstrates the complex interchange of preconceptions of women's behaviour. On the one hand there are claims that women are too easily labelled as mentally ill. Women are disproportionately represented among those voluntarily detained for psychiatric treatment (Fegan and Fennell (1998: 74)). There is a preconception that women are mentally fragile and therefore especially prone to mental illness (Goudsmit (1995)). Further it is claimed that women whose sexual behaviour is regarded as abnormal are as seen as exhibiting mental illness. On the other hand there are claims that mental health professionals do not take seriously the mental health problems women face. Unhappiness, self-deprecation, or unfulfillment are regarded by health care professionals as normal for women, some critics claim. This last point has led some to suggest that rather than examining more carefully the social and economic factors that cause women to suffer these feelings, they are treated with drugs. We are, as one commentator has put it, seeing the 'medicalisation of female unhappiness' (Scambler (2003d: 139)). It is certainly true that one study has suggested that women are two and a half times more likely to be treated for depression than men (Scambler (2003d: 140)) Although whether that reflects the reluctance of men to seek help for mental health issues or the over-willingness of doctors to diagnose depression among women is a matter for debate.

There are certainly some mental conditions which it is possible to regard as a reaction to oppression faced by women within society: anorexia nervosa may be a good example. But some

---

99 Bartlett and Sandland (2007).

101 Mind/University College London (2003).

100 Mind (1997) and PACE (1998).

102 Unreported, discussed in Cho (2002).

feminist commentators argue that it is dangerous to regard all conditions in this way because it can inhibit proper research into women's mental health issues. For example, premenstrual tension or syndrome is little understood. Indeed patients in hospital suffering manic depression find dramatic improvements in their condition on menstruation (Fegan and Fennell (1998: 79)).

A final point is that it may be suggested that the concept of mental health is gendered. At present women are over-represented as users of the mental health services but this is because we do not regard violence, alcohol misuse, or child abuse as indicative of a mental illness. If we did the gender balance would shift. This raises the whole issue of how we define mental illness, a question to which we shall return shortly.

8.4 Shortfalls in provision on the ground

Users of mental health and their carers or supporters have complained about shortfalls in the provision of mental health services.[103] The complaints have been summarized by the Chief Executive of the Sainsbury Centre for Mental Health thus:

> It would be surprising if a public service was tolerated when it was feared by its customers (whom it puts at risk), unable to show evidence of its effectiveness and paying its staff uncompetitive rates. It would be astonishing if, nevertheless, such a service could not cope with demand. Yet this is a recognizable picture of acute mental health care in the NHS.[104]

We have already mentioned the various ways in which it might be argued discrimination is exhibited. But there are other concerns too. Some complain about the difficulty in obtaining medicine. A report from the Zito Trust[105] found that despite clear evidence that newer atypical antipsychotic drugs provided an effective treatment for schizophrenia, they were not widely available on the NHS, and the extent of their use varied across the country. NICE guidance recommending their use may improve the situation. There also appear to be problems in the provision for dealing with crises. The Healthcare Commission found that across all trusts less than a half of all service users had the phone number of someone in the mental health service that they could call out of hours.[106] The same report found that only half the service users had been given a copy of their care plan, and only a half had received at least one care review in the previous 12 months. The assistance for users with wider social issues was weak. Only a third of users had had help finding accommodation and less than a third with finding a job.

A consistent complaint is that individuals needing assistance in the community with mental health issues find it difficult to access the help they need, and it is only when their condition reaches crisis point and they require detention that they receive it.[107] One study found 28 per cent of those with mental disorders had been 'shunned' when they first sought help.[108] This leads to ever increasing 'crisis management' costs, and to mental health services with decreasing funds and effort available for the care in the community of the less seriously ill. In other words, too little effort and funding is available for work designed to prevent people having to be taken into hospital for mental illness, and too much on dealing with them when they are there. This explains, some claim, why there has been a 30 per cent increase in the number of people detained under the

---

103 Dobson (2004). 104 Muijen, quoted in Rethink (2005).
105 Zito Trust (2004). 106 Healthcare Commission (2004b).
107 King's Fund (2003a). 108 Rethink (2003).

Mental Health Act in the past decade.[109] It may also partly explain the 'revolving door' syndrome with people being released from hospital into the community, but due to the lack of support having to be readmitted into the hospital a short time later.[110] The total spent on mental health services was £4.7 billion in 2005/6.[111] The money does not seem to be providing an adequate service.[112]

This is reflected in acute staff shortages, and difficulties in staff retention across the service.[113] There have also been complaints about the quality of in-patient care with lack of staff, inadequate facilities, and overcrowding being common sources of complaint.[114] All of this seems a long way from the BMA's principles[115] as to how patients suffering mental ill health should be treated:

- *Liberty*. Patients should be free from interventions that inhibit liberty or the capacity to enjoy life unless such intervention is necessary to prevent a greater harm to the patient or to others. Treatment options should be the least restrictive effective option. Appropriate justification must be shown for the use of restraints and it is inappropriate for restrictive measures to be used as an alternative to adequate staffing levels.

- *Autonomy*. Patients' autonomy should be promoted in a manner that is consistent with their needs and wishes.

- *Dignity*. Patients should be treated with respect and courtesy, and their social and cultural values respected. Their views should be taken into account, even when they are considered legally incapable of determining what happens.

- *Privacy*. Patients should be free from any medical procedures unless there are good therapeutic reasons for them.

- *Confidentiality*. Personal health information should be treated confidentially.

- *Having their health needs met*. Health needs should be met as fully as practicable, while recognizing that the availability of resources may limit treatment options.

- *Freedom from unfair discrimination*. Treatment options should be considered on the basis of the patient's need; patients should not be treated differently solely because of the condition that gives rise to the incapacity.

- *The views of the patient should be taken into account* This applies even when they are not entitled in law to make decisions on behalf of the patient.

The picture should not be regarded as all negative. The Healthcare Commission's patient survey[116] suggested that less than 10 per cent of users rated the care they received as poor or very poor; 77 per cent rated it as good, very good or excellent. However, a dominant theme was the desire for users to be involved far more in decision-making about their treatment and provided with more information about medication.

8.5 Social exclusion

There is concern at the degree of social exclusion that can be faced by those with mental health problems. This is manifested in a number of different ways:

---

[109] Rethink (2005: 3).   [110] Rethink (2005: 6).

[111] Oxford Economics (2007). Although for evidence of the financial strain facing many Mental Health Trusts see Sainsbury Centre for Mental Health (2006).

[112] Rankin (2004).   [113] King's Fund (2003a).   [114] Rethink (2005: 1).

[115] BMA (2004: 100).   [116] Healthcare Commission (2005).

- Only 24 per cent of adults with long-term mental health problems are in work. In a Government survey, fewer than four in ten employers said that they would consider employing someone with a history of mental health problems.[117] Nearly a million people are receiving incapacity benefit due to mental ill health.[118]

- Forty-four per cent of people with mental health problems felt that they had experienced discrimination from GPs because of their condition.[119] The Government has recognized that mental health service users as a group are one of the most excluded groups in society.[120]

- Social isolation is an important factor linked to deterioration of mental health and suicide.

- Carers of those suffering mental illness are twice as likely to have mental health problems themselves.[121]

- The Government reports that those suffering mental health problems struggle to find decent housing and transport.

Behind these problems lies a lack of understanding and support among the general public for those suffering mental health difficulties. The perception of danger, which some say is stoked by the Government's rhetoric, makes it difficult for users to fit into the wider community.

8.6 Life on psychiatric wards

Perhaps it would be unrealistic to expect any report on life on psychiatric wards to be glowing. However, the evidence we have indicates a number of issues which cause concern.[122] Rethink, a pressure group supporting mental health service users, suggests that their research finds acute in-patient care to be neither safe nor therapeutic. There are particular concerns with violence and bullying in psychiatric wards.[123] In 2003 a report found disturbing evidence of bullying, violence, and abuse of women at Broadmoor.[124] A study by MIND found that 51 per cent of in-patients reported violence or threats while in hospital.[125] Seventy-eight per cent of staff have reported being assaulted.[126] There is a severe shortage of staff on many wards.[127] A report in 1998 by the Sainsbury Centre for Mental Health[128] found that wards were dirty, cramped, poorly ventilated, and had a constant blare of noise from a television or radio. Further, there was 'institutional aimlessness': a complete lack of anything for patients to do.[129] Staff expect unquestioning obedience and substance misuse is rife.[130] In 2003–04, 94 people died from unnatural causes while being detained under the Mental Health Act (the vast majority being suicide).[131] Despite all of these problems, a number of studies have shown that the majority of patients found their stay in hospital beneficial.[132]

[117] Social Exclusion Unit (2005).   [118] Oxford Economics (2007).
[119] Office of the Deputy Prime Minister (2004).
[120] Social Exclusion Unit (2004). See also Dunn (1999).
[121] See Yates (2007) for a discussion of the law of attention paid to the carers of those with mental illness.
[122] See also Sainsbury Centre (2005).
[123] Ireland and Snowden (2002); Rethink (2004). See BBC Newsonline (10 July 2006) for reports of over 100 sexual assualts in mental health units over a two-year period.
[124] BBC Newsonline (7 March 2003).   [125] MIND (2005).   [126] MIND (2005).
[127] Cole (2005).   [128] Sainsbury Centre for Mental Health (1998).
[129] National Institute for Mental Health in England (2004).   [130] Rethink (2005: 17).
[131] Mental Health Act Commission (2005).   [132] Bartlett and Sandland (2007).

8.7 Coercion/consent

As already mentioned, a large number of patients are detained in mental hospitals not under the Mental Health Act, but because they are voluntary patients, or under the necessity principle. However, there is reason to question whether such consent is genuine. Studies of voluntary patients have shown that many of them are not aware of their status or to what they have consented. Fifty per cent were unclear of their legal status[133] (ie whether they were there voluntarily or whether they had been sectioned); 2/3 did not know the purpose of medication they were taking; 9/10 did not know the side effects of their medication; few questioned realized they had a choice about whether or not to take their medication.[134] It is perhaps inevitable that a person suffering mental health problems will consent to medical treatment and being admitted to hospital for fear of being 'sectioned' or of not being offered treatment.[135]

8.8 Prisons

Around 70 per cent of sentenced prisoners have identifiable mental health problems.[136] In the first half of 2007 there were 50 suicides.[137] The mental health services received by prisoners has been said to be notably worse than that available under the NHS,[138] an issue the Government claims to be addressing.[139] However, inevitably there are concerns that people who should be receiving treatment for their mental disorders are instead being detained in prison for offences committed because they have not received the treatment that they should have.[140]

8.9 Care in the community

There is a concern about the level of support offered to patients in the community. If a patient has been discharged under the MHA 1983 then she or he has an entitlement to after-care under section 117 of the Act.[141] This requires the health authority in their area to provide patients with after-care services until they are not required.[142] However, in *R v Islington and Camden HA*[143] the Court of Appeal accepted that in meeting that obligation, the authority would be required to consider competing claims on its resources.

Patients requiring support or supervision in the community should be given a Care Programme. This involves a system for cooperation between health and social services to ensure that an assessment is made of patients' needs and any risk they may present. A programme of care should be agreed between the health and social services, and a care coordinator should be appointed to oversee its implementation of the programme. The programme should be regularly reviewed. There is evidence that the Care Programme approach is not working as it should, with patients either not having a plan or not knowing what it was.[144] Bartlett and Sandland, summarizing the reports into violent crimes

---

133 Bartlett and Sandland (2007).   134 Billcliff, McCabe and Brown (2001).
135 Bonsack and Borgeat (2005).   136 SEU (2002).
137 BBC Newsonline (12 July 2007).   138 Reed (2002).   139 Social Exclusion Unit (2005).
140 Stephenson (2004); Sainsbury Centre for Mental Health (2007).
141 The likelihood of a successful tort action if an authority fails to supply services appears remote. See Chap 2.
142 *R v Ealing DHA ex p Fox* [1993] 3 All ER 129.
143 [2001] EWCA 240.   144 Rethink (2003).

committed by those being cared for in the community, write 'the independent reports paint a depressing picture of overstretched, under-resourced and under-staffed community mental health teams, unable to maintain contact with patients who have little wish to cooperate with their "care plan" '.[145]

There is relatively little that can be done to compel a patient in the community to act in a particular way, outside the powers of detention under the Mental Health Act. One alternative is guardianship, which was discussed at page 528.

9 Critics of mental health

So far we have been discussing the concept of mental health without really getting to grips with defining it or challenging the very concept of mental health. The concept is in fact highly problematic. Society's understanding of mental illness is fluid. Tony Hope refers to a condition diagnosed by Dr Samuel Cartwright in 1851 called 'drapetomania' which was described as the tendency of Negro slaves to run away from their masters.[146] Until recently homosexuality was considered a psychological disorder.[147] As these examples show, today's mental illness may be tomorrow's normality.

Observations of this kind have led to a school of thought known as anti-psychiatry. Although there are relatively few commentators who accept the extreme tendencies of its leading proponents, their arguments are important because at the very least they reveal how the concept of mental illness is contestable. The leading proponent of anti-psychiatry is Thomas Szasz.[148] He argues that psychiatric disorders are not illnesses, but rather a description of behaviour which offends or annoys people. We have an image of how people 'ought' to behave and if they do not we label them as suffering from a mental illness.[149] As such, when our understanding of what kinds of behaviour are 'normal' changes so does our concept of what constitutes mental illness. The example of homosexuality could be used to demonstrate this point. Seen in this way psychiatry is a means of exercising social control over the 'different' and Szasz has even claimed psychiatry is analogous to slavery.[150] He firmly rejects claims that mentally ill people are not responsible for their actions. A person does not, he claims, lose all control over every movement when they suffer a mental illness.[151] A person who hears voices and acts in response to them, chooses to do so, says Szasz, and is therefore responsible for their actions.[152] In a moderate tone Richard Bentall[153] suggests that hallucinations and delusions are exaggerated forms of mental foibles which we all experience.

A rather different critique of psychiatry is to claim that mental health problems are (or nearly always are) the reaction of normal people to abnormal social pressures or oppressive family institutions.[154] For example, when a women who has suffered years of abuse kills her partner in desperation, some psychiatrists might claim that she suffered from 'battered women's syndrome', whilst others will classify it as an understandable and reasonable reaction to an extreme situation, and not indicative of mental disorder.[155]

[145] Bartlett and Sandland (2007).   [146] Hope (2005: 75).   [147] Kennedy (1981: Chap 1).
[148] Szasz (1972, 2002).   [149] Szasz (1972).   [150] Szasz (2002).
[151] Szasz (2001). See the reply in Brassington (2002).
[152] Szasz (2001). Indeed he suggests the voices may be an expression of the person's true desires which she or he does not want to accept.
[153] Bentall (2004)   [154] Laing (1959).   [155] Kaganas (2003).

These issues can present problems for those diagnosed with mental conditions. Those who accept that they have a mental illness and are willing to receive treatment are seen as on the road to recovery. Those who dispute their diagnosis and deny any illness are regarded as problematic and in need of further treatment.[156]

Those who disagree with the anti-psychiatrists accept that, in the past, the concept of mental health has been misused, and perhaps there are conditions currently regarded as being a manifestation of mental ill-health which will not be so regarded in the future; however, they maintain that we should not throw out the baby with the bathwater. There are people who are genuinely suffering and for whom mental health services offer real help for which they are extremely grateful. To follow Szasz's line and not recognize their illness and to leave them without treatment would be cruel. Szasz, in reply, would challenge any evidence that psychiatry does anyone any 'good', save rendering their behaviour more acceptable by rendering them comatose. Critics of Szasz might accept that there is a danger of conflating 'abnormal behaviour' with 'mentally ill behaviour', but that to some extent this can be overcome by asking if the behaviour is normal for the particular individual. If it is, that might be regarded as indicative of a mental illness.[157] Indeed one of the messages that must be taken seriously from Szasz's writing is the need to be clear, when a person is being detained under the MHA 1983, as to what the purpose for doing so is: is it to protect the public; protect the patient's carers; or to protect the interests of the patient?[158]

At the heart of the debate may be the extent to which an individual diagnosed as mentally disordered can exercise autonomy. To Szasz a person diagnosed as 'mentally ill' is in fact responsible and able to take decisions. To opponents they are not fully autonomous agents, their 'manifestations' of intent do not reflect the 'true wishes' of the individual.[159] After all if we accept there is such a thing as the mind, must we not accept that the mind can become ill?[160]

If we accept there is a concept of mental illness there then comes the difficulty of defining and classifying it. Many now take the view that mental health is better regarded as a spectrum rather than two separate boxes. We are all more or less sane or insane, depending on how you would rather see it. Certainly it is difficult if not impossible to draw a sharp line between sanity and insanity.[161] Most definitions are based on the disturbance of mental functioning, which could involve disruption of thought processes, emotions or motivations.[162] The definition of mental disorder is problematic. Is a violent person to be regarded as mentally ill? What about a person with strong paedophilic desires? If so where does this leave responsibility for criminal actions? With the current climate in the United Kingdom of fear of the dangerously mentally ill, there is a danger that being dangerous becomes synonymous with being mentally ill.[163] There is also a debate over whether it is possible to draw a sharp line between physical illness and mental illness. This becomes particularly relevant when the law seeks to prevent disability discrimination. In the medical profession, there tends to be a clear line between psychiatrists who deal with mental illness, and physicians who deal with physical illness. However, increasing the interaction of bodily and mental health indicates that line is difficult to draw.

---

[156] See discussion Cavadino (1989: 30). [157] Adshead (2003). [158] McMillan (2003a).
[159] See McMillan (2003a), Sayers (2003). [160] Brassington (2002). [161] Kornll (2003).
[162] Kornll (2003). [163] Eldergill (2003).

10 Dangerousness

As has been indicated, a key issue in the current law and debate over reform is over the 'dangerousness' of the mentally ill. This focus has been criticized by those who see a shift in Government policy from a culture of welfare to a culture of control.[164]

10.1 Are the mentally ill dangerous?

The media sometimes portray the mentally disordered as a violent and dangerous group who could attack at any time. But in fact the majority of those with psychiatric problems are not dangerous.[165] When there is an attack by a mentally ill person, the media gives the case extensive coverage.[166] This is not to belittle the occasions where that occurs, but the danger must be put in perspective. Eldergill states:

> People are more likely to win the National Lottery jackpot than they are to die at the hand of a stranger with a mental illness.[167]

He goes on to point out that:

> people suffering from schizophrenia are one hundred times more likely to kill themselves than someone else, and those with a mood disorder are one thousand times more likely.[168]

Indeed there is evidence that people suffering from mental disorder are far more likely to be the victims of violence themselves than an average member of the public.[169] Despite this, the Government has pointed out that of the 500 or so homicides each year, around 15 per cent are committed by those with a mental illness.[170] However, despite greater use of community care, there has been a gradual 3 per cent annual decline in the proportion of homicides committed by people with mental disorders from 1957 to 1995.[171] The strongest link to homicides is not mental illness, but alcohol or drug misuse.[172]

10.2 Can we predict dangerousness?

The prediction of dangerousness is problematic.[173] For example, in one research survey in only four out of 16 research projects were 60 per cent or more of psychiatrists able to agree on whether an individual was dangerous.[174] Of the many attempts that have been made to develop an accurate way of assessing dangerousness probably the most successful has been the MacArthur Violence Risk Assessment study:[175] this used 106 variables to assess dangerousness.[176] Looking at 939 people, the researchers divided them into five risk bands, ranging from the most likely to be violent to the least. In the band of those labelled most likely to be violent, just over three quarters were indeed violent. This is significantly better than most other studies. However, if all those in the highest risk

---

[164] Farnham and James (2001).   [165] Bowden (1996).

[166] BBC Newsonline (2 September 2005; 22 June 2005; 19 May 2005a; and 19 April 2005).

[167] Eldergill (2003: 333).   [168] Eldergill (2003: 333).   [169] Walsh et al (2003).

[170] DoH (2005p: para 14).   [171] Taylor and Gunn (1999).

[172] Shaw et al (2004).   [173] Munro and Rumgay (2000).

[174] Montadon and Harding (1984).   [175] Monahan (2001).

[176] Bartlett (2003a) suggests the test is too complex to use in a clinical setting.

band were detained that would mean that nearly one in four of those detained would not in fact have been dangerous if not detained. Further if only those in the higher band were detained only 27 per cent of those in the sample who were violent would have been detained. To halve the number of violent incidents it would be necessary to include the top two bands which would mean 36 per cent of those detained would not have been violent.[177]

10.3 If we can predict dangerousness, does it justify detention?

On the assumption that it is possible to identify a mentally ill individual as dangerous, does this justify detaining her or him? To some it does. The state has an obligation to protect its citizens from death.[178] Indeed, this might be regarded as one of the primary duties of the state and required under article 2 of the European Convention. Any interference in the rights of the person detained is justified because the state is acting to protect the even greater rights of citizens not to suffer death or serious injury.

Opponents argue that we do not normally detain people who are not mentally ill, even if they have been classified as dangerous. Having a propensity to commit a crime is very different from committing it.[179] Until a person has committed a criminal act, predictions as to dangerousness do not normally justify detention. Why should we regard the mentally ill in any way differently from those with no mental disorder? To do so would be discriminatory.[180] Supporters of preventative detention of the mentally ill could reply to such an argument in several ways. They may argue that we should detain all people predicted to be dangerous, whether they are mentally ill or not. They may alternatively seek to justify the discrimination by arguing, for example, that because the behaviour of mentally ill people is more difficult to predict such people are more dangerous, or that mentally ill people can be cured and this provides a distinction. However, there is little evidence to suggest that dangerous mentally ill people are any more unpredictable or curable than non-mentally ill dangerous people.

The argument in favour of detention based on the prevention of harm and saving lives could also justify the outlawing of the use of cars and the drinking of alcohol. Both of these measures would, no doubt, save far more lives than preventative detention, yet most people would balk at these suggestions.[181] But is that because we are happy to see interference in the rights of 'them' (the mentally disabled) but not to see an interference in 'our' own rights? It has been estimated that approximately 10 per cent of people with a mental disorder show an increased risk of violence.[182] To put that in context; in a US study it was found that 16 per cent of men aged 18–24 from low socio-economic classes were violent. That was a far higher percentage than those found suffering from mental disorder. Arguably a stronger case for preventative detention might be put for locking up all poor young men, rather than those with mental illnesses. Would that be acceptable?

There is another issue here. If the dangerously mentally ill are to be detained for the purpose of prevention: where, how, and by whom? Doctors are unlikely to be willing to simply oversee people who are not being detained for treatment but prevention,[183] but non-medically qualified 'guards' may lack the experience and skills to care for those

---

177 This summary is taken from Bartlett (2003a).
178 The Government emphasized this in DoH (2005p: para 14).
179 Szasz (2003).   180 Hope (2004: 80); The Richardson Committee (1999).
181 White (2002).   182 Walsh and Fahy (2002).   183 Bartlett (2003), White (2002).

detained. Bartlett argues that hospitals are willing to care for the physically disabled even where nothing can be done for them, and the same attitude could be taken towards the mentally ill who have to be detained.[184]

One final point is that whatever the theoretical issues, dangerousness must be taken into account. That may be because political reality requires that any mental health legislation reassures the public that they are protected from the widely perceived danger of the mentally ill. Also, because any professional deciding whether a person should be detained is bound to consider dangerousness. Few professionals will be willing to release an individual into the community whom they believe will be likely to be violent.[185] In other words, however the criteria for detention are framed, dangerousness will be a relevant factor. If that is so, is it better to be open about this and define clearly the degree of risk that will justify detention, and what factors can be taken into account in assessing that risk?[186]

11 Paternalism as the ground for detention?

If we do not accept dangerousness as a ground for detention on its own, what alternative justifications could there be? One is paternalism. We could simply say that treatment for mental illness is justified because that is best for the patient. This would especially be so where an effective treatment would be available.[187] However, this is generally regarded as a justification in cases where the patient is incompetent; where the patient is competent and refuses treatment it is not. We do not allow treatment for physical conditions to be given to competent patients on the basis of paternalism, why should it be any different if the illness is mental?

One approach that has support in academic circles is that the test of treatment and detention should be based on capacity alone.[188] Compulsory treatment and detention is only permissible under civil law if the patient is competent and consents to treatment. If she or he is incompetent then treatment and detention can be given if that is in the patient's best interests. To treat mentally ill competent people differently from non-mentally ill competent people is to discriminate on the grounds of mental illness. Bartlett emphasizes the wrong that is done to a competent person who receives mental health treatment against their wishes in this way:

> The violation of autonomy consequent on enforced treatment of a person with capacity is considerable. The introduction of psychiatric medication into an individual's body results in fundamental and substantial changes to the person's self. These changes are, of course, the objective of the treatment, and have social benefits. Many patients will also willingly consent to them, as they are perceived to have benefits to them too. That in no way alters the extraordinary nature of the intervention, however, and it is difficult to see that it should be provided to a patient with capacity who refuses it.[189]

There is much be said for this view. There are, however, problems. The first is that it might be said to be politically unacceptable. It would, in theory, require a doctor to

---

[184] Bartlett (2003).
[185] The decision of the Canadian Supreme Court in *Starson v Swayze* [2003] 1 SCR 722 shows the difficulties in determining whether a dangerous individual is competent.
[186] Bartlett (2003).　　　　　　　　　　　　　　　　　　[187] Stone (1975).
[188] See eg Bellhouse et al (2003); Buchanan (2002); and Gunn (2000).　　[189] Bartlett (2003).

release into the community a dangerous, but competent individual. Politicians would find it difficult to defend this before the general public. The second and linked point has been already alluded to and that is that the definition of 'capacity' is vague; it would arguably be inevitable that a person regarded as dangerous by a professional would be 'deemed' incompetent, rather than being released to the public. If this is so, the argument goes, we should have dangerousness as an open factor with clear guidance as to how dangerousness should be assessed and the level of dangerousness required. The third danger of the capacity approach is that the hurdle for capacity is set high so that only clearly rational people meet it. But that would restrict the rights of many who at present might be regarded as competent. Set the hurdle too low and it would be mean too many people who would be generally regarded as suitable for treatment would not receive it.[190] A final point has been made by Peter Bartlett: many supporters of the capacity approach accept that once a person has committed a criminal act, this justifies preventative detention. But he argues that whether someone has committed a crime is a red herring. The crime may tell us nothing about their dangerousness and non-criminal acts may be far more indicative of dangerousness than criminal one. There may be an argument that having committed an offence they, to some extent, forfeit rights to liberty but that would need some careful argumentation.

12 Conclusion

As this chapter demonstrates there is difficulty in striking the correct balance between protecting the public from the perceived threat of mentally disordered people, and protecting the rights of those who suffer mental illness. The debate over that balance has, however, meant that other issues have too easily been overlooked: abuse and violence in psychiatric in-patient facilities; the under-resourcing of community care; the lack of protection of mentally disordered people from abuse of various kinds; and the absence of an effective legal recognition of the position of those who care for the mentally ill.

QUESTIONS

1. C.S. Lewis (1953: 228) wrote: 'To be cured against one's will and cured of states which we may not regard as disease is to be put on a level with those who have not yet reached the age of reason or those who never will; to be classed with infants, imbeciles and domestic animals.' Is it ever justifiable to treat a competent person without their consent for a mental disorder?

2. In early 2005, media attention focused on the case of a man weighing 33 stones who suffered from Prader-Willi syndrome, an inherited condition which leads to over eating. He was detained for assessment by social services under the Mental Health Act 1983. It appeared that the major concern of the social services was that the patient's condition was not improving and he had lost control over his eating (Prader-Willi Syndrome Association (2005)). Was this a misuse of the MHA? How would the press have reacted if the individual had died?

---

[190] Bartlett (2003: 337 et seq).

3. Often the argument is made that we need to protect the general public from the mentally ill. Are not the mentally ill members of the general public?

4. Is muttering to oneself and not responding to questions signs of a mental disorder? When does behaviour cease to be 'eccentric' and become the symptoms of an illness?

5. One mental service user wrote that her medication delivered a 'nothingness which was dull and sweet' (Cardinal (1996: 108)). Is that a cure? Have we too easily forgotten the power of the drug industry?

FURTHER READING

For useful general discussion on mental health law and policy see:

Bartlett, P. and Sandland, R. (2007) *Mental Health Law* (Oxford University Press).

Glover-Thomas, N. (2003) *Reconstructing Mental Health Laws and Policy* (Butterworths).

Laurance, J. (2003) *Pure Madness* (Routledge).

Peay, J. (2003) *Decisions and Dilemmas* (Hart).

Richardson, G. (1999) *Richardson Committee: Review of the Mental Health Act 1983* (DoH).

Richardson, G. (2002) '"Autonomy, Guardianship and Mental Disorder" One problem, two solutions' *Modern Law Review* 65: 702.

Rogers, A. and Pilgrim, D. (2001) *Mental Health Policy in Britain: A Critical Introduction* (Palgrave).

Yates, V. (2007) 'Ambivalence, Contradiction, and Symbiosis: Carers' and Mental Health Users' Rights' *Law and Policy* 29: 435.

For discussion of reforms to the law see:

Fennell, P. (2005) 'Convention Compliance, Public Safety, and the Social Inclusion of Mentally Disordered People' *Journal of Law and Society* 32: 90.

Richardson, G. (2002) 'Autonomy, Guardianship and Mental Disorder' One problem, two solutions *Modern Law Review* 65: 702.

On anti-psychiatry see:

Adshead, G. (2003) 'Commentary on Szasz' *Journal of Medical Ethics* 29: 230.

Bentall, R. (2004) *Madness Explained* (Penguin).

Double, D. (2006) *Critical Psychiatry* (Palgrave).

Szasz, T. (2001) 'Mental illness: psychiatry's phlogiston' *Journal of Medical Ethics* 27: 297.

Szasz, T. (2002) *Liberation by Oppression: A Comparative Study of Slavery and Psychiatry* (Transaction).

Szasz, T. (2005) '"Idiots, infants, and the insane": mental illness and legal incompetence' *Journal of Medical Ethics* 31: 78.

11 Research

INTRODUCTION

This chapter will consider health care research.[1] Generally, there is no legal regulation of health care research unless it involves one of the following:

- human participants
- human gametes (sperm or ova)
- human embryos
- animals
- data relating to individuals

So a scientist adding chemicals together in a laboratory will not face regulation of the kind discussed in this chapter. However, where experiments are carried out on patients, a host of issues arise: Is there adequate consent? Can the scientist be sued for negligence if the participant is harmed? Are there some forms of research that are illegal on ethical grounds, even if the participants have consented? How can research be conducted in a way which protects the confidentiality and data protection rights of the participants?

Overshadowing the law on medical research is the knowledge that under the Nazi regime medical research was performed by doctors on people without their consent. Such horrors have led to a widespread acceptance that medical research involving humans needs careful regulation, and that great care needs to be taken to ensure that the participants are consenting.[2] The law recognizes the danger that researchers desperate to advance medicine will be tempted to fudge the requirement that participants in research must consent.

One key distinction in this topic is drawn between therapeutic and non-therapeutic use of medical drugs or procedures. A doctor may use an untested drug on a patient who is suffering from a particular disease, believing the drug to be the best (or perhaps only) hope of a cure. In such a case the use is therapeutic. The drug is being given for the benefit of that patient. By contrast, if a doctor seeks healthy volunteers upon which to test a drug's possible side effects, the use is non-therapeutic. The drug is not being given to the volunteers to improve their health, but rather to test the drug to see if it can be used on other people. Of course, the distinction is not always that clear. If the drug which is being tested might be of some benefit, it is less clear whether this is therapeutic or non-therapeutic treatment. What is clear is that cases of non-therapeutic use of treatments are far more controversial than therapeutic ones.

---

[1] Research involving animals will not be included in this book.
[2] Although there are allegations that such testing still takes place on prisoners in North Korea (BBC Newsonline (28 July 2004)) and more generally Plomer (2005).

The tension running through this topic is between the wish to promote medical advances only achievable through research, and the wish to protect participants. Of course, many of the medical advances which now save countless lives are only possible because of medical research using human subjects. Indeed it has been said that society has a duty to engage in research.[3] Medicines can only be released as available for general use when we are confident that they are safe to use. We can only be sure of that if tests have been carried out on a sufficient number of volunteers. Imposing regulations on consent which are too strict will hinder this important work, while too lax regulation will lead to research being used where 'volunteers' have not effectively consented or have been treated in an inappropriate way. For example, the inquiry into the children's heart surgery at the Bristol Royal Infirmary found that untried novel procedures were being used without full consent from parents or the approval of the Local Research Ethics Committee. The inquiry found that a higher number of children died following surgery with the new techniques than in hospitals using traditional forms of surgery. As this case shows, however, there is not a clear line between research and providing what a doctor genuinely believes is the best treatment. The doctors believed the novel form of treatment they were offering was the best available. On the other hand, as we shall see shortly, it is claimed by some that increasing regulation of medical research is making the cost prohibitive for academic and/or charity-based researchers, leaving research the preserve of large corporations.

The assumption that medical research is a good that must be promoted is not supported by everyone. It has been noted that restricting medical research does not cause anyone harm, at most it fails to materialize a good.[4] This means, some argue, that in deciding whether research should be restricted, it is not necessary to show that the harm to participants will be greater than the harm that people will suffer from the disease under investigation if the research is not carried out. Rather a lower threshold is required. Others argue that placing too great a weight on the interests of research participants fails to protect the rights of those suffering from illnesses for which research could find a cure.

1 The legal regulation of research

The regulation of research involving humans is governed by a patchwork of legislation, common law, and international regulation.[5] The main sources of the law governing research are the following.

(i) The Declaration of Helsinki

The World Medical Association has developed the Declaration of Helsinki, which was originally agreed in 1964, but is regularly revised. Although the declaration is not binding in English law, according to one leading commentator it 'has become the benchmark against which current UK research projects are measured'.[6] This declaration includes a number of important principles:

- The need for consent for all competent participants in research.
- The rights of subjects to withdraw from the research.

---

[3] Fried (2001).   [4] Jonas (1998: 916).   [5] Mclean (2002).   [6] Mclean (2002: 607).

- Human experimentation is to be used as a last resort where other forms of research not involving human subjects are not possible.

- There must be proportionality between the benefits of the research and the risks run by the subjects.

Paragraph 5 of the Declaration contains an over-arching principle:

In medical research on human subjects, considerations related to the well-being of the human subject should take precedence over the interests of science and society.

This means that if there is ever a clash between the rights of the human subjects of research and the interests of society, the rights of the subject prevail. If, for example, a scientist believed that by carrying out an experiment on someone without their consent it would be possible to find a cure to a chronic or terminal disease, it would not be permissible to do so. This might be thought to take too absolutist a stance: if it were possible to find a cure for AIDS by taking one blood sample from a single non-consenting person, would it not be justifiable to do so? Is it not taking individual rights too far not to permit such a minor infringement of someone's bodily integrity in order to make such a significant gain for society? To others the temptation to infringe rights in the name of medical advance is so great that an absolutist approach must be taken.

(ii) The criminal law

To touch someone, or to administer to them a noxious substance, without their consent is a criminal offence. However, in some circumstances the consent of the victim to the administration or the touching can provide a defence. So, of course, there is no offence if a doctor touches a patient with their consent in the course of treatment. Is the same true in the case of medical research? The Law Commission suggests: a person should not be guilty of an offence if he causes injury to another, of whatever degree, if such injury is caused during the course of properly approved medical research (ie approved by a Local Research Ethics Committee (LREC)) and with the consent of that other person.[7]

Notice here that the research must be properly approved. So if the doctor is conducting her or his own study, but has not had it approved by an Ethics Committee, she or he could still be guilty of a criminal offence if she or he caused the patient harm, even if the patient had consented.

(iii) Legislation

A variety of pieces of legislation can impact on the performance of medical research including the following: Human Fertilisation and Embryology Act 1990; Data Protection Act 1998; Health and Social Care Act 2001; Human Tissue Act 2004; Mental Capacity Act 2005. There are also the Medicines for Human Use (Clinical Trials) Regulations 2004, which give effect to the EC directive.[8]

(iv) The Human Rights Act 1998

To perform a human experiment on patients without their consent or other legal authorization could infringe patients' rights under the European Convention on Human Rights, articles 3 or 8.[9] A Research Committee would be a public authority and would be required to ensure that any approved research did not infringe participants' human rights.

---

[7] Law Commission Report No 231 (1995: 8.38–52).
[8] EC directive 2001/20/EC.   [9] *X v Denmark* (1983) 32 DR 282.

(v) The common law (tort or contract)

A researcher will owe a participant a duty of care in the tort of negligence and could be sued for damages if she or he breaches that duty. It would be very unlikely for there to be a contract between a researcher and participant, but in such a case there is the possibility of a claim for breach of contract.

(vi) Professional and governmental guidance

The Government and Professional Bodies have produced guidance on the conduct of research.[10] Breach of the guidance could lead to disciplinary measures being taken against them. Funders of research or local hospitals may also have particular requirements they impose in relation to research.

(vii) Local and multi-centre ethics committees

These committees have been created to regulate and oversee research in their particular areas. We will be examining their work later. The committees can refuse to authorize a research project or place conditions on its operation. In practice, a researcher whose research proposal has been passed by a Local Research Committee is likely to feel that their research will not face legal challenges, although approval by an Ethics Committee does not guarantee that the research is lawful.

Research from a legal point of view will fall into one of three categories:

- Research which is illegal and if conducted would amount to a criminal offence.
- Research which is lawful but is regulated. If the regulatory requirements are not fulfilled it would amount to a crime or a tort.
- Research which is lawful and is unregulated.

We shall be considering these categories separately.

2 Research which is outlawed on the grounds of public policy

Under this heading we will consider research projects which are unlawful as contrary to public policy.

2.1 Research which harm participants

Even if participants were willing to undergo research which endangered their lives, it is highly unlikely such research would be lawful. But where is the line to be drawn? How risky does research have to be before it is outlawed?

There is no explicit guidance to be found on this in the decisions of English courts. Perhaps the starting point is the decision of the House of Lords in *R v Brown*[11] where a group of men were engaged in sado-masochistic practices. They inflicted on each other a variety of injuries and were charged with assaults occasioning actual bodily harm and inflicting grievous bodily harm. Their defence was based on the fact that the 'victims' had consented to the injuries being done to them. The House of Lords held that in

---

[10] See eg GMC (2002); DoH (2005h).   [11] [1994] 1 AC 242.

cases involving injuries amounting to actual bodily harm or worse, the consent of the victims did not provide a defence unless the conduct fell into an 'exceptional' category of cases where the activities promoted the public good: sport, medical procedures, and ritual circumcision were some examples. Sado-masochism could not be said to be in the public good.

The reasoning used in that case suggests that as long as the medical research involved is in the public interest, consent may provide a defence to even serious injuries. But this still leaves unanswered the question of where the line would be drawn. Of course euthanasia is unlawful and so a participant could not agree to be killed as part of a research project. But what about a small risk of death or a higher risk of serious harm? A court considering where the line is to be drawn would, no doubt, take account of the following points.

(i) *Paragraph 18 of the Helsinki Declaration* states medical research involving human subjects should only be conducted if the importance of the objective outweighs the inherent risks and burdens to the subject. This is especially important when the human subjects are healthy volunteers.

Europe's Protocol to the Convention on Human Rights and Biomedicine concerning biomedical research has a similar provision and adds:

> where the research does not have the potential to produce results of direct benefit to the health of the research participant, such research may only be undertaken if the research entails no more than acceptable risk and acceptable burden for the research participant (Article 6(2)).

There are two points worth noting about these articles. First, a risk of harm to a participant is only permissible where the research has important benefits. Research into finding a cure for AIDS or malaria may justify a risk of harm to the participants, but it is unlikely that such a risk would be acceptable to find a solution to male hair loss. Second, a distinction is drawn between research that may directly benefit the participant and that which will not. So where the participant suffers from a condition and the research project is aimed at finding a treatment for that condition, then a higher level of risk may be legitimate than otherwise. However, ultimately on the question of how much harm can be caused to a consenting participant the Convention ends up placing weight on the phrase 'an acceptable risk' and that provides little guidance.

(ii) *Professional guidance.* The Royal College of Physicians[12] suggests that where volunteers are healthy they should be subject to no more than a minimal risk. A minimal risk is one which is very remote and may be ignored: the kind of risk or harm involved in driving a car; a chance of more than one in a million.[13]

(iii) *Academic writings.* It has been suggested by some ethicists that research is only acceptable if the harms faced by the subject are no more likely or no more severe than the subject would be likely to meet in everyday life.[14] That test, however, has been criticized for being ambiguous and poorly defined. Different people at different stages of their lives are willing to take different kinds of risks.[15] Hope and McMillan interpret the 'everyday life' test to mean that a research participant should not be facing graver risks to her or his life than she or he did carrying on her or his normal life.[16] This would allow

---

[12] Royal College of Physicians (2007).   [13] Royal College of Physicians (1996: para 7.2).
[14] Hope and McMillan (2004).   [15] Resnik (2005).   [16] Hope and McMillan (2004).

different people to take different levels of risk, depending on their lifestyles. Another suggestion is that the test should be phrased in the following way:

> the probability and magnitude of the harm or discomfort anticipated in research are not greater than those encountered during the performance of routine physical or psychological examinations or tests.[17]

Other commentators have focused on the fact that we allow people to undertake activities that carry a high risk of serious injury, such as rock-climbing or motor bike racing. If we allow people to do these things we should certainly allow them to take risks in the name of medicine. However, it might be argued that the difference with medical research is that it is funded and encouraged by the state. It is one thing to allow people to do dangerous things in their spare time; it is another to permit the state to sponsor such activities. To supporters of research, however, the point of the comparison with other dangerous activities is that we allow them even though they produce far less public benefit than medical research does, and so the case for allowing risk-taking in medical research is stronger. We shall now consider some of the kinds of research projects which are potentially harmful to participants and which cause particular problems.

2.2 'Challenge studies'

These studies involve intentionally infecting healthy people in order to study the development of the disease and treatment of it.[18] These are important in the study of medicine and in particular of vaccines. The Medical Research Council has regularly infected healthy people with the common cold to investigate possible treatments.[19] To many such forms of research are ethically more troublesome than other forms of research where one is testing, for example, a trial drug on a group of people. In 'challenge studies' the researcher is doing an act with the intent of causing the participant a harm, albeit a minor one and one for which a cure will immediately be offered. In other kinds of research the effect of the medication is unknown and there is no intent to cause the participant harm. Even if the researcher is aware that the drug may have unpleasant side effects, it is not her or his intent that the participant suffers them.[20]

2.3 Placebos

Some forms of medical research involve giving participants a placebo medication. The placebo will look like medication, but in fact be a harmless substance which has no medically significant content. The reason for using a placebo is to measure the psychological impact of taking what a patient believes to be medicine. Often researchers will give one sample group the trial drug, another sample group a placebo, and a third sample no medication at all. The sample that takes the trial drug may do better than the sample who take nothing, but if they do as well as those who took the placebo this will indicate it was the psychological impact of taking a substance, rather than the effect of the drug itself, which had the impact.

However, there are some legal and ethical difficulties in using the placebos. First, there is the issue of consent. If a patient is led by a researcher to believe she or he is taking

---

[17] Resnik (2005).   [18] Hope and McMillan (2004).
[19] Jackson (1989).   [20] Hope and McMillan (2004).

a medicine, when in fact it is a placebo, has the participant been misled? Can she or he be said to have consented to taking the placebo? If a patient is told that they are taking a placebo this may well negate the usefulness of the experiment which is designed to find out the psychological benefits of taking what one believes is medicine. One solution is to inform participants that they may be taking a placebo, although this may still have some impact on the effectiveness of the research. This would not provide a solution in cases where researchers wish to use a 'single blind placebo' when every participant in the sample is given a placebo for a period of time. This is often done at the start of research and is used where patients are currently taking medication and researchers wish to record their medical state if they are taking no medication at all. In such a case, telling participants that they may be taking a placebo is misleading because they definitely will be, while telling them they are taking the placebo might negate the effectiveness of the project. To some, telling such participants that they may at some time during the study be taking a placebo is at most blurring the truth and is not an outright lie, and therefore is justifiable given the benefits of such research. To others, such a response does not take the duty to be candid with research participants seriously enough, and they believe that the only ethically acceptable option is to make it clear to participants that they will all, at some stage of the research, be taking a placebo.[21]

A second issue is whether it is legitimate to offer a treatment which is providing no benefit, particularly if the researcher believes that there is treatment on offer which will benefit patients. In other words, if a patient is suffering from a medical condition and drug A is available to provide some relief, but researchers wish to test drug B to see if it is an improvement on drug A, then giving a participant a placebo (when if they were not participating they would be receiving drug A) could be said to be harming them. That said, there is evidence that a placebo drug can have beneficial effects for patients, presumably through its psychological impact.[22]

The use of placebos has been considered by the World Medical Association (WMA) who have issued the following note of clarification attached to the Declaration of Helsinki:

> The WMA hereby reaffirms its position that extreme care must be taken in making use of a placebo-controlled trial and that in general this methodology should only be used in the absence of existing proven therapy. However, a placebo-controlled trial may be ethically acceptable, even if proven therapy is available, under the following circumstances:
>
> — Where for compelling and scientifically sound methodological reasons its use is necessary to determine the efficacy or safety of a prophylactic, diagnostic or therapeutic method; or
>
> — Where a prophylactic, diagnostic or therapeutic method is being investigated for a minor condition and the patients who receive the placebo will not be subject to any additional risk of serious or irreversible harm.
>
> — All other provisions of the Declaration of Helsinki must be adhered to, especially the need for appropriate ethical and scientific review.[23]

As these passages from the Declaration indicate, the use of placebos in research is problematic where there are known therapies available. This is because by being involved in research the participants receiving the placebo will be receiving treatment less advantageous to them than they would if they were not participating.[24]

---

[21] Evans (2000).   [22] Lichtenberg et al (2004).
[23] World Medical Association (2002).   [24] Hoffman (2001).

Even more problematic than placebo drugs is 'placebo' surgery:[25]

SHOCK TO THE SYSTEM

Placebo surgery

In some quarters horror has greeted reports of placebo surgery. This is based on the same principle as placebo medicine: it is an attempt to ascertain the psychological impact that having surgery has. So some participants in the research will have an operation, others will have what they believe is surgery, but in fact no surgery is done, although they may be cut open so a scar is produced, giving the appearance of surgery. In one study into Parkinson's disease, for example, 20 patients had the stem cells of aborted human foetuses put into their brains via a hole drilled into their skulls; and the other 20 had just the holes drilled (although for them the dura was not penetrated) (Freed et al (2001)). Of course, in that study the patients or their representatives were aware that they may be receiving the treatment or the placebo. But should that be permitted? With placebo medicine at least no harm is done to the patient, but with placebo surgery some harm is done. But if it is consented to and it plays an important part in the progress of science should it not be permitted? The issues are discussed further in Albin (2005); Dekkers and Boer (2001); and Freeman et al (1999).

3 Research involving children

At first the notion of using children who cannot consent or object to being used as research subjects seems unacceptable. However, there may be no alternative when it comes to research seeking to find treatment for childhood illnesses or assessing the effect of a drug on children. Indeed it has been argued that the failure to undertake sufficient research involving children has meant that children have been given drugs which have only been tested on adults, a practice which endangers children.

3.1 The general approach of the law

There is little explicit guidance on the legality of using children in medical research.[26] If the normal laws governing the medical treatment of children (see Chapter 4) apply to research, then a doctor could carry out medical research involving a child if the research was otherwise lawful and she or he had the consent of either a *Gillick* competent child or someone with parental responsibility for the child.[27] However, it is unclear whether the normal rules dealing with children and medical treatment apply in this context. There are two reasons why:

(i) In *Re W*[28] Lord Donaldson thought it highly improbable that a *Gillick* competent child could consent to a medical procedure which did not benefit the child. That would be the case in non-therapeutic research.

(ii) It is not clear whether a parent can exercise parental responsibility by consenting to a procedure which is clearly not in the child's best interests. There is an argument

[25] The issue is discussed in Albin (2005); Dekkers and Boer (2001); and Freeman et al (1999).
[26] For a useful discussion see Hunter and Pierscionek (2007).
[27] MRC (2004b: 5.1.4).   [28] [1992] 4 All ER 627.

that parental responsibility only gives parents the authority to consent to procedures which are in the child's best interests.

Critics of this view might make two points. First, we do in fact allow parents to make decisions which harm children. Parents are allowed to feed their children unhealthy food, watch too much television, and so forth as long as the child is not suffering significant harm, at which point the child can be taken into care. Being involved in medical research, even if slightly harming the child, does not do so significantly. Second, it might be said that in fact involving a child in medical research benefits the child. It teaches the child altruism and the benefits of being part of a community project.[29]

However doubtful the precedent, it is clear that research involving children does take place. It is difficult to imagine a judge deciding that it would be unlawful for a doctor to carry out research which was shown to be clearly in the public interest. The Helsinki Declaration also clearly envisions research being lawful, paragraph 16 stating:

> When a subject deemed legally incompetent, such as a minor child, is able to give assent to decisions about participation in research, the investigator must obtain that assent in addition to the consent of the legally authorized representative.

Any research which poses more than a minimal risk to children is of questionable legality, even where the child's parent have consented, unless that research can be said to directly benefit the child.[30]

3.2 Clinical trials involving children

Where the research involves a clinical trial of a drug the Medicines for Human Use (Clinical Trials) Regulations 2004[31] apply and there are special rules that operate in relation to children. Under the Regulations a minor is a person under the age of 16.[32] Prior to the involvement of minor in a trial, consent must be obtained from a parent or a person with parental responsibility.[33] In the case of trials of emergency treatments, if no person with parental responsibility is available, a 'personal legal representative' can give consent. The representative must be a person who is not connected with the trial; is willing to act as a representative; and is suitable to do so because of their relationship with the child. If no such person is available then a 'professional legal representative' can be used. They will be someone nominated by the health care provider who is unconnected with the trial. To clarify, then, there is hierarchy of who can provide consent:

(1) The person with parental responsibility.

(2) The personal legal representative.

(3) The professional legal representative.

It is only permissible to rely on the consent of a representative if there is no one higher up the list available. So if the parents refuse to consent to the child's participation, it is not possible to rely on a legal representative for consent.

Controversially, it is possible to conduct research on a minor even if she or he objects. However, the Regulations[34] state that researchers should consider the objections of a minor who is capable of assessing information about the research.

---

[29] Montgomery (2003: 365).   [30] Institute of Medical Ethics (1986).
[31] SI 2004/1031.   [32] Reg 2.   [33] Sch 1, part 4.   [34] Sch 1, part 4.

Hopefully a researcher would not be willing to involve a child who strongly objected to being involved in the project, particularly where that child was competent.

The regulations also require that a Research Ethics Committee approves the research involving children and must do so having received advice from an expert in paediatrics.

3.3 Professional guidance

The BMA accepts the legality of research involving children, but suggests it should only be used where research involving consenting adults could not be used:

> Babies, children, and people with severe mental health problems should be involved only when, for example, a particular disease affects only this group or because people in these categories respond differently to therapies already proven effective in trials involving consenting adults.[35]

The BMA guidance suggests that research on children is legitimate if it is not contrary to their interests (ie does not harm them). This means that research is permissible even if it does not benefit the children, as long as it does not harm them either. However, others suggest this is too lenient and it cannot be justifiable to carry out research on children in a way that is not positively in their interests because that would be to use a child as a means to an end.[36]

The Royal College of Paediatrics and Child Health have produced some useful guidelines on the ethical conduct of research involving young children.[37] These are based on six key principles:

- Research involving children is important for the benefit of all children and should be supported, encouraged, and conducted in an ethical manner.

- Children are not small adults; they have an additional, unique set of interests.

- Research should only be done on children if comparable research on adults could not answer the same question.

- A research procedure which is not intended directly to benefit the child subject is not necessarily either unethical or illegal.

- All proposals involving medical research on children should be submitted to a Research Ethics Committee.

- Legally valid consent should be obtained from the child, parent, or guardian as appropriate. When parental consent is obtained, the agreement of school age children should also be requested by researchers.

3.4 Ethical issues

Given the concern about using non-consenting research participants, the burden of justifying research involving children lies on its supporters. Indeed some ethicists take the view that it is never appropriate to do research using participants without their consent. The difficulty with that approach in this context is that, as already mentioned, the only way to properly test treatments for childhood illnesses, or to check the effect on children

---

[35] BMA (2004: 506).   [36] Edwards and McNamee (2005).
[37] The Royal College of Paediatrics and Child Health (1992). The MRC (2004b) has similar guidelines.

of medicines approved for use on adults, is to involve children.[38] Even if research is permissible, the BMA has emphasized that special care must be taken of child participants. They are easily bewildered and are not in a position always to express their needs or defend their interests.[39]

Some commentators have argued that we should presume that children will want to be involved in research because there is a moral obligation to participate in research.[40] It has even been suggested that research involving children should be permitted, even if the parents object.[41] This is part of a wider argument about duties to participate in research to which we will return later in this chapter.

4 Research involving incompetent adults

Is it lawful to carry out research on incompetent adults?[42] Some of the issues raised are similar to those relating to children. There is a conflict between the principle of not involving individuals in research without their consent, and the desire to ensure that there are effective medicines to deal with serious mental illness.

4.1 Mental Capacity Act 2005

The provisions dealing with research involving incompetent adults are found in the Mental Capacity Act 2005, sections 30–34. Research involving clinical trials for medicines is dealt with by the Medicines for Human Use Regulations 2004 (which will be discussed shortly). The Draft Code of Practice for the 2005 Act states:

> The Act and the Code of Practice aim to establish the right balance between the need for research to bring benefit or information, and the need for protection against exploitation and abuse. It also seeks to ensure that any increased risk of the research, over and above that risk associated with the condition or treatment itself, is either proportionate to the potential benefit to that individual, or, in the case of research to provide knowledge, the risk is minimal.[43]

The Act regulates research which is 'intrusive'; that is it would be unlawful if carried out in relation to a person who had the capacity to consent, but had not consented.[44] So research that involved any kind of touching or administration of a substance would fall within the category of 'intrusive', while simply watching someone and recording their movements would probably not be.[45] That said, watching someone for a prolonged period of time through a two-way mirror might be regarded as 'intrusive'.[46] Under section 30 'intrusive research'[47] can only be lawfully carried out on a person who lacks capacity[48] (P) if the following conditions are met:

---

[38] Kirby (2004).   [39] BMA (2004: 511).   [40] Harris and Holm (2003).
[41] Evans (2004).   [42] McHale (2006b).   [43] Para 12.3.   [44] S 30(2).
[45] Although there is an argument that this could amount to an offence contrary to the Protection from Harassment Act 1997.
[46] DoH (2005b).
[47] This phrase does not include a clinical trial subject to the Medicines for Human Use (Clinical Trials) Regulations 2004, SI 2004/1031.
[48] There must be a proper assessment that P is incompetent before these provisions can be relied upon.

(i) The research project has been approved by an 'appropriate body'. This will normally be the Local Ethics Committee.

(ii) The research is connected to 'an impairing condition' from which P suffers or its treatment.[49]

(iii) There must be reasonable grounds for believing that research of comparable effectiveness cannot be carried out if the project has to be confined to, or relate only to, persons who have capacity to consent to taking part in it.[50]

(iv) The research must either:

(a) have the potential to benefit P and not impose a burden on P which is disproportionate to the benefit, *or*

(b) be intended to provide assistance in the treatment or care of people suffering from a similar condition, as long as the risk to P from the research is negligible and does not interfere with P's freedom, action, or privacy in a significant way so as to be unduly invasive.[51]

(v) Reasonable steps must have been taken by the researcher to identify a person who is P's carer or interested in P's welfare.[52] The researcher must provide the carer with information about the project and ask her or him whether P should take part and what she or he thinks P's wishes and feelings would be. If the carer replies that P would not want to take part in the project then P must not take part in the project;[53]

(vi) Research may not be carried out on P if she or he has made an effective advance decision or other statement indicating that she or he did not want to be part of the research.[54]

(vii) Nothing may be done to P in the course of research to which P appears to object, unless it is necessary to protect P from harm.[55]

(viii) Appropriate means must be used to maximize P's understanding of the research process and if possible enable P to be a part of the decision-making process. This might involve, for example, giving information in a simplified format.

(ix) The normal requirements which attach to research generally are satisfied.

As these conditions show the legislation is strict in its requirements. But the provisions are not uncontroversial. The controversial issues include the following:

(i) They permit research to be carried out on incompetent people even if it is not going to benefit the patients themselves. To some it is never justifiable to treat incompetent people against their best interests. Jonas argues:

What is wrong with making a person an experimental subject is not so much that we make him thereby a means (which happens in social contexts of all kinds), as that we make him a thing—a passive thing merely to be acted on, and passive not even for real

---

[49] S 31. S 31(3) explains that 'impairing condition' means 'a condition which is (or may be) attributable to, or which causes or contributes to (or may cause or contribute to), the impairment of, or disturbance in the functioning of, the mind or brain'.

[50] S 31(4).   [51] S 31(5), (6).

[52] This is not someone who is paid to care for P. If such a person cannot be found then the researcher can nominate a person who is willing to be consulted by the researcher about P: s 32(2).

[53] S 32.   [54] S 33(2).   [55] S 33(2).

action, but for token action whose token object he is. His being is reduced to that of a mere token or 'sample'.[56]

Against this principle must be weighed the concern that if research cannot be conducted on incompetent people then medical advances will be severely restricted. Should research into Alzheimer's not take place because it cannot be shown that an effective treatment is so close at hand that participants in research are likely themselves to benefit?

(ii) The legislation only regulates research that is 'intrusive'. It would appear to permit observing behaviour, changing diet, and perhaps even taking a urine sample (if no touching was involved). It might be thought that conduct which is not otherwise a criminal offence involves such a minor wrong, if a wrong at all, to the incompetent person that we should not be concerned about it. However, critics would argue that apparently trivial interferences with the interests of the incompetent individuals may not appear trivial to a vulnerable and frightened incompetent person, especially if the research involves a diversion from their ordinary routine.[57]

(iii) The research cannot be carried out if at any time P appears to object. In the case of a mentally ill person this may be a difficult requirement to interpret. It certainly makes researchers' jobs more difficult.

(iv) The legislation could be said to be ambiguous. Section 30 states that the research will be 'unlawful unless...' and then lists the conditions which are included within those listed above. However, the Act does not make it clear that as long as the conditions are satisfied the research will be lawful. Researchers may be concerned that even if they comply with all the requirements in the Act it is still possible that their actions will be unlawful.

(v) Much depends on the effectiveness of the Local Ethics Committees. Before approving research involving incompetent people they will need to consider *inter alia*:

- whether the outcome of the research is of potential benefit to the person or others with a similar disorder;
- the justification for including participants who may lack capacity to consent in the research and whether the research could be done solely involving those with capacity;
- the assessment of each participant's capacity as part of the consent procedure and how that will be assessed and documented;
- how the Research Group proposes to identify and consult an appropriate third party (such as a carer);
- whether sufficient safeguards are in place in circumstances where it is not possible to identify a third party to represent the participant's interests;
- whether it is clear who is responsible for identifying whether the person objects to any part of the research (whether by showing signs of resistance or otherwise) and so should be withdrawn.[58]

4.2 Incompetent people and clinical trial regulations

The Medicines for Human Use Regulations 2004 make special provision for clinical trials involving incompetent people.[59] For the purpose of the Regulations an incapable

---

[56] Jonas (1969: 235).   [57] Annas and Glantz (1986).   [58] DoH (2005b: 130).
[59] These implement EU Clinical Trials Directive 2001/20/EC; discussed in Liddell et al (2006).

adult is 'an *adult unable by virtue of physical or mental incapacity to give informed consent*'. Clinical trials involving such a person are only permitted where there is the consent of a 'Personal Legal Representative', but where such a person cannot be found then the consent of a 'Professional Legal Representative' can be relied upon. What does this mean?

- *Personal Legal Representative.* This is someone who:
  - (i) is not connected with the conduct of the trial;
  - (ii) is suitable to act as the person's legal representative due to their relationship with the individual;
  - (iii) is willing to act as a personal legal representative.

  This is likely to be a close relation or friend of the individual who is willing to make decisions on their behalf.

- *Professional Legal Representative.* This is someone who:
  - (i) is not connected with the conduct of the trial;
  - (ii) is either (a) the doctor primarily responsible for the adult's medical treatment, or (b) a person nominated by the relevant health care provider.

Before a Research Ethics Committee gives consent for a clinical trial involving incompetent people it must obtain advice on the clinical, ethical and psychosocial problems that may arise in relation to the trial.

Part 5 of Schedule 1 of the 2004 Regulations also contains a number of important restrictions on trials involving incompetent adults. These include the following:

- The subject has received information according to her or his capacity of understanding regarding the trial, its risks and its benefits.

- The investigator must consider the explicit wish of a subject not to participate in the project or to withdraw from it. However, that is only required if the subject is capable of forming an opinion and assessing the information referred to in the previous paragraph.

- There are grounds for expecting that administering the medicinal product to be tested in the trial will produce a benefit to the subject outweighing the risks or produce no risk at all.

- The clinical trial is essential to validate data obtained—
  - (a) in other clinical trials involving persons able to give informed consent, or
  - (b) by other research methods.

- The clinical trial relates directly to a life-threatening or debilitating clinical condition from which the subject suffers.

- The clinical trial has been designed to minimize pain, discomfort, fear, and any other foreseeable risk in relation to the disease and the cognitive abilities of the patient.

- The interests of the patient always prevail over those of science and society.

It is worth emphasizing that the objection of the incompetent adult to participation is not a bar to their involvement, but should be considered by the investigator. It is hoped that it would be highly unlikely that an incompetent individual would be forced against their will to be involved.

4.3 Ethical issues

Your response to the use of incompetent adults in research depends largely on your response to the general question of how decisions should be made in relation to incompetent people. We have discussed that question in Chapter 4. But for now we will summarize how some of the views would apply in this context.[60]

(i) *Best interests.* If we take the view that decisions about incompetent adults should be based simply on what is in their best interests it appears to follow that unless research will directly benefit the individual (eg it is research into a condition from which the individual suffers and the research is likely to produce a treatment for that condition in the near future) it is not justifiable.

Some, however, argue that relying on a best interests approach can, in fact, justify a far wider range of research than the previous paragraph would suggest. This is because being involved in research is a 'good thing' to do. Altruism is generally praised in our society. Allowing an incompetent person to play their part in society allows them to live a good life which is to their benefit. We should therefore allow research to involve incompetent people if the burdens are reasonable ones to expect citizens to undertake. Critics of this argument reply that although being altruistic can benefit a person, it can only do so if they have sufficient understanding of what they are doing. If they have no awareness of the good they have done, or the esteem within which they are held by others, then there are no tangible benefits of altruism. Even if the rather intangible benefits of altruism are accepted they are unlikely to outweigh anything more than a small amount of harm in a research project.

(ii) *Substituted judgment.* This approach suggests that we consider what the person concerned, had they been competent, would have decided. This is of course a difficult question, especially where the individual never has been competent. Some using such an approach argue that as most people do not involve themselves in research we should assume a person does not wish to be involved. However, it might be said that where a person suffers from a particular condition and is asked to participate in research which will assist in finding a treatment for that condition, most people do participate. This might suggest an approach whereby we assume consent if the research concerns a condition from which the individual suffers, but not if the individual has no connection with the condition.

(iii) *Society's interests.* It might be argued that in relation to incompetent people the interests of the wider community can sometimes justify involving them in research even if they are not in a position to consent or object. The main objection to such an argument is that it is not applied to competent people. If the importance of research to our society is so great that it justifies involving incompetent people without their consent, does it not also justify involving competent people without their consent?[61] However, there may be an argument that research on a person who is neither consenting nor objecting is not as wrong as research on a person who is objecting.

---

[60] Lewis (2002) provide an excellent discussion of these issues.   [61] Lewis (2002).

5 Research in the context of emergency treatments

There are particular problems where doctors wish to research treatment designed to deal with emergency situations (eg treatment for a heart attack). In such a case it is not always possible to gain the consent of the patient to the treatment. If the emergency is predictable (eg it is foreseen that a patient may require resuscitation at some time in the future) then consent may be sought in advance for a novel form of treatment.[62] In the case of unpredictable emergencies we are left with the option of either permitting research on participants without their consent or leaving emergency treatment untested. Neither option is attractive.

6 Experimental treatment

What is the legal position where a doctor wishes to try out treatment which is in essence experimental, in the sense that there is insufficient research to indicate what the effect of the treatment is likely to be? It must be admitted that the line between experimental treatment and research is not clear-cut. Mason and Laurie[63] suggest:

> Research implies a predetermined protocol with a clearly defined end-point. Experimentation by contrast, involves a more speculative, ad hoc, approach to an individual subject. The distinction is significant in that an experiment may be modified to take into account the individual's response; a research programme however, is, by definition, bound to tie the researcher to a particular course of action until such time as its general ineffectiveness is satisfactorily demonstrated.

The significance of the distinction is this. If the project is research then it will need to go through the regulatory procedure, including approval by an Ethics Committee, as discussed above. If, however, it is regarded as treatment, and the doctor is simply offering what she or he believes to be the best treatment for the patient, given the current state of know-how, then it can be classified as treatment.

The issue of experimental treatment was considered in the following case:[64]

KEY CASE   Simms v Simms [2003] 1 All ER 669

JS (aged 18) and JA (aged 16) suffered from variant Creutzfeldt-Jakob Disease (v-CJD). Their parents sought declaratory relief that it was lawful for the proposed treatment to be given to them. Both JS and JA were incompetent to consent to it. The proposed treatment was new and had not been tested on humans. The treatment required surgery under general anaesthetic. The medical evidence was unanimous that in both cases the individuals would die without treatment. There was also unanimity that the effectiveness of the treatment was unknown, but that it would not be irresponsible to use it. The experts did divide on whether they themselves would be willing to use the treatment on a patient.

---

[62] BMA (2004: 510). See also article 19 of the Additional Protocol to the European Convention on Human Rights and Biomedicine Concerning Biomedical Research.
[63] Mason and Laurie (2006: 651).   [64] Harrington (2003).

Butler Sloss P held that it was lawful to offer the treatment. Because the two young people were incompetent to make the decision, the question was whether the proposed treatment would be in their best interests. She held it would be. There was no responsible body of opinion which thought it irresponsible to provide the proposed treatment. In reaching this conclusion she referred to the *Bolam* test (see Chapter 3). Although there was a 5 per cent chance of haemorrhage as a result of the procedure, this was within the reasonable bounds of risk given the situation the patients were in. The proposed treatment was of benefit to the patients even if there was no hope of recovery, and the hope was that the treatment would slow down deterioration or prolong life. Even though the chance of improvement was slight it was a risk worth taking. As she pointed out:

> the concept of 'benefit' to a patient suffering from v-CJD does encompass an improvement from the present state of illness, or a continuation of the existing state of illness, without deterioration for a longer period than might otherwise have occurred.

Here the condition was fatal and progressive; it was therefore reasonable to attempt experimental treatment with unknown risks and benefits. She stated:

> A patient who is not able to consent to pioneering treatment ought not to be deprived of the chance in circumstances where he would have been likely to consent if he had been competent.

When considering what was in the patients' best interests their futures with and without the treatment, as well as the views of their families should be taken into account. The parents' support of the proposed treatment was said to carry 'considerable weight'.

Supporters of this decision will welcome the acknowledgement that to deny experimental treatment to the patients in the perilous conditions that they found themselves would be cruel. Opponents might suggest that what we have seen in these cases is doctors wanting to try out experimental treatments, rather than really seeking to improve the conditions of the individuals.[65] To opponents the case is an example of the worst kind of human guinea pig. Similar concerns may attach to *B NHS Trust v J*[66] where use of a new drug on a PVS patient was authorized by the court. This was despite the fact the drug offered only a 'very slim outside chance' of success and it having been used on a very small number of patients previously. Sir Mark Potter held that the patient should not be denied the 'glimmer of hope' the treatment offered.

Paragraph 32 of the Helsinki protocol supports the use of experimental treatment, where it offers hope of saving life or alleviating suffering:

> In the treatment of a patient, where proven prophylactic, diagnostic and therapeutic methods do not exist or have been ineffective, the physician, with informed consent from the patient, must be free to use unproven or new prophylactic, diagnostic and therapeutic measures, if in the physician's judgement it offers hope of saving life, re-establishing health or alleviating suffering. Where possible, these measures should be made the object of research, designed to evaluate their safety and efficacy. In all cases,

---

[65] Maclean (2002). See Price (2005b) for an excellent discussion of the issues.
[66] [2006] EWHC 3152 (Fam).

new information should be recorded and, where appropriate, published. The other relevant guidelines of this Declaration should be followed.

7 Consent to research

As has been emphasized throughout this chapter, the question of whether or not the participant consents to being involved in the research is key. Where the participant does not want to be involved only rarely will research be permissible. But what does consent mean? This was discussed in detail in Chapter 4, but it is worth mentioning two issues that are particularly likely to arise in the research context.

7.1 Duress/undue influence

It is highly unlikely that a medical professional will deliberately try and force her or his patients into a research project, but the power relationship between professional and patient can be such that patients feel they have no choice. They may feel they owe it to their doctor to participate; or they feel they will receive less adequate treatment if they refuse; or they simply do not realize that they are being invited to participate in research and interpret the doctor to be making a demand.[67] Further, if a patient is facing a terminal illness with no known cure, but is invited to participate in a research project involving a new untested drug, is the patient really in a position to make a genuine choice?

Paragraph 23 of the Helsinki Declaration[68] is alive to these issues:

> When obtaining informed consent for the research project, the physician should be particularly cautious if the subject is in a dependent relationship with the physician or may consent under duress. In that case the informed consent should be obtained by a well-informed physician who is not engaged in the investigation and who is completely independent of this relationship.

The concern of patients that they will receive less effective treatment if they refuse to participate in research is addressed in paragraph 28 of the Helsinki Declaration: 'The refusal of a patient to participate in a study must never interfere with the patient–physician relationship.' Of course, whether the patient believes that is another matter.

7.2 Informed consent

How much information must be given to participants in research for their consent to be sufficiently informed to be legally effective? Paragraph 22 of the Helsinki Declaration states:

> In any research on human beings, each potential subject must be adequately informed of the aims, methods, sources of funding, any possible conflicts of interest, institutional affiliations of the researcher, the anticipated benefits and potential risks of the study and the discomfort it may entail.

[67] Iltis (2005a).
[68] See also article 12, The Additional Protocol to the European Convention on Human Rights and Biomedicine.

The BMA guidance has provided a list of the information which should be given to research participants:[69]

- the purpose of the research and confirmation of its ethical approval;
- whether the participant stands to benefit directly and, if so, the difference between research and treatment;
- the meaning of relevant research terms (such as placebos);
- the nature of each procedure, and how often or for how long each may occur, the processes involved, such as randomization;
- the potential benefits and harms (both immediate and long term);
- arrangements for reporting adverse events;
- the legal rights and safeguards for participants;
- details of compensation if harm results from their participation, how their health data will be stored, used, and published;
- if samples of human material are donated, whether they will be used for any other research or purpose;
- whether and how DNA will be extracted, stored, or disposed of;
- the name of the researcher they can contact with enquiries;
- if the researcher stands to benefit (for example, financially);[70]
- the name of the doctor directly responsible for their care;
- how they can withdraw from the project;
- what information they will receive about the outcome;
- that withdrawal will not affect the quality of their health care.

The Medicines for Human Use Regulations 2004 requires the participant to have given informed consent. Paragraph 3(1) of Part 1 of Schedule 1 explains:

A person gives informed consent to take part in a clinical trial only if his decision:

(a) is given freely after that person is informed of the nature, significance, implications and risks of the trial; and

(b) either:

  (i) is evidenced in writing, dated and signed, or otherwise marked, by that person so as to indicate his consent, or

  (ii) if the person is unable to sign or to mark a document so as to indicate his consent, is given orally in the presence of at least one witness and recorded in writing.

The person must have met with the researcher and been informed of 'the objectives, risks and inconveniences of the trial and the conditions under which it is to be conducted'.

These guidelines appear to indicate that a higher standard for informed consent is required in the case of research than in the case of medical treatment,[71] although we

---

[69] BMA (2004: 499).

[70] Kim et al (2004) found in a survey a clear majority of potential participants in research wanted to know if the researchers had any financial interest in the outcome of the research.

[71] Chalmers and Lindley (2001).

are yet to have a case which makes that clear.[72] In deciding the legal requirements as to how much information must be disclosed a judge may well refer to the guidelines and protocols we have just discussed. One test that might appeal is that a researcher must disclose all relevant facts which a reasonable subject would want to know.[73]

Against such a strict approach, it might be feared that giving potential participants a long list of all the potential dangers of research, however small, will put people off volunteering, to the detriment of scientific progress.[74] One survey found that a shorter form which contained less information was more effective than a longer form that contains more information.[75] There are also difficulties where different participants in the trial are going to be treated differently: eg where some are to be given an experimental treatment and others the traditional treatment. It may be important that participants do not know which treatment they are receiving.[76] Of course in such a case it is no doubt sufficient if the patient is made aware of the alternative ways in which she or he may be treated during the research. But even that, some researchers fear, can distort findings.[77] Further, there are concerns that providing too much information to participants will lead to 'information overload' and mean that participants will be unable to make an effective decision.[78]

The extent to which participants in research fully understand the risks they are taking and the forms of treatment trialled may well be open to debate. The little research that has been done on this suggests a low level of comprehension of risk among participants.[79] A different concern is that researchers keen to get a good number of participants may be encouraged to 'shade the truth' by 'glossing over' the details of the risks.[80]

7.3 Right to withdraw

There is widespread agreement that participants in research have the right to withdraw from the project at any time, and this is made clear in the 2004 Regulations and the International Declarations. However, Sarah Edwards has argued in favour of only a conditional right to withdraw.[81] Those who withdraw can have a negative impact on the research and can lead to researchers trying to 'weed out' at an early stage participants who may be tempted to withdraw. This can have a negative impact on the aim of having a broad cross section of people. Edwards suggests that at least research staff should have the ability to 'push' participants who are considering withdrawing into staying the course. As long as it is made clear to participants that they will not simply be able to leave on a whim when they enter the research, the objections to a more restricted right to withdraw may be less.

7.4 Health Services Research

The issue of consent is problematic in Health Services Research.[82] This is research not looking at the effectiveness of a particular treatment, but at the delivery of healthcare. For example, a study might look at the effectiveness of screening patients for STDs, or

---

[72] Montgomery (2003: 361).   [73] Fox (1998b: 119).   [74] Pullman (2002).
[75] Hamilton et al (2007).   [76] Tobias and Souhani (1993).   [77] Kottow (2004).
[78] See Iltis (2006) who questions the ability of most people to understand and appreciate risks and therefore to be able to give informed consent.
[79] Joffe et al (2001).   [80] Kottow (2004).   [81] Edwards (2005).
[82] Cassell and Young (2002).

look at alternative ways post-natal care can be offered. The difficulty is that such studies tend to involve looking at geographical data. For example, the NHS might want to research how best to provide treatment and advice for STDs and use a trial whereby one part of the country receives one mode of provision and another a different one. In such a case obtaining consent is problematic because if an individual does not consent to be involved there is no realistic way alternative provision can be made.

SHOCK TO THE SYSTEM

Research horror stories

At the start of this chapter we referred to the non-consensual medical research that took place under the Nazi regime. The horror that greeted the discovery of these practices led many to say that never again should such 'research' take place. However, to this day there are horror stories of research practices which harm individuals. Here are a sample:

• The following allegations appeared in a BBC report (BBC Newsonline (30 November 2004)). In the 1990s HIV positive children who had been taken into care in New York City were tested with experimental and highly toxic drugs. Claims have been made that when their carers reported serious side effects of the drugs (such as inability to walk, persistent vomiting) they were told that this was because of their HIV infection, rather than the truth, which was that the drugs were having these side effects. Neither the children, their relatives, nor their guardians were informed that the children were being used as part of a secret trial.

The Alliance of Human Research Protection claims this has been happening across the United States with a total of 13,878 children being involved since the late 1980s, and between 5 and 10 per cent of those children being in foster care. According to the Associated Press Report: 'In one study (testing the drug dapsone) at least 10 children died from a variety of causes, including four from blood poisoning, and researchers said they were unable to determine a safe, useful dosage. They said the deaths didn't appear to be 'directly attributable' to dapsone but nonetheless were 'disturbing'. 'Overall mortality while receiving the study drug was significantly higher in the daily dapsone group. This finding remains unexplained,' the researchers concluded (Associated Press (2005)).

• In 2000 the Griffiths Report looked into research at the North Staffordshire Hospital NHS Trust carried out between 1990 and 1999 (Griffiths (2000)). It found that researchers were not adequately getting the consent of participants. Some people were not given adequate information about the research and others did not fully appreciate that they had a choice as to whether or not to be involved. There was evidence that on some consent forms signatures were forged.

• In September 1999 Jesse Gelinger, an 18-year-old student, died after taking part in a gene therapy trial in the US. His death was said to be caused by 'an atypical reaction to the experimental agent'. Earlier studies using the drugs on animals had found a link with liver failure which had caused death, but participants were not told this. The principal investigator, it was claimed, had a $13 million interest in the company marketing the drug (Kong (2005)).

• In March 2006 six volunteers for a drug trial at Northwick Park Hospital, London were taken seriously ill. Their conditions were described as life threatening. They suffered organ failure and their immune systems were sent into overdrive. The worst affected had to have his finger tips amputated. The incident led to a major investigation into the way clinical trials were conducted (Expert Scientific Group on Phase one Clinical Trials (2007)).

8 Payment

Is it ever appropriate to pay people to participate in research? It is certainly permitted in England and Wales.[83] It took me only a few seconds on the internet to find advertisements offering payments of thousands of pounds to be a participant in research.

The Royal College of Physicians[84] supports the payment of volunteers but these should not be at such a level as to persuade people to volunteer against their better judgment. Payment may be particularly appropriate where individuals are not just the 'subject' of research but are actively involved as a partner in research (eg in filling in paperwork and recording results). The benefits of payment are that it encourages people to volunteer to be involved, particularly if the project requires a considerable amount of time or effort on behalf of the participants. It may also discourage people from withdrawing from a project. Even if there is no payment for a person's time, at least their expenses should be paid.

Commentators, not surprisingly, are divided on the issue.[85] Opponents argue that society owes a special obligation towards those who participate in research and in particular to ensure that their consent to be involved is full and free. Once payments are allowed, this adds to the murkiness surrounding consent. Supporters might point to other situations where payments are made to those undertaking dangerous activities.

In a survey of unpaid volunteers, just over 43 per cent agreed with paying participants in research.[86] Amongst supporters payment was seen as acceptable to reimburse costs; as a public recognition of their time and effort; and to encourage the recruitment of volunteers where that had been problematic.[87] Opponents of payment took the view that volunteering should be motivated by a desire to help others, not receive money.

9 Licensing of research

The Government have made it clear that proper governance of research is essential if there is to be public confidence in the quality of research and the protection of the rights of participants.[88] Indeed this is required by the European Convention on Human Rights and Biomedicine (articles 7–11) and the Helsinki Declaration (paragraph 13). The licensing and regulation of research is governed by the following:

- The Government's Research Governance Framework, which applies to all research undertaken by the Department of Health or the NHS, as well as research undertaken by industries, charities, and universities.[89] In effect it covers any large scale research project.

- The Medicines for Human Use (Clinical Trials) Regulations 2004 govern the conduct of clinical trials and make it clear that any clinical trial must be approved by an Ethics Committee and authorized by the licensing authority.

---

[83] See Involve (2002).   [84] Royal College of Physicians (2007).
[85] Compare Wilkinson and Moore (1997) and McNeill (1993).
[86] Russell et al (2000).
[87] For evidence that payment can increase the number of volunteers see: Bentley and Thacker (2004).
[88] DoH (2005h).   [89] DoH (2005h).

We shall consider first the work of Research Ethics Committees, whose approval is required for all kinds of research. We shall then consider the special regulations that apply in respect of clinical trials under the 2004 Regulations.

9.1 Research Ethics Committees

The Ethics Committee will consider a wide range of factors when considering the research proposal including the following:

- That there are adequate arrangements to ensure the full consent of all participants or, where the participants are incompetent, that the legal requirements are met. The committee will look at the information that will be provided to the participants.

- That the legal requirements are met. For example, that the Human Tissue Act 2004 and any guidance issued by the Human Tissue Authority has been complied with.

- That the study has scientific validity. The Committee will look at the conduct and design of the study. It will need to be persuaded that the research has not already been adequately done elsewhere and that the study will add something useful to the state of knowledge. Expert advice will be taken when considering these issues.

- That the study will not cause the participants undue pain or discomfort and that any pain or discomfort is in proportion to the benefits of the research.[90]

- That the arrangements for recruitment of research participants are adequate, in particular that there is a good range of participants in terms of gender, ethnic background, age etc.

- That the arrangements for the care and protection of research participants are adequate.

- That the participants' rights of confidentiality are adequately protected.

- That the impact of the research on the wider community has been taken into account.[91]

The work of the Research Ethics Committees (RECs) is overseen by the UK Ethics Committee Authority, which is part of the National Patient Safety Authority.[92] The committees are required to be independent, so much so that the Department of Health and the NHS are not entitled to interfere with decisions of the RECs. Although RECs will consider the legality of research, they are not expected to give legal advice, nor are they responsible if the research turns out to be unlawful.[93] Researchers should keep RECs informed of the progress of their studies.[94] The primary purpose of the RECs is 'to protect the dignity, rights, safety and well-being of all actual or potential research participants'.[95] However, as of secondary importance, the interests and needs of researchers should be taken into account.[96]

An REC should have between seven and 18 members, and represent a broad range of experience and expertise. This should include expertise in scientific, clinical, pharmacological, statistical, and methodological aspects of the research. If necessary, a specialist

[90] Para 2.2.8.   [91] DoH (2005b).
[92] The Central Office for Research Ethics Committees (COREC) became subsumed within the National Patient Safety Authority in 2005.
[93] DoH (2005p: 3.12.7).   [94] DoH (2005p: 3.12.8).
[95] DoH (2001a: para 2.1).   [96] DoH (2001a: 2.1).

referee can be asked to give advice on a project.[97] There should be lay members as well as experts, and the REC membership should have a variety of age, gender, and ethnic background. At least three members of the committee must be independent of any organization where research is likely to take place. At least a third of the membership should be independent of the NHS, and their primary personal or professional interest should not be in the research area.

If the research is based in a particular locality the local REC will consider the matter, but if the project involves five or more sites (ie working in areas covered by more than five health authority boundaries) then an application can be made to a Multi-centre Research Ethics Committee. This saves researchers having to apply to a large number of separate Ethics Committees and the delay that could result.

There has been much concern over the way RECs' systems work. Some of these have been met by attempts to standardize and streamline the work of the committees. However there are several outstanding complaints:

(i) The lack of on-going monitoring of research. Although there is a careful vetting of research before it is started there is little monitoring of how the research is actually carried out. It is true that the RECs will consider the reports from the researchers as the research progresses, but there is no pro-active supervision.[98] Whether RECs could take on the role of monitoring research projects is a matter for debate. Some believe that the volunteers on these committees already suffer under a substantial overload and monitoring would impact adversely on the relationship between committees and researchers.[99]

(ii) The workload for these committees can be considerable. The members are volunteers who are not paid and there is even difficulty finding funding for training. It has been said that this contrasts notably with the funding available for such committees in other countries.[100] There are reports of some RECs finding it difficult to be quorate.[101]

(iii) At one time there were concerns over the variations in approaches taken between committees.[102] There were complaints that the same research project was rejected by one REC and approved by another.[103] Some see this as a reflection of the problems over the selection and training of committee members. The creation in 2004 of the UK Ethics Committees Authority (UKECA) meant greater consistency and a tighter control over the performance of committees. Although technically the UKECA only governs committees considering medical products it is likely to have an impact on the way RECs deal with all kinds of applications. The National Patient Safety Authority took on oversight of the RECs in 2005.[104] However the 2005 review acknowledges that there was still a problem with consistency of decisions.[105]

(iv) Some feel that RECs lack accountability for their decisions.[106] There are few ways of challenging a decision of the REC. Although the decision of an REC can be subject

---

[97] DoH (2001a: para 6.1–6.17).   [98] DoH (2004f).

[99] Pickworth (2000).   [100] Pickworth (2000).

[101] Ad Hoc Advisory Group on the Operation of NHS Research Ethics Committees (2005) and Central Office for Research Ethics Committees (2006).

[102] Alderson et al (1995).

[103] See Sayers (2007) and Edwards et al (2004) for an argument that this should not cause concern.

[104] Ad Hoc Advisory Group on the Operation of NHS Research Ethics Committees (2005).

[105] Ad Hoc Advisory Group on the Operation of NHS Research Ethics Committees (2005). See Angell et al (2006) for an empirical study supporting claims of inconsistency.

[106] Brazier (1990b).

to judicial review it is unlikely such an application would succeed.[107] As a public authority the REC is required to act in a way which is compliant with individuals' human rights under the Human Rights Act 1998, although again it would be unlikely that any action would successfully brought against an REC.

(v) Complaint has been made that RECs are too paternalistic. These complaints tend to be made by those who support a liberal approach towards research, and argue that if members of the public are willing to be involved in a project that involves risks, they should be allowed to participate and it is not for an REC to protect the participants against themselves. This complaint in particular has been made by people suffering from AIDS, believing that RECs have denied them the opportunity to be part of a research project into possible cures for AIDS.[108]

(vi) Concern has been expressed at the dominance of the professionals involved in the committees.[109] Although lay members are required to be present on the panel to represent the views of 'ordinary members' of the public, they may find it difficult to assert their views against the views of experts on the committee.

(vii) Some researchers have complained that those on the committee lack the expertise to properly understand the nature and purpose of their research. This has led to complaints that research proposals have been rejected on an unfounded basis. A Department of Health review[110] suggested that Ethics Committees should follow expert advice on technical/scientific issues and this should mean such errors occur rarely.

(viii) The members of the RECs tend to be older and from a professional background. The ethnic mix does not reflect that of the wider society.[111]

In response to these concerns, reforms have been proposed.[112] At the heart of these proposals is the suggestion that a 'national research ethics advisor' should initially consider all proposals. Where there are no serious ethical concerns, approval can be given without the proposal needing to be considered by a full REC. Similarly if there are proposals that clearly have a flaw, they can be immediately referred back for amendment, without having to wait for a full REC meeting. The aim is that this will produce a speedier and more effective system.[113]

9.2 Medicines for Human Use (Clinical Trials) Regulations 2004

EUROPEAN ANGLES

These regulations were passed to give effect to the two European Directives: Clinical Trials Directive 2001 and Good Clinical Practice Directive 2005. They set out in detail the procedures that must be undertaken before a clinical trial of a new medicine can be started. Before commencing a clinical trial involving the testing of medicines on people, the sponsor must obtain clinical trial authorization (CTA) from the Medicines and Healthcare products Regulatory

---

[107] *R v Ethical Committee of St Mary's Hospital (Manchester) ex p Harriott* [1988] 1 FLR 512.
[108] Edwards et al (2004).   [109] McNeill (1993: 95).
[110] Ad Hoc Advisory Group on the Operation of NHS Research Ethics Committees (2005).
[111] Ad Hoc Advisory Group on the Operation of NHS Research Ethics Committees (2005).
[112] Central Office for Research Ethics Committees (2006).
[113] See Hunter (2007) for scepticism about the new scheme's effectiveness.

Agency (MHRA).[114] The CTA application may be made in parallel with an REC application. It is not necessary to have a CTA in order to obtain a favourable opinion, but the REC should be provided with a copy of the CTA when available.[115] The key points in the Regulations are:

- to establish the Ethics Committee system on a statutory basis (Regulations 5 to 10, and Schedule 2);

- to require all clinical trials to be conducted in accordance with the principles of good clinical practice (Regulations 28 to 31, and Schedules 1 and 5);

- to provide additional protection for minors and physically or mentally incapacitated adults who are candidates for clinical trials, as discussed above (Regulations 14 to 16 and Parts 3 and 5 of Schedule 1 for incapacitated adults and Regulation 15 and Part 4 of Schedule 1 for minors);

- to require sponsors to provide trial medicines free of charge to patients if they are not covered by a prescription charge (Regulation 28);

- to provide for inspection by the MHRA for good clinical practice and to help ensure those standards are maintained (Regulations 47 to 52, Parts 2 and 3 of Schedule 7, and Schedule 9); and

- to provide for enforcement of these new provisions (Regulations 47 to 52 and Schedule 9).

The Regulations set out in Schedule 1 state 16 principles of good practice which must be observed by all clinical trials:[116]

Principles based on Articles 2 to 5 of the GCP Directive

1. The rights, safety and well-being of the trial subjects shall prevail over the interests of science and society.

2. Each individual involved in conducting a trial shall be qualified by education, training and experience to perform his tasks.

3. Clinical trials shall be scientifically sound and guided by ethical principles in all their aspects.

4. The necessary procedures to secure the quality of every aspect of the trial shall be complied with.

5. The available non-clinical and clinical information on an investigational medicinal product shall be adequate to support the proposed clinical trial.

6. Clinical trials shall be conducted in accordance with the principles of the Declaration of Helsinki.

7. The protocol shall provide for the definition of inclusion and exclusion of subjects participating in a clinical trial, monitoring and publication policy.

8. The investigator and sponsor shall consider all relevant guidance with respect to commencing and conducting a clinical trial.

9. All clinical information shall be recorded, handled and stored in such a way that it can be accurately reported, interpreted and verified, while the confidentiality of records of the trial subjects remains protected.

[114] Medicines for Human Use (Clinical Trials) Regulations 2004.
[115] DoH (2004g).   116 Reg 28.

Conditions based on Article 3 of the Directive

10. Before the trial is initiated, foreseeable risks and inconveniences have been weighed against the anticipated benefit for the individual trial subject and other present and future patients. A trial should be initiated and continued only if the anticipated benefits justify the risks.

11. The medical care given to, and medical decisions made on behalf of, subjects shall always be the responsibility of an appropriately qualified doctor or, when appropriate, of a qualified dentist.

12. A trial shall be initiated only if an ethics committee and the licensing authority comes to the conclusion that the anticipated therapeutic and public health benefits justify the risks and may be continued only if compliance with this requirement is permanently monitored.

13. The rights of each subject to physical and mental integrity, to privacy and to the protection of the data concerning him in accordance with the Data Protection Act 1998 are safeguarded.

14. Provision has been made for insurance or indemnity to cover the liability of the investigator and sponsor which may arise in relation to the clinical trial.

The Regulations have given rise to criticisms. Charities have been vociferous in their complaints that the extra bureaucratic requirements will hinder research.[117] It has been claimed:

> If this directive had been introduced forty years ago, many of the most critical advances in cancer treatment would not have been made. Women with breast cancer would still have to lose their breasts, and patients with throat cancer their voice boxes. Childhood leukaemia would still be a death sentence rather than a great success story of cancer research.[118]

The concerns particularly apply to those who are engaging in non-commercial research where the extra costs involved will be particularly onerous.[119] There appears to have been a gradual decrease in the number of research clinical trials carried out by non-commercial bodies since 2000.[120] In part this may be due to a decrease in funding. The decrease in non-commercial research is a particular concern given fears of bias in commercially sponsored research.[121]

Supporters of the Regulations argue that they will provide a standardized approach to clinical trials throughout the UK.[122] They will be particularly useful where someone wants to do research which covers several European countries. The Regulations are also seen as an important part of ensuring consistency in the regulation of research, and limiting the difference in approach between RECs. The Regulations also impose a higher standard of control over what happens during the study itself than that for other research projects. This all causes Michael Allen to conclude: 'Research will be more difficult to perform but better in quality: this fits in pretty well with the way of the modern world.'[123] Indeed the dangers of inadequate supervision by Ethics Committees can be seen in the rare, but tragic deaths of participants.[124] Indeed some European countries

---

[117] MRC (2004a).   [118] Cancer Research (2005).
[119] See the discussion in Liddell et al (2006).
[120] Garrow (2005).   [121] Lexchin et al (2003).   [122] Allen (2004).
[123] Allen (2004).   [124] Savulescu (2002a).

have applied the directives to all areas of medical research, rather than, as England and Wales have done, only to medicines.

10 Selecting participants

Where the product or procedure which is to be trialled offers hope to patients who are suffering from a condition for which there is no effective treatment, there may be competition among patients over who can be a participant in the research project.[125] There is little guidance or regulation in the law on how researchers should select participants where demand outstrips available places. Where the experimental treatment is very risky, one suggestion is that preference should be given to those volunteers whose life expectancy is very low, the argument being that if the trial is disastrous and the trialled treatment kills this patient, this will be less of harm if the participants have a low life expectancy any way. Hence it has been suggested that trials for xenotransplantation should be first undertaken on patients suffering PVS.[126] However, such arguments are open to the criticism that they indicate we view the lives of patients with PVS or low life expectancy as dispensable, or at least of less worth than other people's lives. Further, there is increased campaigning from patient's pressure groups who seek access to drugs for which early trials indicate some effectiveness.[127] Regulations now require those organizing a research project to have clear protocols on who will be included or excluded from research.[128] These will be considered by the REC when considering whether to approve the project as a whole. As long as the protocol is non-discriminatory and has a logical basis, the committee is likely to approve it.

11 Publication fraud

All is not well in the field of published medical research. 'Research fraud' is said to be common and there is a lack of effective sanction against it.[129] A slightly different concern is that if the research is not demonstrating a result which is pleasing to the funders of the research the work is simply not written up or made public.[130]

Some papers are published which are based on pure fiction. In one notorious case articles co-authored by the then President of the Royal College of Obstetricians and Gynaecologists were found to be based on cases which simply did not exist, leading to his resignation.[131] In fact a close reading of that case reveals another problem which is 'gift authorship', whereby a person's name appears as an author of the article, even though their contribution to the article is minimal. The pressure to be seen to be publishing a large number of articles can lead to a seemingly endless list of names of authors for some articles in medical journals. That same pressure leads to short cuts being taken with, at best, sloppy recording and, at worst, outright fabrication of the results. Indeed one survey suggested that even among experienced researchers there was a grey zone where it was unclear whether or not certain forms of research were ethically appropriate.[132]

---

[125] Fovargue (2007).   [126] Ravelingien et al (2004).   [127] Fovargue (2007).
[128] The Medicines for Human Use (Clinical Trials) Amendment Regulations 2006, SI 2006/1928.
[129] Freeland Judson (2004); O'Reilly (1990). This is even a problem with writing on ethics!!: Schüklenk (2007).
[130] Fox (1998b: 120).   [131] See Smith (2003).   [132] Lynoe et al (1999).

It is, for example, clear that researchers should publish all the findings of their study that are relevant, even if a particular finding does not fit the general picture or the line the researchers wish to take. However, whether a result which is regarded as 'rogue' or 'obviously false' needs to be included is more debatable. In addition to outright fraud there is a concern that research funded by the pharmaceutical industry is more likely to favour the sponsor's own product.[133]

Remarkably it was not until March 2005 that a UK agency (the UK Panel for Health and Biomedical Research Integrity) was created specifically to combat research misconduct.[134] Before then COPE (Committee on Public Ethics), a pressure group, were the leading figures investigating allegations of fraud in research. Its annual reports are replete with worrying examples. It is clear that only a handful of cases reach the professional bodies.[135] The GMC from 2000 heard only 16 cases of research fraud.[136] One survey[137] of newly appointed consultants found that just over 55 per cent of them had witnessed some kind of research misconduct. The most common form of this was connected with authorship: either the inclusion of names which should not have been included, or the omissions of names that should. Just over 10 per cent had witnessed the deliberate fabrication or alteration of data. A survey of American scientists found that over a third had engaged in serious research misconduct.[138]

One explanation for the lack of investigation for research fraud may be the fear of being sued for libel if one falsely alleges research has been fraudulently carried out. Indeed those most likely to be aware of research fraud will be junior researchers assisting a more senior figure; concern for their professional futures may cause them to be wary of 'whistleblowing'.[139] One researcher pointed out that when he submitted articles claiming a scientific breakthrough, no journal asked for proof of what he claimed, but when he wrote an article alleging research fraud the journal's lawyers wanted proof of every word.[140]

Clearly there is a problem. The wariness that is felt about medical research involving humans is only heightened when there are doubts over the validity of the research produced. One difficulty in scientific research is the difficulty in spotting fraud. Without replication of the testing it is difficult, if not impossible, to establish there has been fraud.[141]

Of course, nothing in this section should cast doubt on the enormous benefits that have been achieved through medical research. The majority of research is not affected by fraud of the kind we have been discussing. However, if medical research is to keep its good name, it is necessary to ensure that there is an effective deterrent against fraud.

12 An obligation to participate?

A rather more radical approach to the issues surrounding medical research is to claim that individuals have an obligation to participate in medical research.[142] At first this seems startling, but it has been pointed out[143] that our society is willing on occasion to

---

[133] Lexchin et al (2003).   [134] White (2005).   [135] Eg Dyer (2003); Dyer (1997a).
[136] O'Brien (2003).   [137] Geggie (2001).
[138] Martinson, Anderson, and de Vries (2005).   [139] Ferriman (2003).
[140] Ferriman (2003) referring to the work of Peter Wilmshurst.
[141] MRC (2000).   [142] Plomer (2001).
[143] Harris (2005b). See Brassington (2007) and Shapshay and Pimple (2007) for responses to Harris's arguments.

restrict people's freedom in the interest of the wider social goals: jury service; compulsory education; compulsory vaccinations; quarantine regulations; compulsory military service. It might be argued that participation in medical research should be added to the list, this being part of our basic duty to assist those in need.[144]

Harris argues that we can state that research is presumed to be in someone's best interests:

> There are dangers in being too conservative about what does or does not benefit someone, or in defining someone's interests too narrowly. Everyone benefits from living in a society, and, indeed, in a world in which medical research is carried out and which utilizes the benefits of past research. It is both of benefit to patients and research subjects and in their interests, to be in a society which pursues and actively accepts the benefits of research and where research and its fruits are given a high priority. We all also benefit from the knowledge that research is ongoing into diseases or conditions from which we do not currently suffer but to which we may succumb. It makes us feel more secure and gives us hope for the future, for ourselves, and our descendants, and others for whom we care. If this is right, then I have a strong general interest that there be research, and in all wellfounded research; not excluding but not exclusively, research on me and on my condition, or on conditions which are likely to affect me and mine. All such research is also of clear benefit to me. A narrow interpretation of the requirement that research be of benefit to the subject of the research is therefore perverse.[145]

Because he believes that involvement in research is clearly in an individual's best interests, we do not have to be stringent in requiring that any consent given is fully informed and free. When people consent to procedures which are in their best interests we are understandably less suspicious that there may not be consent.

Harris also supports the obligation to participate in research as an aspect of fairness. We enjoy the benefits of medical advances and so we should be willing to support the research that enables those advances to be made. Few, he points out, are willing to participate in research, but fewer will refuse to take advantage of the medical advances that are thereby produced. However, critics might reply that it is difficult in our society to avoid taking the benefits of research; they are an everyday part of life.[146]

A slightly different argument Harris makes is that even if we say that research does not benefit an individual we should not assume that the interests of the subject should override the interest of others in society, because that is to say that the interests of one individual are more important than the interests of another. In particular, we should not accept that the interests of a person not wanting to participate in research are necessarily more weighty than the interests of a person suffering from an illness for which a cure will be discovered through the research. This kind of argument is consequentialist and may be rejected by those supportive of human rights.

With all of these arguments, Harris restricts his claim to saying that there is a moral obligation to participate, rather than suggesting that there be a legally enforceable obligation. However, he accepts his arguments would justify mandatory participation. A moment's thought about the consequences of mandatory participation will lead many to reject the idea. The image of people being dragged to hospital by the police or the army in order to undergo medical testing against their wishes is shocking to most. Indeed some commentators have argued that although Harris has shown that it would

---

[144] Harris (2005).   [145] Harris (2005b: 244).   [146] Shapshay and Pimple (2007).

be good for us to participate in research, he has not shown that there is an obligation to do so.[147]

Another claim is that there is a right to participate in research. Imagine that you are suffering from a serious illness for which there is as yet no known cure, but you hear that a drug has been developed which is believed might cure the illness, but it is as yet untested. Can you demand you be given the treatment?[148] Consider, for example, this comment from a father on discovering that some sick babies in a unit were receiving experimental treatment and others not:

> Why are they playing around with babies' lives?...Who gives them the right to sit there with say ten babies and think well this one here will...suit the trial, you know. Why not all ten of them? Why isn't it available everyone so everybody has a fair chance?[149]

QUESTIONS

1. Consider how a utilitarian approach to human research ethics would differ from one based on human rights.

2. 'The history of experimentation with human beings testifies to physician-scientists' real and caring dedication to the alleviation of mankind's pain and suffering from the ravages of disease. It also testifies to the carelessness with which human beings have been recruited for participation in research, a carelessness that has been too readily obscured by the caring dimension of scientists' work' (Katz (1993: 51)). Which is the greater fear, that participants in research will be misused or that research will be hindered by over-regulation of research?

3. Would you want your children to be involved in medical research? Under what conditions? Would you want your children to be given medicine which had not been tested on children?

4. Early on in a trial testing two alternative drugs on two samples it becomes clear that one drug is far more effective than the other; should the research be stopped and all participants be given the more successful? Or should the trial be continued until its full length to ensure the accuracy of the findings? (See Hope (2000) for a discussion of this issue).

5. Buchanan and Miller (2006) argue that commentators have tended to see research ethics as a matter of individual rights for participants and failed to appreciate that the issue is one of public health. Using public health ethics might lead you to conclude there is a duty to research and a duty to stop if early studies show the treatment is effective. The costs to society of not researching would need to be emphasized. Do you find the public health angle a useful one for viewing research ethics, or is it a dangerous one?

---

[147] Shapshay and Pimple (2007).   [148] Dresser (2001).
[149] Snowdon, Garcia, and Elbourne (2002).

FURTHER READING

The following provide useful discussion on the issues covered in this chapter:

Beyleveld, D., Townend, D., and Wright, J. (eds) *Research Ethics Committees* (Ashgate).

Edwards, S. and McNamee, M. (2005) 'Ethical concerns regarding guidelines for the conduct of clinical research on children' *Journal of Medical Ethics* 31: 351.

Ferguson, P. (2003) 'Legal and ethical aspects of clinical trials: the views of researchers' *Medical Law Review* 11: 48.

Foster, C. (2001) *The Ethics of Medical Research on Humans* (Cambridge University Press).

Fovargue, S. (2007) '"Oh pick me, pick me"—Selecting participants for xenotransplant clinical trials' *Medical Law Review* 15: 176.

Harris, J. (2005b) 'Scientific research is a moral duty' *Journal of Medical Ethics* 31: 242.

Lewis, P. (2002) 'Procedures that are against the medical interests of the incompetent person' *Oxford Journal of Legal Studies* 12: 575.

McHale, J. (2006b) 'Law Reform, Clinical Research and Adults without Mental Capacity' in S. McLean (ed) *First do no Harm* (Ashgate).

Morrison, D. (2005) 'A Holistic Approach to Clinical and Research Decision-Making' *Medical Law Review* 13: 45.

Plomer, A. (2005) *The Law and Ethics of Medical Research* (Cavendish).

Price, D. (2005b) 'Remodelling the regulation of postmodern innovation in medicine' *International Journal of Law in Context* 1: 121.

Bibliography and Further Reading

Aasi, G-H. (2003) 'Islamic legal and ethical views on organ transplantation and donation' *Zygon* 38: 725.

Abdallah, H., Shenfield, F. and Latarche, E. (1998) 'Statutory information for the children born of oocyte donation in the UK' *Human Reproduction* 13: 1106.

Abdallah, S., Daar, S. and Khitamy, A. (2001) 'Islamic Bioethics' *Canadian Medical Association Journal* 9: 164.

Abortion Law Reform Association, (1997) *A Report on NHS Abortion Services* (ALRA).

Abortion Rights (2004) *Eroding Women's Rights To Abortion Rights* (Abortion Rights).

Abortion Rights (2007) *Campaign for a Modern Abortion Law Launched as Poll Confirms Overwhelming Public Support* (Abortion Rights).

ACC (2004) *Annual Report* (ACC).

Ackernman, J. (1998) 'Assisted suicide, terminal illness, severe disability, and the double standard' in M. Battin, R. Rhodes and A. Silvers (ed) *Physician Assisted Suicide* (Routledge).

Action for ME (2005) *'The Times Reports on Biological Research'* (Action for ME).

Ad Hoc Advisory Group on the Operation of NHS Research Ethics Committees (2005) *Report* (DoH).

Adams, T., Budden, M., Hoare, C., Sanderson, H. (2004) 'Lessons from the central Hampshire electronic health record pilot project: issues of data protection and consent' *British Medical Journal* 328: 871.

Admiral, P. (1996) 'Voluntary euthanasia' in S. McLean (ed) *Death Dying and the Law* (Dartmouth).

Adshead, G. (2003) 'Commentary on Szasz' *Journal of Medical Ethics* 29: 230.

Advisory Group on the Ethics of Xenotransplantation (1996) *Report (DoH)*.

Agar, N. (2004) *Liberal Eugenics* (Cambridge University Press).

Agar, N. (2007) 'Embryonic potential and stem cells' *Bioethics* 21: 198.

Age Concern (1999) *Debate of the Age* (Age Concern).

Agich, G. (2003) *Dependence and Autonomy in Old Age: An Ethical Framework for Long Term Care* (Cambridge University Press).

Agich, G. and Siemionov, M. (2005) 'Until they have faces: the ethics of facial allograft Transplantation' *Journal of Medical Ethics* 31: 707.

Ahuja, K.K., Mostyn, B.J. and Simons, E.G. (1997) 'Egg sharing and egg donation: Attitudes of British egg donors and recipients' *Human Reproduction* 12: 2845.

Ajaj, A., Singh, M., Abdulla A. (2001) 'Should elderly patients be told they have cancer?' *British Medical Journal* 323: 1160.

Akker, van der, O. (1999) 'Organizational selection and assessment of women entering a surrogacy agreement in the UK' *Human Reproduction* 14: 262.

Alan Guttmacher Institute (1998) *Sharing Responsibility: Women, Society and Abortion Worldwide* (AGI).

Alan Guttmacher Institute (2004) *Adding it Up* (AGI).

Albin, R. (2005) 'Sham surgery controls are mitigated trolleys' *Journal of Medical Ethics* 31: 149.

Allen, M. (2007) 'Re-detention after recent discharge: a role for judicial review?' *Medical Law Review* 15: 253.

Allen, M. (2004) 'The clinical trial directive will improve trial quality' in *Healthwatch Newsletter* 53: 1.

Alcohol Concern (2002) *Alcohol and Teenage Pregnancy* (Alcohol Concern).

Alderson, P. (1993) *Children's Consent to Surgery* (Open University Press).

Alderson, P. (2002) 'Prenatal counselling and images of disability' in D. Dickenson (ed) *Ethics Issues in Maternal-Foetal Medicine* (Cambridge University Press).

Alderson, P. (2003) *Children's Consent to Surgery* (Oxford University Press).

Alderson, P., Madden, M., Oakley, A., and Wilkins, R. (1995) 'Access and multicentre research' *Journal of Medical Ethics* 105: 13.

Alghrani, A. (2005) 'Deciding the fate of frozen embryos' *Medical Law Review* 13: 244.

Alghrani, A. and Harris, J. (2006) 'Reproductive liberty: should the foundation of families be regulated' *Child and Family Law Quarterly* 18: 191.

Alldridge, P. (1994) 'Who wants to live for ever?' in S. Lee and D. Morgan *Death Rites* (Routledge).

Alldridge, P. and Morgan, D. (1992) 'Ending life' *New Law Journal* 142: 1536.

Allen, N. (2007) 'Re-detention after recent discharge: a role for judicial review?' *Medical Law Review* 15: 253.

Allmark, P. (2002) 'Can there be an ethics of care?' in K. Fulford, D. Dickenson and T. Murray (eds) *Healthcare Ethics and Human Values* (Blackwell).

Allsop. J. and Mulcahy, L. (1998) 'Maintaining professional identity: doctors' responses to complaints' *Sociology of Health and Illness* 20: 802.

Almqvist, E. (1999) 'A worldwide assessment of the frequency of suicide, suicide attempts, or psychiatric hospitalization after predictive testing for Huntingdon Disease' *American Journal of Human Genetics* 64: 1293.

Al-Shahi, R. and Warlow, C. (2000) 'Using patient identifiable data for observational reseach and audit' *British Medical Journal* 321: 1031.

Alward, P. (2002) 'Thomson, the right to life, and partial birth abortion or two MULES for Sister Sarah' *Journal of Medical Ethics* 28: 99.

Amarasekara, K. and Bagaric, M. (2002) *Euthanasia, Morality and the Law* (Peter Lang).

Anderson, M. (2006) 'Xenotransplantation: a bioethical evaluation' *Journal of Medical Ethics* 32: 205.

Anderson, P. (1992) 'Good death' *Tricycle* 36.

Andorno, R. (2004) 'The right not to know: an autonomy based approach' *Journal of Medical Ethics* 30: 435.

Andrews, K. (1989) 'Recovery of patients after four months or more in the persistent vegetative state' *British Medical Journal* 306: 1600.

Andrews, K., Murhpy, L., Munday, R. and Littlewood, C. (1996) 'Misdiagnosis of the vegetative state' *British Medical Journal* 313: 13.

Andrews, L. (2001) *Future Perfect: Confronting Decision about Genetics* (Cambridge University Press).

Andrews, L. and Nelkin, D. (2001a) *Body Bazaar: The Market for Human Tissue* (Crown).

Angell, E., Sutton, A., Windridge, K., and Dixon-Woods, M. (2006) 'Consistency in decision making by research ethics committees: a controlled comparison' *Journal of Medical Ethics* 32: 662.

Annas, G. (1986) 'Pregnant Women as Fetal Containers' *Hastings Centre Report* 16: 13.

Annas, G. (1998) 'The bell tolls for right to assisted suicide' in L. Emanuel (ed) *Regulating How We Die* (Harvard University Press).

Annas, G. (1990) 'Nancy Cruzon and the right to die' *New England Journal of Medicine* 323: 670.

Annas, G. and Glantz, L. (1986) 'Rules for research in nursing homes' *New English Journal of Medicine* 315: 1157.

Anon (2003a) 'What's wrong with that?' *British Medical Journal* 327: E1 15.

Anon (2003b) 'Big Boob by Doctors' *The Sun* 23 August 2003.

Anon (2004a) 'Young girls seek IVF2' 7 July 2004 *Bionews*.

Anon (2004b) 'Woman denied IVF because of wrong hair colour' 19 July 2004 *Bionews*.

Anon (2005) 'Fears over UK egg and sperm donor shortages' 29 March 2005 *Bionews*.

Anscombe, G. (1981) 'Ethical problems in the management of some severely handicapped children' *Journal of Medical Ethics* 7: 122.

Anstey, K. (2002) 'Are attempts to have impaired children justifiable?' *Journal of Medical Ethics* 28: 286.

Applebe, G. and Wingfield, J. (2005) *Dale and Applebe's Pharmacy Law and Ethics* (Pharmaceutical Press).

April, C. and Parker, M. (2007) 'End of life decision-making in neonatal care' *Journal of Medical Ethics* 33: 126.

Ardagh, M. (2000) 'Futility has no utility in resuscitation medicine' *Journal of Medical Ethics* 26: 396.

Aries, P. (1974) *Western Attitudes Towards Death from the Middle Ages to the Present* (John Hopkins University Press).

Aries, P. (1983) *The Hour of our Death* (Penguin).

Aries, P. (2000) 'Death denied' in D. Dickenson, M. Johnson and J. Samson Katz (eds) *Death, Dying and Bereavement* (Sage).

Armstrong, D. (2004) 'The rise of surveillance medicine' in G. Scambler (ed) *Major Themes in Health and Social Welfare: Medical Sociology* (Routledge).

Arnes, M. (1996) 'Euthanasia: Buddhist principles' *British Medical Bulletin* 52: 369.

Arras, J. (1997) 'Physician-assisted suicide: a tragic view' *Journal of Contemporary Health Law and Policy* 361.

Asch, A. and Wasserman, D. (2007) 'A Response to Nelson and Mahowald' *Cambridge Quarterly of Healthcare Ethics* 16: 468.

Asche, A. (2003) 'Disability equality and prenatal testing: contradictory or 630 compatible?' *Florida State University Law Review* 30: 315.

Ashe, M. (1988) 'Law-language of maternity; discourse holding nature in contempt' *New England Law Review* 22: 521.

Ashton, J. and Seymour, H. (1988) *The New Public Health* (Oxford University Press).

Ashworth, M. (2004) 'How are the primary care organizations using financial incentives to influence prescribing?' *Journal of Public Health* 26: 48.

Associated Press (2005) *A National Scandal: AIDS Drug Experiments on Foster Care Children* (Associated Press).

Association of the British Pharmaceutical Industry (2007) *Health and Medicines Factsheet* (ABPI).

Asthma UK (2005) *The Asthma Audit* (Asthma UK).

Atiyah, P. (1982) 'Economic duress and the "overborne will"' *Law Quarterly Review* 98: 197.

Attell-Thompson, L. (2005) 'Consumer directed health care: Ethical limits to choice and responsibility' *Journal of Medicine and Philosophy* 30: 207.

Audit Commission (1995) *Setting the Record Straight* (HMSO).

Audit Commission (2003) *Achieving the NHS Plan* (DoH).

Bachelard, S. (2002) 'On euthanasia: blind sport in the argument from mercy' *Journal of Applied Philosophy* 19: 131.

Bagheri, A. (2007) 'Individual choice in the definition of death' *Journal of Medical Ethics* 33: 146.

Bagshaw, R. and McBride, N. (2005) *Tort Law* (Pearson).

Baker, R., Shields, C., Stevenson, K., Fraser, R., Stone, M. (2000) 'What proportion of patients refuse consent to data collection from their records for research purposes?' *British Journal of General Practice* 50: 655.

Baldwin, T. (2005) 'Reproductive liberty and elitist contempt' *Journal of Medical Ethics* 31: 288.

Bailey-Harris, R. (2000) 'Patient Autonomy—a turn in the tide?' in M. Freeman and A. Lewis (eds) *Law and Medicine* (Oxford University Press).

Bainham, A. (1987) 'Handicapped girls and judicial parents' *Law Quarterly Review* 103: 334.

Bainham, A. (1992) 'The Judge and the competent minor' *Law Quarterly Review* 108: 194.

Bainham, A. (1996) 'Sex education: a family lawyer's perspective' in N. Harris, (ed) *Children, Sex Education and the Law* (National Children's Bureau).

Bainham, A. (2005) *The Modern Law of Children* (Jordans).

Baird, D. and Glasier, A. (1999) 'Science medicine and the future: contraception' *British Medical Journal* 319: 969.

Baird, D. and Glasier, A. (1999) 'Science medicine and the future: contraception' *British Medical Journal* 319: 961.

Baker, P. (2004) 'Research in obstetrics and gynaecology' Association of Research Ethics Committees Newsletter.

Barber, K., Falvey, S., Hamilton, C., Collett, D., and Rudge, C. (2006) 'Potential for organ donation in the United Kingdom: audit of intensive care records' *British Medical Journal* 332: 1124.

Barron, K. (2005) 'When will the full NICE guidelines on infertility treatment be implemented?' 3 April *Bionews*.

Bartlett, P. (1997) 'Doctors as fiduciaries; Equitable regulation of the doctor-patient relationship' *Medical Law Review* 193.

Bartlett, P. (2003a) 'Adults, mental illness and incapacity' *Journal of Welfare and Family Law* 25: 341.

Bartlett, P. (2003b) 'The test of compulsion in mental health law: capacity, therapeutic benefit and dangerousness as possible criteria' *Medical Law Review* 11: 326.

Bartlett, P. (2005) *The Mental Capacity Act* (Oxford University Press).

Bartlett, P. (2006) 'Psychiatric treatment: in the absence of law?' *Medical Law Review* 14: 124.

Bartlett, P. and Sandland, R. (2007) *Mental Health Law* (Oxford University Press).

Barth, K. (1998) 'Parents and children' in M. Lammers and A. Verhey (eds) *On Moral Medicine* (Eerdmans).

Battin, M. (1980) 'Suicide a fundamental human right' in M. Battin and D. Mayo *Suicide: The Philosophical Issues* (Routledge).

Battin, M. (1992) 'Voluntary euthanasia and the risk of abuse' 20 *Law Medicine and Health Care* 133.

Battin, M. (1995) *Ethical Issues in Suicide* (Prentice Hall).

Battin, M. (1998) 'Physician-assisted suicide: safe, legal, rare?' in M. Battin, R. Rhodes and A. Silvers (eds) *Physician Assisted Suicide* (Routledge).

Battin, M. (2005) *Ending Life* (Oxford University Press).

Battin, M., van der Heide, A., Ganzini,L., van der Wal, G., Onwuteaka-Philipsen, B. (2007) 'Legal physician-assisted dying in Oregon and the Netherlands: evidence concerning the impact on patients in "vulnerable" groups' *Journal of Medical Ethics* 33: 591.

Baumrin, B. (1998) 'Physician stay thy hand' in M. Battin, R. Rhodes and A. Silvers, *Physician Assisted Suicide* (Routledge).

Baylis, F. (2002) 'Human cloning: three mistakes and an alternative' *Journal of Medicine and Philosophy* 27: 319.

Bayne, T. (2003) 'Gamete donation and parental responsibility' *Journal of Applied Philosophy* 20: 77.

BBC Newsonline (16 November 1998) 'GPs "help" 27,000 patients to die'.

BBC Newsonline (12 December 1999) 'Gay couple become fathers'.

BBC Newsonline (2 March 2001) 'One in ten "harmed" in hospital'.

BBC Newsonline (23 February 2001) '£20,000 for extra IVF baby'.

BBC Newsonline (1 November 2001) 'Health Patients "benefit from Prayer"'.

BBC Newsonline (24 January 2003) 'Suicide man's "dignified death"'.

BBC Newsonline (7 March 2003) 'Broadmoor women faced sex abuse'.

BBC Newsonline (4 April 2003) 'Pill linked to cervical cancer risk'.

BBC Newsonline (3 July 2003) 'Mixed-sex human embryo created'.

BBC Newsonline (18 August 2003) 'Doctor slang is dying'.

BBC Newsonline (21 October 2003) 'UK considers bulk sperm imports'.

BBC Newsonline (9 December 2003) 'Health Records put on Internet'.

BBC Newsonline (9 February 2004) 'Morning-after Pill scheme grows'.

BBC Newsonline (16 March 2004) '40% of pregnancies unplanned'.

BBC Newsonline (20 March 2004) 'Compensation Culture under fire'.

BBC Newsonline (26 April 2004) 'Kidney father auction keeps organ'.

BBC Newsonline (15 June 2004) 'NHS staff reject own hospitals'.

BBC Newsonline (30 June 2004) 'EU faces fertility tourism threat'.

BBC Newsonline (19 July 2004) 'NHS refuses couples IVF treatment'.

BBC Newsonline (22 July 2004) 'Drug watchdog costs too much'.

BBC Newsonline (26 July 2004) 'Twins born to own gran fly home'.

BBC Newsonline (28 July 2004) 'We hear a terrible tale from a modern day Dr Mengele'.

BBC Newsonline (22 August 2004) 'Would-be organ donors stay silent'.

BBC Newsonline (1 September 2004) 'Pig organs may be safe for humans'.

BBC Newsonline (2 September 2004) 'Coma patient's shock pregnancy'.

BBC Newsonline (29 September 2004) 'Sex abuse trials open on Pitcairn'.

BBC Newsonline (21 October 2004) 'UK considers bulk sperm imports'.

BBC Newsonline (30 November 2004) 'New York's HIV experiment'.

BBC Newsonline (1 December 2004) 'Tough challenges remain in AIDS fight'.

BBC Newsonline (10 December 2004) 'Fertility watchdog "incompetent"'.

BBC Newsonline (2 February 2005) 'Patient GP ratio "varies widely"'.

BBC Newsonline (9 February 2005) 'Tissue from dead woman helps 20'.

BBC Newsonline (24 February 2005) 'Teen pregnancy "hotspots" tackled'.

BBC Newsonline (27 February 2005) 'Euthanasia doctor is struck off'.

BBC Newsonline (10 March 2005) 'NHS "not dealing with complaints"'.

BBC Newsonline (21 March 2005) 'Hospital withheld patients' food'.

BBC Newsonline (29 March 2005) 'Odd accidents affect one million'.

BBC Newsonline (31 March 2005) 'DNA profiling of babies rejected'.

BBC Newsonline (1 April 2005) 'Couples face long waits for IVF'.

BBC Newsonline (8 April 2005) 'Depression "top sick leave cause"'.

BBC Newsonline (19 April 2005) 'More cash for mental health urged'.

BBC Newsonline (19 April 2005) 'Mother Cures Daughter of Diabetes'.

BBC Newsonline (28 April 2005) 'Lords back "designer baby choice"'.

BBC Newsonline (29 April 2005) 'Life expectancy gap "widening"'.

BBC Newsonline (3 May 2005) 'Woman, 67, to be "oldest mum yet"'.

BBC Newsonline (8 May 2005) '"Get to grips" call over sickies'.

BBC Newsonline (9 May 2005) 'Girls aged 10 are taking the Pill'.

BBC Newsonline (9 May 2005) 'Care refusal spread TM to others'.

BBC Newsonline (17 May 2005) 'Med journals too close to firms'.

BBC Newsonline (18 May 2005) 'Child drug research plea renewed'.

BBC Newsonline (19 May 2005a) 'Police killer held indefinitely'.

BBC Newsonline (19 May 2005b) 'UK scientists clone human embryo'.

BBC Newsonline (19 May 2005c) '"Make IVF genetic screen routine"'.

BBC Newsonline (20 May 2005) 'UK scientists clone human embryo'.

BBC Newsonline (24 May 2005) 'Fertility Success Gulf Revealed'.

BBC Newsonline (26 May 2005) 'Parents "must tackle teen births"'.

BBC Newsonline (29 May 2005) 'Fast-freeze "boosts egg survival"'.

BBC Newsonline (30 May 2005) 'Living Organ Donor Drive Launched'.

BBC Newsonline (1 June 2005) '"Artificial heart saved my life"'.

BBC Newsonline (13 June 2005a) 'Hospital blamed for tough births'.

BBC Newsonline (13 June 2005b) 'Men warned about obesity problem'.

BBC Newsonline (13 June 2005c) 'Intoxication rife among doctors'.

BBC Newsonline (22 June 2005) 'Hospital criticised after killing'.

BBC Newsonline (23 June 2005) 'Obese Mums harm baby's fertility'.

BBC Newsonline (10 May 2006) 'Doctors oppose right to die law'.

BBC Newsonline (1 June 2006) 'Hospices "face financial deficit"'.

BBC Newsonline (15 June 2006) 'The genius sperm bank'.

BBC Newsonline (26 June 2006) 'Doctors change euthanasia stance'.

BBC Newsonline (8 July 2006) 'Briton becomes new mother at 62'.

BBC Newsonline (10 July 2006) 'Mental unit sex assaults "rife"'.

BBC Newsonline (15 July 2005) 'Prayer "no aid to heart patients"'.

BBC Newsonline (17 July 2005) 'Public Split on new hate laws'.

BBC Newsonline (18 July 2005) 'Warning over maternity care risk'.

BBC Newsonline (19 July 2005) 'NHS 'refuses couples IVF treatment'.

BBC Newsonline (21 July 2005) 'Breast cancer drug fast-tracked'.

BBC Newsonline (4 August 2005) 'Brain-dead woman dies after birth'.

BBC Newsonline (9 August 2005) '"Rationed" bowel cancer drug fear'.

BBC Newsonline (11 August 2005) 'Health inequality gap "widening"'.

BBC Newsonline (24 August 2005) 'Placebo sparks brain pain killers'.

BBC Newsonline (1 September 2005) 'Pig organs may be safe for humans'.

BBC Newsonline (2 September 2005) 'Row erupts over dyslexia "denial"'.

BBC Newsonline (2 September 2005) 'Child murder suspect is sectioned'.

BBC Newsonline (8 September 2005) 'Yes to cloning with two mothers'.

BBC Newsonline (12 September 2006) 'NHS management bills "soars"'.

BBC Newsonline (16 September 2005) 'Sperm ships for fertility seekers'.

BBC Newsonline (22 September 2005) 'Fast-track drug appraisal'.

BBC Newsonline (27 September 2005) 'Euthanasia doctor is struck off'.

BBC Newsonline (29 September 2005) 'Sex Abuse Trials Open on Pitcairn'.

BBC Newsonline (30 September 2005) 'Mother, 53, has baby for daughter'.

BBC Newsonline (3 October 2005) 'Nurse wins breast cancer drug row'.

BBC Newsonline (6 October 2005) '"Pay more" to sperm, egg donors'.

BBC Newsonline (15 December 2006) 'Obesity "could bankrupt the NHS"'.

BBC Newsonline (4 January 2007) 'Treatment keeps girl child sized'.

BBC Newsonline (22 January 2007) 'Seven week wait for abortion'.

BBC Newsonline (5 March 2007) 'Hot baths may cut male fertility'.

BBC Newsonline (14 March 2007) 'No such thing as naughty anymore'.

BBC Newsonline (11 May 2007) 'Body parts sale man avoids jail'.

BBC Newsonline (3 June 2007) 'Cancer-drug refund scheme backed'.

BBC Newsonline (2 July 2007) '25% of virgins ignore safe sex'.

BBC Newsonline (3 July 2007) 'Girl could give birth to sister'.

BBC Newsonline (12 July 2007) 'Inmate suicide rate "increasing"'.

BBC Newsonline (6 August 2007) 'Free IVF care "denied to many"'.

BBC Newsonline (9 September 2007) 'More detained in secure hospitals'.

BBC Newsonline (2 October 2007) 'North Carolina pair feud over leg'.

BBC Newsonline (4 October 2007) 'Couples swap kidneys in UK first'.

BBC Newsonline (8 October 2007) 'Children Donor Awareness Rejected'.

BBC Newsonline (14 November 2007) 'Breakthrough in primate cloning'.

Beauchamp, T. (1978) 'A reply to rachels on active and passive euthanasia' in T. Beauchamp and S. Perlin (eds) *Ethical Issues in Death and Dying* (Prentice Hall).

Beauchamp, T. (1995) 'Principlism and its alleged competitors' *Kennedy Institute of Ethics Journal* 5: 181.

Beauchamp, T. (1999) 'The failure of theories of personhood' *Kennedy Institute of Ethics Journal* 9: 309.

Beauchamp, T. (2004) 'Does ethical theory have a future in bioethics?' *Journal of Law, Medicine and Ethics* 32: 209.

Beauchamp, T. and Childress, J. (2003) *Principles of Biomedical Ethics* (Oxford University Press).

Becker, C. (1990) 'Buddhist views of suicide and euthanasia' *Philosophy East and West* 40: 543.

Becker, C. (1993) *Breaking the circle: death and the afterlife in Buddhism* (Southern Illinois University Press).

Beckwith, F. (1992) 'Personal bodily rights, abortion, and unplugging the violinist' *International Philosophical Quarterly* 32: 105.

Beckwith, F. (2005) 'Of souls, selves, and cerebrums' *Journal of Medical Ethics* 31: 56.

Beecham, L. (2004) 'BMA annual representative meeting: Aborted babies born alive should receive full care' *British Medical Journal* 329: 72.

Bell, A. (2005) *Anti-Depressants being 'over-prescribed'* (Norwich Union Health).

Bell, D. (2006) 'The UK Human Tissue Act and consent: surrendering a fundamental principle to transplantation needs?' *Journal of Medical Ethics* 32: 283.

Bell, D. and Bennett, G. (2001) 'Genetic secrets and the family' *Medical Law Review* 9: 130.

Bellantoni, L. (2003) 'What good is a pragmatic bioethic?' *Journal of Medicine and Philosophy* 28: 615.

Bellhouse, J., Holland, A., Clare, I., Gunn, M., and Watson, P. (2003) 'Capacity-based mental health legislation and its impact on clinical practice' *Journal of Mental Health Law* 9.

Beloff, M. (2003) *Life, Death and the Law* (Royal College of Surgeons).

Belshaw, C. (2005) *10 Good Questions about Life and Death* (Blackwells).

Benatar, D. (1999) 'The unbearable lightness of bringing into being' *Journal of Applied Philosophy* 16: 173.

Benatar, D. (2006a) 'Bioethics and health and human rights: a critical view' *Journal of Medical Ethics* 32: 17.

Benatar, D. (2006b) *Better never to have been: the harm of coming into existence* (Oxford University Press).

Benatar, D. (2007) 'Moral theories may have some role in teaching applied ethics' *Journal of Medical Ethics* 37: 361.

Benatar, S. (2004) 'Blinkered bioethics' *Journal of Medical Ethics* 30: 291.

Bender, L. (1992) 'A feminist analysis of physician-assisted dying and voluntary active euthanasia' *Tennessee Law Review* 59: 519.

Bennett, J. (1966) 'Whatever the consequences' *Analysis* 26: 83.

Bennett, R. (2004) 'Human reproduction: irrational but in most cases morally defensible' *Journal of Medical Ethics* 30: 379.

Bennett, R. (2007) 'Routine antenatal HIV testing and informed consent: an unworkable marriage' *Journal of Medical Ethics* 33: 446.

Bennett, R. and Erin, A. (eds) (2001) *HIV and AIDS, Testing, Screening, and Confidentiality* (Oxford University Press).

Bennion, F. (1994) 'Legal death of brain damaged persons' HL Paper (1993–4) 28-III.

Benson, J. and Britten, N. (1996) 'Respecting the autonomy of cancer patients when talking with their families' *British Medical Journal* 313: 729.

Bentall, R. (2004) *Madness Explained* (Penguin).

Bently, L. and Sherman, B. (1995) 'The ethics of patenting: Towards a transgenic patent system' *Medical Law Review* 3: 275.

Bentley, J. and Thacker, P. (2004) 'The influence of risk and monetary payment on the research participation decision making process' *Journal of Medical Ethics* 30: 293.

Benyon, H. (1982) 'Doctors as murderers' *Criminal Law Review* 17.

Berg, J. (2001) 'Grave secrets: legal and ethical analysis of postmortem confidentiality' *Connecticut Law Review* 34: 81.

Beswick, J. (2007) 'A first class service? Setting the standard of care for the contemporary NHS' *Medical Law Review* 15: 245.

Better Regulation Task Force (2004) *Better Routes to Redress* (TSO).

Bevan, H. (1989) *Child Law* (Butterworths).

Beyleveld, D. and Brownsword, R. (2001) *Human Dignity in Bioethics and Biolaw.* (Oxford University Press).

Beyleveld, D. and Brownsword, R. (2007) *Consent in the Law* (Hart).

Beyleveld, D. (2002) 'Law, ethics and research ethics committees' *Medicine and Law* 21: 57.

Beyleveld D. and Histed E. (2000) 'Betrayal of confidence in the Court of Appeal' *Medical Law International* 4: 277.

Beyleveld, D. and Haker, H. (2000) *The Ethics of Genetics in Human Procreation* (Ashgate).

Beyleveld, D., Townend, D., and Wright, J. (eds) (2007) *Research Ethics Committees* (Ashgate).

Bickenbach, J. (1998) 'Disability and lifeending decisions' in M. Battin, R. Rhodes, and A. Silvers (eds) *Physician Assisted Suicide* (Routledge).

Biegler, P. (2003) 'Should patient consent be required to write a do not resuscitate Order?' *Journal of Medical Ethics* 29: 359.

Biggs, H. (1996) 'Euthanasia and death with dignity' *Criminal Law Review* 878.

Biggs, H. (1998) 'I don't want to be a Burden! A feminist reflects on women's experiences of death and dying' in S. Sheldon and M. Thomson (eds) *Feminist Perspectives on Health Care Law* (Cavendish).

Biggs, H. (2001) *Euthanasia* (Hart).

Biggs, H. (2002) 'Forever and ever amen: life and death in perpetuity' *Res Publica* 8: 93.

Biggs, H. (2003) 'A pretty fine line: life, death, autonomy and letting it b' *Feminist Legal Studies* 11: 291.

Biggs, H. (2007a) ' "Taking account of the views of the patient" ', but only if the clinician (and the court) agrees' *Child and Family Law Quarterly* 19: 225.

Biggs, H. (2007b) 'The quest for the perfect child' in K. Horsey and H.Biggs (eds) *Human Fertilization and Embryology: Reprodcing Regulation* (Routledge).

Biggs, H. (2007c) 'Criminalizing carers: death desires and assisted dying outlaws' in in B. Brooks-Gordon, F.Ebtehaj, J. Herring, M. Johnson, and M. Richards (eds) *Death Rights and Rites* (Hart).

Biggs, H. and Diesfeld, K. (1995) 'Assisted suicide for people with depressions: an advocate's perspective' *Medical Law International* 2: 23.

Billcliff, N., McCabe, E., and Brown, J. (2001) 'Informed consent to medication in long-term psychiatric inpatients' *Psychiatric Bulletin* 25: 132.

Biller-Andorno, N. and Schauenberg, H. (2001) 'It's only love? Some pitfalls in emotionally related organ donation' *Journal of Medical Ethics* 27: 162.

Bingol, N., Schuster, C., Fuchs, M., Iosub, S., Turner, G., Stoner, R., and Gromisch, J. (1987) 'The influence of socio-economic factors on the occurrence of fetal alcohol syndrome' *Advances in Alcohol and Substance Abuse* 6: 105.

Bjorkman, B. (2007) 'Why we are not allowed to sell that which we are encouraged to donate' *Cambridge Quarterly of Healthcare Ethics* 15: 60.

Bjorkman, B. and Hansson, S. (2006) 'Bodily rights and property rights' *Journal of Medical Ethics* 32: 209.

Blackford, R. (2006) 'Sinning against nature: the theory of background conditions' *Journal of Medical Ethics* 32: 326.

Blake, M. (1997) 'Physician assisted suicide: a criminal offence or a patient's right' *Medical Law Review* 5: 294.

Blank, R. (1991) *Fertility Control: New Techniques New Policy Issues* (Greenwood Press).

Blank, K., Robison, J., Prigerson, H. and Schwartz, H. (2001) 'Instability of attitudes about euthanasia and physician assisted suicide in depressed older hospitalized patients' *General Hospital Psychiatry* 23: 326.

Blyth, A. (1990) 'Audit of terminal care in a general practice' *British Medical Journal* 300: 983.

Blyth, E. (2003) 'Fertility rights: will the UK's Human Rights Act make any difference to access to assisted conception treatment' in J. Gunning and H. Szoke *The Regulation of Assisted Reproductive Technology* (Ashgate).

Blyth, E. (2007) 'Conceptions of welfare' in K. Horsey and H.Biggs (eds) *Human Fertilization and Embryology: Reprodcing Regulation* (Routledge).

Blyth, E. and Farrand, A. (2005) 'Reproductive tourism—a price worth paying for reproductive autonomy?' *Critical Social Policy* 25: 91.

Blyth, E., Crawshaw, M. and Speirs, J. (eds) (1998) *Truth and the Child 10 years on: Information Exchange in Donor Assisted Conception* (British Association of Social Workers).

Blyth, E. and Potter, C. (2003) 'Paying for it? Surrogacy, market forces, assisted conception' in R. Cook, S. Day Sclater and F. Kaganas (eds) *Surrogate Motherhood* (Hart).

BMA (1996) *News Review* (BMA).

BMA (1999) *Withholding and Withdrawing Life-Prolonging Medical Treatment. Guidance for Decision Making* (BMA).

BMA (2001) *Consent, Rights and Choices in Health Care for Children and Young People* (BMA).

BMA (2001b) *Gene Patenting* (BMA).

BMA (2004) *Medical Ethics Today* (BMA).

BMA (2005) *Organ Donation—Presumed Consent for Organ Donation* (BMA).

BMA (2006) *Child and Adolescent Mental Health* (BMA).

BMA (2007a) *A Rational Way Forwaard for the NHS* (BMA).

BMA (2007b) *Withholding and Withdrawing Life-Prolonging Medical Treatment* (BMA).

BMA Medico-Legal Committee (2001) *Mediation, clinical negligence claims & the medical profession* (BMA).

BMA and Law Society (2004) *Assessment of Mental Capacity* (BMJ).

Board of Social Responsibility, Church of England (2000) *On Dying Well* (Church House Publishing).

Boddington, P. (1998) 'Organ donation after death—should I decide, or my family' *Journal of Applied Philosophy* 15: 69.

Boddington, P. and Podpadec, T. (2002) 'Measuring quality of life in theory and in practice' *Bioethics* 6: 201.

Boonin, D. (2000) 'How to argue against active euthanasia' *Journal of Applied Philosophy* 17: 157.

Boonin, D. (2002) *A Defense of Abortion* (Cambridge University Press).

Bonsack, C. and Borgeat, F. (2005) 'Perceived coercion and need for hospitalization related to psychiatric admission' *International Journal of Law and Psychiatry* 28: 342.

Boozang, K. (1997) 'An intimate passing: restoring the role of family and religion in dying' *University of Pittsburgh Law Review*.

Bortolotti, L. and Harris, J. (2006) 'Embryos and eagles: symbolic value in research and reproduction' *Cambridge Quarterly of Healthcare Ethics* 15: 22.

Bovens, L. (2007) 'The rhythm method and embryonic death' *Journal of Medical Ethics* 32: 355.

Bowden, P. (1996) 'Violence and mental disorder' in N. Walker (ed) *Dangerous People* (Blackstone).

Bowman, K. (2004) 'What are the limits of bioethics in a culturally pluralistic society?' *Journal of Law, Medicine and Ethics* 32: 664.

Boyd, K. (1992) 'HIV Infection and AIDS' *Journal of Medical Ethics* 18: 173.

Boyd, K. (1998) 'Euthanasia: back to the future' in J. Keown (ed) *Euthanasia Examined* (Cambridge University Press).

Boyd, K. (2002) 'Mrs Pretty and Ms B' *Journal of Medical Ethics* 28: 211.

Boyd, P. (2003) 'The requirements of the Data Protection Act for the processing of medical data' *Journal of Medical Ethics* 29: 34.

Boyd, K. (2005) 'Medical ethics: principles, persons and perspectives' *Journal of Medical Ethics* 31: 481.

Boyle, J. (1997) 'A case for sometimes feeding patients in PVS' in J. Keown (ed) *Euthanasia Examined* (Cambridge University Press).

Boyle, K. (1999) 'Personal responsibility in health care' in M. Chery (ed) *Persons and Their Bodies* (Kluwer).

Boyd, K. (2005) 'Medical ethics: principles, persons, and perspectives: from controversy to conversation' *Journal of Medical Ethics* 31: 481.

BPAS (1999) *Pricelist of Services* (BPAS).

BPAS (2006) *Poll Shows Majority Support for Legal Abortion* (BPAS).

Bradbury, M. (2000) 'The good death?' in D. Dickenson, M. Johnson and J. Samson Katz, *Death, Dying and Bereavement* (Sage).

Bradley, G. (1993) 'Life's dominion: a review Essay' *Notre Dame Law Review* 69: 329.

Brahams, D. (1989) 'Kidney for sale by live donor' *The Lancet* 1989: 285.

Braidotti, R. (1994) *Nomadic Subjects* (Columbia University Press).

Brassington, I. (2002) 'Actions, causes, and psychiatry: a reply to Szasz' *Journal of Medical Ethics* 28: 120.

Brassington, I. (2007) 'John Harris' argument for a duty to research' *Bioethics* 21: 160.

Braunack-Mayer, J. (2001) 'What makes a problem an ethical problem?' *Australian Journal of Medical Ethics* 27: 98.

Brazier, M. (1987) 'Patient autonomy and consent to treatment: the role of law?' *Legal Studies* 7: 169.

Brazier, M. (1988) "Embryo's 'rights': abortion and research' in M. Freeman (ed), *Medicine, Ethics and Law* (Stevens).

Brazier, M. (1990a) 'The challenge for parliament' in A. Dyson and J. Harris (eds) *Experiments on Embryos* (Routledge).

Brazier, M. (1990b) 'Liability of ethics committee and their members' *Personal Negligence* 186.

Brazier, M. (1997) 'Prenatal responsibilities, foetal welfare and children's Health' in C. Bridge (ed) *Family Law Towards the Millennium* (Butterworths).

Brazier, M. (1998) 'Reproductive rights: feminism or patriarchy?' in J. Harris and

S. Holm (1998) *The Future of Human Reproduction* (Oxford University Press).

Brazier, M. (1999a) 'Regulating the reproduction business' *Medical Law Review* 7: 166.

Brazier, M. (1999b) 'Liberty, responsibility, maternity' *Current Legal Problems* 52: 359.

Brazier, M. (1999c) 'Can you buy children?' *Child Family Law Quarterly* 11: 345.

Brazier, M. (2002) 'Retained organs: ethics and humanity' *Legal Studies* 22: 550.

Brazier, M. (2003a) 'Organ retention and return: problems of consent' *Journal of Medical Ethics* 29: 30.

Brazier, M. (2003b) *Medicine, Patients and the Law* (Penguin).

Brazier, M. (2005a) 'Times of change' *Medical Law Review* 13: 1.

Brazier, M. (2005b) 'An intractable dispute: when parents and professionals disagree' *Medical Law Review* 13: 412.

Brazier, M. (2006a) 'Do no harm—Do patients have responsibilities too?' *Cambridge Law Journal* 65: 397.

Brazier, M. (2006b) 'Human(s) (as) medicine(s)' in S. McLean (ed) *First do no Harm* (Ashgate).

Brazier, M. and Beswick, J. (2006) 'Who's caring for me?' *Medical Law International* 7: 183.

Brazier, M. and Cave, E. (2007) *Medicine, Patients and the Law* (Penguin).

Brazier, M. and Miola, J. (2000) 'Bye-bye bolam: a medical litigation revolution' *Medical Law Review* 85.

Brazier, M. and Glover, N. (2000) 'Does medical law have a future?' in D. Hayton (ed) *Law's Futures* (Hart).

Brecher, B. (1994) 'Organs for transplant: donation or payment?' in R. Gillon (ed) *Principles of Health Care Ethics* (John Wiley and Sons).

Breck, J. (2002) 'Sacredness and sanctity of human life' in N. Messer (ed) *Theological Issues in Bioethics* (Darton Longman and Todd).

Breitbart, W. and Rosenfeld, B. (1999) 'Physician-assisted suicide: the influence of psychosocial issues' *Cancer Control Journal* 6: 146.

Brennan, T., Laird, L., Localio, H., Lawthers, A., Newhouse, J., Weiler, P., and Hiatt, H. (1991) 'Incidence of adverse events and negligence in hopsitalized patients' *New England Journal of Medicine* 324: 370.

Bresnahan, J. (1998) 'Catholic spirituality and medical Interventions and dying' in S. Lammers and A. Verhey (eds) *On Moral Medicine* (Eerdmans).

Brewaeys, A. (2003) 'Lesbian couples in DI practice' in J. Gunning and H. Szoke (eds) *The Regulation of Assisted Reproductive Technology* (Ashgate).

Brewaeys, A., Ponjaert, I., van Hall, E., Golombok, S. (1997) 'Donor insemination: child development and family functioning in lesbian mother families' *Human Reproduction* 12: 1349.

Brickman, P. and Coates, D. (1978) 'Lottery winners and accident victims: is happiness relative' *Journal of Personality and Social Psychology* 36: 917.

Bridge, C. (2002) 'Religion, culture and the body of the child' in *Body Lore and Laws* (Hart).

Bridge, S. (1999) 'Assisted reproduction and parentage in law' in A. Bainham, S. Day Sclater, and M. Richards (eds) *What is a Parent?* (Hart).

Bridgeman, J. (1998) 'Because we care? The medical treatment of children' in S. Sheldon and M. Thomson, *Feminist Perspectives on Health Care* (Cavendish).

Bridgeman, J. (2006) 'Young people and sexual health: Whose rights? Whose responsibilities?' *Medical Law Review* 14: 418.

Bridgeman, J. and Millns, A. (1998) *Feminist Perspectives on Law* (Sweet and Maxwell).

Brinsden, P., Appleton, T., Murray, E., Hussein, M., Akagbosu, F. and Marcus, S. (2000) 'Treatment by in vitro fertilisation with surrogacy: experience of one British centre' *British Medical Journal* 320: 924.

Bristol Royal Infirmary Inquiry (2001) *Learning from Bristol* (DoH).

Bristow, J. (2002) 'In Praise of the Pill' 6 March 2002 *Spiked*.

British Fertility Society (1996) *Payment of Semen Donors* (BFS).

British Fertility Society (2004) *UK study shows 29% drop in sperm concentration* (BFS).

British Market Research Bureau (2003) *Evaluation of the Teenage Pregnancy Strategy* (BMRB).

British Medical Association (1998a) *Philosophy and Practice of Medical Ethics* (BMA).

British Medical Association (1998b) *Human Genetics: Choice and Responsibility* (BMA).

British Medical Association (1999) *Withholding and Withdrawing Life-Prolonging Medical Treatment. Guidance for Decision Making* (BMA).

British Medical Association (2001) *Withholding and Withdrawing Life-Prolonging Medical Treatment: Guidance for Decision Makers, 2nd ed* (BMA).

British Medical Association (2004) *Medical Ethics Today* (BMJ).

British Psychological Society (2002) *Guidelines on Confidentiality and Record Keeping* (BPS).

British Transplant Society (1995) *Report of the BTS Working Party on Organ Transplantation* (BTS).

British Transplant Society (2000) *United Kingdom guidelines for living donor kidney transplantation* (BTS).

British Transplant Society (2005) *Approved Position Statements* (BTS).

Brock, D. (1992) 'Voluntary active euthanasia' *Hastings Center Report* 22: 10.

Brock, D. and Griffiths, J. (2002) *Trends in Suicide by method in England and Wales 1979 to 2001* (ONS).

Brockopp, I (2002) 'Islamic ethics of saving life: a comparative perspective' *Medicine and Law* 21: 225.

Brody, B. (1975) *Abortion and the Sanctity of Human Life* (Harvard University Press).

Broeckaert, B. and Olarte, J. (2002) 'Sedation in palliative care: fact and concepts' in H. ten Have and D. Clark (eds) *The Ethics of Palliative Care* (Open University Press).

Brogden, M. (2001) *Geronticide: Killing the Elderly* (Jessica Kingsley).

Brook Advisory Centres (1999) *You think they won't tell anyone. Well you hope they won't* (Brook Advisory Centres).

Brooke, J. (2004) 'Commentary on: The person, the soul and genetic engineering' *Journal of Medical Ethics* 30: 597.

Brooks-Gordan, B., Ebtehaj, F., Herring, J., Johnson, M., and Richards, M. (eds) (2007) *Death Rights and Rites* (Hart).

Brown, B. (2002) 'Human cloning and genetic engineering: the case for proceeding cautiously' *Albany Law Review* 65: 649.

Brown, C. (2005) '"Postcode prescribing" is still alive and well in NHS-funded infertility treatment' 5 April 2005 *Bionews*.

Brown, M. (2000) 'The morality of abortion and the deprivation of futures' *Journal of Medical Ethics* 26: 103.

Brown, G. and Moskowitz, E. (1997) 'Moral and policy issues in long acting contraception' *Annual Review of Public Health* 18: 379.

Browne, A. (2000) 'Lives ruined as NHS leaks patients' dated 25 June 2000, *The Observer*.

Brownsword, R. (2002) 'Stem cells, superman, and the report of the select committee' *Modern Law Review* 65: 568.

Brownsword, R. (2003a) 'Review' *Modern Law Review* 66: 156.

Brownsword, R. (2003b) 'An interest in human dignity as the basis for genomic torts' *Washburn Law Journal* 42: 413.

Brownsword, R. (2003c) 'Bioethics today, bioethics tomorrow: stem cell research and the "dignitarian alliance"' *Notre Dame Journal of Law, Ethics and Public Policy* 15.

Buchanan, A. (1998) 'Advance directives and the personal identity problems' *Philosophy and Public Affairs* 17: 277.

Buchanan, A. (2002) 'Psychiatric detention and treatment: a suggested criterion' *Journal of Mental Health Law* 6: 35.

Buchanan, A., Brock, D, Daniels, N. and Wikler, D. (2000) *From Chance to Choice* (Cambridge University Press).

Buchanan, A. and Brock, C. (1990) *Deciding for Others. The Ethics of Surrogate Decision Making* (Cambridge University Press).

Buchanan, D. (2000) *An Ethic for Health Promotion: Rethinking the Sources of Human Well-Being* (Oxford University Press).

Buchanan, D. and Miller, F. (2006) 'A public health perspective on research ethics' *Journal of Medical Ethics* 32: 739.

Buetow, S. and Elwyn, G. (2006) 'Are patients morally responsible for their errors? *Journal of Medical Ethics* 32: 260.

Burgermeister, J. (2004) 'French wine makers face legal action over birth defects' *British Medical Journal* 329: 368.

Burley, J. (1998) 'The price of eggs' in J. Harris and S. Holm, *The Future of Human Reproduction* (Oxford University Press).

Burley, J. and Harris, J. (1999) 'Human cloning and child welfare' *Journal of Medical Ethics* 25: 108.

Burley, J. and Harris, J. (eds) (2002) *A Companion to Genetics: Philosophy and the Genetic Resolution*. (Blackwells).

Burrows, J. (2001) 'Telling tales and saving lives' *Medical Law Review* 9: 110.

Burtchaell, J. (1998) 'Human life and human love' in A. Lammers and A. Verhey (eds) *On Moral Medicine* (Eerdmans).

Butcher, J. (2007) 'Controversial mental health bill reaches the finishing line' *The Lancet* 370: 117.

Burton, B. (2004) New Zealand widens access to 'no fault' compensation for Medical mishap *British Medical Journal* 328: 729.

Butler, J. (1999) *The Ethics of Health Care Rationing: Principles and Practices* (Cassell).

Byrne, P. and Rinkowski (1999) '"Brain death" is false' *Linacre Quarterly* 42.

Caldicott, F. (1997) *Report of the Review of Patient-identifiable Information* (DoH).

Callahan, D. (1989) 'Can we return death to disease?' *Hastings Center Report* 4: 5.

Callahan, D. (1990a) 'Afterword' in P. Homer and M. Holstein (eds) *A Good Old Age* (Simon and Schuster).

Callahan, D. (1990b) *Setting Limits: What Kind of Life* (Simon and Schuster).

Callahan, D. (1992a) 'When self determination runs amock' *Hastings Center Report* 22: 52.

Callahan, D. (1992b) 'Bioethics and Fatherhood' *Utah Law Review* 3: 735.

Callahan, D. (1993) *The Troubled Dream of Life* (Simon and Schuster).

Callahan, D. (1983) 'On feeding the dying' *Hastings Center Report* 13: 22.

Callahan, D. (2003) 'Principlism and communitarianism' *Journal of Medical Ethics* 29: 287.

Callahan, D. and White, M. (1996) 'The legalization of physician-assisted suicide: creating a regulatory potemkin village' *University of Richmond Law Review* 30: 1.

Callahan, J. (1987) 'On harming the dead' *Ethics* 97: 341.

Callahan, J. and Roberts, D. (1996) 'A feminist social justice approach to reproduction assisting technologies' *Kentucky Law Journal* 84: 1197.

Callahan, S. (1995) 'Case against self determined dying in assisted suicide and euthanasia' *Studies in Pro-Life Feminism* 1: 303.

Callus, T. (2007) 'Patient perception of the Human Fertilisation and Embryology Authority' *Medical Law Review* 15: 62.

Calman, K., Hunter, D., and May, A. (2004) *Lost in Translation* (Durham University).

Calvert-Smith, D. (2003) 'Legislative technique and human rights' *Criminal Law Review* 384.

Cambridge Health Informatics Ltd (2001a) *Designing Future Systems to Support Confidentiality* (NHS).

Cambridge Health Informatics Ltd (2001b) *Gaining Patient Consent to Disclosure* (NHS).

Cameron, C. and Williamson, R. (2005) 'In the world of Dolly, when does a human embryo acquire respect?' *Journal of Medical Ethics* 31: 215.

Campbell, A. (2003) 'The virtues (and vices) of the four principles' *Journal of Medical Ethics* 29: 292.

Campbell, C. (2004) 'Harvesting the living?: separating "brain death" and organ transplantation' *Kennedy Institute of Ethics Journal* 14: 301.

Cancer Research (2005) *Letter* <http://www.saveeuropeanresearch.org>.

Canadian Biotechnology Advisory Committee on Patenting of Higher Life Forms (2002) *Patenting of Higher Life Forms* (CBAC).

Canadian Biotechnology Advisory Committee (2004) *Protecting Privacy In An Age Of Genetic Information* (CBAC).

Canadian Royal Commission (1993) *New Reproductive Technologies* (Canadian Government).

Cane, P. (2006) *Atiyah's Accidents, Compensation and the Law* (Butterworths).

Cane, P. (2004) 'Another failed sterilisation' *Law Quarterly Review* 120: 189.

Cantor, N. (1996) 'Discarding substituted judgment and best interests' *Rutgers Law Review* 48: 1193.

Cantor, N. (2005) *Making Medical Decisions for the Profoundly Mentally Disabled* (MIT Press).

Cantor, N. and Thomas III, G. (2000) 'The legal bounds of physician conduct hastening death' *Buffalo Law Review* 83.

Canvin, K., Bartlett, A., and Pinfold, V. (2005) 'Acceptability of compulsory powers in the community: the ethical considerations of mental health service users on supervised discharge and guardianship' *Journal of Medical Ethics* 31: 457.

Caplan, A. (1992) 'Is xenografting morally wrong?' *Transplantation Proceedings* 24: 722.

Cappelen, A. and Norheim, O. (2005) 'Responsibility in health care: a liberal egalitarian approach' *Journal of Medical Ethics* 31: 476.

Capron, A. (1986) 'Legal and ethical problems in decisions for death' *Law and Medical Health Care* 14: 141.

Capron, A. (1991) 'Protection of research subjects' *Law, Medicine and Healthcare* 19: 184.

Capstick, B. (2004) 'The future of clinical negligence litigation?' *British Medical Journal* 328: 457.

Card, R. (2006) 'Two puzzles for Marquis's conservative view on abortion' *Bioethics* 20: 264.

Cardinal, M. (1996) 'The words to say it' in S. Dunn, B. Morrison and M. Roberts (eds) *Mind Readings* (Minerva).

Care Not Killing (2006) *What is really happening in Oregon?* (Care not Killing).

Carlisle, J., Shickle, D., Cork, M., McDonagh, A. (2007) 'Concerns over confidentiality may deter adolescents from consulting their doctors. A qualitative exploration' *Journal of Medical Ethics* 32: 133.

Carmel, S. (2001) 'The will to live: gender differences among elderly persons' (2001) *Social Science and Medicine* 52: 949.

Carson, D. (1986) 'The symbolic significance of giving to eat and drink' in J. Lynn (ed) *By No Extraordinary Means* (Indiana University Press 1986).

Case, P. (2003) 'Confidence matters: The rise and fall of informational autonomy in medical law' *Medical Law Review* 11: 208.

Case, P. (2004) 'Secondary iatrogenic harm: claims for psychiatric damage following a death caused by medical error' *Modern Law Review* 67: 561.

Cases-Becerra, L. (1997) 'Women prosecuted and imprisoned for abortion in chile' *Reproductive Health Matters* 9: 29.

Cassell, J. and Young, A. (2002) 'Why we should not seek individual informed consent for participation in health services research' *Journal of Medical Ethics* 28: 313.

Cassileth, B. et al (1980) 'Informed consent—Why are its goals imperfectly realized?' *New England Journal of Medicine* 302: 896.

Castonguay, K. (1999) 'Pro-life feminism' in J. Kourany, J. Sterba and R. Tong (eds) *Feminist Philosophies* (Prentice Hall).

Castro, de, L. (2003a) 'Human organs from prisoners' *Journal of Medical Ethics* 29: 171.

Castro, de, L. (2003b) 'Commodification and exploitation: arguments in favour of compensated organ donation' *Journal of Medical Ethics* 29: 142.

Cater, S. and Coleman, L. (2006) *'Planned' Teenage Pregnancy* (Policy Press).

Catholic Bishops' Conference (2003) *Response to the Draft Mental Incapacity Bill* (Linacre Centre).

Catholic Bishop' Conference (2004) *Joint submission to the Science and Technology Committee* (TSO).

Cavadino, M. (1989) *Mental Health Law in Context* (Dartmouth).

Cave, E. (2004) *The Mother of all Crimes* (Ashgate).

Central Office for Research Ethics Committees (2006) *Building on improvement: implementing the recommendations of the report of the Ad Hoc Advisory Group on the Operation of NHS Research Ethics Committees* (COREC).

Cepko, R. (1993) 'Involuntary sterilisation of mentally disabled women' *Berkley Women's Law Journal* 8: 122.

Chadwick, R. (1994) 'Corpses, recycling and therapeutic purposes' in R. Lee and D. Morgans (eds) *Death* Rites (Routledge).

Chadwick, R. (1999) 'The Icelandic database' *British Medical Journal* 319: 41.

Chalmers, I. and Lindley, R. (2001) 'Double standards in informed consent' in L. Doyal and J. Tobias (eds) *Informed Consent In Medical Research* (British Medical Journal).

Chalmers, J. and Muir, R. (2003) 'Patient, privacy and confidentiality' *British Medical Journal* 326: 725.

Chapple, A., Ziebland, S., McPherson, A., and Herxheimer, A. (2006) 'What people close to death say about euthanasia and assisted suicide: a qualitative study' *Journal of Medical Ethics* 32: 706.

Chapstick, B. (2004) 'The future of clinical negligence litigation?' *British Medical Journal* 328: 487.

Charlesworth, M. (2005) 'Don't blame the "bio"—blame the "ethics": varieties of (bio)ethics and the challenge of pluralism' 2(1) *Journal of Bioethical Inquiry* 10.

Charny M. and Lewis P. (1989) 'Which of two individuals do you treat when only their ages are different and you can't treat both' *Journal of Medical Ethics* 15: 28.

Chau, P-L. and Herring, J. (2007) 'The meaning of death' in B. Brooks-Gordan, F. Ebthaj, J. Herring, M. Johnson, and M. Richards (eds) *Death Rights and Rites* (Hart).

Cherry, M. (1999) 'Persons and their bodies: rights, responsibilities, and the sale of organs' in M. Cherry (ed) *Persons and Their Bodies* (Kluwer).

Cherry, M. (2005) *Kidney for Sale by Owner* (Georgetown University Press).

Chester, M. (2003) 'Abused by the NHS: patient consent and confidentiality' *Consumer Policy Review* 13: 38.

Chico, V. (2006) 'Saviour siblings: Trauma and tort law' *Medical Law Review* 14: 180.

Chief Medical Officer (2001) *The Removal, Retention and use of Human Organs and Tissue from Post-Mortem Examination* (TSO).

Chief Medical Officer (2003) *Making Amends* (DoH).

Chief Medical Officer (2006a) *Good Doctors, Safer Patients* (DoH).

Chief Medical Officer (2006b) Annual Report (DoH).

Childress, J. and Bernheim, R. (2003) 'Beyond the liberal and communitarian impasse: a framework and vision for public health' *Florida Law Review* 55: 1191.

Chin, A., Hedber, K., Higginson, J., and Fleming, D. (1999) 'Legalized physician assisted suicide in oregon—the first year's experience' *New England Journal of Medicine* 340: 577.

Chisholm, G. (1988) 'Time to end softly softly approach on harvesting organs for transplantation' *British Medical Journal* 296: 1419.

Cho, N. (2002) 'Nearest relatives of gay and lesbian patients' *Journal of Mental Health Law* 323.

Cholbi, M. (2007) 'Self-manslaughter and the forensic classification of self-inflicted death' *Journal of Medical Ethics* 33: 155.

Choo, K. (1995) 'UK Shariah Council approves organ transplants' *The Lancet* 346: 303.

Chochinov, H., Tataryn, D., Clinch, J., and Dudgeon, D. (1999) 'Will to live in the terminal dying' *The Lancet* 354: 816.

Choudhry, S., Daar, A., Radcliffe-Richards, J., Guttmann, R., Hoffenberg, R., Lock, M., Sells, R., and Tilney, N. (2003) 'Unrelated living organ donation: ULTRA needs to go' *Journal of Medical Ethics* 29: 169.

Chouhan, P. and Draper, H. (2003) 'Modified mandated consent for organ procurement' *Journal of Medical Ethics* 29: 157.

Christman, J. (2004) 'Relational autonomy liberal individualism and the social constitution of selves' *Philosophical Studies* 143.

Church of England (2005) *Science, Medicine Technology and the Environment* (CoE).

Church of England House of Bishops and Roman Catholic Bishops' Conference, (2005) *Joint submission to the House of Lords Select Committee on Medical Ethics* (TSO).

Cica, N. (1993) 'Sterilising the intellectually disabled' *Medical Law Review* 1: 186.

Clark, B. (1979) *Whose Life is it Anyway?* (Mead).

Clark, D. and Seymour, J. (1999) *Reflections on Palliative Care* (Open University Press).

Clark, D., Dickinson, G., Lancester, C., Noble, T., Ahmedai, S., and Philp, I. (2001) 'UK

Geriatricians' attitudes to active voluntary euthanasia and physician assisted death' *Journal of Medical Ethics* 30: 395.

Clark, D., ten Have, H., and Janssens, R. (2002a) 'Palliative care service developments in seven european countries' in H. ten Have and D. Clark (eds) *The Ethics of Palliative Care* (Open University Press).

Clark, D., ten Have, H., and Janssens, R. (2002b) 'Conceptual tensions in European palliative care' in H. ten Have and D. Clark (eds) *The Ethics of Palliative Care* (Open University Press).

Clarke, C. (2002) 'Trust in medicine' *Journal of Medicine and Philosophy* 27: 11.

Clarke, L. (1989) 'Abortion: a rights issue?' in R. Lee and D. Morgan (eds) *Birthrights: Law and Ethics at the Beginning of Life* (Routledge).

Claxton, K. and Culyer, A. (2006) 'Wickedness or folly? The ethics of NICE's decisions' *Journal of Medical Ethics* 32: 375.

Claxton, K and Culyer, A. (2007) 'Rights, responsibilities and NICE: a rejoinder to Harris' *Journal of Medical Ethics* 33: 462.

Cleft Lip and Palate Association (2005) *Cleft Lip and Palate?* (CLPA).

Cleveland, S. (1997) 'Sterilization of the mentally disabled: applying error cost analysis to the "best interest" inquiry' *Georgetown Law Journal* 86: 137.

Clews, G. (2002) 'Doctors back patients' rights to refuse treatment' (2002) *BMA News* 30 March 2002, 12.

Clouser, K. and Gert, B. (1990) 'A critique of principalism' *Journal of Medicine and Philosophy* 15: 219.

Coady, C. (2002) 'Religious meddling: a comment on Skene and Parker' *Journal of Medical Ethics* 28: 221.

Cockerham, W. (2001) 'Medical sociology and sociological theory' in W. Cockerham, *The Blackwell Companion to Medical Sociology* (Blackwell).

Codd, H. (2007) 'The slippery slope to sperm smuggling: prisoners, artificial insemination and human rights' *Medical Law Review* 15: 220.

Coggon, J. (2006) 'Could the right to die with dignity represent a new right to die in English law?' *Medical Law Review* 14: 219.

Coggon, J. (2007) 'Ignoring the moral and intellectual shape of the law after bland: the unintended side-effect of a sorry compromise' *Legal Studies* 27: 100.

Cohen, G. (1986) 'Self-ownership and equality' in F. Lucash (ed) *Justice and Equality Here and Now* (Cornell University Press).

Cohen, C. (1992) 'The case for presumed consent to transplant human organs after death' *Transplantation Proc* 24: 2168.

Cohen, C. (1998) 'Christian perspective on assisted suicide and euthanasia' in M. Battin, R. Rhodes and A. Silvers (eds) *Physician Assisted Suicide* (Routledge).

Cohen, C. (2007) *Renewing the Stuff of Life: Stem Cells, Ethics, and Public Policy* (Oxford University Press).

Cohen-Almagor, R. (2001) *The Right To Die With Dignity* (Rutgers University Press).

Cohen-Almagor, R. (2002a) 'Dutch perspectives on palliative care in the Netherlands' *Issues in Law and Medicine* 111.

Cohen-Almagor, R. (2002b) 'A critique of Callahan's utilitarian approach to resource allocation in health care' *Issues in Law and Medicine* 17: 247.

Cohen-Almagor, R. (2004) *Euthanasia in the Netherlands* (Kluwer).

Cohen-Almagor, R. and Hartman, M. (2001) 'The Oregon death with dignity Act: review and proposals for improvement' *Journal of Legislation* 27: 269.

Cole, A. (2005) 'Community care has led to loss of staff from psychiatric wards' *British Medical Journal* 330: 1227.

Coleman, D. and Drake, S. (2002) 'A disability perspective from the United States on Ms B' *Journal of Medical Ethics* 28: 240.

Commission for Health Improvement (CHI) (2005) *Lessons from CHI Investigations 2000–2003* (CHI).

Committee of Public Accounts (2005) *Tackling Obesity in England* (Hansard).

Coneghan, D. and Mansell, W. (1999) *The Wrongs of Tort* (Pluto).

Congregation for the Doctrine of the Faith (1990) *Donum Vitae* (Roman Catholic Church).

Conwell, Y. and Caine, E. (1999) 'Rational suicide and the right to die' *New England Journal of Medicine* 325: 1101.

Cook, R. (2002) 'Villain, hero or masked stranger' in A. Bainham, S. Day Sclater, and M. Richards *Body Lore and Laws* (Hart).

Cook, R., Day Sclater, S., and Kaganas, F. (2003) 'Introduction' in R. Cook, S. Day Sclater and F. Kaganas (eds) *Surrogate Motherhood* (Hart).

Cook, R. and Golombok, S. (1996) 'A Survey of semen donation' *Human Reproduction* 10: 951.

Cookson, R. (2005) 'QALYs and capabilities' *Health Economics* 14: 1287.

Cookson, R. and Dolan, P. (1999) 'Public views on health care rationing: a group discussion study' *Health Policy* 49: 63.

Cookson, R. and Dolan, P. (2000) 'Principles of justice in health care rationing' *Journal of Medical Ethics* 26: 323.

Cookson, R., McDaid, D., and Maynard, A. (2001) 'Wrong SIGN, NICE mess: Is national guidance distorting allocation of resources?' *British Medical Journal* 323: 743.

Cooper, L. (2002) 'Myalgic encephalomyelitis and the medical encounter' in S. Nettleton and U. Gustafsson (eds) *The Sociology of Health and Illness Reader* (Polity).

Cordess, C. (ed) (2001) *Confidentiality and Mental Health* (Jessica Kingsley).

Corea, G. (1985) *The Mother Machine* (The Women's Press).

Coulson, J. (1996) 'Till death us do part' *BMA News Review* 23.

Coulter, A. and Ham, C. (eds) (2000) *Global Challenge of Healthcare Rationing* (Oxford University Press).

Council of Europe (2003) *Euthanasia* (Council of Europe).

Counterpoint Research (2001) *Young People's Perceptions of Contraception and Seeking Contraceptive Advice* (Counterpoint).

Cowling, D. (2005) 'Opinion polls: Movement on the issues?' *Bionews* 3 May 2005.

Cramb, A. (1998) 'Schoolgirls are left holding the virtual baby' *Electronic Telegraph*, Issue 1084.

Cranford, R. (1996) 'Misdiagnosing the persistent vegetative state' *British Medical Journal* 313: 5.

Cranford, R. and Smith, D. (1987) 'Consciousness: The most critical moral (constitutional) standard for human personhood' *American Journal of Law and Medicine* 13: 233.

Creek, van de, L., Miars, R., Herzog, C. (1987) 'Client anticipations and preferences for confidentiality of records' *Journal of Counselling and Psychology* 34: 62.

Cribb, A. (2005) *Health and the Good Society* (Oxford University Press).

Cromwell, S. (2003) *Hindu Bioethics in the Twenty-First Century* (NYU Press).

Cronin, A. (2007) 'Transplants save lives, defending the double veto does not: a reply to Wilkinson' *Journal of Medical Ethics* 33: 219.

Crouch, C. and Elliott, C. (1998) 'Moral agency and the family' *Cambridge Quarterly of Healthcare Ethics* 8: 275.

Culver, C. and Gert, B. (1982) *Philosophy in Medicine* (Oxford University Press).

Curran, C. (1982) 'The contraceptive revolution and the human condition' *American Journal of Philosophy and Theology* 3: 42.

Cutas, D. (2007) 'Postmenopausal motherhood: immoral, illegal? A case study' *Bioethics* 21: 458.

Daar, A. and Khitamy, A. (2001) 'Bioethics for clinicians: Islamic bioethics' *Canadian Medical Association Journal* 164: 1.

Daar, J. (1999) 'Assisted reproductive technologies and the pregnancy process: Developing an equality model to protect reproductive liberties' *American Journal of Law and Medicine* 25: 455.

Dahl, E. and Levy, N. (2006) 'The case for physician assisted suicide: how can it possibly be proven?' *Journal of Medical Ethics* 32: 335.

Daily Telegraph, (2005) 'Every sperm donor recruited costs public £6,250 say critics' *Daily Telegraph* 3 July 2005.

Daniels, C. and Golden, J. (2000) 'The politics of paternity' in M. Freeman and A. Lewis (eds), *Law and Medicine* (Oxford University Press).

Daniels, K. (2000) 'To give or sell human gametes—the interplay between pragmatics, policy and ethics' *Journal of Medical Ethics* 26: 206.

Daniels, N. (1985) *Just Health Care* (Oxford University Press).

Daniels, N. (1996) *Justice and Justification: Reflective Equilibriumin Theory and Practice* (Cambridge University Press).

Daniels, N. (2001) 'Health-care needs and distributive justice' in J. Harris (ed) *Bio-ethics* (Oxford University Press).

Davey Smith, G., Chaturvedi, N., Harding, S., Nazroo, J., and Williams, R. (2002) 'Ethnic inequalities in health' in S. Nettleton and U. Gustafasson, *The Sociology of Health and Illness Reader* (Polity).

Davey, J. and Coggon, J. (2006) 'Life assurance and consensual death: Law making for the rationally suicidal' *Cambridge Law Journal* 65: 521.

Davidson, L. (2002) 'Human rights vs. public protection' *International Journal of Law and Psychiatry* 25: 198.

Davies C., Wetherell, M., and Barnett, E. (2006) *Citizens at the Centre: Deliberative Participation in Healthcare Decisions* (Policy Press).

Davies, C., Wetherell, M., Barnett, E., and Seymour-Smith, S. (2005) *Opening the Box* (NICE).

Davies, J. (1988) 'Raping and making love are different concepts: So are killing and voluntary euthanasia' *Journal of Medical Ethics* 14: 148.

Davies, J. (1998) 'The case for legalising voluntary euthanasia' in J. Keown (ed) *Euthanasia Examined* (Cambridge University Press).

Davies, J. (1999) 'Commentary' *Cambridge Quarterly of Healthcare Ethics* 8: 435.

Davies, M. and Naffine, N. (2001) *Are Persons Property?* (Ashgate).

Davis, K. (1988) *Power under the Microscope: Towards a Grounded Theory of Gender Relations in Medical Encounters* (Foris).

Dawson, A. and Garrard, E. (2006) 'In defence of moral imperialism: four equal and universal prima facie principles' *Journal of Medical Ethics* 32: 200.

Deckers, J. (2007a) 'Why Eberl is wrong. Reflections on the beginning of personhood' *Bioethics* 21: 270.

Deckers, J. (2007b) 'Why two arguments from probability fail and one argument from Thomson's analogy of the violinist succeeds in justifying embryo destruction in some situations' *Journal of Medical Ethics* 33: 160.

Deckers, J. (2007c) 'Are those who subscribe to the view that early embryos are persons irrational and inconsistent? A reply to Brock' *Journal of Medical Ethics* 33: 102.

De Cruz, P. (2001) *Comparative Healthcare Law* (Cavendish).

De Cruz, P. (2007) 'The terminally ill patient and the right to life' *Modern Law Review* 70: 294.

Deech, R. (1998) 'Family law and genetics' *Modern Law Review* 697.

Deech, R. (2003) 'The HFEA—ten years on' in J. Gunning and H. Szoke (eds) *The Regulation of Assisted Reproductive Technology* (Ashgate).

Deech, R.and Smajdor, A. (2007) *From IVF to Immortality* (Oxford University Press).

De Gama, K. (1993) 'A brave new world? Rights discourse and the politics of reproductive autonomy' *Journal of Law and Society* 20: 114.

De Gama, K. (1998) 'Posthumous pregnancies: some thoughts on "life" and "death"' in S. Sheldon and M. Thomson (eds) *Feminist Perspectives on Health Care Law* (Cavendish).

Deigh, J. (1998) 'Physician assisted suicide and voluntary euthanasia: some relevant differences' *Journal of Criminal Law and Criminology* 1155.

Dekkers, W. and Boer, G. (2001) 'Sham neurosurgery in patients with Parkinson's disease: is it morally acceptable?' *Journal of Medical Ethics* 27: 151.

Dekkers, W., Sandman, L. and Webb, P. (2002) *Good Death or Good Life as a Goal of Palliative Care* (Open University Press).

Delatycki, M. (2005) 'Response to Spriggs: Is conceiving a child to benefit another against the interest of the new child?' *Journal of Medical Ethics* 31: 343.

Dell, S. (1984) *Murder into Manslaughter* (Oxford University Press).

Department of Constitutional Affairs (DCA) (2007) *Mental Capacity Act Code of Practice* (TSO).

Department of Human Services (2003) *Fifth Annual Report on Oregon's Death with Dignity Act* (DHS, Oregon).

Department of Human Services (2007) *Annual Report* (DHS, Oregon).

Deuraseh, N. (2003) 'Is birth control permissible by Islamic law (Shari'ah)?' *Arab Law Quarterly* 18: 90.

De Vries, R. (2004) 'The warp of evidence-based medicine: Lessons from Dutch maternity care' *International Journal of Health Services Research* 34: 595.

Devereux. J. (2006) 'Continuing conundrms in competency' in S. McLean (ed) *First do no Harm* (Ashgate).

Devettere, R. (1990) 'Neocortical death and human death' *Law and Medical Health Care* 18: 96.

Devlin, N., and Parkin, D. (2003) 'Does NICE have a cost-effectiveness threshold and what factors influence its decisions? A discrete choice analysis' (unpublished).

Devolder, K. and Savulescu, J. (2006) 'The moral imperative to conduct embryonic stem cell and cloning research' *Cambridge Quarterly of Healthcare Ethics* 15: 7.

De Vries, R. (2004) 'How can we help? From "sociology in" to "sociology of" bioethics' *Journal of Law, Medicine and Ethics* 32: 279.

Dickens, B. (1997) 'The control of living body materials' *University of Toronto Law Journal* 27: 142.

Dickens, B. (2002) 'Can sex selection be ethically tolerated? *Journal of Medical Ethics* 28: 335.

Dickenson, D. (2000) 'Are medical ethicists out of touch?' *Journal of Medical Ethics* 26: 254.

Dickenson, N., Paul, C., Herbison, P., and Silva, P. (1998) 'First sexual intercourse: age, coercion and later regrets' *British Medical Journal* 316: 29.

Diduck, A. (1993) 'Legislating ideologies of motherhood' *Social and Legal Studies* 2: 461.

Dieterle, J. (2007) 'Physician assisted suicide: a new look at the arguments' *Bioethics* 21: 127.

Dingwall, R. (1995) 'Negligence litigation research and the practice of midwifery' in J. Alexander, V. Levy and S. Roch (eds) *Midwifery Practice: A Research-based Approach* (Macmillan).

Dixon, K. (1994) 'Oppressive limits: Callahan's foundation myth' *Journal of Medicine and Philosophy* 19: 613.

Dobson, R. (2004) 'Trust's mental health services are threadbare, says CHI' *British Medical Journal* 328: 662.

Dodd, G. (2003) 'Surrogacy and the law in Britain: users' perspectives' in R. Cook, S. Day Sclater, and F. Kaganas (eds) *Surrogate Motherhood* (Hart).

Dodds, S. (2000) 'Choice and control in feminist bioethics' in C. Mackenzie and N. Stoljar (eds) *Relational Autonomy* (Oxford University Press).

Dodds, S. (2005) 'Gender, ageing, and injustice: social and political contexts of bioethics' *Journal of Medical Ethics* 31: 295.

DoH (1989) *Changing Childbirth* (HMSO).

DoH (1992) *The Health of the Nation* (HMSO).

DoH (1993) *AIDS: HIV Infected Health Care Workers* (HMSO).

DoH (1994) *Abortion Act 1967, Compendium of Guidance* (DoH).

DoH (1996a) *The Protection and the Use of Patient Information* (HMSO).

DoH (1996b) *Guidelines for Pre-test Discussion on HIV Testing* (DoH).

DoH (1998) *Code of Practice for the Diagnosis of Brain Stem Death* (DoH).

DoH (1999a) *Working Together (HMSO).*

DoH (1999b) *Organ Donation. Everything you need to Know* (DoH).

DoH (1999c) *Framework of Mental Health* (DoH).

DoH (2000a) *Working Towards Ending The Postcode Lottery Of Infertility Treatment* (DoH).

DoH (2000b) *Press Release* (DoH).

DoH (2000c) *An Organisation with a Memory* (TSO).

DoH (2000d) *The NHS plan. A plan for Investment* (TSO).

DoH (2000e) *An Investigation into Conditional Organ Donation* (DoH).

DoH (2000f) *Committee Announces Decision on use of Genetic Test Results for Hungington's Disease by Insurers* (DoH).

DoH (2004i) *Best Practice Guidance for Doctors and Other Health Care Professionals on the Provision of Advice and Treatment to Young People under 16 on Contraception, Sexual and Reproductive Health* (DoH).

DoH (2001a) *Shifting the Balance of Power within the NHS* (DoH).

DoH (2001b) *Consent—What you have a right to expect. A guide for parents* (DoH).

DoH (2001c) *Good Practice in Consent 2001* (DoH).

DoH (2001d) *Seeking Consent: Working with Children* (DoH).

DoH (2001e) *Reference Guide to Consent to Examination or Treatment (DoH).*

DoH (2001h) *Report of a census of organs and tissues retained by pathology in England* (TSO).

DoH (2002a) *Guidance Note for Completing the Abortion Notification Form HAS 4* London (DHSS).

DoH (2002b) *HIV Infected Health Care Workers* (DoH).

DoH (2002c) *Action To Ensure £50 Million Investment In Palliative Care Delivers The Best Services For Patients* (DoH).

DoH (2002e) *Human Bodies, Human Choices* (DoH).

DoH (2002f) *Priorities and Planning Framework* (DoH).

DoH (2003a) *Confidentiality: NHS Code of Practice* (DoH).

DoH (2003b) *Information sheet on palliative care and hospices* (DoH).

DoH (2003c) *Patient Choice* (DoH).

DoH (2004a) *The NHS Improvement Plan* (DoH).

DoH (2004b) *The Protection and Use of Patient Information* (DoH).

DoH (2004c) *Research Governance Framework for Health and Social Care* (DoH).

DoH (2004d) *Human Tissue Act 2004 Explanatory Notes* (TSO).

DoH (2004e) *Reconfiguring the Department of Health's Arm's Length Bodies* (DoH).

DoH (2004f) *Standard Operating Procedures for Research Ethics Committees* (DoH).

DoH (2004g) *Advice on the Decision of the European Court of Human Rights in the Case of HL v UK (The 'Bournewood' Case)* (DoH).

DoH (2004h) *Improving Mental Health Law* (DoH).

DoH (2004i) *Government Rules out Presumed Consent* (DoH).

DoH (2004m) *Continuing Care: Review, Revision and Restitution* (DoH).

DoH (2005a) *Creating a Patient-led NHS* (DoH).

DoH (2005b) *Draft Code of Practice, Mental Capacity Act* (DoH).

DoH (2005c) *Mental Capacity Bill Memorandum submitted to the Joint Committee on Human Rights in response to their letter of 18 November 2004 as published in their 23rd Report* (DoH).

DoH (2005d) *Health Survey 2003* (DoH).

DoH (2005e) *Government Response to the Report from the House of Commons Science and Technology Committee: Human Reproductive Technologies and the Law* (DoH).

DoH (2005f) *Review of the Human Fertilisation and Embryology Act* (DoH).

DoH (2005g) *Maintaining High Professional Standards in the Modern NHS* (DoH).

DOH (2005h) *Responsibilities, Liabilities And Risk Management In Clinical Trials Of Medicines* (DoH).

DoH (2005i) *Annual Review* (DoH).

DoH (2005j) *Lowest suicide rate for young men for nearly 20 years* (DoH).

DoH (2005k) *Government Response to House of Commons Health Committee Report on Palliative Care Fourth Report of Session 2003–04* (DoH).

DoH (2005m) *Guide to the Human Tissue Act* (DoH).

DoH (2005p) *Bournewood consultation* (DoH).

DoH (2006a) *Xenotransplantation Guidance* (DoH).

DoH (2006b) *The NHS in England: the operating framework for 2007/08* (DoH).

DoH (2006c) *Health Survey of England* (DoH).

DoH (2006d) *Safety First* (DoH).

DoH (2006e) *Teenage Pregnancy: Accelerating the Strategy to 2010* (DoH).

DoH (2006f) *Review of the Human Fertilisation and Embryology Act: Proposals for revised legislation (including establishment of the Regulatory Authority for Tissue and Embryos* (TSO).

DoH (2006g) *Our Health, Our Care, Our Say* (DoH).

DoH (2007a) *Review of parts 2, 5 and 6 of the Public Health (Control of Disease) Act 1984: A consultation* (DoH).

DoH (2007b) *Statistical Bulletin: Abortion Statistics* (DoH).

DoH (2007c) *Trust, Assurance and Safety* (DoH).

DoH (2007d) *Teenage Parents: Next Steps* (DoH).

DoH (2007e) *Making Experiences Count: A new approach to responding to complaints* (DoH).

DoH (2007f) *Draft revised Mental Health Act 1983 Code of Practice* (DoH).

Donchin, A. (2000) 'Autonomy, interdependence and assisted suicide' *Bioethics* 14: 187.

Dochin, A. (2001) 'Understanding autonomy relationally' *Journal of Medicine and Philosophy* 26: 365.

Dodds, S. (2000) 'Choice and control in feminist bioethics' in C. Mackenzie and N. Stoljar, *Relational Autonomy* (Oxford University Press).

Donnelly, J. (1998) *Suicide: Right or Wrong?* (Prometheus Books).

Donohoe, M. (1996) 'Our epidemic of unnecessary caesarean sections' *Wisconsin Women's Law Journal* 11: 197.

Dorff, E. (1998) 'Symposium on cloning: human cloning: a Jewish perspective' *Southern California Interdisciplinary Law Journal* 8: 117.

Double, D. (2006) *Critical Psychiatry* (Palgrave).

Douglas, C. (1992) 'For all the saints' *British Medical Journal* 304: 579.

Douglas, G. (1991) *Law, Fertility and Reproduction* (Sweet and Maxwell).

Douglas, G. (1993) 'Assisted reproduction and the welfare of the child' *Current Legal Problems* 46: 53.

Douglas, T. (1995) *Scapegoats: Transferring Blame* (Routledge).

Downie, R. (1988) 'Traditional medical ethics and economics in health care: a critique' in G. Mooney and A. McGuire (eds) *Medical Ethics and Economics in Health Care* (Oxford University Press).

Downie, J. (2000) 'The contested lessons of euthanasia in the Netherlands,' *Health Law Journal* 8: 119.

Downie, J. and Sherwin, S. (1996) 'A feminist exploration of issues around assisted death' *Saint Louis University Public Law Review* 303.

Downie, R. and Macnaughton, J. (2007) *Bioethics and the Humanities* (Routledge).

Doyle, L. (1990) 'Medical ethics and moral indeterminacy' *Journal of Law and Society* 17: 1.

Doyal, L. (1999) 'The moral character of clinicians or the best interests of patients' *British Medical Journal* 318: 1432.

Doyle, L. and Doyle, L. (2001) 'Why active euthanasia and physician assisted suicide should be legalised' *British Medical Journal* 323: 1079.

Draper, H. (1996) 'Women, forced caesarean and ante-natal responsibilities' 22 *Journal of Medical Ethics* 22: 327.

Draper, H. (2007) 'Paying gamete donors does not wrong the future child' in K. Horsey and H.Biggs (eds) *Human Fertilization and Embryology: Reproducing Regulation* (Routledge).

Dresser, R. (1992) 'Wanted: single, white male for medical research' *Hastings Center Report* 22: 24.

Dresser, R. (1994) 'Missing persons: legal perceptions of incompetent patients.' *Rutgers Law Review* 46: 609.

Dresser, R. (1995) 'Dworkin on dementia: elegant theory, questionable policy' *Hastings Center Report* 25: 32.

Dresser, R. (2001) 'Hope versus hypothesis testing: expanded access to experimental interventions' in R. Dresser (ed) *When science offers salvation* (Oxford University Press).

Dresser, R. (2003) 'Precommitment: a misguided strategy for securing death with dignity' *Texas Law Review* 81: 1823.

Dresser, R. and Robertson, J. (1989) 'Quality-of-life and non-treatment decisions for incompetent patients' *Law Medicine and Health Care* 17: 234.

DTI (1999) *Biotechnology Clusters* (HMSO).

DuBois, J. (1999) 'Physician-assisted suicide and public virtue: a reply to the liberty thesis of "the philosophers" brief' *Issues in Law and Medicine* 15: 159.

DuBois, J. (2002) 'Is organ procurement causing the death of patients?' *Issues in Law and Medicine* 18: 21.

Du Bois-Pedain, A. (2007) 'Is there a human right to die?' in B. Brooks-Gordan, F.Ebtehaj, J. Herring, M. Johnson, and M. Richards (eds) *Death Rights and Rites* (Hart).

Du Boulay, S. (1994) *Cicely Saunders* (Hodder & Stoughton).

Ducharme, H. (2000) 'Thrift-euthanasia, In theory and in practice: a critique of non-heart-beating organ harvesting' in M. Freeman and A. Lewis *Law and Medicine* (Oxford University Press).

Dunn, S. (1999) *Creating Accepting Communities* (MIND).

Durkheim, E. (1952) *Suicide: A Study in Sociology* (Routledge).

Dutch Government (2003) *Replies of the Government of the Netherlands to the concerns expressed by the Human Rights Committee* (Dutch Government).

Dworkin, G. (1970) 'The law relating to organ transplantation in England' *Modern Law Review* 33: 353.

Dworkin, G. (1978) 'Legality of consent to non-therapeutic medical research on infants and young children' *Archives of Diseases in Childhood* 51: 443.

Dworkin, G. and Kennedy, I. (1993) 'Human tissue: rights in the body and its parts' *Medical Law Review* 1: 29.

Dworkin, G., Frey, R., and Bok, S. (1998) *Euthanasia and Physician-Assisted Suicide* (Cambridge University Press).

Dworkin, R. (1993) *Life's Dominion* (Harper Collins).

Dworkin, R. (1998) 'Euthanasia, morality, and law transcript' *Loyola Los Angeles Law Review* 31: 1147.

Dworkin, R., Nagel, T., Nozick, R., Rawls, J., Scanlon, T., and Jarvis Thomson, J. (1998) 'The philosophers' brief' in M. Battin, R. Rhodes, and A. Silvers (eds) *Physician Assisted Suicide* (Routledge).

Dyck, A. (1975) 'A good Samaritan Ideal and beneficent euthanasia' *Linacre Quarterly* 42: 176.

Dyer, C. (1990) 'GMC's decision on "kidneys for sale"' *British Medical Journal* 300: 961.

Dyer, C. (1997a) 'Consultant struck off over research fraud' *British Medical Journal* 315: 205.

Dyer, C. (1997b) 'Gynaecologist admonished for removing ovaries without consent' *British Medical Journal* 315: 831.

Dyer, C. (1997c) 'Hillsborough survivor emerges from permanent vegetative state' *British Medical Journal* 314: 993.

Dyer, C. (1999) 'British GP cleared of murder charge' *British Medical Journal* 318: 1306.

Dyer, C. (2000) 'Triplets' parents win right to damages for extra child' *British Medical Journal* 321: 1306.

Dyer, C. (2003) 'GMC reprimands doctor for research fraud' *British Medical Journal* 326: 730.

Dyer, C. (2003) 'New powers for CHI "threaten patient confidentiality"' *British Medical Journal* 327: 580.

Dyer, O. (2002) 'GP struck off after offering to "fix" kidney sale' *British Medical Journal* 325: 510.

Eastday.com (29 May 2002) 'Male pregnancy now an option, Beijing surgeon says'.

Eberl, J. (2000) 'The beginning of personhood' *Bioethics* 14: 134.

Eberl, J. (2007) 'A Thomasist perspective on the beginning of personhood: redux' *Bioethics* 21: 283.

Ebrahim, A. (2000) 'Status of the embryo in the light of Islamic jurisprudence' in A. Lewis and M. Freeman (eds) *Law and Medicine* (Oxford University Press).

Edwards, J. (1999) 'Explicit connections' in J. Edwards, S. Franklin, E. Hirsch, F. Price, and M. Strathern (eds) *Technologies of Procreation* (Routledge).

Edwards, S. (2005) 'Research participation and the right to withdraw' *Bioethics* 19: 192.

Edwards, S., Kirchin, S., and Huxtable, R. (2004) 'Research ethics committees and paternalism' *Journal of Medical Ethics* 30: 88.

Edwards, S., Ashcroft, R., and Kirchin, S. (2004) 'Research ethics committees: differences and moral judgement' *Bioethics* 18: 401.

Edwards, S. and McNamee, M. (2005) 'Ethical concerns regarding guidelines for the conduct of clinical research on children' *Journal of Medical Ethics* 31: 351.

Eekelaar, J. (1988) 'Does a mother have legal duties to her unborn child?' in P. Byrne (ed)

Medical Law and Ethics (Oxford University Press).

Eekelaar, J. (1986) 'The eclipse of parental rights' *Law Quarterly Review* 102: 4.

Eekelaar, J. (1994) 'The interests of the child and the child's wishes: the role of dynamic self-determinism' *International Journal of Law, Policy and the Family* 8: 42.

Elam, G. (2000) *Consent to Organ and Tissue Retention at Post-Mortem Examination and Disposal of Human Materials* (DoH).

Eldergill, A. (2003) 'Is anyone safe? Civil compulsion under the Draft Mental Health Bill' *Journal of Mental Health Law* 331.

Elliott, K. (2007) 'An ironic *reductio* for a 'pro-life' argument: Hurlbut's proposal for stem cell research' *Bioethics* 21: 98.

Emmanuel, E. (1999) 'What is the great benefit of legalizing euthanasia or physician-assisted suicide?' *Ethics* 109: 629.

Emanuel, E. (1998) 'The future of euthanasia and physician-assisted suicide: beyond rights talk to informed public policy' *Minnesota Law Review* 82: 983.

Emer, N. (2001) *Self-esteem: The costs and causes of low self-worth* (JRF).

Engleheart, H. (1999) 'The body for fun, beneficence, and profit: A variation on a postmodern theme' in M. Cherry (ed) *Persons and Their Bodies* (Kluwer).

Englert, Y. (1995) *Organ and Tissue Transplantation in the European Union* (Martinus Nijhoff).

English, J. (1984) 'Abortion and the concept of a person' in J. Feinberg (ed) *The Problem of Abortion* (Wadsworth).

English, R. (2001) 'No rights to last rites' *New Law Journal* 151: 1844.

English, V. (2006) 'Autonomy versus protection—who benefits from the regulation of IVF' *Human Reproduction* 24: 3044.

English, V., Gardner, J., Romano-Critchley, G., and Sommerville, A. (2001) 'Legislation on euthanasia' *Journal of Medical Ethics* 27: 284.

English, V., Mussell, R., Sheather, J., and Sommerville, A. (2006) 'Autonomy and its limits' in S. McLean (ed) *First do no Harm* (Ashgate).

English, V. and Sommerville, A. (2003) 'Presumed consent for transplantation:

a dead issue after Alder Hey' *Journal of Medical Ethics* 29: 147.

Epstein, M. (2006) 'Why effective consent presupposes autonomous authorisation: a counterorthodox argument' *Journal of Medical Ethics* 32: 342.

Epstein, M. (2007) 'Legitimizing the shameful: end-of-life ethics and the political economy of death' *Bioethics* 21: 233.

Epstein, R. (1997) *Mortal Peril: Our Inalienable Right to Health Care?* (Addison Wesley).

Eriksson, M. (1993) 'Family planning as a human rights issue' in J. Eekelaar and P. Sarcevic (eds) *Parenthood in Modern Society* (Kluwer).

Erin, C. and Harris J. (2003) 'An ethical market in organs' *Journal of Medical Ethics* 29: 137.

Erin, C. and Harris, J. (1999) 'Presumed consent or contracting out' *Journal of Medical Ethics* 25: 365.

Erin, C. and Harris, J. (1994) 'A monopsonistic market' in I. Robinson (ed) *Life and Death under High Technology Medicine* (Manchester University Press).

ESHRE (2004) 'Assisted reproduction technology in Europe' *Human Reproduction* 19: 490.

European Parliamentary Assembly, Social, Family Affairs and Health Committee (2003) *Euthanasia* (European Parliament).

Evans, M. (1990) 'A plea for the heart' *Bioethics* 3: 227.

Evans, M. (1994) 'Against the definition of brainstem death' in D. Morgan and R. Lee (eds) *Death Rites* (Routledge).

Evans, M. (2000) 'Justified deception? The single blind placebo in drug research' *Journal of Medical Ethics* 26: 188.

Evans, J. (2003) 'Commodifying life? a pilot study of opinions regarding financial incentives for organ donation' *Journal of Health Politics, Policy and Law* 28: 1.

Evans, H. (2004) 'Should patients be allowed to veto their participation in clinical research?' *Journal of Medical Ethics* 30: 198.

Evans, T. and Harris, J. (2004) 'Citizenship, social exclusion and confidentiality' *British Journal of Social Work* 34: 69.

Expert Advisory Group on Cancer (1995) *A Policy Framework for Commissioning*

Cancer Services (DoH).Expert Scientific Group on Phase one Clinical Trials (2007) *Final Report* (TSO).

Fabre, C. (2006) *Whose Body is it Anyway?* (Oxford University Press).

Fadel, H. (2002) 'Religious values and legal dilemmas in bioethics' *Fordham Urban Law Journal* 30: 147.

Fagerlin, A. and Schneider, C. (2004) 'Enough: the failure of the living will,' *Hastings Center Report* 34: 30.

Fahey, T., Montgomery, A., Barnes, J. and Protheroe, J. (2003) 'Quality of care for elderly residents in nursing homes and elderly people living at home: controlled observational study' *British Medical Journal* 326: 580.

Faludi, S. (1992) *Backlash* (Chatto and Windus).

Family and Youth Concern (2004) *Sex Education or Indoctrination* (Family and Youth Concern).

Fan, R. and Tao, J. (2004) 'Consent to medical treatment' *Journal of Medicine and Philosophy* 29: 139.

Farnham, F. and James, D. (2001) '"Dangerousness" and dangerous law' *The Lancet* 358: 1926.

Farrell, A.-M. (2006) 'Is the gift still good? Examining the politics and regulation of blood safety in the European Union' *Medical Law Review* 14: 155.

Farrelly, C. (2004) 'Genes and equality' *Journal of Medical Ethics* 30: 587.

Feder Kittay, E. (2005) 'At the margins of moral personhood' *Ethics* 116: 100.

Feenan, D. (1996) 'Common law access to medical records' *Modern Law Review* 59: 101.

Feenan, D. (1997) 'A good harvest?' *Child and Family Law Quarterly* 305.

Fegan, M. and Fennell, P. (1998) 'Feminist perspectives on mental health law' in S. Sheldon and M. Thomson (eds) *Feminist Perspectives on Health Care Law* (Cavendish).

Feinberg, J. (1992) *Freedom and Fulfilment* (Princeton University Press).

Feinberg, J. (1984) *The Moral Limits of the Criminal Law* (Oxford University Press).

Feldman, D. (2002) *Civil Liberties and Human Rights in England and Wales* (Oxford University Press).

Feng, T. (1987) 'Failure of medical advice: Trespass or Negligence?' *Legal Studies* 7: 149.

Fenn, P., Deacon, S., Gray, S., Hodges, R., and Rickman, N. (2000) 'Current cost of medical negligence in the NHS Hospitals: analysis of claims database' *British Medical Journal* 320: 1567.

Fennell, P. (2005) 'Convention compliance, public safety, and the social inclusion of mentally disordered people' *Journal of Law and Society* 32: 90.

Fenwick, A. (1998) 'Applying the best interests to persistent vegetative state—a principled distortion?' *Journal of Medical Ethics* 24: 86.

Fenwick, A. (1999) '*Re S (Medical Treatment: Adult Sterilisation)* Retrenching on risk—revising the lawful boundaries of sterilisation' *Child and Family Law Quarterly* 313.

Ferguson, P. (2002) 'Selecting participants when testing new drugs' *Medico-Legal* 70: 130.

Ferguson, P. (2003) 'Legal and ethical aspects of clinical trials: the views of researchers' *Medical Law Review* 11: 48.

Ferriman, A. (2003) 'Have editors got their priorities right?' *British Medical Journal* 1113: 327.

Field, D., Hockey, J., and Small, N. (1997) *Death Gender and Ethnicity* (Routledge).

Field, D. and Addington-Hall, J. (2000) 'Extending specialist palliative care to all?' in D. Dickenson, M. Johnson and J. Samson Katz (eds) *Death, Dying and Bereavement* (Sage).

Field, M. (1993) 'Killing "the handicapped" before and after birth' *Harvard Women's Law Journal* 16: 79.

Fineman, M. (2004) *The Autonomy Myth* (Oxford University Press).

Finnis, J. (1973) 'The rights and wrongs of abortion' *Philosophy and Public Affairs* 2: 117.

Finnis, J. (1991) 'Intention and side-effects' in R. Frey and C. Morris (eds) *Liability and Responsibility* (Oxford University Press).

Finnis, J. (1993) 'Bland: crossing the Rubicon?' *Law Quarterly Review* 109: 329.

Finnis, J. (1994) 'Abortion and health care ethics' in R. Gillon (ed) *Principles of Health Care Ethics* (John Wiley and Sons).

Finnis, J. (1995a) 'A philosophical case against euthanasia' in J. Keown (ed) *Euthanasia Examined* (Cambridge University Press).

Finnis, J. (1995b) 'The fragile case for euthanasia: a reply to John Harris' in J. Keown *Euthanasia Examined* (Cambridge University Press).

Finnis, J. (1995c) 'Misunderstanding the case against euthanasia: a response to Harris's first reply' in J. Keown (ed) *Euthanasia Examined* (Cambridge University Press).

Finnis, J. (1998a) 'Public reason, abortion, and cloning' 32 *Valparaiso University Law Review* 32: 361.

Finnis, J. (1998b) 'Euthanasia, morality, and the law' *Loyala Los Angeles Law Review* 1465.

Finlay, I. (2001) 'UK strategies for palliative care' *Journal of the Royal Society of Medicine* 94: 437.

Fitzpatrick, R. (2003) 'Society and changing patterns of disease' in G. Scrambler (ed) *Sociology as Applied to Medicine* (Saunders).

Fitzsimons, S. 'Too posh to push?' *The Guardian* 14 June 2001.

Flamme, A. and Forster, H. (2000) 'Legal limits: when does autonomy in health care prevail' in A. Lewis and M. Freeman (eds) *Law and Medicine* (Oxford University Press).

Flanagan, O. (1991) *Varieties of Moral Personality* (Harvard University Press).

Florovsky, G. (1976) *Creation and Redemption* (Norland).

Foley, E. (2002) 'Human cloning and the right to reproduce' *Albany Law Review* 65: 625.

Foot, P. (1976) 'The problem of abortion and the doctrine of double effect' in S. Gorovitz et al (eds) *Moral Problems in Medicine* (Prentice Hall).

Foot, P. (2001) *Natural Goodness* (Oxford University Press).

Ford, M. (2005a) 'The personhood paradox and the "right to die"' *Medical Law Review* 13: 80.

Ford, M. (2005b) 'A property model of pregnancy' *International Journal of Law in Context* 1: 261.

Ford, M. and Morgan, D. (2003) '*Leeds Teaching NHS Trust v A*—Addressing a misconception' *Child and Family Law Quarterly* 15: 199.

Ford, M. and Morgan, D. (2004) 'Misconceived conceptions' *Journal of Medical Ethics* 30: 478.

Ford, N. (2002) *The Prenatal Person* (Blackwell).

Fordham, S. and Dowrick, C. (1999) 'Is care of the dying improving? The contribution of specialist and non-specialist to palliative care' *Family Practice* 16: 573.

Foresight (2007) *Tackling Obesities* (Department of Innovation, Universities and Skills).

Fortin, J. (1988) 'Legal protection for the unborn child' *Modern Law Review* 51: 54.

Fost, N. (1999) 'The unimportance of death' in A. Youngner and J. Shapiro (eds) *The Definition of Death* (Hopkins University Press).

Foster, C. (2001) *The Ethics of Medical Research on Humans* (Cambridge University Press).

Foster, C. (2007) 'Simple rationality? The law of healthcare resource allocation in England' *Journal of Medical Ethics* 33: 404.

Foster, P. (1995) *Women and the Health Care Industry* (Open University Press).

Foster, P. (1998) 'Informed consent in practice' in S. Sheldon and M. Thomson (eds) *Feminist Perspectives on Health Care Law* (Cavendish).

Fovargue, S. (2002) 'The law's response to pregnancy and childbirth; consistency, conflict or compromise' *Modern Law Review* 65: 290.

Fovargue, S. (2005) 'Consenting to bio-risk: xenotransplantation and the law' *Legal Studies* 25: 404.

Fovargue, S (2006) 'Assisting conception for the single infertile' *child and family law quarterly* 18: 423.

Fovargue, S. (2007) '"Oh pick me, pick me"—Selecting participants for xenotransplant clinical trials' *Medical Law Review* 15: 176.

Fovargue, S. and Miola, S. (1998) 'Policing pregnancy: implications of the AttorneyGeneral's Reference (No 3 of 1994)' *Medical Law Review* 6: 265–296.

Fox, M. (1994) 'Animal rights and wrongs' in R. Lee and D. Morgan (eds) *Death Rites* (Routledge).

Fox, M. (1998a) 'Abortion decision making—taking men's needs seriously' in E. Lee *Abortion Law and Politics* (Palgrave).

Fox, M. (1998b) 'Research bodies: feminist perspectives on clinical research' in S. Sheldon and M. Thomson (eds) *Feminist Perspectives on Health Care Law* (Cavendish).

Fox, M. and McHale, J. (1998) 'Xenotransplantation: the ethical and legal ramifications' *Medical Law Review* 6: 42.

Fox, M. and Thomson, M. (2005) 'A covenant with the status quo? Male circumcision and the new BMA guidance to doctors' *Journal of Medical Ethics* 31: 463.

Fox-Rushby, J. (2002) *Disability Adjusted Life Years (DALYs) for Decision-Making?* (Office of Health Economics).

Franklin, S. (1997) *Embodies Progress: A Cultural Account of Assisted Conception* (Routledge).

Freed, C., Greene, P., and Breeze, R. (2001) 'Transplantation of embryonic dopamine neurons for severe Parkinson's disease' *New England Journal of Medicine* 344: 710.

Freeland Judson, H. (2004) *The Great Betrayal* (Harcourt).

Freeman, M. (1988) 'Sterilising the mentally handicapped' in M. Freeman (ed) *Medicine, Ethics and the Law* (Stevans).

Freeman, M. (1997) 'Taking the body seriously?' in K. Stern and P. Walsh *Property Rights in the Human Body* (Kings College London).

Freeman, M. (1999) 'Does surrogacy have a future after Brazier?' *Medical Law Review* 7: 1.

Freeman, M. (2000) 'Can we leave the best interests of very sick children to their parents' in M. Freeman and A. Lewis, *Law and Medicine* (Oxford University Press).

Freeman, M. (2002) 'Denying death its dominion: Thoughts on the Diane Pretty Case' *Medical Law Review* 10: 245.

Freeman, M. (2006) 'Saviour siblings' in S. McLean (ed) *First do no Harm* (Ashgate).

Freeman, M. and Jaoude, P. (2007) 'Justifying surgery's last taboo: the ethics of face transplants' *Journal of Medical Ethics* 33: 76.

Freeman, T., Vawter, D., Leaverton, P., Godbold, J. Hauser, R., and Goetz, C. (1999). 'Use of placebo surgery in controlled trials of a cellular-based therapy for Parkinson's disease' *New England Journal of Medicine* 341: 988.

Freud, S. (1911) *Psychopathology of Everyday Life* (Fisher Unwin).

Fried, E. (2001) 'Physician duties in the conduct of human subject research' *Accountability in Research* 8: 349.

Frileux, S., Lelievre, C., Munoz Sastre, M., Mullet, E., and Sorum, P. (2003) 'When is physician assisted suicide or euthanasia acceptable?' *Journal of Medical Ethics* 29: 330.

Fulcher, J. and Scott, J. (2003) *Sociology* (Oxford University Press).

Fulford, K. (2001) '"What is (mental) disease?": an open letter to Christopher Boorse' *Journal of Medical Ethics* 27: 80.

Fulford, K., Dickenson, D. and Murray, T. (2002) *Healthcare Ethics and Human Values* (Blackwell).

Fulford, K. (2005) 'The paradoxes of confidentiality' in C. Cordess (ed) *Confidentiality and Mental Health* (Jessica Kinglsey).

Furedi, A. (1998) 'Wrong but the right thing to do: public opinion and abortion' in E. Lee (ed) *Abortion Law and Politics Today* (Macmillan).

Furedi, A. (2000) *Abortion: A Provider's Perspective* (University of Westminster).

Furedi, A. (2001) '"Disability cleansing" or Reasonable Choice?' *Spiked* 29 August 2001.

Furedi, A. and Lee, E. (2001) 'Defending abortion in law and practice' *Spiked* 8 March 2001.

Gallagher, J. (1987) 'Prenatal invasions and interventions: what's wrong with fetal rights' *Harvard Women's Law Journal* 10: 9.

Gallagher, J. (1995) 'Collective bad faith; "Protecting the fetus"' in J. Callaghan (ed) *Reproduction, Ethics and the Law: Feminist Responses* (Indiana University Press).

Gampel, E. (2006) 'Does professional autonomy protect medical futility judgments?' *Bioethics* 20: 92.

Garcia, J. (1997) 'Intentions in medical ethics' in D. Oderberg and J. Laing (eds) *Human Lives* (Oxford University Press).

Gard, M. and Wright, J. (2005) *The Obesity Epidemic* (Routledge).

Gardner, B., Theocleous, F., Watt, J., and Krishnan, K. (1985) 'Ventilation or dignified death for patients with high tetraplegia' *British Medical Journal* 291: 1620.

Gardner, R. (2003) *Therapeutic and Reproductive Cloning* (Cardiff Centre for Ethics, Law and Society).

Gardiner, P. (2003) 'A virtue ethics approach to moral dilemmas in medicine' *Journal of Medical Ethics* 29: 297.

Garrard, E. and Wilkinson, S. (2005) 'Passive euthanasia' *Journal of Medical Ethics* 31: 64.

Garrow, A. (2005) *What is the current trend in clinical trials sponsored by NHS, MRC and charities?* (Healthwatch).

Garwood-Gowers, A. (1999) *Key Legal and Ethical Issues in Living Donor Organ Transplantation* (Ashgate).

Garwood-Gowers, A. (2001) 'Extraction and use of body materials for transplantation and research purposes: the impact of the Human Rights Act 1998' in A. Garwood-Gowers, J. Tingle, and T. Lewis (eds), *Healthcare Law: The Impact of the Human Rights Act 1998* (Cavendish).

Garwood-Gowers, A. (2005) 'The proper limits for medical intervention that harms the therapeutic interests of incompetents' in A. Garwood-Gowers, J. Tingel, and K. Wheat (eds) *Contemporary Issues in Healthcare Law and Ethics* (Elsevier).

Garwood-Gowers, A. and Tingle, J. (2001) 'The Human Rights Act 1998: a potent tool for changing healthcare law and practice' in A. Garwood-Gowers, J. Tingle, and T. Lewis (eds) *Healthcare Law: The Impact of the Human Rights Act* (Cavendish).

Gastmans, C., van Neste, F., and Schotsmans, P. (2004) 'Forcing requests for euthanasia: a clinical practice guide' *Journal of Medical Ethics* 30: 212.

Gavaghan, C. (2007) *Defending the Genetic Supermarket* (Cambridge University Press).

Geggie, D. (2001) 'A survey of newly appointed consultants' attitudes towards research fraud' *Journal of Medical Ethics* 27: 344.

Gelder, P. (2002) *Boys and Young Men—half the solution to the issue of teenage pregnancy* (DoH).

Genetic Interest Group (1998) *Confidentiality Guidelines* (Genetic Interest Group).

Genetic Interest Group (2004) *Human Bodies, Human Choices, A Response from the Genetic Interest Group* (Genetic Interest Group).

Gentzler, J. (2003) 'What is a death with dignity?' *Journal of Medicine and Philosophy* 28: 461.

George, K. (2007) 'A woman's choice? The gendered risks of voluntary euthanasia and physician-assisted suicide' *Medical Law Review* 15: 1.

George, T. (2005) 'The case against kidney sale' *Indian Journal of Medical Ethics* 1.

Gervais, K. (1986) *Redefining Death* (Yale University Press).

Gibbons, S. (2007) 'Are UK genetic databases governed adequately? A comparative legal analysis' *Legal Studies* 27: 312.

Gibson, S. (2007) 'Uses of respect and uses of the human embryo' *Bioethics* 21: 370.

Giesen, D. (1997) 'Artificial reproduction revisited' in C. Bridge (ed) *Family Law Towards the Millennium* (Sweet and Maxwell).

Gilbar, R. (2004) 'Medical confidentiality within the family' *International Journal of Law Policy and the Family* 18: 194.

Gilbar, R. (2005) *The Status of the Family in Law and Bioethics: The Genetic Context* (Ashgate).

Gilbert, D., Walley, T., and New, B. (2000) 'Lifestyle medicines' *British Medical Journal* 321: 1341.

Gilder, G. (1986) *Men and Marriage* (Pelican).

Gilhooley, M. and McGee, S. (1991) 'Medical records' *Journal of Medical Ethics* 17: 138.

Gill, M. (2004) 'Presumed consent, autonomy and organ donation' *Journal of Medicine and Philosophy* 29: 37.

Gillett, G. (1988) 'Euthanasia letting die and the pause' *Journal of Medical Ethics* 14: 61.

Gilley, J. (2000) 'Intimacy and terminal care' in D. Dickenson, M. Johnson and J. Samson Katz (eds) *Death, Dying and Bereavement* (Sage).

Gilligan, C. (1982) *In a Different Voice: Psychological Theory and Women's Development* (Harvard University Press).

Gillon, R. (1985) *Philosophical Medical Ethics* (John Wiley).

Gillon, R. (1986) *Philosophical Medical Ethics* (John Wiley).

Gillon, R. (1987) 'AIDS and medical confidentiality' *British Medical Journal* 294: 1675.

Gillon, R. (1989) 'Editor's reply' to C. Strong and G. Anderson 'The moral status of the near term fetus' *Journal of Medical Ethics* 15: 25.

Gillon, R. (1990) 'Death' *Journal of Medical Ethics* 16: 3.

Gillon, R. (1995) 'On giving preference to prior volunteers when allocating organs for transplantation' *Journal of Medical Ethics* 21: 195.

Gillon, R. (1998) 'Persistent vegetative state, withdrawal of artificial nuitrition and hydration, and the patient's best interests' *Journal of Medical Ethics* 24: 75.

Gillon, R. (1999a) 'Foreseeing is not necessarily the same thing as intending' *British Medical Journal* 318: 1431.

Gillon, R. (1999b) 'Euthanasia in the Netherlands' *Journal of Medical Ethics* 25: 34.

Gillon, R. (1999c) 'When doctors might kill their patients' *British Medical Journal* 318: 1431.

Gillon, R. (2001a) 'Is there "a new ethics of abortion"?' *Journal of Medical Ethics* 27: 885.

Gillon, R. (2001b) 'Telling the truth, confidentiality, consent and respect for autonomy' in J. Harris (ed) *Bioethics* (Oxford University Press).

Gillon, R. (2003) 'Ethics needs principles—four can encompass the rest—and respect for autonomy should be "first among equals"' *Journal of Medical Ethics* 29: 307.

Gillon, R. (2004) 'Why the GMC is right to appeal over life prolonging treatment' *British Medical Journal* 329: 810.

Glaisier, A. and Baird, T. (1998) 'The effects of self-administering emergency contraception' *New England Journal of Medicine* 39: 1.

Glannon, W. (2001) *Genes and Future People* (Westview).

Glannon, W. (2003) 'Do the sick have a right to cadaveric organs?' *Journal of Medical Ethics* 29: 153.

Glannon, W. (2005) *Biomedical Ethics* (Oxford University Press).

Glannon, W. and Ross, L. (2002) 'Do genetic relationships create moral obligations in organ transplantation?' *Cambridge Quarterly of Healthcare Ethics* 11: 153.

Glover, J. (1998) 'Eugenics: some lessons from the Nazi experiments' in J. Harris and S. Holm, *The Future of Human Reproduction* (Oxford University Press).

Glover, J. (1977) *Causing Death and Saving Lives* (Penguin).

Glover-Thomas, N. (2003) *Reconstructing Mental Health Laws and Policy* (Butterworths).

Glynne, J. and Gomez, D. (2005) *Fitness to Practise: Health Care Regulatory Law, Principle, and Process* (Thomson, Sweet & Maxwell).

GMC (1992) *Transplantation of Organs from Live Donors* (GMC).

GMC (1993) *HIV Notification and AIDS: The Ethical Considerations* (GMC).

GMC (1997) *Serious Communicable Diseases* (GMC).

GMC (1998) *Seeking Patients' Consent* (GMC).

GMC (2000) *Confidentiality: Protecting and Providing Information* (GMC).

GMC (2002) *Research: The Role and Responsibilities of Doctors* (GMC).

GMC (2004) *Confidentiality. Protecting and Providing Information* (GMC).

GMC (2005) *Developing Medical Regulation* (GMC).

GMC (2007) *Good Medical Practice* (GMC).

Godiwala, S. (2002) 'Killing the scapegoat: how the poor are manipulated in the right to die debate' *Georgetown Journal on Poverty Law and Policy* 453.

Goff, Lord (1995) 'A matter of life and death' *Medical Law Review* 3: 1.

Gold, E. (1996) *Body Parts: Property Rights and the Ownership of Human Biological Material* (Georgetown University Press).

Golombok, S. (2002) 'Parenting and contemporary reproductive technologies' in M. Bornstein (ed) *Handbook of Parenting* (Lawrence Erlbaum Associates).

Golombok, S., Braewaeys, A., Cook, R., Giavazi, M., Guerra, D., Mantovani, A., van Hall E., Crosignani, P., and Dexeus, S. (1996) 'The European study of assisted reproduction families' *Human Reproduction* 1: 2324.

Golombok, S., Jadva, V., Lycett, E., Murray, C., and MacCallum, F. (2005) 'Families created by gamete donation: follow-up at age 2' *Human Reproduction* 20: 286.

Golton, R. and Doyal, L. (1998) 'Goodbye Dolly? The ethics of human cloning' *Journal of Medical Ethics* 24: 279.

Goodwin, B. (1992) *Justice by Lottery* (University of Chicago Press).

Goodwin, M. (2007) *Black Markets* (Cambridge University Press).

Goold, S. (1996) 'Allocating health care: cost-utility analysis, informed democratic decision making or the veil of ignorance?' *Journal of Health Politics, Policy and Law* 21: 69.

Gordijn, B., Crul, B., and Zylicz, Z. (2002) 'Euthanasia and physician-assisted suicide' in H. ten Have and D. Clarke (eds) *The Ethics of Palliative Care* (Open University Press).

Gormally, L. (1995) 'Walton, Davies, Boyd and the legalization of euthanasia' in J. Keown (ed) *Euthanasia Examined* (Cambridge University Press).

Gormally, L. (1997) *Euthanasia and Assisted Suicide: seven reasons why they should not be legalised* (Linacre Centre).

Gormally, L. (1997b) *Contraception and Catholic Sexual Ethics* (Linacre Centre).

Gormally, L. (2002) 'Commentary on Skene and Parker: the role of the church in developing the law' *Journal of Medical Ethics* 28: 224.

Gormally, L. (2004) *Obstetrics and Gynaecology in a multi-cultural society: the Catholic view* (Linacre Centre).

Gorsuch, N. (2000) 'The right to assisted suicide and euthanasia' *Harvard Journal of Law and Public Policy* 599.

Gorsuch, N. (2006) *The Future of Assisted Suicide and Euthanasia* (Princeton University Press).

Gosden, R. (1999) *Designer Babies* (Victor Gallancz).

Gostin, L. (2000) 'Human rights of persons with mental disabilities. The European Convention on Human Rights' *International Journal of Law and Psychiatry* 23: 125.

Gostin, L. (1995) 'Health information privacy' *Cornell Law Review* 80: 451.

Gostin, L. and Hodge, J. (1998) 'Piercing the veil of secrecy in HIV/AIDS and other sexually transmitted diseases: theories of privacy and disclosure in partner notification' *Duke Journal of Gender, Law and Policy* 5: 9.

Gostin, L. and Hodge, J. (1999) 'Genetic privacy and the law: an end to genetics exceptionalism' (1999) 40 *Jurimentrics* 21.

Gostin, L., Hodge, J. and Burghardt, M. (2002) 'Balancing communal goods and personal privacy under a national health informational privacy rule' *St Louis University Law Journal* 46: 5.

Gostin, L., Burris, S. and Lazzarini, Z. (1999) 'The law and the public's health: a study of infectious disease law in the United States' *Columbia Law Review* 99: 59.

Goudsmit, E. (1995) 'All in her mind! Sterotyptic views and the psychologisation of women's illness' in S. Wilkinson and C. Kitzinger (eds) *Women and Health* (Taylor and Francis).

Government of the Netherlands (2003) *Replies to the concerns expressed by the Human Rights Committee* (Government of the Netherlands).

Government Statistical Service (2005) *Abortion Statistics England and Wales* (GSS).

Graber, M. and Tansey, J. (2005) 'Autonomy, consent, and limiting healthcare costs' *Journal of Medical Ethics* 31: 424.

Grabrick, D., Hartmann, L., Cerhan, J., Vierkant, R., Therneau, T., Vahov, C., Olson, J., Couch, F., Anderson, K., Pankratz, V., and Sleers, T. (2000) 'Risk of breast cancer with oral contraceptive use in women with a family history of breast cancer' *Journal of American Medical Association* 283: 1791.

Graham, H. (2002) 'Socio-economic change and inequalities in men and women's health in the UK' in S. Nettleton and U. Gustafsson (eds) *The Sociology of Health and Illness Reader* (Polity).

Graham, W., Smith, S., Kamal, P., Fitzmaurice, A., Smith, N., Hamilton, N. and Qyat, J. (2000) 'Randomised controlled trial comparing effectiveness of touch screen system with leaflet for providing women with information on prenatal tests' *British Medical Journal* 320: 155.

Grayling, A. (2005) 'Right to die' *British Medical Journal* 330: 799.

Greaves, D. (2002) 'Reflections on a new medical cosmology' *Journal of Medical Ethics* 28: 81.

Green, S. (2006) 'Coherence of medical negligence cases: A game of doctors and purses' *Medical Law Review* 14: 1.

Griffiths, C. and Brock, A. (2004) *Twentieth Century Mortality Trends in England and Wales* (ONS).

Griffiths, J. Bood, A., and Weyers, H. (1998) *Euthanasia and Law in the Netherlands* (Amsterdam University Press).

Griffiths, R. (2000) *Report of a Review of Research Framework* (NHS).

Grisez, G. and Boyle, J. (1971) *Life and Death with Liberty and Justice* (University of Notre Dame Press).

Grisez, G., Boyle, J., Finnis, J., and May, M. (1988) '"Every marital act ought to be open to new life" Toward a clearer understanding' *The Thomist* 52: 365.

Grol, R., Wensing, M., Mainz, J. et al (1999) 'Patient's priorities with respect to general practice care' *Family Practice* 16: 4.

Grubb, A. (1990) 'Abortion law in England: the medicalisation of a crime' *Law Medicine and Health Care* 18: 146.

Grubb, A. (1991) 'The new law of abortion: clarification or ambiguity?' *Criminal Law Review* 659.

Grubb A. (1994) 'The doctor as fiduciary' *Current Legal Problems* 311.

Grubb, A. (1995) 'Commentary' *Medical Law Review* 3: 83.

Grubb, A. (1997) 'The persistent vegetative state: a duty (not) to treat and conscientious objection' *European Journal of Health Law* 4: 157.

Grubb, A. (1998a) 'Negligence, causation and Bolam' *Medical Law Review* 6: 37.

Grubb, A. (1998b) 'I, Me, Mine': bodies, parts and property' *Medical law International* 3: 299.

Grubb, A. (1999) 'Medical negligence: Duty to third party' *Medical Law Review* 331: 7.

Grubb, A (2000) Breach of confidence: anonymised information' *Medical Law Review* 8: 115.

Grubb, A., Walsh, P., Lambe, N., Murrells, T., and Robins, S. (1997) *Doctor's Views and the Management of Patients in Persistent Vegetative State* (Centre of Medical Law and Ethics, King's College London).

Grunseit, A. and Kippax, S. (1994) *Effects of Sex Education on Young People's Sexual Behaviour* (Macquarie University Australia).

Guardian, The (3 May 2007) 'One in four GPs shuns abortion, survey finds'.

Guardian, The (2005) 'Net closes on firms draining NHS lifeblood' *The Guardian* 2 June 2005.

Gunn, M. (1994) 'The meaning of incapacity' *Medical Law Review* 2: 8.

Gunn, M. (2000) 'Reforms of the Mental Health Act 1983: the relevance of capacity to make decisions' *Journal of Mental Health Law* 3: 39.

Gunn, M. and Holland, T. (2002) 'Some thoughts on the proposed Mental Health Act' *Mental Health Law Journal* 360.

Gunnell, D. and Ewings, P. (1994) 'Infertility prevalence, needs assessment and purchasing' *Journal of Public Health Medicine* 16: 29.

Gunning, J. and Stoke, H. (2003) *The Regulation of Assisted Reproductive Technology* (Ashgate).

Gurnham, D. (2007) 'The ethics of side effects: sanctity of life and doctrine of double effect as political rhetoric' *Asian Journal of WTO & International Health Law and Policy* 2: 141.

Guroian, V. (2002) *Incarnate Love: Essays in Orthodox Ethics* (University of Notre Dame Press).

Gurry, F. (1985) *Breach of Confidence* (Oxford University Press).

Guttmann, A. and Guttman, R. (1993) 'Attitudes of health care professionals and the public towards the sale of kidneys for transplantation' *Journal of Medical Ethics* 19: 148.

Habiba, M. (2000) 'Examining consent within the patient-doctor relationship' *Journal of Medical Ethics* 26: 183.

Hackett, E., Francis, S. (2003) '"Death was a blessing"—should it ever be pharmaceutically hastened? British pharmacists' views' *Pharmacology World Science* 25: 288.

Haddow, G. (2005) 'The phenomenology of death, embodiment and organ transplantation' *Sociology of Health & Illness* 27: 92.

Hagelin, J., Nilstun, T., Hau, J., Carlsson, H-E. (2004) 'Surveys on attitudes towards legalisation of euthanasia: importance of question phrasing' *Journal of Medical Ethics* 30: 521.

Haimes, E. and Weiner, K. (2000) '"Everybody's got a dad...". Issues for lesbian families in the management of donor insemination' *Sociology of Health and Illness* 22: 480.

Haker, H. and Beyeveld, D. (2000) *The Ethics of Genetics in Human Reproduction* (Ashgate).

Hale, B. (1996) *From the Test Tube to the Coffin* (Sweet and Maxwell).

Hale, B. (2003) 'A pretty pass: when is there a right to die?' *Common Law World Review* 1.

Hall, M. (2002) 'Law, medicine, and trust' *Stanford Law Review* 55: 463.

Halliday, S. (2004) 'A comparative approach to the regulation of human embryonic stem cell research in Europe' *Medical Law Review* 12: 40.

Halliday, S. (2005) 'Regulating active voluntary euthanasia' in A. Garwood-Gowers, J. Tingel and K. Wheat *Contemporary Issues in Healthcare Law and Ethics* (Elsevier).

Hamer, C. and Rivlin, S. (2002) 'A stronger policy of organ retrieval from cadaveric donors' *Journal of Medical Law* 29: 196.

Hamilton, S., Heppter, J., Hanby, A., and Hewison, J. (2007) 'Consent gained from patients after breast surgery for the use of surplus tissue in research: an exploration' *Journal of Medical Ethics* 33: 229.

Hamoda, H., Critchley, H., Paterson, K., Guthrie, K., Rodger, M., and Penney, G. (2005) 'The acceptability of home medical abortion to women in UK settings' *British Journal of Obstetrics and Gynaecology* 112: 781.

Hanser, M. (1999) 'Killing, letting die and preventing people from being saved' *Utilitas* 11: 277.

Hardwig, J. (1997) 'Is there a duty to die?' *Hastings Center Report* 27: 34.

Hardy, E. and Yolanda Makuch, M. (2001) 'Gender, infertility and ART' *Current Practices and Controversies in Assisted Reproduction* (WHO).

Hardcastle, R. (2007) *Law and the Human Body* (Hart).

Hare, R. (1975) 'Abortion and the golden rule' *Philosophy and Public Affairs* 4: 201.

Harman, E. (1999) 'Creation ethics' *Philosophy and Public Affairs* 28: 310.

Harman, E. (2007) 'How is the ethics of stem cell research different from the ethics of abortion?' *Metaphilosophy* 38: 207.

Harman, G. and Thompson, J.J. (1996) *Moral Relativism and Moral Objectivity* (Blackwell).

Harrington, J. (1996) 'Privileging the medical norms: liberalism, self-determination and refusal of treatment' *Legal Studies* 16: 348.

Harrington, J. (2003) 'Deciding best interests: medical progress, clinical judgment and the "good family"' *Web Journal of Current Legal Issues* 3.

Harris, H. (1995) 'Final thoughts on final acts' in J. Keown (ed), *Euthanasia Examined* (Cambridge University Press).

Harris, J. (1975) 'The survival lottery' *Philosophy* 50: 191.

Harris, J. (1984) *The Value of Law* (Oxford University Press).

Harris, J. (1987) 'QALYfying the value of life' *Journal of Medical Ethics* 3: 117.

Harris, J. (1992) *The Value of Life* (Routledge).

Harris, J. (1995a) 'Euthanasia and the value of life' in J. Keown (ed), *Euthanasia Examined* (Cambridge University Press).

Harris, J. (1995b) 'The philosophical case against the philosophical case against euthanasia' in J. Keown (ed), *Euthanasia Examined* (Cambridge University Press).

Harris, J. (1995d) 'Double jeopardy and the veil of ignorance—a reply' *Journal of Medical Ethics* 21: 151.

Harris, J. (1997) 'The injustice of compensation for victims of medical accidents' *British Medical Journal* 314: 1821.

Harris, J. (1998) *Clones, Genes and Immortality* (Oxford University Press).

Harris, J. (1998a) 'Rights and reproductive choice' in J. Harris and S. Holm (eds) *The Future of Human Reproduction: Choice and Regulation* (Oxford University Press).

Harris, J. (1998b) 'Blood, sperm and posthumous parenting' in J. Harris and S. Holm (eds) *The Future of Human Reproduction: Choice and Regulation* (Oxford University Press).

Harris, J. (1999) 'The concept of the person and the value of life' *Kennedy Institute of Ethics Journal* 9: 293.

Harris, J. (2000) 'Research on human subjects, exploitation, and global principles of ethics' in M. Freeman and A. Lewis, *Medicine and Law* (Oxford University Press).

Harris, J. (2001) 'One principle and three fallacies of disability studies' *Journal of Medical Ethics* 27: 383.

Harris, J. (2002) 'Law and regulation of retained organs: The ethical issues' *Legal Studies* 527.

Harris, J. (2003a) '(ARTBs) Assisted reproductive technological blunders' *Journal of Medical Ethics* 29: 205.

Harris, J. (2003b) 'Organ procurement: dead interests, living needs' *Journal of Medical Ethics* 31: 242.

Harris, J. (2003c) 'In praise of unprincipled ethics' *Journal of Medical Ethics* 29: 303.

Harris, J. (2004a) 'Intimations of immortality' *Current Legal Problems* 65.

Harris, J. (2004b) *On Cloning* (Routledge).

Harris, J. (2005a) 'Sex selection and regulated hatred' *Journal of Medical Ethics* 31: 291.

Harris, J. (2005b) 'Scientific research is a moral duty' *Journal of Medical Ethics* 31: 242.

Harris, J. (2005c) 'It's not NICE to discriminate' *Journal of Medical Ethics* 31: 373.

Harris, J. (2005d) 'No sex selection please, we're British' *Journal of Medical Ethics* 31: 286.

Harris, J. (2005e) 'The right to die lives! There is no personhood paradox' *Medical Law Review* 13: 386.

Harris, J. (2006) 'NICE is not cost effective' *Journal of Medical Ethics* 32: 378.

Harris, J. (2007) 'NICE rejoinder' *Journal of Medical Ethics* 33: 467.

Harris, J. and Burley, J. (2002) *A Companion to Genetics* (Blackwell).

Harris, J. and Erin, C. (2002) 'An ethically defensible market in organs' *British Medical Journal* 325: 114.

Harris, J. and Holm, S. (1995) 'Is there a moral obligation not to infect others?' *British Medical Journal* 311: 1215.

Harris, J. and Holm, S. (2002) 'Commentary on Skene and Parker: the role of a church (or other ideologically based interest group) in developing the law—a plea for ethereal intervention' *Journal of Medical Ethics* 28: 219.

Harris, J. and Holm S. (2002) 'Extending human lifespan and the precautionary Paradox' *Journal of Medicine and Philosophy* 27: 355.

Harris, J. and Holm, S. (2003) 'Should we presume moral turpitude in our children?—Small children and consent to medical research' *Theoretical Medicine and Bioethics* 24: 121.

Harris, J. and Holm, S. (2004) *The Future of Reproduction* (Oxford University Press).

Harris, J. and Stanton, C. (2005) 'The moral status of the embryo post-Dolly' *Journal of Medical Ethics* 31: 221.

Harris, J.W. (1996) *Property and Justice* (Oxford University Press).

Harris-Short, S. (2004) 'An "identity crisis" in the international law of human rights? The challenge of reproductive cloning' *International Journal of Children's Rights* 11: 333.

Harrison, B. (1998) 'A feminist-liberation view of abortion' in D. Lammers and A. Verhey (eds) *On Moral Medicine* (Eerdmans).

Harrison, C. (2002) 'Neither *Moore* nor the market: alternative models for compensating contributors of human tissue' *American Journal of Law and Medicine* 28: 77.

Harrison, S. (1998) 'The politics of evidence based medicine in the United Kingdom' *Policy and Politics* 26: 15.

Harrison, S. and Ahmad, W. (2000) 'Medical autonomy and the UK state 1975 to 2025' *Sociology* 34: 129.

Hart, J. (1998) 'Expectations of health care: promoted, managed or shared?' *Health Expectations* 1: 3.

Hart, G. and Wellings, K. (2002) 'Sexual behaviour and its medicalisation: in sickness and in health' *British Medical Journal* 324: 896.

Hasman, A., Hope, T., and Østerdal, L. (2006) 'Health care need: three interpretations' *Journal of Applied Philosophy* 23: 145.

Hauerwas, S. (1998) 'Rational suicide and reasons for living' in S. Lammers and A. Verhey (eds) *On Moral Medicine* (Eerdmans).

Hausman, D. (2006) 'Valuing health' *Philosophy and Public Affairs* 34: 246.

Have, T. H. and Anssens, R. (2002) 'Futility limits and palliative care' in H. ten Have and D. Clark (eds) *The Ethics of Palliative Care* (Open University Press).

Have, T. H. and Clark, D. (eds) (2002) *The Ethics of Palliative Care* (Open University Press).

Häyry, M. (2004) 'A rational cure for pre-reproductive stress syndrome' *Journal of Medical Ethics* 30: 377.

Häyry, M. (2006) 'Public health and human values' *Journal of Medical Ethics* 32: 706.

Hayward, S. and O'Hanlon, T. (2003) 'Kidneys for sale…on net' 27 April 2003 *Sunday Mirror*.

Healthcare Commission (2004a) *Responses to the Healthcare Commission Consultation on Complaints* (Healthcare Commission).

Healthcare Commission (2004b) *Patient Survey Report* (DoH).

Healthcare Commission (2004c) *Reforming the NHS Complaints Procedure* (DoH).

Healthcare Commission (2005) *Evidence of Health Inequalities* (TSO).

Healthcare Commission (2006) *Investigation into 10 Maternal Deaths* (DoH).

Healthcare Commission (2007a) *The Views of Hospital Patients in England* (DoH).

Healthcare Commission (2007b) *Annual Report* (DoH).

Health Development Agency (2001) *Teenage Pregnancy* (DoH).

Health Economics Research Inc. (1999) *Evolution of the Oregon Plan* (HER).

Heitman, E. (2002) 'Social and ethical aspects of in vitro fertilization' in S. Nettleton and U. Gustafsson, *The Sociology of Health and Illness Reader* (Polity).

Held, V. (2006) *The Ethics of Care* (Oxford University Press).

Hellema, H. (1991) 'Euthanasia—2% of Dutch deaths' *British Medical Journal* 303: 877.

Hellema, H. (1993) 'Dutch doctors support life termination in dementia' *British Medical Journal* 306: 1364.

Heller, M. and Eisenberg, R. (1998) 'Can patents deter innovation?' *Science* 280: 698.

Hendin, H. (1998) *Seduced by Death* (Norton & Co).

Hendin, H. (1999) 'Euthanasia consultants or facilitators' *Medical Journal of Australia* 170: 351.

Hendricks, S. (2003) 'Lifts are not the only place of breach of confidentiality' *British Medical Journal* 327: 1024.

Henshaw, R. and Templeton, A. (1992) 'Mifepristone: separating fact from fiction' *Drugs* 44: 531.

Hermsen, M. and Have, H. (2002) 'Euthanasia in palliative care journals' *Journal of Pain and Symptom Management* 23: 517.

Herring, J. (1997) 'Caesarean sections, phobias and foetal rights' *Cambridge Law Journal* 509.

Herring, J. (1997b) 'Children's abortion rights' *Medical Law Review* 5: 257.

Herring, J. (1998) 'Caesarean sections and the right of autonomy' *Cambridge Law Journal* 438.

Herring, J. (1999) 'The welfare principle and parents' rights' in A. Bainham, S. Day Sclater and M. Richards (eds) *What is a Parent?* (Hart).

Herring, J. (2000) 'The caesarean section cases and the supremacy of autonomy' in M. Freeman and A. Lewis, *Law and Medicine* (Oxford University Press).

Herring, J. (2002) 'Giving, selling and sharing bodies' in A. Bainham, S. Day Sclater and M. Richards *Body Lore and Laws* (Hart).

Herring, J. (2005) 'Mistaken sex' *Criminal Law Review* 511.

Herring, J. (2006) *Criminal Law* (Oxford University Press).

Herring, J. (2007a) 'Where are the carers in healthcare law and ethics?' *Legal Studies* 27: 51.

Herring, J. (2007b) *Family Law* (Pearson).

Herring, J. (2007c) 'Crimes against the dead' in B. Brooks-Gordon, F. Ebtehaj,

J. Herring, M. Johnson, and M. Richards (eds) *Death Rights and Rites* (Hart).

Herring, J. (2008) 'The place of carers' in M. Freeman, *Law and Bioethics* (Oxford University Press).

Herring, J. and Chau, P-L (2002) 'R (On the application of Quintavalle v Secretary of State for Health—are cloned embryos embryos?' *Child and Family Law Quarterly* 315.

Herring, J. and Chau, P-L (2007) 'My body, your body, our bodies' *Medical Law Review* 15: 34.

Herissone-Kelly, P. (2006) 'The prohibition of sex selection for social reasons in the United Kingdom: Public opinion trumps reproductive liberty?' *Cambridge Quarterly of Healthcare Ethics* 15: 261.

Herissone-Kelly, P. (2007) 'Parental love and the ethics of sex selection' *Bioethics* 16: 326.

Hesketh, W. (2005) 'Medico-crime in the UK' in A. Garwood-Gowers, J. Tingel and K. Wheat (2005) *Contemporary Issues in Healthcare Law and Ethics* (Elsevier).

Hester, D. (2003) 'Is pragmatism well-suited to bioethics?' *Journal of Medicine and Philosophy* 28: 545.

Hewitt, P. (2005) *Speech to NHS Confederation* (DoH).

Hewlett, S. (1996) 'Consent to clinical research—adequately voluntary or substantially influenced' *Journal of Medical Ethics* 22: 232.

HFEA (1996) *Annual Report* (HFEA).

HFEA (2000a) *Ninth Annual Report & Accounts* (HFEA).

HFEA (2000b) *National Data Statistics* (HFEA).

HFEA (2003) *HFEA Update: Embryo donation to single women* (HFEA).

HFEA (2004a) *Code of Practice* (HFEA).

HFEA (2004b) *Sex Selection* (HFEA).

HFEA (2004c) *Preimplantation Tissue Typing Report* (HFEA).

HFEA (2005a) *Tomorrow's Children* (HFEA).

HFEA (2005b) *The Regulation of Donor Assisted Conception* (HFEA).

HFEA (2005c) *SEED Report* (HFEA).

HFEA (2006) *Standards for Assisted Conception Centres* (HFEA).

HFEA (2007a) *Number of Sperm Donors Up Following Anonymity Law Changes* (HFEA).

HFEA (2007b) *Facts and Figures* (HFEA).

HFEA (2007c) Code of Practice (HFEA).

HFEA (2007e) *Number Sperm and Egg Donors* (HFEA).

HFEA (2007f) *HFEA statement on its decision regarding hybrid embryos* (HFEA).

Hietala, M., Hakonen, A., Aro, A., Niemela, P., Peltonen, L., and Aula, P. (1995) 'Attitudes toward genetic testing among the general population and relatives of patients with a severe genetic disease' *American Journal of Human Genetics* 56: 1493.

Higginson, I., Finlay, I., Goodwin, D., Cook, A., Hood, K., Edwards, A., Douglas, H.-R., and Normand, C. (2002) 'Do hospital-based palliative care teams improve care for patients or families at the end of life?' *Journal of Pain and Symptom Management* 23: 96.

Higgs, P. (2003) 'Older people, health care and society' in G. Scrambler (ed) *Sociology as Applied to Medicine* (Saunders).

Hill, C. (1994) 'The note' in H. Kuhse (ed) *Willing to Listen; Wanting to Die* (Penguin).

Hill, L. (1991) 'What does it mean to be a "parent"? The claims of Biology as the Basis for Parental right' *New York University Law Review* 66: 353.

Hill, S., Garattini, S., Leonhout, J., O'Brien, B. and Joncheere, K. (2003) *Technology Appraisal Programme of the National Institute for Clinical Excellence* (WHO).

Hill, T. (1991) *Autonomy and Self-Respect* (Cambridge University Press).

Hillier, S. (2003) 'The health and health care of ethnic minority groups' in G. Scrambler (ed), *Sociology as Applied to Medicine* (Saunders).

Himma, K. (1999) 'Thomson's violinist and conjoined twins' *Cambridge Quarterly of Healthcare Ethics* 8: 428.

Himmelweit, S. (1998) 'More than "a woman's right to choose"' *Feminist Review* 38: 29.

HM Government (2007a) *Government Response to the Report from the Joint Committee on the Human Tissue and Embryos (Draft) Bill* (TSO).

HM Government (2007b) *The Government Response to the Health Committee Report on the Electronic Patient Record* (TSO).

HM Treasury (2007) *2007 Pre-Budget Report and Comprehensive Spending Review* (TSO).

Hoffenberg, R. (1987) *Report of the Working Party on the Supply of Donor Organs for Transplantation* (HMSO).

Hoffman, S. (2001) 'The use of placebos in clinical trials: responsible research or unethical practice?' *Connecticut Law Review* 33: 449.

Hoffmann, D. and Tarzian, A. (2001) 'The girl who cried pain. Bias against women in the treatment of pain' *Journal of Law Medicine and Ethics* 29: 13.

Hoffman, Lord (2005) 'Causation' *Law Quarterly Review* 121: 592.

Hoffmaster, B. (1992) 'Between the sacred and the profane: bodies, property and patents in the Moore Case' *Intellectual Property Journal* 7: 116.

Holbrook, J. (2003) 'The trouble with *Making Amends*' *Spiked* 22 August 2003.

Holland, S. (2003) *Bioethics* (Polity).

Holm, S. (1995) 'Not just autonomy: the principles of American biomedical ethics' *Journal of Medical Ethics* 12: 332.

Holm, S. (1998) 'A life in the shadow' *Cambridge Quarterly of Healthcare Ethics* 7: 160.

Holm, S. (1998) 'Ethical issues in preimplantation diagnosis' in J. Harris and S. Holm (eds) *The Future of Human Reproduction* (Oxford University Press).

Holm, S. (2001) 'Is society responsible for my health?' in R. Bennett and C. Erin, *HIV and AIDS, Testing, Screening, and Confidentiality* (Oxford University Press).

Holm, S. (2005) *Forgetting to be NICE* (Cardiff Centre for Ethics, Law and Society).

Holm, S. (2006) Self inflicted harm—NICE in ethical self destruct mode?' *Journal of Medical Ethics* 32: 125.

Hope, T. (2000) 'The best is the enemy of the good—can research ethics learn from rationing?' *Journal of Medical Ethics* 26: 417.

Hope, T. (2005) *A Very Short Introduction to Medical Ethics* (Oxford University Press).

Hope, T., Savulescu, J., and Hendrick, J. (2003) *Medical Ethics and Law* (Churchill Livingstone).

Hope, T. and McMillan, J. (2004) 'Challenge studies of human volunteers: ethical issues' *Journal of Medical Ethics* 30: 110.

Hopwood, V. (2001) 'Legal Moves' *Liability Risk Insurance* 138: 19.

Horder, J. (1988) 'Mercy killings—some reflections on Beecham's Case' *Journal of Criminal Law* 309.

Hornell, M. (1999) 'Profession awaits guidelines for treating terminally ill patients' *The Times*, 12 May 1999.

Horsey, K. (2007) 'Unconsidered inconsistencies' in K. Horsey and H. Biggs (eds) *Human Fertilization and Embryology: Reproducing Regulation* (Routledge).

Horsey, K. and Biggs, H. (eds) (2007) *Human Fertilization and Embryology: Reproducing Regulation* (Routledge).

Hospice Information (2003) *Hospice and Palliative Care Facts and Figures 2003* (Hospice Information).

House of Commons Health Committee (1995) *Priority setting in the NHS* (HMSO).

House of Commons Constitutional Affairs Committee (2006) *Compensation Culture* (TSO).

House of Commons Science and Technology Committee (2005) *Human Reproductive Technologies and the Law* (TSO).

House of Commons Science and Technology Committee (2007) *Scientific Developments Relating to the Abortion Act 1967* (TSO).

House of Lords Select Committee on Medical Ethics (1994) *Paper No 21* (HMSO).

House of Lords Select Committee (2005) *On the Assisted Dying for the Terminally Ill Bill* (TSO).

Hoyano, L. (2002) 'Misconceptions about wrongful conception' *Modern Law Review* 65: 883.

Hudson Jones, A. (1999) 'Literary perspectives on ageing' *The Lancet* 34: 51.

Hughes, J. and Keown, D. (1995) 'Buddhism and medical ethics' *Journal of Buddhist Ethics* 2.

Hughes, P. (1998) 'Exploitation, autonomy, and the case for organ sales' *International Journal of Applied Philosophy* 12: 89.

Hull, R. (2006) 'Cheap listening—Reflections on the concept of wrongful disability' *Bioethics* 20: 55.

Hultman, C., Sparen, P., Takei, N., Murray, R., and Cnattingius, S. (1999) 'Prenatal and perinatal risk factors for schizophrenia, affective psychosis, and reactive psychosis of early onset: case-control study' *British Medial Journal* 318: 421.

Human Genome Organisation's Ethics Committee (2000) *Statement on Benefit Sharing* (HUGO).

Human Genome Organisation's Ethics Committee (2000) *Public Attitudes to Human Genetic Information* (HUGO).

Human Genetic Council (2002) *Inside Information* (HGC).

Human Genetics Commission (2006) *Making Babies* (HGC).

Human Tissue Authority (2005) *Draft Codes of Practice* (TSO).

Human Tissue Authority (2006a) *Guidance — Public Display* (TSO).

Human Tissue Authority (2006b) *Information about Living-donor Transplants* (TSO).

Human Tissue Authority (2006c) *Non-consensual DNA Analysis* (HTA).

Human Tissue Authority (2006d) Code of Practice—Consent (HTA).

Human Tissue Authority (2006e) *Code of Pratice—Donation of Organs, Tissue and Cells for Transplantation* (HTA).

Human Tissue Authority (2007a) *Annual Report* (TSO).

Hunter, D. (2007) 'Efficiency and the proposed reforms to the NHS research ethics system' *Journal of Medical Ethics* 33: 651.

Hunter, D. and Pierscionek, B. (2007) 'Children, Gillick competency and consent for involvement in research' *Journal of Medical Ethics* 33: 659.

Hursthouse, R. (1987) *Beginning Lives* (Blackwells).

Hursthouse, R. (1999) *On Virtue Ethics* (Oxford University Press).

Huxtable, R. (2004) 'Get out of jail free?' *Palliative Medicine* 18: 62.

Huxtable, R. and Möller, M. (2007) 'Setting a principled boundary? Euthanasia as a response to "life fatigue"' *Bioethics* 21: 117.

Huxtable R. and Woodley J. (2005) 'Gaining face or losing face? The debate on face transplants' *Bioethics* 19: 505.

Huxtable, R. and Woodley, J. (2006) '(When) will they have faces? A response to Agich and Siemionov' *Journal of Medical Ethics* 32: 403.

Ibrahim (2000) *Abortion* (RIFI).

Iltis, A. (2005a) 'Timing invitation to participate in clinical research' *Journal of Medicine and Philosophy* 30: 89.

Iltis, A. (2005b) 'Patient ethics and responsibilities' *Journal of Medicine and Philosophy* 30: 131.

Iltis, A. (2006) 'Lay concepts in informed consent to biomedical research: The capacity to understand and appreciate risk' *Bioethics* 20: 180.

Ince, S. (1984) 'Inside the surrogate industry' in R. Arditti, R. Duelli Klein and S. Minden, *Test-Tube Women* (Pandora Press).

Independent Advisory Group on Teenage Pregnancy (2005) *Annual Report* (DoE).

Information Centre (2007a) *Guardianship under the Mental Health Act 1983* (NHS).

Information Centre (2007b) *Staff in the NHS* (NHS).

Information Commissioner (2002) *Use and Disclosure of Health Data: Guidance on the Application of the Data Protection at 1998* (TSO).

Information Policy Unit (2004) *A strategy for the NHS* (TSO).

Ingham, R. (2000) 'Doctors should advise adolescents to abstain from sex: Anti' *British Medical Journal* 332: 1520.

Ingham, R., Clement, S., and Gillibrand, R. (2000) *Teenage Pregnancy Unit Advisory Document* (HMSO).

Innes, J. (2002) 'Mercy death husband walks free' *The Scotsman* 7 September 2002.

Institute of Medical Ethics (1986) *Medical Research with Children* (Institute of Medical Ethics).

International Planned Parenthood Federation (IPPF) (1999) 'Nepal: fighting to change a harsh abortion law' *Real Lives* 3: 1.

International Planned Parenthood Federation (2003) *Facts on Sexual and Reproductive Rights* (IPPF).

Involve (2002) *A guide to paying members of the public who are actively involved in research* (Involve).

Inwald, D., Jacobovits, I., and Petros, A. (2000) 'Brain stem death' *British Medical Journal* 320: 1266.

IOM Committee (1999) *To Err is Human* (IOM).

IPPR (2006) *Great Expectations* (IPPR).

Iqbal, Z., Pryce, A., and Afza, M. (2006) 'Rationalizing rationing in health care: experience of two primary care trusts' *Journal of Public Health* 28: 125.

Ireland, J. and Snowden, P. (2002) 'Bullying in secure hospitals' *Journal of Forensic Psychiatry* 13: 538.

Irving, Lord (1999) 'The patient, the doctor, their lawyers and the judge: rights and duties' *Medical Law Review* 7: 255.

Islamic Medical Association (2004) *Care at the End of Life* (IMA).

Ives, J. and Draper, H. (2005) 'What is a father?' *Bionews* 323.

Jackson G. (1989) 'The Medical Research Council Common Cold Unit' *Review of Infectious Disease* 11: 1020.

Jackson, J. (1999) 'Can older women cope with motherhood' in H. Khue and P. Singer, *Bioethics* (Blackwells).

Jackson, E. (2000) 'Abortion, autonomy and prenatal diagnosis' *Social and Legal Studies* 9: 468.

Jackson, E. (2001) *Regulating Reproduction* (Hart).

Jackson, E. (2006) '"Informed consent" to medical treatment and the importance of tort' in S. McLean (ed) *First do no Harm* (Ashgate).

Jackson, E. (2007) 'Death, euthanasia and the medical profession' in Brooks-Gordan, B., Ebtehaj, F., Herring, J., Johnson, M. and Richards, M. (eds) *Death Rights and Rites* (Hart).

Jackson, J. (2006) *Ethics in Medicine* (Polity Press).

Jaggar, A. (1983) *Feminist Politics and Human Nature* (Rowman and Allenheld).

James, N. (1994) 'From vision to system: the maturing of the hospice movement' in R. Lee and D. Morgan (eds) *Death Rites* (Routledge).

James, N. and Field, D. (1992) 'The routinization of hospice: Charisma and bureaucratization' *Social Science and Medicine* 34: 1363.

Jamrozik, K. (2000) 'The case for a new system for oversight of research on human subjects' *Australian Journal of Medical Ethics* 26: 334.

Jandoo, R. and Harland, W. (1984) 'Legally aided blackmail' *New Law Journal* 134: 402.

Janssens, R., ten Have, H., Broeckaert, B., Clark, D., Gracia, D., Illhardt, F-J., Lantz, G., Privitera, S., and Schotsmans, P. (2002) 'Moral values in palliative care: a European comparison' in H. ten Have and D. Clark (eds) *The Ethics of Palliative Care* (Open University Press).

Jansen-van der Weide, M, Onwuteaka-Philipsen, B., and van der Wal, G. (2005) 'Granted, undecided, withdrawn and refused requests for euthanasia and physician-assisted suicide' *Archives of Internal Medicine* 165: 1698.

Jarvis, R. (1995) 'Join the club' *Journal of Medical Ethics* 21: 199.

Jadva, V., Murray, C., Lycett, E., MacCallum, F., and Golombok, S. (2003) 'Surrogacy: the experiences of surrogate mothers' *Human Reproduction* 2196.

Jecker, N. (1993) 'Privacy beliefs and the violent family' *Journal of the American Medical Association* 269: 776.

Jennett, B. and Plum, F. (1972) 'Persistent vegetative state after brain damage' *Lancet* 1: 734.

Jennet, R. (1997) 'Letting vegetables die' in J. Keown (ed) *Euthanasia Examined* (Cambridge University Press).

Jervey, T. and McHale, J. (2004) *Health Law and the European Union* (Cambridge University Press).

Jochemsen, H. and Keown, J. (1999) 'Voluntary euthanasia under control?' *Journal of Medical Ethics* 25: 16.

Joffe, S., Cook, E., Cleary, P., Clark, J., and Weeks, J. (2001) 'Quality of informed consent in cancer trials' *The Lancet* 358: 1772.

Johnsen, D. (1986) 'The creation of fetal rights: conflicts with women's constitutional rights to liberty, privacy and equal protection' *Yale Law Journal* 95: 599.

Johnson, M. (2004) *Speech on National Infertility Day* (DoH).

Johnson, M. (2007) 'Escaping the tyranny of the embryo? A new approach to ART regulation based on UK and Australian experiences' *Human Reproduction* 21: 2756.

Johnston, G. and Abraham, C. (1995) 'The WHO objectives for palliative care: to what extent are we achieving them?' *Palliative Medicine* 9: 123.

Joint Committee (2007) *Report from the Joint Committee on The Human Tissue and Embryos (Draft) Bill* (TSO).

Jonas, H. (1969) 'Philosophical reflections on experimenting with human subjects' *Daedalus* 98: 219.

Jonas, H. (1998) 'Philosophical reflections on experimenting with human subjects' in S. Lammers and A. Verhy *On Moral Medicine* (Eerdmans).

Jones, A. (1986) 'Casuitry and clinical ethics' *Theoretical Medicine* 7: 67.

Jones, M. and Morris, A. (1989) 'Defensive medicine: myths and facts' *Journal of the Medical Defence Union* 5: 40.

Jones, M. (1990) 'Medical confidentiality' *Professional Negligence* 16.

Jones, D. (1996) *Medical Negligence* (Sweet and Maxwell).

Jones, M. (1999) 'Informed consent and other fairy stories' *Medical Law Review* 7: 103.

Jones, D. (2000) *Speaking for the Dead* (Ashgate).

Jones, C. (2003) 'The utilitarian argument for medical confidentiality: a pilot study of patients' views' *Journal of Medical Ethics* 29: 348.

Jonsen, A. and Garland, M. (1976) 'A moral policy for life/death decisions in the intensive care nursery' in A. Jonsen and M. Garland, *Ethics of Newborn Intensive Care* (University of California Press).

Jonsen, A. (2003) *The Birth of Bioethics* (Oxford University Press).

Jordan, C. (2002) 'First *Moore*, then *Hecht* isn't it time we recognize a property interest in tissues, cells, and gametes?' *Real Property, Probate and Trusts Journal* 37: 151.

Joseph Rowntree Foundation (1999) *Response to consultation on teenage pregnancy* (JRF).

Jost, T. and Mendelson, D. (2003) 'A comparative study of the law of palliative care and end-of-life treatment' *Journal of Law Medicine and Ethics* 31: 130.

Jowell, R., Curtice, J., Park, A., Brook, L., Ahrendt, D. and Thomson, K. (1996) *British Social Attitudes* (Dartmouth).

Jowell, T. (2004) *Speech,* 25 February 2004 (DoH).

Kafetz, K. (2002) 'What happens when elderly people die?' *Journal of the Royal Society of Medicine* 95: 536.

Kaganas, F. (2003) 'Domestic homicide, gender and the expert' in A. Bainham, S. Day Sclater, and M. Richards (eds) *Body Lore and Laws* Oxford: Hart.

Kant, I. (1993) *Grounding for the Metaphysics of Morals* (Hackett).

Kamisar, Y, (1998) 'The problems presented by the compelling, heart-wrenching case' *Journal of Criminal Law and Criminology* 88: 1121.

Kamm, F. (1992) *Creation and Abortion* (Oxford University Press).

Kamm, F. (1993) *Morality, Mortality: Death and Whom to Save From It* (Oxford University Press).

Kamm, F. (1998) 'Physician-assisted suicide, euthanasia, and intending death' in M. Battin, R. Rhodes, and A. Silvers (eds) *Physician Assisted Suicide* (Routledge).

Kaplan, D. (1999) 'Prenatal screening and its impact on persons with disabilities' in H. Khuse and P. Singer (eds) *Bioethics* (Blackwell).

Kaplan, C. and Hepworth, S. (2004) 'Supporting health service staff involved in a complaint incident or claim' *NHSLA Journal* 3: 11.

Karakatsanis, K. and Tsanakas, J. (2002) 'A critique on the concept of "brain death"' *Issues in Law and Medicine* 127.

Kass, L. (1998) 'The wisdom of repugnance: why we should ban the cloning of humans' *Valparaiso University Law Review* 32: 679.

Katz, J. (1993) 'Human experimentation and human rights' *Saint Louis University Law Journal* 7.

Katz, J. (2002) *The Silent World of Doctor and Patient* (John Hopkins).

Kelly, G. (1951) 'The duty to preserve life' *Theological Studies* 12 Dec.: 550.

Kennedy, I. (1969) 'Alive or dead' *Current Legal Problems* 22: 102.

Kennedy, I. (1981) *The Unmasking of Medicine* (Allen and Unwin).

Kennedy, I. (1987) 'Malpractice litigation crisis? what crisis?' in P. Byrne (ed) *Medicine in Contemporary Society* (King's Fund).

Kennedy, I. (1977) 'Switching off life support machines' [1977] *Criminal Law Review* 443.

Kennedy, I. (1991a) *Treat me Right* (Oxford University Press).

Kennedy, I. (1991b) 'Patient doctors and human rights' in R. Blackburn and J. Taylor (eds) *Human Rights of the 1990s* (Mansell).

Kennedy, I. (1992) 'Consent to treatment: the capable person' in C. Dyer (ed) *Doctors, Patients and the Law* (Blackwell).

Kennedy, I. and Grubb, A. (1989) 'Testing for HIV infection: the legal framework' *Law Society Gazette* 86: 30–5.

Kennedy, I. and Grubb, A. (2000) *Medical Law* (Butterworths).

Kenny, D. (1982) 'Confidentiality: the confusion continues' *Journal of Medical Ethics* 8: 9.

Kent, A. (2003) 'Consent and confidentiality in genetics: whose information is it anyway?' *Journal of Medical Ethics* 29: 16.

Keown, D. (1995) *Buddhism and Bioethics* (Macmillan).

Keown, D. (1999) 'Attitudes to euthanasia in the Vinaya and commentary' *Journal of Buddhist Ethics* 6: 262.

Keown, J. (1984) 'Miscarriage: a medicolegal analysis' *Criminal Law Review* 608.

Keown, J. (1987) 'Selective reduction of multiple pregnancy' *New Law Journal* 1165.

Keown, J. (1988) *Abortion, Doctors and the Law* (Cambridge University Press).

Keown, J. (1989a) 'AIDS: should it be made a notifiable disease?' *Professional Negligence* 121.

Keown J. (1989b) 'The ashes of AIDS and the phoenix of informed consent' *Modern Law Review* 52: 790.

Keown, J. (1992) 'The law and practice of euthanasia in the Netherlands' *Law Quarterly Review* 108: 51.

Keown, J. (1994a) 'Applying Bland' *Cambridge Law Journal* 53: 456.

Keown, J. (1994b) 'Publication review life's dominion: an argument about abortion and euthanasia' *Law Quarterly Review* 110: 671.

Keown, J. (1994c) 'Some reflections on euthanasia in the Netherlands' in L. Gormally (ed) *Euthanasia, Clinical Practice and the Law* (Linacre Centre).

Keown, J. (1994d) 'Further reflections on euthanasia in the Netherlands in the light of the Remmelink Report and the Van der Maas Survey' in L. Gormally (ed) *Euthanasia, Clinical Practice and the Law* (Linacre Centre).

Keown, J. (1997a) 'Restoring moral and intellectual shape to the law after Bland' *Law Quarterly Review* 113: 481.

Keown, J. (1997b) 'The gift of love in Europe' *Journal of Medical Ethics* 23: 96.

Keown, J. (1998) 'The legal revolution: from "sanctity of life" to "quality of life" and "autonomy"' *Journal of Contemporary Health Law and Policy* 14: 253.

Keown, J. (2000) 'Beyond Bland: a critique of the BMA guidance on withholding medical treatment' *Legal Studies* 66.

Keown, J. (2001) 'Dehydration and human rights' *Cambridge Law Journal* 60: 53.

Keown, J. (2002) *Euthanasia, Ethics and Public Policy* (Cambridge University Press).

Keown, J. (2005a) '"Morning after" pills, "miscarriage" and muddle' *Legal Studies* 296.

Keown, J. (2005b) 'A futile defence of Bland' *Medical Law Review* 13: 393.

Keown, J. (2006a) 'Mr Marty's muddle: a superficial and selective case for euthanasia in Europe' *Journal of Medical Ethics* 32: 29.

Keown, J. (2006b) *Considering Physician-Assisted Suicide* (Care not Killing).

Keown, J. (2006c) 'Restoring the sanctity of life and replacing the caricature:a reply to David Price' *Legal Studies* 26: 109.

Keown, J. (2007) 'Physician assisted suicide. Lord Joffe's slippery bill' *Medical Law Review* 15: 126.

Keown, J. and Gormally, L. (1999) 'Human dignity, autonomy and mentally incapacitated patients: A Critique of *Who Decides?*' *Web Journal of Current Legal Issues* 4.

Kerridge, I., Saul, P., and Lowe, M., McPhee, J. and Williams, D. (2002) 'Death dying and donation' *Journal of Medical Ethics* 28: 89.

Kessler, D., Summerton, N., and Graham, J. (2006) 'Effects of the medical liability system in Australia, the UK and the USA' *Lancet* 368: 240.

Keville, T. (1994) 'Gender bias in medical research and clinical testing' *Women's Rights Law Reporter* 16: 18.

Keywood, K. (1998) 'Sterilising the woman with learning difficulties—in her best interests?' in J. Bridgeman and S. Millns (eds) *Law and Body Politics* (Dartmouth).

Keywood, K. (2002) 'Disabling sex: some legal thinking about sterilisation, learning disability and embodiment', in A. Morris and S. Nott (eds), *The Gendered Nature of Health Care Provision* (Dartmouth).

Khan, F. (2002) 'Religious teachings and reflections on advance directives: an Islamic perspective' *Fordham Urban Law Journal* 30: 267.

Khan, M., Robson, M., and Swift, K. (2002) *Clinical Negligence* (Cavendish).

Khoury, L. (2006) *Uncertain Causation in Medical Liability* (Hart).

Kiernan, K. (1995) *Transition to Parenthood* (LSE).

Kim, S., Millard, R., Nisbet, P., Cox, C., and Caine, E. (2004) 'Potential research participants' views regarding researcher and institutional financial conflicts of interest' *Journal of Medical Ethics* 30: 73.

King, D. (1999) 'Preimplantation genetic diagnosis and the new eugenics' *Journal of Medical Ethics* 25: 176.

King, J. (2007) 'The justiciability of resource allocation' *Modern Law Review* 70: 197.

King, P. and Wolf, L. (1998) 'Lessons for physician-assisted suicide from the African American Experience' in M. Battin, R. Rhodes, and A. Silvers (eds) *Physician-assisted suicide* (Routledge).

King's Fund (2003a) *London's State of Mind* (King's Fund).

King's Fund (2003b) *What is the real choice of more patient choice?* (King's Fund).

King's Fund (2004) *Prevention Rather than Cure* (King's Fund).

King's Fund (2005) *An Independent Audit of the NHS Under Labour* (King's Fund).

King's Fund (2006) *Local Variation in NHS Spending Priorities* (King's Fund).

Kingdom, E. (1991) *What's Wrong with Rights?* (Edinburgh University Press).

Kingston, J. (1999) 'Human rights: the solution to the abortion dilemma' in C. Gearty and A. Tomkins (eds) *Understanding Human Rights* (Pinter).

Kinnell, H. (2000) 'Serial homicide by doctors' *British Medical Journal* 321: 1594.

Kipnis, K (2006) 'A defense of unqualified medical confidentiality' *American Journal of Bioethics* 6: 7.

Kirby P. (2004) *A guide to actively involving young people in research* (INVOLVE).

Kishore, R. (2005) 'Human organs, scarcities, and sale: morality revisited' *Journal of Medical Ethics* 31: 362.

Kissane, D. (2002) 'Deadly days in Darwin' (2002) in K. Foley and H. Hendin (eds) *The Case Against Assisted Suicide* (John Hopkins University Press).

Kissane, D., Clarke, D., and Street, A. (2001) 'Demoralisation Syndrome—a Relevant Psychiatric Diagnosis for Palliative Care' *Journal of Palliative Care* 17: 12.

Kirklin, D. (2004) 'The Role of Medical Imaging in the Abortion Debate' *Journal of Medical Ethics* 30: 426.

Kitwood, T. and Bredin, K. (1992) 'Towards a theory of dementia care: personhood and wellbeing' *Ageing and Society* 12: 269.

Klein, R. and Williams, A. (2000) 'Setting priorities: what is holding us back—inadequate information or inadequate institutions?' in A. Coulter and C. Ham (eds) *The Global Challenge of Health Care Rationing* (Open University Press).

Klein, R., Day, P. and Redmayne, S. (1996) *Managing Scarcity* (Open University Press).

Klein, R. (2001) *The New Politics of the NHS* (Prentice Hall).

Klotzo, J. (2004) *A Clone of Your Own* (Oxford University Press).

Kluge, E-H. (1999) 'Organ donation and retrieval: whose body is it anyway?' in H. Kuhse and P. Singer (eds) *Bioethics* (Blackwell).

Kmietowicz, Z. (2001) 'Reform of NICE needed to boost its credibility' *British Medical Journal* 323: 1324.

Kmietowicz, Z. (2004) 'Admissions to hospital under the Mental Health Act rise by 30% over 10 years' *British Medical Journal* 328: 854.

Knowles, A. and McMahon, M. (1995) 'Expectations and preferences regarding confidentiality in the psychologist-client relationship' *Australian Psychologist* 30: 175.

Koch, T. (2003) 'Absent virtues: the poacher becomes gamekeeper' *Journal of Medical Ethics* 29: 337.

Koch, T. (2005) 'The challenge of Terri Schiavo: lessons for bioethics' *Journal of Medical Ethics* 31: 376.

Kohn, L., Corrigan, J. and Donaldson, M. (eds) (2000) *To Err is Human* (National Academy Press).

Kolker A. and Burke B. (1994) *Prenatal Testing: A Sociological Perspective* (Bergin & Garvey).

Kolnai, A. (1995) 'Dignity' in R. Dillon (ed) *Dignity, Character and Self-Respect* (Routledge).

Kong, M. (2005) 'Legitimate requests and indecent proposals: matters of justice in the ethical assessment of phase I trials involving competent patients' *Journal of Medical Ethics* 31: 205.

Koop, C. (1978) 'A physician looks at abortion' in R. Ganz. (ed) *Thou Shalt Not Kill: The Christian Case Against Abortion* (Arlington House Publishers).

Korcz, K. (2002) 'Two Moral Strategies Relating to Abortion' *Journal of Social Philosophy* 33: 581.

Kornll, J. (2003) 'Crazy (mental illness under ADA)' *University of Michigan Journal of Law Reform* 36: 585.

Kottow, M. (2004) 'The battering of informed consent' *Journal of Medical Ethics* 30: 565.

Kounougeri-Manoledaki, E. (2000) 'Assisted reproduction and human rights in Greece' in A. Bainham (ed) *International Survey of Family Law* (Jordans).

Kranenburg, L., Zuidema, W., Weimar, W., IJzermans, J., Passchier, J., Hilhorst, M. and Busschbach, J. (2005) 'Postmortal or living related donor: preferences of kidney patients' *Transplant International* 18: 519.

Kuczewski, M. (1994) 'Whose will is it anyway? A discussion of advance directives, personal identity and consensus in medical ethics' *Bioethics* 8: 27.

Kuhse, H. (1984) 'A modern myth: that letting die is not the international causation of death' *Journal of Applied Philosophy* 1: 21.

Kuhse, H. (1985a) 'Euthanasia—again' *Medical Journal of Australia* 142: 610.

Kuhse, H. (1987) *The Sanctity of Life Doctrine in Medicine* (Oxford University Press).

Kuhse, H. (1988) 'A report from Australia: when a human life has not yet begun—according to the law' *Bioethics* 2: 334.

Kuhse, H. (1998) 'Why killing is not always worse—and sometimes better—than letting die' *Cambridge Quarterly of Healthcare Ethics* 7: 371.

Kuhse, H. (1998) 'From intention to consent' in M. Battin, R. Rhodes and A. Silvers *Physician Assisted Suicide* (Oxford University Press).

Kuhse, H. (1999) 'Some reflections on the problem of advance directives, personhood, and personal identity subjects' *Kennedy Institute of Ethics Journal* 9: 347.

Kuhse, H. and Singer, P. (1985) *Should the baby live?* (Oxford University Press).

Kuhse, H. and Singer, P. (2001) 'Killing and letting die' in J. Harris (ed) *Bioethics* (Oxford University Press).

Kuhse, H., Singer, P., Baurne, P., Clark, M., and Richard, M. (1998) 'End-of-Life decisions in Australian medical practice' *Medical Journal of Australia* 116: 191.

Kunich, J. (2002) 'The naked clone' *Kentucky Law Journal* 91: 1.

Kunin, J. (2003) 'Withholding artificial feeding from the severely demented: merciful or immoral? Contrasts between secular and Jewish perspectives' *Journal of Medical Ethics* 29: 208.

LaFleur, W. (1992) *Liquid Life* (Princeton University Press).

Laing, J. (2003) 'Reforming mental health law and the ECHR' *Journal of Social Welfare and Family Law* 25: 325.

Laing, J. (2006) 'Artificial reproduction, blood relatedness and human identity' *The Monist* 10 January.

Laing, R. (1959) *The Divided Self* (Penguin).

Laing, J and Oderberg, D. (2005) 'Artificial reproduction, the "welfare principle", and the common good' *Medical Law Review* 13: 328.

Lalos, J., Daniels, K., Gotlieb, C., and Lalos, O. (2003) 'Recruitment and motivation of semen providers in Sweden' *Human Reproduction* 18: 212.

Lamb, D. (1985) *Death, Brain Death and Ethics* (State University of New York).

Lamb, D. (1987) *Death, Brain Death and Ethics* (Routledge).

Lamb, D. (1988) *Down the Slippery Slope* (Croon Helm).

Lamb, D. (1990) 'Wanting it both ways' *Journal of Medical Ethics* 16: 8.

Lamb, D. (1994) 'What is death?' in R. Gillon (ed) *Principles of Health Care Ethics* (John Wiley and Sons).

Lamb, D. (1995) 'Autonomy and the refusal of life-prolonging therapy' *Res Publica* 1: 147.

Lamb, D. (1996) *Transplantation and Ethics* (Avebury).

Lammers, M. and Verhey, A. (eds) (1998) *On Moral Medicine* (Eerdmans).

Land, W. and Cohen, B. (1992) 'Postmortem living organ donation in Europe' *Transplantation Proceedings* 24: 2165.

Landes, E. and Posner, R. (1978) 'The economics of the baby shortage' *Journal Legal Studies* 7: 323.

Landis, S., Schoenbach, V., and Weber, D. (1992) 'Results of a randomized trial of partner notificaiton in cases of HIV infection in North Carolina' *New England Journal of Medicine* 326: 101.

Lane, R. (2007) 'Safety, identity and consent: a limited defense of reproductive human cloning' *Bioethics* 20: 125.

Lanham, D. (1971) 'Transplants and the Human Tissue Act 1961' *Medicine, Science and the Law* 11: 16.

Lanham, D. (1990) 'The right to choose to die with dignity' *Criminal Law Journal* 14: 401.

Larijani, B., Zahedi, F. and Ghafouri-Fard, S. (2004) 'Rewarded gift for living renal donors' *Transplantation Proceedings* 36: 2539.

Laurance, J. (2000) 'The booming baby market' *The Independent on Sunday* 7 April 2000.

Laurance, J. (2003) *Pure Madness* (Routledge).

Laurence, L. and Weinhouse, B. (1997) *Outrageous Practices* (Rutgers University Press).

Laurie, G. (1997) 'Biotechnology: facing the problems of patent law' in H. MacQueen and B. Bain (eds) *Innovation, Incentive and Reward* (Edinburgh University Press).

Laurie, G. (2002) *Genetic Privacy: A Challenge to Medico-Legal Norms* (Cambridge University Press).

Lavery, R. (1990) 'Routine medical treatment of children' *Journal of Social Welfare and Family Law* 375.

Lavi, S. (2001) 'The problem of pain and the right to die' in A. Sarat (ed) *Pain, Death and the Law* (University of Michigan Press).

Law Commission Report 110 (1981) *Breach of Confidence* (Law Commission).

Law Commission Consultation Paper 139 (1995) *Consent in the Criminal Law* (Law Commission).

Law Commission Report No 231 (1995) *Mental Incapacity* (Law Commission).

Law Commission Report No 257 (1999) *Damages for Personal Injury: NonPecuniary Loss* (Law Commission).

Lawlor, R. (2007) 'Moral theories in teaching applied ethics' *Journal of Medical Ethics* 33: 370.

Lawton, J. (2000) *The Dying Process* (Routledge).

Leathard, A. (1980) *The Fight For Family Planning* (Macmillan).

Leatherman, S. and Sutherland, K. (2005) *The Quest for Quality in the NHS* (DOH).

Leder, D. (1999) 'Whose body? What body' in M. Cherry (ed) *Persons and Their Bodies* (Kluwer).

Lee, E. (2002) *Why Abortion Law Matters* (Pro-Choice Forum).

Lee, E. (2003) 'Tensions in the regulation of abortion in Britain' *Journal of Law and Society* 30: 532.

Lee, E. (2004) 'We still need abortion as early as possible, as late as necessary' *Spiked* 9 July 2004.

Lee, E. (2007) 'The abortion debate today' in K. Horsey and H. Biggs (eds) *Human Fertilization and Embryology: Reproducing Regulation* (Routledge).

Lee, E. and Davey, J. (1998) *Attitudes to Abortion for Fetal Abnormality* (Pro-Choice Forum).

Lee, E., Clements, S., Ingham, R., and Stone, N. (2004) *A Matter of Choice?* (Joseph Rowntree Trust).

Lee, P. (1996) *Abortion and Unborn Human Life* (Catholic University of American Press).

Lee, P. (2004) 'A Christian philosopher's view of recent directions in the abortion debate' *Christian Bioethics* 10: 7.

Lee, P. (2007) 'Substantial identity and the right to life: a rejoinder to Dean Stretton' *Bioethics* 21: 93.

Lee, R. (1994) 'Deathly silence; doctors' duty to disclose dangers of death' in R. Lee and D. Morgan (eds) *Death Rights* (Routledge).

Lee, R. and Morgan, D. (1988) 'Sterilisation and mental handicap: sapping the strength of the state' *Journal of Legal Studies* 229.

Lee, R. and Morgan, D. (2000) *Human Fertilisation and Embryology Act 1990: A Guide* (Blackwell).

Lee, S. (1987) 'Towards a jurisprudence of consent' in J. Eekelaar and J. Bell (eds) *Oxford Essays in Jurisprudence* (Oxford University Press).

Lee, S., Ralston, H., Drey, E., Partridge, J., Rosen, M. (2005) 'Fetal pain' *Journal of the American Medical Association* 294: 947.

Legal Services Commission (2007) *Annual Report* (LSC).

Leigh, B. (2004) 'What's the problem?' *British Medical Journal* 328: 460.

Lenaghan, J. (1997) 'The rationing debate: Central government should have a greater role in rationing decisions—The case for' *British Medical Journal* 314: 967.

Leng, R. (1982) 'Mercy killing and the CLRC' *New Law Journal* 132: 76.

Levitt, M. (1999) 'The ethics and impact on behaviour of knowledge about one's own genome' *British Medical Journal* 319: 1283.

Lewis, C. (1953) 'The Humanitarian Theory of Punishment' *University of Melbourne Law Review* 228.

Lewis, P. (2001) 'Rights discourse and assisted suicide' *American Journal of Law and Medicine* 45.

Lewis, P. (2002) 'Procedures that are against the medical interests of the incompetent person' *Oxford Journal of Legal Studies* 12: 575.

Lewis, P. (2006) 'Assisted dying in France. The evolution of assisted dying in France: a third way?' *Medical Law Review* 14: 44.

Lewis, P. (2007a) 'The empirical slippery slope from voluntary to non-voluntary euthanasia' *Journal of Law Medicine and Ethics* 197.

Lewis, P. (2007b) 'Withdrawal of treatment from a patient in a permanent vegetative state: Judicial involvement and innovative 'treatment'' *Medical Law Review* 15: 392.

Lewis, P. (2007c) *Assisted Dying and Legal Change* (Oxford University Press).

Lewis, R. (2005) *The Sound of Silence* (Public Finance).

Lexchin, J., Bero, L., Djulbegovic, B., and Clark, O. (2003) 'Pharmaceutical industry sponsorship and research outcome and quality: systematic review' *British Medical Journal* 326: 1167.

Liao, A. (2003) *Mental Health Teenage Motherhood and Age at first Birth among British Women in the 1990s* (Institute of Economic Research).

Lichtenberg, P., Heresco-Levy, U. and Nitzan, U. (2004) 'The ethics of the placebo in clinical practice' *Journal of Medical Ethics* 30: 551.

Liddell, K. and Hall, A. (2005) 'Beyond Bristol and Alder Hey: the future regulation of human tissue' *Medical Law Review* 13: 170.

Liddell, K., Bion, J., Chamberlain, D., Druml, C., Kompanje, E., Lemaire, F., Menon, D., Vrhovac, B., and Wiedermann, C. (2006) 'Medical research involving incapacitated adults: Implications of the EU Clinical Trials Directive 2001/20/EC' *Medical Law Review* 14: 467.

Lie, R., Emanuel, E., Grady, C., and Wendler, D. (2004) 'The standard of care debate: the Declaration of Helsinki versus the international consensus opinion' *Journal of Medical Ethics* 30: 190.

Lieberman, B. (2005) 'Egg sharing: a misnomer?' *Bionews* 25 April 2005.

Light, D. (1997) 'The real ethics of rationing' *British Medical Journal* 315: 112.

Lillehammer, H. (2002) 'Voluntary euthanasia and the logical slippery slope argument' *Cambridge Law Journal* 545.

Linacre Centre (1994) 'Submission to the House of Lords Select Committee on Medical Ethics' in L. Gormally (ed) *Euthanasia, Clinical Practice and the Law* (Linacre Centre).

Linacre Centre (1998) *Witholding and Withdrawing Treatment* (Linacre Centre).

Linacre Centre (2002) *Response to Human Bodies, Human Choices: a Consultation Report of the Department of Health* (Linacre Centre).

Lind, C. (2003) '*Re R (Paternity of IVF Baby)*—Unmarried paternity under the Human Fertilisation and Embryology Act 1990' *Child and Family Law Quarterly* 327.

Lind, (2006) 'Evans v United Kingdom: Judgments of Solomon: power, gender and procreation' *Child and Family Law Quarterly* 437.

Lindemann Nelson, J. (2007) 'Testing, terminating and discriminating' *Cambridge Quarterly of Healthcare Ethics* 462.

Litman, M. (1997) 'The legal status of genetic material' in B. Knoppers, C. Laberge and M. Hirtle (eds) *Human DNA: Law and Policy* (Kluwer).

Little, G. (1997) 'Comparing German and English law on non-consensual sterilisation: a difference in approach' *Medical Law Review* 5: 269.

Lizza, J. (2006) *Persons, Humanity and the Definition of Death* (John Hopkins University Press).

Lock, M. (2002) *Twice Dead* (University of California Press).

Lockwood, M. (1988) 'Quality of life and resource allocation' in J. Bell and S. Mendus, *Philosophy and Medical Welfare* (Cambridge University Press).

Lockwood, M. (ed) (1985) *Moral Dilemmas in Modern Medicine* (Oxford University Press).

Logue, B. (1996) 'Physician-assisted suicide: a social science perspective on international trends' in S. Maclean (ed) *Death, Dying and the Law* (Dartmouth).

Logue, B. (1994) 'When hospice fails: the limits of palliative care' *Omega Journal of Death and Dying* 29: 1.

Lombardo, P. (1996) 'Medicine, eugenics and the Supreme Court: from coercive sterilization to reproductive freedom' 13 *Journal of Contemporary Health Law and Policy* 13: 1.

Long, R. (1993) 'Abortion abandonment and positive rights' *Social Philosophy and Policy* 10: 166.

Loughrey, J. (2003) 'Medical information, confidentiality and a child's right to privacy' *Legal Studies* 510.

Low, L. (1993) 'Genetic discrimination in life insurance' *British Medical Journal* 317: 1632.

Lowe, N. and Juss, S. (1993) 'Medical treatment—pragmatism and the search for principle' *Modern Law Review* 56: 865.

Lublin, N. (1998) *Pandora's Box: Feminism Confronts Reproductive Technology* (Rowman and Littlefield).

Lucassen, A. and Kaye, J. (2006) 'Genetic testing without consent: the implications of the new Human Tissue Act 2004' *Journal of Medical Ethics* 32: 690.

Lupton, D. (1994) *Medicine as Culture* (Thousand Oaks).

Lynoe, N., Jacobsson, L., and Lundgren, E. (1999) 'Fraud, misconduct or normal science in medical research—an empirical study of demarcation' *Journal of Medical Ethics* 6: 510.

Lyons, D. (1965) *The Forms and Limits of Utilitarianism* (Oxford University Press).

Maclean Massie, A. (1995) 'Regulating choice: a constitutional law response to Professor John A Roberts' *Washington and Lee Law Review* 52: 135.

Maclean, A. (1993) *The elimination of morality* (Oxford University Press).

Maclean, A. (2006) 'Advance directives, future selves and decision-making' *Medical Law Review* 14: 291.

MacCallum, F., Lycett, E., Murray, C., Jadva, V., and Golombok, S. (2003) 'Surrogacy: the experience of commission couples' *Human Reproduction* 1334.

MacCallum, F. and Golombok, S. (2004) 'Children raised in fatherless families from infancy: A follow-up of children of lesbian and single heterosexual mothers at early adolescence' *Journal of Child Psychology and Psychiatry* 45: 1407.

MacDonald, S. (2006) 'A suicidal woman, roaming pigs and a noisy trampolinist: refining the ASBO's definition of 'anti-social behaviour' *Modern Law Review* 69: 183.

Machado, N. (1998) *Using the Bodies of the Dead* (Ashgate).

Machado, C., Korein, J., Ferrer, Y., Portela, L., Garcia, M., Manero, M. (2007) 'The concept of brain death did not evolve to benefit organ transplants' *Journal of Medical Ethics* 33: 197.

Macintyre, A. (1984) *After Virtue* (University of Notre Dame Press).

Macintosh, K. (2005) *Illegal Human Beings* (Cambridge University Press).

Mackenzie, C. (1992) 'Abortion and embodiment' *Australasian Journal of Philosophy* 70: 136.

Mackenzie, C. (2007) 'Feminist bioethics and genetic termination' *Bioethics* 21: 515.

Mackenzie, C. and Stoljar, N. (2000) *Relational Autonomy* (Oxford University Press).

Mackenzie, R. and Cox, S. (2007) 'Transableism, disability and paternalism in public health ethics: taxonomies, identity disorders and persistent unexplained physical symptoms' *International Journal of Law in Context* 2: 363.

Mackenzie, R. (2007) 'Beyond genetic and gestational dualities' in K. Horsey and H.Biggs (eds) Human *Fertilization and Embryology: Reprodcing Regulation* (Routledge).

Mackinnon, C. (1987) *Feminism Unmodified* (Harvard University Press).

Mackinnon, C. (1991) *Towards a Feminist Theory of the State* (Harvard University Press).

Maclean, A. (2000) 'The Human Rights Act 1998 and the individual's right to treatment' *Medical Law International* 5: 205.

Maclean, A. (2001) 'A crossing of the Rubicon on the Human Rights Ferry' *Modern Law Review* 64: 775.

Maclean, A. (2002) 'Beyond Bolam and Bolitho' *Medical Law International* 5: 205.

Magnusson, R. (1998) 'Property Rights in human corpses' in N Palmer and E McKendrick (eds) *Interests in Goods* (LLP London).

Magnusson, R. (2004) '"Underground euthanasia" and the harm minimization debate' *Journal of Law, Medicine and Ethics* 32: 486.

Maguire, D. and Burtchaell, J. (1998) 'The Catholic legacy and abortion' in M. Lammers and A. Verhey (eds) *On Moral Medicine* (Eerdmans).

Mahowald, M. (2006) *Bioethics and Women* (Oxford University Press).

Mahowald, M. (2007) 'Prenatal testing for selection against disabilities' *Cambridge Quarterly of Healthcare Ethics* 457.

Mak, Y., Elwyn, G., and Finlay, I. 'Patients' voices are needed in debates on euthanasia' *British Medical Journal* 327: 213.

Malek, M. (2003) 'Implementing QALYs' *Aventis* 6.

Maloney, A. (1995) 'You say you want a revolution? Pro-life philosophy and feminism' *Studies in Pro-Life Feminism* 22 September 1995.

Mann, J. (1998) 'The neurobiology of suicide' *Nature Medicine* 4: 25.

Mann, P. (1998) 'Meanings of death' in M. Battin (ed) *Physician Assisted Suicide* (Routledge).

Marie Stopes International (2002) *Annual Review* (MSI).

Markowitz, S. (1990) 'Abortion and feminism' *Social Theory and Practice* 16: 1.

Marquis, D. (1989) 'Why abortion is immoral' *Journal of Philosophy* 86: 183.

Marquis, D. (2002) 'A defence of the potential future of value theory' *Journal of Medical Ethics* 28: 198–201.

Marquis, D. (2006) 'Abortion and the beginning and end of human life' *Journal of Law, Medicine and Ethics* 17.

Marteau, T. and Richards, M.P.M. (1996) *The Troubled Helix* (Cambridge University Press).

Martinson, B., Anderson, M., and de Vries, R. (2005) 'Scientists behaving badly' *Nature* 434: 737.

Mason, J. and Laurie, G. (2001) 'Consent or property—dealing with the body and its parts in the shadow of Bristol and Alder Hey' *Modern Law Review* 64: 710.

Mason, K. (2005) 'What is in a name? The vagaries of Vo v France' *Child and Family Law Quarterly* 16: 97.

Mason, K. and Laurie, G. (2006) *Law and Medical Ethics* (Oxford University Press).

Maternity Care Working Party (2001) *Modernizing Maternity Care* (RCOG).

Matthews, P. (1995) 'The man of property' *Medical Law Review* 3: 251.

Martin, R. (2006) 'The exercise of public health powers in cases of infectious disease: human rights implieations' *Medical Law Review* 14: 132.

Mayor, S. (2001) 'Health department to fund interferon beta' *British Medical Journal* 323: 1087.

McCall Smith, A. (1999) 'Euthanasia: the strength of the middle ground' *Medical Law Review* 7: 194.

McCall Smith, A. (1997) 'Beyond autonomy' *Journal of Contemporary Health Law and Policy* 14: 23.

McCarthy, D. (2001) 'Why sex selection should be legal' *Journal of Medical Ethics* 27: 302.

McCormack, P. (1998) 'Quality of life and the right to die: An ethical dilemma' *Journal of Advanced Nursing* 28: 63.

McDonagh, E. (1996) *Breaking the Abortion Deadlock* (Oxford University Press).

McGee, A. (2005) 'Finding a way through the ethical and legal maze withdrawal of medical treatment and euthanasia' *Medical Law Review* 3: 357.

McGee, G. (2003) *Pragmatic Bioethics* (MIT Press).

McGlennan, T. (2000) *Genetics and Insurance* (BIOS).

McHale, J. (2006a) '"Appropriate consent" and the use of human material for research purposes: the competent adult' *Clinical Ethics* 1: 95.S

McHale, J. (2006b) 'Law reform, clinical research and adults without mental capacity' in S. McLean (ed) *First do no Harm* (Ashgate).

McHale, J. (2007) 'Rights to medical treatment in EU Law' *Medical Law Review* 15: 99.

Mckie, J., Kuhse, H., Richardson, J., and Singer, P. (2002) 'Allocating heath care by QALYs' *Cambridge Quarterly of Healthcare Ethics* 5: 534.

McLachlin J. (1998) 'Negligence law—proving the connection' in N.J. Mullany and A.M. Linden (eds) *Torts Tomorrow: A Tribute to John Fleming* (The Law Book Company).

McLachlan, H. (2005) 'Justice and the NHS: a comment on Culyer' *Journal of Medical Ethics* 31: 379.

Mclean, J. (1998) 'Human cloning: A dangerous dilemma' *Journal of Law Society of Scotland* 43: 24.

McLean, S. (1999) *Old Law, New Medicine* (Pandora).

McLean, S. (ed) (2002) *Medical Law and Ethics* (Ashgate).

McLean, S. (2006) 'From Bland to Burke' in S. McLean (ed) *First do no Harm* (Ashgate).

McLean, S. and Britton, A. (1996) *Sometimes a Small Victory* (Glasgow University).

McLean, S., Campbell, A., Gutridge, K., and Harper, H. (2006) 'Human tissue legislation and medical practice' *Medical Law International* 8: 1.

McLean, S. and Williamson, L. (2005) *Xenotransplantation—Law and Ethics* (Ashgate).

McLean, S. and Williamson, L. (2007) 'The demise of UKXIRA and the regulation of solid-organ xenotransplantation in the UK' *Journal of Medical Ethics* 33: 373.

McMahan, J. (1995) 'The metaphysics of brain death' *Bioethics* 9: 91.

McMahan, J. (2002) *The Ethics of Killing* (Oxford University Press).

McMillan, J. (2003a) 'Dangerousness, mental disorder, and responsibility' *Journal of Medical Ethics* 29: 232.

McMillan, J. (2003b) 'NICE and the draft fertility guidance' *Journal of Medical Ethics* 29: 313.

McNamara, B. (2001) *Fragile Lives: Death, Dying and Care* (Allen and Unwin).

McNamara, B. (2004) '"Good enough" death: Autonomy and choice in Australian palliative care' *Social Science and Medicine* 58: 929.

McNeill, P. (1993) *The Ethics and Politics of Human Experimentation* (Cambridge University Press).

McWhinnie, A. (2001) 'Gamete donation and anonymity' *Human Reproduction* 16: 807.

MDU (2004) *MDU objects to GMC disclosure plan* (MDU).

Medical Research Council (MRC) (2000) *Public Perceptions of the Collection of Human Biological Samples* (MRC).

Medical Research Council (MRC) (2004a) *Human Tissue Bill—Views of the Medical Research Council* (MRC).

Medical Research Council (MRC) (2004b) *Medical Research Involving Children* (MRC).

Meier, D. (1998) 'A national survey of physician-assisted suicide and euthanasia in the United States' *New England Journal of Medicine* 338: 1193.

Meilaender, G. (1998) *Bioethics: a Primer for Christians* (Eerdmans).

Melo-Martín, I. (2006) 'Furthering injustices against women: genetic information, Moral obligations, and gender' *Bioethics* 20: 301.

Mental Health Act Commission (2005) *Annual Report* (Mental Health Act Commission).

Mental Health Strategies (2005) *The 2004/05 National Survey Of Investment In Mental Health Services* (Mental Health Strategies).

Mental Health Alliance Foundation (2005) Press Release.

Mental Health Foundation (2007) *Statistics on Mental Health* (MHF).

Menzel, P. (1994) 'Rescuing lives: Can't we count?' *Hastings Center Report* 24: 22.

Meredith, S. (2005) *Policing Pregnancy: The Law and Ethics of Obstetric Conflict* (Ashgate).

Merry, A. and McCall Smith, A. (2001) *Errors Medicare and the Law* (Cambridge University Press).

Meschede D. and Horst, J. (1997) 'Sex chromosomal anomalies in pregnancies conceived through intracytoplasmic sperm injection: a case for genetic counselling' *Human Reproduction* 12: 112.

Messer, N. (2002) *Theological Issues in Bioethics* (Darton Longman and Todd).

Meyers, D. and Mason, J. (1999) 'Physician-Assisted Suicide: A Second View from Mid-Atlantic' *Anglo-American Law Review* 28: 265.

Michalowski, S (1999) 'Court-Authorised Caesarean Sections—The End of a Trend?' *Child and Family Law Quarterly* 62: 115.

Michalowski, S. (2001) 'Reversal of fortune: *Re A (Conjoined Twins)*' *Health Law Journal* 9: 149.

Michalowski, S. (2004) *Medical Confidentiality and Crime* (Oxford University Press).

Michalowski, S. (2005) 'Advance refusals of life-sustaining medical treatment: The relativity of an absolute right' *Modern Law Review* 68: 958.

Michalowski, S. (2007) 'Trial and error at the end of life—no harm done?' *Oxford Journal of Legal Studies* 27: 257.

Miles, A. (1991) *Women, Health and Medicine* (Open University Press).

Millburn, A. (1999) *Modern Services, Modern Decisions* (DoH).

MIND (1997) *Without prejudice* (MIND).

MIND (2005) *Ward Watch* (MIND).

MIND/University College London (2003) *Report on the Mental Health of Lesbian, Gay and Bisexual People* (MIND).

Miers, D. (1996) 'Liability for injuries caused by violent patients' *Journal of Personal Injury Litigation* 314.

Minow, M. (1997) 'Which question? which lie? Reflections on the physician-assisted suicide cases' *Supreme Court Review* 1.

Miola, J. (2006) 'Autonomy rued OK?' *Medical Law Review* 14: 108.

Miola, J. (2007) *Medical Ethics and Medical Law* (Hart).

Moazam, F. (2004) 'Feminist discourse on sex screening and selective abortion of female foetuses' *Bioethics* 18: 205.

Modernisation Board (2005) *Annual Report* (DoH).

Mohindra, R. (2007) 'Medical futility: a conceptual model' *Journal of Medical Ethics* 33: 71.

Monahan, J. (2001) 'Major mental disorder and violence: Epidemiology and risk assessment' in G. Pinard and L. Pagani (eds) *Clinical Assessment of Dangerousness: Empirical Contributions* (Cambridge University Press).

Moncrieff, J. (2003) 'The politics of a new Mental Health Act' *British Journal of Psychiatry* 183: 8.

Monitor (2005) *Annual Report* (TSO).

Montadon, C. and Harding, T. (1984) 'The reliability of dangerousness assessments. A decision making exercise' *The British Journal of Psychiatry* 144: 149.

Montgomery, J. (1987) 'Confidentiality and the immature minor' *Family Law* 101.

Montgomery, J. (1988) 'Children as property' *Modern Law Review* 51: 323.

Montgomery, J. (1989) 'Rhetoric and welfare' *Oxford Journal of Legal Studies* 9: 395.

Montgomery, J. (1990) 'Rights, restraint and pragmatism' *Modern Law Review* 52: 524.

Montgomery, J. (1998) 'Professional regulation a gendered phenomenon' in Sheldon, S. and Thomson, P. (ed) *Feminist Perspective on Healthcare Law* (Cavendish).

Montgomery, J. (1999) 'Medical law in transition' *Current Legal Problems* 52: 251.

Montgomery, J. (2000) 'Time for paradigm shift' *Current Legal Problems* 53: 363.

Montgomery, J. (2003) *Health Care Law* (Oxford University Press).

Montgomery, J. (2006) 'Law and the demoralization of medicine' Legal Studies 26: 185.

Montgomery, J. (2006b) 'The Legitimacy of Medical Law' in S. McLean (ed) *First do no Harm* (Ashgate).

Moore, G. (2001) *The Body in Context* (Cambridge University Press).

Moreham, N. (2005) 'Privacy in the common law: a doctrinal and theoretical analysis' *Law Quarterly Review* 121: 628.

Moreland, J. and Rae, S. (2000) *Body and Soul* (Intervarsity Press).

Morgan, D. (1998) 'Frameworks of analysis for feminisms' account of reproductive technology' in S. Sheldon and M. Thompson *Feminist Perspectives on Health Care Law* (Cavendish).

Morgan, D. (2001) *Issues in Medical Law and Ethics* (Cavendish).

Morgan, D. and Ford, M. (2004) 'Cell phoney: human cloning after Quintavalle' *Journal of Medical Ethics* 30: 524.

Morgan, D. and Lee, R. (1997) 'In the name of the father?' *Modern Law Review* 60: 840.

Morgan, L.M. and Michaels, M.W. (1999) *Fetal Subjects, Feminist Positions* (University of Pennsylvania Press).

Morgan, M. (2003) 'The doctor-patient relationship' in G. Scambler (ed) *Sociology as Applied to Medicine* (Saunders).

MORI (2001) *Doctors Win Overwhelming Vote of Confidence from the Public* (MORI).

Morris, A. (2007) 'Spiralling or stabilising? The compensation culture and our propensity to claim damages for personal Injury' *Modern Law Review* 70: 349.

Morris, A. (2000) 'Easing the passing: end of life decisions and the Medical Treatment (Prevention of Euthanasia) Bill' *Medical Law Review* 8: 300.

Morris, A. and Nott, J. (2002) *Well Women: Women's Access to Health Care* (Oxford University Press).

Morris, C. (2007) 'Evans v United Kingdon: Paradigms of parenting' *Modern Law Review* 70: 979.

Morris, F. and Ashead, G. (1997) 'Liability of psychiatrists for the violent acts of their patients' *New Law Journal* 558.

Morrison, B. (1997) *As If* (Granta).

Morrison, D. (2005) 'A holistic approach to clinical and research decision-making' *Medical Law Review* 13: 45.

Moynihan, R. (2002) 'Too much medicine' *British Medical Journal* 324: 859.

Moynihan, R., Heath, I., and Henry, D. (2002) 'Selling sickness' *British Medical Journal* 324: 886.

Muir, D. and Griffin, G. (2001) *Infection risks in Xentransplantation* (DoH).

Mulcahy, L. (2003) *Disputing Doctors: The Socio-Legal Dynamics of Complaints about Doctors* (Open University Press).

Mulcahy, L., Selwood, M., Summerfield, M., and Netten, A. (1999) *Mediating Medical Negligence Claims* (University of London).

Mulgan, T. (2006) *Future People* (Oxford University Press).

Mulheron, R. (2007) 'Medical negligence, secondary victims and psychiactric illness' in R. Probert (ed) *Family Life and the Law* (Ashgate).

Mullender R. (1996) 'Judicial review and the rule of law' *Law Quarterly Review* 112: 182.

Mumford, S. (1998) 'Bone marrow donation—the law in context' *Child and Family Law Quarterly* 135.

Munro, E. and Rumgay, J. (2000) 'Role of risk assessment in reducing homicides by people with mental illness' *British Journal of Psychiatry* 176: 116.

Munzer, S. (1994) 'An uneasy case against property rights in body parts' in E. Paul, F. Miller and J. Paul (eds) *Property Rights* (Cambridge University Press).

Munzer, M. (1999) 'The special case of property rights in umbilical cord blood for transplantation' *Rutgers Law Review* 51: 493.

Murphy, J. (1991) 'Cosmetics, eugenics ambivalence' *Journal of Social Welfare and Family Law* 375.

Murphy, T. (1998) 'Health confidentiality in the age of talk' in S. Sheldon and M. Thomson *Feminist Perspectives on Health Care Law* (Cavendish).

Murphy, T and Veatch, R. (2006) 'Members first: the ethics of donating organs and tissues to groups' *Cambridge Quarterly of Healthcare Ethics* 15: 59.

Murphy, T. and Younger, S. (2003) 'Organ salvage policies' in K. Fulford, D. Dickenson, and T. Murray, *Healthcare Ethics and Human Values* (Blackwell).

Myers, D. (1990) *The Human Body and The Law* (Edinburgh University Press).

Nadel, M. and Nadel, C. (2005) 'Using reciprocity to motivate organ donations' *Yale Journal of Health Policy, Law & Ethics* 5: 293.

Naffine, N. (1997) 'The body bag' in N. Naffine and R.J. Owens (eds) *Sexing the Subject of Law* (LBC).

Nathanson, B. (1979) *Aborting America* (Doubleday).

National Academy of Sciences (2002) *Scientific and Medical Aspects of Human Reproductive Cloning* (NAS).

National Audit Office (2001a) *Tackling Obesity in England* (TSO).

National Audit Office (2001b) *Handling Clinical Negligence Claims in England* (TSO).

National Audit Office (2004) *Tackling Cancer* (NAO).

National Audit Office (2005a) *A Safer Place for Patients* (TSO).

National Audit Office (2005b) *Managing the Financial Implications of NICE Guidance* (NAO).

National Collaborating Centre for Women's and Children's Health (2004) *Fertility* (RCOG).

National Institute for Mental Health in England (2004) *Cases for Change: Hospital Services* (TSO).

National Institute for Mental Health in England (2007) *National Suicide Prevention Programme for England* (DoH).

National Patient Safety Agency (2007) *The National Patient Safety Agency Annual Report and Accounts 2006/07* (TSO).

National Statistics (2000) *Abortion Statistics 1999* (TSO).

National Statistics (2003) *Health Statistics Quarterly Autumn* (ONS).

National Statistics (2004) *Life Expectancy* (ONS).

National Statistics (2006) *General Household Survey* (ONS).

National Statistics (2007a) *Contraception and Sexual Health 2006/07* (ONS).

National Statistics (2007b) *Death Registration* (ONS).

National Statistics (2007c) *Health Statistics Quarterly* (ONS).

National Statistics (2007d) *Suicide* (ONS).

National Statistics (2007e) *Attitudes to Mental Illness* (ONS).

Nelson, H. (2000) 'Feminist Bioethics: Where we've been, Where we're going' *Metaphilosophy* 31: 492.

Nesbitt, W. (1995) 'Is killing no worse than letting die?' *Journal of Applied Philosophy* 12: 101.

Nettleton, S. (2001) *The Sociology of Health and Illness* (Blackwell).

New, B. Solomon, M., Dingwall, R. and McHale, J. (1994) *A Question of Give and Take* (King's Fund Institute).

Newdick, C. (1995) 'Strict liability for defective drugs in the pharmaceutical industry' *Law Quarterly Review* 101: 405.

Newdick, C. (2005) *Who Should we Treat?* (Oxford University Press).

Newdick, C. (2007) 'Judicial review: Low-priority treatment and exceptional case review' *Medical Law Review* 15: 236.

Newson, A. and Smajdor, A. (2005) 'Artificial gametes: new paths to parenthood?' *Journal of Medical Ethics* 31: 184.

Ngwana, C. and Chadwick, R. (1993) 'Genetic diagnostic information and the duty of confidentiality: ethics and the law' *Medical Law International* 73.

NHS (1997) *The New NHS* (DoH).

NHS (2001) *NHS Cancer Care in England and Wales* (DoH).

NHS (2005a) *About the NHS* (DoH).

NHS (2005b) *Prescriptions Dispensed In The Community* (NHS).

NHS (2007a) *NHS Contraceptive Services 2006–7* (NHS).

NHS (2007b) *NHS Core Principles* (NHS).

NHS (2007c) *How the NHS Works* (NHS).

NHS Confederation (2005) *Improving End of Life Care* (NHS).

NHS Conferation (2007) *In Sickness and in Health* (NHS).

NHS Executive (1996) *NHS Indemnity* (NHS).

NHS Information Authority (2002) *Share with Care!* (NHSIA).

NHS Institute (2005) *Prospectus* (NHS Institute).

NHS Litigation Authority (2007) Annual Report (NHSLA).

NHS Management Executive (1991) *Assessing Healthcare Needs* (NHSME).

NHS Networks (2007) *Organ donation* (NHS).

NHS Ombudsman (2005) *Making Things Better?* (TSO).

NICE (1999) *Framework Document* (NICE).

NICE (2000) *Response to Letter in BMJ* (NICE).

NICE (2002a) *NICE responds to criticisms over guidance on colorectal cancer drugs* (NICE).

NICE (2002b) *Memorandum of Evidence to the Health Committee* (NICE).

NICE (2004a) *Improving supportive and palliative care for adults with cancer* (NICE).

NICE (2004b) *Guide to the Methods of Technology Appraisal* (NICE).

NICE (2004c) *Caesarean Sections* (NICE).

NICE (2005a) *Social Value Judgments— Principles for the Development of NICE Guidance* (NICE).

NICE (2005b) *Long-Acting Reversible Contraception* (NICE).

Nicholson, M. and Bradley, J. (1999) 'Renal transplantation from living donors' *British Medical Journal* 318: 409.

Nietzsche, F. (1968) *Twilight of the Idols and the Antichrist* (Penguin).

Nobbs, C. (2007) 'Probability potentiality' *Cambridge Quarterly of Healthcare Ethics* 16: 240.

Noonan, J. (1970) 'An almost absolute value in history' in J. Noonan (ed) *The Morality of Abortion* (Harvard University Press).

Noonan, J. (1991) 'How to argue about abortion' in J. Sterba (ed) *Morality in Practice* (Wadsworth).

Nord, E. (1999) *Cost-Value Analysis in Healthcare* (Cambridge University Press).

North, R. and Rothenberg, K. (1994) 'Partner notification and the threat of domestic violence against women with HIV infection' *New England Journal of Medicine* 329: 1194.

North, K. and Golding, J. (2000) 'A maternal vegetarian diet in pregnancy is associated with hypospadias' *British Journal of Urology International* 85: 107.

Norrie, K. (1991) *Family Planning Practice and the Law* (Dartmouth).

Norrie, K. (2000) 'Protecting the unborn child from its drug or alcohol abusing mother' in M. Freeman and A. Lewis, *Law and Medicine* (Oxford University Press).

Nuffield Council (2004) *Nuffield Council expresses concerns about Human Tissue Bill* (Nuffield Council).

Nuffield Council on Bioethics (1993) *Genetic Screening: Ethical Issues* (Nuffield Council).

Nuffield Council on Bioethics (1995) *Human Tissue: Ethical and Legal Issues* (Nuffield Council).

Nuffield Council on Bioethics (1996) *Animal to Human Transplants* (Nuffield Council).

Nuffield Council on Bioethics (2002) *The Ethics of Patenting DNA* (Nuffield Council).

Nuffield Council on Bioethics (2007) *Critical Care Decisions in Fetal and Neonatal Medicine: Ethical Issues* (Nuffield Council on Bioethics).

Nuland, S. (1993) *How We Die: Reflections on Life's Final Chapter* (Vintage).

Nursing and Midwifery Council (2002) *Code of Professional Conduct* (NMC).

Nursing Times (2003) 'Nurses divided over assisted suicide' *Nursing Times* 5 February 2003.

Nussbaum, M. (1988) 'Non-relative virtues: an Aristotelian approach' in P. French, T. Uehling, and H. Wettstein (eds) *Ethical Theory, Character, and Virtue* (University of Notre Dame Press).

Nyboe Andersen, A., Gianaroli, L. and Nygren, K. (2004) 'Assisted reproductive technology in Europe' *Human Reproduction* 19: 490.

Nys, T. (1996) 'Desirable characteristics of living donation transplant legislation' in D. Price and H. Akveld (eds) *Living Organ Donation in the Nineties* (EUROTOL).

Oakley, A. (1980) *Women Confined* (Oxford University Press).

Oehmichen, M. and Meissner, C. (2003) 'Active euthanasia and physician assisted suicide: the german discussion' *Legal Medicine* 5: 20.

Oregon Department of Administrative Services (1999) *Assessment of the Oregon Health Plan Medicaid Demonstration* (Office for Oregon Health Plan Policy and Research).

Oregon Health Services Commission (2007) *Prioritization of Health Services* (Oregon Health Services Commission).

OCPS (2004) Registrar General's Supplement on Abortion 1973 (London HMSO).

O'Brien, J. (2003) The COPE report 2003: *A view from the GMC* (GMC).

O'Brien, J. and Chantler, C. (2003) 'Confidentiality and the duty of care' *Journal of Medical Ethics* 23: 36.

O'Donovan, K. (1989) 'What shall we tell the children?' in R. Lee and D. Morgan (eds) *Birthrights: Law and Ethics at the Beginnings of Life* (Routledge).

O'Donovan, K. (2006) 'Taking a neutral stance on the legal protection of the fetus' *Medical Law Review* 14: 155.

Office of the Deputy Prime Minister (2004) *Action on Mental Health* (TSO).

Office of National Statistics (1998) *Living in Britain* (TSO).

Office of National Statistics (1997) *Abortion Statistics* (TSO).

Office of National Statistics (2003) *Conceptions in England and Wales 2001* (TSO).

Office of National Statistics (2004) *Living in Britain* (TSO).

Office of National Statistics (2005) *Mental health of children and young people in Great Britain* (Palgrave).

Office of National Statistics (2007) *Contraception and Sexual Health 2006/07* (TSO).

O'Grady, K-A. and Nolan, T. (2004) 'Privacy: bad for your health' *Medical Journal of Australia* 180: 307.

Okin, S. (1998) 'Feminism, moral development, and the virtues' in R. Crisp (ed) *How Should One Live?* (Oxford University Press).

Okino Sawada, N., Mendes, I., Correia, F., and Coleta, J. (1996) 'Personal and territorial space of the patients' *Medicine and Law* 15: 261.

Oliphant, K. (2007) 'Beyond misadventure: Compensation for medical injuries in New Zealand' *Medical Law Review* 15: 357.

O'Neill, O. (1979) 'Begetting, bearing, and rearing' in O. O'Neill and W. Ruddick (eds) *Having Children* (Oxford University Press).

O'Neill, O. (1984) 'Paternalism and partial autonomy' *Journal of Medical Ethics* 10: 177.

O'Neill, O. (2002) *Autonomy and Trust in Bioethics* (Cambridge University Press).

O'Neill, O. (2003) 'Some limits of informed consent' *Journal of Medical Ethics* 29: 4.

Onwuteaka-Philipsen, B., van der Heide, A., Koper, D., Keij-Deerenberg, I., Rietjens, I., Rurup, M., Vrakking, A., Georges, J., Muller, M., Van der Wal, G., and van der Maas, P. (2003) 'Euthanasia and other end of life decisions in the Netherlands 1990, 1995 and 2001' *The Lancet* 17 June 2003: 1.

Onwuteaka-Philipsen, B., van der Heide, A., Muller, M., Rurup, M., Rietjens, C., Georges, J., Vrakking, A., Cuperus-Bosma, J., van der Wal, G., and van der Maas, P. (2005) 'Dutch experience of monitoring euthanasia' *British Medical Journal* 331: 24.

Opinion Research Business (2003) *Survey on Euthanasia and Assisted Suicide* (ORB).

Oregon Health Services Commission (2007) *Prioritization of Health Services* (Oregon Health Services Commission).

Organisation for Economic Co-Operation and Development (1987) *Financing and Delivering Health Care* Paris (OECD).

Ormerod, D. (2005) *Criminal Law* (Oxford University Press).

O'Reilly, J. (1990) 'More gold and more fleece: improving the legal sanctions against medical research fraud' *Administrative Law Review* 42: 393.

Orentlicher, D. (2000) 'Beyond cloning: expanding reproductive options for same sex couples' *Brooklyn Law Review* 66: 3.

O'Rourke, N., Barrett, A., Jones, R., Featherstone, C., Hughes, V. (2001) 'Patients rarely regret optimism' *British Medical Journal* 322: 1062.

Orr, R. and Siegler, M. (2002) 'Is posthumous semen retrieval ethically permissible?' *Journal of Medical Ethics* 28: 299.

Oshana, M. (1998) 'Personal autonomy and society' *Journal of Social Philosophy* 29: 81.

Ost, S. (2004) *An Analytical Study of the Legal, Moral, and Ethical Aspects of the Living Phenomenon of Euthanasia* (Edwin Mellen Press).

O'Sullivan, D. (1998) 'The allocation of scarce resources and the right to life under the European convention on human rights' *Public Law* 389.

Otlowski, M. (1997) *Voluntary Euthanasia and the Common Law* (Oxford University Press).

Otlowski, M. (2002) 'Review of H. Biggs, euthanasia: death with dignity and the law' *Medical Law Review* 238.

Øverland, G. (2007) 'Survival lotteries reconsidered' *Bioethics* 21: 355.

Oxford Economics (2007) *Mental Health and the UK Economy* (Oxford Economics).

Pacheco, J., Hershberger, P., Markert, R., Kumar, G. (2003) 'A longitudinal study of attitudes toward physician-assisted suicide and euthanasia among patients with non-curable malignancy' *American Journal of Hospice and Palliative Care* 99.

Padela, A. (2007) 'Islamic medical ethics: a primer' *Bioethics* 21: 169.

Pallis, C. (1990) 'Return to Elsinore' *Journal of Medical Ethics* 16: 10.

Pallis, C. and Harley, D. (1996) *ABC of Brain Stem Death* (BMJ).

Palmboom, G., Willems, D., Janssen, N., and de Haes, J. (2007) 'Doctor's views on disclosing or withholding information on low risks of complication' *Journal of Medical Ethics* 33: 67.

Palmer, H. (1957) 'Dr Adams' Trial for Murder' *Criminal Law Review* 365.

Palmer, E. (2000) 'Resource Allocation Welfare Rights' *Oxford Journal of Legal Studies* 20: 63.

Palmer, K. (2006) *NHS Reform. Getting Back on Track* (King's Fund).

Pappworth, M. (1967) *Human guinea pigs: experimentation on man* (Routledge).

Parens, E. (1998) *Enhancing Human Traits* (Georgetown University Press).

Parens, E. and Asch, A. (2003) 'The disability rights critique of prenatal genetic testing' in E. Parens and A. Asch (eds) *Prenatal Testing and Disability Rights* (Georgetown University Press).

Parfit, D. (1984) *Reasons and Persons* (Oxford University Press).

Paris, J. and Moreland, M. (1998) 'A Catholic perspective on physician-assisted suicide' in M. Battin, R. Rhodes, and A. Silvers *Physician Assisted Suicide* (Routledge).

Park, A. (2007) British Attitudes Survey (National Centre for Social Research).

Parker, M. (2002) 'A deliberative approach to bioethics' in K. Fulford, D. Dickenson, and T. Murray (eds) *Healthcare Ethics and Human Values* (Blackwell).

Parker, M. (2004) 'Response to Orr and Siegler—collective intentionality and procreative desires: the permissible view on consent to posthumous conception' *Journal of Medical Ethics* 30: 389.

Parker, M. (2007) 'The best possible child' *Journal of Medical Ethics* 33: 279.

Parliamentary and National Health Services Ombudsman (2005) *NHS funding for the long-term care of elderly and disabled people* (TSO).

Parliamentary and Health Services Ombudsman (2007) *Putting Principles into Practice* (TSO).

Parliamentary Office of Science and Technology (2004) *Organ Transplants* (POST).

Parnes, E. (2000) *Enhancing Human Traits* (Georgetown University Press).

Parry, B., Zimmern, R., Hall, A., and Liddell, K. (2004) *A Critique of the Human Tissue Bill* (King's College, London).

Partridge, E. (1981) 'Posthumous interests and posthumous Respect' *Ethics* 91: 43.

Patient Advisory Group (2007) *Annual Report* (Patient Advisory Group).

Pattenden, R. (2003) *The Law on Professional Client Confidentiality* (Oxford University Press).

Paterson, I. (2001) 'Consent to cancer registration—an unnecessary burden' *British Medical Journal* 322: 1130.

Pattinson, S. (2002a) 'Undue influence in the context of medical treatment' *Medical Law International* 5: 305.

Pattinson, S. (2002b) *Influencing Traits Before Birth* (Dartmouth).

Pattinson, S. (2003) 'Paying living organ providers' *Web Journal of Current Legal Issues.*

Pattinson, S. (2006) *Medical Law and Ethics* (Sweet and Maxwell).

Pearlman, R., Cain, K., Patrick, D., AppelbaucMaizel Starks, H., Jecker, N. and Uhlmann, R. (1993) 'Insights pertaining to patient assessments of states worse than death' *Journal of Clinical Ethics* 4: 33.

Peart, N., Campbell, A., Manara, A. (2000) 'Maintaining a pregnancy following loss of capacity' *Medical Law Review* 8: 275.

Pearson, V., Owen, M., Phillips, D., Pereira Gray, D., and Marshall, M. (1995) 'Pregnant teenagers' knowledge and use of emergency contraception' *British Medical Journal* 310: 1644.

Peay, J. (2003) *Decisions and Dilemmas* (Hart).

Pedain, A. (2003) 'The human rights dimension of the Diane Pretty Case' *Cambridge Law Journal* 181.

Pedain, A. (2005) 'Doctors, parents and the courts: Legitimising restrictions on the continued provision of life-span-maximising treatments for severely handicapped nondying babies' *Child and Family Law Quarterly* 335.

Peel, E. (2005) 'Loss of a chance in medical negligence' *Law Quarterly Review* 121: 364.

Peery, T. and Miller, F. (1971) *Pathology* (Little Brown).

Pelligrino, E. and Thomasma, D. (1988) *For the Patient's Own Good* (Oxford University Press).

Pellegino, E. (1995) 'Towards a virtue-based normative ethics for the health professions' *Kennedy Institute of Ethics Journal* 5: 253.

Pence, G. (2002) *Brave New Bioethics* (Rowman and Littlefield).

Pennings, G. (2002) 'Reproductive tourism as moral pluralism in motion EU faces fertility tourism threat' *Journal of Medical Ethics* 28: 337.

Pennings, G. (2007) 'Directed organ donation: Discrimination or autonomy?' *Journal of Applied Philosophy* 24: 41.

Perry, M. (2001) 'Religion, politics, and abortion' *University of Detroit Mercy Law Review* 79: 1.

Petchesky, R. (1979) 'Reproductive freedom: beyond "a woman's right to choose,"' *Journal of Women in Culture and Society* 5: 661.

Petcheksy, R. (1984) *Abortion and Woman's Choice* (Longman).

Peterson, K. (1996) 'Private decisions and public scrutiny' in S. McLean (ed) *Contemporary Issues in Law, Medicine and Ethics* (Dartmouth).

Petersen, T. (2005a) 'Just diagnosis? Preimplantation genetic diagnosis and injustices to disabled people' *Journal of Medical Ethics* 31: 231.

Peterson, M. (2005b) 'Assisted reproductive technologies and equity of access issues' *Journal of Medical Ethics* 31: 280.

Peynser, J. (1995) 'Health care litigation; examination, diagnosis and prognosis' *Journal of Personal Injury Litigation* 91.

Phillips, M. (2002) 'Sex and social suicide' *Daily Mail* 14 December 2002.

Phillipson, G. (2003) 'Transforming breach of confidence? Towards a common law right of privacy under the Human Rights Act' *Modern Law Review* 66: 726.

Pickworth, E. (2000) 'Should local research ethics committees monitor research they have approved?' *Journal of Medical Ethics* 26: 330.

Pijnenborg, L., van der Maas, P., van Delden, J., and Looman, C. (1993) 'Life-terminating acts without explicit request of patient' *The Lancet* 314: 1196.

Pinfold, V. and Bindman, J. (2001) 'Is compulsory community treatment ever justified?' *Psychiatric Bulletin* 25: 268.

Pleschberger, S. (2007) 'Dignity and the challenge of dying in nursing homes: the residents' view' *Age and Ageing* 36: 197.

Plummer A. (1998) 'Judicially enforced Caesareans and the sanctity of life' *Anglo American Law Review* 27: 235.

Plomer, A. (2001) 'Medical research, consent and the European Convention on Human Rights and Biomedicine' in A. Garwood Gowers, J. Tingle, and A. Lewis *Healthcare Law: The Impact of the Human Rights Act 1998* (Cavendish).

Plomer, A. (2005) *The Law and Ethics of Medical Research* (Cavendish).

Polkinghorne, J. (1989) *Review of the Guidance on the Research Use of Fetuses and Fetal Material* (HMSO).

Polkinghorne, J. (2004) 'The person, the soul, and genetic engineering' *Journal of Medical Ethics* 30: 593.

Pollock, S. (1985) 'Sex and the contraceptive act' in H. Homans (ed) *The Sexual Politics of Reproduction* (Gower Press).

Pollock, K. and Grime, J. (2002) 'Patients' perceptions of entitlement to time in general practice consultations for depression: qualitative study' *British Medical Journal* 325: 687.

Pontifical Academy for Life (2000) *The Dignity of the Dying Person* (Vatican).

Pope Paul VI (1968) *Of Human Life. Encyclical Letter of His Holiness on the Regulation of Birth* (Vatican).

Pope Paul VI (1977) *Respect for Life in the Women* (Vatican).

Porat, A. and Stein, A. (2001) *Tort Liability Under Uncertainty* (Oxford University Press).

Porter, R. (1997) *The Cambridge History of Medicine* (Cambridge University Press).

POST (2005) *Omnibus Survey* (POST).

Prader-Willi Syndrome Association (2005) *Press Release* (PWSA).

Prado, C. (1998) 'Effects of gender differences on physician-assisted suicide: practice and regulation' *Southern California Review of Law and Women's Studies* 101.

Prainsack, B. and Spector, T. (2006) 'Twins: a cloning experience' *Social Science & Medicine* 63: 2739.

President's Commission for the Study of Ethical Problems in Medical and Biomedical and Behavioral Research Report (1983) *Deciding to Forgo Life-Sustaining Treatment* (Washington).

President's Council on Bioethics (2002) *Human Cloning and Human Dignity* (Washington).

Priaulx, N. (2004) 'Joy to the world! A (healthy) child is born! Reconceptualizing "harm" in wrongful conception' *Social and Legal Studies* 13: 5.

Priaulx, N. (2007a) *The Harm Paradox: Tort Law and the Unwanted Child in an Era of Choice* (Routledge).

Priaulx, N. (2007b) 'Beyond health and disability' in K. Horsey and H. Biggs (eds) *Human Fertilization and Embryology: Reproducing Regulation* (Routledge).

Price, D. (1988) 'Selective reduction and feticide: the parameters of abortion' *Criminal Law Review* 199.

Price, D. (1996) 'Assisted suicide and refusing medical treatment: linguistic, morals and legal contortions' *Medical Law Review* 4: 270.

Price, F. (1993) 'Beyond expectation: clinical practices and clinical concerns. Solutions for life and growth?' in J. Edwards, S. Franklin, R. Hirsch, F. Price, and M. Strathern (eds) *Technologies of Procreation* (Routledge).

Price, D. (1996) 'Lessons for health care rationing from the case of child B' *British Medical Journal* 312: 167.

Price, D. (1997a) 'Organ transplant initiatives: The twilight zone' *Journal of Medical Ethics* 23: 170.

Price D. (1997b) 'Euthanasia, Pain Relief and Double Effect' *Legal Studies* 17: 323.

Price, D. (2000a) *Legal and Ethical Aspects of Organ Transplantation* (Cambridge University Press).

Price, D. (2000b) 'Choices without reasons: citizens' juries and policy evaluation' *Journal of Medical Ethics* 26: 272.

Price, D. (2003) 'From Cosmos and Damian to Van Velzen: The Human Tissue Saga Continues' *Medical Law Review* 1.

Price, D. (2005a) 'The Human Tissue Act 2004' *Modern Law Review* 68: 798.

Price, D. (2005b) 'Remodelling the regulation of postmodern innovation in medicine' *International Journal of Law in Context* 1: 121.

Price, D. (2007) 'Property, harm and the corpse' in B. Brooks-Gordan, F. Ebtehaj, J. Herring, M. Johnson, and M. Richards (eds) *Death Rights and Rites* (Hart).

Pierce, P. (1993) 'Deciding on breast cancer treatment' *Nursing Research* 42: 20.

Probert, R. (2004) 'Families, assisted reproduction and the law' *Child and Family Law Quarterly* 274.

Pullen, I. (1990) 'Patients, families and Genetic Information' in E. Sutherland and A. McCall Smith (eds) *Family Rights: Family Law and Medical Advance* (Edinburgh: Edinburgh University Press).

Pullman, D. (2002) 'Conflicting interests, social justice and proxy consent to research' *Journal of Medical Philosophy* 27: 523.

Purdy, L. (1989) 'Surrogate mothering: exploitation or empowerment' *Bioethics* 3: 18.

Purdy, L. (1990) 'Are pregnant women fetal containers?' *Bioethics* 4: 273.

Purdy, L. (1996) 'A feminist view of health' in S. Wolf *Feminism and Bioethics* (Oxford University Press).

Purdy, (1999) 'Genetics and reproductive risk: can having children be immoral?' in H. Khuse and P. Singer (eds) *Bioethics* (Blackwell).

Purdy, L. (2006) 'Women's reproductive autonomy: medicalisation and beyond' *Journal of Medical Ethics* 32: 287.

Project for Advice, Counselling and Education (PACE) (1998) *Diagnosis: homophobic—the experiences of lesbians, gay men and bisexuals in mental health services* (PACE).

Pro-Life Alliance (2007) *Pro-Life Alliance welcomes result of Public Opinion Poll on Abortion* (Pro-Life Alliance).

Quah, S. (2001) 'Health and Culture' in W. Cockerham (ed) *The Blackwell Companion to Medical Sociology* (Blackwell).

Quick, O. (2006a) 'Outing medical errors: Questions of trust and responsibility' *Medical Law Review* 14: 22.

Quick, O. (2006b) 'Prosecuting "Gross" medical negligence: manslaughter, discretion and the crown prosecution service' *Journal of Law and Society* 33: 421.

Quigley, M. (2007a) 'Property and the body: Applying Honore' *Journal of Medical Ethics* 33: 631.

Quigley, M. (2007b) 'A NICE fallacy' *Journal of Medical Ethics* 3: 465.

Quill, T. (1993) 'The ambiguity of clinical intentions' *New England Journal of Medicine* 329: 1039.

Quinn, W. (1984) 'Abortion identity and loss' *Philosophy and Public Affairs* 13: 24.

Quante, M. (1999) 'Autonomy and personal identity' *Kennedy Institute of Ethics Journal* 9: 365.

Rachels, J. (1975) 'Active and passive euthanasia' *New England Journal of Medicine* 78.

Rachels, J. (1986) *The End of Life* (Oxford University Press).

Rachels, J. (1999) *The Elements Of Moral Philosophy* (McGraw-Hill).

Radcliffe-Richards, J., Daar, A., Guttmann, R., Hoffenberg, R., Kennedy, I., Lock, M., Sells, R., and Tilney, N. (1998) 'The case for allowing kidney sales' *The Lancet* 351: 1950.

Radick, G. (2001) 'Discovering and patenting human genes' in A. Bainham, S. Day Sclater, M. Richards *Body Lore and Laws* (Hart).

Rae, W., Sullivan, J., Razo, N., George, C., and Ramirex, J. (2002) 'Adolescent health risk behaviour' *Journal of Pediatric Psychology* 27: 549.

Raftery, J. (2001) 'NICE: faster access to modern treatments? Analysis of guidance on health technologies' *British Medical Journal* 323: 1300.

Rai, A. (1997) 'Rationing through choice: a new approach to cost-effectiveness analysis in health care' *Indiana Law Journal* 72: 1015.

Ramrakha, S., Caspi, A., Dickon, N., Moffitt, T., and Paul, C. (2000) 'Psychiatric disorders and risky sexual behaviour in young adulthood' *British Medical Journal* 321: 263.

Ramsey, P. (1970) *The Patient as a Person* (Yale University Press).

Ramsay, P. (1978) *Ethics at the Edges of Life* (Yale University Press).

Randall, F. and Downie, R.(2006) *The Philosophy of Palliative Care* (Oxford University Press).

Rankin, J. (2004) *Developments and Trends in Mental Health Policy* (IPPR).

Rao, R. (2000) 'Property, privacy and the human body' *Boston University Law Review* 80: 359.

Rao, R. (2002) 'Conceiving a code for creation: the legal debate surrounding human cloning: what's so strange about human cloning?' *Hastings Law Journal* 53: 1007.

Raphael-Leff, J. (2002) 'The "kinder egg": some intrapsychic, interpersonal and ethical implications of infertility treatment and gamete' in K. Fulford, D. Dickenson, and T. Murray (eds) *Healthcare Ethics and Human Values* (Blackwell).

Ravelingien, A., Mortier, F., Mortier, E., Kerremans, I., and Braeckman, J. (2004) 'Proceeding with clinical trials of animal to human organ transplantation: a way out of the dilemma' *Journal of Medical Ethics* 30: 92.

Rawlins, M. (2004) 'National Institute for Clinical Excellence and its value judgments' *British Medical Journal* 329: 224.

Rawlinson Commission, The (1994) *The Physical and Psycho-Social Effects of Abortion on Women* (HMSO).

Raymond, J. (1993) *Women as Wombs* (Harper Collins).

Raymond, D. (1999) 'Fatal practices: a feminist analysis of physician assisted suicide and euthanasia' *Hypatia* 14: 1.

Raymont, V., Bingley, W., Cuchanan A., David, A., Hayward, P., Wessley, S., and Hotopf, M. (2004) 'Prevalence of mental incapacity in medical inpatients and associated risk factors: Cross sectional study' 364 *The Lancet* 1421.

Read, J., Mosher, L., and Bentall, R. (2004) *Models of Madness* (Blackwells).

Reed, J. (2002) 'Delivering psychiatric care to prisoners' *Advanced Psychiatric Treatment* 8: 117.

Rees Jones, I. (2003) 'Health promotion and the new public health' in G. Scambler (ed) *Sociology As Applied to Medicine* (Saunders).

Regan, D. (1979) 'Rewriting Roe v. Wade,' *Michigan Law Review* 77.

Reiman, J. (2007) 'The pro-life argument from substantial identity and the pro-choice argument from asymmetric value: a reply to Patrick Lee' *Bioethics* 21: 329.

Research Works Ltd (2004) *Patient Access to Health Records London: Health Records and Data Protection Review Group* (DOH).

Resnik, D. (2004) 'The precautionary principle and medical decision making' *Journal of Medicine and Philosophy* 29: 281.

Resnik, D. (2005) 'Eliminating the daily life risks standard from the definition of minimal risk' *Journal of Medical Ethics* 31: 35.

Resnicoff, S. (1999) 'Jewish law perspectives on suicide and physician-assisted dying' *Journal of Law and Religion* 289.

Resuscitation Council (2001) *Decisions Relating to Cardiopulmonary Resuscitation* (Resuscitation Council).

Retained Organs Commission (2005) *Response to Department of Health Consultation Report—Human Bodies, Human Choices* (DoH).

Rethink (2003) *Just One Percent?* (Rethink).

Rethink (2005) *The Draft Mental Health Bill 2004* (Rethink).

Rhoden, N. (1987) 'Caesareans and Samaritans' *Law Medicine and Health Care* 15: 118.

Rhodes, R. Battin, M. and Silvers, A. (2005) *Medicine and Social Justice* (Oxford University Press).

Rich, B. (1993) 'Postmodern medicine: deconstructing the Hippocratic Oath' *University of Colorado Law Review* 65: 77.

Rich, B. (1998) 'Personhood, patienthood, and clinical practice: reassessing advance directives' *Psychology, Public Policy, and Law* 610.

Richards, M. (1999) 'Future bodies: human genetic selection' in H. Kuhse and P. Singer (eds) *Bioethics* (Blackwell).

Richardson, A. and Mmata, C. (2007) *NHS Maternity Statistics, England: 2005–06* (Information Centre).

Richardson, G. (1999) *Richardson Committee: Review of the Mental Health Act 1983* (DoH).

Richardson, G. (2002) 'Autonomy, guardianship and mental disorder' One problem, two solutions *Modern Law Review* 65: 702.

Richardson, G. (2005) 'The European convention on mental health law in England

and Wales: Moving beyond process?' *International Journal of Law and Psychiatry* 28: 127.

Richardson, K. (1998) 'Religious, philosophical, and ethical perspectives on cloning: human reproduction by cloning in theological perspective' (1998) 32 *Valapraiso University Law Review* 32: 739.

Ridley, S. (2000) 'Sudden death from suicide' in D. Dickenson (ed) *Death Dying and Bereavement* (Sage).

Riley, L. (2007) 'Equality of access to NHS-funded IVF treatment in England and Wales' in K. Horsey and H. Biggs (eds) *Human Fertilization and Embryology: Reproducing Regulation* (Routledge).

Rix, B. (1990) 'Danish Ethics Council Rejects Brain Death as the Criterion of Death' *Journal of Medical Ethics* 16: 5.

Roberts, D. (1996) 'Reconstructing the patient: starting with women of color' in S. Wolf (1996) *Feminism and Bioethics* (Oxford University Press).

Roberts, M. (2000) 'Children by donation: Do they have a claim to their genetic parentage?' in J. Bridgeman and D. Monk (2000) *Feminist Perspectives on Child Law* (Cavendish).

Roberts, S. (1986) 'Warnock and surrogate motherhood: sentiment or argument' in P. Byrne (ed) *Rights and Wrongs in Medicine* (Oxford University Press).

Robertson, G. (1981) 'Informed consent to medical treatment' *Law Quarterly Review* 97: 102.

Robertson, J. (1983) 'Procreative liberty and the control of conception, pregnancy and childbirth' *Virginia Law Review* 69: 405.

Robertson, J. (1986) 'Embryos, families, and procreative liberty: the legal structure of the new reproduction' *Southern California Law Review* 59: 939.

Robertson, J. (1988) 'Fetal tissue transplants' *Washington University Law Quarterly* 66: 443.

Robertson, J. (1990) 'The ethical acceptability of fetal tissue transplants' *Transplant Proceedings* 22: 1025.

Robertson, J. (1991) 'Second thought on living wills' *Hastings Center Report* 21: 6.

Robertson, J. (1994a) 'Posthumous reproduction' *Indiana Law Journal* 69: 1027.

Robertson, J. (1994b) *Children of Choice* (Princeton University Press).

Robertson, J. (1997) 'Respect for life in bioethical dilemmas—the case of physicianassisted suicide' *Cleveland State Law Review* 329.

Robertson J (2003) 'Extending preimplantation genetic diagnosis: the ethical debate. Ethical issues in new uses of preimplantation genetic diagnosis' *Human Reproduction* 18: 456.

Robling, M., Hood, K., Houston, H., Pill, R., Fay, J., and Evans, H. (2004) 'Public attitudes towards the use of primary care patient record data in medical research without consent: a qualitative study' *Journal of Medical Ethics* 30: 104.

Robinson, R. (2003) 'ECT and the Human Rights Act' *Journal of Mental Health Law* 66.

Rodwin, M. (2001) 'The politics of evidence based medicine' *Journal of Health Politics, Policy and Law* 26: 439–446.

Roff, S. (2007) 'Self-interest, self-abnegation and self-esteem: towards a new moral economy of non-directed kidney donation' *Journal of Medical Ethics* 33: 437.

Rogers, A. and Draper H. (2003) 'Confidentiality and the ethics of medical ethics' *BMJ* 29: 220.

Rogers, A. and Pilgrim, D. (2001) *Mental Health Policy in Britain: A Critical Introduction* (Palgrave).

Rogers, W. (2006) 'Feminism and public health ethics' *Journal of Medical Ethics* 32: 351.

Rogers, W., Ballantyne, A., and Draper, H. (2007) 'Is sex-selective abortion morally justified and should it be prohibited?' *Bioethics* 9: 520.

Ronson, J. (2002) 'Blood sacrifice' *The Guardian* 6 April 2002.

Rosato, J. (2004) 'The children of art (assisted reproductive technology): should the law protect them from harm?' *Utah Law Review* 57.

Rose, A. (1999) 'Reproductive misconception: why cloning is not just another assisted reproductive technology' *Duke Law Journal* 48: 1133.

Ross, A. (1986) 'The case against showing patients their records' *British Medical Journal* 310: 578.

Ross, L (1993) 'Moral grounding for the participation of children as organ donors' *Journal of Law and Medical Ethics* 21: 251.

Rothstein, M. (1998) 'Genetic privacy and confidentiality: why they are so hard to protect' *Journal of Law, Medicine and Ethics* 26: 198.

Rout, G. (1992) 'Elective ventilation for Organ donation—the case against' 8 *Care of the Critically Ill* 60.

Rowlands, S. and Hannaford, P. (2003) 'The incidence of sterilisation in the UK' *British Journal of Obstetrics and Gynaecology* 110: 819.

Royal College of General Practitioners (2000) *Confidentiality 2000* (GMC).

Royal College of Nursing (1986) *Practical Aspects of Confidentiality Relating to the Health of Employees* (RCN).

Royal College of Obstetricians and Gynaecologists (RCOG) (1996) *Termination of Pregnancy for Fetal Abnormality* (RCOG).

Royal College of Obstetricians and Gynaecologists (RCOG) (1998) *A Consideration of the Law and Ethics in Relation to Late Termination for Fetal Abnormality* (RCOG).

Royal College of Obstetricians and Gynaecologists (RCOG) (1999) *Male and Female Sterilisation* (RCOG).

Royal College of Obstetricians and Gynecologists (RCOG) (2001a) *Further Issues Relating to Late Abortion, Fetal Viability and Registration of Births and Deaths* (RCOG).

Royal College of Obstetricians and Gynecologists (RCOG) (2001b) *The Care of Women Requesting Induced Abortion* (RCOG).

Royal College of Obstetricians and Gynecologists (RCOG) (2001c) *National Audit of Induced Abortion* (RCOG).

Royal College of Paediatrics and Child Health (1992) *Guidelines For The Ethical Conduct of Medical Research Involving Children* (RCPCH).

Royal College of Paediatrics and Child Health (1997) *Withholding or Withdrawing Life Saving Treatment in Children* (RCPCH).

Royal College of Physicians (2007) *Guidelines on the practice of ethics committees in medical research with human participants* (RCP).

Royal College of Psychiatrists (2006) *Assisted Dying for the Terminally Ill Bill—Statement from the Royal College of Psychiatrists on Physician Assisted Suicide* (RCP).

Royal College of Surgeons (2002) *Good Surgical Practice* (RCS).

Rubinstein, H. (1999) 'If I am only for myself, what am I? A communitarian look at the privacy stalemate' *American Journal of Law and Medicine* 25: 203.

Runciman, B., Merry, A., and McCall Smith, A. (2001) 'Improving patients' safety by gathering information' *British Medical Journal* 323: 298.

Russell, J. (2003) 'Confidentiality of patients' information must be guaranteed' *British Medical Journal* 327: 812.

Russell, M., Moralego, D., and Burgess, E. (2000) 'Paying research subjects: participants' perspectives' *Journal of Medical Ethics* 26: 126.

Ryan, C. (2000) 'Betting your life' in D. Dickenson et al (eds) *Death Dying and Bereavement* (Sage).

Sacred Congregation for the Doctrine of The Faith (1980) *Declaration on Euthanasia* (The Vatican).

Salek, S. (2005) 'Health economics and access to treatment' in J. Gunning and S. Holm *Ethics, Law and Society* (Ashgate).

Sainsbury Centre for Mental Health (1998) *Acute problems* (Sainsbury Centre for Mental Health).

Sainsbury Centre for Mental Health (2005) *Back on Track?* (Sainsbury Centre for Mental Health).

Sainsbury Centre for Mental Health (2006) *Under Pressure: The Finances of Mental Health Trusts in 2006* (The Sainsbury Centre for Mental Health).

Sainsbury Centre for Mental Health (2007) *Mental Health in Prisons* (The Sainsbury Centre for Mental Health).

Samanta, A., Mello, M., Foster, C., Tingle, J., and Samanta, J. (2006) 'The role of clinical guidelines in medical negligence litigation: a shift from the Bolam standard?' *Medical Law Review* 14: 321.

Sander, W. (1993) 'Catholicism and marriage in the United States' *Demography* 30: 373.

Sandland, R. (2007) 'Freedom of the press and the confidentiality of medical records' *Medical Law Review* 15: 400.

Sanger, A. (2004) *Beyond Choice* (Public Affairs).

Sankar, P., Moran, S., Merz, J., and Jones, N. (2003) 'Patient Perspectives on Medical Confidentiality' *Journal of General Internal Medicine* 18: 659.

Sapiro, J. and Ungoed-Thomas, A. (1998) 'Euthanasia and the Human Rights Act 1998' in A. Garwood-Gorwers, J. Tingle, and T. Lewis (eds) *Healthcare Law: The Impact of the Human Rights Act 1998* (Cavendish).

Sapiro, J. and Ungoed-Thomas, A. (2001) 'Euthanasia and the Human Rights Act' in J. Tingle, J. Griffiths, and A. Garwood-Gowers (eds) *Healthcare: the Impact of the Human Rights Act 1998* (Cavendish).

Satz, A. (2002) 'The case against assisted suicide reexamined' *Michigan Law Review* 1380.

Satz Nugent, J. (2003) '"Walking into the sea" of legal fiction: an examination of the European Court of Human Rights, *Pretty v United Kingdom* and the universal right to die' *Journal of Transnational Law and Policy* 183.

Saunders, C. (2001) 'The evolution of palliative care' *Journal of the Royal Society of Medicine* 94: 430.

Saunders, J. (1994) 'Medical futility: CPR' in R. Lee and D. Morgan (eds) *Death Rites* (Routledge).

Savulescu, J. (1994) 'Rational desires and the limitation of life-sustaining treatment' *Bioethics* 8: 191.

Savulescu, J. (1997) 'Liberal rationalism and medical decision making' *Bioethics* 11: 115.

Savulescu, J. (2001a) 'Is current practice around late termination of pregnancy eugenic and discriminatory? Maternal interests and abortion' *Journal of Medical Ethics* 27: 165.

Savulescu, J. (2001b) 'Resources, Down's syndrome, and cardiac surgery' *British Medical Journal* 322: 875.

Savulescu, J. (2001c) 'Procreative beneficence: Why we should select the best children' *Journal of Medical Ethics* 5: 413.

Savulescu, J. (2002a) 'Two deaths and two lessons: Is it time to review the structure and function of research ethics committees?' *Journal of Medical Ethics* 28: 1.

Savulescu, J. (2002b) 'Abortion, embryo destruction and the future of value argument' *Journal of Medical Ethics* 28: 133.

Savulescu, J. (2003a) 'The public interest in embryos' in J. Gunning and H. Szoke (eds) *The Regulation of Assisted Reproductive Technology* (Ashgate).

Savulescu, J. (2003b) 'Is the sale of body parts wrong?' *Journal of Medical Ethics* 29: 29.

Savulescu, J. (2005) 'Equality, cloning and clonism: why we must clone' *Bionews* 16 May 2005.

Savulescu, J. (2006) 'In defence of procreative beneficence' *Journal of Medical Ethics* 33: 284.

Savulescu, J. and Momeyer, R. (1997) 'Should informed consent be based on rational beliefs?' *Journal of Medical Ethics* 23: 282.

Sayers, G. (2003) 'Psychiatry and the control of dangerousness: a comment' *Journal of Medical Ethics* 29: 235.

Sayers, G. (2007) 'Should research ethics committees be told how to think' *Journal of Medical Ethics* 33: 39.

Sayers, G. and Perera, S. (2002) 'Withholding life prolonging treatment and selfdeception' *Journal of Medical Ethics* 28: 347.

Scambler, G. (2003a) 'Deviance, sick role and stigma' in G. Scambler (ed) *Sociology as Applied to Medicine* (Saunders).

Scambler, G. (2003b) 'Death, dying and bereavement' in G. Scambler (ed) *Sociology as Applied to Medicine* (Saunders).

Scambler, G. (2003c) 'Health and illness behaviour' in G. Scambler (ed) *Sociology as Applied to Medicine* (Saunders).

Scambler, G. (2003d) 'Women and health' in G. Scambler (ed) *Sociology as Applied to Medicine* (Saunders).

Scambler, G. and Blane, D. (2003) 'Inequality and social class' in G. Scambler (ed) *Sociology as Applied to Medicine* (Saunders).

Schildmann, J., Doyal, L., Cushing, A., and Vollmann J. (2006) 'Decisions at the end of life: an empirical study on the involvement, legal understanding and ethical views of pre-registration house officers' *Journal of Medical Ethics* 32: 567.

Schmidt, V. (2004) 'Models of healthcare rationing' *Current Sociology* 52: 962.

Schneider, C. (1998) *The Practice of Autonomy* (Oxford University Press).

Schneider, C. and Farrell, M. (2000) 'Information, decisions, and the limits of informed consent' in A. Lewis and M. Freeman (eds) *Law and Medicine* (Oxford University Press).

Schotsmans, P. (2002) 'Palliative care: a relational approach' in H. ten Have and D. Clarke (eds) *The Ethics of Palliative Care* (Open University Press).

Schramme, T. (2007) 'Should we prevent non-therapeutic mutilation and extreme body modification?' *Bioethics* 9.

Schüklenk, U. (2007) 'Index 2007: names of plagiarists': Is naming and shaming the answer?' *Bioethics* 21: ii.

Schwab, A. (2007) 'Formal and effective autonomy in healthcare' *Journal of Medical Ethics* 32: 575.

Scott, C. (2000) 'Is too much privacy bad for your health?' 17 *Georgia State University Law Review* 481.

Scott, E. (1986) 'Sterilization of mentally retarded persons' *Duke Law Journal* 806.

Scott, R. (2002) *Rights Duties and the Body. Law and Ethics of the Maternal-Fetal Conflict* (Hart).

Scott, R. (2003) 'Prenatal screening, autonomy and reasons: The relationship between the law of abortion and wrongful birth' *Medical Law Review* 11: 265.

Scott, R. (2005) 'Interpreting the disability ground of the Abortion Act' *Cambridge Law Journal* 64: 388.

Scott, R. (2006) 'Choosing between possible lives: Legal and ethical issues in pre-implantation genetic diagnosis' *Oxford Journal of Legal Studies* 26: 153.

Scott, R., Williams, C., Ehrich, K. and Farsides, B. (2007) 'The appropriate extent of pre-implantation genetic diagnosis: health professionals' and scientists' views on the requirement for a 'significant risk of a serious genetic condition' *Medical Law Review* 15: 320.

Scott-Moncrieff, L. (2006) 'Unnoticed incapacity, illusory rights' *Medical Law Review* 14: 238.

Scowen, E. (1990) 'The human body—whose property and whose profit' *Dispatches* 1: 1.

Scroggie, F. (1998) 'Why do parents want their children sterilised?' *Journal of Child Law* 17: 35.

Scully, J. (2004) 'What is a disease' *EMBO Reports* 5: 650.

Seale, C. (1989) 'What happens in hospices: a review of research evidence' *Social Science and Medicine* 28: 551.

Seale, C. (1998) *Constructing Death* (Cambridge University Press).

Seale, C. (2000) 'Changing patterns of death and dying' *Social Science and Medicine* 51: 917.

Seale, C. (2006) 'National survey of end-of-life decisions made by UK medical practitioners' *Palliative Medicine* 20: 1.

Seale, C. and Kelly, M. (1997) 'A comparison of hospice and hospital care for those who die: views of the surviving spouse' *Palliative Medicine* 11: 93.

Seale, C. and Addington-Hall, J. (1994) 'Euthanasia: Why people what to die earlier' *Social Science and Medicine* 39: 647.

Seavillekein, V. and Sherwin, S. (2007) 'The myth of the gendered chromosome' *Cambridge Quarterly of Healthcare Ethics* 16: 7.

Seehouse, D. (1992) 'Does the National Health Service have a purpose?' in A. Grubb (ed) *Challenges in Medical Care* (Wiley).

Sen, A. (2002) 'Health: perception versus observation' *British Medical Journal* 324: 859.

Seymour, J. (2000) *Childbirth and the Law* (Oxford University Press).

Shakespeare, T. (1999) '"Losing the plot" medical and activist discourses of contemporary genetics and disability' *Sociology of Health and Illness* 21: 669.

Shapshay, S. and Pimple, K. (2007) 'Participation in biomedical research is an imperfect moral duty: a response to John Harris' *Journal of Medical Ethics* 33: 414.

Shrage, L. (2003) *Abortion and Social Responsibility* (Oxford University Press).

Shaw, A. (1994) 'In defence of ageism' *Journal of Medical Ethics* 20: 188.

Shaw, A. (2002) 'Two challenges to the double effect doctrine: euthanasia and abortion' *Journal of Medical Ethics* 28: 102.

Shaw, D. (2007) 'The body as unwarranted life support: a new perspective on euthanasia' *Journal of Medical Ethics* 33: 519.

Shaw, J., Amos, T., Hunt, I., Flynn, S., Turnbull, P., Kapur, N., and Appleby, L. (2004) 'Mental illness in people who kill strangers: longitudinal study and national clinical survey' *British Medical Journal* 328: 734.

Sheldon, S. (1997) *Beyond Control Medical Power and Abortion Law* (Pluto).

Sheldon, S. (1998) '"A responsible body of medical men skilled in that particular art..." Rethinking the Bolam test' in S. Sheldon and M. Thomson (eds) *Feminist Perspectives on Healthcare Law* (Cavendish).

Sheldon, S. (2004) '*Evans v Amicus Healthcare*—Revealing cracks in the "twin pillars"?' *Child and Family Law Quarterly* 437.

Sheldon, S. and Thomson, M. (1998) 'Health care law and feminism: A developing relationship' in S. Sheldon and M. Thomson (eds) *Feminist Perspectives on Healthcare Law* (Cavendish).

Sheldon, S. and Wilkinson, S. (2001) 'Termination of pregnancy for reason of foetal disability' *Medical Law Review* 9: 85.

Sheldon, T. (2001) 'Dutch GP found guilty of murder faces no penalty' *British Medical Journal* 509.

Sheldon, T. (2004) 'New penalties for dutch doctors who flout euthanasia law' *British Medical Journal* 329: 131.

Shenfield, F. (2000) 'Consent and intent: the legal differences in assisted reproductive treatments' in M. Freeman and A. Lewis *Medicine and Law* (Oxford University Press).

Sherwin, S. (1996) 'Feminism and bioethics' in S. Wolf (ed) *Feminism and Bioethics* (Oxford University Press).

Sherwin, S. (1998) *The Politics of Women's Health: Exploring Agency and Autonomy* (Temple University Press).

Shewmon, D. (1998) '"Brainstem death", "brain death" and death: A critical reevaluation of the purported evidence' *Issues in Law and Medicine* 14: 125.

Shildrick, M. (1997) *Leaky Bodies and Boundaries. Feminism, Postmodernism and (Bio)ethics* (Routledge).

Siegler, M. (1982) 'Confidentiality in medicine—a decrepit concept' *New England Journal of Medicine* 307: 1518.

Silvers, A. (1998) 'Protecting the innocents from physician-assisted suicide' in M. Battin, R. Rhodes, and A. Silvers *Physician Assisted Suicide* (Routledge).

Sinclair, D. (2003) *Jewish Biomedical Law* (Oxford University Press).

Sinclair, D. (2005) *Jewish Medical Ethics* (Oxford University Press).

Singer, P. (1972) 'Famine, affluence and Morality' *Philosophy and Public Affairs* 1: 229.

Singer, P. (1993) *Practical Ethics* (Cambridge University Press).

Singer, P. (1994) *Rethinking Life and Death* (Oxford University Press).

Singer, P. (1995) 'Is the sanctity of life ethic terminally ill?' *Bioethics* 9: 307.

Singer, P. (2002) 'Ms B and Diane Pretty; a commentary' *Journal of Medical Ethics* 28: 236.

Singer, P. (2003) 'Voluntary euthanasia: a utilitarian perspective' *Bioethics* 17: 526.

Simanowitz, A. (1995) 'Law reform and medical negligence litigation: the UK position' in S. McLean (ed) *Law Reform and Medical Injury Litigation* (Dartmouth).

Simanowitz, A. (1987) 'Medical accidents: the problem and the challenge' in P. Byrne (ed) *Medicine in Contemporary Society* (King's Fund).

Simanowitz, A. (1998) 'Defensive medicine: Myth or reality?' in P. Byrne (ed) *Health, Rights and Resources* (Oxford University Press).

Sindell, M., Katz, J., and Komaromy, C. (2000) 'The case for palliative care in residential and nursing homes' in D. Dickenson, M. Johnson, and J. Samson (eds) *Death, Dying and Bereavement* (Sage).

Singer, P. (1992) 'Xenotransplantation and speciesism' *Transplantation Proceedings* 24: 728.

Sirrat, G. and Gill, R. (2005) 'Autonomy in medical ethics after O'Neill' *Journal of Medical Ethics* 31: 127.

Skegg, P. (1974) 'Irreversibly comatose individuals; alive or dead?' *Cambridge Law Journal* 130.

Skegg, P. (1985) *Law Ethics and Medicine* (Oxford University Press).

Skegg, P. (1999) 'English medical law and "informed consent": An antipodean assessment and alternative' *Medical Law Review* 7: 135.

Skene, L. (1998) 'patient's rights or family responsibilities' *Medical Law Review* 6: 1.

Skene, L. (2001) 'Genetic secrets and the family' *Medical Law Review* 9: 162.

Skene, L. (2002) 'Proprietary rights in human bodies, body parts and tissue' *Legal Studies* 102.

Skene, L. and Parker, M. (2002) 'The role of the church in developing the law' *Journal of Medical Ethics* 28: 215.

Small, N. (2001) 'Social work and palliative care' *British Journal of Social Work* 31: 961.

Smart, C. and Neale, B. (1999) *Family Fragments* (Polity).

Smart, J. (1993) *Utilitarianism: For and Against* (Cambridge University Press).

Smith II, G. (1996) 'Our hearts were once young and gay: health care rationing and the elderly' *University of Florida Journal of Law and Public Policy* 8: 1.

Smith II, G. (2002) 'Distributive justice and health care' *Journal of Contemporary Health Law and Policy* 18: 421.

Smith II, G. (2005) *The Christian Religion and Biotechnology* (Springer).

Smith II, G. (2007) *When Mercy Seasons Justice* (Columbus School of Law).

Smith, T. (1993) 'Influence of socioeconomic factors for attaining targets on reducing teenage pregnancies' *British Medical Journal* 306: 1232.

Smith, R. (2000a) 'The failings of NICE' *British Medical Journal* 321: 1363.

Smith, J. (2000b) 'A comment on Moor's Case' *Criminal Law Review* 566.

Smith, J. (2002a) *The Shipman Inquiry* (HMSO).

Smith, R. (2002b) 'In search of "non-disease"' *British Medical Journal* 324: 883.

Smith, R. (2003) 'Editorial accountability' in COPE, *2003 COPE Report* (COPE).

Smith, S. (2005) 'Evidence for the practical slippery slope in the debate on physician assisted suicide and euthanasia' *Medical Law Review* 13: 17.

Smolin, D. (2002) 'Should a ban on reproductive cloning include a ban on cloning for purposes of research or therapy?' *Cumberland Law Review* 32: 487.

Snow, R., Garcia, S., and Kureshy, N. (1996) *Investigating Women's Preferences for Contraceptive Technology* (Harvard School of Public Health).

Snowdon C., Elbourne D., Garcia J. (2002) 'Decisions, decisions: How do parents view the decision they made about a randomised controlled trial?' in K. Fulford, D. Dickenson, T. Murray (eds) *Healthcare Ethics and Human Values* (Blackwell).

Social and Community Planning Research (1996) *British Social Attitudes Survey* (SCPR).

Social Exclusion Unit (1999) *Teenage Pregnancy* (TSO).

Social Exclusion Unit (2002) *Reducing Reoffending: National Action Plan* (SEU).

Social Exclusion Unit (2005) *Mental Health: Key Facts and Figures* (SEU).

Social Issues Research Centre (2005) *Poverty and Obesity* (SIRC).

Social Services Committee (1990) *Tenth Report. Abortion Act 1967 'Conscience Clause'* (Hansard).

Sokol, D. (2006) 'Dissecting Deception' *Cambridge Quarterly of Healthcare Ethics* 15: 457.

Sokol, D., Car, J. (2006) 'Patient confidentiality and telephone consultations: time for a password' *Journal of Medical Ethics* 32: 688.

Sokolowski, R. (1991) 'The fiduciary relationship and the nature of professions', in E.D. Pellegrino, R.M. Veatch and J.P. Langan (eds) *Ethics, Trust, and the Professions* (Georgetown University Press).

Sommerville, M. (1986) 'Pain and suffering at the interfaces of medicine and the law' *University of Toronto Law Journal* 36: 186.

Sommerville, A. (1996) 'Are advance directives really the answer? and what was the question?' in S. McLean (ed) *Death Dying and the Law* (Dartmouth).

Sommerville, M. (2001) *Death Talk* (McGillQueen's University Press).

Sommerville, M. (2002) 'Deathbed disputation' *Canadian Medical Association Journal* 167: 651.

Sommerville, A. (2003) 'Juggling law, ethics, and intuition: practical answers to awkward questions' *Journal of Medical Ethics* 29: 281.

Special Committee of the Canadian Senate (1995) *Of Life and Death* (Canadian Government).

Spencer, J. (2005) 'Damages for lost chances; lost for good?' *Cambridge Law Journal* 282.

Sperling, D. (2006) *Management of Post-Mortem Pregnancy: Legal and Philosophical Aspects* (Aldershot).

Spial, J. (2003) 'Response to "do genetic relationships create moral obligations in organ transplantation?"' *Cambridge Quarterly of Healthcare Ethics* 12: 116.

Spriggs, M. (2004) 'Canaries in the mines: children, risk, non-therapeutic research, and justice' *Journal of Medical Ethics* 30: 176.

Spriggs, M. (2005) 'Is conceiving a child to benefit another against the interests of the new child?' *Journal of Medical Ethics* 31: 341.

Sprung, C., Cohen, S., Sjokvist, P., Baras, M., Bulow, H-H., Hovilehto, S., Ledoux, D., Lippert, A., Maia, P., Phelan, D, Schobersberger, W., Wennberg, E., and Woodcock, T. (2003) 'End-of-life practices in European intensive care units' *Journal of American Medical Association* 290: 270.

SPUC (2000) *HFEA 'Shows Lack of Respect for Human Life'* (SPUC).

Sque, M., Long, T., and Payne, S. (2005) *Families who did not donate organs: Methods for recruiting potential participants* (Transplant UK).

Stacey Taylor, J. (2005) *Stakes and kidneys: Why markets in human body parts are morally imperative* (Ashgate).

Staden, van, C. and Krüger, C. (2003) 'Incapacity to give informed consent owing to mental incapacity' *Journal of Medical Ethics* 29: 41.

Stammers, T. (2000) 'Doctors should advise adolescents to abstain from sex: For' *British Medical Journal* 32: 1520.

Stanley, J. (1987) 'More fiddling with the definition of death?' *Journal of Medical Ethics* 13: 21.

Stanton, C. and Harris, J. (2005) 'The moral status of the embryo post-Dolly' *Journal of Medical Ethics* 31: 221.

Stanworth, M. (1988) 'Reproductive technologies and the deconstruction of motherhood' in M. Stanworth (ed) *Reproductive Technologies: Gender, Motherhood and Medicine* (Polity).

Stapleton, J. (2005) 'Loss of the chance of cure from cancer' *Modern Law Review* 68: 1015.

Stapleton, J. (2006) 'Occam's razor reveals an orthodox basis for *Chester v Afshar*' *Law Quarterly Review* 426.

Starzl, T., Fung, J., and Tzakis, A. (1993) 'Baboon to human liver transplant' *The Lancet* 341: 65.

Statham, H., Solomou, W., and Green, J. (2006) 'Late termination of pregnancy: law, policy and decision making in four English fetal medicine units' *British Journal of Obstetrics and Gynaecology* 1402.

Stauch, M. (1995) 'Rationality and the refusal of medical treatment: a critique of the recent approach of the English courts' *Journal of Medical Ethics* 21: 162.

Stauch, M. (1998) 'Court-authorised caesareans and the principle of patient autonomy' *Nottingham Law Journal* 79.

Stauch, M. (2000) 'Causal authorship and the equality principle: a defence of the acts/omissions distinction in euthanasia' *Journal of Medical Ethics* 26: 237.

Stauch, M. (2001) 'Pregnancy and the Human Rights Act 1998' in A. Garwood-Gowers, J. Tingle and T. Lewis (eds) *Health Law: The Impact of the Human Rights Act 1998* (Cavendish).

Stauch, M. (2002) 'Comment on Re B' *Journal of Medical Ethics* 28: 232.

Stauch, M. and Wheat, K. (2004) *Sourcebook on Medical Law* (Cavendish).

Steinbock, B. (1988) 'Surrogate motherhood as prenatal adoption' *Law Medicine and Healthcare* 16: 44.

Steinbock, B. (1992) *Life Before Birth* (Oxford University Press).

Steinbock, B. (2000) 'The ethics of human cloning' in M. Freeman and A. Lewis

Medicine and Law (Oxford University Press).

Steinbock B. (2005) 'The case for physician assisted suicide: not (yet) proven' *Journal of Medical Ethics* 31: 235.

Steiner, H. (1997) 'Property in the body: a philosophical perspective' in K. Stern and P. Walsh (eds) *Property Rights in the Human Body* (King's College London).

Stephenson, P. (2004) 'Mentally ill offenders are being wrongly held in prisons' *British Medical Journal* 328: 1095.

Strasser, M. (1998) 'The futility of futility? On life, death, and reasoned public policy' *Maryland Law Review* 505.

Street, A. and Kissane D. (2000) 'Dispensing death, desiring death' *Omega* 41: 231.

Stern, K. (1994) 'Advance directives' *Medical Law Review* 57.

Stretton, D. (2000) 'The argument from intrinsic value: a critique' *Bioethics* 14: 228.

Stevens, R. (2005) 'An opportunity to reflect' *Law Quarterly Review* 121: 189.

Stone, A. (1975) *Mental Health and the Law* (National Institute of Mental Health).

Stone, D. (2001) 'Confidentiality, access to health records and the HRA 1998' in A. Garwood-Gowers, J. Tingle, and T. Lewis (eds) *Healthcare Law: The Impact of the Human Rights Act 1998* (Cavendish).

Stychin C. (1998) 'Body talk: rethinking autonomy, commodification and the embodied legal self' in S. Sheldon and M. Thomson (eds) *Feminist Perspectives on Health Care Law* (Cavendish).

Sullivan, R, Menapace, L., and White R. (2001) 'Truth-telling and patient diagnoses' *Journal of Medical Ethics* 27: 192.

Sunstein, C. (2004) 'Lives, life-years, and willingness to pay' *Columbia Law Review* 104: 205.

Suter, S. (2004) 'Disentangling privacy from property: toward a deeper understanding of genetic privacy' *George Washington Law Review* 72: 737.

Sutherland, E. (2003) '"Man not included"—single women, infertile couples and procreative freedom in the UK' *Child and Family Law Quarterly* 15: 155.

Syrett, K. (2002) 'NICE work: rationing, review and the "legitimacy problem" in the new NHS' *Medical Law Review* 10.

Syrett, K. (2003) 'A technocratic fix to the "legitimacy problem"? The Blair government and health care rationing in the United Kingdom' *Journal of Health Politics, Policy and Law* 28: 715.

Syrett, K. (2005) 'Does it pay to be NICE?' in A. Garwood-Gowers, J. Tingle, and K. Wheat (eds) *Contemporary Issues in Healthcare Law and Ethics* (Elsevier).

Syrett, K. (2006) 'Deconstructing deliberation in the appraisal of medical technologies: NICEly does it?' *Modern Law Review* 69: 869.

Szasz, T. (1972) *The Myth of Mental Illness* (Oxford University Press).

Szasz, T. (2001) 'Mental illness: psychiatry's phlogiston' *Journal of Medical Ethics* 27: 297.

Szasz, T. (2002) *Liberation by Oppression: A Comparative Study of Slavery and Psychiatry* (Transaction).

Szasz, T. (2005) '"Idiots, infants, and the insane": mental illness and legal incompetence' *Journal of Medical Ethics* 31: 78.

Tabberer, S., Hall, C., Prendergast, S., and Webster, A. (2000) *Teenage pregnancy and choice: Abortion or motherhood: influences on the decision* (Joseph Rowntree Foundation).

Takala, T. (1999) 'The right to genetic ignorance confirmed' *Bioethics* 13: 288.

Tallis, R. (2004) *Hippocratic Oaths: Medicine and Its Discontents* (Atlantic Books).

Tang, W-R., Aaronson, L., and Forbes, S. (2003) 'Quality of life in hospice patients with terminal illness' *Western Journal of Nursing Research* 26: 113.

Tauber, A. (2003) 'Sick autonomy' *Perspectives in Biology and Medicine* 46: 484.

Taylor, P. and Gunn, J. (1999) 'Homicides by people with mental illness: myth and reality' *The British Journal of Psychiatry* 174: 9.

Taylor, R. (2007) 'Reversing the retreat from *Gillick*?' *Child and Family Law Quarterly* 19: 81.

Tearfund (2007) *Churchgoing in the UK Today* (Tearfund).

Teather, D. (2002) 'Lesbian couple have deaf baby by choice' *The Guardian*, April 8 2002.

Teenage Pregnancy Unit (2000) *Teenage Pregnancy National Campaign* (DoH).

Teenage Pregnancy Unit (2007) Teenage conception statistics for England 1998–2005 (DoH).

Teff, H. (1998) 'The standard of care in medical negligence—Moving on from Bolam' *Oxford Journal of Legal Studies* 18: 473.

Templeton, A. (2000) 'Infertility and the establishment of pregnancy' *British Medical Bulletin* 56: 577.

Tengs, T., Meyer, G., Siegel, J., Pliskin, J., Graham, J., and Weinstein, M. (1996) 'Oregon's Medicaid ranking and cost-effectiveness' *Medical Decision Making* 16: 99.

The, A-M., Hak, T., Koëter, G., and van der Wal, G. (2000) 'Collusion in doctor-patient communication about imminent death' *British Medical Journal* 321: 1376.

Thomas, K. (2003) *Caring for the Dying at Home: Companions on the Journey* (Radcliffe Medical Press).

Thomas, P. (2004) 'Compulsion and psychiatry—the role of advance statements' *British Medical Journal* 329: 122.

Thomasma, D., Kimbrough-Kushner, T., Kimsma, G., and Ciesielski-Carlucci, C. (eds) (1998) *Asking to Die* (Kluwer).

Thomson, J. (1971) 'A defense of abortion' *Philosophy and Public Affairs* 1: 47.

Thomson, M. (1998) *Reproducing Narrative* (Dartmouth).

Thunder, J. (2003) 'Quiet killings in medical facilities: detection and prevention' *Issues in Law and Medicine* 18: 211.

Tobias, J. and Souhani, R. (1993) 'Fully informed consent can be needlessly cruel' *British Medical Journal* 307: 1199.

Toft, B. (2004) *Independent review of the circumstances surrounding four adverse events that occurred in the Reproductive Medicine Units at The Leeds Teaching Hospitals NHS Trust, West Yorkshire* (DoH).

Tomlinson, S. (1999) 'Genetic testing for cystic fibrosis' *Harvard Journal of Law and Technology* 11: 551.

Tong, R. (1996) 'Feminist approaches to Bioethics' in S. Wolf (ed) *Feminism and Bioethics* (Oxford University Press).

Tong, R. (1997) *Feminist approaches to Bioethics: Theoretical reflections and practical applications* (Westview Press).

Tong, R. (2004) *Linking Visions* (Rowman and Littlefield).

Tooley, M. (1980) 'An irrelevant consideration: Killing versus letting die' in B. Steinbock (ed) *Killing and Letting Die* (Forham University Press).

Tooley, M. (1983) *Abortion and Infanticide* (Oxford University Press).

Toombs, S. (1999) 'What does it meant to be *somebody*' in M. Chery (ed) *Persons and Their Bodies* (Kluwer).

Torrance, I. (2003) 'Confidentiality and its limits' *Journal of Medical Ethics* 29: 8.

Toulson, R. and Phipps, C. (1996) *Confidentiality* (Sweet and Maxwell).

Towse, A., Fenn, P., Grey, A., Rickman, N., and Salinas, R. (2004) *Reducing Harm to Patients in the National Health Service. Will the Government's compensation proposals help?* (Office of Health Economics).

Transplantation Society Council (1985) 'Commercialisation in transplantation' *The Lancet* 715.

Tribe, L. (1998) 'On not banning cloning for the wrong reasons', in M. Nussbaum and C. Sunstein (eds) *Clones and Clones* (W W Norton).

Truog, R. (1997) 'Is it time to abandon brain death' *Hastings Center Report* 27: 29.

Truog R., Robinson, W. (2003) 'Role of brain death and the dead-donor rule in the ethics of organ transplantation' *Critical Care Medicine* 31: 2391.

Tsai, D. (2005) 'The bioethical principles and Confucius' moral philosophy' *Journal of Medical Ethics* 31: 159.

Tur, R. (2002) 'Special defence based on the ethics of doctors. "The Doctor's Defence and Professional ethics"' *King's College Law Journal* 13: 75.

Tur, R. (2003a) 'Legislative technique and human rights: the sad case of assisted suicide' *Criminal Law Review* 3.

Tur, R. (2003b) 'Just how unlawful is euthanasia' *Journal of applied philosophy* 19: 220.

Turnberg, L. (2003) 'Common sense and common consent in communicable disease surveillance' *Journal of Medical Ethics* 29: 27.

Turner, A. and Coyle, A. (2001) 'What does it mean to be a donor offspring?' *Human Reproduction* 15: 2041.

Turner, L. (2004) 'Bioethics needs to rethink its agenda' *British Medical Journal* 328: 175.

Twycross, R. (1990) 'Assisted death: a reply' *The Lancet* 336: 796.

Twycross, R. (1998) 'Where there is hope, there is life: a view from the hospice' in J. Keown (ed) *Euthanasia Re-examined* (Cambridge University Press).

UKCC (1996) *Guidelines for Professional Practice* (UKCC).

UK Transplant (2004a) *A Review Of The Impact Of Three Initiatives For Improving Donation Rates In The UK* (UK Transplant).

UK Transplant (2004b) *Opt in or opt out?* (UK Transplant).

UK Transplant (2004c) *Organ donation and religious perspectives* (UK Transplant).

UK Transplant (2005) *TV more talked about than matters of life and death* (UK Transplant).

UK Transplant (2007) *Transplant Activity in the UK* (UK Transplant).

ULTRA (2003) *Annual Report* (DoH).

Underhill, K., Montgomery, P., and Operario, D. (2007) 'Sexual abstinence only programmes to prevent HIV infection in high income countries: systematic review' *British Medical Journal* 335: 248.

Underwood, M. and Bailey, J. (1993) 'Coronary bypass surgery should not be offered to smokers' *British Medical Journal* 306: 1047.

UNESCO (1989) *Human Rights Aspects of Traffic in Body Parts and Human Fetuses for Research and/or Therapeutic Purposes* (UNESCO).

United Nations Human Rights Committee (2001) *Concluding Observations of the Human Rights Committee: Netherlands* (CCPR/CO/72/NET) (UN).

United States President's Commission for the Study of Ethical Problems in Medicine (1981) *Defining Death* (US Government).

United States' President's Commission on Bioethics (2002) *Human Cloning and Human Dignity*.

United States Task Force on Organ Transplantation (1986) *Organ Transplantation: Issues and Recommendations* (US Government).

Uren, Z., Sheers, D., and Dattani, N. (2007) 'Teenage conceptions by small area deprivation in England and Wales' in National Statistics, *Health Statistics Quarterly* (Palgrave).

Van Delden J. (1999) 'Slippery slopes in flat countries—a response' *Journal of Medical Ethics* 25: 22.

Van Delden J., Pijnenborg, L., van der Maas, P. (1993) 'Dances with data' *Bioethics* 7: 323.

Van der Heide, A., Deliens, L., Faisst, K., Nilstun, T., Norup, M., Paci, E., van der Wal, G., and van der Maas P. (2003) 'End of life decisions in six European countries' *British Medical Journal* 362: 345.

Van der Heide, A., Onwuteaka-Philipsen, B., Rurup, M. Buiting, H. van Delden, J., Hanssen-de Wolf, J., Janssen, A. Pasman, R., Rietjens, J., Prins, C., Deerenberg, I., Gevers, J., van der Maas, P., and van der Wal, G. (2007) 'End-of-life practices in the Netherlands under the euthanasia' *New England Journal of Medicine* 356: 1957.

Van der Maas, P. (1996) 'Euthanasia, physician assisted suicide and other medical practices involving the end of life in the Netherlands 1990–1995' *New England Journal of Medicine* 335: 1699.

Van der Maas, P., van Delden, J., and Pijnenborg, L. (1991) 'Euthanasia and other medical decisions concerning the end of life' *The Lancet* 338: 669.

Van der Maas, P., van Delden, J. and Pijnenborg, L. (1992) *Euthanasia and Other Medical Decisions Concerning the End of Life* (Elsevier).

Van Tilld, A. and Borouill, D. (1975) 'How dead can you be?' *Medicine, Science and Law* 133.

Van Zyl, L. (2000) *Death and Compassion: A Virtue-based Approach to Euthanasia* (Ashgate).

Varelius, J. (2007) 'Illness, suffering and voluntary euthanasia' *Bioethics* 21: 75.

Veatch, R. (1989) *Death Dying and the Biological Revolution* (Yale University Press).

Veatch, R. (1993) 'The impending collapse of the whole-brain definition of death' *Hasting Center Report* 23: 4.

Veatch, R. (1999) 'The conscience cause: How much individual choice in defining death can our society tolerate?' in S. Youngner,

R. Arnold, and R. Schapiro (eds) *The Definition of Death* (Baltimore).

Veatch, R. (2000) 'Doctor does not know best' *Philosophy and Medicine* 25: 701.

Veatch, R. (2003a) 'Why liberals should accept financial incentives for organ procurement' *Kennedy Institute of Ethics Journal* 13: 19.

Veatch, R. (2003b) 'Is there a common morality?' *Kennedy Institute of Ethics Journal* 13: 189.

Veatch, R. (2004) 'Abandon the dead donor rule or change the definition of death?' *Kennedy Institute of Ethics Journal* 14: 261.

Veatch, R. (2005) 'The death of whole-brain death' *Journal of Medicine and Philosophy* 30: 353.

Veitch, K (2006) 'Medical law and the power of life and death' *International Journal of Law in Context* 2: 137.

Veldink, J., Wokke, J. and van der Wal, G. (2002) 'Euthanasia and physician-assisted suicide among patients with amyotrophic lateral sclerosis in the Netherlands' *New England Journal of Medicine* 346: 1638.

Velleman, D. (1999) 'A right to selftermination' *Ethics* 109: 606.

Vigod, S., Bell, C., and Bohnen, M. (2003) 'Privacy of patients' information in hospital lifts: observational study' *British Medical Journal* 327: 1024.

Vikan, A., Camino, C. and Biaggio, A. (2005) 'Note on a cross-cultural test of Gilligan's ethic of care' *Journal of Moral Education* 34: 107.

Vincent, C., Neale, G. and Woloshynowych, M. (2001) 'Adverse events in British hospitals: preliminary retrospective record review' *British Medical Journal* 2001: 517.

Volokh, E. (2007) 'Medical self-defense, prohibited experimentatal therapies, and payment for organs' *Harvard Law Review* 120: 1814.

Voluntary Euthanasia Society (2003) *Public Opinion* (VES).

Wade, T. (2001) 'Ethical issues in diagnosis and management of patients in the permanent vegetative state' *British Medical Journal* 322: 352.

Wade, D. and Halligan, P. (2004) 'Do biomedical models of illness make for good healthcare systems?' *British Medical Journal* 329: 1398.

Walker, A. (2003) 'Should there be limits on who may access assisted reproductive services? A legal perspective' in J. Gunning and H. Szoke *The Regulation of Assisted Reproductive Technology* (Ashgate).

Wallbank, J. (2004) 'Reconstructing the HFEA 1990: is blood really thicker than water?' *Child and Family Law Quarterly* 387.

Walsh, E. and Fahy, T. (2002) 'Violence in Society' *British Medical Journal* 325: 507.

Walsh, E., Moran P., Scott, C., McKenzie, K., Burns, T., Creed, F., Tyrer, P., Murray, R., and Fahy, T. (2003) 'Prevalence of violent victimisation in severe mental illness' *British Journal of Psychiatry* 183: 233.

Walsh, P. (ed) (1999) *The Vegetative State* (Centre of Medical Law and Ethics).

Walsh, V. (1980) 'Contraception: the growth of technology' in The Brighton Women and Science Group (eds) *Alice through the Microscope* (Virago).

Walter, T., Littlewood, J., and Pickering, M. (2000) 'Death in the News' in D. Dickenson, M. Johnson, and J. Samson Katz (eds) *Death, Dying and Bereavement* (Sage).

Walton, D. (1992) *Slippery Slope Arguments* (Oxford University Press).

Wanlass, D. (2006) *Securing Good Care for Older People* (King's Fund).

Ward, B. and Tate, P. (1994) 'Attitudes among NHS Doctors to Requests for Euthanasia' *British Medical Journal* 308: 1332.

Ward, K. (1989) 'An irresolvable debate' in A. Dyson and J. Harris *Experiments on Embryos* (Routledge).

Warner, Lord (2004) HL Deb vol 664 col 370, 22 July 2004.

Warnock, M. (1984) *Report of the Inquiry into Human Fertilisation and Embryology* (DoH).

Warnock, M. (1992) *The Uses of Philosophy* (Blackwell).

Warnock, M. (1998) 'Informed consent—a publisher's duty' *British Medical Journal* 316: 1002.

Warnock, M. (2001) *An Intelligent Person's Guide to Ethics* (Duckbacks).

Warnock, M. (2002) *Making Babies* (Oxford University Press).

Warren, M. (1973) 'On the moral and legal status of abortion' in L. Schwartz (ed) *Arguing About Abortion* (Bemon Wadsworth).

Warren, M. (1997) *Moral Status: Obligations to Persons and their Living Things* (Oxford University Press).

Watt, H. (2002a) *Euthanasia: Unpacking the Debate (Lincare* Centre).

Watt, H. (2002b) *Living Together: Pregnancy and Parenthood* (Linacre Centre).

Watt, H. (2003) *Thinking Twice: Cloning and In Vitro Fertilisation* (Linacre Centre).

Watt, H. (2007) 'Embryos and pseudoembryos: parthenotes, reprogrammed oocytes and headless clones' *Journal of Medical Ethics* 33: 554.

Weait, M. (2005) 'Knowledge autonomy and consent: *R v Konzani*' *Criminal Law Review* 763.

Weait, M. (2007) 'On being responsible' in V. Munro and C. Stychin (eds) *Sexuality and the Law* (Routledge).

Weaver, J. (2002) 'Court ordered Cacsarean sections' in A. Bainham, S. Day Sclater, and M. Richards (eds) *Body Lore and Laws* (Hart).

Webster, C. (1998) *The National Health Service: A Political History* (Oxford University Press).

Weir, T. (2000) *A Casebook on Tort* (Sweet and Maxwell).

Weir, T (2000b) 'The unwanted child' *Cambridge Law Journal* 59: 238.

Weiss, B. (1982) 'Confidentiality. expectations of patients, physicians and medical students' *Journal of American Medical Association* 247: 2695.

Wellcome Trust (1998) *Public Perspectives on Human Cloning: A Social Research Study* (Wellcome Trust).

Welcome Trust and Medical Research Council (2001) *Human Tissue and Biological Samples for Research* (MRC).

Weller, M. and Brahams (2004) 'The UK Draft Mental Health Bill 2004: a compromise that pleases no one' *The Lancet* 364: 1651.

Wellings, K., Field, J. and Johnson, A. (1994) *Sexual Behaviour in Britain* (Penguin).

Wells, C. (1989) 'Otherwise kill me' in R. Lee and D. Morgan *Birthrights: Law and Ethics at the Beginnings of Life* (Routledge).

Wells, A. (1994) 'Patenting new life forms' *European Intellectual Property Review* 3: 111.

Wells, C. (1998) 'On the outside looking in; perspectives on enforced caesareans' in S. Shledon and M. Thomson (eds) *Feminist Perspectives on Health Care Law* (Cavendish).

Wert de, G. (1998) 'The post-menopause' in J. Harris and S. Holm (eds) *The Future of Human Reproduction* (Oxford University Press).

West, R. (1985) 'Authority autonomy and choice' *Harvard Law Review* 384.

West, R. (1997) *Caring for Justice* (New York University Press).

Weyers, H. (2006) 'Explaining the emergence of euthanasia law in the Netherlands: How the sociology of law can help the sociology of bioethics' *Sociology of Health & Illness* 28: 802.

Wheat, K. (1997) 'Can paternalism ever justify a breach of confidence?' *Health Care Risk Report* 3: 12.

Wheat, K. (2000) 'The law's treatment of the suicidal' *Medical Law Review* 182.

White, C. (2005) 'UK agency to combat research misconduct' *British Medical Journal* 330: 616.

White, S. (2002) 'Preventive detention must be resisted by the medical profession' *Journal of Medical Ethics* 28: 95.

Whitfield, A. (1990) 'Informed consent: does the doctrine benefit patients in the United Kingdom' in D. Brahams (ed) *Medicine and the Law* (Royal College of Physicians).

Whitty, N. (1998) '"In a perfect world": feminism and health care resource allocation' in S. Sheldon and M. Thomson (eds) *Feminist Perspective on Health Care Law* (Cavendish).

WHO (1948) *Constitution of the WHO* (WHO).

WHO (1978) *Risk Approach for Maternal and Child Health Care* (WHO).

WHO (1991) *Human Organ Transplantation* (WHO).

WHO (1994) *Guiding Principles on Human Organ Transplantation* (WHO).

WHO (1998) *World Health Report* (WHO).

WHO (2003) *Technology appraisal programme of the National Institute of Clinical Excellence* (WHO).

Wicks, E. (2001) 'The right to refuse medical treatment under the European Convention on Human Rights' *Medical Law Review* 9: 17.

Wicks, E. (2007) *Human Rights and Healthcare* (Hart).

Widdett, J. and Thomson, M. (1997) 'Justifying treatment and other stories' *Feminist Legal Studies* 5: 77.

Wight, D., Henderson, M., Raab, G., Abraham, C., Buston, K., Scott, S., and Hart, G. (2003) 'Extent of regretted sexual intercourse among young teenagers in Scotland' *British Medical Journal* 320: 1243.

Wight, J., Jakubovic, M., Walters, S., Maheswaran, R., White, P., and Lennon, V. (2004) 'Variation in cadaveric organ donor rates in the UK' *Nephrology Dialysis Transplantation* 19: 963.

Wiland, E. (2000) 'Unconscious violinists and the use of analogies in moral argument' *Journal of Medical Ethics* 26: 466.

Wilkins, R. (1993) 'Does the fetus have a right to life?' *Journal of Social Philosophy* 24: 123.

Wilkinson, M. and Moore, A. (1999) 'Inducements revisited' Bioethics 13: 114.

Wilkinson, S. (2000) 'Palliative care and the doctrine of double effect' in D. Dickenson, M. Johnson, and J. Samson Katz, *Death, Dying and Bereavement* (Sage).

Wilkinson, T. (2003) 'What's not wrong with conditional organ donation' *Journal of Medical Ethics* 29: 163.

Wilkinson, S. (2003b) *Bodies for Sale* (Routledge).

Wilkinson, T. (2005) 'Individual and family consent to organ and tissue donation: is the current position coherent ?' *Journal of Medical Ethics* 31: 587.

Wilkinson, T. (2007a) 'Racist organ donors and saving lives' *Bioethics* 21: 63.

Wilkinson, T. (2007b) 'Individual and family decisions about organ donation' *Journal of Applied Philosophy* 24: 26.

Williams, A. (1997) 'Intergenerational equity' *Health Economics* 6: 117.

Williams C. (1995) 'Contraceptive failure may be a major factor in teenage pregnancy' *British Medical Journal* 311: 807.

Williams, C., Alderson, P. and Farsides, R. (2002) '"Drawing the line" in prenatal screening and testing' *Health Risk and Society* 4: 61.

Williams, G. (1957) *The Sanctity of Life and the Criminal Law* (Faber and Faber).

Williams, G. (1978) *Textbook of Criminal Law* (Stevens).

Williams, G. (1994) 'The fetus and the right to life' *Cambridge Law Journal* 53: 71.

Williams, G. (2001) 'The principle of double effect and terminal sedation' *Medical Law Review* 9: 41.

Williams, G. (2007) *Intention and Causation in Medical Non-Killing* (Routledge).

Williams, K. (2001) 'Medical Samaritans. Is there a duty to treat?' *Oxford Journal of Legal Studies* 21: 393.

Williams, K. (2003) 'Doctors as Good Samaritans' *Journal of Law and Society* 30.

Williams, K. (2007) 'Litigation against English NHS ambulance services and the rule in Kent v. Griffiths' *Medical Law Review* 15: 153.

Williams, M. (2005) 'Death rites: assisted suicide and existential rights' *International Journal of Law in Context* 1: 183.

Williamson, R. (1999) 'Human reproductive cloning is unethical because it undermines autonomy: Commentary on Savulescu' *Journal of Medical Ethics* 25: 96.

Willison, D., Kashavjee, K., Nair, K., Goldsmith C., and Holbrook A. (2003) 'Patients' consent preferences for research uses of information in electronic medical records' *British Medical Journal* 326: 373.

Wilson, L. (1999) *Living Wills* (Nursing Times).

Wilson, K., Curran, D., and McPherson, C. 'A burden to others: A common source of distress for the terminally ill' *Cognitive Behaviour Therapy* 34: 115.

Wilton, J. (2007) 'An anatomist's perspective on the Human Tissue Act 2004' in Brooks-Gordan, B., Ebtehaj, F., Herring, J., Johnson, M., and Richards, M. (eds) *Death Rights and Rites* (Hart).

Winn, S., Roker, D., and Coleman, J. (1998) 'Young people's sexual knowledge' in

J. Coleman and D. Roker (eds) *Teenage Sexuality* (Harwood Academics).

Winick, B., Kress, K., and Schopp, R. (2003) 'Outpatient civil commitment' *Psychology, Public Policy and the Law* 9: 33.

Winston, R. (2005) *Memorandum to Select Committee on Science and Technology* (TSO).

Winter, B. and Cohen, S. (1999) 'ABC of intensive care. Withdrawal of care' *British Medical Journal* 319: 316.

Witting, C. (2001) 'National Health Service Rationing' *Oxford Journal of Legal Studies* 21: 443.

Wolf, N. (1995) 'Our bodies, our souls' *The New Republic* 16 October 1995.

Wolf, S. (1996) 'Introduction: gender and feminism in bioethics' in S. Wolfe (ed) *Feminism and Bioethics* (Oxford University Press).

Wolf, S. (1996) 'Gender, feminism and death: physician-assisted suicide and euthanasia' in S. Wolf (ed) *Feminism and Bioethics* (Oxford University Press).

Wolf-Devine, C. (1989) 'Abortion and the "feminine voice"' in J. Pojman and F. Beckwith (eds) *The Abortion Controversy* (Jones and Bartlett).

Wolpe, P. (1998) 'The triumph of autonomy in American bioethics: a sociological view' in R. Devries and J. Subedi (eds) *Bioethics and society* (Prentice Hall).

Woods, K. and McNamara, J. (1980) 'Confidentiality: its effect on interviewee behaviour' *Professional Psychology* 11: 714.

Woods, S. (2002) 'Respect for autonomy and palliative care' in H. ten Have and D. Clark *The Ethics of Palliative Care* (Open University Press).

Woolf, Lord (2000) 'Clinical negligence; what is the solution? How can we provide justice for doctors and patients?' *Medical Law International* 4: 133.

Woolf, Lord (2001) 'Are the courts excessively deferential to the medical profession?' *Medical Law Review* 9: 1–16.

World Medical Association (2002) *Declaration of Helsinki* (WMA).

Wright, D., Henderson, M., Raab, G., Abraham, C., Buston, K., Scott, S., and Hart, G. (2000) 'Extent of regretted sexual intercourse among young teenagers in Scotland' *British Medical Journal* 321: 1243.

Wrigley, A. (2007) 'Proxy consent: moral authority misconceived' *Journal of Medical Ethics* 33: 527.

Wyatt, J. (2000) *Medical Paternalism and the Fetus* (BPAS).

Yamey, G. (1999) 'Sexual and reproductive health: what about boys and men?' *British Medical Journal* 319: 1315.

Yates, V. (2007) 'Ambivalence, contradiction, and symbiosis: carers' and mental health users' rights' *Law and Policy* 29: 435.

Zilberberg, J. (2007) 'Sex selection and restricting abortion and sex determination' *Bioethics* 9: 517–519.

Zimmern, R., Hall, A., and Liddell, K. (2004) *The Human Tissue Bill following its third reading in the House of Commons* (Cambridge Genetics Knowledge Park).

Zinn, C. (2001) 'A third of surgeons in New South Wales admit to euthanasia' *British Medical Journal* 323: 1268.

Zinn, C. (2003) 'Wife wins case against GPs who did not disclose husband's HIV status' *British Medical Journal* 326: 1286.

Zito Trust (2004) *Looking Forward to a World Class Mental Health Service* (Zito Trust).

Zohar, N. (1998) 'Jewish deliberation on suicide' in M. Battin, R. Rhodes and A. Silvers (eds) *Physician Assisted Suicide* (Routledge).

Zyl, van, L. (2000) *Death and Compassion* (Ashgate).

Zyic, Z. (1998) 'Palliative care' in D. Thomasma (ed) *Asking to Die* (Kluwer).

Index